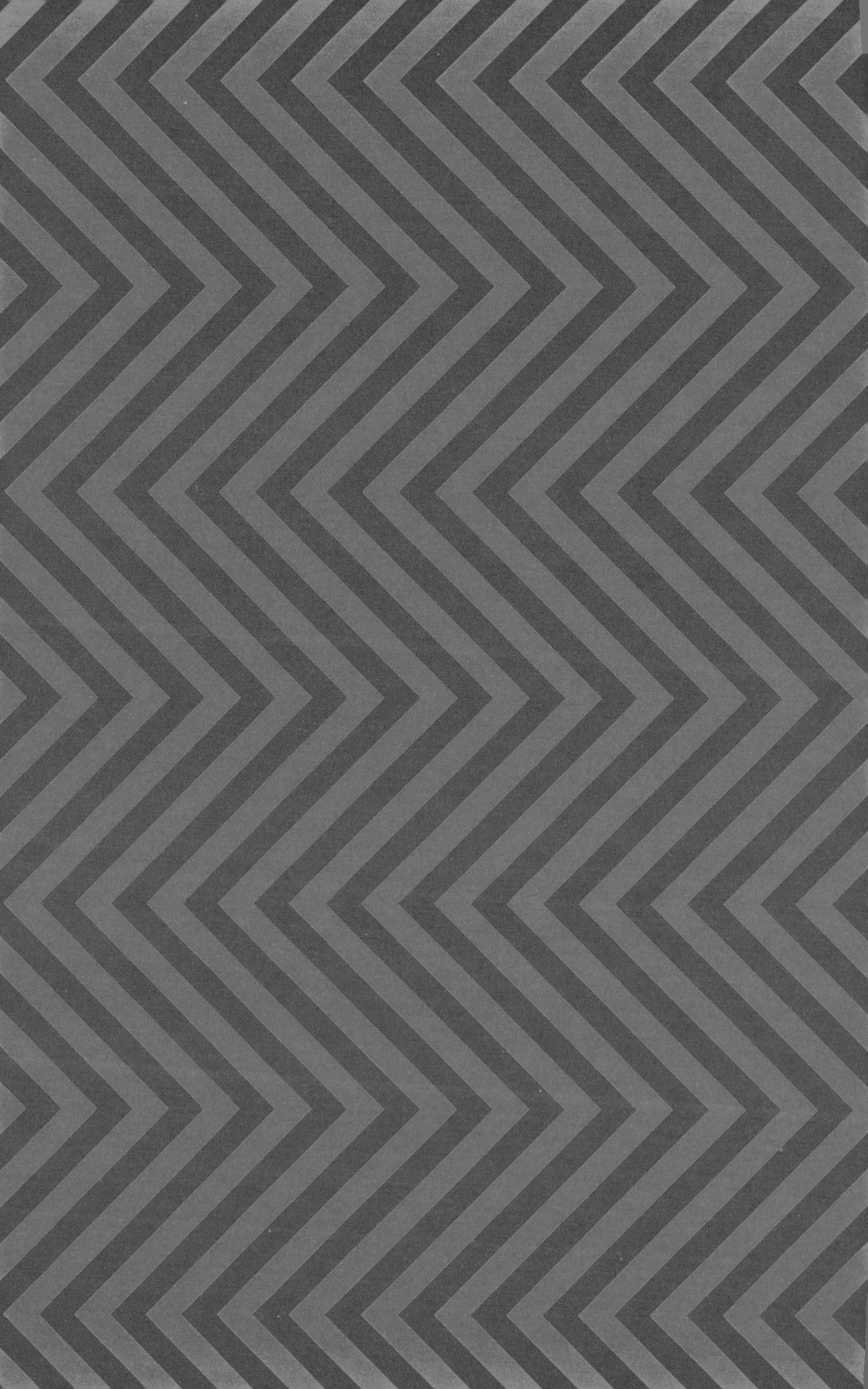

Pet Shop Boys
Volume

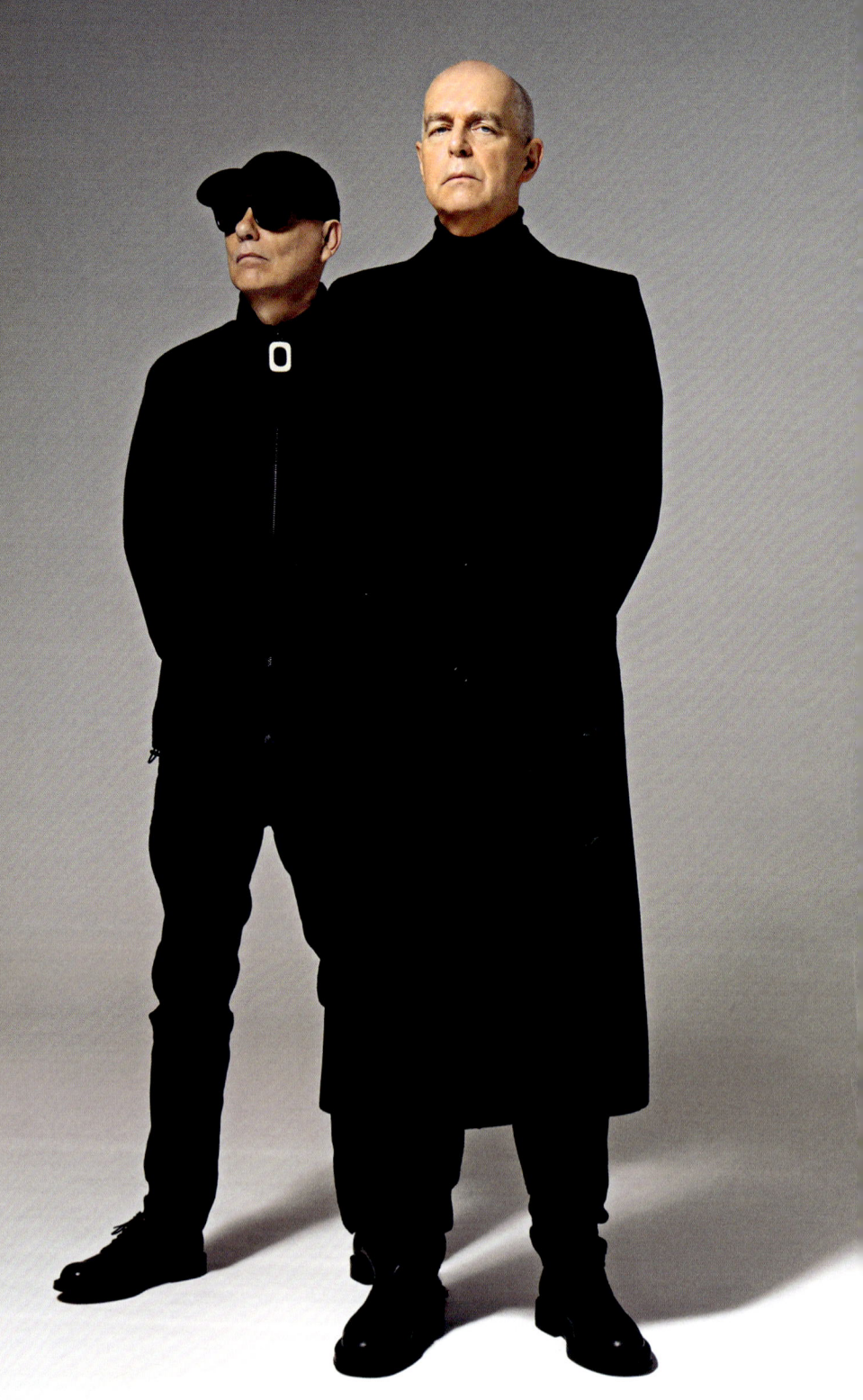

Pet Shop Boys Volume

The complete visual record
1984–2024

Chris Heath
with Philip Hoare

Foreword by
Jeremy Deller

and an introduction by
Libby Sellers

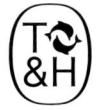

Contents

Pet Shop Boys are always on my mind
Jeremy Deller 8

Pet Shop Boys, practice
Philip Hoare 10

Pet Shop Boys, design
Libby Sellers 18

Pet Shop Boys, catalogue 1984–2024

West End girls (first release) 34
One more chance 36
Opportunities (let's make lots of money)
    (first release) 38
West End girls (second release) 44
Love comes quickly 52
Please 58
Opportunities (let's make lots of money)
    (second release) 62
Suburbia 66
Paninaro 74
Disco 78
Television 80
It's a sin 82
What have I done to deserve this? 86
Actually 90
Rent 94
Always on my mind 98
It couldn't happen here 104
Heart 106
Pet Shop Boys, annually 110
Domino dancing 112
Showbusiness / I like it here,
    wherever it is 116
Introspective 118
Left to my own devices 122
It's alright 126
MCMLXXXIX tour 130
Projections 134
Pet Shop Boys, Literally 136
So hard 138
Behaviour 142
Being boring 144

Where the streets have no name
    (I can't take my eyes off you) / How can
    you expect to be taken seriously? 148
Performance tour 154
Jealousy 158
Promotion 162
DJ culture 164
Discography / Videography 168
Was it worth it? 170
Can you forgive her? 174
Go west 180
Very 184
Very Relentless 188
Pet Shop Boys versus America 192
I wouldn't normally do this kind of thing 194
Liberation 198
Yesterday, when I was mad 202
Disco 2 206
Discovery tour 208
Various 212
Paninaro '95 214
Alternative 220
Before 222
Se a vida é (That's the way life is) 226
Bilingual 234
Single-Bilingual / Discoteca 236
A red letter day 240
Somewhere – In concert
    at the Savoy Theatre 244
Somewhere 248
I don't know what you want
    but I can't give it any more 252
New York City boy 258
Creamfields 264
Nightlife 266
Nightlife tour 268
You only tell me you love me
    when you're drunk 272
Pet Shop Boys Catalogue 1986–1996 276
Closer to Heaven 278
Home and dry 280
University tour 284
Release 286
Release tour 288

I get along 292
London 296
Disco 3 300
Miracles 302
PopArt 306
Flamboyant 310
Battleship Potemkin 314
Back To Mine: Pet Shop Boys 318
I'm with stupid 320
Fundamental 324
Fundamental tour 328
Minimal 332
Pet Shop Boys Catalogue 336
Numb 338
A Life in Pop 342
Concrete 344
Integral 346
Disco Four 350
Pet Shop Boys Story 352
Love etc. 354
Yes 358
Did you see me coming? 364
Pandemonium tour 368
Beautiful people 372
Pet Shop Boys Party / Christmas 374
Love life 376
Together 378
Ultimate 382
The Most Incredible Thing 384
Format 386
Winner 388
Elysium 392
Leaving 394
Memory of the future 398
Electric tour 402
Axis 406
Vocal 410
Electric 414
Love is a bourgeois construct 418
Thursday 420
Fluorescent 424
A Man from the Future 426
The pop kids 428
Super 432

Twenty-something 436
Super tour 440
Inner sanctum 444
Say it to me 446
Pet Shop Boys Catalogue 1999–2012 448
Undertow 450
Agenda 452
Musik 458
Dreamland 460
Burning the heather 464
Monkey business 468
Hotspot 472
Two books about Pet Shop Boys 476
My Beautiful Laundrette 478
I don't wanna 480
Cricket wife 484
Dreamworld tour 488
Lost 492
Smash 496
Relentless 502
Loneliness 506
Dancing star 510
Nonetheless 514
A new bohemia 520
Feel 524
New London boy / All the young dudes 528
Christmas cards 532
Literally / Annually 544

Pet Shop Boys in conversation
    with Chris Heath, April 2006 550

A further conversation
    with Chris Heath, October 2024 562

Discography 572
Biographies 585
Index 590
Photographers' and
    contributors' credits 592

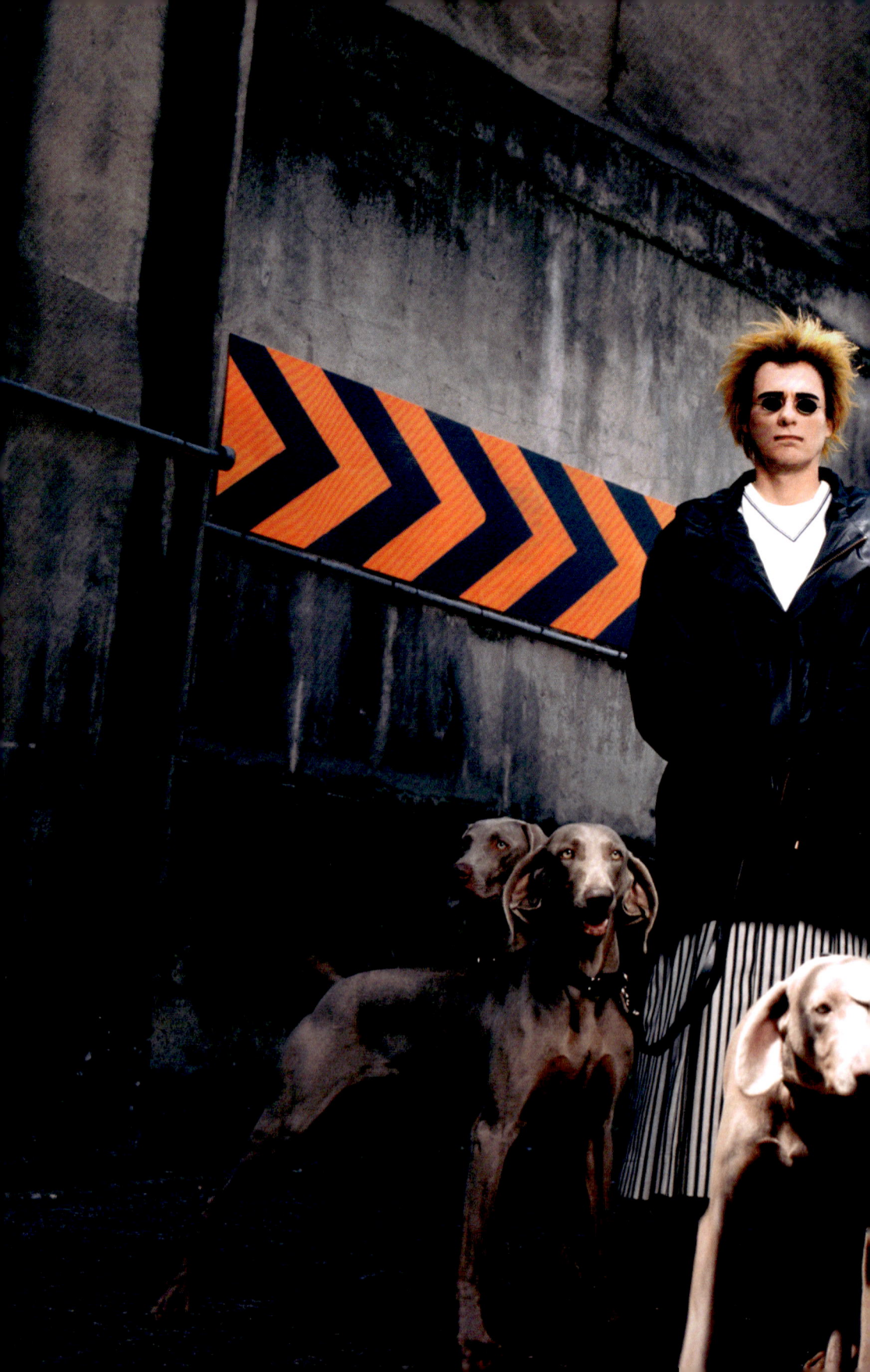

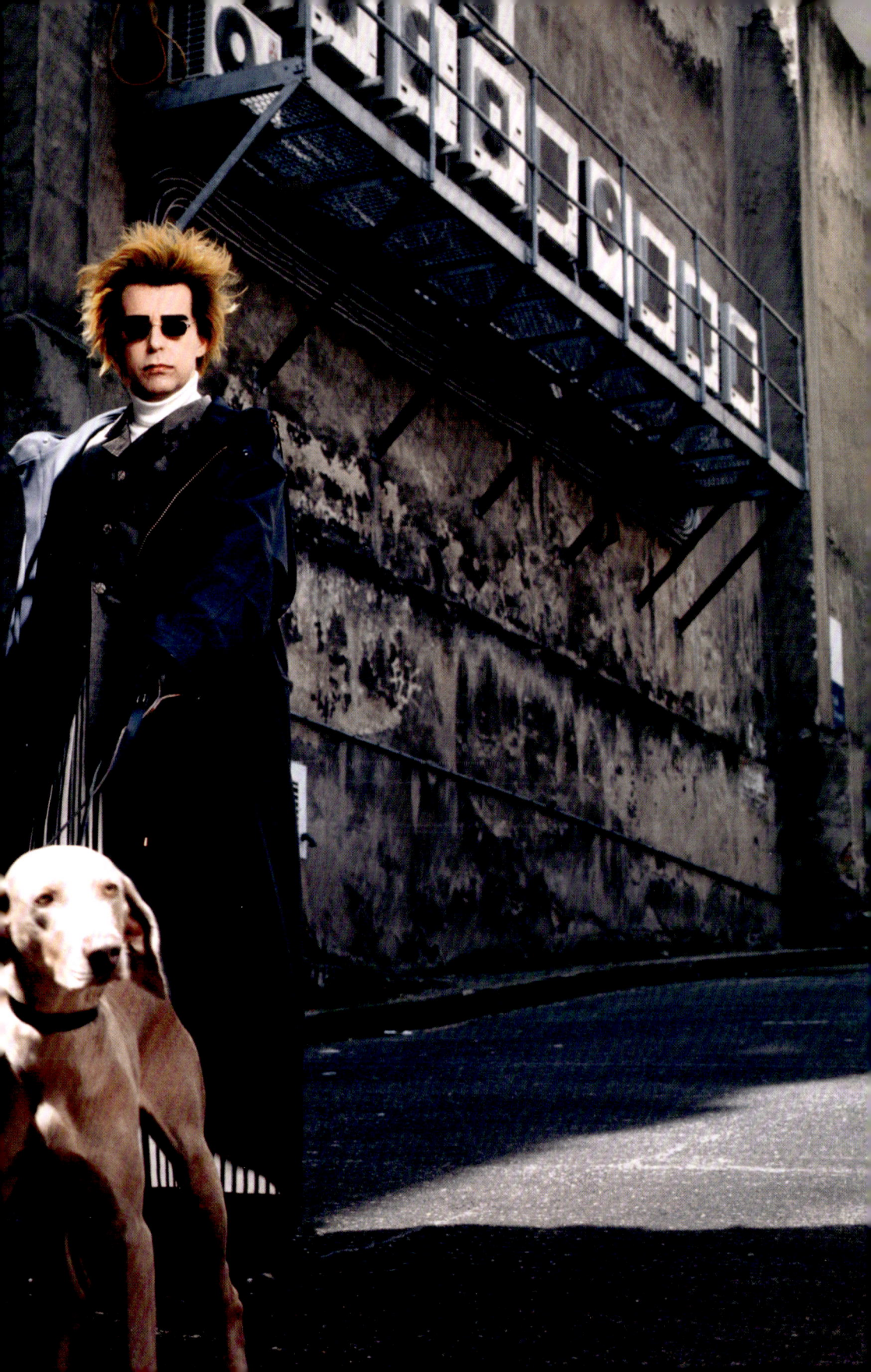

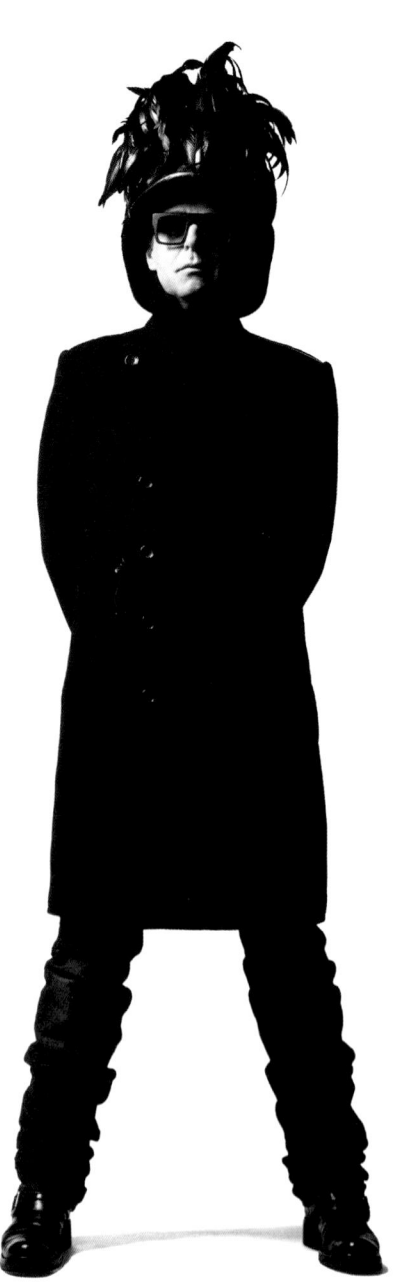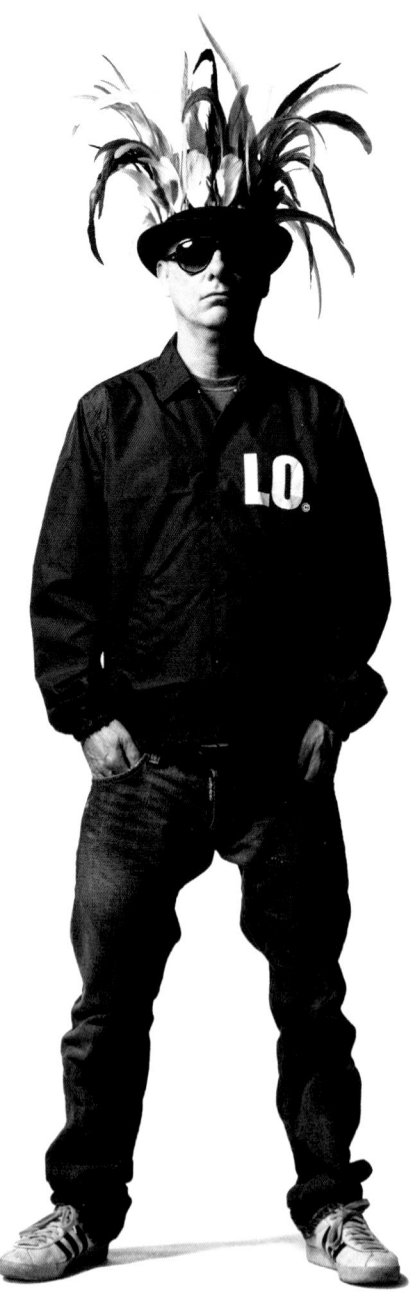

Pet Shop Boys are always on my mind
Jeremy Deller

The book in your hands is part of the ongoing artwork that is Pet Shop Boys. A total artwork or, as the Germans put it, a *Gesamtkunstwerk*. For is not pop music the predominant late twentieth-century art form? An art form, at once both mass media and profoundly personal, that has changed lives and reimagined societies time and again. I have always thought that being avant-garde was easy compared with the alchemy involved in making an enduring pop song. Few musicians can claim to have achieved that. It happens when a group takes an aesthetic position, creates a world of their own, and then consistently adheres to it. Roxy Music and Kraftwerk managed it in the 1970s. And Pet Shop Boys have done so since 1984.

    The ability to bend reality through cover versions is part of this. A good cover version is so much more than a clever musical reinterpretation. It can be a moment where something you have taken for granted is transformed, to the point where you see things in a different way. It is a form of storytelling. In the right hands, a cover version can articulate the need for change in society, by presenting often difficult conversations around race and identity. As examples of adaptability and new possibilities, they are effective expressions of hope. Tennant and Lowe are masters of the cover version.

    Pet Shop Boys have been a presence in my life since my teens, but I did not properly understand them until I saw them live at the Royal Opera House in 2018. (It is no coincidence that opera is the original western total artwork.) To say that it was a revelation is an understatement. Initially, I could not work out what was happening to me. Then I realized that I was having an experience similar to that of being in a retrospective exhibition of a great visual artist, where their career reveals itself as you walk from room to room, and afterwards the world seems a different place. The effect was what I would call euphoric melancholy. By the end of that night, I had a better understanding of them and of myself.

    We look to artists for many things. One is that they tell us that it is OK to be who you are, to be different, that you are not alone. From the beginning, Pet Shop Boys did that by speaking directly to individual after individual, making that loneliest of decades bearable for many. No matter where you have come from, no matter to whom you are attracted, you can find and lose yourself in their world. They are a broad church.

    When we talk about music, we are actually talking about ourselves. Popular music allows us to enjoy an ideal of friendship, love, and shared experience outside of sport. Pet Shop Boys have created a place where all of us can feel at home. And for that I say thank you.

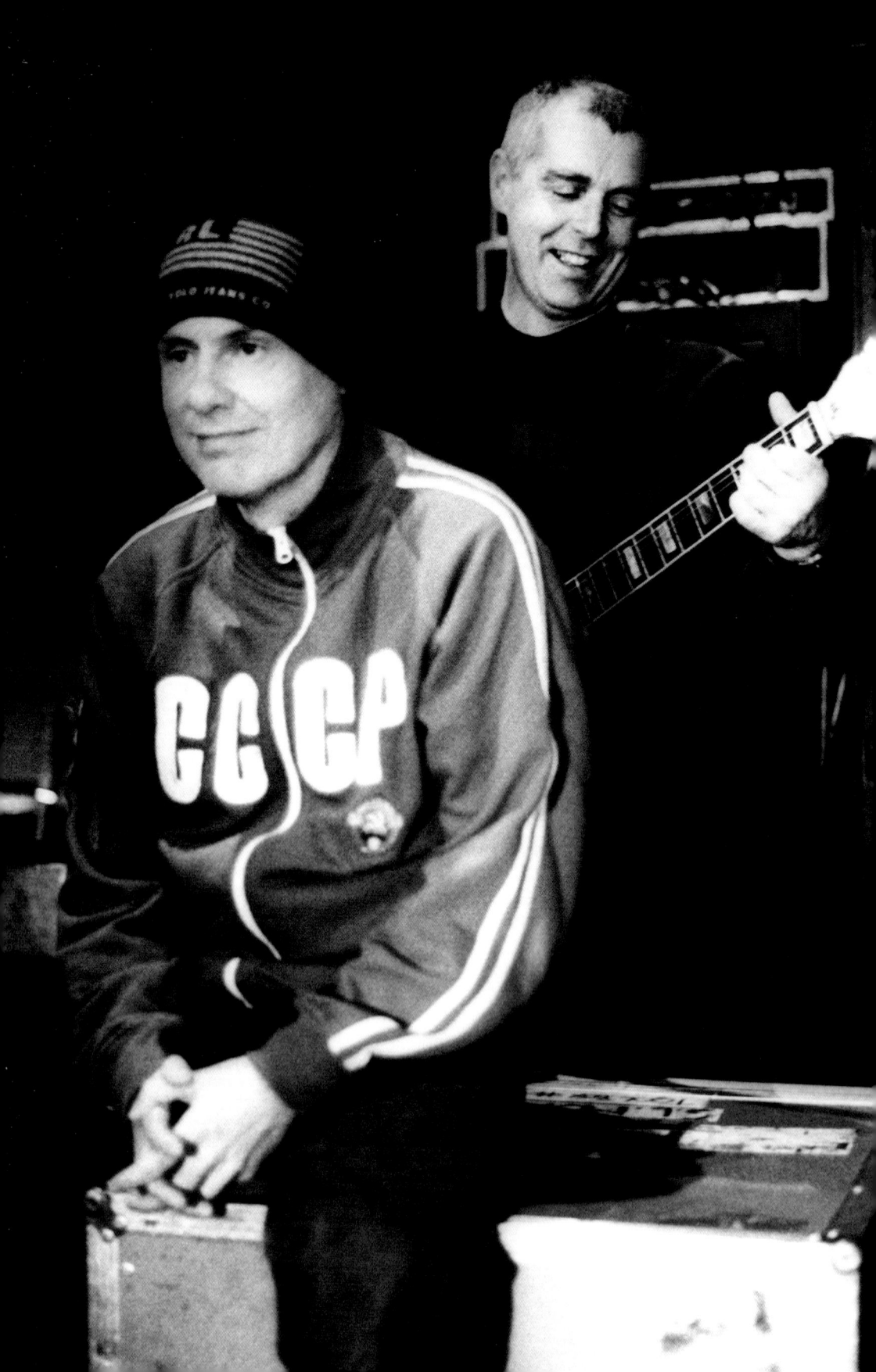

Pet Shop Boys, practice
Philip Hoare

'It's all a question of masks, really: brittle, painted masks.
We all wear them as a form of protection; modern life forces us to.'
Noël Coward, *Design for Living*, 1933

'Are Pet Shop Boys art or are they, in fact, dead arty?' Michael Bracewell and Jon Wilde asked in *Blitz* magazine in 1991. Such questions surround the group, and have done since their inception. 'My opinion is that you shouldn't think about it', Tennant told them, all but waving a schoolmasterly finger. '"Arty", to me, means imitation of the style of an artist. I don't think we are about imitation. I just think there's a fundamental problem with pop music thinking of itself as art. This idea seems to ruin it.... There's a different intellectual motive going on. Pop music is presented largely as being about style. Essentially, the style of thinking about yourself as an artist. When pop music gets weighed down with a load of theories which art seems to have written into it, it seems to destroy what it is that makes pop music.'

As with everything in life and art, that which you observe, you destroy. And yet, in that same interview, Tennant went on to put the group into a literary and cultural context. 'I see us in the tradition of Joe Orton and Noël Coward in that we are serious, comic, light-hearted, sentimental and brittle, all at the same time.... We are of the middle class and, at the same time, we attack that kind of life. Just as we are of pop music and we attack it at the same time. Also, we do it with wit, humour and our very own individual style. There's a mocking edge to our music. We're mocking ourselves, as well as just about everybody else.'

That sense of self-awareness has defined the way Pet Shop Boys have been perceived throughout their career. In the two-dimensional world of pop music, Pet Shop Boys occupy a subversive new zone of their own; both part of that world, and apart from it. Indeed, the cyberworld of the twenty-first century, which to some extent they anticipated in their video and sleeve imagery of the 1990s, eminently suits the ambivalence with which they still approach the business of being Pet Shop Boys. Gradually, their public image morphed from 'real' group members to fantastical marionettes, like some modern-day *commedia dell'arte* figures. As pop artists, Tennant and Lowe have often proposed the notion that they step back from public performance and appearance, to be replaced by increasing technological simulacra; the idea being to retreat into a kind of remote-control creation – as proposed, and indeed carried out, by Kraftwerk in their use of stage robots, or in Damon Albarn's cartoon Gorillaz project.

And yet the essential paradox – the abiding paradox of being Pet Shop Boys – is that, for all the artificiality of pop, and of the images they choose to project, they do not effect this retreat. The interface between them and their audience – visually represented by the work in this book – remains intact. Far from retreating from public view, the group remains resolutely in the public eye, engaged in public and cultural discourse. It is why, for instance, their court case against Roger Scruton in 1999 represented a key moment in the public assertion of their art and its *authenticity*. Scruton raised a doubt as to whether

Pet Shop Boys 'made more than a minimal contribution' to the making of their records. The argument touched on a crucial point: Pet Shop Boys' emotional investment as artists; what we think of them, what they think of us. It is a matter of context, and it is a surprisingly emotional one – considering the ironic personae imposed upon them by their critics and would-be detractors.

Much of this paradox is implicit in the public characters of Tennant and Lowe themselves. Critics would like to see them as caricatures of themselves, puppets created by some omnipotent *eminence grise* to dangle from a Svengali's strings – a prejudice that has its roots in the group's provenance. In part this is because Pet Shop Boys emerged from the media and the mediated arts. The pre-life of the group – a journalist and an architecture student – represented an immediate bone of contention with respect to their presumptuous ambition to make great pop records. It is difficult to imagine a scenario more calculated to arouse suspicion, and envy, in their peers. Indeed, it is this origin that gives the group its bite; its sense of determined cussedness, as embodied by that wagging finger, by those fists dug in the pockets of a pair of jeans. It is an essentially Northern attitude – hence, perhaps, the early description of the group as 'The Smiths you can dance to'.

Given the contrast between their private lives and their public incarnation, Pet Shop Boys were, and are, suspected of arch artistic and perhaps commercial control. It is this situation that wrapped early Pet Shop Boys in accusations of distance – if not diffidence – and to some extent still does. It was assumed that theirs were formulated gestures in a medium supposed to be known for its emotional and impulsive expression; just as they would be perpetually suspected of adopting an ironic stance: 'A lot of what we do is very literal', as Tennant comments now – so literal that it is presumed it must be ironic. Yet to accuse the group of artificiality (a suspicion further underlined by their use of electronic – therefore 'tricksy' – instruments) is to deny the constructed nature of pop itself, and especially the lineage of art and glamour that reaches back through Roxy Music and David Bowie to Andy Warhol and Richard Hamilton – what musician and surrealist George Melly, perhaps the first serious analyst of post-war pop culture, called in his 1970 book a 'revolt into style'.

Pet Shop Boys' aesthetic has its roots in the early Eighties. In a post-punk period, the notion of DIY had been refined and glamorized by the New Romantic movement and the explosion of high-quality British pop that followed. Bands such as Culture Club, ABC, Human League, Spandau Ballet, and Duran Duran projected a highly stylized sense of glamour, founded in street fashion but with an added gloss. These were pop cultural currents of which Tennant in particular was a part, through his editorial involvement on *Smash Hits* magazine at a time when pop had become both grown up (as the punk generation aged) and yet more escapist in a decade dedicated to consumerism. This was the heady legacy that Pet Shop Boys inherited.

It would have been unconscionable, in 1983, to create a pop group and not have an image that could mediate your message – if you had a message, that is; and clearly Pet Shop Boys did. Taking elements of English post-punk and *i-D* street fashion and melding them with the New York style that the pair had picked up during their initial work with disco record producer Bobby 'O', the look of Pet Shop Boys evolved in a manner quite as determined as that of the groups whom they would soon be regarding as their peers. Yet, crucially, the group was purposefully conceived as a 'self-conscious reaction to those groups', as Tennant says. 'They were about a dialectic between punk and show business.

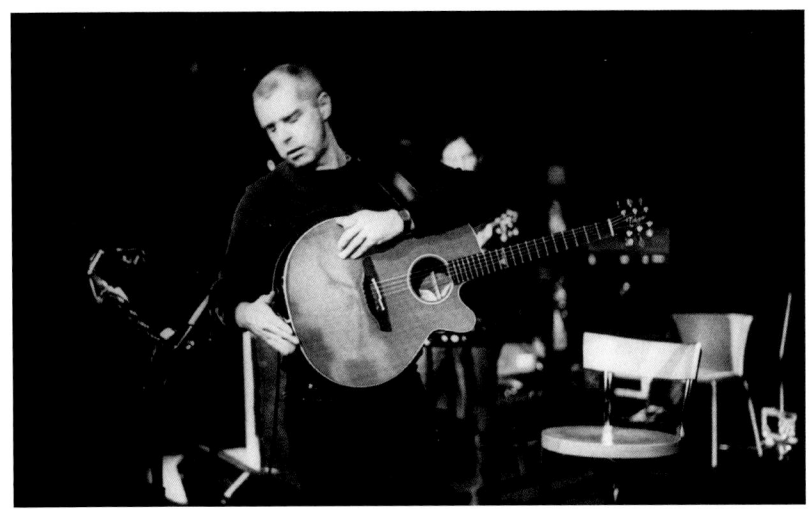

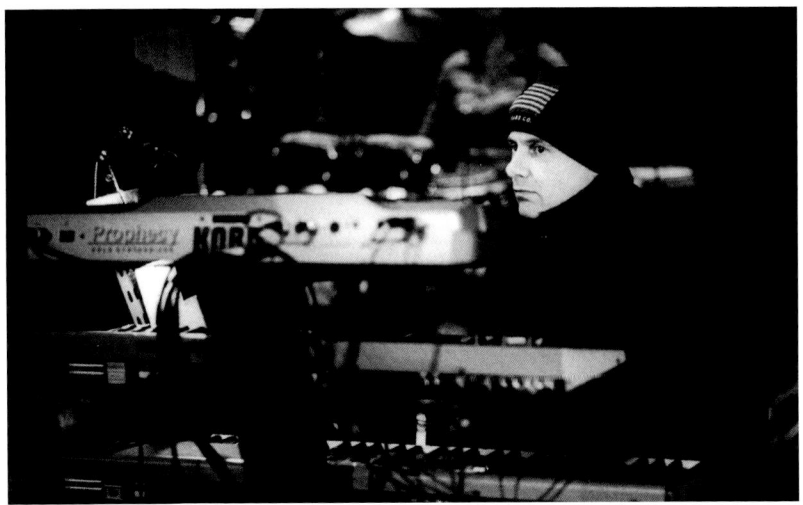

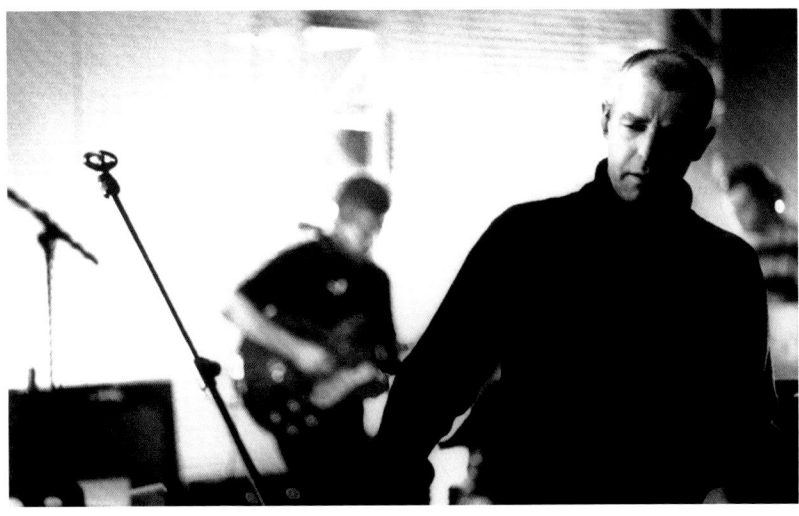

Pet Shop Boys, practice

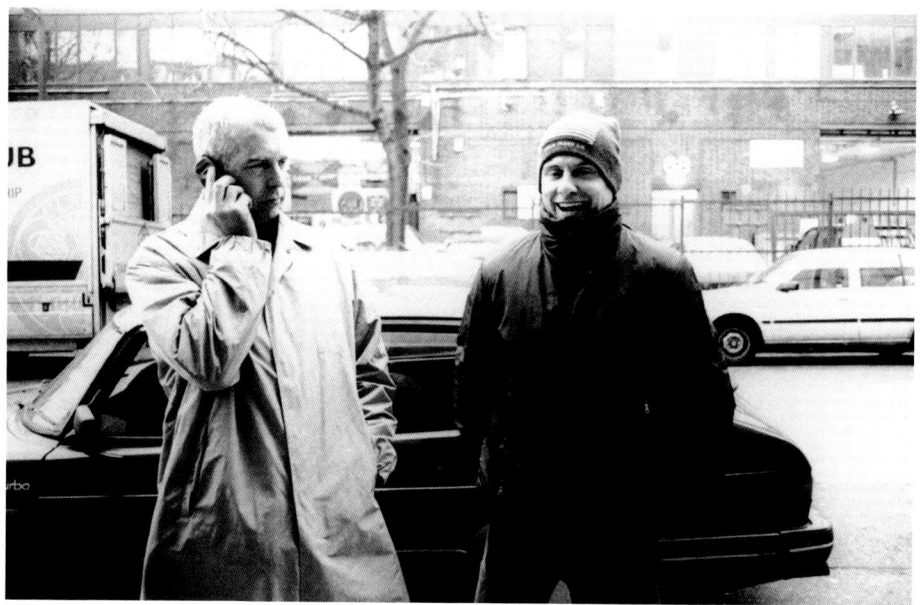

Pet Shop Boys took out that kind of fake showbiz quality. We were just being us – we were reacting against that fake rock notion of "life's a party".'

With this intent, Pet Shop Boys invested the process of pop with a sense of self-awareness, defiance, and intellect that drew upon their own experience – specifically Tennant's involvement in pop publishing and Lowe's training both as a student of architecture and as a musician, as well as his love of dance music: 'Che Guevara and Debussy to a disco beat', as Tennant would sing in 'Left to my own devices' in 1988. Capitalizing on these experiences – transmuting them, too – they benefited from, and reacted to, the precise moment of their emergence on the scene: heirs of punk, disco, glam, and, now, a burgeoning new golden era of British pop.

They achieved this through the now familiar but then still new media mix of photography, design, typography, fashion, and video. Using these powerful tools of pop propaganda, the artists of the early Eighties followed the punk ethic of taking control. Indeed, that sense of hypercontrol is refined and almost defined by the Pet Shop Boys' method. Specifically they were working in the period when Paul Morley – another journalist-turned-pop artist – was directing the highly influential output of the ZTT record label founded by producer Trevor Horn. It was a connection underlined by the fact that the early Pet Shop Boys releases were designed by XL Design, who had worked on the Frankie Goes To Hollywood sleeves for ZTT.

As influential were the groundbreaking designs of Factory Records, overseen by the Mancunian impresario and TV journalist Tony Wilson, and created by Peter Saville. Again, it is no coincidence that another Mancunian, Mark Farrow, started out designing covers for Factory Records, before joining XL and becoming the designer who almost single-handedly created the graphic identity of Pet Shop Boys. Also critical in the artistic development of the group was their new manager, as Kimberley Leston of *The Face* reported in that magazine's first full-length article on Pet Shop Boys, in February 1986: 'The time seemed appropriate to acquire a manager and Tom Watkins ... was drafted in. By now his company XL had been responsible for designing the Frankie Goes To Hollywood package, the interiors of Trevor Horn's two studios and the fittings in Terminal Two at Heathrow Airport. "We needed someone with a big mouth."'

But to others, it was clear that there were other, potent influences on the group, in the arena of contemporary art. 'It's tempting to imagine that Chris and Neil actually sat down and designed the Pet Shop Boys – rather like Gilbert and George, the artists, created Gilbert and George – as an efficient piece of pop art', Michael Bracewell wrote in 1995. 'We quite liked the fact that we were compared to Gilbert and George', Tennant says now. 'That sense that when you put two people together and make one thing of them, they become a kind of trademark.' To Bracewell, as to others, the notion of Pet Shop Boys as performance owed something to the practice of Gilbert and George. And just as those two now middle-aged men from Spitalfields are, separately, the very picture of an ordinary, bourgeois sensibility in their three-button suits (exuding the same middle-classness of which Neil speaks), but together present an altogether odder aspect, so the twinning of Pet Shop Boys represents an image that is more than the sum of its parts. There are many precedents for such cultural duos – from Castor and Pollux to Ron and Russell Mael of Sparks, via Morecambe and Wise. But the bottom line for Pet Shop Boys is the position of creative strength. Together, they present a united front, an intransigent attitude – some might call it truculence – which in other artists of their status would be the mark of a prima donna, but in their case is the pursuit of perfection.

In 1993, the writer and friend of the group Dave Rimmer noted in the *Guardian* that, 'Everything one now thinks of as the Pet Shop Boys – silent Chris walking two steps behind singing Neil, and so on – stems from discussions the group had with photographer / videomaker Eric Watson at the very beginning of their career.' As is evident from this book, it is Watson's work that created and reflected that powerful visual tension. On one hand, we have the socially deft figure of Neil, moving easily through the world; and on the other, the faintly disruptive figure of Chris, perpetually at odds with it.

Appearance in pop is all. And so we have the early Pet Shop Boys in casual clothes, lounging like Wham! on the cover of 'One more chance', or posing as if for a *Face* fashion spread for the first release of 'Opportunities'. Already the dynamic is established: Neil in a suit, Chris in a hat. And that, essentially, is the way it stayed – from the almost aggressive denial of folded arms and blanked-out eyes of 'Suburbia' to the lush, psychosexual extravaganza of 'It's a sin' and the tour that followed it (and the Catholicism that seeded it), when Pet Shop Boys worked with their first fine artist, Derek Jarman, a collaboration that teased out the latent hedonism in the group, as if it had been bursting to get out all along. In many ways, working with Jarman on stage liberated Pet Shop Boys from the graphic two dimensions of product presented by a record company for public consumption and enabled them to become something much more interesting.

That aesthetic overload – transcending any notion of being merely a pop group – reached its glorious crescendo in 1991 with the *Performance* tour, whose title called to mind Nicolas Roeg's 1971 film of the same name starring Mick Jagger and Edward Fox, a fevered depiction of early Seventies decadence. Though the connection is unintentional, the *Performance* concert reflects Roeg's film in another way too. Both evoke Tennant's own theory of the pop dynamic, as expressed in his foreword to the catalogue of the exhibition *Icons of Pop* at London's National Portrait Gallery in 1999: 'The thrill of emergence, the quasi-royal ubiquitousness of established fame, the imperial phase of world domination, the disciplined strategies of survival.'

Reflecting that narrative and the notion of performance itself, the tour combined music, art, design, and performance in a manner to which only opera could do justice – and so the group collaborated with the direction and designs, respectively, of the English National Opera's David Alden and David Fielding. As I followed its progress from the dress rehearsal at Brixton Academy to New York's Radio City Music Hall, Prague, Blackpool, and back to London, it seemed to me that *Performance* presented an invented Pet Shop Boys world, from wanking schoolboys to surfing Edwardians: a synoptic, political, yet purely personal voyage into their collective imaginations. It was as though Fielding and Alden had somehow tapped into the creative circuits of Tennant's and Lowe's brains, and magically transformed them into phantasmagoric theatre.

The consequences of what was perhaps the most satisfying spectacle in modern pop music are still being felt, not least by the group themselves. Their graphic, cartoon-like personae of the early Nineties – the pointy hats and the astronautical jumpsuits designed by Fielding – were an artful riposte to the 'reality' adopted elsewhere, especially in the grunge rock of Nirvana and the 'latent hippieness' of the late rave scene. Later, on the release of their 1996 album *Bilingual*, with its defiantly European aesthetic, Tennant would note that one reason 'for doing the album like this was as a reaction against Britpop. We like being part of Europe; we are a very international group and we like that fact.' Equally, their love of the glamorous and the international resulted in another collaboration, this time with American photographer Bruce Weber, who has shot three videos for Pet Shop Boys. The result exemplifies the transatlantic tension that the group had represented since their early days (and which would elsewhere emerge, graphically, in their cover version of, and video for, the Village People's 'Go west').

It was, perhaps, preordained that the group's aesthetic concerns – as expressed in the increasingly minimal yet lavish graphics of Mark Farrow and his associates – would find fellow feeling in the new young British art scene of the period. That empathy was directly reflected in the staging of their 1997 *Somewhere* residency in the silver art-deco proscenium arch of the Savoy Theatre, to a backdrop of interactive films made by the young British artist Sam Taylor-Wood. But the staging was also another framing device: historical and contemporary, an artistic presentation wholly self-knowing and self-referential and yet entirely emotional; the distance between the artifice they adopted and the exquisite happy-sadness of their songs. The warmth that greeted Neil and Chris as they stepped out of the screens and onto the stage was tangible in the intimate auditorium.

If it seemed that the group could not surpass the rich visual impact of the *Performance* tour, they would, as ever, defy expectations. In 1999, directed by the talented new theatre designer Ian MacNeil, the group appeared in the extraordinary guise of the boot-boy samurai costumes of the *Nightlife* album: the shock-headed wigs, skirt-like culottes, Kabuki-style make-up whose unsettling yet historical and cultural references were thrown into even sharper contrast by the group's latest artistic collaboration, with the architect Zaha Hadid. The set that she designed for that tour created an angular yet otherworldly platform for performance: part architectural utopia/dystopia, part futuristic repertory theatre.

To an extent, these different incarnations are disguises to deal with fame. 'I've always wanted to do no promotion at all – to do nothing, really', Chris said in 1998. 'The more we've gone on, the more I've covered up my face; I'm shocked, now, when

I see a picture of myself without my glasses on or the hat. I mean, I wouldn't dream of going to a photo session now without a hat or glasses.' Conversely, Neil assumes a more open persona, elegantly fielding enquiries with the air of a modern Wilde, moving through his chosen society like an ambassador for the subversive project upon which he and Lowe are embarked. Yet even then it's difficult to know the truth of what they portray. As Coward wrote, 'It's all a question of masks, really: brittle, painted masks. We all wear them as a form of protection; modern life forces us to.'

Those masks seemed to fall away in the stripped-down *University* and *Release* tours of 2002. Interestingly, these appearances were themselves a throwback to the group's very first reviewed appearance – not in a rock venue, but in an art gallery. 'It was quite interesting because Pet Shop Boys have never presented themselves as being musicians before on stage, with the exception of when we played at the ICA in 1984', Tennant remarked during the *Release* tour. 'We've always presented ourselves within a visual context on stage, which has been what we've become well known for, and all of a sudden we thought it would be quite interesting to present ourselves as musicians.' And as Tennant says now, 'our masks are in fact reality; the mask is our real face'. Yet even in that minimal but cabaret-style presentation, which reconfigured their back catalogue in a new rock aesthetic – an almost Stalinist reinvention of their own past – it was evident that the group remained determined to confound expectation. It was as if, after all these years, they were still provoking as many questions as they answer; that which keeps them together sets them apart. And it is that ongoing dialogue – with themselves, and with the rest of us – that drives the art of Pet Shop Boys.

This text was originally published in *Pet Shop Boys Catalogue* (2006). The photographs were taken by Pennie Smith during rehearsals for Pet Shop Boys' *University* tour in 2002.

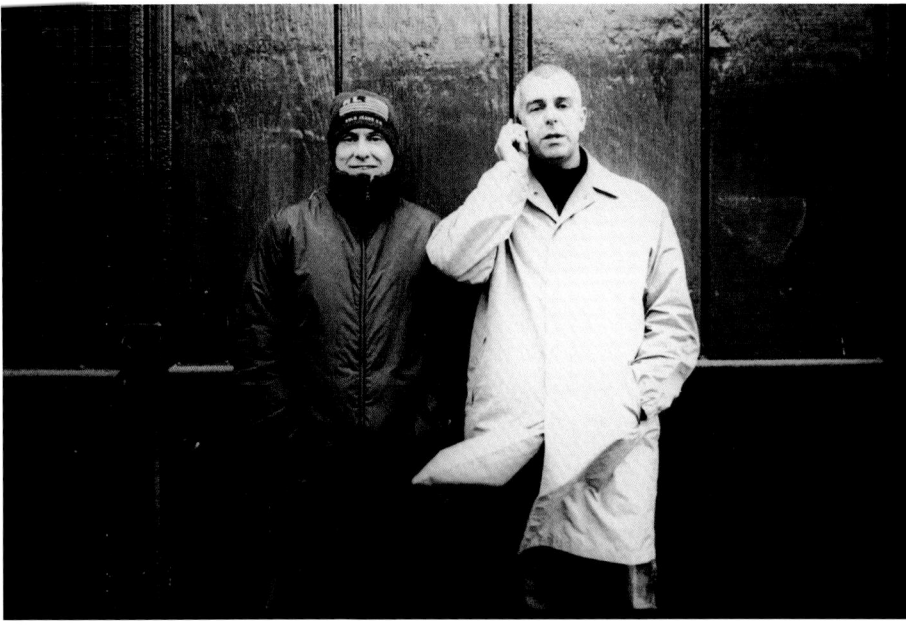

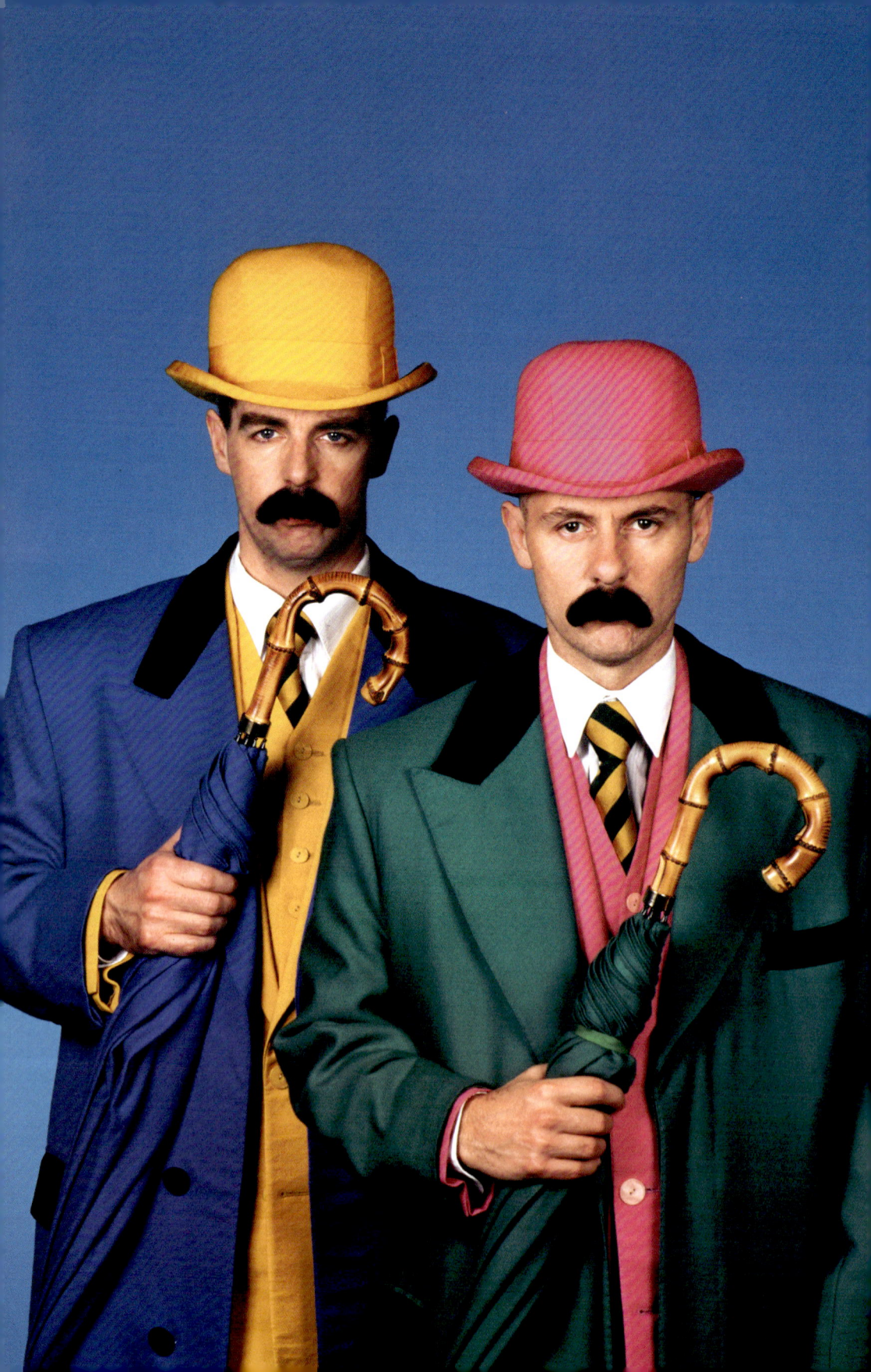

Pet Shop Boys, design
Libby Sellers

Much is made of the 'happenstance' and 'serendipity' of that moment in 1981 when Neil Tennant first met Chris Lowe in a King's Road hi-fi shop. As the story goes, the two fell into chance conversation while Tennant waited for a jack plug to be welded for his Korg synthesizer. A friendship formed over their shared musical passions and the rest, as they themselves say, is 'Pet Shop Boys history'.

Was their meeting really accidental though? As The Beatles prophesized in 1967, 'There's nowhere you can be that isn't where you're meant to be.' And if not by chance, then what of that destination on London's King's Road? Kismet? Cause and effect? An appropriately post-punk example of situational determinism? After all, the shop's fusion of music, technology, and design was the perfect inception point for a partnership celebrated for its fusion of music, technology, and design.

With the scent of sintered metal lingering in the air, that 1981 encounter – both its form and its function – is redolent of the DIY spirit and creative ingenuity that permeated the era. In 1977, the zine *Sideburn* had advised its readers: 'This is a chord. This is another. This is a third. Now form a band.' With a few simple strokes, an entire generation was awakened to the commercial opportunities afforded by restraint. It is an ethos that Tennant holds close: 'Punk was essentially about meaning over form, ability and technique…. There's a wonderful economy to it.' And while parsimony can be liberating, it has its logical limitations. As Tennant continued: 'When you took that punk ideology and applied it without any fear of market or of fashion … that's where interesting things happen, and that's where the Pet Shop Boys come from.' They were not alone on the journey. In 1981, that same significant year, similarly emboldened provocations were infiltrating all creative spheres, which, in turn, both effected and reflected transformations in ours.

A few miles away in London's Covent Garden, architect Ron Arad was launching 'One Off' – a commercial workshop for designs by an anarchic cohort including himself, Tom Dixon, Nick Jones, and Mark Brazier-Jones. Against the dual backdrops of a fiercely guarded furniture industry and Britain's all-pervading social, economic, and political destabilization, they forged entire careers from scavenged remains. With little more than youthful intuition and a spot welder between them, they alchemically transmuted pilfered coal-hole covers, reclaimed cast-iron railings, and abandoned car seats into highly sculptural, and now highly collectible, furniture.

Nearby at *The Face*, art director Neville Brody was readying to launch a new graphic style onto the magazine's nascent readership. His self-produced typefaces and confrontational page layouts reinterpreted Soviet-era, constructivist agitprop for

Pet Shop Boys in their colourful 'Thompson Twins' outfits from the 1991 *Performance* tour (photo: Derek Ridgers)

a new generation. In Paris, by way of Tokyo, Comme des Garçons and Yohji Yamamoto were stirring cultural insurrections of their own, though this time against the prevailing trends for overtly gendered and sexualized fashion. With their respective 1981 debuts came cerebral, dark, and androgynous fashion collections that liberated through refusal and rebellion. While in New York, still the same year, Keith Haring's graffitied doodles were crawling their way up from the city's subways and onto the white galleried walls of Tribeca.

The desire to deconstruct, to strip everything back to a few chords, some welded scrap metal, or a bolt of distressed fabric was a deliberate reaction against the hyper-saturated and ornamental excesses of their time. Framed within these chronicles, certain early Pet Shop Boys' traits are instantly recognizable: the juxtaposition of shiny pop and urban decay in photographer/videographer Eric Watson's imagery, the masterful austerity of their first *Top of the Pops* performances, and the elegantly detached, minimalist aesthetic of Pet Shop Boys' record sleeves, designed by Mark Farrow, first at XL Design and 3, then at Farrow Design, and now at Farrow.

Attaching an image to a piece of music is an obvious though relatively modern idea, dating from the late 1930s, when Columbia Records in New York hired commercial artist Alex Steinweiss as its first art director. His innovation – swapping industry-standard, plain paper wrappers for elaborately illustrated sleeves – saw a near 900% sales increase over those for the same record in basic packaging. Steinweiss's preference for taking direct inspiration from the music itself pioneered cover art as an expression of creative intent, and prototyped the modern album sleeve as we know it today.

There have been several exceptional musician-designer partnerships (including Pink Floyd and Hipgnosis, Grace Jones and Jean-Paul Goude, Joy Division/New Order and Peter Saville), yet few capture the music through the sleeve design as consistently as do Pet Shop Boys and Farrow. Testament to their close creative alliance is an ability to distil the tone or narrative of a song or album into one artwork, and to do so with such integrity that it remains in our memory as the abiding image of that project. It is there in that self-conscious yawn and arch comma of *Actually* (1987; pages 90–1), *Very*'s sophisticated masterclass in collaborative reinvention (1993; pages 184–7), the perfumed, bucolic idyll of 'Miracles' (2003; pages 302–3), the brooding darkness of *Fundamental* (2006; pages 324–7), the blue, blue, euphoric blue of *Electric* (2013; pages 414–17) … all the way through to the complete reset offered by 2024's *Nonetheless* (pages 514–19), which reads like a purposeful mirroring of their mid-Eighties aesthetic.

'History', as Mark Twain concluded, 'does not repeat itself, but it often rhymes.' On the artwork for *Nonetheless*, Tennant and Lowe's formal attire, photographer Tim Walker's framing devices, and Farrow's centralized serif type all coordinate to create a visual resonance with their previous covers. For a band not normally given to nostalgia, these quotations from an earlier era are noteworthy. Certainly, a modernist linear trajectory, devoid of any historical referencing, was never their intention. Yet this time the visual references are drawn from their own remarkable past. Perhaps, as Lowe has said, 'It's like going round a roundabout and taking different exits.' Any new exit cannot fail to be informed by those that came before.

In his introduction to the 2006 book *Pet Shop Boys Catalogue*, reproduced here, Philip Hoare establishes this trajectory of about-turns and exits. His juxtapositions of their real/unreal and masked/unmasked personae highlight a particularly postmodern embrace of the 'and/or' – an invitation to pivot, revisit, retreat, and reinvent as desired; and often to do so all at the same time. That this trajectory continues only confirms

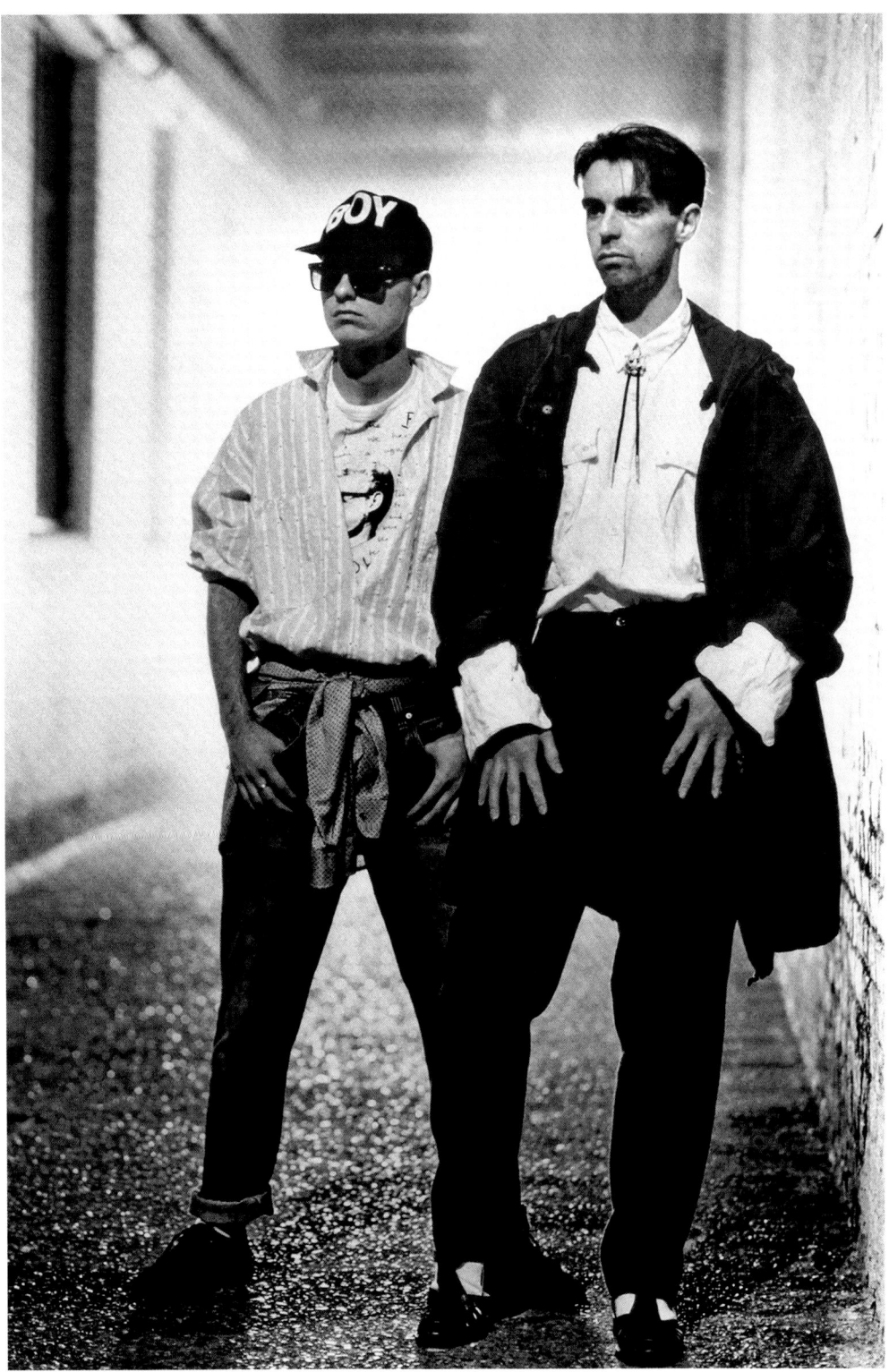
A photograph by Eric Watson from October 1984, used for the sleeve of 'West End girls' the following year

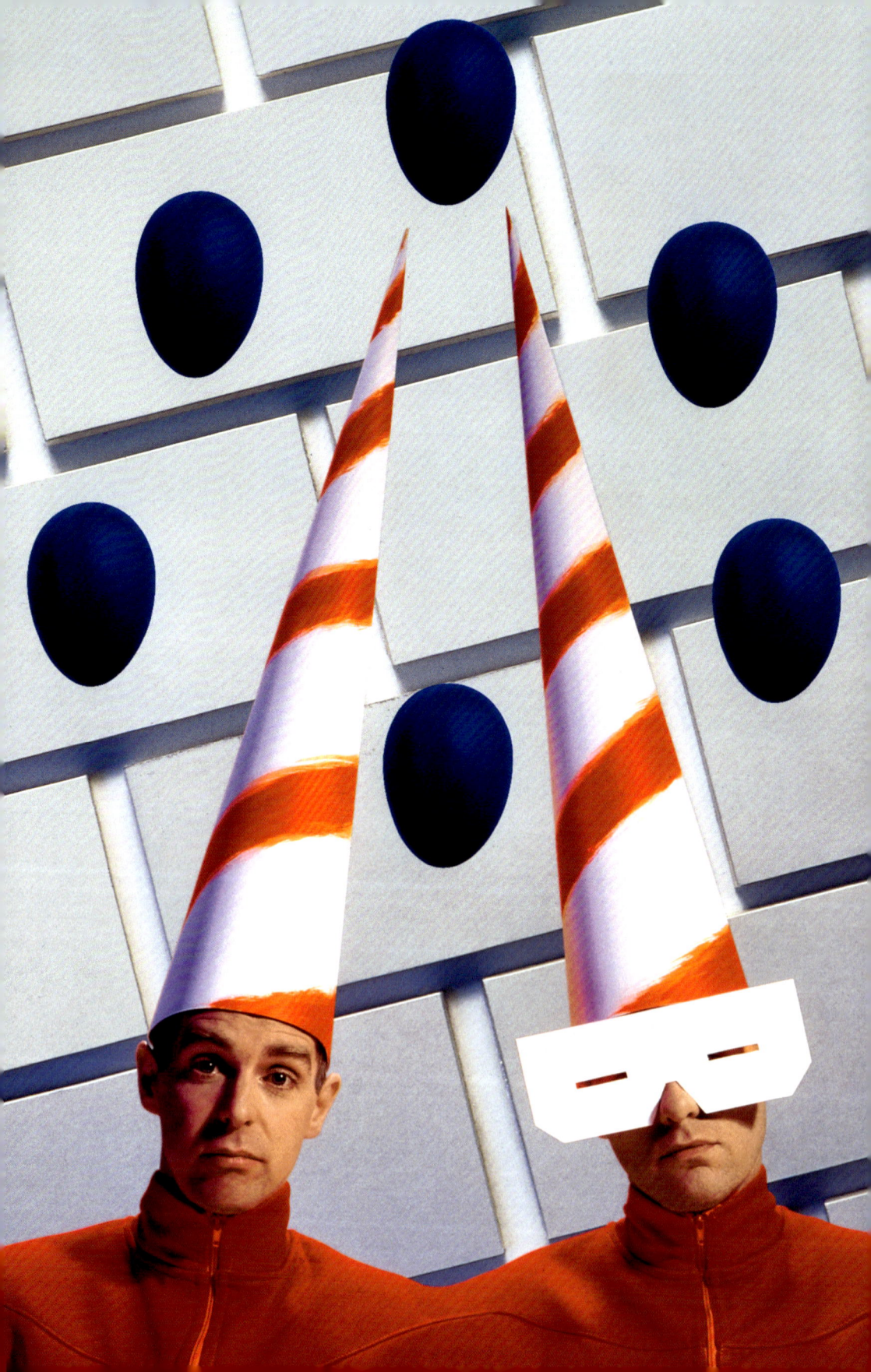

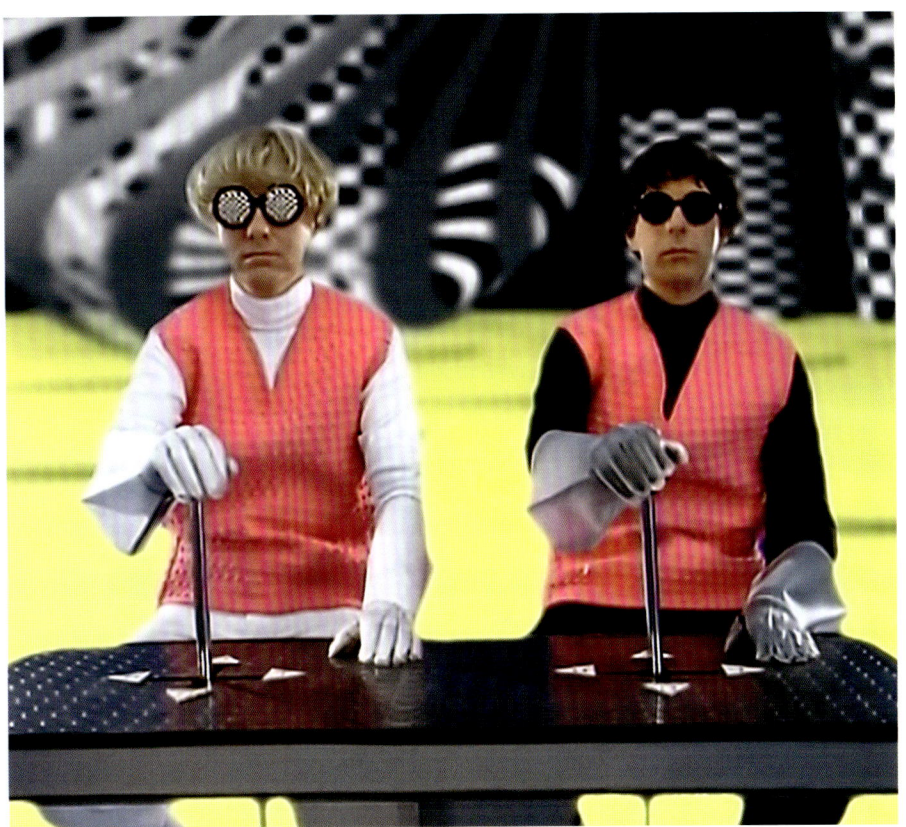

above A still from Howard Greenhalgh's video for 'I wouldn't normally do this kind of thing' from 1993, part of the *Very*-era reinvention of Pet Shop Boys' look

opposite Chris Nash's promotional photographs of Pet Shop Boys in their celebrated pointy hats for the 1993 release of 'Can you forgive her?', which heralded the dramatic change in the group's aesthetic

Tennant's conviction when, in conversation with the duo's biographer Chris Heath, he said: 'To stop creating the world would be to start doing something utterly ordinary. It's a life less ordinary we're trying to create.' When asked to describe that world, Tennant simply points to a copy of *Catalogue* – the visual representation of the years 1984 to 2004 – which this publication, *Volume*, incorporates and from which it progresses.

While the pair's core creativity has carried on uninterrupted, the materiality of their music, the way we consume it, has undergone numerous design pivots of its own ever since. The release of *Yes* in 2009 coincided with a revival of vinyl prompted by the retro-curious and sustained by diehard collectors. Like the vinyl expansion of the Eighties when the opportunities to 'rejig the format' were countless, what was perceived as 'simple marketing' by the record companies was for Pet Shop Boys 'an excuse to keep creating, to do new things'. Inspired by German artist Gerhard Richter's *4900 Colours*, the coloured blocks of the album's titular affirmative tick went through a detailed construction process, before being broken down again and dispersed across an ambitious series of iterated assets (overleaf and pages 358–63).

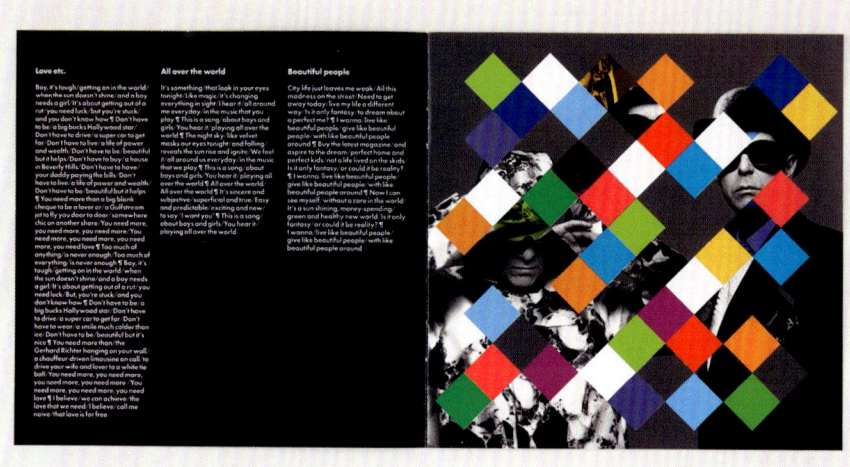

The coloured diamonds created by Farrow for the release of *Yes* in 2009 appeared across the album's various formats and associated singles, including inside the special-edition CD booklet.

For Farrow, the diamonds were an 'alphabet or visual language' that, like Richter's squares, achieved a 'sense of boundlessness' across the various formats: from the variations designed for different retailers, online platforms, and international markets, across the album's associated singles and remixes, through the *Pandemonium* tour programme and merchandise, even into the physical staging and costumes for the tour, as designed by Es Devlin and Jeffrey Bryant respectively. According to Tennant, *Yes* was 'pure design product'. When the special vinyl edition of the album, housed in a black perspex box, was nominated for the London Design Museum's annual awards, the physicality of music, its thingness, resumed its place in a broader cultural discussion.

That the discussion required resuming at all was indicative of a larger fissure in the century-old music industry, initiated by the challenges posed by new (and not always legal) modes of music distribution. By 2017, and within a decade of launching, the revenue earned by music streaming platforms such as Apple Music and Spotify overtook physical sales of CD and vinyl for the first time. With their infinite supply of music on digital demand, both our expectations and experiences of music were irrevocably transformed.

For all the criticisms levelled at streaming platforms – be they algorithmic or economic – they did not, as anticipated, eventuate in the death of vinyl. Conversely, they have been credited for the year-on-year increase in physical sales as fans pursue more from their music appreciation than intangible audio files could offer. Proof, if any is needed here, that our relationship with music often goes beyond the auditory. It also highlights an early oversight by streaming services. By prioritizing function over form,

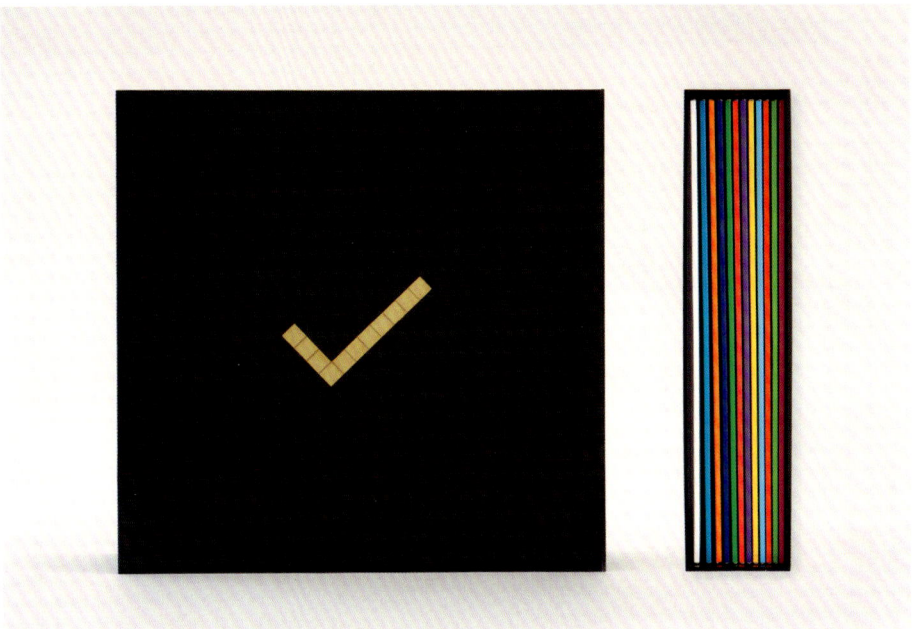

The transparent black perspex box of the eleven-disc special edition of *Yes*, produced with The Vinyl Factory in an edition of three hundred copies (pages 361–3)

they missed a significant trick to add value that played to their specific strengths. The next obvious step was to introduce compelling and interactive user experiences as appropriate for their digital world. We may never be able to carry these experiences out of a shop, or display them like a badge of loyalty, yet these new layers of digital design have the potential to complement (if not compete with) the physical.

When Spotify launched 'canvases' – mini video loops on the service's app – Pet Shop Boys were quick to respond. For the 2023 reissue of *Relentless*, they commissioned a series of canvases from video and projection designers Luke Halls Studio. Taking inspiration from the arcade and computer games that Lowe remembers fondly from his Blackpool youth, these looping videos relocate the *Very*-era Pet Shop Boys simulacra into Pac-Man's maze, parkouring across Super Mario Bros' skylines, and tumbling down Donkey Kong's ladders (pages 504–5). As Tennant sings in 'Left to my own devices', Che Guevara 'reads about a new device and takes to the stage in a secret life'. It was a classic Pet Shop Boys meta manoeuvre, a witty, tongue-in-cheek reappropriation of their own reinvented selves. And one received enthusiastically by both those for whom the visual clues were similarly evocative and those weaned on TikTok-style instant gratification.

There is a fleetness afforded by streaming that suits Pet Shop Boys' particular take on pop, holding it to higher standards through their merger of high-art ideals with everyday experiences. The pace with which they could release via YouTube the highly topical, Vladimir Putin-inspired 'Living in the past (home demo)' in 2023 (pages 494–5) was, in Tennant's words, 'the kind of immediate response vinyl would never allow'. And yet Pet Shop Boys have always employed video to visualize their interests, political or

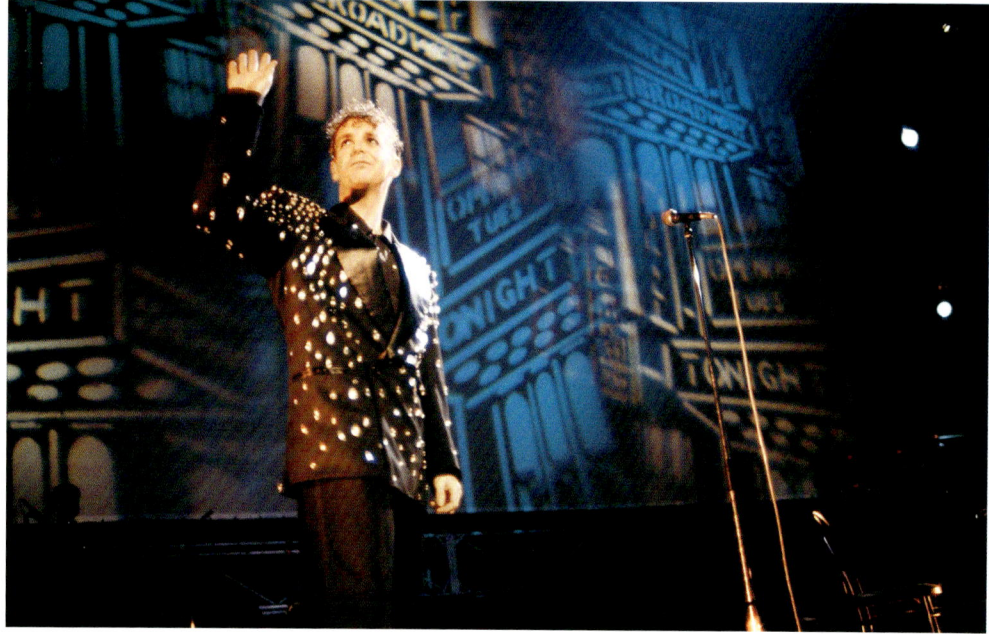

Neil Tennant in front of one of the video projections from the MCMLXXXIX tour of 1989

otherwise. From the 'teased out latent hedonism' that Philip Hoare identifies in their collaborations with Derek Jarman, through Bruce Weber's achingly beautiful celebrations of love, loss, and longing and Howard Greenhalgh's Dada-ist flights into computer-generated, otherworldly fantasy, to the Eadweard Muybridge-esque archival sampling in Luke Halls Studio's videos – all have visualized Pet Shop Boys' world as erudite, engaged, and, most crucially, theatrical.

Like live television performances on *The Ed Sullivan Show* or *Top of the Pops*, the emergence of music videos helped forge connections with fans, offering prime facetime with national and international audiences. As pop promos and the channels available for them matured throughout the Eighties, they altered the landscape of music, transforming the experience into a twenty-four-hour visual spectacle. More recently, the role of video has segued to merge the demands of live performance and pre-recorded visuals. As advanced digital technologies enable music venues to be completely wrapped in LED screens, bands have increasingly engaged video and projection design to augment and wrap their live performances. Syncopated with time-coded set lists, pyrotechnics, lighting, choreography, and costume changes, they provide a sequence of genuinely astonishing and immersive visual effects that elevate the gig experience into a total work of art. And while this brings a hitherto-unimagined degree of opulence and pageantry, the premise of projection as framing device is something Pet Shop Boys have pioneered since their first tour, *MCMLXXXIX* of 1989, colloquially entitled 'the Derek Jarman tour'.

On the topic of performance, Tennant maintains that, 'In British pop, people's style has always been created by their limitations. Ours is based on the limitation of us as performers. We had to build something around the two of us, something that

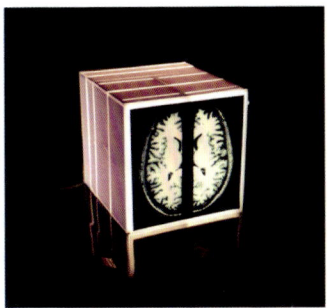 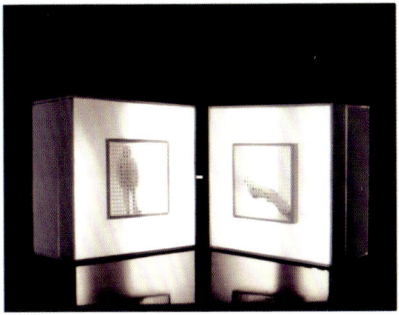

Two of designer Es Devlin's preparatory sketches for the staging of the *Fundamental* tour of 2006–7

makes us look interesting within it. And also, of course, to make the most of what talents we've got.' From Jarman's collaborations (pages 134–5) through to Tom Scutt's 2022 *Dreamworld* tour (pages 488–91), Pet Shop Boys have made a point of working with theatre directors and designers to build that something 'interesting' around them. Correspondingly, their live shows are conceived in the theatrical convention of clearly defined acts, underlining a preference for music as dramatic narrative device (opposed to the autobiographical content that dominates so much of contemporary pop).

For long-term collaborator Es Devlin, each of her stage designs began with the set list, a pencil, and a blank piece of paper. Discussing her work with Pet Shop Boys in the 2024 BBC *Imagine* documentary 'Pet Shop Boys: Then and Now', she states, 'What I've found with Neil and Chris is everything has been proved already; the songs are already in the popular imagination. So, if we want to craft something, whether it succeeds or fails … the songs are there to support us in our continuing enquiries and curiosities.'

Her enquiries, like Farrow's graphics, have been consummate. Similar to reading the libretto of an opera, Devlin takes the concept behind the lyrics and music and visually modulates them to tell the story, enabling the audience to feel, breathe, and inhabit the narrative through her manipulation of space. For the *Fundamental* tour of 2006–7 (pages 328–31), she and a cast of creatives deployed an X-ray image of a divided brain to evoke both the relationship between Tennant and Lowe (their rational and emotional respective selves) and, conversely, the collective 'cognitive dissonance' of its era, remembered for an unjustifiable war, rising surveillance culture, and threat of authoritarian control. The brief for the *Electric* tour of 2013–15 (following pages and pages 402–5) was 'analogue chaos'. Devlin's response merged piercing lasers with

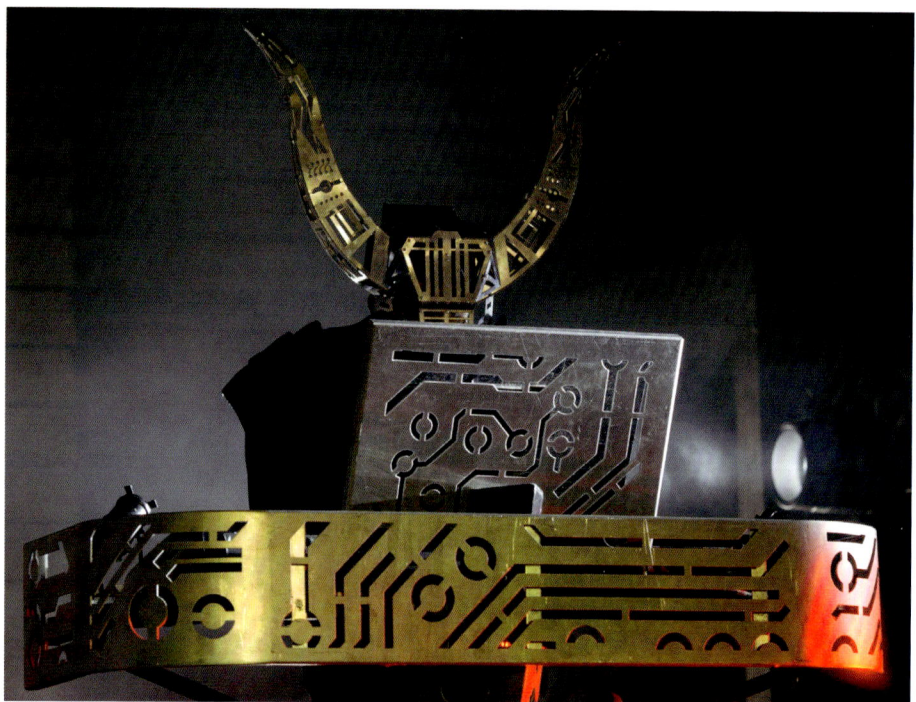

Chris Lowe at his 'circuit board' keyboard riser and wearing one of the Minotaur headpieces designed by Robert Allsopp for the *Electric* tour of 2013–15

Robert Allsopp-designed Minotaur headpieces and a series of digital mazes inspired by the printed circuit boards at 'the heart of the band's synthesizers'. The combined effect represented for Devlin the 'division between man and the machine', evoking both 'primal desire and constructed artifice', Sigmund Freud's 'id' meets William Gibson's *Neuromancer*.

The complexity of designing for varying scales of venue – from clubs, theatres, arenas, and festivals – has finely honed Pet Shop Boys' live productions over recent decades. Having long ago cast off unwieldy props and architecturally engineered metal structures (along with any insecurities of themselves as performers), the band launched the *Dreamworld* tour with seemingly little more than a pair of lamp posts, Lowe's keyboard riser, and an automated LED curtain wall. Within that sublimely minimalist set (designed by Scutt, with video content again by Luke Halls), a single visual, digital line was taken for a walk through the band's greatest hits – both musical and visual. Interspersed throughout was a procession of references to the many iconic costumes and characters that they have assumed over the years. From interpretations of their many sci-fi-inspired headgear from the 'Go west' period, the whirling dervishes from the *Discovery* tour, the mirrored costumes of the *Electric* tour, the Stephen Linard-designed coat worn by Tennant in their earliest videos, photo shoots, and television performances, through Lowe's BOY cap and streetwear obsession ... each a subtle nod to Pet Shop Boys' rich sartorial legacy and their frequent journeys into the bizarre. 'I admire the artifice of performance, the creation of a persona through costume', Tennant said in conversation with author Katie Baron. 'Extreme is part of our iconography.'

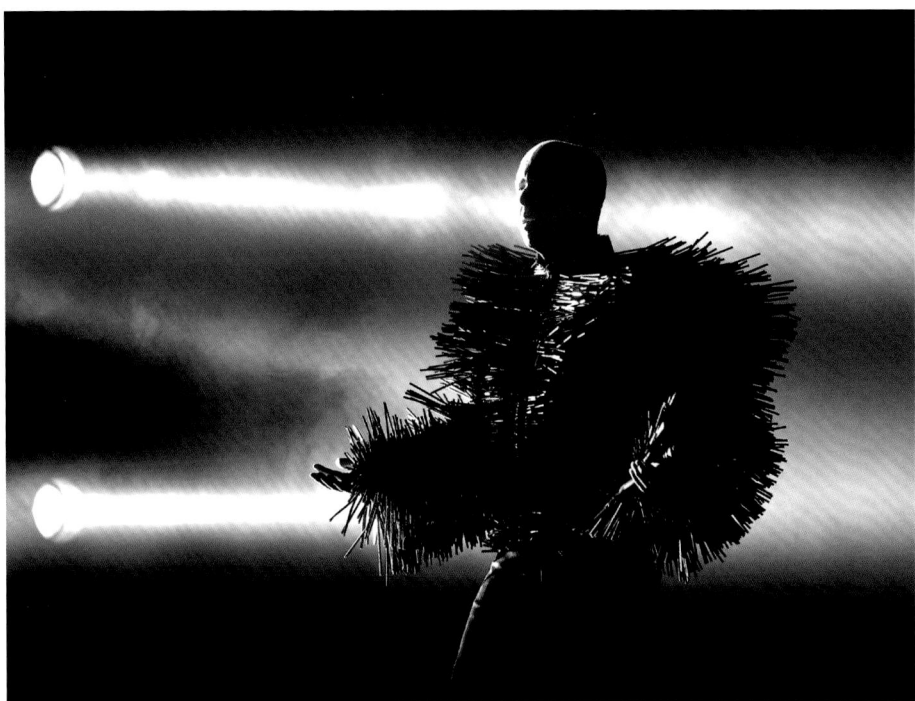

Neil Tennant in one of the 'drinking straw' jackets designed by Jeffrey Bryant for the *Electric* tour
overleaf Tom Scutt's *Dreamworld* tour set, with a pair of lamp posts in front of a large wall of video projections

The trail of visual clues offered by these costumes leads a direct path back to the subversive, post-punk spirit when characters like Leigh Bowery, Princess Julia, and Trojan were crafting outrageous personages from scavenged materials and pound-shop finds for club nights at London's Taboo and Kinky Gerlinky. Extreme was the strict dress code of every given night. 'Would you let you in?', asks Princess Julia on the Superchumbo remix of the Pet Shop Boys' 2024 song 'Party in the Blitz'.

An exuberant and constant fixture of that underground scene, Jeffrey Bryant literally cut his cloth transforming bedsheets, breakfast cereal boxes, and detergent bottles into idiosyncratic and outré costumes for himself and his tribe of nocturnal allies. The city's clubs and parties were his apprentice's workshop, helping to hone his sense of theatricality through creative salvage and a tailor's mastery of complex sculptural garments. Bryant's long-standing alliance with Pet Shop Boys has, according to Baron, 'given rise to a vast catalogue of experimental costuming bearing a sci-fi-like agelessness', including his inflatable Bowery-esque dayglo suits and full-face helmets made from mixing bowls for the *Super* tour of 2016–19 (pages 440–3), or the thousands of black drinking straws used to sculpt Tennant and Lowe's extraordinary *Electric* tour jackets. 'Ridicule', as Tennant fondly reminisces, 'is nothing to be scared of.'

And with that, we have all of a sudden returned to that 1981 moment, with the new bohemians, Blitz Kids, and a countercultural elite fuelling a defiant and DIY embrace of music, art, design, and performance. Five decades might feel a lifetime for some, though through a twist of fate, a carefully curated sense of self, and an absolute dedication to their art, Pet Shop Boys have made the leap seem timeless.

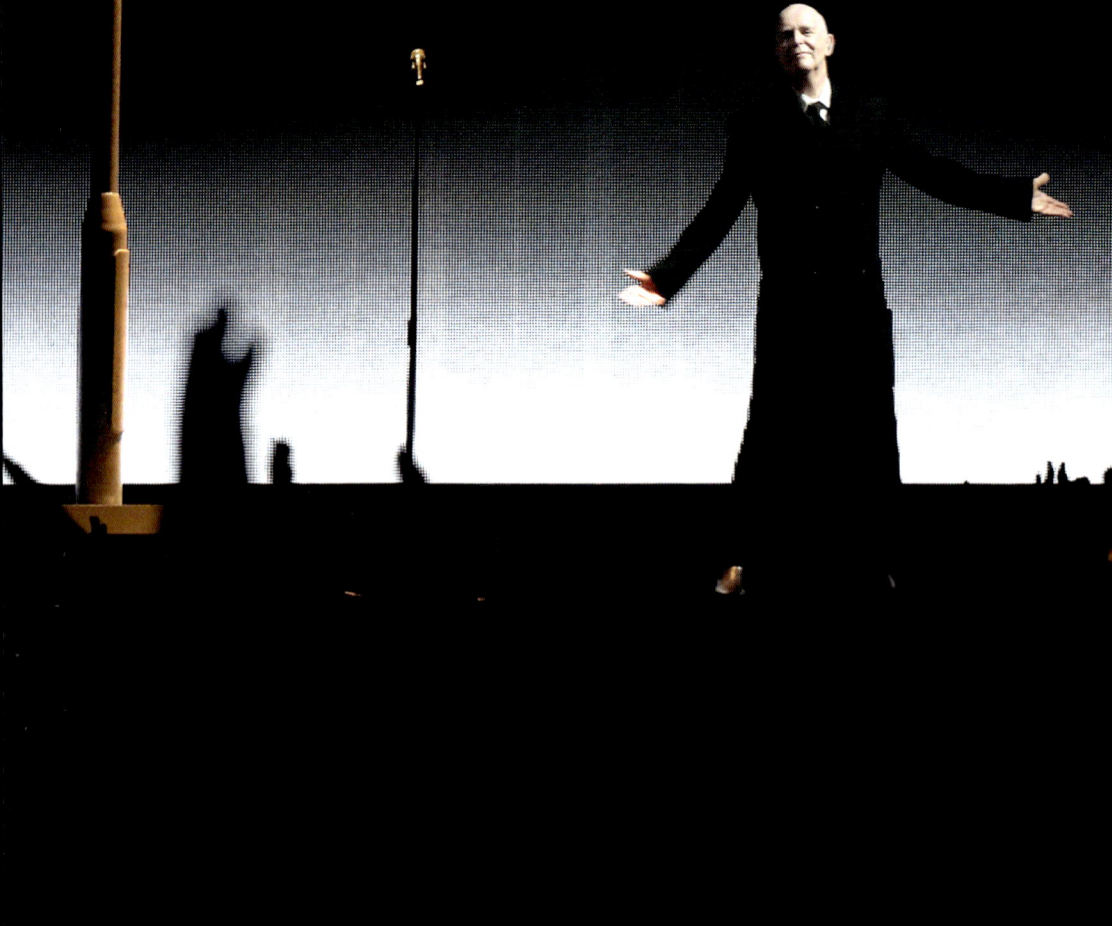

TURN IT ON

Pet Shop Boys, catalogue

1984–2024

West End girls

(first release)
release 9 April 1984
formats 7" / 7" promo / 12" / 12" promo
photographer Eric Watson
design XL Design (except US 12")

By the time 'West End girls' was first released on Epic, Pet Shop Boys already had a refined sense of image, one that was decidedly transatlantic. 'We'd been to New York twice and developed a wardrobe of New York clothes', Neil recalls. The photo on the sleeve was by Eric Watson – whom Neil had known from Newcastle and with whom he was working regularly at *Smash Hits* – and came from the first Pet Shop Boys session the previous August. 'We hadn't got any money, of course. I was working at *Smash Hits* and wasn't paid very well. Eric said if we were going to make a record for Bobby 'O', we'd need some photos, and that's why they were taken.' It was at another session for *Smash Hits*, during which Watson was playing the 'West End girls' demo, that Gordon Charlton of Epic heard and liked it.

Staying in New York – where he was setting up a US version of *Smash Hits* – Neil picked up other style clues. 'I remember a messenger came into the office with a parcel, and I asked him, "How do you do the laces like that so you don't have to fasten them?" People were breakdancing on the street on cardboard.... We used to go to Danceteria.... Madonna might be there, in her earlier incarnation.' Neil and Chris then thought of Pet Shop Boys as a 'British rap group' – to the extent that they would later appear on *Soul Train*. American style was crucial to early Pet Shop Boys. 'Our first year of success was very much skewed towards America', Neil recalls.

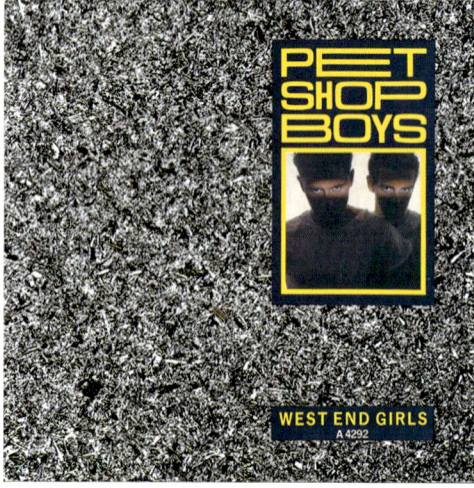

7", front

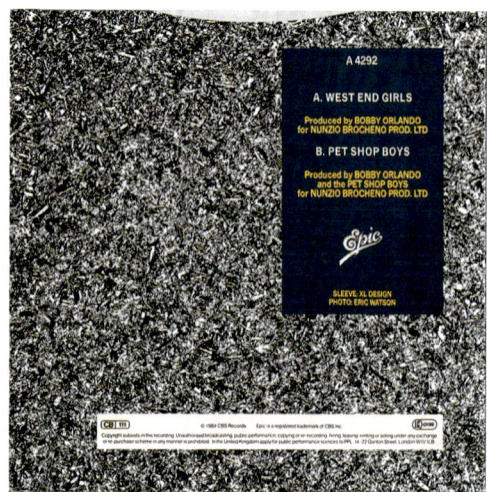

7", back

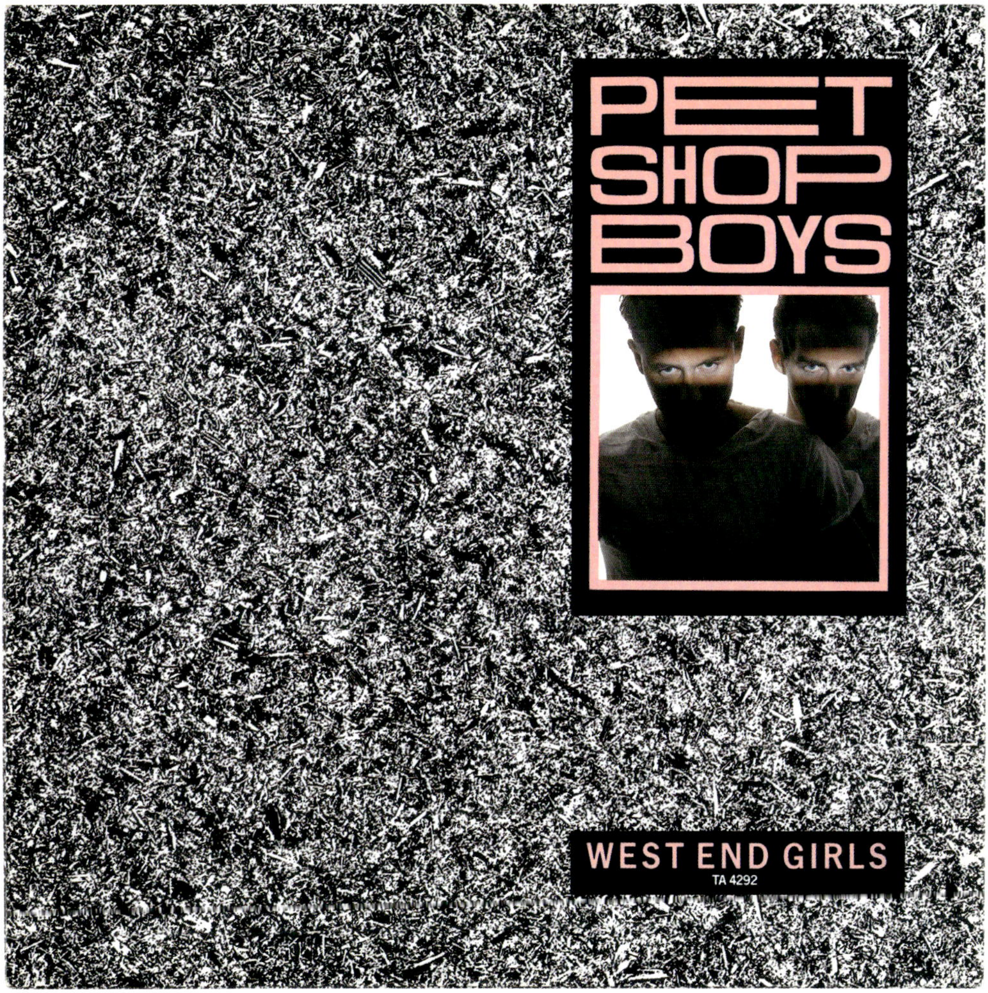

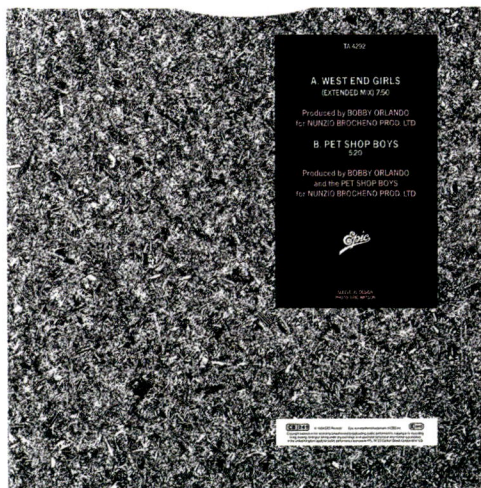

12", front

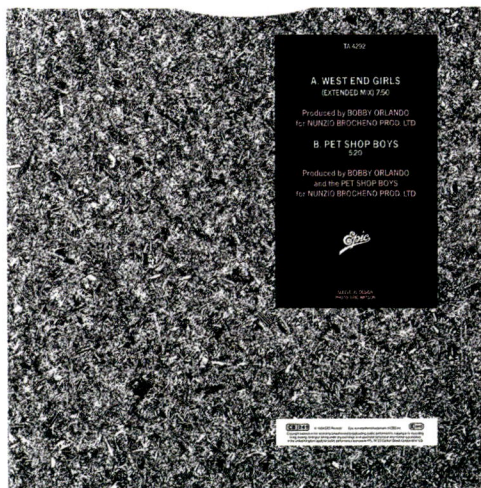

12", back

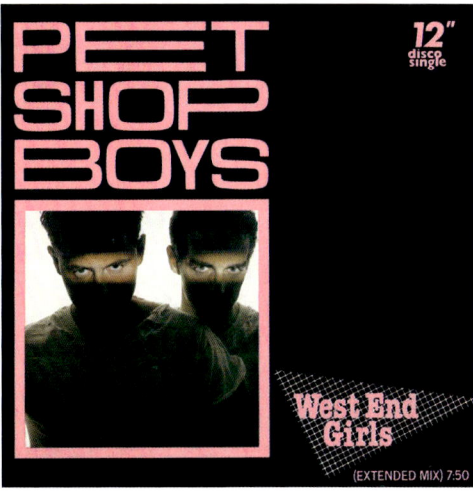

12", Belgium, front

West End girls 1984

One more chance

release Autumn 1984 (exact date unknown)
formats 7" (Sweden) / 12" (Belgium, Denmark, Germany, Netherlands)
photographer Eric Watson
design In-house record company designers

The photograph on the German twelve inch was the same as that on the first release of 'West End girls'. In that first session, Chris posed cradling his tennis racket, but those images ended up not being used for the sleeve. Even so, the sports look turned out to be prophetic. 'This was a year before Wham! and their shuttlecocks, remember', notes Neil, who had already had his own brief flirtation with 'the cycling thing', wearing professional cyclists' highly coloured zip-up tops (ABC had worn these on their London debut at Legends). 'And of course white socks, which everyone wore in the Eighties.... I used to like ski pants with little stirrups. I wore those relentlessly for two years.' Although decidedly unsporty, Neil is still drawn to the appeal of sportswear. 'I always liked hooded tops – I bought my first one in New York in 1983.'

The photograph on the Belgian twelve inch – the 'speakers' sleeve – was taken later in 1984, by which time Chris had had his hair permed. Again, the image was influenced by New York street fashion. 'Those Nike anoraks, which seemed terribly hip, were difficult to get in England. We loved them.' Both the German and Belgian sleeves also repeated the typography of the words 'Pet Shop Boys' that XL Design had created for the first 'West End girls' sleeve and that would reappear on the later release of that song, soon becoming a kind of logo for the group.

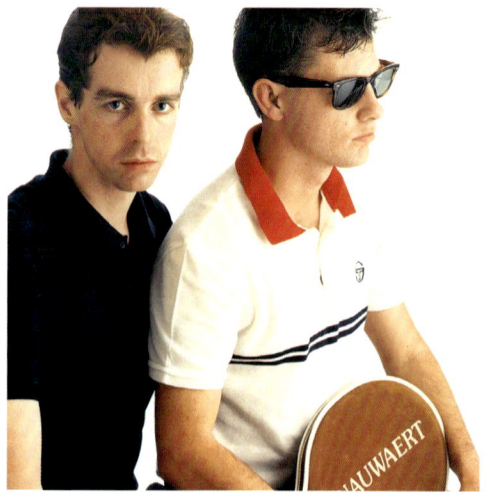

From the first Eric Watson photo session, August 1983

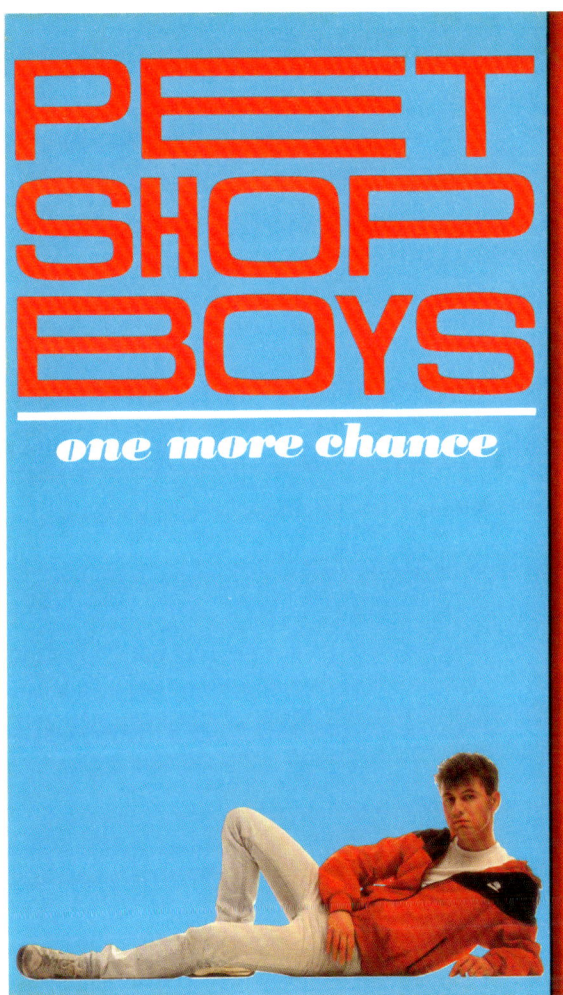
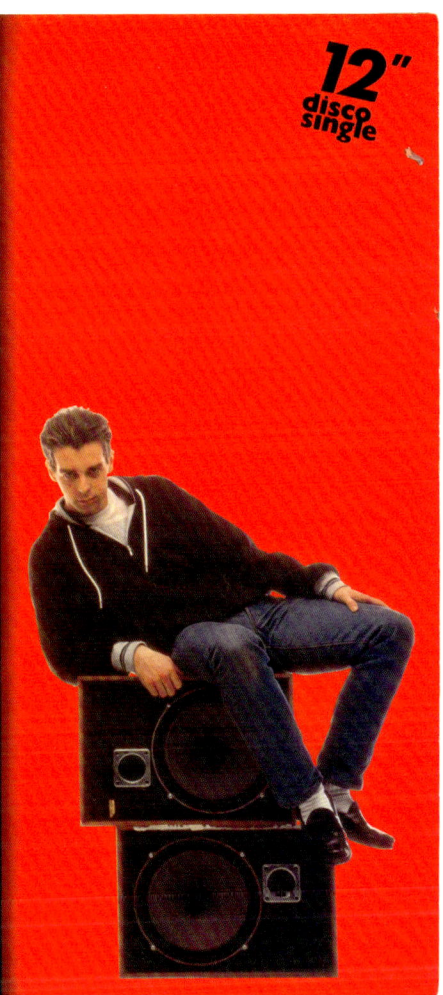

12", Belgium, front

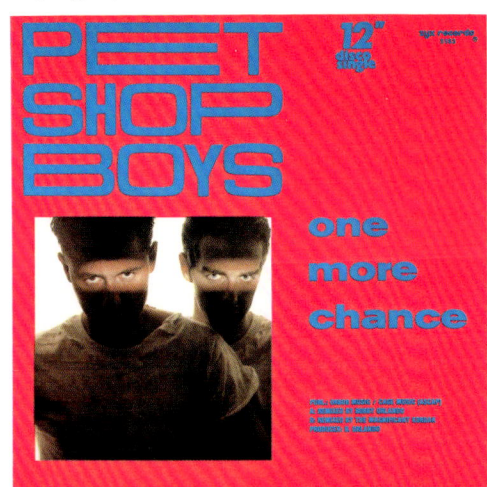

12", Germany, front

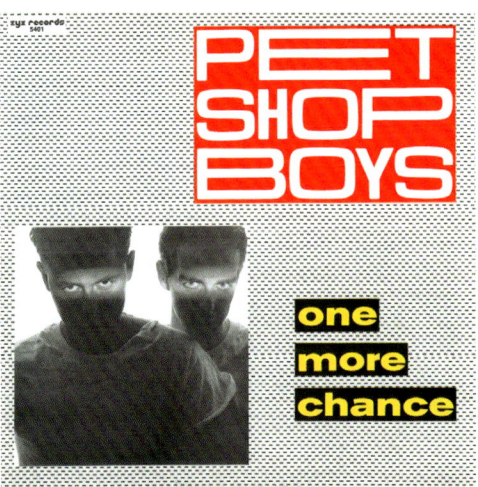

12", Germany (1986 re-release), front

One more chance 1984 37

Opportunities (let's make lots of money)

(first release)
release 1 July 1985
formats 7" / 7" promo / 12" × 2 / 12" promo
photographer Eric Watson
design XL Design
video Eric Watson and Andy Morahan

In late 1984, Pet Shop Boys moved from Epic, and the following year they signed with Parlophone. 'Opportunities (let's make lots of money)' was their first single on the new label. The look with which the group would become associated in their early years – Neil in formal wear and Chris in jeans and a hat – was established with this release. Again, Eric Watson was the photographer. For several days, the pair were photographed at various locations in east London. In the end, two close-up portraits were selected for use on all formats of the record: Neil with dishevelled, curly, floppy hair, big shirt collar, dark tie, and dollar sign on his overcoat lapel; Chris with a peaked cap, open-necked Fifties-style shirt and American leather jacket, and T-shirt and gold chain. The pre-release twelve-inch promo featured the same images but reproduced with a 'photocopy' quality.

    This release also saw the first use of oversized six-inch picture labels (on the twelve-inch mixes, with matt black sleeves and spot varnish lettering). Inspired by Italian disco records, they were an effective use of design space. Italy had a great influence on the early evolution of the group. On the re-release of 'West End girls', Neil told *Blitz* magazine – in a spread that reproduced the so-called 'ugly pictures' (page 48) full page – 'Italian disco is one of the great undiscovered areas. They get these beautiful sad melodies with a disco beat.'

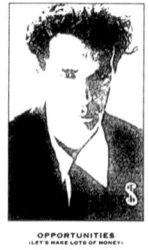

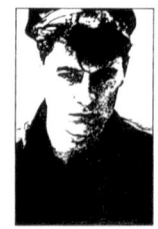

12" promo, front   12" promo, back

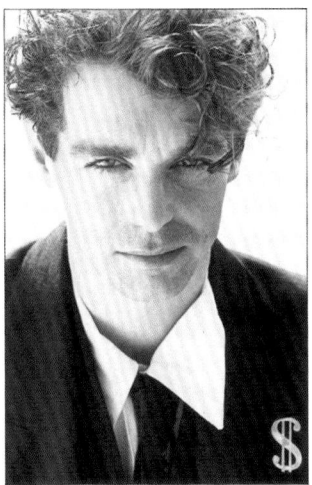

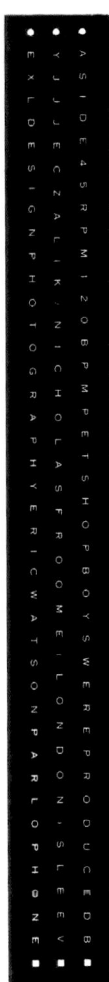

12", front

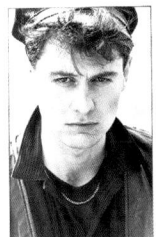

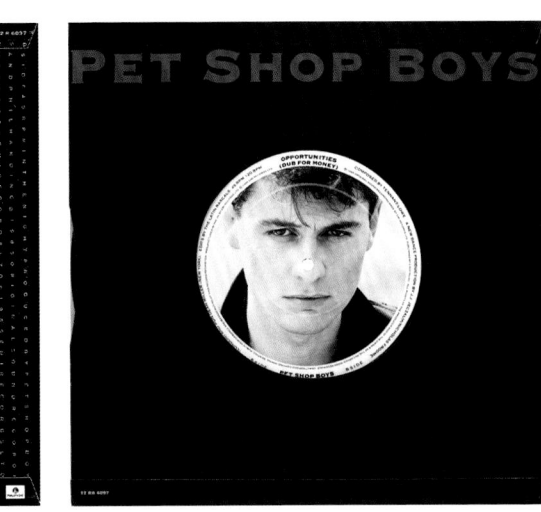

12", back   12" (die-cut with 6" picture label on record), back

Opportunities (let's make lots of money)   1985

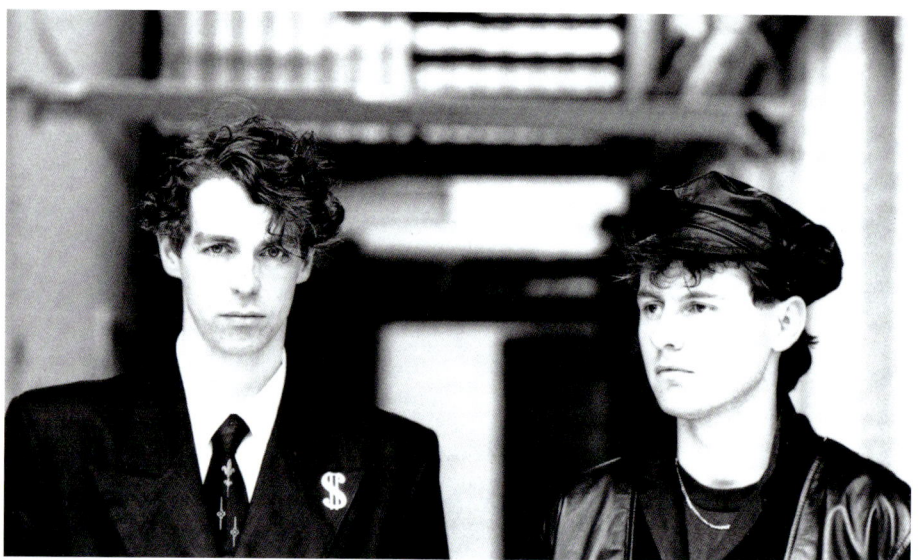

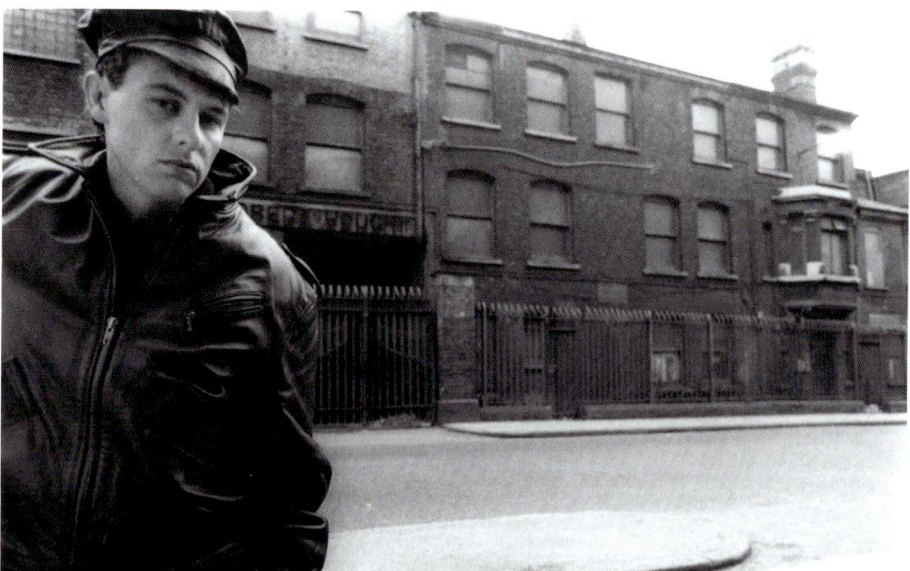

above and opposite Images and contact sheet from the first 'Opportunities' session with Eric Watson

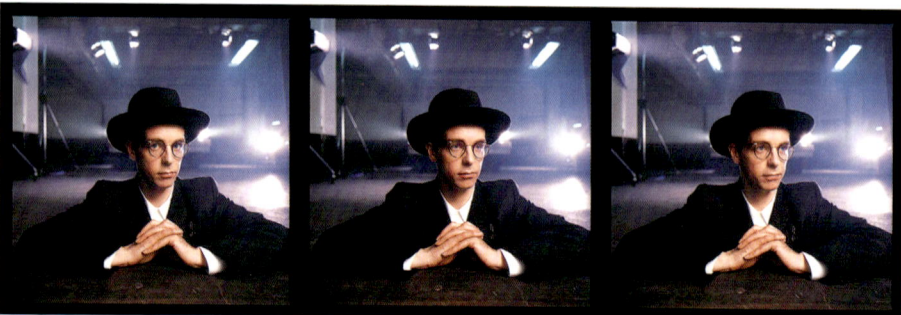

On the set of the video for 'Opportunities (let's make lots of money)' (photo: Paul Rider)

40   Opportunities (let's make lots of money) 1985

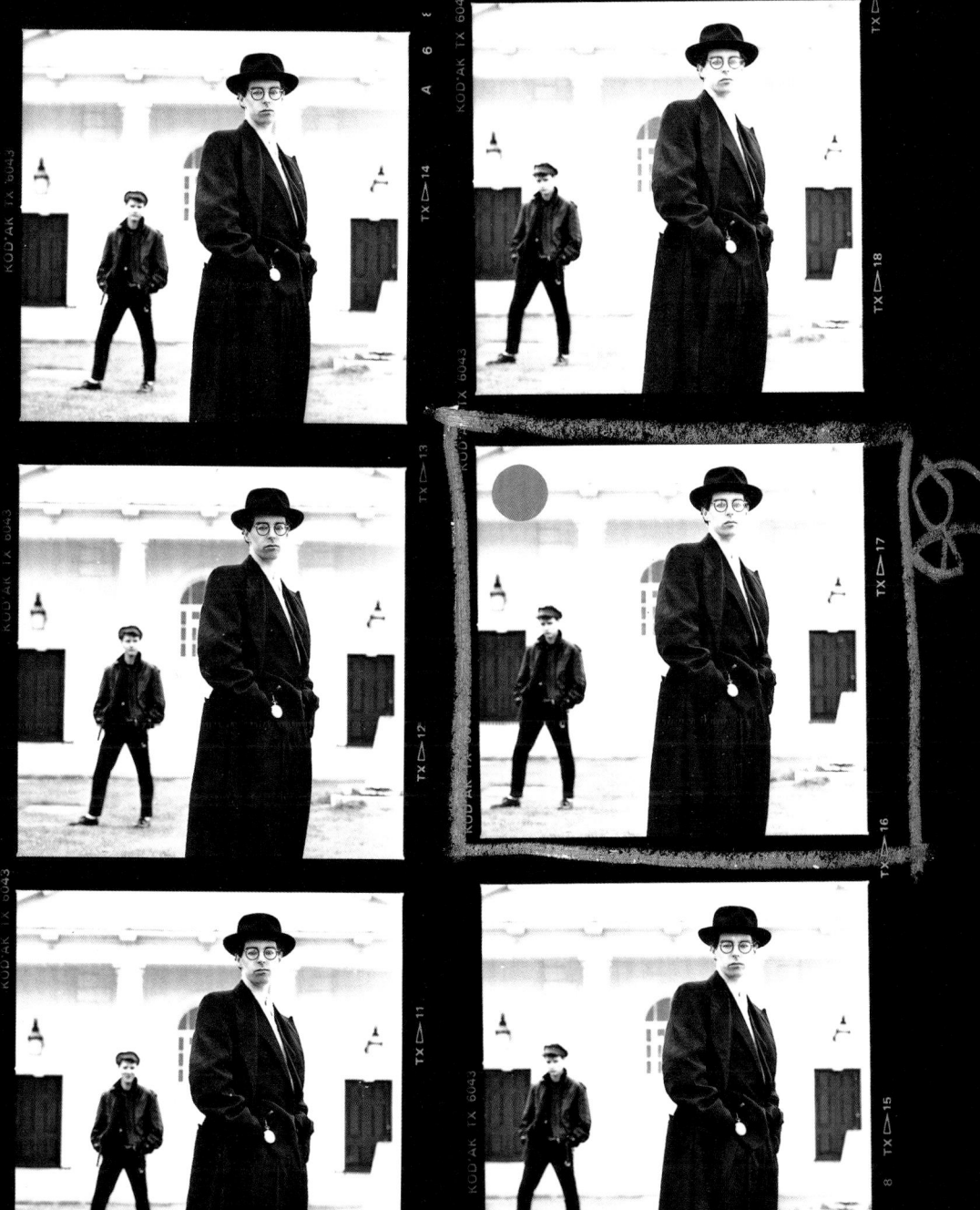

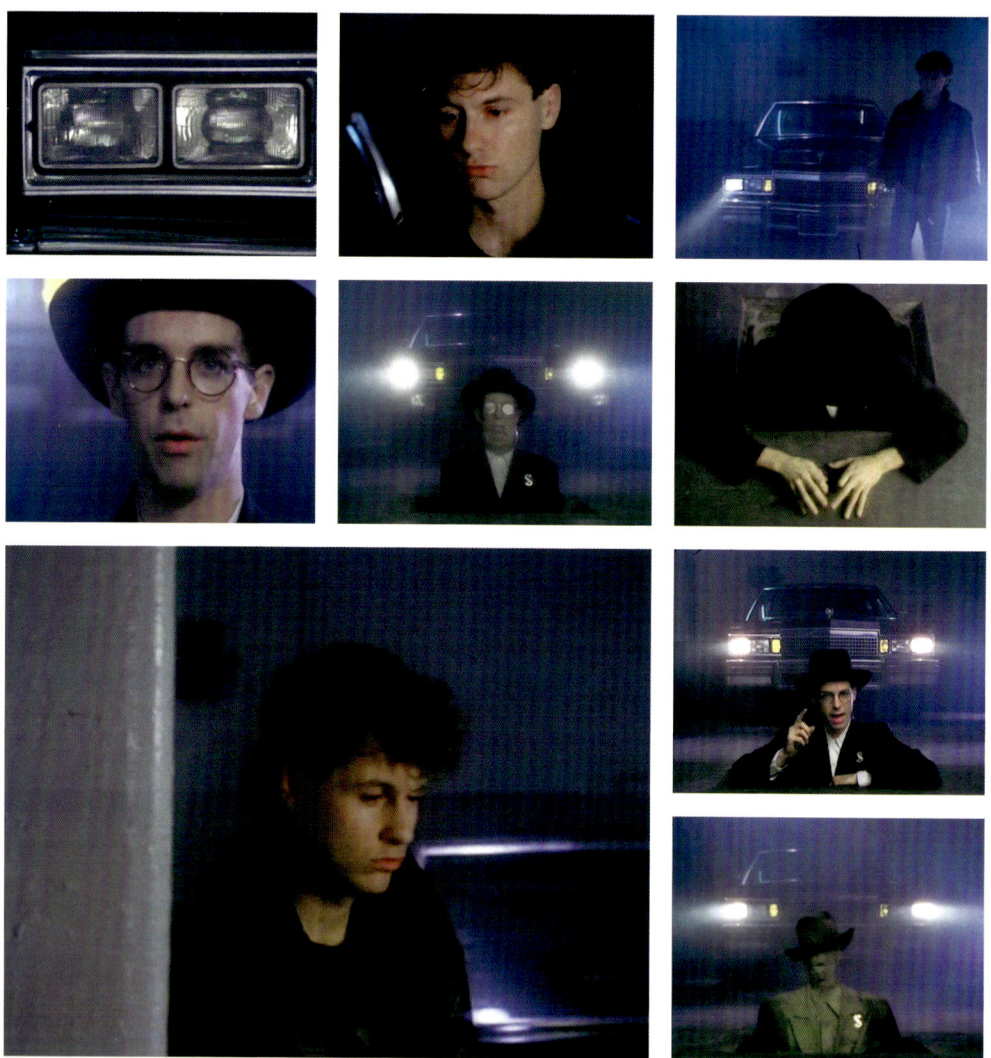

In the group's first video, Neil is seen sunken in the pit of a dark garage, dressed vaguely like a Hasidic Jew in round spectacles, hat, and long funereal coat, with the dollar sign again on his lapel, illuminated by the headlights of a car parked behind him. Chris hovers in the background, and in close-up, as a dumb mechanic. At the end, Neil's body crumbles to dust and the car drives off. There are overtones of Samuel Beckett and David Lynch in this dark, troglodytic vision. Eric Watson cited John Huston's film *Wiseblood*, based on Flannery O'Connor's southern Gothic tale, as an influence; he saw Neil as playing the fake preacher from the film (played by Harry Dean Stanton). 'Neil's character reminds me of the main character in the film and the novel, standing on the street corner, saying they believe in God but just getting money out of people', Watson said in 1992. 'At the time, I was so cynical that I believed that everybody who was involved in culture was just making a fast buck.'

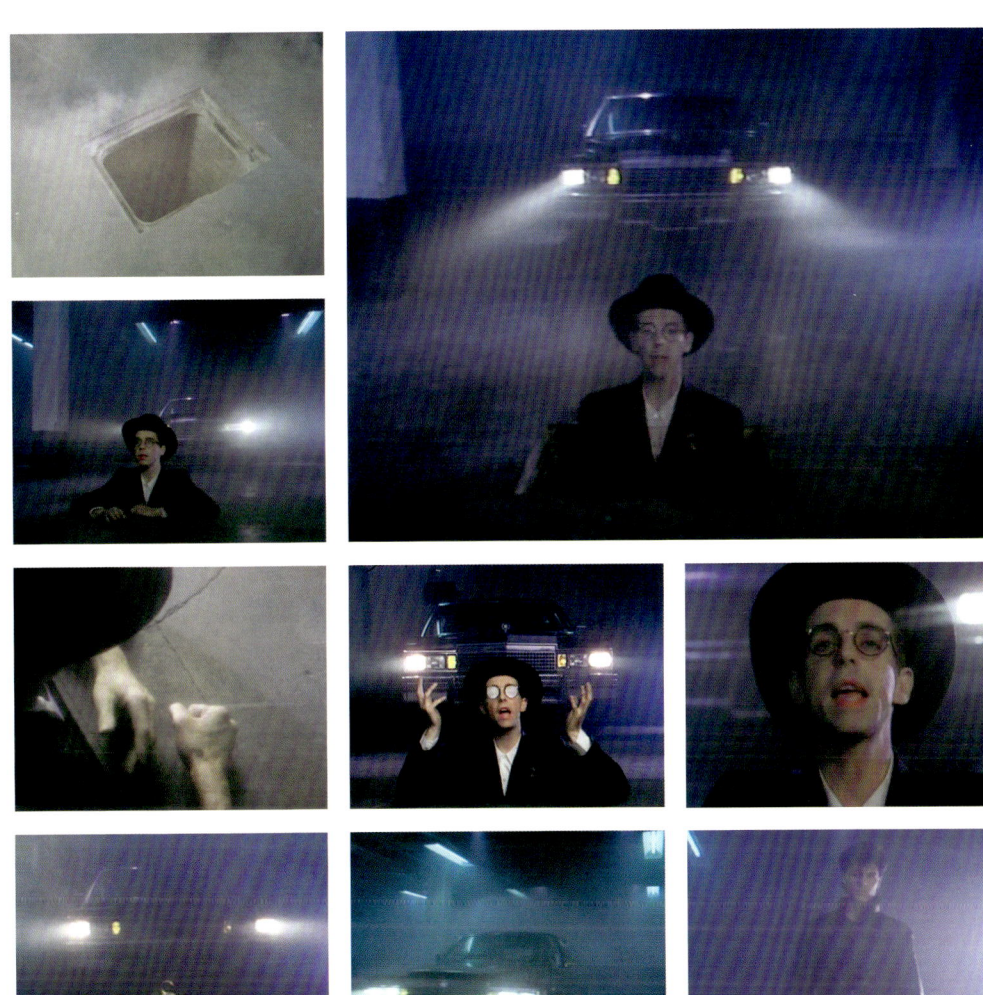

Opportunities (let's make lots of money) 1985

West End girls

(second release)
release 28 October 1985
formats 7" / 10" collectors' edition / 12" × 3 /
12" promo × 2 / cassette (United States, Canada)
photographer Eric Watson
design XL Design and Chris Lowe
video Eric Watson and Andy Morahan

The design of Pet Shop Boys' breakthrough number-one single marked the distillation of the group's look at the midpoint of the Eighties. In a youth culture led by the *haute* street fashion of publications such as *The Face*, *i-D*, and *Blitz*, design and style were more than ever essential aspects of promotion. The statements made in the packaging of the reissued 'West End girls' were thus key to the formation of the group's image. Crucially, the cover for the single was again designed by XL Design, with Chris also having an input. It was a pivotal moment: there was a sense of the group's aesthetic finding its feet. '"West End girls" became a hit so slowly', says Neil, 'that there were endless formats to jig the charts.'

The look of the single was also influenced by the left-field but high-glamour structuralist aesthetic pioneered by Scritti Politti, whose covers mimicked the packaging of Christian Dior's Eau Sauvage. 'We were influenced by that idea of looking like a brand, a perfume bottle or whatever.' But in their case, the style became refined to pure structure, with colour and form stripped down to bare essentials. The twelve inch's sleeve was partly designed by Chris. It has a marked relationship to the design of New Order's 'Blue Monday' twelve inch by Peter Saville – which brought Neil close to tears when it arrived at *Smash Hits*, so liberally did it seem to borrow from the style of their favourite producer, Bobby 'O'.

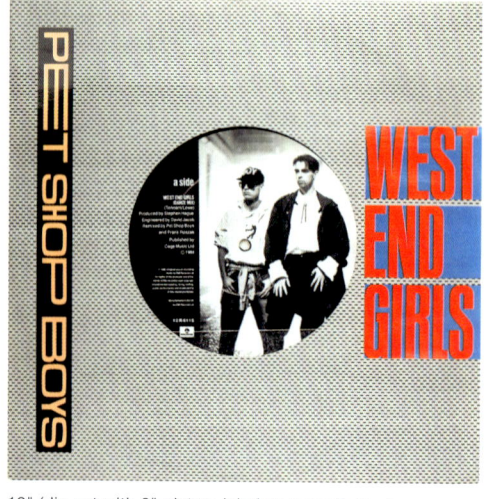

12" (die-cut with 6" picture label on record), front

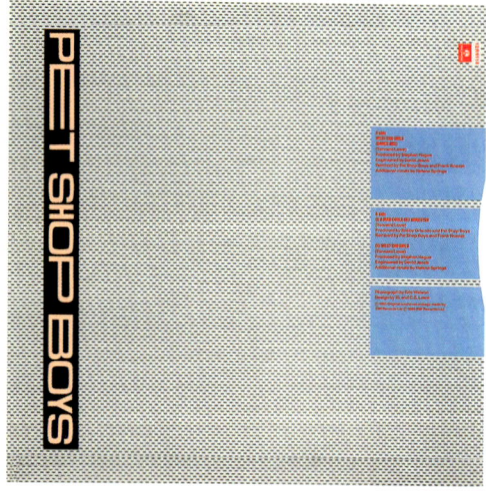

12" (die-cut with 6" picture label on record), back

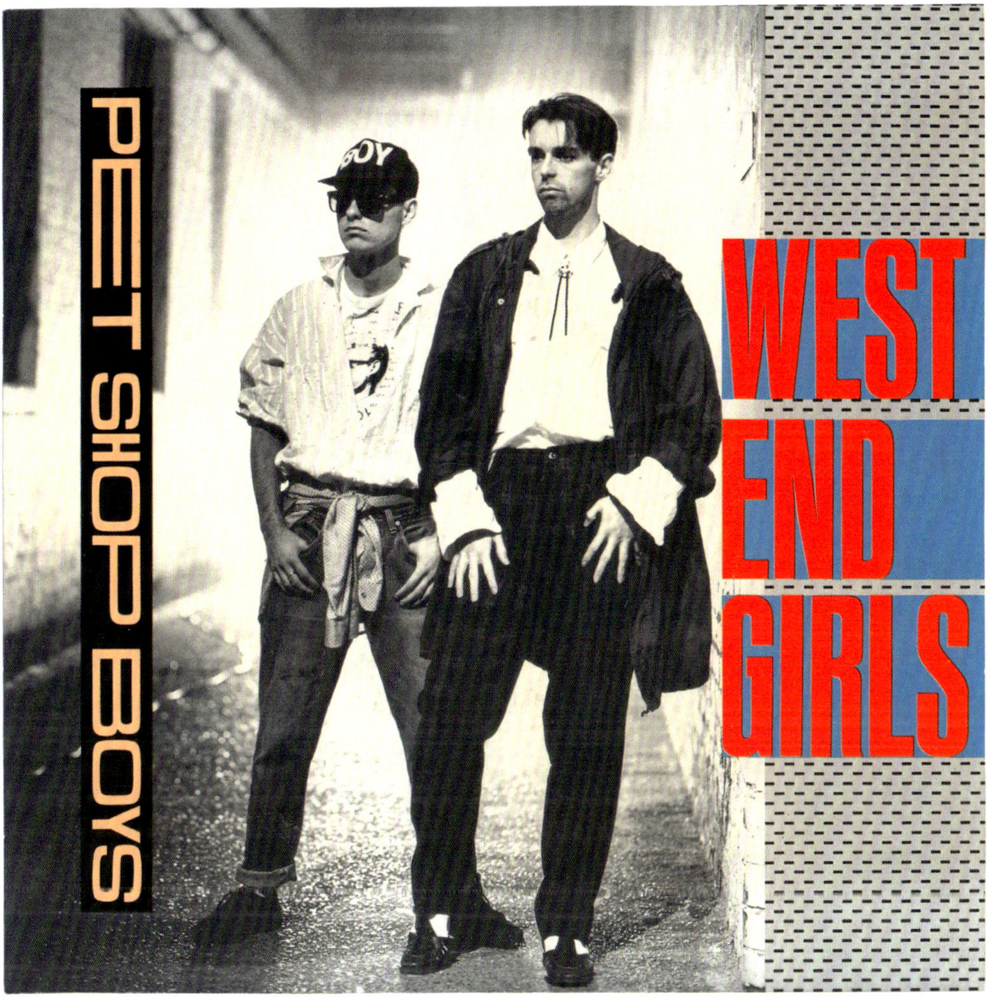

7", front

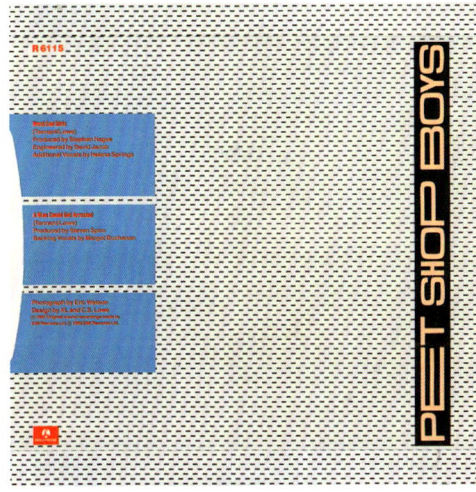

7", back

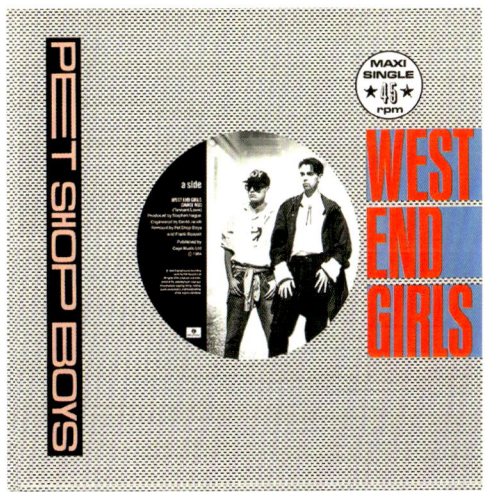

12", Germany (with 6" picture printed on sleeve), front

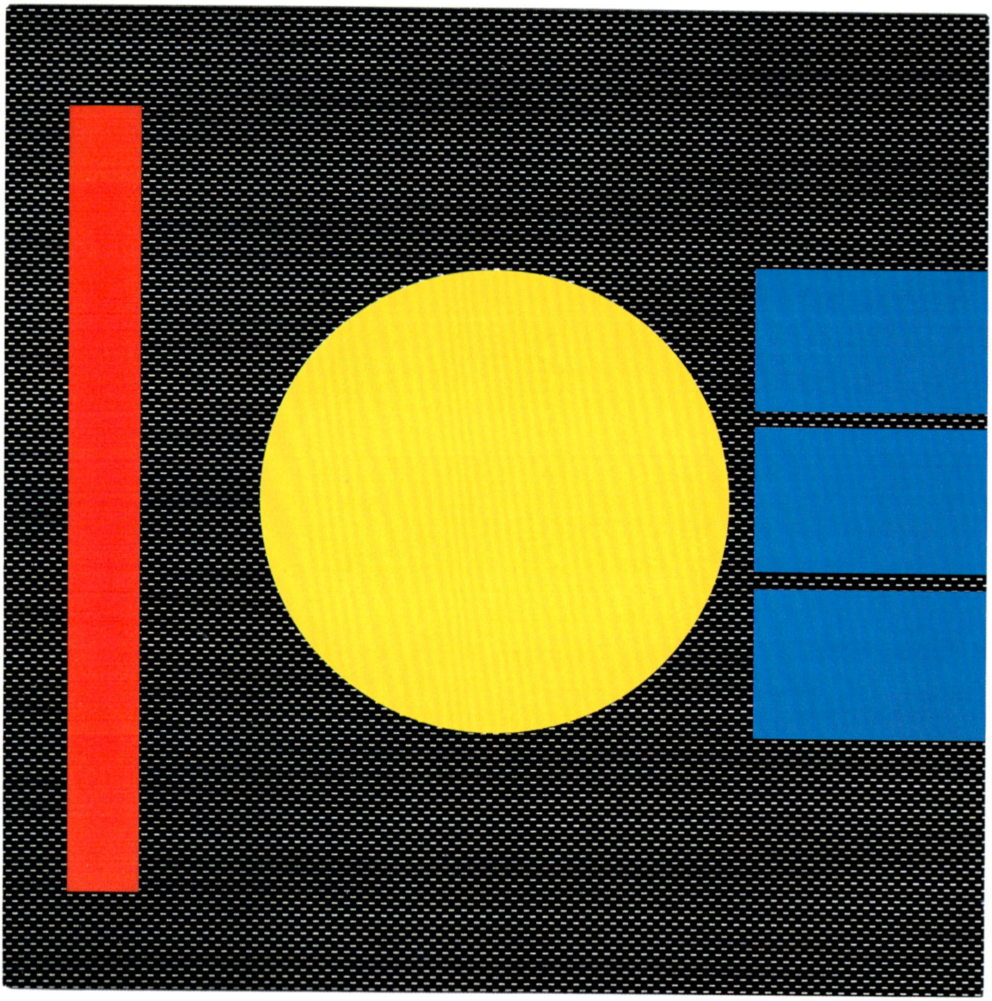

12" Shep Pettibone Mastermix (with 6" yellow centre printed on sleeve), front

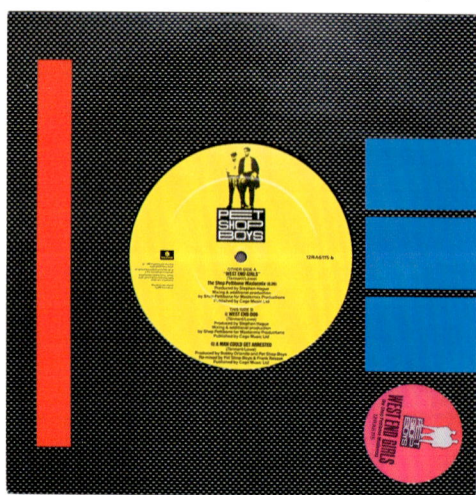

12" Shep Pettibone Mastermix (die-cut with 6" label), front

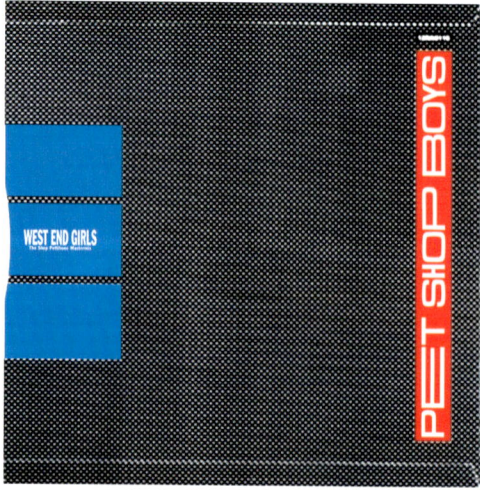

12" Shep Pettibone Mastermix (die-cut with 6" label), back

West End girls 1985

The twelve-inch remix, released in January 1986 was the first Pet Shop Boys sleeve to be designed by Mark Farrow, who had moved from Manchester to London and joined XL Design. 'I hated the original sleeve – the fact that there were two typefaces, one had three sizes, just everything about it I loathed. I had the Factory ethic in my head. So the first thing I did was strip all the type off so we just had the coloured blocks and background.' As Neil recalls, 'As we did new formats, we got more confident, until we were just using blocks of colour – partly designed by Chris.' Indeed, the industrial-style 'dash' background was a particular favourite of Chris's. Together with the bright, primary colours, it was also a nod towards the Italian designer Ettore Sottsass and his influential group Memphis, whose work was collected by the group's new manager, Tom Watkins.

Farrow also designed the ten-inch collectors' edition, although EMI had provided the wrong template, which is why the flaps do not meet in the middle and a sticker was needed to bridge the gap. With its fold-out circular sleeve, revealing a new image of the group beneath, it artfully played with the sense of collectorship among Pet Shop Boys' growing fan base. Within that core of dedicated supporters, the duo had taken on a unique profile in which the two men themselves represented a binary recognition. As Neil comments, 'We were starting to use one of the photographs as a kind of logo.'

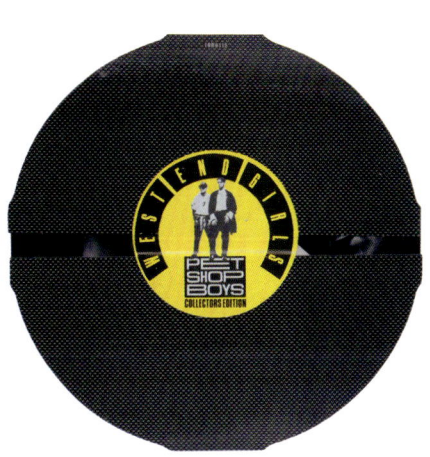
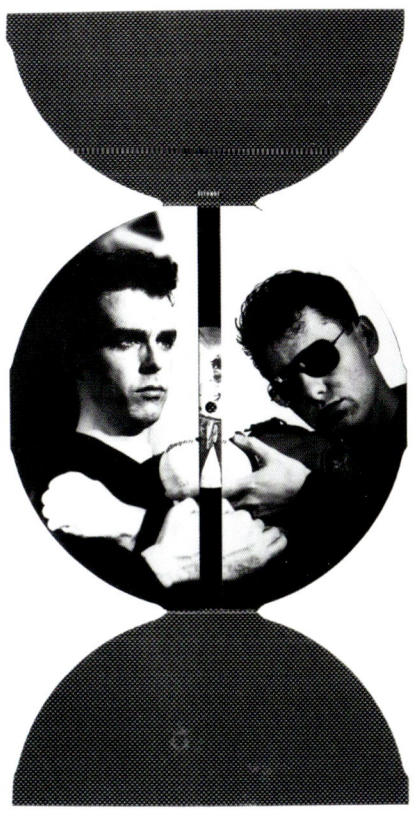

10" collectors' edition, folded (above) with the sticker to keep the sleeve closed and unfolded (right) showing a photograph of Neil and Chris and the picture label on the record

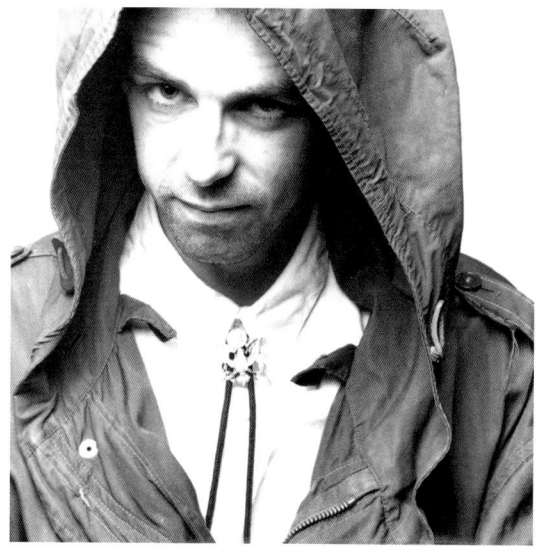 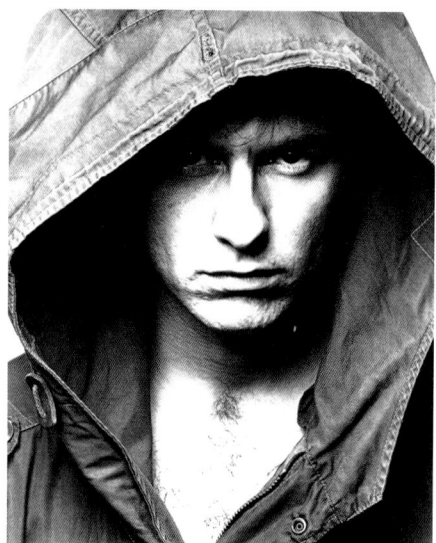

From the October 1984 session with Eric Watson

After being taken up by Tom Watkins and his management company Massive, Pet Shop Boys' style had changed. 'Tom said we had to get a stylist', Neil recalls. 'We'd been dropped by Epic and I'd met Tom.... Suddenly "West End girls" was in the Top 30 in Belgium ... and we were asked us to go and do a TV appearance there. Tom persuaded Massive to lend us some money, and Iain R. Webb [fashion editor and former New Romantic / Blitz Kid] took us shopping in King's Road. He complained that all Chris wanted to do was buy a gold chain.' The result was to make the group look more glamorous. Neil continues: 'Webb suggested we mix new things with vintage clothing – Chris and I were very sniffy about that. My contribution was the BOY hat and T-shirt because I lived opposite the shop on the King's Road. The hat made all the difference. And of course, I was already going bald – there was a bald patch on top of my head – so hats hid that.' Chris wore the hat in October 1984 for the photo session that provided the 'West End girls' sleeve. Neil refers to the hooded shots as 'the famous "ugly pictures"' – complete with stubble and chest hair.

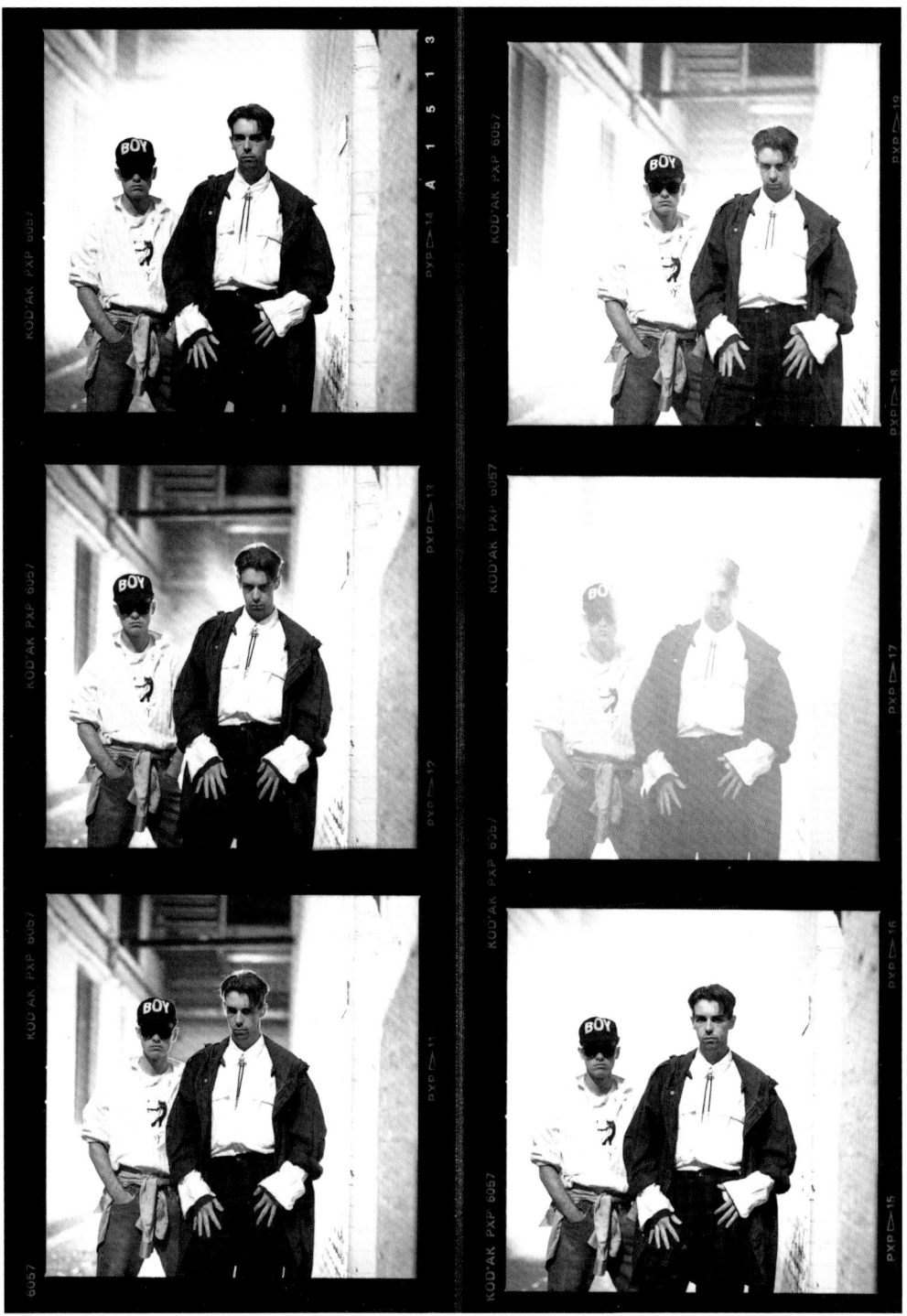

Contact sheet from the October 1984 session with Eric Watson

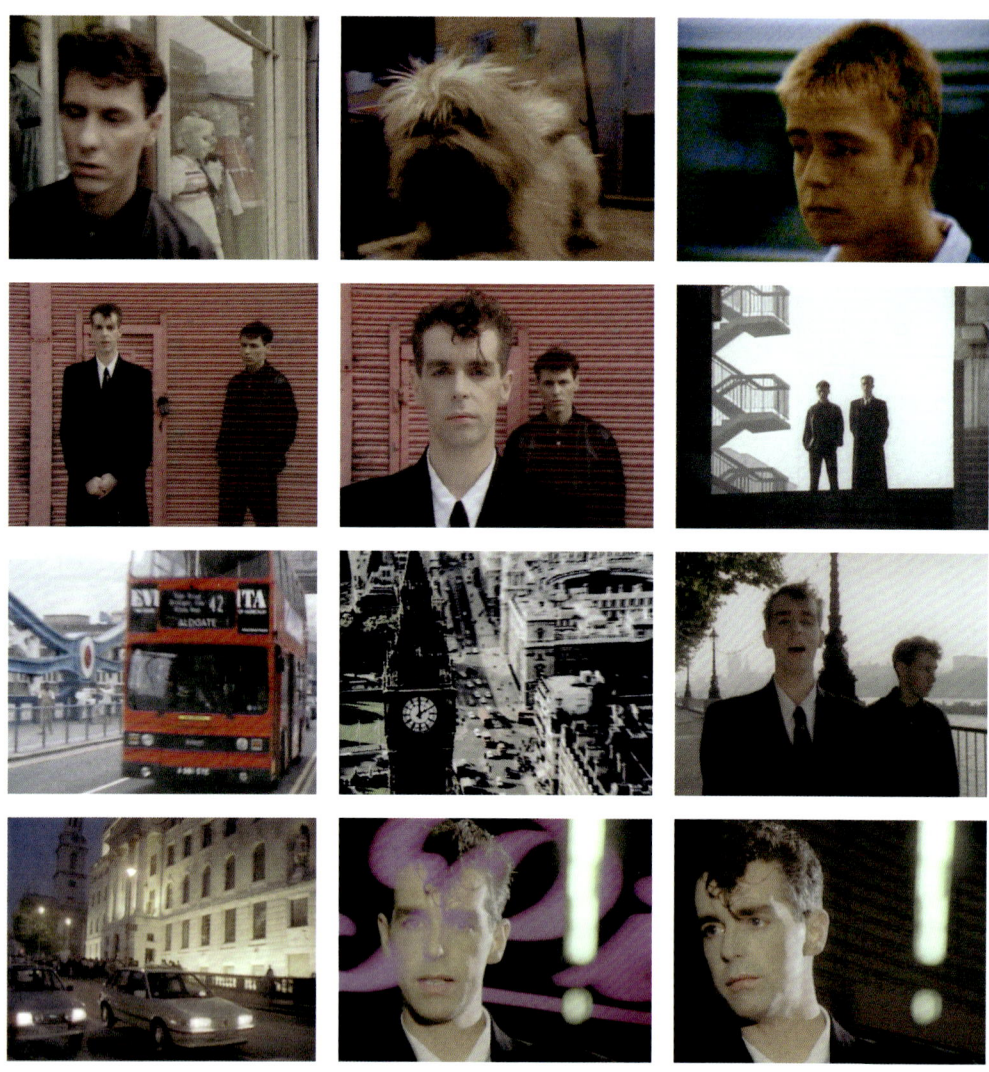

The 'West End girls' video was shot in London by Eric Watson with Andy Morahan, who had been responsible for Wham!'s videos. We follow Neil and Chris along dawn streets of the East End, with a gang of skinheads, through walkways and crowds and subways, across the concourse of Waterloo Station, and along the Embankment to the neon lights and cinemas of the West End (via aerial views of the city, and shots of the anti-apartheid demonstration outside South Africa House on Trafalgar Square).

'It was pretty literal. We began in the morning in the East End and ended in the West End. It was all shot in one day', says Neil. This sense of extempore progress allowed for accidental felicities. 'When we started in the East End, a tramp appeared, walking in sync with us.' 'Tom Watkins had said "We've got to do some kind of travelogue around London"', Watson recalled. 'Andy and I went out about six o'clock one

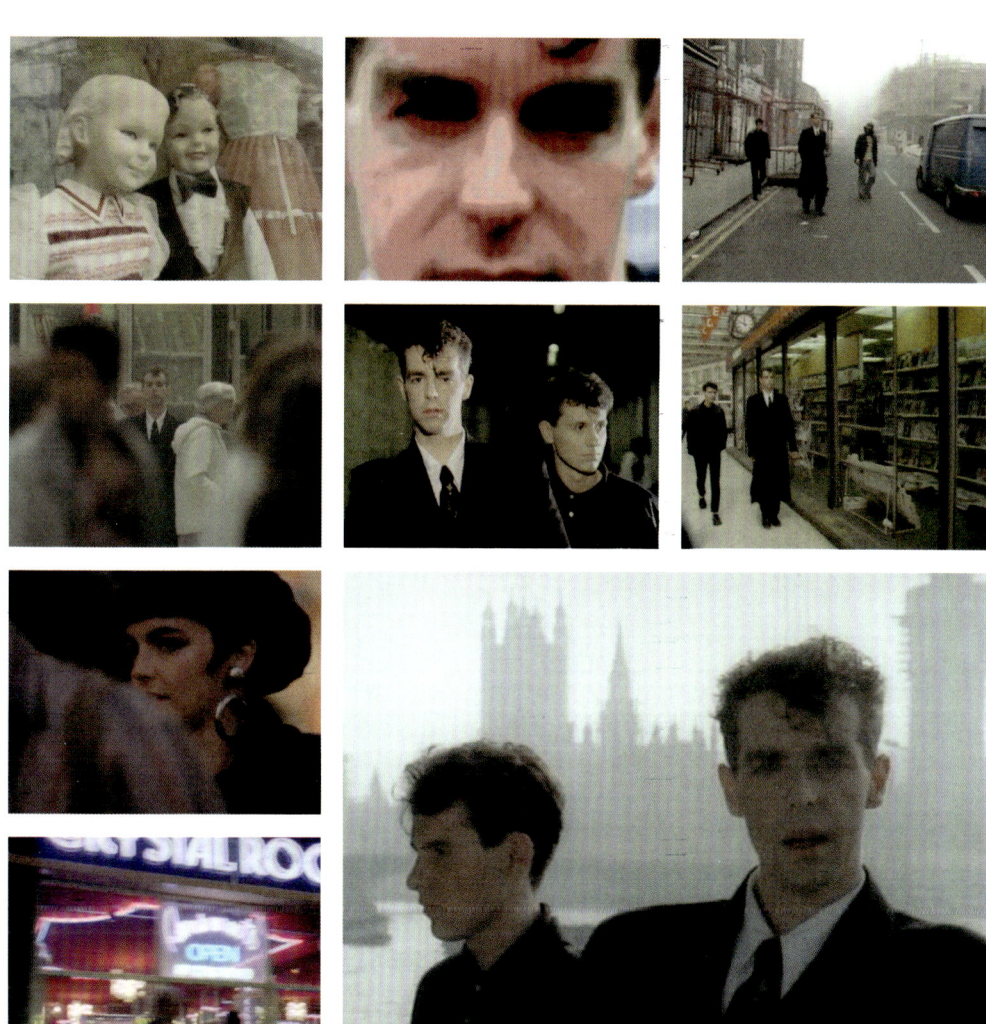

morning with video 8 cameras and went round Aldgate and places like that, filming. Chris didn't want to be seen playing keyboards or anything, and we realized there was something about someone singing and someone else doing nothing – just looking, then looking away – that adds a hideous tension. It's creepy but also, I suppose, charming. It was only later we realized we'd created a … product.' The video was crucial in creating the image of the group in the public imagination. The duo were seen as an urbane, existential, observational pair, somewhat removed from and yet part of the action.

Love comes quickly

release 24 February 1986
formats 7" / 7" promo / 10" collectors' edition / 12" × 3
photographer Eric Watson
design Mark Farrow at 3 and Chris Lowe
video Eric Watson and Andy Morahan

This release saw the refinement of Chris in a hat as the Pet Shop Boys icon; with only the lower part of his face visible, it is a confrontational, tough look that complements the minimal design of the twelve inch. 'I can become Chris Lowe from the Pet Shop Boys just by putting a hat on', he told the *Sunday Correspondent* in 1990. Five years later, Neil remarked to Michael Bracewell, writing for the *Guardian*, 'Chris actually pioneered a kind of street-type look…. [He] invented what a keyboard player was meant to look like … a baseball cap and scowling.' Mark Farrow comments: 'At the time, not putting any type on the sleeve was quite a big thing to do. I'm not sure that anyone had actually done it at that point on something as commercial as this. My argument was that Chris in the BOY cap *was* kind of a logo. "West End girls" had been number one, and he'd worn that outfit and to me it was pretty obviously a Pet Shop Boys record and so it didn't need anything else.' The American release had to carry the title, as did the UK seven inch. The ten-inch collectors' edition has a clear plastic sleeve and white lettering, over a backlit photograph of Neil and Chris. The subsequent photo session with Robert Mapplethorpe (following pages) was remarkably restrained for the photographer's work, which was often highly sexualized. Neil is now more concerned that the trousers on which Mapplethorpe had insisted did not go with the jacket he wore.

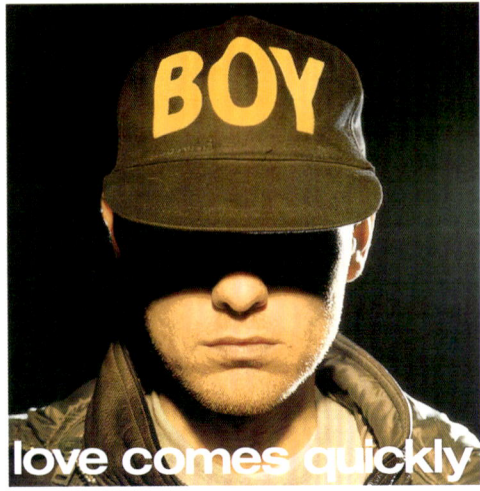

7", front

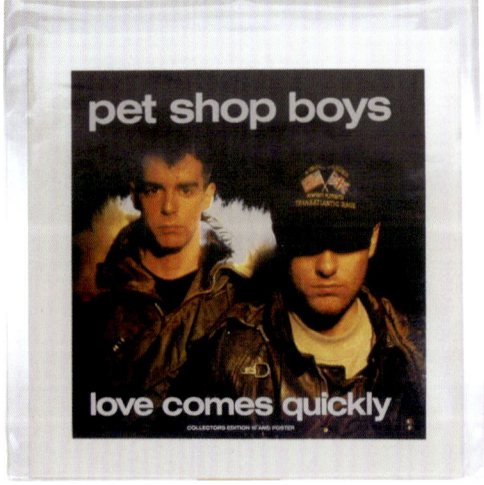

10" collectors' edition, front

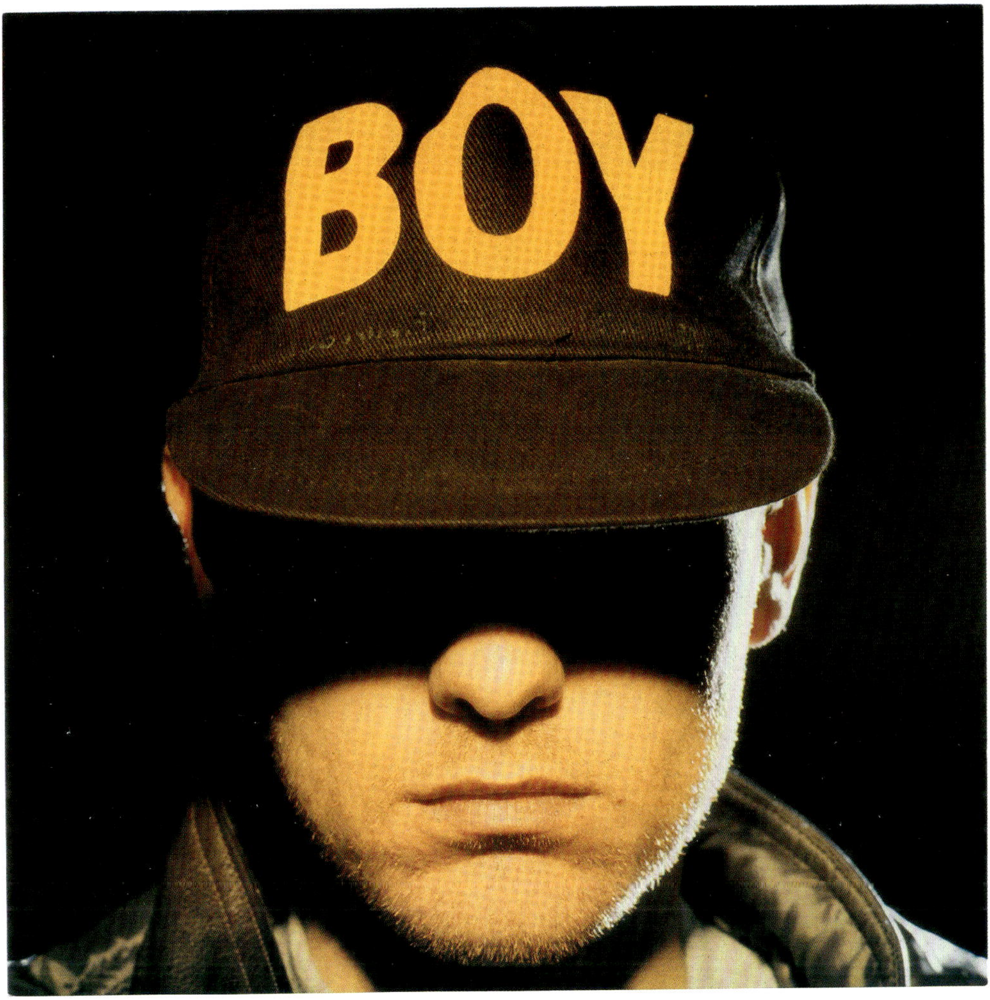

12", front

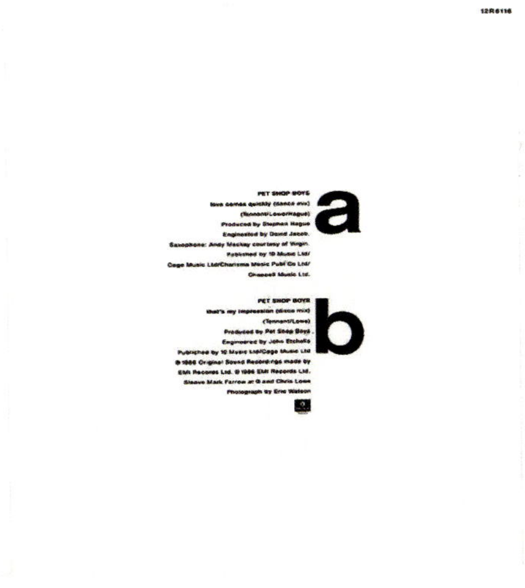

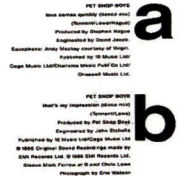

12", back

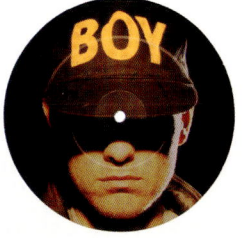

12" (die-cut with 6" picture label on record), front

Love comes quickly 1986 53

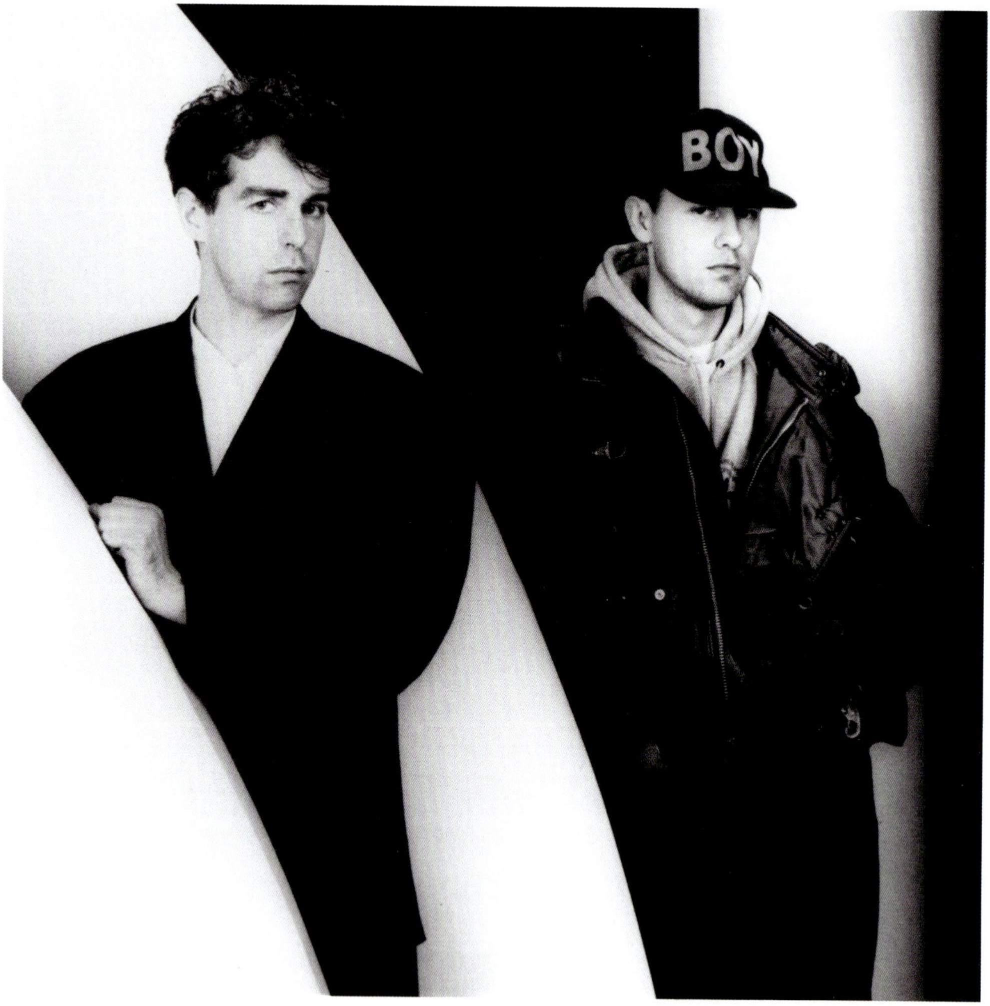

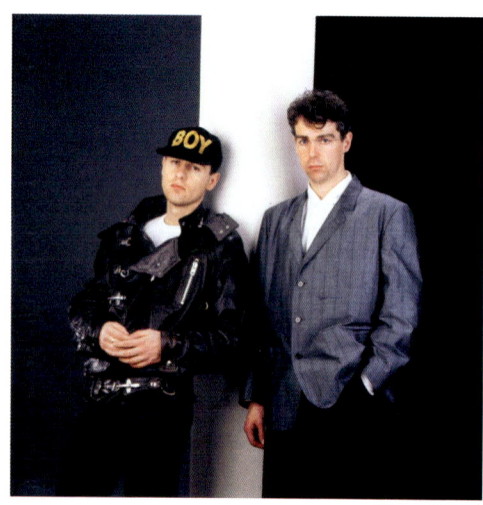
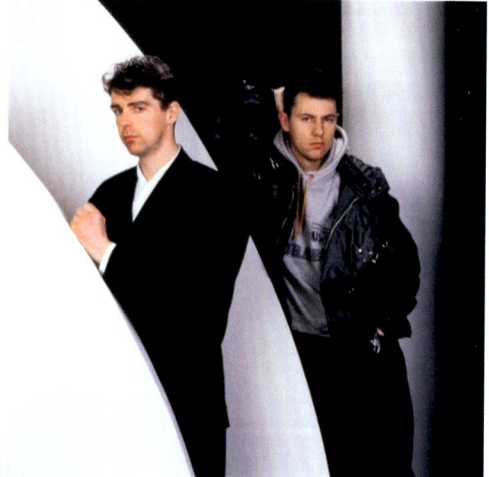

54 Love comes quickly 1986

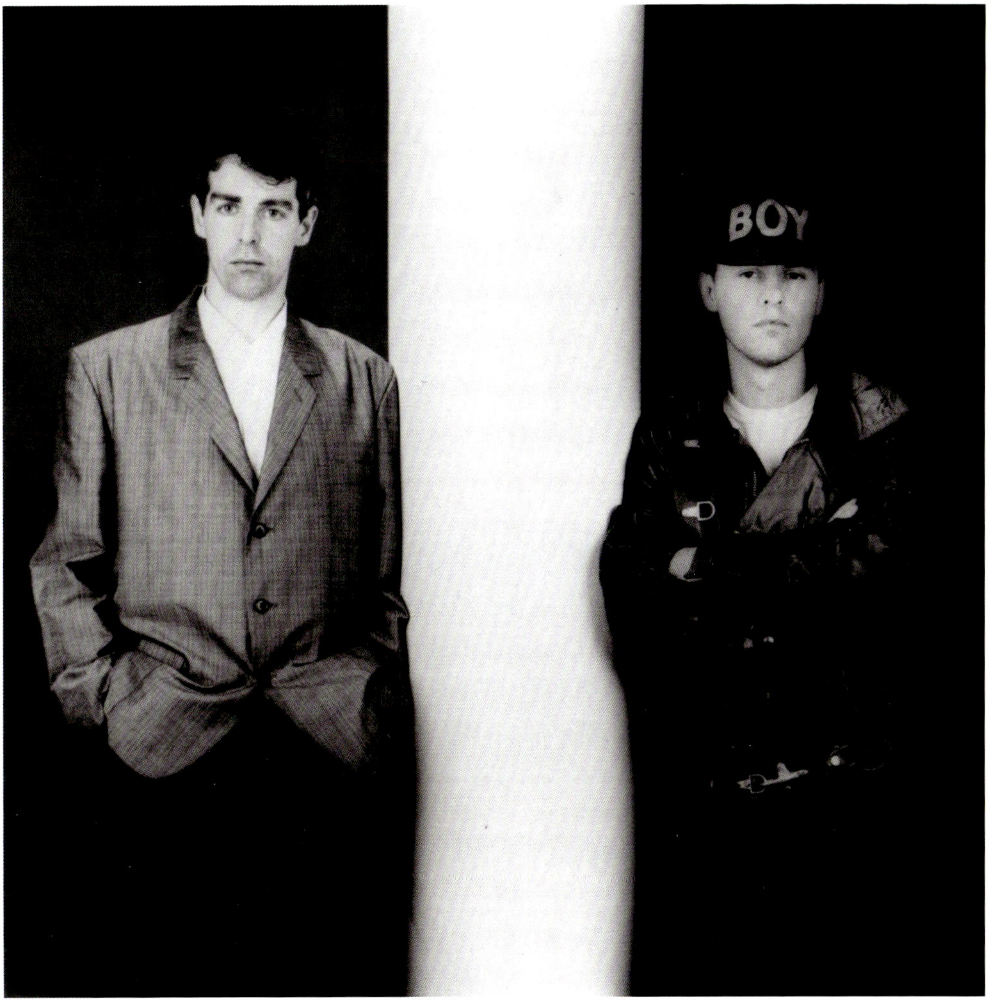

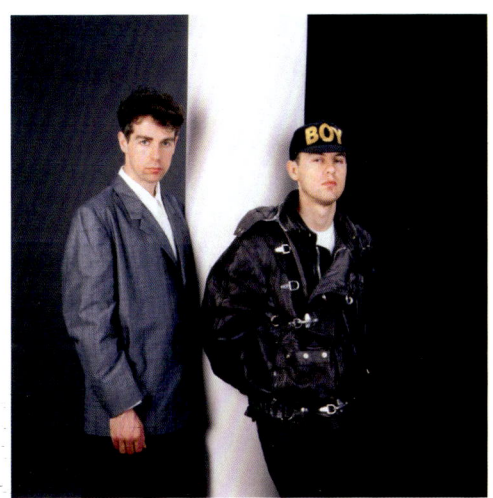
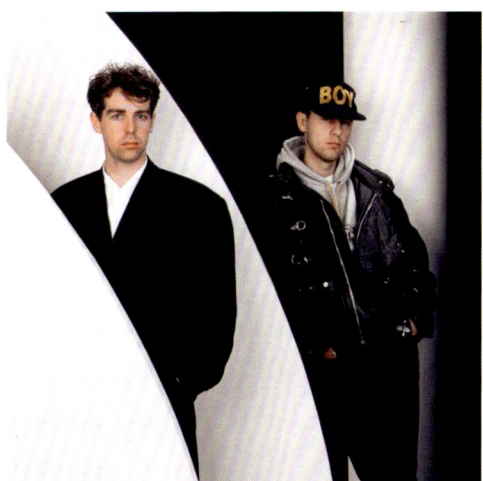

From the Robert Mapplethorpe photo session, March 1986

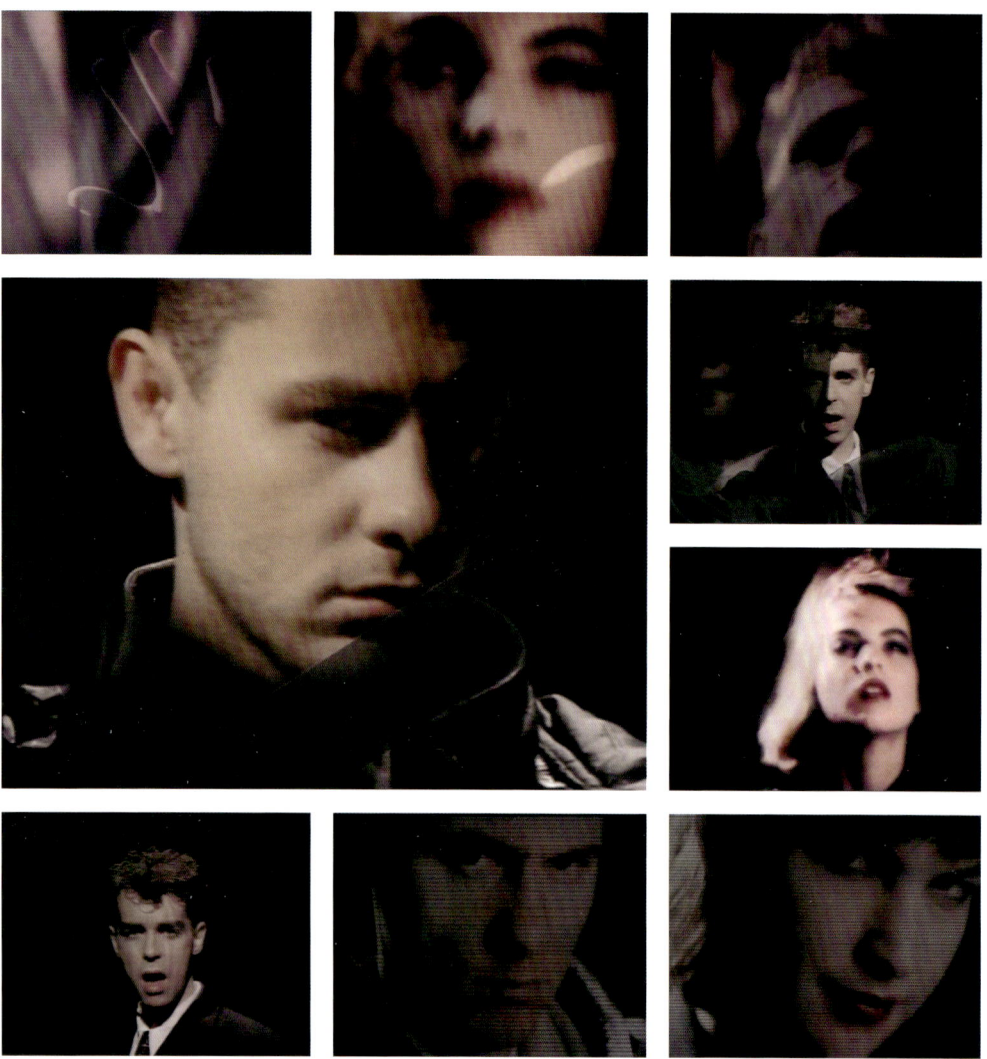

Anonymous faces of beautiful boys and girls blur as Neil and Chris are seen through an imposed grid, as if imprisoned by love. 'We went out with Eric to buy a suit to wear in the "Loves comes quickly" video', Neil recalls. 'I bought this gorgeous suit by Jean-Paul Gaultier.... I could suddenly afford to buy expensive suits. So from that moment on, that's what I wore.' The video is very much studio- and effect-based. It was also evidently inexpensive to produce. In Eric Watson's hindsight, it was 'a complete disaster. I wanted an image of Chris whirling over on this giant webbing, with Neil just a singing head. It was all supposed to be disconnected, because the song was all floaty and ethereal, but the technique defeated us. And when we shot it, there wasn't a great deal of Chris in it, so it had to be re-edited. It's nowhere near as good as the song.'

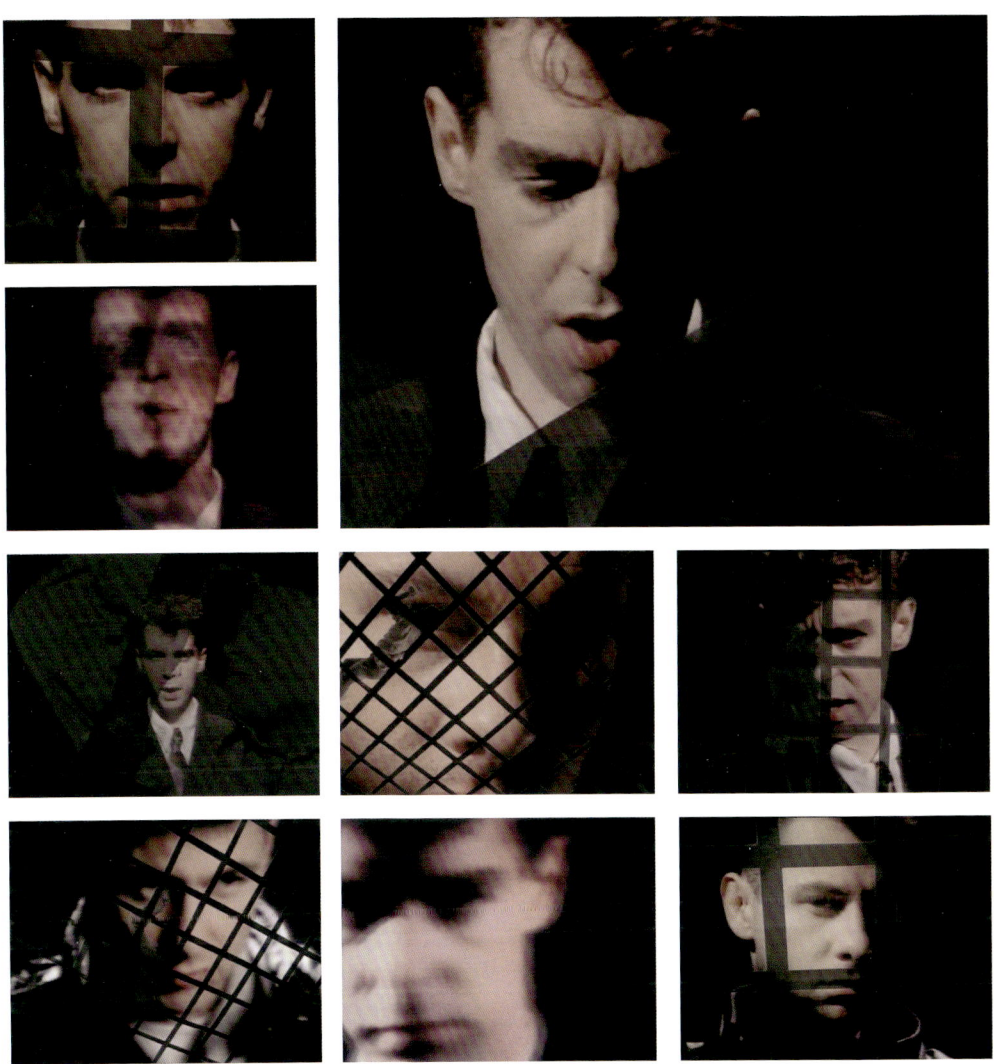

Love comes quickly 1986

Please

release 24 March 1986
formats LP / cassette / CD
photographer Eric Watson and others
design Mark Farrow at 3 and PSB

The design of *Please*, released in March 1986, was as minimal as its title. Virtually every detail was stripped away, leaving only an image barely bigger than a postage stamp, with the group's name and album title below. The effect was to draw the viewer in, towards what is ostensibly an innocent imageW but is in fact one of seductive desire. Mark Farrow had designed a sleeve at Factory Records for the group Section 25 with a tiny photo on it, and had liked the way it looked. 'It's almost the starting point, when I design a cover, that it shouldn't look like a cover', says Farrow. 'It's "how can this look different from anything else?" But not wilfully, for the sheer hell of it – there's got to be a good reason. My idea was that it was reverse marketing – the virtue of the fact that you would have this big white expanse and a tiny picture, when every other sleeve was full of photos or information, was that it demanded your attention and drew you in.' They chose a photo by Eric Watson because the white towels and T-shirts worked with the white background. The back cover text was confined to a small block that echoes the design of the front – although when the credits were changed at the last minute the text no longer formed a perfect square. The inner sleeve (following pages) has ninety-eight different images, each the same size as the front cover image. For the CD it was decided that, instead of reducing the LP sleeve proportionately, as is the usual practice, the photo and text should be exactly the same size as on the LP, with the white space greatly reduced.

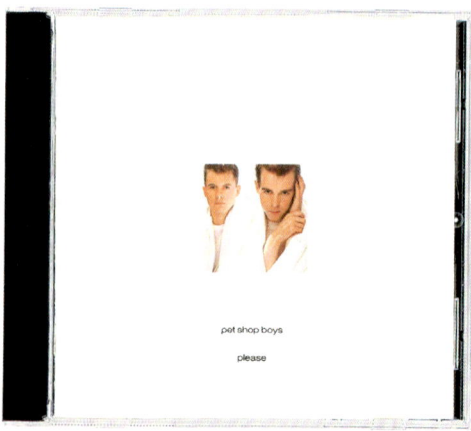

CD, front

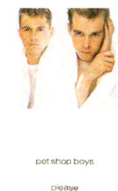

LP, outer sleeve, front

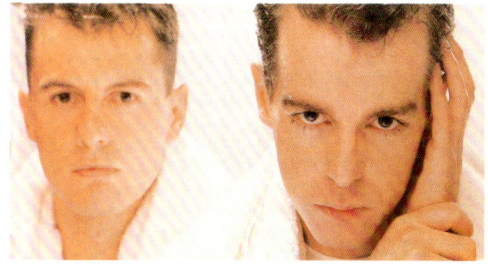

LP, outer sleeve, back

LP, Spain, outer sleeve, front

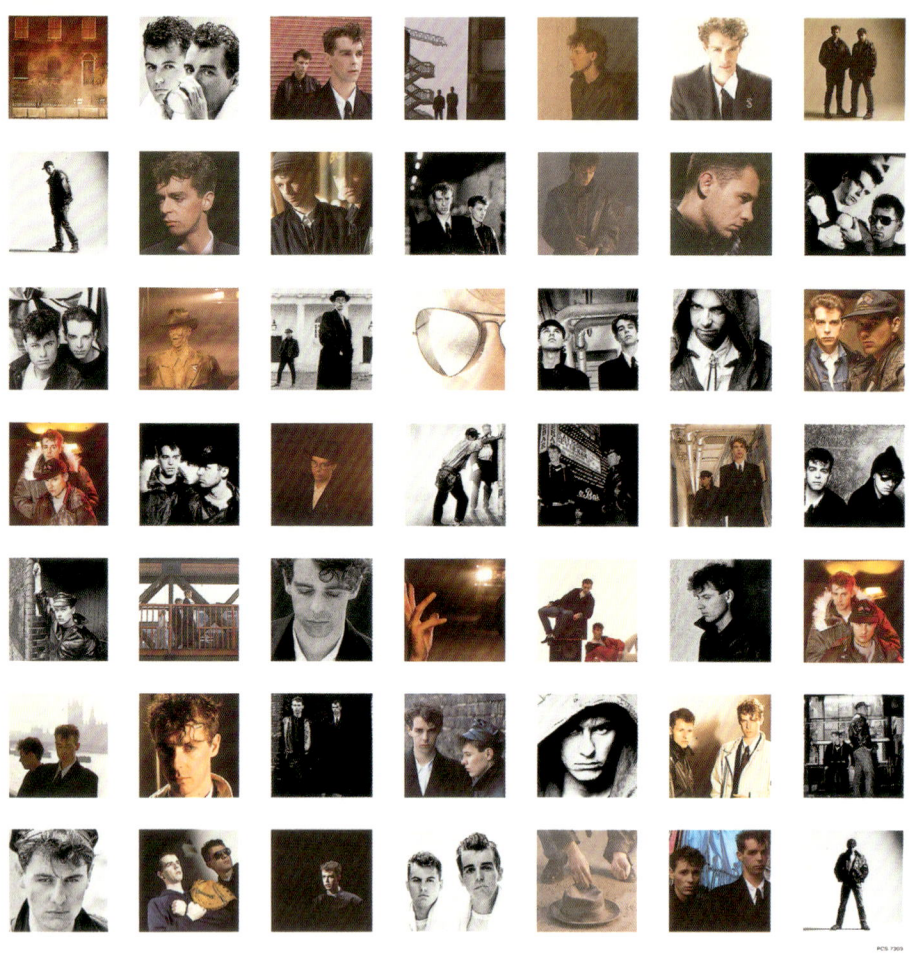

LP, inner sleeve, front (photos: Eric Watson, Paul Rider, John Stoddard, Brian Aris, Joe Shutter, Ian Hooton, Chris Burscough)

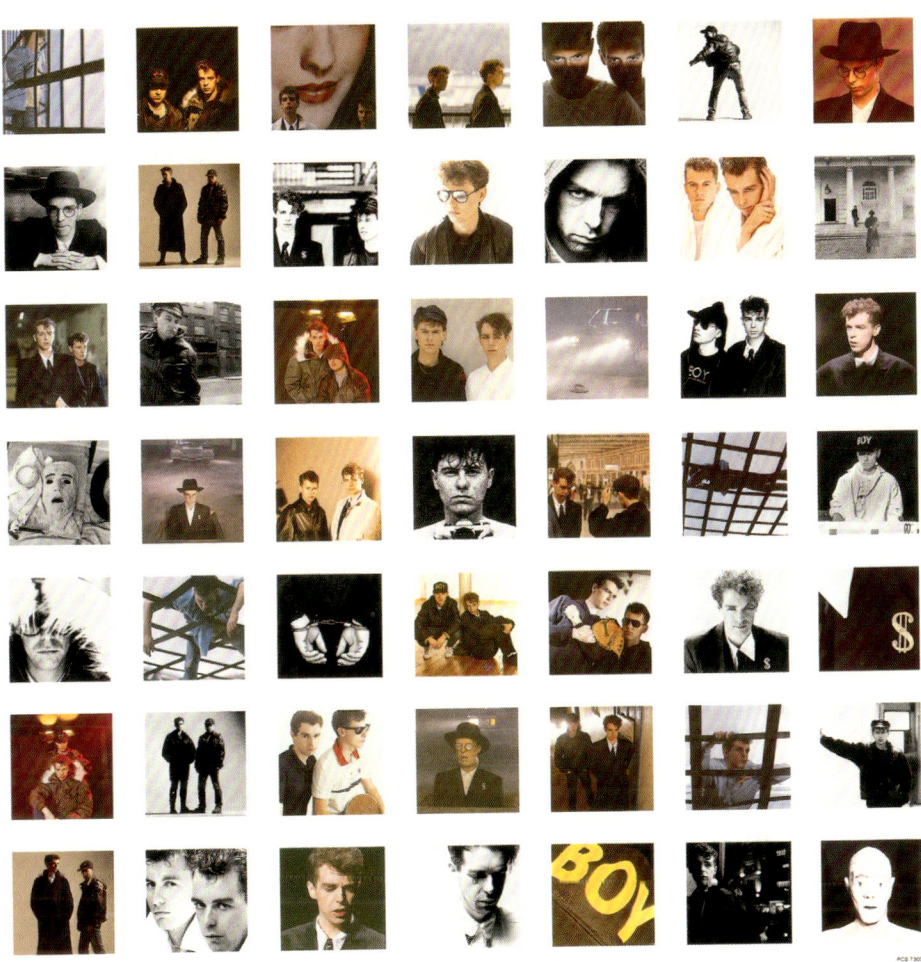

LP, inner sleeve, back (photos: Eric Watson, Paul Rider, John Stoddard, Brian Aris, Joe Shutter, Ian Hooton, Chris Burscough, Chris Lowe)

Opportunities (let's make lots of money)

(second release)
release 19 May 1986
formats 7" / 12" × 3 / 12" promo / cassette
design Mark Farrow at 3 and PSB
video Zbigniew Rybczynski

Here the image of the group has become subordinate to, or subsumed by, their graphic; as if their style had been reduced to typography. Farrow's design is extraordinarily bold, in keeping, perhaps, with the apparently bold statement of the song title. Yet, just as the song is ironical, so the absence of the Pet Shop Boys' image here is itself ambiguous – especially in an era in which image and content had become confused, and, at the same time, more important than ever as part of the capitalistic system. This, like the second release of 'West End girls', was also a re-recording of the song. 'It's kind of a Factory sleeve, really', says Mark Farrow. 'It was gold and silver because that's what money is. I don't remember there being any big decision about there not being a photo on it.'

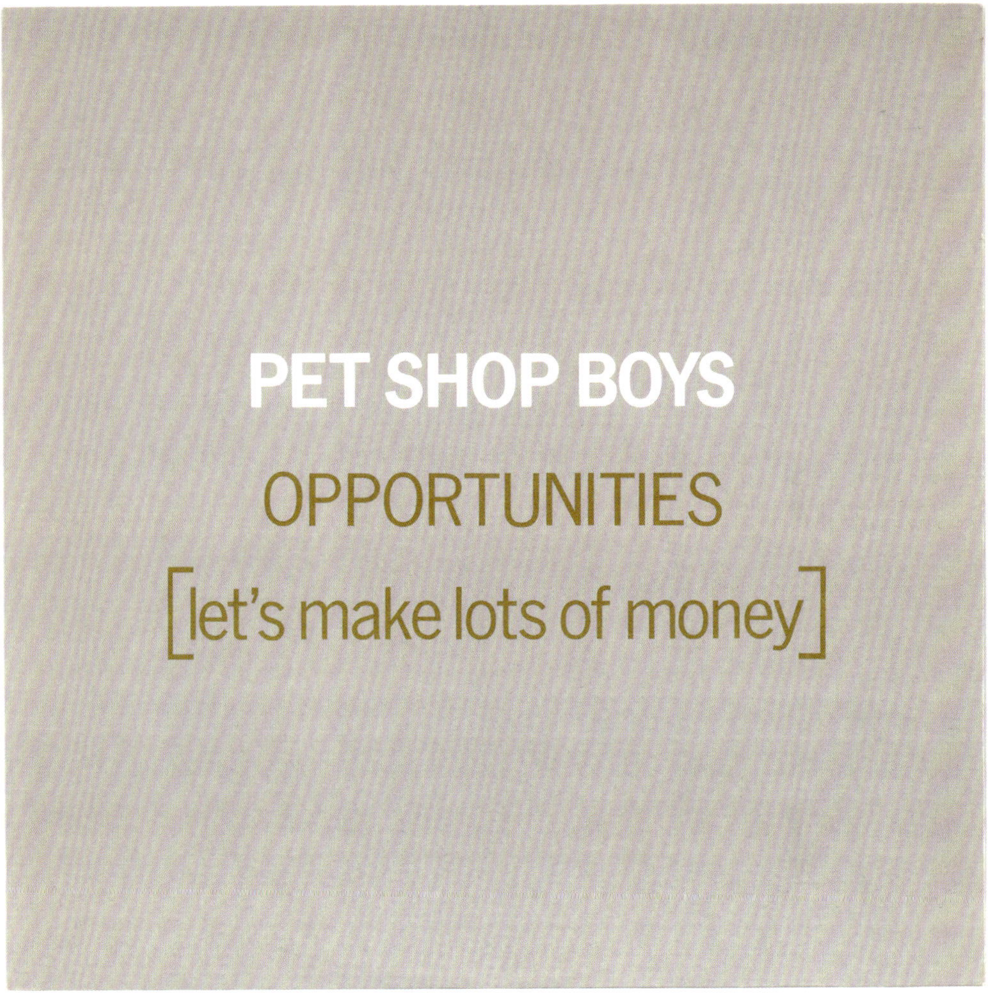

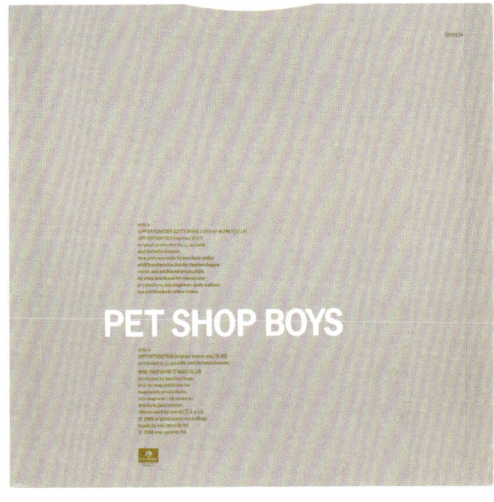

12", front

12", back

Opportunities (let's make lots of money) 1986

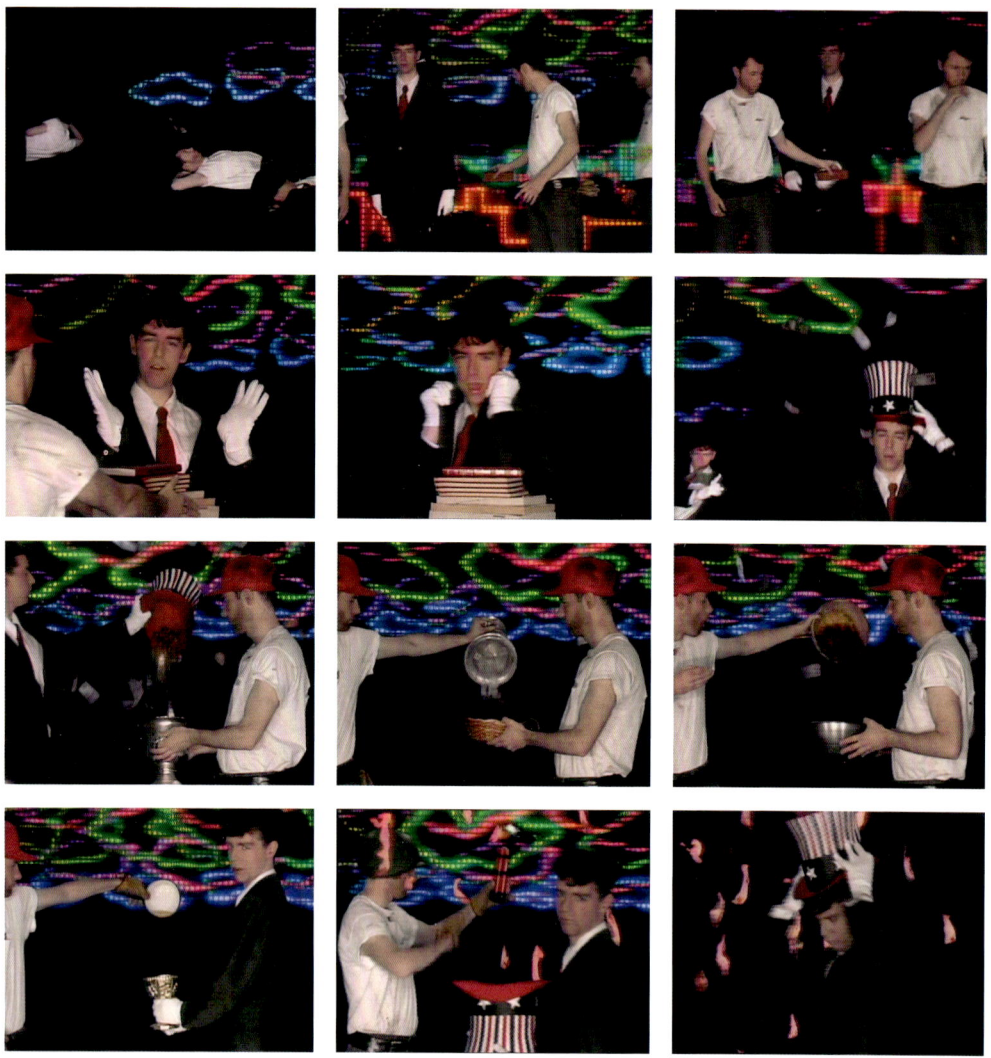

In studio-black limbo, with video game graphics running an illuminated panorama of clouds and city skylines behind them, Neil – dressed in a shiny suit – and Chris – in T-shirt and jeans and leather gloves, as a builder or scaffolder – pass objects between them: a case, a brick, books, an urn, a petrol can, etcetera. Meanwhile, bank notes fall from the sky and start to burn. Neil doffs his Uncle Sam top hat (an image to be reprised, tangentially, for 'Go west' in 1993), which Chris fills with a silvery liquid.

The video effects, which now seem quite primitive, were considered highly innovative at the time, while the iconic nature of the imagery seems deeply ironical. Here Pet Shop Boys' early love affair with America has taken a more nuanced turn, as the omnipotent dollar is satirized by Neil's hat. There is even a shot of a red electric guitar. 'I think the director, Zbig, knew that we hated guitars', commented Neil. 'For us, anyway, it was a joke: we were making a video for America and we had an electric guitar.'

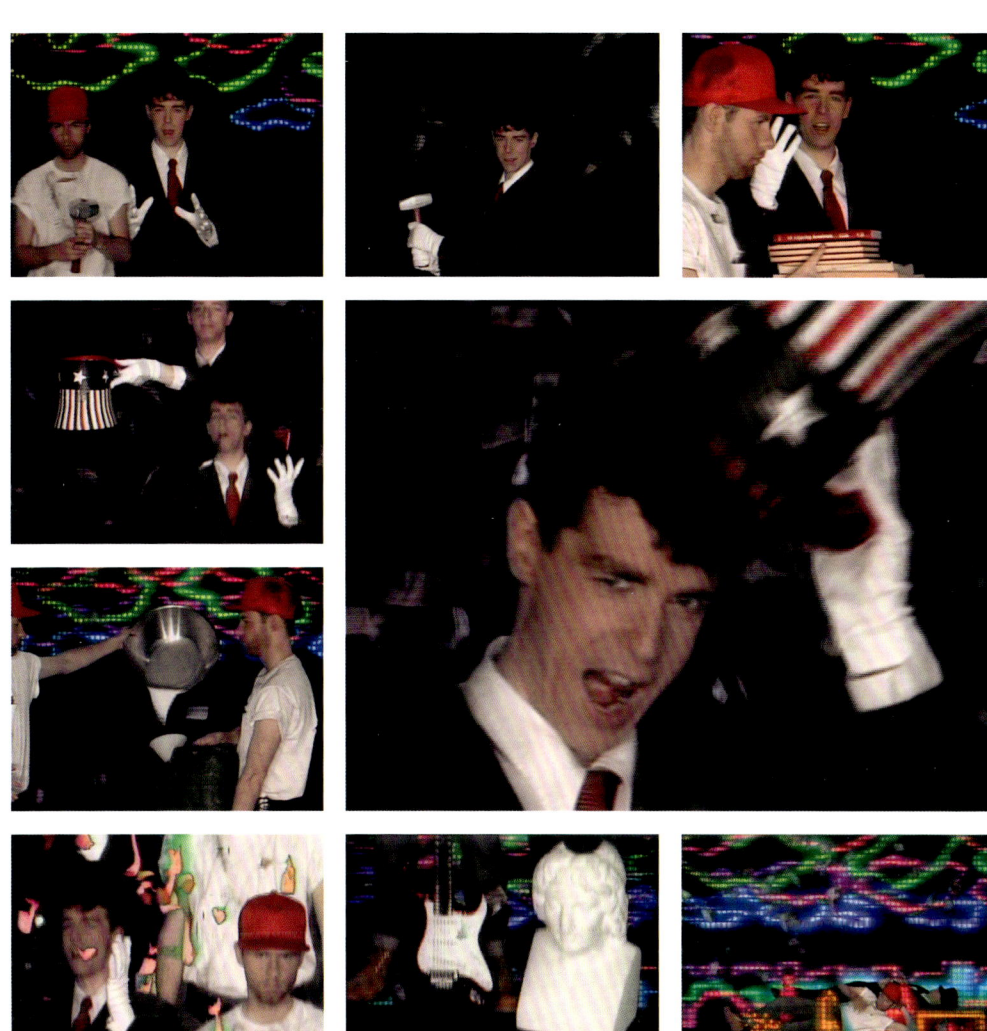

Opportunities (let's make lots of money) 1986

Suburbia

release 22 September 1986
formats 7" / double 7" gatefold / 12" / cassette
photographer Eric Watson
design Mark Farrow at 3 and PSB
video Eric Watson

The most visually arresting of all the early Pet Shop Boys releases, 'Suburbia' was also the first single with inner and outer sleeves. The cover of the twelve inch went on to win a D&AD design award. Chris is wearing a Poshboy T-shirt, cap, and flip-up Issey Miyake 'venetian-blind' sunglasses; Neil is in round aviator shades and black T-shirt, reflecting the minimal design. The insert of the twelve inch and the gatefold inner of the seven inch uses blurred photos of Neil grabbing Chris around the neck in a mock fight that resembled a Francis Bacon painting. The gatefold sleeve (following pages) has a white band containing the credits, purposefully echoing a film poster (the credit for Penelope Spheeris's film *Suburbia*, an inspiration for the song, was added to imply that the release had a relationship to the movie).

Neil recalls that Chris had bought his T-shirt and cap, then tried on the Issey Miyake glasses. 'They were very expensive', he says, 'but I said they'd look great in a photo session.' Neil's sunglasses were blacked-in with tape so as not to reflect the photographer's lights. The throttling shot was Eric Watson's idea – he had already done test shots with some other people. Neil and Chris were originally keen to use photographs from a piece just published in *The Face* that year of kids rampaging around the outskirts of Dublin. Mark Farrow recalls: 'Stealing cars, and setting them on fire and jumping on them, kids riding ponies down the street …'. Farrow was supposed to track them down, but dragged his heels: 'I am absolutely hopeless at doing things like that.' Meanwhile, photos from the Eric Watson session (pages 70–1) were sent over so that Farrow could put them on the back of the sleeve. 'And I just thought that that picture of Chris with those glasses and that T-shirt on was one of the best photographs I'd ever seen. It's everything about Pet Shop Boys summed up to me in a photo. That's something I've never backed away from – I've always thought that if the photograph is strong enough to do the work on its own, then I don't really need to do anything. In my mind at that time Chris was the logo, if you like', says Farrow: 'the way Chris looked was the logo of the Pet Shop Boys.'

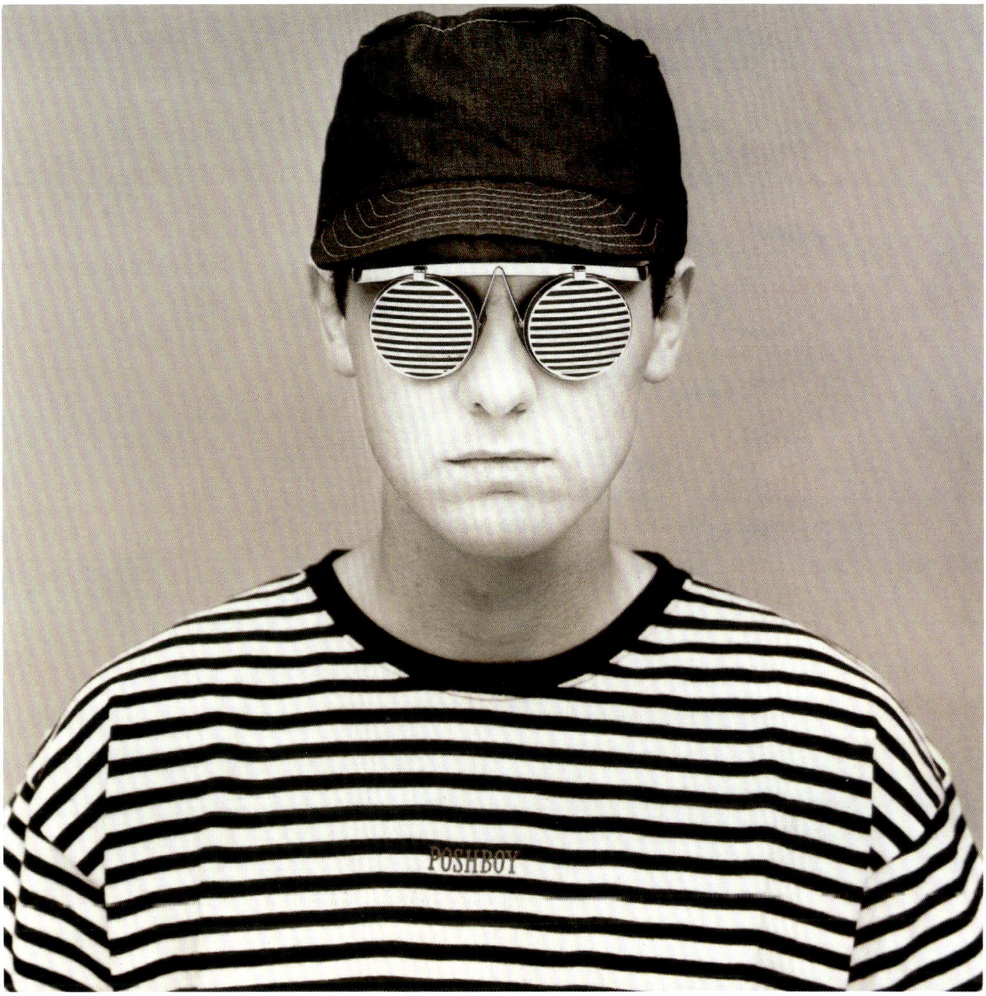

12", outer sleeve, front

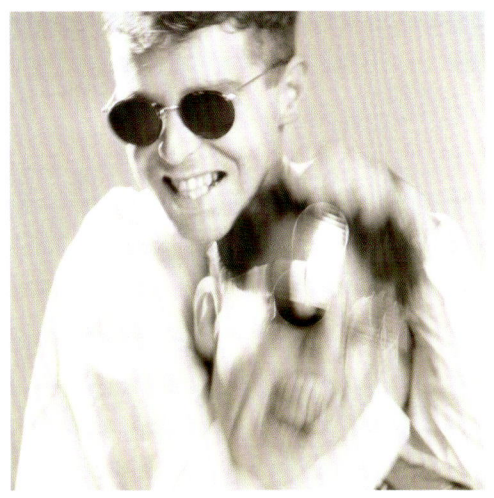

12", inner sleeve, front

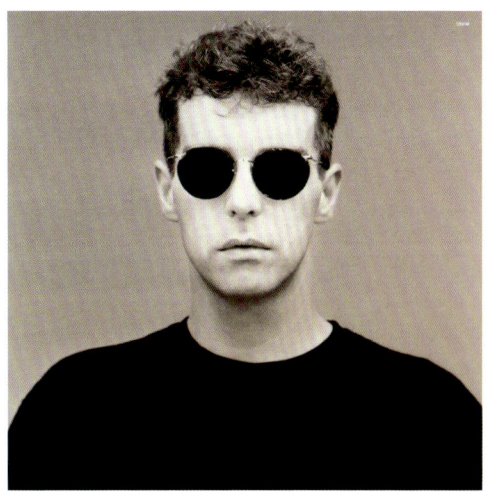

12", outer sleeve, back

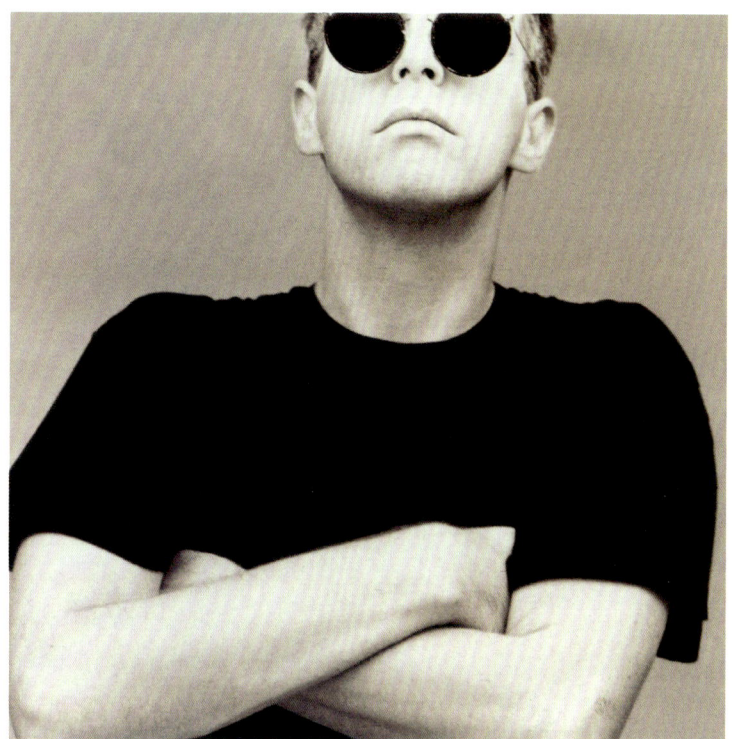

7", gatefold (closed), front

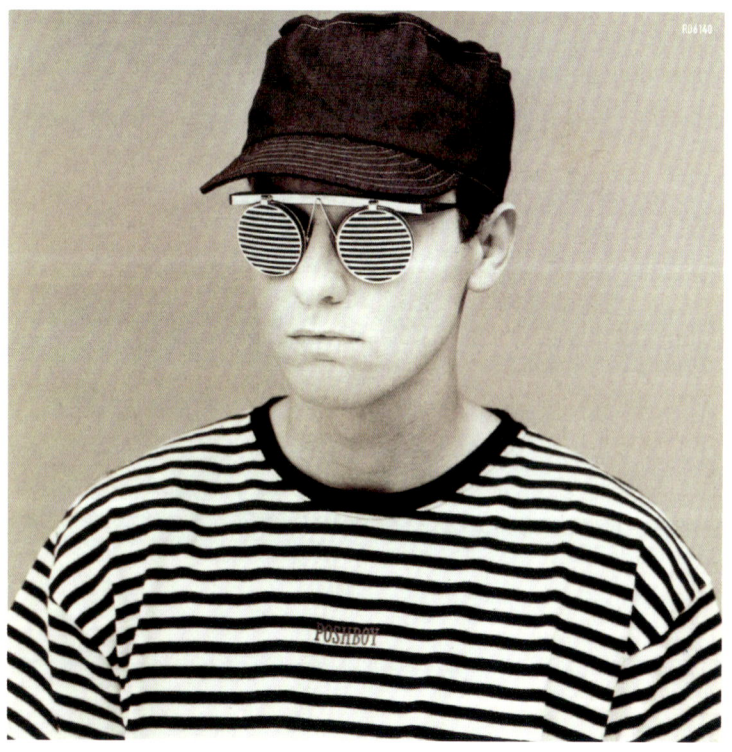

7", gatefold (closed), back

68 Suburbia 1986

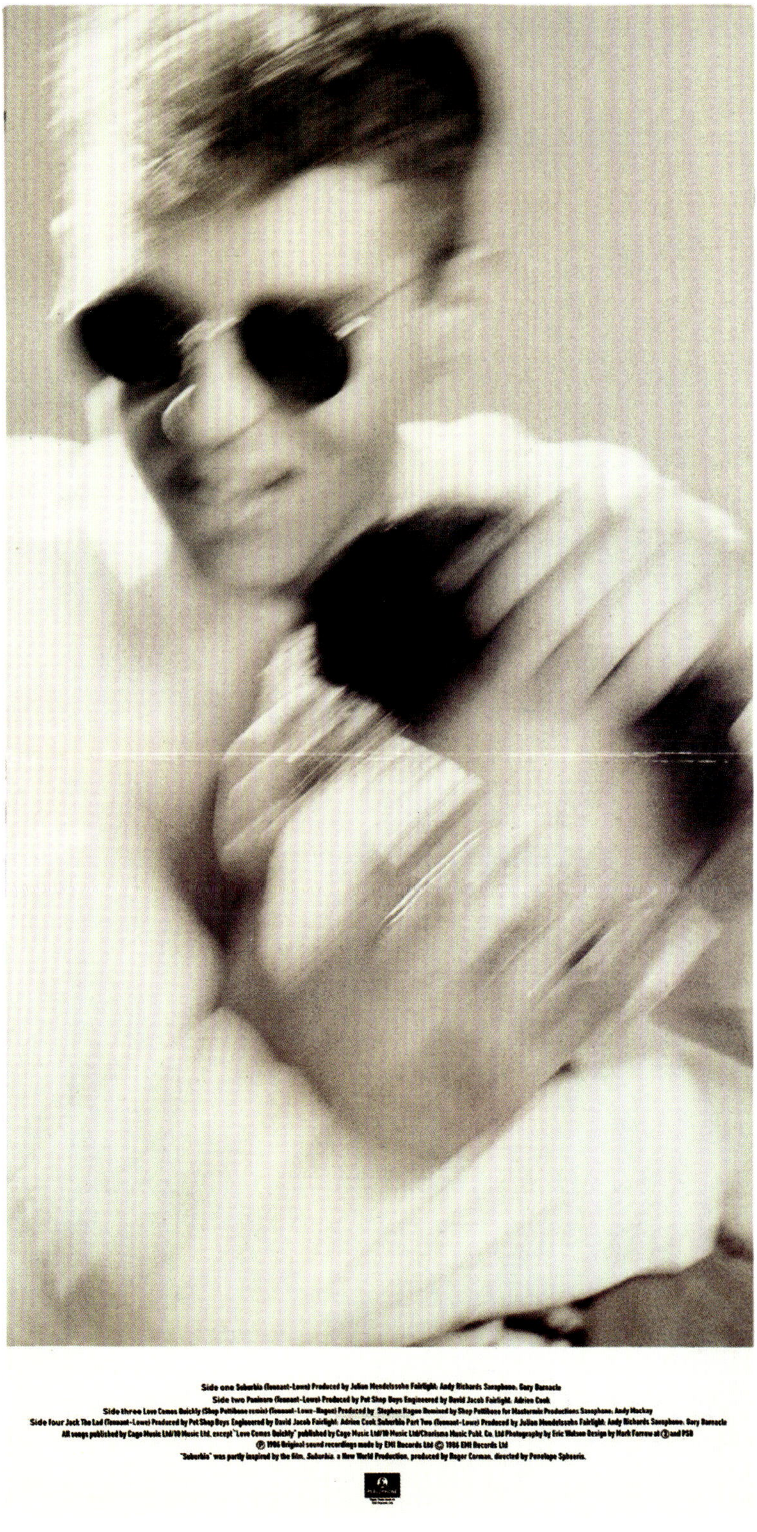

7", gatefold (open), inside

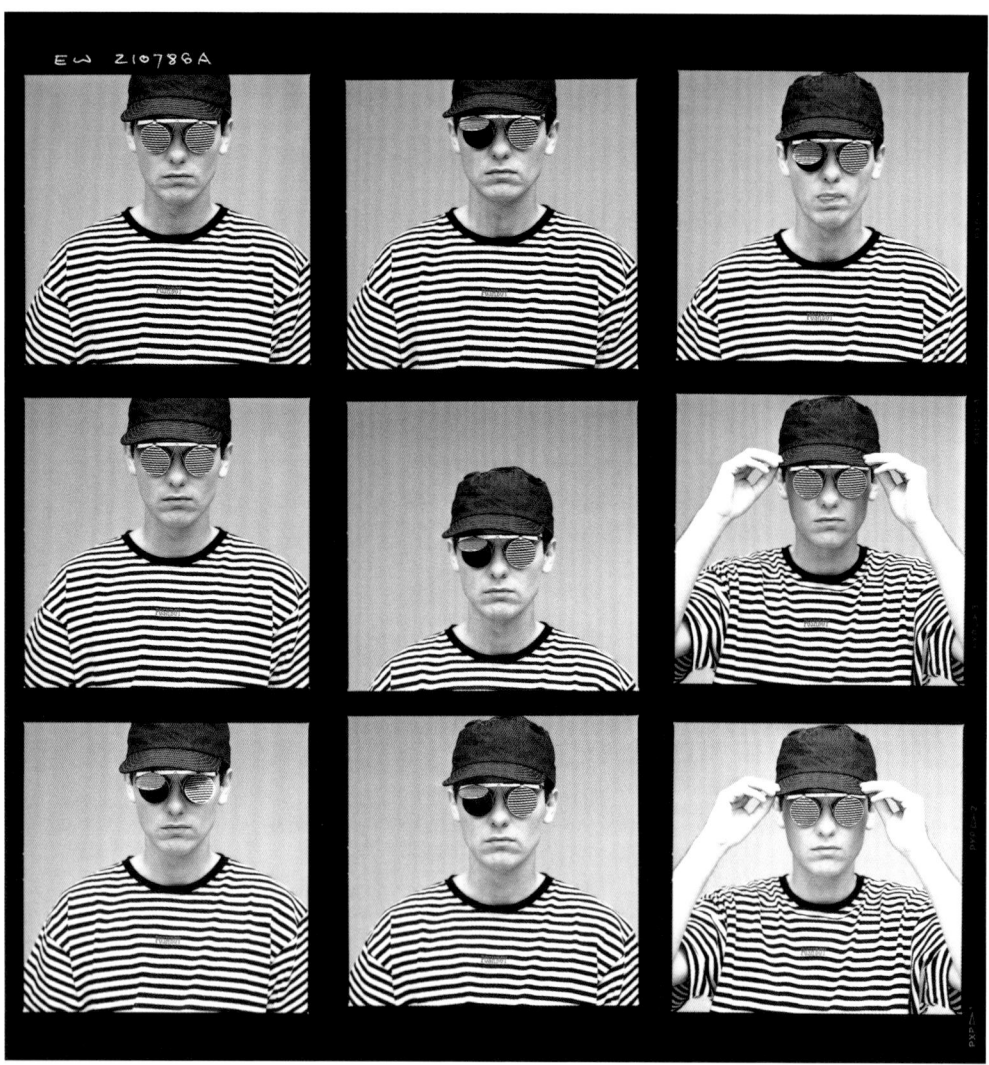

Contact sheet from the 'Suburbia' photo session with Eric Watson, 20 July 1986

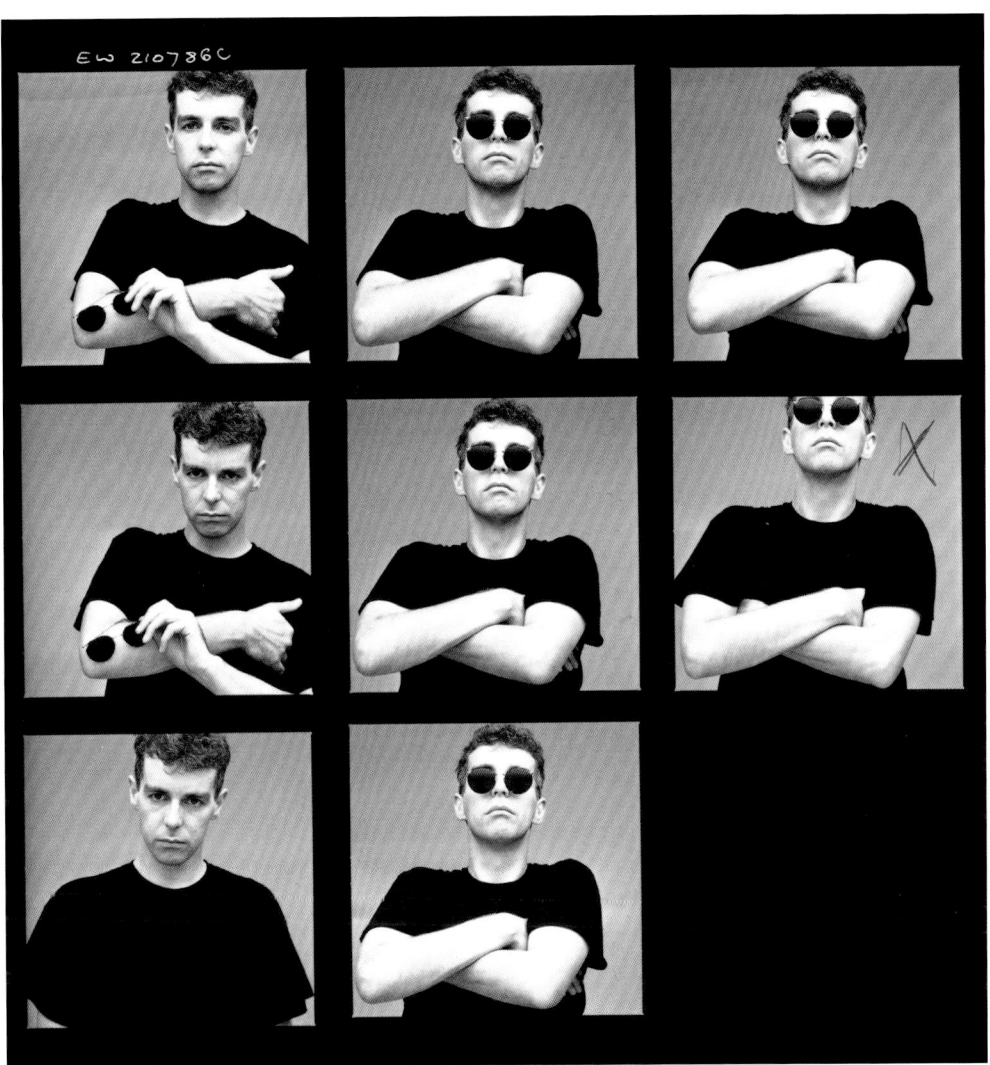

Contact sheet from the 'Suburbia' photo session with Eric Watson, 20 July 1986

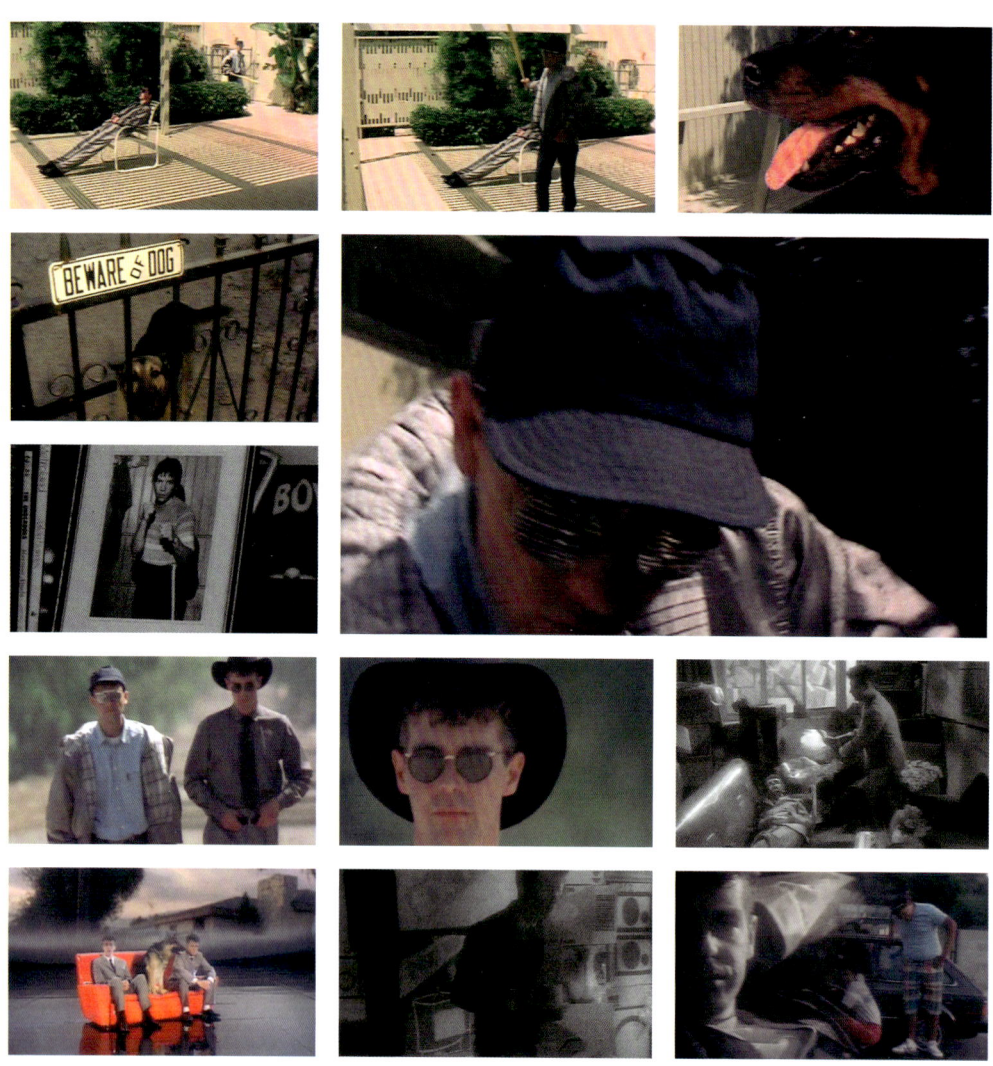

In the stratified sharp light of California, we see Chris fighting with a German shepherd dog, and Neil in stetson and shades. Cut to English suburbia, where Neil and Chris in grey suits sit in a suburban front room, frustrated by the newspapers and the television (which is playing the 'Opportunities' video). Rows of semi-detached English houses contrast with the suburbs of Los Angeles and their Hispanic inhabitants. Chris wields a baseball bat; Neil sprays flies. Their red sofa is suddenly seen in isolation, and we cut to more shots of Californian underclass. 'The light was fantastic for the LA stuff', recalls Chris. It was one of Eric Watson's favourite videos. 'I'd been raving about Penelope Spheeris's film for years, in particular the poster, which was a little punk kid with a mohawk on a tricycle with a rifle outside a suburban home. It was such a great image. We wanted the video to be partly suburban Los Angeles and partly suburban London, so it was shot in a town north of Pasadena and in

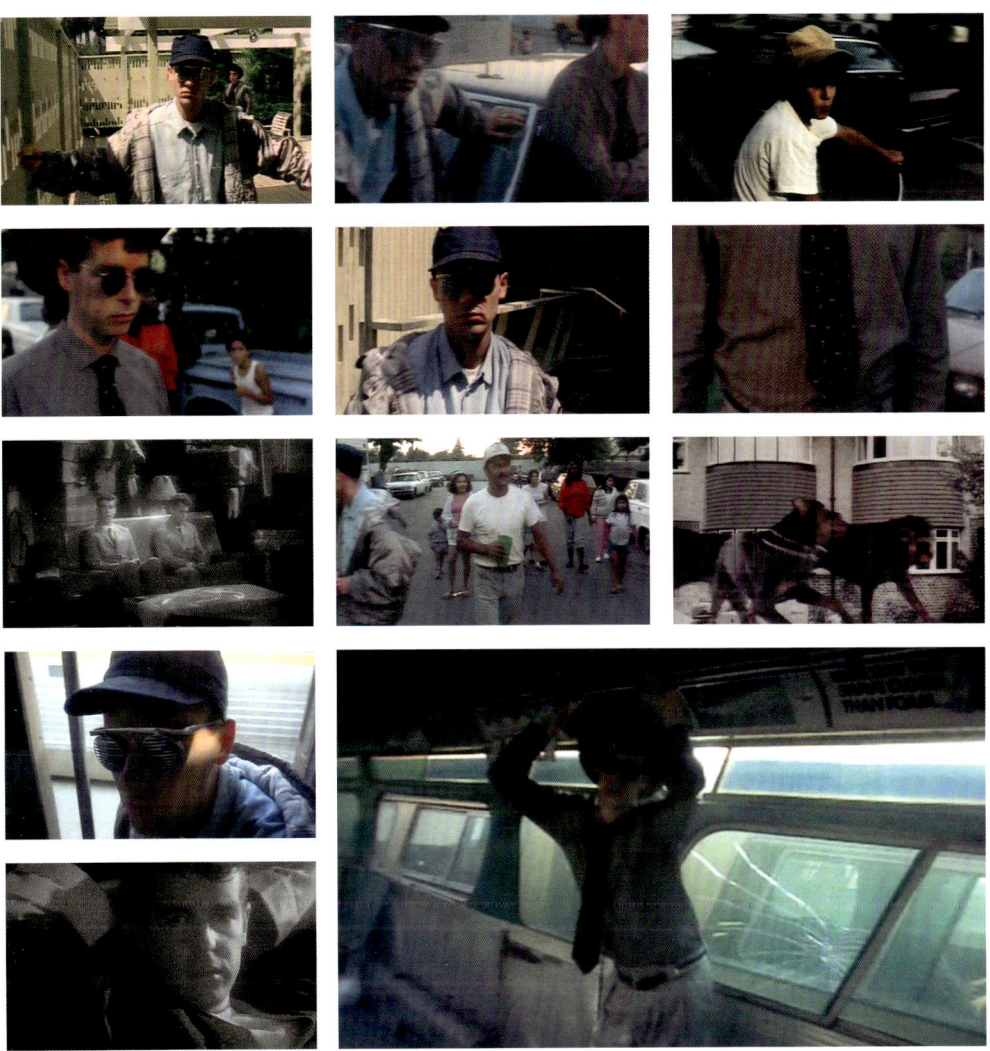

Kingston-upon-Thames, and it goes here–there, here–there. I don't think anyone noticed, but you can see all these boxes, partially open, and the idea was that we'd suddenly become really wealthy but didn't have time to get the things out of the box.' This was a visual trope to which the group would return in their *Performance* tour of 1991.

Paninaro

release Autumn 1986 (exact date unknown)
format 12" (Italy)
design Mark Farrow at 3 and PSB
video PSB

Pet Shop Boys' attraction to Italian youth culture was underlined by their anthemic tribute to a new cult, as noted in *i-D* magazine's 'encyclopaedia of the '80s', *A Decade of i-Deas*: 'In '86 Italian streets from Milan to Rome were full of teenagers wearing rolled-up 501 jeans, bright padded ski jackets, Timberland shoes, checked shirts, preppy blazers, white trousers, backpacks, Ray-Bans, Charro belts, and beige driving gloves for their loud trail bikes. They called themselves "Paninari", literally translated from the word "sandwich", although they gathered outside burger bars and lived on a diet of fast food. So strong was the trend that it even had its own magazines: comic-book A5 manuals like *Preppy*, *Paninaro*, and *Wild Boys* depicted violent *Rambo*-like escapades as well as ads for quilted ski jackets and massive buckle belts. Paninari music included Duran Duran, Patsy Kensit, Madonna, Spandau Ballet and the Pet Shop Boys (who adopted the look and made a record called "Paninaro"), and its fashion spread throughout Europe.'

'Paninaro' was released as a standalone twelve-inch single, whose lettering mirrored that of 'Suburbia', but only in Italy, as Pet Shop Boys intended. 'We always had this bizarre ambition that we wanted to be big in Italy more than anywhere else', said Neil. 'We never were, of course.' 'We tried hard though', said Chris.

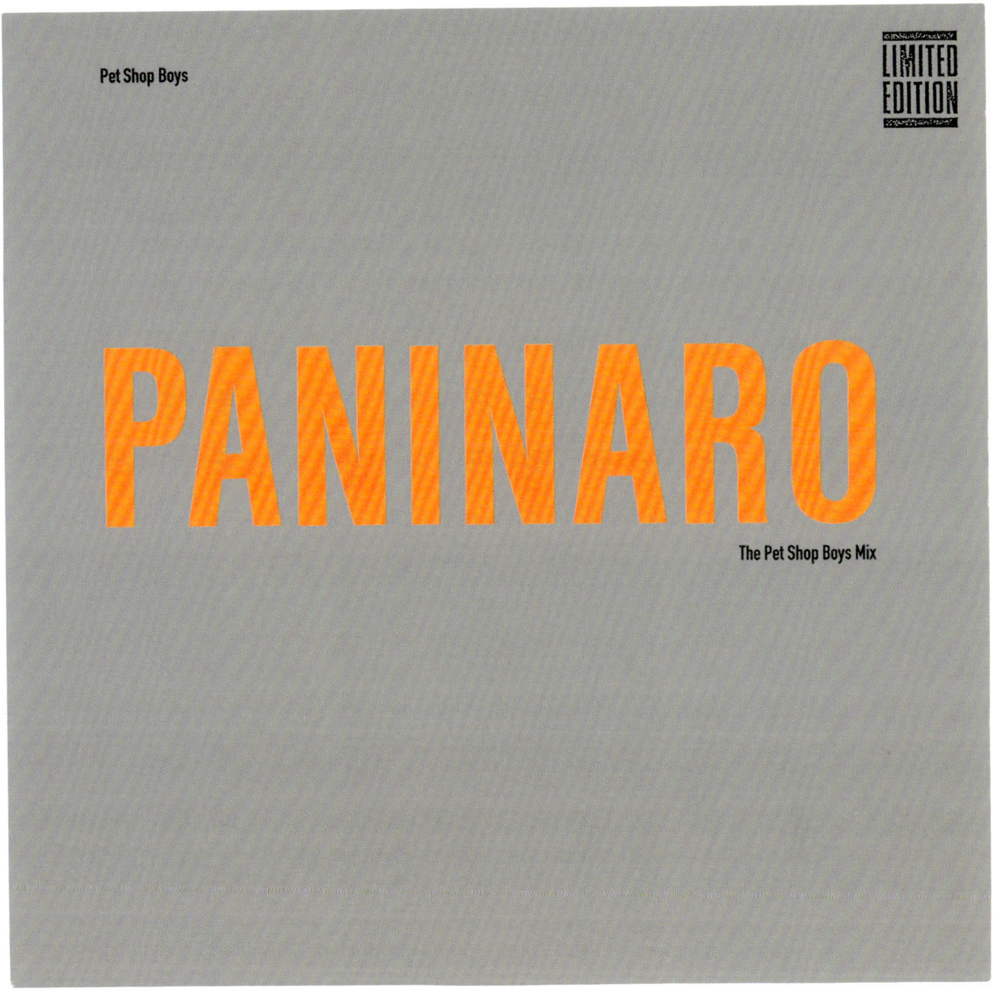

12", Italy, front

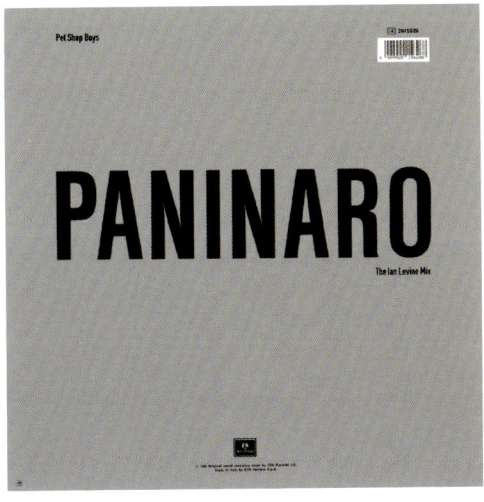

12", Italy, back

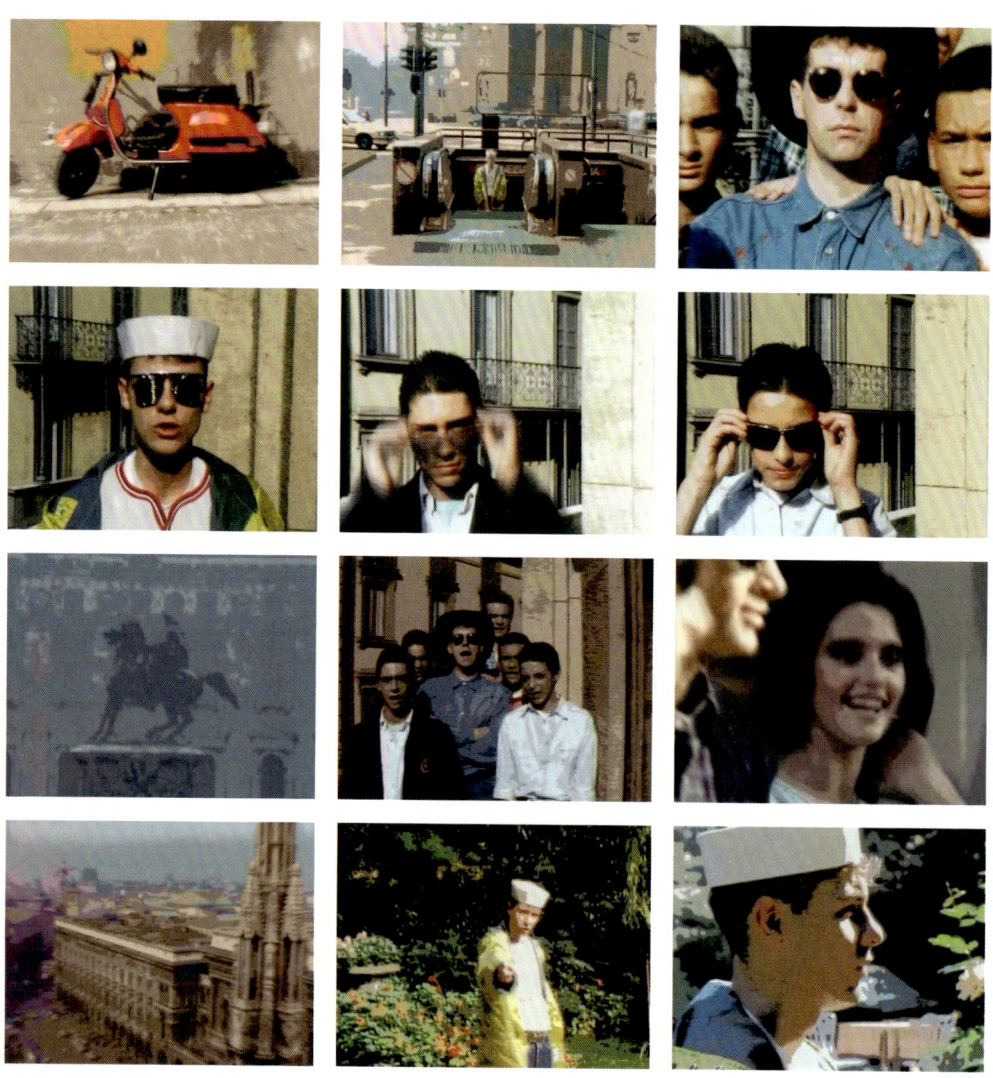

Chris emerges onto an Italian street from a subway escalator, dressed in jeans, yellow jacket, and a white sailor's hat. Solarized shots of Italian youth cut to Chris surrounded by a gang as he raps, and they sing the chorus. Neil is seen likewise, but wearing stetson, denim shirt, and round aviator shades. Lots of attitude: Chris dances, and so do his flip-up Issey Miyake 'Suburbia' shades. More shots of stylish Italian kids wearing designer clothes and shades mix with images of Emporio Armani posters and scenes of historical Milan. Owing to the lack of a budget, Neil and Chris filmed the video themselves in Milan, using a 'very cheap' video camera that they were given in Japan, and also did their own editing.

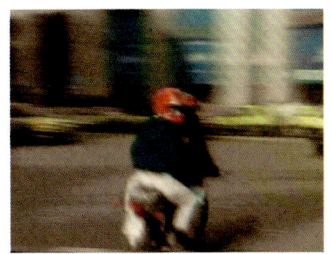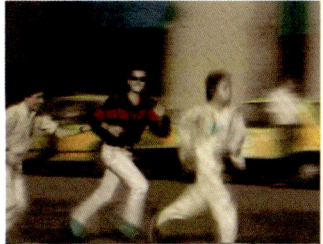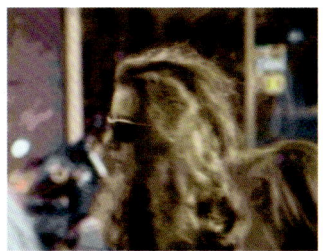
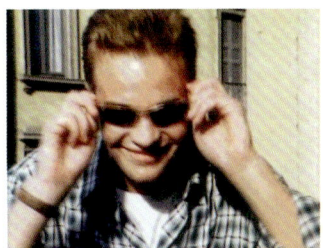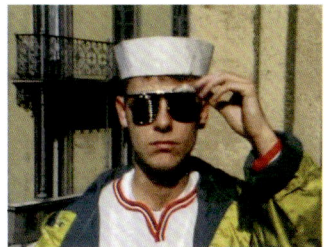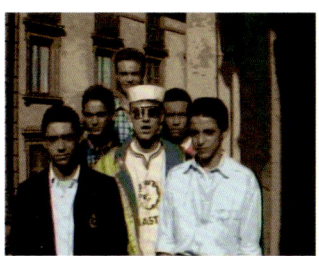
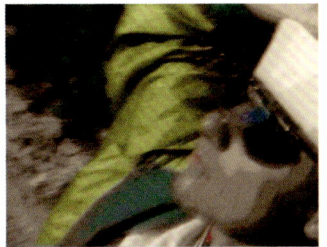
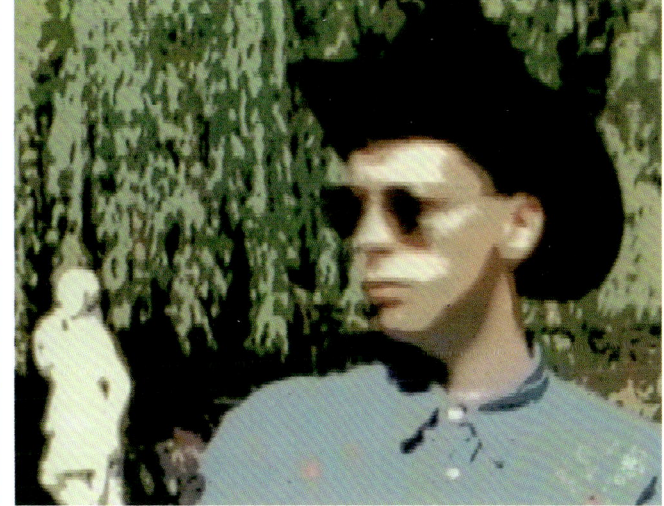
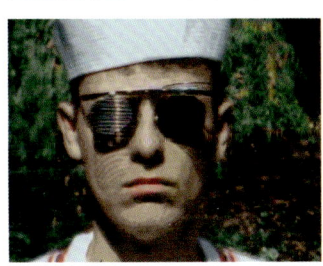

Paninaro 1986

Disco

release 17 November 1986
formats LP / cassette / CD
design Mark Farrow at 3 and PSB

Disco was first of a series of Pet Shop Boys albums to contain extended dance mixes of recent hits and a new song, in the tradition of Soft Cell's *Non Stop Ecstatic Dancing*. Its title was something of a provocation and a defiant show of pride in the face of an American culture that still deemed the word 'disco' an insult, connoting music that was shallow, passionless, and worthless.

Chris particularly liked the way he had looked in the 'Paninaro' video. So Mark Farrow went into an edit suite with Liz Flowers of Picture Music International (Pet Shop Boys' video publishers) to take off some stills. The blurred front image of Chris playing keyboards in his yellow jacket and striped 'Suburbia' T-shirt seemed to fit, since it looked 'like it was in a club'. The inner sleeve photos of Chris and Neil were also taken from the same video.

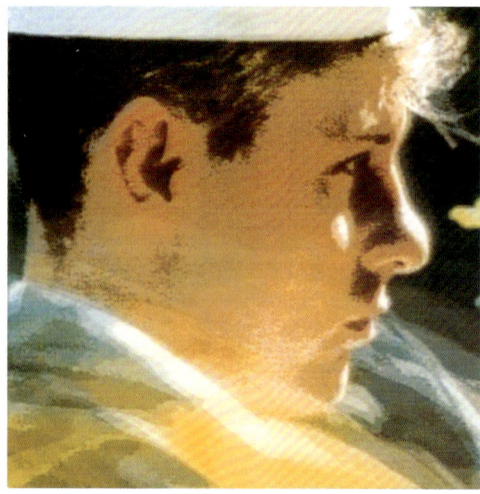

LP, inner sleeve, front

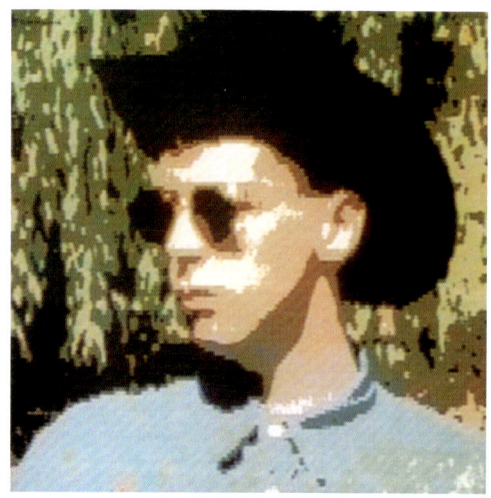

LP, inner sleeve, back

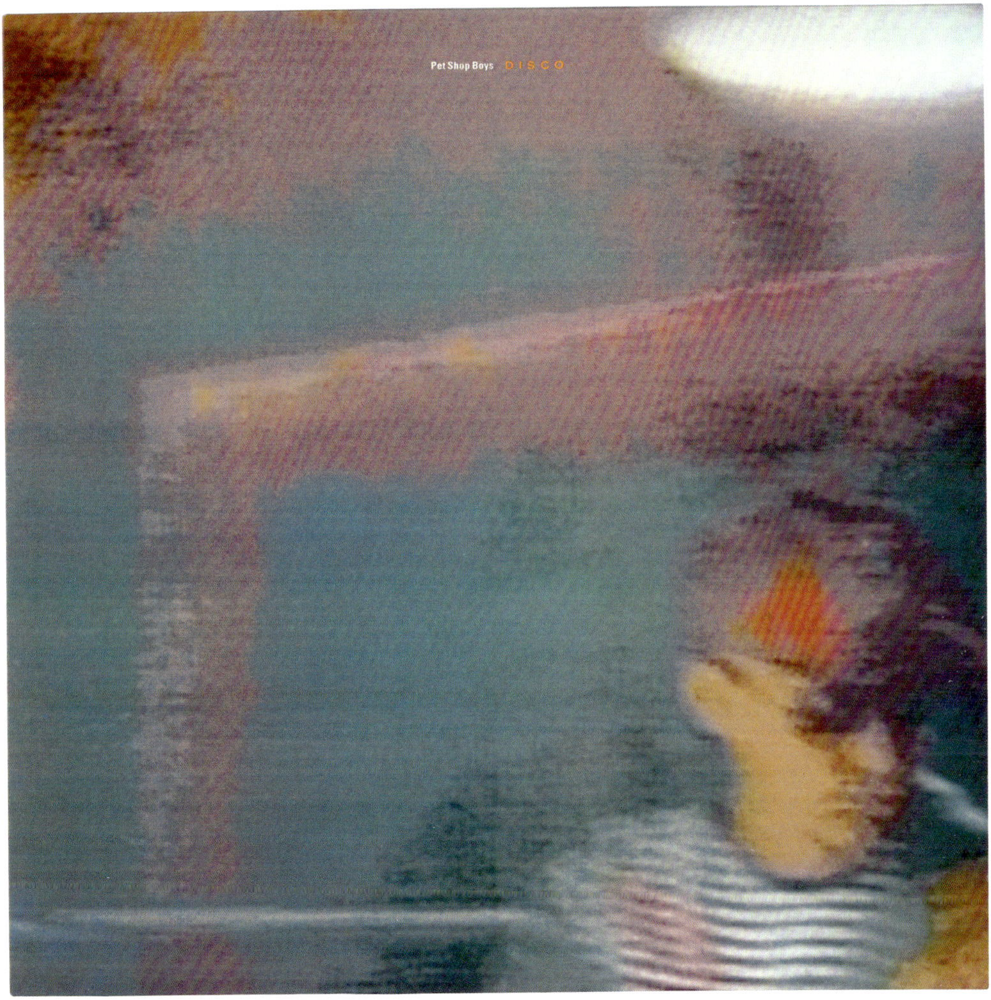

LP, outer sleeve, front

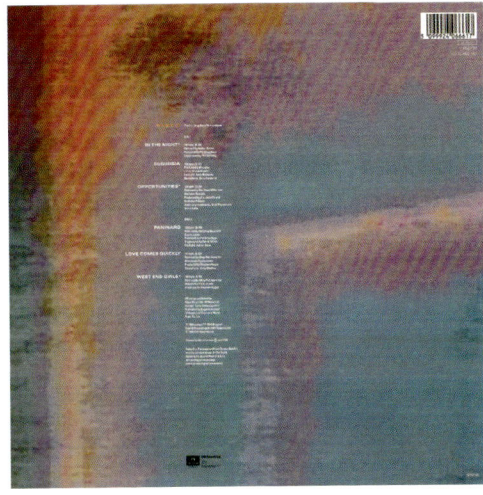

LP, outer sleeve, back

Disco 1986

Television

release 1 December 1986
formats VHS / Beta / laserdisc
design Mark Farrow at 3 and PSB

Television was a compilation of Pet Shop Boys' first promotional videos, which also included some brief extracts from notable early TV appearances. In some of the interstitial moments between songs, we see them establishing their distance from, and attitude towards, the medium. From the start, they were resistant to the clichés forced upon pop musicians whenever a TV camera was pointed in their direction. They refused to be bamboozled by other people's lazy expectations into doing something shameful. As Neil commented to David Toop in an *Elle* magazine interview coinciding with the release of their second studio album, *Actually*, 'When somebody points a film camera at you, they normally say "Right, start." And I say, "I don't know what to do."'

The collection includes the famous interview in which Chris offers the definitive statement of attitude that they subsequently sampled and used on 'Paninaro': 'I don't like country and western, I don't like rock music, I don't like rockabilly ... I don't like much really, do I? But what I do like, I love passionately.' Its sleeve reused the two images from the 'Paninaro' video that had previously been used on the *Disco* inner sleeve: 'It covered *Please* and it covered *Disco*,' says Mark Farrow, 'so the cover has the pictures from the inside sleeve of *Disco* presented like the picture on the front of *Please*.'

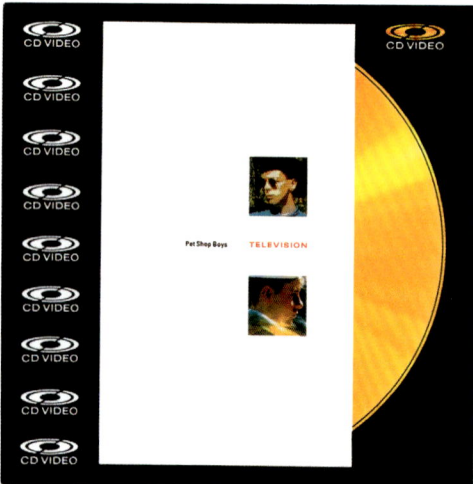

Laserdisc, front

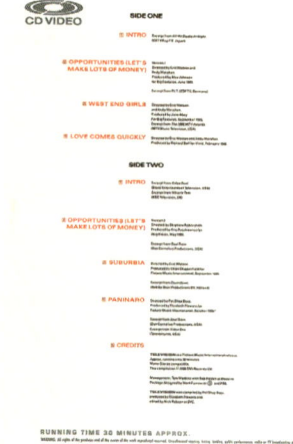

Laserdisc, back

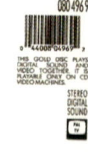

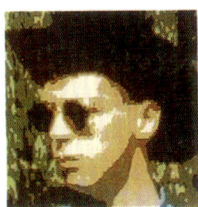

Pet Shop Boys **TELEVISION**

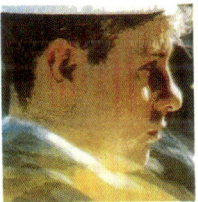

VHS, front

It's a sin

release 15 June 1987
formats 7" / cassette / CD / 12" / 12" remix
photographer Eric Watson
design Mark Farrow at 3 and PSB
video Derek Jarman

The photographs were shot in the eighteenth-century Christ Church, Spitalfields. (Gilbert and George live on the same street.) The main shot that appeared on both the seven inch and the inner sleeve of the twelve inch was taken in the abandoned sacristy. The outer sleeve of the twelve inch has full-length photographs of Neil and Chris standing inside the church. The empty, cavernous spaces reflect the oppressive nature of the song's themes. The cover of the twelve-inch remix is a close-up of Chris from the video, in which he plays a medieval jailer. It is a deliberately obscure image that again references the darker ideas of the song itself.

It was Neil's idea to put the title in inverted commas 'like a Victorian book illustration'. The main cover photograph reminds him of Walter Sickert's painting *Ennui* (c. 1914) ; while the hooded figures of the video echo Francisco de Zurbarán's *St Francis in Meditation* (1635–9). One correspondent to *Literally*, the Pet Shop Boys fan-club magazine, noted, 'In his book *Ways of Seeing*, John Berger suggests that many contemporary advertisements (mostly magazine ads) are modelled from medieval and Renaissance paintings. The cover for "It's a sin" seems to resemble the cluttered voguishness of such paintings.' Neil replied that while Eric Watson certainly 'read a lot of Berger ... we did photos in a church because we felt like it'.

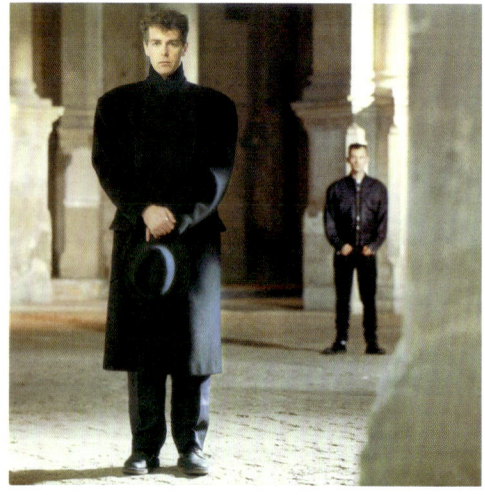

12", outer sleeve, front

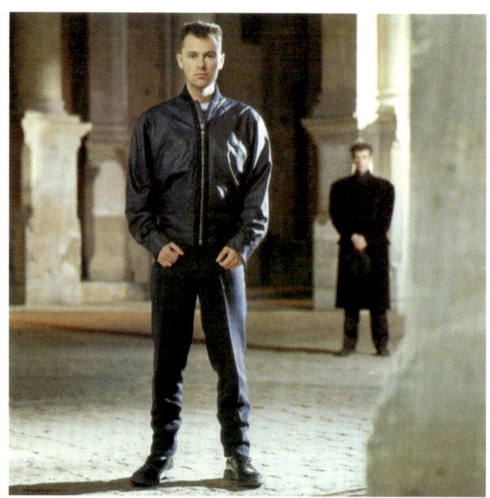

12", outer sleeve, back

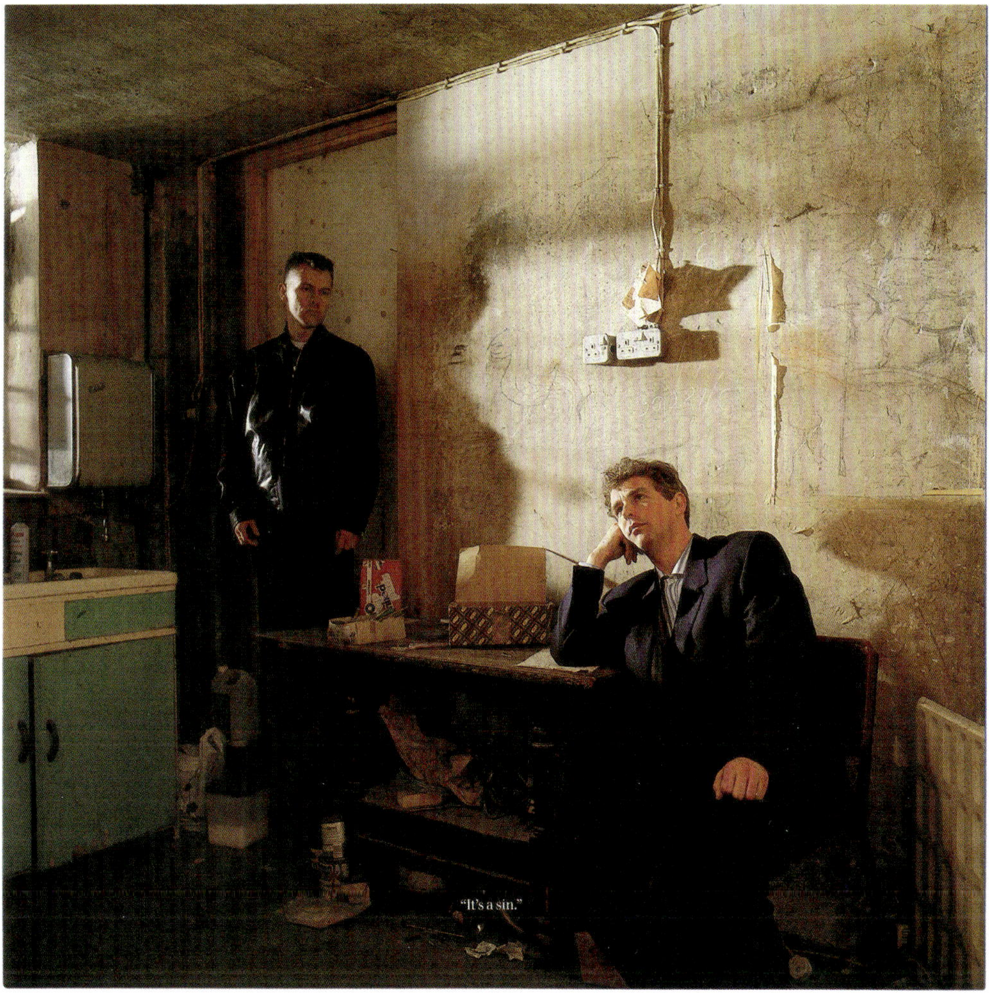

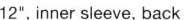

12", inner sleeve, front

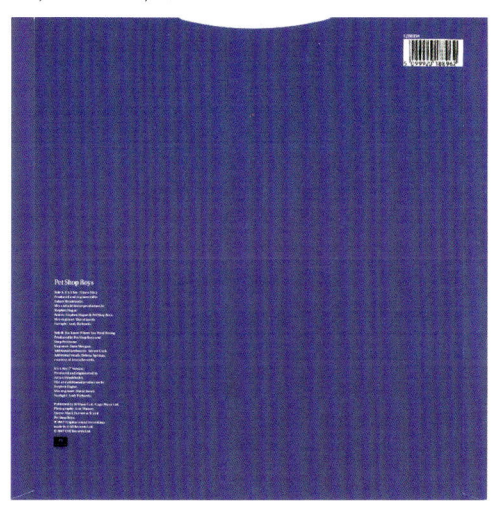

12", inner sleeve, back

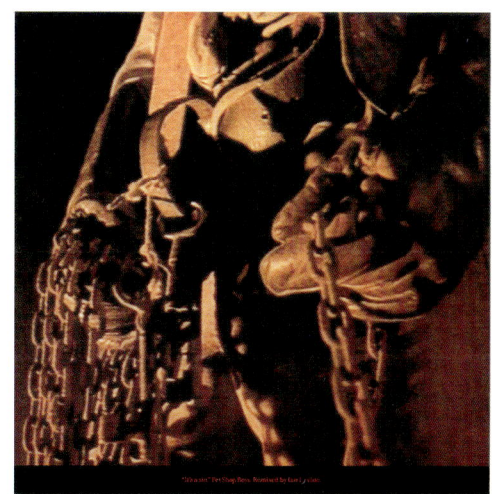

12" remix, front

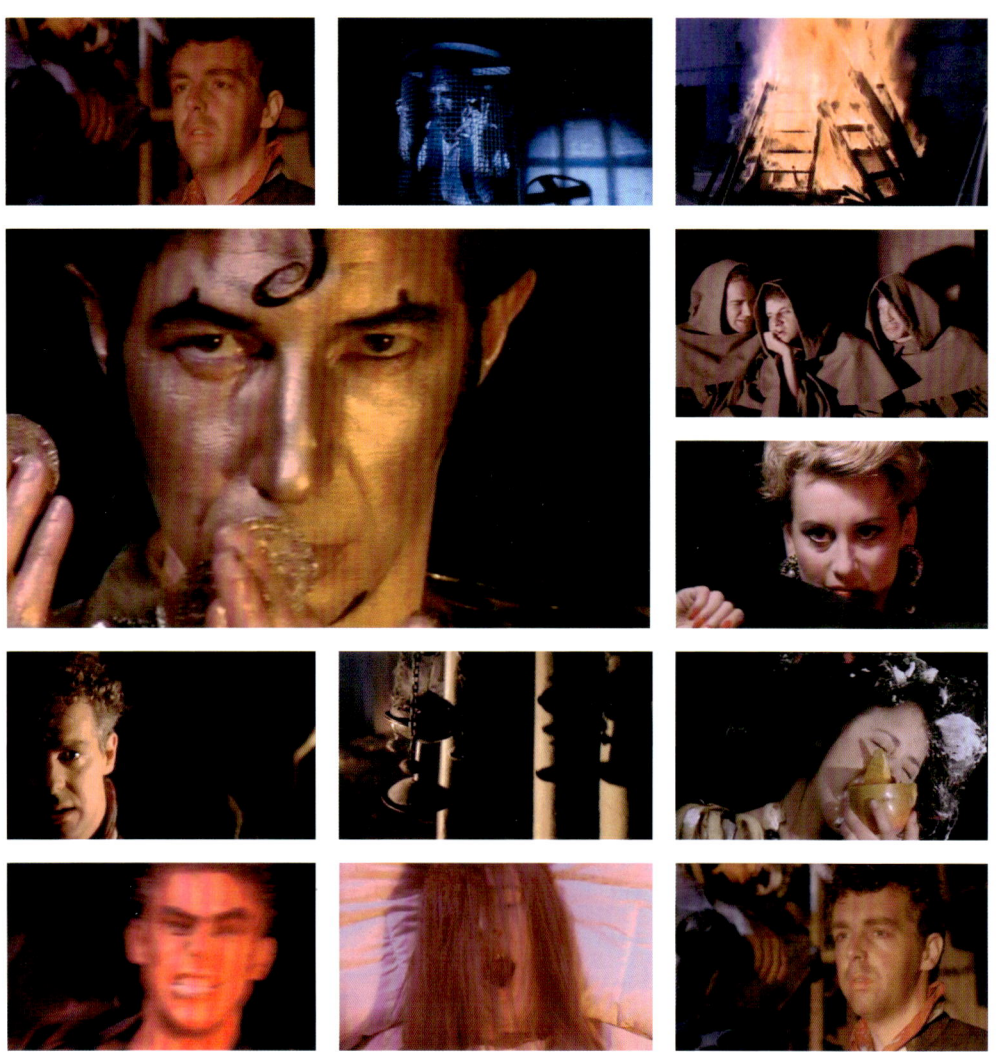

In a medieval dungeon, hooded monks process with candles. A bonfire is lit, and Neil appears as a prisoner in peasant clothes. Chris is the jailer, holding chains in heavy gauntlets. Shadows and flames cut with faces that represent the seven deadly sins. It seems that Neil is being tried by the Inquisition for his (undefined) sins. It was the first time they worked with the British film director and artist Derek Jarman. 'I just thought of it initially as another pop video', said Jarman, who had made videos for Marianne Faithfull, Bryan Ferry, and The Smiths, among others. 'Of all the music people I've worked with they put the most trust in me. [They have] a knowledge of theatre and know that having asked people to do something you have to leave them free to do what they want if you're going to get good results. I dressed Chris up in some old rags. He still says it felt the most comfortable of all the costumes he's worn.' Neil adds that the video was filmed in London's as-yet undeveloped

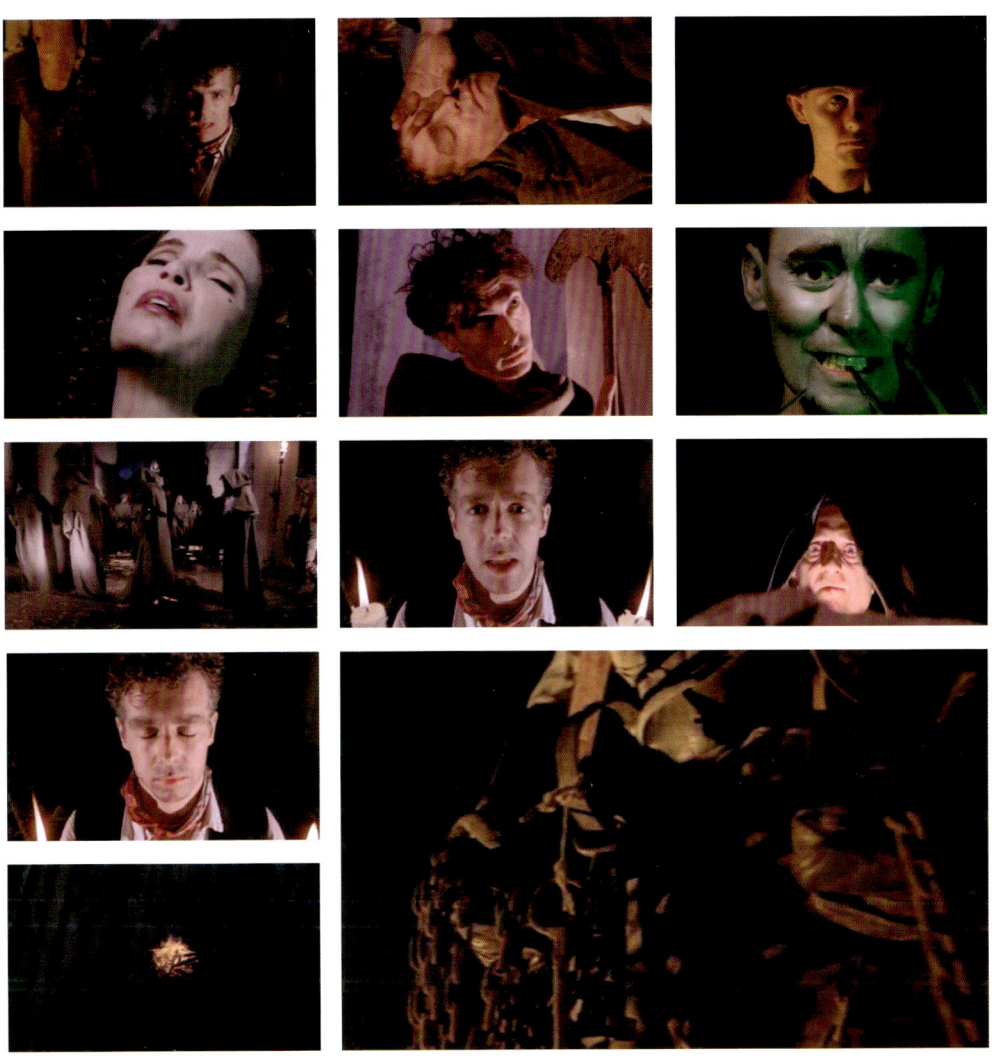

Docklands, 'in a wharf where Kubrick had just shot *Full Metal Jacket* ... I didn't want it to look like we were taking the mickey out of religion. We were very anxious to have this mood – beautiful, serious, and dry.' Personalities playing the seven deadly sins included actor Ron Moody, fashion designer Stephen Linard, and painter Duggie Fields.

What have I done to deserve this?

release 10 August 1987
formats 7" / 7" promo / 12" / 12" double A-side with 'Rent' (US) / 12" promo / cassette / CD
photographers Eric Watson and Val Wilmer
design Mark Farrow at 3 and PSB
video Eric Watson

Eric Watson photographed Neil and Chris in front of a blow-up vintage photo of Dusty Springfield, the iconic Sixties pop star who was about to undergo a revival as a result of this, her duet with Pet Shop Boys. 'It's funny to think that we had a huge blow-up of the Dusty photograph and stood in front of it', Neil notes. 'Now that would be entirely done by computer.' This was the first sleeve where Mark Farrow was involved in the planning of the photo shoot. He suggested they use an old picture, and tracked down Val Wilmer, the original photographer from 1964, and went through her archive and chose this image. At Watson's studio, Farrow was all set on Neil and Chris being photographed on either side of the shot of Dusty 'in that deadpan way that they look'. But by chance there was a Harley Davidson parked outside the studio; Watson and Neil and Chris decided to borrow it. 'I remember being completely crestfallen and thinking it was a terrible idea', says Farrow. 'It wasn't what Pet Shop Boys was about. I was really upset that they wanted to do it, and even more upset when they chose it as the cover. It clearly was a prop. He's not holding the handlebars or anything. That felt like a "pop picture" to me, and although Pet Shop Boys were pop, we didn't present them in a pop way and they didn't present themselves in a pop way, and it just felt they were pandering there. It looks all right now.'

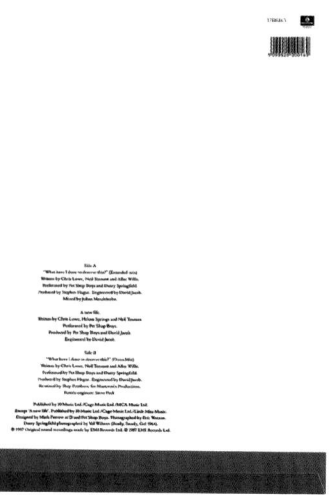

12", back

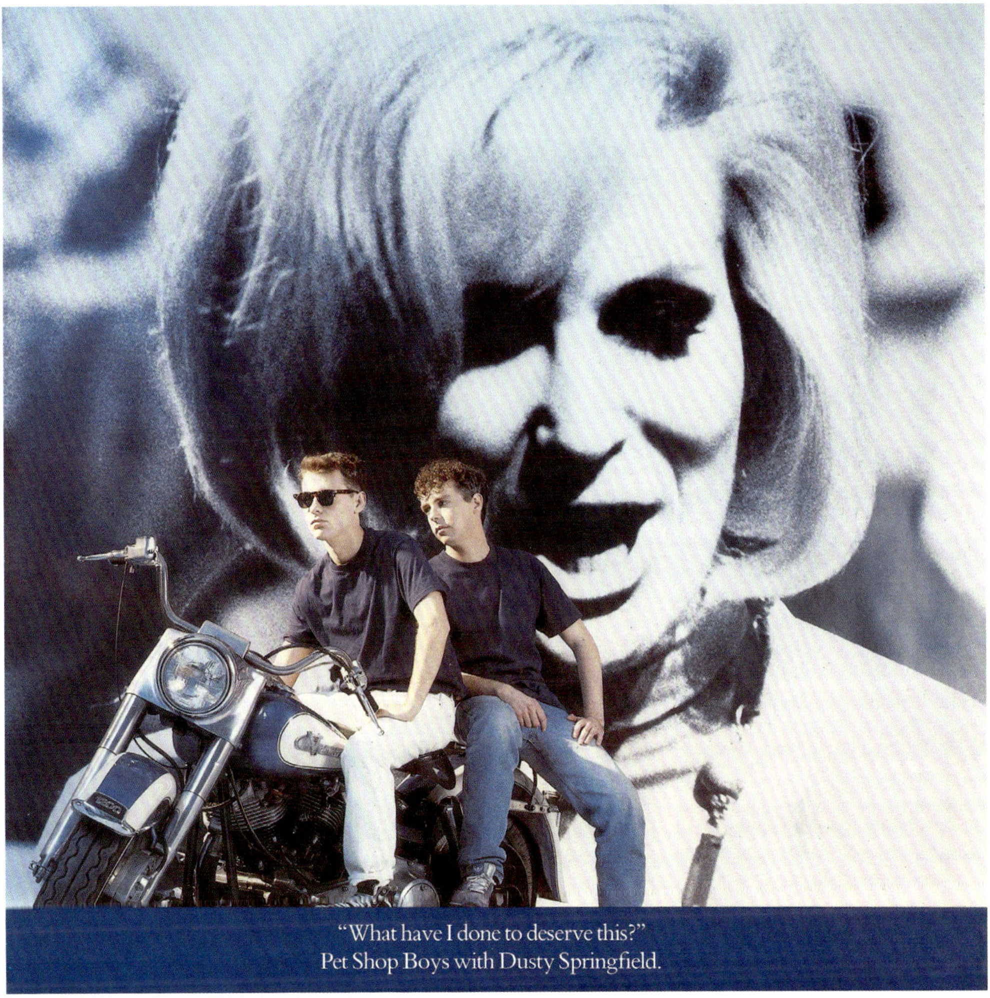

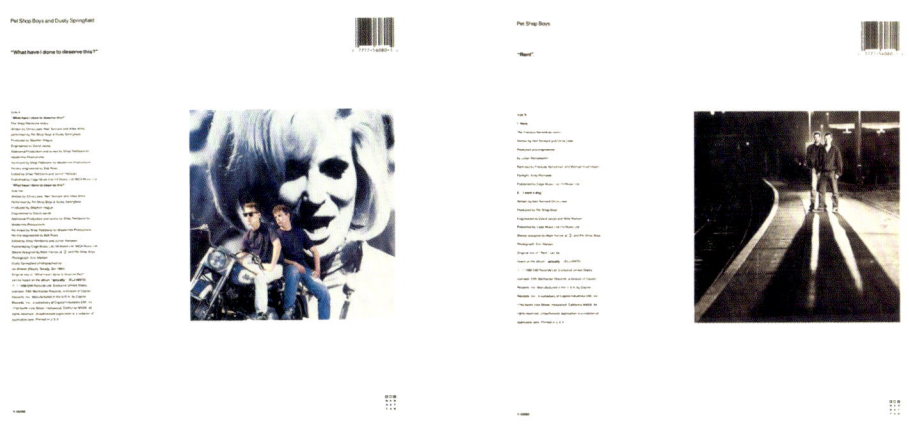

12", front

12", United States, double A-side, front

12", United States, double A-side, back

What have I done to deserve this? 1987 87

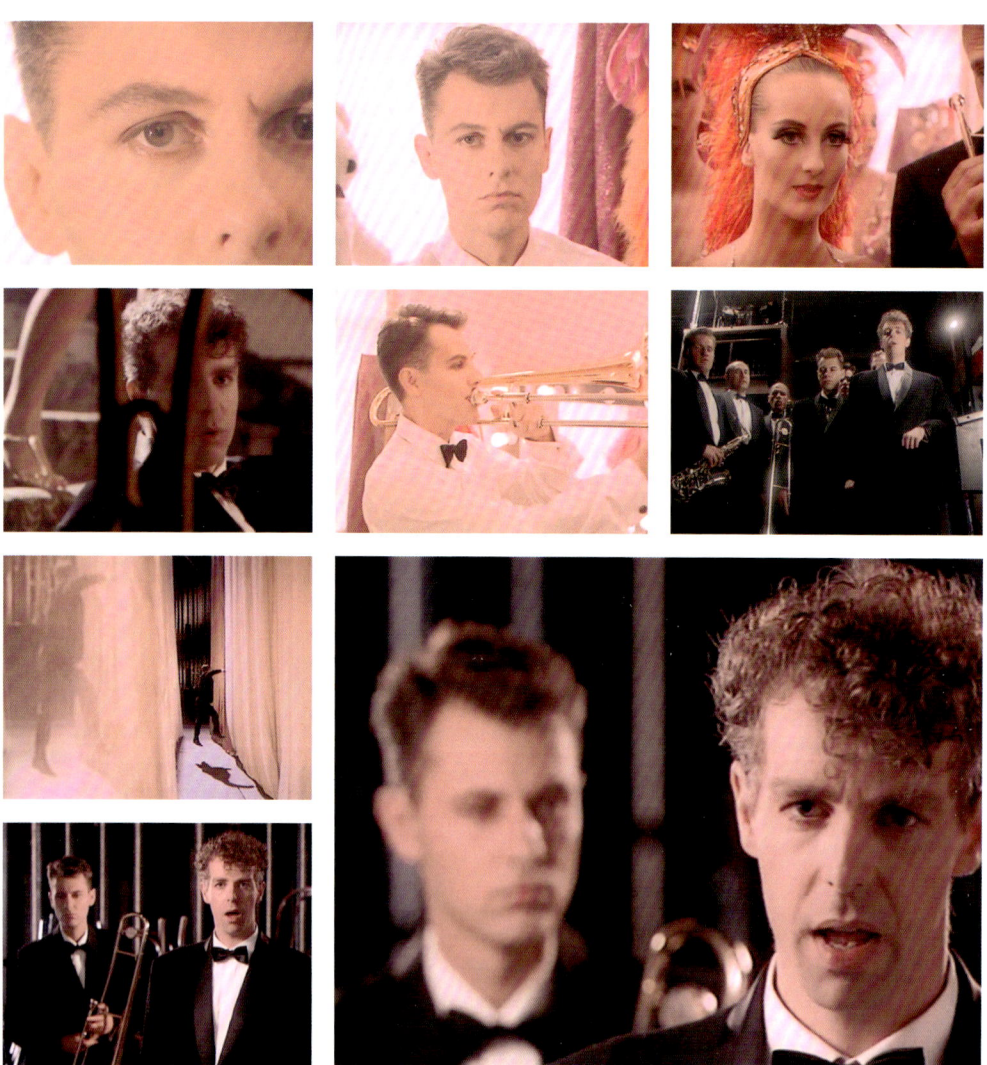

In a dressing room, plumed and sequinned showgirls get ready to go on stage while the band, in evening dress, tune up. One girl takes off her heavy-rimmed spectacles; Chris, as the trombonist, is momentarily left behind. The performers – among them Neil, also in evening wear, singing – descend the curved stairs of the nightclub (in fact, Brixton Academy), while Chris breaks free and dances between two huge curtains on which the shadows of the showgirls are seen. Meanwhile, Dusty Springfield appears in a head-and-shoulders shot to sing each chorus.

This was the first appearance of showgirls in the Pet Shop Boys' world – *Sunday Night at the London Palladium* meets Eighties glam pop via Brecht and Weil. 'This is utterly fab', recalled Eric Watson. 'It had some good gags, like the girl with the thick glasses. We wanted to do something about show business, but in a terrible sort of English way. Because of Dusty, I guess. First there are people getting ready and then it's this show with

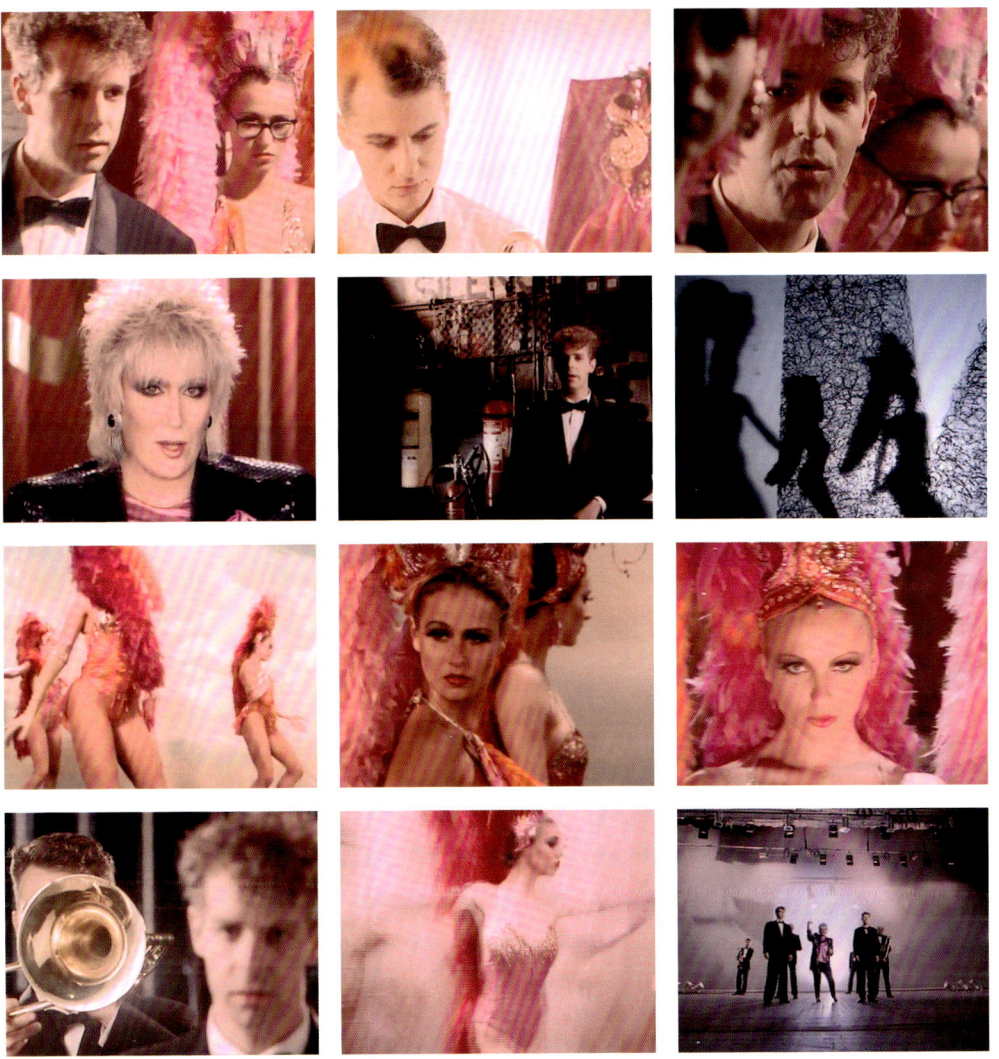

all these layers.' 'Chris especially wanted to do a video in which he danced – he wanted a specific role, not just wander around', said Neil. But, characteristically, Chris does his dance backstage, as though he would only leap and spin if no one were looking. And, in fact, this was the case – he asked for most of the crew to be removed for this scene. 'I'm very shy', he said. The trombone is Chris's own; he used to play the instrument as a teenager and played it in one of the first Pet Shop Boys shows, at the ICA in London.

Actually

release 7 September 1987
formats LP / cassette / CD
photographers Cindy Palmano and Eric Watson
design Mark Farrow at 3 and PSB

Neil and Chris had thought of the title for their second studio album, *Actually*, early on and then, typically, went off it. Eventually they came back round. 'It was so English and kind of arch. It was also a kind of joke and something we said a lot', says Neil. 'And also it could almost be a sentence – 'Pet Shop Boys, actually' – which echoed *Please*.' They had nothing to put on the sleeve, however. Neil had the idea of using a painting, and they commissioned Alison Watt, who had just won the National Portrait Gallery annual portrait prize, to paint them. She wanted them to sit for three weeks, which they could not do, so she worked from photos taken by Eric Watson in her Glasgow flat. Chris hated himself in the finished portrait (page 92), however, and Neil didn't think it was the right cover anyway, so the idea was dropped.

Next they did another session with Eric. They liked the results but didn't think they were strong enough for the cover, although one photo was used on the inner sleeve and another became the sleeve of 'Rent' (page 95). They began searching through recent photographs. They realized that the best was one that Cindy Palmano had taken on the set of the 'What have I done to deserve this?' video. She had also been asked to shoot a session for the cover of *Smash Hits*. She sat them with a waist-high piece of reflecting metal in front and another hanging behind (page 93). Their favourite photo was the very first, when Neil was yawning. But it had already been sent to *Smash Hits*, which was on press the next day. Desperate calls were made, and Pet Shop Boys agreed to do a new session that evening for the magazine, and got back the yawning image.

Mark Farrow then suggested that it would be even stronger if they removed the reflective background and made it white. 'As soon as we got the proof we knew it was right', Neil remembers. 'It was very un-whatever everyone else was doing and not a "please, please buy me" image' – which did not mean that Chris liked it. 'I can't stand the way I look in it. Straight after that, I had my hair cropped.' 'It's very much the defining image of Pet Shop Boys', Neil reflects. 'Ennui', says Chris. Farrow laughed when he saw the photos. They summed up Neil and Chris's downtime personalities: 'Neil's bored and yawning and Chris looks pissed off.'

Pet Shop Boys, actually.

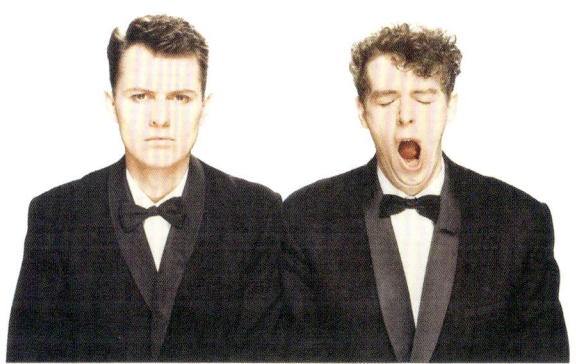

LP, outer sleeve, front (photo: Cindy Palmano)

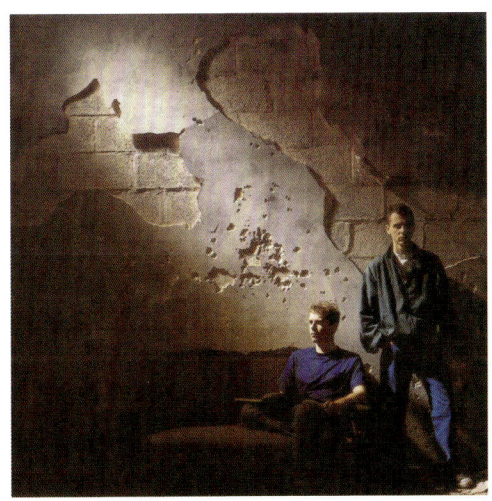

LP, inner sleeve, front (photo: Eric Watson)

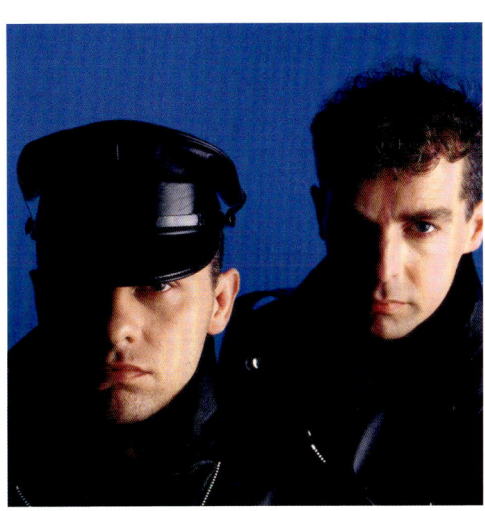

The new session for *Smash Hits* (photo: Andrew Catlin)

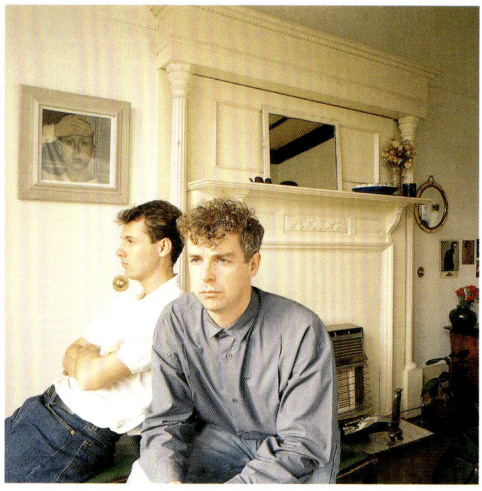 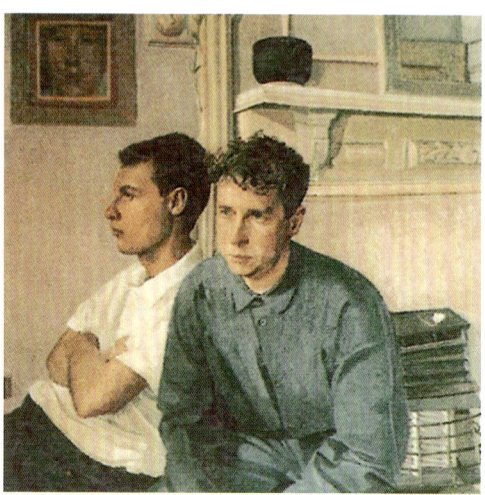

From the shoot in Alison Watt's flat (photo: Eric Watson)   Alison Watt's painting of Pet Shop Boys

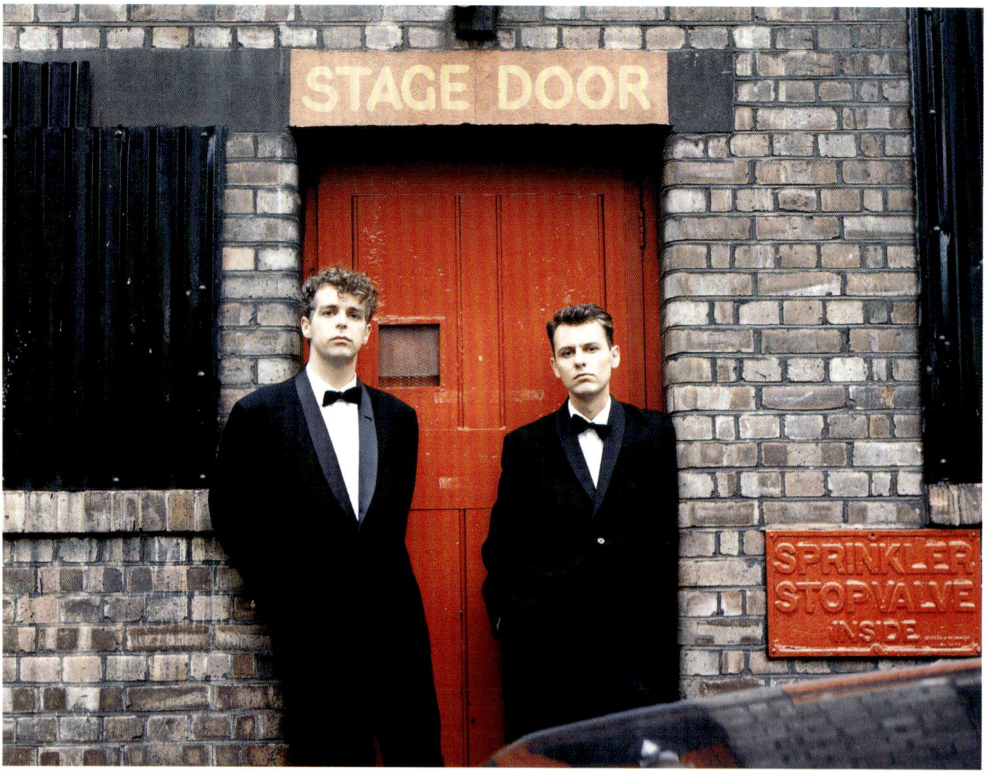

above On the set of the 'What have I done to deserve this?' video, taken at the same time as the image used for *Actually* (photo: Cindy Palmano)

opposite Contact sheet from the 'What have I done to deserve this?' video shoot from which the *Actually* cover image came (photos: Cindy Palmano)

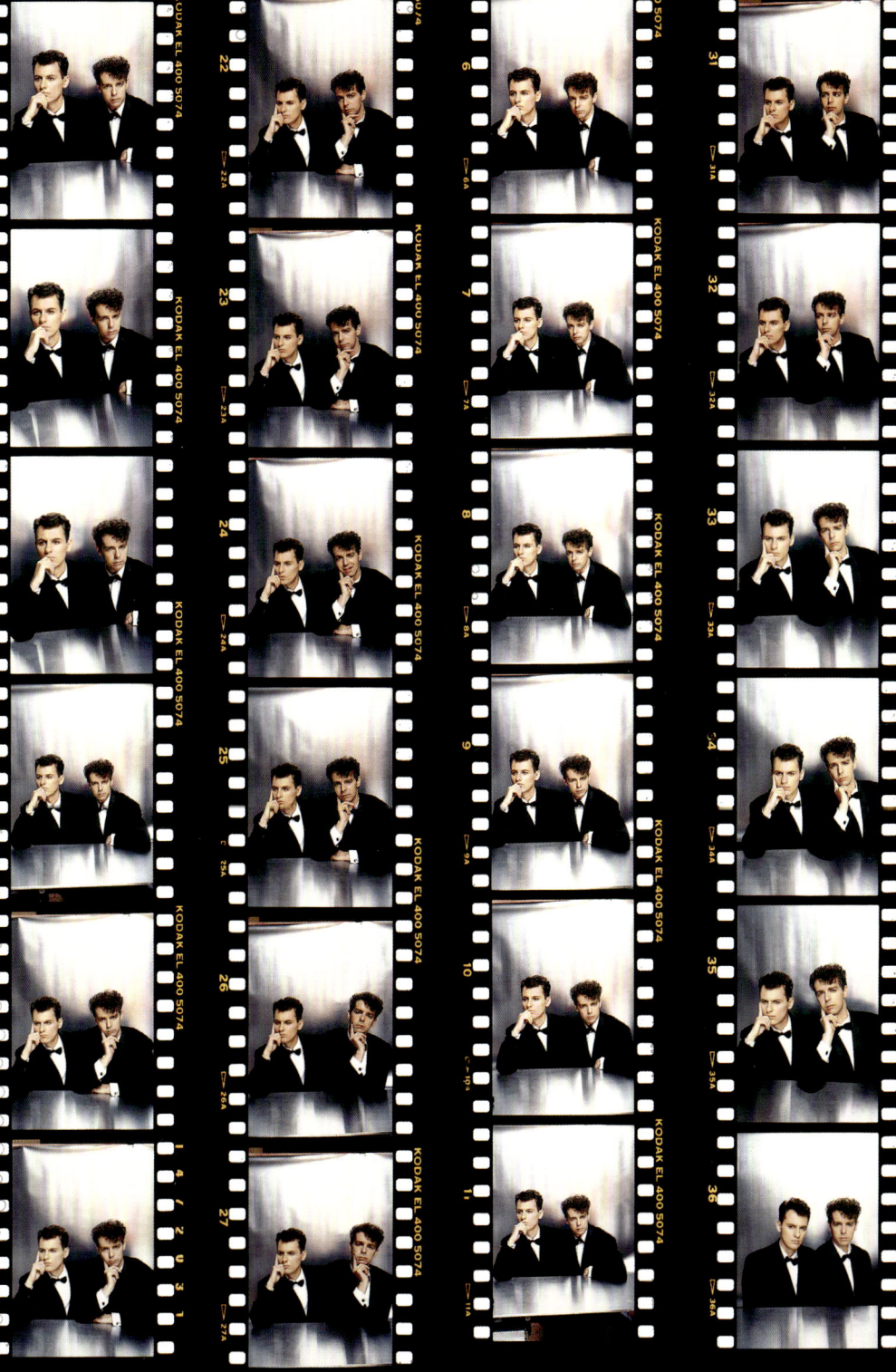

Rent

release 12 October 1987
formats 7" / 7" promo / 12" / 12" promo / 12" double A-side
with 'What have I done to deserve this?' (US) / cassette / CD
photographer Eric Watson
design Mark Farrow at 3 and PSB
video Derek Jarman

The photograph on the sleeve of both the seven inch and the twelve inch was shot, rather speedily, on a railway platform at King's Cross Station. The light behind the two figures was being held in position by Peter Andreas, Neil and Chris's friend. The image has a direct relationship to the Derek Jarman film made for the single, although it was was shot long before. The photograph just seemed to fit the atmosphere of the song: 'the whole seedy, night-time King's Cross'.

They had been shooting all day in Eric Watson's studio and decided at the last minute to shoot some more at King's Cross in the evening, after first going back to Neil's house so that he could lend Mark Farrow an anorak he had worn on *Top of the Pops* to keep out the cold. 'We walked down and bought platform tickets', says Farrow.

When the sleeve was designed, Neil and Chris were in New York, and Mark Farrow finagled his first trip to New York simply to show them the proof. Farrow's combination of the black-and-white photo and orange type gave the sleeve a decidedly retro and yet thoroughly current feel. Reviewing the single, *No.* 1 magazine saluted Neil and Chris with the phrase 'hats off to the obsessive spinsters of pop', a comment they rather liked. '"The obsessive spinsters of pop" is how we present ourselves in a way', Neil noted.

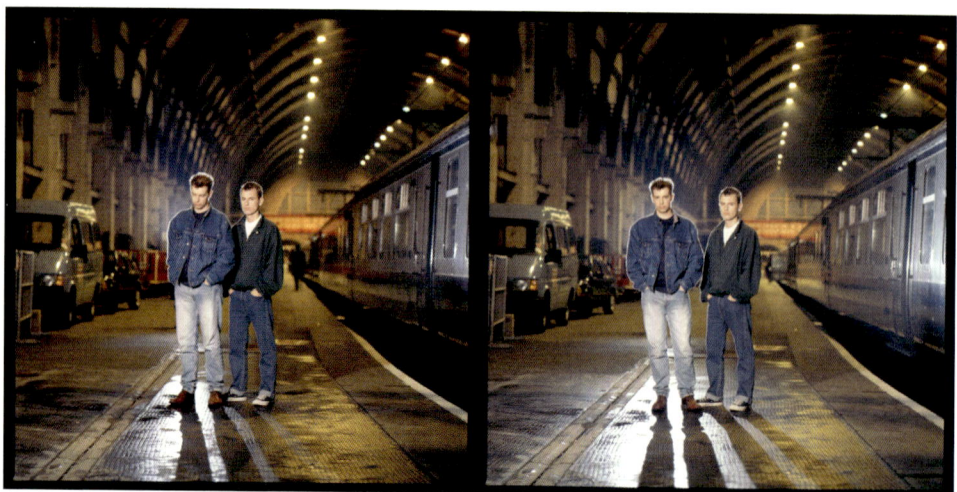

From the Eric Watson photo shoot at King's Cross Station

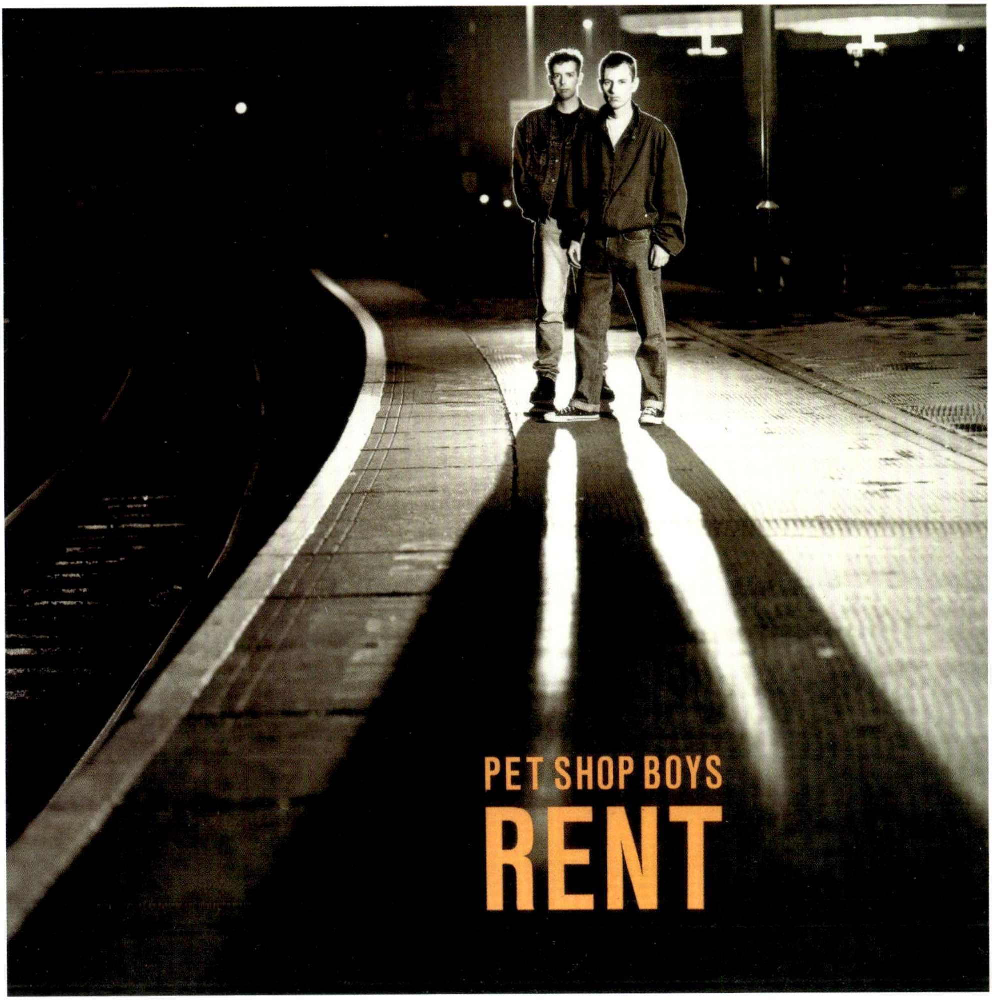

12", front

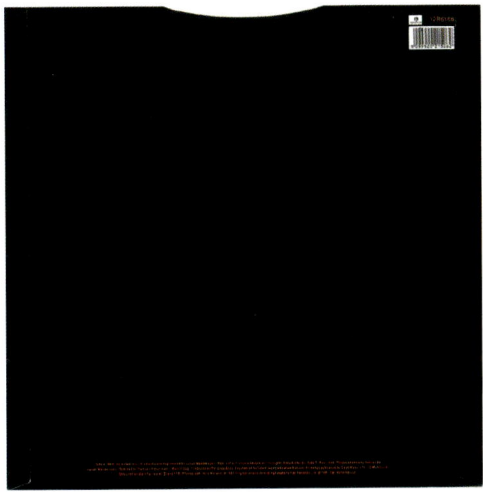

12", back

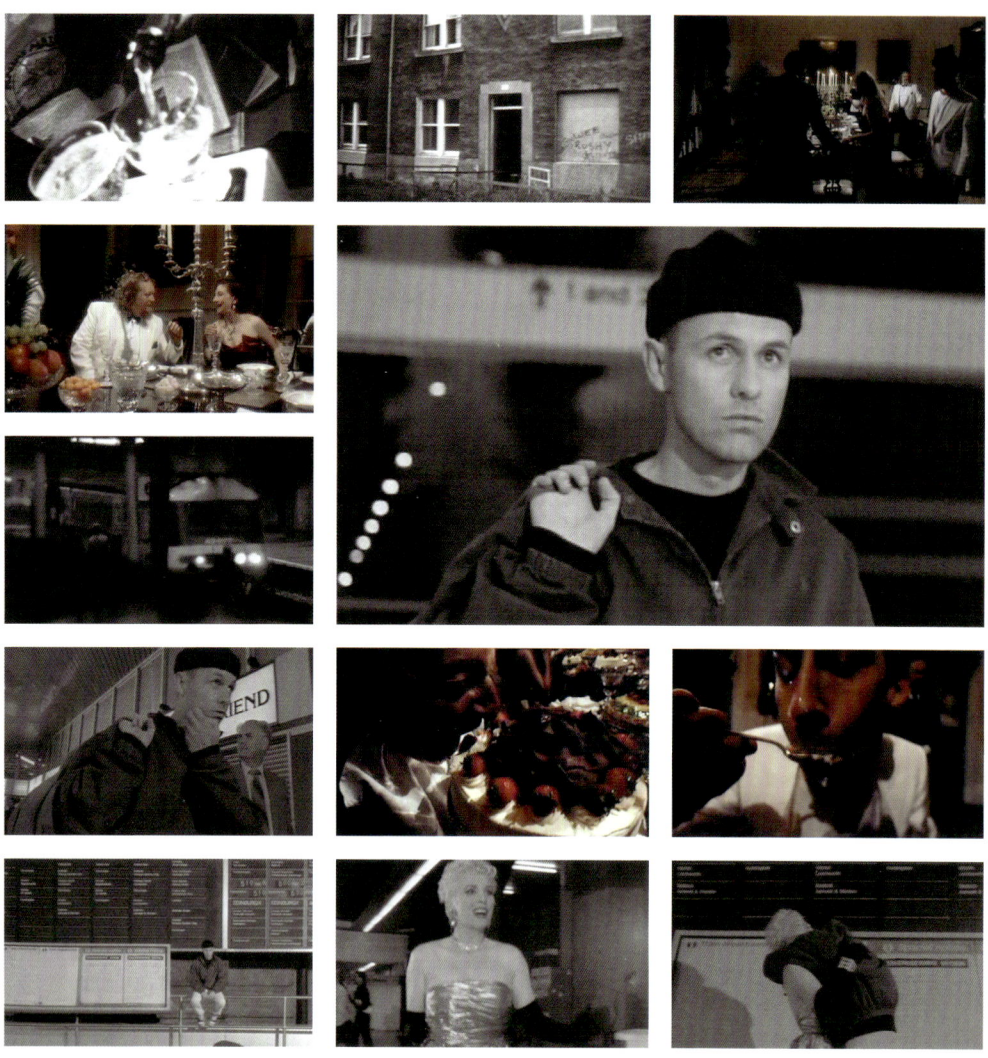

At a posh dinner, Margi Clarke is entertained by her corpulent and bearded lover/husband, while outside, Neil, dressed in the peaked cap of a chauffeur, waits by the car, singing. Chris is seen in a woolly hat, bag slung over a shoulder, as he gets off a train at King's Cross Station. Margi storms out of the dinner, driven off by Neil; the remaining diners eat disgustingly. Delivered by Neil to the station, Margi runs in to find Chris sitting under the platform indicator. They embrace and laugh, and he puts his coat protectively over her bare shoulders. 'I just thought of someone immensely rich and this slightly overblown dinner party and a young woman escaping back to her roots', said Derek Jarman. 'Margi was good because people associated her with Liverpool.' 'Jarman had this idea: the classic Sixties thing is that you come from the deprived North and go to Swinging London,' says Neil, 'so in this video it's the opposite way round: you leave for the Swinging North.'

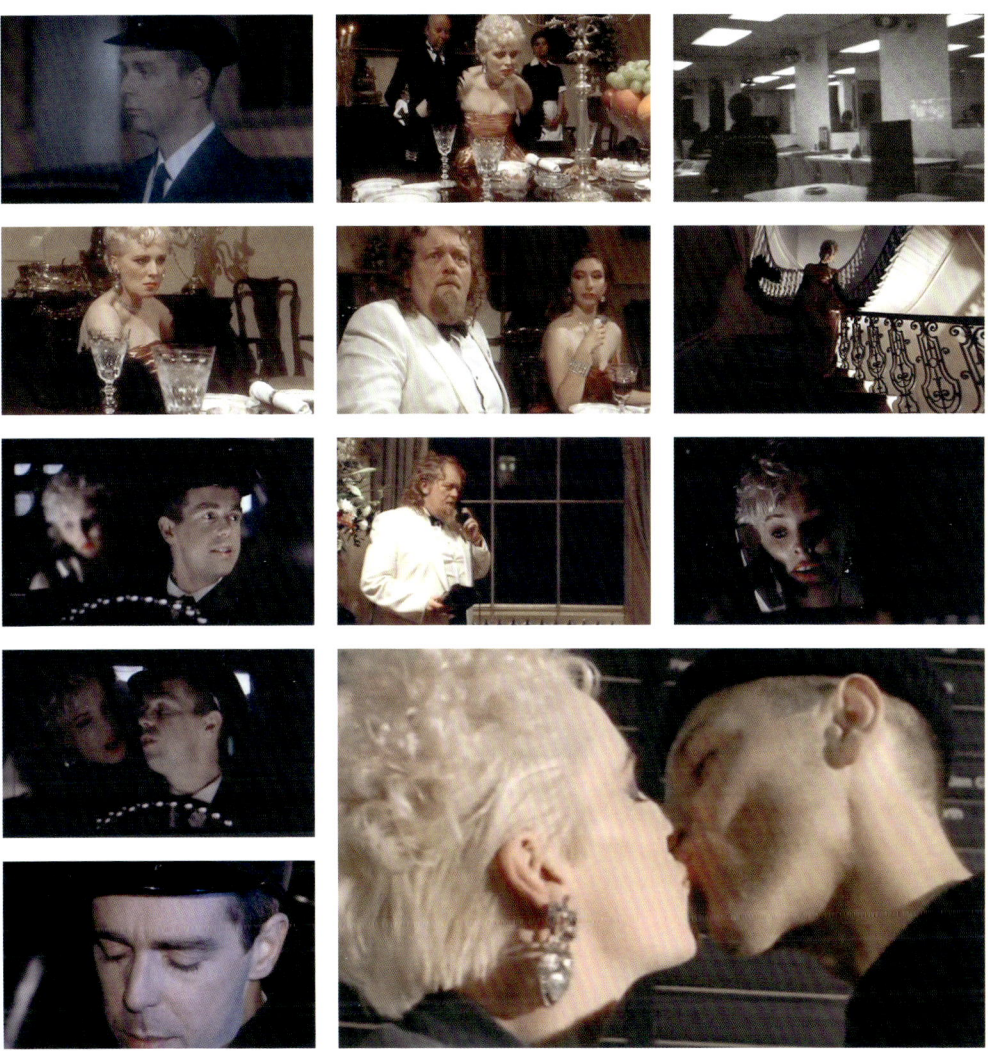

Originally they wanted the limousine to be driving through a riot, so that the wealth and power within contrasted with the anarchy outside. 'But the budget wasn't big enough for rioting.' When they arrived at King's Cross, they were greeted by a sign on the platform information board: 'King's Cross Welcomes The Pet Shop Boys'. Jarman had friends dressed up as tramps, and the British Rail PR kept trying to have them moved out of shot. Chris, kept waiting by the film crew, stormed off at one point and Pet Shop Boys split up – for an evening.

Always on my mind

release 30 November 1987
formats 7" / 12" / 12" remix / cassette / CD
photographer Eric Watson
design Mark Farrow at 3 and PSB
video Jack Bond

The twelve inch of 'Always on my mind', Pet Shop Boys' cover of the Elvis Presley song, was released in a plain white outer sleeve in the style of *Please*. A rectangular photo appears in the top left-hand corner, a still from their soon-to-be-released film *It couldn't happen here* (pages 104–5), which had been shot in the same month. Chris is driving and Neil (with white scarf) is in the passenger seat. The tiny picture was placed where it was, and the exact size it was, to match the barcode on the reverse. The lettering of the title of the song and the group's name is ranged to the right. The reverse is also entirely white, with the text ranged left and running down the length of the sleeve. On both sides of the inner sleeve appears a full-bleed image – Chris in woolly hat and leather jacket on one side; Neil in evening clothes on a quayside on the other – again, both are stills from *It couldn't happen here*. Cropped versions of these two images were repeated on the reverse of the remix twelve-inch, which had stark, oversized typography on the front.

The US sleeve featured Eric Watson photographs with make-up by Pierre LaRoche, the French make-up artist famous for creating the *Aladdin Sane* cover for David Bowie. 'Pierre made me undo my shirt collar,' Neil recalls, 'which I would never normally do.' 'We'd just come back from some good shopping in Japan', says Chris.

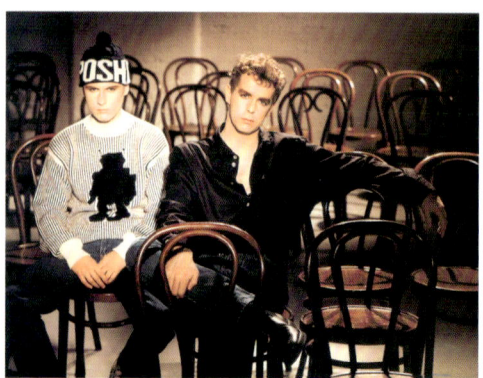

12", United States, front   12" remix, front

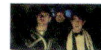

"Always on my mind."

Pet Shop Boys

12", outer sleeve, front

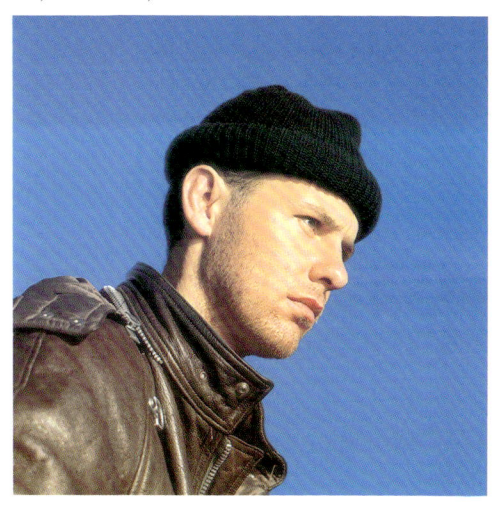

12", inner sleeve, front

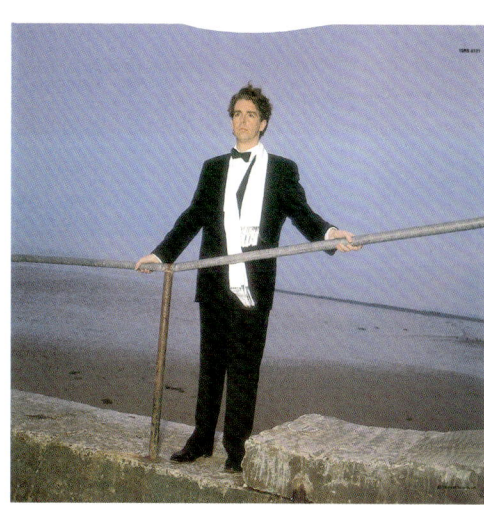

12", inner sleeve, back

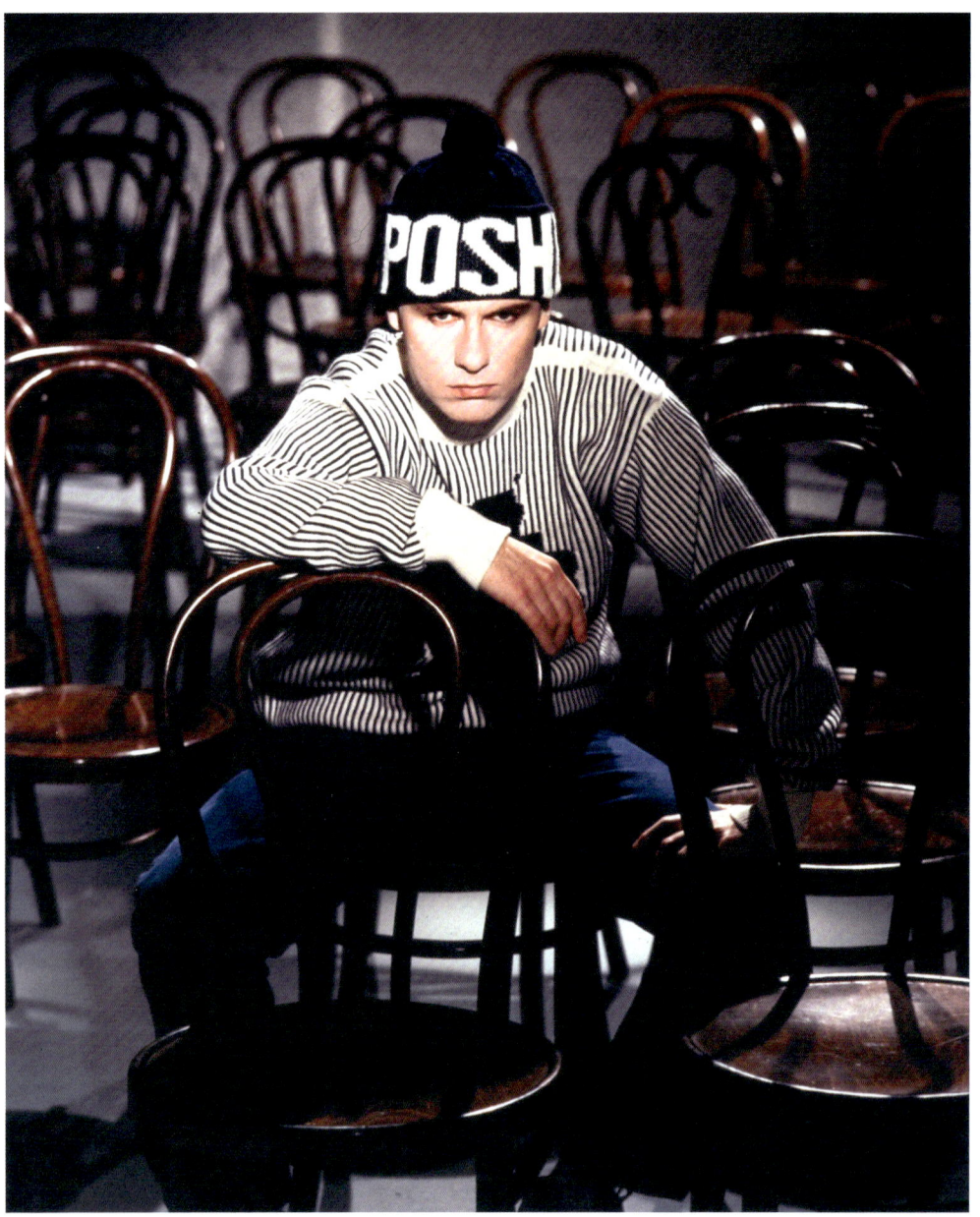

The photo shoot in which Neil and Chris wear make-up by Pierre LaRoche (photos: Eric Watson)

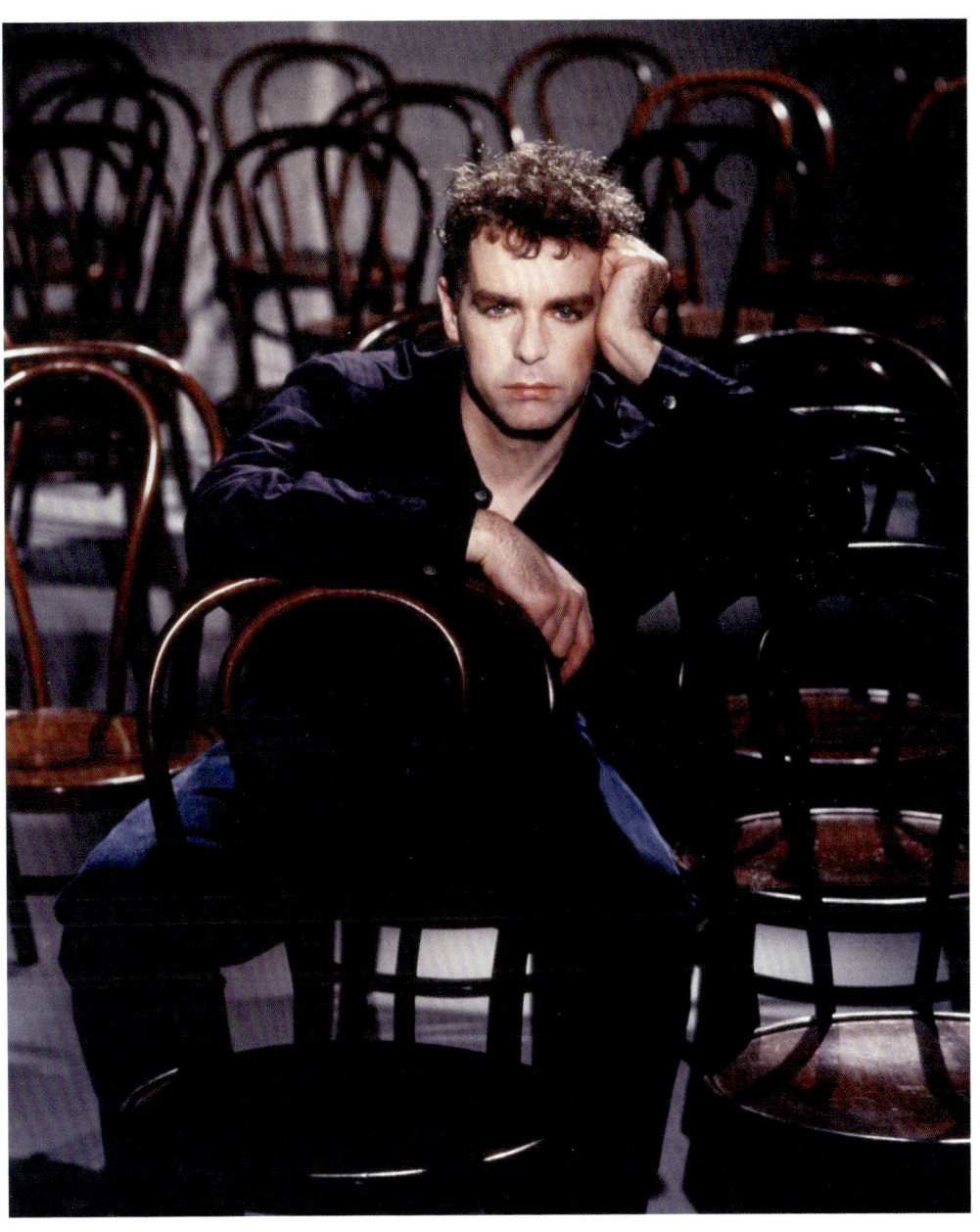

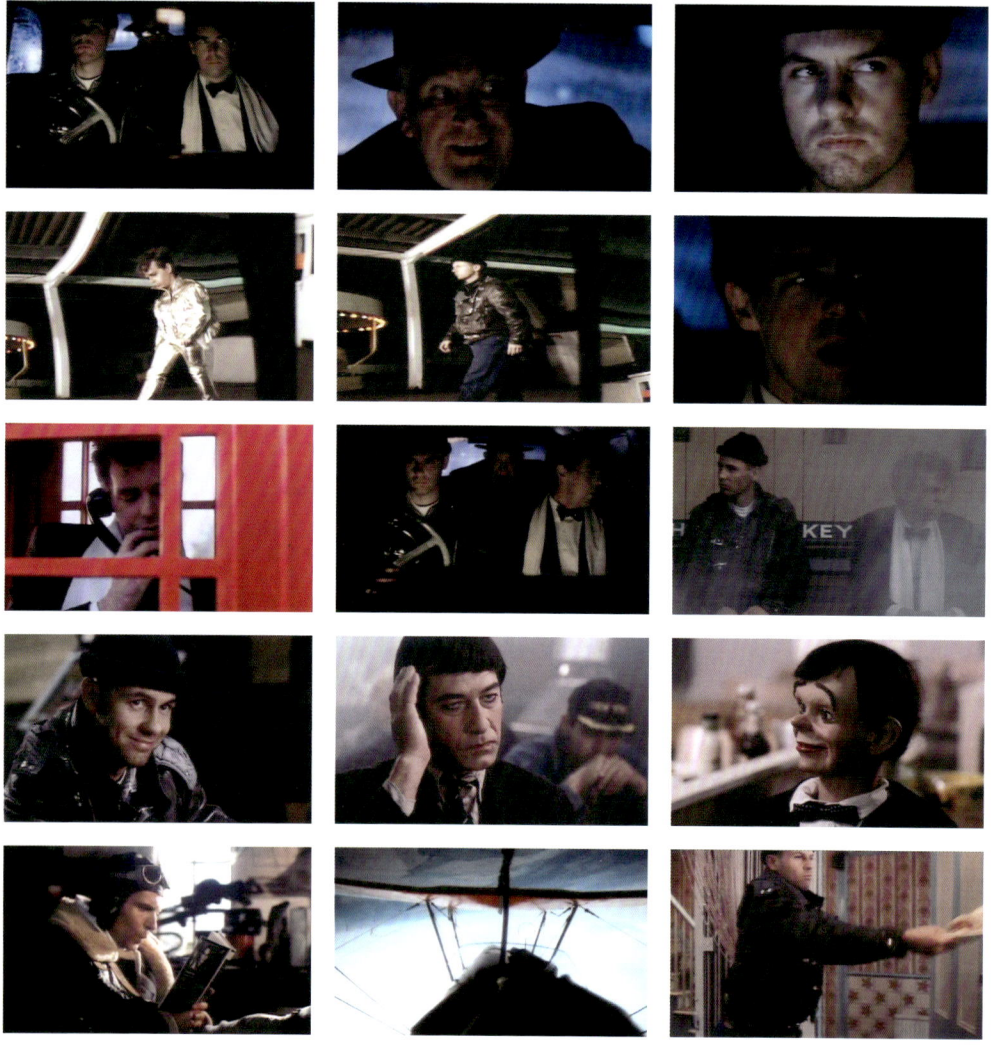

The video is adapted from a scene in *It couldn't happen here* (pages 104–5), interspersed with other episodes from the film. Pet Shop Boys are driving an old car they have just bought and hear on the radio about a hitchhiker who has hacked to death three people who have given him lifts. Chris stops for a girl hitchhiker, but when the car door opens it is a man fitting the murderer's description (played by Joss Ackland) who gets in. Clips from the film appear between moments from the car scene. After babbling manically, sometimes echoing the words of the song, and also quoting lines from 'What have I done to deserve this?', Ackland asks to be let out and Pet Shop Boys continue on their journey, untouched. 'Always on my mind' was scheduled as a single while they were filming the movie, and this new scene had to be written speedily so that it could appear in the film. Midway through, Chris smiles for the first time in a video. 'It caused a lot of comment at the time', says Neil.

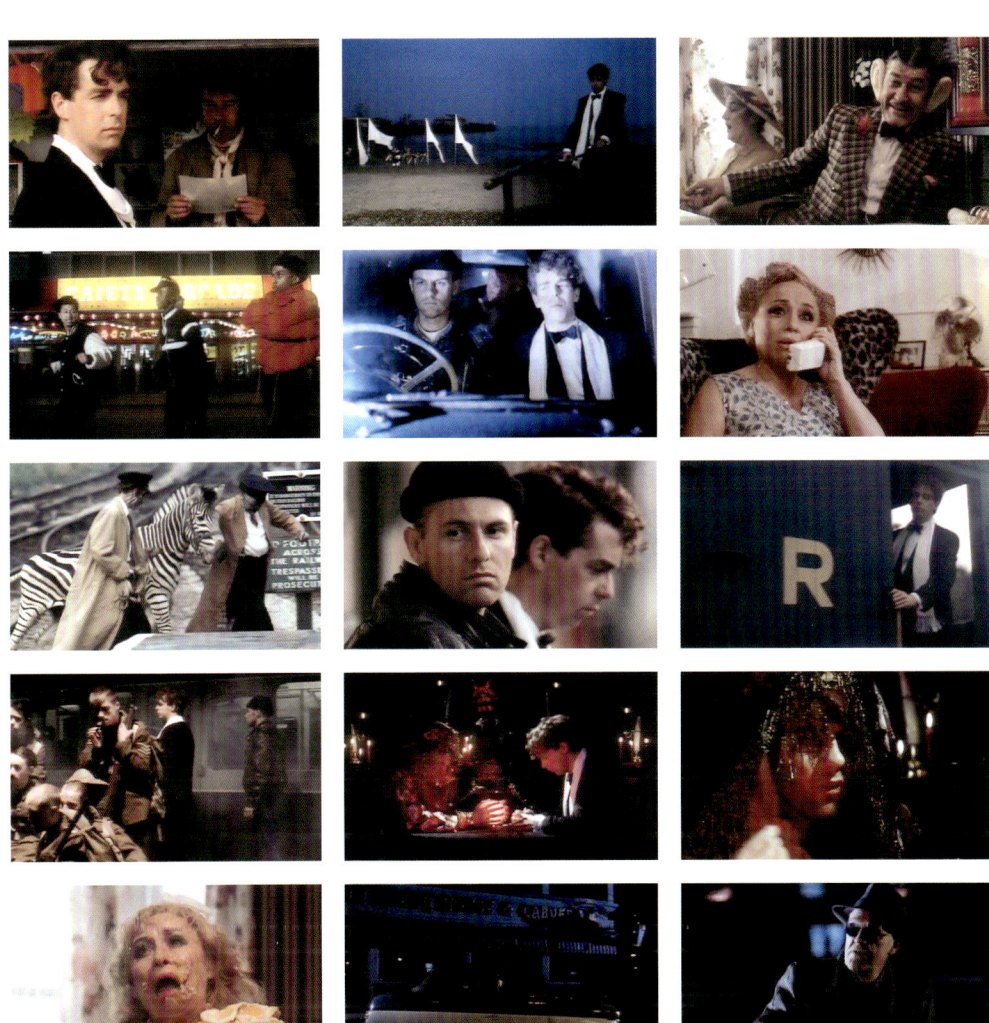

Always on my mind 1987

It couldn't happen here

filmed November 1987
release 8 July 1988 (theatres) / 1 December 1989 (VHS and laserdisc)
formats VHS / laserdisc (Japan, United States)
director Jack Bond
design Video Collection International

Shot in November 1987, this was Pet Shop Boys' first and only feature film, an exercise in seaside surrealism. Its style is quirky, and it follows the tradition of British directors such as Michael Powell and films such as *Brighton Rock*. Directed by Jack Bond, starring Barbara Windsor, Joss Ackland, Gareth Hunt, and Neil Dickson, and filmed over three weeks in Clacton and south London, the project had originally been conceived as an hour-long video based on the *Actually* album. 'We just do what we normally do in videos', Chris said: 'Walk around, me a few paces behind Neil.' The film won an award at the Houston film festival.

During the course of the film we see a number of bizarre scenes: Victorian 'what-the-butler-saw' images; Joss Ackland as a murderous hitchhiker; a bed-and-breakfast run by Barbara Windsor; schoolboys in shorts led by a blind priest (Ackland); Neil in a gold lamé suit *à la* Elvis; a casino; Neil in dinner jacket in a phone box; Gareth Hunt as, variously, an ageing ventriloquist and burger-bar owner; Neil having his fortune read by a fortune-teller (Chris); two zebras being led across a railway track by two men with zebra-striped faces; a wartime station on which stand soldiers in khaki and a band plays; Neil, still in dinner jacket, pushing his bicycle out of the sea; Neil Dickson as a literature-reading pilot; and shots of a Tiger Moth plane flying above the English countryside.

'The story is basically us playing our songs as we drive to London in this car and meet phantom-like figures', said Neil. 'I always think it should be called "Escape from Suburbia" because we're really escaping – escaping from figures of authority: a priest, a mother figure, a con man and so on.' Jack Bond – chosen by the group because they had liked a *South Bank Show* film that he had made about Roald Dahl – commented that, 'The journey is obviously physically a journey across England, but which England? In a sense it's a dreamworld of England, almost a journey through the psyche of England, which is very varied and strange.' In particular, Bond saw the Pet Shop Boys as the kind of adventurous, radical product of England's repressiveness. 'In our country there's this repressiveness and fascism and conservatism and they squeeze and out come these slices of imagination that no one can stop. For me, the Pet Shop Boys represent a vulnerable creativity that got through, and they got through on a massive scale. In the film, they're almost always untouched and they almost never react – I think that's how they've succeeded. Non-reaction is the most powerful form of reaction.'

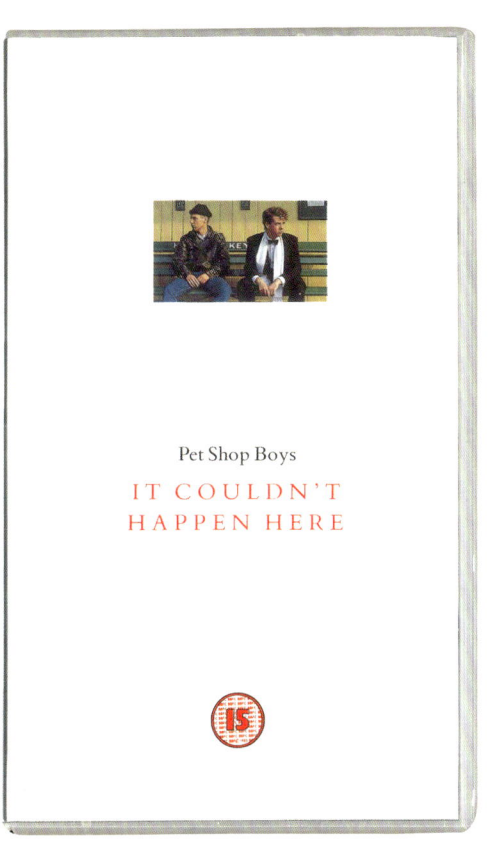

VHS, front

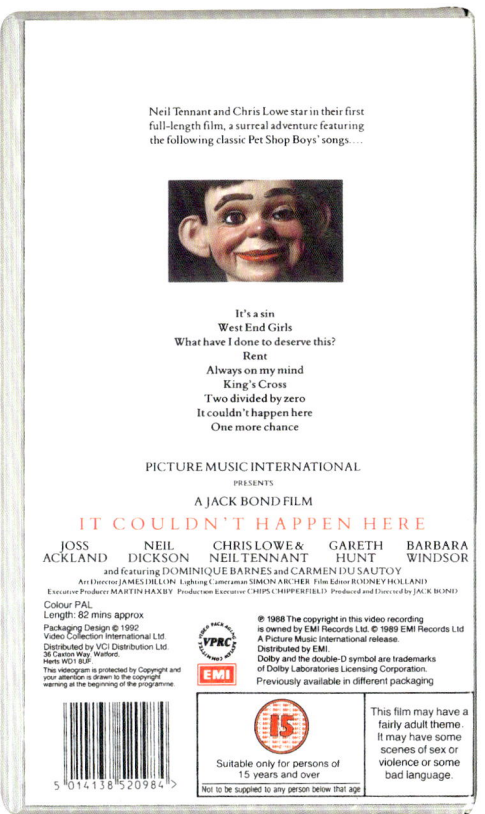

VHS, back

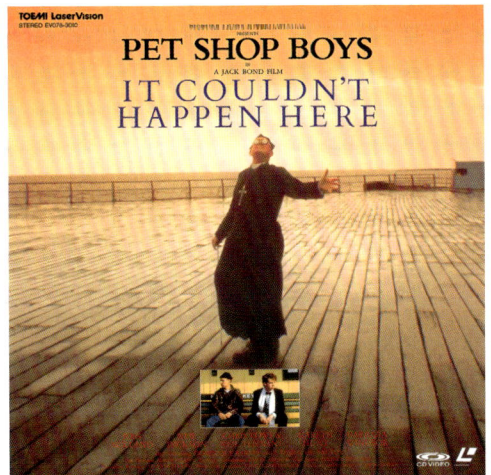

Laserdisc, front

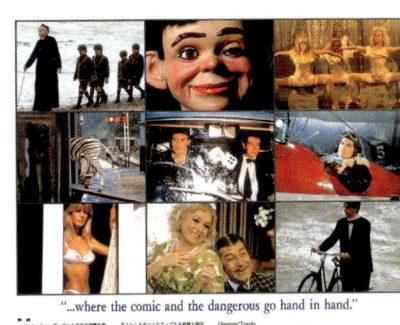

Laserdisc, back

It couldn't happen here 1987 105

Heart

release 21 March 1988
formats 7" × 2 / 7" promo / 12" × 2 / 12" remix /
12" promo × 2 / cassette / CD
photographer Eric Watson
design Mark Farrow at Three Associates and PSB
video Jack Bond

'Heart' was originally written for Madonna but never presented to her. Instead, it became Pet Shop Boys' fourth UK number-one single, following 'West End girls', 'It's a sin', and 'Always on my mind'. The images used were characteristically those where the group were simply photographed in some new clothes. 'Eric had this great idea of how to photograph us in them,' said Chris. The result was a solemn Edwardian look. 'I did have a relationship with hats', Neil notes of his bowler hat – headgear that would be reprised in colourful fashion on the 1991 *Performance* tour.

'The pictures were a gift', says Farrow. The word HEART was printed large in Helvetica Bold Condensed to mirror the way the word was repeated in the song. 'It looked like an art statement somehow.' He had the idea to replace it with the word REMIX on the twelve-inch remix. Two seven-inch records of the single were released, one showing Neil in his suit seated, looking down, and holding his hands on his lap, against a striated background; the other had Chris in the same position wearing his rubber coat and hat and industrial-style dungarees. On both of the seven-inch sleeves, the images were reproduced brown. For the CD and the twelve-inch remix, the same photograph of Neil appears before a blurred figure of a standing Chris, waving his arms in a fashion reminiscent of a Francis Bacon painting. Once again, the image has a brown cast on the twelve inch; on the CD it is reproduced blue.

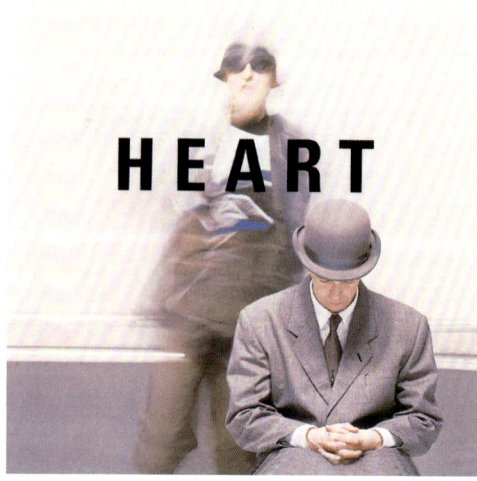

CD, front

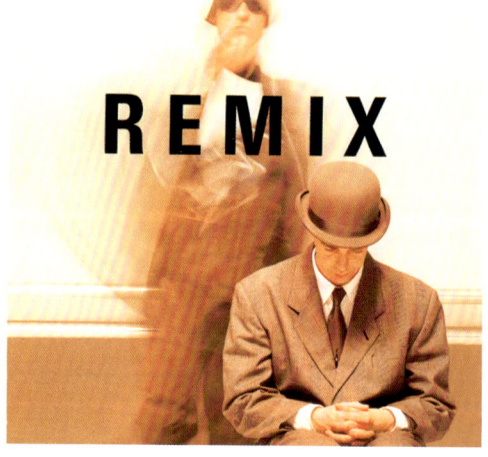

12" remix, front

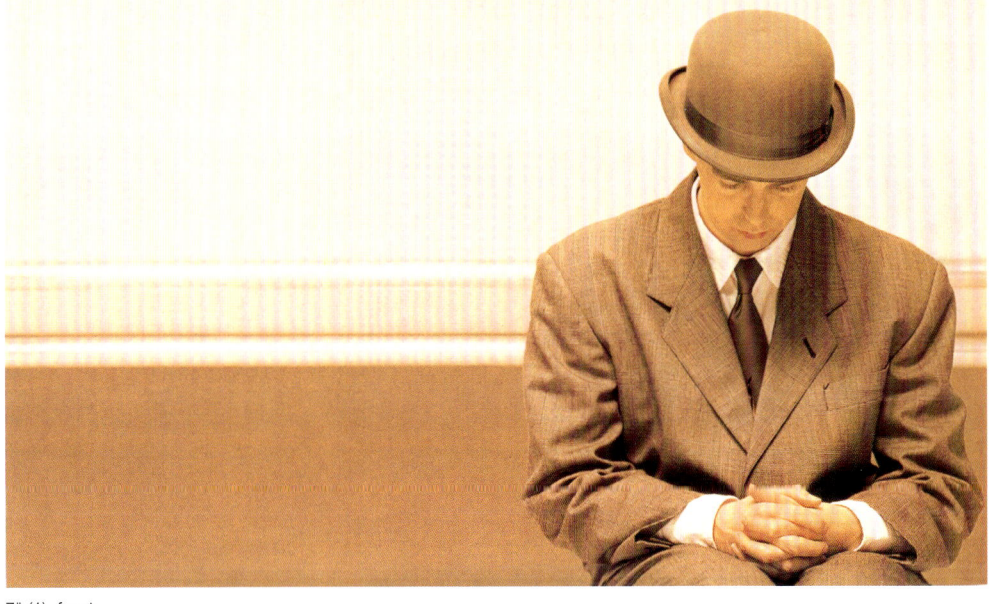

7" (1), front

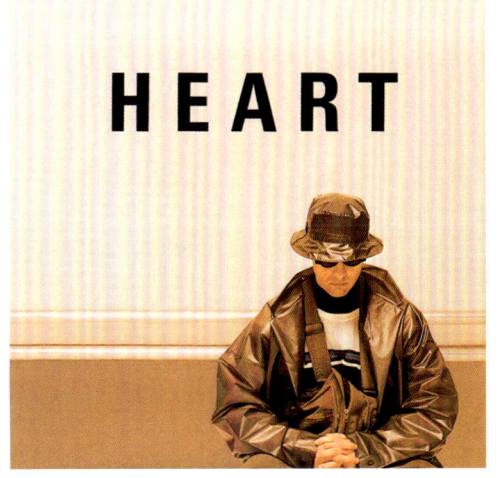

7" (2), front

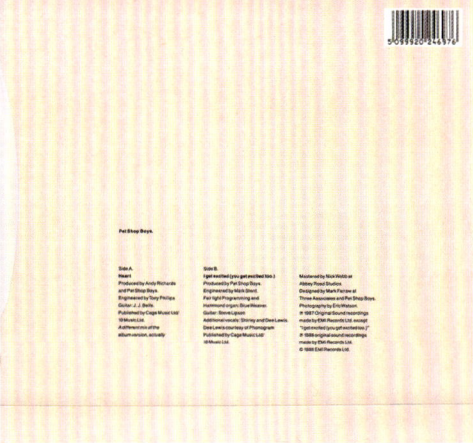

7", back

Heart 1988 107

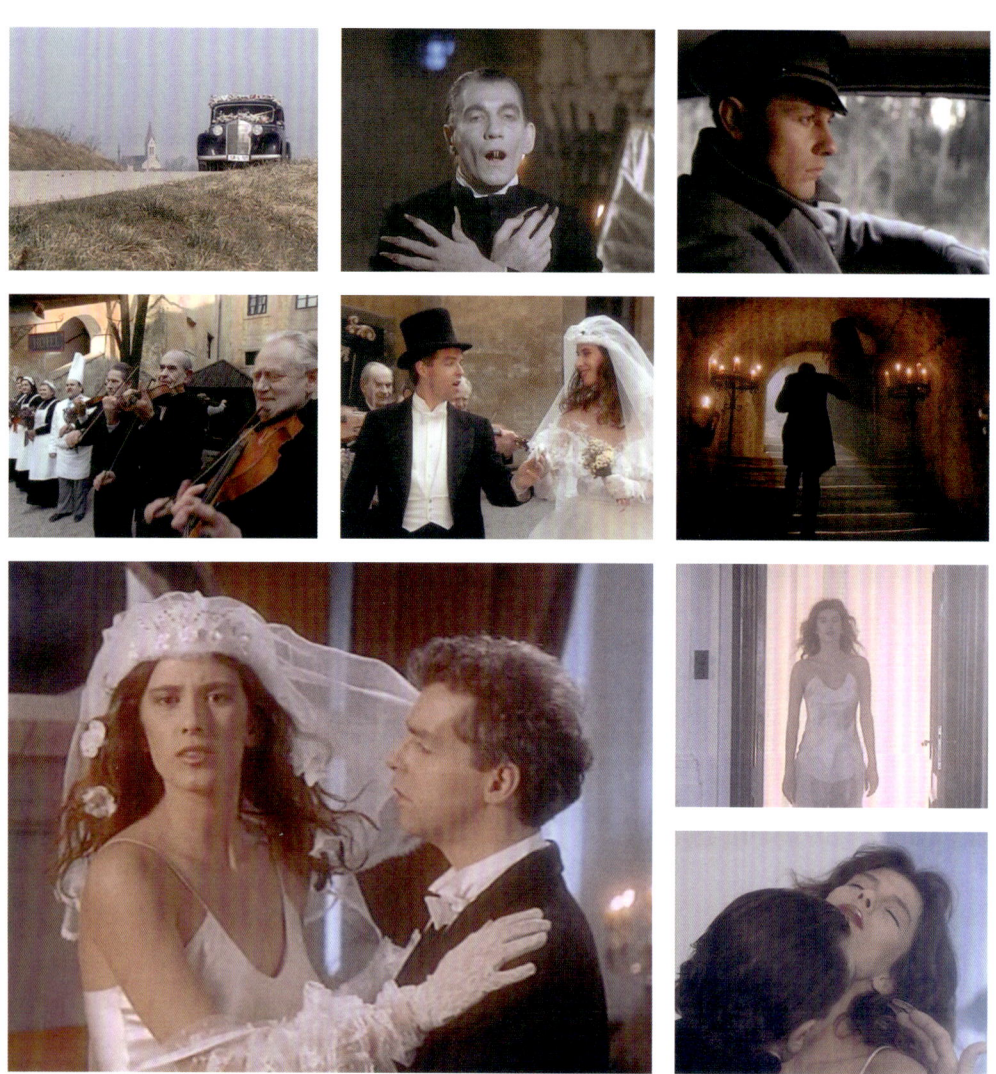

A resetting of the Dracula story as schlock-horror-pantomime, the video featured acclaimed British actor Ian McKellen in the title role. McKellen, with two needle teeth, lurks in his Transylvanian castle, his shadow cast on the walls like Nosferatu, while a wedding party, driven by Chris and consisting of Neil and his bride, arrives by limousine. Chris is seen in the newlyweds' room, throwing clothes out of a suitcase, while Neil undresses his bride. However, the Count soon seduces her to dance with him – and then bites into her neck, before being driven off with his conquest by Chris. In the last sequence, Neil is left in the castle to become a vampire himself and, presumably, to continue the story. '"Heart" was the director Jack Bond's idea', Neil comments. It was filmed in a castle in Slovenia that had become a hotel; Tito had stayed in the room they were using as a dressing room. 'Jack claimed that the shadowy flying bat was a piece of film given to him by Werner Herzog

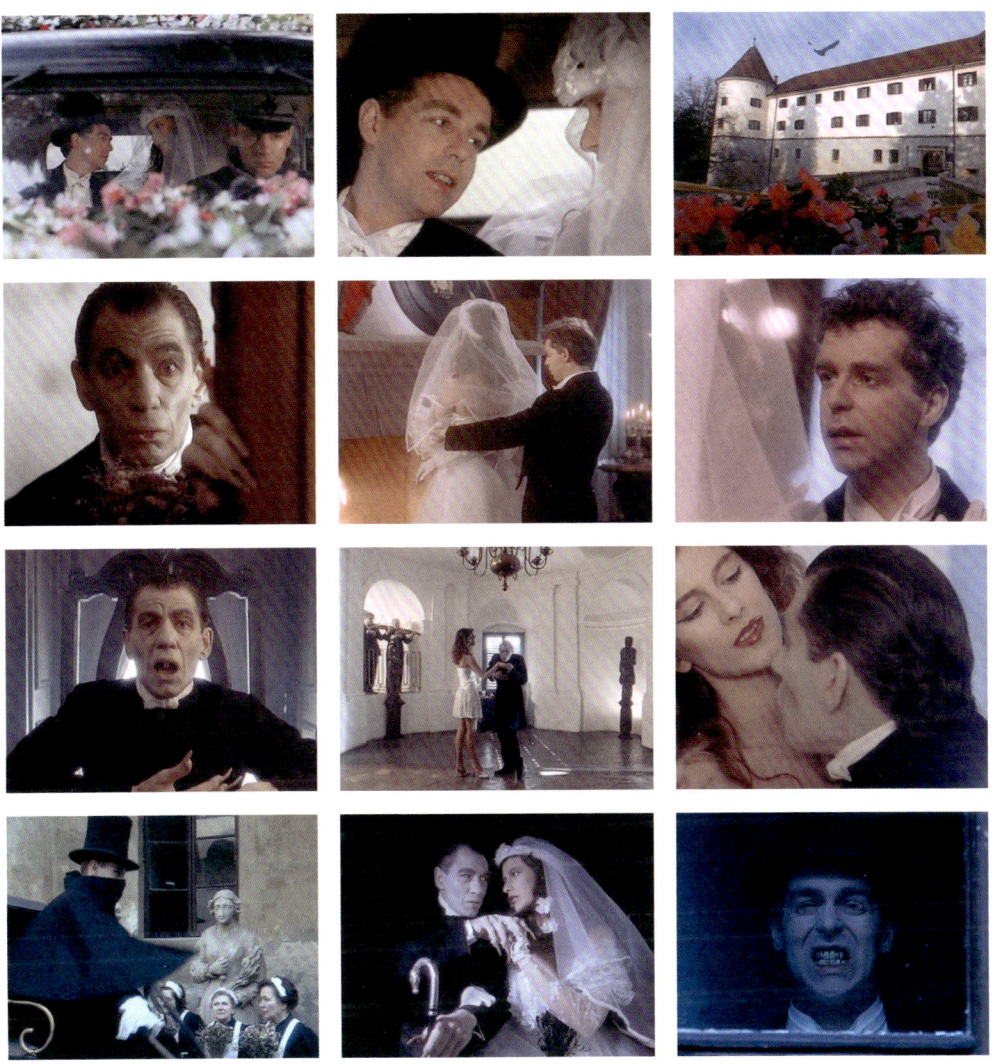

(who made *Nosferatu* with Klaus Kinski).' McKellen can be heard singing over the track in the video, and Bond can be seen near the beginning – the man with a horse who removes his hat. 'It's the full story of Dracula in four and a quarter minutes', said Neil. 'It's another in the series of costume dramas that started with "It's a sin"', added Chris.

Pet Shop Boys, annually

release August 1988 (exact date unknown)
format 64-page hardback book
authors Chris Heath and PSB
design Jaqui Doyle and Mark Farrow (cover)

In the tradition of Christmas annuals, *Pet Shop Boys, annually* was a glossy manual to Pet Shop Boys' world. It was designed by Jaqui Doyle, who designed the fan-club magazine *Literally* (Mark Farrow designed the cover). As well as showing the record sleeves, video stills, and a selection of photographs to date, it featured pages showing Neil's suits and Chris's sunglasses. It also had Polaroids taken on the group's travels and their favourite records. In response to a query from a fan in the April 2003 edition of *Literally*, Chris said, 'I'm not good at archiving. I live in a tiny flat and I've not got much storage space. I sometimes find I have twenty of one record and none of another.' To which Neil added, 'I do have most things, but I'm not convinced that I have a copy of *Pet Shop Boys, annually*, so if any reader has two copies and would like to send one in I'd be very grateful, because every time I sign that book I think how beautifully done it was.' Its cover combined two Eric Watson photographs from the 'Heart' session (pages 106–7) in the style of the *Actually* cover.

Pet Shop Boys, annually.

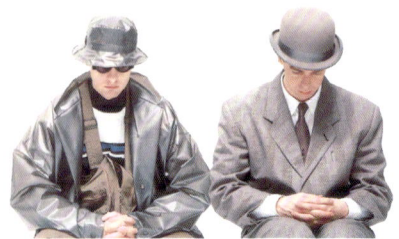

Front cover

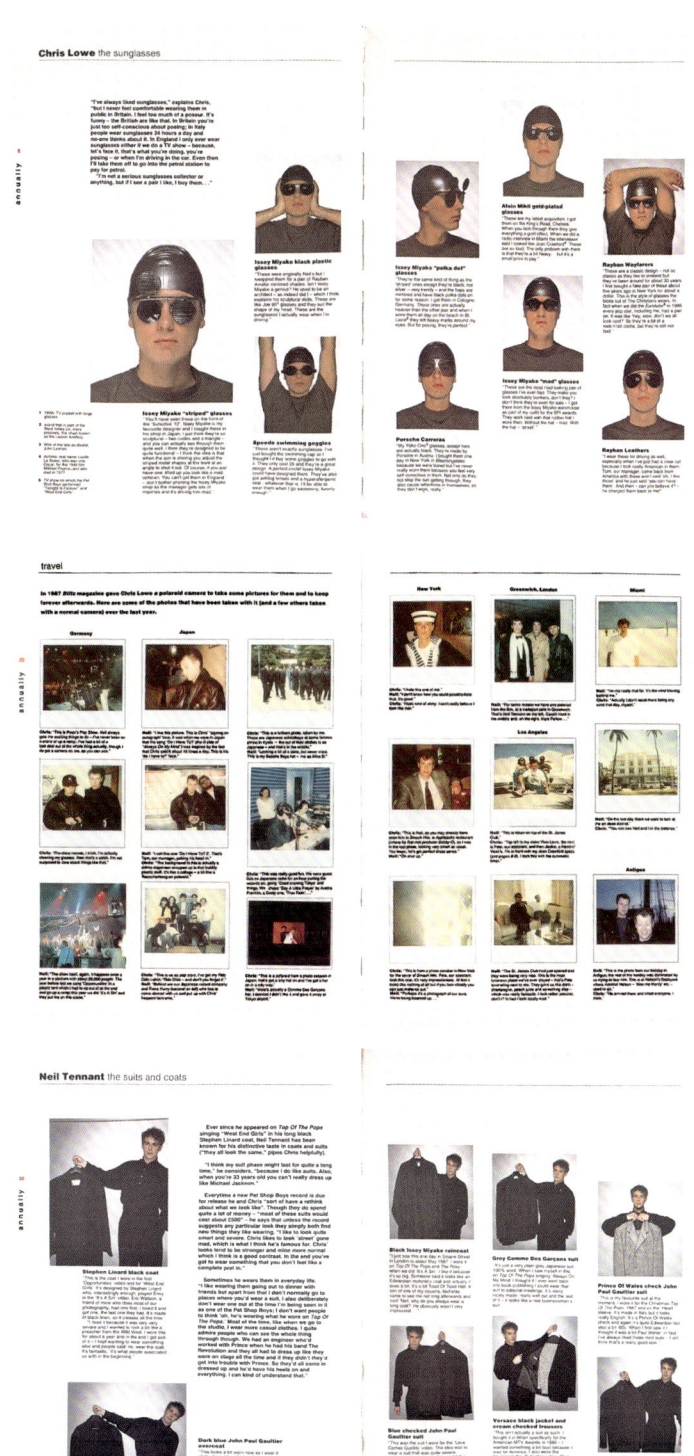

Domino dancing

release 12 September 1988
formats 7" / 7" promo / 12" / 12" remix / 12" promo / cassette / CD
photographer Peter Andreas
design Mark Farrow at Three Associates and PSB
video Eric Watson

The sleeves of both the seven-inch and twelve-inch releases featured a picture of Neil and Chris taken on holiday in Miami by their friend Peter Andreas – who had inspired the track by using the phrase 'domino dancing' on a Caribbean holiday. 'I like that the horizon looks slightly drunken', says Neil. 'That's his style', adds Chris. 'It is on a bit of a slant and I could have straightened it up but I was quite determined it should stay on a slant ... the remix sleeve is also on the same slant', says Mark Farrow. 'Again, that's like a Factory sleeve, but rather than finding something really obscure, it was a Polaroid of Neil and Chris. It was presenting everything to do with the record in a very matter-of-fact way.' In keeping with this simple approach, none of the sleeves had any identifying text on the front, the first time since 'Suburbia'. The back of the seven inch, the reverse of the twelve inch's outer sleeve, and both sides of the twelve inch's inner sleeve showed the information read-out from a mixing desk's computer. The remix twelve inch had a simple track listing.

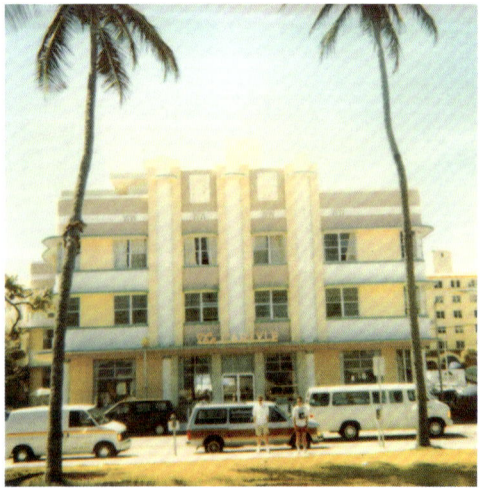
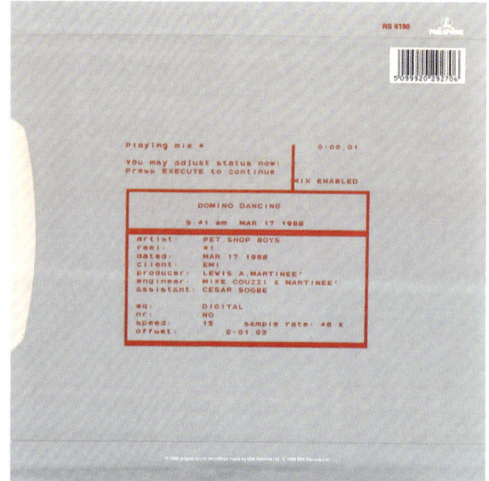

12" remix, front   7", back

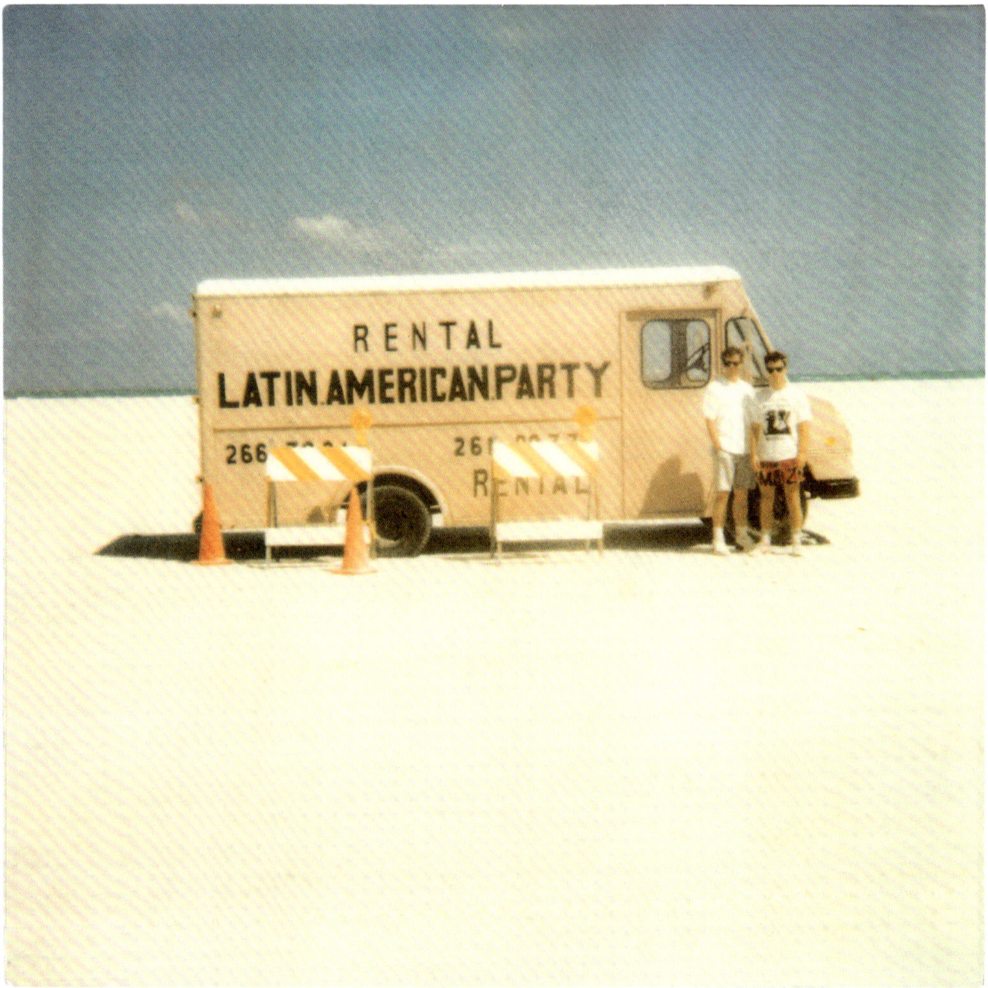

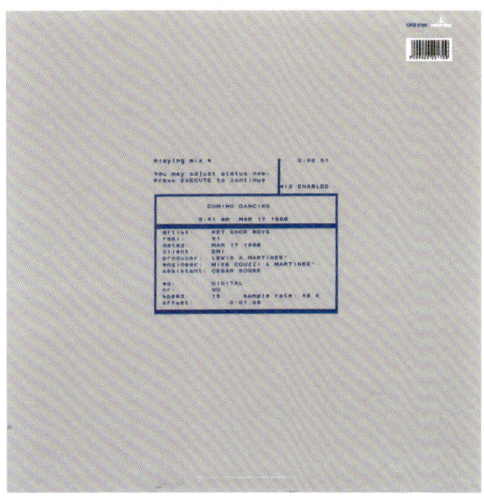

12", outer sleeve, front

12", outer sleeve, back

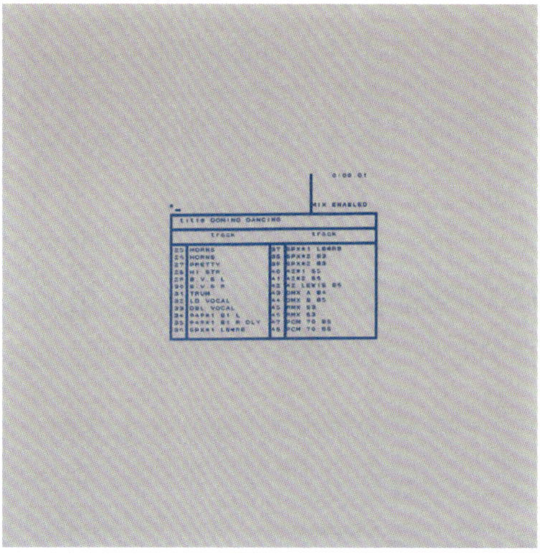

12", inner sleeve, front

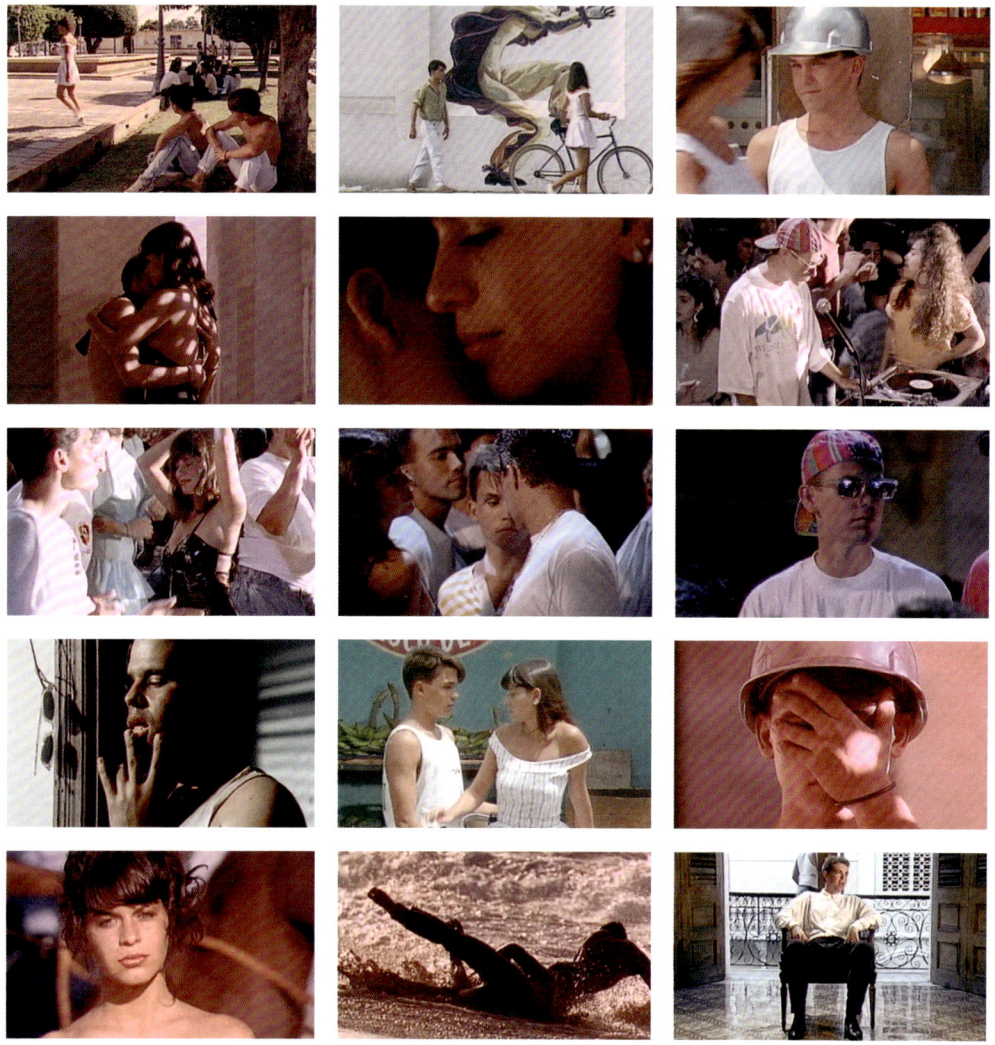

Two good-looking young boys lounge in the park and gaze at a beautiful passing girl; shots of street murals and a deserted colonnade can be seen reflected in Chris's sunglasses. One of the boys follows and ends up dancing tenderly with the girl. Later, in a disco, Chris is the DJ and Neil sings as the crowd dances. The boy comes looking for his new girlfriend but she dances suggestively with another boy and ignores him. In the next scene, the second boy and the girl embrace in a waterfall, passionately. Then the two boys are seen fighting over the girl in the surf on the beach, while the girl walks around without a care. 'We wanted somewhere full of really pretty young people so I suggested Puerto Rico', said Eric Watson. The video was filmed in about four days in the historic colonial district of Old San Juan in the north of the island. One of the locations that was featured is the Santa María Magdalena de Pazzis Cemetery. All the lead actors were Puerto Rican and cast by Pet Shop Boys.

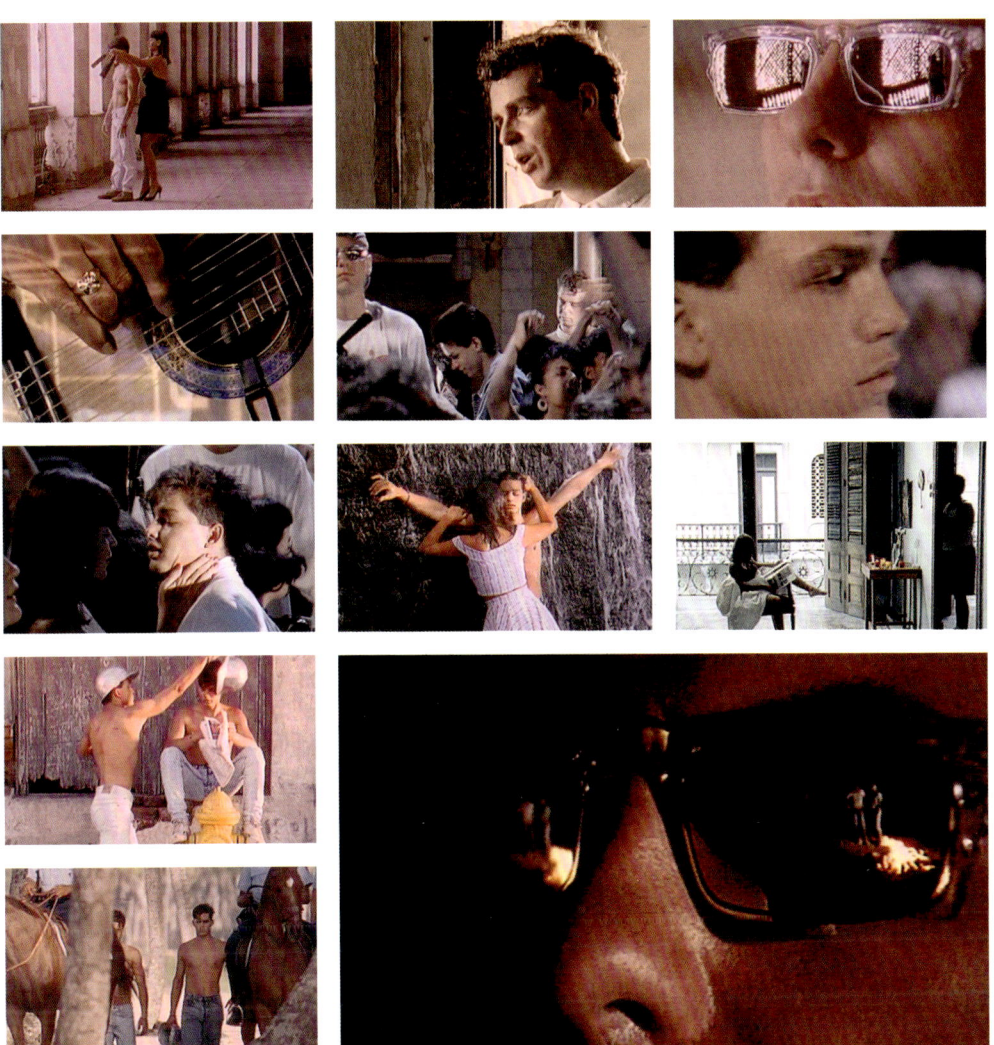

'I had this bee in my bonnet about women being objects, so I did this thing about this girl older than the boys having them both on', Watson remembered. It was a bit like those magazine photo stories, but more stylish. It was the video that everyone liked. Neil and Chris pop up every so often. They were basically sunbathing, and every now and then they would turn up and say "This is good fun", and an hour later they would go away again.'

Showbusiness / I like it here, wherever it is

release 1 December 1988
formats VHS / laserdisc (*I like it here, wherever it is* only)
photographer Cindy Palmano
design Mark Farrow at Three Associates and PSB

The second Pet Shop Boys video compilation after *Television* (pages 80–1), *Showbusiness* featured all the promotional videos made between 'It's a sin' and 'Domino dancing' – the group's costume-drama era. Its cover was a photograph taken by Cindy Palmano on the set of the video for 'What have I done to deserve this?' (pages 88–9). The showgirls' costumes were secondhand and had previously appeared in the James Bond movie *Octopussy*. As with *Television*, Mark Farrow designed the VHS box and also did the title sequence, his first, on the video itself. In Japan, Pet Shop Boys released a different format, with a slightly different running order, on both VHS and laserdisc, calling it *I like it here, wherever it is*, a quote by Joss Ackland taken from the car scene of their film *It couldn't happen here* (pages 104–5). It was to be the first of several Japan-only Pet Shop Boys releases. Again, the sleeve featured a photograph from the 'What have I done to deserve this?' video set.

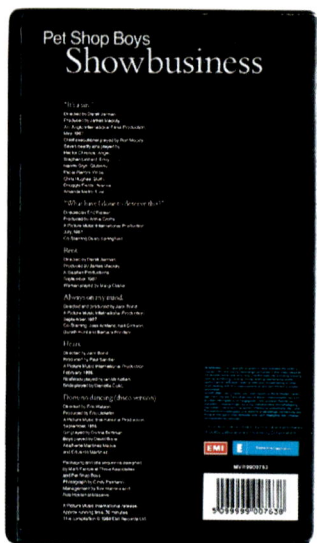

VHS, back

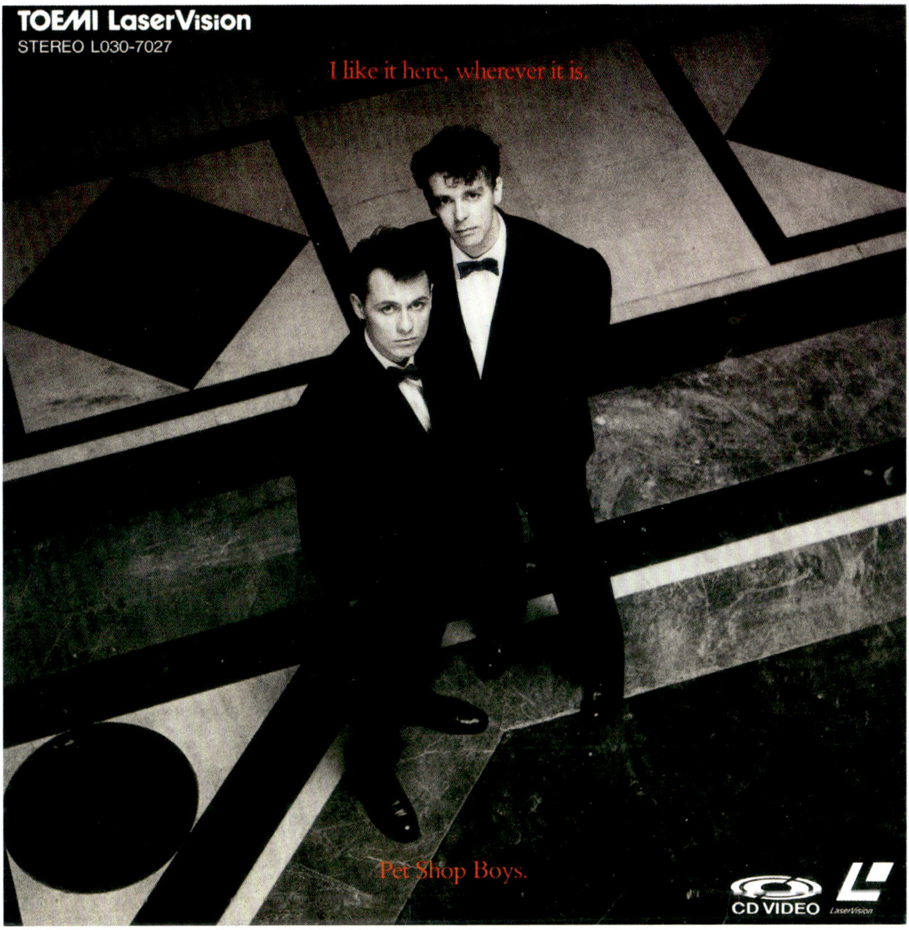

Laserdisc, front

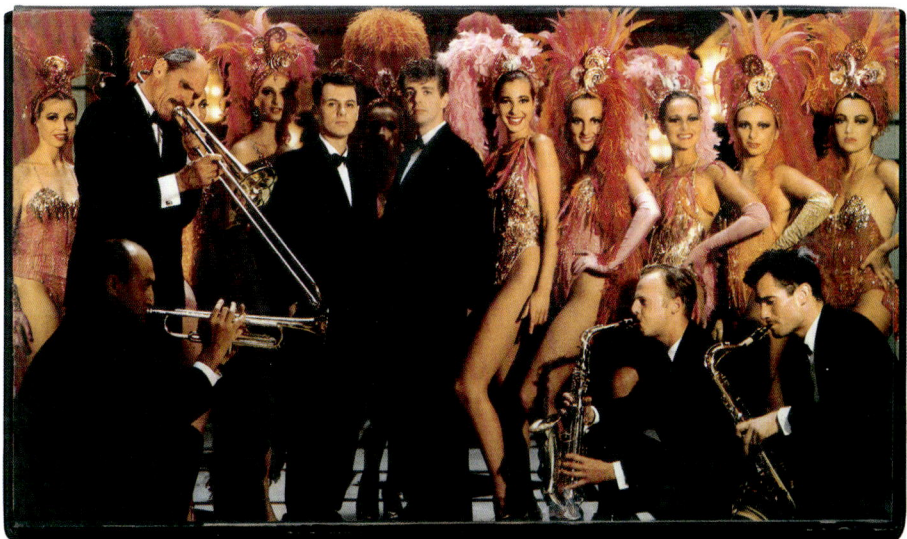

VHS, front

Introspective

release 10 October 1988
formats LP / limited-edition triple-disc LP / cassette / CD
photographers Eric Watson, Peter Andreas,
Michael Roberts, and Cindy Palmano
design Mark Farrow at Three Associates and PSB

Mark Farrow and Christophe Gowabs were looking through a designer's book of colour combinations and saw these colours. 'For once, we were not taking it and trying to turn it into another idea but thought "that's what we're going to do."' They took it exactly as it appeared in the book. The cassette and CD used different colours. 'But the vinyl was always the strongest set. It got called the gay flag, which it wasn't, and the testcard, which it wasn't either. It was just literally an idea of what colours could go together.' 'It was probably the first sleeve we designed as a CD rather than as a record sleeve', recalls Neil. 'Actually, it's our least favourite sleeve.' The regular LP has yellow, green, pink, red, yellow again, purple, and blue stripes, with the title printed on the sleeve. Chris remembers that Tom Watkins thought that whenever people saw the testcard on the television they would think, 'Oh, I must go out and buy that *Introspective* album.' The inner-sleeve photograph by Eric Watson shows Neil and Chris wearing yellow T-shirts dyed to match the background colour, and cuddling Booblies, a friend's Yorkshire terrier. It was a happy accident that Chris was wearing a stripey cap.

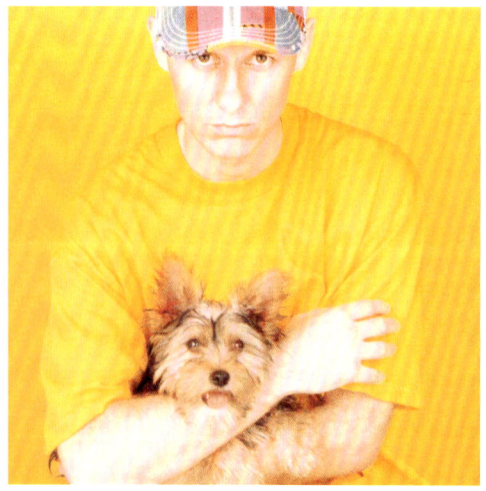

LP, inner sleeve, front

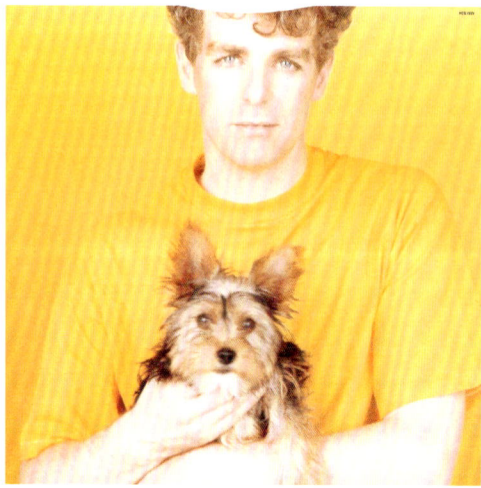

LP, inner sleeve, back

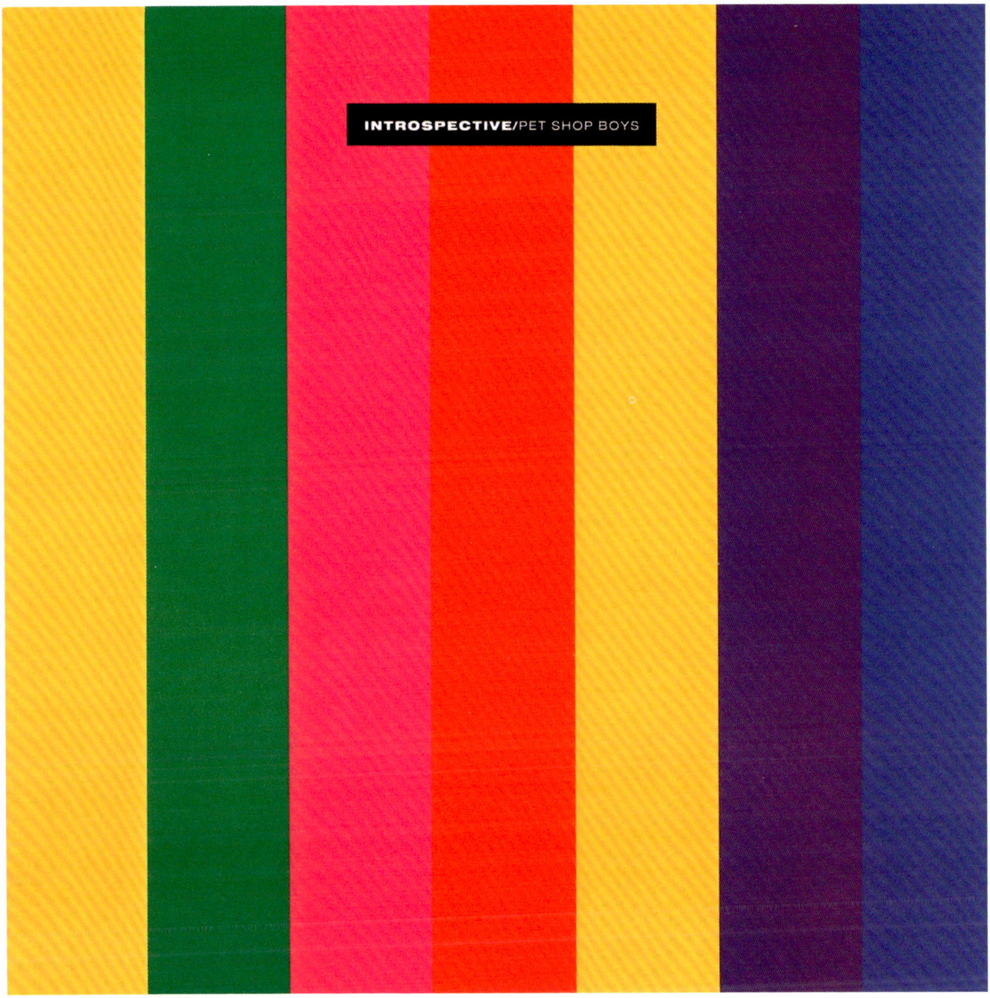

LP, outer sleeve, front

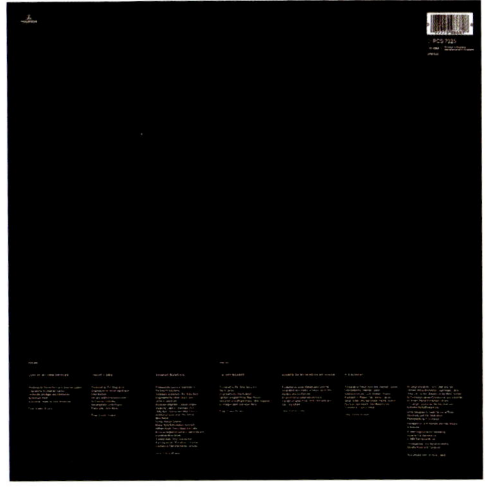

LP, outer sleeve, back

Introspective 1988

The limited-edition triple-disc LP of *Introspective* is a wonderful, glossy compendium of pop and high-fashion styling, characteristically referencing the past, present, and future. The outer sleeve has six stripes, one fewer than the regular LP, to match the number of songs and the track information on the reverse, and has no text on the front – just a bellyband for the title. The highly effective 'big label' idea, which Pet Shop Boys had used since the first release of 'Opportunities (let's make lots of money)' (pages 38–9), was first used by Alexander Robotnik for Italian disco tracks. Pierre LaRoche again did the make-up for the 'I want a dog' and 'Always on my mind / In my house' picture labels. He was also the make-up artist on the first Pet Shop Boys tour. Neil recalls that their tour manager Ivan Kushlick imposed a strict discipline.

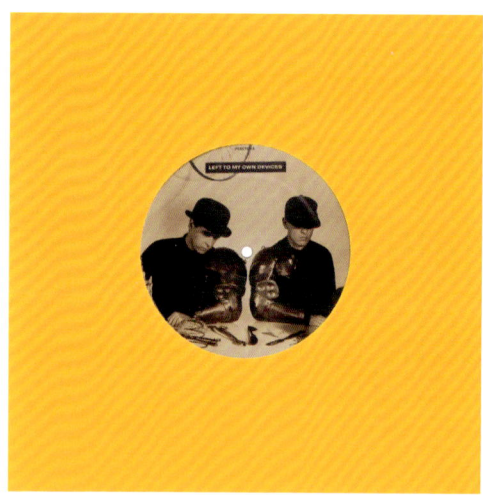

Limited-edition triple-disc LP, side A, inner sleeve, front (photo: Michael Roberts)

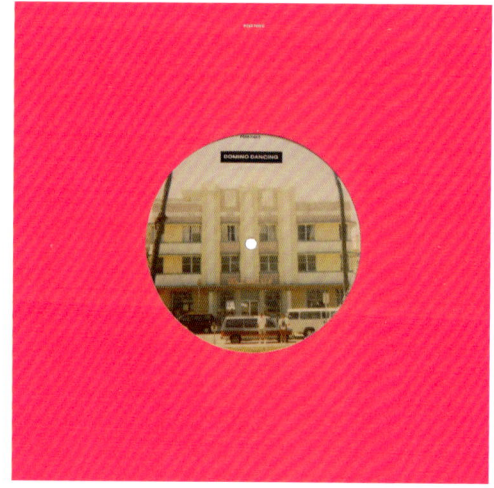

Limited-edition triple-disc LP, side C, inner sleeve, front (photo: Peter Andreas)

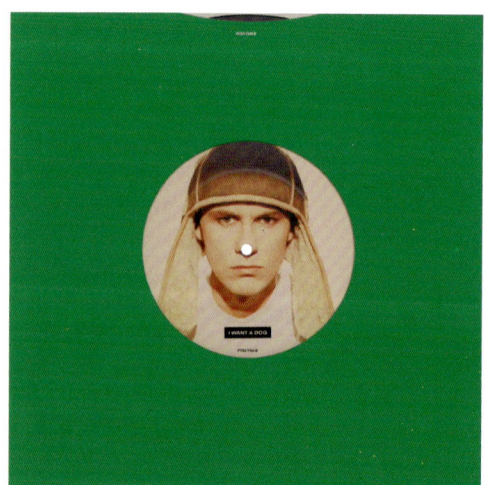

Limited-edition triple-disc LP, side B, inner sleeve, back (photo: Eric Watson)

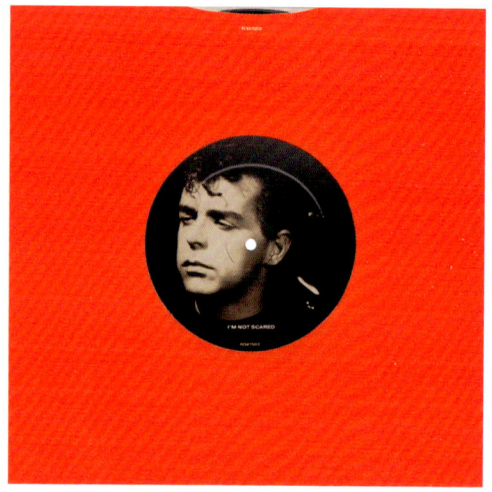

Limited-edition triple-disc LP, side D, inner sleeve, back (photo: Michael Roberts)

'Ivan said if anyone was late they would be fined £100 a minute, and the proceeds would go to an AIDS charity. Pierre said, "It is such a good cause I think we all 'ave a duty to be late."' (Sadly, LaRoche himself would later die of an AIDS-related illness.)

The Michael Roberts photograph for the 'Left to my own devices' label was the same image that appeared on the seven-inch release of that song (page 123). Roberts' shot of Neil for 'I'm not scared' also had a specific historical reference: it was based on a photograph of Dmitri Shostakovich – actually, from a film by Tony Palmer of an actor playing Shostakovich sitting in an empty room after being denounced by someone. The baby in the 'It's alright' photograph was Buster Palmano, Cindy Palmano's son.

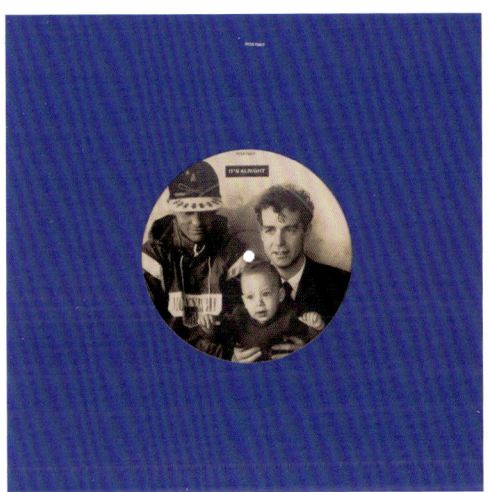

Limited-edition triple-disc LP, side E, inner sleeve, back (photo: Eric Watson)

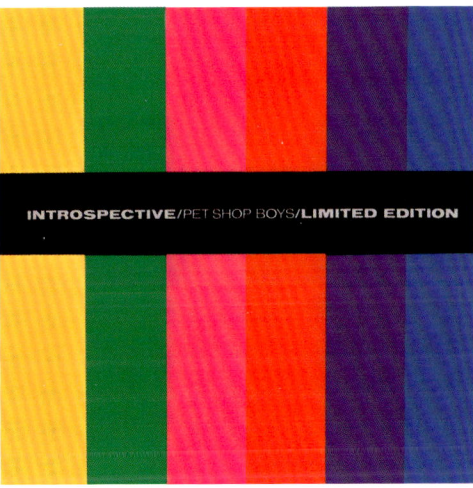

Limited-edition triple-disc LP, outer sleeve, front

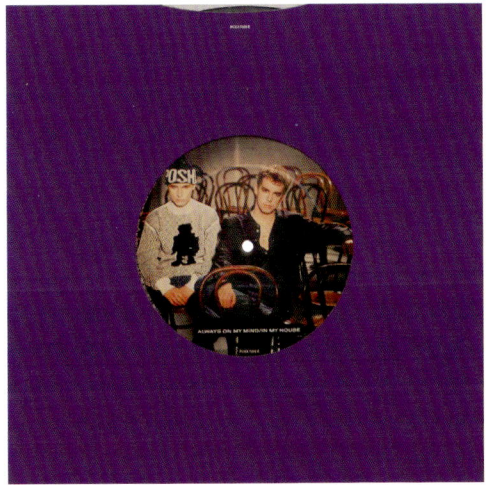

Limited-edition triple-disc LP, side F, inner sleeve, front (photo: Cindy Palmano)

Left to my own devices

release 14 November 1988
formats 7" / 7" promo / 12" × 2 / 12" promo / cassette / CD
photographer Michael Roberts
design Mark Farrow at Three Associates and PSB
video Eric Watson

The Michael Roberts photographs, in which Chris and Neil pose with medieval armour, with a suspended bicycle wheel overhead, have a surrealist or dadaist overtone, and reference the work of artists such as Marcel Duchamp, who famously set a bicycle wheel on a stool. Roberts, then fashion editor for *Tatler*, defined that magazine's influential look in the Eighties. He was renowned for his use of models off the street (although these were usually public schoolboys with Bruce Weber looks) and for referencing vintage themes. The 'sleeve within a sleeve' was 'totally Mark Farrow', says Neil. 'I hated these pictures, which I thought were really contrived and pretentious, so I covered them up', Farrow explains. The sleeve mimicked an American map he had bought that had come in a yellow envelope with a cut at the top; he copied it and the type layout.

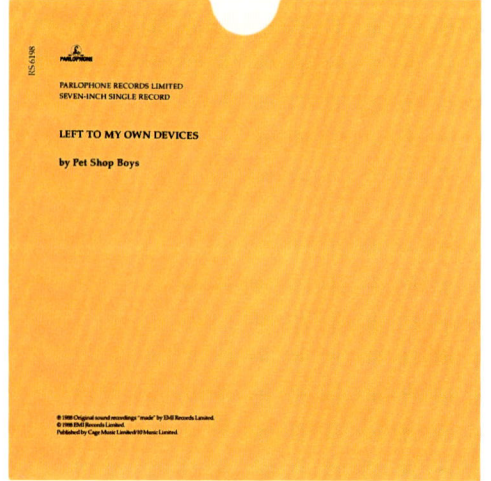

12", outer sleeve, front

12", outer sleeve, back

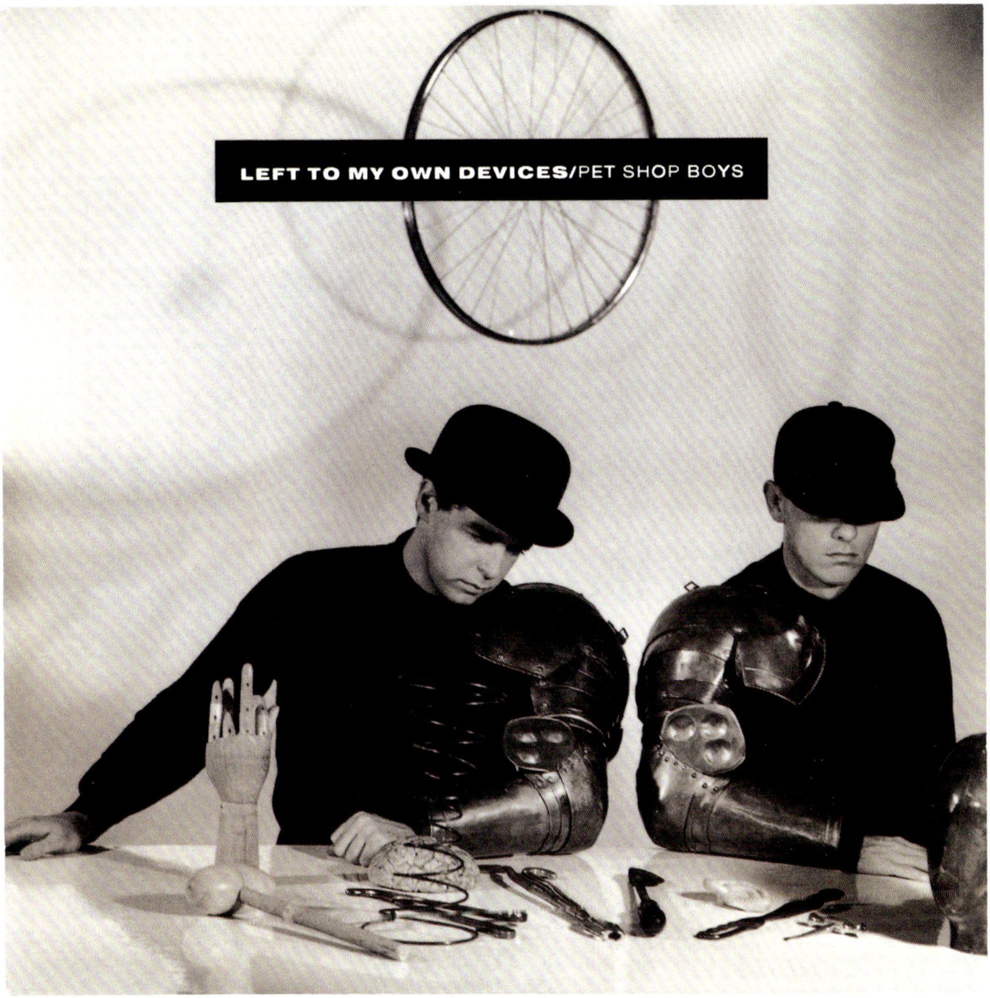

7", inner sleeve, front

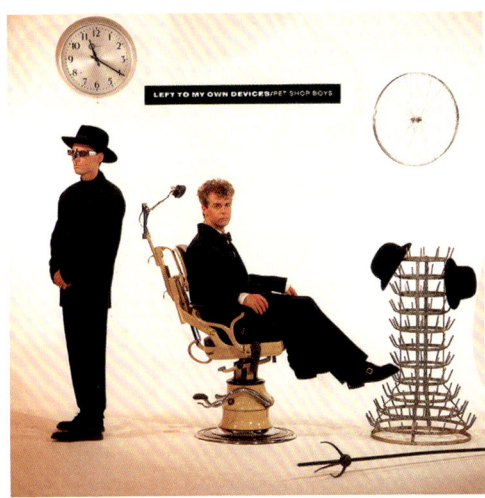

12", inner sleeve, front

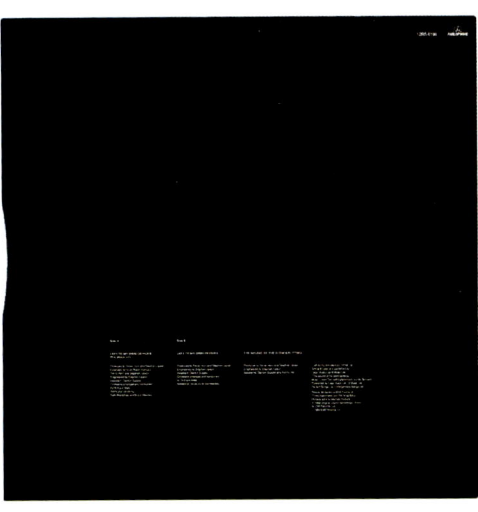

12", inner sleeve, back

Left to my own devices 1988

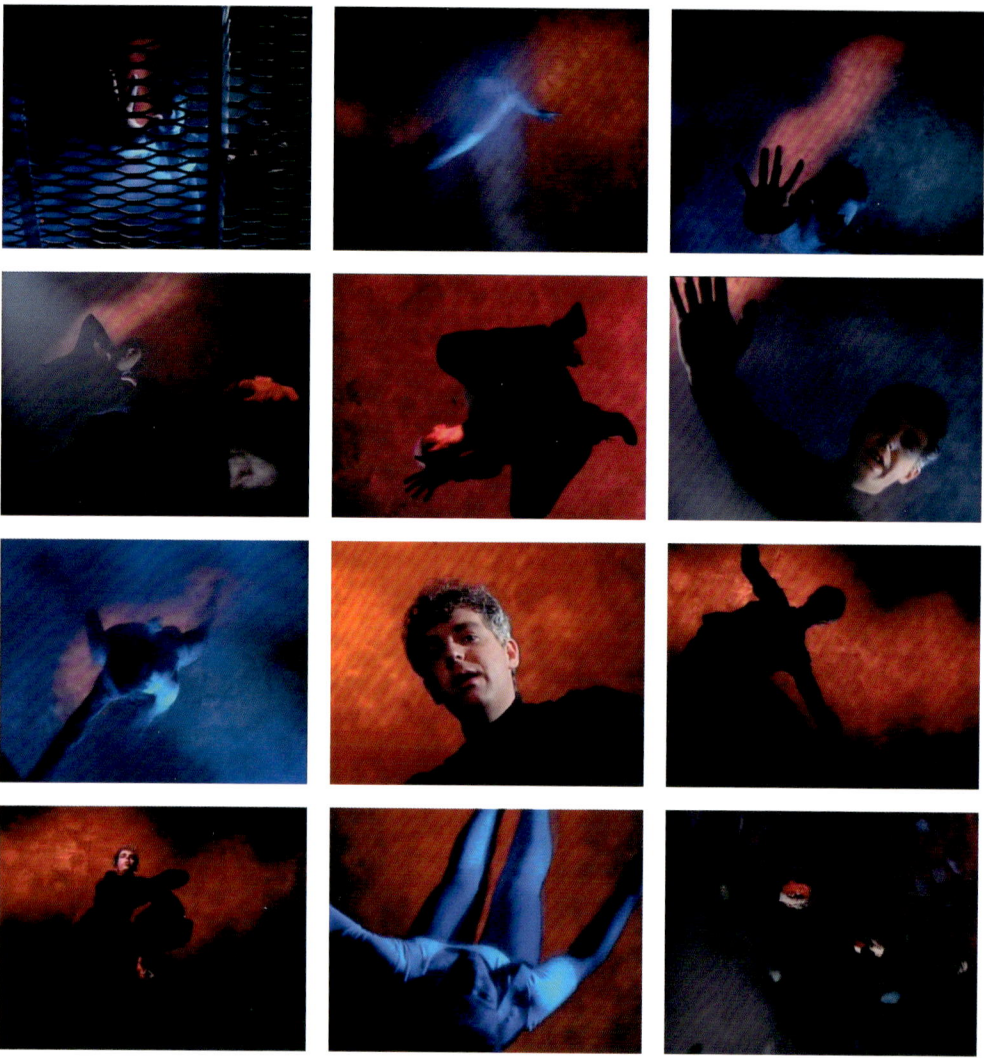

An impressionistic scene: a metal grille through which acrobats are seen from below as they swing and leap vertiginously. Neil, in black clothes sings, while Chris, also dressed entirely in black, dances and strikes poses, all seen from beneath, as if they were on a glass floor. The video is a clever, glorious reflection of the song's atmosphere. However, 'I got into trouble for this', recalled Eric Watson. 'I wanted to create a sort of Dante's Inferno, everybody walking on space. I wanted it to be like a painting; keep the same point of view with events running through it. But someone said it was a terrible piece of negativism because at the end the Pet Shop Boys are stamping over everyone. I thought it was funny, but it didn't appeal to a lot of people's sense of humour.' He later edited a longer version of the video for US clubs, including 'lots of very literal inserts (the phrase "party animal", for instance, is illustrated by a shot of Chairman Mao)'. Owing to the use of copyright material, it was never shown in Britain.

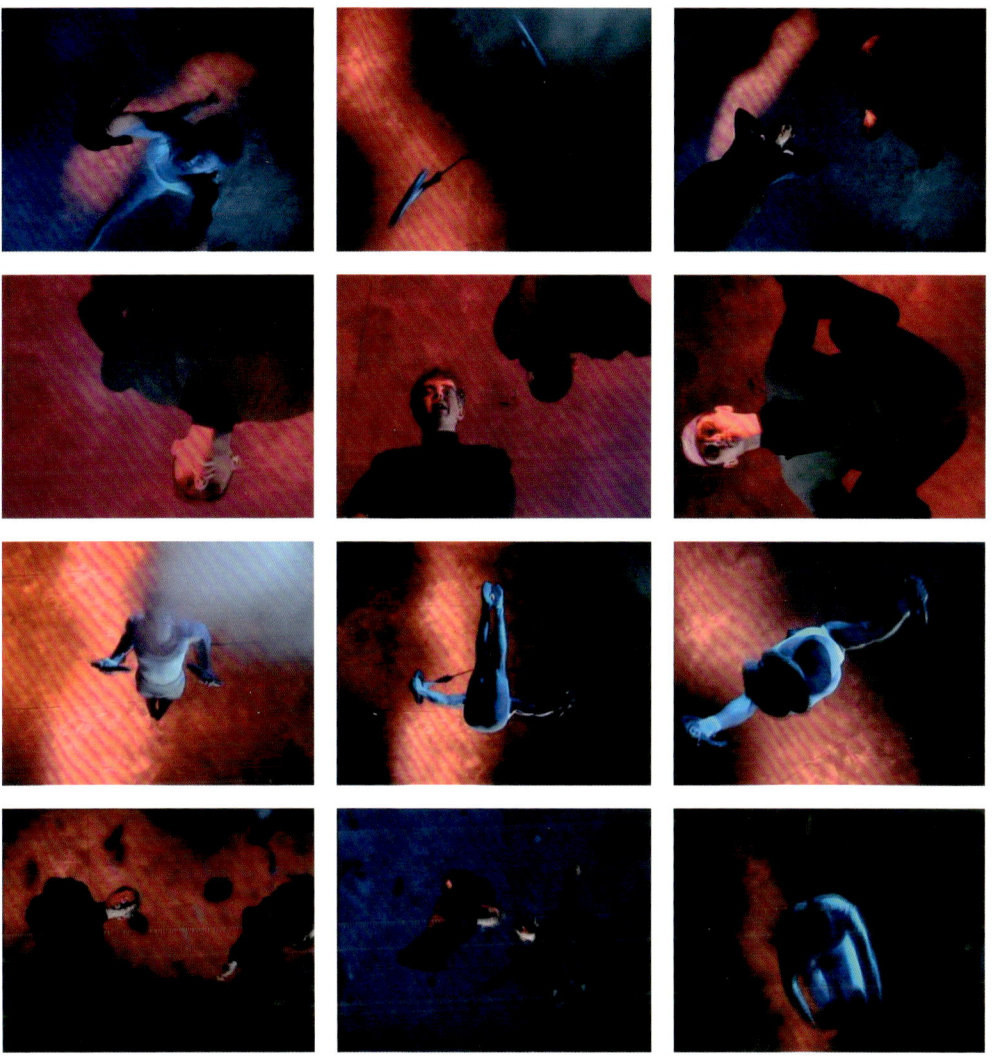

It's alright

release 26 June 1989
formats 7" × 2 / 10" / 12" × 2 / 12" remix / 12" promo / cassette / CD
photographer Eric Watson
design Mark Farrow at 3a
video Eric Watson

Originally the 'Batman' shoot by Cindy Palmano (page 133) was to be used for the cover of 'It's alright', but at the last moment the 'optometrist' shots, taken by Eric Watson (again with characteristic Pierre LaRoche make-up) for a twelve-inch remix, were used for the regular seven-inch and twelve-inch releases instead.

At that time, talking about the unusual care Pet Shop Boys took with their sleeves, Neil said, 'I quite often look through our records and think how fantastic they look…. You want to make the record something special. It's not just nothing, the sleeve. I personally think it's as important as the music. You're buying an object, so you want it to be a beautiful object. I also think a sleeve should give you things to wonder about. You can get the "It's alright" sleeve and spend hours wondering about Chris's glasses.'

The fluoro-colours used on the twelve-inch bellyband and the typographic limited-edition formats echoed those used in the forthcoming *MCMLXXXIX* tour merchandise and in the stage show itself (pages 130–3). 'It was a housey, dancey, acieedy kind of thing', says Farrow. The ten-inch remix format also included an inserted poster showing the 'optometrist' photos of Neil and Chris combined into one image.

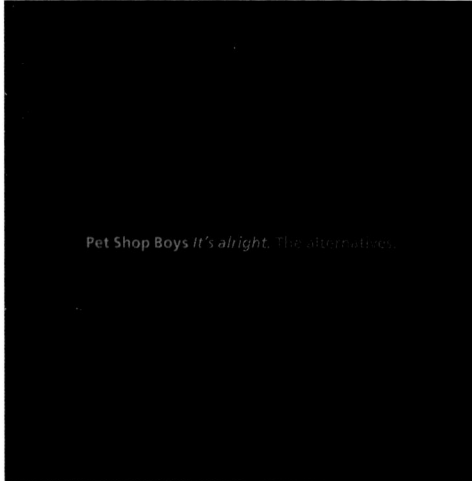

10" remix, front

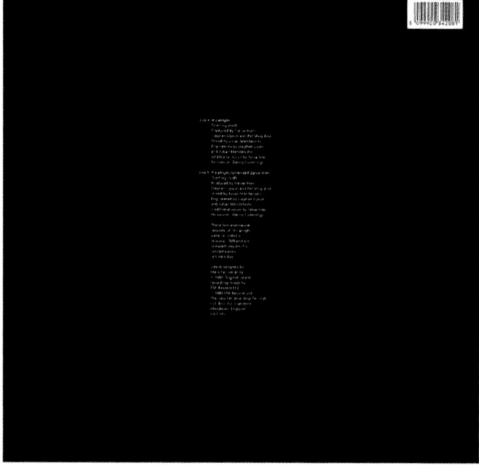

10" remix, back

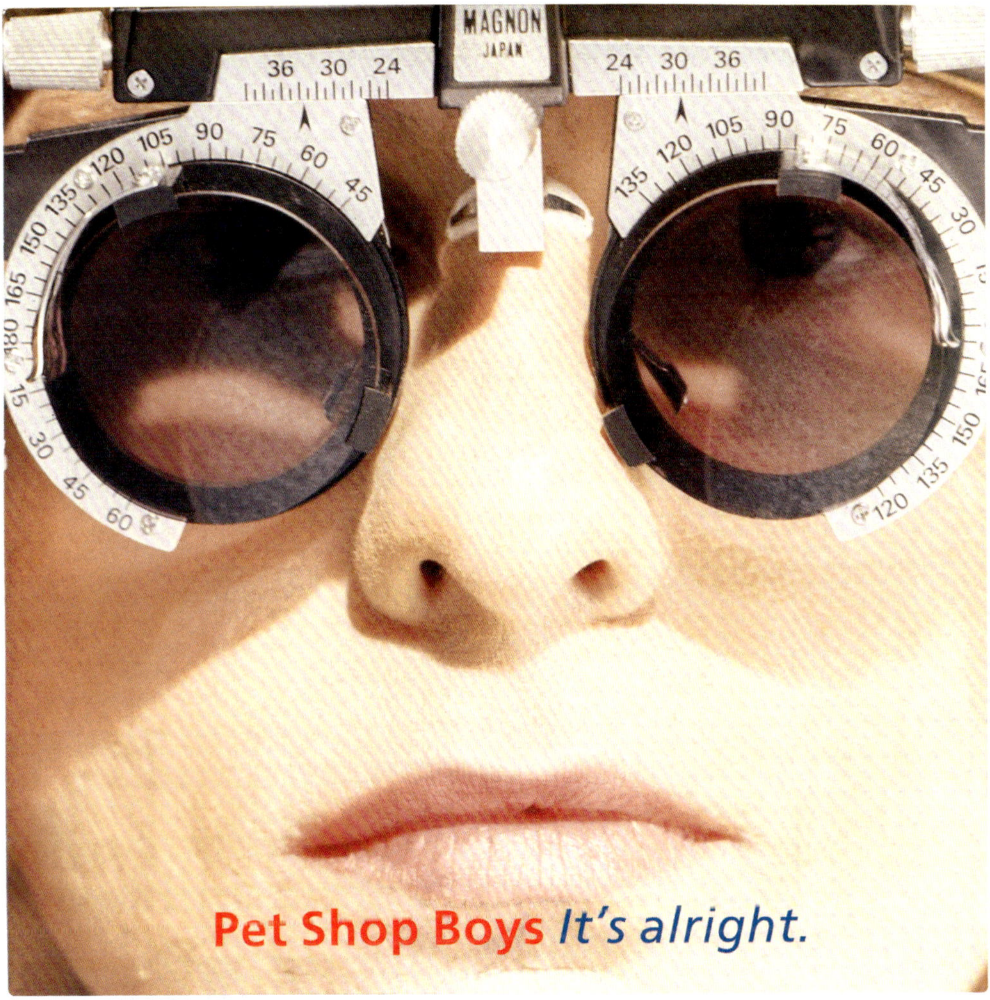

7", front

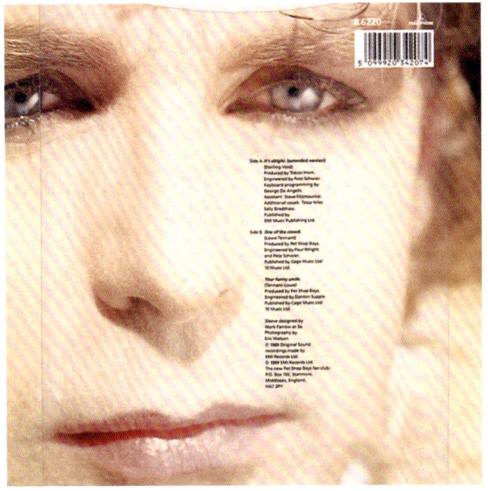

7", back

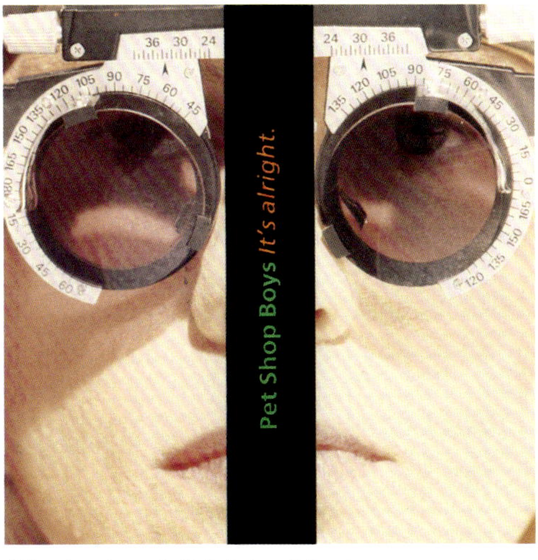

12", outer sleeve (with bellyband), front

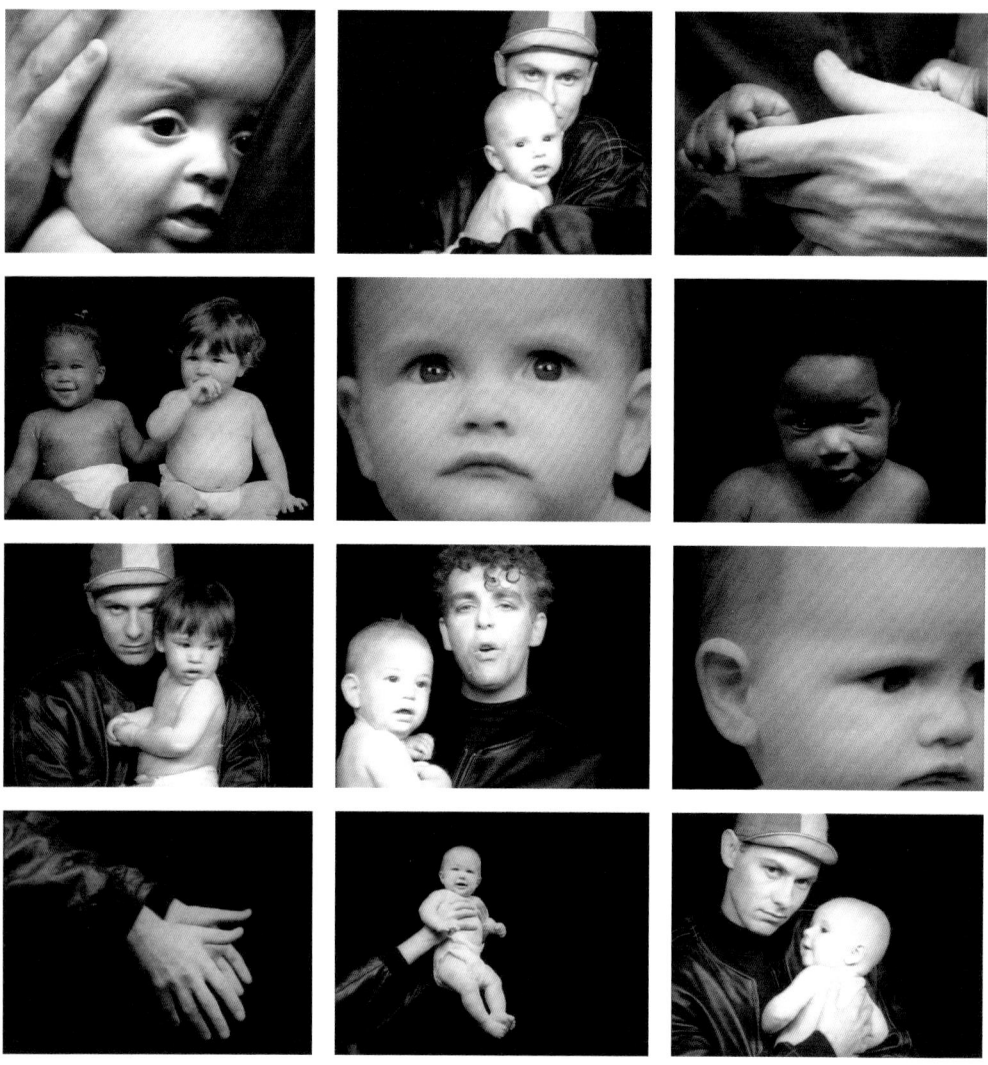

In soft but sharp black and white, black leather and white skin contrast: Neil and Chris cradle babies against a velvet-black background. The result is hypnotic yet optimistic. Eric Watson again directed the video, for which no fewer than 110 babies were gathered, after a suggestion by Chris. 'I thought of babies because when you think what the song's about, whatever we do affects the generation that follows.' The photography was inspired by the lighting in a Mapplethorpe portrait of Warhol, 'in which ... he looks like he's glowing'. 'The idea was that all you'd ever see would be babies, except for men in leather jackets', said Watson. 'Chris and Neil were there for the wide shots, but for the close-ups it was my assistants in the same clothes holding the babies.' This was a necessary precaution. 'In one of the shots Neil is singing and there's a baby at the front with his hands over his ears.' Among the babies used was the photographer's own son, Eugene, seen sitting on Chris's lap (top row, second from the left).

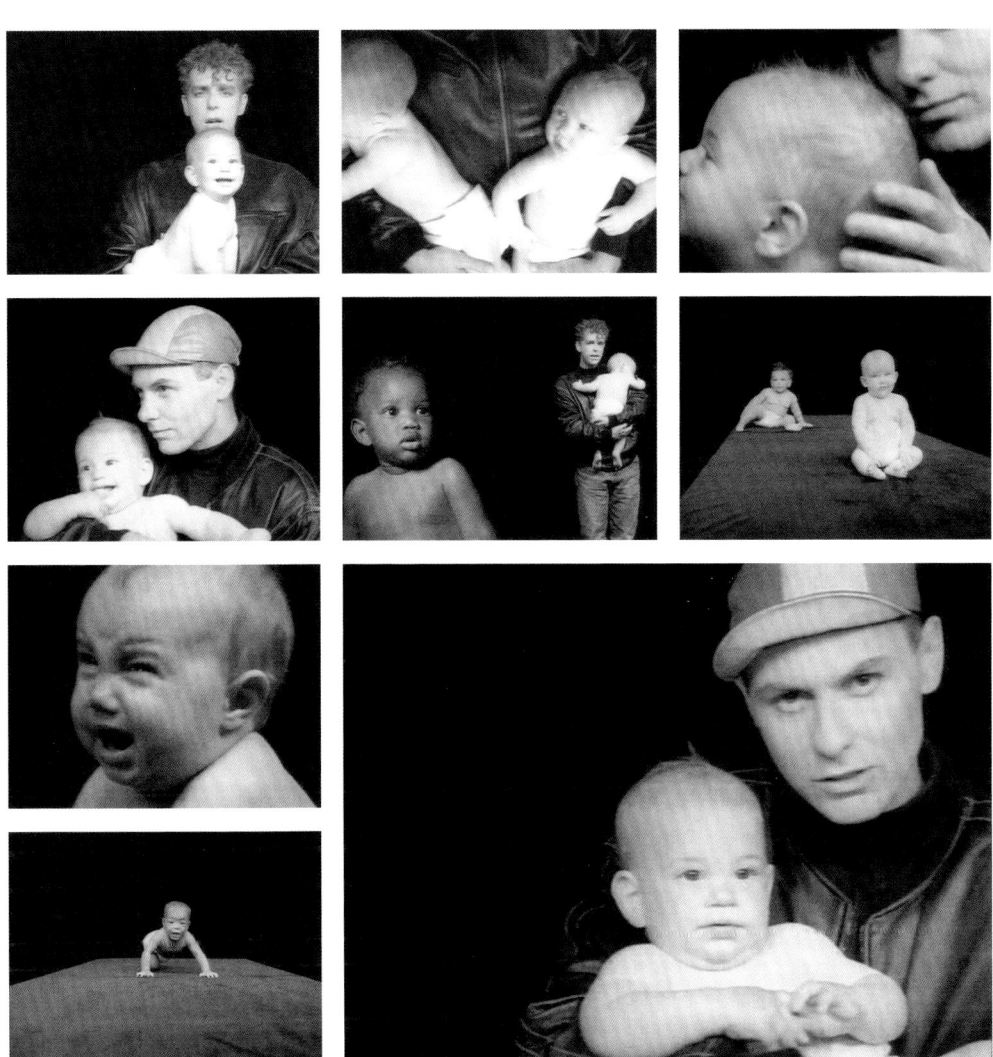

It's alright 1989

MCMLXXXIX tour

dates 29 June – 21 July 1989
director Derek Jarman
film projections Derek Jarman
photographer Lawrence Watson

Probably the most extravagant and flamboyant tour since David Bowie's *Diamond Dogs*, *MCMLXXXIX*'s visual keynote was set by Derek Jarman, who directed this lavish theatrical spectacle and whose own feature films followed much the same themes. 'We wanted a lot to happen on stage', observed Neil at the time. 'One evening we went to see *Requiem*, Derek Jarman's film based on Benjamin Britten's "War Requiem", and we knew that Derek had recently directed an opera in Florence and we decided there and then that we'd ask him if he'd like to direct our tour.… Derek shot a film specially, which will be back-projected onto a screen behind us (pages 134–5) and we have six dancers – hopefully the film and the dancers serve to create an atmosphere. The dancing amplifies the rhythmic elements and the film amplifies what the songs are about or provides a backdrop for their performance.'

'They asked for a theatrical concert and that's what we're doing', said Jarman. 'I suppose some people think pop music and theatre shouldn't mix but I think pop music is theatre.… There are two ways of doing it: you either just sit there and sing on a stool and do it the simple way or you go for it.'

'Before this we hadn't toured because we didn't see any reason for us to tour in a naturalistic way.… [It] was an attempt to get around that by putting on a film multimedia show.… We wanted to put on a theatrical event', Chris said. 'That was our motivation. And actually I think that some of the costumes in that show were some of the best we ever had – not the ones we wore but the ones the extras wore. The costumes for "It's a sin" of the seven deadly sins, combined with the films and the dancers from New York and the way we were doing the music, was a triumph.' 'I think the version of "It's a sin" on that tour is the best live thing we've ever done', Neil added. 'It has to be said, the starting point for all of our tours has been the fact that the way we make music means you don't have to have the stage full of musicians, as we have computers playing live, so you could do whatever you wanted on stage.'

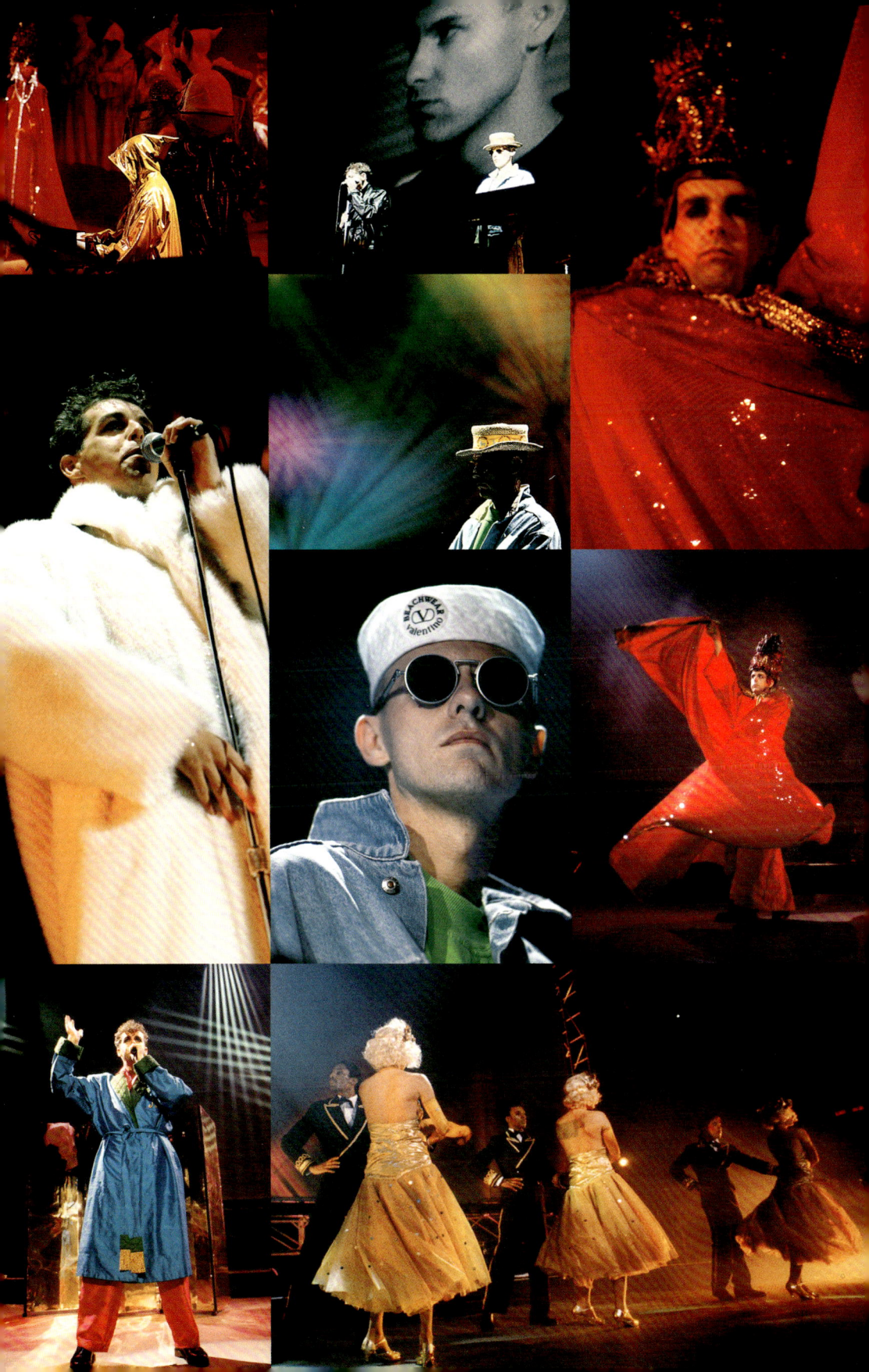

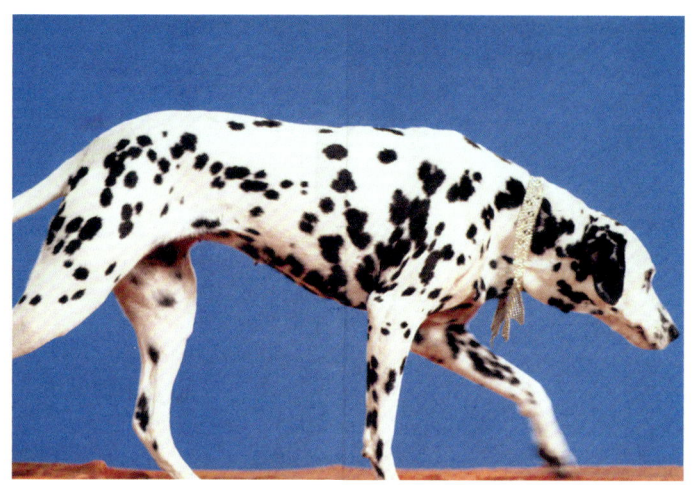
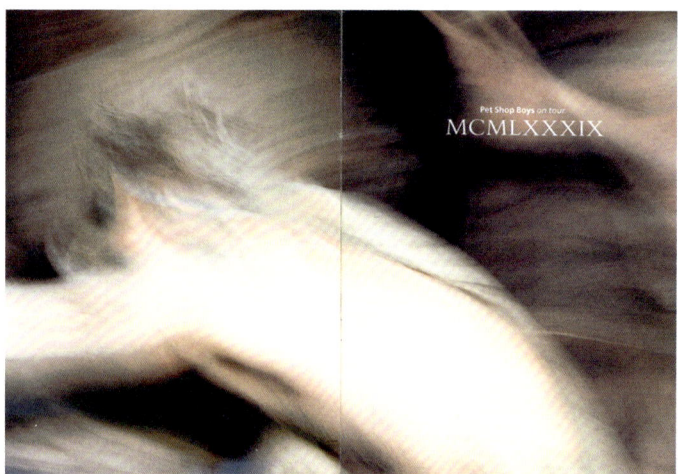
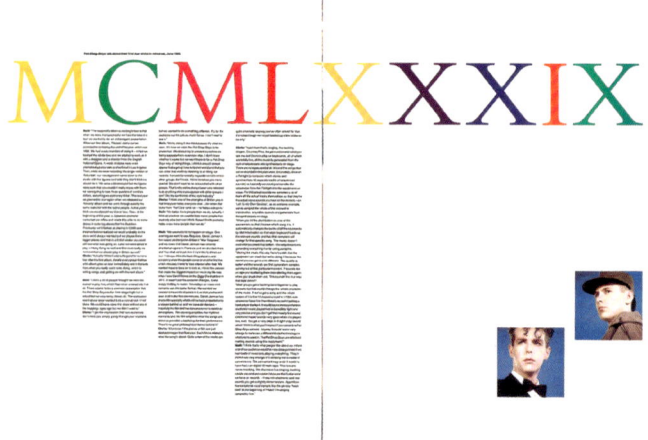

top Tour programme, front and back cover
centre Title page   above First page of interview

Mark Farrow designed the programme in a large 338 × 246 mm format that would be used for several subsequent Pet Shop Boys tour programmes. It, too, featured some of the themes of Jarman's projections, such as the dalmatian in 'Paninaro'. It used the high-key colours that first appeared on the *Introspective* album cover (pages 118–21). The programme also set the pattern of future tour programmes by including an interview between Neil and Chris and journalist Chris Heath.

Jarman filmed the concert at Wembley Arena. Pet Shop Boys were persuaded, against their better instincts, that it would be fine to save money by shooting it on video rather than on film. Jarman considered even video unnecessary. 'I'm a technophobe', he noted during the shoot. 'Why don't we do it all on Super 8? It's totally ridiculous and mad. All these wires. There's no communication with the cameras. Soon the director won't even be there, he'll be editing it from the moon.' When Neil and Chris saw the edited footage, they were disappointed both in the way the show had been captured and in how they themselves looked, and agreed to allow only the eight songs they thought worked best to be released – hence the title, *Highlights*. The full show has never appeared.

To coincide with the Japanese leg of the tour, Pet Shop Boys released another Japan-only product: *In Depth* was a mini-album of recent hits and B-sides. Its cover featured one of Cindy Palmano's 'Batman' images that had been intended for 'It's alright' (pages 126–7). The shoot was originally done for *The Face* in the build-up to the keenly anticipated release of Tim Burton's *Batman* movie. The pose was to 'suggest Batman and Robin without being too literal', Chris noted. Only the black-and-white version worked, and as *The Face* did not want a black-and-white cover, the photographs were used for *In Depth* and for tour material instead. The typography matched that of the 'It's alright' releases.

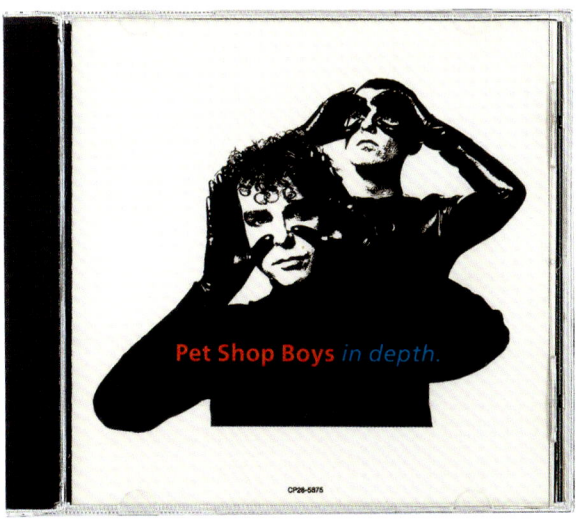

In Depth, CD, front

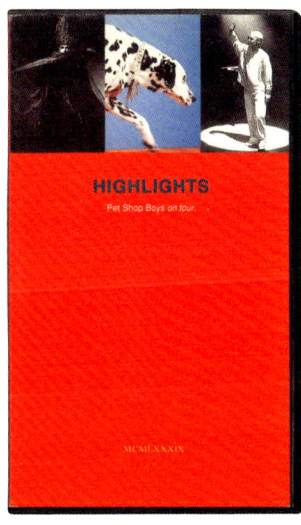

Highlights, VHS, front

Projections

filmed May and June 1989
release 1 December 1993
format VHS
director Derek Jarman

Derek Jarman's projections for *MCMLXXXIX* were eventually released in 1993. 'Each film is related to what the song's about', Chris notes. 'Quite a few of the tracks are cinematic anyway; we've often aimed for that. It's not as though we've just flashed up a few slides to be arty.' 'We've actually managed to come up with the best Super 8 imagery I've ever done', said Jarman. 'I decided there was no point illustrating the songs literally or it would just become laboured. For instance, "Paninaro" refers to a particular type of motor-scooter kid in Italy – we took that theme and instead made some film which looked like old washed-out postcards of Italy, of statues and clouds and ceilings and Italian hustlers from another age. In each song there's a taking-off point for the imagery I use. They're parallel.' The richness of that imagery had much to do with Jarman's own visual archive – filmic, as well as mental; the result was characteristically self-referential Jarman, obsessively recycling his own aesthetic. 'No one else could have done this film within a budget like this because I think I'm the only film-maker who has a huge film library, 400 hours of imagery which I can pirate…. The Italian footage, for instance, is holiday film from 1985.' Others were specifically shot for the tour, often with actor- and dancer-friends of Jarman's: to accompany 'Heart', for example, he filmed dancers, including himself (second row, far right), at Benjy's nightclub in east London.

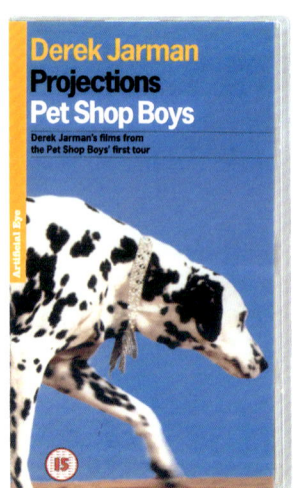

VHS, front (design: Artificial Eye)

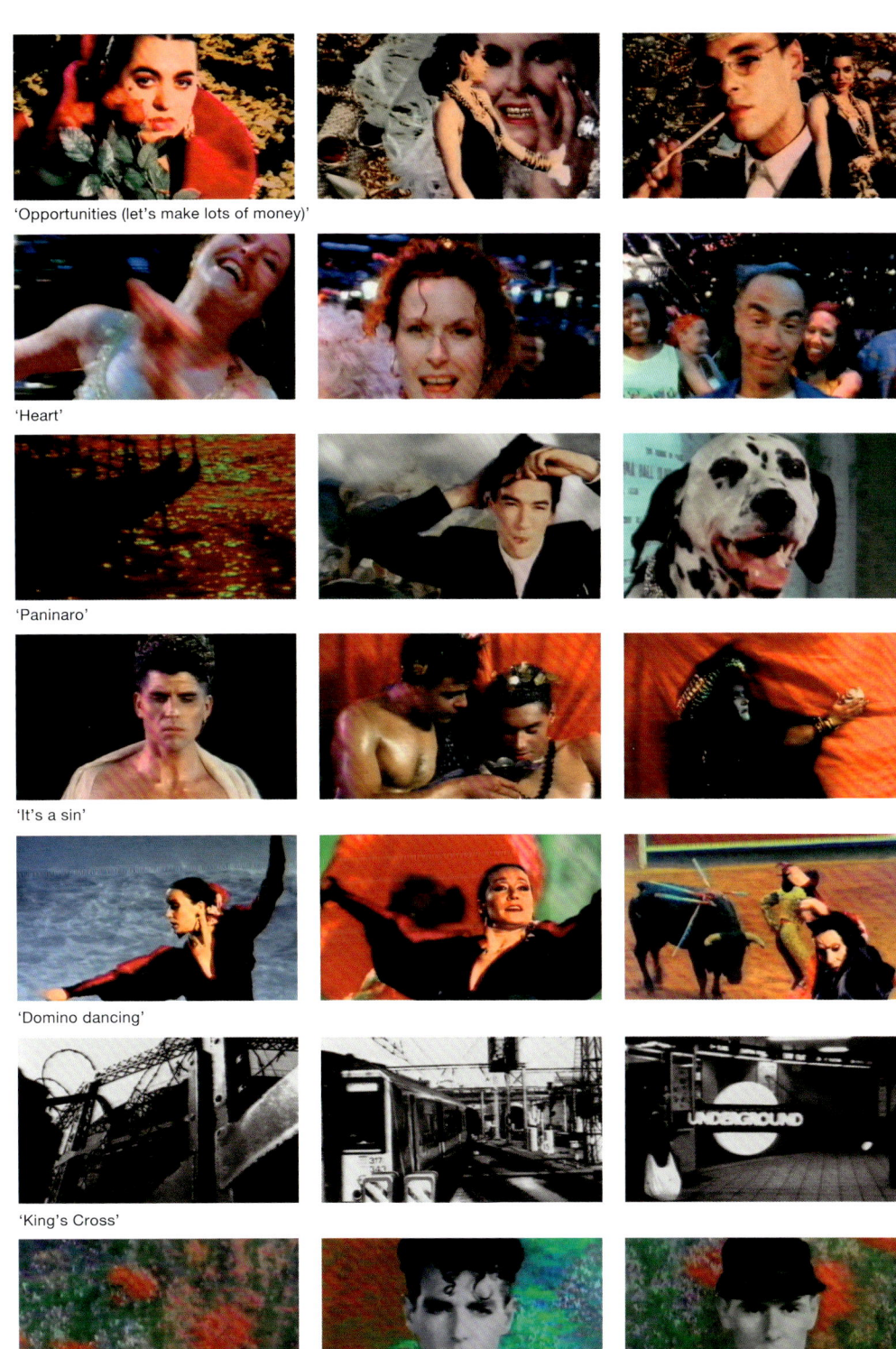

'Opportunities (let's make lots of money)'

'Heart'

'Paninaro'

'It's a sin'

'Domino dancing'

'King's Cross'

'Always on my mind'

Pet Shop Boys, Literally

release 12 November 1990
formats 340-page hardback and paperback book
author Chris Heath
photographers Lawrence Watson, Eric Watson (UK cover),
and The Douglas Brothers (US cover)
design Mark Farrow

When Pet Shop Boys invited Chris Heath to join them on their long-awaited first tour, it was with a vague plan for him to write the text for a photo book, but he set his sights on something more ambitious. Throughout the tour, he shadowed them closely and recorded what was happening, wherever they were and whatever they were doing: as they sped-change costumes mid-set at the back of the stage, relaxed or worried or argued in hotel rooms, wandered foreign streets, or dealt with promoters and press and managers and each other. He even took notes at their shoulders as they unwound on nightclub dancefloors.

The book's clearest inspiration was Michael Braun's obsessive, close-up but matter-of-fact account of The Beatles' early travels, *Love Me Do!* (Braun was thanked at the beginning of *Literally* for this reason), and it was written in the conviction that such a forensically detailed and anthropological narrative could reveal and explain far more than it might at first appear to. Neil and Chris were horrified in places by such an unvarnished account, but also relished the distinctiveness of an approved pop-star book that was not a superficial hagiography.

For the cover, one of Eric Watson's 'It's alright' photos was used (replaced by a Douglas Brothers' photograph for the later United States paperback edition), and inside were images by the tour photographer Lawrence Watson. The book borrowed its title from the recently started Pet Shop Boys fan-club magazine.

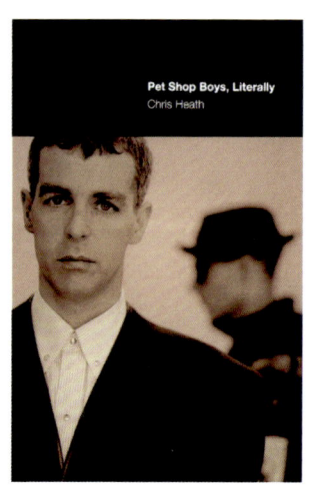

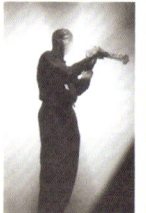

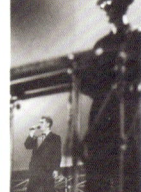

Pet Shop Boys, *Literally*
Chris Heath

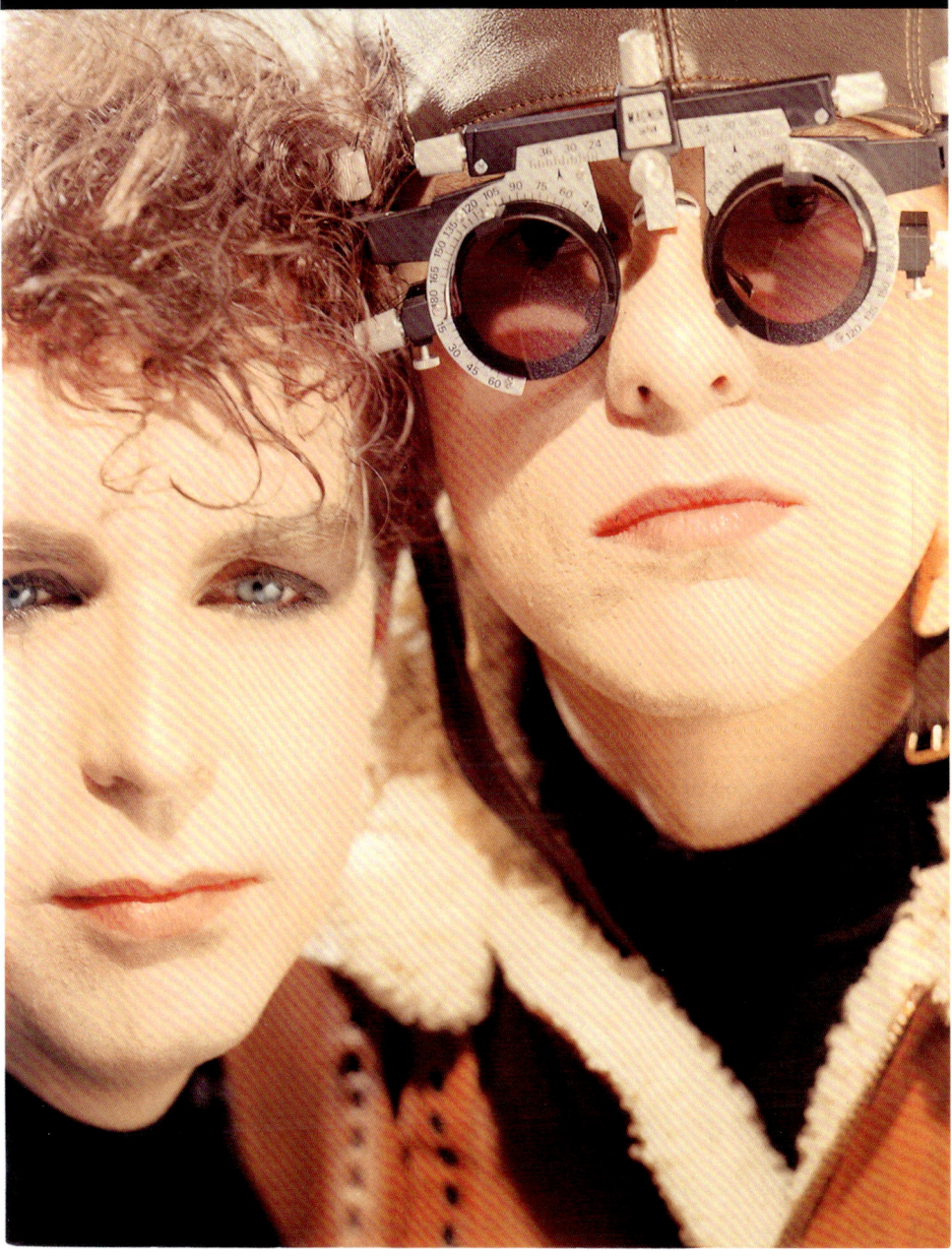

above Hardback, front jacket
opposite left Paperback, United States, front cover
opposite right Paperback, pages 244–5 (with photos by Lawrence Watson)

So hard

release 24 September 1990
formats 7" / 12" / 12" remix / cassette / CD
photographer Eric Watson
design Mark Farrow/3a and PSB
video Eric Watson

'So hard' – 'a true story of deceit', according to Neil – appeared after the longest gap between Pet Shop Boys singles since their first hit in 1985. It marked the beginning of a period in which the design of Pet Shop Boys sleeves seemed to be tugged in two directions, in part continuing and further elaborating the aesthetic they had developed in the Eighties and in part looking to outside contemporary influences, in particular the explosion of rave culture.

Speaking about the design, Mark Farrow says 'I remember it all being about the typography, and this typography feeling very of the era. Around this time I was doing lots of dance stuff for Deconstruction Records and all that was very faceless – there were no images of bands. This sleeve in many ways feels like it fits in with what I was doing outside Pet Shop Boys, whereas previously what I did with Pet Shop Boys set the agenda for everything else. It's more about the typography, and there's a picture of them on it in the same way that there's a picture of mountains on a chocolate box. I remember being a lot more bothered at this period about what the remix sleeve looked like than what the actual sleeve looked like. Nonetheless those pictures were great. I think it was just "I like the Chris one with the apple", as straightforward as that.' Neil adds, 'Chris is eating an apple just because he was eating an apple'.

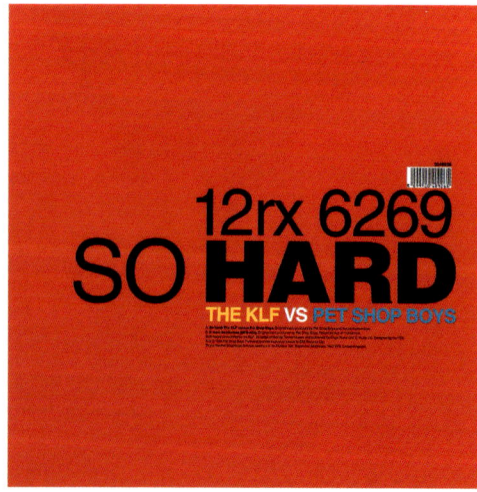

12" remix, front

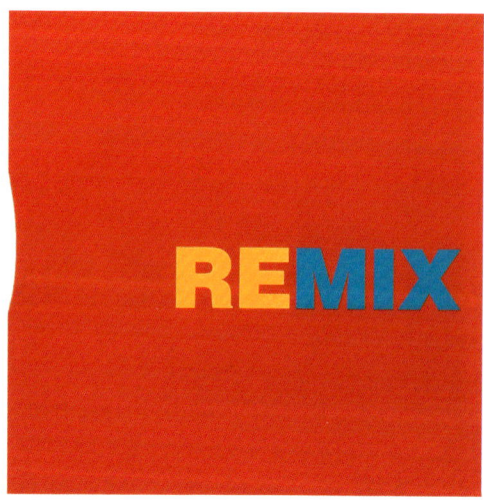

12" remix, back

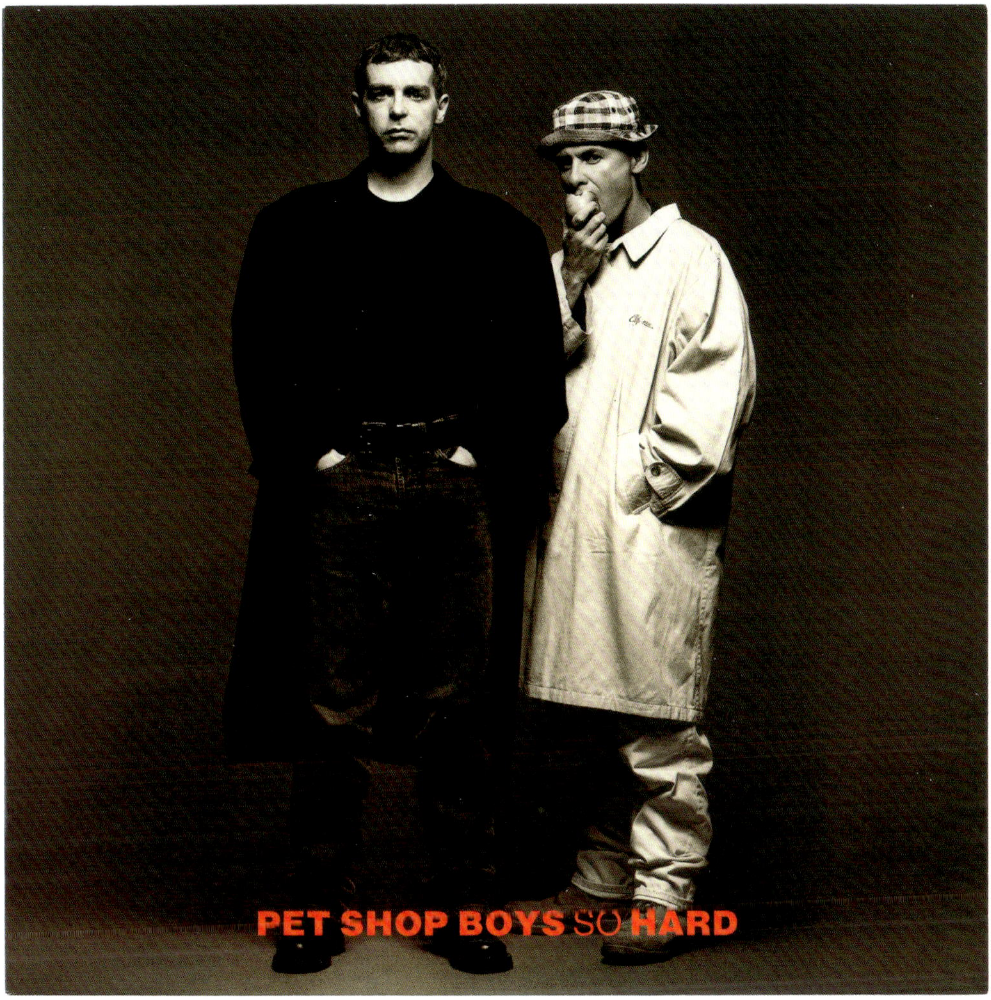

12", front

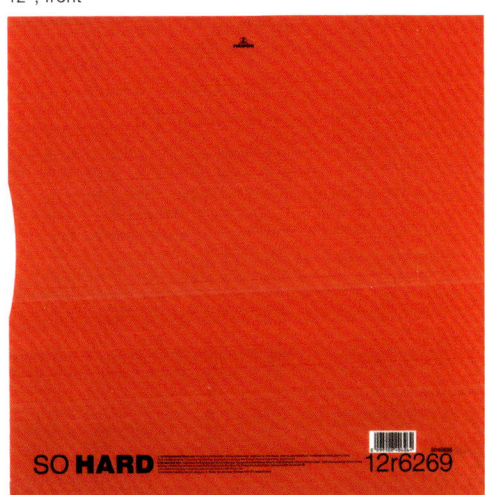

12", back

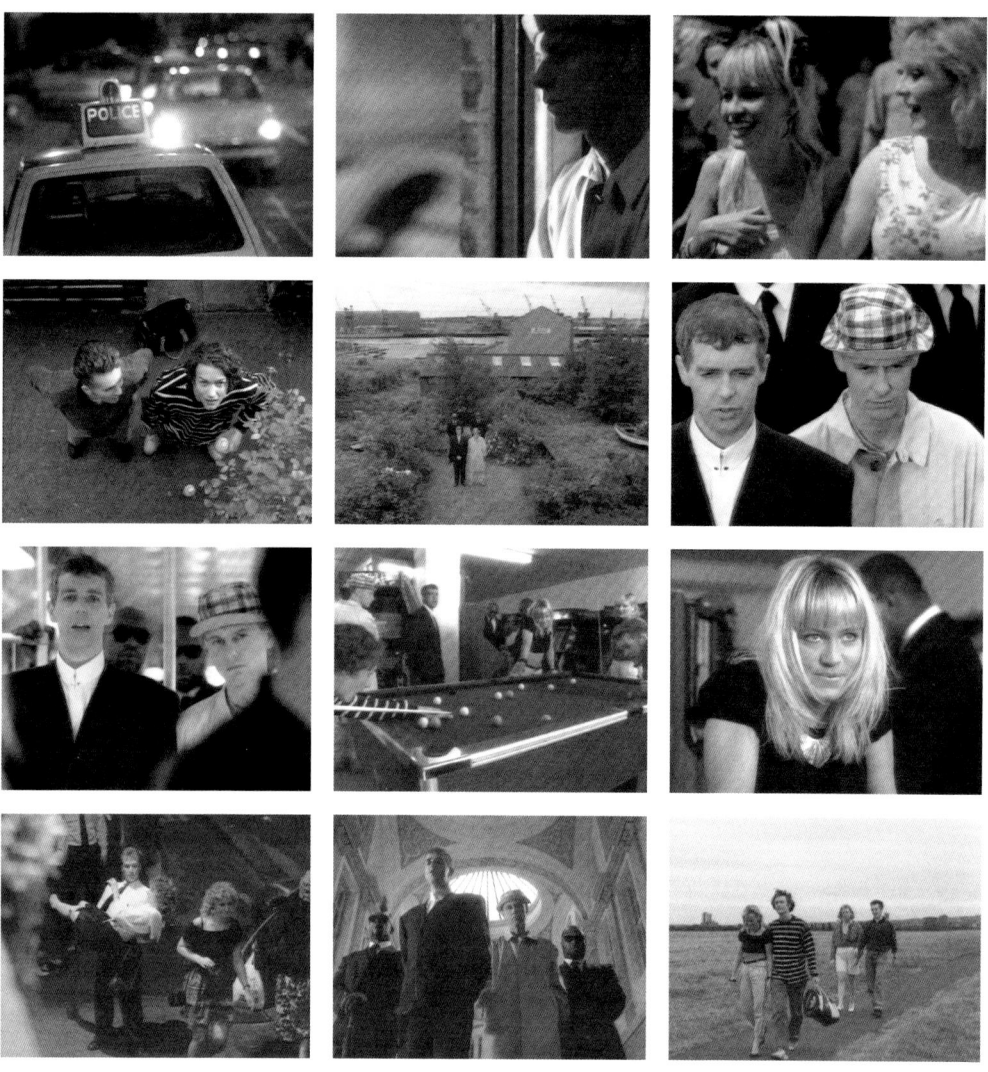

Boys gather at a girl's window, then go off into the streets of Newcastle. Neil and Chris appear, flanked by two unmoving minders. We see them in a car and on the bus, shadowing the main characters. At night, Newcastle comes to life. Later, one of the girls slaps one of the boys and walks off. 'Suddenly we go Northern', says Neil. The film was shot in black and white, with the distinctive silhouette of the Tyne Bridge, and features Anna Marie Gascoigne, sister of footballer Paul, and Dainton Connell, the group's personal assistant (standing behind Chris). The narrative follows the subject of the song, which is about 'two people being totally unfaithful to each other but both pretending they are faithful and then catching each other out'. It was filmed over two days by Eric Watson, with cameraman Pascal Lebec, who had shot Madonna's 'Vogue' video. 'It's about going out, boys meet girls on Friday and Saturday nights', Chris explained. 'It's very Pet Shop Boys', Neil added. They appear as

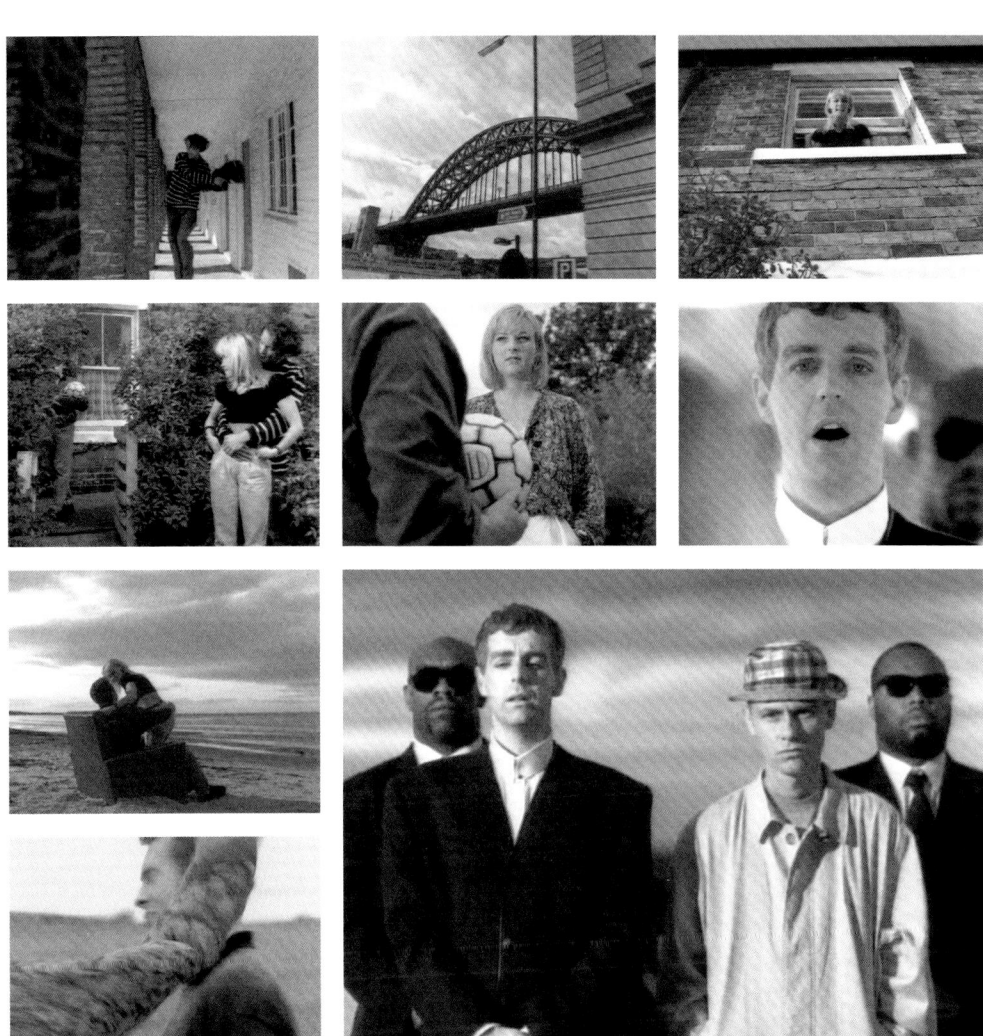

'an alien presence' in the film, always flanked by Dainton and Chopper. Newcastle – home town to both Neil and Watson – was chosen because of its famous Bigmarket nightlife. Watson remarked that the video was 'billed to the record company as "Domino dancing goes north". Gritty realism and all that, and we wanted to do a story. But when you go to Newcastle it's quite a heavy place, especially on a Friday night. People like the exotic, and trying to sell them cranes instead of palm trees is difficult.'

Behaviour

release 22 October 1990
formats LP / cassette / CD
photographer Eric Watson
design Mark Farrow/3a and PSB

In a refinement of previous album designs that used large areas of white space, here the central image has been expanded to include four photos arranged in a rectangle: Neil and Chris holding oversize bunches of roses; Neil full-face; the back of Chris's newly shorn head; and an empty chair with roses on the floor. 'I always thought the portrait of Chris's head was incredibly strong', notes Mark Farrow.

It was the third consecutive Pet Shop Boys studio album sleeve, after *Please* and *Actually*, with a white background. 'I think it had become a prerequisite at that point', says Farrow. 'I always felt with *Behaviour* there is a sort of story implied', Neil commented of the sleeve design. Not only is the inner sleeve pure red, the *inside* of the outer sleeve is red too. The lushness of the printing contrasts with the otherwise minimal design in a manner that echoes the content of the album, the group's most mature work to date. The US formats differ crucially in the American spelling of 'Behavior'. In Japan, the CD was released in a white velvet box, a fantastically impractical and almost fetishistic object to rival Factory Record's celebrated *The Return of the Durutti Column*, which came clad in sandpaper. 'It was so refreshing to get that Japanese edition where they'd used a furry cover and foil-blocked type', says Farrow. 'It felt like for once somebody who had an empathy with what we do had picked up the ball and run with it.'

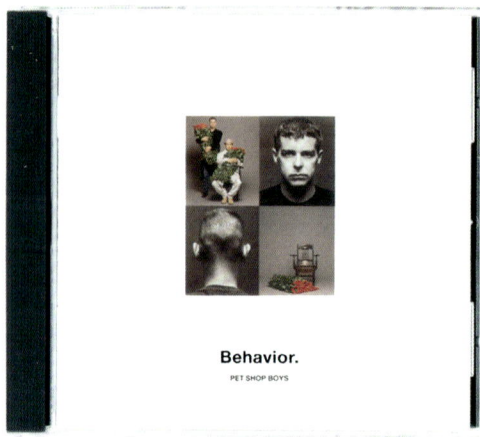

CD, United States, front

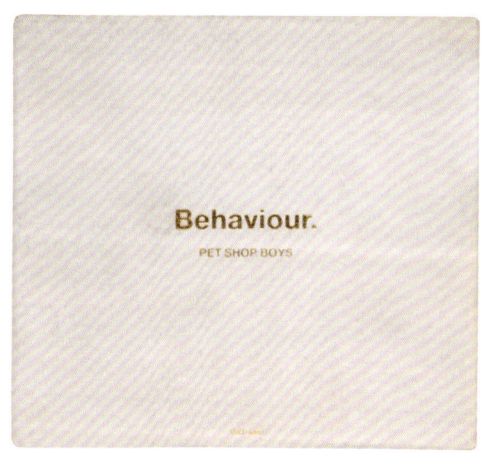

CD, Japan, outer box

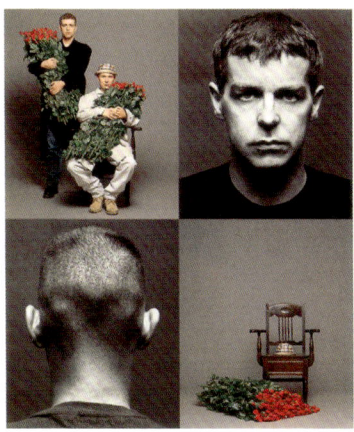

Behaviour.
PET SHOP BOYS

LP, outer sleeve, front

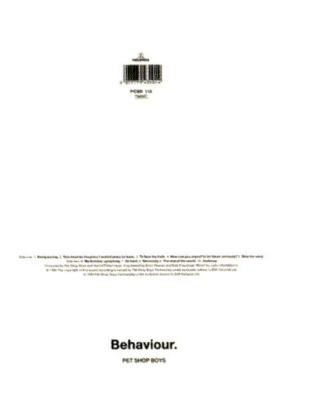

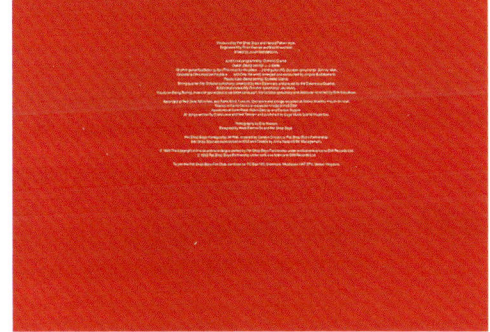

LP, outer sleeve, back

LP, inner sleeve, back

Being boring

release 12 November 1990
formats 7" / 12" / 12" remix / 12" promo × 2 / cassette / CD × 2
photographer The Douglas Brothers
design Mark Farrow/3a and PSB
video Bruce Weber

Neil wears the same Thierry Mugler suit he wore for the 'So hard' video; Chris wears a Mitchko inflatable coat and Jean-Paul Gaultier sunglasses. The Douglas Brothers were the photographers of the moment, specializing in obscure images that referenced the work of such nineteenth-century photographers as Julia Margaret Cameron and Eadweard Muybridge. The session was shot in Pet Shop Boys' west London offices at Pembridge Villas, an extraordinary modern, architect-designed space with a high vaulted room spanned by a glass and metal bridge. 'The way they work is quite unusual', Neil said. 'While one of them sets up the shot, the other photographs.' The photographs were originally taken for the American magazine *Creem*, but the group liked the shots so much that they bought some of them. In the magazine, Chris was described as looking like 'a B-boy from Pluto'.

The design, says Mark Farrow, was 'to all intents and purposes exactly the same as *Behaviour*, but it had two pictures on it instead of four.' It was Farrow who thought of calling the second twelve-inch single 'Being Remixed'. On the back of the sleeve, he repeated the motif of enlarging the catalogue number, which he had first done on the 'So hard' remix (page 138).

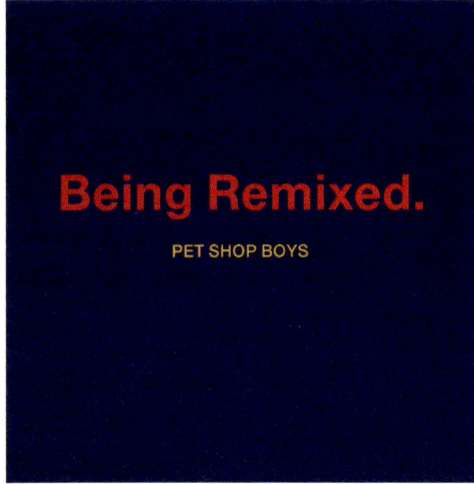

12" remix, front

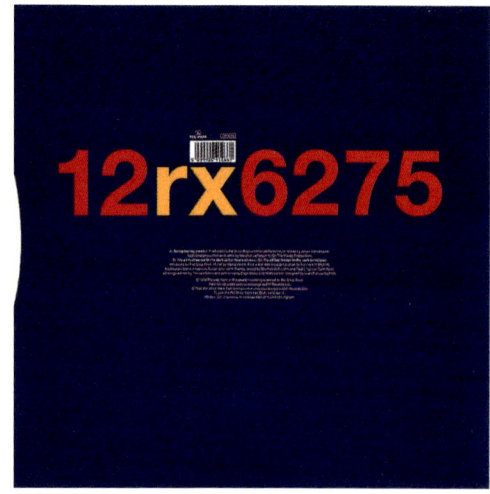

12" remix, back

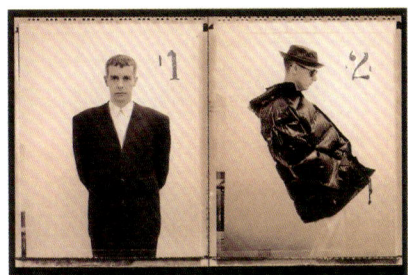

12", front

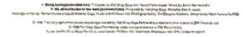

12", back

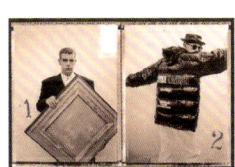

7", front

Being boring 1990

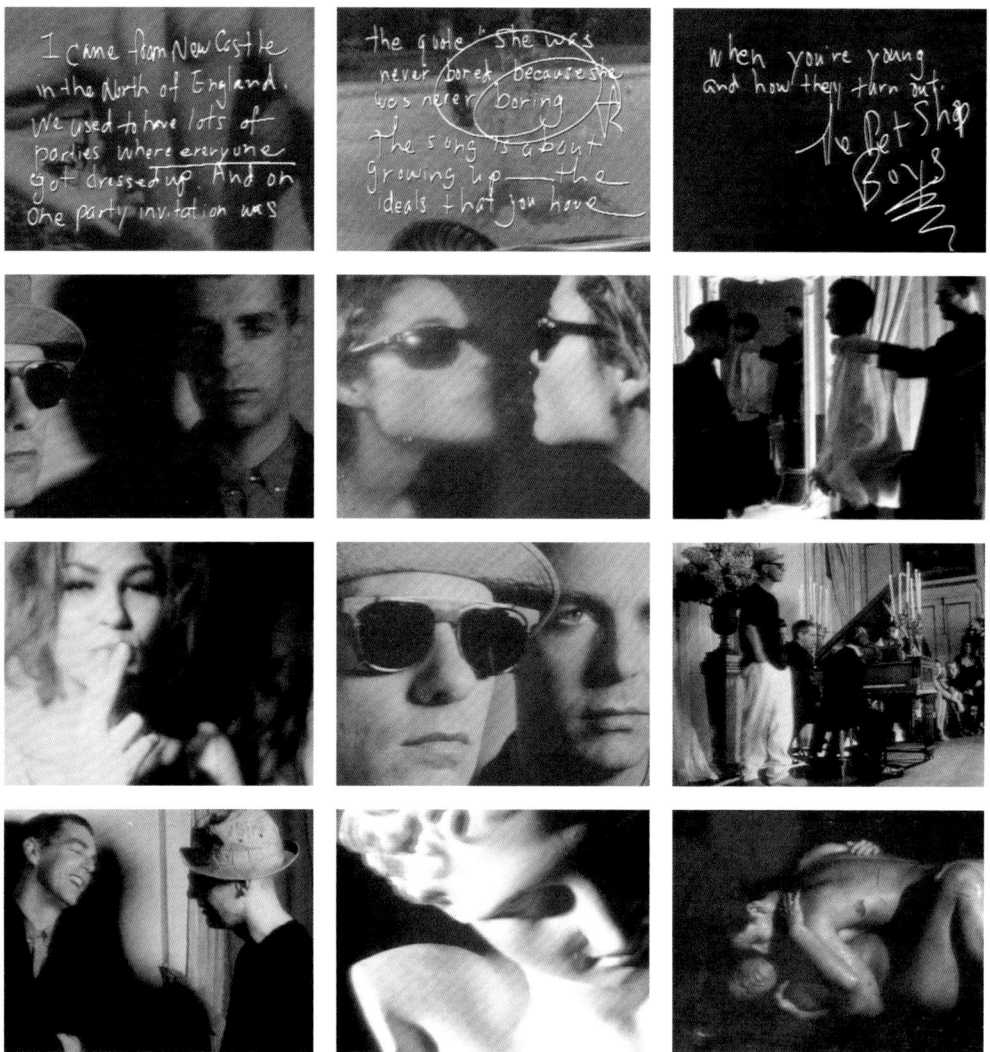

A naked boy climbs out of a pool and bounces on a trampoline. We see more naked, tanned people in the bath and in the shower, covered in foam; one boy shaves his chest. Neil and Chris are seen in portrait, not singing. Room-swapping in a big house; a horse is led, surreally, indoors. Dancers perform skitteringly on the stairs. A girl in a tutu; bikes are ridden indoors, round a circular sofa; abandoned dancing at a mad party; everyone is beautiful, having a good time. They all are seen crashed out on the stairs, Neil and Chris among them. Neil and Chris are caught off guard, laughing and joking. A naked couple clinches on the beach at night.

'As we wrote "Being boring", we thought of Bruce Weber to make the video', Neil commented at the time. 'His work has this innocent quality, and you also never know whether it's in the past or the present. It has this timelessness.' It was the first video Weber had directed. Inspired by the song – which took its title from a party invitation from Neil's Newcastle

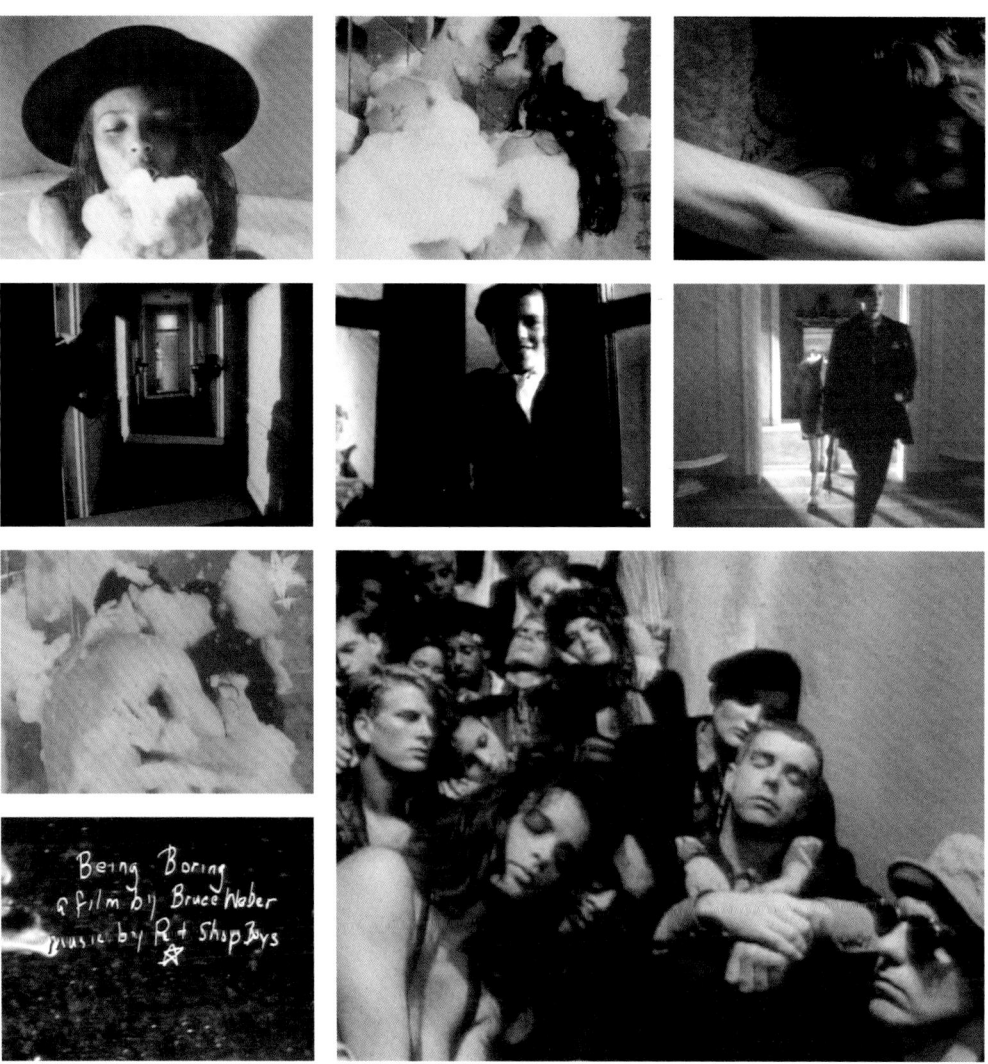

days that quoted Zelda Fitzgerald's line 'She was never bored, mainly because she was never boring' – the video was shot in one day at a house in Long Island, chosen for its associations with F. Scott Fitzgerald and *The Great Gatsby*. Weber 'wanted it to be like this beautiful party', and the cast included a selection of his beautiful friends – and a horse and a chimpanzee on roller-skates. The video was 'really inspired by the attitude of the way parties were in European films when I was growing up, the kind of things where people would stay for days'. It looked back to a pre-AIDS era of knowing innocence, of decadent naivity. Characteristic of Weber's work is the use of his handwritten captions, and here used as a kind of journal of the song's creation. The words came from an interview Weber conducted with Neil. Although MTV in America and several British television programmes refused to show it because it included scenes of nudity, it won *Music Week*'s 'Best Video of the Year Award'.

Where the streets have no name
(I can't take my eyes off you)

release 11 March 1991
formats 7" / 12" / 12" remix / cassette / CD
photographer Lawrence Watson, Paul Rider
(12" remix), and George Mott (US CD)
design Mark Farrow/3a and PSB
video Liam Kan

Pet Shop Boys' cover of U2's 'Where the streets have no name', mixed with the Frankie Valli hit 'I can't take my eyes off you', was released in most formats as a double A-side with a radically remixed *Behaviour* track, 'How can you expect to be taken seriously?' The principal releases featured a photo of Neil and Chris at Japan's Narita airport taken by Lawrence Watson on 3 July 1989 during their *MCMLXXXIX* tour. The image worked with the theme of the songs, which were intended as tongue-in-cheek comments on the inflated egos of some rock stars, 'because the photo looked very rock star-ish with the flowers and dark glasses', as Neil recalled. At first they used this image on the US twelve-inch version of 'How can you expect to be taken seriously?' 'Then we decided to use it for "Where the streets have no name" as well', says Neil. For the UK sleeves, Mark Farrow chose to black out the Japanese girl seen behind Neil's head on the earlier US twelve-inch because he thought it would look stronger. The twelve-inch remix used a different image altogether: an angled close-up shot of Chris's keyboards. All of the principal releases also featured Farrow's first use of three different weights of the same typeface for the words 'Pet Shop Boys', which would reappear on several of the subsequent releases.

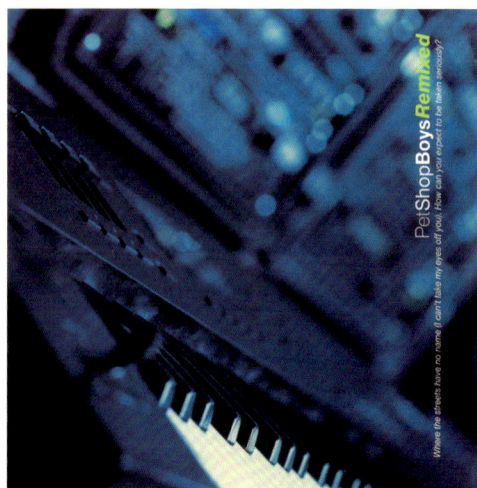

12" remix, front

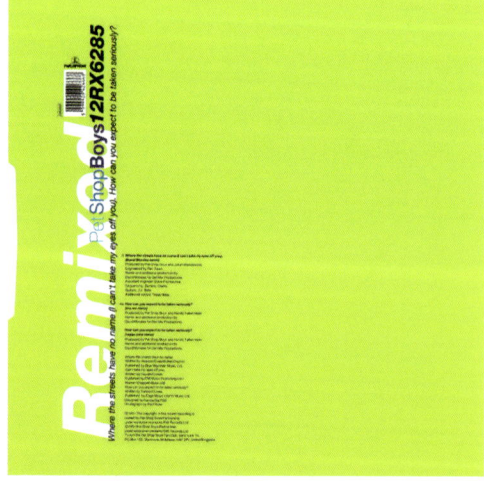

12" remix, back

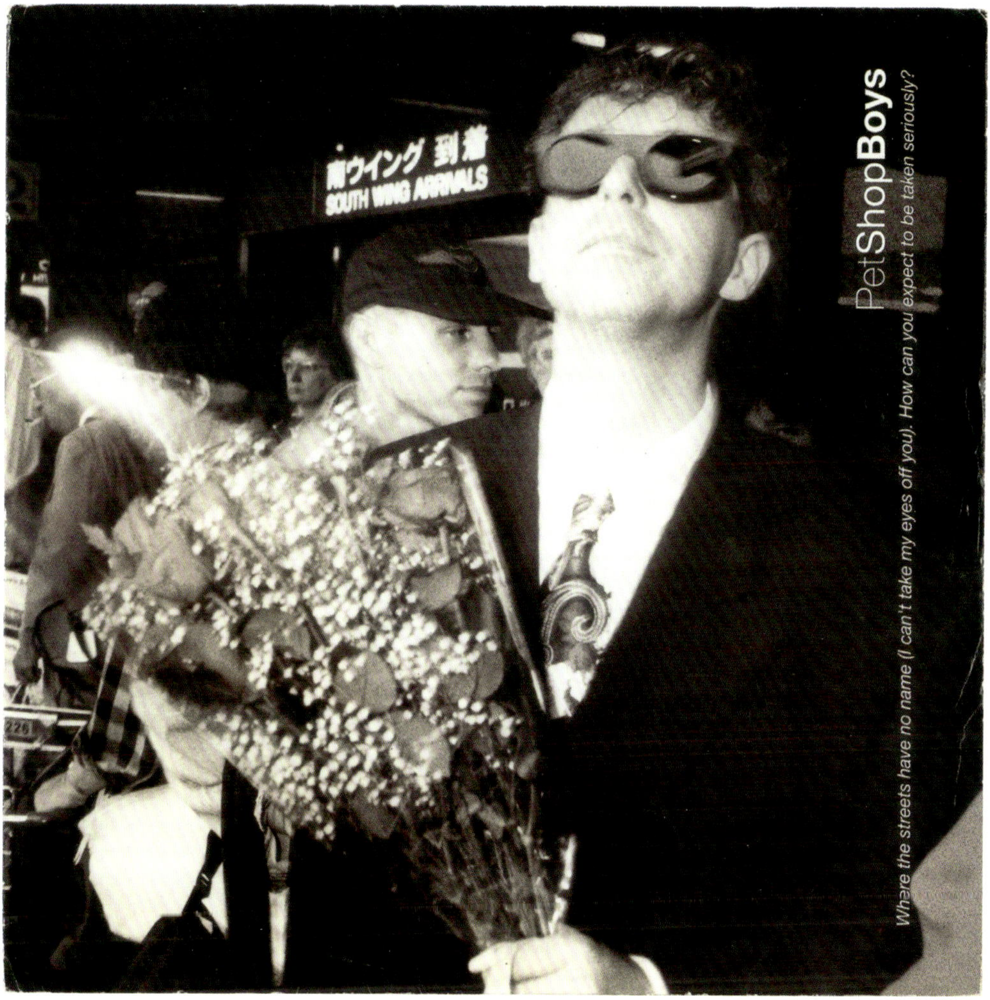

12", outer sleeve, front

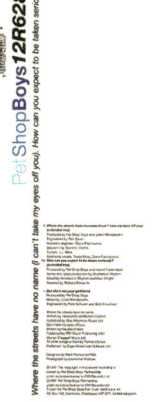

12", outer sleeve, back

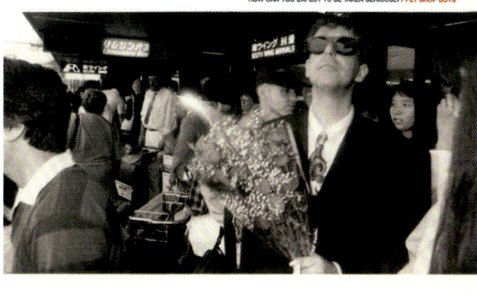

'How can you expect to be taken seriously?' 12", US, front

Where the streets have no name (I can't take my eyes off you) 1991

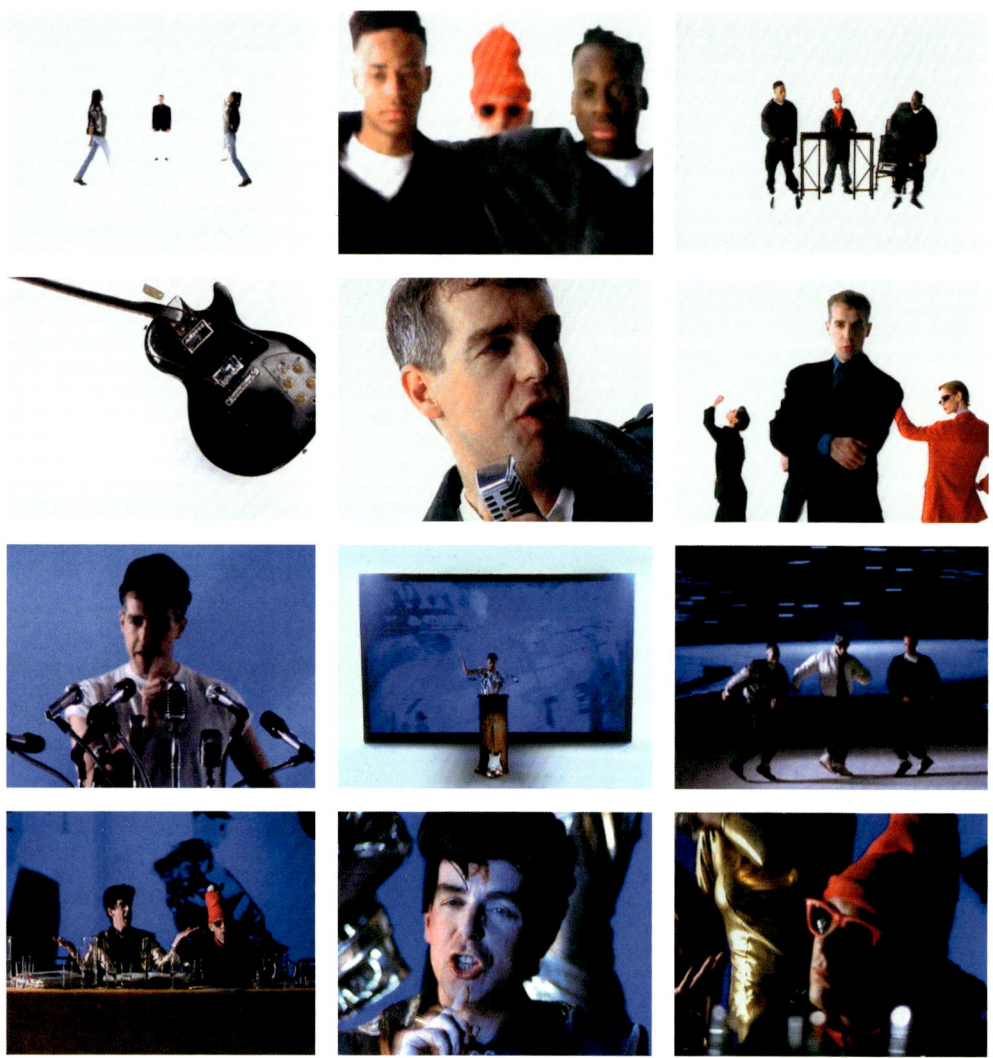

The complementary videos for 'How can you expect to be taken seriously?' and 'Where the streets have no name' were deliberately made together with the same director and cast to emphasize the connection between the two songs. 'How can you …?' is a satire on global pop stars who overreach their sense of self-importance. The two street dancers used in the videos, Trevor Henry and Mark Martin, were later invited to join the *Performance* tour as angelic hip-hop boys (and to be recorded, as 'Ignorants', for the Pet Shop Boys' label Spaghetti). In a white space, the dancers and sharply dressed women pose and perform. Chris is at a keyboard, wearing a tall red bobble hat and oversized coat and red glasses; at other times, he wears a blue Champion hat, green shades and white jacket. Neil sings, dressed variously in dark jacket and white jeans or leather jacket and blue jeans with a BOY belt buckle. He lectures from a press podium, to a bank of microphones, in front of a screen showing

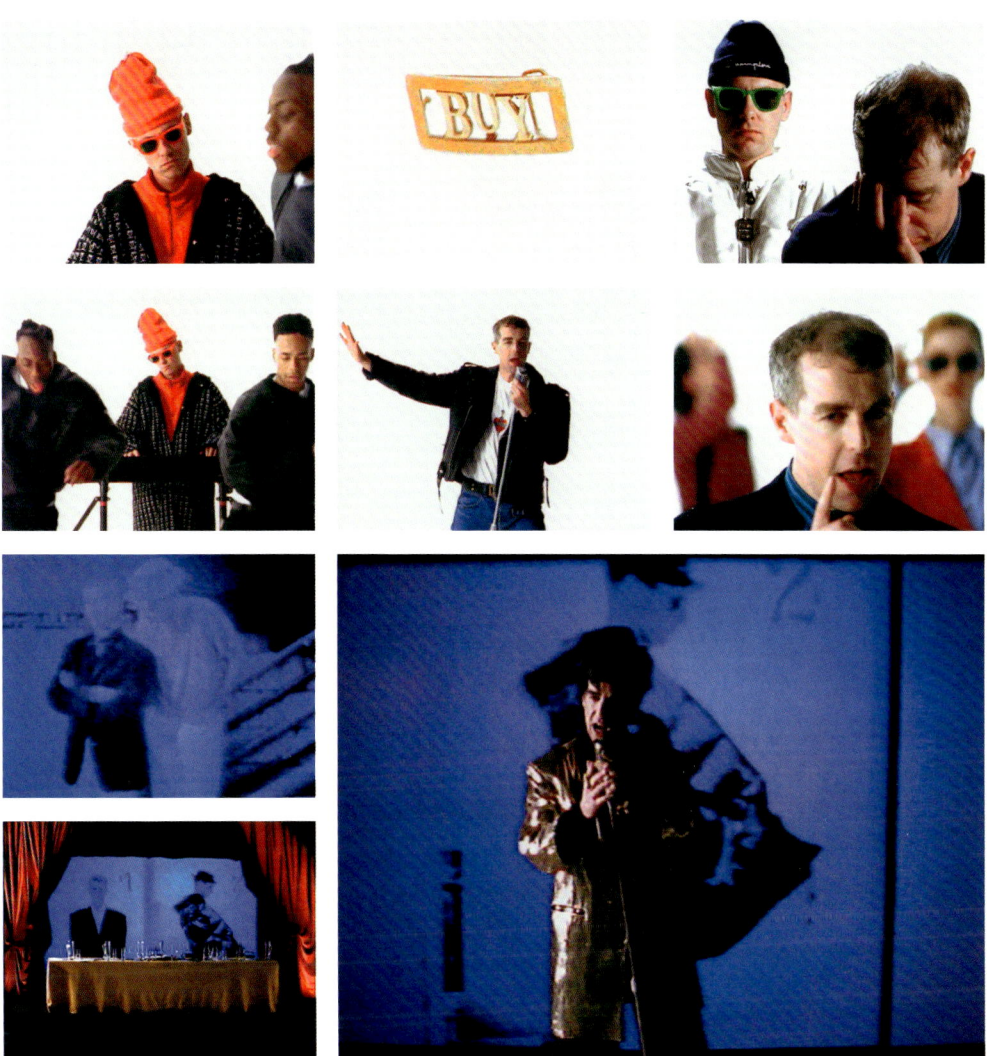

images of the group. A girl dances; Chris dances in step with the boys. Finally, Neil appears in Elvis lamé drape-coat and black wig (a look he would reprise in *Performance*), with Chris at his side, at a press conference in front of blow-ups of the Douglas Brothers photos for 'Being boring' (pages 144–5). Radically for Pet Shop Boys, an electric guitar makes a rare appearance, as in the second 'Opportunities (let's make lots of money)' video (pages 64–5), although here it is smashed in a mock rock outburst.

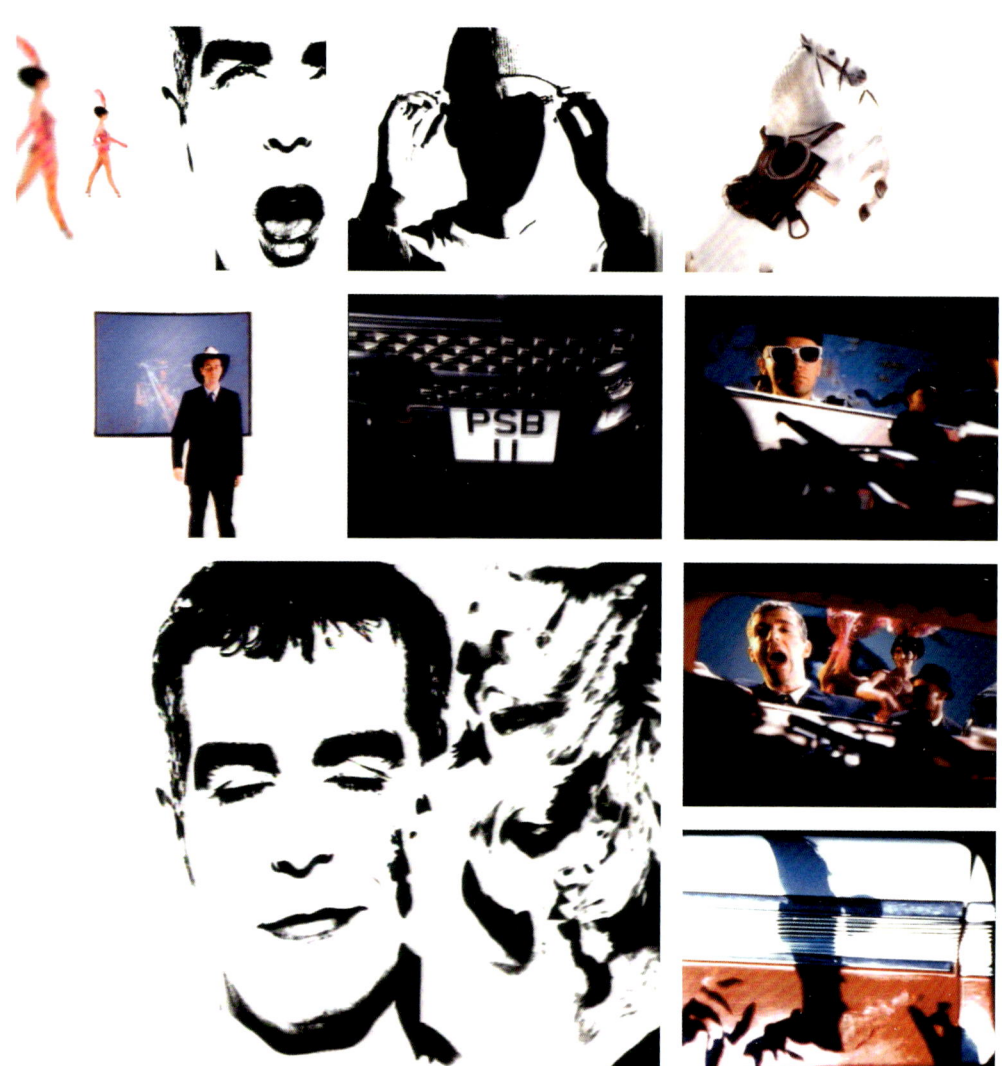

At the beginning of 'Where the streets have no name', the entire video for 'How can you expect to be taken seriously?' is run at high speed. Showgirls then parade across the screen, as Neil and Chris, reduced to black-and-white graphic images, sing and perform. Trevor Henry and Mark Martin dance; a white horse rears; a film screen shows moving landscapes of modern cities and streets and skies and desert plains. Cowgirls strut; Neil drives his crew in a Cadillac; he is kissed by a Marilyn Monroe lookalike; and he dances. Filming for both videos was done in a warehouse in north-west London, during tour rehearsals, using back-projection screens. The original idea, Chris said, 'was to make a video in America, driving down an empty road in the desert. But we didn't have time to do that.' The group were filmed sitting in a classic US 1950s convertible Cadillac – with the number plate 'PSB 11'; Chris quipped that the video couldn't be shown on a children's TV show because they weren't wearing seat belts.

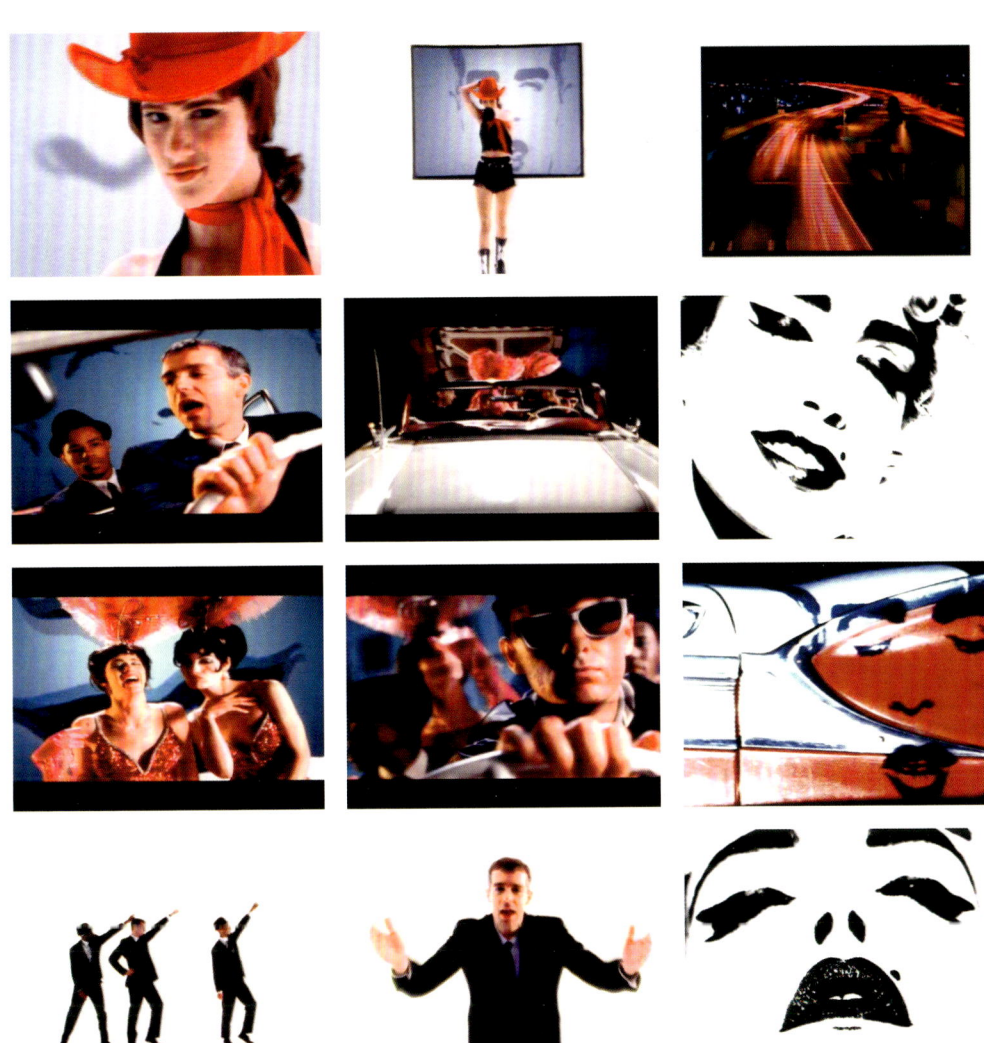

Where the streets have no name (I can't take my eyes off you) 1991

Performance tour

dates 11 March – 17 June 1991
director David Alden
film projections David Fielding
photographer George Mott and Pennie Smith

'Having done the last tour, we realized how much further we could go', Neil told Michael Bracewell in 1991. 'The second tour was the theatrical performance we'd always wanted to do. We wanted to define a way Pet Shop Boys could perform live, without turning into a rock band.' The most overtly theatrical outing by the group, Performance was more opera than rock concert. Indeed, it was designed and directed by David Fielding and David Alden, renowned for their work with the English National Opera. 'They put together this show with a very vague narrative,' Neil said, 'a journey – but the idea was that every song was visualized as a scene with Chris and me travelling through it. At the time, touring it, it seemed very tough because there were so many people involved, and technically it was so difficult because there were so many lights and costumes and scene changes, but I'm always meeting people who remember it as something very special. It's a show I feel really proud of. I think it changed the idea of how people saw rock shows, and I think it's been copied quite a bit since. In retrospect, with that show we really went as far as we could.'

   Resembling a cartoon cross between Tintin's Thompson Twins and the artists Gilbert and George via René Magritte, the 'English look' of the bowler hats, moustaches, and umbrellas (pages 18 and 157) was, Neil recalls, quite accidental. On stage, the effect was made yet more surreal when these pastel-clad Edwardian everymen took to surf boards. It was also cartoon-like, in a manner reflected in an image on the cover of the tour programme, showing David Fielding's pre-production model (page 156). This concept presaged the artificial virtual reality of the work that Fielding would go on to do for 'Can you forgive her?' (pages 174–9).

   'There's a kind of biography but obviously it's not realistic', Alden said of the show's narrative. 'It's almost like a cartoon reality of people who start out young, trapped in a school, then go out on the road and taste strange and forbidden adventures – then land in a terrible nightmarish psychiatrist's ward.' Fielding and Alden projected a gothic, dystopian imagination onto the very theatrical fantasy that they created for the tour. 'We also have this idea that there's a subtext in the show; there's a war almost between God and the Devil; a war between Heaven and Hell … and the whole fate of the world is being decided by what happens to Pet Shop Boys on their journey … the sense that during the course of this there are godlike and demonic forces at work, watching over their journey and fighting for their souls.'

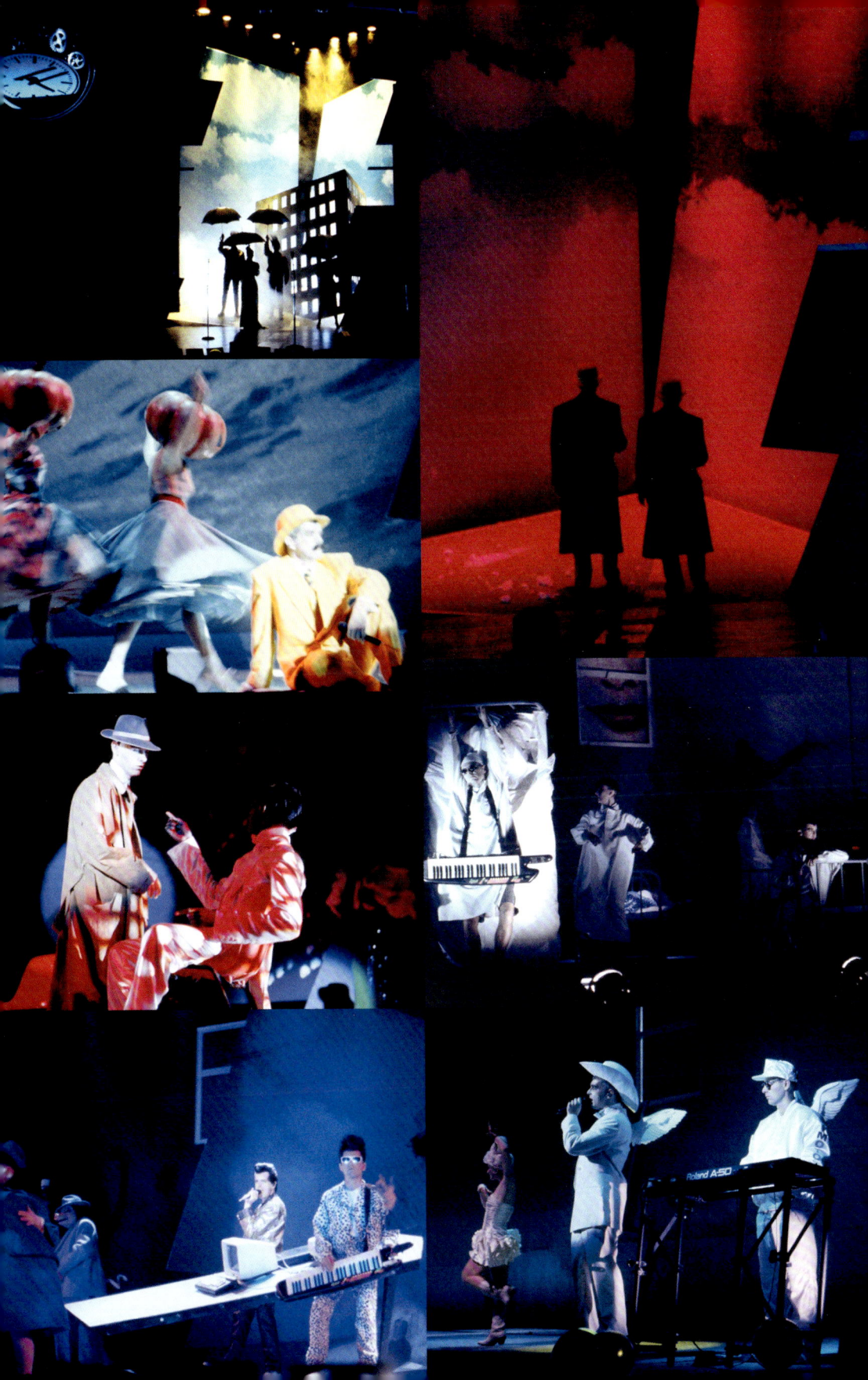

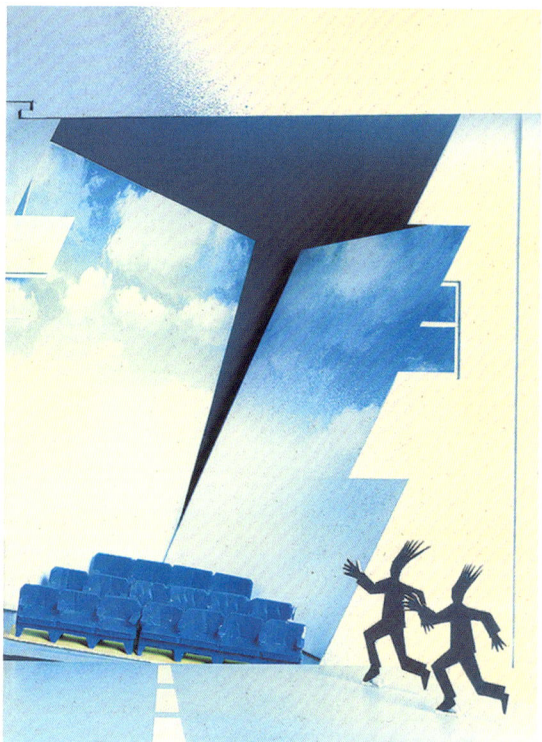

Tour programme, front cover

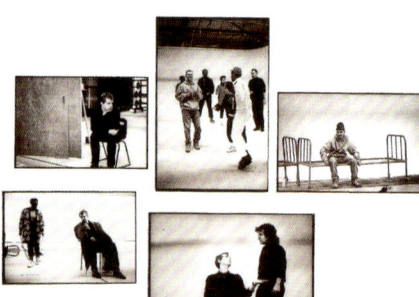

In Rehearsal

Interview page with photos of rehearsals for the concert

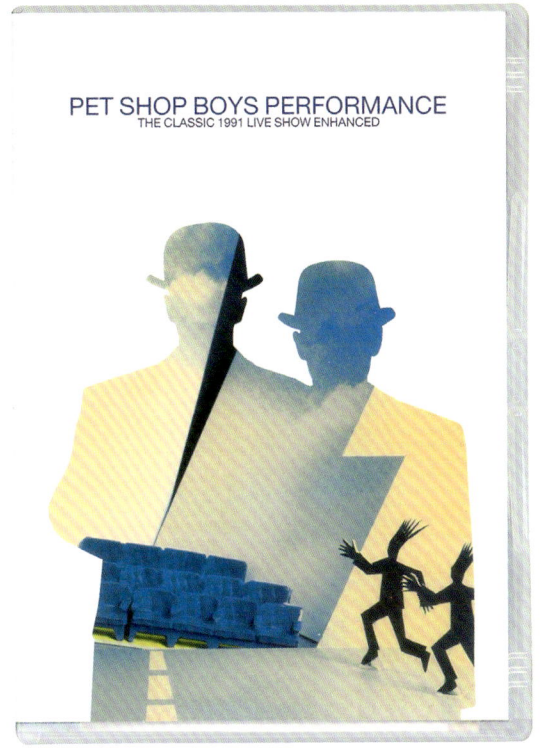 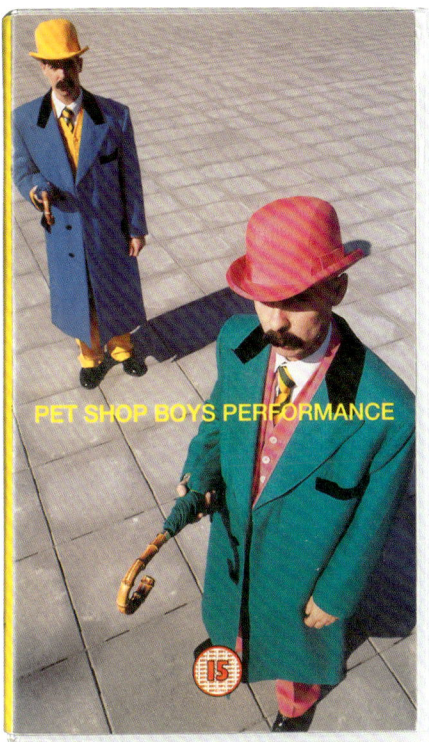

DVD, front   VHS, front

As with *MCMLXXXIX*, Mark Farrow designed a large programme to accompany the tour. The cover featured a photograph of the original model of the stage set, while inside appeared an interview between Neil and Chris and Chris Heath, biographies of the cast and crew of the tour, and photographs of the rehearsals, with a commentary from David Fielding and David Alden explaining their vision and inspiration. 'David Fielding and I have a style we have evolved over the years', Alden said during the pre-production, 'a sort of dark surrealistic nightmarish vision of the modern world which we've used in various operas and theatre pieces. Somehow the Pet Shop Boys' songs seem to cry out for the same sort of visual treatment.'

    The subsequent film of the concert at Birmingham's NEC (directed by Eric Watson) was later released on VHS, with Neil and Chris in their highly coloured and surreal 'Thompson Twins' outfits appearing on the cover. The photograph was taken by Derek Ridgers during the European leg of the tour for the cover of, and a feature in, London's *Time Out* magazine. In September 2004, an enhanced version of the film was released on DVD. As well as the original film footage, it also featured Neil and Chris's commentary over the film as the concert progressed, recorded with Chris Heath. The cover, like the original, was designed by Farrow, and combined the outline of Neil and Chris with the model of the stage set.

Jealousy

release 28 May 1991
formats 7" / 12" / 12" promo / cassette / CD × 2
photographer Eric Watson and George Mott
design Mark Farrow/3a and PSB
video Eric Watson

This was a new version of the track that had originally appeared on *Behaviour*. The high-fashion colours of Chris in sportswear on the twelve-inch sleeve contrast with the more dour image of Neil on the seven-inch single. 'Eric is famous for "not smiling" portraits', says Neil. (Both pictures would appear on a UK CD sleeve.) The graphic, bleached-out colours were based on an idea from Chris, 'where the photographs were a few steps removed from reality'. During the same session they were photographed with a helicopter, but the advent of the first Gulf War made their use problematic.

Mark Farrow now thinks that 'the type doesn't feel like it works with the song "Jealousy". This period here does really seem to belong to an era. I remember looking at Motocross clothing and stuff like that – that's where the influence for all this type came from. But it doesn't seem to sit comfortably.' In the photograph, Chris's fillings were retouched, as Neil's had been for the cover of *Actually* (page 91). On another CD version, the gatefold packaging shows Neil and Chris in their white 'angel' costumes from the *Performance* tour, photographed by George Mott.

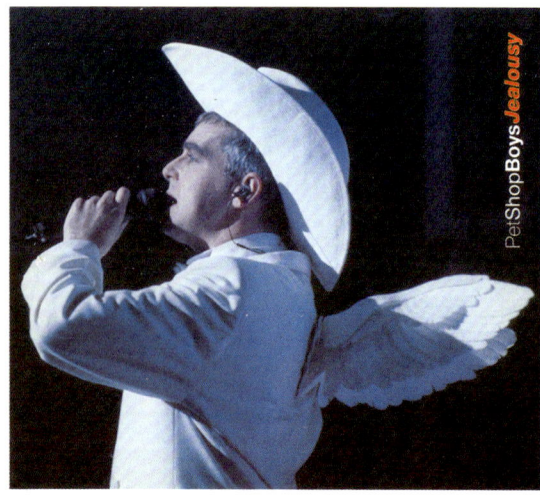

CD 2, front

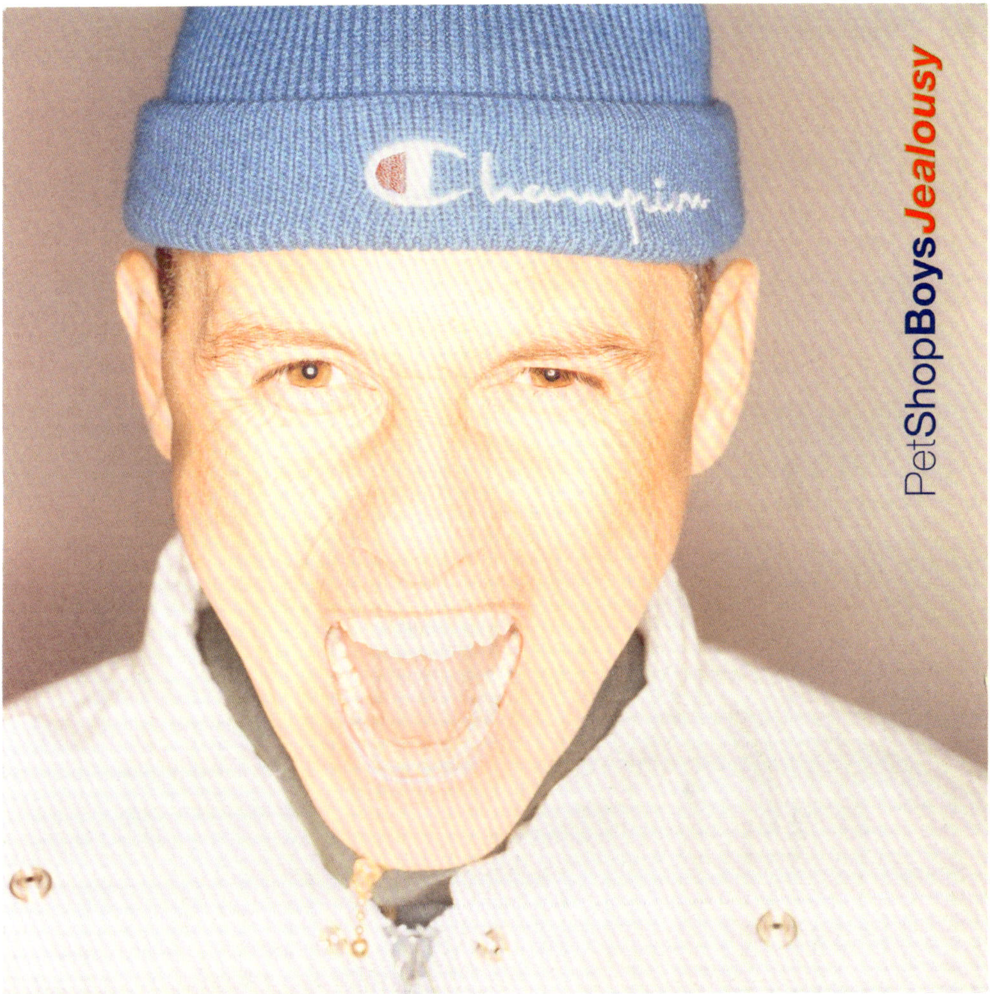

12", front

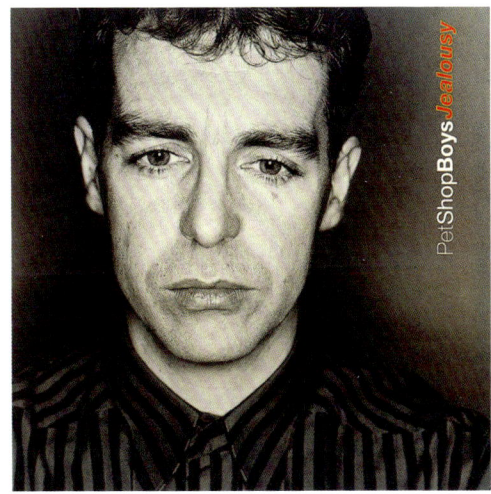

7", front

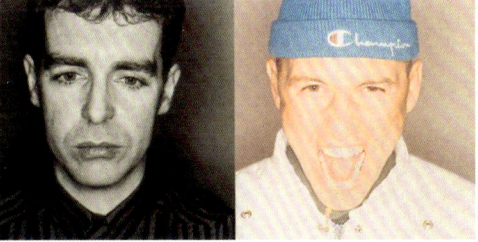

CD 1, front

Jealousy 1991

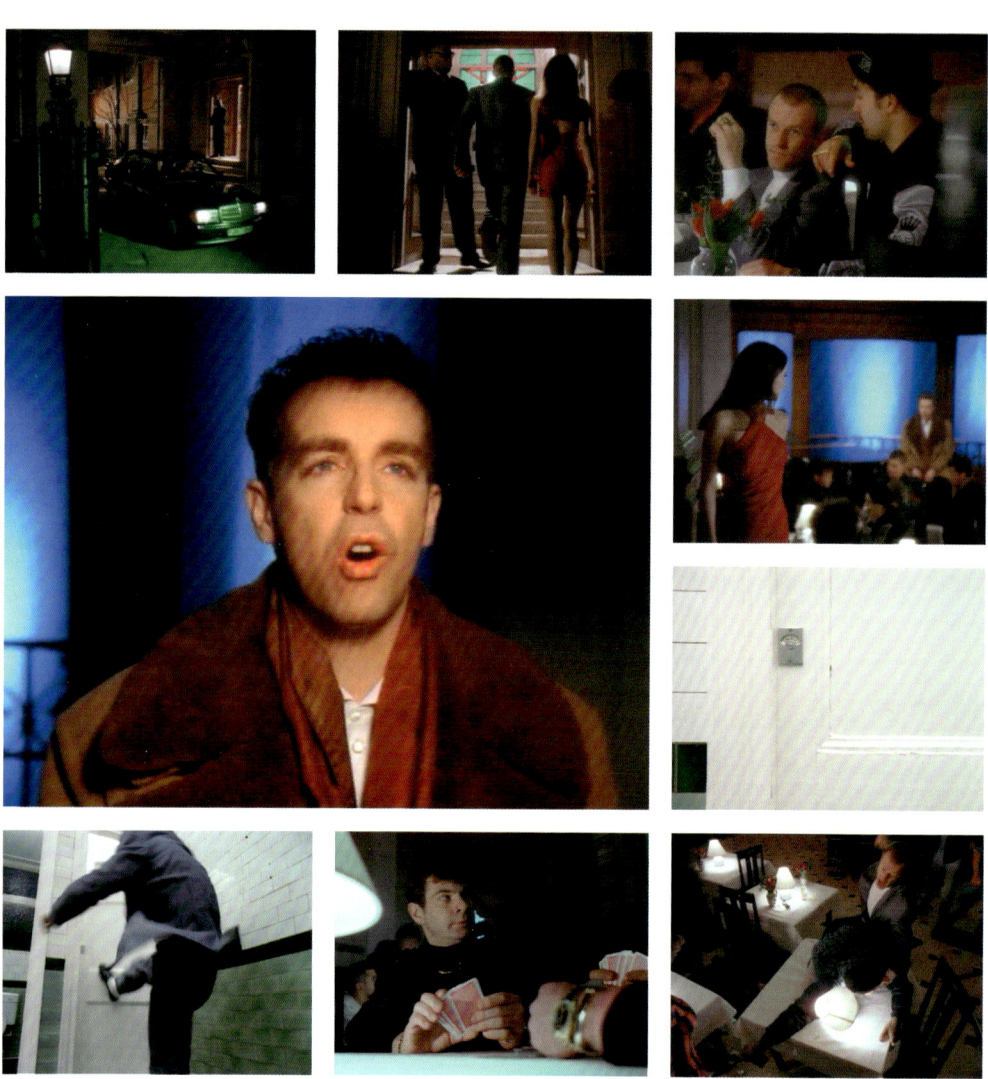

Another highly narrative filmic video, this was shot in a former car showroom in west London. Dainton Connell and Peter Andreas have cameo roles. 'We're performing the song in a nightclub with villains in it: one of them picks up another's girlfriend and at the orchestral break at the end a huge fight breaks out.' Chris plays a grand piano, clad in flight jacket and cap and shades; Neil sings, in a fur-collared Armani coat reminiscent of Oscar Wilde. The illicit couple cavort in the toilets; violence ensues in slow motion, and Dainton closes the doors on the action inside. Appropriately, the scene is bathed in a green glow, a jealous cast that recurs throughout the video. Eric Watson noted that, 'At the time the record industry was doing all this self-censorship, so I wanted things in there about race, and also this terrible violence. Which was terribly negative, but a hell of lot of violence does go on, and most videos quite happily skip over it and just have the word "ecstasy" in them all the time.'

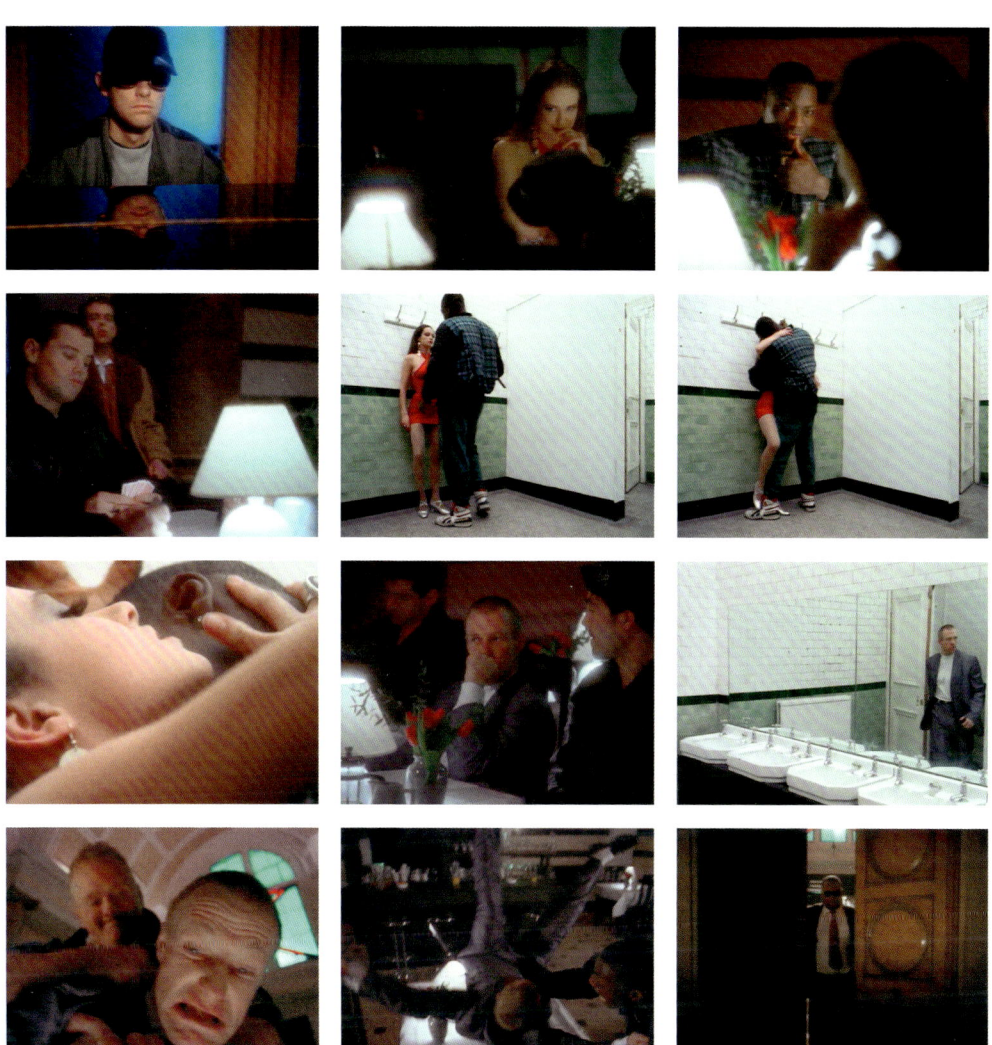

Promotion

release 3 June 1991
formats VHS / laserdisc (Japan)
design 3a and PSB

The next compilation of Pet Shop Boys videos, from 'Left to my own devices' to 'Jealousy', was called *Promotion* 'because videos are called promotional clips and it fits in with the other very literal titles we've used … Also, they *are* promotion; that's why they're made.' The sleeve photograph is an image from the video of 'Where the streets have no name' (pages 152–3). 'It's *Promotion*, and he feels like a salesman in that picture', says Farrow, who designed the cover with the same three-weight typography he had first used on the sleeves of 'Where the streets have no name' (pages 148–9).

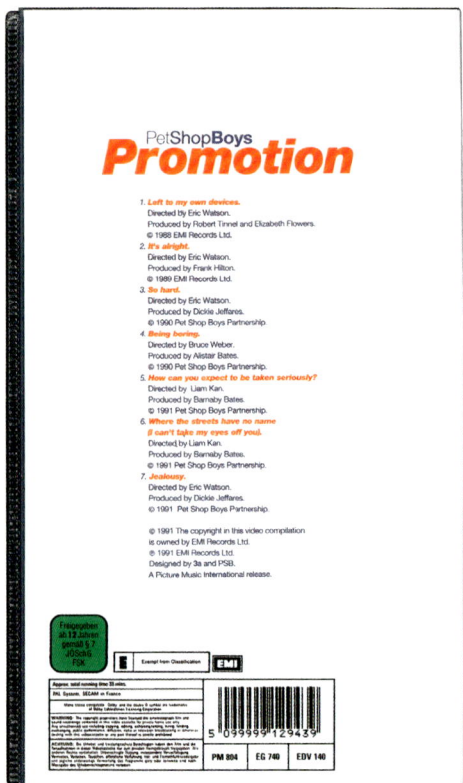

VHS, back

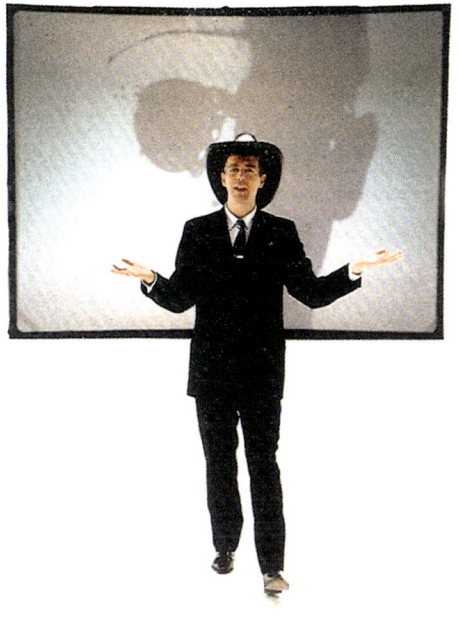

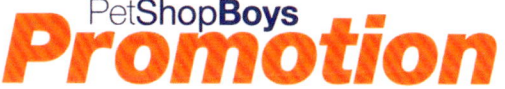

VHS, front

DJ culture

release 14 October 1991
formats 7" / 12" / 12" remix / cassette × 2 / CD × 2
photographer Eric Watson
design Mark Farrow/3a and PSB
video Eric Watson

The photograph on the front of 'DJ culture' was taken in Eric Watson's studio, in front of electronic DJ equipment (Mark Farrow recalls that during their tour he had told them they should be photographed in front of Chris's rack of gear). 'We're *being* DJs', notes Chris. 'Just technology', says Neil. 'It was difficult to do because to get the lights on the machinery to glow we had to be photographed with a flash and then stand there for eleven seconds totally still, totally in the dark, apart from the lights on the machinery.' The remix sleeve used some images of TV static. 'A lot of those sleeves, like that remix, set the agenda for the stuff that was coming out at that period of time', says Farrow: 'Pet Shop Boys sleeves that looked like dance sleeves.'

The song is a counterpoint to 'It's alright'. As Neil puts it, 'It is about how facile and pretentious modern life is. Just as in DJ records everything is sampled to sound authentic, so in a lot of aspects of modern life – for instance in politics – it is almost as though attitudes are sampled. People pretend to sound concerned, or have that empty positivism which is everywhere at the moment.... The whole thing is sort of fake.'

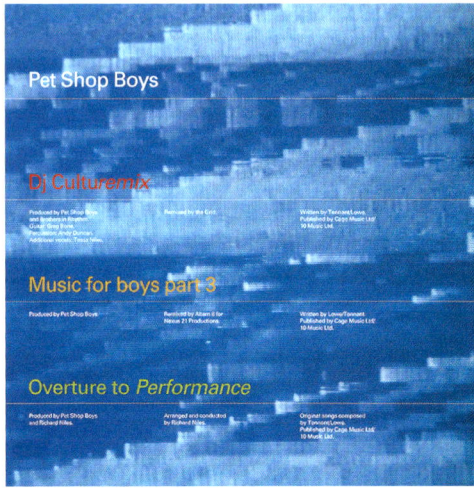

12" remix, front

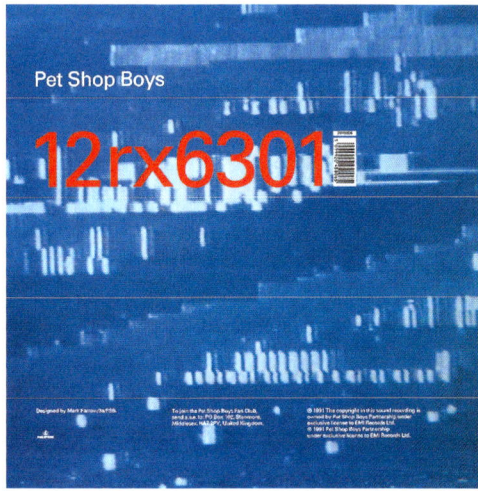

12" remix, back

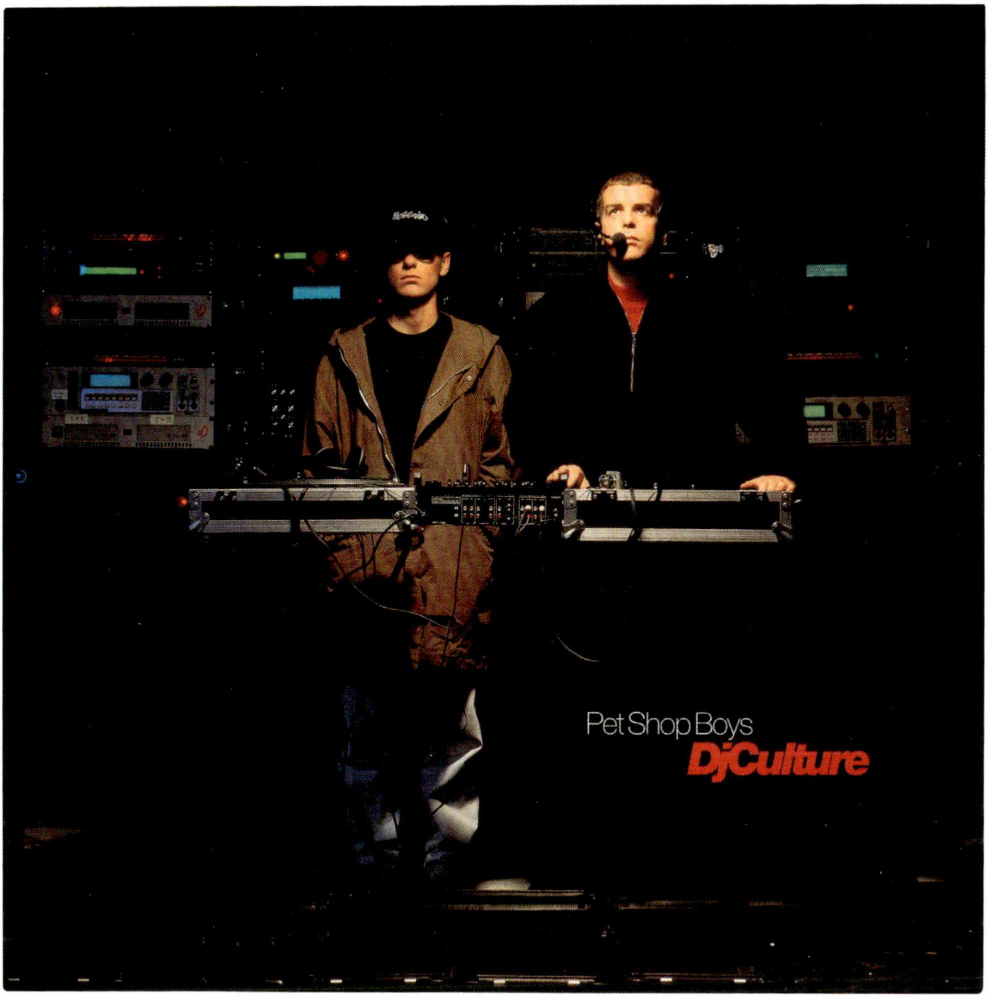

12", front

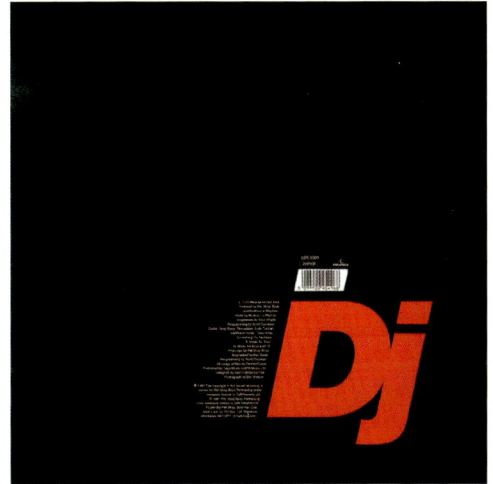

12", back

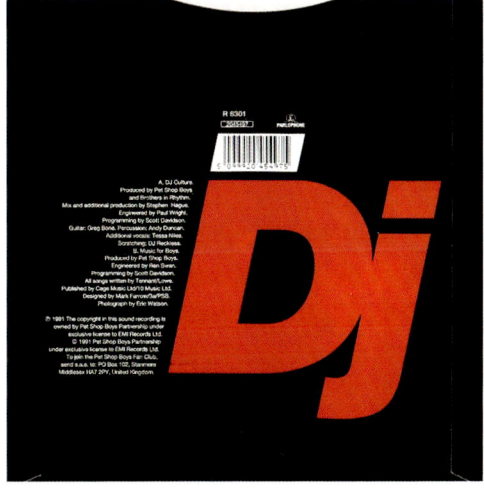

7", back

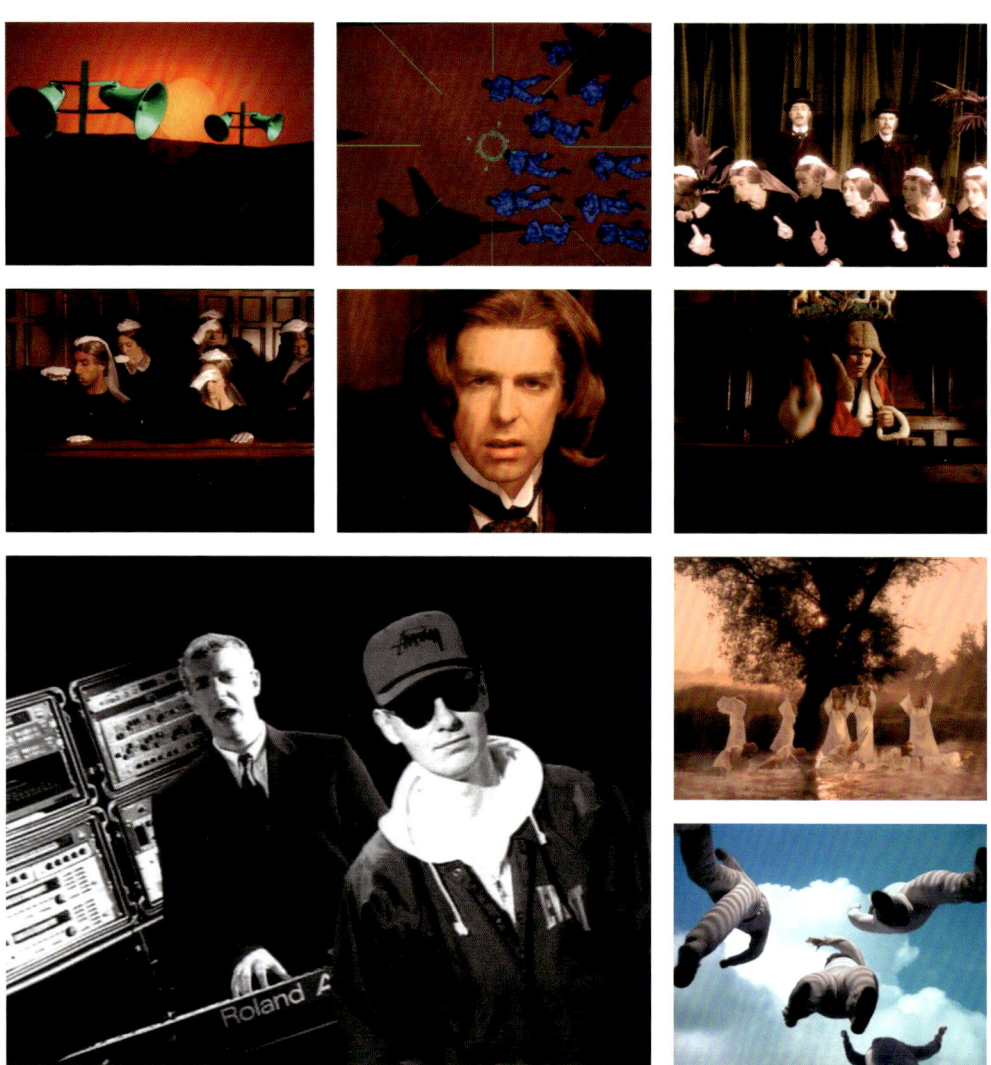

Tannoys broadcast announcements as a video war game plays; a row of Queen Victorias (idiosyncratically choreographed by Jacob Marley, choreographer on the *Performance* tour) are watched by Neil and Chris dressed as top-hatted Victorian gents. Neil referees a football match, then plays Oscar Wilde on trial at the Old Bailey, with Chris as the judge – a visualization of the song's line that quotes Wilde's heartfelt cry 'And I, my lord, may I say nothing?' Robed dancers embrace on a river; models strike poses; Chris swings a football rattle; both Neil and Chris become doctors in the 'Betty Ford Clinic'. And in an echo of the first Gulf War – and an augury of the second – they are seen as soldiers in desert camouflage fatigues. The video was their most expensive to date, costing £150,000. Shot over two days on a site in north-west London, it was triggered by the observation of their American manager at the time, Arma Andon, that 'their videos

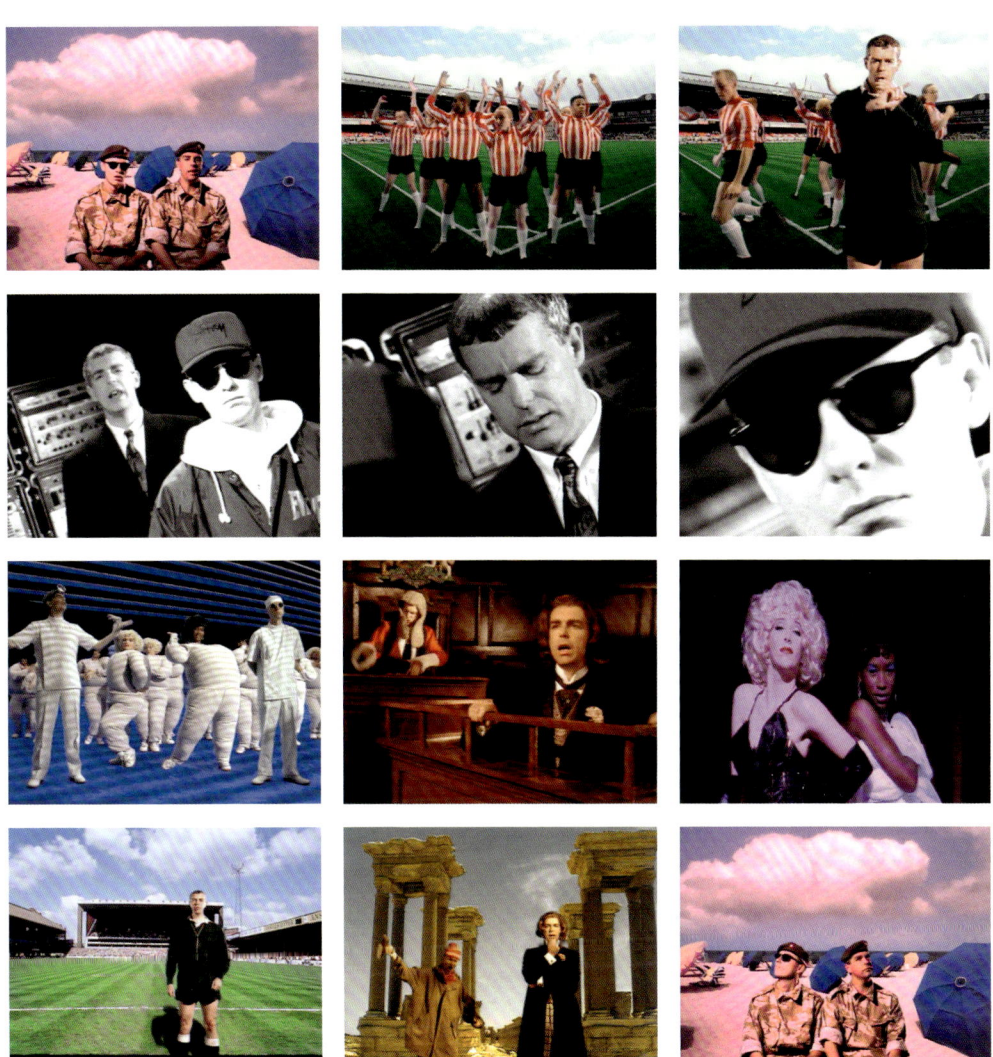

weren't at all like their stage show'. Eric Watson saw it as 'an extravaganza that cost a lot of money. It's a line-by-line interpretation of the lyrics, completely literal. I was using all the things I'd learned about Computer Graphic Television – one of those shots of hippies in the river is a composite of something like fifteen different elements. When it gets to some of the montages at the end, I did ridiculous things like having Neil as Oscar Wilde in front of the Acropolis with Chris in the background as a football fan shouting "Arsenal!"'

Discography / Videography

release 4 November 1991
formats LP / cassette / CD / VHS / laserdisc (Austria, Japan, US)
photographer Eric Watson
design Mark Farrow, Rob Petrie/3a and PSB

In an image that reprises the group's poses on *Actually*, the front of the first Pet Shop Boys 'greatest hits' album, *Discography*, has Chris wearing a 'foldaway' hat from Miami, Junior Gaultier sunglasses, and a Versace jacket, while Neil wears a Gaultier black suit and tie and a Daks white shirt. The reverse of the inner sleeve has eighteen photographs, one for each single release – a collage that was originally considered for the sleeve itself. Seeing a poster for the album, a friend told Neil that his raised eyebrow summed up Pet Shop Boys in one gesture.

It was Neil and Chris who suggested that the cover should be an updated version of *Actually*, their most famous image. 'The rest of it was typographic gymnastics, really', adds Farrow. 'It was fun working with them because you had the chart positions and the credits and so on, and it's a joy how rigorous they are, so we were never short of information to fill things up with. To be given all that information and asked to do a typographical layout with it was sheer enjoyment.' The album cover treatment was repeated for the video equivalent, *Videography*.

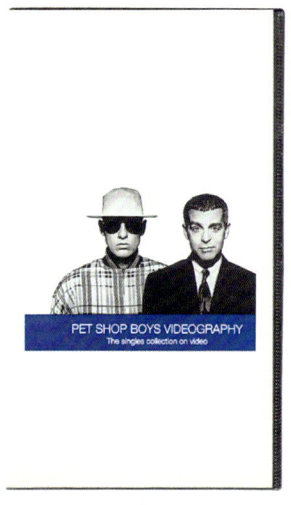

Videography, VHS, front

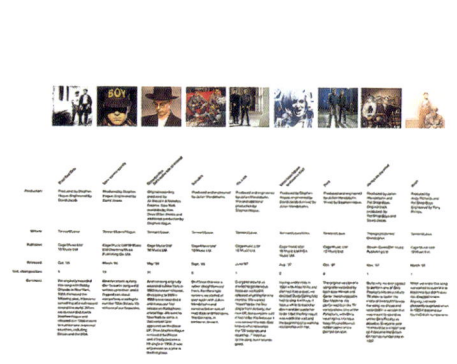

LP, Side 1, inner sleeve, back

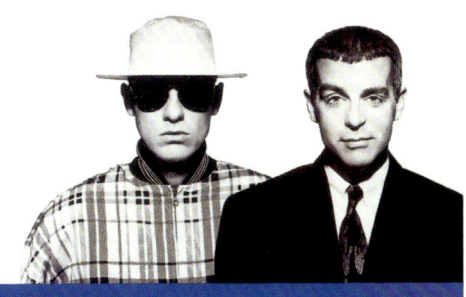

LP, outer sleeve, front

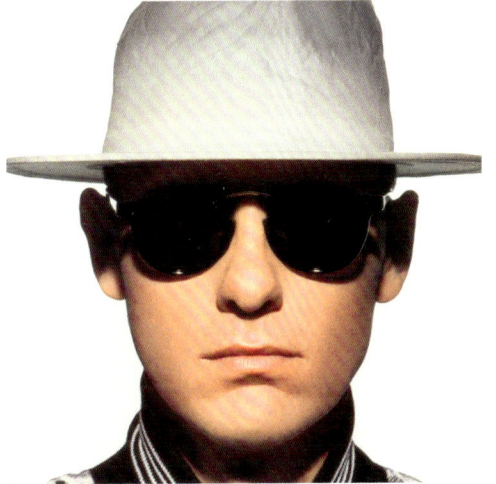

LP, Side 1, inner sleeve, front

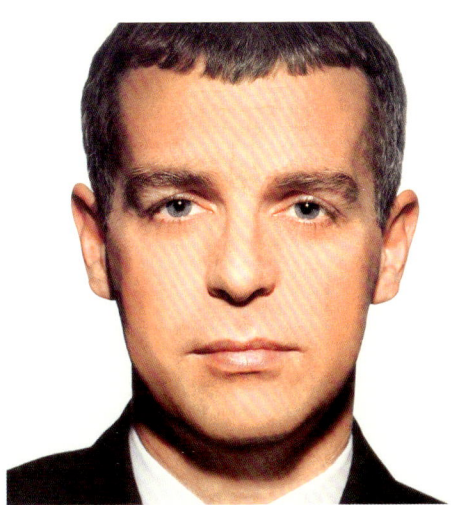

LP, Side 2, inner sleeve, front

Was it worth it?

release 9 December 1991
formats 7" / 12" / 12" promo / cassette / CD × 2
dolls Toshima Tada
photographer Robert Shackleton
design Farrow/3a and PSB
video Eric Watson

This was the first single sleeve not to feature a photograph of the group since the second release of 'Opportunities' (pages 62–3). Instead, they used a photograph showing dolls of Neil and Chris – seen as the real Pet Shop Boys had been in the *Behaviour* session (pages 142–3), holding bunches of red roses. They were made by a Japanese fan, Toshima Tada. Neil liked the way Chris's doll looks cross. 'We thought they were really fantastic.... They seemed to capture something about us', said Neil. The same dolls were used for that year's Pet Shop Boys Christmas card, produced as a mobile to hang from the ceiling (page 533). 'In Japan, the Pet Shop Boys are frequently given pictures of themselves', noted a newspaper interview in 1990. 'They are represented as little dolls with huge eyes. One had Lowe crying and being comforted by Tennant, another had them in a car holding steering wheels pointed in opposite directions. Mostly, though, they are shown kissing. "Very Japanese", says Tennant. "All the drawings they do of you in Japan always present you in this same strange way, with big eyes, and we've always liked that."' Both the seven inch and the twelve inch had the same artwork for the front cover. The reverse of the twelve inch shows red roses against a blue background, while on the seven inch they are against chrome yellow, the highly saturated colour reminiscent of David Lynch's films.

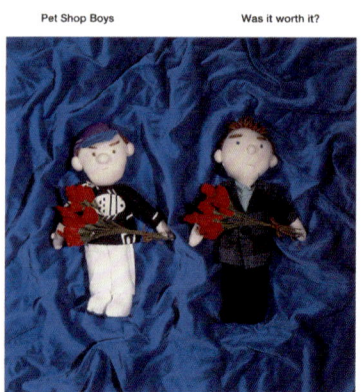

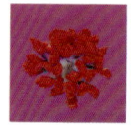

CD, front　　　　　　　　　　　　CD, back

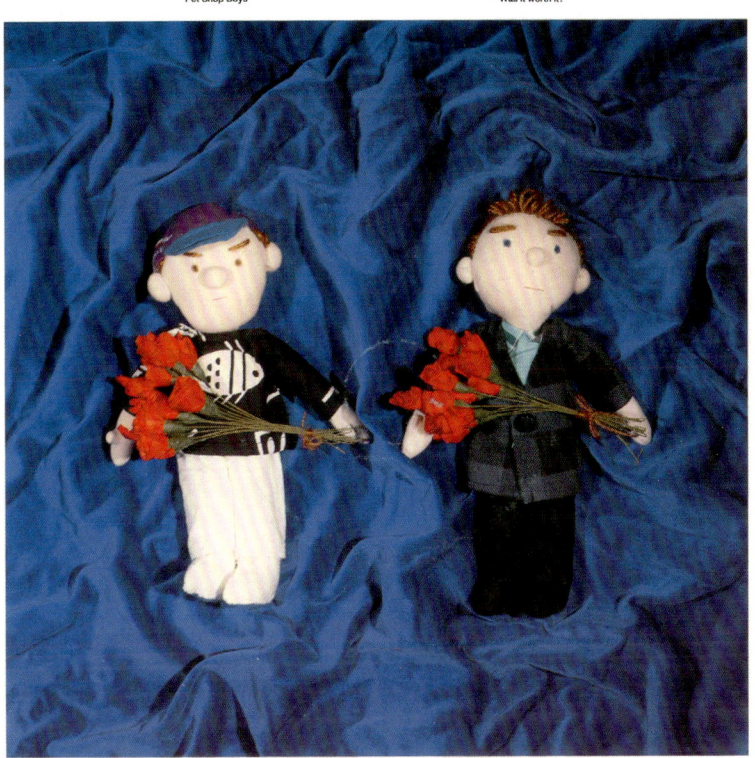

12", front

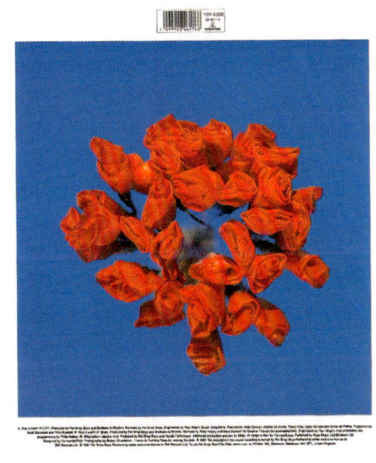

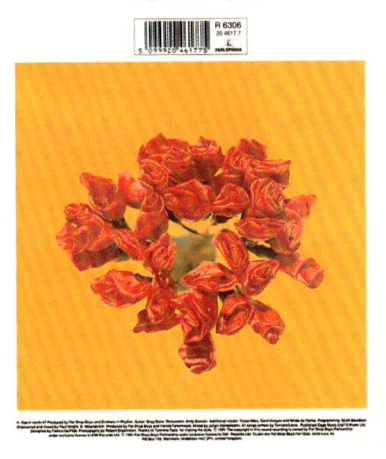

12", back   7", back

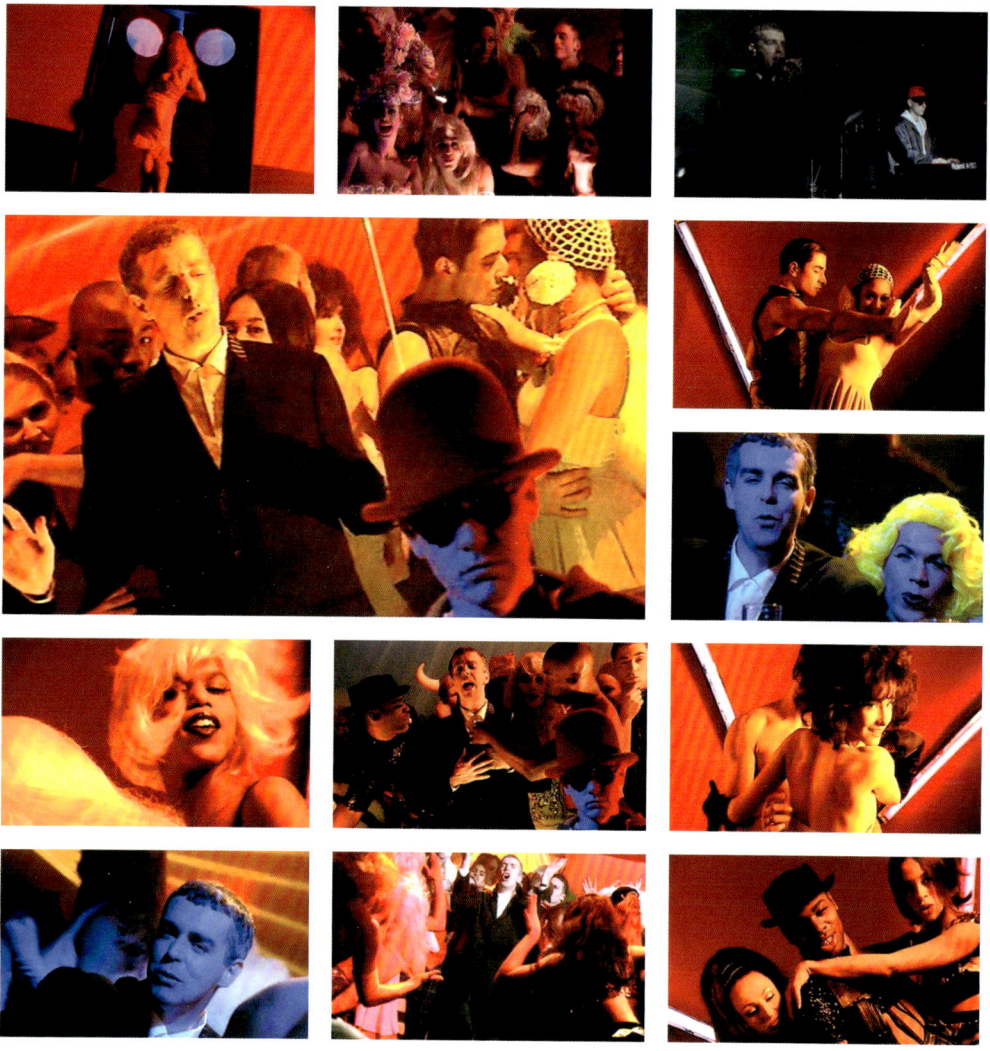

Live on stage, Pet Shop Boys seem to perform to a nightclub crowd clad in extravagant costumes, including a Warhol-style Monroe in drag, as they strike 'vogueing' poses; couples embrace with *joie de vivre*. The last video shot for Pet Shop Boys by Eric Watson, it mixes footage from a recent Heaven gig with shots of Neil and Chris and a cast recruited from Kinky Gerlinky – a moveable London club of transvestites and street fashion in the tradition of Blitz and Taboo, hosted by Michael and Gerlinda Costiff, who also ran the eclectic boutique World, off Charing Cross Road. 'The Stock Aitken & Waterman revival', commented Watson. He had been watching dance films such as *Saturday Night Fever*, and John Waters' *Hairspray*, and wondered, 'What's good about them?' 'And we were all going down to Kinky Gerlinky and it seemed really vibrant and a bit of a laugh, all the cross-dressing. And I also had this thing about creating completely unnatural lighting.' The result was

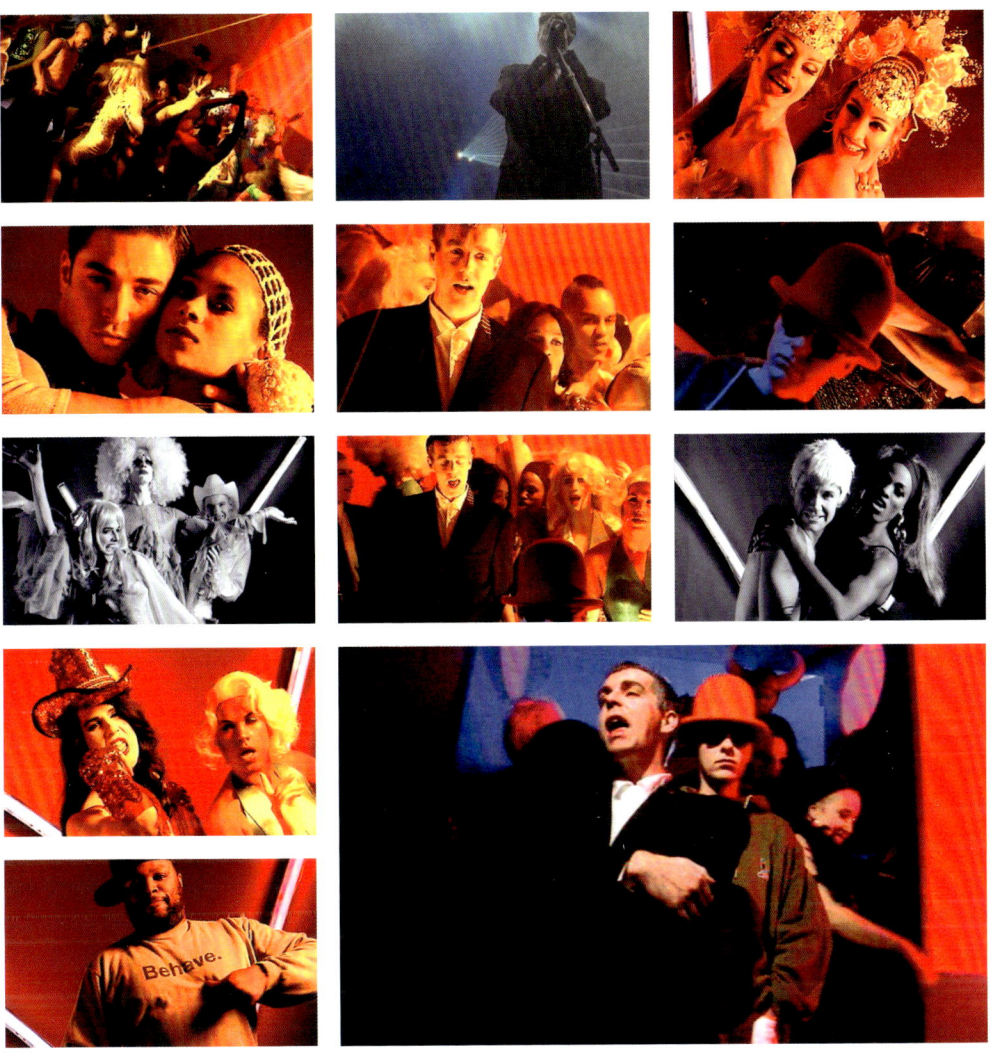

'a good-time dance film', although, as Watson said to Neil afterwards, 'How can it *just* be a good-time dance film when half of the women are men?' 'I've got a great hat on there', recalls Chris. 'It's a Diddyman hat.' 'Actually, it was a woman's hat', says Neil, 'from Kenzo.' 'Again you get Chris doing nothing on one side of a piece of glass while everyone else is having a good time,' added Watson, 'but he was wearing that high orange hat so he didn't really need to do anything whatsoever.'

Can you forgive her?

release 31 May 1993
formats 7" / 7" promo / 12" (not UK) / 12" remix /
12" promo / cassette / cassette promo / CD /
limited-edition double CD
photographer Chris Nash
design Farrow / PSB
video Howard Greenhalgh

'Can you forgive her?' was the first single from the next album, *Very*, the first after the highly theatrical *Performance* tour. For this phase of their career, Pet Shop Boys decided to change the way they presented themselves almost entirely. They were tired of being naturalistic, of being 'themselves'. As Arma Andon had pointed out, they staged these elaborate, costumed, theatrical fantasies in concert but rarely explored the same kind of presentation in videos or for records. 'Also', says Neil, 'I think we thought we'd done to death the classic Pet Shop Boys thing, and it was finally summed up on the cover of *Discography* (pages 168–9), Chris stony-faced and me with an ironically arched eyebrow. We thought: right, we've just completely done that now. We wanted to do something that is the opposite of what everyone else is doing. Everyone else is being "real", so we're being artificial.' They were also reacting against the other dominant musical current of the era. 'Everyone was being grungy', Chris remembers. 'Everyone was just dressing in baggy jeans and T-shirt and sweatshirt, that Nirvana thing, looking ordinary. We didn't want to look ordinary. We didn't want to be fashion either. We wanted to be unique, outside of it.' Another influence was the rise of increasingly realistic computer games. Chris continues: 'I thought wouldn't it be great if we became this thing removed from reality and existing in a non-real world?'

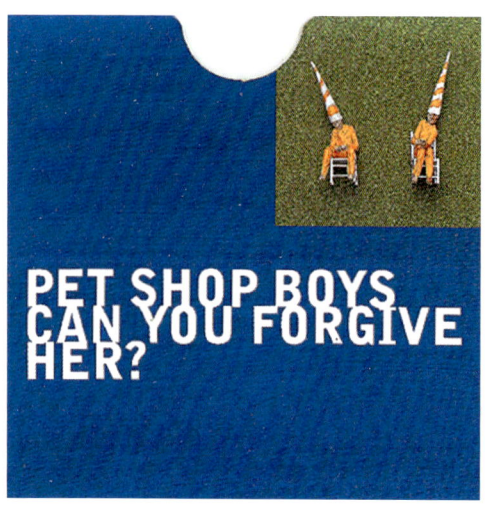

Limited-edition double CD, outer sleeve, front

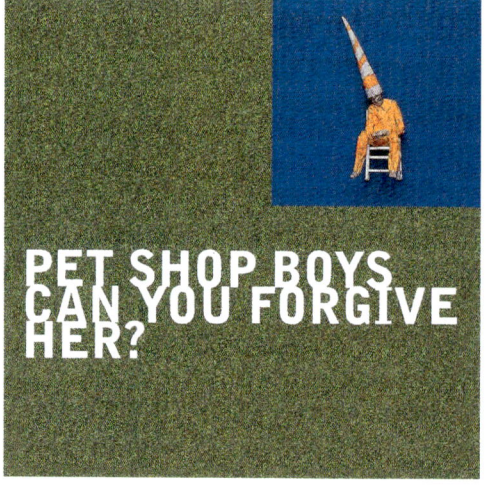

Limited-edition double CD (CD 1), inner sleeve, front

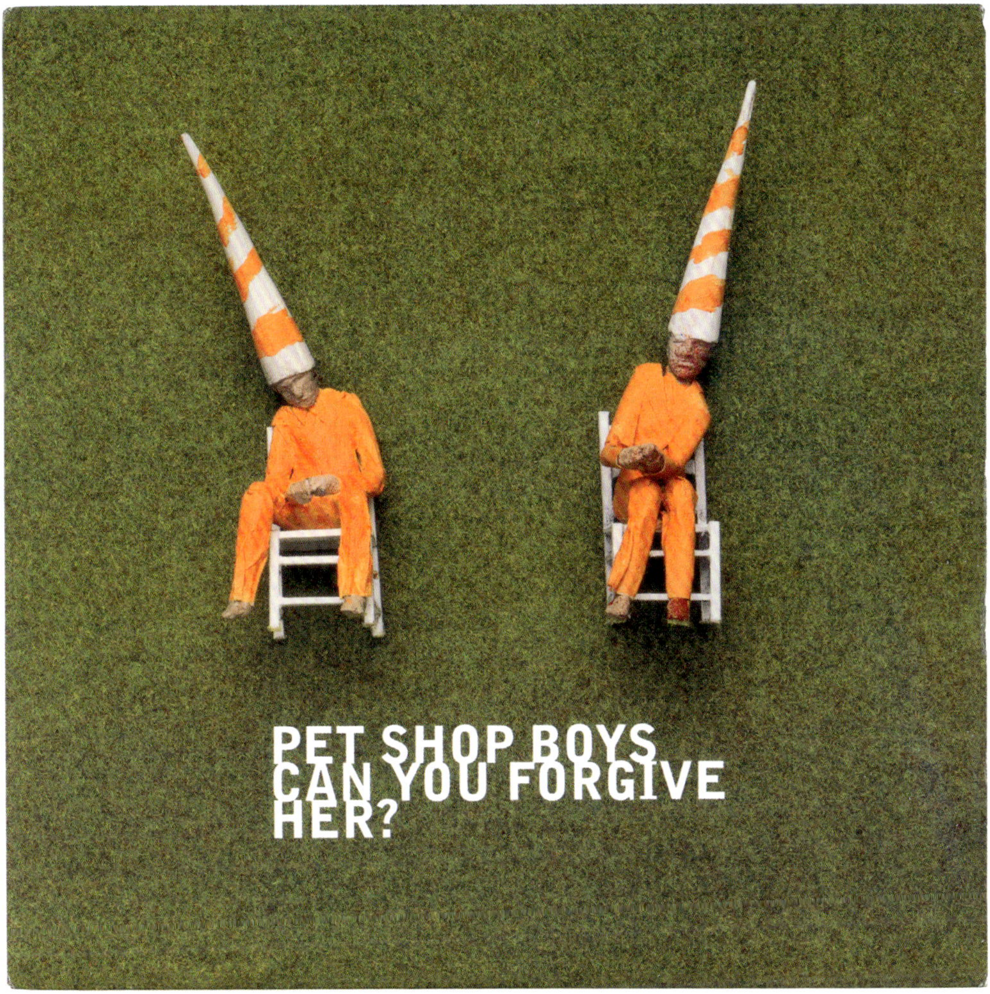

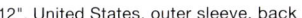

12", United States, outer sleeve, front

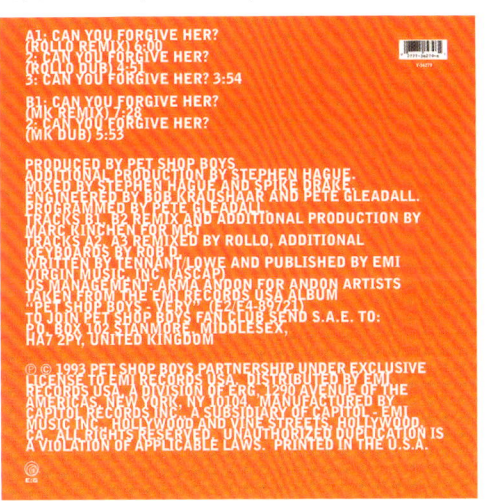

12", United States, outer sleeve, back

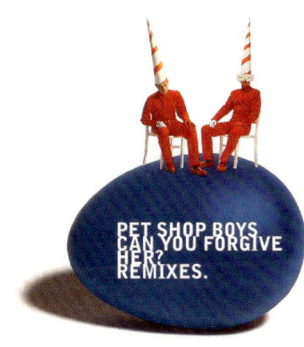

12" remix, front

Can you forgive her? 1993 175

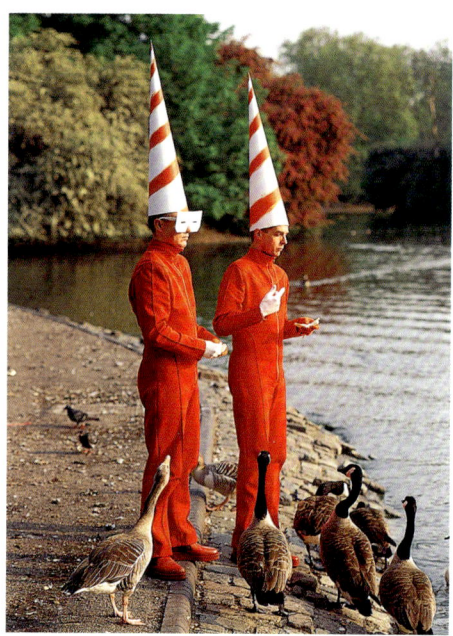

above and opposite From the photo shoot by Chris Nash

And so they asked David Fielding to come up with some concepts as an extension of the *Performance* aesthetic. 'David brought about six different looks into the office,' according to Neil, 'and we chose this one, because it was simple, and you could use it in different kinds of ways. I remember when we got the models in, Jill Carrington, our then manager, didn't like them at all. There was always a worry about looking ludicrous. If you see the *Top of the Pops* performance, it's just incredible. The sheer nerve. I'm sitting on a pair of stepladders wearing an orange jumpsuit with a stripey pointy hat. Chris, meanwhile, is behind a giant blue egg with a telescope wearing the same outfit.'

The small models were used on the single sleeves simply because that was the only representation of their new look that was available at the time. 'Nothing was ready', Farrow remembers. 'All we had was the models. There was nothing else.' So he had them photographed. By the time Farrow did the remix twelve inch, the Chris Nash photos were ready (including the one opposite). They were photographed against a white background: a huge white curved surface that no one else could tread on without removing their shoes, so that dark scuff marks would not show up on film. Neil was photographed first, up a ladder, and then Chris. The photos were then combined by computer with other photographs that Nash had already taken to create Fielding's original design. The typography was influenced by the work being done at *Raygun* magazine in America. 'This was kind of my take on that, this type bumping into itself. It was a deliberate move away from anything we'd done before – probably pushed by Neil and Chris in a "we must not use Helvetica again" kind of way. Chris more than Neil, I think.'

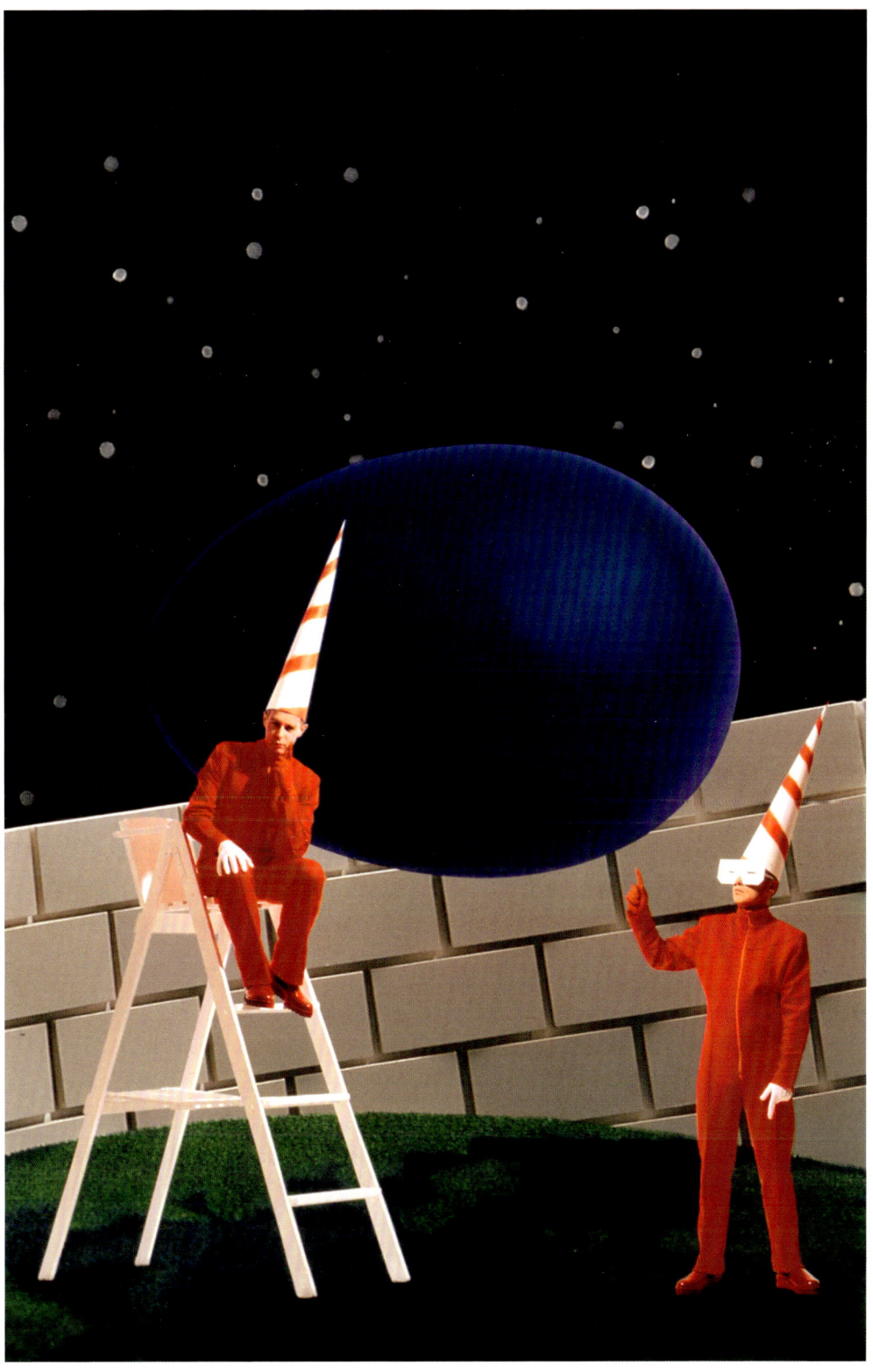

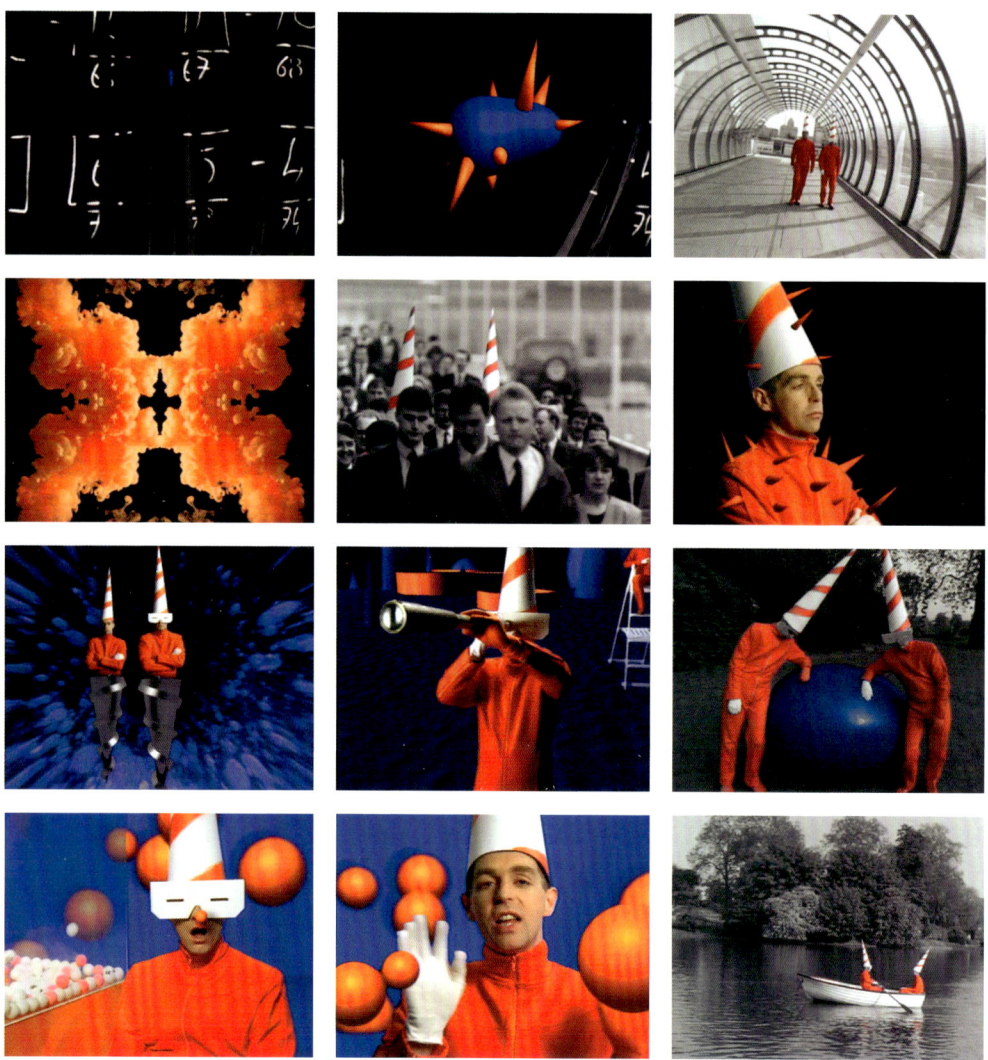

Fielding's original concept was carried through into the video: 'What we've done is create a storyline about two characters who are born from an egg. I wanted to create a metaphor about being born and being brought up in what seems like an alien landscape on the Earth, and looking out beyond, looking at the heavens, and thinking "why are we here?" Chris will have a telescope for looking at the stars.... There are images connected with school games, an element in the song, which is about growing up at school and finding one's sexuality during that period of development behind the bicycle sheds or cricket pavilions.... I thought it would be nice if it had an abstract surrealistic quality to it.'

Neil and Chris walk through a futuristic architectural tube in orange jumpsuits and striped pointy hats as spiky and spherical objects float around them, morphing in this cyberworld. Chris is seen captured in a flying orange box. Neil is seen on an umpire's high chair, while Chris peers

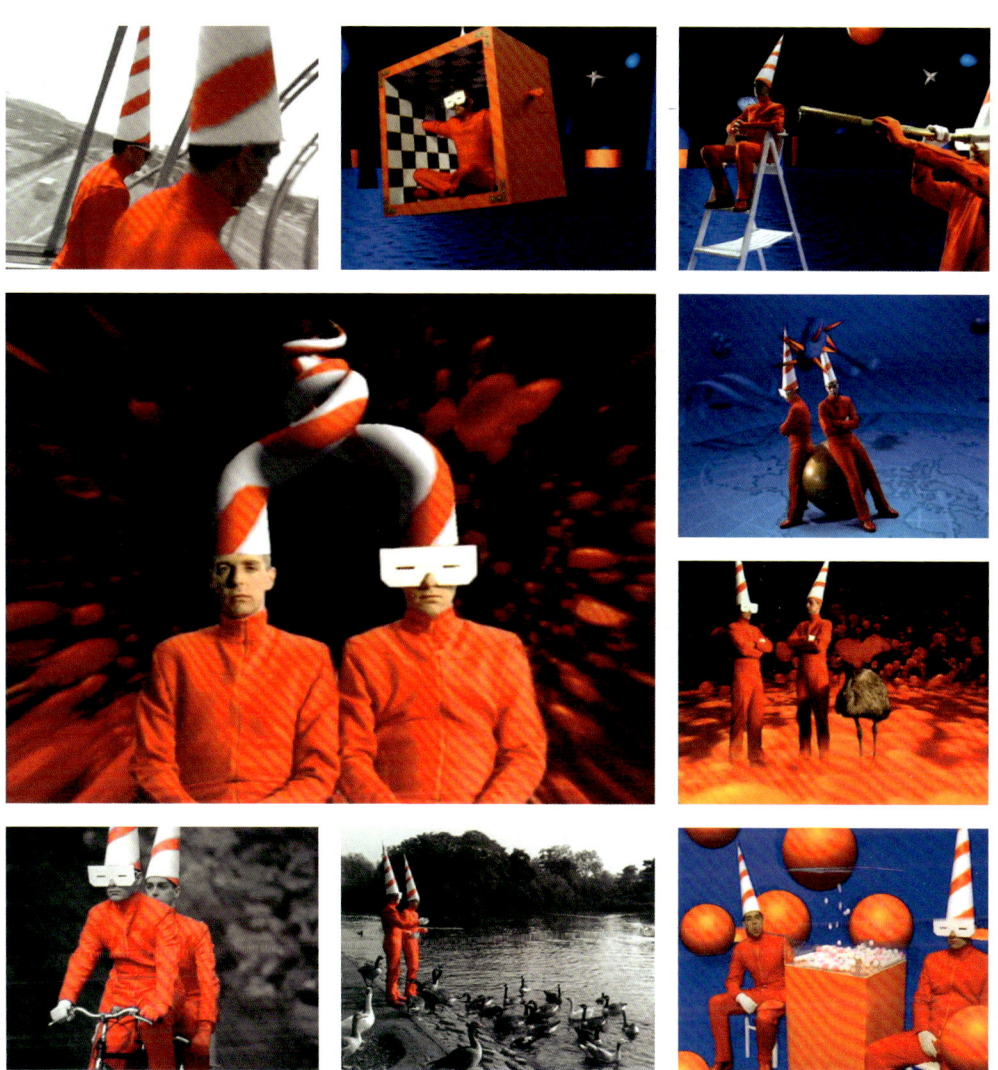

through a telescope. They appear as incongruous figures in a commuter crowd, the only coloured elements in an otherwise black-and-white scene; their hats entwine. They also appear on the top of the Monument in Pudding Lane, in the City of London, as weird screwlike forms, and next to a glowing blue egg while a pair of emus stalk around them. Orange balls pop out of Chris's mouth. They row on a boating lake; cycle a tandem; feed the ducks; and then a curtain with arithmetic symbols closes. Howard Greenhalgh explained in *The Face* in 1993: 'For "Can you forgive her?", we were presented with a concept. David Fielding brought in this model of a *Top of the Pops* set he was going to do, with Neil and Chris in the uniforms and hats sat on a globe structure, and they said they wanted to make this look work as a video. So we had this big blue egg shape and just did bizarre things with computer graphics. It's like Dada, nonsense really – it's nothing to do with the track.'

Go west

release 6 September 1993
formats 7" / 12" / 12" promo × 2 / cassette / CD
photographer Chris Nash
design Farrow / PSB
video Howard Greenhalgh

The idea to record the Village People's 'Go west' came from Chris, who saw it as 'a song about an idealistic, gay utopia ... And I knew that the way Neil would sing it would make it all sound hopeless.' The American symbolism of the cover images and colours – created while the US presidential election was underway and based on real campaign badges – is subverted by the communistic overtones of the design, and of the video for the song, shot in Moscow's Red Square. The tension in the visual presentation of the song – both on the cover and in the video – counterpoints the innocent naiveté of the subject matter. The costumes were 'supposed to look military', Chris said. 'We decided to be one-dimensional', Neil told *The Face*. 'David had this idea of having a look for each single that would tie in with how the album looked and also give us something to do on television. [On *Top of the Pops*] we went with a choreographer, a designer, our costume people, make-up people.' In the *Guardian*, Dave Rimmer noted: 'No more mini costume dramas, no more Chris walking two steps behind. Their videos are no longer "about" anything. Instead there are simple shapes and strong colours, SF costumes in non-naturalistic computer-animated realities, an absence of narrative or personality. The current Pet Shop Boys image is as abstract as the digital money that also flies from market to market by satellite.'

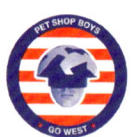
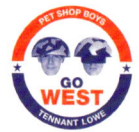

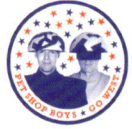
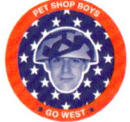

7", front   7", back

180

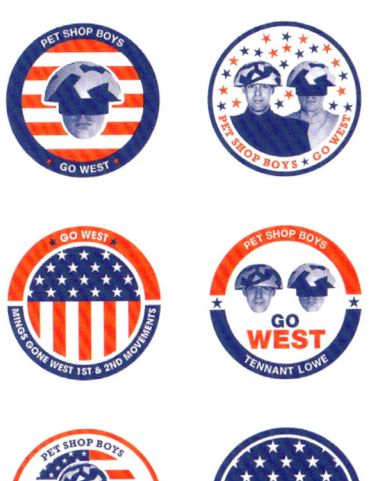

12", front

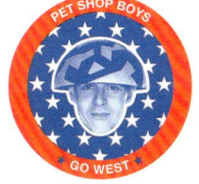

12", back

CD, front

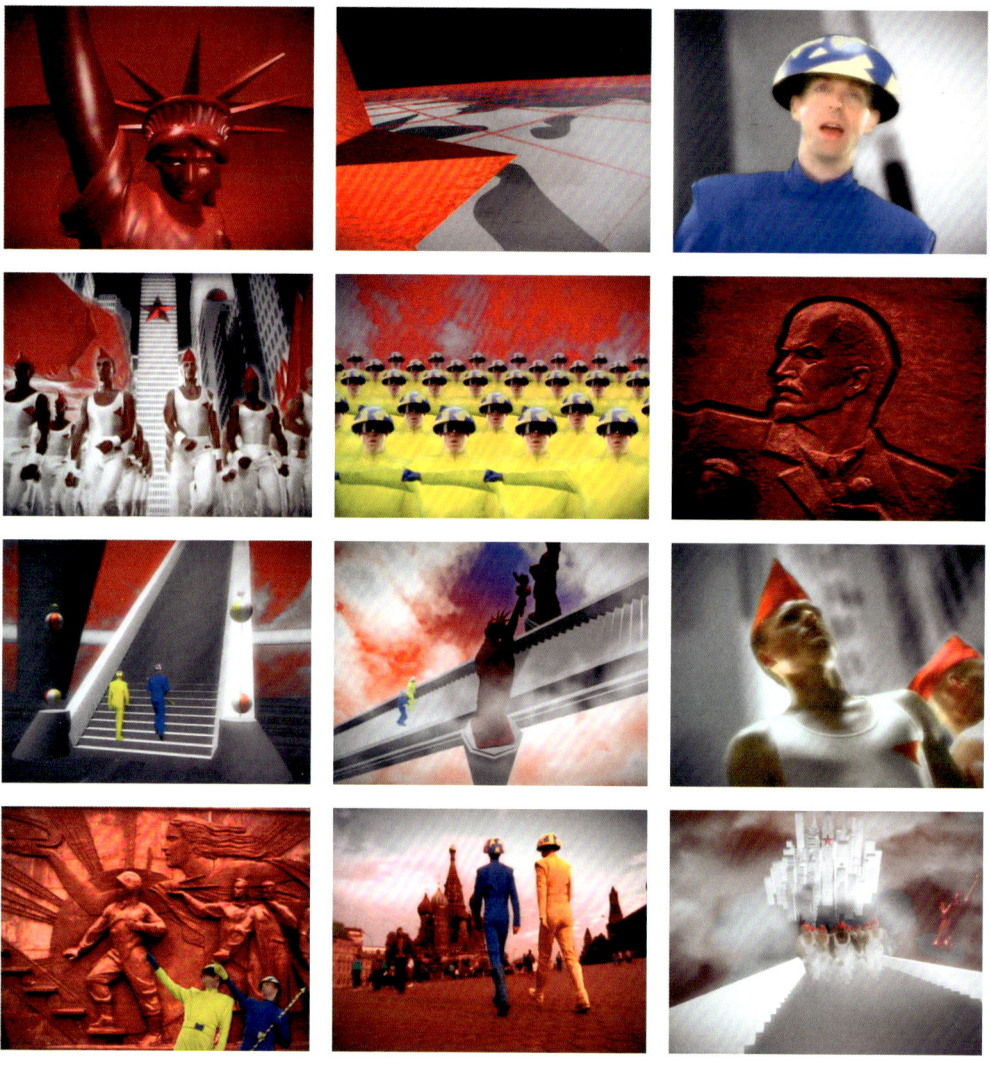

The Statue of Liberty radiates red stars across the Atlantic. Marching Soviet athletes carry flags; Neil and Chris appear in blue and yellow jumpsuits. Soviet-era statues vie with Liberty on either side of a moving stairway; Neil steps off it and through a door in the sky. Chris surfs on a yellow board. Guards march past the Tomb of the Unknown Soldier at the Kremlin; Neil and Chris appear in costume in front of St Basil's Cathedral. The clouds give way to a final image of Liberty. 'The bright, clean colours and computer graphics were Chris's idea', says Neil. The Russian footage came about 'completely by coincidence. We'd been invited to launch MTV Russia, and we thought, since the song was about going west, the best place to go west from would be Moscow. But the cameras were impounded when we got there, so we ended up having only three hours to shoot.' No one had bothered to get permission to film. In that post-*Glasnost* era, 'Russia was going through a remarkable *laissez-faire* period', says Neil.

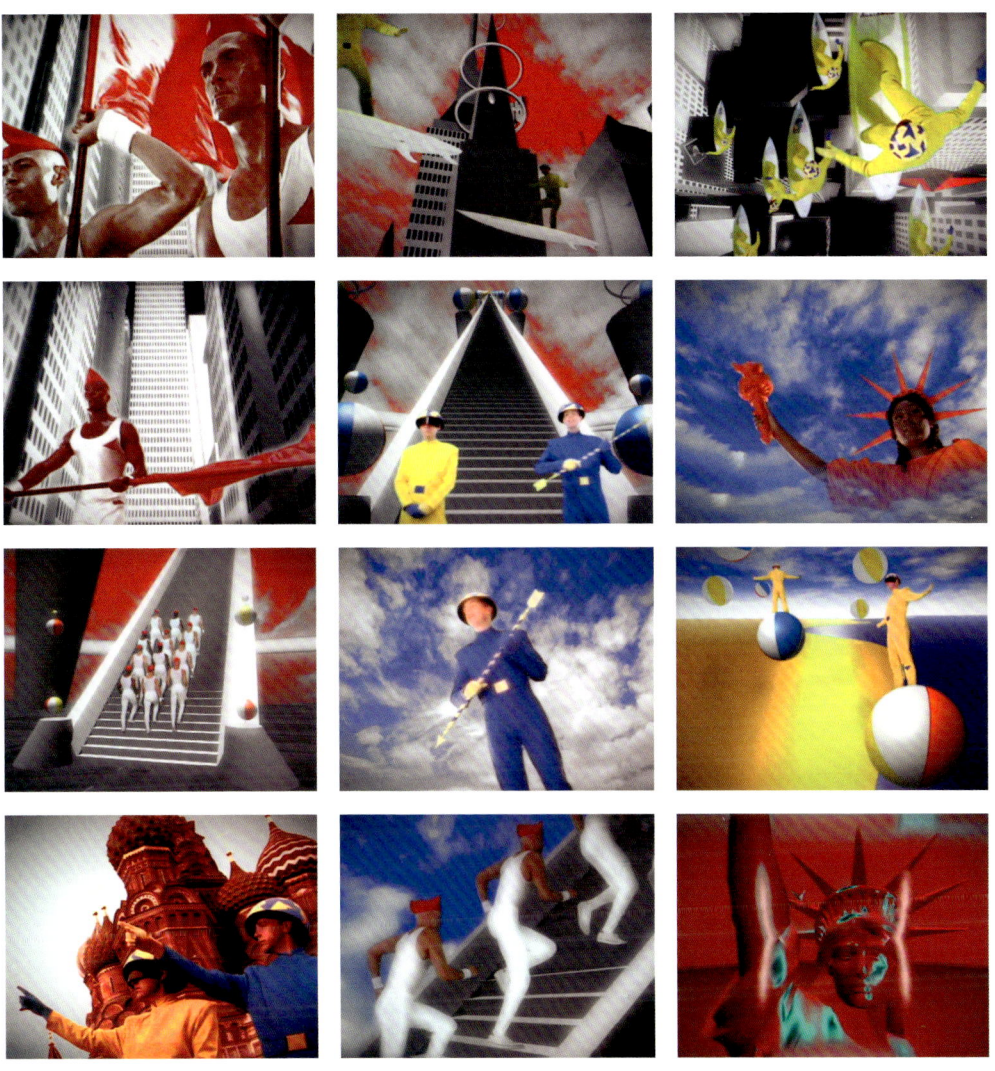

He and Chris merely drove up to Red Square in a limousine, wearing their costumes, got out and started walking. Howard Greenhalgh then sped round shooting Communist-era symbols. 'It was a very expensive video – so much of it was done in post-production', says Neil. The steps were inspired by the 1946 film *A Matter of Life and Death*, by British directors Michael Powell and Emeric Pressburger, in which an RAF pilot is shot down and mistakenly summoned to Heaven before his time on a giant moving staircase.

Very

release 27 September 1993
formats LP / cassette / CD × 2 / picture disc (Mexico)
costume design David Fielding
photographer Chris Nash and Trevor Key
packaging design Pentagram
graphic design Farrow / PSB

For their next studio album, *Very* – their only number-one album – Pet Shop Boys approached Pentagram and asked them to reconceptualize the CD box. 'We thought it was pathetic that, because of CDs, record design has just become a booklet behind a piece of transparent plastic', Neil noted. 'We'd got fed up with the fact that CD packaging all boiled down to the booklet,' added Chris, 'so the obvious way around it was to make the actual box the cover.' Daniel Weil came up with the 'Lego' concept. It was 'tactile', Chris said at the time.

 'I remember being vaguely disappointed that it was still just a CD box', recalls Mark Farrow. 'Neil and Chris and I were the kind of editors on it.' He worked on the graphic elements of the package, while Chris Nash contributed photographs to the booklet. 'Neil said, "This is the poppiest we've ever done and it's all about pop and it's got to be bright and it's got to be mad."' Farrow made a conscious effort to meet that spirit. Of the overall *Very* period, Farrow says, 'I felt my job was to curate the whole thing, and make it coherent. But part of that was to not make it coherent – to go a bit mad. Being let out of my tight, rigorous Helvetica cage.' The CD label and sticker on the back of the box were aerial views of one of the 'Go west' helmets. When the original run of orange boxes ran out, it was replaced by a Trevor Key photograph of the box on a blue background. The reverse of the alternative CD was a high-key pink.

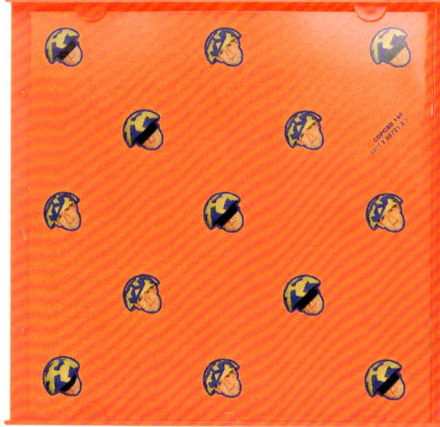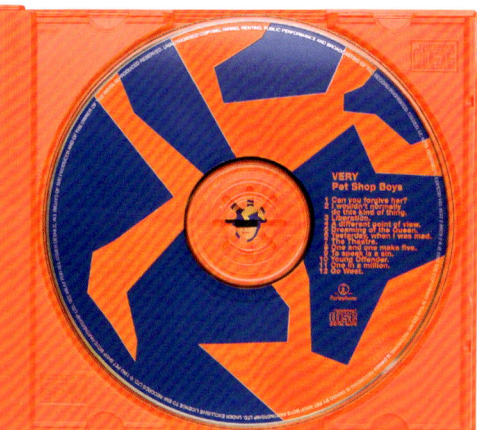

CD, open

CD, front

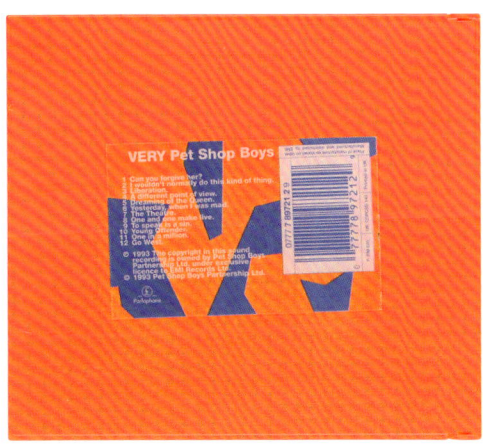

CD, back

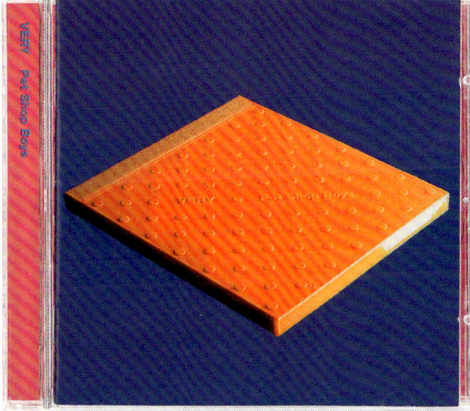

CD, second issue, front

Very 1993

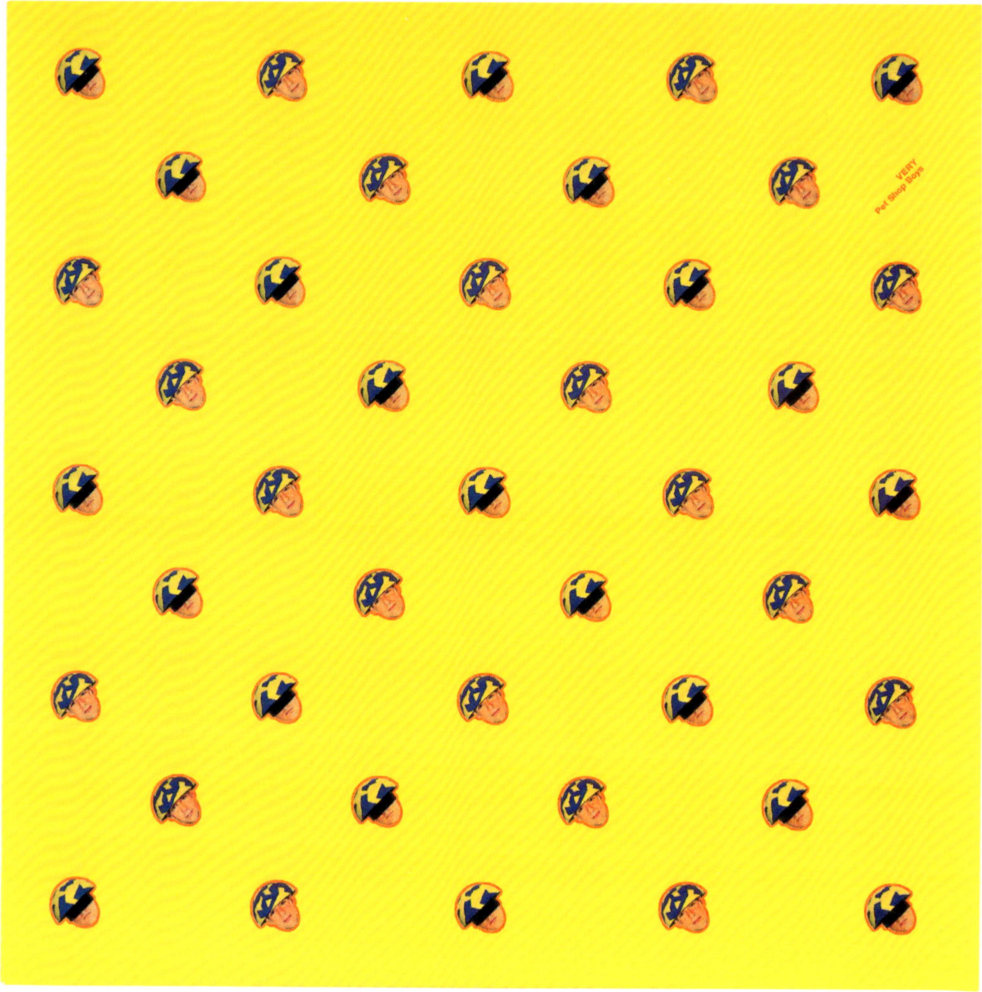

LP, outer sleeve, front

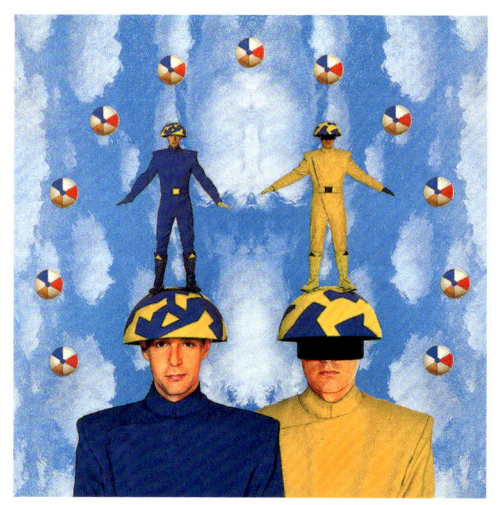

LP, inner sleeve, front

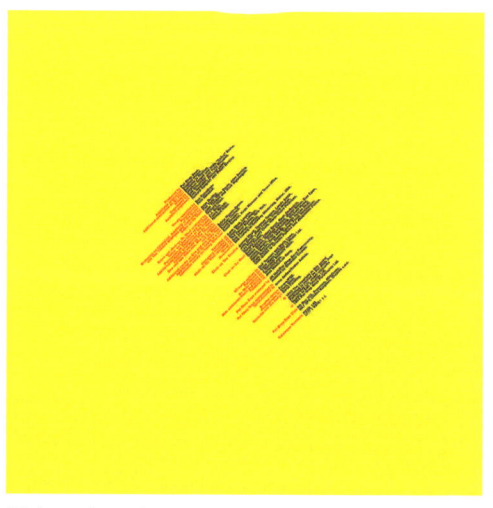

LP, inner sleeve, back

'It was pretty poptastic, that whole campaign', says Farrow. 'The box was the product, and the box was in the ads, and we had [Neil and Chris] flying through space on the boxes. It was very strong. It was about being bothered.' But each of the special CD packages cost Neil and Chris forty pence, which was deducted from their royalties. It was not practical to reproduce the 'Lego' effect on the cover of the LP, so Farrow replaced the grid of circular dots on the outside of the orange case with small disembodied Pet Shop Boys heads in the semi-spherical 'Go west' hats. The background colour was also changed to yellow to match the colour of the hats. On the back of the outer sleeve, the heads were repeated, with the track listings typeset obliquely in between. On the front of the inner sleeve was one of Chris Nash's 'Go west' promotional photographs, while on the reverse, the credits were set on an angle, not only so they would match the heads and text on the outer sleeve, but also to continue the sense of the design elements flying through space. This treatment also calls to mind early avant-garde Soviet art, poster design, and typography, continuing the references to Russia established with the 'Go west' release. The Mexican record company imaginatively turned Farrow's design into a picture disc, although here the heads and text are turned upright, and the album's title is translated into Spanish: 'Muy'.

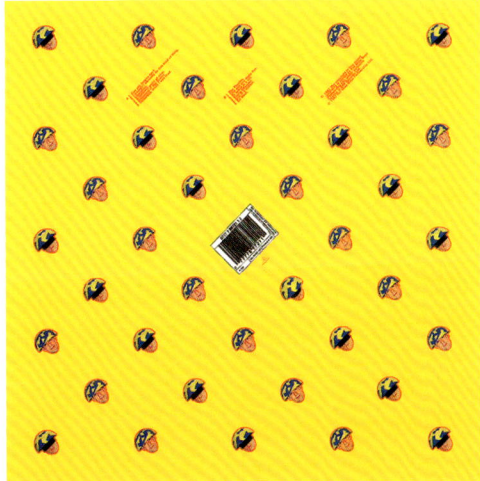

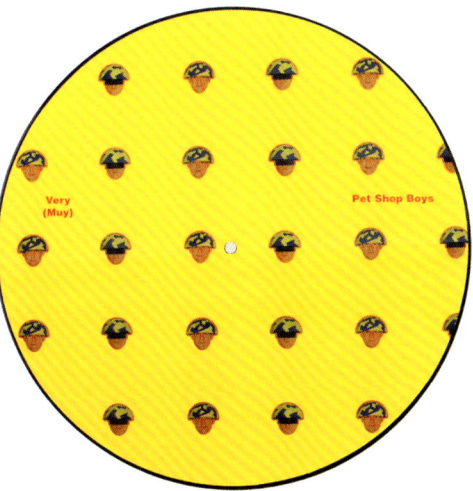

LP, outer sleeve, back

Picture disc, Mexico, front

Very Relentless

release 27 September 1993
formats Limited-edition triple-disc LP /
limited-edition double CD
costume design David Fielding
photographer Chris Nash
packaging design Pentagram
design Farrow / PSB

Very Relentless was a limited-edition release that included *Very* and a bonus six-track album, *Relentless*, of mainly instrumental songs. The fold-out plastic bubble outer sleeve for the CD had been Pentagram's alternative suggestion when the Pet Shop Boys had proposed that they rethink the conventional packaging of CDs. Once again, the disembodied 'Go west' heads were used, as they had been on the LP, for the cardboard inner sleeves, small and set at an angle in a grid. A larger single head was used on the front and back of the booklet, Neil on one side and a vibrating Chris on the other. 'The idea was that Neil's head represented *Very*', says Farrow, 'and *Relentless* was represented by Chris's head vibrating to dance music.'

An even more limited edition of *Relentless* was produced as an LP, in the form of three coloured twelve-inch records (following pages). Each side contained just one of the tracks, and each record was the produced in the same colour as its sleeve: one came in pink, one was in light blue, and one was in bright yellow. On the outer sleeve, now both Neil's and Chris's heads are wobbling. And, in a clever device, their heads are used on the labels of the records themselves to indicate the side: one head for side 1, two for side 2, and so on. 'It was Mark's idea to make the heads wobbly', says Neil. 'The limited-edition twelve inch is worth a fortune now.'

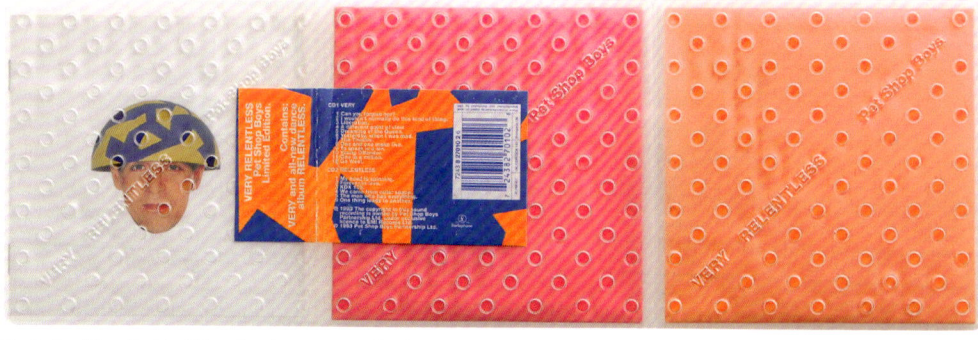

Limited-edition double CD, outer sleeve, open, front

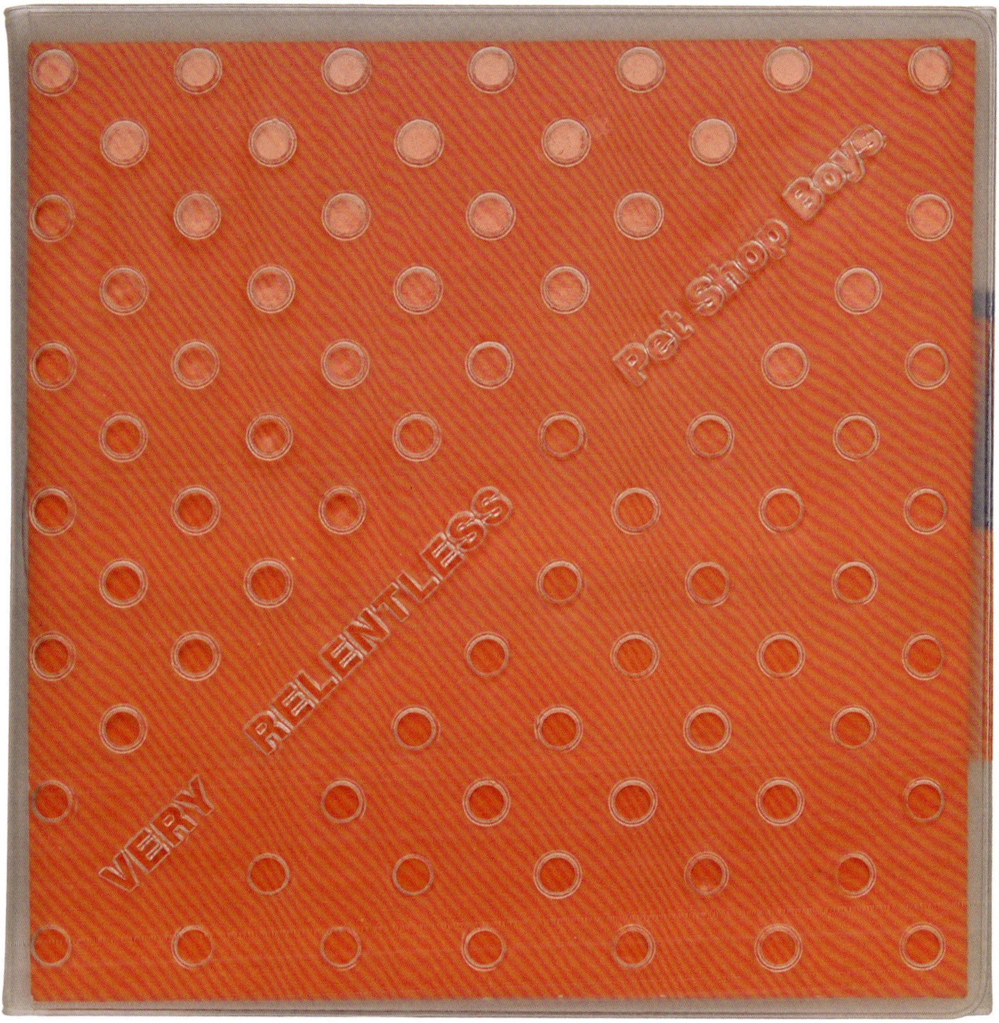

Limited-edition double CD, outer sleeve, closed

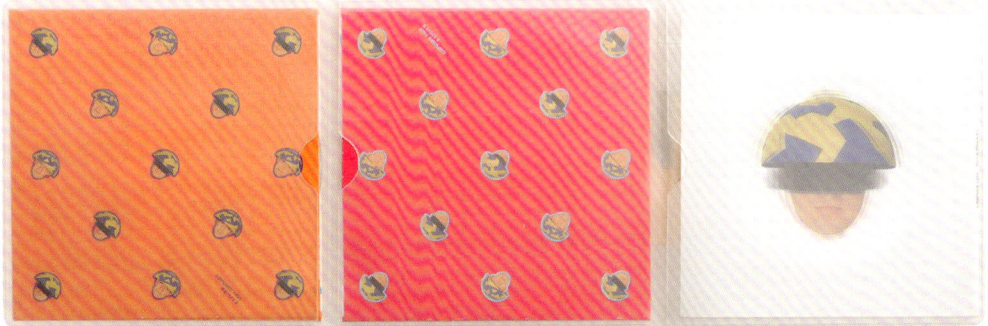

Limited-edition double CD, outer sleeve, open, inside

Very Relentless 1993

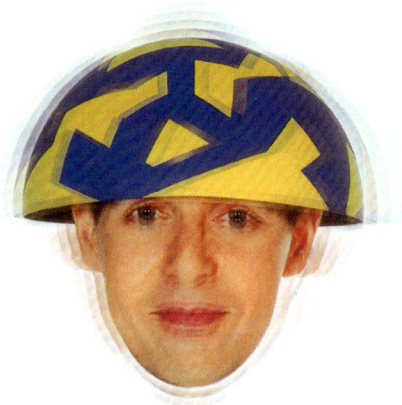

Limited-edition triple-disc LP, outer sleeve, front

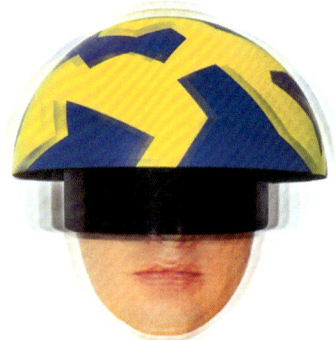

Limited-edition triple-disc LP, outer sleeve, back

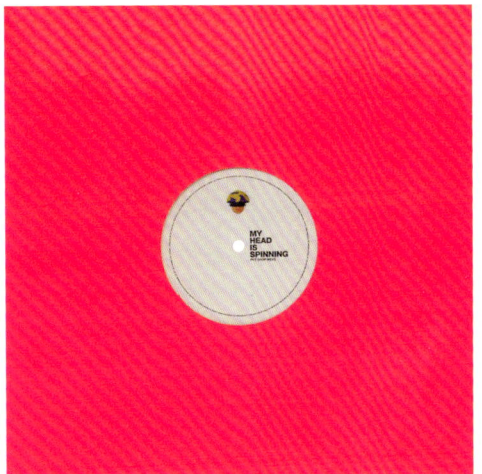
Limited-edition triple-disc LP, Side 1, inner sleeve

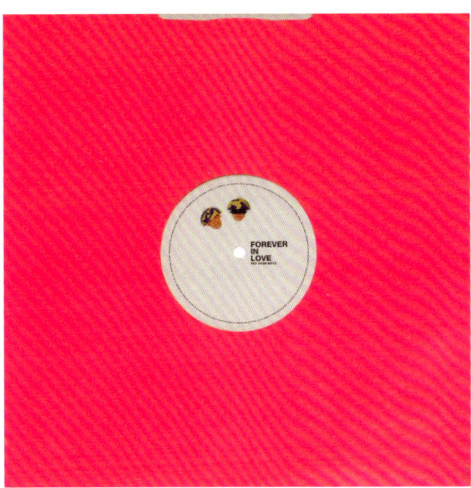
Limited-edition triple-disc LP, Side 2, inner sleeve

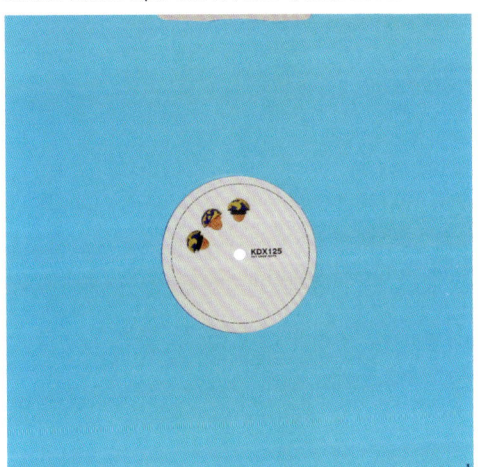
Limited-edition triple-disc LP, Side 3, inner sleeve

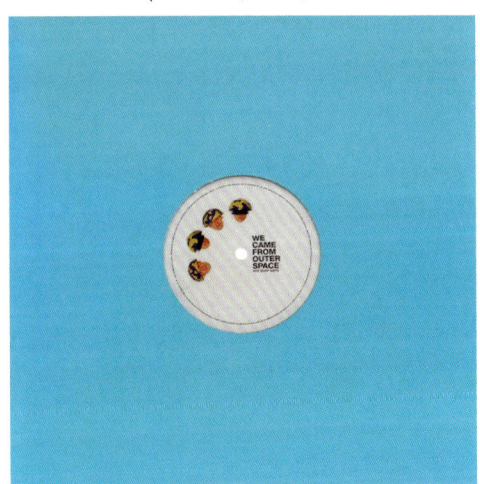
Limited-edition triple-disc LP, Side 4, inner sleeve

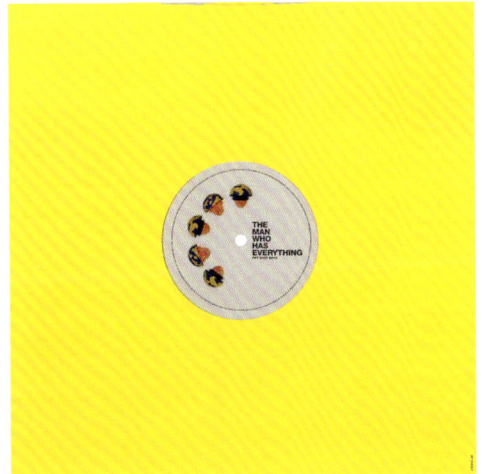
Limited-edition triple-disc LP, Side 5, inner sleeve

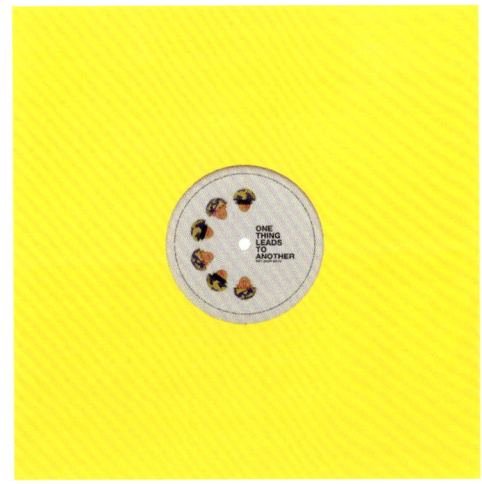
Limited-edition triple-disc LP, Side 6, inner sleeve

Pet Shop Boys versus America

release 4 November 1993
formats 250-page hardback and paperback book
author Chris Heath
photographer Pennie Smith
design Mark Farrow

Originally planned as a photo book with extended captions, the project evolved into a narrative following the adventures of the group and their entourage as they took the *Performance* tour across America. 'The book is so well observed,' says Neil, 'it really brings back the flavour of that time.' Pennie Smith – famous for her iconic photographs of The Clash, among others – was official photographer on the tour; her black-and-white images were placed next to Chris Heath's text and form a complementary narrative of their own. 'The whole show happens chronologically through the book', Neil observes; the two-hour-long spectacle of the onstage event is thus stilled in time, as if in the photographer's flashlight.

The design of the book was entirely Mark Farrow's. Its reportage feel owes something to publications such as *Picture Post* and *Life*. Smith's work has an immediacy that conveys the mayhem of touring, with the inevitable *longueurs* that sit between moments of intense excitement. That snatched yet composed sensibility – a sharp contrast to the perceived 'high life' of being in a pop group on the road, and its inexorable, often frantic momentum – gives the book its reflective quality, as well as conveying the long periods of 'downtime' that touring involves.

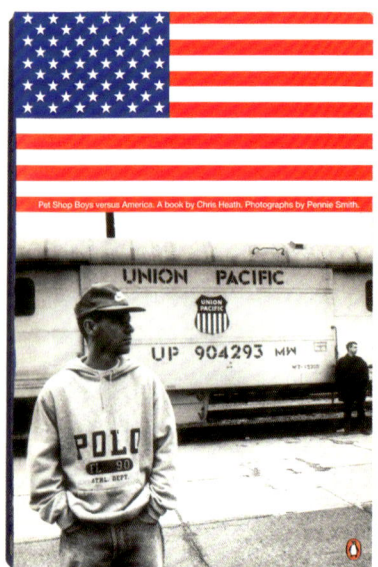

Paperback, front cover

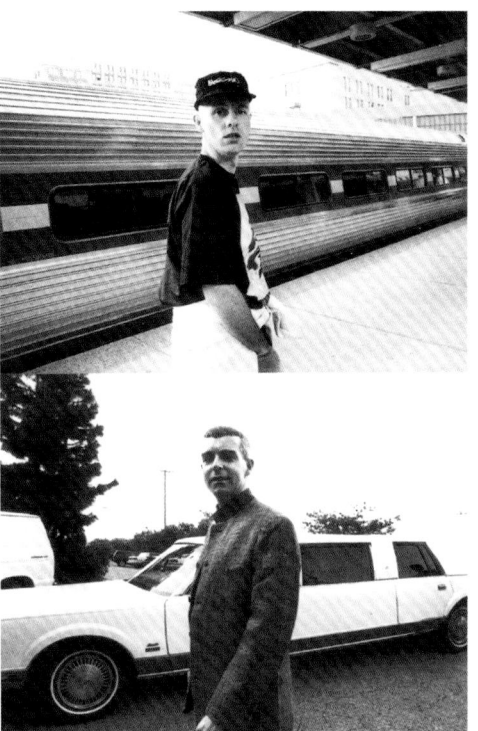

Sunday, 17 March

Coconut Grove, Miami, a suburb of boutiques with pastel pink and green awnings. The Pet Shop Boys and entourage are staying at the Mayfair House Hotel. Everyone is booked under their own names except for Neil (C. Heston) and Chris (R. Welch). Across the road from the hotel Grove Calloways is holding a ZZ Top Hot Legs Contest. 'Men and women'. For the finest legs, free ZZ Top concert tickets.

On the first night in America Chris and Neil host a tour party barbecue on the hotel roof. It looks like the party scene in *Spinal Tap*, someone says. Spirits are high. They talk about Japan: amusing mishaps, the return of their number-one fan Eiko, Mr Udo, the promoter they had duelled with on their last tour there. He apparently praised the show, but didn't come to see it. He threw them a party, but didn't turn up. I have just flown in. Joining a tour after it has begun is like arriving late at a party: you feel that everyone has drunk more than you and is talking about something they understand but which you yourself can't quite grasp.

In Japan they went to see one of George Michael's cover version concerts.

'We were asked backstage beforehand,' said Neil, 'and Chris made a remark about his haircut.'

'I said I really liked "Careless Whisper",' says Chris. 'And I asked, "You do 'Killer'?" and he said, "I'll do it first so you can go." '

'He always puts himself down,' says Neil. 'He tells you it's half-empty.'

Chris scowls when he is told that their new British single, 'Where the Streets Have No Name (I Can't Take My Eyes off You)', which melds a U2 song and an old Frankie Valli tune into a high-energy stomper, has entered the charts at number seven. The mid-week prediction had been number three. That afternoon Neil has been to see the film everyone is talking about, *The Doors*. No good. He says he saw it so that he would have something to talk about in interviews.

Record Mirror, 16 March, 'Strange Behaviour', an interview with Tim Nicholson:
'This tour is going to be even more theatrical than the last one,' explains Neil. 'The last

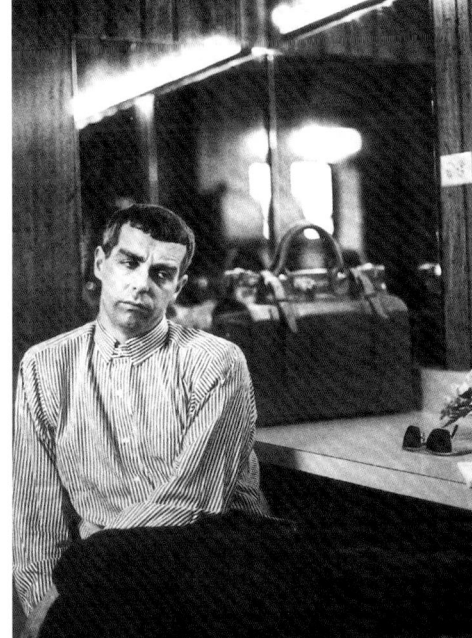

'We've got Trevor and Mark,' points out Neil.

'Yeah,' says Chris, 'but that's not that different. For the Arsenio Hall show we had a scratch video made and banks of video screens and we had our attitude sorted out. We can't just plonk ourselves in front of a bunch of musicians. I don't want to be presented as us and a band. It's the wrong thing.' He thinks. 'We want lots of dry ice and smoke.'

Neil nods. 'It's got to look very...'

'... moody,' says Chris.

'Technical,' says Neil.

'Like we look like,' says Chris.

'We should be right next to each other,' adds Neil. 'We have to establish that we are a duo. We have to look like a duo.'

A man comes laden with bowls of salad. Neil and Chris tell him they don't want it and ask him to take it away, but he categorically refuses. 'I have to stick all this stuff in here,' he insists. 'You gotta tell someone big or else I'll get in trouble.' So they give in, he deposits the food and leaves.

'You can't not have food in your dressing-room,' huffs Neil. 'It's absolutely *de rigueur*.'

Downstairs there is a soundcheck. They go through 'Rent' over and over, Sylvia unhappy with Derek's harmonies, and Derek unhappy with Sylvia's criticisms.

'You always tell me different things,' he huffs.

'I'm not saying it's wrong,' she pacifies him, 'it's just not right.'

Chris is on the telephone in the production office, talking to the art director of *The Tonight Show* in Los Angeles.

'What we want out of it is something that looks like the Pet Shop Boys show – moody, lots of white light, maybe something extra like a flower strobe or a laser... Everything. As much as you've got, throw at us... I really don't know what your show looks like... If you're going for any image, kind of modern, industrial, technical. We usually perform in front of banks of video screens, but we haven't got anything to project on them now... It's a duo with a few extras, not a band...'

He re-joins Neil in the catering room. 'I had a word with the art director for *The Tonight Show*.'

'Who is he?' asks Neil.

'No one knows his name,' misquotes Chris. 'He said, "You have no creative

I wouldn't normally do this kind of thing

release 15 November 1993
formats 7" / 12" / 12" remix / 12" promo × 2 / cassette / CD × 2
photographer Andy Earl
design Farrow / PSB
video Howard Greenhalgh

This song is about 'a reserved Englishman falling in love and going bonkers. He decides he couldn't care less any more, and throws caution to the wind. It's a funny song, but it's sincere', Neil said at the time. 'I'm so bored with people seeing us as ironic that I'm quite keen on being sincere at the moment.' 'We've always wanted to wear wigs', he told the *Independent*. 'The inspiration was The Byrds, or *Rubber Soul*-period Beatles, where the fringe comes down to your eyes.... It's extraordinary how it changes your personality, wearing a wig. As the song is a little Sixties, we thought it would be nice to have the transparent boots and gloves.' 'It's a reaction against everything that's going on – grunge and dressing down', Chris added. 'It was the continuation of the *Very* look', says Farrow. 'We knew what we wanted to do – them dancing round each other's heads – so we photographed them in different positions, and then they were all stripped together.' The bubble sleeve from *Very Relentless* (pages 188–9) was repeated for one of the CDs.

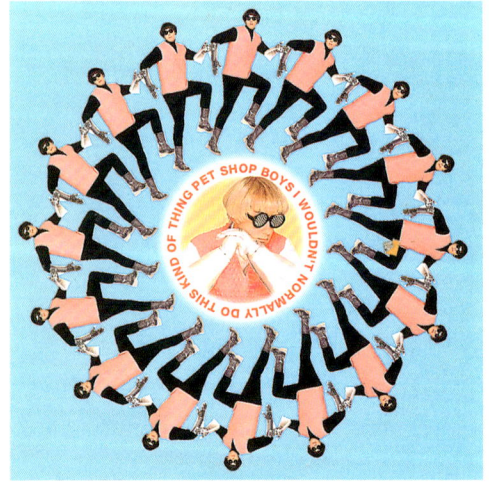

CD 1, front

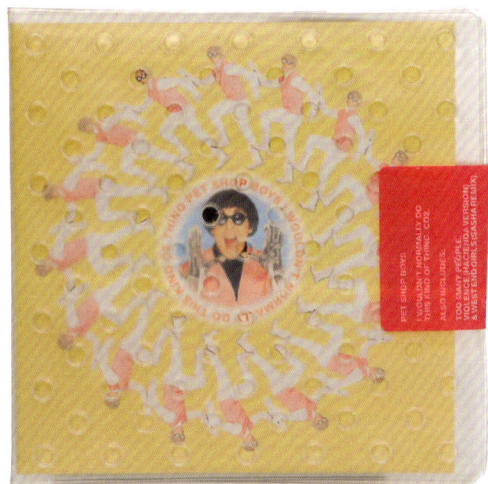

CD 2, front

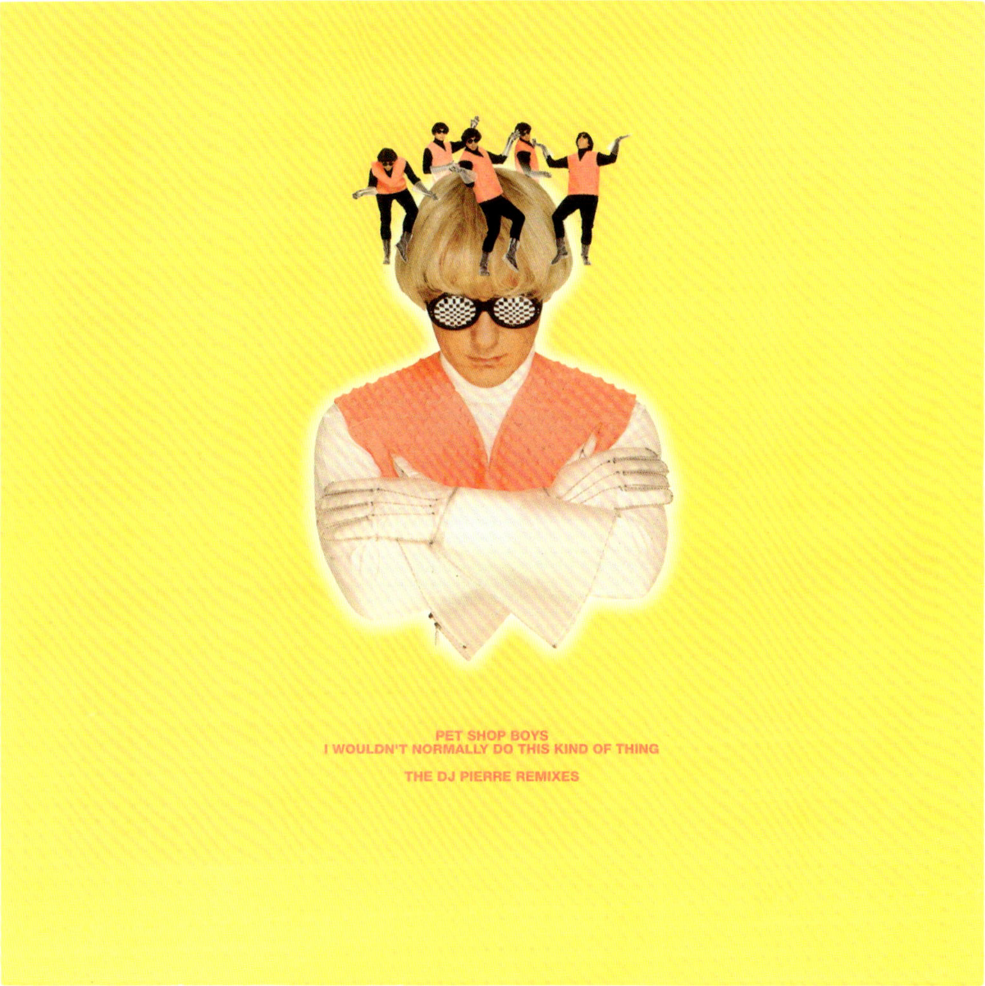

PET SHOP BOYS
I WOULDN'T NORMALLY DO THIS KIND OF THING

THE DJ PIERRE REMIXES

12" remix, front

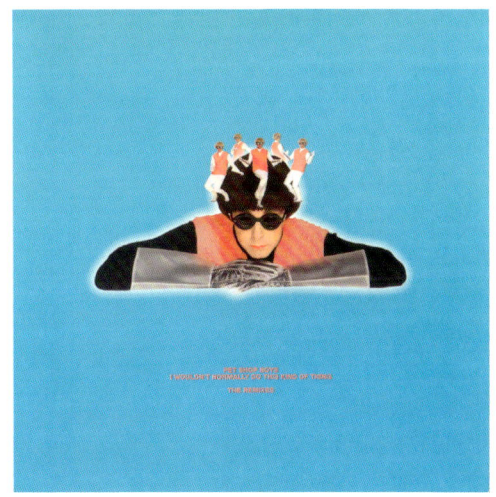

12", front

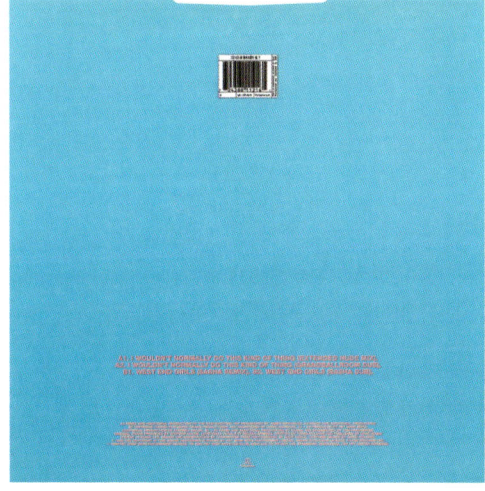

12", back

I wouldn't normally do this kind of thing 1993 195

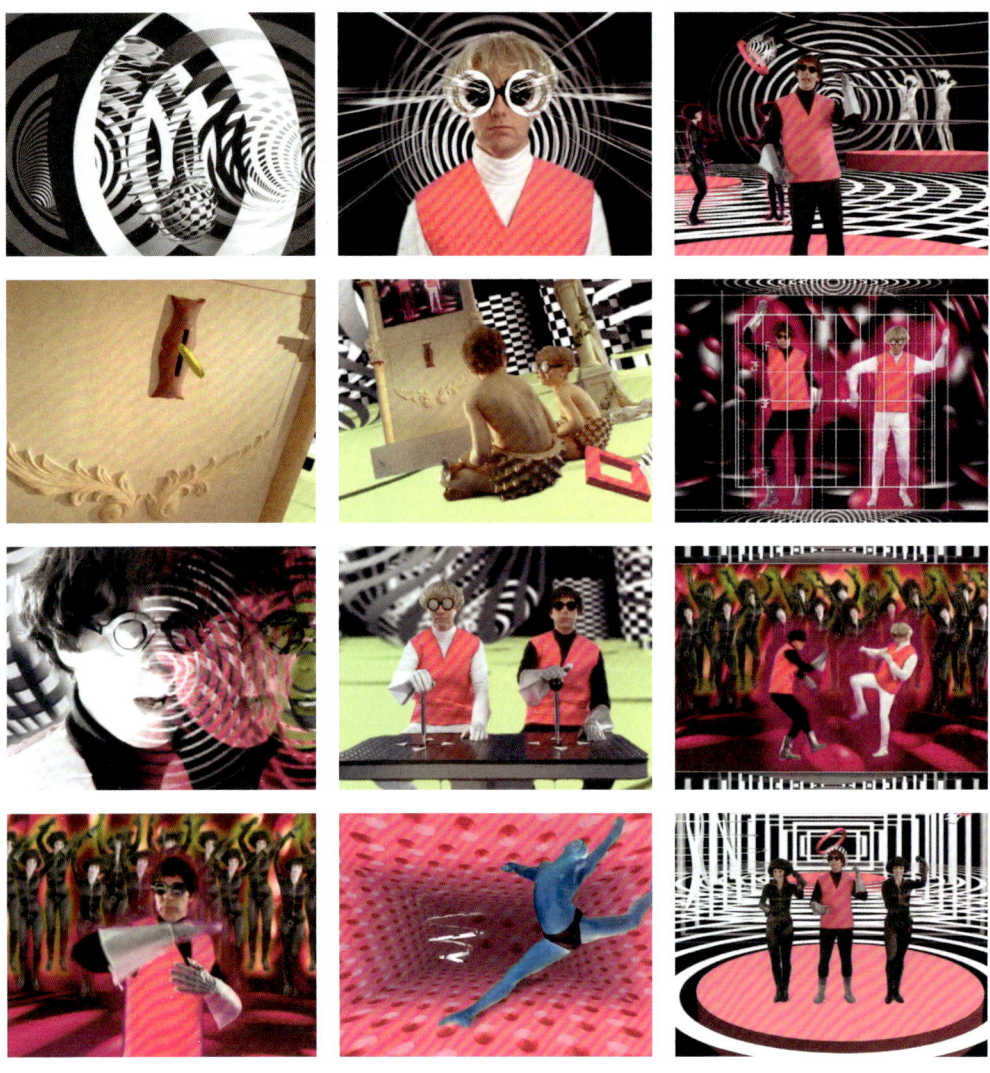

Swirling black-and-white patterns form tunnels and vortexes in this boldly coloured and at once futuristic and retro video, framing Neil and Chris in bobbed wigs, Sixties glasses, and pink, black, and white outfits (the knobbly tunics echo the 'Lego' packaging of *Very*). They do things they wouldn't normally do – dancing vigorously, fighting, wearing silly wigs – against a background inspired by the British Op Art artist Bridget Riley and computer games. Cat-suited and Mary Quant Sixties-style girls dance. Chris flips a coin into an amusement machine that displays their own virtual representations on video (the actions of which they control by wiggling large joysticks). Two small-boy versions of the pair in spiky rubber pants sit and watch the video of the virtual Neil and Chris dancing before playing toy trumpets. Neil and Chris then kick-box; a dancer takes all his clothes off (reflecting a line in the song) and leaps across the screen; and Neil and Chris finish by doing a static Gilbert and George-style dance.

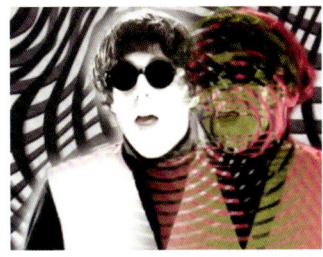 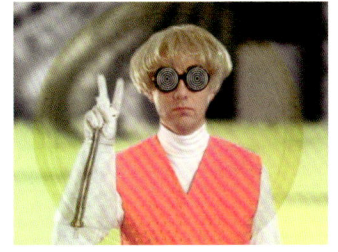 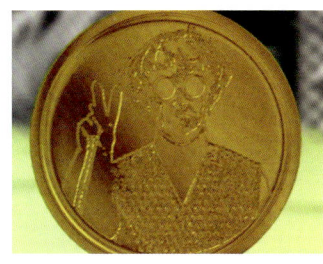
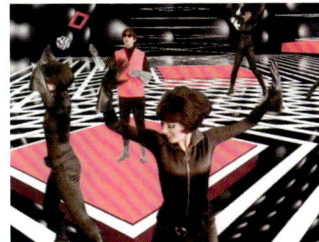 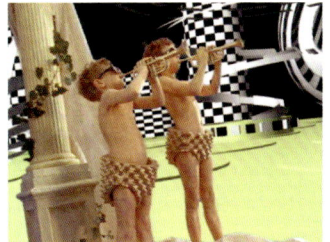 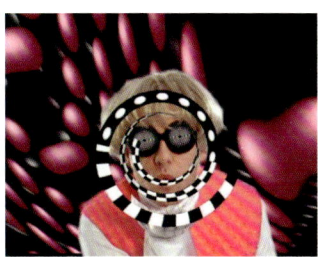
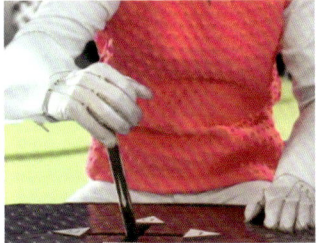 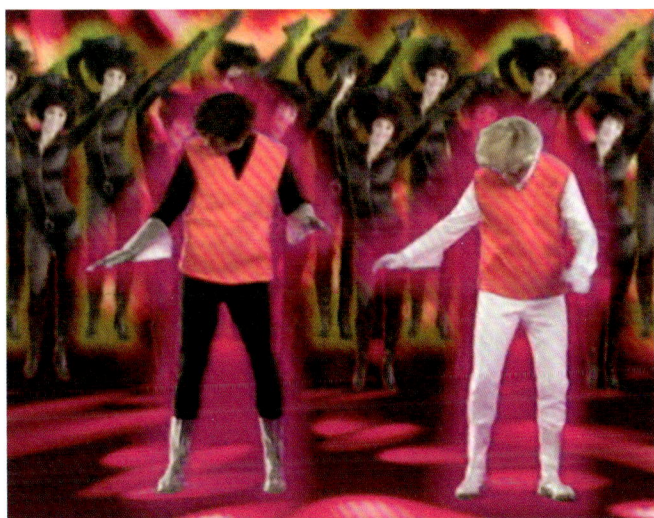
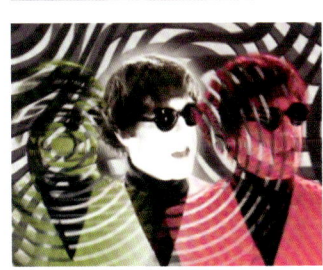

I wouldn't normally do this kind of thing 1993 197

Liberation

release 4 April 1994
formats 7" / 12" double disc / 12" double disc promo / cassette / CD × 2 / CD promo × 2
design Farrow / Why Not Films / Soho 61 FX / David Fielding / IQ Videographics / PSB
video Howard Greenhalgh

The sleeves for the next single taken from *Very* featured computer-generated forms that also appear in the video for the song. They were created by rotating Neil's and Chris's profiles three hundred and sixty degrees to form a solid body (Chris is the orange solid, Neil is the blue). These seemingly spinning computerized portraits evoke Italian artist Renato Bertelli's various continuous sculptures of the Fascist leader Benito Mussolini from 1933, as well as more recent works by the British sculptor Tony Cragg, such as *In Mind* from 2002. The heads were originated for the video and then reused for the sleeves, though they had to be re-rendered at a higher resolution. On the reverse of the CD, the text is placed in boxes that match the colours of the heads on the front, and offset from each other to create a similar impression of spinning. The backgrounds of the two outer sleeves of the double-disc remix twelve inches are tight close-ups of each head that also give the illusion of movement, while the group's name and remix titles appear in a box created from a close-up of the other head.

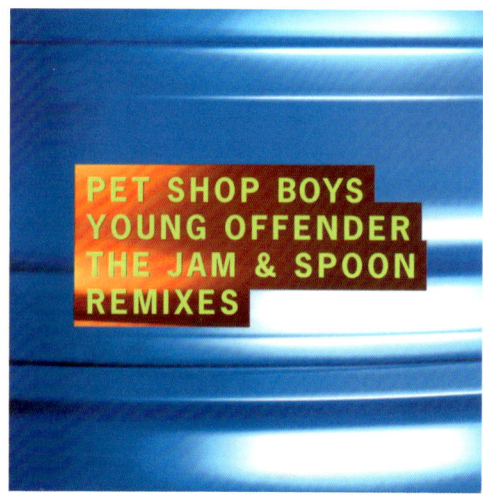

12" double disc, Disc 2, outer sleeve, front

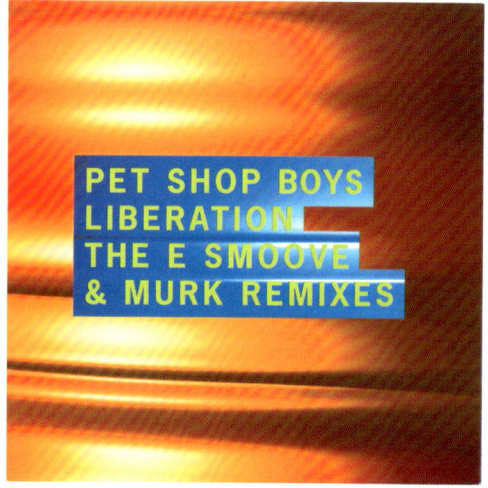

12" double disc, Disc 1, outer sleeve, front

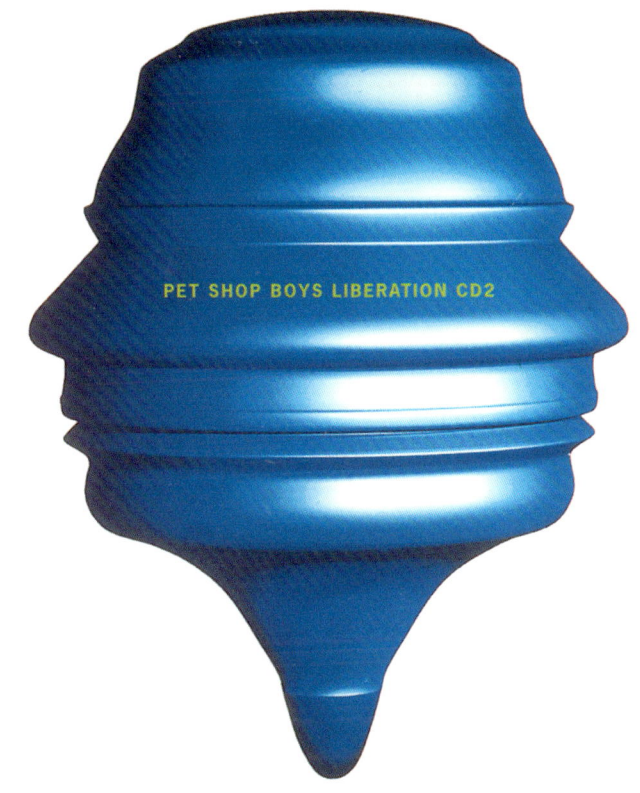

CD 2, front

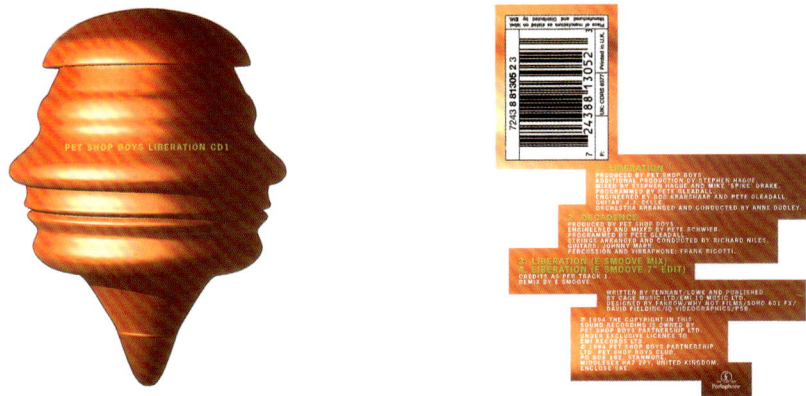

CD 1, front   CD 1, back

Liberation 1994 199

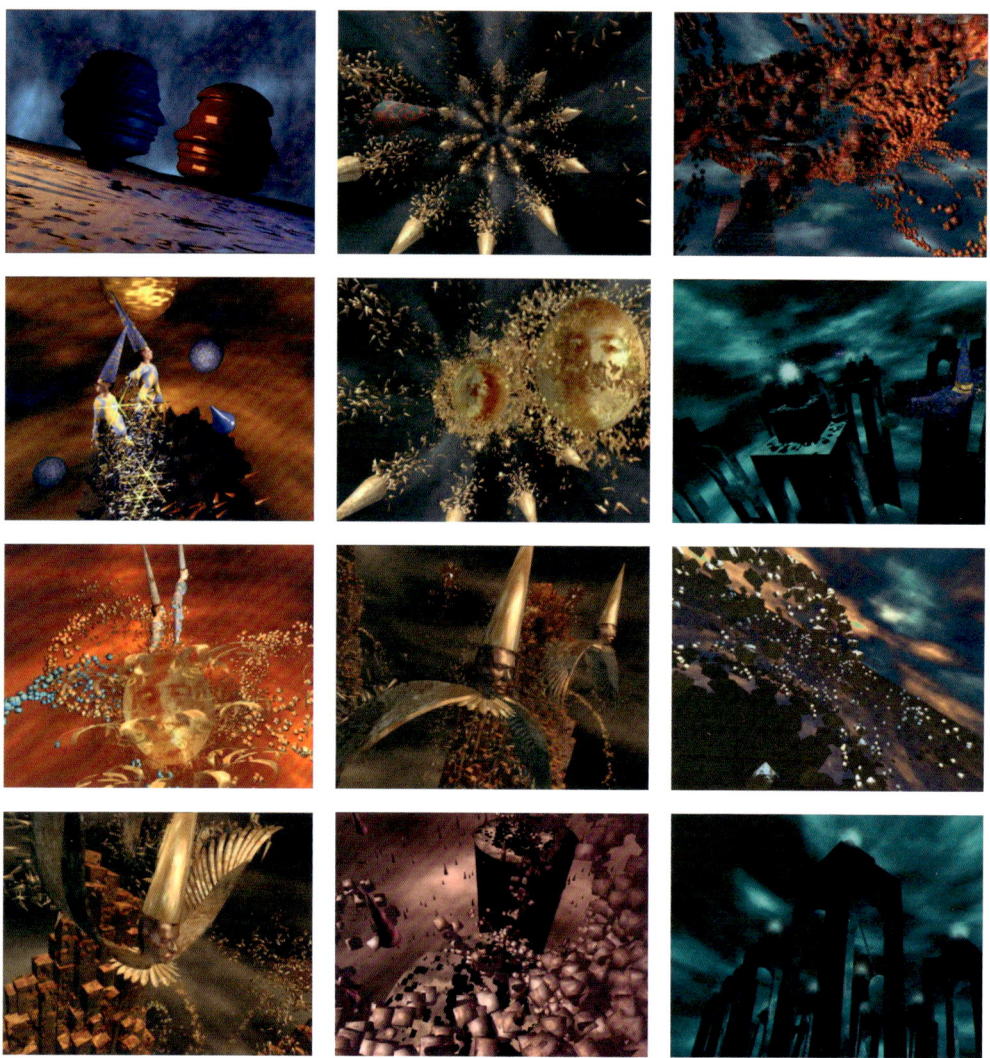

The song's 'live for today' message was reflected in the video, in which Pet Shop Boys are seen in a futuristic landscape. The two spinning head-profiles of Neil and Chris merge with DNA-like swirls and blobby figures, and turn into blue and red spinning tops heading towards a bizarre planet. Neil and Chris then appear as figures in space, wearing blue pointy dunce hats like those worn in the video for 'Can you forgive her?'; Neil's face sings from a golden globe through a fireworky sky. Strange architectural shapes rise up; Neil and Chris, now golden birds, fly through them as disembodied heads with pointy hats and wings shedding golden fragments. Their fourth computer-enhanced collaboration with director Howard Greenhalgh, the video was almost totally computer-generated, apart from the scenes where you can see Neil's face mouthing the song's lyrics. The other images of Pet Shop Boys in various guises were built up from photographs. Its technology and imagery was considered so

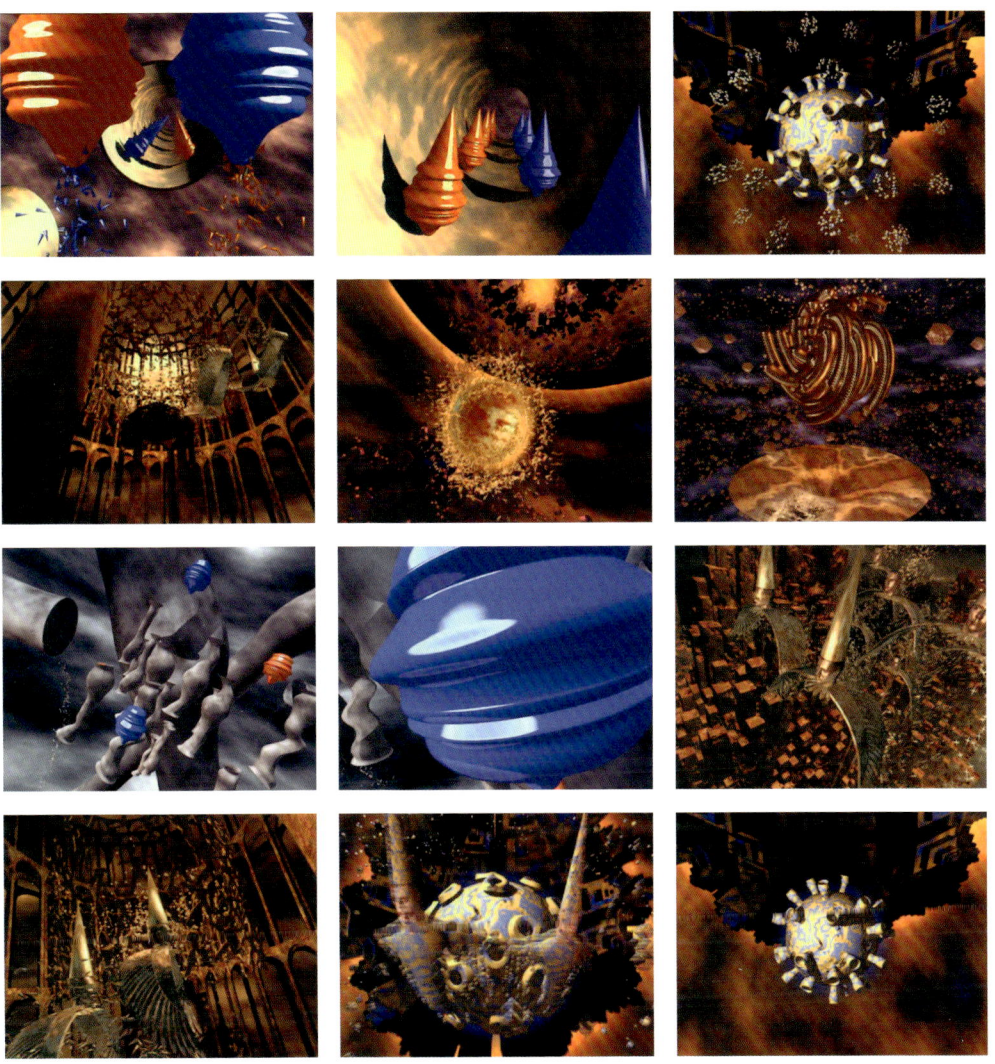

cutting-edge that it was subsequently incorporated into a movie that toured IMAX theatres. 'It's what we've been trying to get towards,' explains Neil, 'being computer-animated.' Kraftwerk had the same aspirations to cyberspatial reinvention, with their use of robots on stage and computer animations on cover images and in videos.

Yesterday, when I was mad

release 29 August 1994
formats 12" / 12" promo / cassette / CD × 2
photographer Richard Burbridge
design Farrow / PSB
video Howard Greenhalgh

'The song's about being on tour – mad in the sense of being angry', Neil says. But for both the sleeve and the video, they leant on the other meaning of mad. For the sleeves, they rented a straitjacket from a costume-hire shop, but apparently it was the authentic article. Initially the group were to be photographed wearing jackets, but in the end, only one jacket was shot. 'They looked really good', Chris said. 'Like an advert for Comme des Garçons.' 'Very spooky', Neil said. 'The video hadn't been made, they weren't around, there was nothing visual to go off, so we hired a straitjacket and photographed it', says Mark Farrow. 'It was a bit spooky and stained and unnerving.' The image 'becomes like texture'. Each format showed a different view of the same jacket. The outer sleeve of the CDs was printed matt to suggest the texture of the straitjacket itself. The sleeve won a D&AD award.

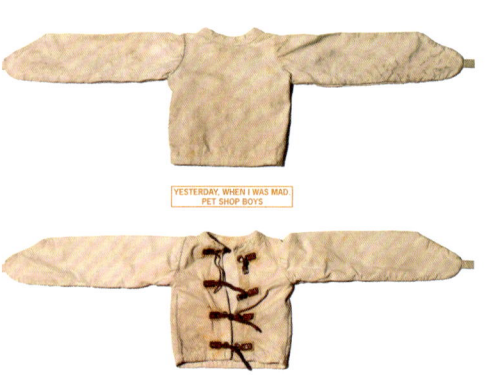

12", front

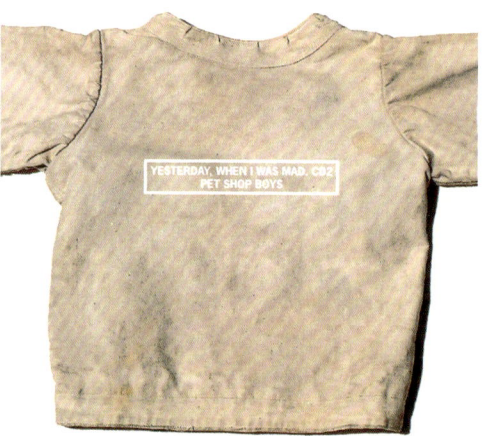

CD 2, inner sleeve, front

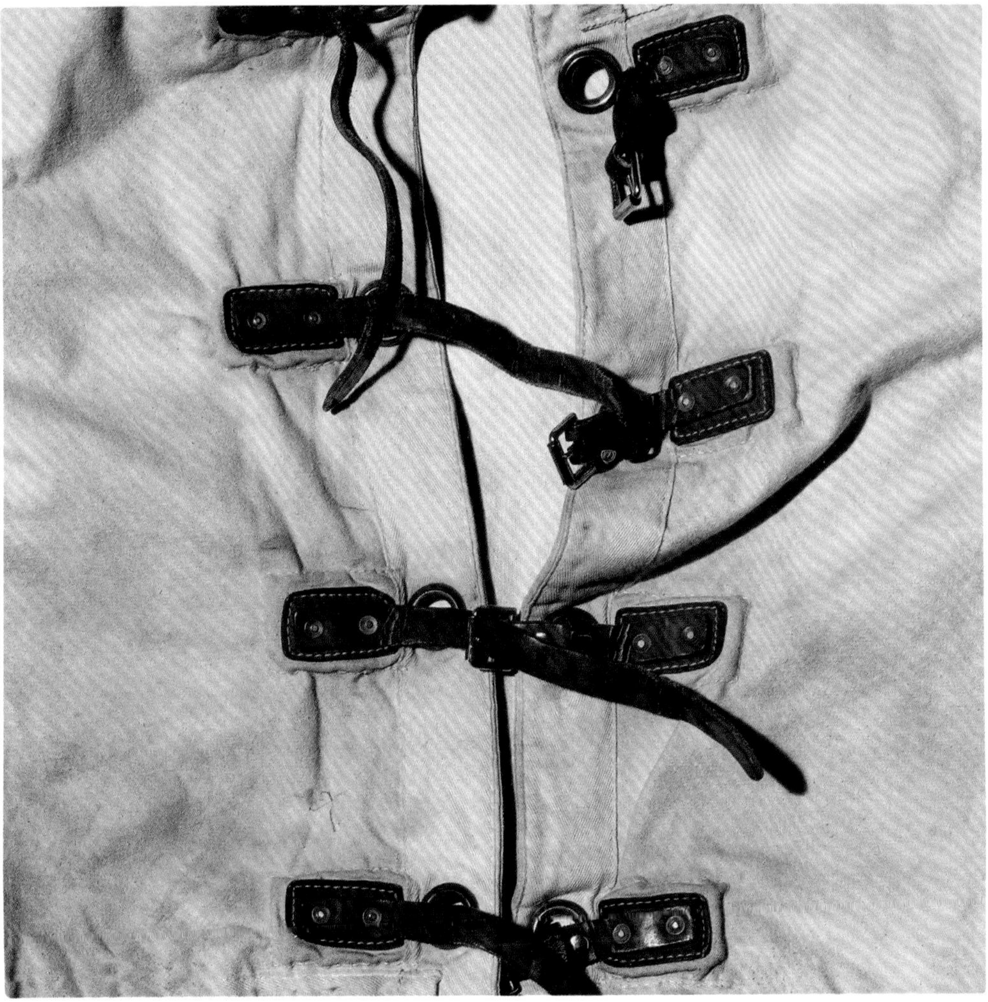

12" promo, front

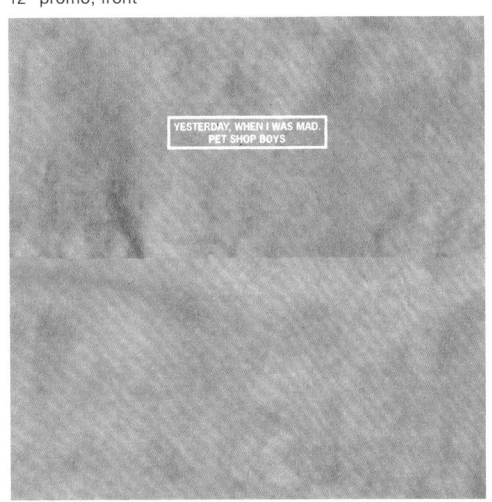

CD, outer sleeve

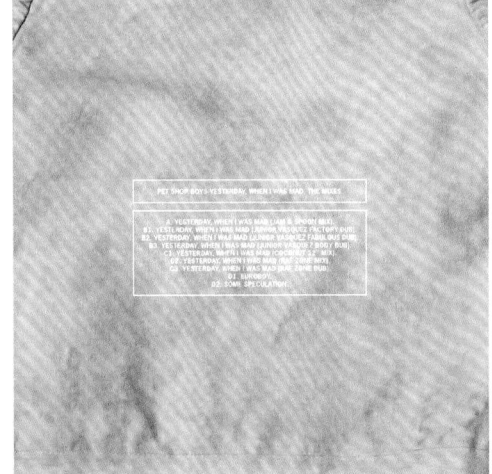

12" promo, back

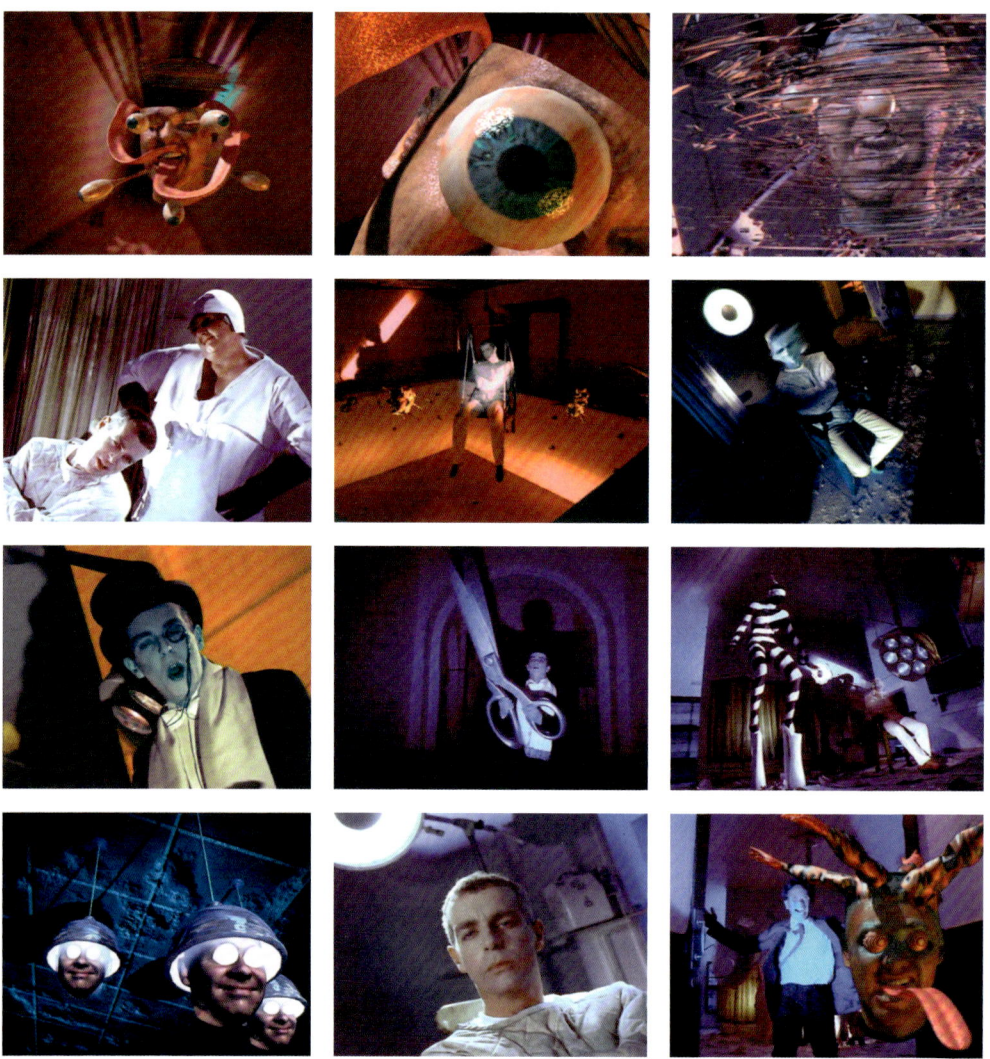

A flying head is deconstructed into boggling eyeballs and long tongue; a top hat walks down a corridor towards a fat nurse in a cyber-hospital. Neil is seen in evening clothes, top hat, monocle, and cane; and then strapped into a straitjacket in a chair. Scenes of madness surround him: giant scissors, two red-headed little girls; a stripey dancer. An Indian family gather round Neil's seated figure. 'Filmed on the day that Tony Blair became leader of the Labour Party', Neil recalls. The video was shot in two London hospitals: Westminster – then closed – and the West Middlesex, still in use. 'This room we were filming in was full of artificial limbs, rather spookily.' During the filming, when Neil came down the corridor with a large pair of scissors, they had to stop when a man was wheeled out of an operating theatre on a trolley, groaning in agony. Chris was away while the video was shot, and so his image was scanned in by computer afterwards. 'This complemented another of the ideas behind the video

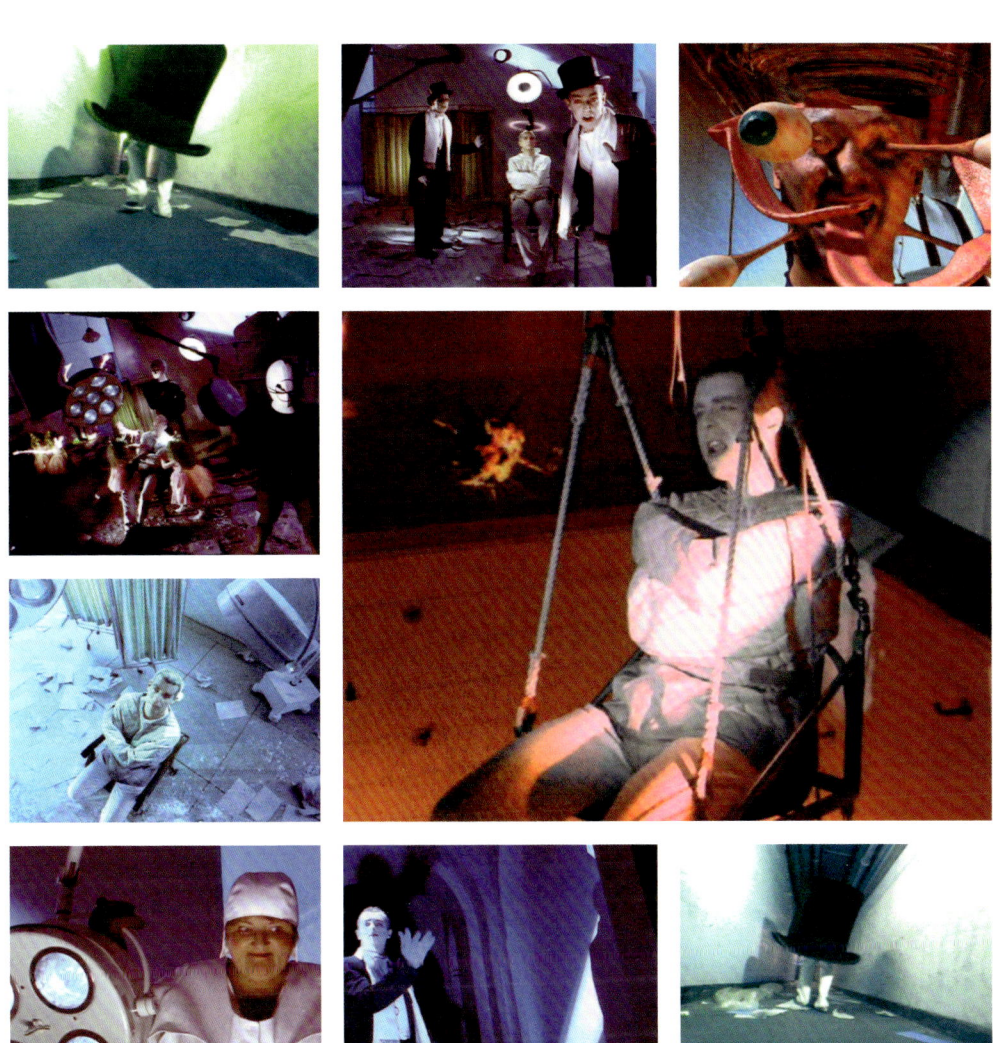

– that after several videos in which the real Pet Shop Boys have been in a computer-generated world, this time there would be computer-generated Pet Shop Boys in the real world.' The process was itself akin to a medical procedure: 'You stand there totally immobile and this scanner goes all the way around you', marvelled Chris. 'The video was surprisingly good', he added. 'I loved being a lampshade…. I look so happy there. Blissfully.'

Disco 2

release 12 September 1994
formats LP / cassette / CD
design Farrow / PSB

The sleeve of the next Pet Shop Boys remix album features a video still of Neil in shades, white fez-like hat, and gloves; Chris appears in the same clothing on the back. A close-up detail of a different still runs down the left-hand side of the cover, where the album's title and the group's name appear in white. This strip is matched on the back by a strip of black containing the track listings and credits. Perversely, perhaps, the black strip and video pattern are repeated *inside* the sleeve, the strip containing further credits. On the CD, the left-hand strip is replaced by the hollow spine of the box, in which is printed the same video detail and text. The image came from a performance by the group of 'Liberation' on an Italian TV show, shot in the same style as the first *Disco* album (pages 78–9). '*Disco* 1 revisited – simple as that, really', says Mark Farrow. This time, though, Neil was on the front cover.

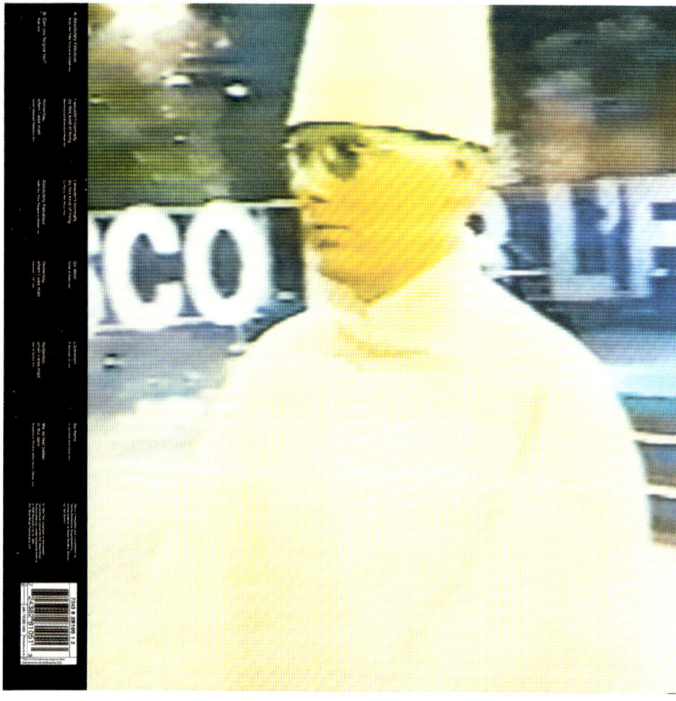

LP, outer sleeve, back

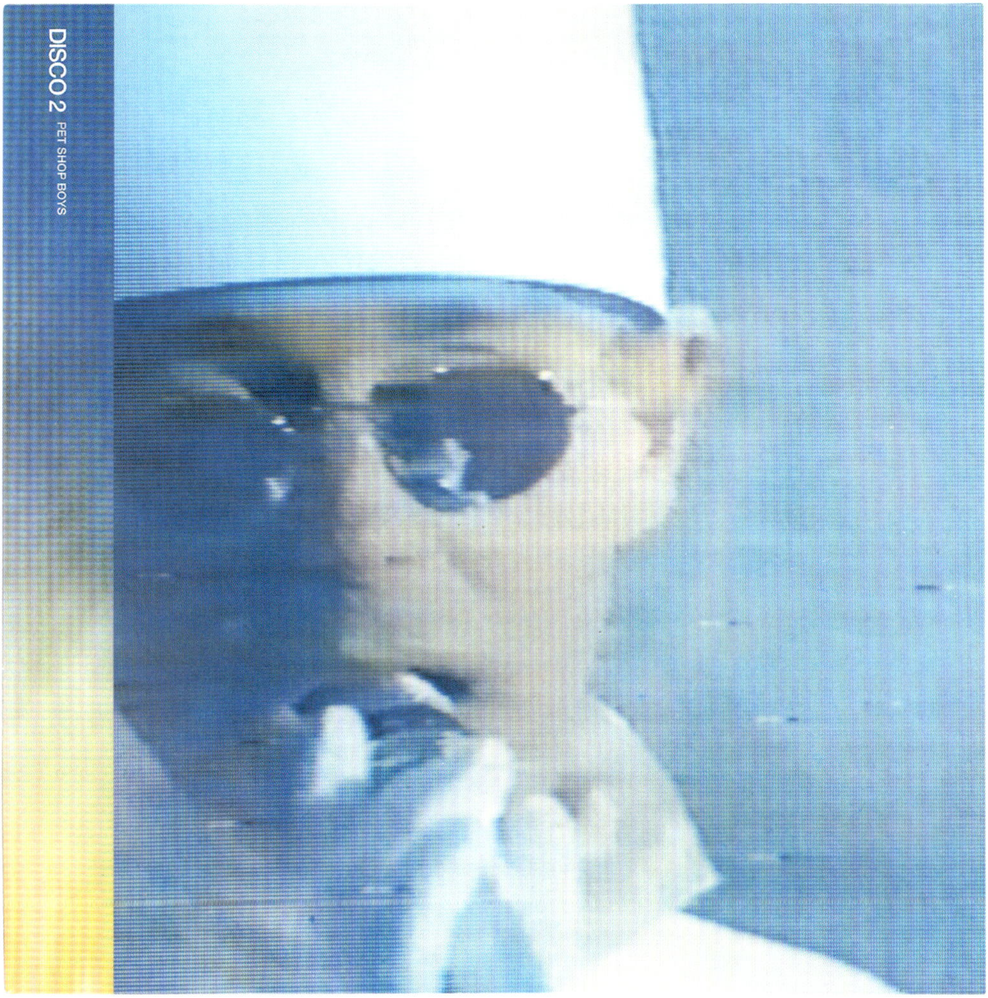

LP, outer sleeve, front

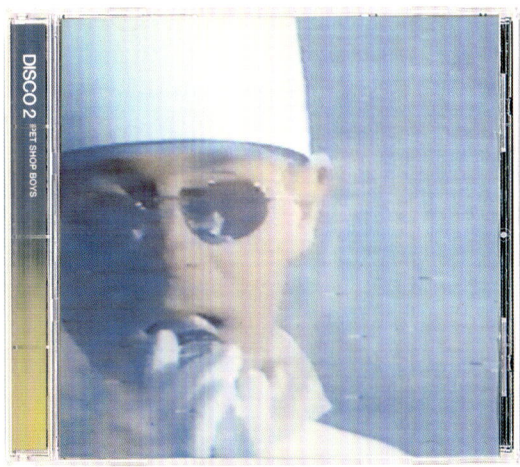

CD, front

Discovery tour

dates 26 October – 11 December 1994
production design Abigail Rosen Holmes
lighting design Abigail Rosen Holmes
choreography Les Child, Claire Eastman

For their *Discovery* tour of Singapore, Australia, and Central and South America, Pet Shop Boys wanted a performance that reflected the sense of sun and sexual liberation that could be found in places like Brazil. 'We went to the Sound Factory bar in New York and we liked the fact that they had live drummers playing along with the music, and they had these naked men go-go dancing with flags around them', Neil noted. 'We totally took both ideas – the percussion and the dancers – from that.' It was 'probably the most popular tour we ever did in terms of the sheer enjoyment factor', Neil recalled. 'That was fun', Chris agreed. 'The whole thing about it was that it was a fun, sexy party show.' 'It was meant to be a party', Neil said. 'We got dancers who were just hired to be like go-go dancers, although of course we then spent weeks choreographing them. And we reused things: some of the Derek Jarman films, some costumes, and sort of brought everything we'd ever done together.' 'It was the most rock 'n' roll show we've done', Chris said. 'It was a straight-up concert in many ways. Apart from the naked people in cages. And the wigs.' 'And the coned hats with lights on', Neil added. 'We're selling pointy hats as merchandise, and we're hoping the audience will wear them', Neil said at the time. 'I'd love to see 8,000 people in pointy hats. It'd be a great feeling.' 'I think this show reflects how we've changed', Chris noted. 'We're more liberated. I think we're more liberated as people.' 'Is that meant seriously?' Neil rejoined. 'It's quite nice if it is, actually.'

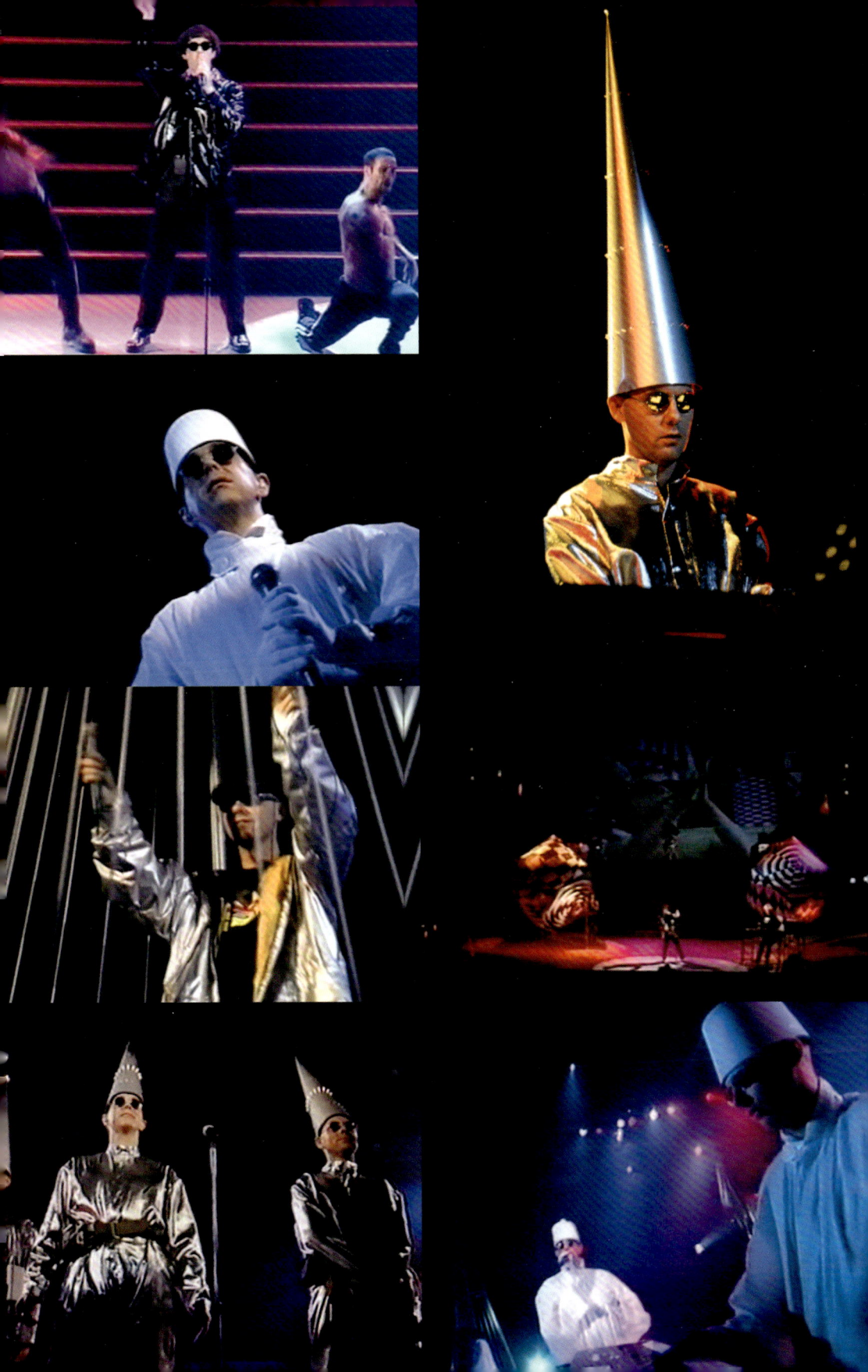

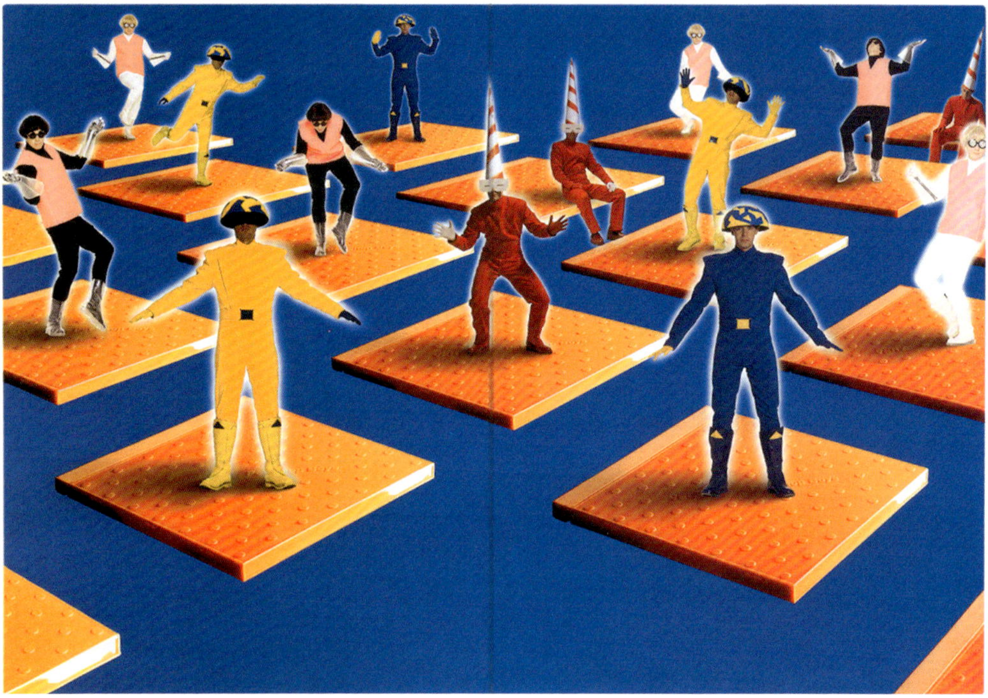

Tour programme, cover

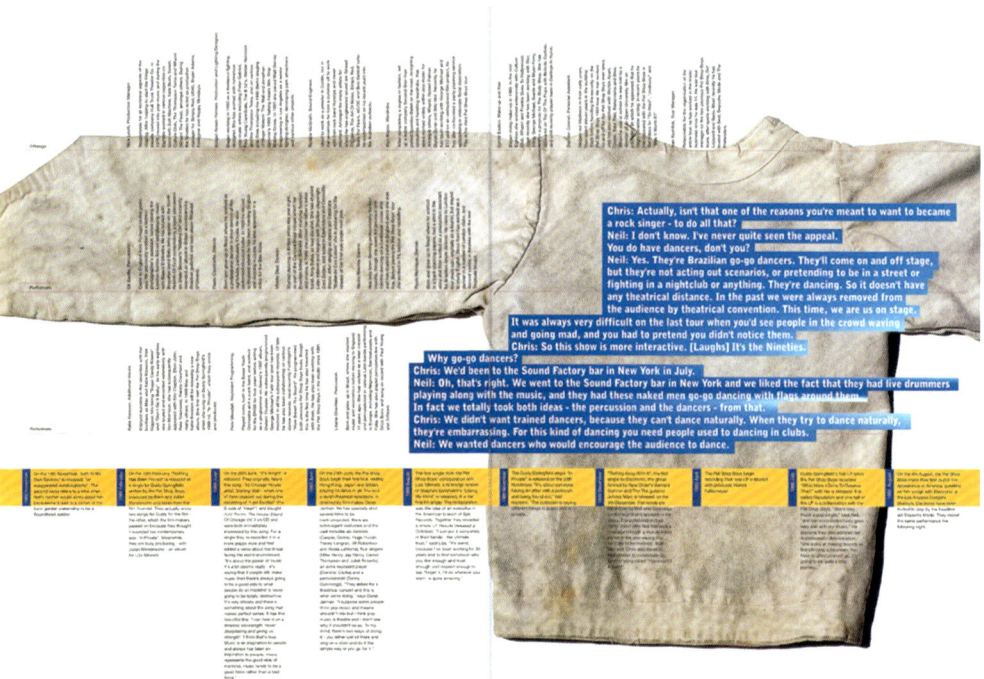

Tour programme, centrefold

210 Discovery tour 1994

The format of the tour programme – designed by Rob Petrie, Mark Farrow, and Phil Sims at Farrow – followed the template set by those of the two previous tours. It reused various design elements that had featured on releases from the *Very* era. Here, the cover is a wraparound compilation of *Very* images originally used in the television advertisement for the album, showing different characters dancing on the 'Lego' CD box. The title page has a different video still from the Italian TV appearance that featured on the cover of *Disco 2* (pages 206–7), showing both Neil and Chris in all-white 'Absolutely fabulous' costumes and fez hats. Other pages mixed elements from recent releases, such as the straitjacket from 'Yesterday, when I was mad' (pages 202–3), with a typographic treatment similar to that on 'Liberation' (pages 198–9).

A video of the Rio de Janeiro date on the *Discovery* tour was shot by a local crew and then edited back in London. The colours of Mark Farrow's cover hint at the Brazilian flag, and the liberated tone of the tour itself. The cover photograph by Andy Earl shows the tips of the metallic pointy hats the Pet Shop Boys wore for 'Go west' at the show's end, which, at a climactic moment (and when surreptiously switched on manually by each Pet Shop Boy wearer) had rings of lights that moved up towards the hats' points, over and over.

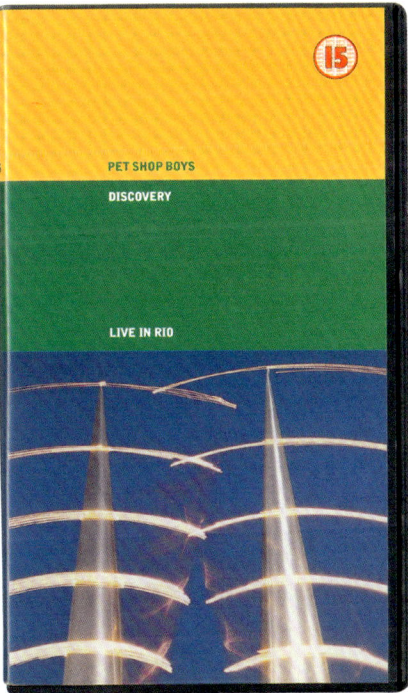

VHS, front

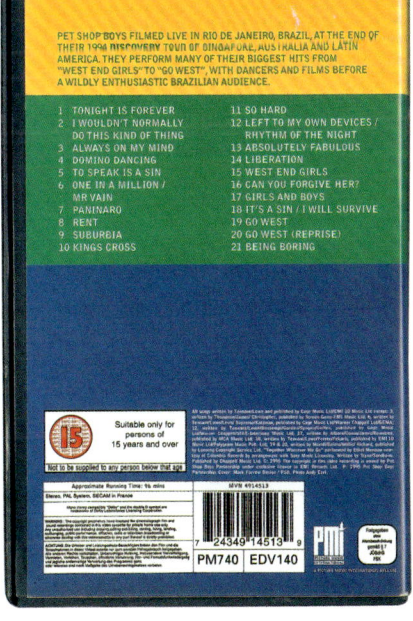

VHS, back

Various

release 6 March 1995
formats VHS / laserdisc (Austria, Japan, US)
photographers Trevor Key, Chris Nash, and Andy Earl
design Farrow

The third collection of Pet Shop Boys' promotional videos, Various covers the Very period, from 'Can you forgive her?' to 'Yesterday, when I was mad', and also includes the video for 'Absolutely fabulous', the group's charity single with the stars of the show of that name, Jennifer Saunders and Joanna Lumley. The cover of Various used a compilation of Very-era images similar to the one that appeared on the Discovery tour programme.

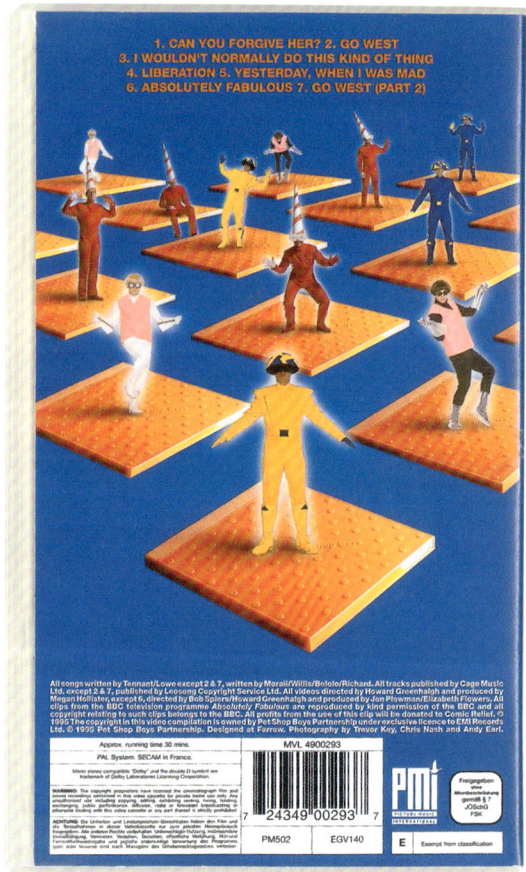

VHS, back

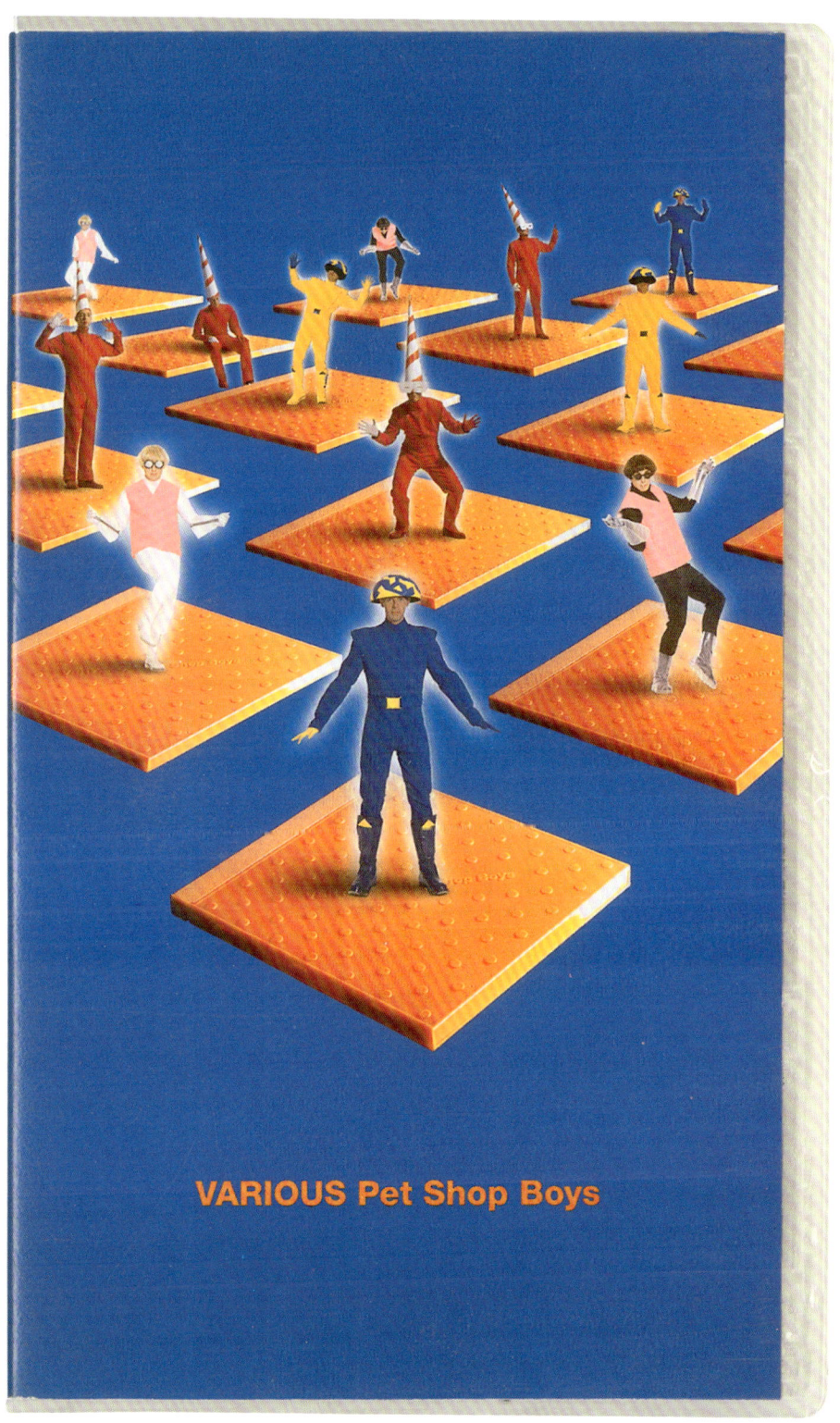

VHS, front

Paninaro '95

release 31 July 1995
formats 12" remix × 2 / 12" promo × 2 /
Limited-edition yellow cassette /
cassette promo / CD × 2 / CD remix
photographer Eric Watson
design Mark Farrow Design / PSB
video Howard Greenhalgh

'Possibly my least favourite PSB cover', says Neil. Based on the live version Chris had performed on the *Discovery* tour, with a new rap in the middle, the song was recorded as a single to coincide with *Alternative* (pages 220–1) after a discussion of what kind of single one could release to promote an album of B-sides: a very Pet Shop Boys dilemma. In designing the CD sleeves, Mark Farrow reasoned that as the song was famous in its earlier version, 'everyone knew passion, love, sex, money'. He cropped into the Eric Watson photographs that he had been supplied, finding a colour or texture that seemed to complement the word in each of the quadrants: 'Passion was red, love was green, and sex was the kind of plasticy outfit that Chris had on.' For the second CD, he simply carried on with the song lyrics – 'Violence, religion, injustice, and death' – choosing different details for each one. Some of these details were also printed on the CD discs, while the complete images were included inside the gatefold box. For the two promo twelve-inch records, Farrow used the same details but, instead of the lyrics, he put the titles of the tracks in each square.

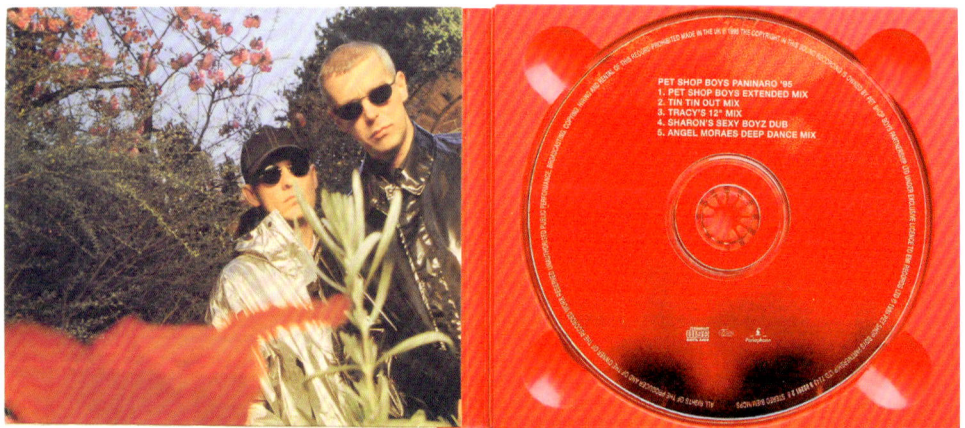

CD 1, inside

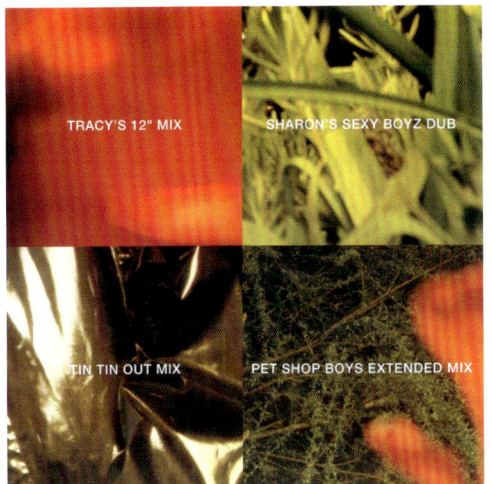

12" promo, Part One, front

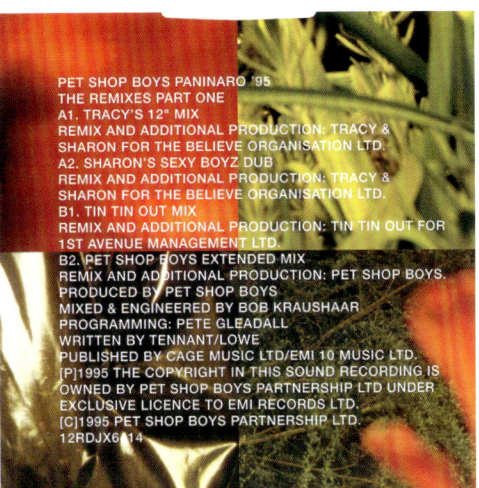

12" promo, Part One, back

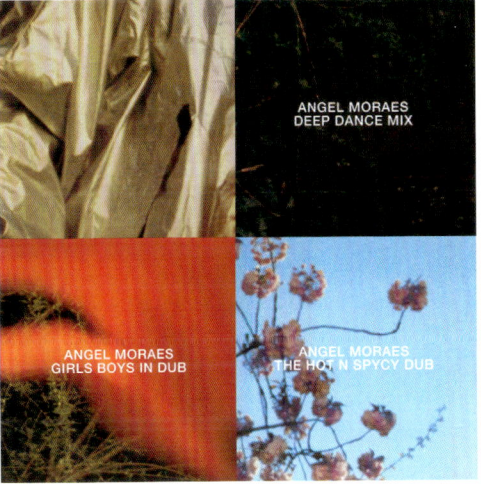

12" promo, Part Two, front

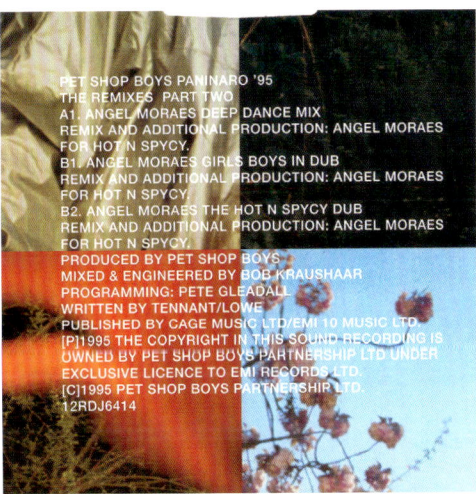

12" promo, Part Two, back

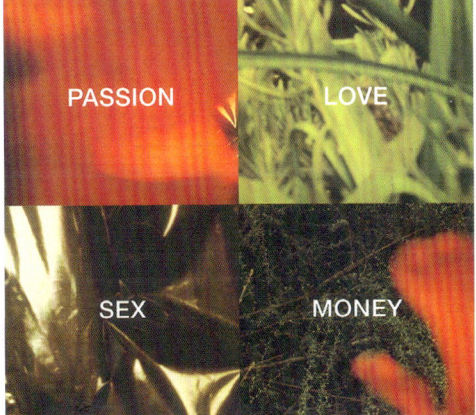

CD 1, front

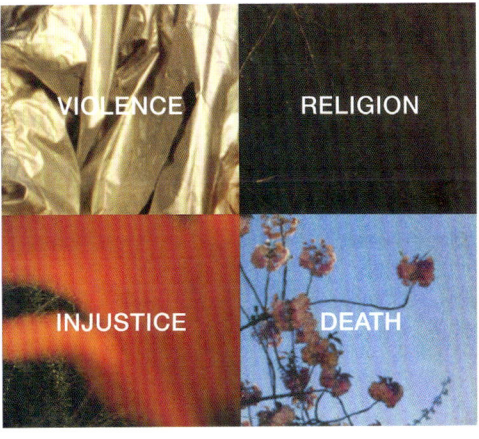

CD 2, front

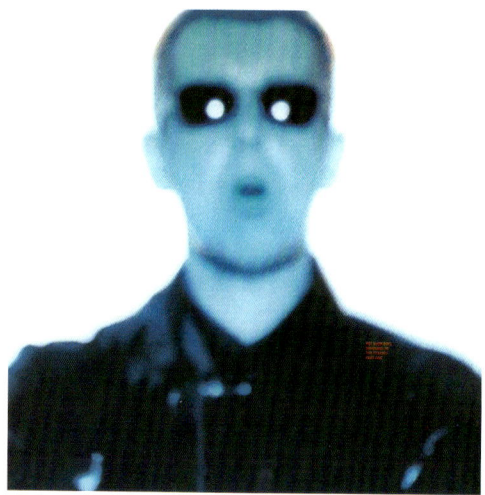
12" remix, Part One, front

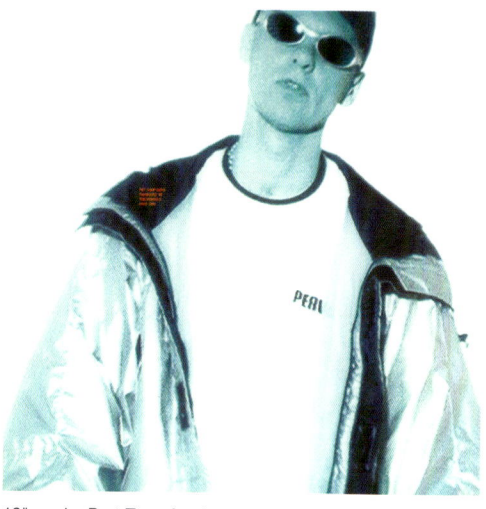
12" remix, Part Two, front

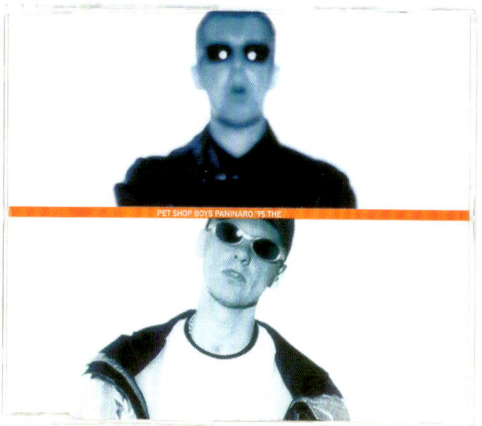
CD remix, front

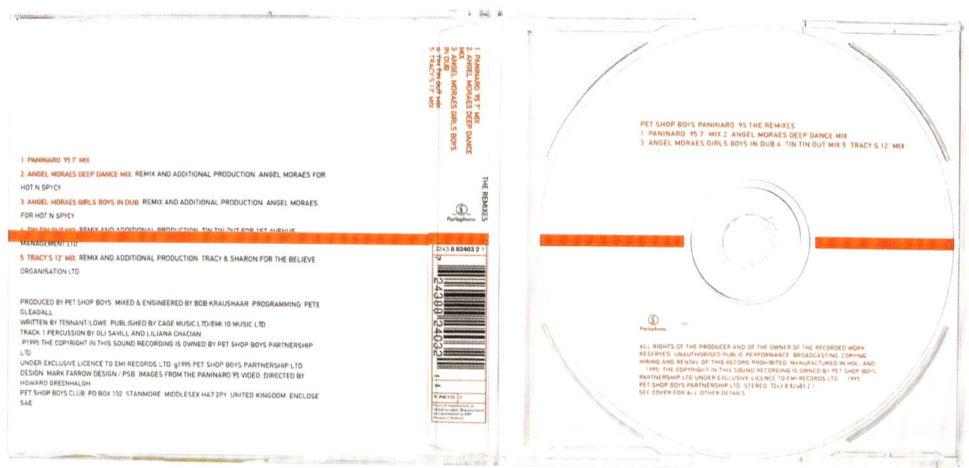
CD remix, inside

The two remix twelve-inch records and CD all used two particularly striking images of Neil and Chris taken from the 'Paninaro '95' video (pages 218–19), which were then cut out and set against a white background. The typography on the twelve-inch records – orange to complement the blue cast of the images – was perhaps the most minimal to date in Pet Shop Boys' output. Not only is it set very small and in not-instantly noticeable positions, but also the information (track listings and credits, etcetera) is kept to the absolute minimum. On the CD, orange once again plays a prominent role, here running as a thin line across the centre of the booklet beneath the jewel case. The lines continues inside the case, running across the centre of the back of the booklet and across the CD itself, which is painted white.

12" remix, Part Two, back

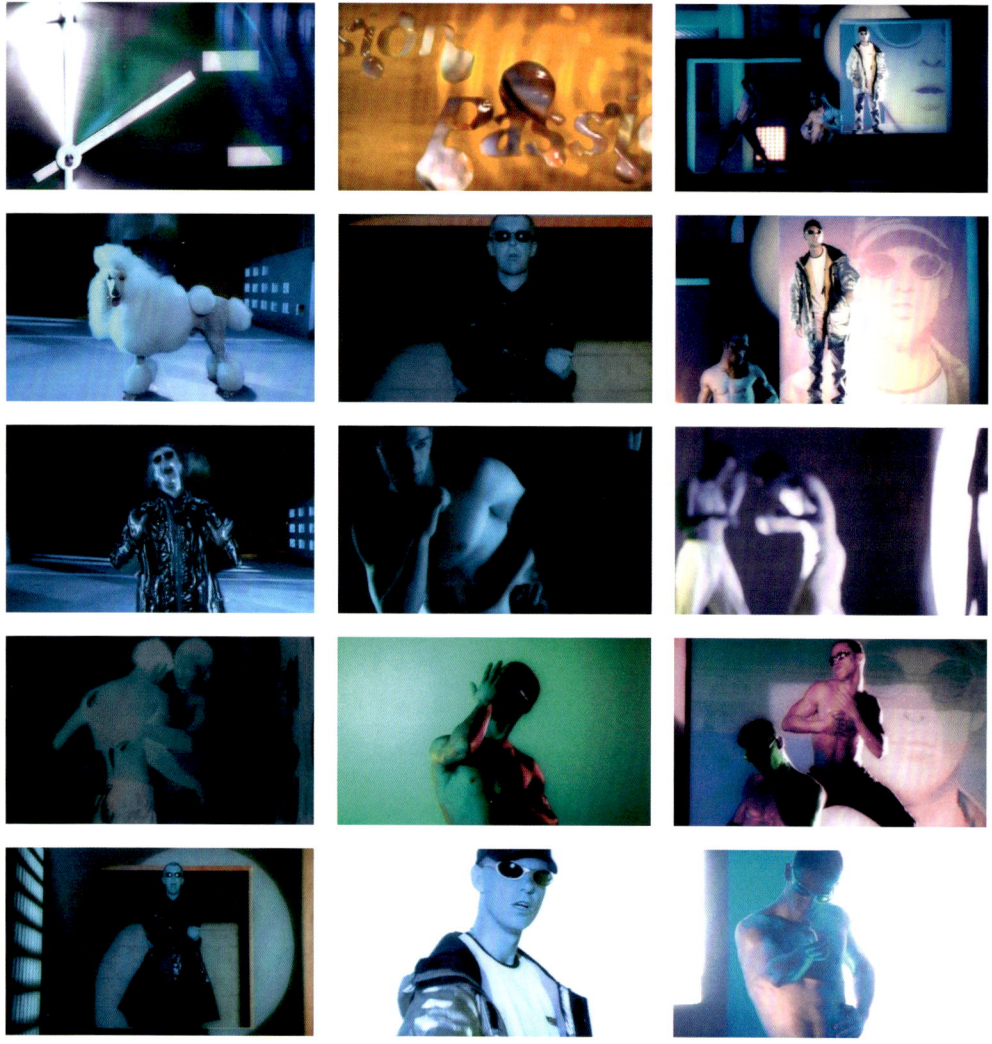

Gauges and shapes resolve into the key words of the song: 'Love, sex, passion, money', and so on. As with the original 'Paninaro' video (pages 76–7), Chris, unusually the lead singer on the track, dominates the action, while Neil is a shadowy figure moving through a dystopian futuristic world, partly another computer generation. Neil and Chris are seen in real life, while liquid muscle men – in the style of *Terminator 2* – dance and pose in an exaggerated fashion. Neil and Chris perform to the camera in boxes. A poodle is seen. At various times, Neil dances and walks across the screen in a shiny mac and gets transformed, *Matrix*-style, into contorted forms, apparently in great pain and anguish before being returned to his original state. Boxers – one of whom, David Walker, is a friend of the group – spar, shirtless, in jogging pants, while other near-naked men gyrate to the music. Chris raps to the camera, close up, his face bathed in warm light. 'I think we went homoerotic on this one', says Neil.

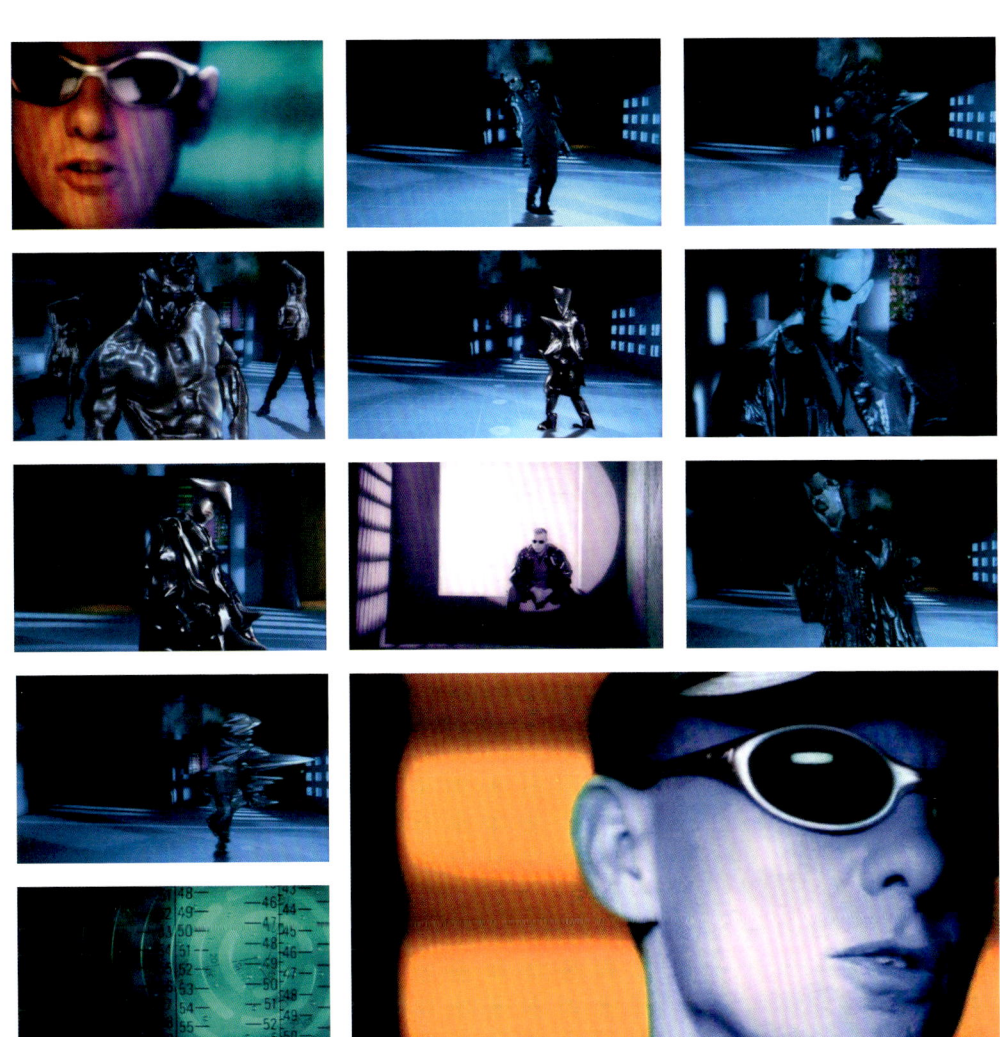

Alternative

release 7 August 1995
formats Triple-disc LP / double cassette / double CD
photographers Richard Burbridge (masks),
Eric Watson (interview portraits)
design concept Phil Sims, Mark Farrow, and
Rob Petrie at Farrow
design Mark Farrow with Pete Mauder at Farrow

Originally this album of B-sides and extra tracks from CD singles was to be entitled 'Besides'. The first copies of the CD, cassette, and LP had a lenticular image that shifted between Neil and Chris, who are wearing fencing masks. They were photographed in the masks by Richard Burbridge. The idea of using a lenticular image that changes back and forth between Neil and Chris was Mark Farrow's response to the title *Alternative*: 'It gave you an alternative – it was that straightforward. It alternated.' The triple-disc LP came in a black box set with elegant embossed silver lettering on the reverse. Inside, the same images, but this time just ordinary photographs, appeared on the three inner sleeves. Also included in the box set was a booklet that contained an interview between Pet Shop Boys and Jon Savage and portaits by Eric Watson.

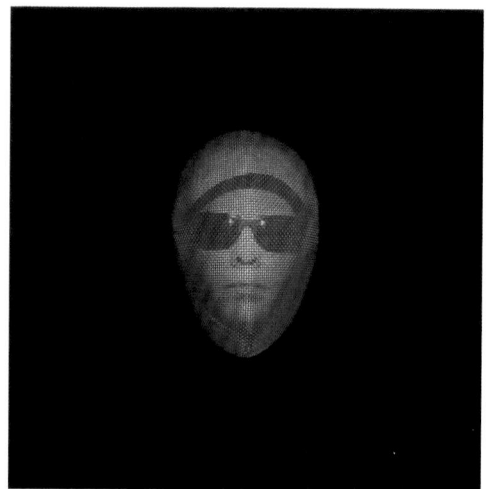
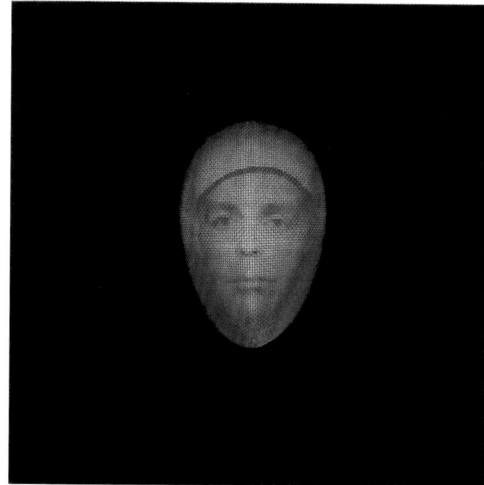

LP, inner sleeve 2, front   LP, inner sleeve 3, front

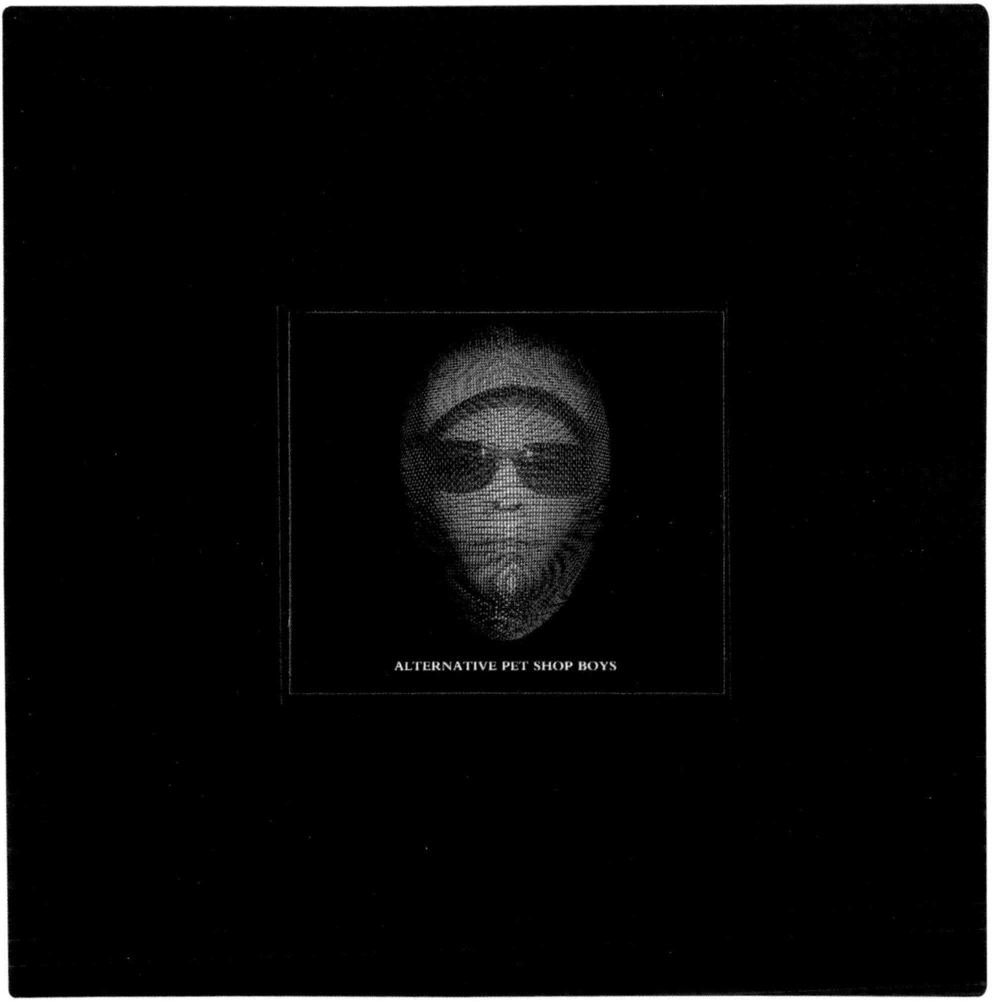

LP, outer box, front

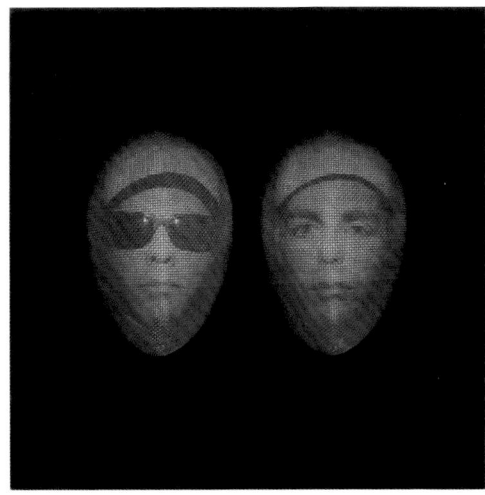

LP, inner sleeve 1, front

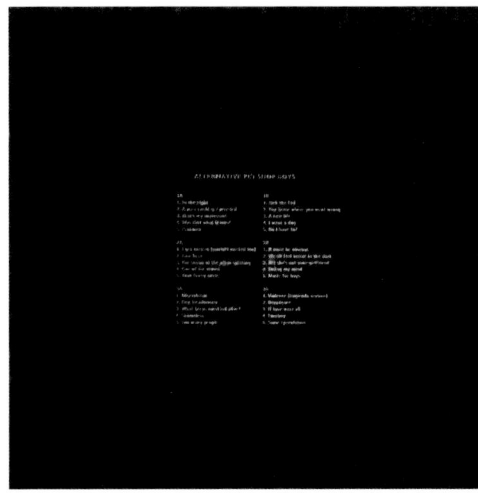

LP, outer box, back

Before

release 22 April 1996
formats 12" promo × 3 / limited-edition 12"
triple-disc box set / cassette / CD × 2 / CD promo
photographer Brad Branson
design Mark Farrow Design / PSB
video Howard Greenhalgh

'Before' was the first single from the next album, *Bilingual*. By this stage, the principal product was almost always the CD, and most of the effort went into designing that format. Brad Branson's portraits of Neil and Chris have a 'solarized' effect, as used by the early twentieth-century artist Man Ray, which gives them a shiny, glossy, almost metallic feel. 'This is where Mark Farrow got into spot varnish', says Neil. Farrow used the varnish to coat the portraits, further accentuating their glossiness, and continued it round inside the CD sleeves where all the track listings and credits appeared. The limited-edition twelve-inch triple-disc box set came in a grey-green box with tiny lettering that matched the typography inside the CD. The inner sleeves were effectively the CD sleeves opened up, with the spot varnish and type in the same places. The twelve-inch promos are among the rarest of all Pet Shop Boys releases, and perhaps the most controversial. The colours again reflect a Warholian sensibility. A single penis is used for the 'Before' promo (representing 'before' sex); two penises together are used for the separately distributed promo of the B-side, 'The truck-driver and his mate'. 'It's a song about male bonding', noted Chris.

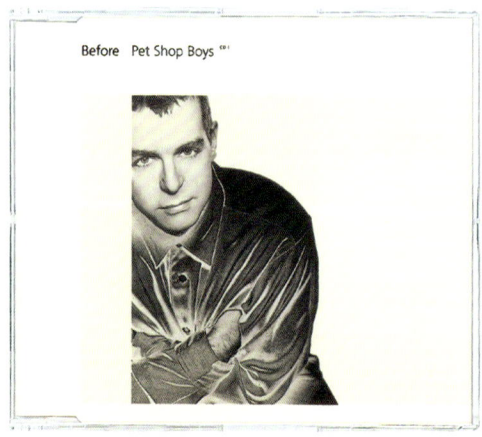

CD 1, front

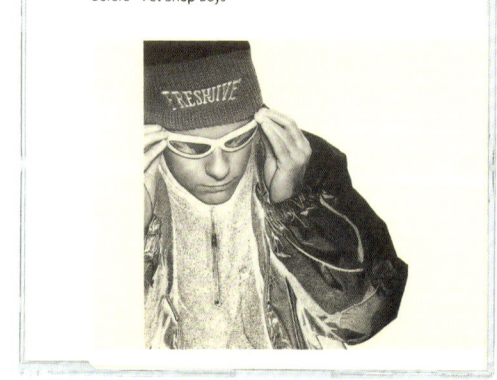

CD 2, front

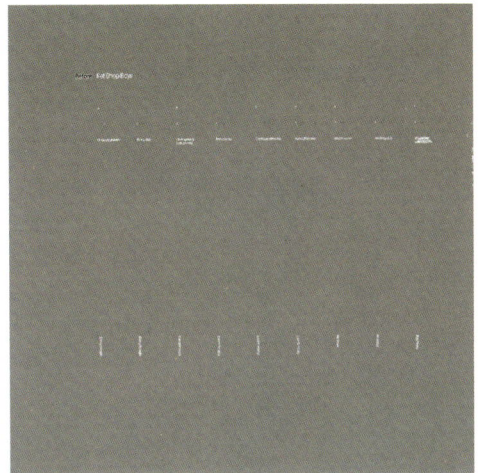

Limited-edition 12" triple-disc box set, front

Limited-edition 12" triple-disc box set, back

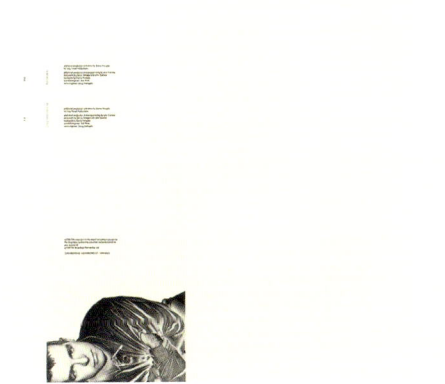

Limited-edition 12" triple-disc box set, Side A, inner sleeve

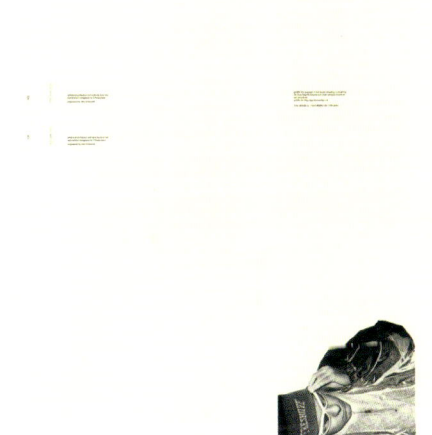

Limited-edition 12" triple-disc box set, Side E, inner sleeve

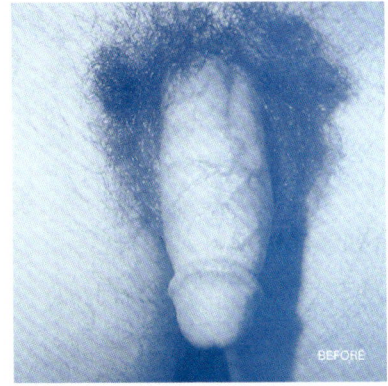

12" promo 1, front

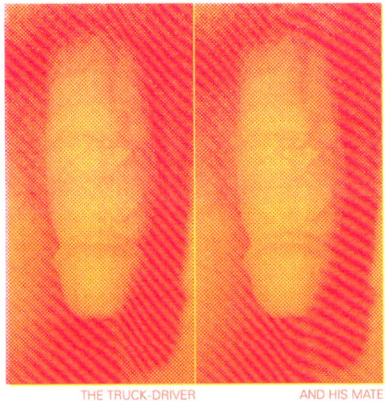

12" promo 3 ('The truck-driver and his mate'), front

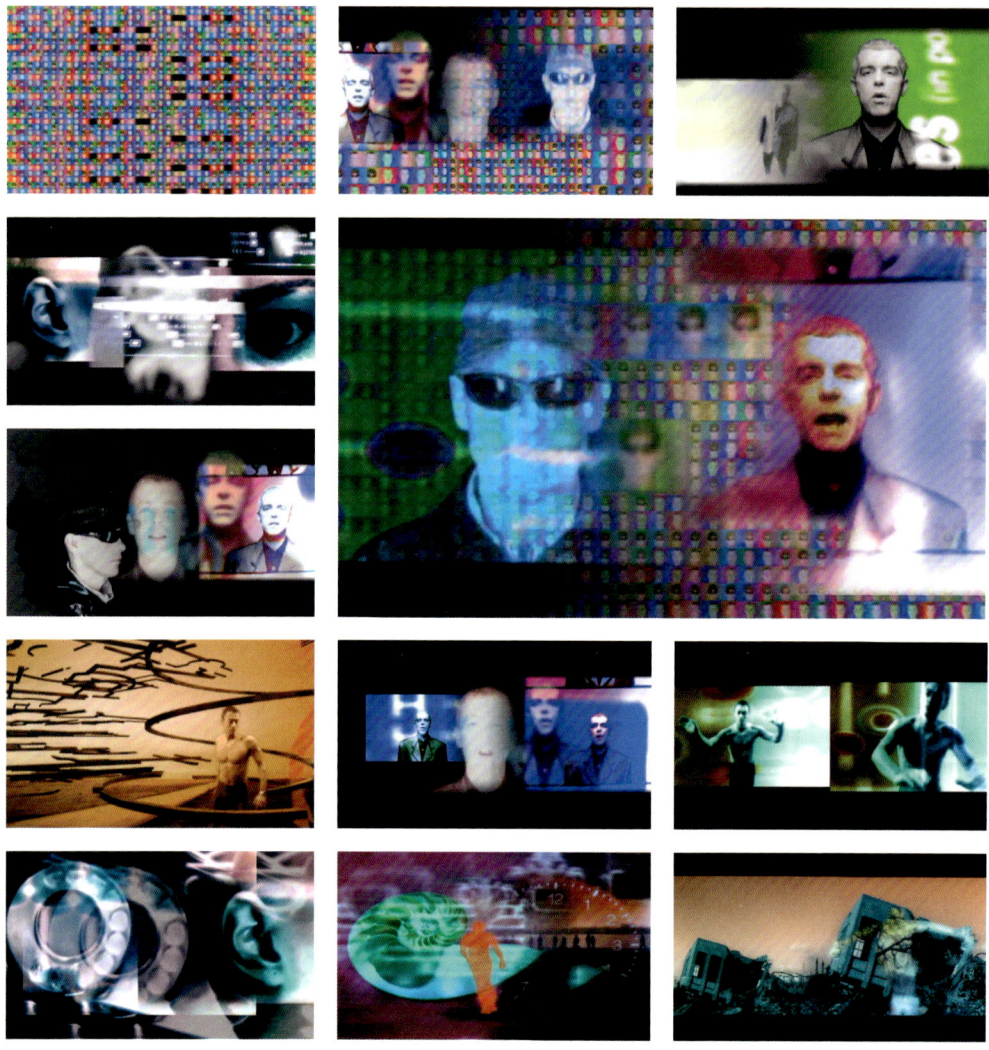

In this extremely complex video, we see desert scenes and topless men; fragmentary figures scattered across the screen, or is it screens? Close-up eyes and old-fashioned telephone dials appear constantly; Neil's and Chris's faces are multiplied ad infinitum towards and away from the viewer. While most of the images were filmed in a studio, some shots are from Dungeness in Kent, close to Derek Jarman's house there, although processed in post-production so that they look as otherworldly as the other images in the video. It is never clear if this is a computerized or real world we are looking at. 'It's really complicated', Neil said at the time. The video also featured the song's three backing singers, Barbara Tucker, Karen Bernard, and Carol Sylvan. 'It was a very quick video', Neil recalls. 'We were only there for four hours.' Howard Greenhalgh – who can be seen in silhouette in the video – developed the group's idea for an incredibly split-screen picture.

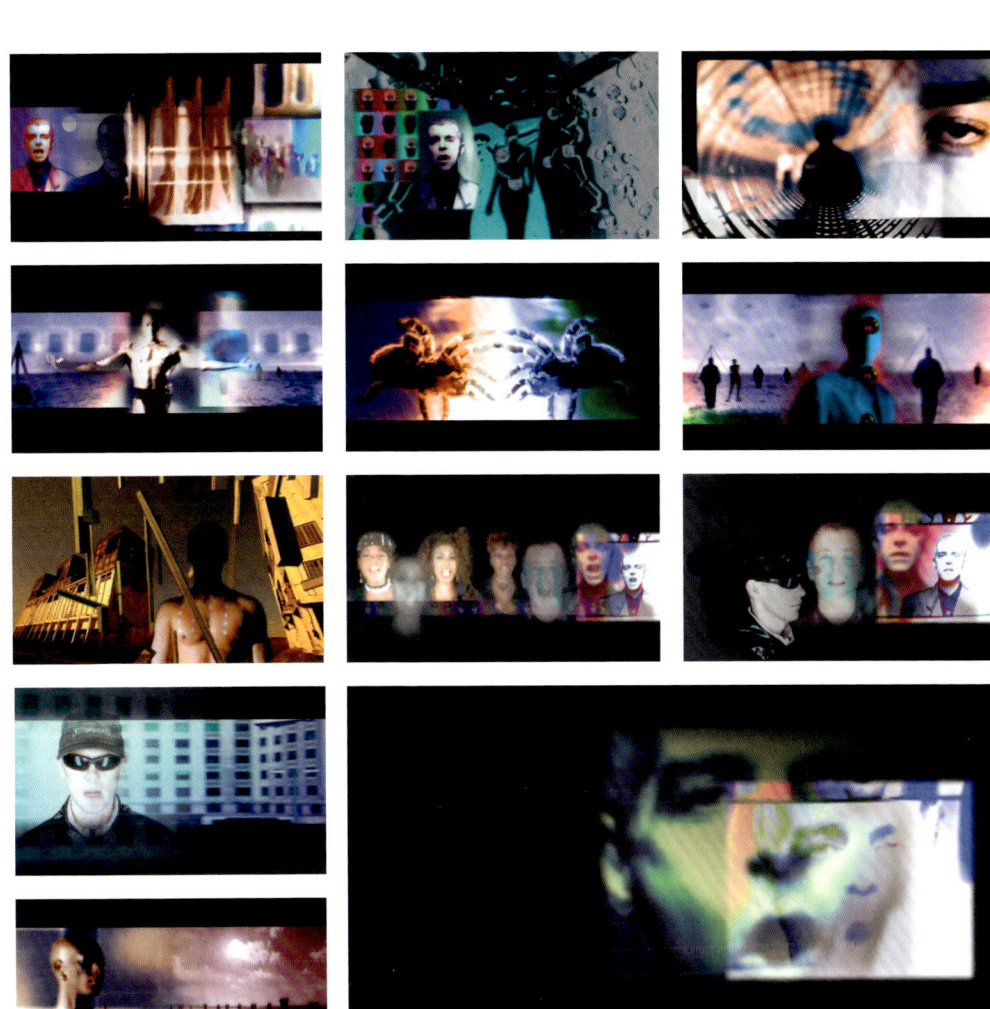

Se a vida é (That's the way life is)

release 12 August 1996
formats Double 12" / 12" promo × 2 / cassette / CD × 2
photographer Lynda Churilla (for Bruce Weber)
design Mark Farrow Design / PSB
video Bruce Weber

As had been the case with 'Before', the principal format of the 'Se a vida é' release was the CD. Here Mark Farrow used a series of photographs taken during the making of the song's video (pages 232–3). 'We're back in Bruce Weber land', says Neil. All of the images came from the video session shot at the Wet 'n' Wild theme park in Florida and were used across the range of CD singles, twelve-inch sleeves, and promos. 'I was just given a big old box of fantastic photographs of fantastic looking people', says Farrow. It was very easy – it was summery and fun and wet and sexy. It was just a joy, that sleeve. It was like the song.' Reflecting the song's summer theme, Farrow employed suitably bright colours for all the formats, packaging the CDs and the discs in vivid yellow and printing the photographs in duotone pink, blue, green, red, and orange with the occasional white panel. He then made elaborate use of flecks of spot varnish to achieve a water-splash effect on the images and white panels. 'Very designed', says Neil. For Farrow, it is 'One of my favourites. From a design point of view it's more or less exactly the same layout as "Before".' The design of the CD fronts is continued inside the sleeves (page 228).

The two-disc twelve inch (pages 228–9) continued the same summery theme of the CDs, but on the outer sleeve Farrow replaced the images with plain panels in the colours in which he had printed the CD photographs. Once again, spot varnish was used to create the water effect. For the inner sleeves, he used mainly different photos from the Wet 'n' Wild session, printing them in the same duotone colours as on the CDs. For this release, the design concept was carried through to the discs themselves, which were pressed in a fluorescent green and yellow vinyl. The labels repeat the coloured-panel device on the outer sleeve, but here are printed in different colours.

The two twelve-inch promos (pages 230–1) featured some of the same photographs that had been used on the two-disc twelve inch and CDs, although here the colours are pared down to just two, with the images being printed in fluorescent yellow and blue-purple. Again the discs were coloured, one in fluorescent yellow, the other in blue-purple.

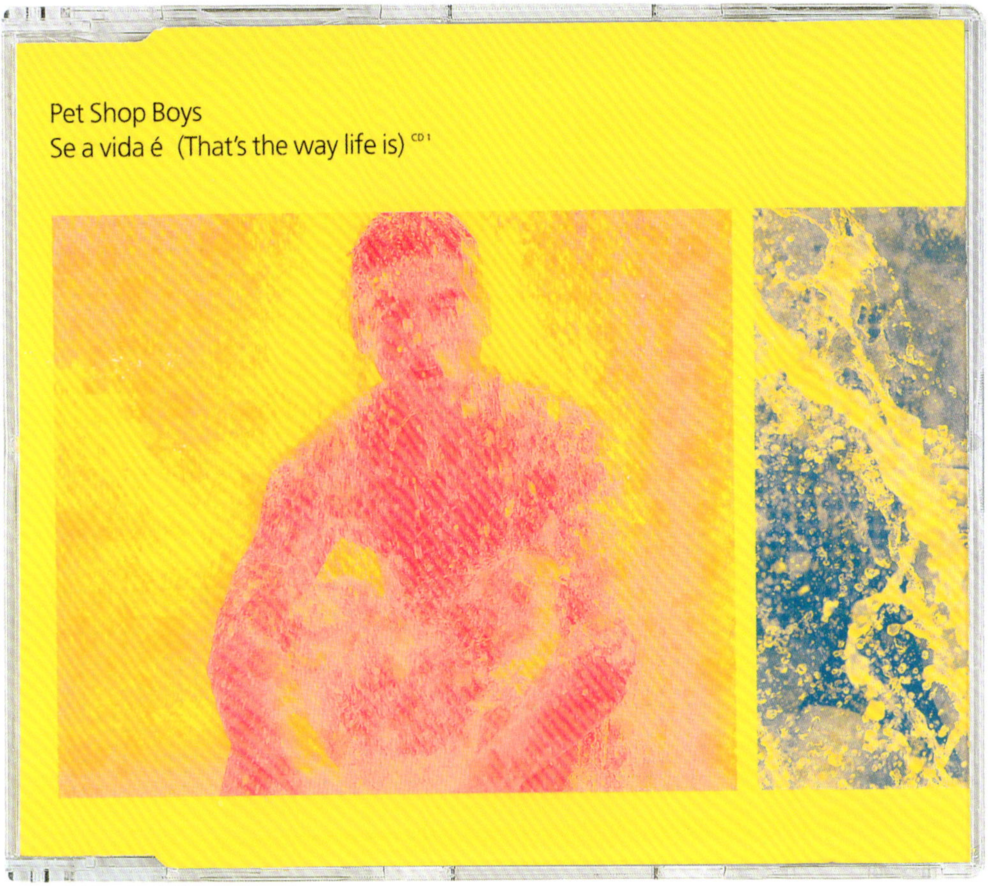

Pet Shop Boys
Se a vida é (That's the way life is) CD 1

CD 1, front

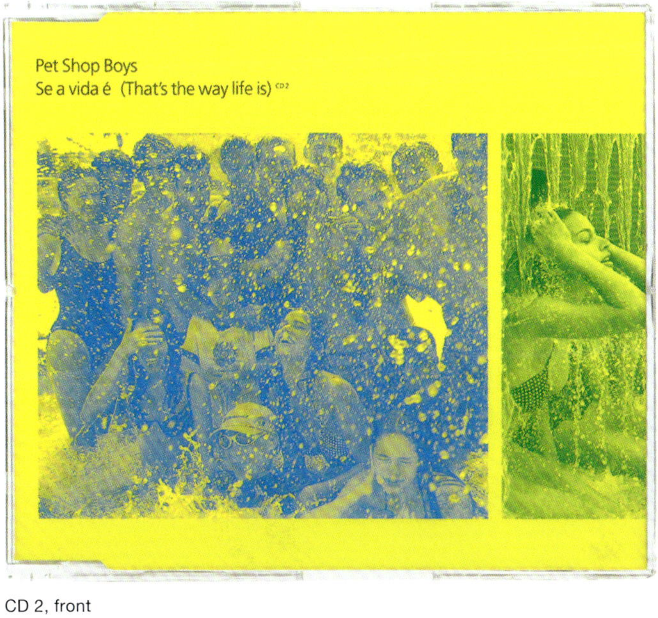

Pet Shop Boys
Se a vida é (That's the way life is) CD 2

CD 2, front

Se a vida é (That's the way life is) 1996 227

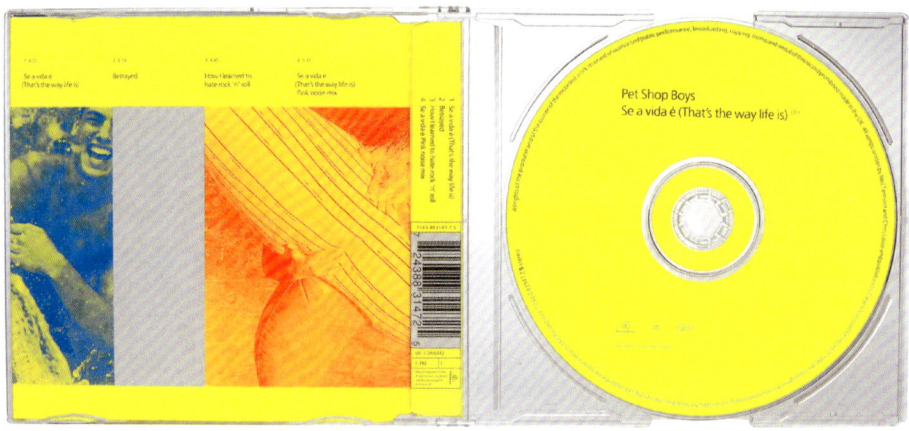

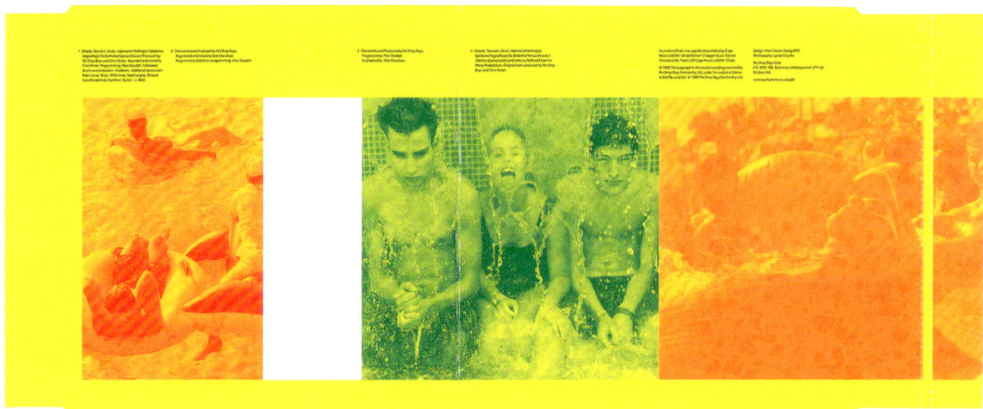

CD 1, inside and inner sleeve (inside)

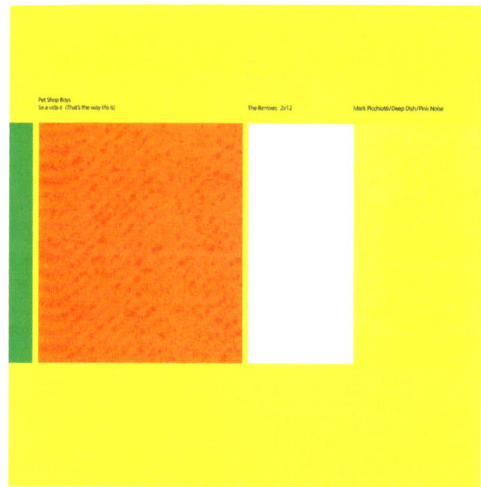

Double 12", outer sleeve, front

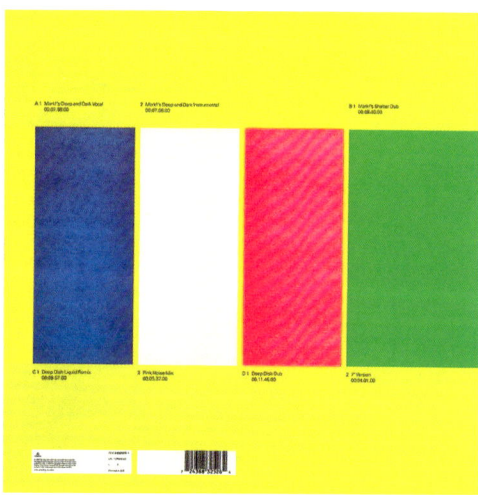

Double 12", outer sleeve, back

Se a vida é (That's the way life is) 1996

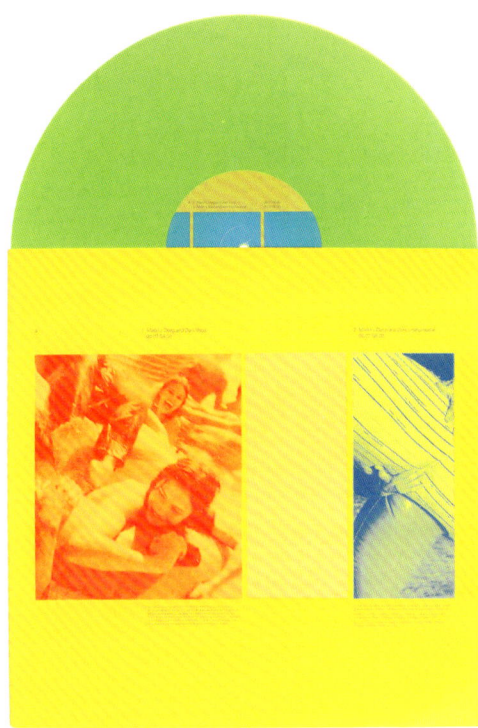

Double 12", Side A/B, inner sleeve, front, and disc

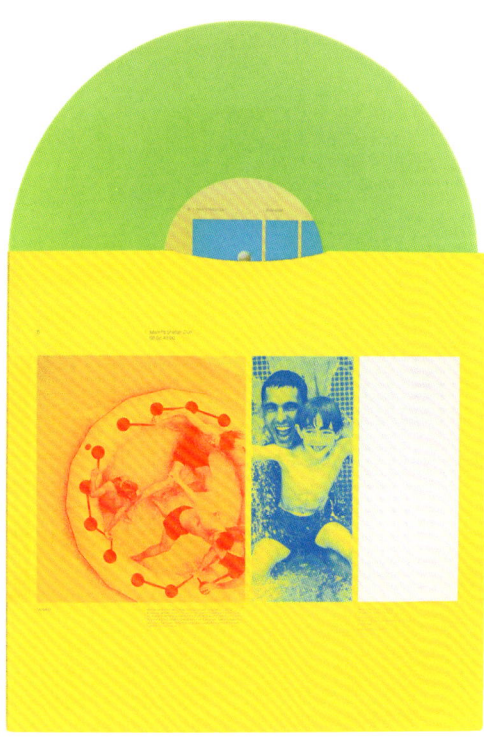

Double 12", Side A/B, inner sleeve, back, and disc

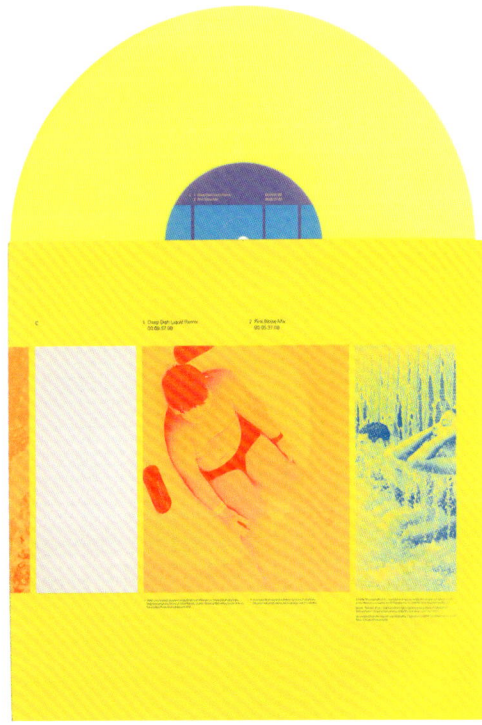

Double 12", Side C/D, inner sleeve, front, and disc

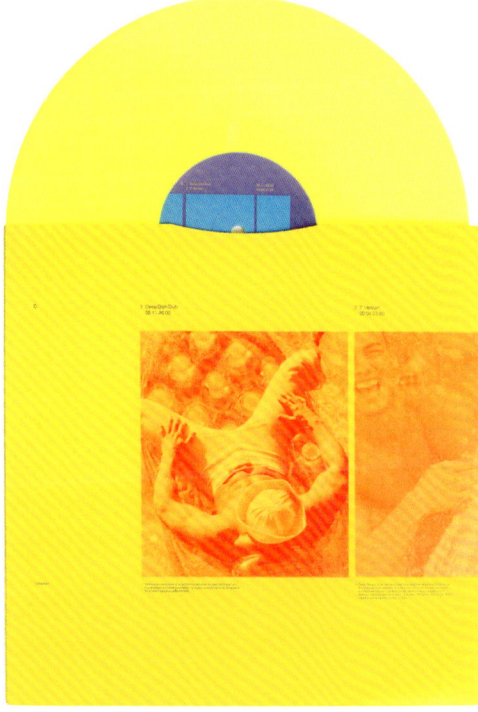

Double 12", Side C/D, inner sleeve, back, and disc

Se a vida é (That's the way life is) 1996

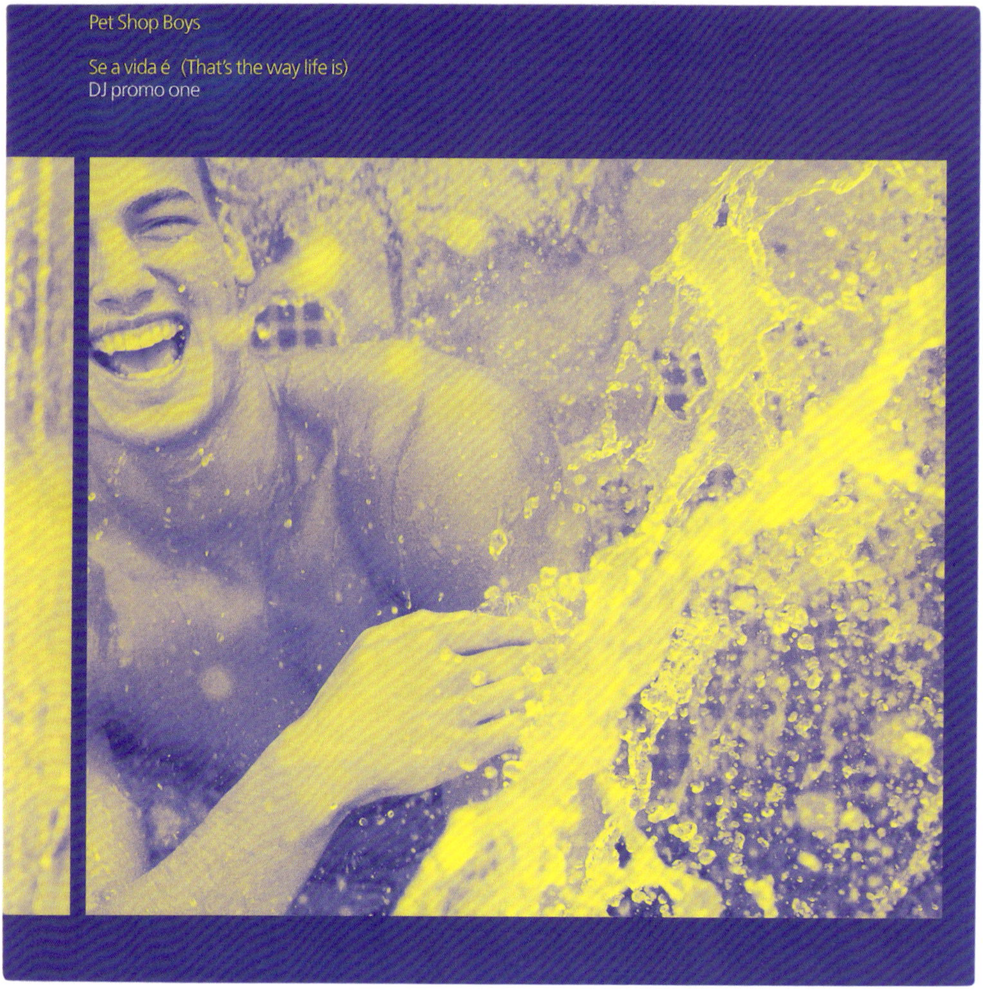

Pet Shop Boys
Se a vida é (That's the way life is)
DJ promo one

12" promo 1, front

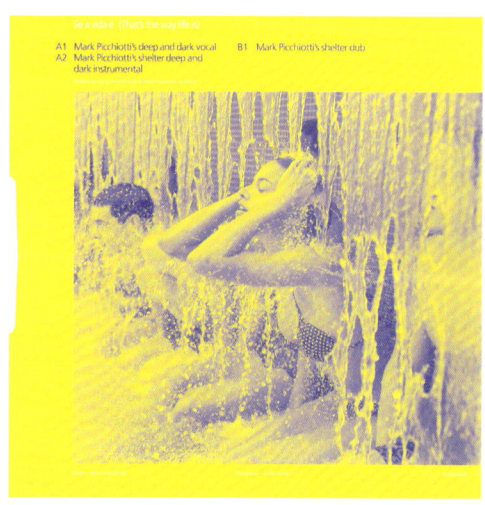

12" promo 1, back

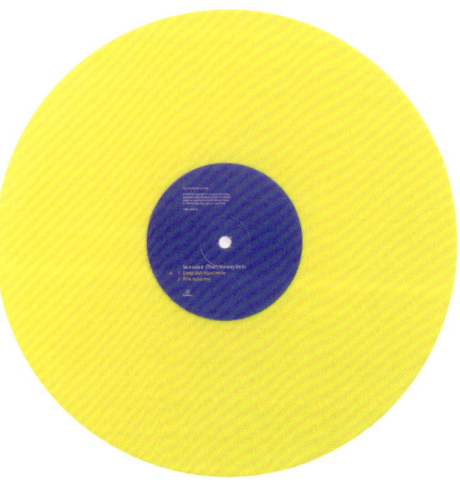

12" promo 2, fluorescent-yellow disc

230   Se a vida é (That's the way life is)   1996

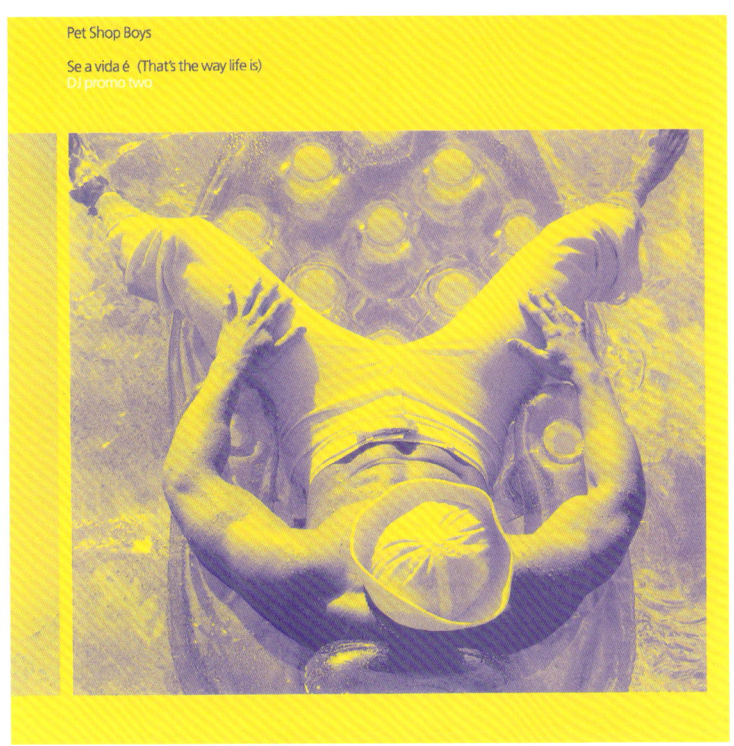

12" promo 2, front

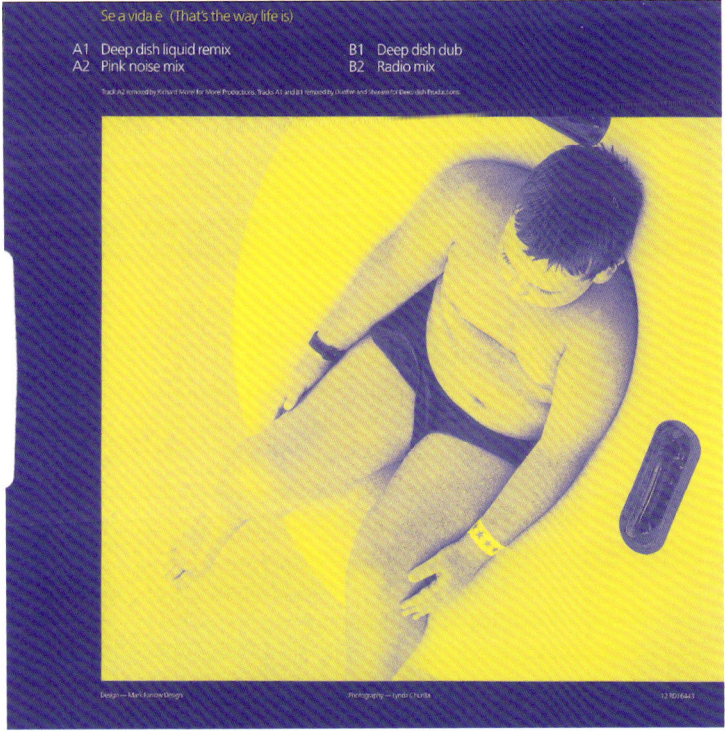

12" promo 2, back

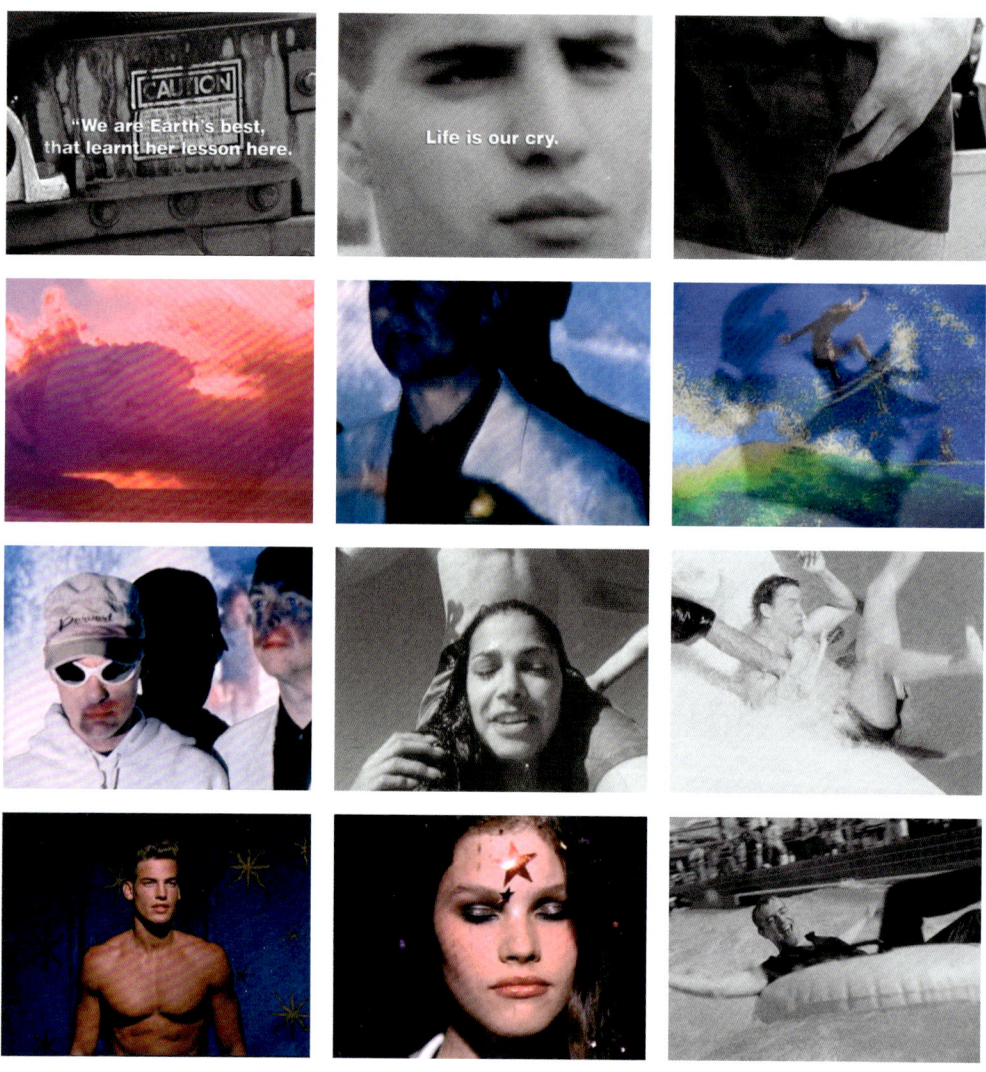

This was the second Pet Shop Boys video to be directed by Bruce Weber and was filmed at the Wet 'n' Wild leisure park in Florida. In slow black and white, the video starts with close-up images of machinery and boys in swimming trunks clutching their crotches as they begin a descent down a water slide, while captions flash up lyrical quotes from poet Rupert Brooke. Suddenly, as the song begins properly, the film erupts into colour. Surfers and kids play. The footage in the park, again in black and white, is highly charged with beautiful tanned bodies, but with 'ordinary' people, too. 'I like the suburban-ness of it, all these people in bathing suits ... the weird attitude of it all', said Weber. Adding more glamour to the scene, he stuck a star to Neil's forehead and a smaller one to Chris's cheek; and then assistants showered them with stars. The two are seen in glimpses, posed, with a film of surfers projected onto their faces and white clothes. Weber became feverishly excited as this was filmed, his

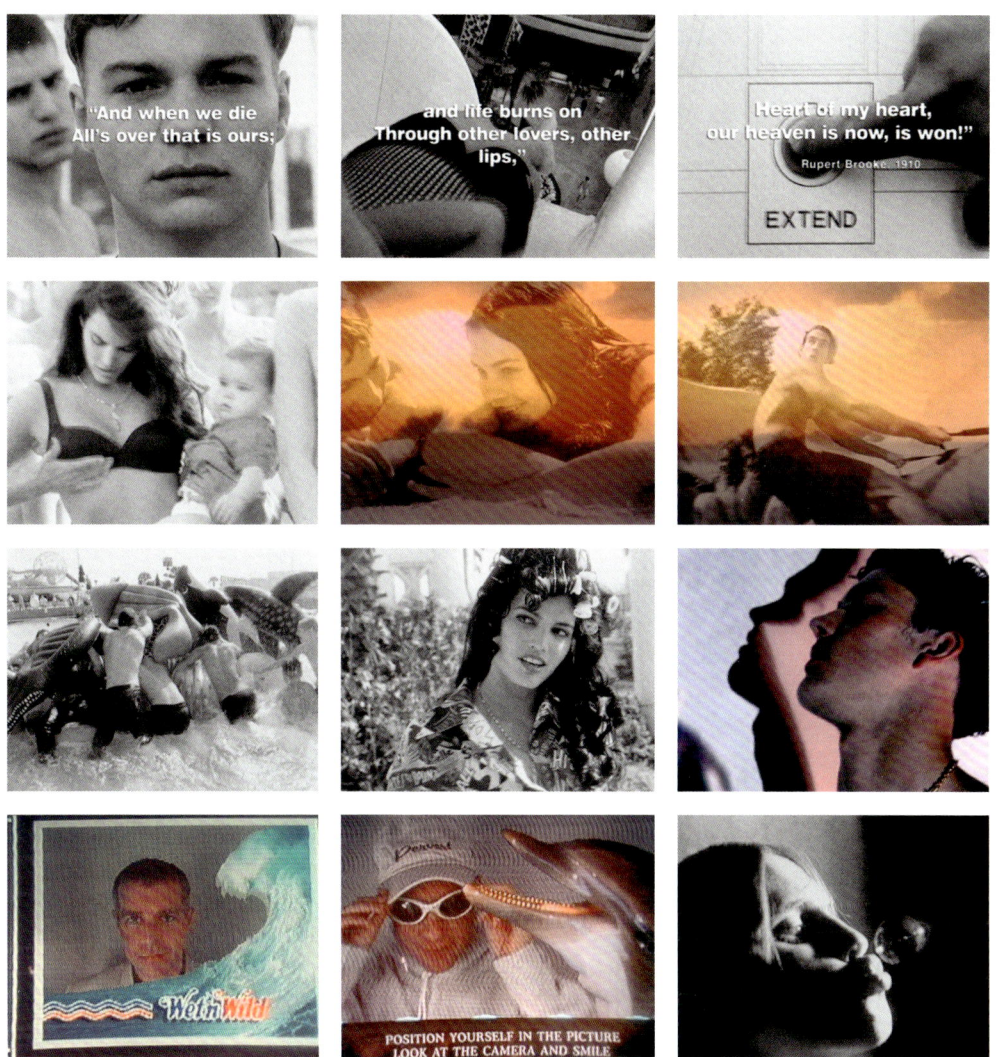

voice reaching a higher and higher pitch: 'Oh beautiful ... Oh, I love it! ... Oh Neil, there's a surfer right on your pocket. I love it, I love it.' He asked them to look upwards and open their mouths, as if gazing at something in wonderment. 'I love it!... It's like kids at the movies.... Beautiful ... It's beautiful.... Just open your mouths.... Beautiful ... Beautiful.' At the end of the video, Neil and Chris take their positions in the Photo Illusion Booth, in which visitors to the leisure park pay $5 to be photographed against selected backgrounds.

Bilingual

release 2 September 1996
formats LP / cassette / CD / special-edition CD
photographer Chris Heath, José Cea, and Andy Earl
design Mark Farrow Design / PSB

The CD case of the next studio album had a semi-opaque frosted surface that formed the single word 'Bilingual' in clear plastic. Underneath can be seen the yellow booklet, with 'Pet Shop Boys' visible beneath the title. The original idea had been that it should look like luxury packaging. Farrow had wanted it to be a pillow pack – a rigid, curved, opaque case. That proved too expensive. Then he wanted a sandblasted front, but that also proved too costly. In the end, the frosted finish is a screenprinted dirty varnish. The LP sleeve was an attempt to emulate the CD case, using a yellow panel and white type and frame instead. The pictures inside were taken by Chris Heath and José Cea on the *Discovery* tour or for the *Literally* fanzine. The images were printed twice to reflect the 'bi-' of 'bilingual'. A special edition was also subsequently released with a photo by Andy Earl on the front, again printed twice, and a yellow frame. Some years later, when discussing an imminent Pet Shop Boys sleeve, someone from the record company offered the following advice: 'This sleeve has got to say "buy me". Unlike *Bilingual*, which said "I'm not for you".'

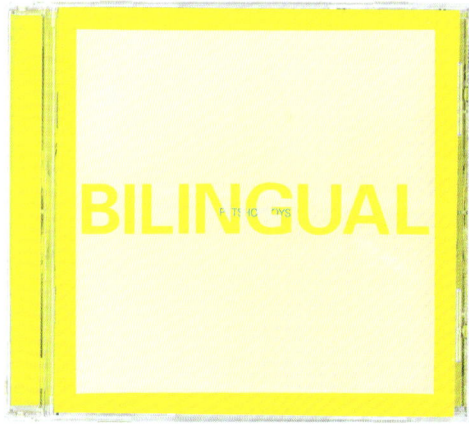

CD, front

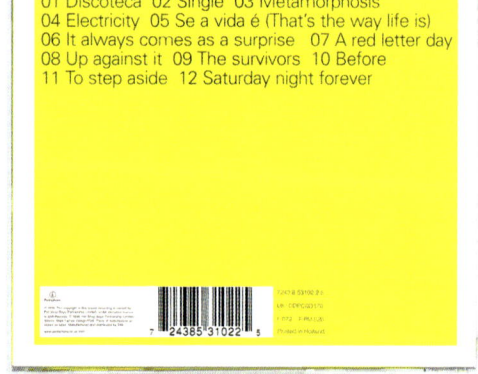

CD, back

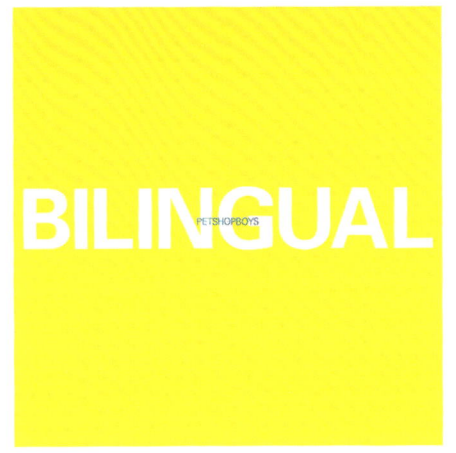

LP, outer sleeve, front

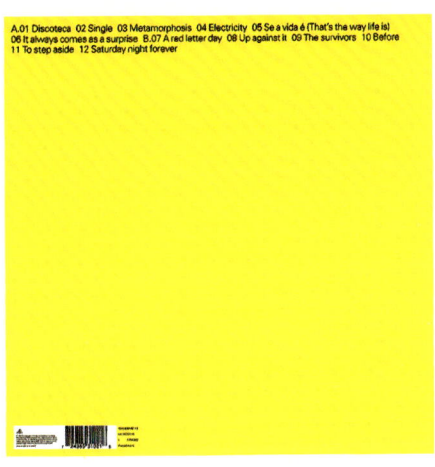

LP, outer sleeve, back

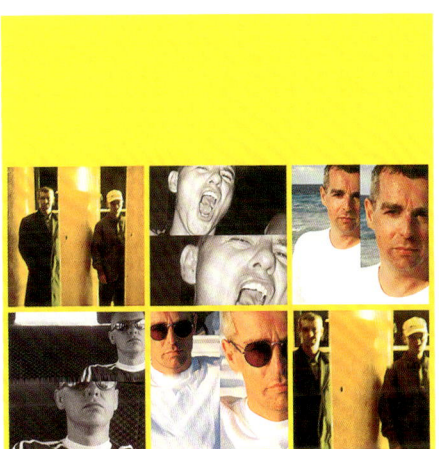

LP, inner sleeve, front

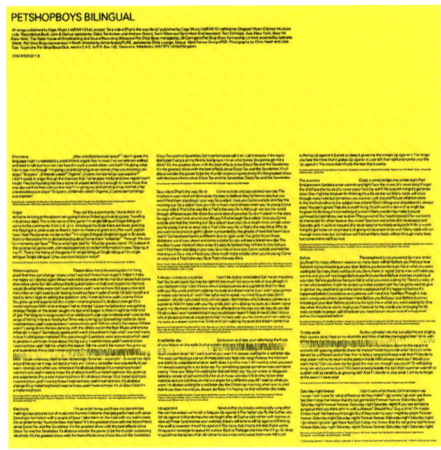

LP, inner sleeve, back

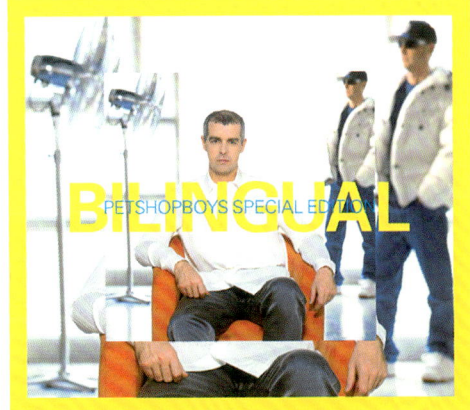

CD, special edition, outer sleeve, front

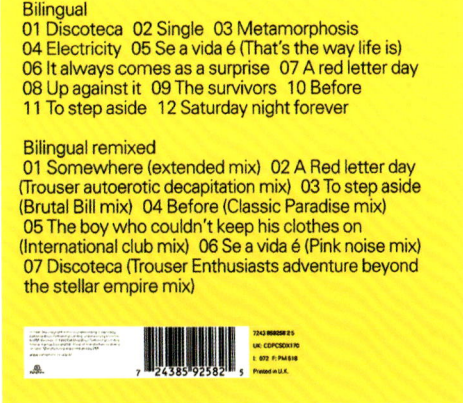

CD, special edition, outer sleeve, back

Single-Bilingual / Discoteca

release 11 November 1996
formats 12" promo × 2 / cassette / CD × 2 / CD promo
design Mark Farrow Design / PSB
video Howard Greenhalgh

On the album *Bilingual*, the song had simply been called 'Single', but by the time it was released on its own, it came soon after a recent Everything But The Girl hit that had had the same name, and so Pet Shop Boys renamed it 'Single-Bilingual'. 'A play on words,' Chris noted. 'It obviously means bisexual.' All formats of the song featured a purely typographic treatment, the first time a Pet Shop Boys single sleeve had had no image since the second release of 'Opportunities' and 'Paninaro' more than ten years earlier (pages 62–3 and 74–5). Farrow used tracing paper for the CD sleeves, a different colour for each one, to achieve a similar effect to the *Bilingual* sleeve, with overlaid words. The song was released on two twelve-inch promos with a new recording of another *Bilingual* track, 'Discoteca' (on the album the two songs are mixed together and segue into one another), which at one point was considered as the third single from the album. On the sleeves of the twelve-inch promos, which repeated the yellow and green colours of the main CDs, the overlay effect was achieved typographically, with a line from 'Discoteca' in English appearing above the Spanish equivalent, and vice versa.

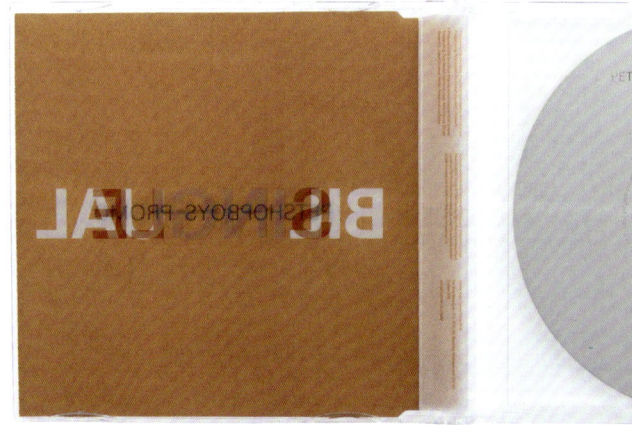
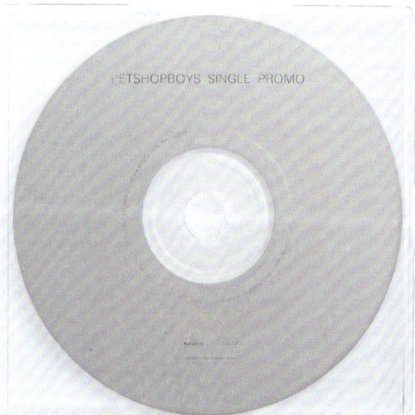

CD promo, inside

12" promo 2, front

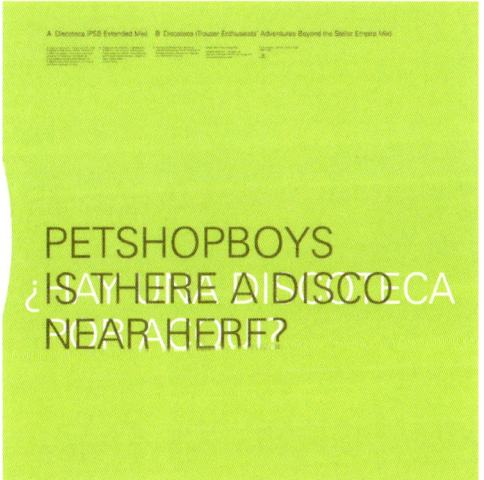

12" promo 2, back

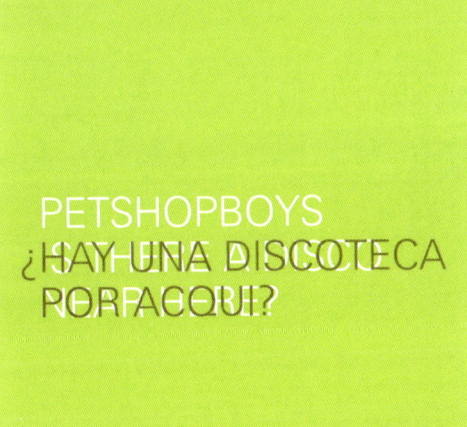

12" promo 1, front

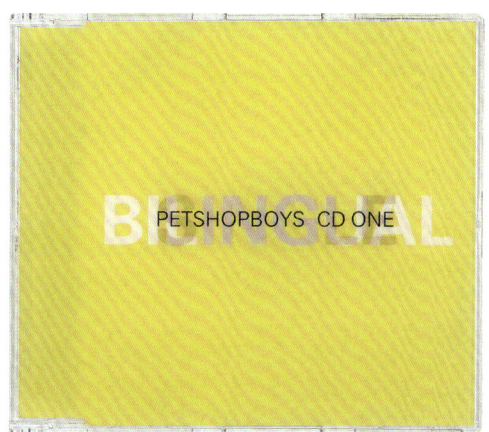

12" promo 1, back

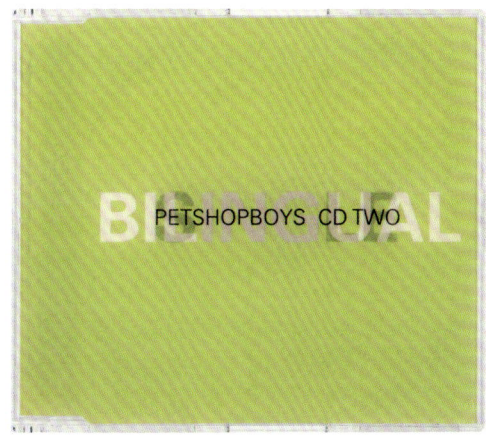

CD 1, front

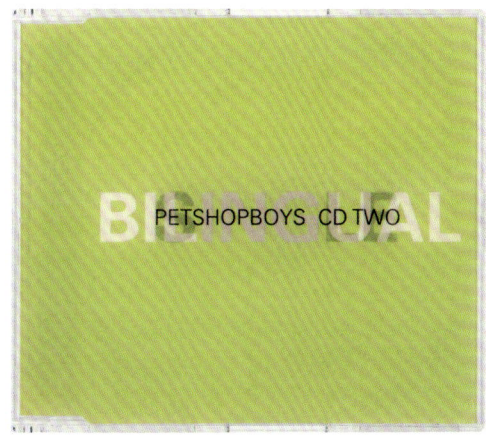

CD 2, front

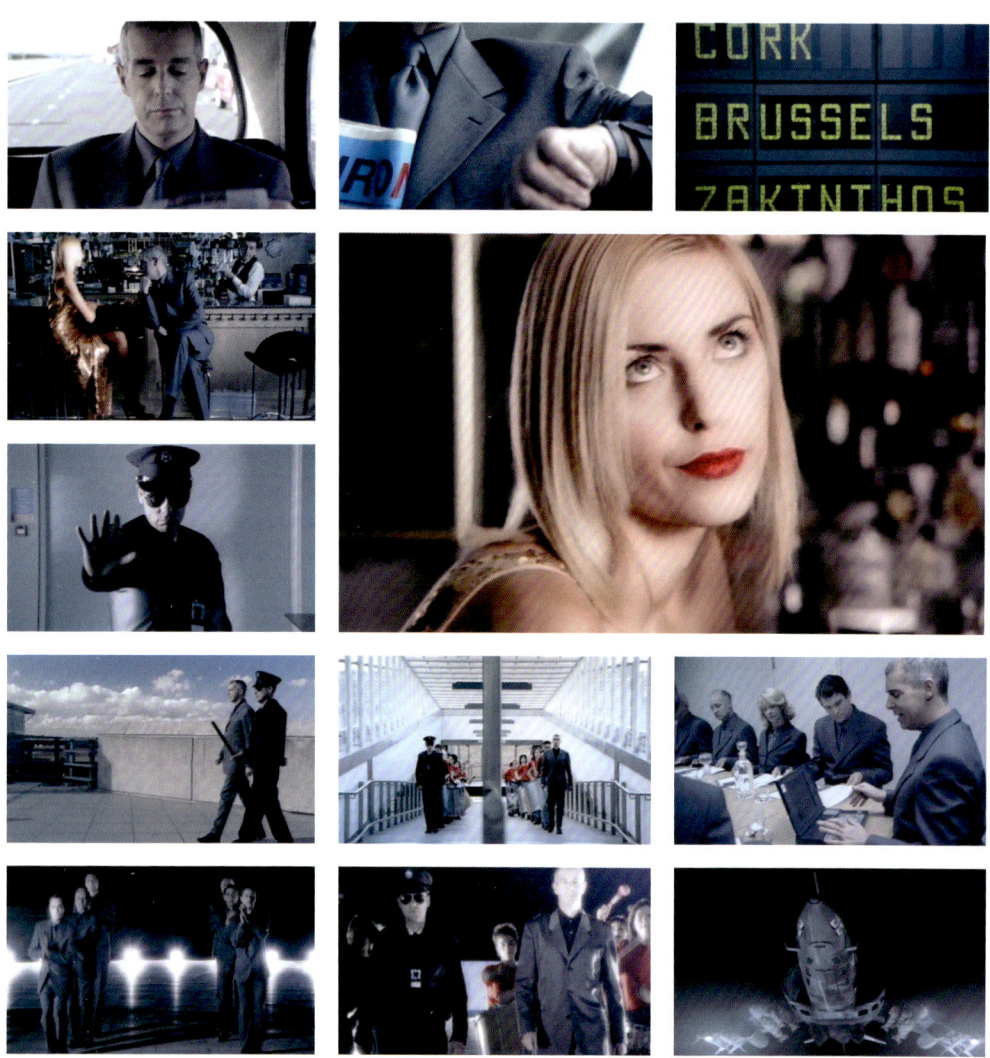

The video – which Pet Shop Boys wanted to resemble an advert – was shot at Stansted Airport. Neil plays the executive-narrator of the song, who flies off to the Continent to do business. We see him arriving at the airport, checking in, finding himself squashed on the plane between two obnoxious men, chatting up an unimpressed blonde in a bar, and tapping on his PC at a meeting. Meanwhile, stuffy businessmen in grey suits start dancing in formation, and drummers from the all-women percussion band SheBoom, who feature on the song, follow Neil and Chris around, their red T-shirts providing a rare touch of colour in an otherwise grey video. Finally, businessmen and women start dancing as the song segues into a reprise of 'Discoteca' and military aircraft fly overhead. 'It's one of our literal videos', Neil said. 'The narrator is a glib Eurocrat who flies business class and likes all his privileges. He tries to pick up chicks. But he's not really communicating, and he knows it. In fact he's a hopeless wreck. That's why

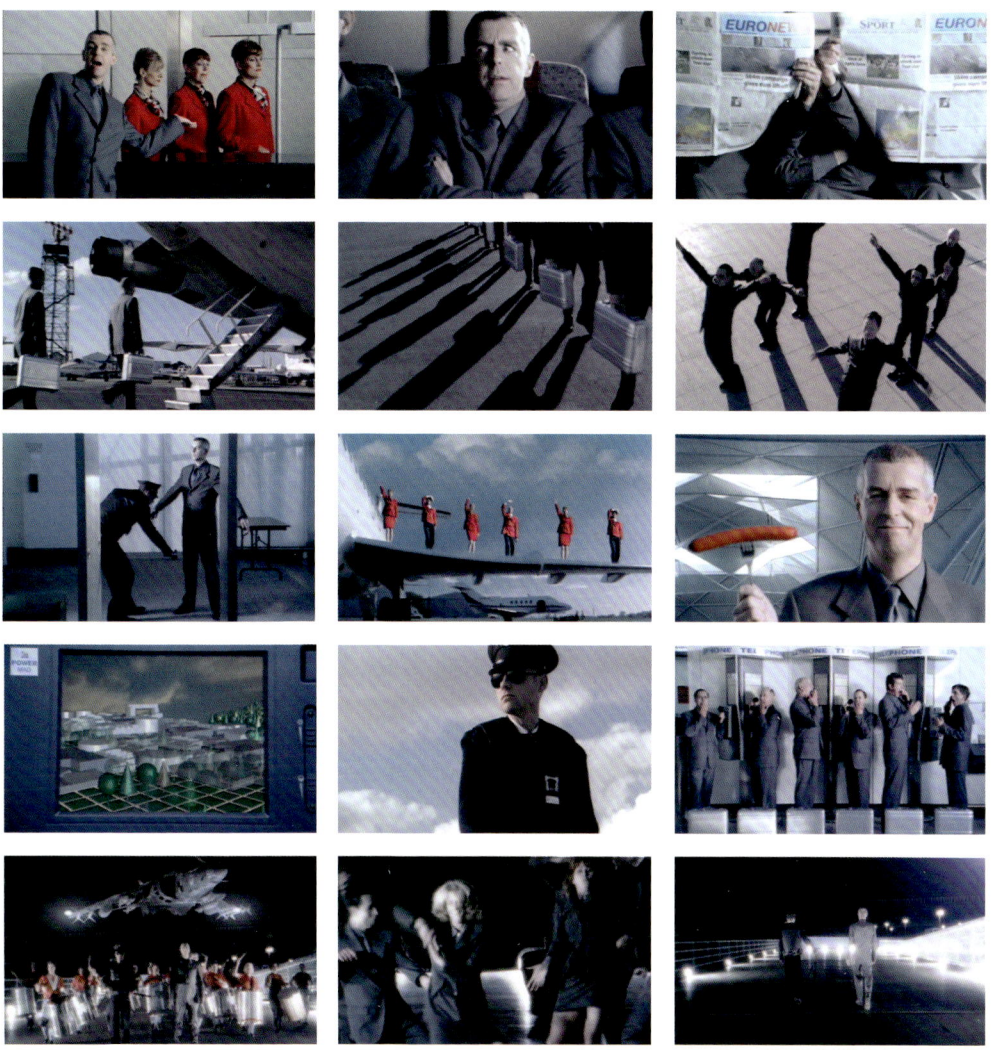

it ends with "Discoteca". He could be literally going to a club, but it's also saying he's a lost and frightened person.' 'I think Neil gives one of the best performances ever in a video', Chris said. 'I think it's absolutely spectacularly brilliant. It's really funny. It brings out Neil's true humour.' 'It's the only video where you get the real me', agreed Neil. 'Behind that sombre face, that's what's there', Chris said. 'Personality.' Chris playing the airport security guard was not the real him, however. 'That's me in a mood.'

A red letter day

release 17 March 1997
formats 12" / 12" promo × 2 / CD × 2 / CD promo
photographers Pennie Smith and Flavio Cecchetto
design Farrow Design / PSB
video Howard Greenhalgh

For the next and final single from *Bilingual*, the design picked up the song's theme of red. The outer sleeve of the twelve inch and the outer sleeve of the CDs (which came with CD 2) were both printed entirely in red, with the words 'Pet Shop Boys' and 'A red letter day' debossed on the surface in capitals. 'It was printed in one red, which was then overprinted, so that in certain areas you were looking at red and then in other areas you were looking at red on red, what's called a double-hit red, which made it even redder', says Mark Farrow. 'And I was having a lot of fun with varnishes.' The inside of the inner sleeve of the twelve inch was also printed in red, while the disc was pressed in the same colour vinyl.

The fronts of the CD inner sleeves, including the promo CD, all featured different photographs of Neil and Chris taken by Pennie Smith on All Saints' Road, west London, close to Sarm West studios, in their downtime during recording. The backs of the inner sleeves, as well as that of the twelve inch, showed pictures by Smith of the pair in the studio, the CDs having three images each and the twelve inch having six.

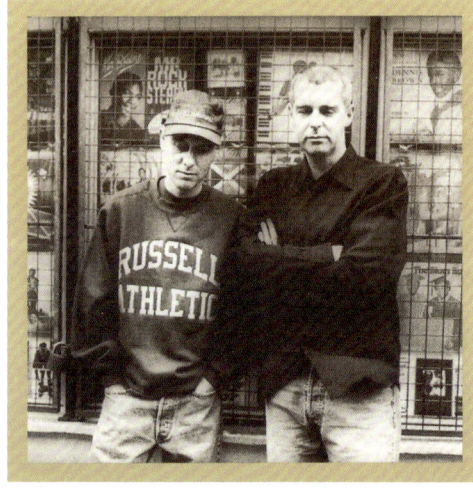

CD 1, inner sleeve, front

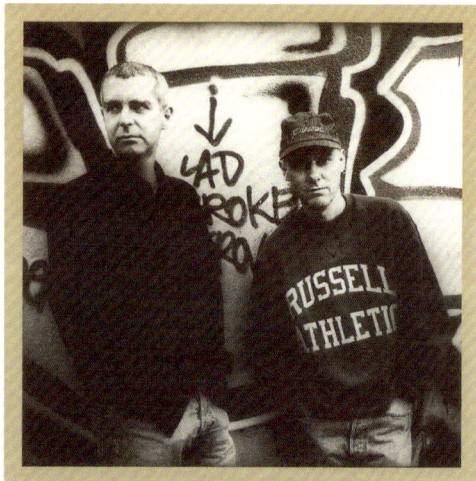

CD 2, inner sleeve, front

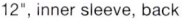
12", outer sleeve, front

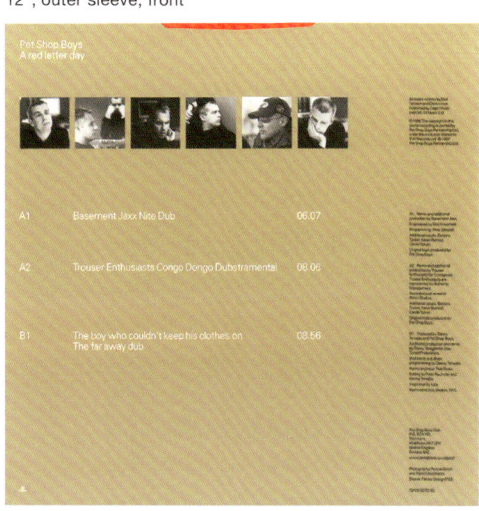
12", inner sleeve, back

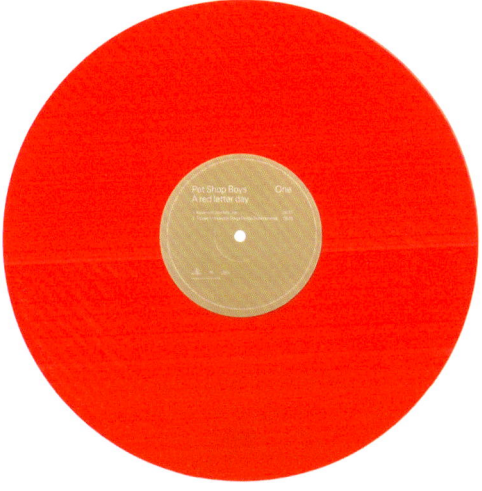
12", disc

A red letter day 1997

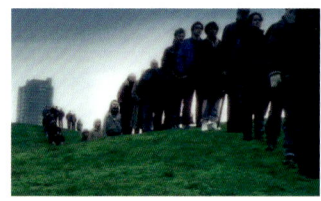 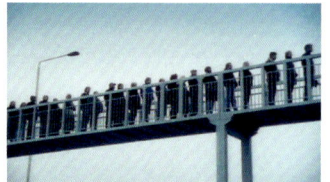 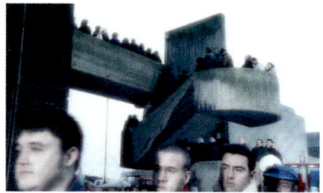
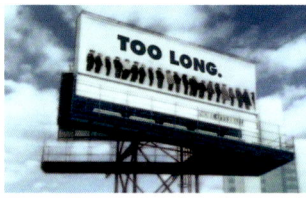 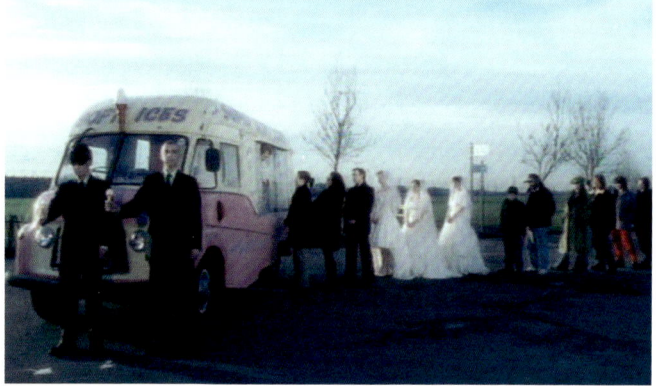
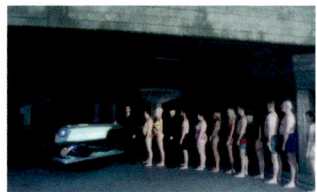
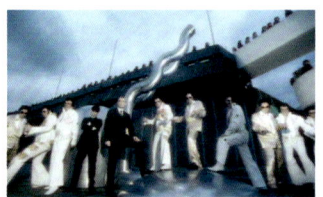 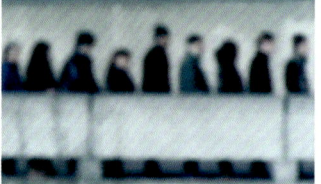 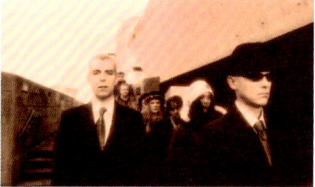
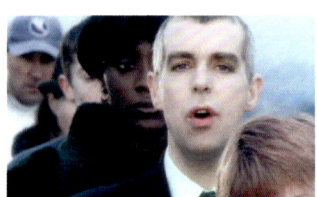 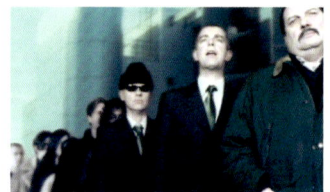 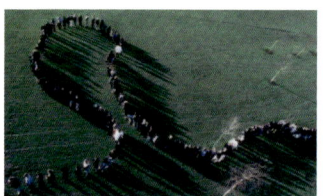

The video for 'A red letter day' was shot mostly at London's Southbank Centre, the arts venue designed by Denys Lasdun. Part of it was also filmed on Hackney Marshes in east London – close to the future sites of the 2012 Olympic Games. The idea for the video came from the key line in the song – 'I'm always waiting for a red letter day' – and features a seemingly never-ending queue of people, including Neil and Chris, forever waiting in line for various underwhelming rewards for their patience: to use a telephone box; to get an ice cream; to go on a sunbed; to look at themselves in a mirror; to jump off a cliff. The queues wind their way round and round the concrete brutalist architecture of the Southbank Centre, while billboards pose the questions the bored queuers must surely be asking themselves – 'Why are we waiting?' 'How long?' – and an electronic board offers them encouragement. 'They let us use the National Theatre sign', marvels Neil. 'It looks a bit like a party political

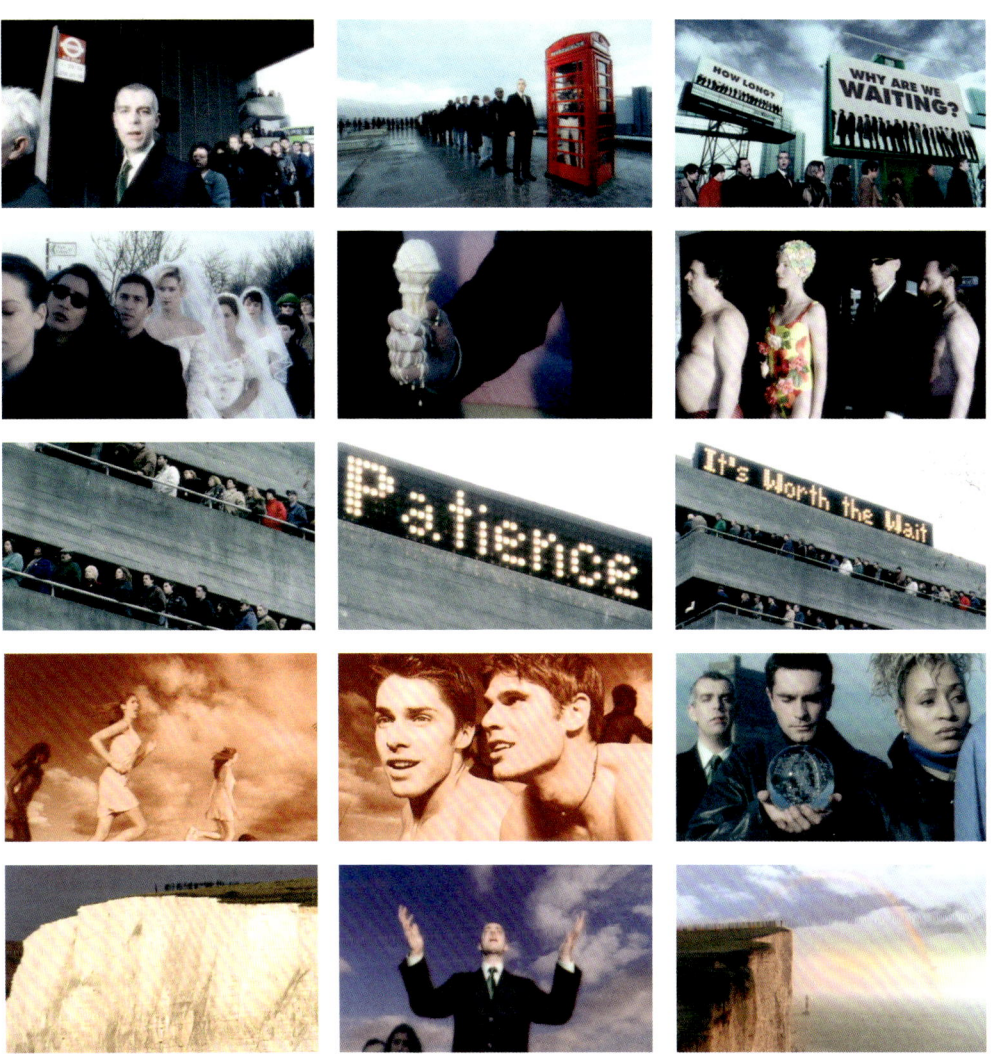

broadcast.' Along the way, several colourful types – Elvis lookalikes, elderly cowboys – attempt to break the tedium. At one point, the video breaks into sepia-tone images of youths playing in an idyllic Arcadian landscape. Dainton Connell makes another Hitchcock-like cameo appearance as one of the queuers.

Somewhere – In concert at the Savoy Theatre

dates 4 – 21 June 1997
design Sam Taylor-Wood, Michael Vale
lighting design Abigail Rosen Holmes
staging/choreography Les Child, Claire Eastman

On 4 June 1997, Pet Shop Boys began a residency at London's Savoy Theatre. They performed on a minimal stage in front of two screens, each showing a film by British artist Sam Taylor-Johnson (then Taylor-Wood), out of which they walked at the beginning of the concert and re-entered halfway through and at the end. 'That's when we did "art"', recalled Chris. 'I very much felt that we were part of the Britart scene.' As Neil says, 'The idea of the show came about because I saw a piece by Sam called *Pent-Up*, which was five video screens – they were all interacting with each other.' Originally, Neil and Chris wanted to have closed-circuit televisions – one in Piccadilly Circus, for instance, and one outside the theatre – but it was too complicated and expensive for this short run. 'Then Sam had the idea of filming a party that we would walk in and out of.' The film is a Warholesque party, shot in a flat in west London. It features key members of the young British art movement and their friends. Taylor-Wood was inspired by the way the Savoy Theatre 'is reminiscent of twenties decadence, with that silvery tinge to everything. The idea came to use people hanging around, lounging on couches, and doing nothing in particular and looking decadent in that Warhol kind of way. I wanted the films to act as a background so that nothing is too overpowering. These fairly curious people, lounge lizards, do not distract from the performance and can merely be glanced at. It is an endless waiting, because the whole thing is shot in real time, unedited.' Halfway through the performance, the films move from black and white to colour.

Reflecting the silver interior of the Savoy Theatre, the concert programme was printed on silvery pages (page 246). The centrefold featured a striking split image made up of portraits by Andy Earl, first seen on *Talk*, a limited-edition interview CD produced to promote *Bilingual*. The subsequent DVD of the concert, shot by Annie Griffin, had a cover image of the special neon sign that Pet Shop Boys commissioned to hang outside the theatre (page 247). The previous year, BBC Radio 1 had broadcast a two-hour documentary, *About Pet Shop Boys*. As well as audio of Neil and Chris as they talked and worked, and interviews with them, it also included interviews with Bobby Orlando, Johnny Marr, Dusty Springfield, Jack Bond, Patsy Kensit, Bernard Sumner, and others, and extracts from previously unheard early demos. After its broadcast, it was subsequently packaged as a two-CD set and sold exclusively at the *Somewhere* concerts (page 247).

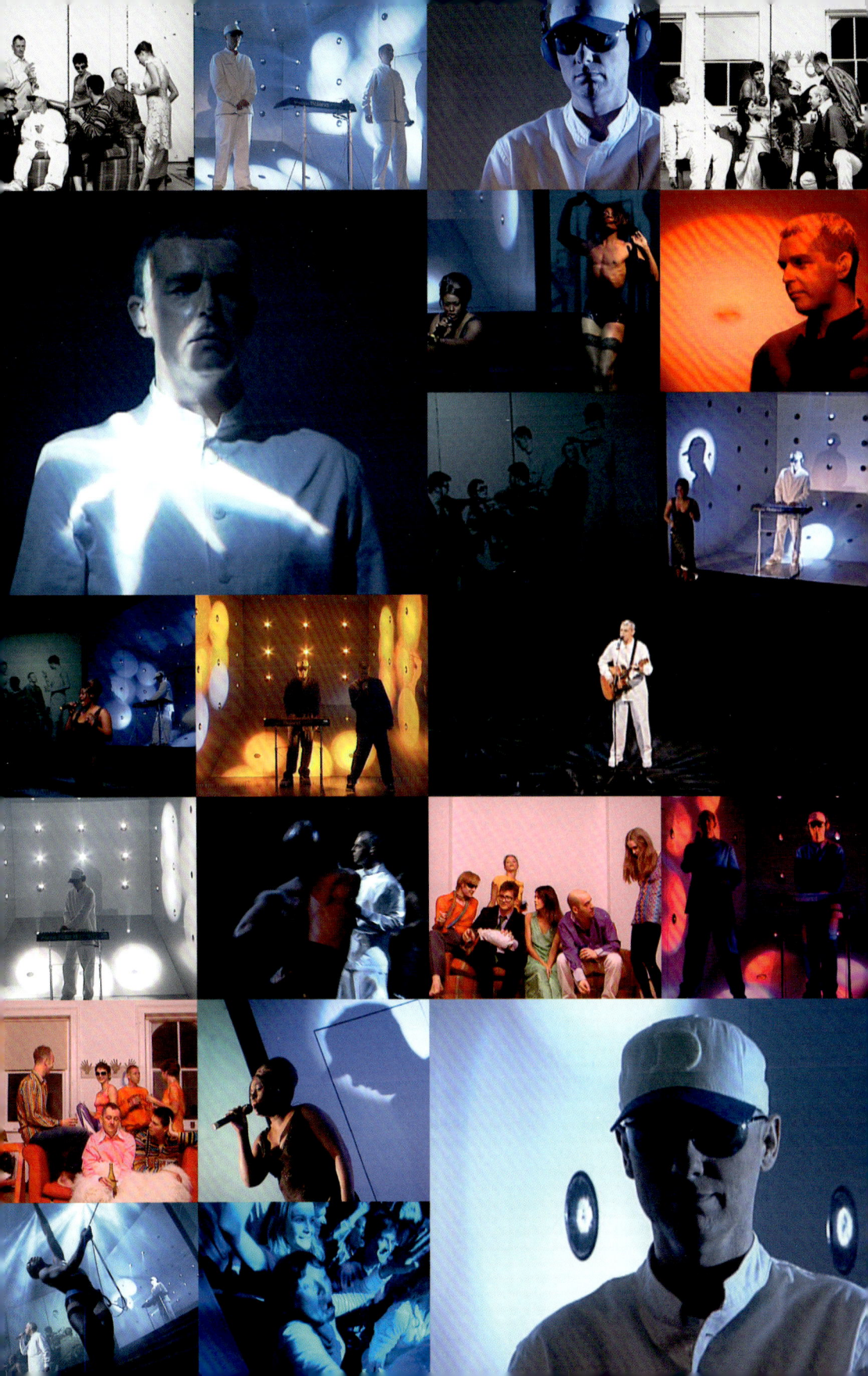

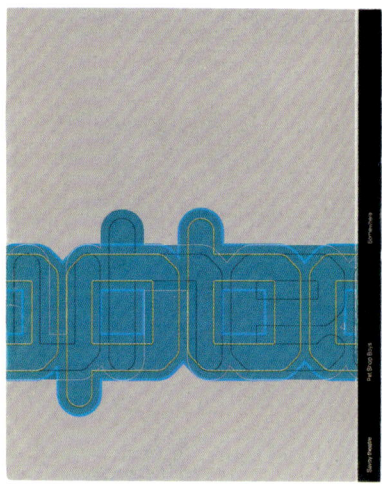

Concert programme, front

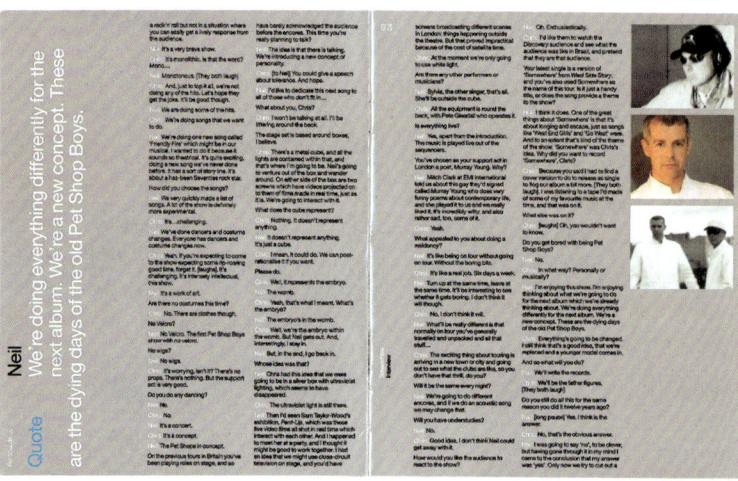

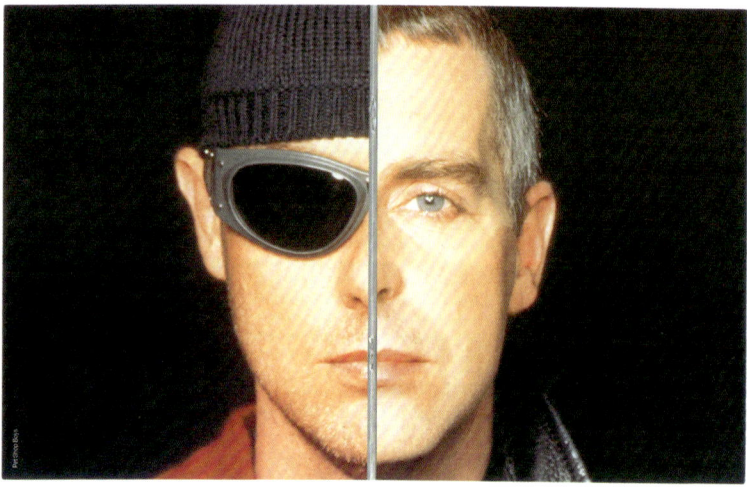

Concert programme, interview and centrefold

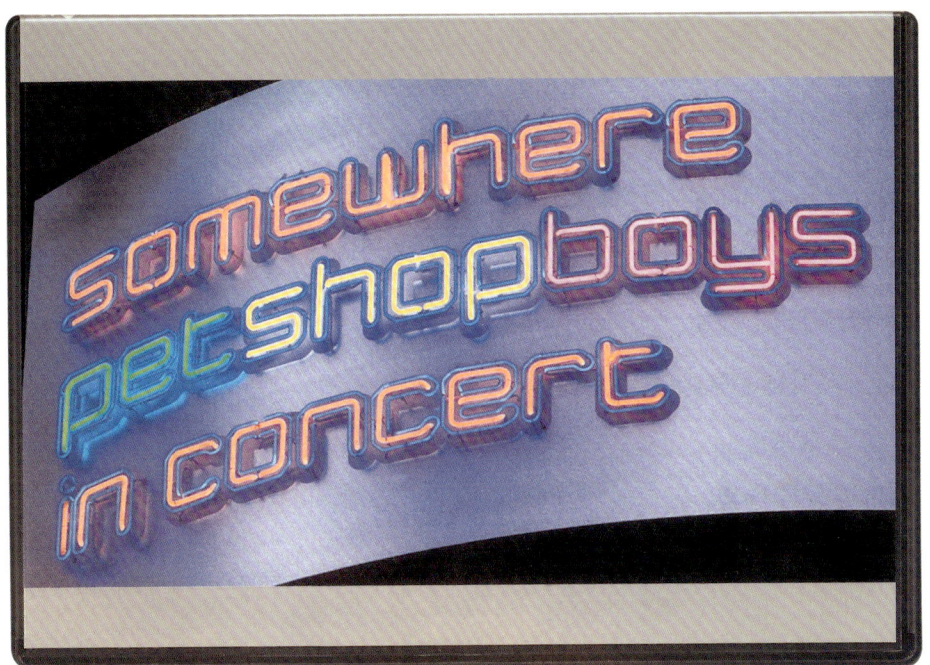

DVD, front

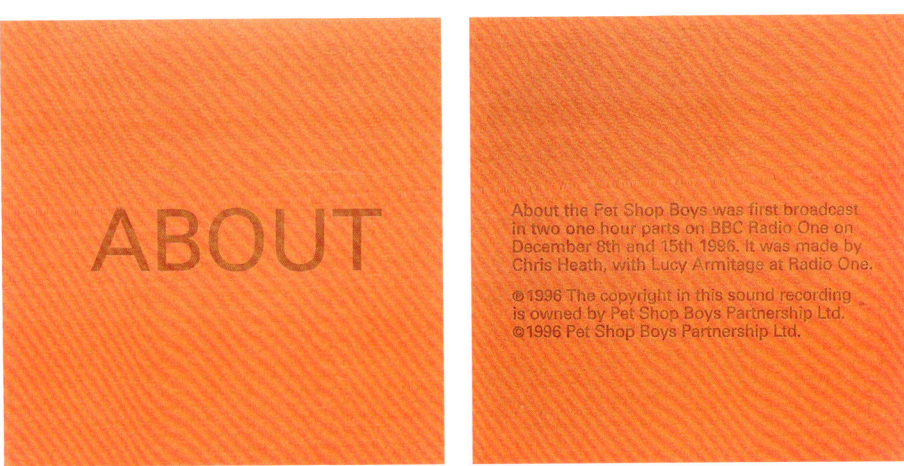

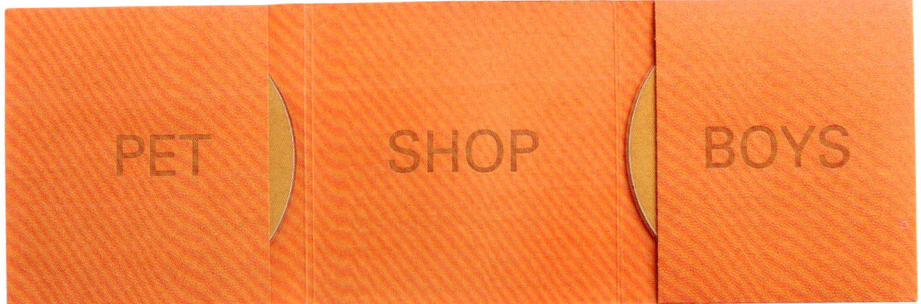

About Pet Shop Boys, CD, front, back and inside

Somewhere

release 23 June 1997
formats 12" promo / cassette / CD × 2 / CD promo
photographer Andy Earl
typeface Farrow Design
design Farrow Design / PSB
video Annie Griffin

For the Savoy Theatre concerts, Farrow created a typeface that was used on everything connected with the show: the neon sign outside the theatre, the programme, and the various sleeves of the single 'Somewhere' (a cover version of the Stephen Sondheim and Leonard Bernstein song from *West Side Story*). 'We created a typeface that was really a modern take on an American college typeface called Princeton', Mark Farrow recalls. The CD cases were designed so that the CDs themselves were exposed and visible from the front. 'We wanted to do something different with them, strip it back as far as we could.' Again, silver was the key colour. 'We did some really clever stuff with the way we printed colours over and under silver, which gave you lots of nice different colours. We also printed transparent ink onto the discs themselves so that you got the metallic coming through.' The information and photography were confined to either side of the CD spine, Chris appearing on one CD, Neil on the other. For the American version, the outside and inside copy and images for the two British CD singles were combined to form one CD sleeve.

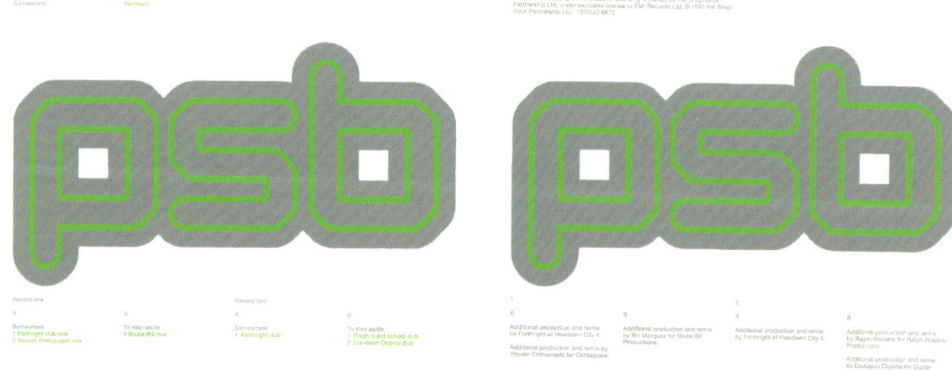

12" promo, outer sleeve, front   12" promo, outer sleeve, back

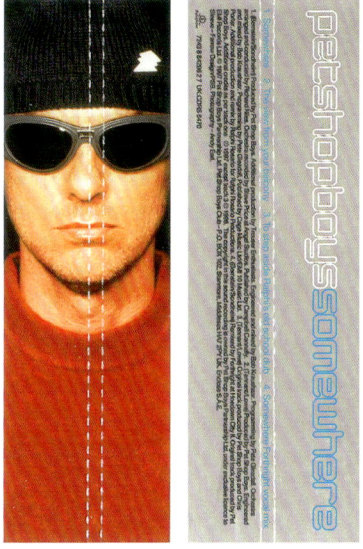 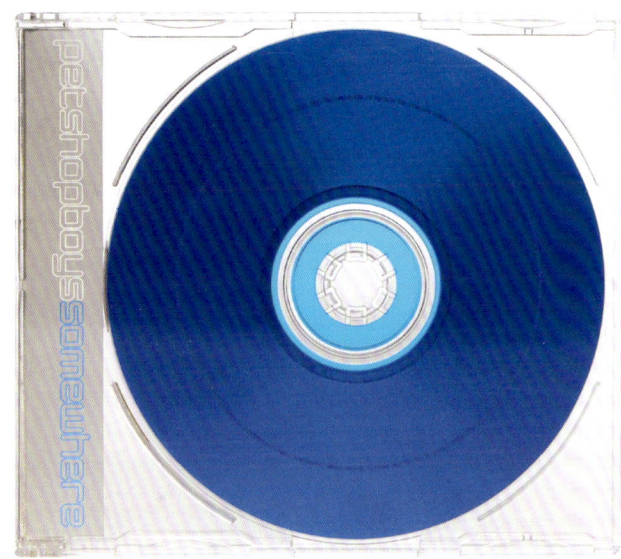

CD 1, spine band, reverse and front   CD 1, front

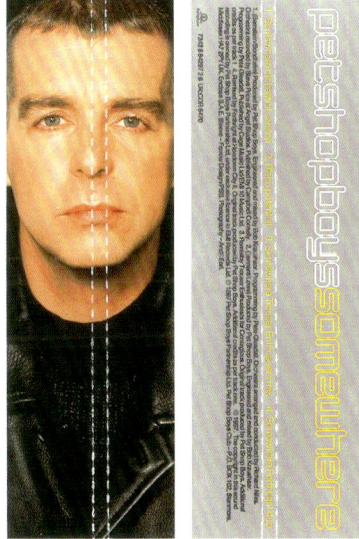 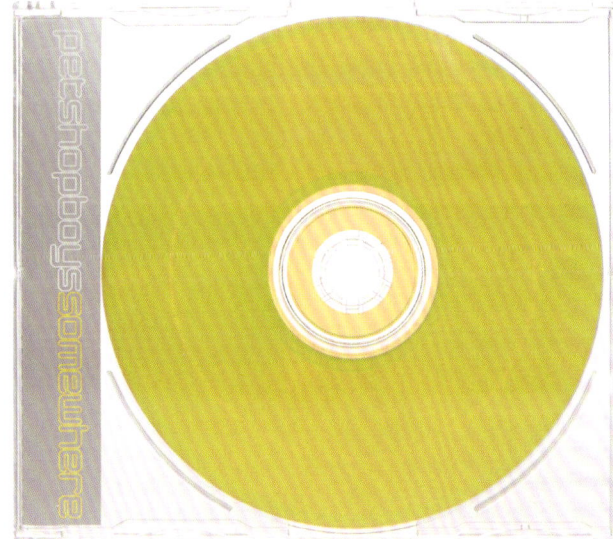

CD 2, spine band, reverse and front   CD 2, front

Somewhere 1997

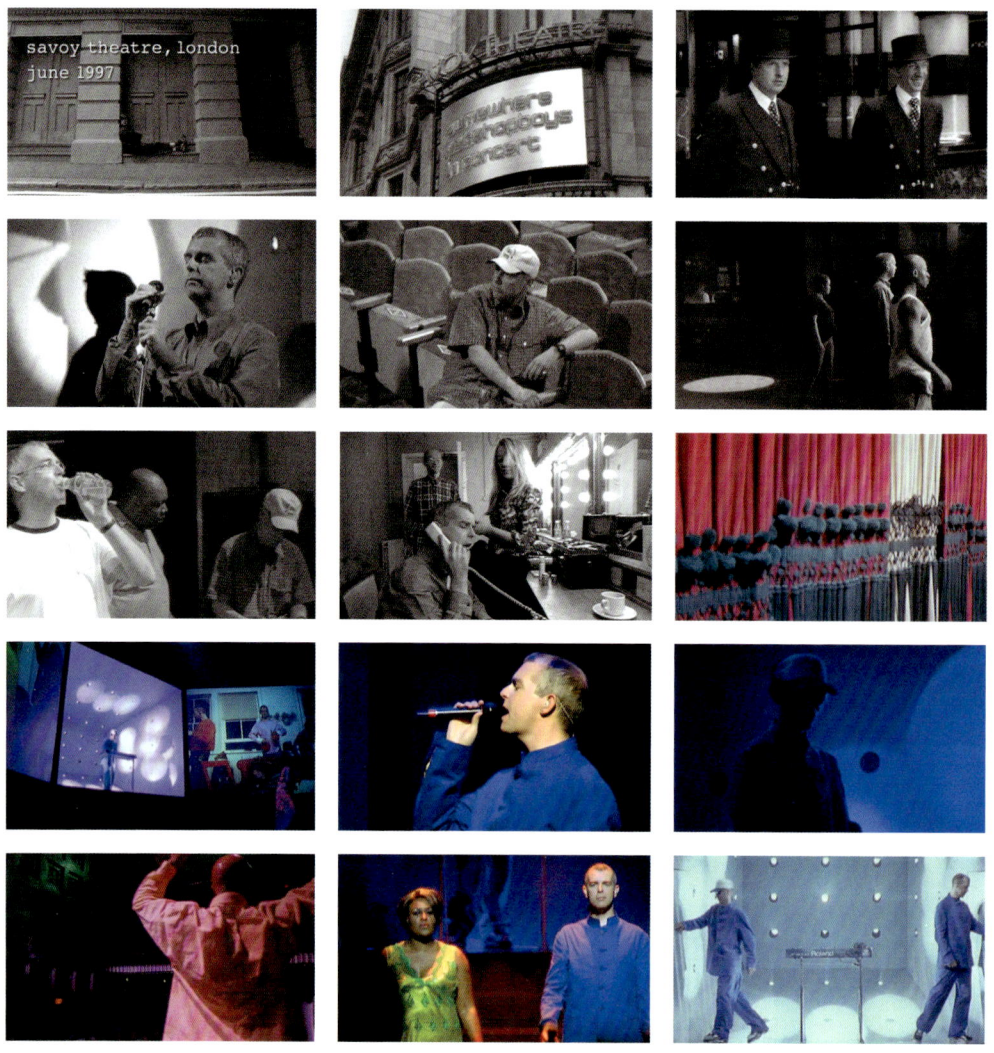

The video for 'Somewhere' is an edited version of the half-hour black-and-white documentary on the staging of the *Somewhere* show at the Savoy Theatre that appears on the DVD of the concert, followed by colour footage of Neil, Chris, and Sylvia Mason-James performing in the show itself. The song can be heard in the background. During the documentary, we see Neil and Chris running through the rehearsals, having tea, relaxing behind the scenes, and preparing for the performance. After the show, they wind down with a drink. Touches of humour run through the video. Chris, in particular, reveals his comic side – normally kept hidden and not part of Pet Shop Boys' image – by poking fun at Neil and pointing out the ridiculous side of the whole affair; at the end of the concert, thinking he is safe behind the curtain, he drops his trousers, only for the curtain to rise more quickly than he had expected.

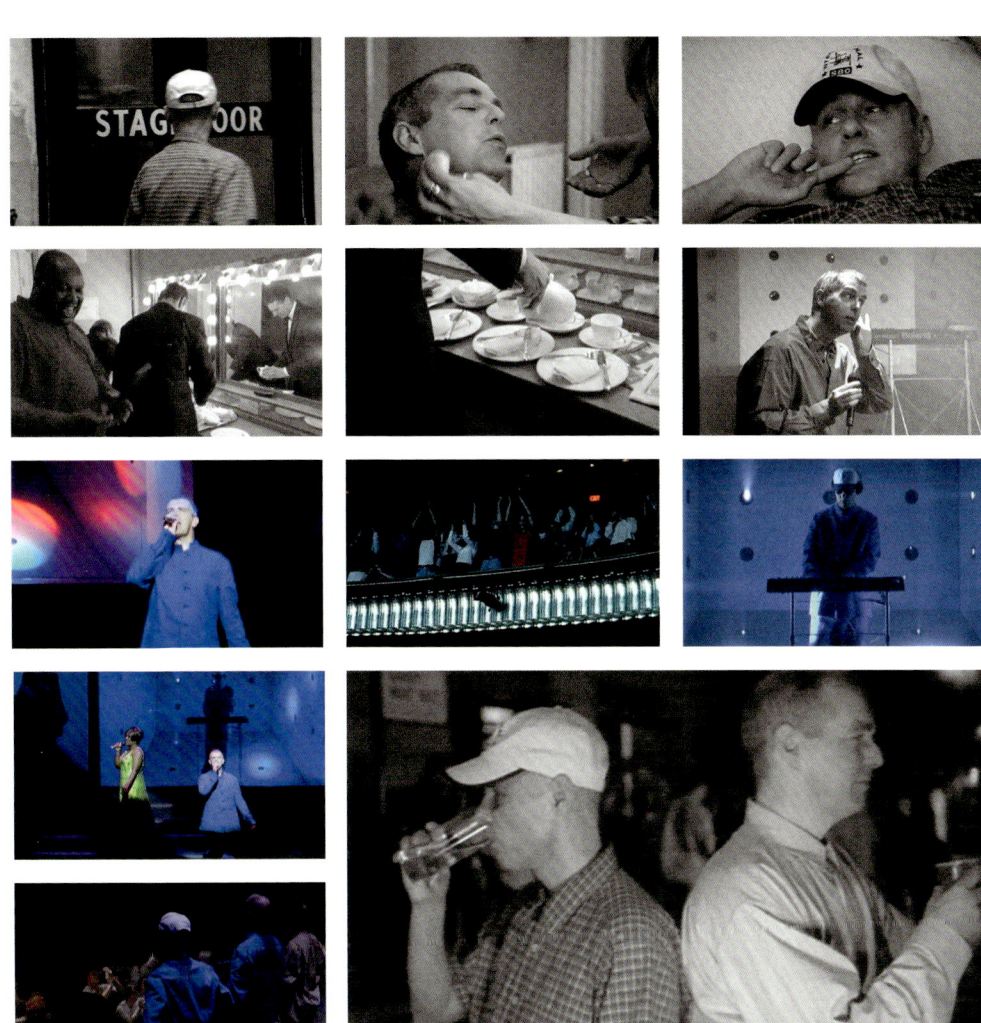

I don't know what you want but I can't give it any more

release 19 July 1999
formats 12" promo / cassette / CD × 2 / CD promo
photographer Eric Watson
design Farrow Design / PSB
video Pedro Romhanyi

For their next album, *Nightlife*, Pet Shop Boys once again transformed their image, this time with shocking effect. As the album was less personal in tone – 'the lyrics are not necessarily reflections of me, Neil Tennant' – they decided to appear less naturalistic, donning orange punk wigs, false eyebrows, dark glasses, and heavily layered and flowing clothes. The look was inspired by photographs in Japanese magazines of men in samurai trousers. 'We didn't want the look to be just fashion, we wanted something that had an element of ritual in it', said Neil. 'I like the way it has a slightly ceremonial look about it.' The costumes were developed with theatre designer Ian MacNeil. The wigs were made of human hair. 'The costumes are a distancing technique – a way of saying that we're nothing to do with anything else that's happening in pop', Neil told Michael Bracewell in an interview for the *Guardian*. 'Also, the Pet Shop Boys have always been obsessed with not being real, because we think we're more interesting.' 'But it can also look grotesque', Chris added. 'It really wasn't designed for daily wear', agreed Neil. He also commented that the costumes were also partly inspired by plans that he and Chris had to make a musical out of Graham Greene's novel *Brighton Rock*. 'I told Ian I wanted these long parkas, trailing on the ground, which the gang would wear.'

Mark Farrow remembers he was 'quite shocked' when he first saw the new look. 'I'm not mad on it, if I'm honest. Those eyebrows didn't do it for me at all.' The cover photos were taken in West Central Street in central London. It was the first time Pet Shop Boys had worked with Eric Watson for some years. The Weimaraner dogs were a last-minute addition: 'We were going to have bicycles originally. We wanted some movement in the picture', said Neil. Watson's image was split between the two CD singles so that the full image could be seen only when they were placed side by side. 'The type was based on a dot-matrix typeface and we put a blur on it so it appeared to be moving', says Farrow.

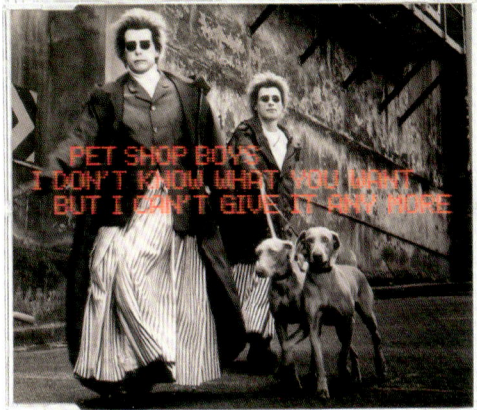

CD 2, front

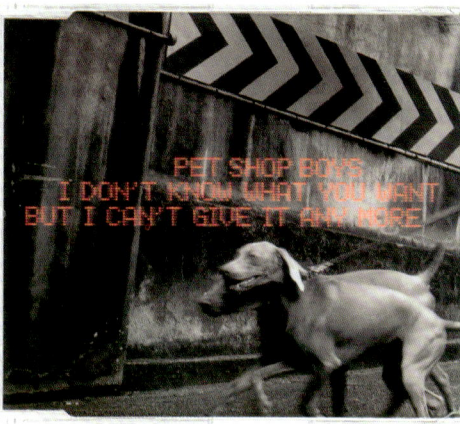

CD 1, front

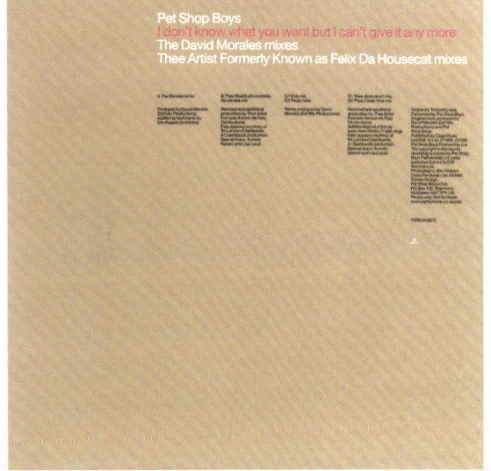

12" promo, outer sleeve, back

CD, United States, back

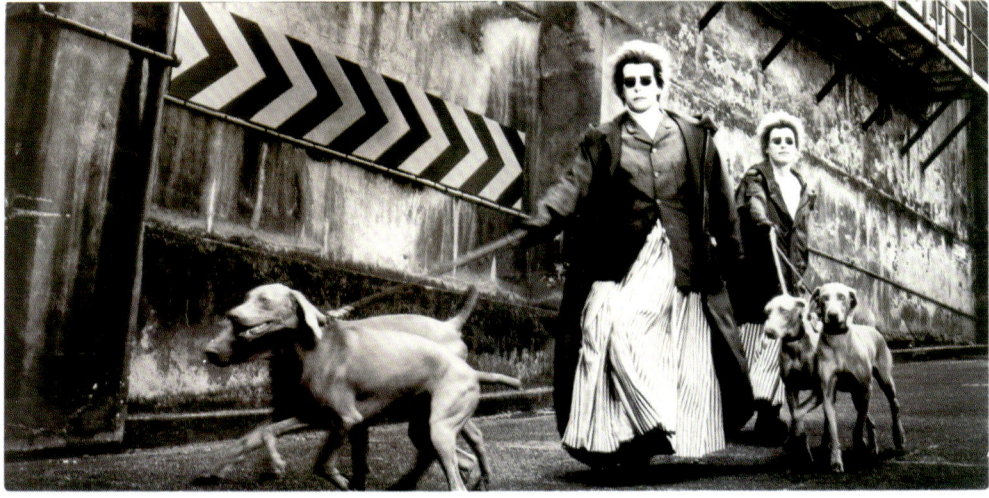

12" promo, gatefold, inside

I don't know what you want but I can't give it any more 1999 253

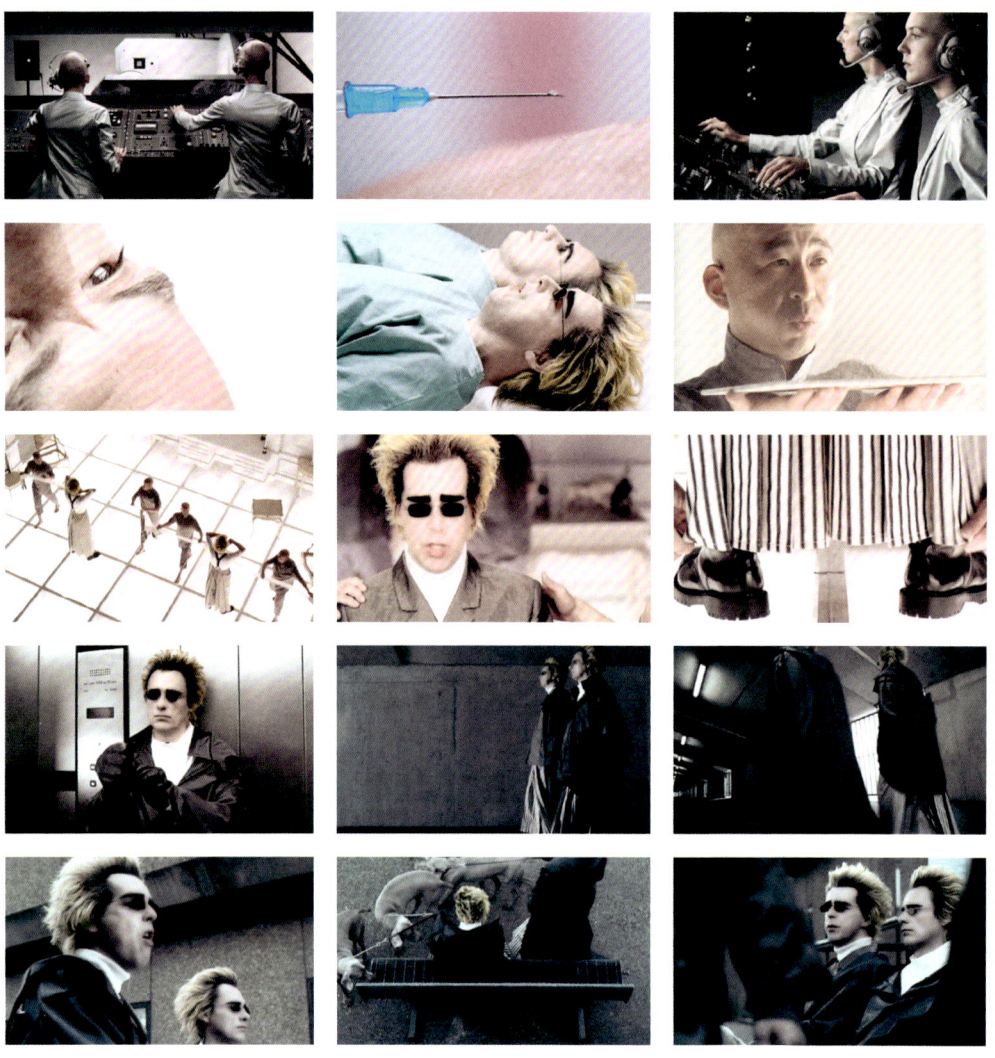

Drawing on various movies – *THX1138*, *Ridicule*, *2001: A Space Odyssey* and *A Clockwork Orange*, and shot, variously, in a west London studio, at Heathland School in Hounslow, and on walkways beneath the stands at Twickenham rugby ground – the video sees the group metamorphosing into their new look, from an operating table to a Regency room, underlit to replicate the final scene in *2001: A Space Odyssey*: 'We wanted the video to look very futuristic and science fiction, and that is the ultimate science-fiction movie.' 'So what does all of this new look mean?' wrote Michael Bracewell. 'Or does it mean anything? To judge from the exterior shots of the video, and the extreme styling of their new image, they are positioning themselves in a vision of the future in which the architectural brutalism of the Seventies has become as weathered as the Victorian neo-Gothicism of Sir George Gilbert Scott's St Pancras Hotel. It is, perhaps, the idea

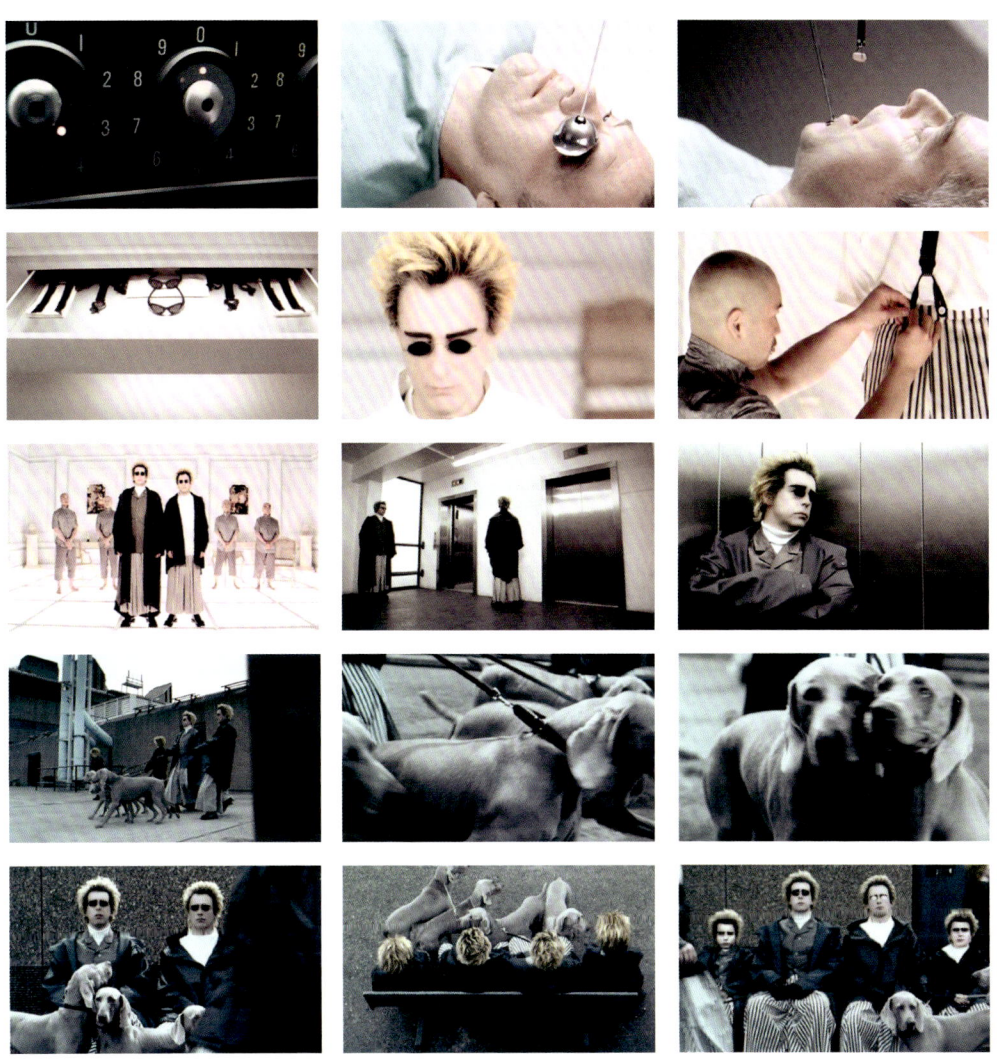

of the future itself appearing antique and old-fashioned, with every adult and child dressed, as revealed at end of the video, in the extraordinary Samurai chic which we had assumed was a sub-cult gang costume – like the Droogs in *A Clockwork Orange* – rather than the mark of complete social conformity. "There is a comment about conformity", says Neil. "But I think that if our previous shows were paintings, they would have been figurative. Whereas this one is definitely abstract."'

As well as the session in central London, Eric Watson also photographed Neil and Chris in their new costumes near his home in Rye in Sussex (the black-and-white shots against the cliffs show them wearing Issey Miyake handbags as hats), and in the empty shell of the former St Pancras Hotel, Gilbert Scott's Victorian gothic masterpiece in King's Cross – itself a Pet Shop Boys' site, being the location for the video for 'Rent', as well as a song title in its own right. The hotel was also the venue for the presentation of the new look to the press. The press interviews were conducted in an upper chamber of the building – which housed hundreds of vacant and decrepit rooms that seemed to echo the decaying interior seen on the 'It's a sin' cover (page 83). Neil and Chris sat in futuristic chairs on an illuminated floor – a reference to Kubrick's ground-breaking film *2001: A Space Odyssey* (but also, perhaps, to the art piece that Pet Shop Boys made for Brian Eno's War Child charity in February 1997, when they re-created the *Saturday Night Fever* illuminated dance floor, which was subsequently auctioned for £7,500). 'At St Pancras Hotel, journalists walked up the main staircase then went through a door', Neil recalls. 'When the door opened, it triggered the sound of barking dogs – quite scary, actually. Then at the end of the corridor the video for 'I don't know what you want …' was playing. Then you turned into the room with the lightbox and Chris and me sitting on it. Ian MacNeil put it together.'

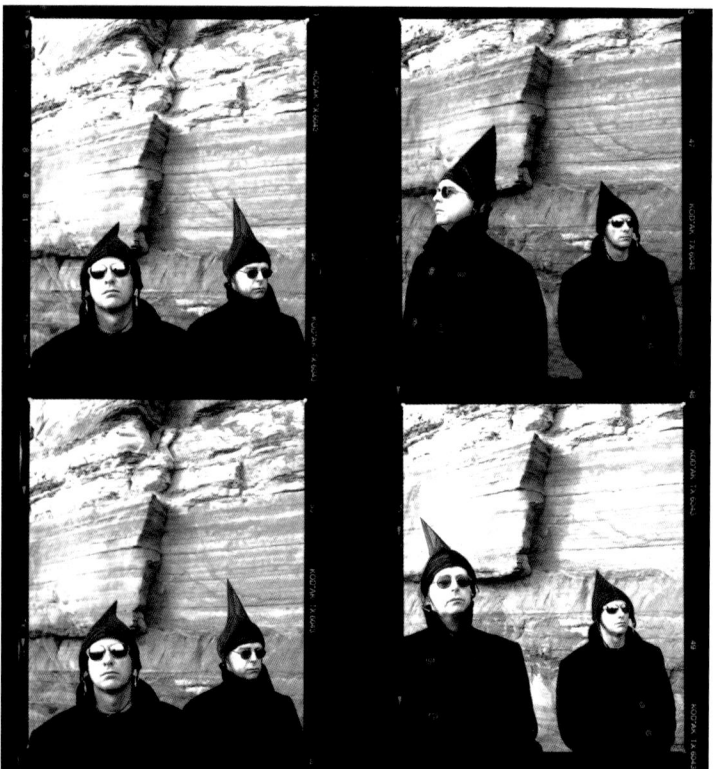

From the Eric Watson photo shoots in Sussex (above) and the St Pancras Hotel (opposite)

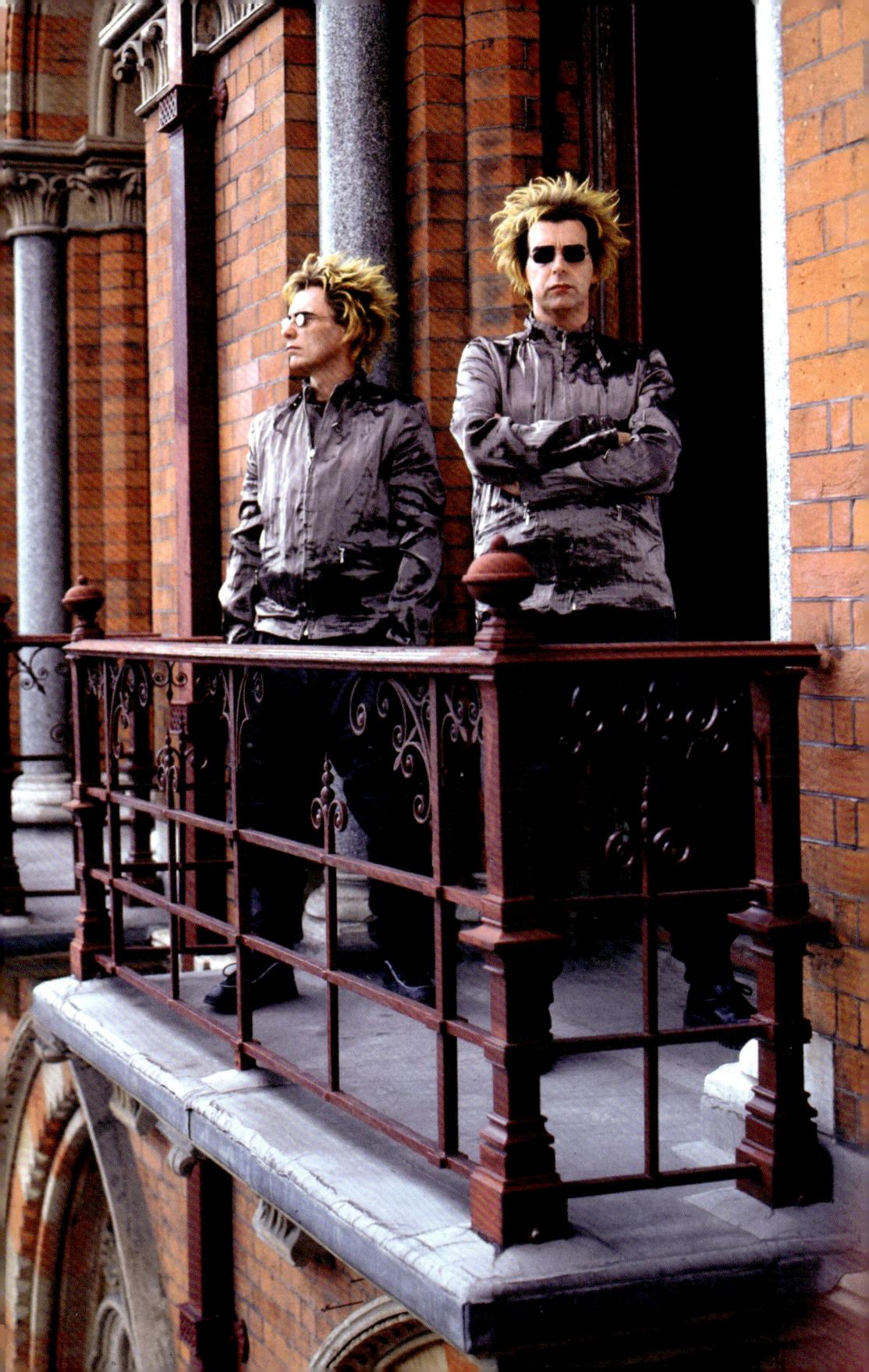

New York City boy

release 27 September 1999
formats Limited-edition two-disc 12" / 12" promo × 4 /
four-disc 12" promo / cassette / CD × 2 / CD promo × 2
photographer Eric Watson
design Farrow Design / PSB
video Howard Greenhalgh

The next single continued to showcase the group's new look.
The photographs were taken by Eric Watson on the same day as the
sleeve photos for 'I don't know what you want …' (pages 6–7 and 253).
They were shot in the same alleyway off West Central Street in London.
The metal foil jackets are by Versace and designed to be breathable.
'We wanted to use a gothic typeface, but Mark Farrow couldn't find one,
so he designed an entirely new typeface of his own', says Neil. Farrow
had seen 'some kind of ticket – a luggage receipt or something like that
– and it had these printed letters in this style, and I'd kept it because
I really liked them. We just drew up the typeface based on ten or twelve
of these letters, because I really liked them. It's odd, because it's got
a mix of upper and lower cases in the type – the 'n' is a lower-case 'n'
– which is not something I'd normally do. We were allowed to do some
pretty lavish stuff on this whole campaign – we did a four-disc twelve-inch
promo (pages 260–1) – and from our point of view as designers those
things are just really good fun. We used a fluorescent ink that we got
mixed especially, and used a metallic colour for the backgrounds, and
got to do those great big numbers on each one: just a licence to go mad
and do something that feels really fresh and new.'

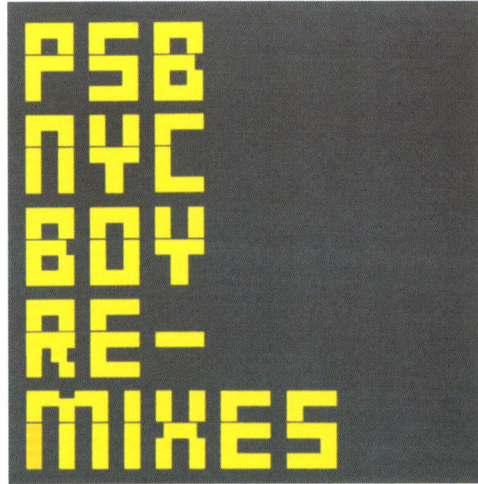

Limited-edition two-disc 12", outer sleeve, front

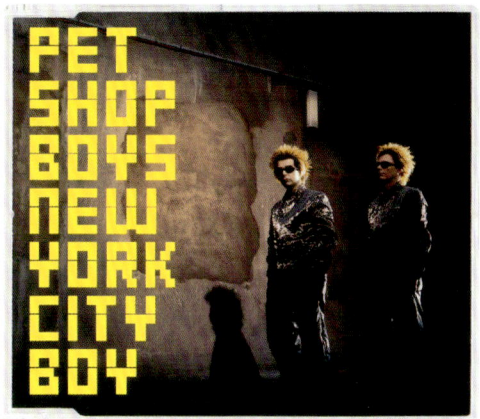

CD 1, front

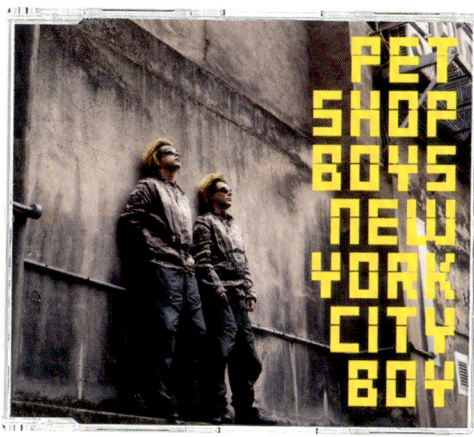

CD 2, front

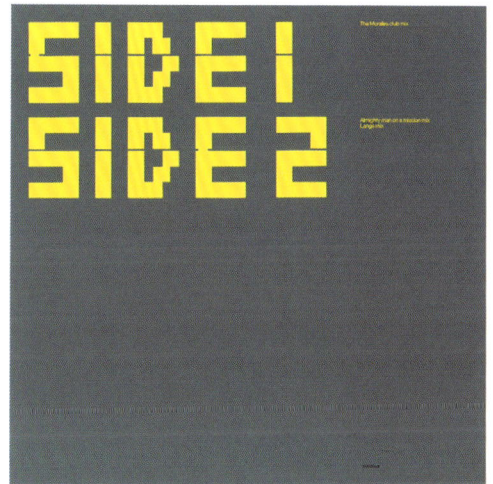

Limited-edition two-disc 12", Side 1/2, inner sleeve, front

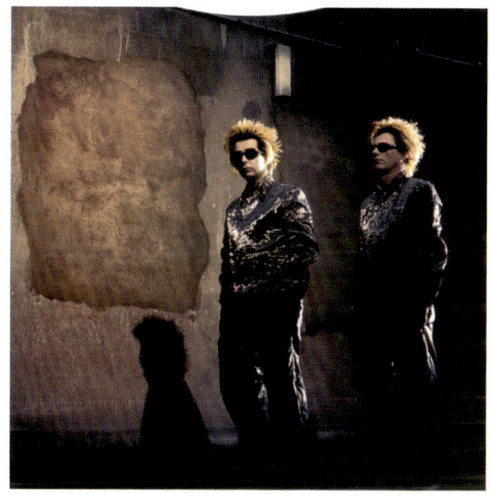

Limited-edition two-disc 12", Side 1/2, inner sleeve, back

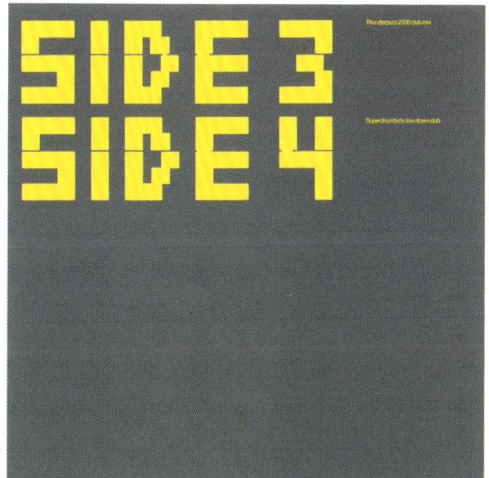

Limited-edition two-disc 12", Side 3/4, inner sleeve, front

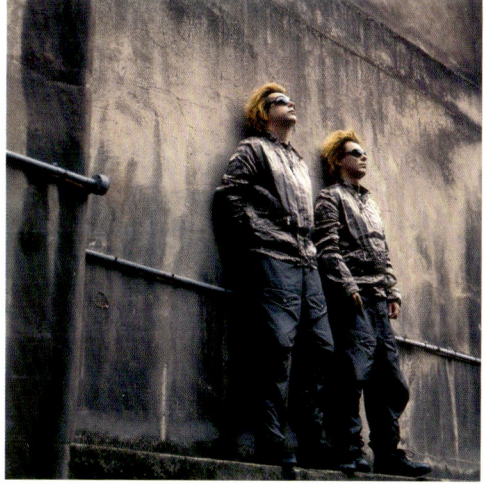

Limited-edition two-disc 12", Side 3/4, inner sleeve, back

New York City boy 1999 259

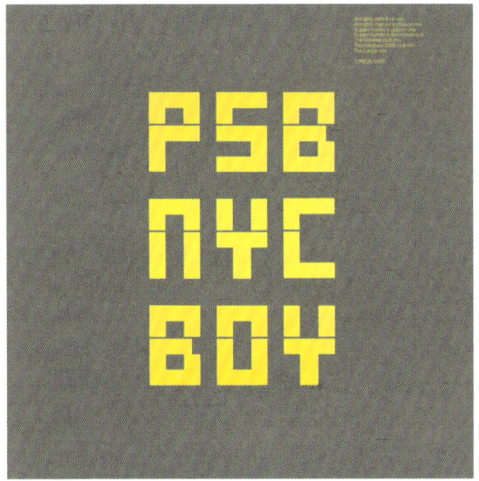

Four-disc 12" promo, outer sleeve, front

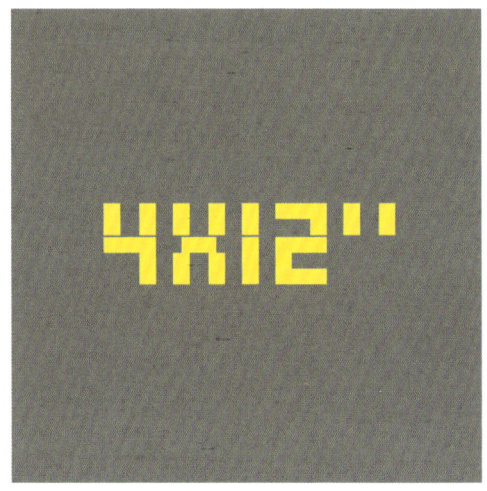

Four-disc 12" promo, outer sleeve, back

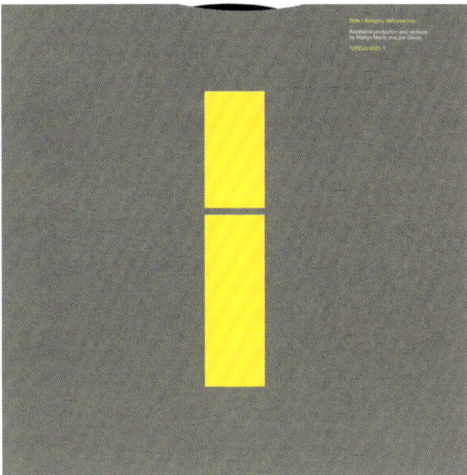

Four-disc 12" promo, Side 1/2, inner sleeve, front

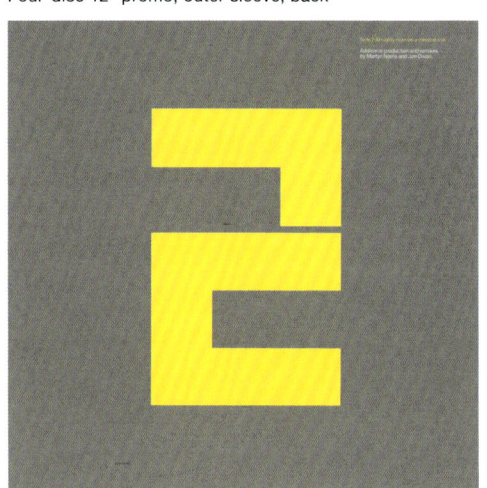

Four-disc 12" promo, Side 1/2, inner sleeve, back

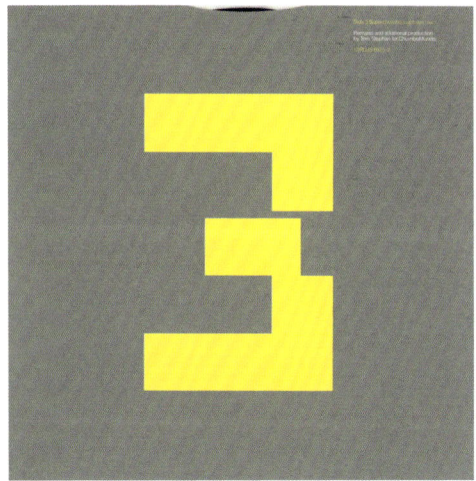

Four-disc 12" promo, Side 3/4, inner sleeve, front

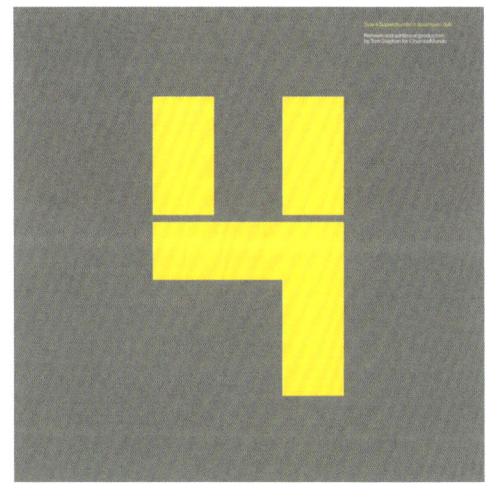

Four-disc 12" promo, Side 3/4, inner sleeve, back

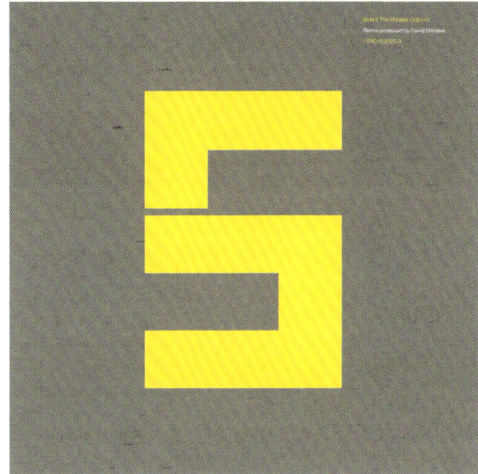
Four-disc 12" promo, Side 5/6, inner sleeve, front

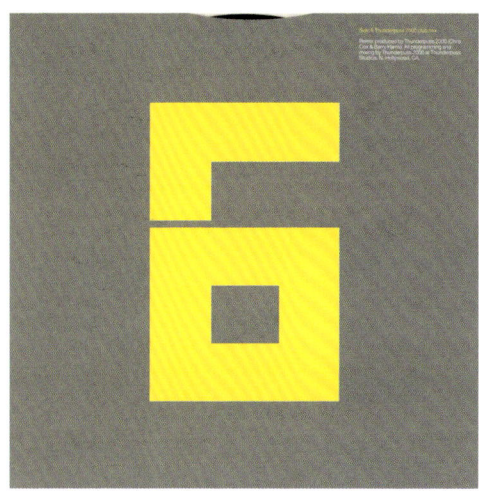
Four-disc 12" promo, Side 5/6, inner sleeve, back

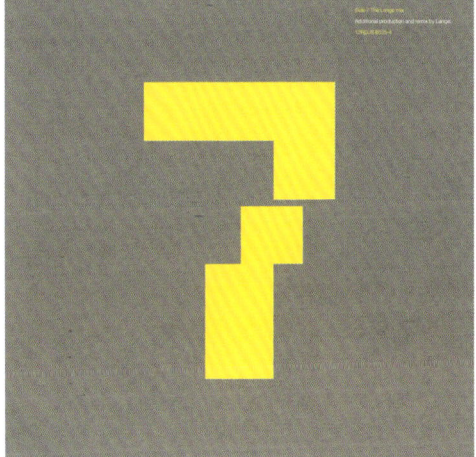
Four-disc 12" promo, Side 7/8, inner sleeve, front

Four-disc 12" promo, Side 7/8, inner sleeve, back

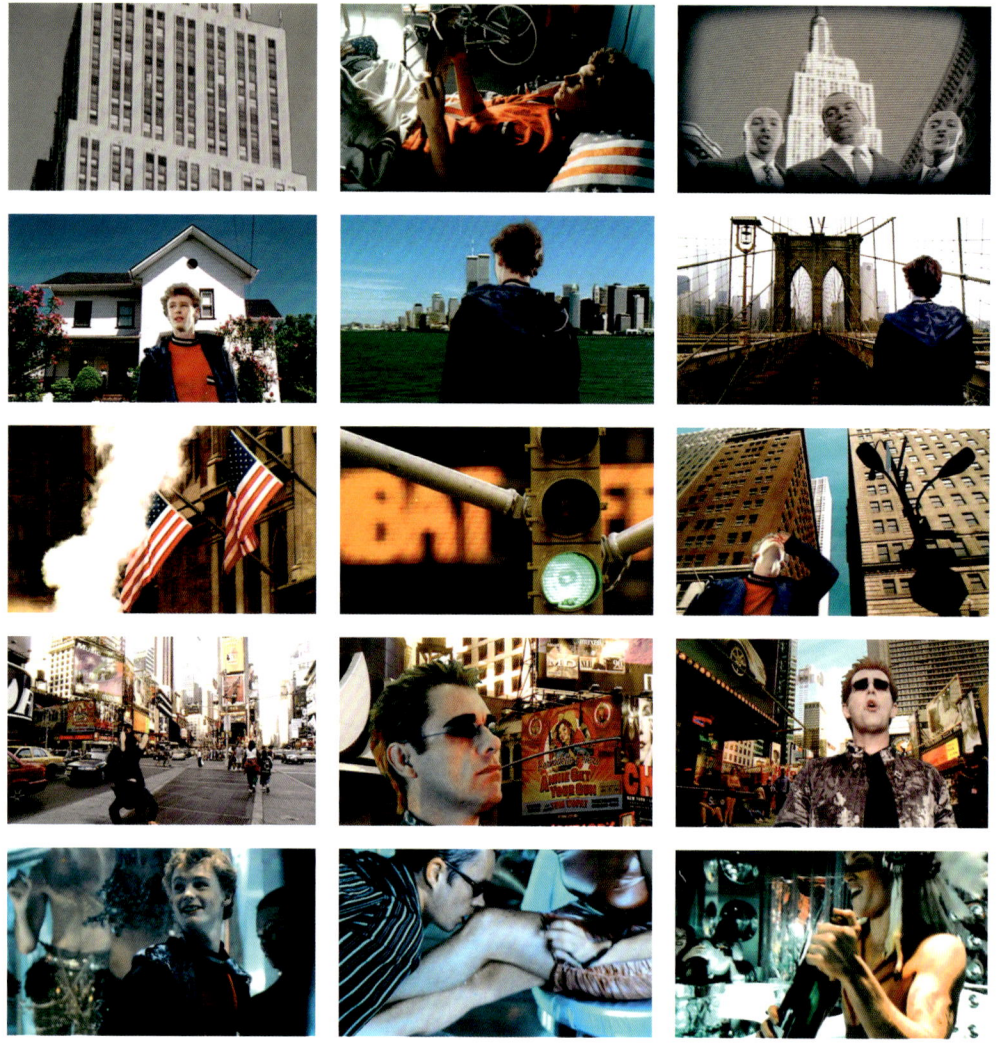

The main character of the video is the boy of the song's title. 'It's the story of the song', Chris said. 'It starts off in this teenage boy's bedroom, and then when he goes to New York it's the New York of all these different eras: the West Side Story bit of the Fifties …'. 'Breakdancing, early Eighties', Neil added. 'The Studio 54 era, late Seventies', Chris said. 'The sailors, late Forties, just after the war', Neil said. The group appears as themselves, in their Versace foil jackets and orange wigs (now cropped), time-travelling. 'We're just us …', Neil said. In the hedonistic Studio 54 sequence, various outrageously dressed and scantily clad revellers, including a Warhol lookalike in blond wig, dance and drink, while Neil sings and Chris looks on. They were in fact filmed in London, and Howard Greenhalgh shot the New York sequences later, melding the two locations together in the final edit. Neil remembers, 'It was the most expensive video we have ever done, although we never actually went to New York.'

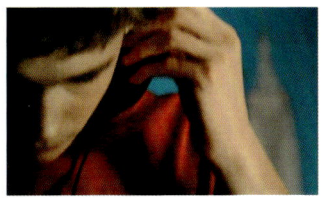
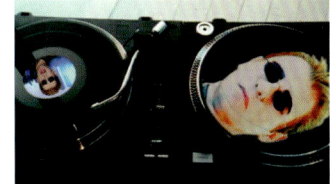
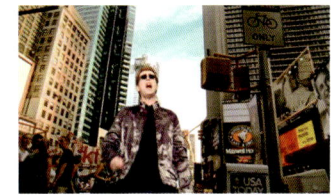
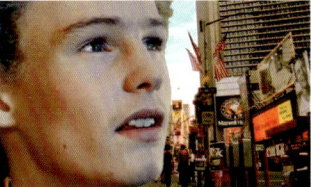
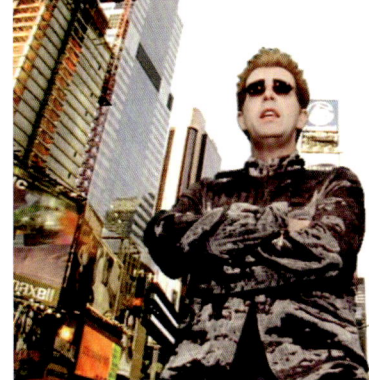
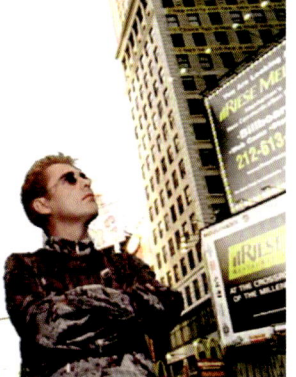
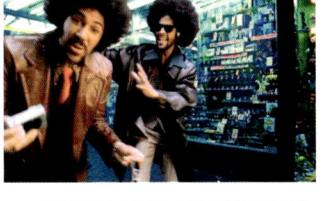
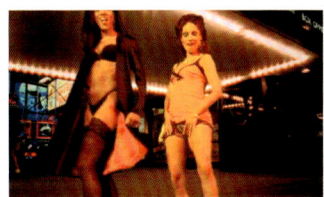
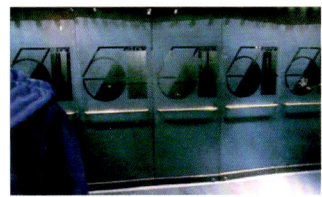
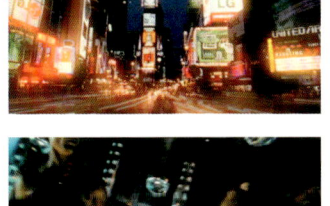
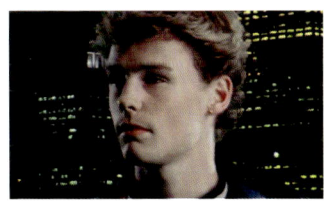
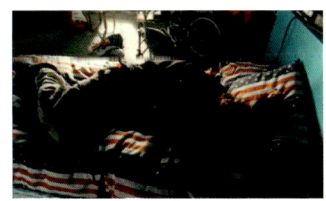

New York City boy 1999

Creamfields

dates 28 August 1999
staging Ian MacNeil
choreography Les Child

Pet Shop Boys were the only live band to play this all-day and all-night dance festival, which took place in six tents near Liverpool on 28 August 1999. They performed in the wigs, make-up, and metal Versace jackets worn in the 'New York City boy' video (pages 262–3), and then in the all-white outfits from the *Somewhere* shows (pages 244–5), on a set designed like a panelled Georgian drawing room (and based on a set in Stanley Kubrick's *2001: A Space Odyssey*). Chris's keyboard was meant to be placed on an old wooden stand to blend in with the anachronistic aesthetic, but it was too wobbly, so a modern one was used instead.

During the performance, the only record of which was a low-quality video filmed on a hand-held camera, two television sets silently played movies: Kubrick's sandals-and-swords saga *Spartacus* and David Lynch's exercise in Victorian surrealism *The Elephant Man*. The group were joined on stage by singer Sylvia Mason-James and dancer Les Child, who performed in a heavy quilted skirt. The strangely disembodied and dramatic air of the performance was reflected in an offhand comment made by Neil at the time. 'We're turning *Waiting for Godot* into a musical. It's our new idea. It's the musical we'll be in.' He then reconsidered, and added, 'Chris can play Godot, so he doesn't have to be there.'

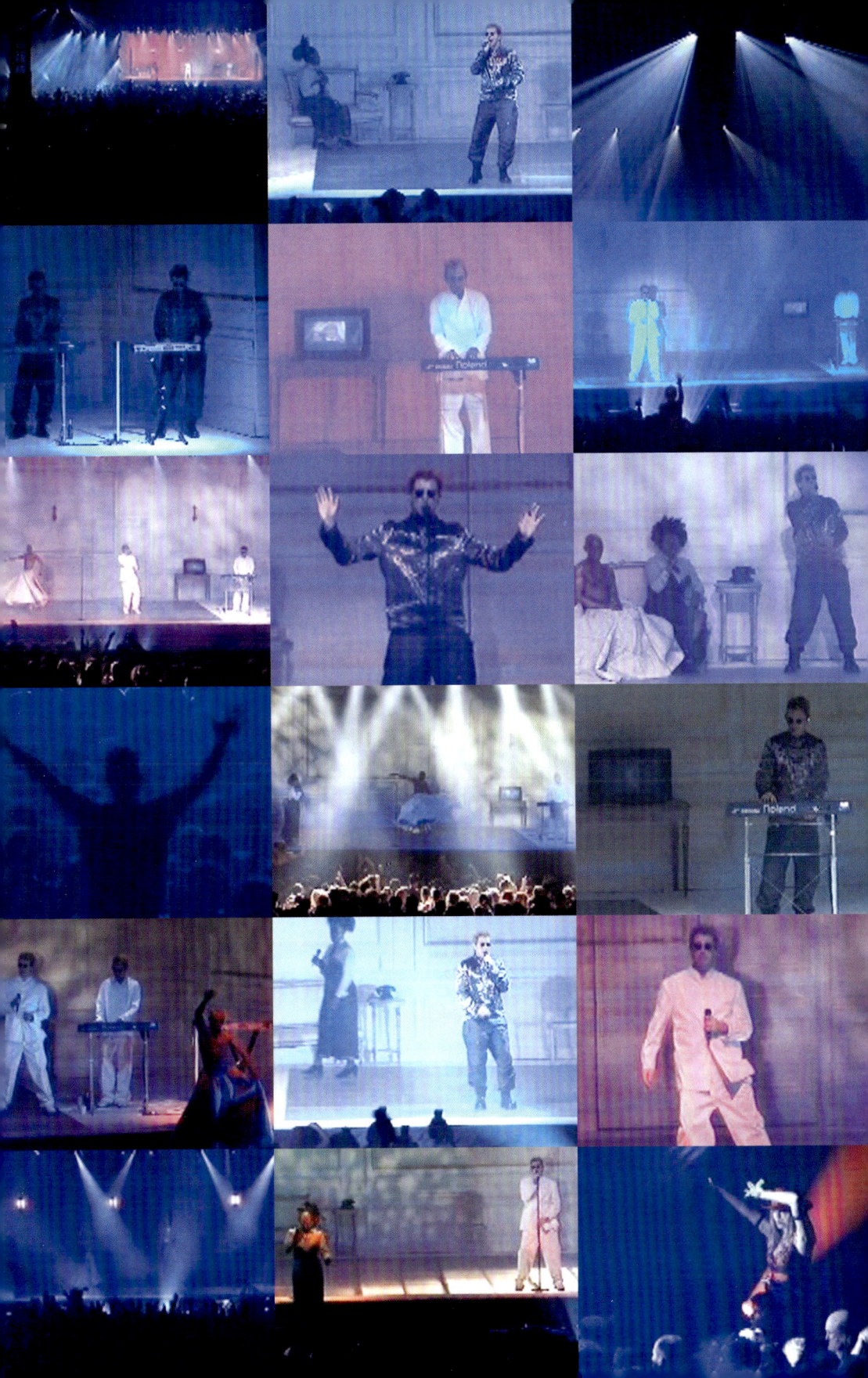

Nightlife

release 11 October 1999
formats LP / cassette / CD / minidisc
photographer Alexei Hay
design Farrow Design / PSB

Alexei Hay was commissioned for the *Nightlife* artwork after the group saw his shot of a girl on the New York subway. He suggested doing the same with Neil and Chris. 'We spent three and a half hours being photographed on the subway', said Neil, 'which is illegal, with lights taped to the hanging rail. We were meant to be going to Coney Island …', '… but we got on the wrong train', recalls Chris. Farrow suggested the blurring of the heads 'to give movement to the shots, like you're on the subway at night', Neil said. 'The photo relates to the idea of nightlife because you're going out.' 'The most exciting time for going out is when you actually live slightly out of town,' Chris said, 'that sense of adventure that you're going to do something great.' According to Farrow, the initial impulse for the blurring was that the unblurred photos offered an unsympathetically intimate view of their new look. 'I would have been happy to go with the pictures as they were, because they were quite striking, but it completely changed the look of it', he says. The album used the same typeface as 'New York City boy' (pages 258–61). 'One version had a plastic case with "Nightlife" printed on it, and it folded out.' A promo CD with an interview about the album was also released.

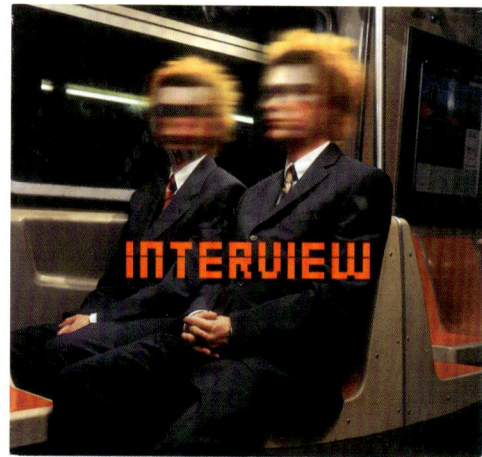

Interview, CD, front

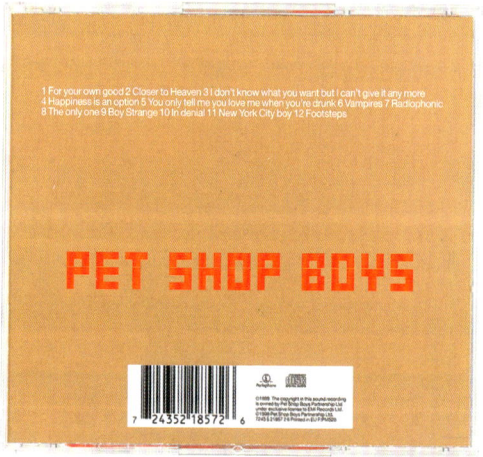

CD, back

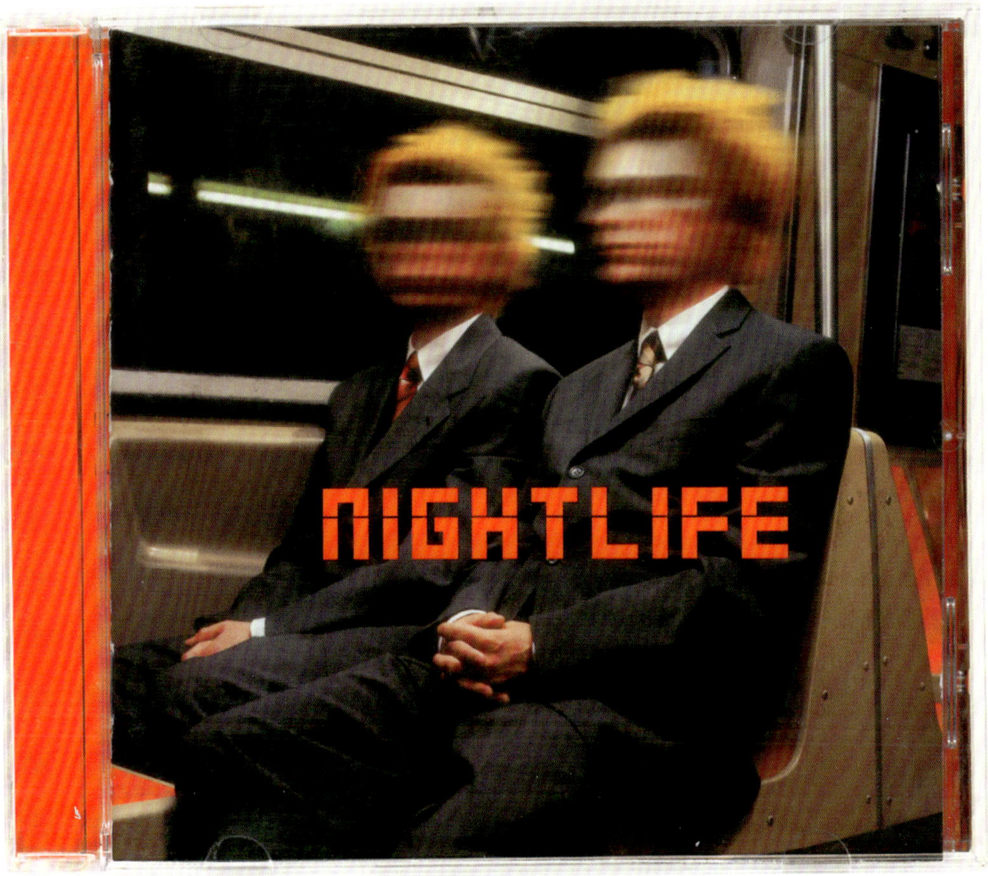

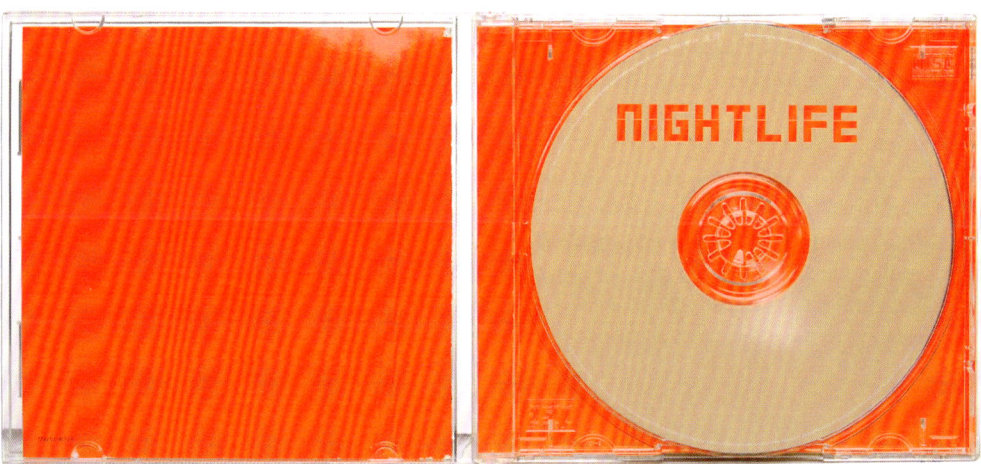

CD, front

CD, inside

Nightlife 1999

Nightlife tour

dates 20 October 1999 – 12 February 2000
set design Zaha Hadid
project architect Oliver Domeisen at Zaha Hadid
costume design/staging Ian MacNeil

'With their new image, record, and forthcoming tour, the Pet Shop Boys are presenting, as usual, an entire theatrical package', wrote Michael Bracewell. 'This time, they have pulled off the considerable coup of collaborating with the visionary architect Zaha Hadid, some of whose buildings have been considered too radical to be constructed....
The Pet Shop Boys are continuing their fascination with presenting artificial environments in which to perform their songs. "Actually, the idea came about because Janet Street-Porter had been working with Zaha Hadid for her television programme," says Neil. "And she said, 'Why don't you get Zaha Hadid to design your new musical?' and we said, 'Because she's an architect and it's a completely different discipline from designing for the theatre.' But then we were in New York and I was flicking through a book of Zaha's designs in the Rizzoli bookshop, and I suddenly saw all of her architectural models as stage sets – wonderful shapes to walk across while holding a microphone, wearing a ludicrous costume and having a wind machine on you."'

Hadid 'liked the architectonic elements' of Pet Shop Boys videos. 'I noticed they were often travelling and walking through these strange spatialities.... I saw the one where they were on the escalators ['Can you forgive her?'] and I thought they must like being on different heights, and that's how I saw them in this particular set.' She conceived the stage as 'a fragment of a building. Not in a literal sense, but a segment. Or it could be seen as a miniature; a shrunken idea of a whole project.' It was able to conform to any size and shape of auditorium. 'It unfolds like a landscape', she said. 'It could hold things inside it, or it could be one volume that rests other things on it. It could change shape during the show itself, as well as throughout the tour.... Obviously it's not a building and it has to be light, to be rigged, to be easily opened and closed. It could be black and white or solid. The performers could appear within the object or outside it.'

Working with architects was a new sensibility for Pet Shop Boys. According to Neil, 'They bring a very rigorous aesthetic to it that they don't want you to trangress, and I really admire that.' Once the design, seen here during rehearsals, was presented, 'they didn't regard this as something to be messed around with; they felt they had established an aesthetic that you had to work with.' It was a very visual tour for the group. 'It's a bit like a mixture of a concert and an art installation,' Neil said at the time, 'because it's also quite influenced by the American artist Bruce Nauman, whose show we saw in the Hayward Gallery last year [1998].'

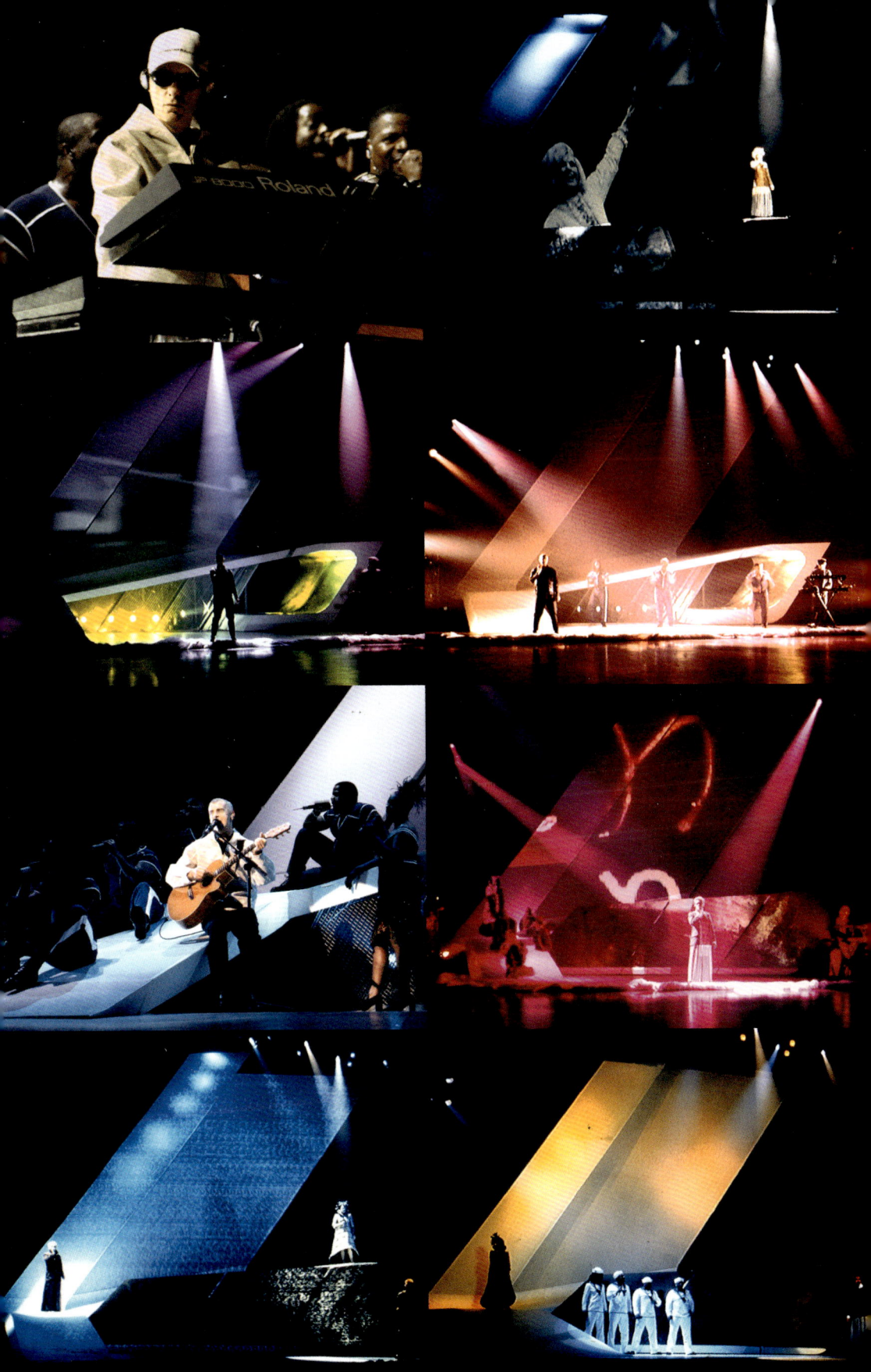

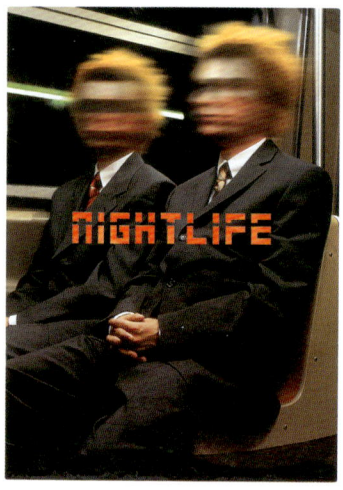
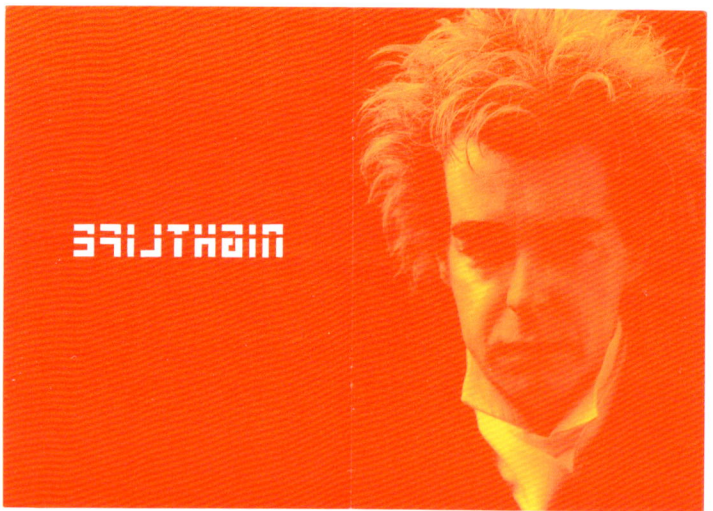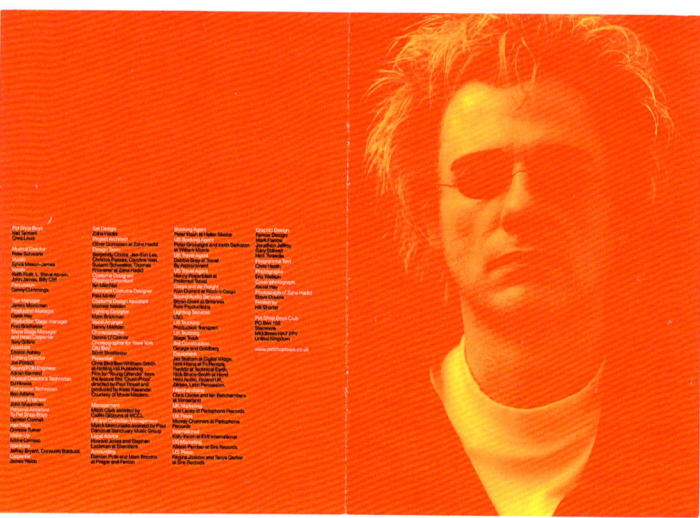

Tour programme, front and back cover (*top*) and inside front and back cover

In keeping with the aesthetic of the concert itself, the tour programme had a futuristic design, using the special typeface that Farrow had created for 'New York City boy' (die cut out of the front cover) and being printed in red and yellow.

The cover of the concert video likewise used Farrow's typeface, with a photo of Neil taken during the show by Lester Cohen. 'It's called *Montage* because it's only based on the concert', Neil noted. 'It's been a long journey.' The film was edited by Warren Meneely. 'We had this idea that at all times there would be three or four things happening on the screen,' said Chris, 'and that's what there is all the way through, so it's like making a new video for every song.' The basic footage was filmed in Dortmund, but the DVD included webcast footage from two other German cities, and from performances in New York and Atlanta; background footage and other material from the *Nightlife* and summer tour of 2000; and additional material from Pet Shop Boys videos, as well as the single videos for 'I don't know what you want …' (pages 254–5), 'New York City boy' (pages 262–3), and 'You only tell me you love me when you're drunk' (pages 274–5).

To tie in with the Japanese tour that year, Pet Shop Boys released a further Japan-only product, *Mini*, which included various songs from the *Nightlife* era as well as live versions of some earlier singles.

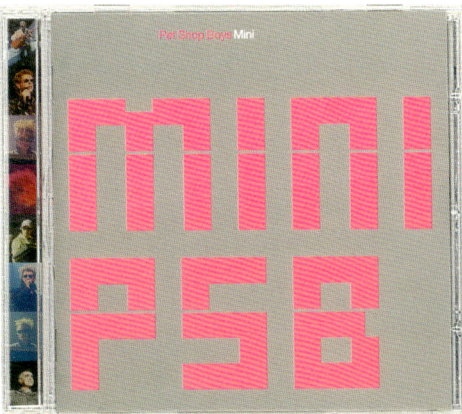

Montage, VHS, front

Mini, CD, front

You only tell me you love me when you're drunk

release 3 January 2000
formats 12" / 12" promo / CD × 3 / cassette /
CD × 2 / CD promo × 3
photographer Harry Borden and Lester Cohen
design Farrow Design
video Pedro Romhanyi

'Promoting the tour with the single,' Neil notes, 'one of our shameful marketing scams.' 'We wouldn't have a book without them', says Chris. 'We should call it "Marketing Scams".' The close-up head photographs were shot by Harry Borden on the set of the 'New York City boy' video (pages 262–3). The eyebrows were never more pronounced than they appear in these images. The other two 'live' photographs were taken by Lester Cohen during the Pet Shop Boys' *Nightlife* concert in Atlanta. CD 1 had a montage of the two heads, while CDs 2 and 3 featured one of the live photographs each. The three CDs were also available in a box set, with thumbnail versions of the three images on the reverse of the box. The orange-brown colour of the packaging was chosen to reflect Neil and Chris's orange wigs.

'I just wanted to write "Drunk" on everything and they didn't, because they loved the idea of "You only tell me you love me when you're drunk", which is a very Pet Shop Boys title', said Mark Farrow. He got his way on the first CD promo and the twelve-inch promo, which had a purely typographic treatment using a plain Helvetica typeface. 'People perceive "You only tell me you love me when you're drunk" as ironic', Neil complained, 'when in fact it's a painful, heartbreaking song to me, because it's so true.'

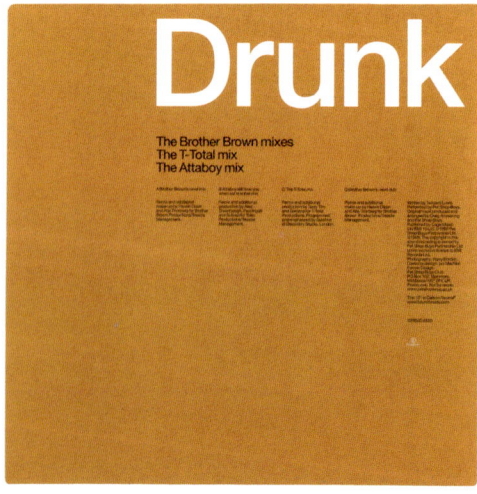

12" promo, outer sleeve, front

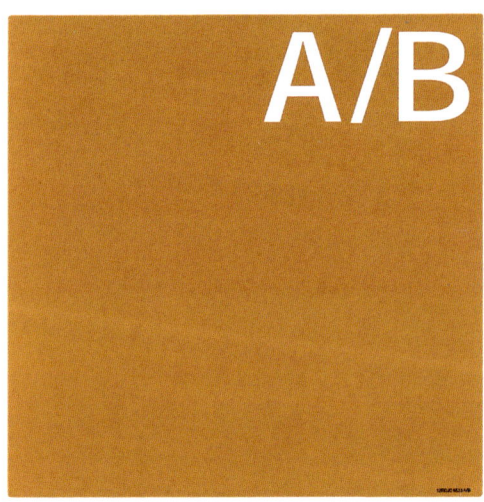

12" promo, Side A/B, inner sleeve, front

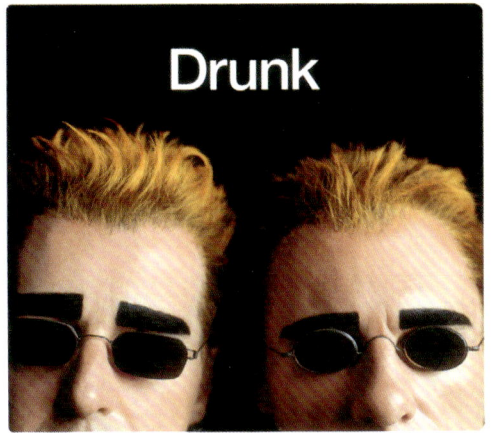
CD promo 1, front

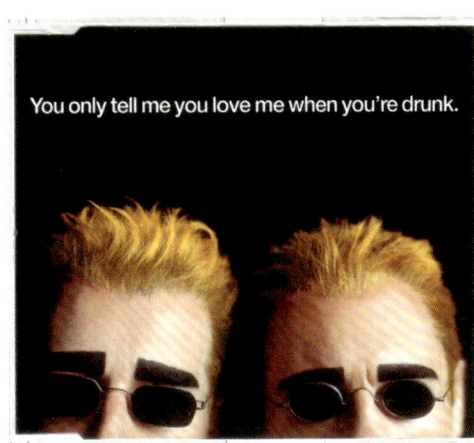
CD 1, front

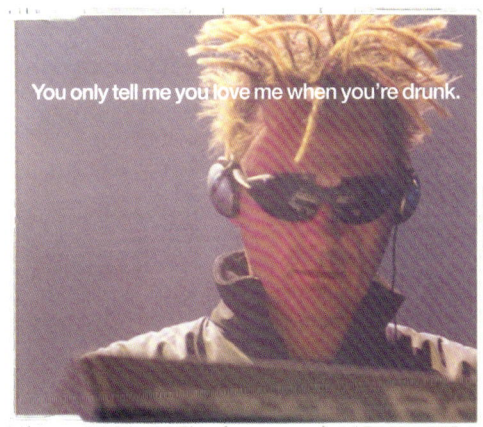
CD 2, front

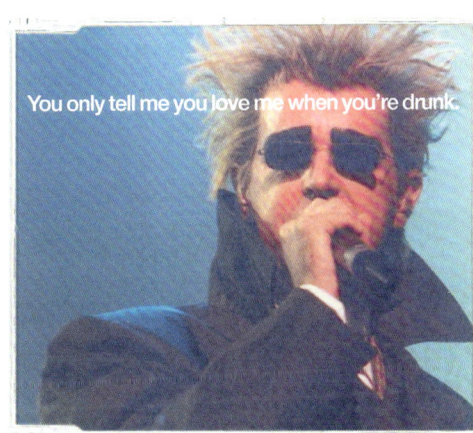
CD 3, front

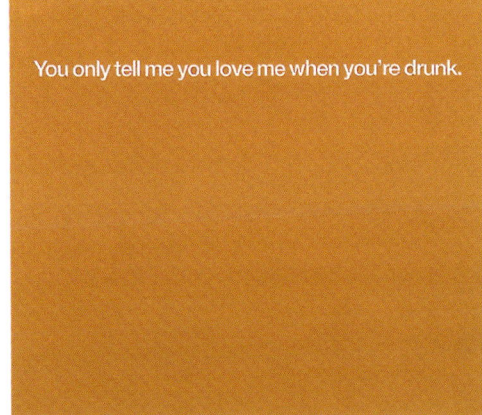
CD box set, front

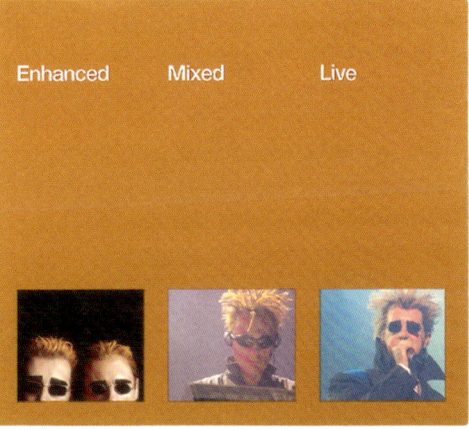
CD box set, back

You only tell me you love me when you're drunk   2000   273

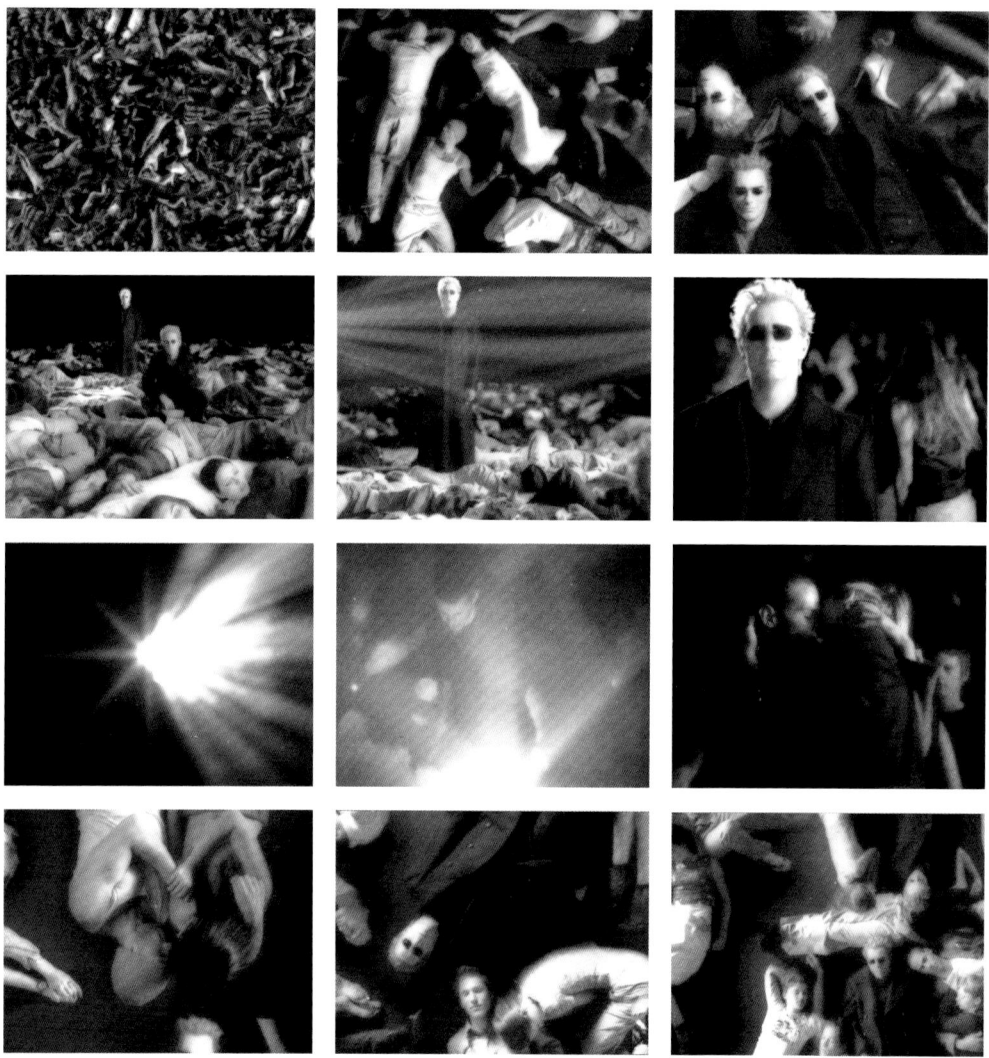

The video for 'You only tell me you love me when you're drunk' was filmed shortly before the start of the *Nightlife* tour. It begins with a distance shot, from high above, of a mass of figures lying down. Having zoomed in, we see that all of these people are sleeping, except for the numerous figures of Neil and Chris, who appear again and again as the camera pans over the crowd. Then they are seen standing or crouching with the sleeping figures at their ankles. Suddenly light floods the scene and the entire crowd wakes from their slumber to party, before sinking back to the floor and deep sleep. 'I think it's a lovely video', Neil says. 'It really encapsulates the mood of the song. It's all these people crashed out at a party, a crowd that goes on for ever.' Pedro Romhanyi used a special camera to shoot from above. 'We just had to lie down', Chris said. 'It was a lying-down video.' 'We had quite a laugh', Neil said. 'There was the excitement of the nude scene, which you can hardly see in the finished video.'

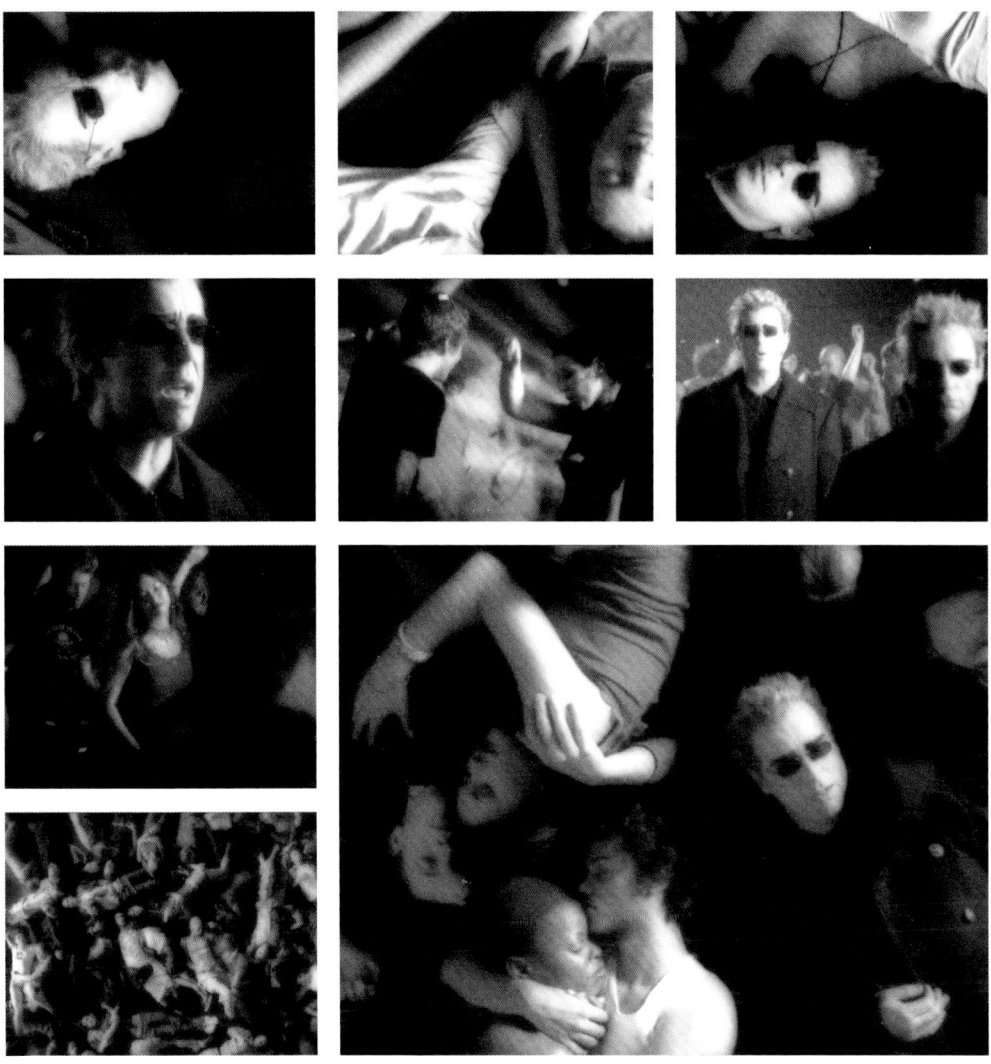

Pet Shop Boys Catalogue 1986–1996

release 4 June 2001
formats CD × 6
photographers Cindy Palmano and Eric Watson
design Farrow Design / PSB

In June 2001, Pet Shop Boys released remastered CD versions of their first six albums, setting aside *Disco* and *Disco 2*. The combined release was called 'Pet Shop Boys Catalogue'. Each album was packaged as a double CD inside a slipcase. The first CD had exactly the same track listing as the original album, and the second CD included songs and mixes, both released and previously unreleased, that had been recorded in the same era as the original album. Each slipcase displayed the original album sleeve design – in the case of *Very* and *Bilingual*, two-dimensional representations of the original three-dimensional or laminated effect – in a square, but with the titles and type stripped from the artwork and placed in the border to left of the sleeve design. The images on *Please* and *Actually* were reduced to reflect the proportions of the original sleeves. In these new cover layouts, it was necessary to decide definitively whether each title should come after the name of the group (*Please, Actually, Behaviour*) or before it (*Introspective, Very, Bilingual*). Each album came with a thirty-six-page booklet including photographs from the time, lyrics, and in-depth commentary by Neil and Chris about each song.

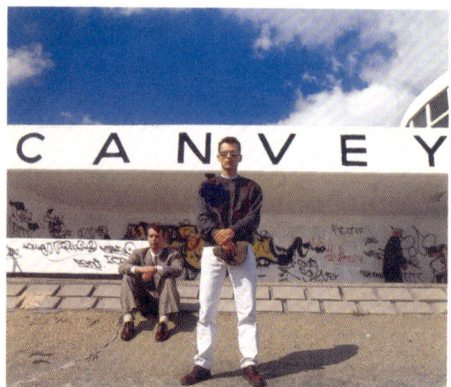

Introspective, booklet, inside pages

Pet Shop Boys
Please

Pet Shop Boys
Actually

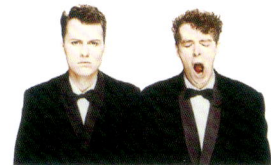

Please, front

Actually, front

Introspective
Pet Shop Boys

Very
Pet Shop Boys

Introspective, front

Very, front

Pet Shop Boys
Behaviour

Bilingual
Pet Shop Boys

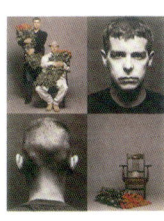

Behaviour, front

Bilingual, front

Pet Shop Boys Catalogue 1986–1996 2001 277

Closer to Heaven

dates 15 May – 13 October 2001 (performances)
release 6 October 2001 (cast recording)
format CD
photographer Paul Wesley Griggs (cover)
and Alastair Muir (cast photography)
design Groupe

Closer to Heaven was the musical written by Pet Shop Boys and playwright Jonathan Harvey. The first public performance was held at the London Arts Theatre on 15 May 2001. It was set in a London club, and its characters included the 'European rock star has-been' Billie Trix (Frances Barber), club owner Vic Christian (David Burt) and his daughter Shell (Stacey Roca), the outrageous manager Bob Saunders (Paul Broughton), Straight Dave (Paul Keating), and Mile End Lee (Tom Walker) – all of whom could have walked out of an updated 'West End girls', and whose subterranean lives are punctuated by hedonism, drugs, and sexual passion.

The show takes place at night – as the dark cover of the cast recording reflects – while the luminous heart echoes the characters' emotional journeys. The stage designer was Es Devlin, who went on to design several Pet Shop Boys tours. She 'wanted to defy the dimensions of the tiny Arts Theatre and to play with the audience's point of view'. One coup was a duet on a perpendicular bed – a breathtaking effect that echoed the upturned beds of the *Performance* tour. 'The music invited bold theatricality, the text invited televisual realism – so scenes were either framed in a room-sized box or escaped up the theatre walls', says Devlin. She was inspired by artist Keith Haring's work in the costumes and choreography for 'Hedonism', while 'the translucent underwear over a lightbox for the bed scene came to me while looking at Glen Luchford's Prada photographs'.

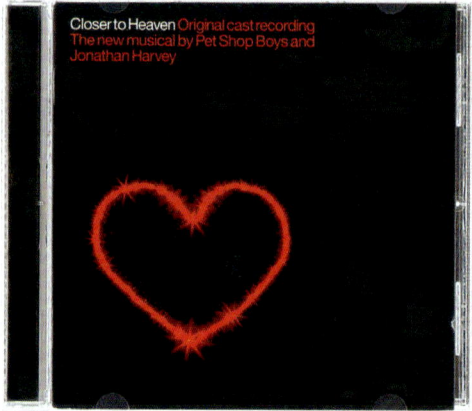

CD, front

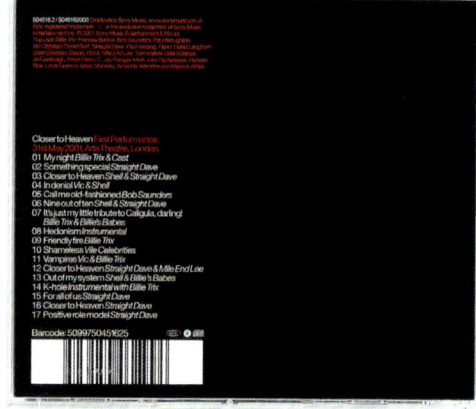

CD, back

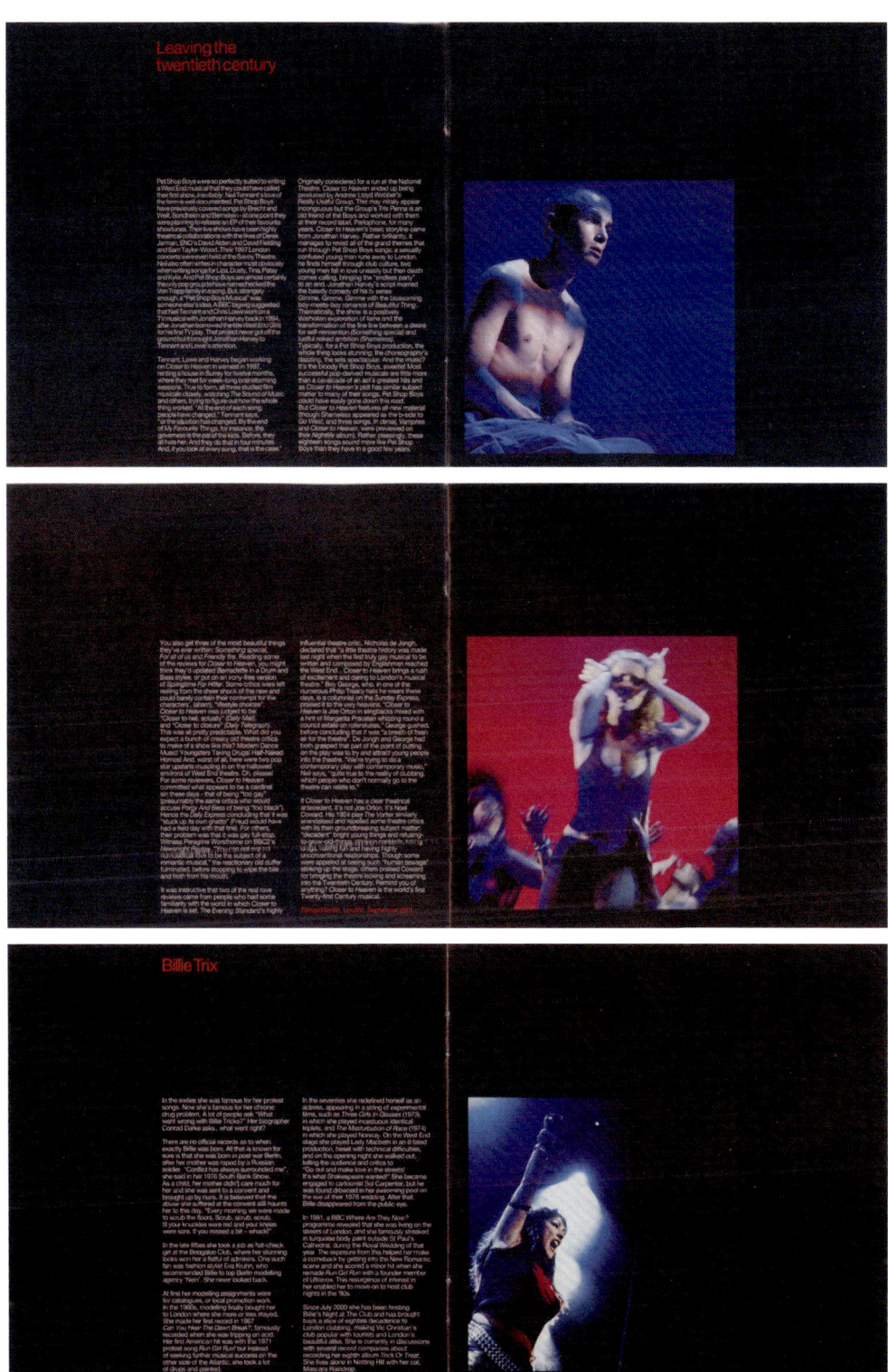

CD, booklet, inside pages

Home and dry

release 18 March 2002
formats 12" promo / CD × 2 / CD promo / DVD
design Scott King (assisted by Patrick Duffy)
video Wolfgang Tillmans

Pet Shop Boys decided to commission a different designer for the various singles from their next album, *Release*, and turned to Scott King, who had been recommended to them simultaneously by Emily King (no relation), design editor of the art magazine *Frieze*, and the artist Wolfgang Tillmans, who would create the video for 'Home and dry'. It was a continuation of Pet Shop Boys' involvement with artists. 'We'd seen this poster he did called "Cher Guevara", which is the picture of Che Guevara with Cher's face on it', said Chris. 'We looked at a lot of his work and liked it.' The first sleeve King designed was for 'Break 4 love', Pet Shop Boys' collaboration with DJ Peter Rauhofer. Chris said of the 'Home and dry' design, 'What I like about it is that he's taken the words "Pet Shop Boys" and made them really big. It's completely the opposite of what we've done in the rest of our career where we've always had really small type, or even just a sticker. He's filled the whole sleeve with real bold colours. It's good to make such a positive statement. It's like a statement of self-belief.'

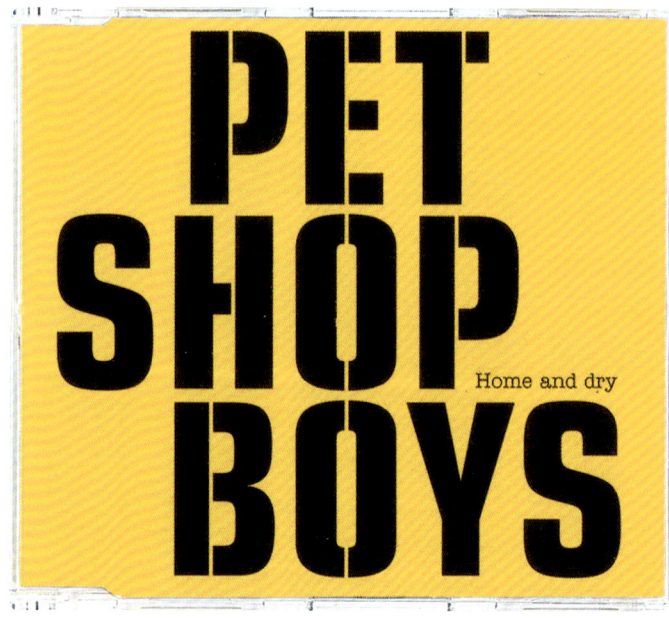

CD 2, front

'Break 4 love' 12" promo, front

12" promo, front

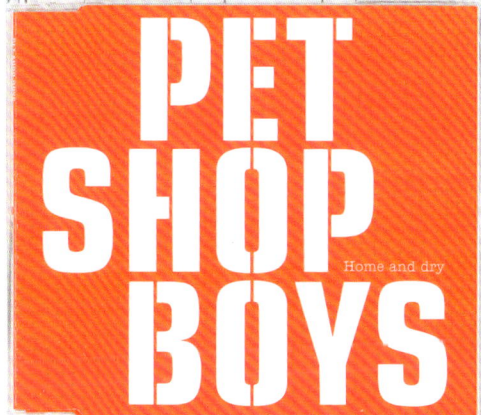

DVD, front

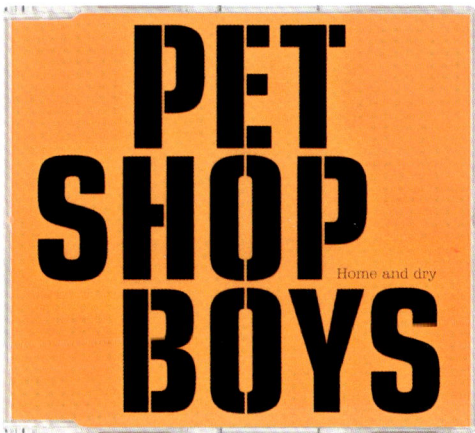

CD 1, front

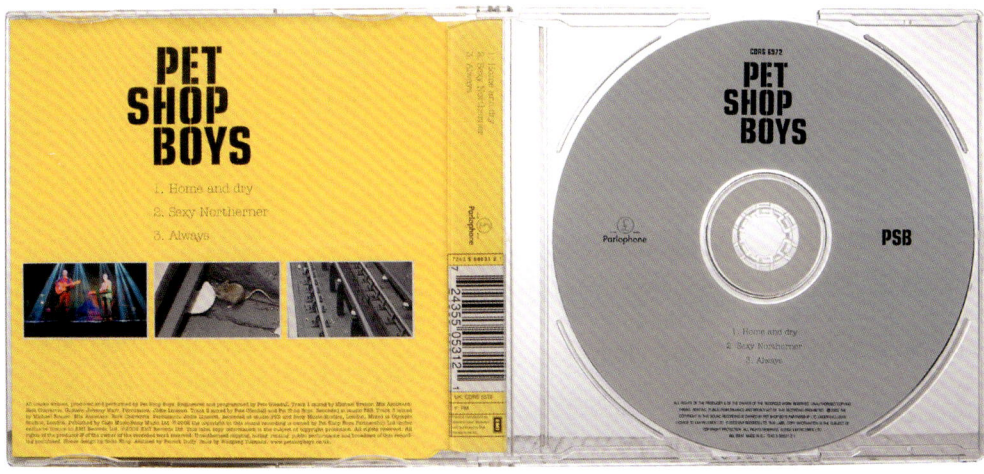

CD 2, inside

Home and dry 2002

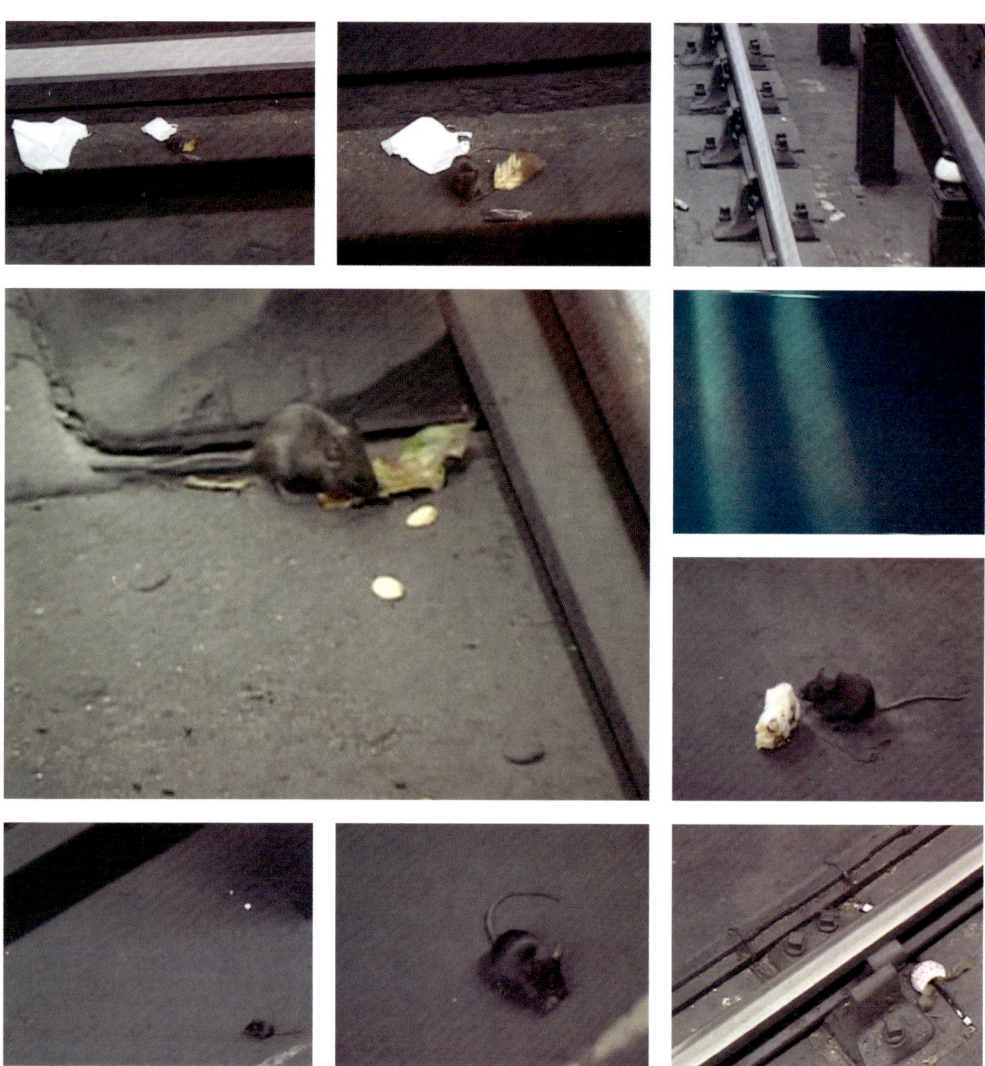

'Having met Wolfgang Tillmans, we suddenly thought maybe he could make a video for us', said Neil. 'A lot of his work concentrates on small details of everyday life turned into larger photographic artworks, and we felt that's what we do: take small details of everyday life and make them into pop songs. They work on different levels, his pictures, as well. Sometimes they have a sexual meaning that isn't necessarily at first apparent.' Tillmans wanted to shoot the video in his flat, showing a man who was missing his girlfriend, looking round at things that reminded him of her. He would cut that with footage of the group performing the song. 'So we filmed the performance', Neil recalls, at the nightclub Heaven, one Sunday afternoon, 'and we went to see him a few days later and he said, "I've completely changed the idea – I hope you don't mind."' And then he showed us what is pretty much the finished video of the mice. He'd spent several days filming mice at Tottenham Court Road

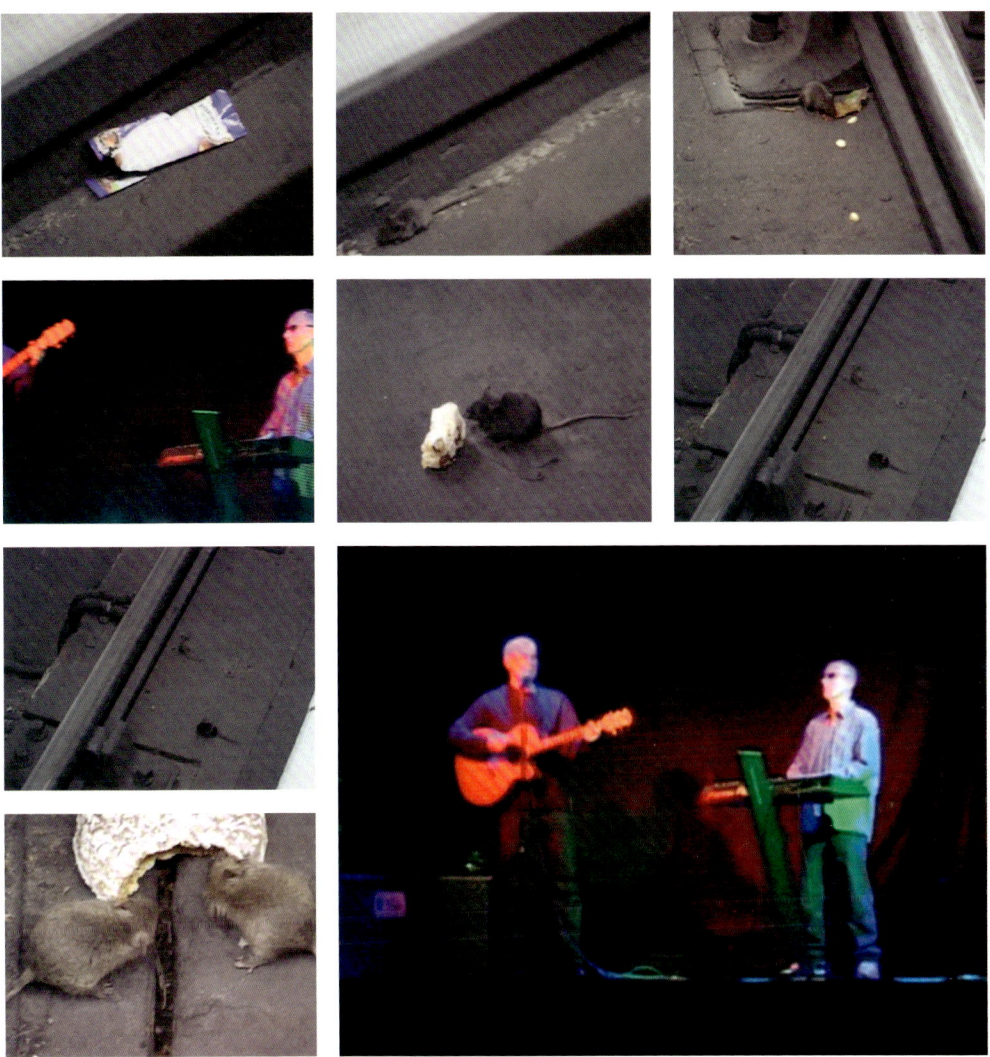

Underground station. It was such an original kind of image. It seemed to sum up the idea. "Home and dry" is about being at home and the idea of travel at the same time.' The video was premiered at insidespace, a gallery within the Selfridges department store. 'It looked great on the wall', Neil said. The group were subsequently told that MTV regarded the video as unbroadcastable. 'I was expecting it', Chris said. 'Our video is actually genuinely shocking, I think, a very brave video.'

University tour

dates 8 – 16 February 2002
set design and lighting Carl Burnett

The short *University* tour, which took in various small venues in Britain (mostly universities) and one in Cologne, Germany (shown here), had an intimate, almost cabaret feel, deliberately low-key – although the stark lighting and use of lateral blinds seemed to reference David Bowie's 1976 *Station to Station* concerts, themselves influenced by the black-and-white photography of Man Ray. Stripped of the grandiose statements of previous tours, it seemed Pet Shop Boys were actually getting nearer and closer to their audiences rather than further away – confronting and escaping at the same time. Most groups begin their careers by working the British university circuit; with characteristic perversity, Pet Shop Boys waited eighteen years to do it.

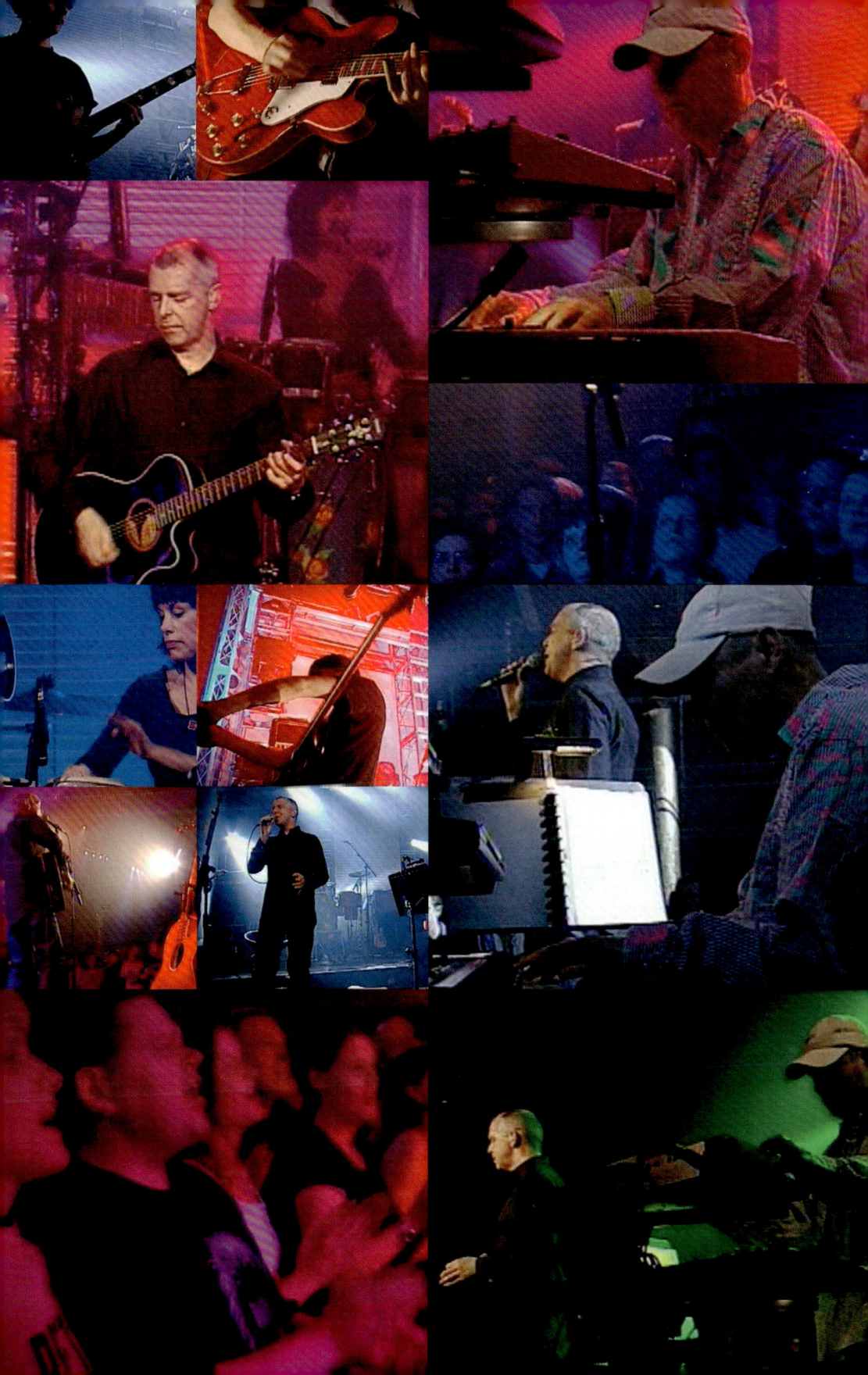

Release

release 1 April 2002
formats LP / cassette / CD × 4
photographers Dan Forbes (flower portraits);
Pennie Smith (group portrait)
design Visionaire Design (art direction: Greg Foley;
production: Jake McCabe; design associate: Tatiana Gaz)

Release was the first Pet Shop Boys album sleeve not designed by Mark Farrow. 'We were keen to experiment with all the details on this album,' Neil noted, 'and we'd worked with Mark and his company for every album, so found it quite difficult to make the break.' New York designers Visionaire are celebrated for their deluxe and eclectic graphic design. They produced four different foil-effect sleeves showing four flowers, each in a different colour – turquoise daisy, grey poppy, pink rose, and red iris – like old botanical prints. 'We thought they would look very beautiful in a row in the record shops', Neil said. The sleeves are in fact slipcases, debossed 'so that they're slightly 3-D'. The jewel case inside reads 'Pet Shop Boys Release' printed in white on white opaque plastic. The LP's outer sleeve shows the tulip in duotone on grey, while the inner sleeve has the full-colour version. The latter also appeared on the front of the Japanese CD. The considered still-life quality of the imagery both complements and counterpoints the album's title, itself suggested by Wolfgang Tillmans: 'There is a sense of emotional release', Neil said. 'Our keyboard technician Paul Beckett saw the artwork and said, "Oh, I get *Release* – it's because the flowers are releasing pollen." I guess some people thinks it sounds slightly sexual too.'

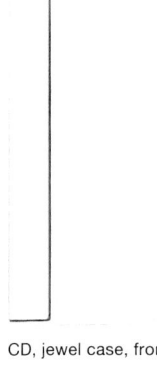

CD, jewel case, front

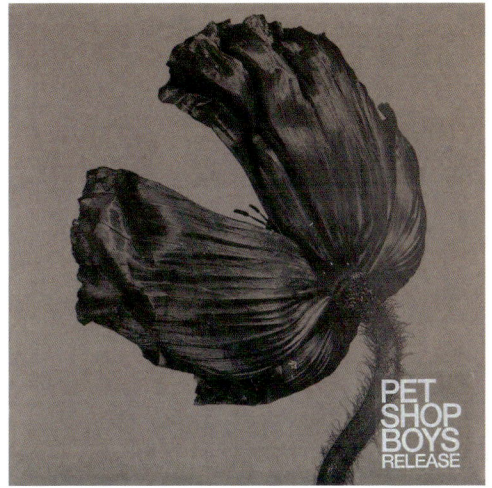

LP, outer sleeve, front

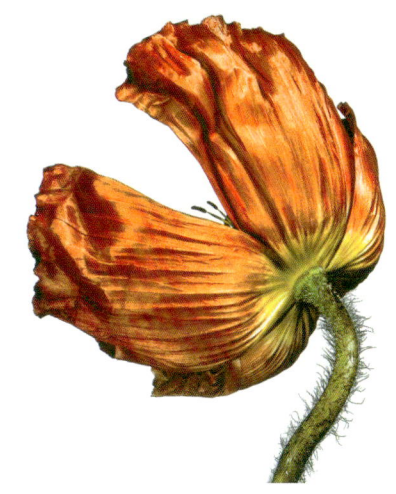

LP, inner sleeve, front

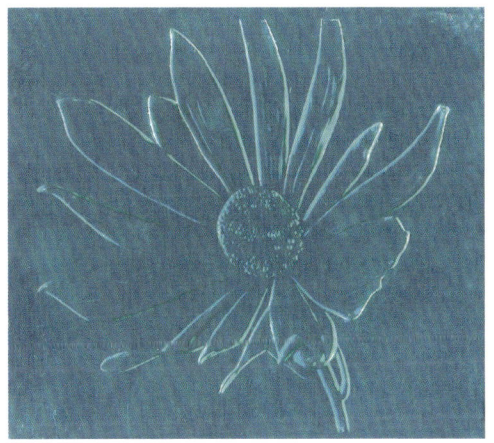

CD 1, slipcase, front

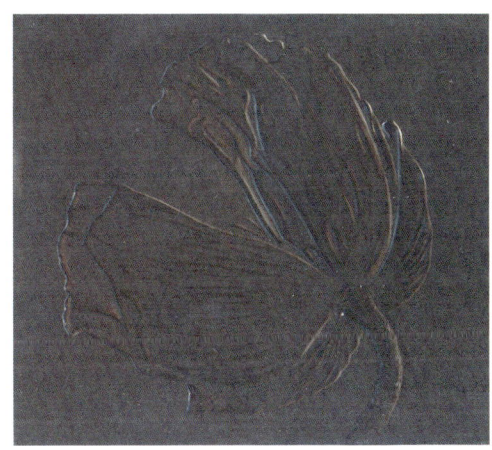

CD 2, slipcase, front

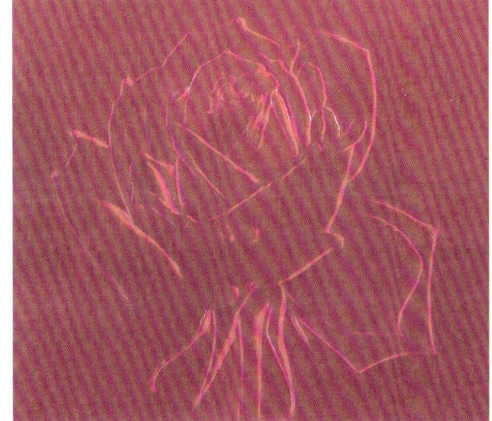

CD 3, slipcase, front

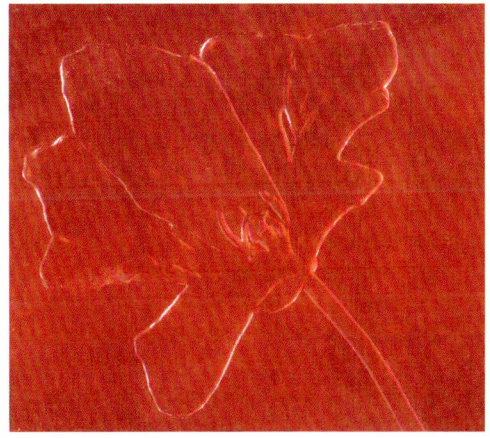

CD 4, slipcase, front

Release tour

dates 14 May – 2 August 2002
set design Ian MacNeil
lighting Carl Burnett

The *Release* tour of 2002 had a similar aesthetic to the *University* tour earlier that year. As Neil explained at the time to Michael Bracewell: 'To us, the enemy used to be rock – like stadium rock in the Eighties, in particular, then during grunge we were doing our pointy hats look and our cartoony videos. Now it seems to me that the enemy is crap pop. It seems to me that most dance music is just industry music, and it's everywhere. Everywhere you go in the world, you'll see a poster for Sasha and Digweed…. So, on *Release*, in terms of presentation, we had, for us, this weird idea that we would present ourselves as musicians – and we've never done that before.'

Pet Shop Boys produced a booklet as a programme for the *Release* tour. Designed by Scott King and with a text by Philip Hoare, it featured photographs shot by the American photographer Valerie Phillips on a cold day in County Durham (following pages). The landscape and townscape of Phillips' photographs, in the limpid northern light, are very much that of Neil's north-east background, and are close to where he had a country house. The photographs also include images of Neil's dog, Kevin, posing with Chris in the car. 'The pool was designed by Victor Pasmore', Neil notes. 'The only pop photo session ever taken in Peterlee new town.' The programme reflects the tone of the *Release* album, which was produced by the group themselves in their studio in the north-east, a fact that had its own influence on the record. 'Up there, we didn't really feel like we were in the middle of some kind of scene', Neil said. 'It is quite a barren landscape, quite bleak, and that is reflected in the type of music we were writing and the way it sounds.'

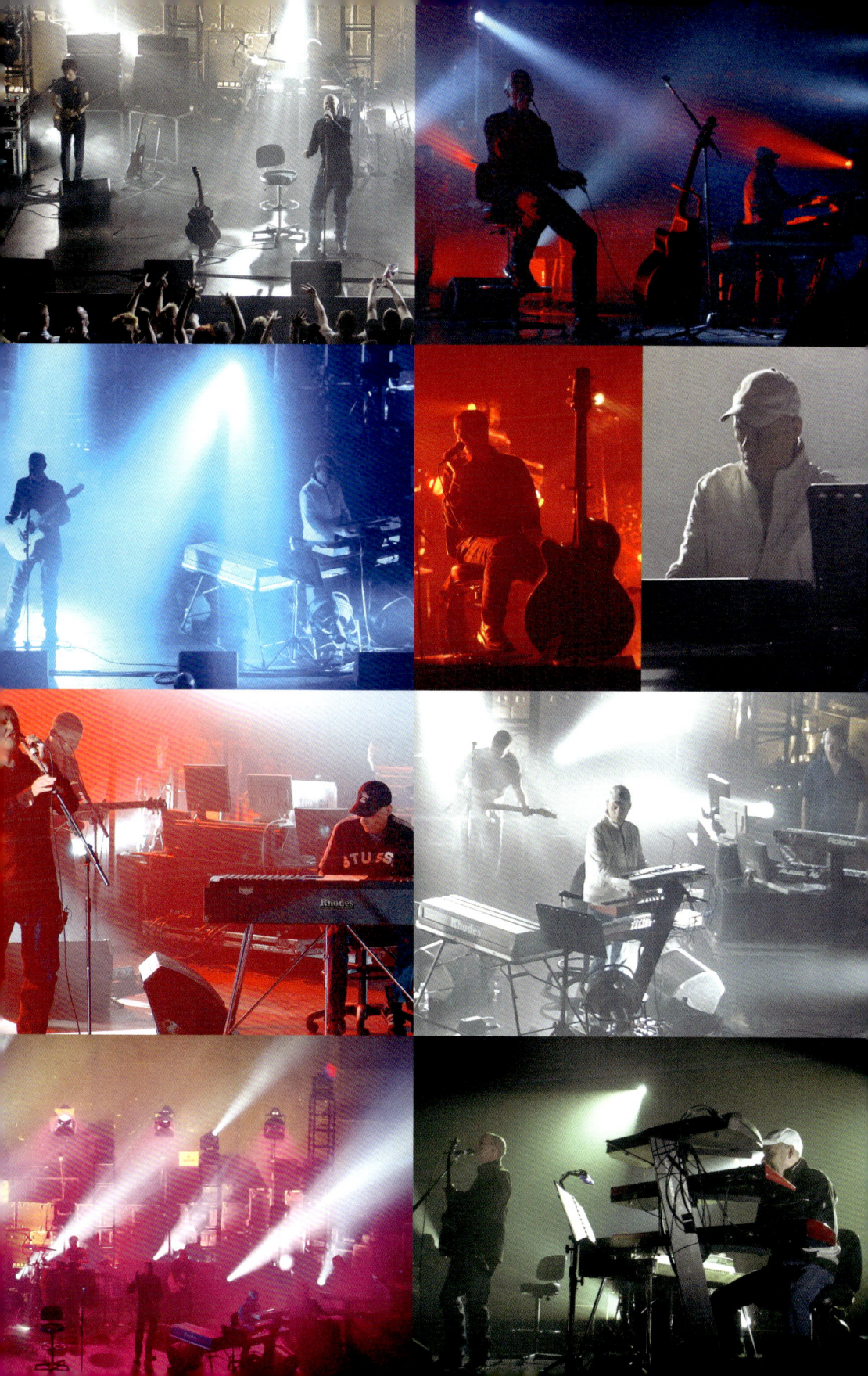

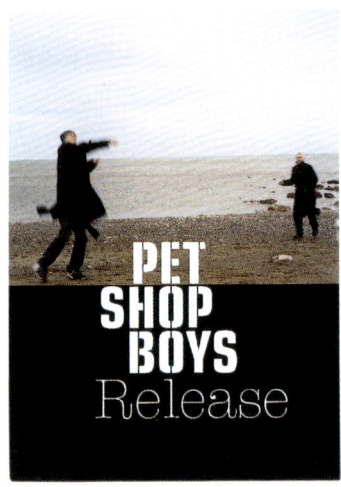

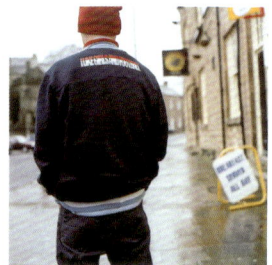

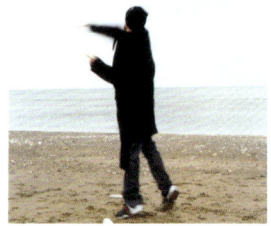
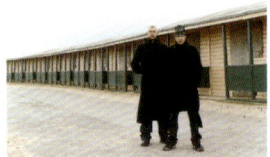

above Tour programme, front cover and inside pages
opposite Some of Valerie Phillips' photos from the programme

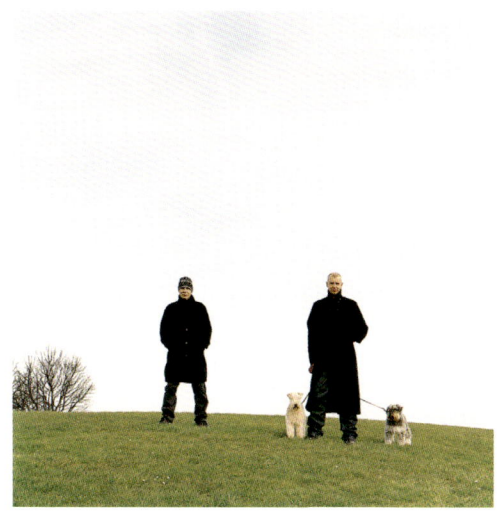
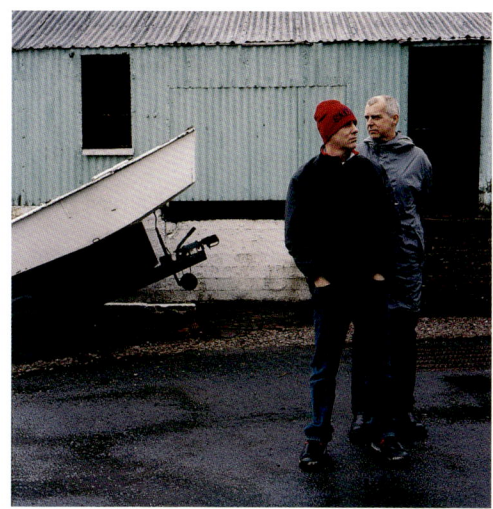
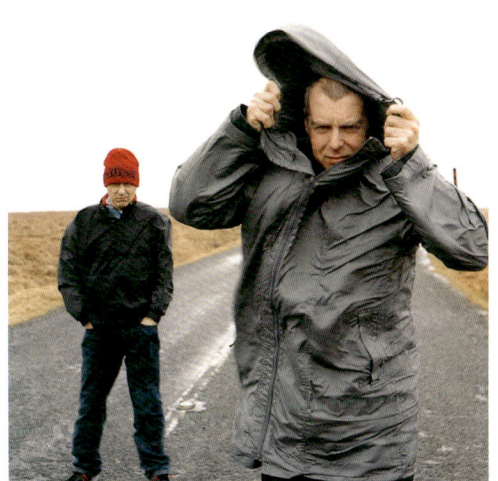
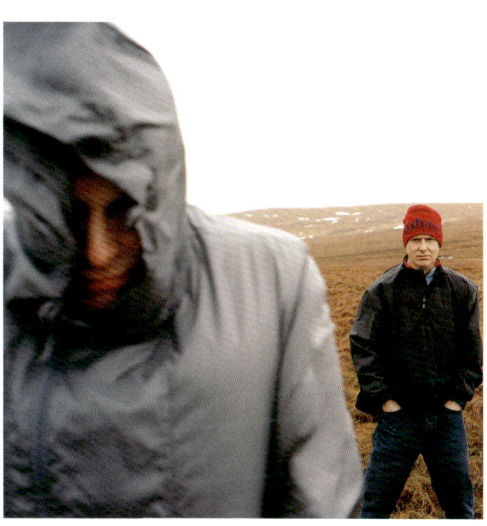
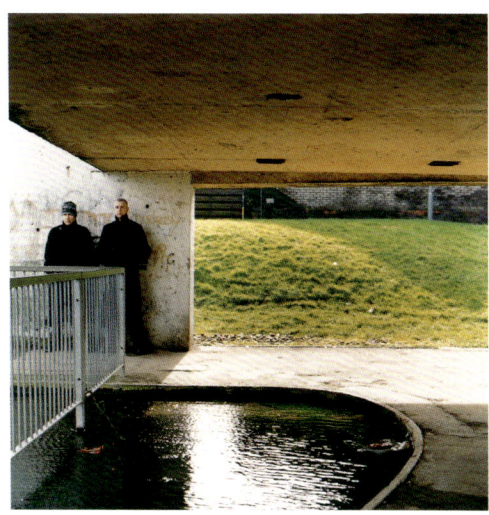
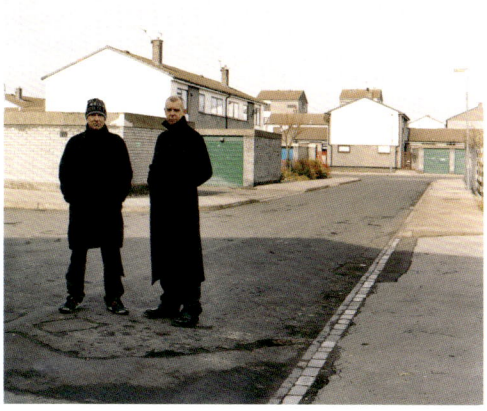

I get along

release 15 July 2002
formats CD × 2 / CD promo / DVD
design Scott King
video Bruce Weber

Scott King also designed the next single from *Release*. 'I think it's hilarious', says Neil. 'It's a pie chart.' The sleeves were based on artwork from King's show in Hoxton in 2002 analysing his emotional state. 'He's adapted that for the idea of the song', Neil explained. 'You have the idea that the person singing the song isn't getting along, so he's got all these sad comments about how the internet's really great. They're all very lonely things.'
King had asked Neil and Chris to write the texts, but they said they preferred it if he would. They include such statements as: 'Is take away food my single greatest friend? It seems so'; 'I hate Thursdays'; 'The weekends seem so long'; 'I must call my Auntie Jean. It's ages since I've spoken to her. I hope she's still alive'; 'I saw a couple in the supermarket today. They were in love. I wonder if they met there? I could go there today ... I am out of fish fingers'; and 'I like spending time on my own. I'm enjoying getting to know myself again. I've never felt so alone, ever.' The song itself was inspired by the relationship between Tony Blair and Peter Mandelson. Mandelson said that when he listened to it, at first he struggled to understand the connection: 'And then the penny dropped. I realized that the song was really about Tony Blair, and I was playing a bit part to the Prime Minister's starring act. The story of my life.'

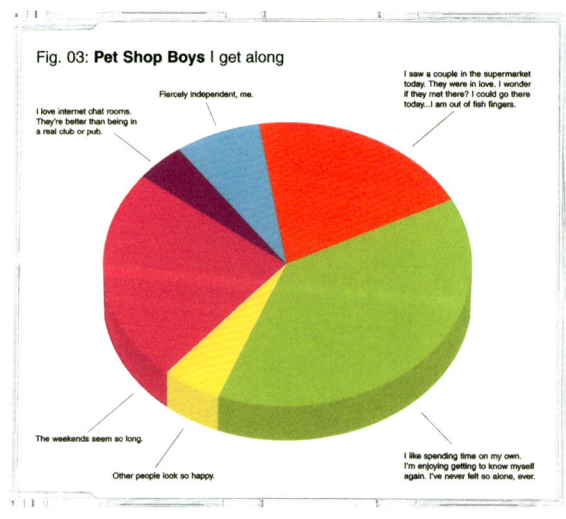

DVD, front

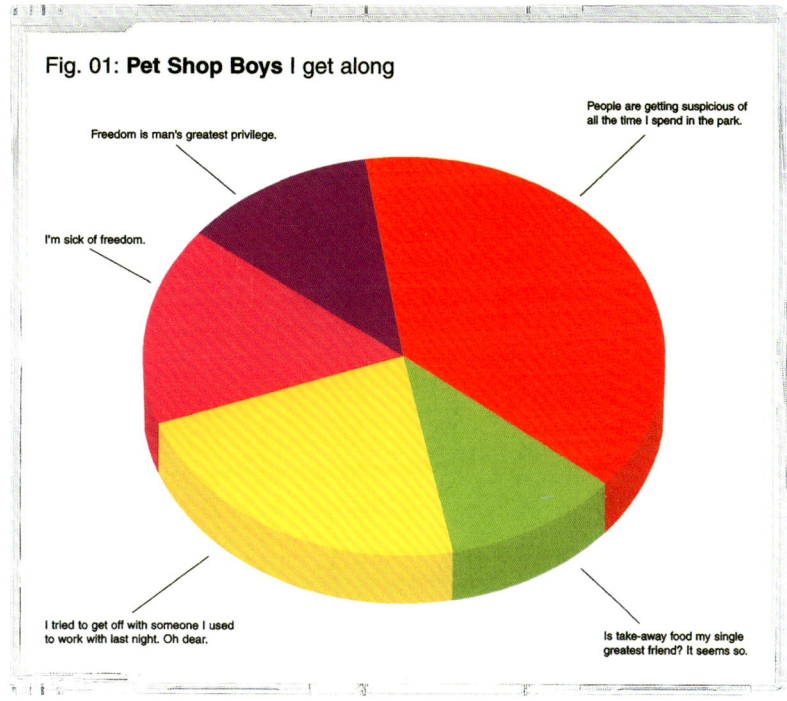

CD 1, front

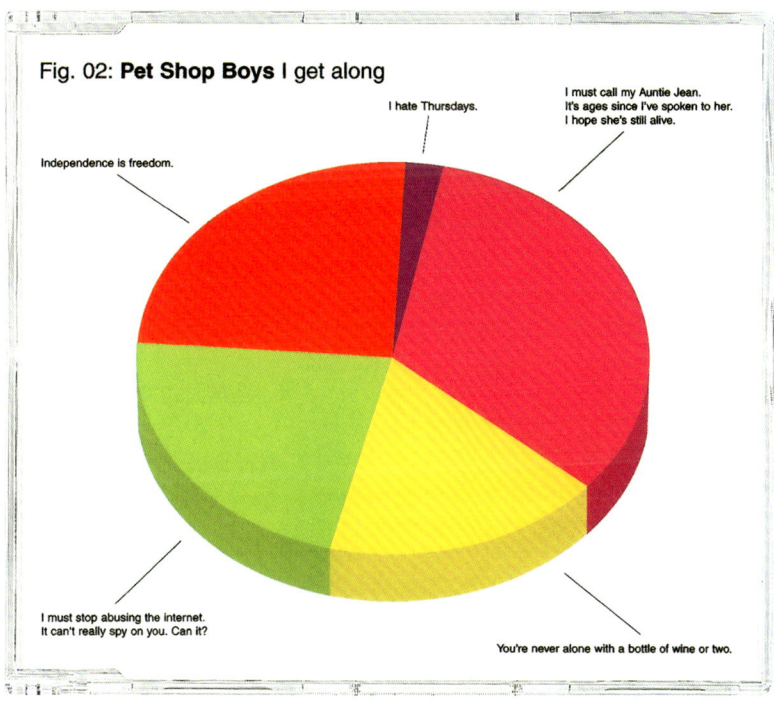

CD 2, front

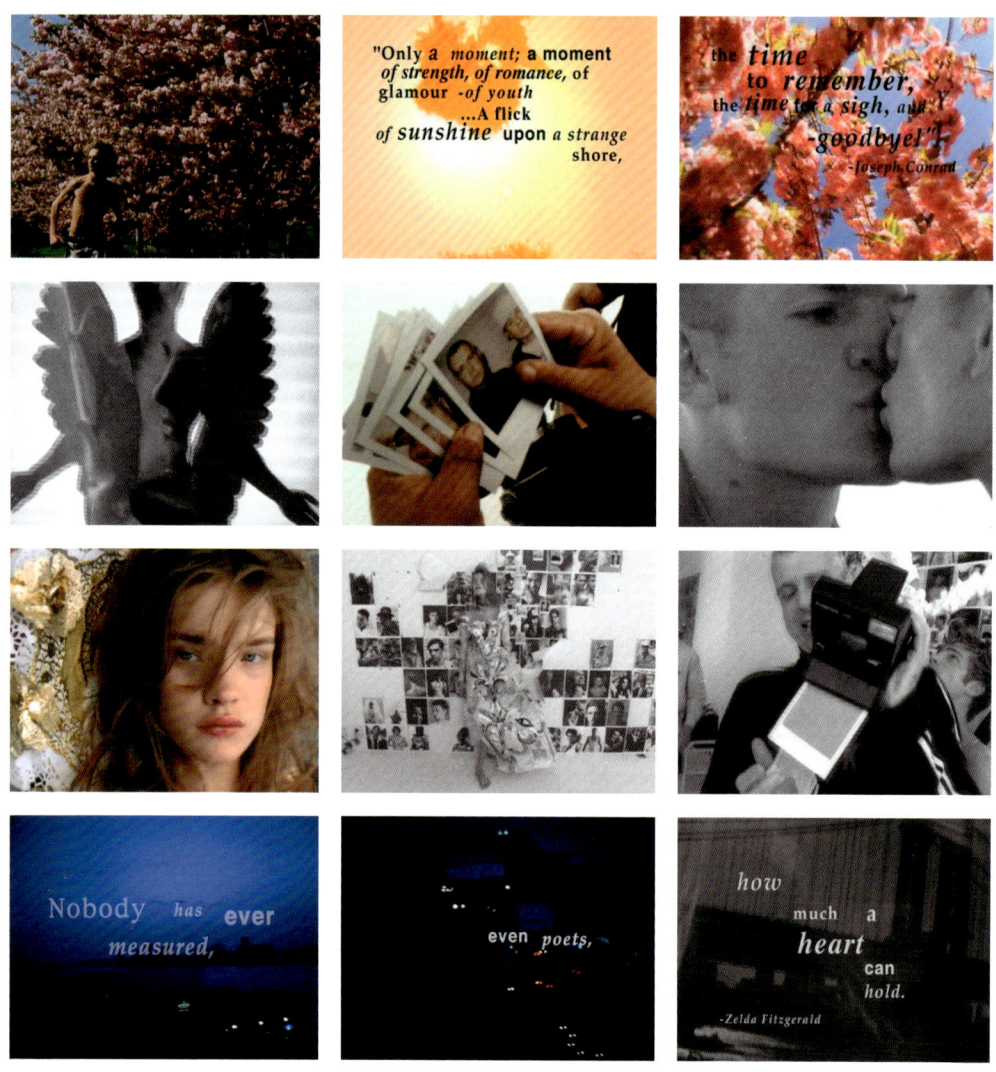

'I get along' was the third video made by Pet Shop Boys with Bruce Weber. 'We like working with him,' Neil said at the time, 'and his work is somewhat timeless. And also we thought it would be good to do something American and glossy which would take away the Britpop overtones that "I get along" has musically, so that it would help you hear the song in a different way. The video makes the song seem more sad. It makes it seem less Beatle-y.' 'It's taking it away from the gritty North', Chris said. 'Bruce said it was going to be a video of a photo shoot in Manhattan.' 'He said he was getting this great Russian model, Natalia Vodianova, and she is gorgeous', Neil added. 'It was the normal Bruce Weber video thing where you went in and then you felt intimidated by the beauty of everyone in the room. And then they all turn out to be really friendly and nice.' As well as being filmed eating lunch and taking Polaroids, Neil and Chris were filmed as they were painted by an artist.

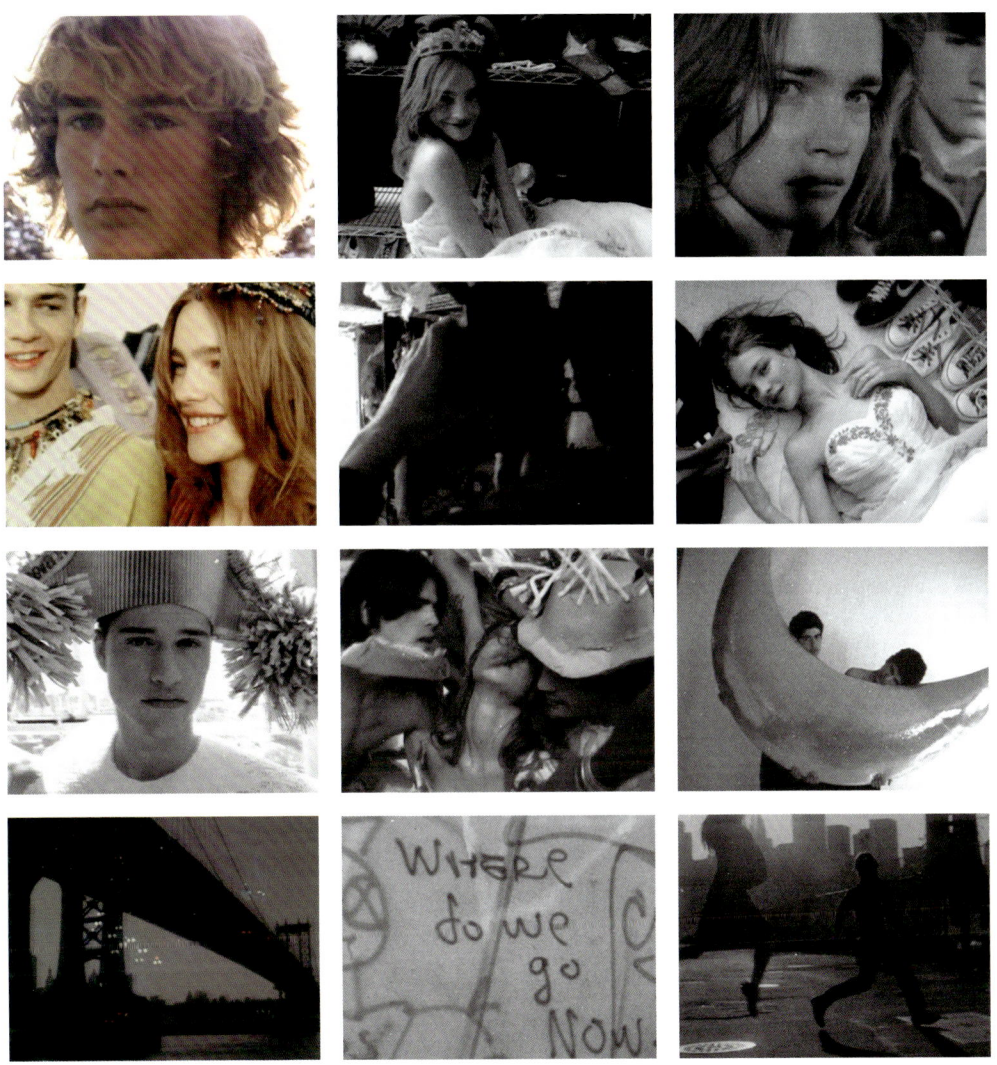

'It was all very relaxed as usual,' Chris said. 'He works with lots of cameras – something's always being filmed, and there's always a lot going on all over the place. The view through the window at the studio is where the Twin Towers would have been.' 'It's all about New York, the whole video', Neil said. 'You can see the cardboard towers collapsing. It's like an elegy for New York.' The 'I get along' video segues into a short Weber video for 'E-mail', another track on *Release*, also shot in New York (bottom row).

London

release 14 October 2002
formats 12" promo / CD × 2 / CD promo × 2
photographer Jonathan de Villiers
art direction and design Scott King
video Martin Parr

Scott King was 'a different kind of designer,' Neil notes, 'rougher. There are lots of jokes. He persuaded us to use the name "Olde English Vinyl"' (for one of Pet Shop Boys' record labels on which they release material by other artists). King returned to the typography that he had first created for 'Break 4 love' and 'Home and dry' (pages 280–1). The bedraggled London pigeon photograph was taken by artist Jonathan de Villiers, a friend of King's. 'Scott thought they were a very good symbol of London', says Neil. 'Pigeons in Trafalgar Square and all the rest of it. And I also think he liked the idea that there were mice in the video for "Home and dry" [pages 282–3] and now we had pigeons: these urban creatures.' The pigeons were photographed especially for these sleeves. The single was released only in Germany.

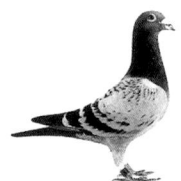

CD promo, front

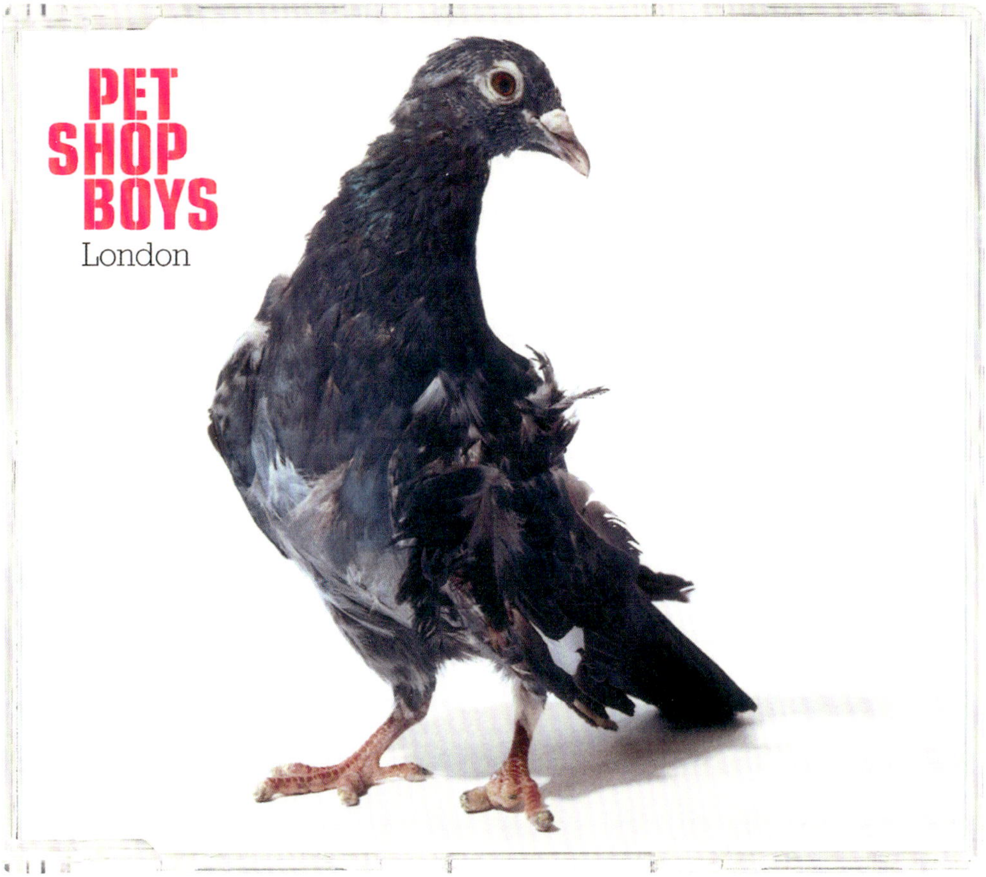

CD 1, Germany, front

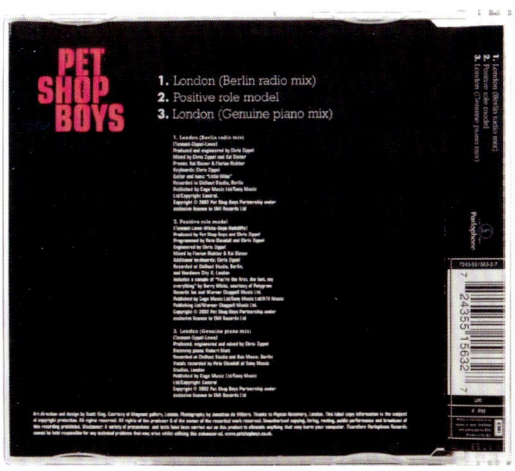

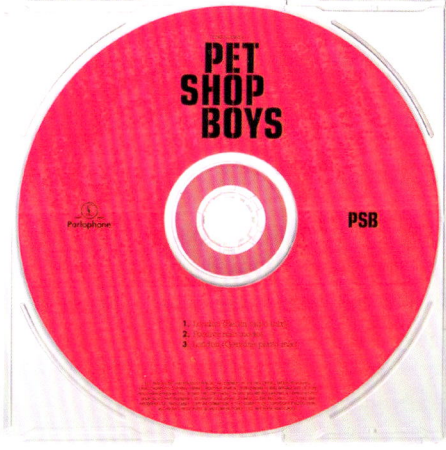

CD 1, Germany, inside

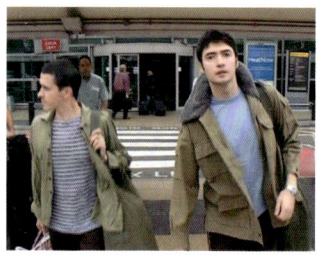 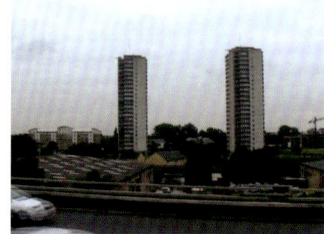 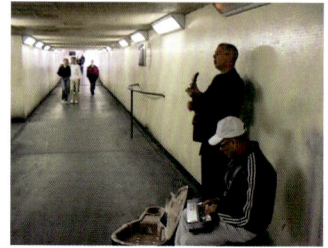
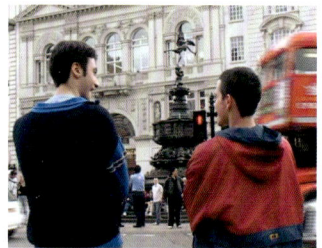 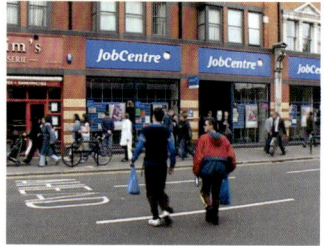 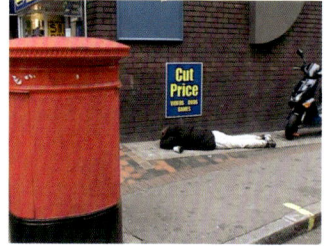
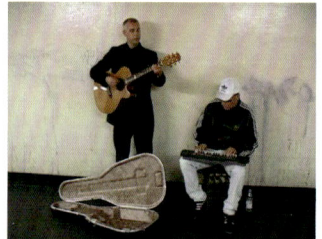 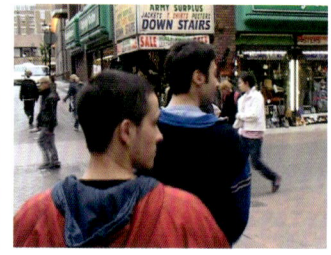 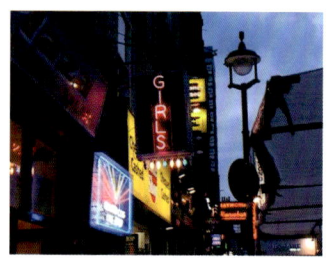
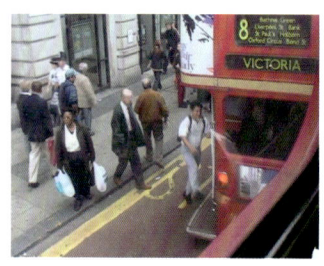 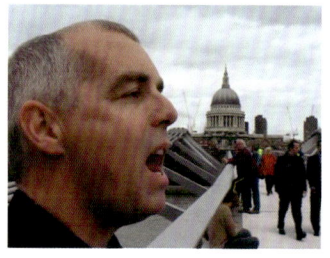 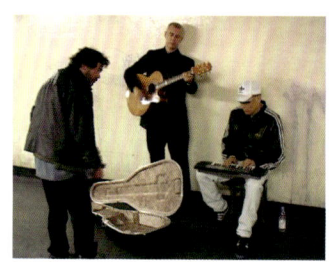

Shot on the streets of London, the video combined Neil and Chris as buskers with images of two Russian boys, as described in the lyrics, at large in the city, looking for work and for fun. The narrative movement of the video eminently suits Martin Parr's quirky sense of observational photography, imbued with a certain pathos. In 1986, Mark Farrow had showed Pet Shop Boys Parr's book *The Last Resort* about the rundown seaside resort of New Brighton in Lancashire. (For a while the group had planned to use one of the book's images – of two kids sitting on a car – as the sleeve of 'Suburbia'.) Neil and Chris spent a day busking around London, beginning at the Millennium Bridge, which connects St Paul's Cathedral with Tate Modern. 'There were some kind of German electroclash kids at one point walking across the bridge', Neil said. 'I just thought, as we were standing there with cameras on us and I was holding a guitar, he was going to say, "Oh, are you the Pet Shop Boys?"'

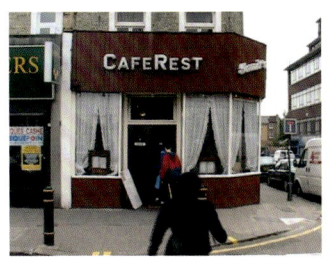 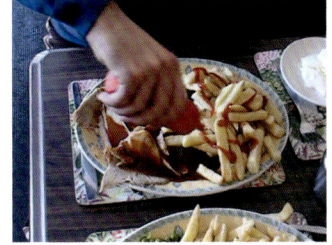 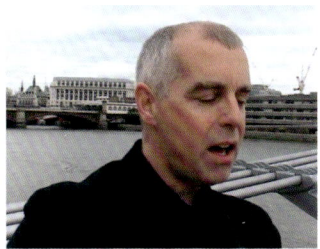
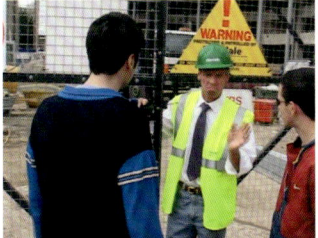 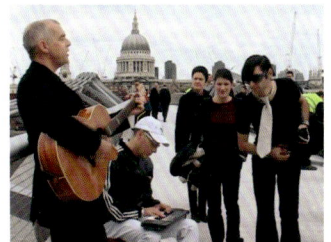 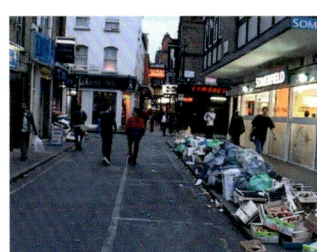
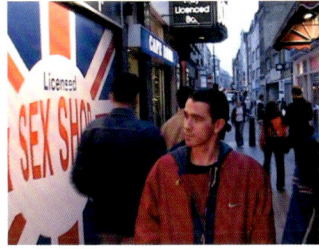
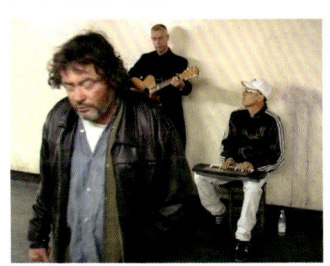 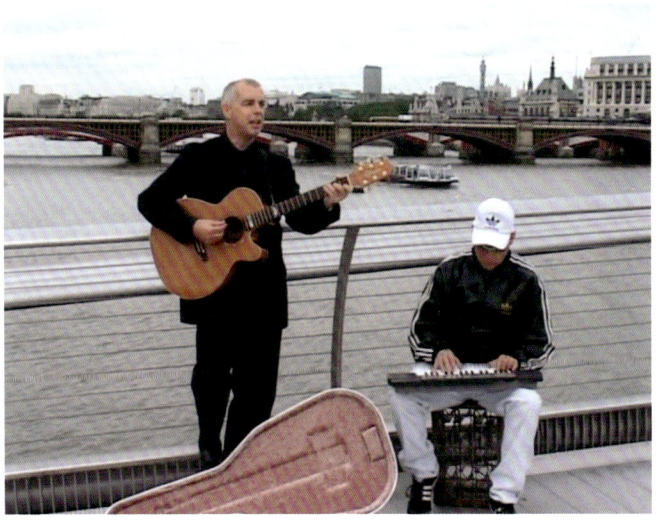

In fact, he said, "Can you tell me where the Science Museum is, please?"' 'You'd have thought, from the way they dressed, that they were going to Tate Modern,' says Chris, 'but that hadn't occurred to them.' 'I said, "You don't want to go there, you want to go to Tate Modern"', Neil recalls. More problematically, when at the Elephant and Castle Underground station, the busking pop stars had to field cries of 'You're a pair of fucking wankers' from passing tramps, one of whom then dropped a coin in their open guitar case.

Disco 3

release 3 February 2003
formats Triple-disc LP / LP promo / cassette / CD
photographer Wolfgang Tillmans
art direction and design Scott King

The fronts of the LP and CD gatefold sleeves of the third Pet Shop Boys *Disco* album featured a night-time cityscape of London shot by Wolfgang Tillmans. Tillmans himself suggested the title, which was originally going to be 'London/Berlin'. When he was working on the sleeve, he said to Neil and Chris, 'As a fan, I don't know why you don't just call this *Disco* 3, because otherwise you have to do so much explaining of what it is, but everybody knows what *Disco* 3 is.' 'What a lovely sleeve that is', rhapsodizes Neil. A promo version of the LP was also released that used the typography of the main formats blown up large. The album was a mixture of new songs, reinterpretations of songs from *Release*, and newly arranged songs from the earliest days of Pet Shop Boys that they had recorded a few months earlier for their first and only John Peel session for BBC Radio.

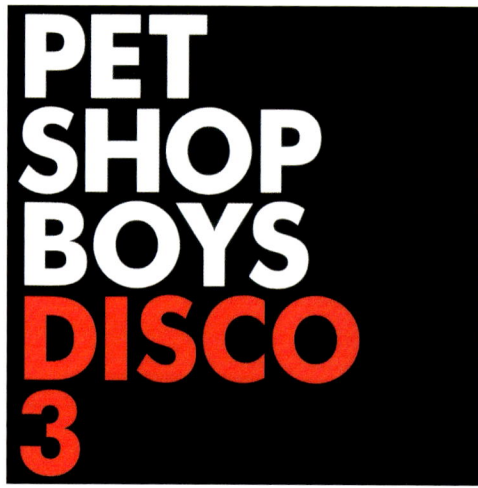

LP promo, front

Triple-disc LP, inner sleeve 3, back

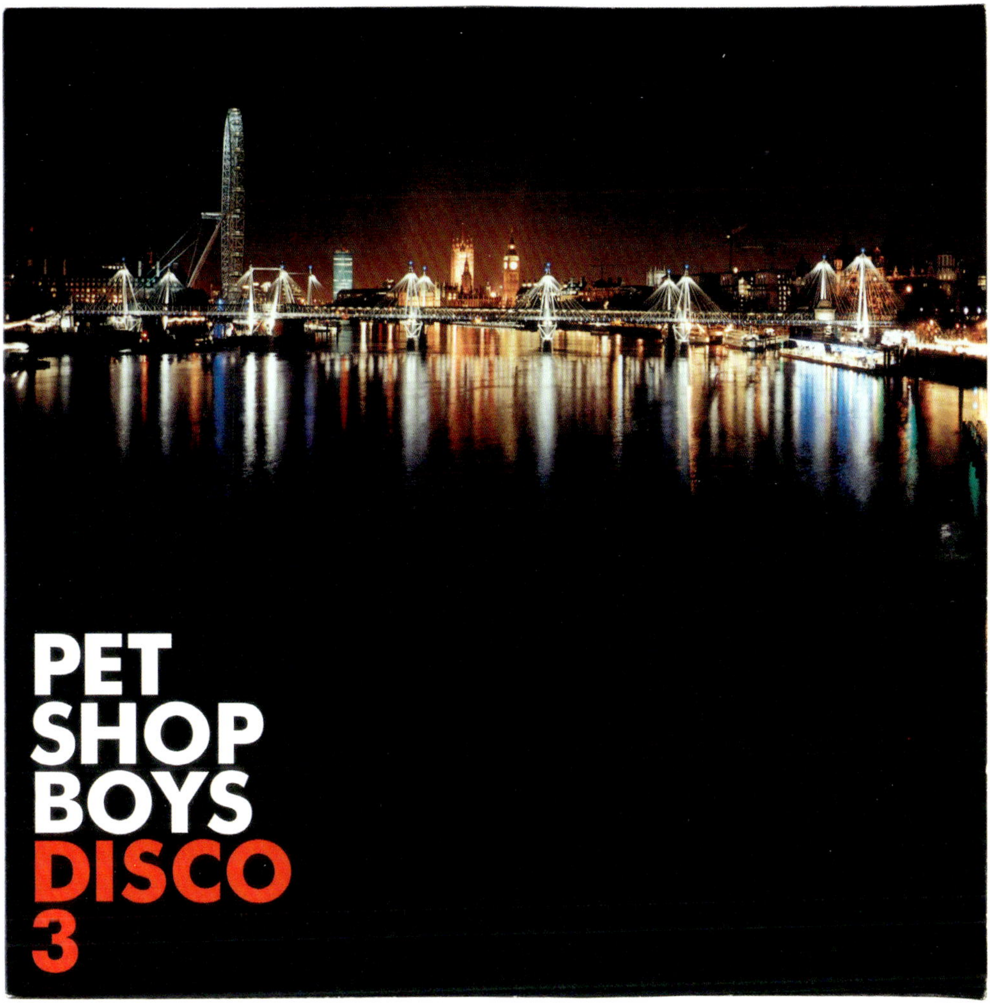

Triple-disc LP, front

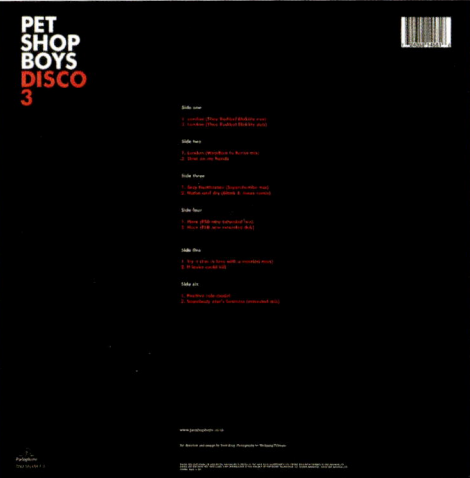

Triple-disc LP, back

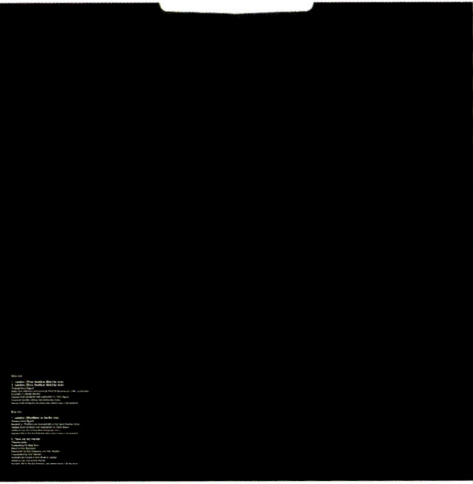

Triple-disc LP, inner sleeve 1, back

Miracles

release 17 November 2003
formats 12" / CD × 2
design Farrow Design / PSB
video Howard Greenhalgh

The sleeve uses die-cut silhouettes of Neil on one side and Chris on the other to reveal pink cherry blossom and blue sky on the inner sleeve. 'It's a love song', Neil explained. 'It's about how, when you're in love with someone, they have a kind of magic and seem to transform everything. "Thunder is silent before you, roses bloom more to adore you." It's almost Shakespearean.' The artwork reflects this notion. The profiles have a sixteenth-century aesthetic: a minimalist version of a religious icon or a cameo of a nobleman made for his lover to wear. 'The return of Mark Farrow', Neil notes. 'Very beautiful, and very English.' The sleeve was inspired by the lyric 'the scent of the jasmine is stronger'. Farrow found pictures of blossom from a photo library and used it on the inside and outside of the inner sleeve, on the label (of the white disc) and on the inside of the outer sleeve. 'This is one instance where it was all about the twelve inch', he says.

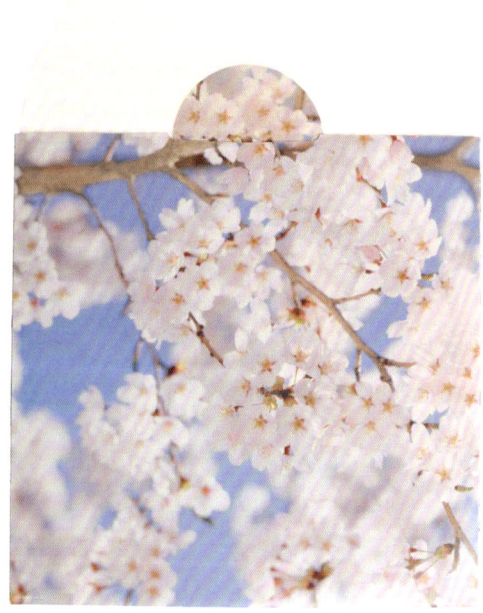

12", inner sleeve and disc

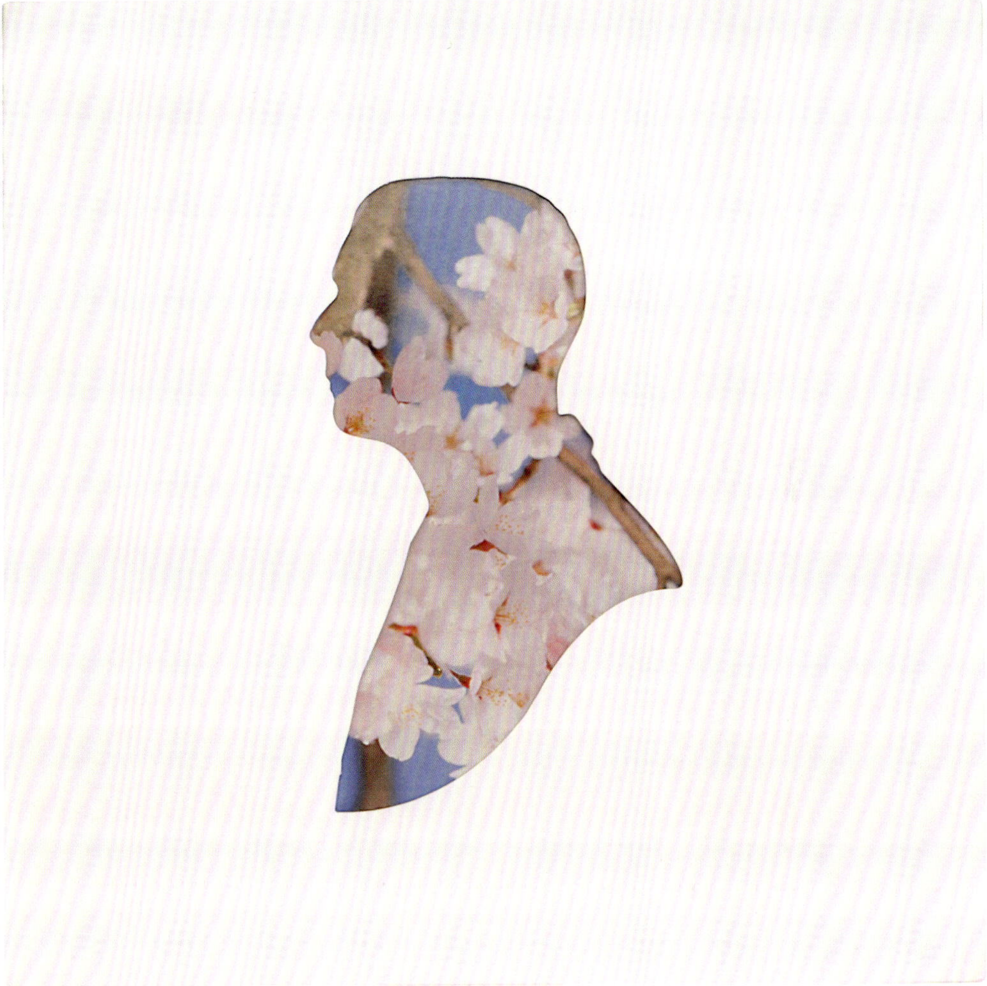

12", outer sleeve, front

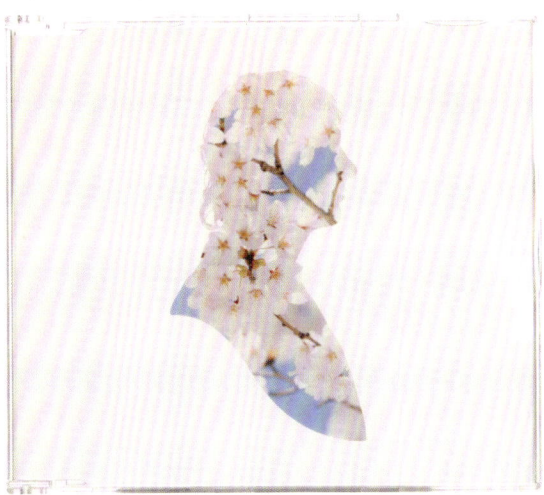

CD 1, front

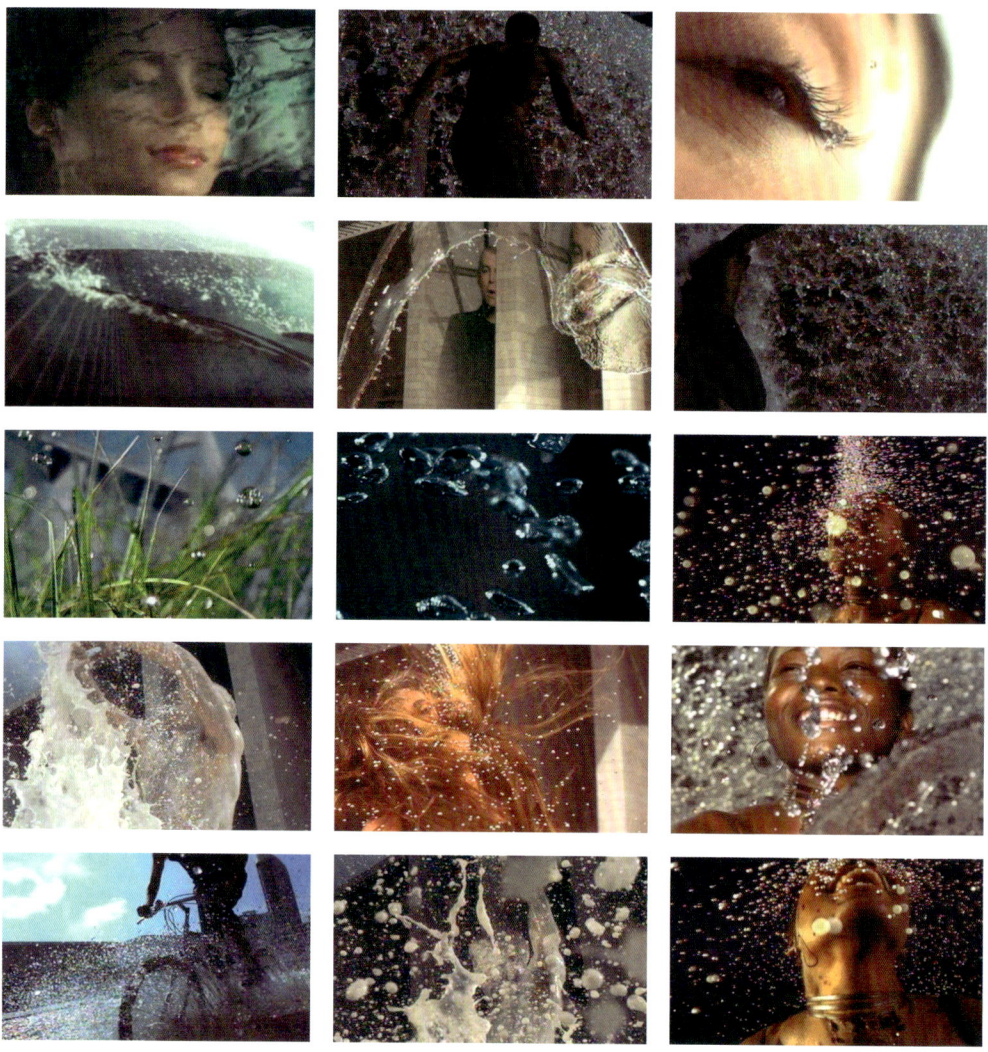

Featuring slow-motion, hyperreal images of near-naked figures dancing, running, and cycling through cascades of clear and milky water, and close-up shots of drops falling on perfect faces, the video continues the theme of the miraculous beauty of nature reflected in the song's lyrics and sleeve design. The film was shot in perfect timing with the pace of the music: the water falls slowly in time with the delicate opening strings and crashes with the beat; and as Neil sings 'sunlight breaks through', the sun bursts from behind a cloud. He and Chris are present only as projections on hard, concrete, industrial-looking architecture. 'The video was based on a camera that can photograph something happening very quickly with extraordinary detail', Neil recalls. 'It was all Howard Greenhalgh's idea. It's a technique-based video. He showed us this new camera where you can show a drop of water falling and breaking up with incredible clarity – it was just using those kind of techniques to get over the miracle idea.'

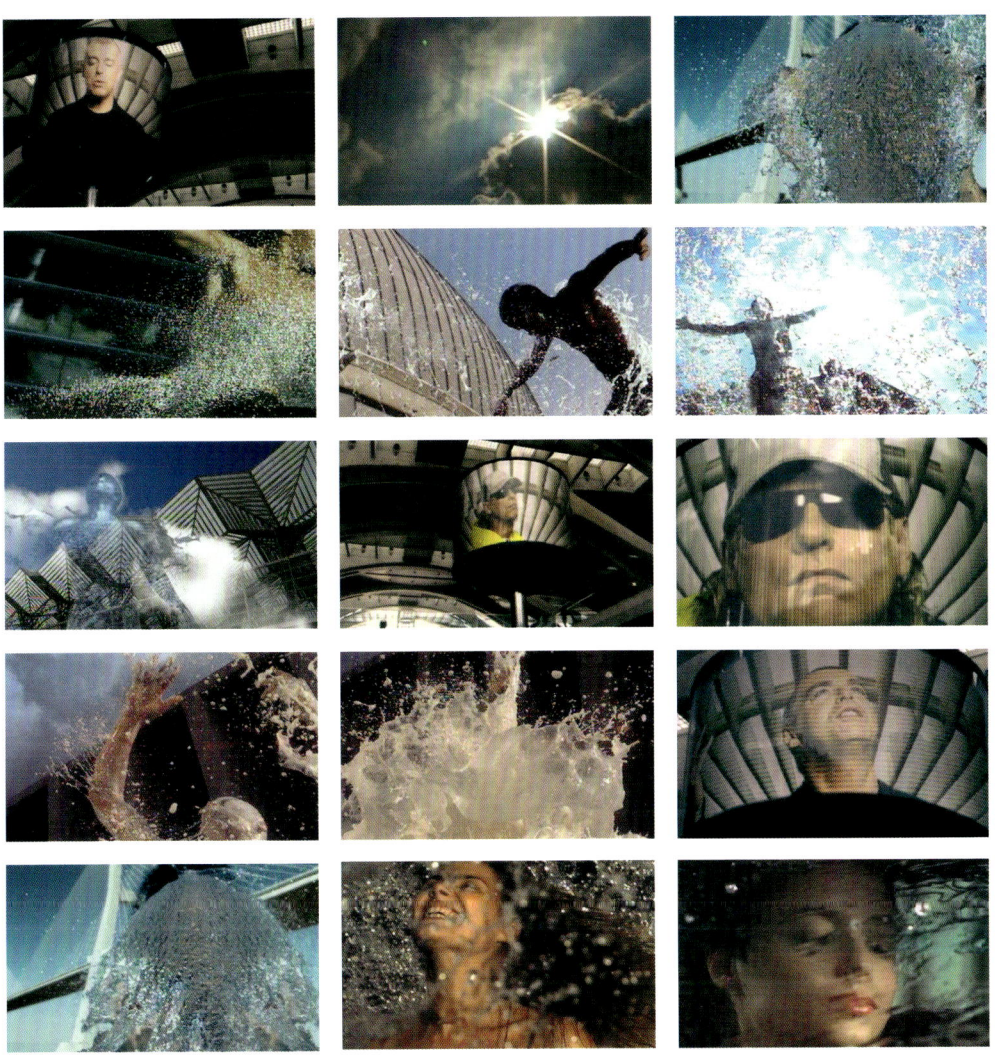

PopArt

release 24 November 2003
formats Limited-edition triple-disc LP in box set /
double CD / limited-edition triple CD / DVD
design Farrow Design / PSB

Although Mark Farrow did not design *Release* and its associated singles, it was always intended that he and his company would design the sleeve for this greatest-hits album. In choosing a picture for the cover, there were discussions about 'what is the ultimate Pet Shop Boys image'. But while they were debating what could be done with the word 'PopArt', Gary Stillwell at Farrow Design came up with the eventual cover design. 'I didn't think there was any chance of them going for a totally graphic cover,' says Farrow, 'but they loved it and the record company went for it as well.' The backgrounds chosen for each word – 'Pop' took its orange-and-white pattern from the 'Can you forgive her?' pointy hats, and 'Art' had the black-and-silver stripes from Chris's sunglasses on the 'Suburbia' sleeve – reflected the title. 'They felt that *Very*, and the stuff around that album, was as pop as they got, and "Suburbia" fitted into their art category', said Farrow. 'So you have the Nineties and the Eighties', Neil said. The artwork inside used a montage of images from the previous twenty years, displayed over the two sides of the concertina CD booklet and the six sides of the vinyl inner sleeves.

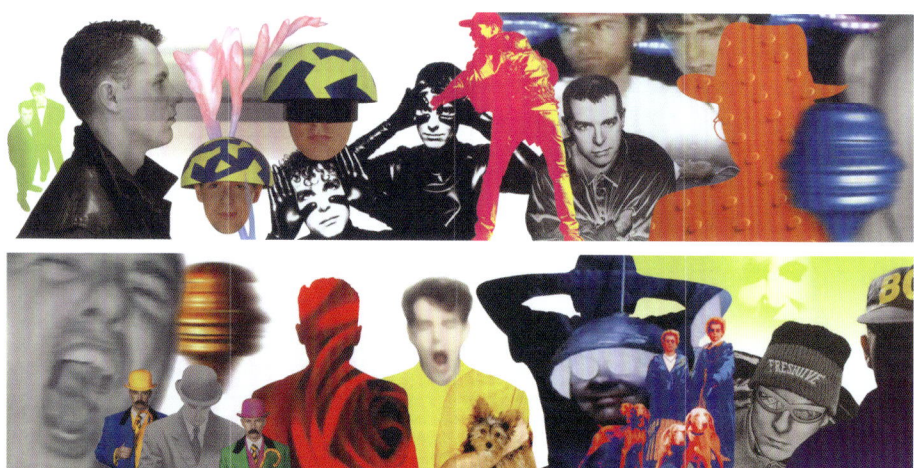

Limited-edition triple CD, concertina booklet, open (front)

Pet Shop Boys
The Hits

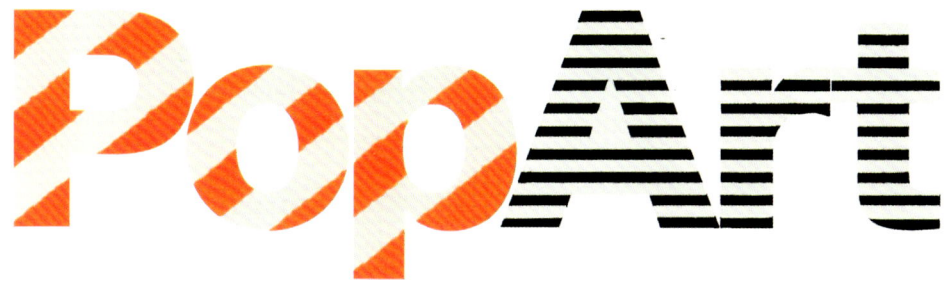

Limited-edition triple-disc LP box set, outer box, front

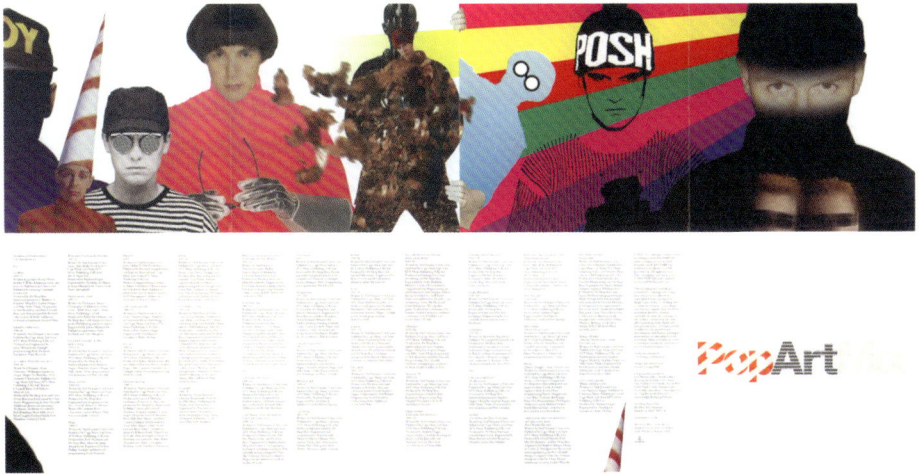

Limited-edition triple CD, concertina booklet, open (back)

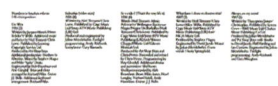
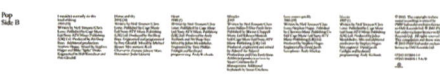

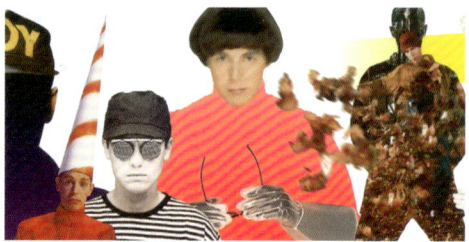

Limited-edition triple-disc LP box set, Side A, inner sleeve

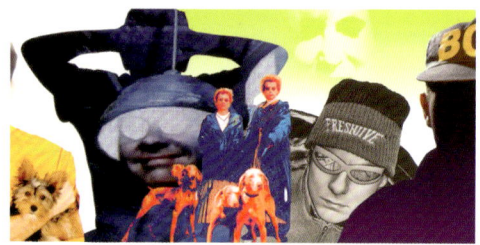

Limited-edition triple-disc LP box set, Side B, inner sleeve

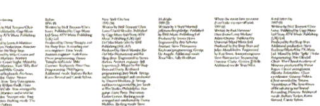
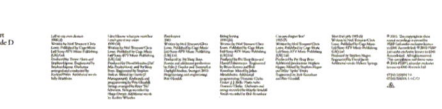

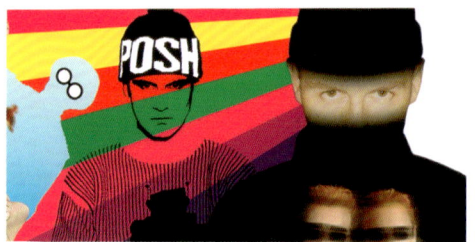

Limited-edition triple-disc LP box set, Side C, inner sleeve

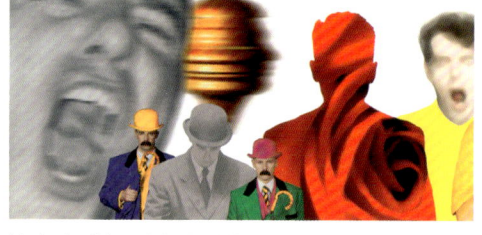

Limited-edition triple-disc LP box set, Side D, inner sleeve

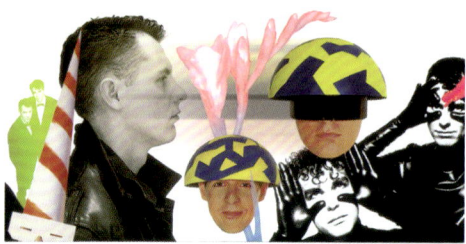

Limited-edition triple-disc LP box set, Side E, inner sleeve

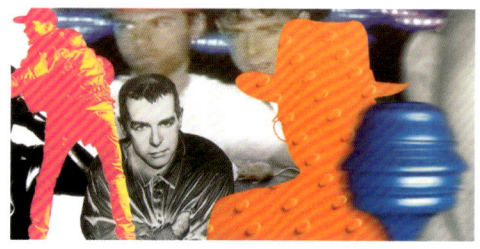

Limited-edition triple-disc LP box set, Side F, inner sleeve

Pet Shop Boys
The Hits

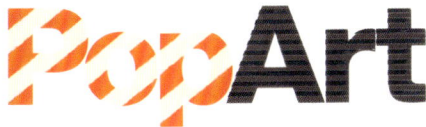

Limited-edition triple CD box set, outer box, front

(CD1) 1 Pop 2 Go West 3 Suburbia 4 Se a vida é (That's the way life is) 5 What have I done to deserve this? 6 Always on my mind 7 I wouldn't normally do this kind of thing 8 Home and dry 9 Heart 10 Miracles 11 Love comes quickly 12 It's a sin 13 Domino dancing 14 Before 15 New York City boy 16 It's alright 17 Where the streets have no name (I can't take my eyes off you) 18 A red letter day

(CD2) 1 Art 2 Left to my own devices 3 I don't know what you want but I can't give it any more 4 Flamboyant 5 Being boring 6 Can you forgive her? 7 West End girls 8 I get along 9 So hard 10 Rent 11 Jealousy 12 DJ culture 13 You only tell me you love me when you're drunk 14 Liberation 15 Paninaro '95 16 Opportunities (Let's make lots of money) 17 Yesterday, when I was mad 18 Single-Bilingual 19 Somewhere

(CD3) 1 Mix 2 Can you forgive her? (Rollo remix) 3 So hard (David Morales Red Zone mix) 4 What have I done to deserve this? (Shep Pettibone mix) 5 West End girls (Sasha mix) 6 Miserablism (Moby Electro mix) 7 Before (Danny Tenaglia Classic Paradise mix) 8 I don't know what you want but I can't give it any more (Peter Rauhoffer New York mix) 9 New York City boy (Lange mix) 10 Young offender (Jam and Spoon Trip-o-matic Fairy tale mix) 11 Love comes quickly (Blank and Jones mix)

Limited-edition triple CD box set, outer box, back

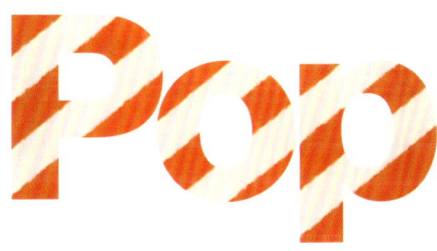

Limited-edition triple CD box set, inner sleeve 1, front

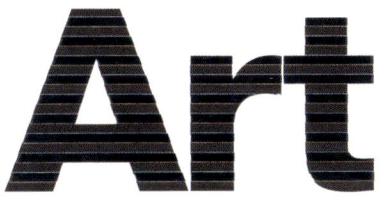

Limited-edition triple CD box set, inner sleeve 2, front

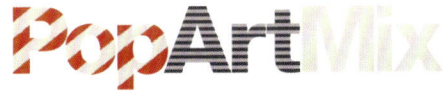

Limited-edition triple CD box set, inner sleeve 3, front

Limited-edition triple CD box set, concertina booklet, closed

Flamboyant

release 29 March 2004
formats 12" / 12" promo × 2 / CD × 2 / CD promo
design Farrow Design / PSB
video Nico Beyer

'Flamboyant' was the second release from *PopArt*, after 'Miracles' (pages 302–5). The song was only included on *PopArt* at the last moment, replacing 'Numb', which was then held for their next album. The sleeve design was chosen to fit in with the Japanese theme of the video, with gold foil-blocked Japanese writing across blurred Pet Shop Boys faces. 'It says "Pet Shop Boys …"', said Neil. 'Well, that's what we think it says', added Chris. The sleeve photos of Neil and Chris were taken from the song's video, and since they were not good enough quality to use as they were, Gary Stillwell at Farrow Design treated them and blurred them. The CDs also have the title and the group's name in English, and continue the gold of the lettering on the discs themselves. The typographic treatment of the inside of the CD sleeves and track information on the discs is identical to that on the CDs of 'Miracles'.

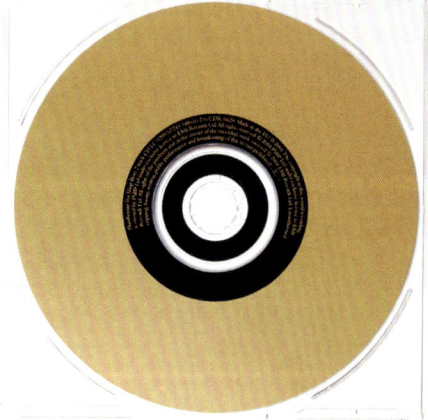

CD 1, inside

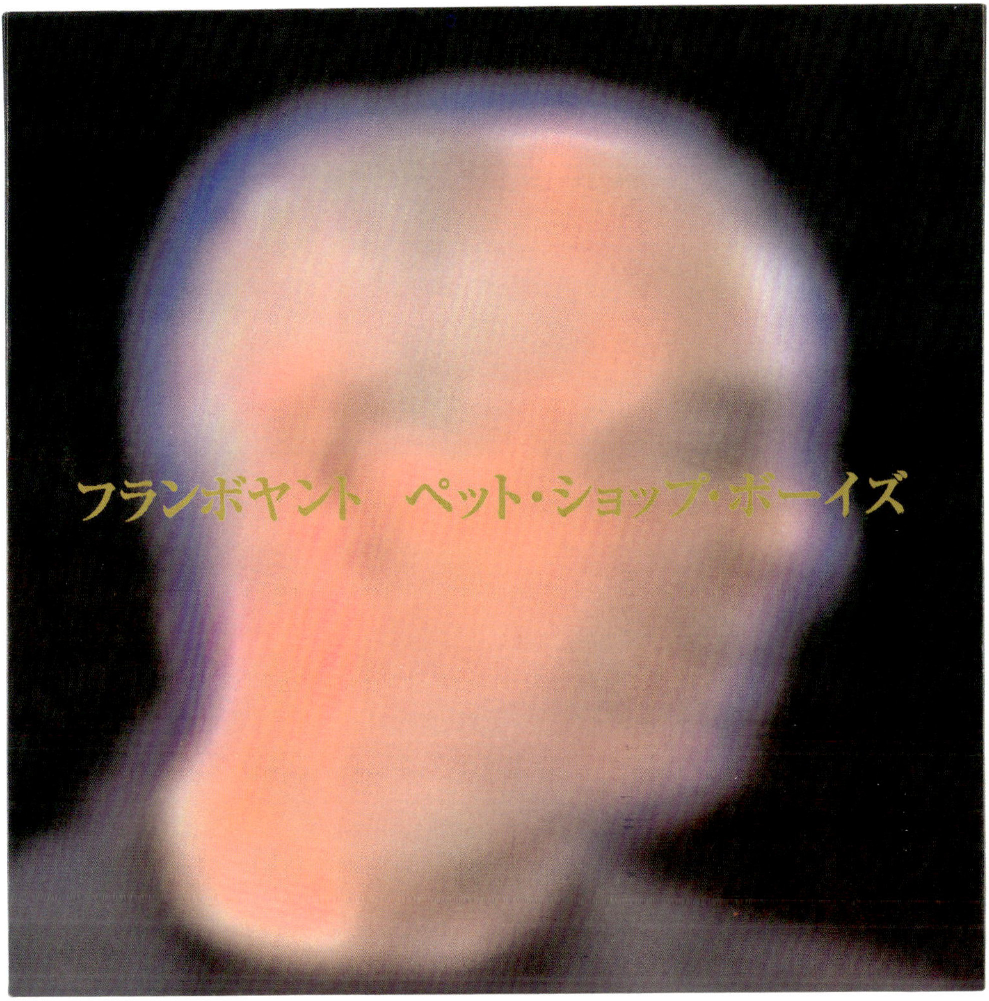

12", outer sleeve, front

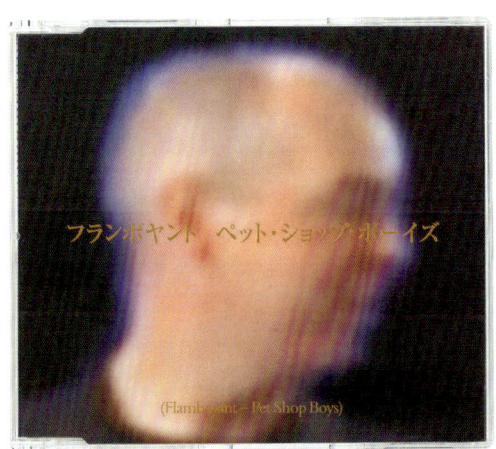

CD 1, front

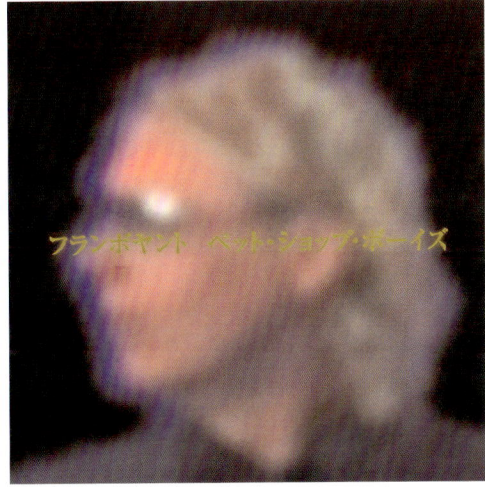

12", outer sleeve, back

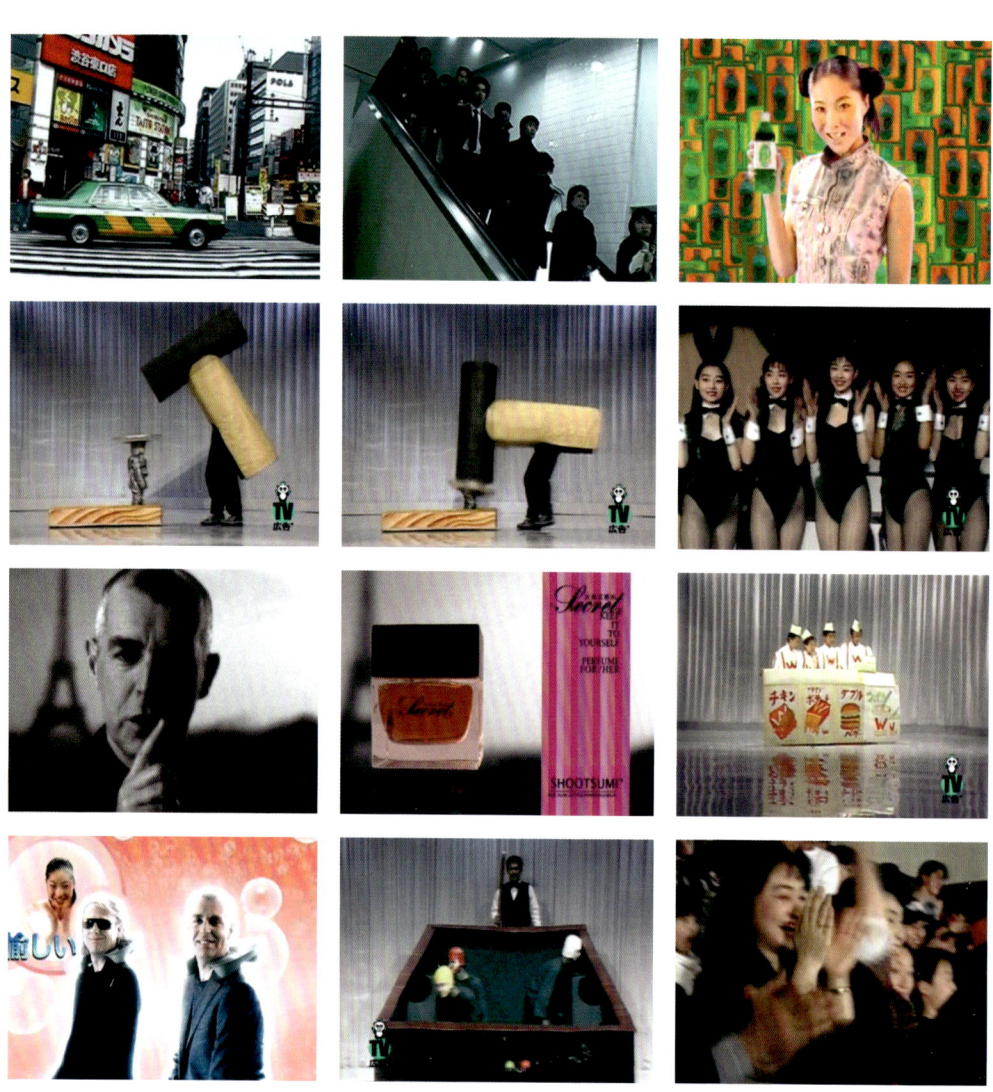

In perhaps Pet Shop Boys' most complex video to date, we follow the efforts of a Japanese office worker and his friends to create the illusion of a snooker game using people dressed as 'balls' – an attempt to win a prize on a popular TV game show dedicated to human versions of non-human objects. We see him watching enviously as one contestant 'hammers' his 'nail' child into a block of wood as applauding *Playboy*-style bunny girls look on; another group, dressed in restaurant uniforms and yellow leggings, mimics an overturned box of fries; while a third group pretends to be a digital stopwatch timing a race. Meanwhile Pet Shop Boys appear in a number of adverts selling authentic Japanese products: mineral water, a shampoo called 'Happy', magically ironed 'dancing shirts', an extraordinarily capacious car, perfume, flat-screen TVs, mobile phones. 'It's a very good video', says Chris. 'We were filmed in Paris against a blue screen.' In an email to the group, the director

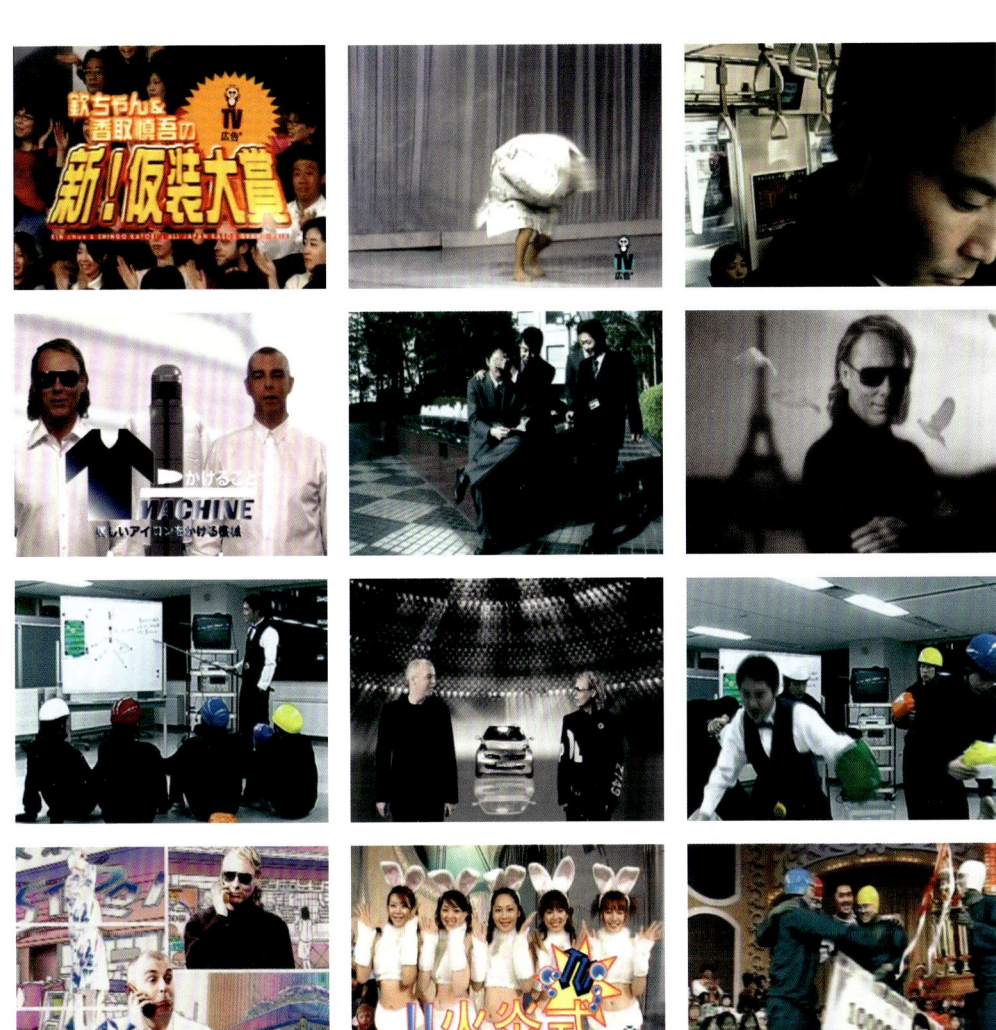

Nico Beyer explained, 'I'm intending to make these commercials as authentic and true to Japanese advertising as possible.... Each commercial will be seven seconds long, which is a true Japanese TV commercial format. Each one should look different and have its own identity and mood: from funny to extroverted, from stylish to romantic.... You are the celebrities and spokesmen within these stories, just as the Japanese very often use Hollywood stars in their campaigns.'

Battleship Potemkin

date 12 September 2004 – 11 January 2008
location London, Frankfurt, Bonn, Berlin, Hamburg, Wallsend, Dresden, Segovia
design (CD) Farrow Design / PSB

In April 2003, the Institute of Contemporary Arts in London (where Pet Shop Boys made one of their first live appearances) asked Neil and Chris to write a new score for the classic 1925 film *Battleship Potemkin* by Russian director Sergei Eisenstein, and perform it as a free concert in London's Trafalgar Square with the film as a backdrop. Eisenstein's film describes the mutiny of the sailors on the battleship *Potemkin* in 1905, an event that involved the local population in Odessa and formed part of Russia's 1905 revolution. Its celebration of political dissent has made it one of the most powerful films of all time.

Encouraged by Eisenstein's remark that he would like a new score written each decade, the group composed music that would be released under the names 'Tennant/Lowe', rather than 'Pet Shop Boys', in accordance with the tradition of publishing classical music under the composers' surnames. They asked German composer Torsten Rasch to orchestrate the work after hearing his song cycle *Mein Herz Brennt*, based on the music of the rock group Rammstein.

The performance took place on a wet Sunday evening, with the Dresdner Sinfoniker accompanying Pet Shop Boys. The film was projected on a gigantic screen erected in front of Nelson's Column. The event opened with a commentary delivered by Simon McBurney, director of the theatre group Complicité, while archive footage was projected onto a screen and the facade of the National Gallery. These images reached back from the poll-tax riot of 1990 to the income-tax demonstration of 1848. Then McBurney seemed to reappear on the roof of St Martin-in-the-Fields church (in fact, it was his body double). Finally, the opening credits of Eisenstein's film began to roll, with its languid scenes of sailors in their hammocks – their striped shirts and muscled arms a homoerotic echo of Herman Melville or Jean Genet – giving way to violent scenes of revolution. The modernity of Eisenstein's vision seemed, in its reshowing, to share an aesthetic link with Tennant and Lowe's composition and the orchestrations by Rasch, as much a tribute to Eisenstein's art as it was to that of Pet Shop Boys. The event attracted 25,000 people. The *Independent* noted that 'this must be the largest audience for an art movie ever recorded'. The performance was restaged in Frankfurt, Bonn, Berlin, and Hamburg in September 2005; at the Swan Hunter shipyard in Wallsend in May 2006; in Dresden as part of the city's 800th anniversary celebrations in July 2006 (page 316) and in Segovia in the same month; and, most recently, in January 2008 at London's Barbican Centre accompanied by the BBC Concert Orchestra.

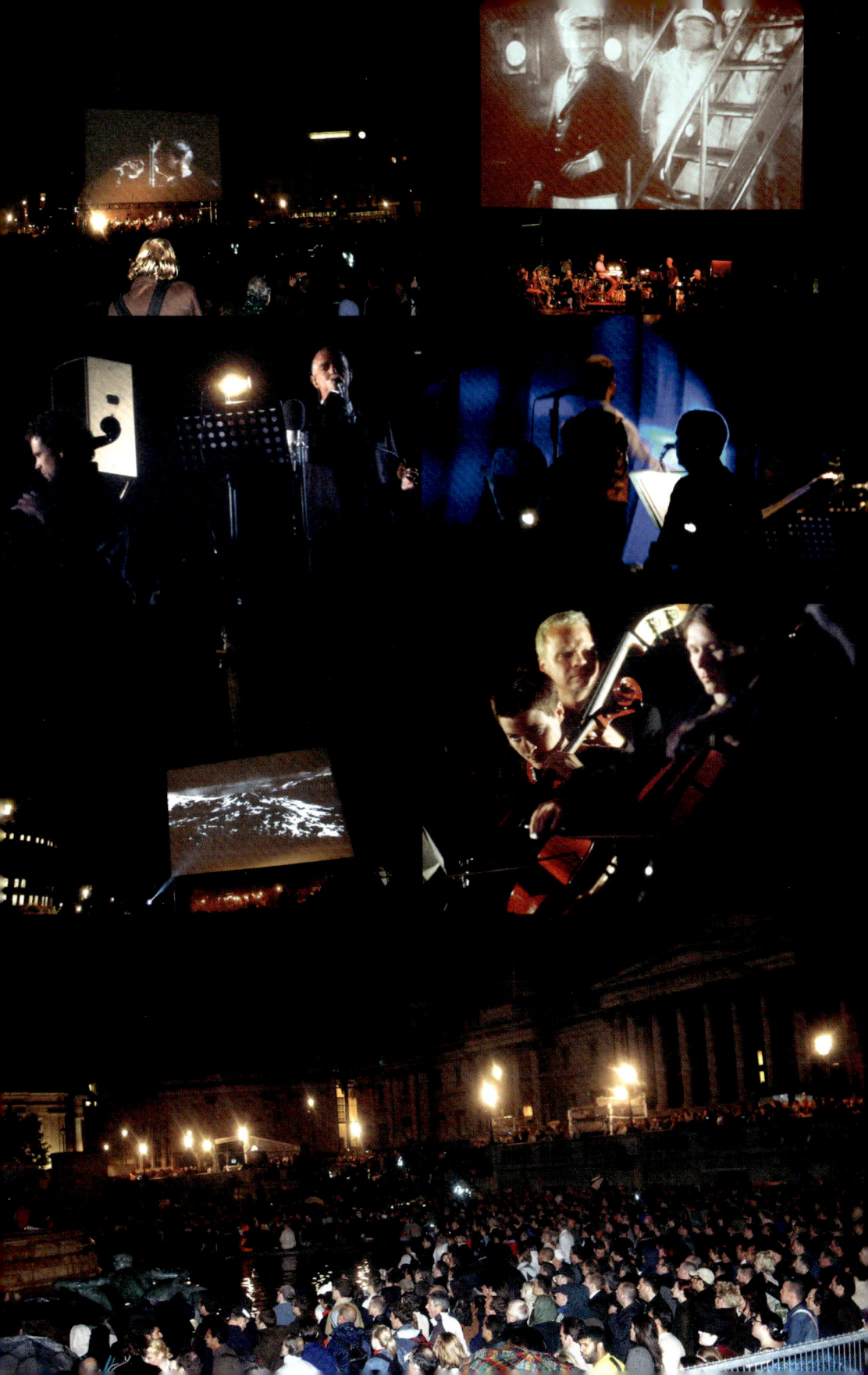

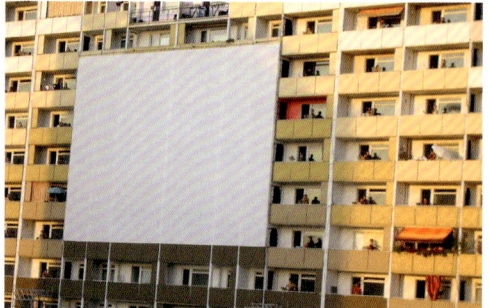 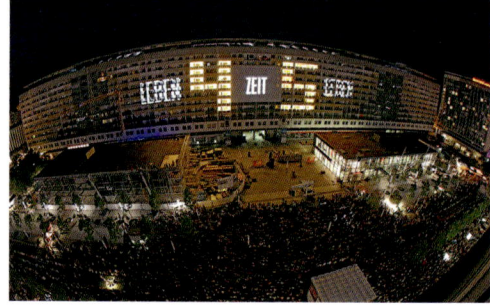

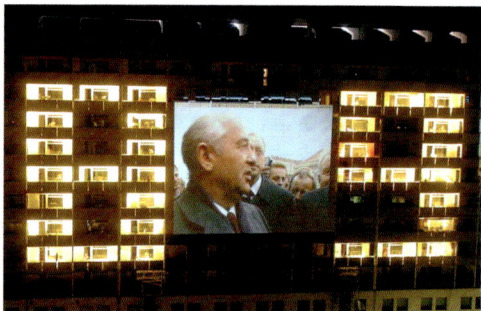 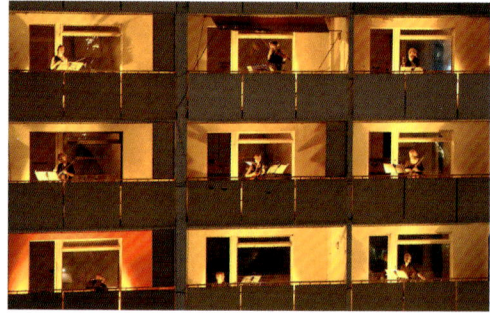

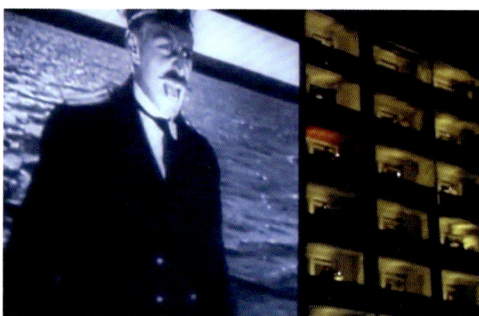 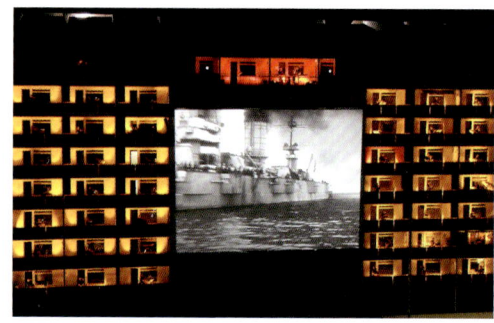

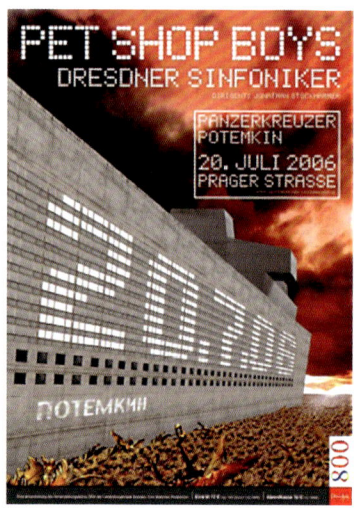

Battleship Potemkin, Dresden poster

For the seventh performance of *Battleship Potemkin*, in front of ten thousand spectators in Dresden, the film was projected onto a screen installed on a Communist-era apartment block on the city's famous Prager Strasse. Musicians from the Dresdner Sinfoniker were positioned on the balconies, one per apartment, in many cases with the residents beside them out of sight. Neil and Chris performed on a balcony at the top of the block above the screen. The conductor, Jonathan Stockhammer, directed the orchestra from a crane in front of the screen. The show was conceived by Markus Rindt and directed by Sven Helbig. Film-maker Bettina Renner produced a sixty-eight-minute documentary about the project, *Hochhaussinfonie* (High-rise symphony). It features on a BluRay edition of *Battleship Potemkin*, synced to Pet Shop Boys' soundtrack, released by the British Film Institute in September 2025.

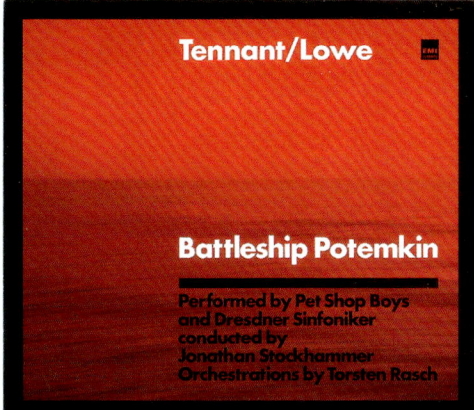

CD, slipcase, front

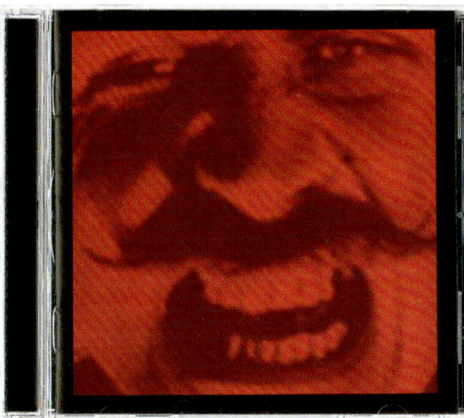

CD, jewel case, front (showing booklet)

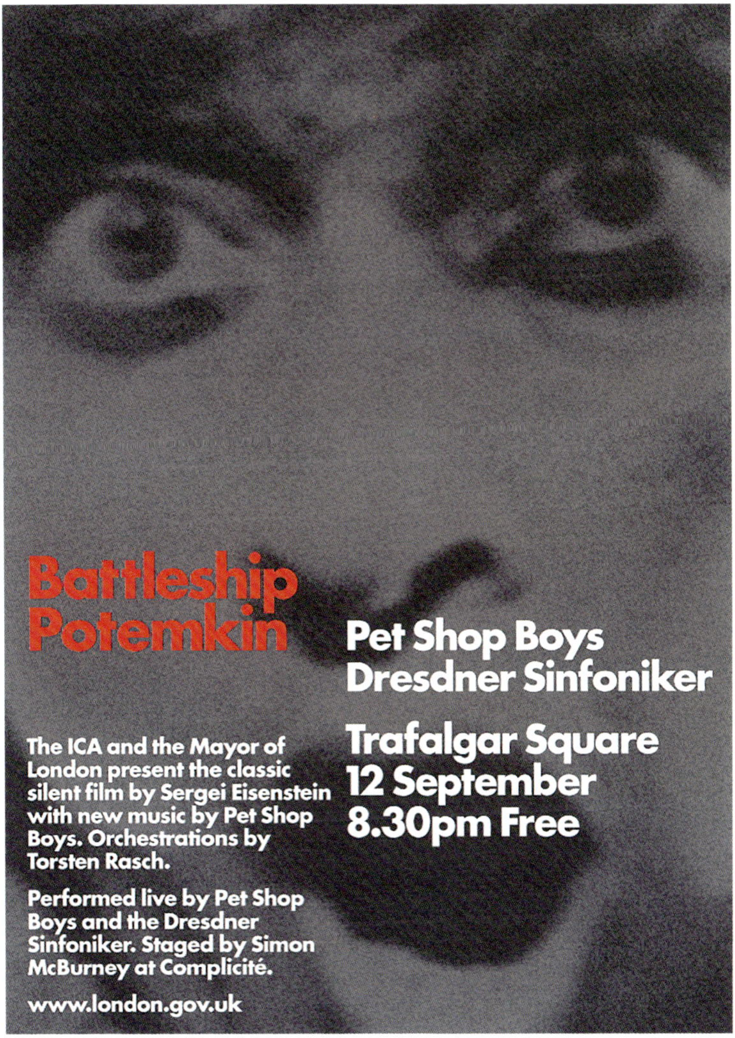

Battleship Potemkin, Trafalgar Square poster

Back To Mine: Pet Shop Boys

release 25 April 2005
formats CD
illustration Gary Stillwell
design Farrow / PSB

The Pet Shop Boys' contribution to the long-running *Back To Mine* CD series of playlists by invited curators differed from its predecessors in two significant ways. For the first time, it was a two-disc set in which Chris and Neil each curated their own separate playlists. ('It's famous for a track that Chris chose – Celestial Choir's "Stand on the word" – that's not available anywhere else', Neil notes. 'I heard it in a record shop in Hoxton', Chris explains.) And its sleeve, rather than fitting in with the series' regular design template, was designed by Farrow as a Pet Shop Boys product.

'It's the start of Gary-at-Farrow's graphic artwork phase', says Neil. Gary Stillwell based the illustration on a photograph by Ripley & Ripley. 'I like it', says Chris. 'It's from the era when I had long blonde hair.' 'The image was created', Stillwell explains, 'by tracing the photograph in Adobe Illustrator, then reducing and simplifying the detail until it became a collection of flat shapes. The colours were adjusted to increase the contrast between shapes – so Neil's jacket was clearly defined against his T-shirt, for instance – which made the image more legible. We changed the colour of Chris's hat as we wanted him to have a brighter colour palette (pink top, yellow hair, green hat) to contrast with Neil's more muted palette.' Stillwell added the key held by Neil: 'The idea was that Pet Shop Boys had invited you "back to mine", and Neil held the key to let you in.'

**BACK TO MINE CD1
CHRIS LOWE**
1 SAVAGE – DON'T CRY TONIGHT
2 MR FLAGIO – TAKE A CHANCE
3 KLEIN & MBO – DIRTY TALK
4 THE FLIRTS – PASSION
5 MATIA BAZAR – TI SENTO
6 JUSTICE VS SIMIAN – NEVER BE ALONE
7 QUEEN – THE SHOW MUST GO ON
8 CELESTIAL CHOIR – STAND ON THE WORD
9 CARL BEAN – I WAS BORN THIS WAY
10 DUSTY SPRINGFIELD – I'D RATHER LEAVE WHILE I'M IN LOVE

**BACK TO MINE CD2
NEIL TENNANT**
1 FAIRMONT – TRAUM
2 HAROLD BUDD, RUBEN GARCIA AND DANIEL LENTZ – PULSE PAUSE REPEAT
3 BIOSPHERE – MICROGRAVITY
4 ENSEMBLE OPUS POSTH – COME IN! (II MOVEMENT) (COMPOSED BY VLADIMIR MARTYNOV)
5 VLADIMIR COSMA – PROMENADE SENTIMENTALE (SENTIMENTAL WALK)
6 ETIENNE DAHO – LA BAIE
7 VESSEL – TINY
8 CRAIG ARMSTRONG – LAURA'S THEME
9 CLOSER MUSIK – ONE TWO THREE NO GRAVITY (DETTINGER MIX)
10 DUSTY SPRINGFIELD – GOIN' BACK
11 LUNZ – LUNZ
12 SIR JOHN BARBIROLLI CONDUCTS THE NEW PHILHARMONIC ORCHESTRA – SOSPIRI OP. 70 (COMPOSED BY EDWARD ELGAR)
13 WWW.JZ-ARKH.CO.UK – DD RHODES
14 VIDEO KID – VIDEO KID
15 LOBE – MOVEMENT
16 JOHN SURMAN – AT DUSK
17 EMIL GILELS – MELODIE OPUS 47 NO. 3 (COMPOSED BY EDVARD GRIEG)

CD, outer sleeve, back

BACK TO MINE
PET SHOP BOYS

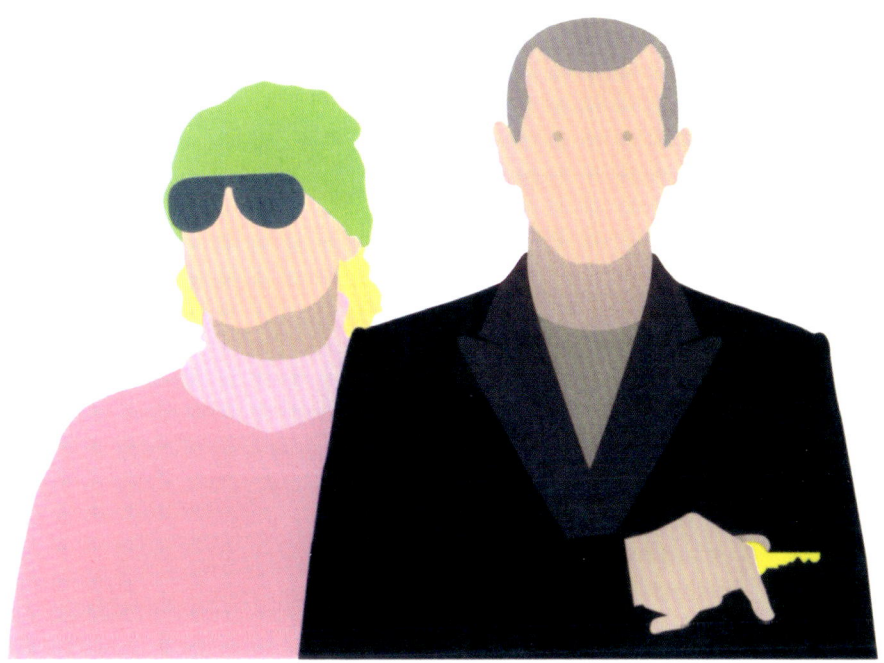

CD, outer sleeve, front

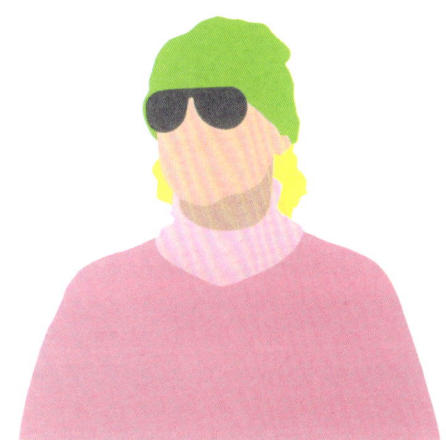

CD 1, inner sleeve, front

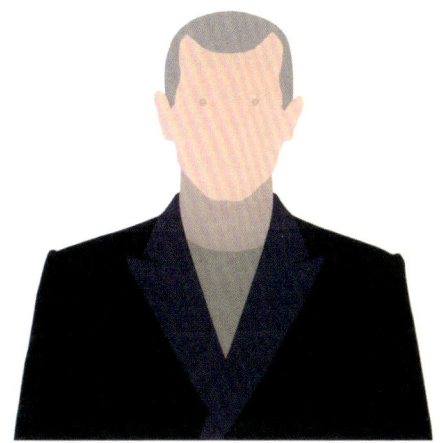

CD 2, inner sleeve, front

I'm with stupid

release 8 May 2006
formats 7" picture disc / 12" (US) / 12" promo × 3 / CD × 2 /
CD promo × 2 / CD-R promo × 6 / DVD / download × 2
photographer John Ross
design and art direction Farrow / PSB
video Rob Leggatt (Blue Source)

'I'm with stupid', the first single from the forthcoming Trevor Horn-produced *Fundamental* album, took its title from the commonplace jokey T-shirts bearing that phrase in combination with an arrow pointing towards the person accompanying the wearer. The song applied the idea to the dynamic between Tony Blair and George Bush. 'It's sort of a satire – Blair thinking Bush is the stupid one', Neil says. 'The pivotal moment in the song is where it says, "Is stupid really stupid, or a different kind of smart?"' The images used on the various versions of the sleeve were shot on the same day as the *Fundamental* sleeve (page 325), here using neon signs fashioned into the traditional 'I'm with stupid' arrows – sometimes pointing at Neil, sometimes at Chris, sometimes at both. 'We just stuck them under the two lights, switched one on, one off', says Mark Farrow. A seven-inch picture disc was released in which, to Neil and Chris's delight, all of the playing surface was as black as a regular vinyl single aside from, on the A-side, the sleeve's red neon arrow, and, on the B-side, its blue neon partner.

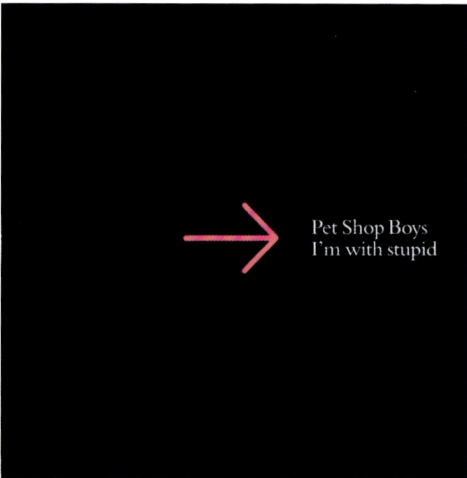

CD promo 1, front

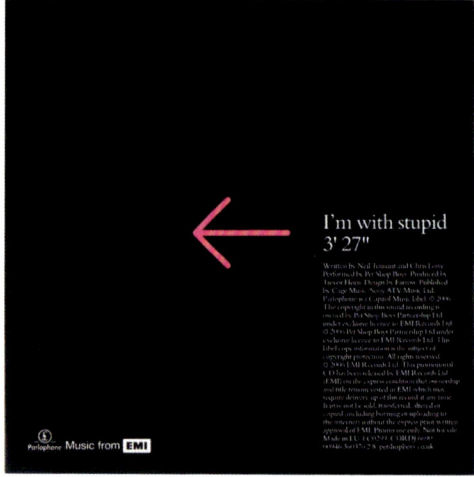

CD promo 1, back

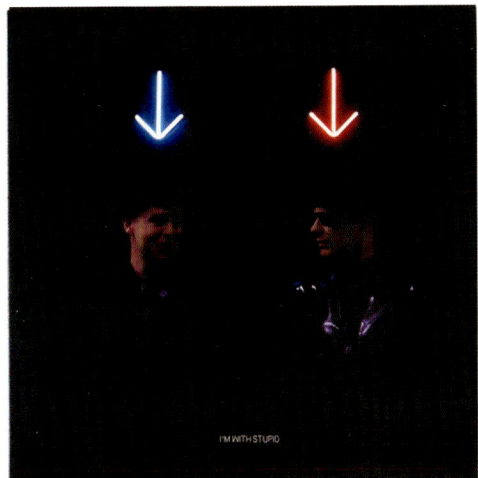

7" picture disc, outer sleeve, front

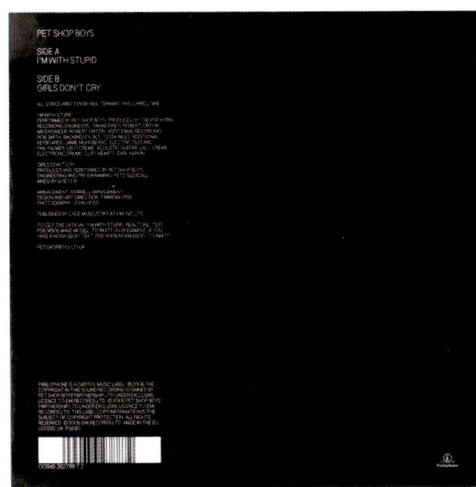

7" picture disc, outer sleeve, back

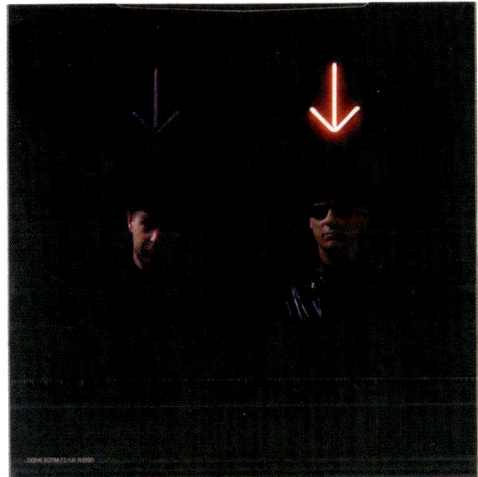

7" picture disc, inner sleeve, front

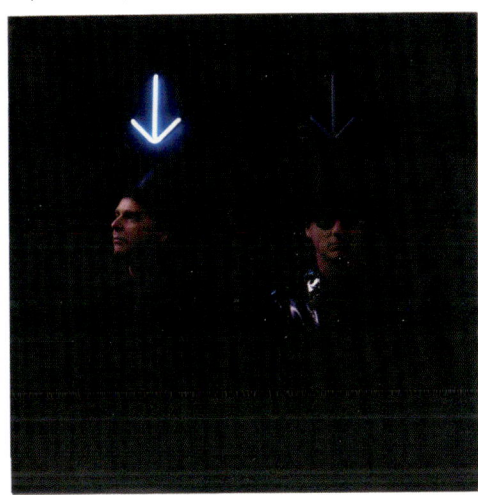

7" picture disc, inner sleeve, back

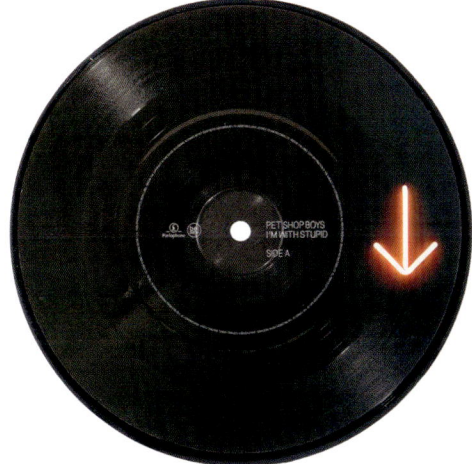

7" picture disc, Side A

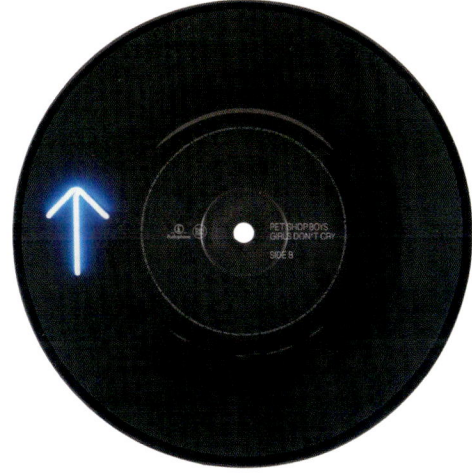

7" picture disc, Side B

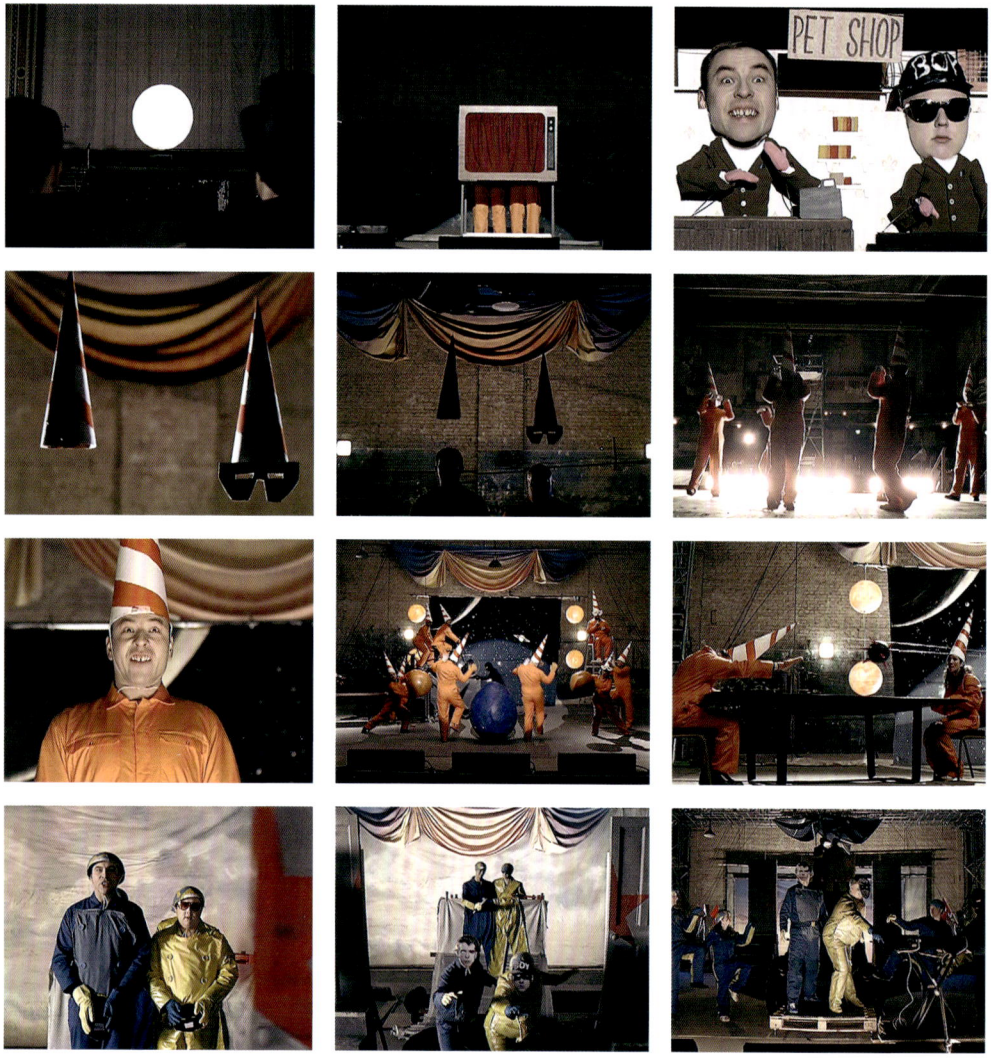

Shot in a disused theatre in London's Alexandra Palace, the video for 'I'm with stupid' featured long-term Pet Shop Boys fans David Walliams and Matt Lucas, then most famous for their TV series *Little Britain*, as the song's notional performers. (Many years earlier, the pair could be seen at the front of the audience during the Pet Shop Boys' performance of 'Liberation' on *Top of the Pops*.) The video's concept, suggested by Lucas, is that – as Neil explains – 'they've kidnapped us and are forcing us to watch *Pet Shop Boys: The Musical*.' To this effect, Walliams' and Lucas's heads appear atop makeshift versions of various iconic Pet Shop Boys looks. The real Pet Shop Boys are shown at the video's end, bound by ropes, literally a captive audience. When this scene was shot, Neil and Chris resisted the director's suggestion that they reacted in animated ways to their predicament. 'I sort of think the Pet Shop Boys, being captured, would be indifferent', Neil reasoned. 'We'd be nonchalant.'

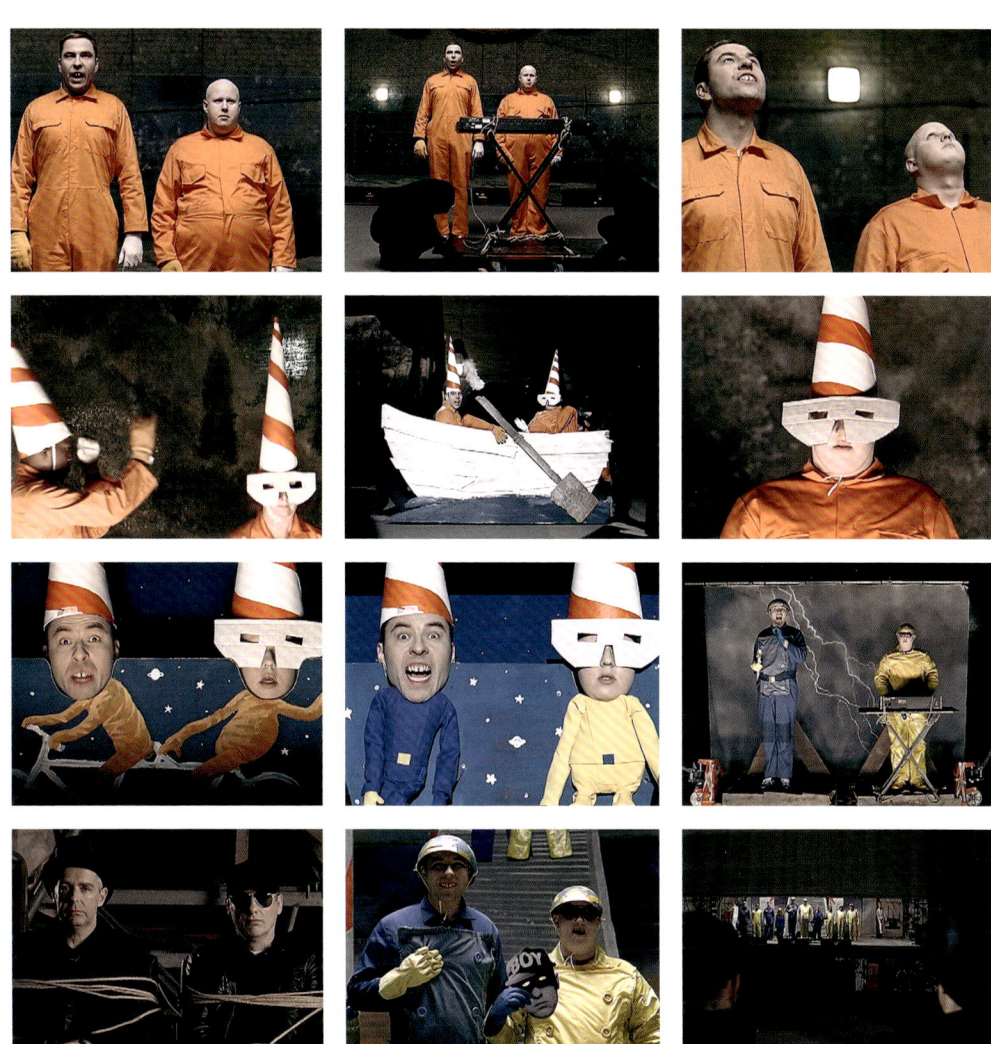

Fundamental

release **22 May 2006**
formats **LP / limited-edition double 12" / CD / limited-edition double CD / download**
photographer **John Ross**
design and art direction **Farrow / PSB**

Fundamental's sleeve shows Neil and Chris, almost completely in the dark, looking up at their name and the album's title in white neon. 'The entire idea of this record', says Neil, 'was a picture of the world post-9/11. I think the light out of darkness thing works with the theme.' The initial suggestion to use neon was Chris's, after he and Neil had seen an exhibition by the American artist Dan Flavin at London's Hayward Gallery. The signs were fabricated at A1 Designs, a company that Farrow found just outside London, not just of the Pet Shop Boys' name and of the word 'FUNDAMENTAL', but also of the album's twelve song titles, each in its own distinctive colour. Not all the signs actually contained neon, however: the various colours required different inert gases. 'It was an amazing experience seeing how they blow the letters', says Farrow. 'We probably could have done it with CGI, but we wanted to do it for real, which we quite often did, historically.' For the front cover, Neil and Chris were photographed in the same frame as the title. 'The idea', says Farrow, 'was that it was essentially a graphic cover, and you might notice that they were in the corner – standing in a seedy doorway, for want of a better term, bathed in the light of just one neon sign – but you might not. So the fact it was more or less all black was very deliberate. Though if it had really been nothing but the light of that sign, they'd have been pitch black, so we cheated a bit, but in camera.' 'The first time I looked at the sleeve, I didn't see us', says Chris, 'which I thought was great.' When studied more closely, the two Pet Shop Boys' styles diverge. 'I wanted to wear slightly Dickensian-looking clothes,' Neil explains, 'because I like the contrast of old and modern.' (His hat is, he notes, a half top hat.) 'I've got a sort of fundamental Chris Lowe look', says Chris. 'It's what I feel comfortable in.'

   The twelve song titles were photographed as a vertical list for use on the album's reverse, in a form redolent of the work of another American artist, Bruce Nauman. Different views of the stacked neon titles appeared elsewhere in the CD and LP artwork. A special limited-edition CD including a second album of remixes and related songs, *Fundamentalism* (also available as two twelve-inch discs), further extended the same visual vocabulary, with photographs of different stacks of neon song titles, some not on the original album. Gary Stillwell at Farrow created a complete bespoke typeface solely for this series of releases, based on the way letters were bent and shaped for neon sign construction, which was used on all the typography throughout the whole project.

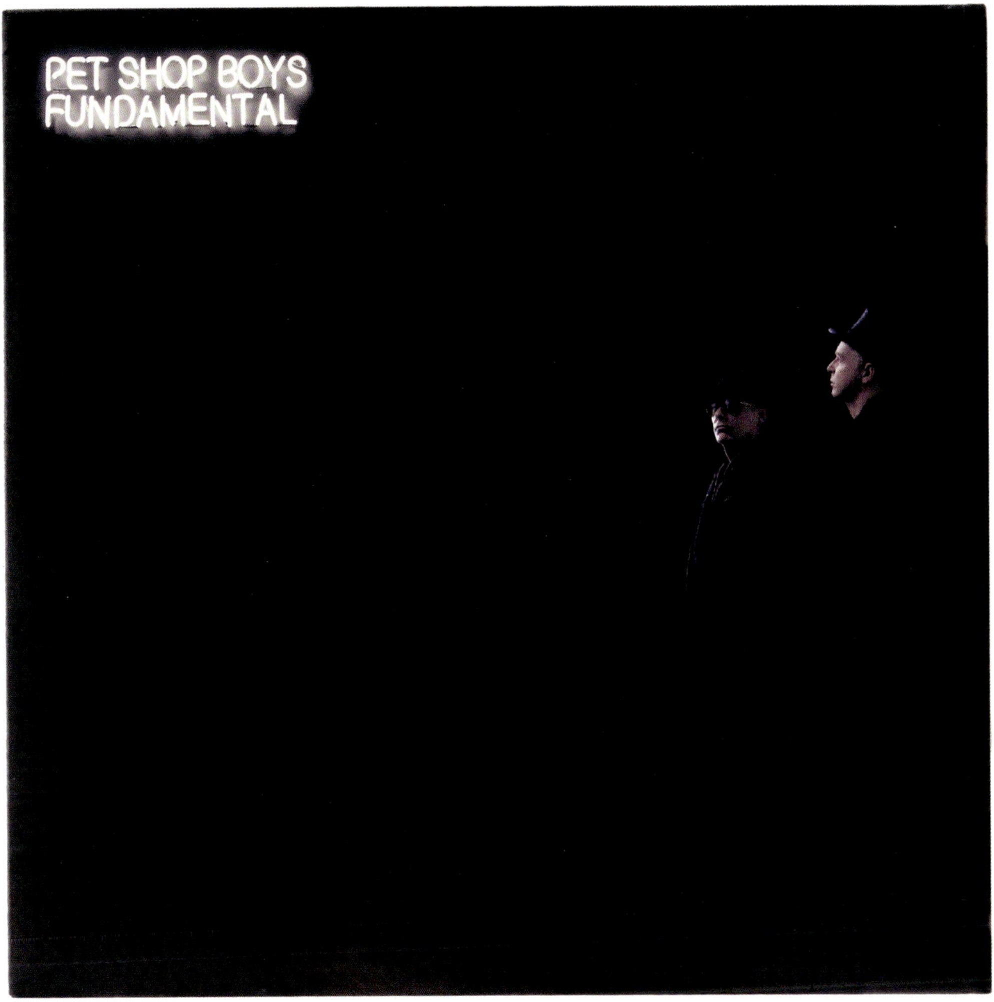

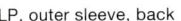

LP, outer sleeve, front

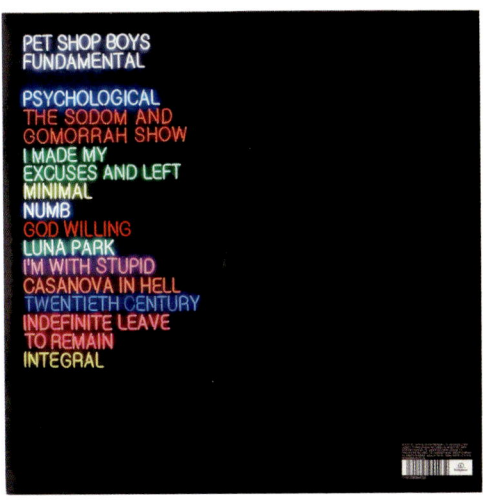

LP, outer sleeve, back

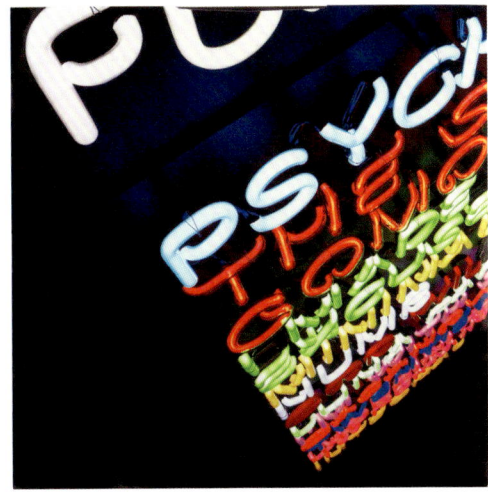

LP, inner sleeve, front

Limited-edition double CD, outer sleeve, back

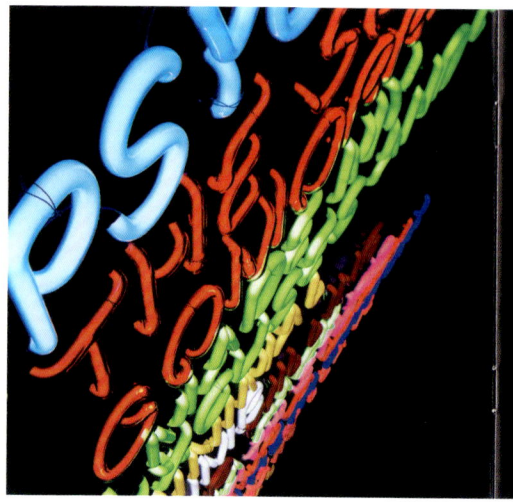

Limited-edition double CD, booklet, inside pages

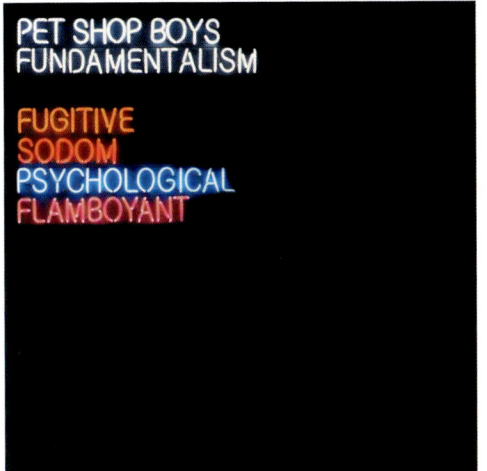
Limited-edition double 12", Part 1, outer sleeve, front

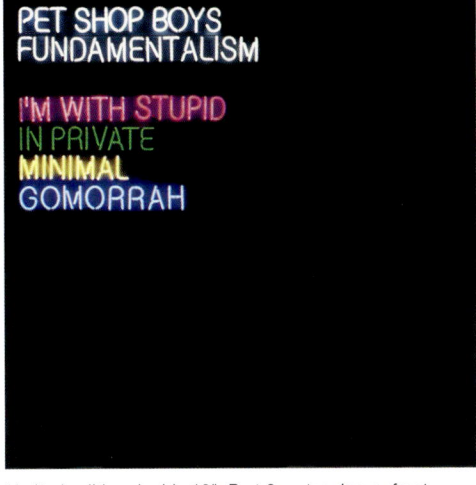
Limited-edition double 12", Part 2, outer sleeve, front

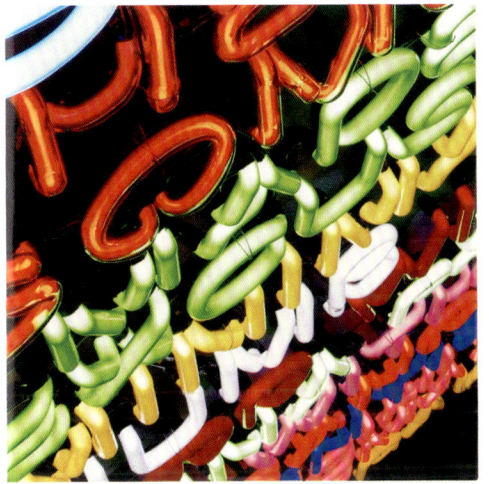
Limited-edition double 12", Part 1, inner sleeve, front

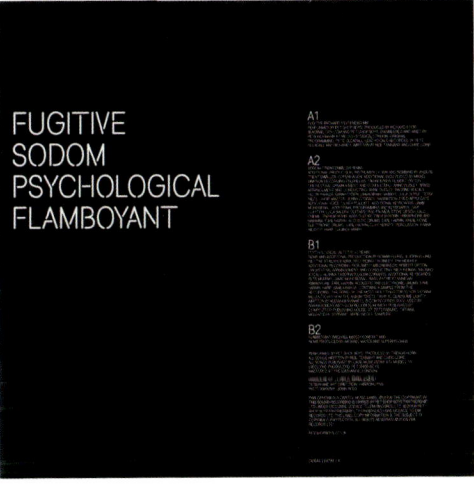
Limited-edition double 12", Part 1, inner sleeve, back

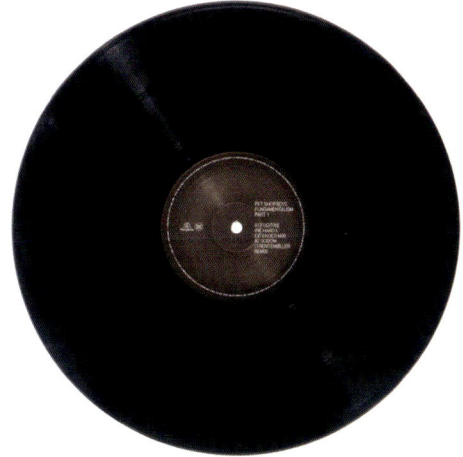
Limited-edition double 12", Part 1, Side A

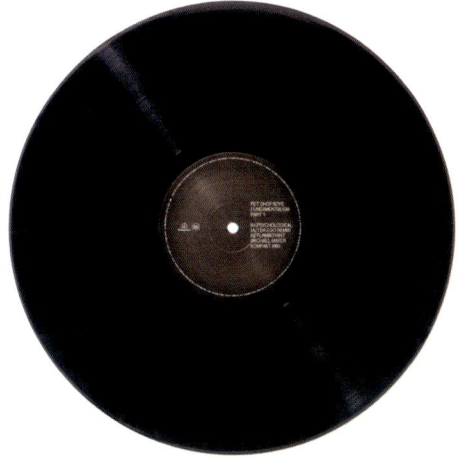
Limited-edition double 12", Part 1, Side B

Fundamental tour

dates 15 June 2006 – 25 November 2007
set design and direction Es Devlin
choreography Hakeem Onibudo

The *Fundamental* tour marked the Pet Shop Boys' first live performance collaboration with director and stage designer Es Devlin. Earlier that year, looking through a book they had found in the National Theatre bookshop about new theatre designers, Neil and Chris were in agreement that there were only two whose work they particularly liked. One was their previous collaborator Ian MacNeil; the second was Es Devlin. Although they had previously worked with Devlin in a very different context – she designed the *Closer to Heaven* musical (her first experience working in pop music; pages 278–9) – they had not previously thought of collaborating with her in this way, but now Neil called her. 'He had a very clear brief,' Devlin recalls, 'which was that the look of the tour should relate to the album artwork – the fluorescent neon tubes, those kinds of colours, that kind of feel.' Devlin came up with a staging centred around a series of squares and cubes. 'I am personally very fascinated by illusion and optical illusion and conjuror's tricks', she says. 'I had the idea of origami, and something that could unfold that would be like a magician's conjuring box.' She was also, she later explained, inspired by the X-ray image of a divided brain that she had seen while witnessing a cerebral angiogram. 'It's all her', says Chris of the design and conceptualization.

The *Fundamental* tour programme (page 330), which showed the Pet Shop Boys photographed by Tim Gutt and interviewed by Chris Heath in and around rehearsals in Bray Studios, Buckinghamshire, reported a conversation after an early run-through. 'Before we discuss anything we should say that was brilliant', Devlin told them, 'That's not our way', Chris pointed out. 'We go straight to the negative', Neil explained.

Several months into the tour's run, on 14 November 2006, their performance was filmed in Mexico City's Auditorio Nacional. The footage, directed by David Barnard, allowed the performers to see their show for the first time. 'I didn't realize how much stuff was going on', says Neil. That concert was subsequently released in May 2007 on DVD, with two different front covers – one showing Chris, the other with Neil – under the title *Cubism* (page 331). Neil would later reflect: 'The reason we're obsessed with cubes is because, as in Cubism, we look at the same thing from many different points of view.'

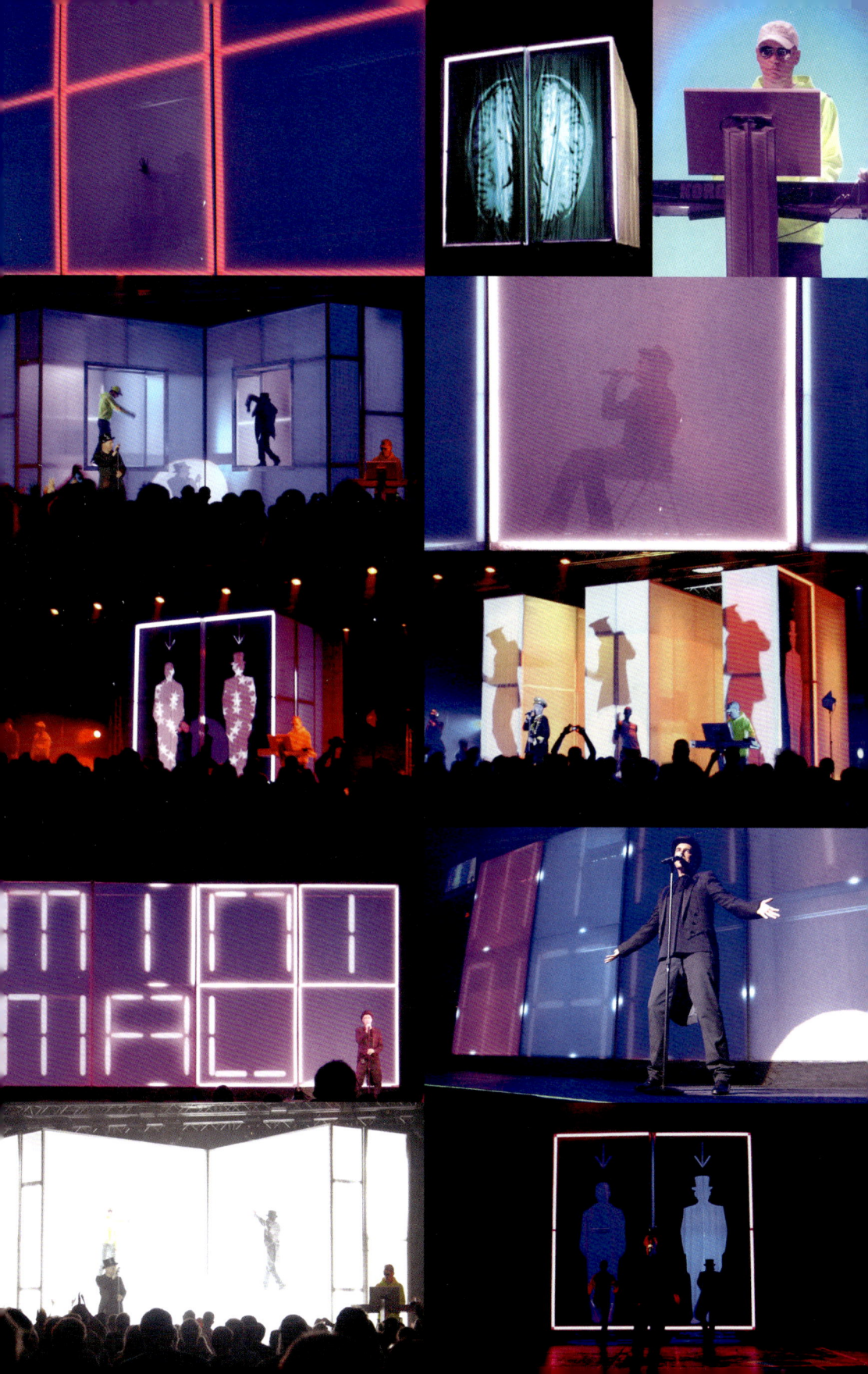

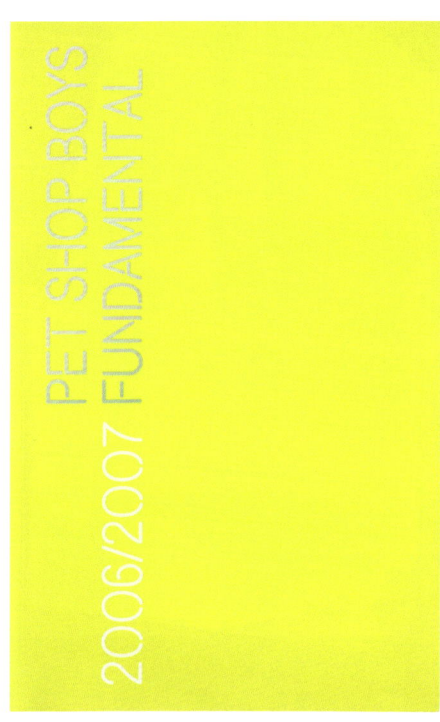
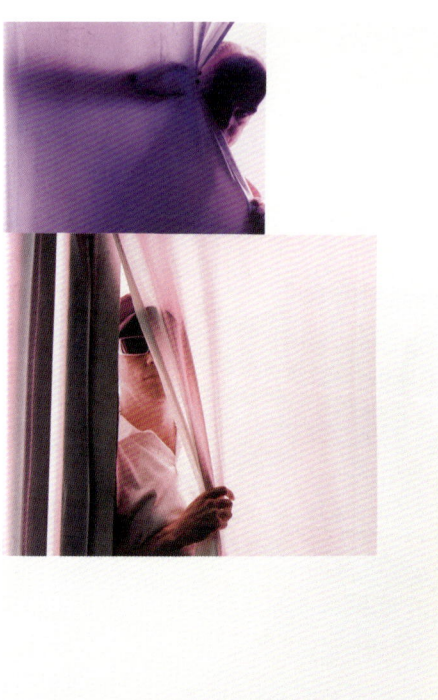

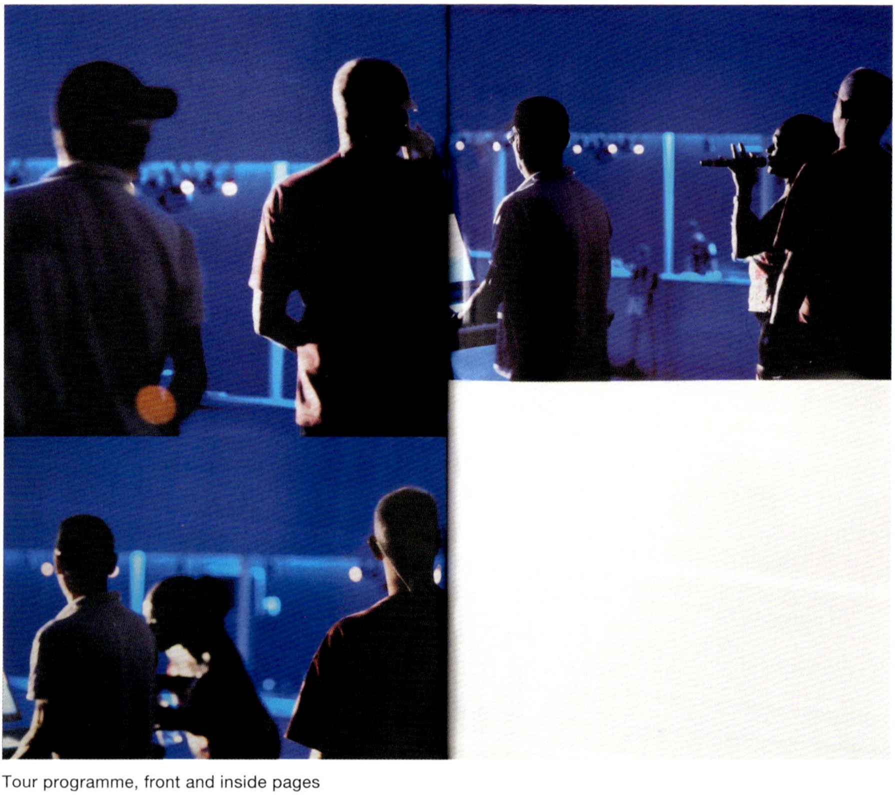

Tour programme, front and inside pages

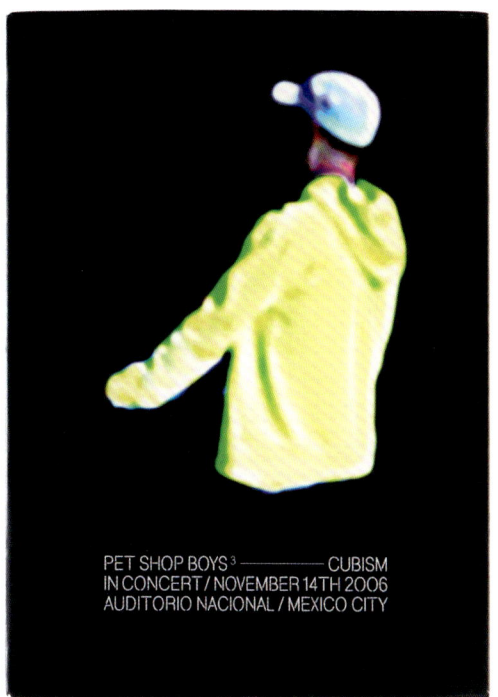

DVD, slipcase 1, front

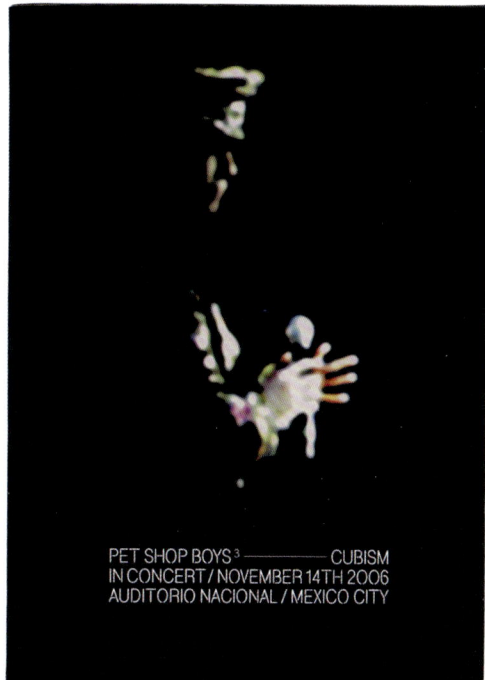

DVD, slipcase 2, front

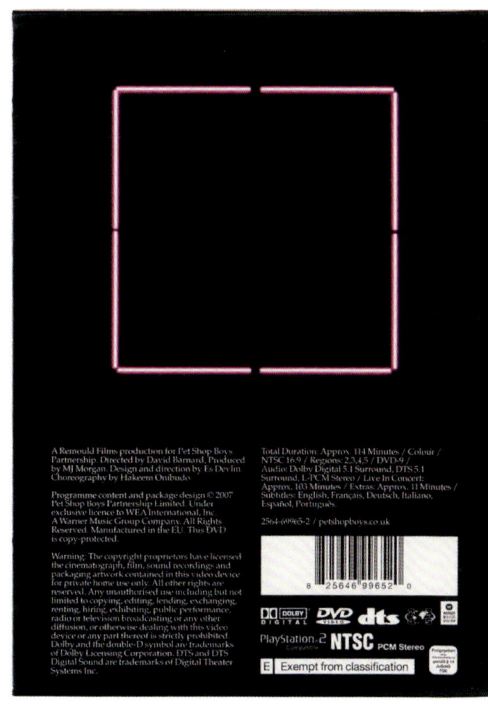

DVD, slipcase, back

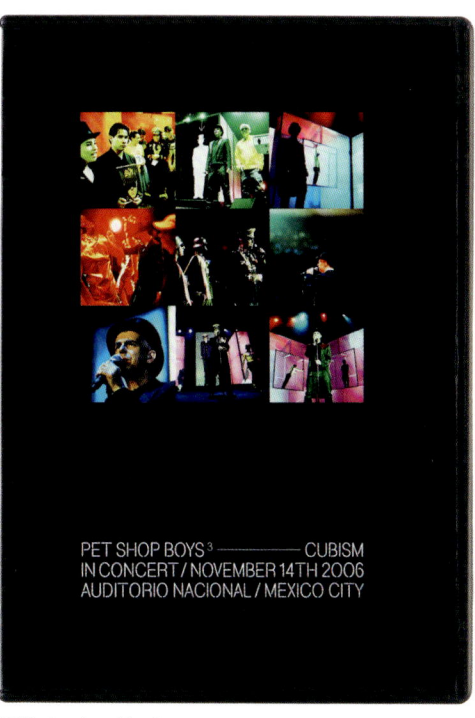

DVD, front and back

Minimal

release 24 July 2006
formats 7" / 12" / 12" promo × 2 / CD × 2 / CD promo /
CD-R promo × 5 / enhanced CD / DVD / download × 2
photographer John Ross
design and art direction Farrow / PSB
video Don Cameron

The various sleeves for *Fundamental*'s second single 'Minimal', produced like the album by Trevor Horn, reimagined the neon-letter imagery in a different (and, indeed, more minimal) way. The song itself had been initially inspired by the distinctive manner, during a September 2004 holiday in Ibiza, in which some Italian friends had expressed their enthusiasm for minimal house music. 'Great record', says Neil. 'It's funny that it's called "Minimal" and yet it's got a huge orchestra on it.' 'Well, it's Trevor, isn't it?' reflects Chris. 'He doesn't do anything minimal.'

When the Farrow team had originally visited the neon sign fabricators, Gary Stillwell recalls, they saw what the neon tubes looked like early in the process of their construction: 'They are all just clear tubes, and we thought how beautiful they were, before they are coloured.' For 'Minimal', they saw an opportunity to use this idea, and a new clear sign was commissioned, then photographed against white and against black at different angles. 'This was my favourite bit of the whole *Fundamental* era', says Mark Farrow. 'That, to me, was a lovely bit of thinking. There's a single called "Minimal", so we'll just do the glass with no gas in it and no colour in it. I was kind of made up with that idea.'

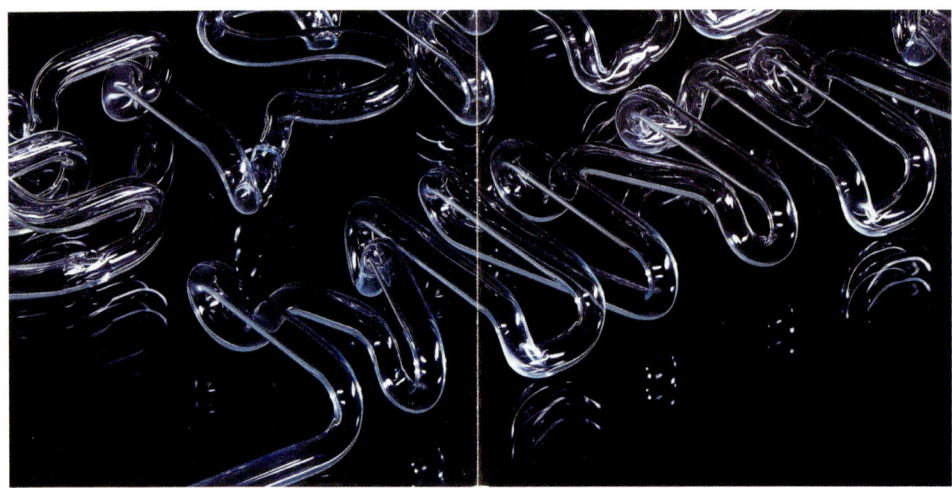

DVD, sleeve, inside

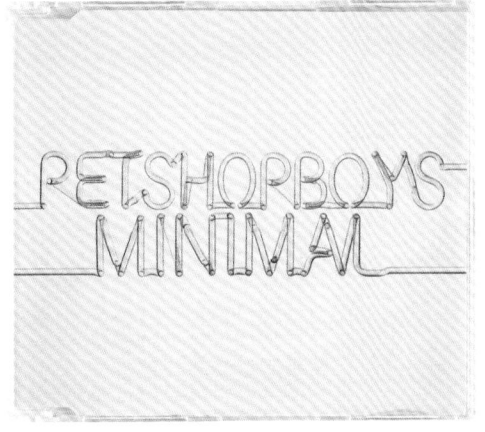

CD, front

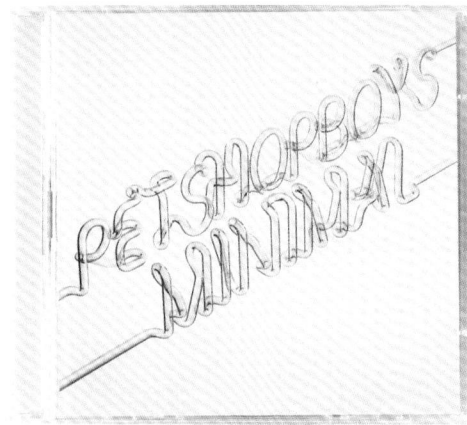

Enhanced CD, front

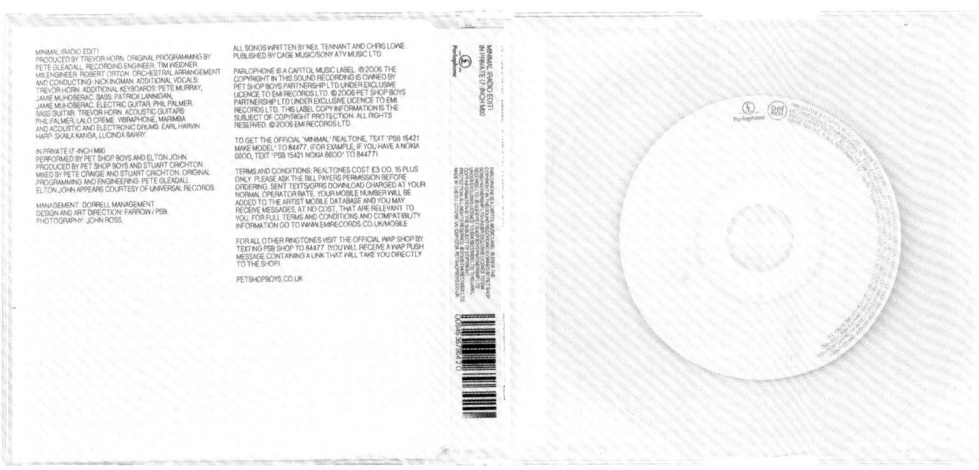

CD, inside

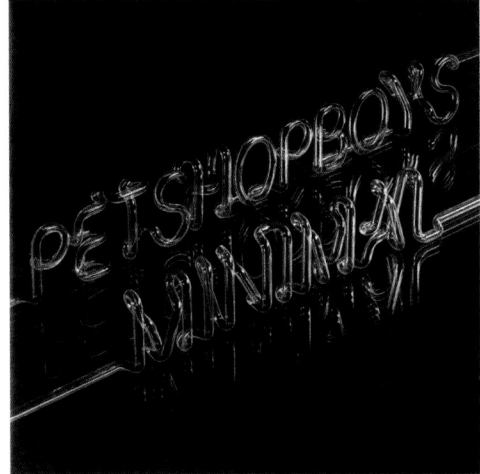

DVD, sleeve, front

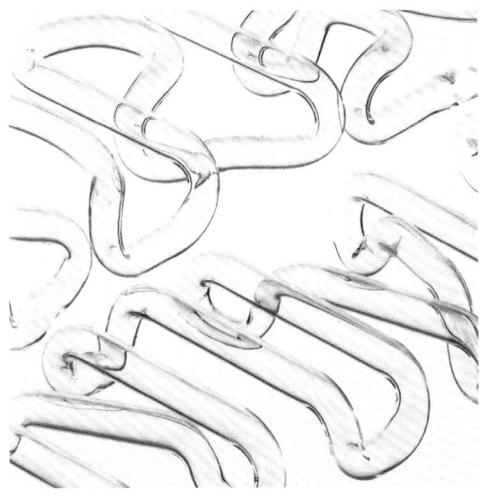

CD remix, front

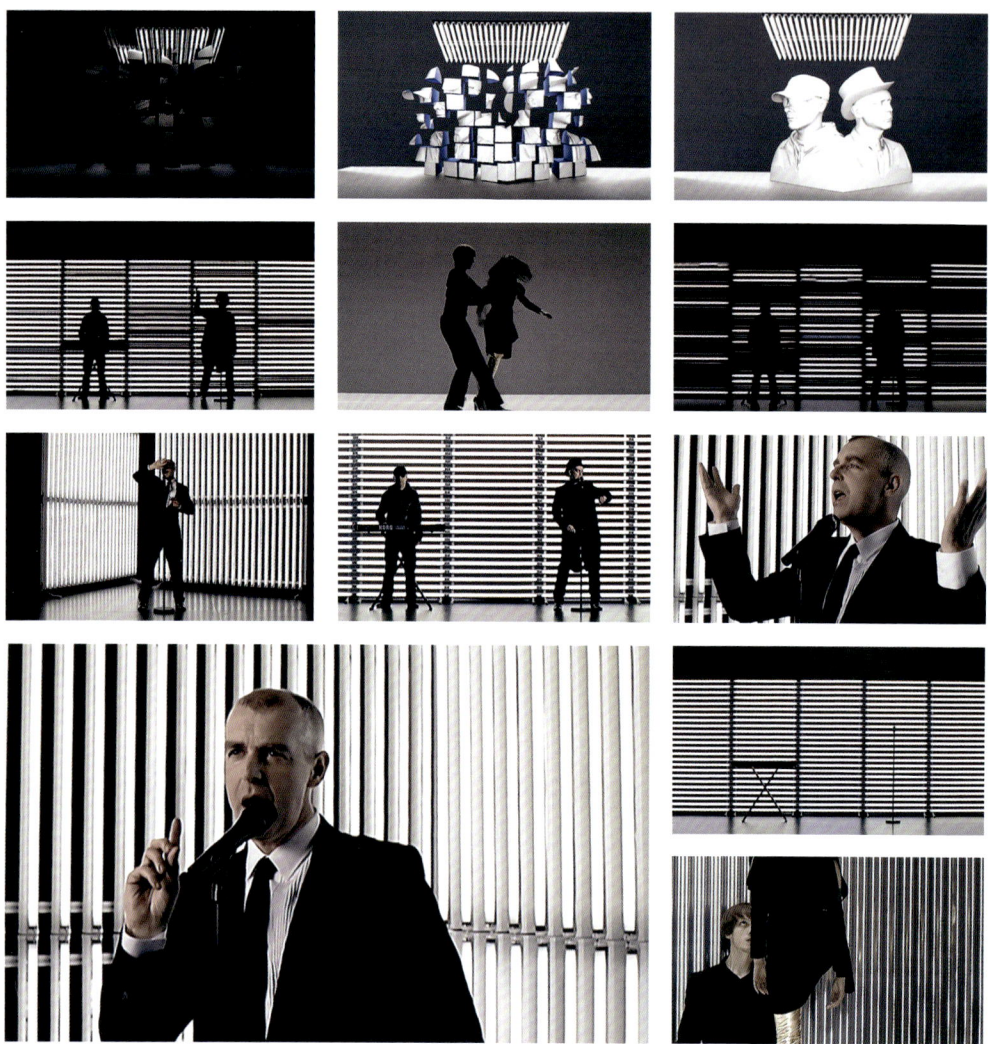

The video for 'Minimal', which was centred around a performance of the song filmed in front of banks of white neon strips, sometimes horizontal, sometimes vertical, was shot just outside Paris by the Australian director Don Cameron. 'It was the video director's idea', says Neil. 'They wanted us to perform, so we're wearing our look of the album. I've got the top hat on. And the two dancers look great. It's a really nice video, actually. But we weren't there very long, shooting it. We went and we came back the same day on the Eurostar. I remember we all broke for lunch and there was wine.' 'It was a union rule',," says Chris. 'We look great in it', says Neil. 'You can't beat those fluorescent tubes, can you?' Chris adds. 'Also,' Neil concludes, 'I look thin, so what's not to like?'

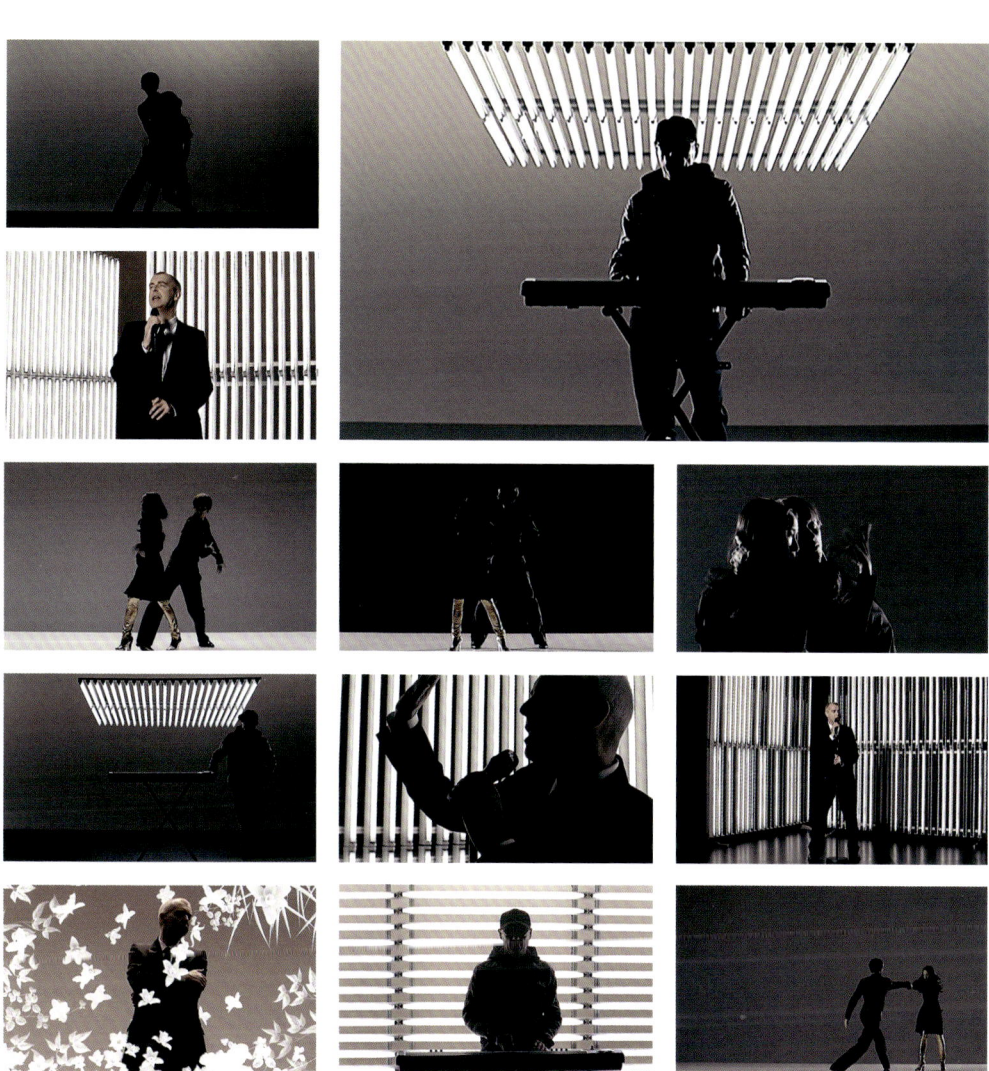

Pet Shop Boys Catalogue

release 16 October 2006
format 336-page hardback book, with dust jacket
authors Philip Hoare and Chris Heath
design Maggi Smith for Thames & Hudson
publisher Thames & Hudson

The initial impetus for a compendium of the Pet Shop Boys' visual history was the proposal from the American curator Terry Myers that a Pet Shop Boys exhibition be shown in American art museums, with an accompanying Thames & Hudson book. The exhibition plan fell through, but the book went ahead, meticulously detailing the visual aspects of the Pet Shop Boys' creative work between 1984 and 2004. Its dust-jacket images of Chris and Neil mirrored Mark Farrow's full-bleed presentation of Eric Watson's portraits from the front and back of the 'Suburbia' twelve-inch single (page 67). Of the image of Chris on the front, which had been suggested by the publisher, Neil says, 'It's the strongest Pet Shop Boys image there is.' 'We had the idea of printing it on silver, which I thought was very Warhol', Chris notes. Beneath the dust jacket, the hardback cover had one of Watson's shots of the Pet Shop Boys with Weimaraner dogs that had been used seven years earlier on the artwork of 'I don't know what you want but I can't give it any more' (page 253), rendered in pinkish tones, which coincidentally had been photographed outside the publisher's then offices in central London. This current book incorporates most of *Catalogue*'s content and builds upon on it.

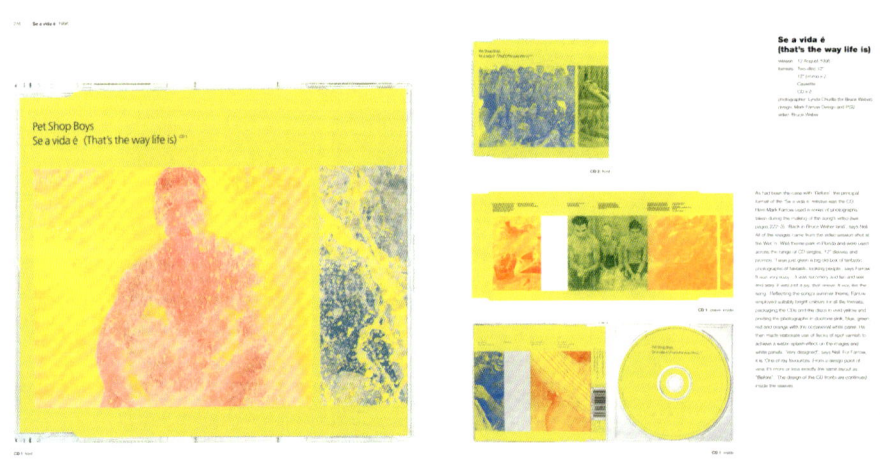

Pages 320–1

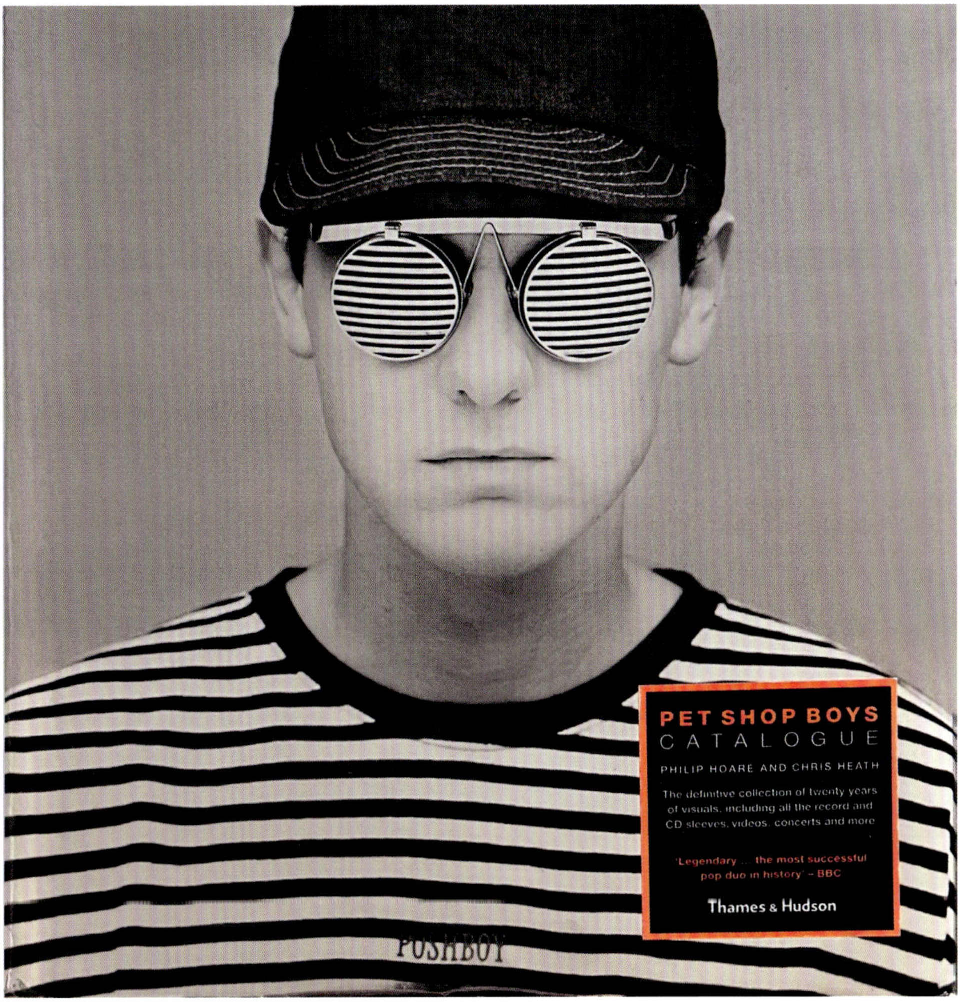

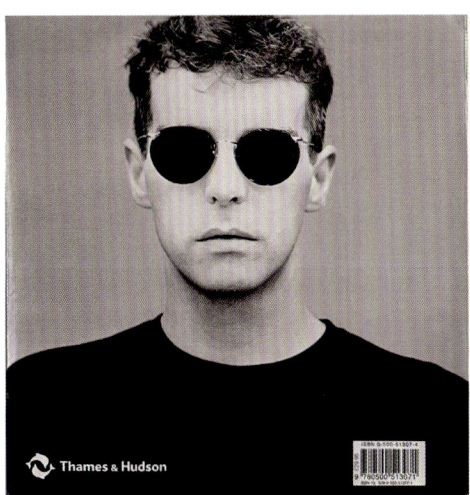
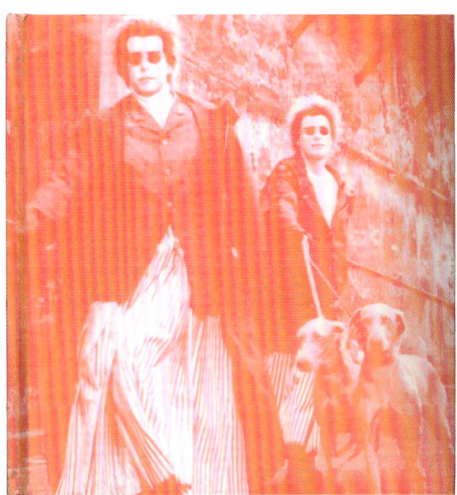

Dust jacket, front (top) and back (above) Cover, front

Pet Shop Boys Catalogue 2006

Numb

release 16 October 2006
formats 7" / 12" / 12" promo / CD / CD promo /
CD-R promo / enhanced CD / download
photographer Sam Taylor-Wood
design and art direction Farrow / PSB
video Julian Gibbs, Julian House, Chris Sayer

'Numb', written by American songwriter Diane Warren, had originally been recorded in 2003 for inclusion on *PopArt* before eventually appearing on *Fundamental*. It was released as a single in a new edit influenced by the way the BBC had used the song that summer as the soundtrack to the montage shown after the England football team had been knocked out of the World Cup. Its principal sleeve shows the Pet Shop Boys photographed by the artist Sam Taylor-Johnson (then Sam Taylor-Wood) at the Jerusalem Tavern in Clerkenwell, London. Neil and Chris are wearing the Doctor of the Plague masks they had bought in Venice some years earlier – masks that Venetians would wear, noses stuffed with spices and herbs, in an attempt to ward off disease. It was some time after the photograph was taken when they realized how well it would fit this new single. 'They just walked in with that photograph', remembers Mark Farrow. The front of the vinyl twelve inch simply shows the song title. 'We took the neon typeface and just blurred it', says Gary Stillwell. 'Numbed it', clarifies Farrow.

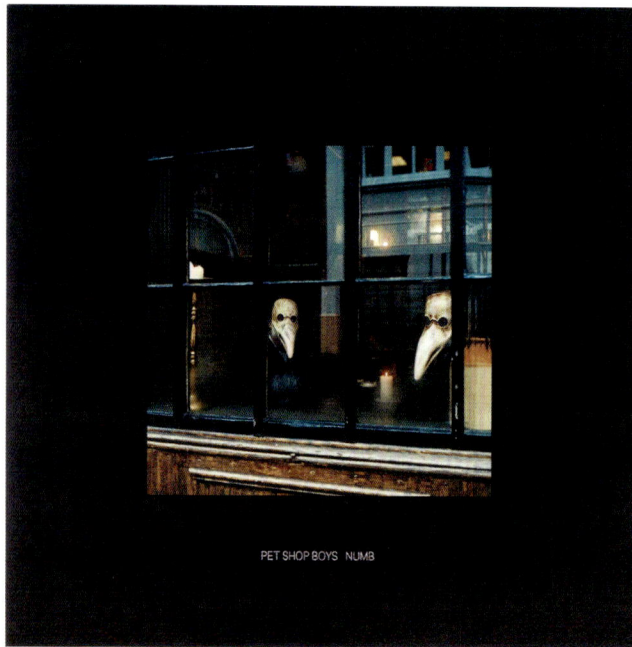

7", front

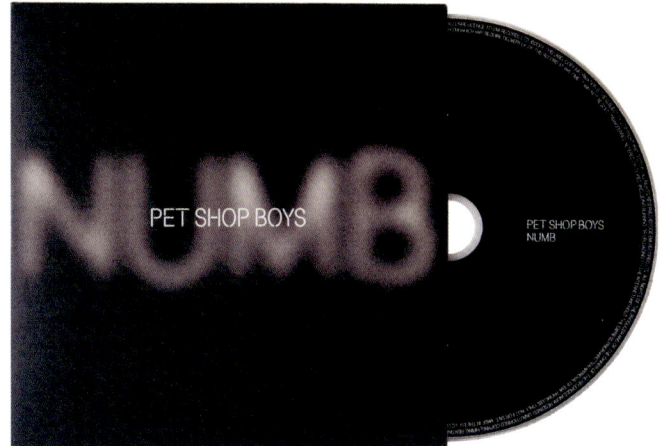

CD promo, card sleeve, front and CD

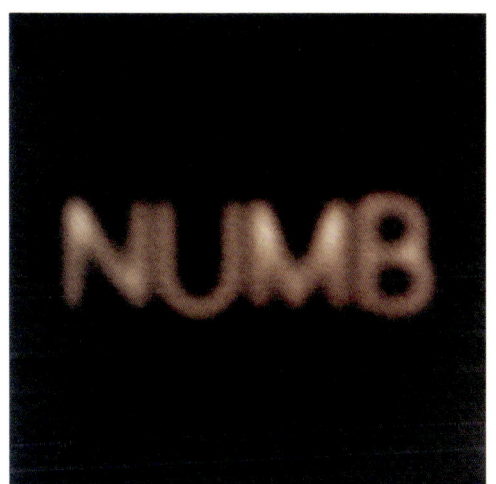

12", outer sleeve, front

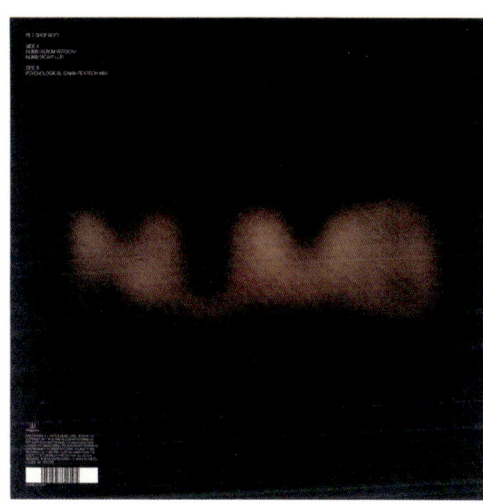

12", outer sleeve, back

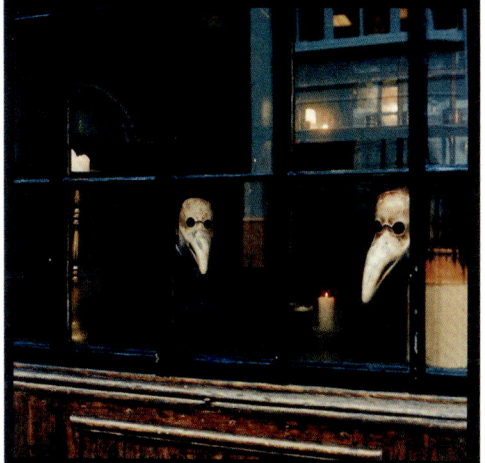

12", inner sleeve, front

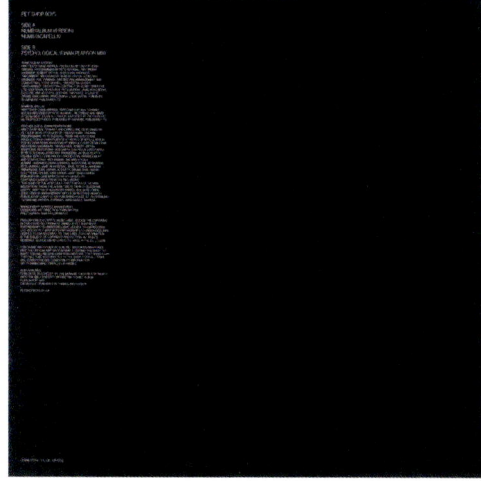

12", inner sleeve, back

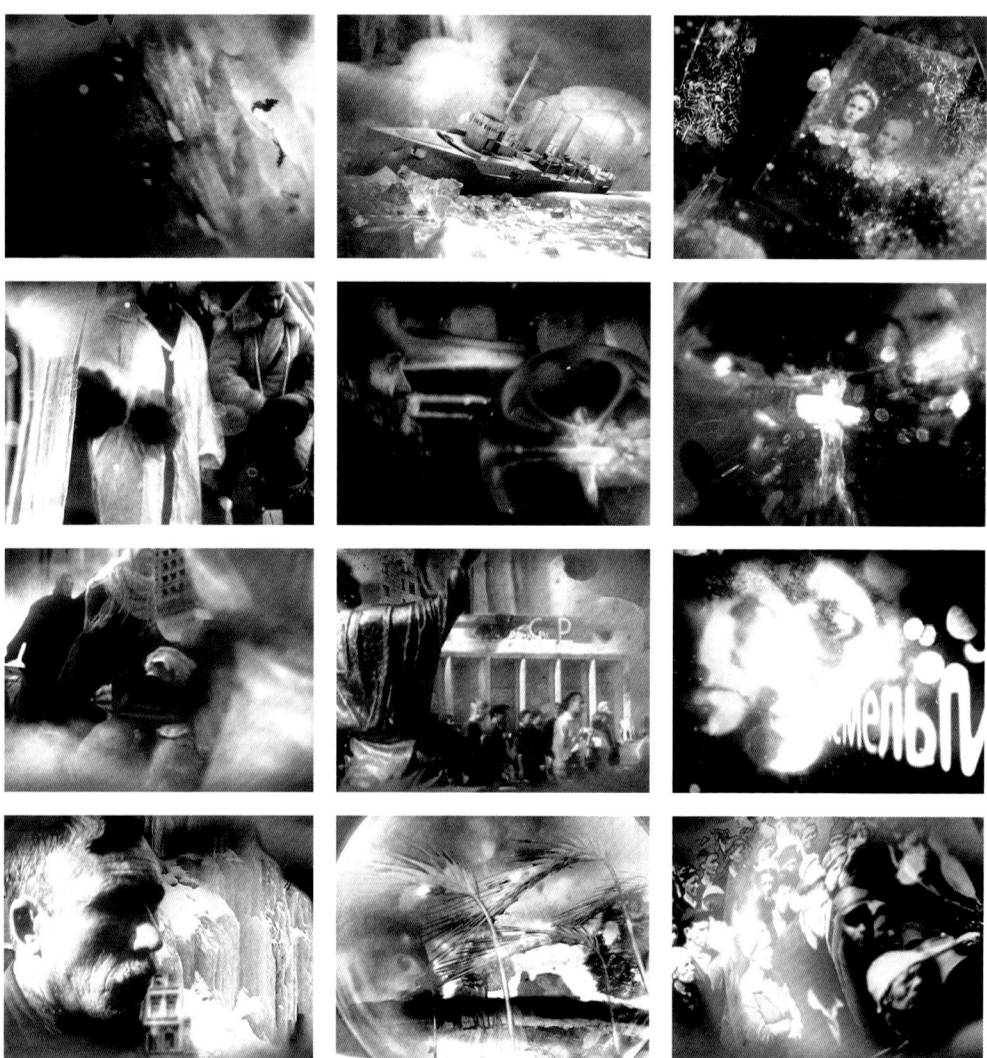

The black-and-white 'Numb' video was made by Julian Gibbs, Julian House, and Chris Sayer. As explained on Sayers' website: 'The video translates the emotional numbness of the song into imagery of a frozen city from archive Russian footage re-collaged together as an icy dream film, following a lone character from a shipwreck to the centre of the city.' Towards the very end, within the collage can be seen fleeting images of Neil and Chris.

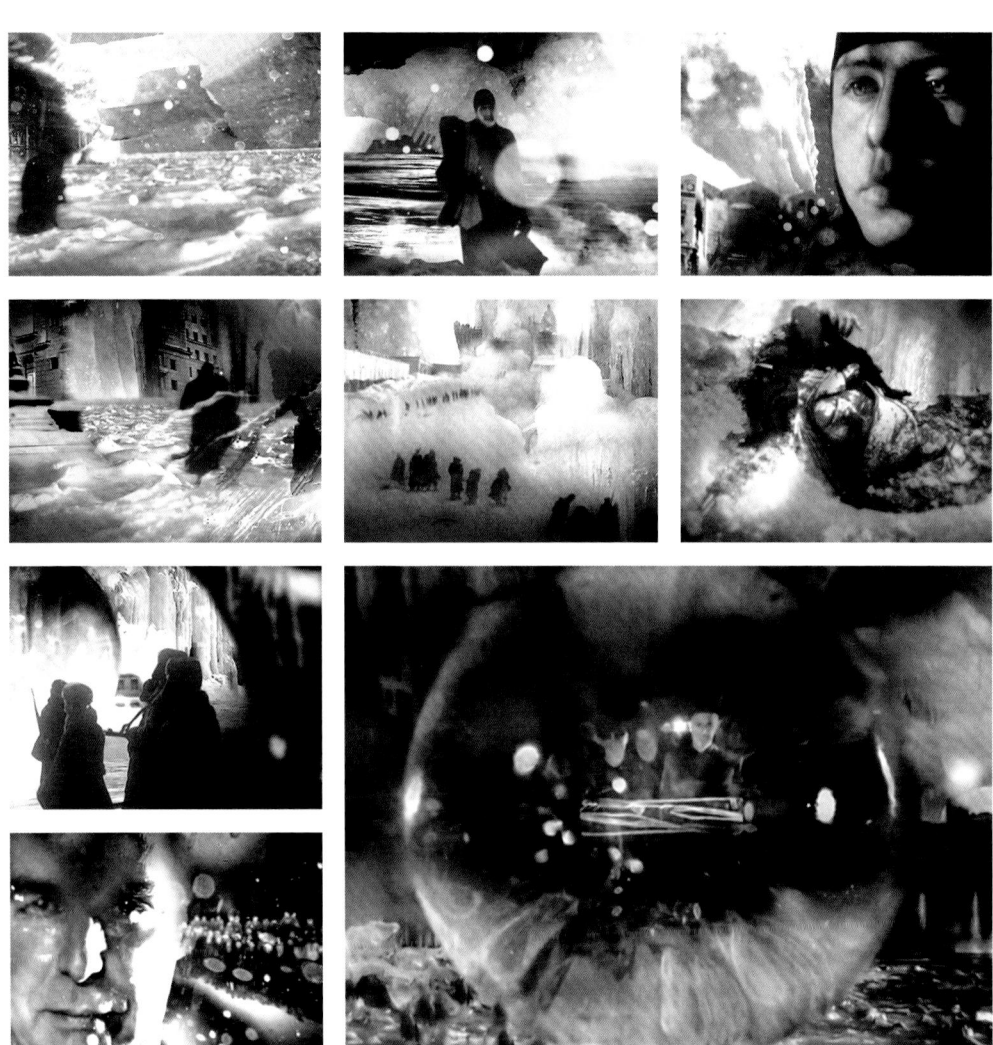

A Life in Pop

release **23 October 2006**
format **DVD**
design **Farrow / PSB**

The television version of George Scott's documentary, just under an hour in length, was broadcast on Channel 4 at 11.05 p.m. on 24 May 2006, but the full version – well over two hours long – was seen only when *A Life in Pop* was released on DVD. As well as a wide cast of collaborators, the two Pet Shop Boys are filmed together and separately (Chris in Blackpool, Neil in Newcastle), reflecting on the past and the present. The front-cover image is taken from an interview conducted in Tate Modern overlooking the River Thames in central London, under their and the documentary's name in the *Fundamental* typeface. Towards the end of the film, Neil says, 'It's unusual for two people to come together and have one creative personality, which is sort of what we've done.' Chris's final words are: 'We aim to be poptastic, I suppose. Whether we succeed or not. And sometimes we disappear along the way.' Within Neil's final statement, he quotes a friend: 'She says "I know what you do: depth through surface." And I guess that is what we do. And that's why it can be taken in in quite a few different ways. And I personally think that's a big strength.' The DVD also included the promo videos for the previous five Pet Shop Boys singles, as well as three landmark TV appearances: performing 'Go west' at the 1994 Brits with a choir of miners; performing 'What have I done to deserve this?' at the 1988 Brits with Dusty Springfield; and their very first TV performance, promoting the Bobby Orlando version of 'West End girls' in 1984, on the Belgian TV show *Hit des Clubs*.

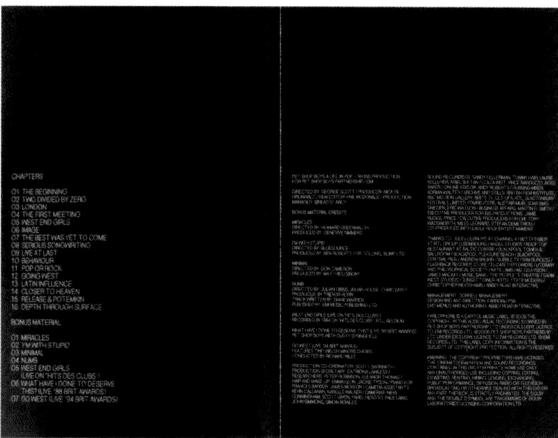

DVD, booklet, inside

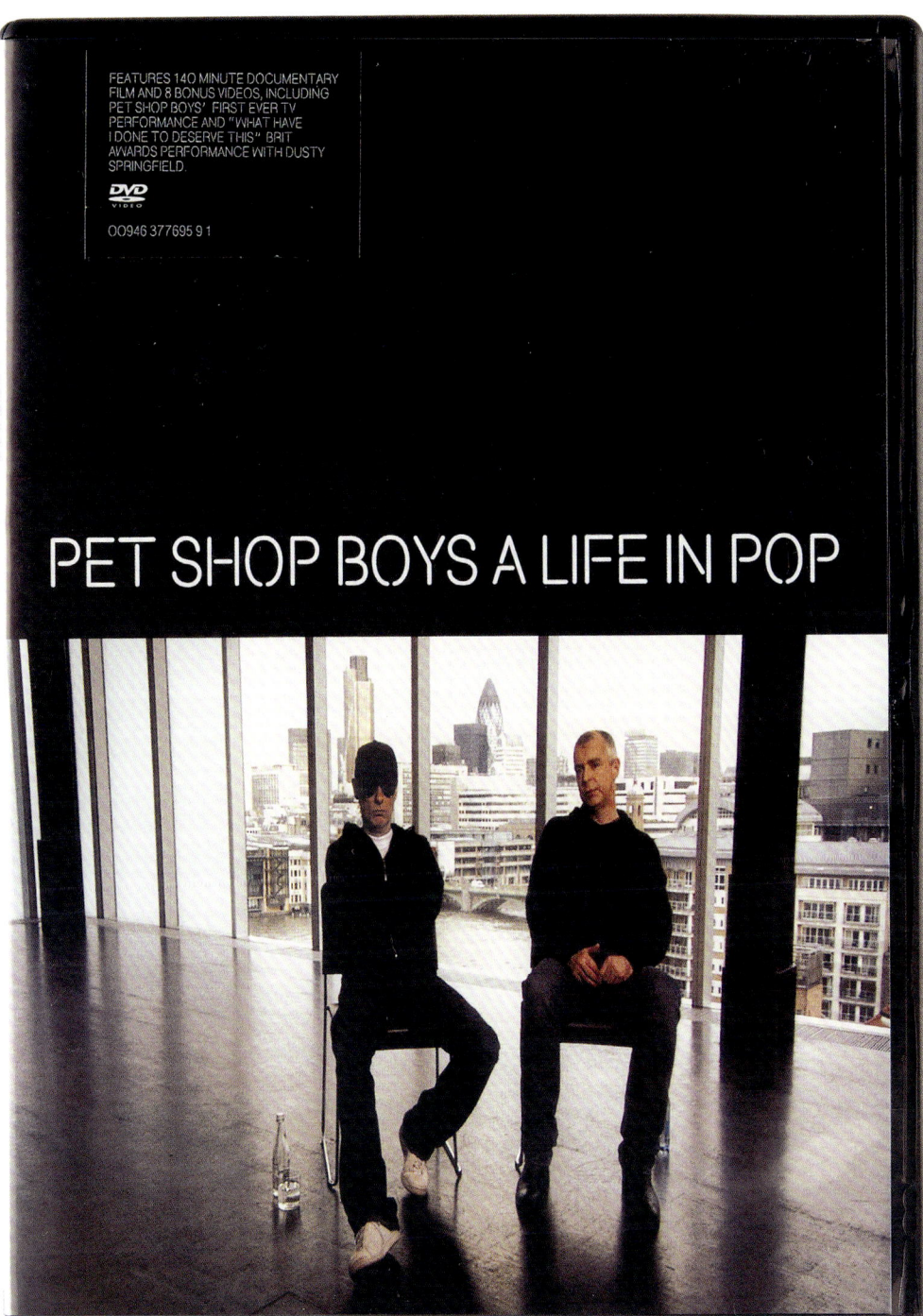

DVD, front

Concrete

release 23 October 2006
format 2 × CD
photographer John Ross and Elliott Franks
design and art direction Farrow / PSB

Earlier in 2006, on 8 May, the Pet Shop Boys had performed a one-off concert with the sixty-piece BBC Concert Orchestra at London's Mermaid Theatre, and a band including Trevor Horn, Anne Dudley, Steve Lipson, and Lol Creme, with guest vocalist spots from Frances Barber, Rufus Wainwright, and Robbie Williams. Highlights from the show had been broadcast on BBC Radio 2, but *Concrete* documented the full performance. Its title was both a nod to the theatre's severe architecture – 'It's a concrete carbuncle', says Chris – and to the convenient fact, says Neil, that the word is also 'almost an anagram of "concert"'. For the sleeve, Mark Farrow asked John Ross to return to the theatre to photograph its predominantly concrete exterior and interior. 'A bit of brutalist architecture', says Farrow, noting, 'You can't go wrong with pictures of architecture on album covers.'

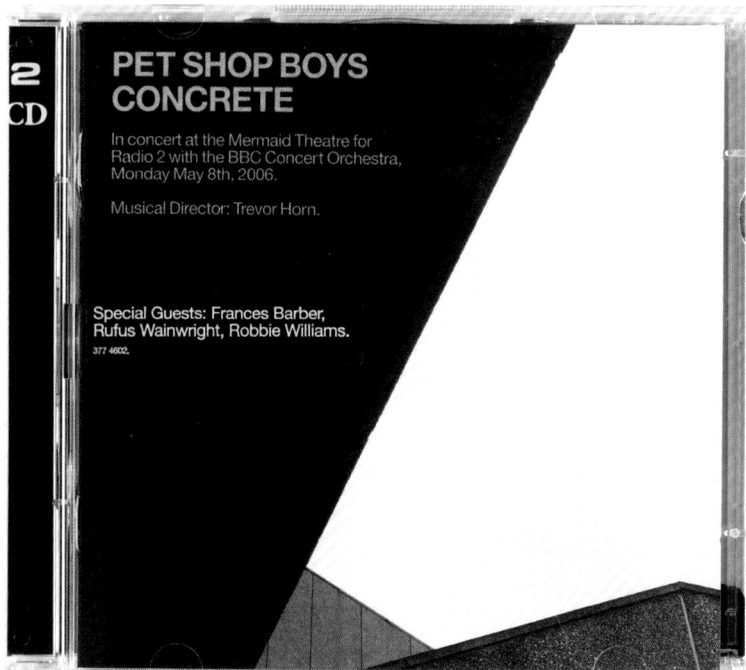

CD, front

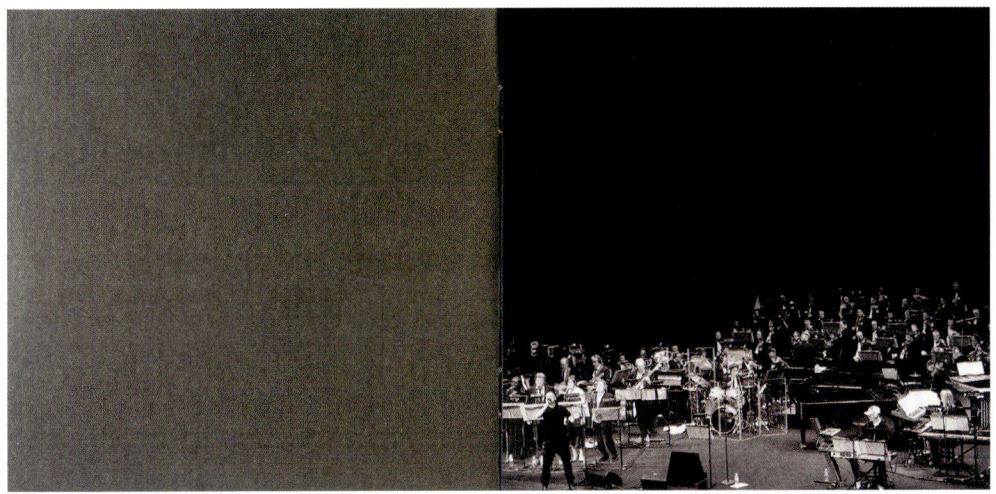

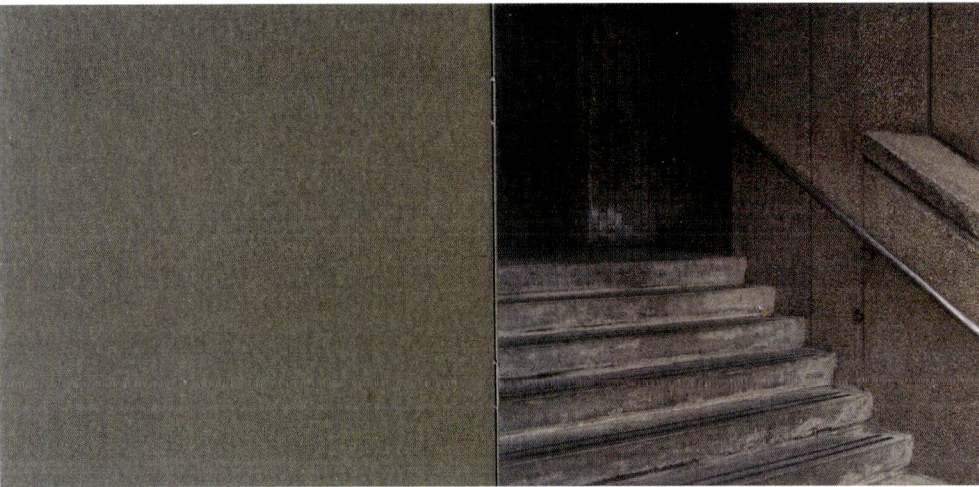

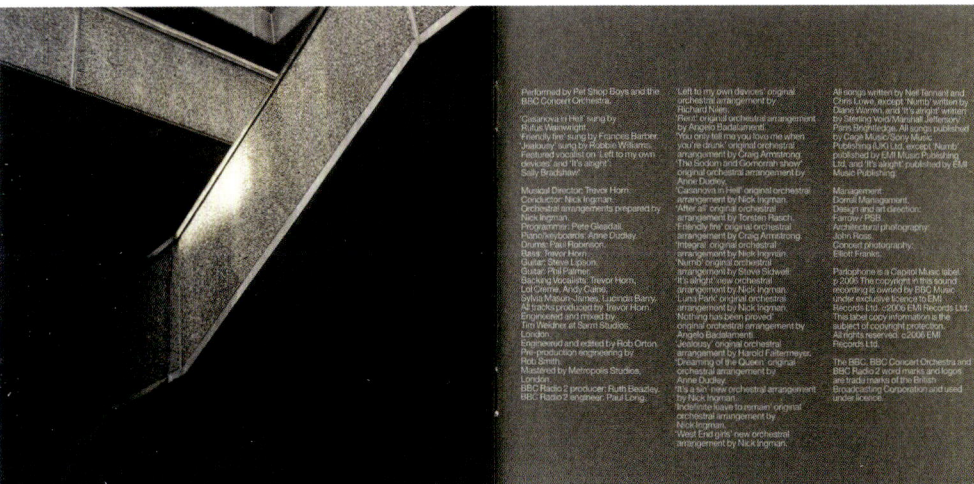

Performed by Pet Shop Boys and the BBC Concert Orchestra.

'Casanova in Hell' sung by Rufus Wainwright.
'Friendly fire' sung by Frances Barber.
'Jealousy' sung by Robbie Williams.
Featured vocalist on 'Left to my own devices' and 'It's alright': Sally Bradshaw.

Musical Director: Trevor Horn.
Conductor: Nick Ingman.
Orchestral arrangements prepared by Nick Ingman.
Programmer: Pete Gleadall.
Piano/keyboards: Anne Dudley.
Drums: Paul Robinson.
Bass: Trevor Horn.
Guitar: Steve Lipson.
Guitar: Phil Palmer.
Backing Vocalists: Trevor Horn, Lol Creme, Andy Caine, Sylvia Mason-James, Lucinda Barry.
All tracks produced by Trevor Horn.
Engineered and mixed by Tim Weidner at Sarm Studios, London.
Engineered and edited by Rob Orton.
Pre-production engineering by Rob Smith.
Mastered by Metropolis Studios, London.
BBC Radio 2 producer: Ruth Beazley.
BBC Radio 2 engineer: Paul Long.

'Left to my own devices' original orchestral arrangement by Richard Niles.
'Rent' original orchestral arrangement by Angelo Badalamenti.
'You only tell me you love me when you're drunk' original orchestral arrangement by Craig Armstrong.
'The Sodom and Gomorrah show' original orchestral arrangement by Anne Dudley.
'Casanova in Hell' original orchestral arrangement by Nick Ingman.
'After all' original orchestral arrangement by Torsten Rasch.
'Friendly fire' original orchestral arrangement by Craig Armstrong.
'Integral' original orchestral arrangement by Nick Ingman.
'Numb' original orchestral arrangement by Steve Sidwell.
'It's alright' new orchestral arrangement by Nick Ingman.
'Luna Park' original orchestral arrangement by Nick Ingman.
'Nothing has been proved' original orchestral arrangement by Angelo Badalamenti.
'Jealousy' original orchestral arrangement by Harold Faltermeyer.
'Dreaming of the Queen' original orchestral arrangement by Anne Dudley.
'It's a sin' new orchestral arrangement by Nick Ingman.
'Indefinite leave to remain' original orchestral arrangement by Nick Ingman.
'West End girls' new orchestral arrangement by Nick Ingman.

All songs written by Neil Tennant and Chris Lowe, except 'Numb' written by Diane Warren, and 'It's alright' written by Sterling Void/Marshall Jefferson/Paris Brightledge. All songs published by Cage Music/Sony Music Publishing (UK) Ltd, except 'Numb' published by EMI Music Publishing Ltd, and 'It's alright' published by EMI Music Publishing.

Management:
Dorrell Management.
Design and art direction:
Farrow / PSB.
Architectural photography:
John Ross.
Concert photography:
Elliott Franks.

Parlophone is a Capitol Music label.
℗ 2006 The copyright in this sound recording is owned by BBC Music under exclusive licence to EMI Records Ltd. ©2006 EMI Records Ltd. This label copy information is the subject of copyright protection. All rights reserved. ©2006 EMI Records Ltd.

The BBC, BBC Concert Orchestra and BBC Radio 2 word marks and logos are trade marks of the British Broadcasting Corporation and used under licence.

CD, booklet, inside pages

Integral

release 4 October 2007
formats CD / CD promo / CD-R promo / download
design Farrow
video Julian Gibbs, Julian House, Chris Sayer

In parallel with the new Pet Shop Boys remix album, *Disco Four* (pages 350–1), a remixed version of 'Integral', a satire of an authoritarian pro-surveillance government state, was released as a promo CD single and digital download, the sleeve of both being a QR code that directs traffic to the Pet Shop Boys website. 'The ideas very much came from them', says Mark Farrow. 'Dave Dorrell, our then manager, discovered the emerging QR code', says Neil. 'I wasn't even clear at the time what he was talking about, I've got to be honest. But when Dave thought something new was happening, you normally thought: well, we might as well go along with it. QR codes are everywhere now, but it took years to get there.' 'Actually, Covid-19 took it to another level', Chris points out.

Download

CD promo, front

CD promo, back

CD promo, disc

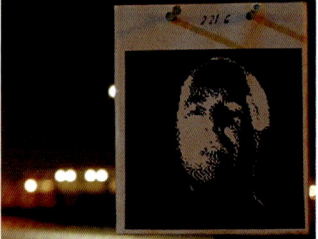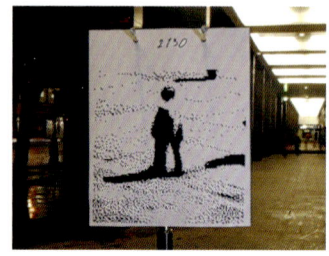
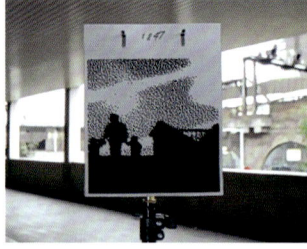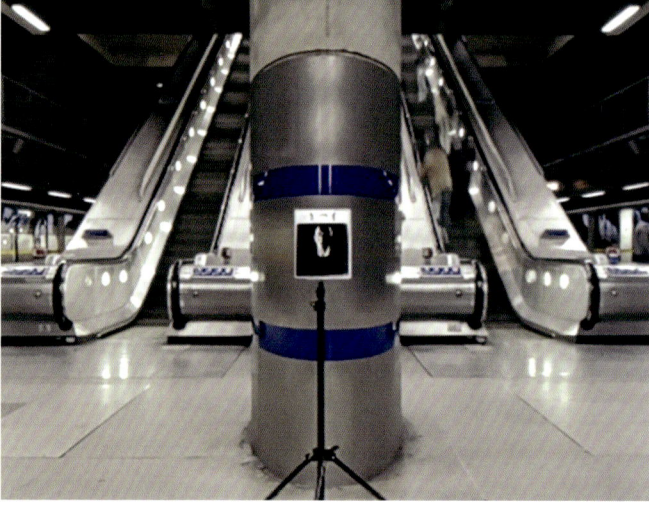
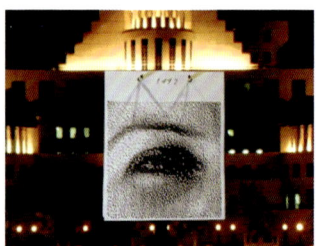
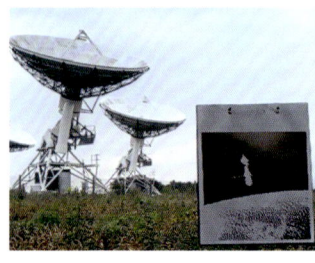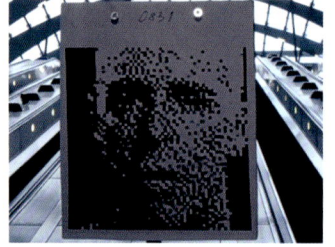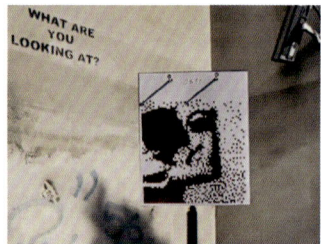

Further QR codes were seeded through the accompanying video of images pixellated to various degrees – one, for instance, directed viewers to the Wikipedia page for George Orwell's classic dystopian novel 1984, and a second went to an organization fighting the introduction of mandatory identity cards. 'We were all about ID cards', says Neil. 'The agenda of the album was Chris and my paranoia about surveillance. And that's what the video is about. Of course, this is right before the smartphone – little did we know that we were going to be carrying around our own surveillance machinery with us.' The video subsequently won the Gold Cyber Lion award at the Cannes International Advertising Festival.

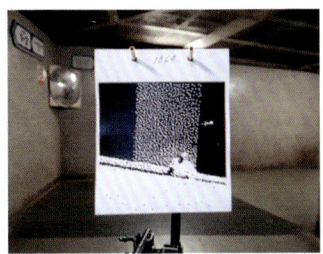
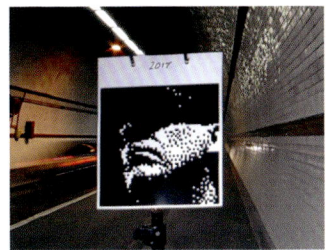
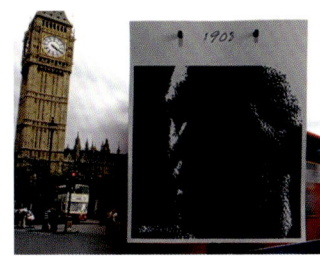
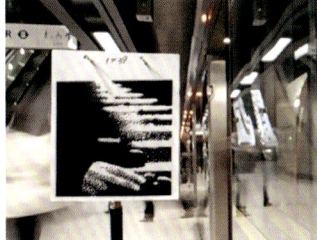
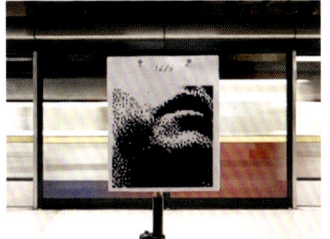

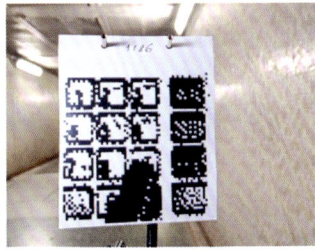
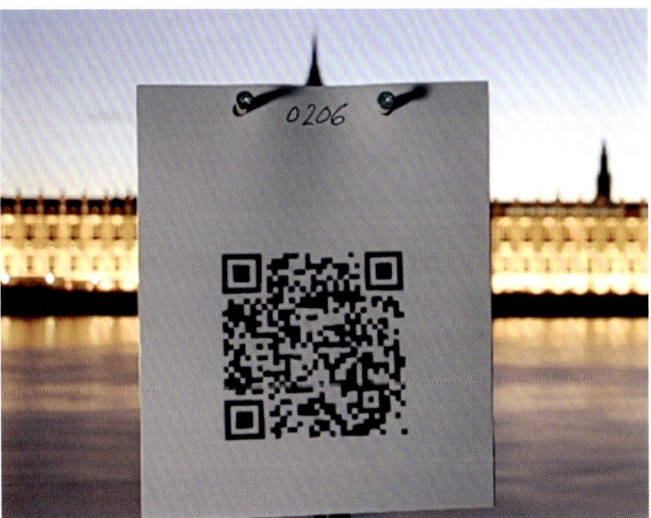
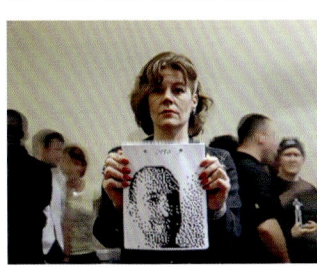

Disco Four

release 8 October 2007
formats 2 × LP / CD / CD promo × 2
photographer John Ross
design and art direction Farrow / PSB

The fourth incarnation of the 'Disco' series differed from the previous three in that this time all the remixes were by the Pet Shop Boys themselves, mostly of songs by other artists: The Killers, David Bowie, Yoko Ono, Madonna, and Atomizer. 'It's a really great album', says Neil. 'The fans all slagged it off because it didn't have any new songs by us on it. But who else has remixed all these people? No one seemed to see that at the time.' 'We're not even DJs', Chris points out.

Disco Four's sleeve was a further iteration of the Fundamental neon concept – in this instance, as Neil and Chris noted, directly in the idiom of Dan Flavin. 'It looks very elegant', Neil says. 'Totally Farrow's idea. It's really simple. One of our best sleeves, in my opinion. Farrow at their best.' 'It's lovely', concurs Chris. 'Beautiful, minimal, clean, fresh, timeless.' The main image was a photograph of white neon tubes in the shape of a figure '4', based on Mark Farrow's realization that four fluorescent tubes would form the number. 'Then', says Gary Stillwell, 'for each of the inner sleeves, we turned a light off.' 'So', explains Farrow, 'you had side one, two, three, and four.' All the text on the sleeve was monochromatic aside from a single word. '"Disco" was in colours', says Farrow, 'because it's disco.' A CD version in a cardboard sleeve showed the four component lights disassembled, a happenstance arrangement noticed at the shoot.

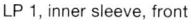

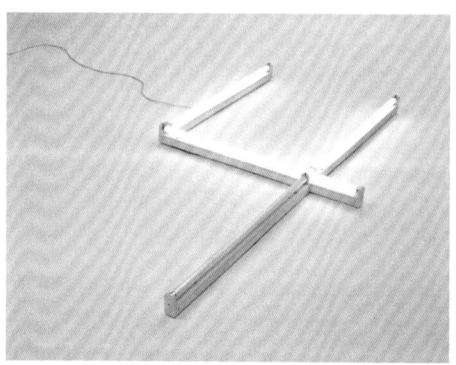 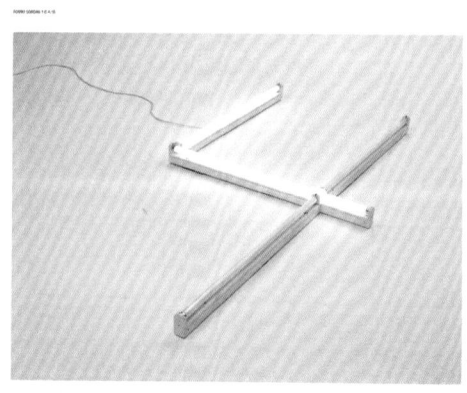

LP 1, inner sleeve, front					LP 1, inner sleeve, back

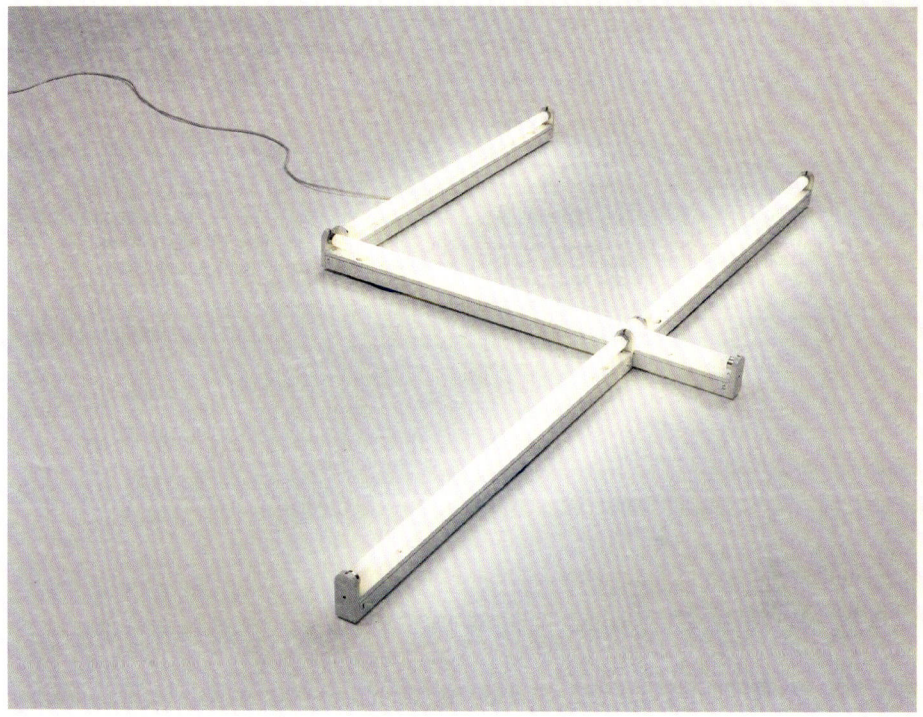

LP, outer sleeve, front

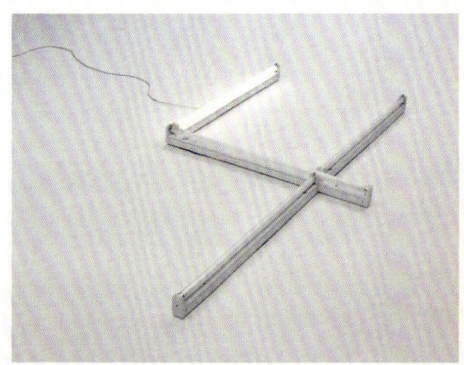

LP 2, inner sleeve, front

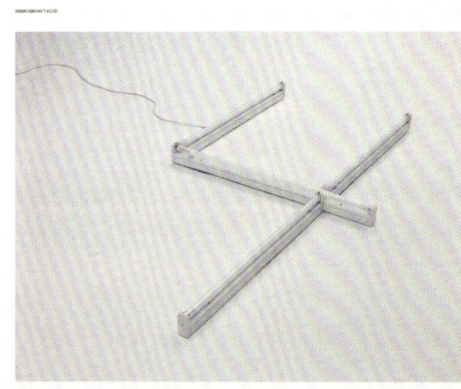

LP 2, inner sleeve, back

Pet Shop Boys Story

release 8 March 2009
formats CD
illustration Gary Stillwell
design and art direction Farrow / PSB

In the brief era when British newspapers semi-regularly commissioned music CDs that they would give away free with each copy of a particular day's issue, the 8 March 2009 edition of the *Mail on Sunday* came with a bespoke Pet Shop Boys compilation, *Pet Shop Boys Story: 25 years of hits* (including, for the first time on CD, 'West End girls (10" version)'). Neil and Chris only agreed to the compilation, which was intended to ramp up excitement ahead of the release of the album *Yes*, on the condition that it would be a true Pet Shop Boys product with its own Farrow-designed artwork. The sleeve, a series of graphic depictions of various Pet Shop Boys looks over the years, had originally been designed by Farrow, using illustrations drawn on computer by Gary Stillwell, for a new B-sides album that had been proposed two or three years previously then cancelled. 'I was just trying to find the twelve most iconic Pet Shop Boys', says Stillwell. 'I seem to remember the roses were quite difficult to get right.' 'I always loved them', says Mark Farrow, of these drawings. When an image was needed for this new collection, these early illustrations came to mind. 'They seemed perfect for this', says Neil.

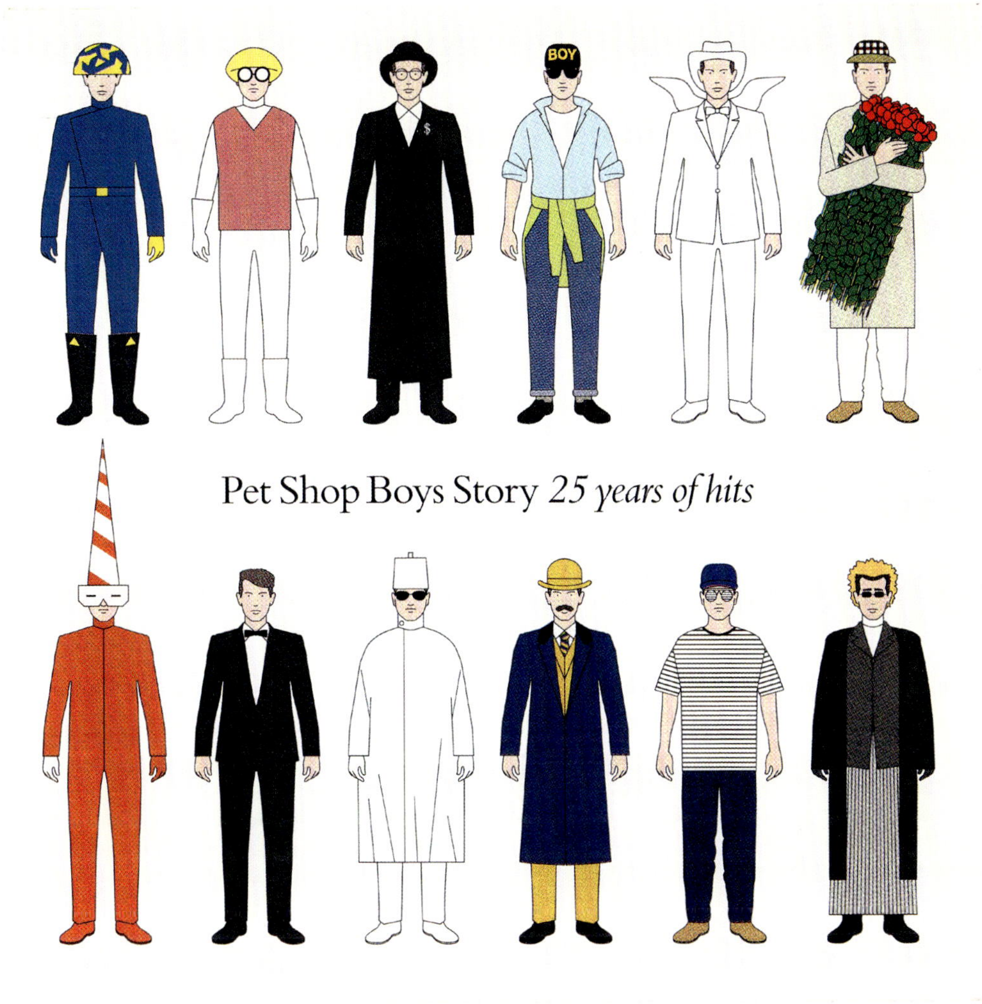

Pet Shop Boys Story *25 years of hits*

CD, front

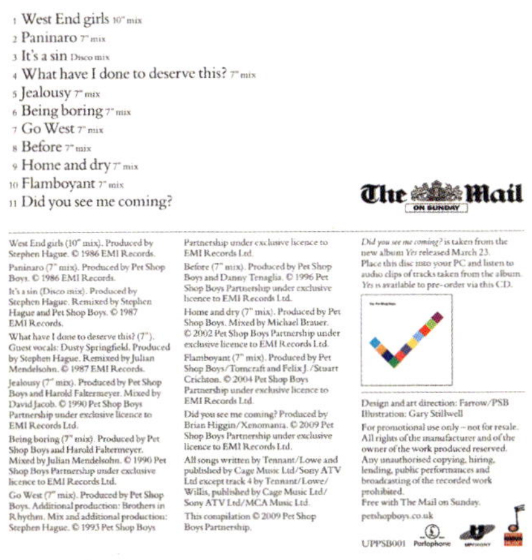

1 West End girls 10" mix
2 Paninaro 7" mix
3 It's a sin Disco mix
4 What have I done to deserve this? 7" mix
5 Jealousy 7" mix
6 Being boring 7" mix
7 Go West 7" mix
8 Before 7" mix
9 Home and dry 7" mix
10 Flamboyant 7" mix
11 Did you see me coming?

West End girls (10" mix). Produced by Stephen Hague. © 1986 EMI Records.
Paninaro (7" mix). Produced by Pet Shop Boys. © 1986 EMI Records.
It's a sin (Disco mix). Produced by Stephen Hague. Remixed by Stephen Hague and Pet Shop Boys. © 1987 EMI Records.
What have I done to deserve this? (7"). Guest vocals: Dusty Springfield. Produced by Stephen Hague. Remixed by Julian Mendelsohn. © 1987 EMI Records.
Jealousy (7" mix). Produced by Pet Shop Boys and Harold Faltermeyer. Mixed by David Jacob. © 1990 Pet Shop Boys Partnership under exclusive licence to EMI Records Ltd.
Being boring (7" mix). Produced by Pet Shop Boys and Harold Faltermeyer. Mixed by Julian Mendelsohn. © 1990 Pet Shop Boys Partnership under exclusive licence to EMI Records Ltd.
Go West (7" mix). Produced by Pet Shop Boys. Additional production: Brothers in Rhythm. Mix and additional production: Stephen Hague. © 1993 Pet Shop Boys

Partnership under exclusive licence to EMI Records Ltd.
Before (7" mix). Produced by Pet Shop Boys and Danny Tenaglia. © 1996 Pet Shop Boys Partnership under exclusive licence to EMI Records Ltd.
Home and dry (7" mix). Produced by Pet Shop Boys. Mixed by Michael Brauer. © 2002 Pet Shop Boys Partnership under exclusive licence to EMI Records Ltd.
Flamboyant (7" mix). Produced by Pet Shop Boys/Tomcraft and Felix J./Stuart Crichton. © 2004 Pet Shop Boys Partnership under exclusive licence to EMI Records Ltd.
Did you see me coming? Produced by Brian Higgin/Xenomania. © 2009 Pet Shop Boys Partnership under exclusive licence to EMI Records Ltd.
All songs written by Tennant/Lowe and published by Cage Music Ltd/Sony ATV Ltd except track 4 by Tennant/Lowe/Willis, published by Cage Music Ltd/Sony ATV Ltd/MCA Music Ltd.
This compilation © 2009 Pet Shop Boys Partnership.

Did you see me coming? is taken from the new album *Yes* released March 23. Place this disc into your PC and listen to audio clips of tracks taken from the album. *Yes* is available to pre-order via this CD.

Design and art direction: Farrow/PSB
Illustration: Gary Stillwell

For promotional use only – not for resale. All rights of the manufacturer and of the owner of the work produced reserved. Any unauthorised copying, hiring, lending, public performances and broadcasting of the recorded work prohibited.

Free with The Mail on Sunday.
petshopboys.co.uk

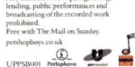
UPPSB001 Parlophone

CD, back

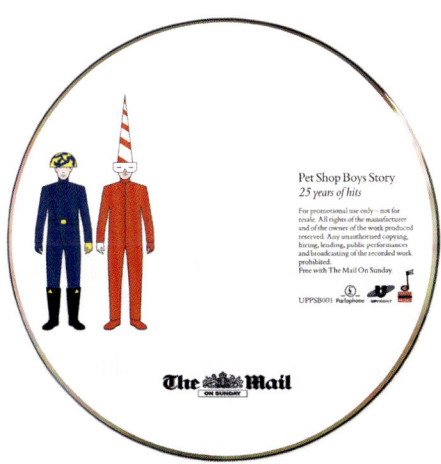

CD, disc

Love etc.

release 17 March 2009
formats 12" promo × 2 / CD / CD remix × 2 /
CD promo × 6 / DVD / download × 2
design and art direction Farrow / PSB
video Han Hoogerbrugge

The first single from the Pet Shop Boys' collaboration with Xenomania, the album *Yes*, was characterized by Neil as 'a post-lifestyle anthem'. Its various sleeves further developed the imagery of the forthcoming but previously completed *Yes* sleeve with its Gerhard Richter-inspired squares (page 359). 'The squares become crosses that are then read as kisses because it's love', says Neil. 'It was another Farrow idea', notes Chris. As well as the white-background, three-kiss first CD single and the black-background second CD equivalent of remixes, there was a promo single using a more complex multicoloured tessellation of squares.

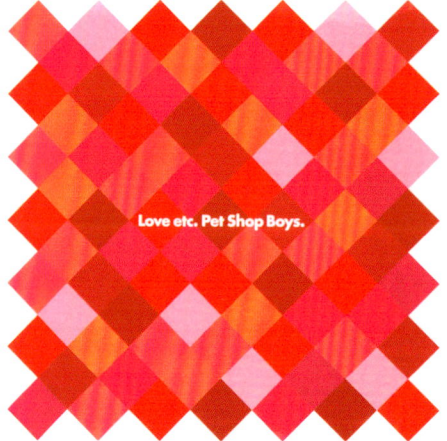

CD promo 1, front

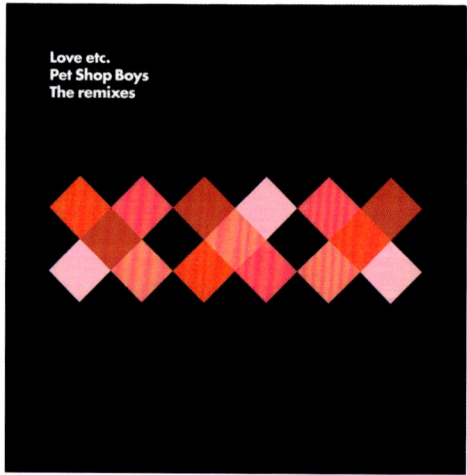

CD remix 1, front

**Love etc.
Pet Shop Boys**

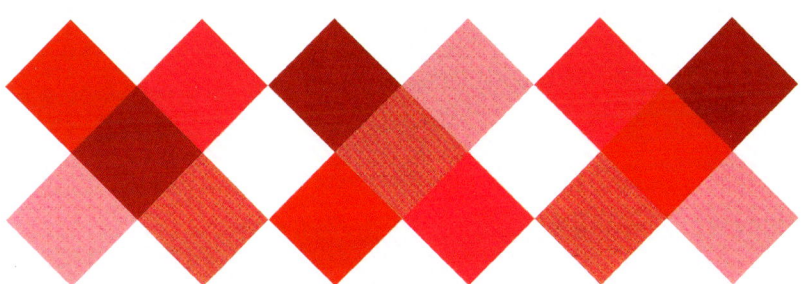

CD, front

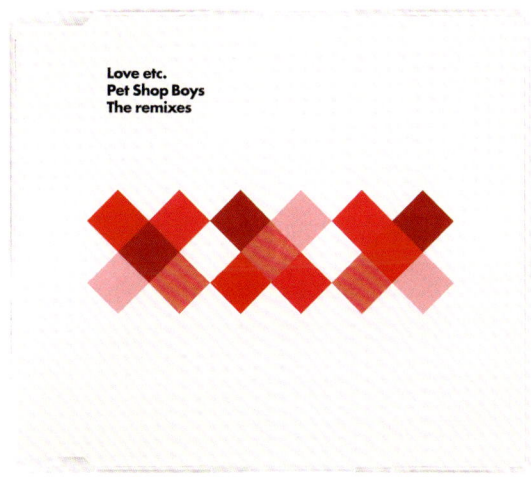

CD remix 2, front

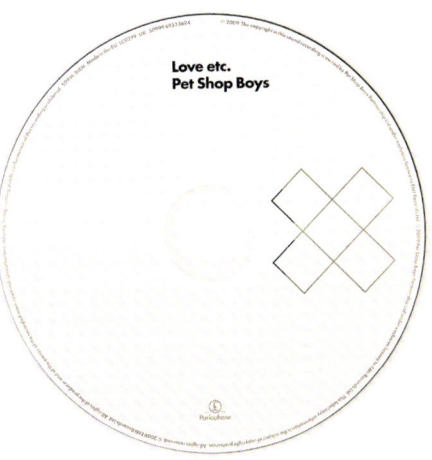

CD remix 2, disc

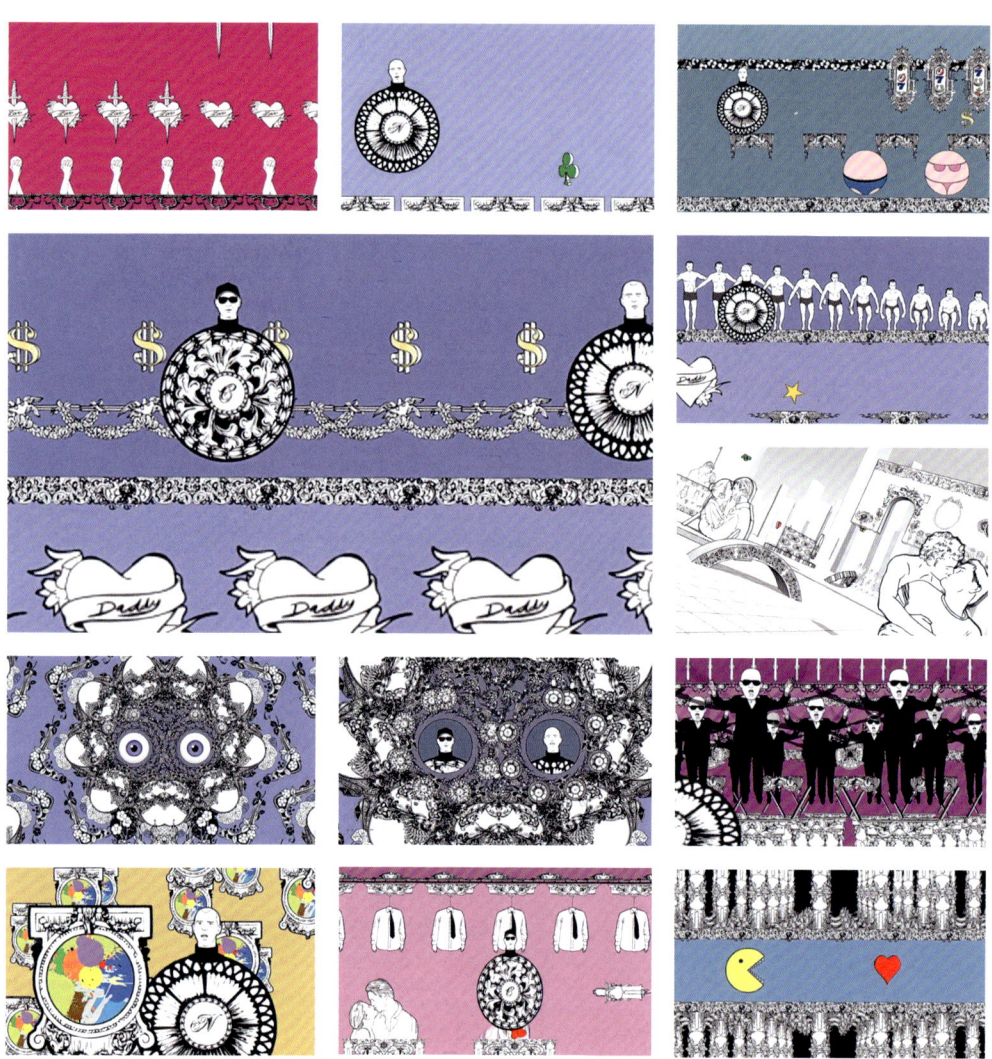

The animated video for 'Love etc.' was made by the Dutch artist Han Hoogerbrugge, who had been recommended to Neil and Chris by Es Devlin. 'It's inspired by computer games, going to different levels', says Chris. 'I think we suggested that we were spacehoppers', says Neil. 'That was because the track, of course, has an undeniable bounce to it.' ('Apart from a bouncing female breast', noted Hoogerbrugge at the time, 'they agreed to everything.') For the Pet Shop Boys' animated avatars, they were filmed from the neck up for about fifteen minutes in January 2009, Neil lip-syncing, and both of them mimicking their reaction to being stretched to help inform their animated facial expressions.

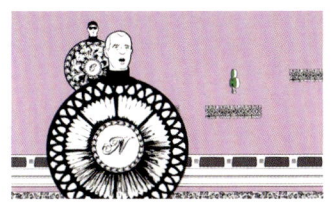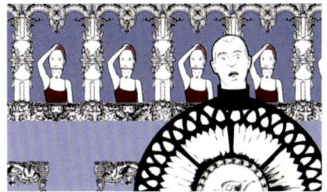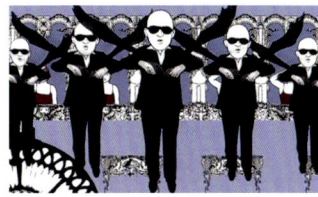
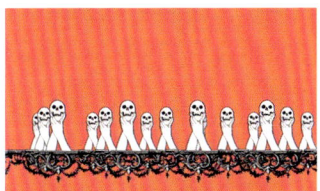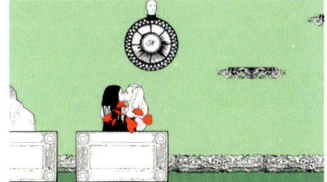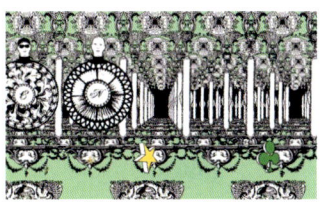
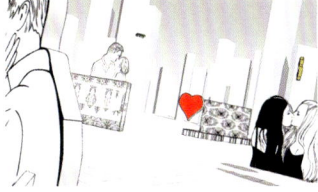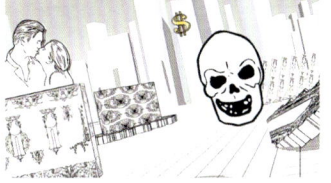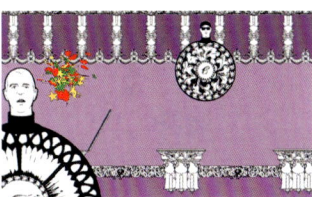
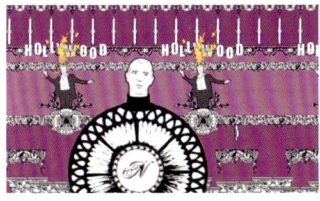
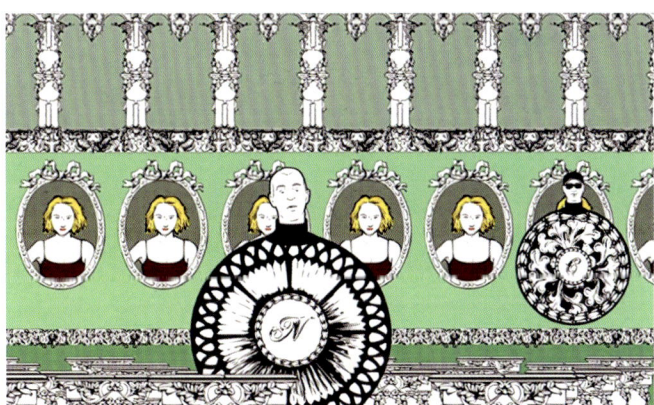
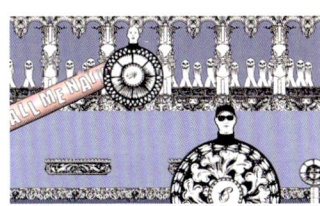

Yes

release 23 March 2009
formats LP / eleven-disc limited-edition LP / CD / double CD special edition / download
photographer Alasdair McLellan
design and art direction Farrow / PSB

'This was a pop album', says Chris, 'so we wanted it to be bright and colourful. Because the last album was all dark and shadowy.' 'I think they came in with a quote, saying that *Fundamental* was neon, and *Yes* is plastic', says Gary Stillwell. 'They liked the idea of it being quite poppy and fun and plastic-y.' For the specific imagery, Gerhard Richter was a key reference point. Neil and Chris had seen his window in Cologne cathedral made of 11,000 coloured squares, and the Serpentine Gallery in London had recently exhibited a complementary work of Richter's, *4900 Colours*. Early versions of the *Yes* sleeve actually involved grids of coloured squares. 'To me, it felt if we do that, it's just going to feel a bit like a variation on *Introspective*', says Mark Farrow. 'That we needed to go further with it.' Next, says Stillwell, they explored ideas using squares 'within a white space, so rather than a big block, they were kind of mixtures of colours'. Then they explored lines of coloured squares on a diagonal, where each differently coloured block represented one of the twelve songs on the album. That's when Farrow had what Neil refers to as 'the brilliant idea'. 'Mark said', remembers Stillwell, '"What if – because it's called *Yes* – that became a tick?"' The twelve coloured blocks were now configured as a tick. 'It was the tick really that suddenly made it', says Chris. 'A symbol that represents the title.' 'It says affirmative', says Neil. 'It says Yes.'

A final adjustment came when, late in the day, Pet Shop Boys vacillated about whether to remove one of the twelve songs, 'This used to be the future', from the main album. 'They got in touch and said, "We're thinking of dropping this track – how would that affect the cover?"' remembers Stillwell. Farrow reported back that the change would actually improve it. 'They said, "Well, that's it"', says Stillwell. 'It looked better as eleven squares', Chris agrees. Farrow also recalls that this was the first time, given the rise of streaming, that they considered a Pet Shop Boys album cover as primarily an online image, and that he petitioned for dropping the words 'Pet Shop Boys' on the digital versions of the screen. 'That was us trying to say: it doesn't need it to say the group's name, because it would be written next to it – you've looked it up', he says. Such thinking was not yet commonplace and, this time, he was rebuffed.

Yes, Pet Shop Boys.

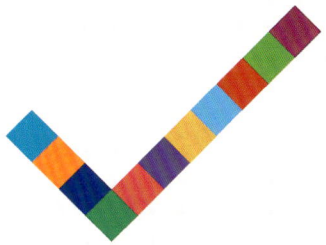

LP, outer sleeve, front

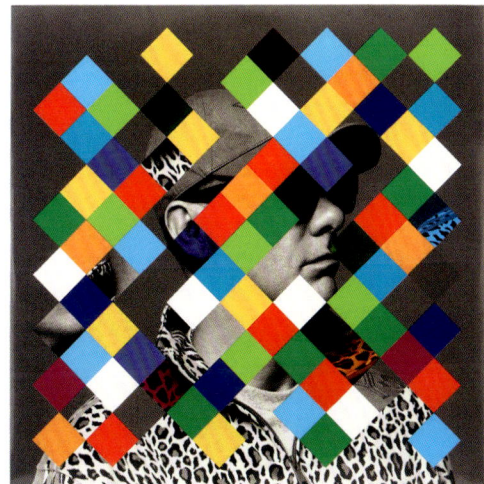

LP, inner sleeve, front

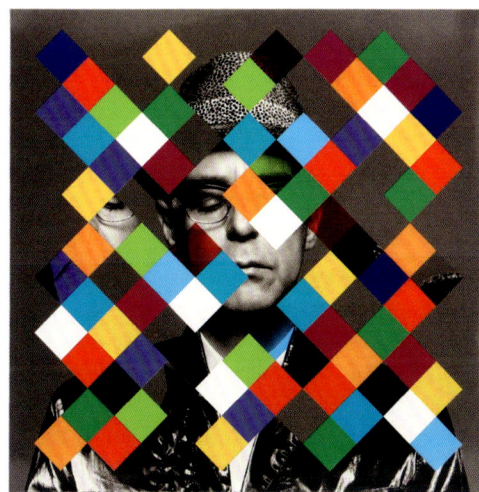

LP, inner sleeve, back

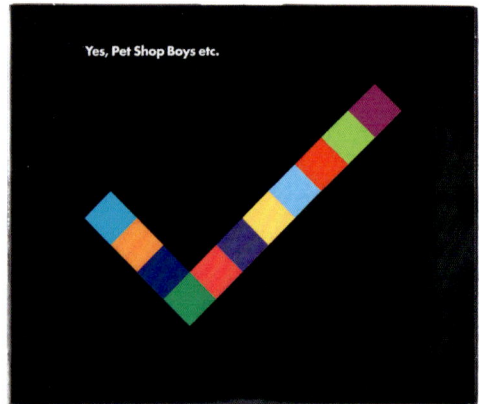
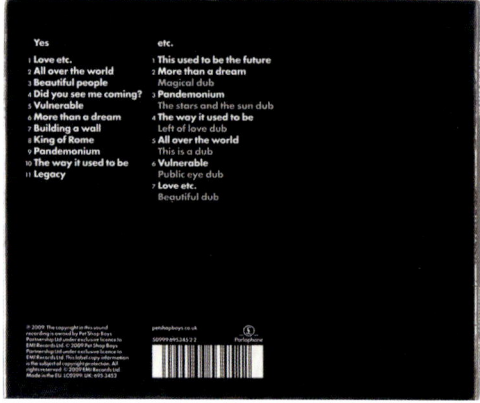
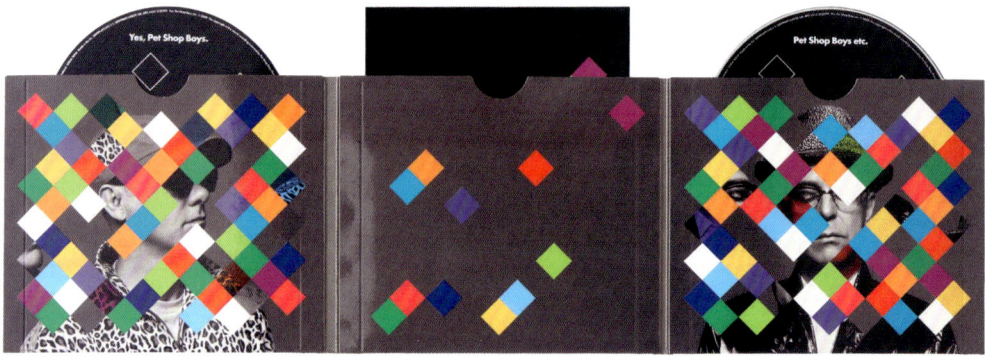

Double CD special edition, front, back, and inside (open)

Two limited editions of *Yes* were released. For the two-CD special edition, entitled *Yes etc.*, Neil and Chris proposed swapping out the white background of *Yes* for black. 'Mark Farrow was so against it', says Neil. 'We had such a battle on the phone when we were on a train to Berlin.' The Pet Shop Boys' only slight disappointment here was that, because *Yes etc.* was fabricated as a folding double-CD cardboard sleeve, this second version is not a perfect square.

There was also a deluxe limited vinyl version produced by The Vinyl Factory in an edition of three hundred copies containing eleven separate twelve-inch singles and a numbered print in a smoked transparent box with a gold *Yes* tick on its front. 'We did everything we wanted to do on this', says Farrow. 'It was a very dark, tinted Perspex box that was like a Seventies hi-fi lid on your record deck. The gold logo on the front was where it would have said Teac or Toshiba or whatever. People think the box is black, but it's not – it's actually transparent, although it is very dark. Each one of the album's tracks gets its own coloured sleeve, which you can lay out as a big tick on the floor, if you want.'

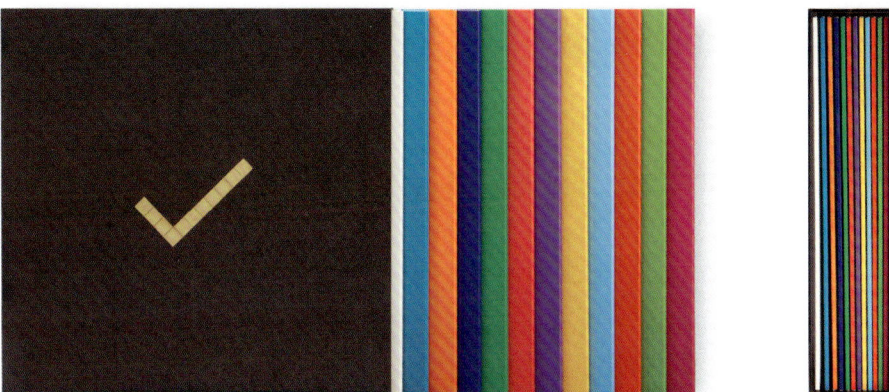
Eleven-disc limited-edition LP, box and outer sleeves

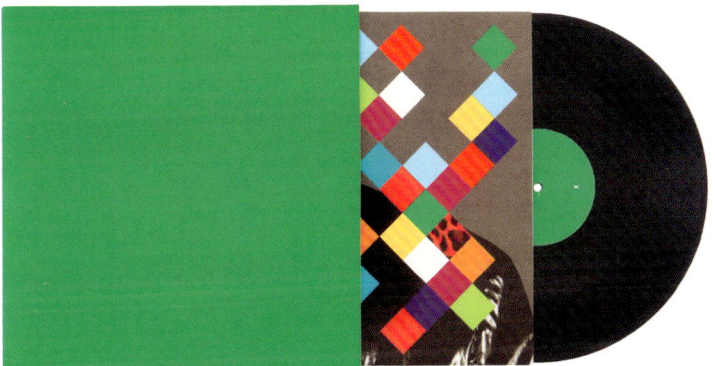
Eleven-disc limited-edition LP, Disc 4, outer sleeve, inner sleeve, and disc

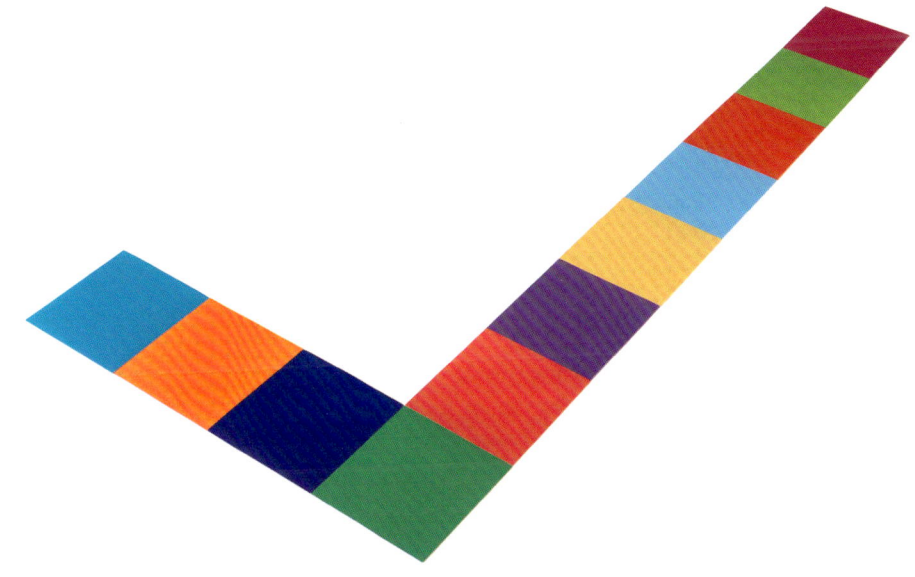
Eleven-disc limited-edition LP, outer sleeves arranged as a tick on the floor

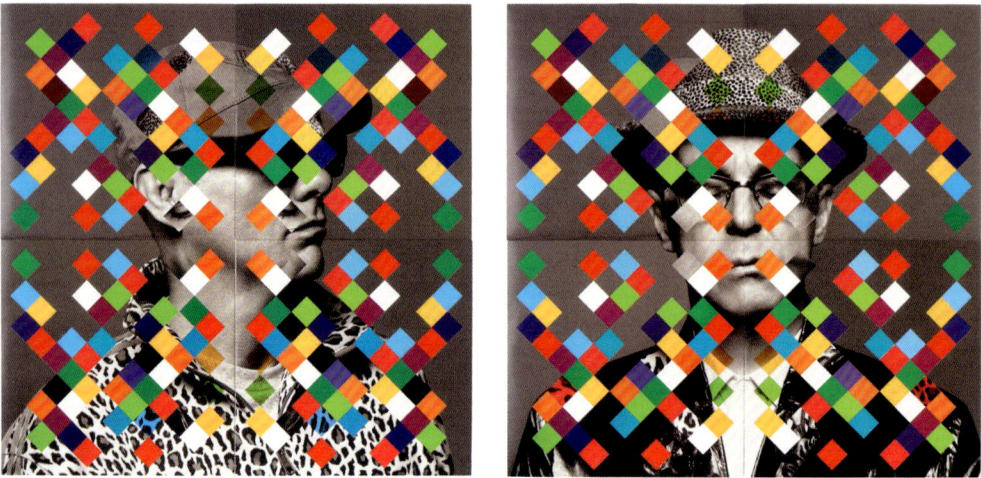

Eleven-disc limited-edition LP, inner sleeves, front: Discs 8–11 (left) and 1–4 (right)

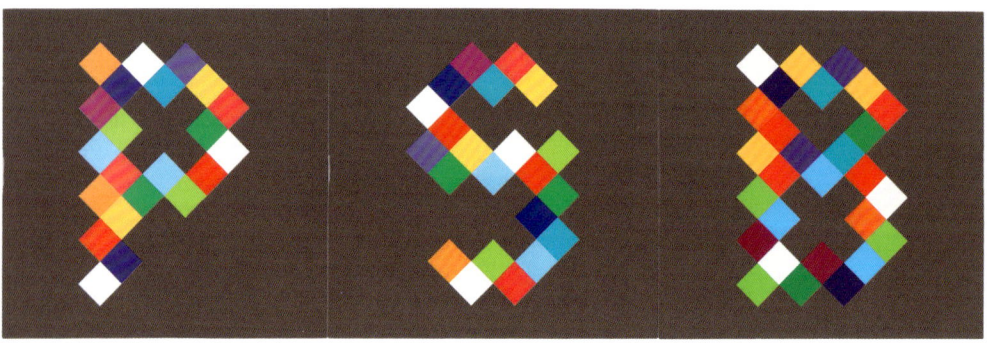

Eleven-disc limited-edition LP, inner sleeves, front: Discs 5–7

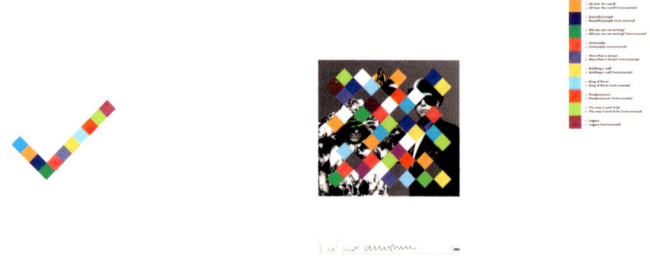

Eleven-disc limited-edition LP, outer sleeve (left) housing signed print (centre) and colour-key track listing (right)

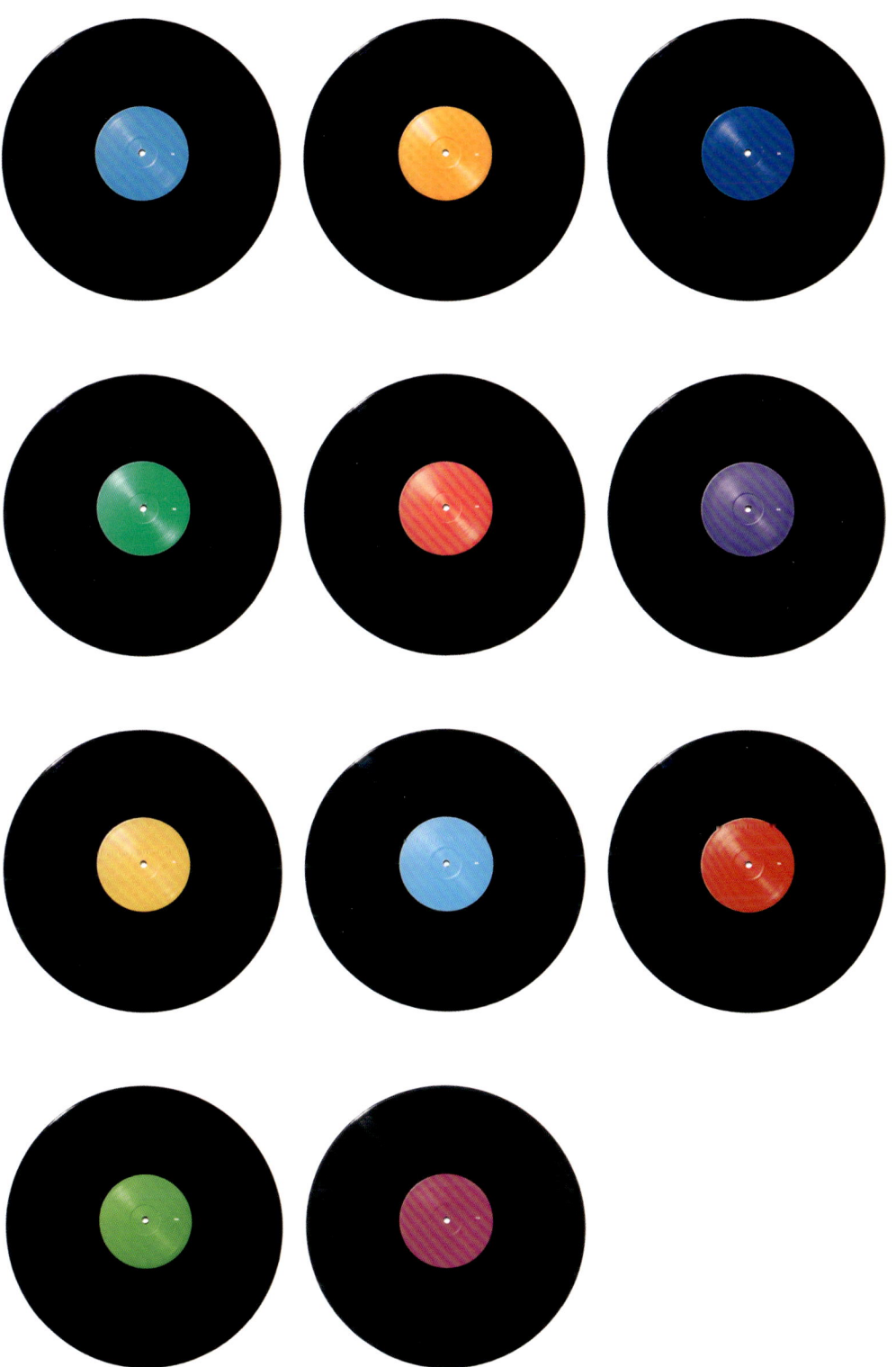

Eleven-disc limited-edition LP, discs

Did you see me coming?

release 1 June 2009
formats 12" remix / CD × 3 / CD-R promo × 5 / download
photographer Alasdair McLellan
design and art direction Farrow / PSB
video Douglas Hart

The various versions of the 'Did you see me coming?' sleeve use portraits from a photo session that Neil and Chris had done with Alasdair McLellan some months earlier, in January 2009. 'I remember being very impressed by the Gareth Pugh stuff hanging on the rack', says Chris of the clothes they were to wear for the shoot. 'It looks so sculptural. The coat I wore literally could stand up on its own. It didn't need the hanger.' That February they had worn the same Gareth Pugh coats for their medley at the Brit Awards, which would be released on one of the digital versions of this single.

In each variation of the 'Did you see me coming?' sleeve, whether solo or together, their faces are almost entirely obscured by Richter-esque coloured squares. 'It's very insulting', says Chris with mock outrage. 'I don't know what they were trying to say, but it's very hurtful.' 'There's often a bit of Chris not wanting to be identified', suggests Mark Farrow, 'He probably asked us, "Can't you put one of those blocks over my head?"' The sleeve of the promo CD removed Neil and Chris altogether, leaving just the two diamonds to stand in for them.

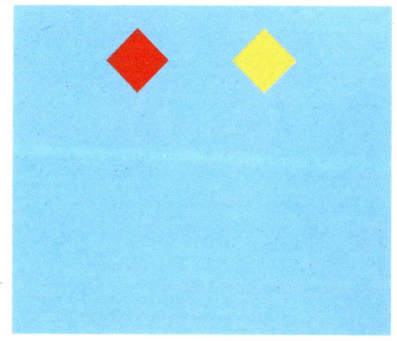

CD promo, front

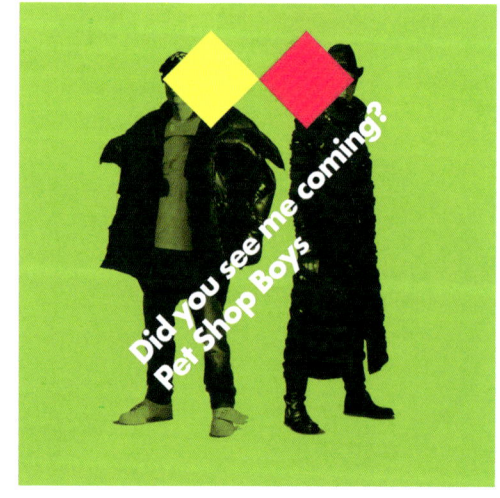

Download

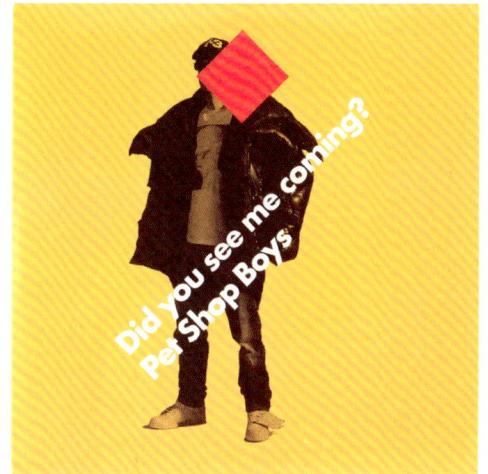
CD 1, front

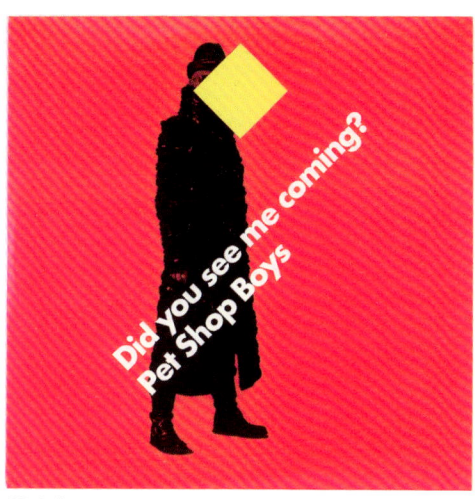
CD 2, front

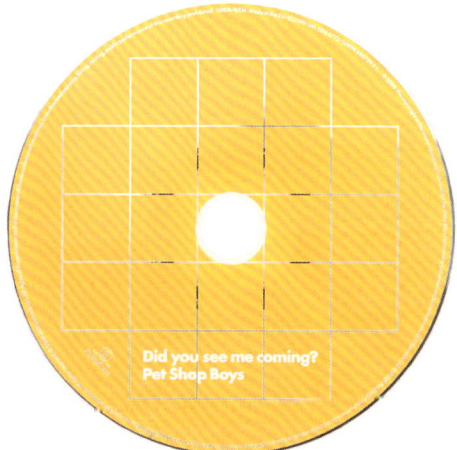
CD 1, disc

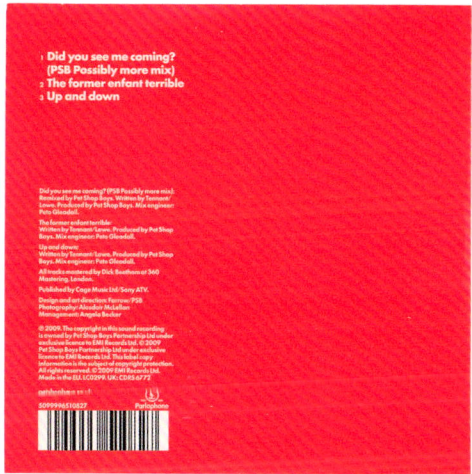
CD 2, back

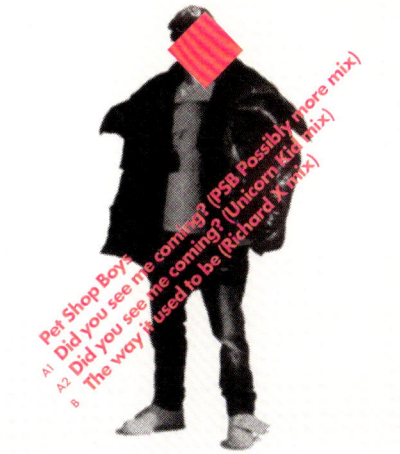
12" remix, front

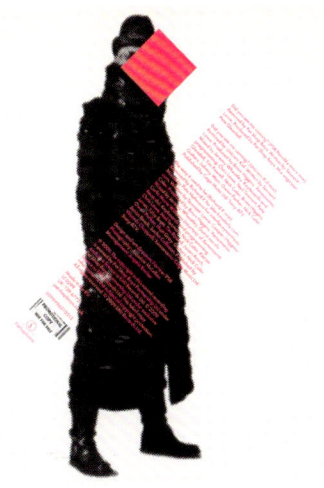
12" remix, back

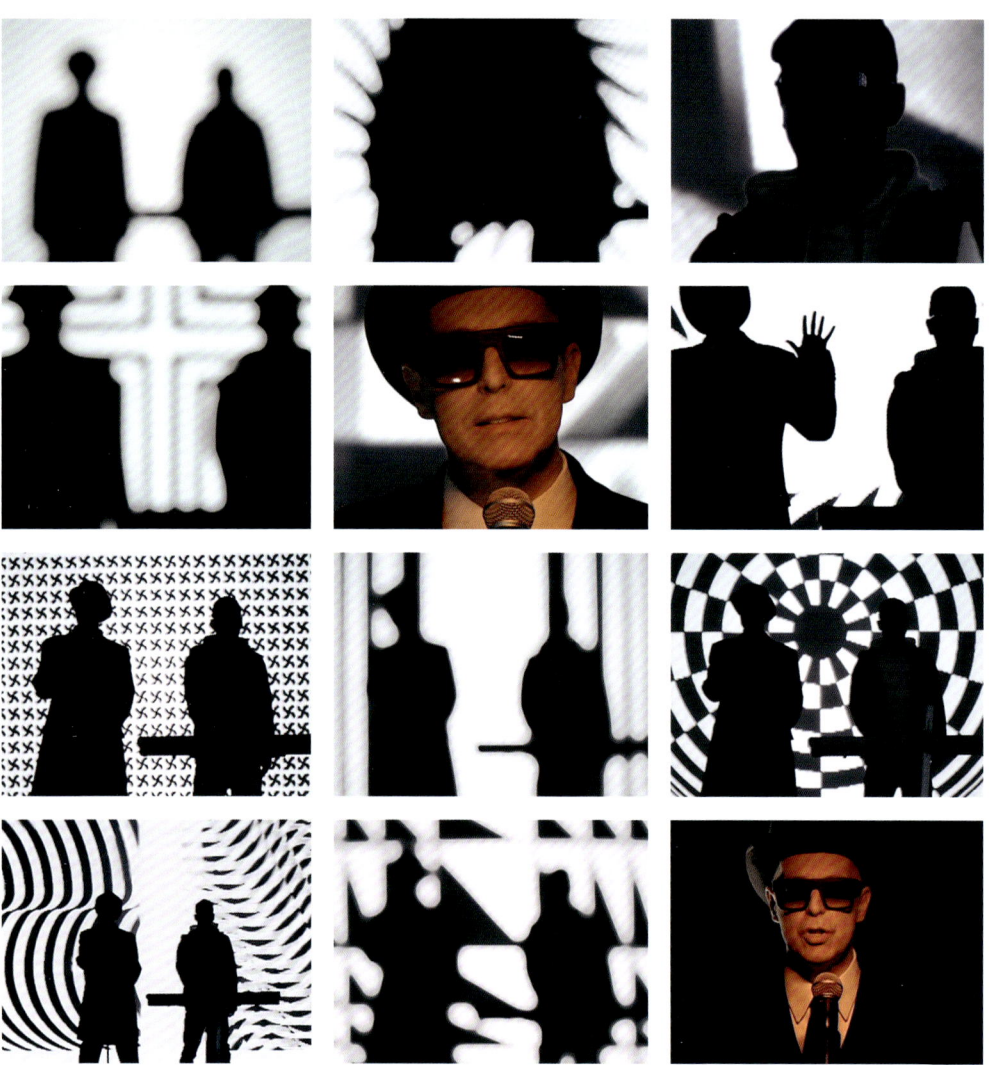

Pet Shop Boys shot a very simple performance video with the director Douglas Hart. 'When we got there, we both thought, isn't this the "Minimal" video all over again, without the dancers?' says Neil. 'We just perform the song in front of a screen', says Chris.

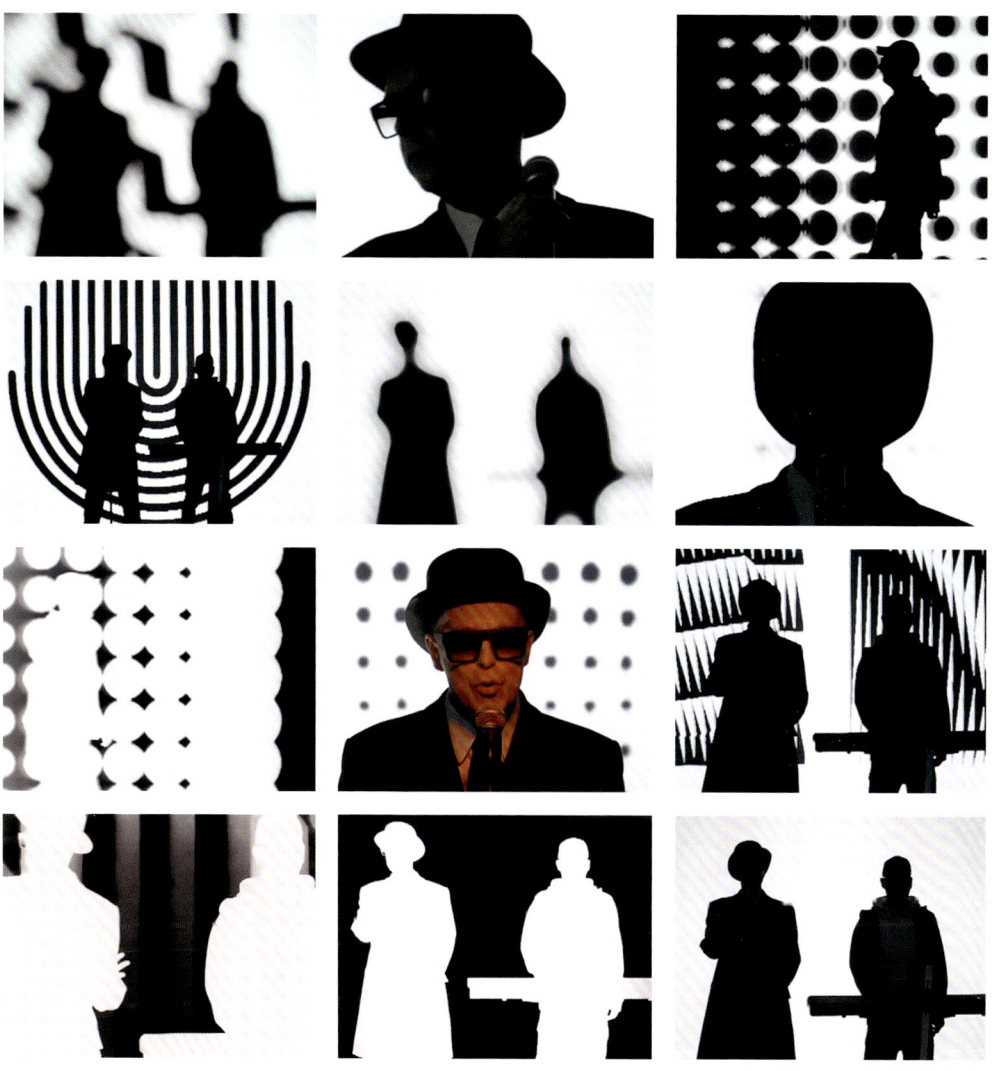

Pandemonium tour

dates 10 June 2009 – July 2011
set design and creative direction Es Devlin
lighting Rob Sinclair
choreography Lynne Page
costumes Jeffrey Bryant / Es Devlin / Carisa Glucksman / PSB

As with the previous tour, *Pandemonium* was designed by Es Devlin. 'Lots of cubes', says Chris. 'Es was famous for cubes', notes Neil. 'She had already done a cube for us on the previous tour.' 'But also', Chris points out, 'the cover for *Yes* is made of squares.' 'She told me, "It's all informed by your sleeves"', says Mark Farrow. 'Which is great because that has gone the other way sometimes – there is stuff that has come from her live things that we have used.' Devlin herself explained: 'We found it refreshing to create the sense of a high-tech video screen and let it crumble into its cheap, low-tech constituents of cardboard boxes.' She noted that, in some ways, this was the sequel to the previous tour: '*Fundamental* started with a single cube that unfolded in an origami sequence of permutations. *Pandemonium* begins with two walls of cubes, each the same 4×4 metre proportion as the *Fundamental* cube, but from there, it develops into a multitude of cubes, including cube-wearing characters. *Fundamental* played with the idea of Pet Shop Boys as two halves of a single band brain with a pair of dancers functioning as alter egos to Neil and Chris. In *Pandemonium*, the role of the dancers has developed into a more complex narrative around the theme of the individual and the system.' 'It's called *Pandemonium*', says Neil, 'and there are elements of chaos in it where the whole thing literally falls down.' The set list was chosen, and structured, in collaboration with Stuart Price. It had four parts: the first was nameless ('something like a performance in an art gallery', says Devlin); the second was 'New York'; the third, 'Ballet'; and the fourth, 'Celebration'.

The tour programme featured photographs by Pelle Crépin. 'We decided to shoot the rehearsals in black and white,' says Farrow, 'and to print the book black and white, entirely.' On the cover is a 'P' in the diamond-based font they had developed for *Yes*. 'There's an entire alphabet. We did it in the colours and just black as well. It's probably the most thorough campaign we ever did for Pet Shop Boys – it developed and developed and developed and turned into a whole campaign, and then an entire range of merchandise.' That July, Gary Stillwell gave a lecture to D&AD students on what they had done. 'Because it was so rigorous', says Farrow. 'It was like a corporate identity.'

On 15 February 2010, a DVD and CD of the tour, entitled *Pandemonium*, was released. The show had been filmed on 21 December 2009 at London's O2 Arena by David Barnard. Between 27 May and 29 July 2011, Pet Shop Boys performed an adapted and edited version of the show while appearing as special guests on Take That's reunion tour with Robbie Williams.

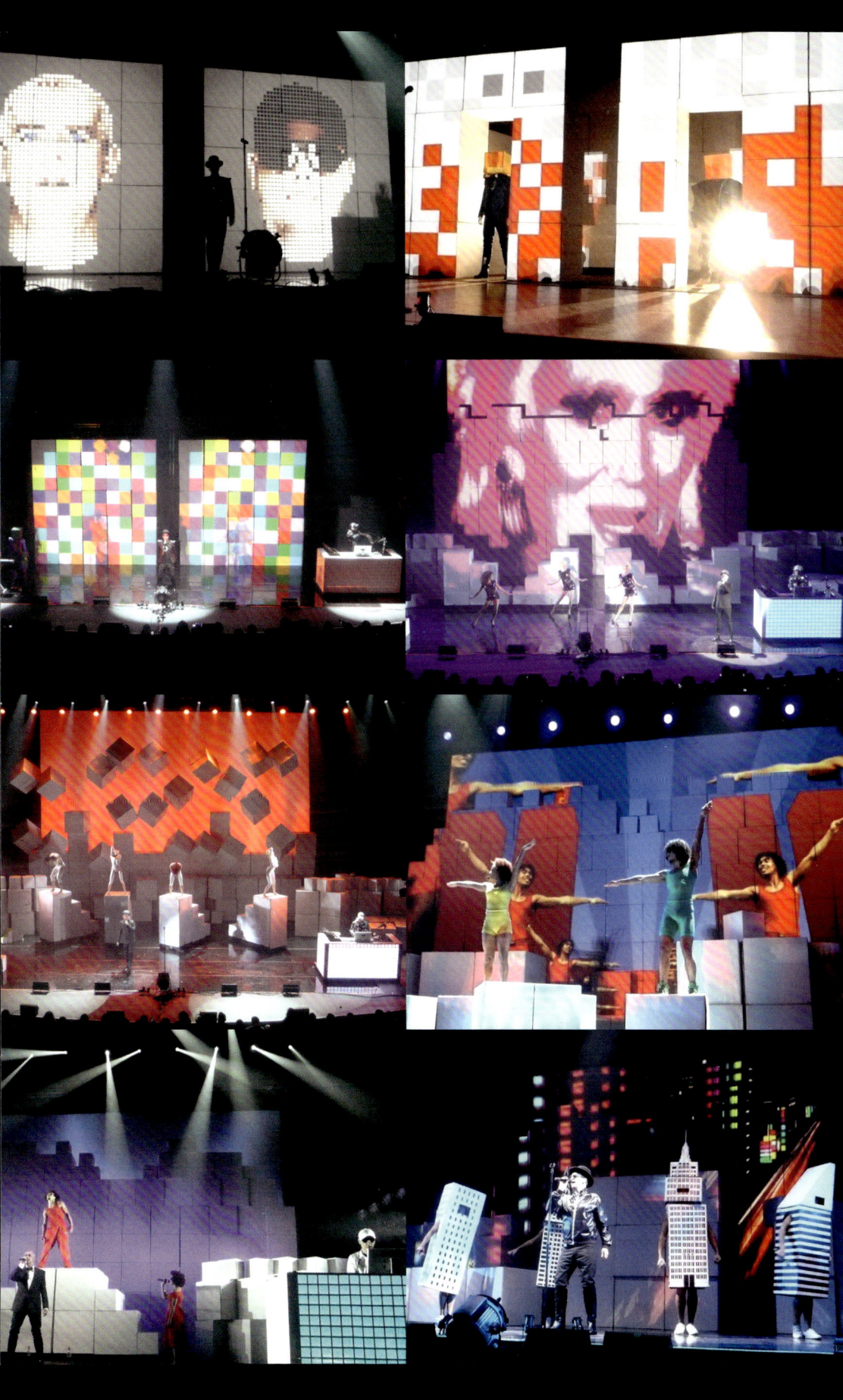

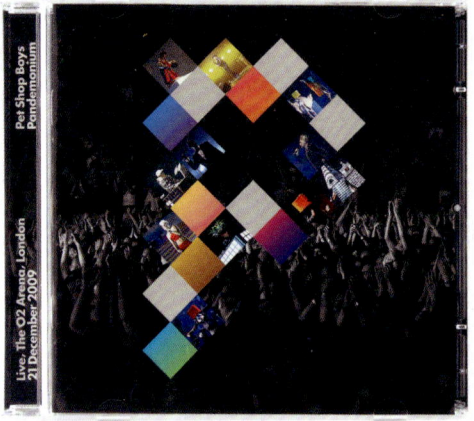

CD/DVD, front

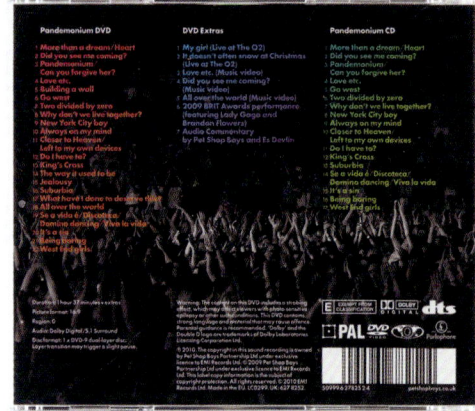

CD/DVD, back

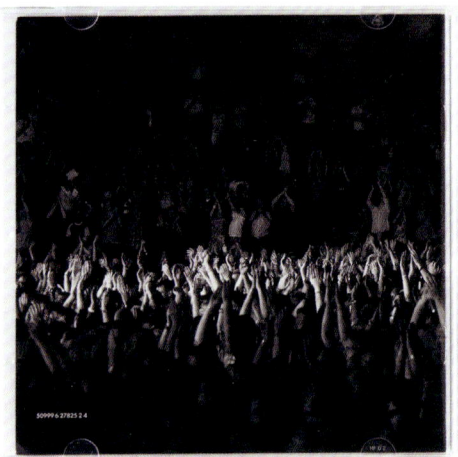
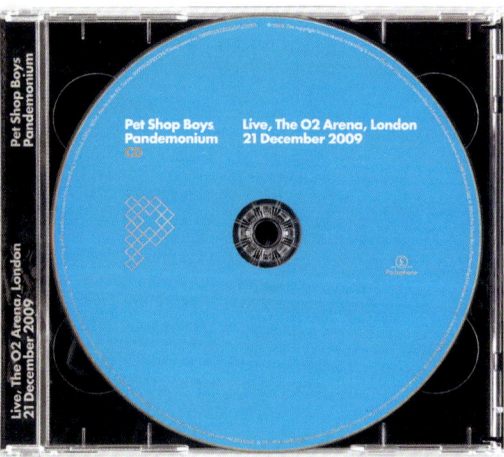

CD/DVD, inside

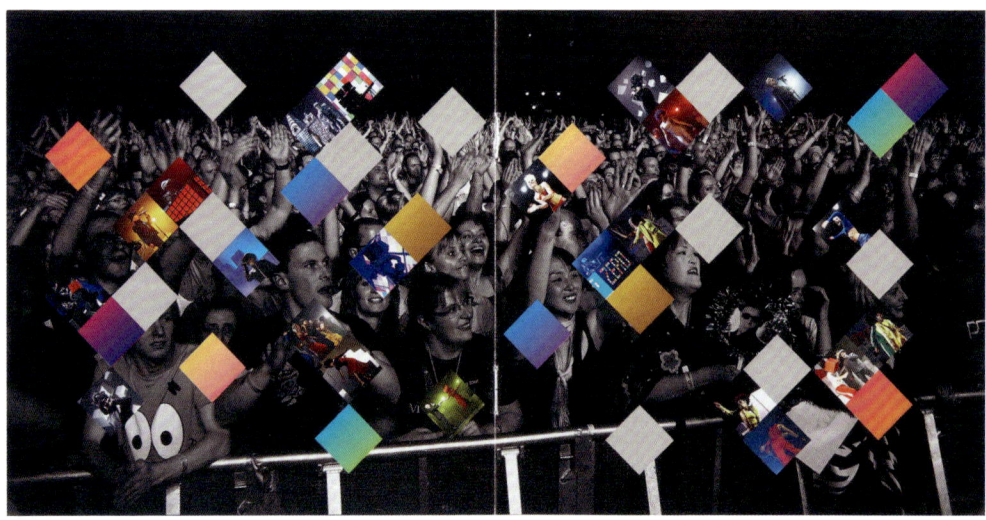

CD/DVD, booklet, inside pages

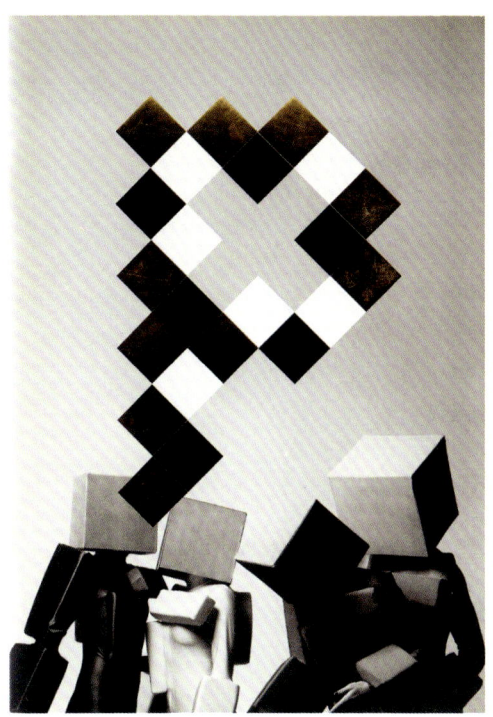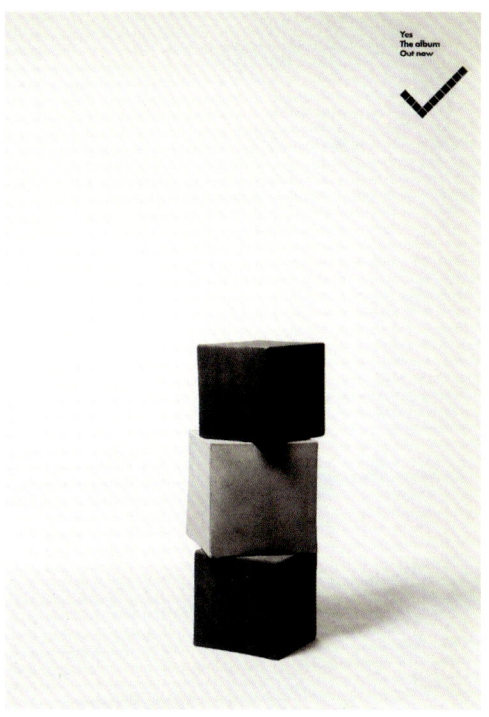

Tour programme, front

Tour programme, back

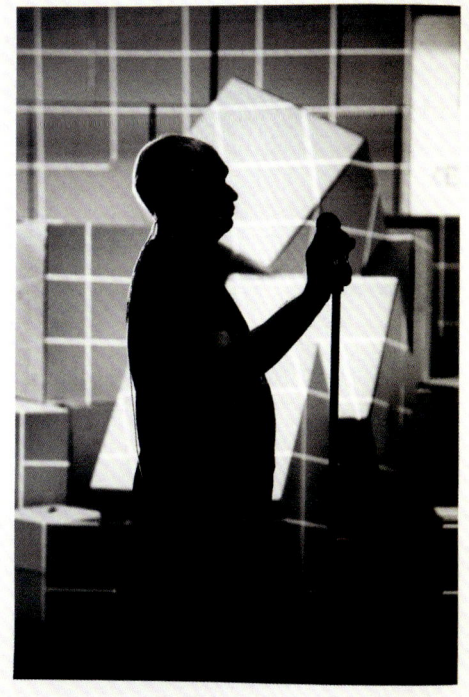

Tour programme, inside pages

Pandemonium tour 2009–2011

Beautiful people

release 2 October 2009
formats 12" promo / CD / CD promo /
CD-R promo / download
design and art direction Farrow / PSB

The *Yes* track 'Beautiful people', originally written as a prospective theme song for a television series by Jonathan Harvey, was released as a German-only single, at the request of the German record company. Its sleeve used the *Yes* squares in a further way, using the diamond typeface that Farrow had developed for the album. 'It was three-dimensional', says Mark Farrow. The sleeve was based on an advertisement that Farrow had created earlier that year for the programme for the White Tie and Tiara Ball, the fundraising event for the Elton John AIDS foundation, which had the message 'LOVE, NEIL AND CHRIS'. There it was a purely white version of the same shadowed typeface, whereas on the 'Beautiful people' sleeve there are occasional sparkles of colour. 'The idea was that the diamonds could become diamantes', says Farrow. 'There is a logic to it.'

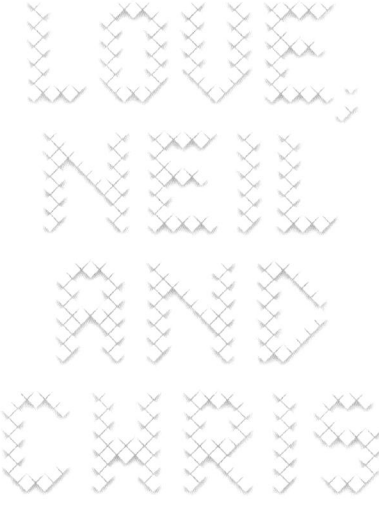

Pet Shop Boys' message in the White Tie and Tiara Ball programme, 2009

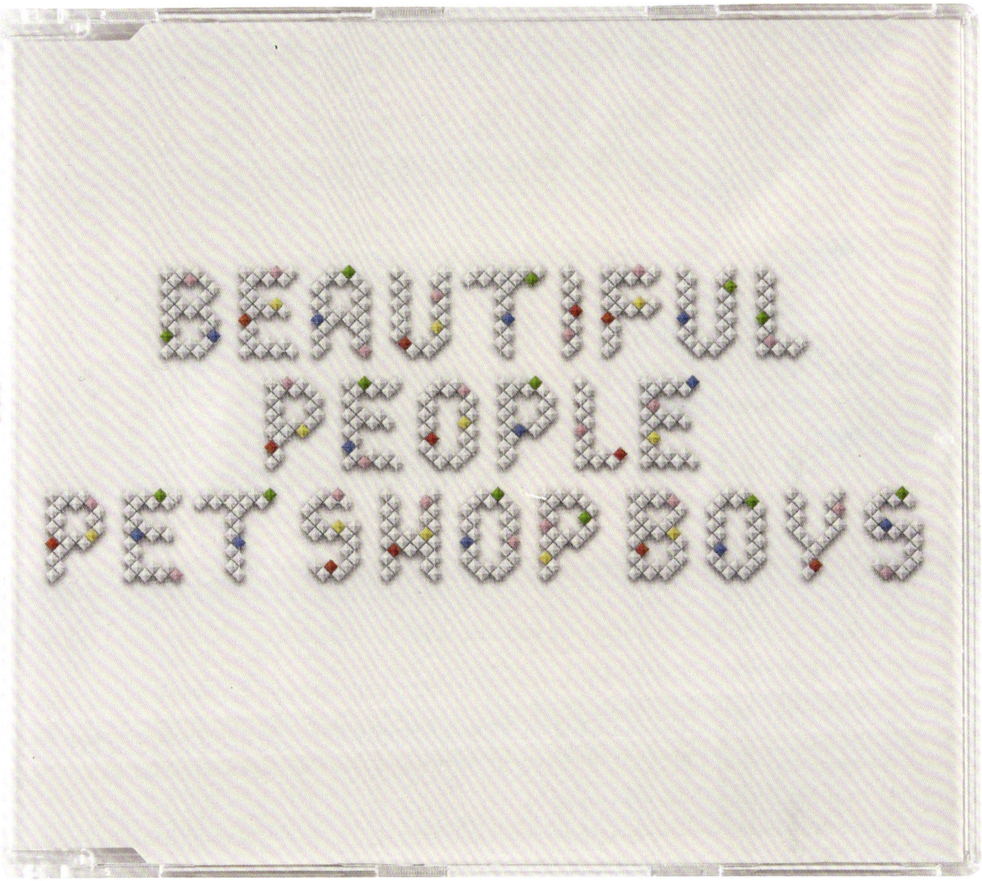

CD, front

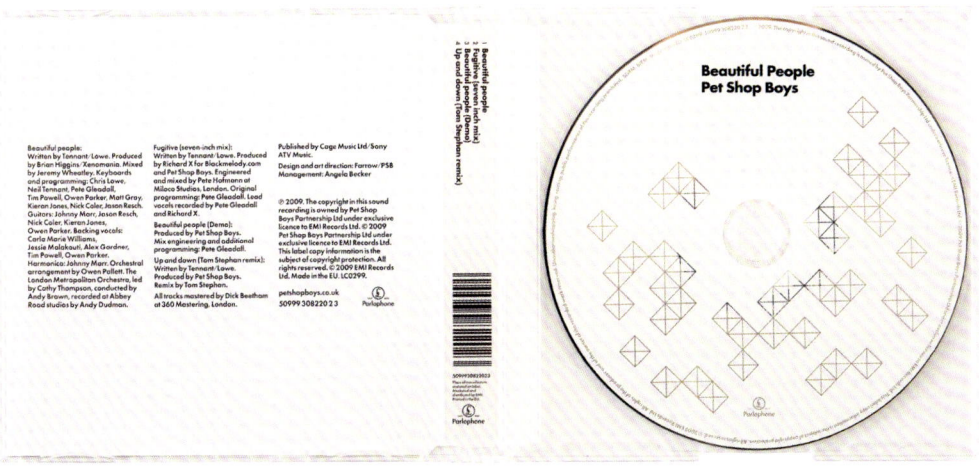

CD, inside

Pet Shop Boys Party / Christmas

release 13 **November** 2009 / 14 December 2009
formats *Party* CD / *Christmas* CD / CD promo × 2
photographer **John Ross** (balloons) and Pelle Crépin (portrait photos)
design and art direction Farrow / PSB

A new compilation, *Pet Shop Boys Party*, was released only in Brazil after it had been explained to Neil and Chris that several of their songs – including, most recently, 'King of Rome' – were famous in Brazil after their use in Brazilian soap operas. The idea for the sleeve, of party balloons festooned with Neil and Chris's heads, was Farrow's. 'It was just literally, "What about if we got balloons printed with their faces and then took photographs of them?"' says Farrow. 'There were about a hundred and fifty of them. We were literally kicking them in the air, and John Ross was just shooting away. We had a great photograph of them all popped, after the event – all these popped balloons with their squished faces on. There were hundreds of shots to choose from.'

When they subsequently released a five-track EP, *Christmas*, in the UK, it was one of these other shots that was used. 'I thought it was a good idea', says Neil, of the overall concept, 'but it didn't look exuberant enough. I think there should be more balloons on the sleeve.' 'More balloons', Chris agrees. 'Also', says Neil, '*Christmas* doesn't look very Christmas-y. Whereas the *Party* actually does look like a party.' Neil further suggests another approach they could have taken: 'We should have got Jeff Koons to do this. We could have got him to make some balloons in shiny metal.' 'I love his little metallic dogs', adds Chris. 'We should use those at some point. For a compilation.' 'Well, I think two of anything looks good', reasons Neil. 'I always wanted to do the salt and pepper set that I had – one of them pointy, the salt one, and the other one round, the pepper one. And it could just say "Pet Shop Boys" underneath.'

01 WEST END GIRLS (TEN INCH MIX) 02 LOVE COMES QUICKLY 03 PANINARO (SEVEN INCH MIX) 04 IT'S A SIN (DISCO MIX) 05 WHAT HAVE I DONE TO DESERVE THIS? 06 ALWAYS ON MY MIND (EXTENDED DANCE VERSION) 07 DOMINO DANCING 08 IT'S ALRIGHT (SEVEN INCH VERSION) 09 BEING BORING 10 GO WEST 11 BEFORE (SINGLE EDIT) 12 NEW YORK CITY BOY 13 HOME AND DRY (RADIO EDIT) 14 MINIMAL (RADIO EDIT) 15 LOVE ETC. 16 KING OF ROME

Party, inner sleeve, inside

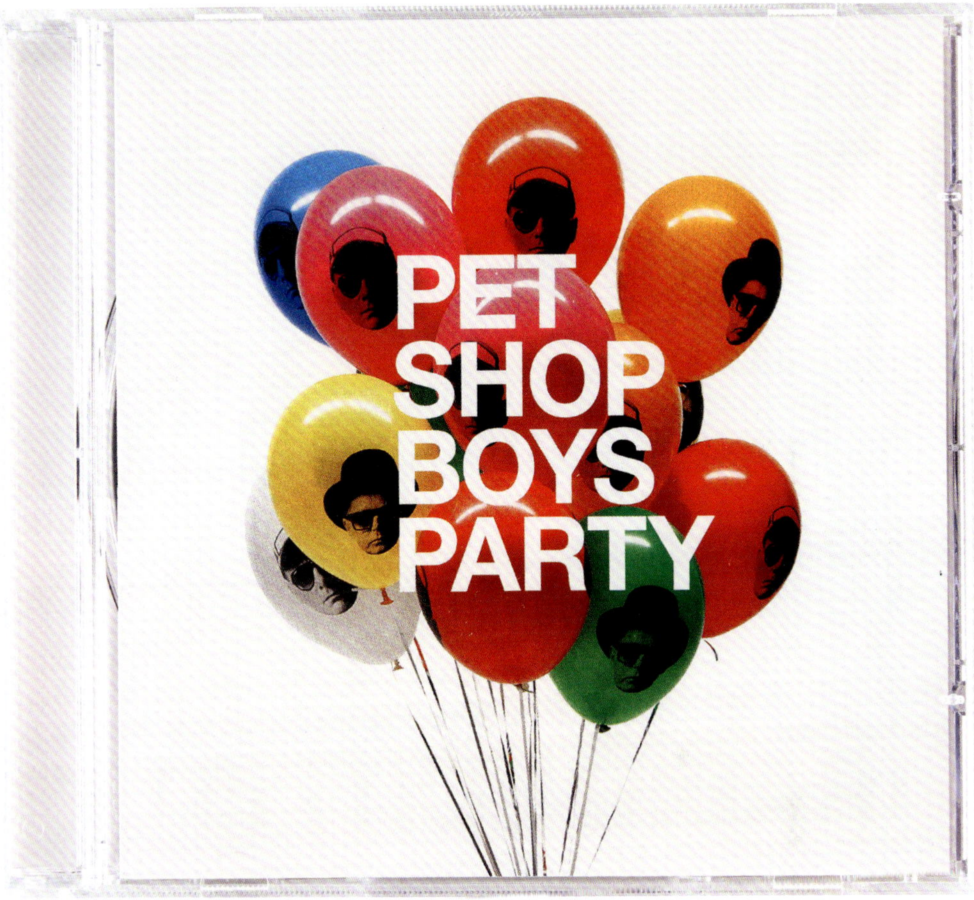

Party, front

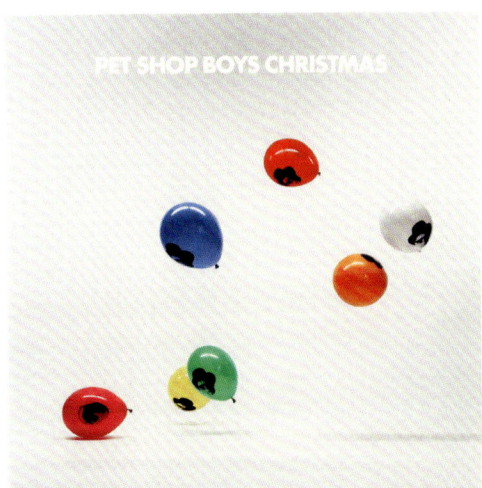

Christmas CD, outer sleeve, front

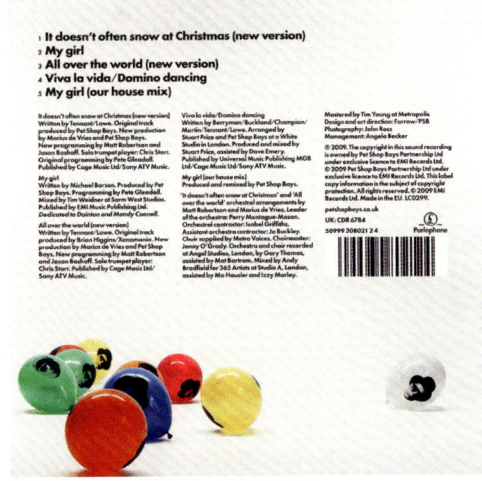

Christmas CD, outer sleeve, back

Love life

release 17 April 2010
formats 7"
design Parlophone

As part of the annual independent record retailers' event Record Store Day, Pet Shop Boys released a one-off limited-edition seven-inch single featuring two unreleased songs: their 2001 demo of 'Love life' (a song that they had given to Swedish group Alcazar) and 'A powerful friend', a song that they had written in 1983 and recorded in around 2002 with *Release* tour guitarists Bic Hayes and Mark Refoy. Atypically, they agreed to use the generic Parlophone sleeves used for all the company's seven-inch single releases on that day. The release was limited to a thousand copies and was exclusive to the independent record shops taking part in the event.

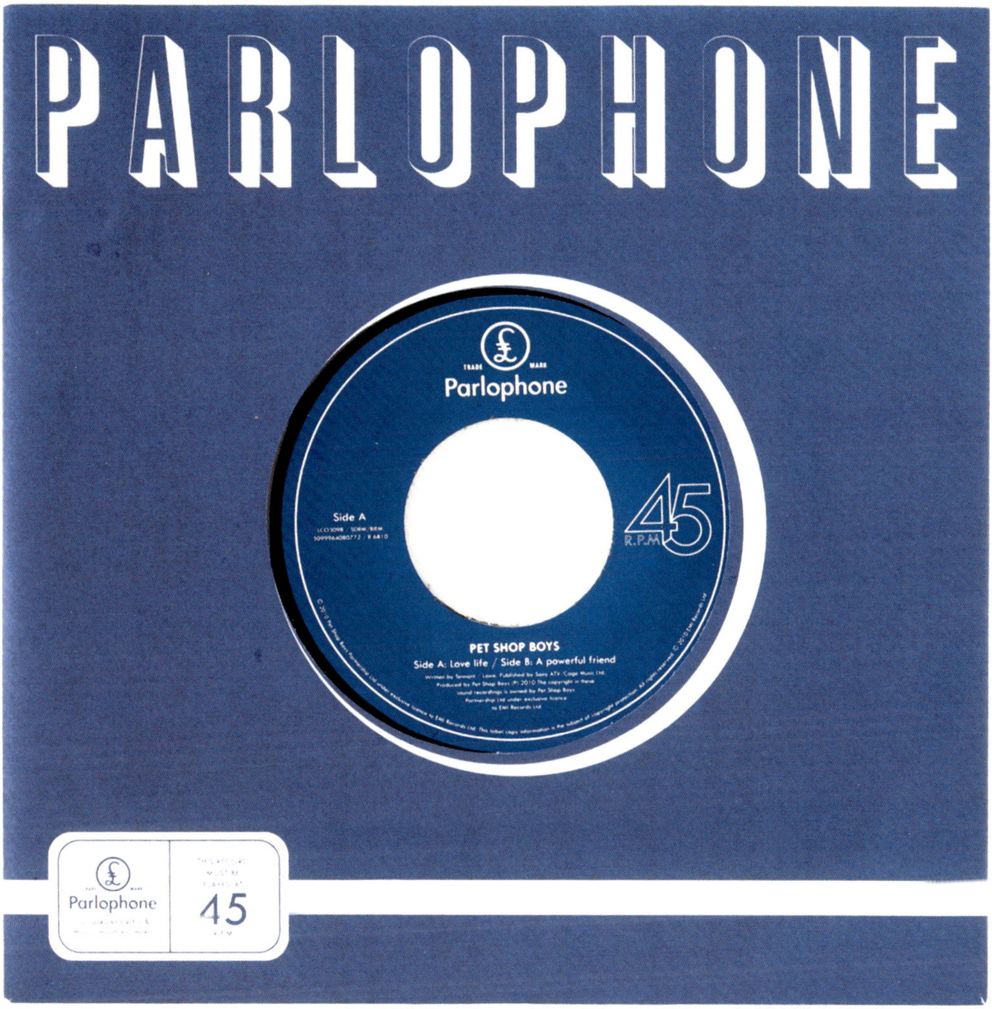

7", front

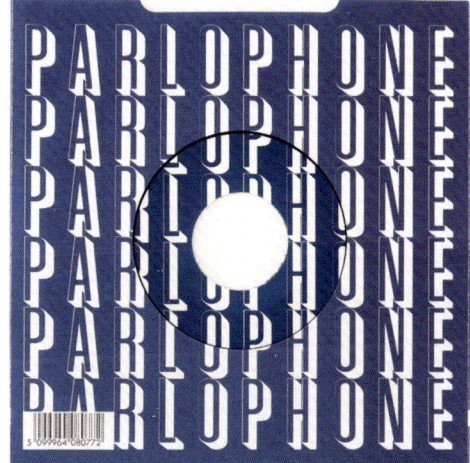

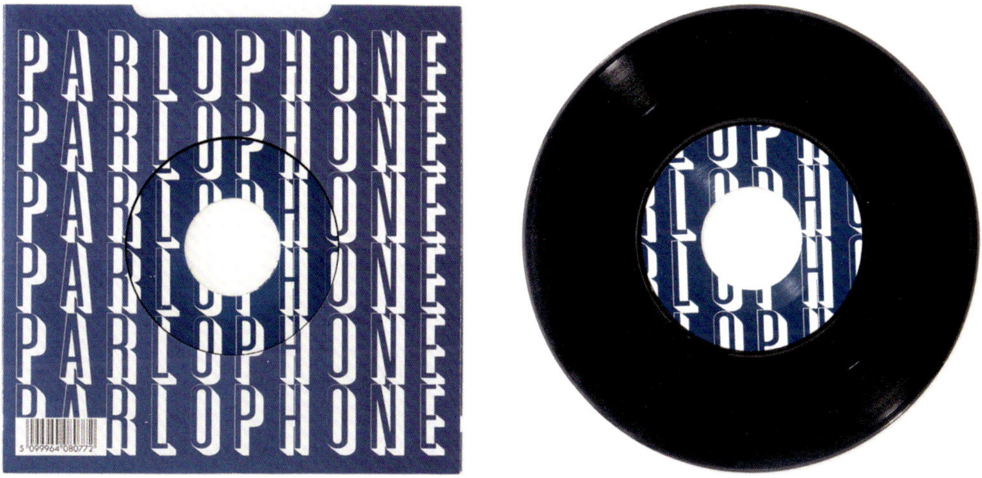

7", back and disc

Love life 2010

Together

release 24 October 2010 (download) / 29 November 2010 (physical formats)
formats CD × 2 / CD promo / download × 5
photographer John Ross
design and art direction Farrow / PSB
video Peeter Rebane

'Together' was a single written for a forthcoming new Pet Shop Boys compilation, Ultimate, its euphoric tune inspired by a revolutionary Portuguese folk song that Neil and Chris once heard someone play in a bar in Porto. In its lyric, Neil says he was 'imagining that there are two people about to have sex for the first time'. The sleeve, showing different images and close-ups of handcuffs, was inspired by a complementary notion that struck Chris one day when he was in a taxi close to home: 'I suddenly thought: I can imagine posters for this release showing just a pair of handcuffs. I thought it was quite a nice idea, being handcuffed together. Also I thought it was a bit kinky as well – I felt we needed to up the kinky factor, which I think has been sadly missing for a while.' 'I think it's the follow-up to the "Yesterday when I was mad" sleeve – the straitjacket', says Neil.

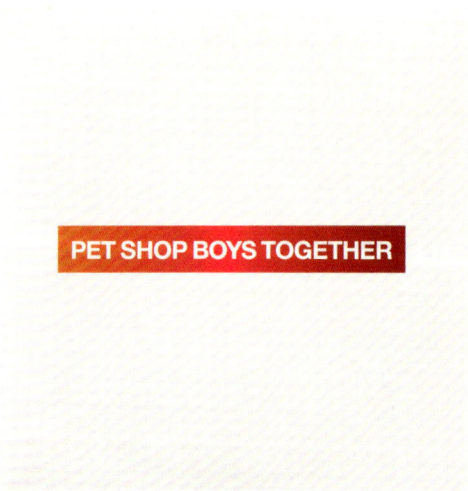

CD promo, front

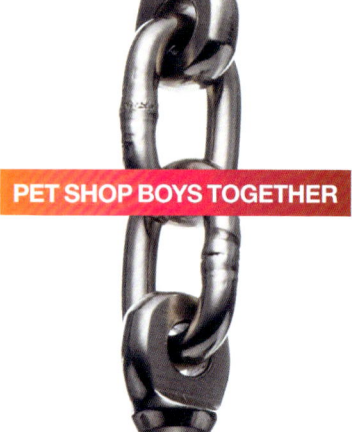

Download

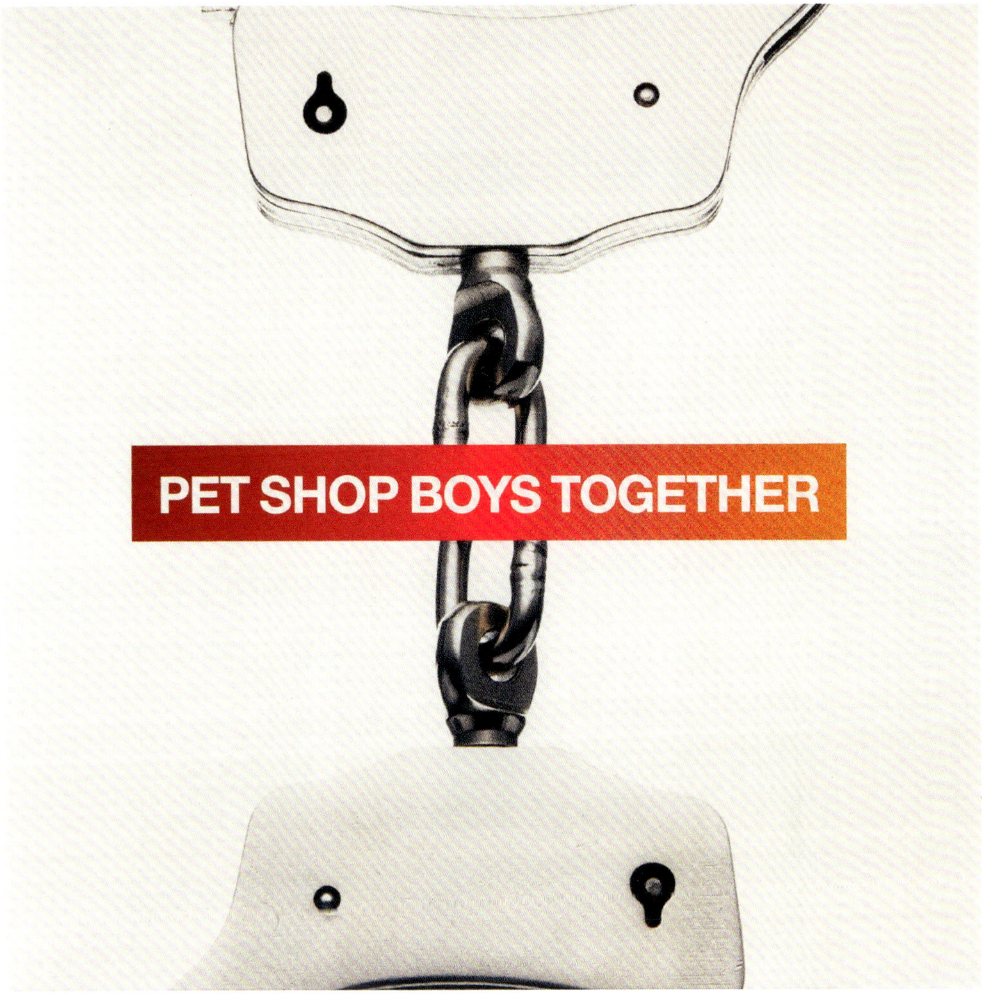

CD 1, front

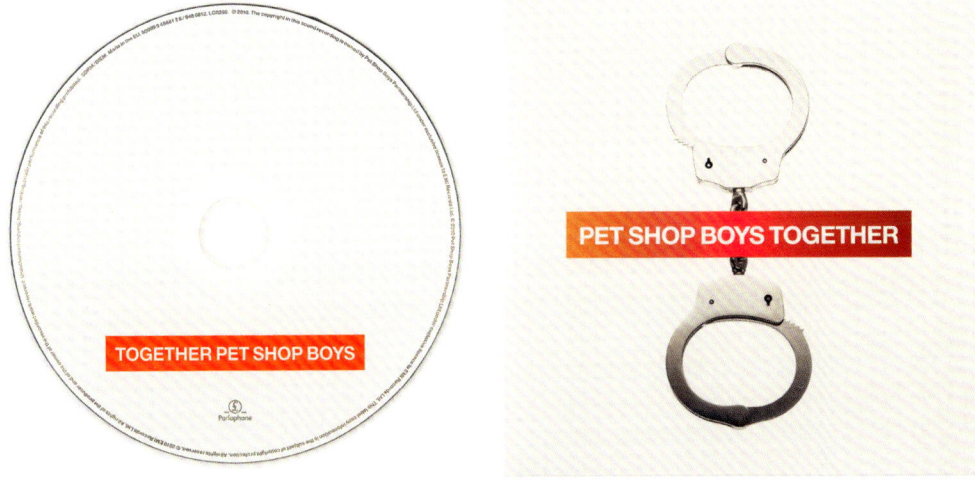

CD 1, disc

CD 2, front

Together 2010

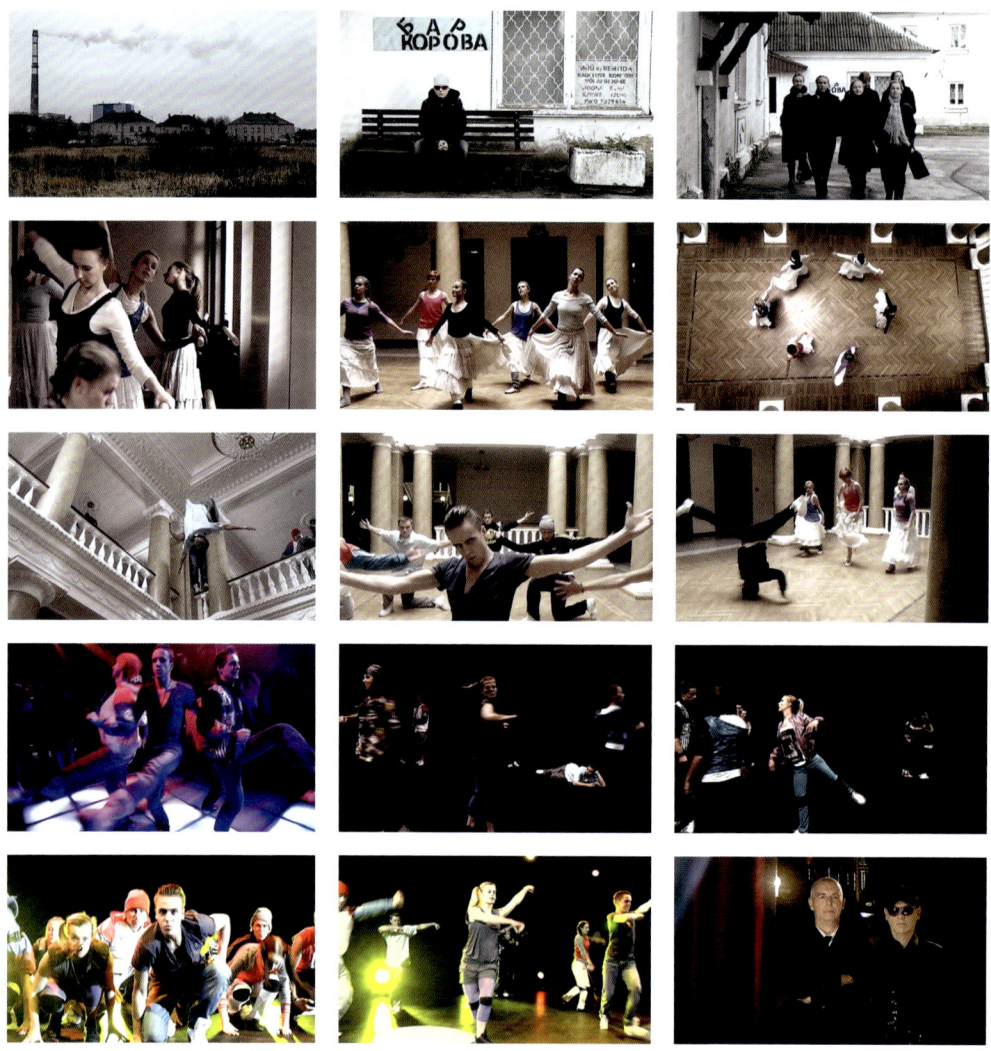

The 'Together' video was made in Estonia by their friend Peeter Rebane. It was based on an idea the Pet Shop Boys had had for some time. 'Ever since', Neil explains, 'we were in a club called Club La Roca in Riga, in Latvia, several years ago. It was a banging techno night and there was a sort of catwalk, and these three Russian boys rushed onto the catwalk and started doing approximately what we would regard as Cossack dancing …' 'With whistles …', Chris interjects. 'To this sort of Scooter-y techno music', Neil continues. 'And we've talked about it ever since.' Rebane wrote a detailed script – 'the only video we've ever made, ever, which has got a complete shooting script from start to finish, like a film', says Neil. 'The idea was to use the techno sound of the riff and the 3/4 time-signature of the music, and so it's like a face-off between some middle-class girls waltzing in some sort of dance school and some Russian boys maybe working on the streets who start doing

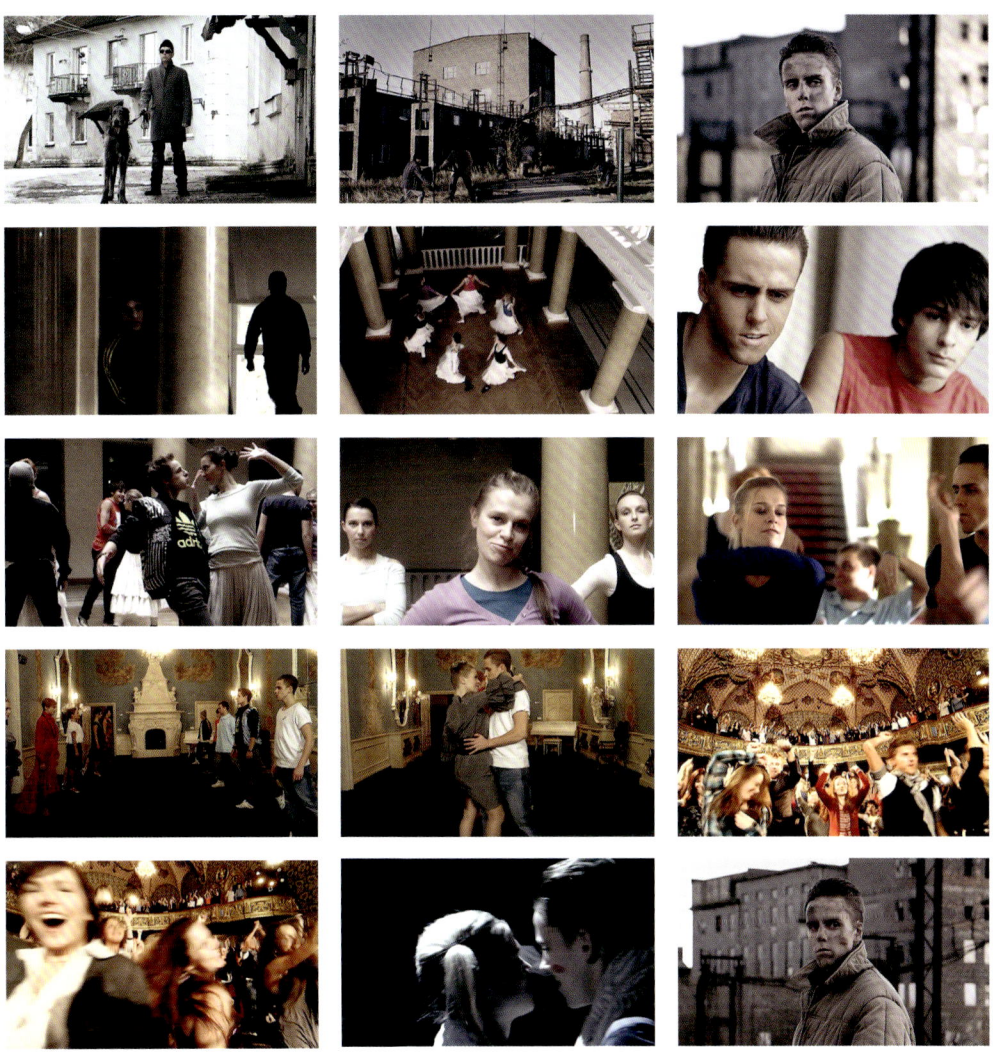

this traditional Cossack dancing. And eventually they end up dancing together.' 'And we're doing our usual wandering through', says Chris. 'It's our concept', says Neil. 'It's sort of based on the video for "It's like that" by Run DMC. We were basically doing an Eastern European version of that.'

Ultimate

release 1 November 2010
formats CD / CD plus DVD deluxe edition / download
photographer Pelle Crépin
design and art direction Farrow / PSB

A new Pet Shop Boys hits compilation had been requested by EMI Records to coincide with the duo's recent resurgent profile. 'The title came about because we wanted a very obvious greatest hits title – we wanted something where you know what it was', said Neil at the time. 'Our last two greatest hits titles, *Discography* and *PopArt*, have been quite sort of arty. So *Ultimate* is meant to be a mass market greatest hits title.' A deluxe edition included a DVD of twenty-seven single performances at the BBC over the years, as well as that year's appearance at Glastonbury.

'I like this sleeve a lot', says Neil. 'Because of the *Pandemonium* tour, we had these great outfits with these hats, which Chris and I bought in Dover Street Market, made by the guy from Kinky Gerlinky.' 'Michael Costiff', says Chris. 'And the pictures are great', says Neil. 'You also get the white background because we're being classic Pet Shop Boys. Greatest hits albums, you have to draw on your history.' 'I think there was some discussion at the time about how it should just be an absolute classic greatest hits album cover', remembers Gary Stillwell. 'That it shouldn't be obscure or weird.' 'A picture of them and a big title, etcetera', says Mark Farrow. 'It was a bit of a nod to *Discography* – that is, the block, the bar. And they were just great photographs. That's just a very strong graphic, powerful image.' The photographs were taken by Pelle Crépin.

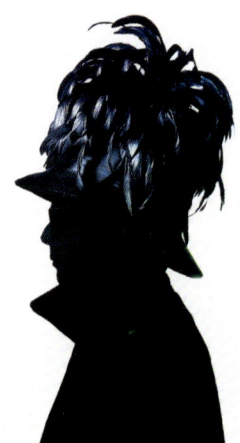 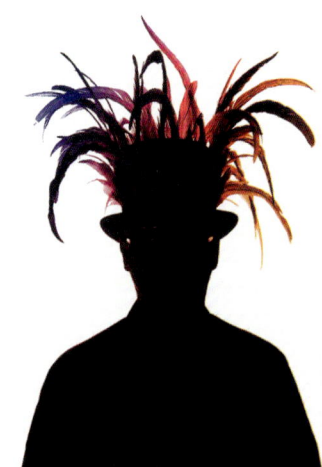

CD, booklet, inside page   CD, booklet, inside page

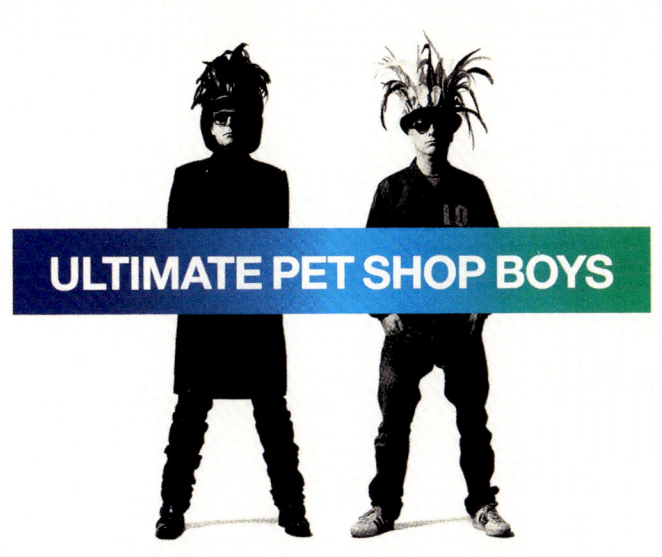

CD, front

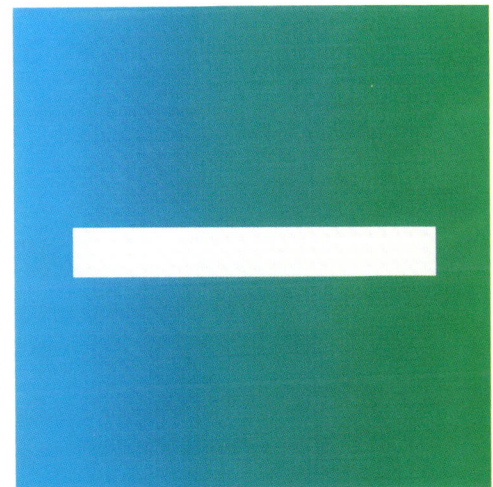

CD, booklet, front

CD plus DVD deluxe edition, booklet, front

The Most Incredible Thing

release 14 March 2011
formats 6 × 12" limited edition / double CD
design Farrow / PSB

The Pet Shop Boys' score to the ballet *The Most Incredible Thing*, four years in the making, was released the week before its first performance at Sadler's Wells in London. *The Most Incredible Thing* was an adaptation of an 1870 fairy tale by Hans Christian Andersen whose potential had been identified by Chris when he read a new translation of the Danish author's stories. He mentioned it to Neil, remarking that it would make a good ballet, in the same week that the Ukrainian dancer Ivan Putrov had phoned Neil to ask if they would write a ballet for him. The two ideas were combined. 'We made the decision that we were going to write for electronics and an orchestra', says Neil. 'It was a voyage of discovery.' The music was released, as was the *Battleship Potemkin* score, under the artist name Tennant/Lowe. A double CD was presented in a hardback sleeve bound like a book. The image on the front cover, of a ballerina, is a silhouette based on an original paper cut by Andersen held in the collection of Odense City Museums in Denmark. 'It just felt very logical', says Mark Farrow. 'And it felt like we could do a really nice treatment on it.' 'Essentially we cleaned it up', says Gary Stillwell. 'Redrew it', adds Farrow.

There was also a limited deluxe edition of five hundred copies, published by The Vinyl Factory. Six twelve-inch discs of the music and the original demos, as well as a print of part of the score, were presented in a large volume within a slipcase. 'It was about its being lavish and beautiful and feeling like a music portfolio', says Farrow. 'It was all covered in silk, foil blocked, and bolted together. It was quite complicated.'

Double CD, inside, showing part of the scenario written by Tennant/Lowe

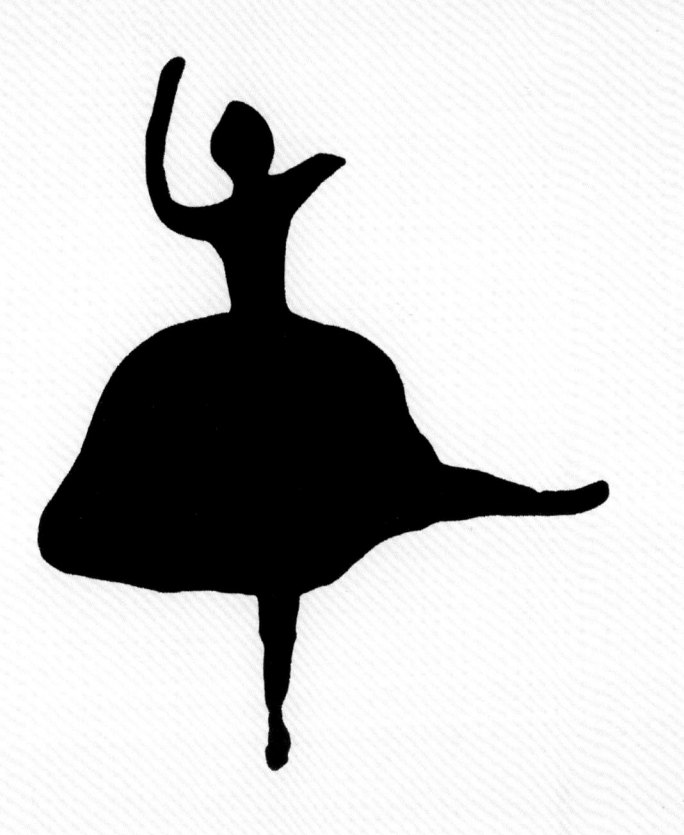

Double CD, front

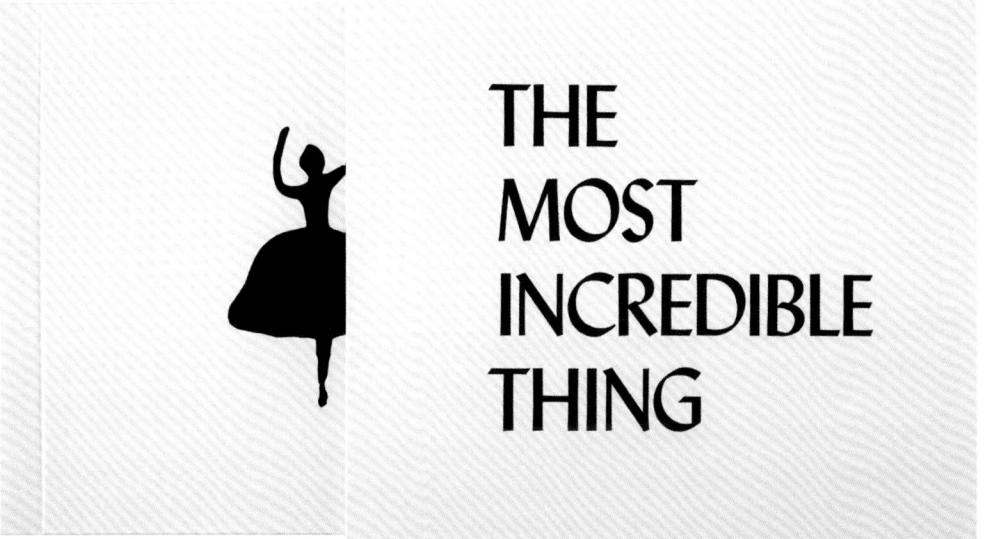

Limited edition, silk-bound slipcase and volume containing 6 × 12" discs and score

Format

release 3 February 2012
formats Double CD / double CD limited edition / 2 × CD promo
design and art direction Farrow / PSB

A sequel to 1995's *Alternative*, *Format* gathered together, as its subtitle made clear, 'B-sides and bonus tracks 1996–2009'. The title was Chris's idea: 'We were driving in Scandinavia and saw this big industrial shed, or shop, and it just had 'Format' written on the side, and I thought, "That's a good album title." And then it became post-rationalized by saying, "Oh, there are all these different formats, therefore it makes sense."'

The cover concept was Farrow's. Each colour block represents a different format: twelve-inch vinyl, seven-inch vinyl, cassette single, or CD single. 'The idea', says Gary Stillwell, 'was to represent each track on the two CDs with the spine of its original format. We ended up with this set of coloured blocks and then tried to arrange them.' 'Most of them are the colours of the original spines', says Mark Farrow. 'But I think we had to do a little bit of cheating.' A problem was posed by the one song that had been available only as a download. Initially Farrow suggested representing it by a wavy line, but Neil and Chris didn't like how that looked. A compliant rationale was soon found. 'If it was a download, it didn't have a physical format', Stillwell explains, 'so we didn't show it.'

For the limited-edition version, the two CDs were housed in larger cardboard box, on which the design curved around the edges. They were accompanied by a booklet including a track-by-track interview with Jon Savage. The two inner sleeves used the same logic as the outer box, each one representing only the formats of the tracks on that particular disc.

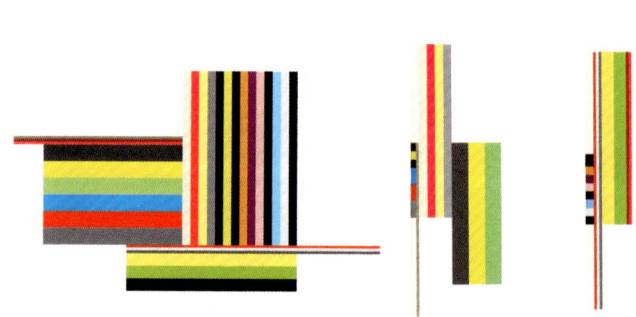

Double CD promo, outer sleeve and two inner sleeves

Pet Shop Boys
Format

B-sides and bonus tracks
1996–2009

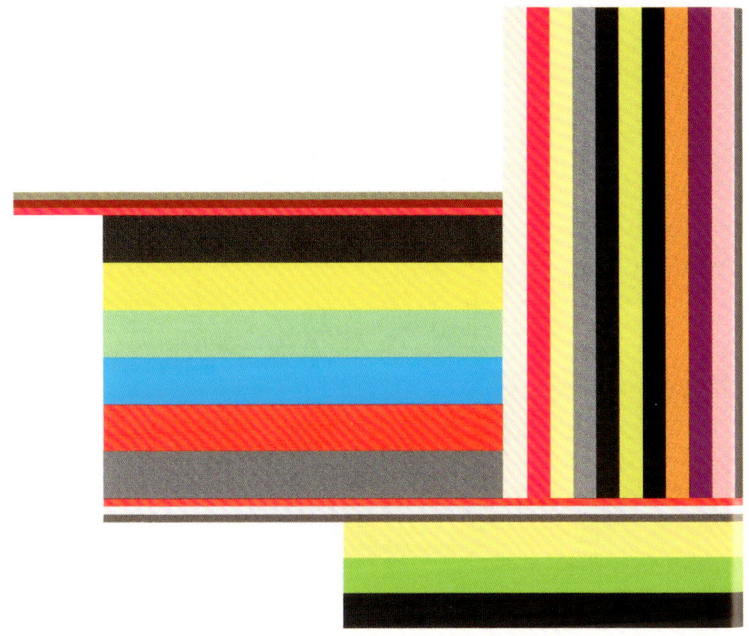

Double CD limited edition, outer box

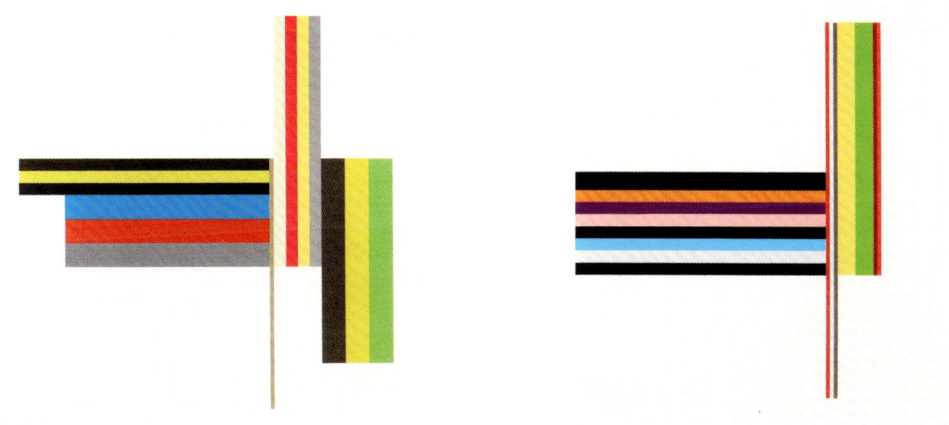

Double CD limited edition, CD One, sleeve   Double CD limited edition, CD Two, sleeve

Winner

release 6 August 2012
formats 7" promo / CD / CD promo × 2 / CD-R promo × 4 /
download × 4 / download remix
model Chiara Ferrari
design and art direction Farrow / PSB
video Surrender Monkeys

'The song is about being in something like the X-Factor or Eurovision Song Contest – coming from nowhere and finding yourself a winner and the crowd is all cheering', says Neil. Or maybe even about something closer to home: 'Me and Chris getting to number one with "West End girls" and knowing that it's going to change our lives. It's a transience-of-fame song, really. It's also saying: it's not where you've got to, it's how you got there that counts.' One reason for releasing 'Winner' as the first single from the forthcoming *Elysium* was the obvious way its lyric dovetailed with the imminent London Olympics. (The Pet Shop Boys would perform 'West End girls' as part of the closing ceremony on 12 August, and then performed three songs, including 'Winner', at the final parade of British athletes through London on 10 September.)

The sleeve, which echoed the Olympic theme with its depiction of an empty podium, evolved from an early concept for the *Elysium* sleeve – a rectangular monolith: 'This idea', says Gary Stillwell, 'of Greek statuary.' As soon as 'Winner' was selected as the first release, 'I don't remember there even being a conversation', says Mark Farrow. 'I knew what we would do. We'd turn the monolith into a podium.' The computer graphic image was designed by Chiara Ferrari. 'She's an architect and interior designer who used to share our studio', says Farrow. 'And she was better at 3D stuff than we were.' Originally the yellow version was intended for a twelve-inch single, but when no physical twelve-inch was released, it was used instead for the download of the remix bundle.

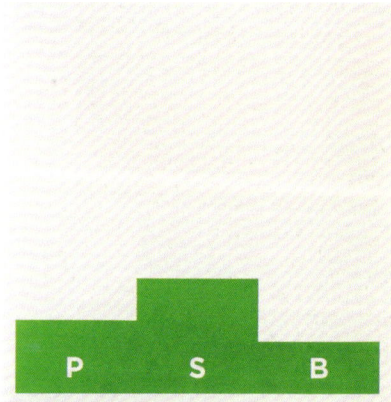

7" promo, outer sleeve

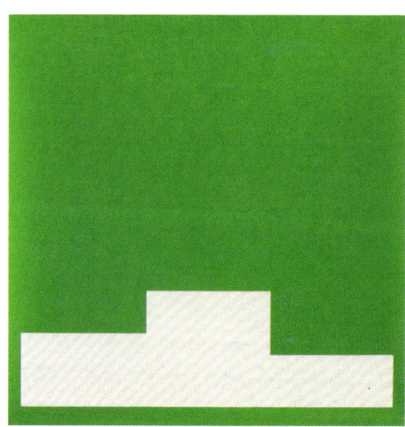

7" promo, inner sleeve

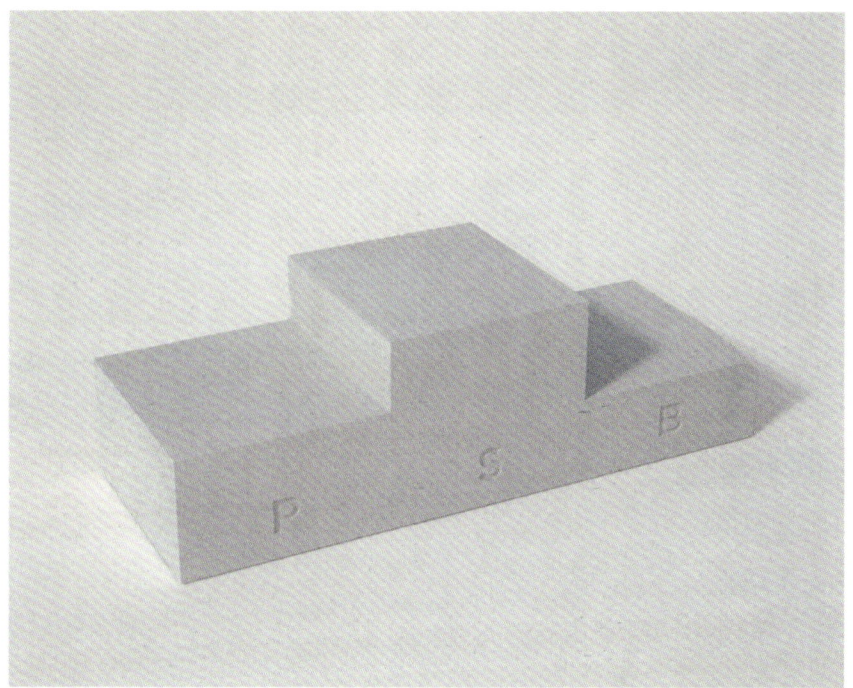

Winner
Pet Shop Boys

CD, front

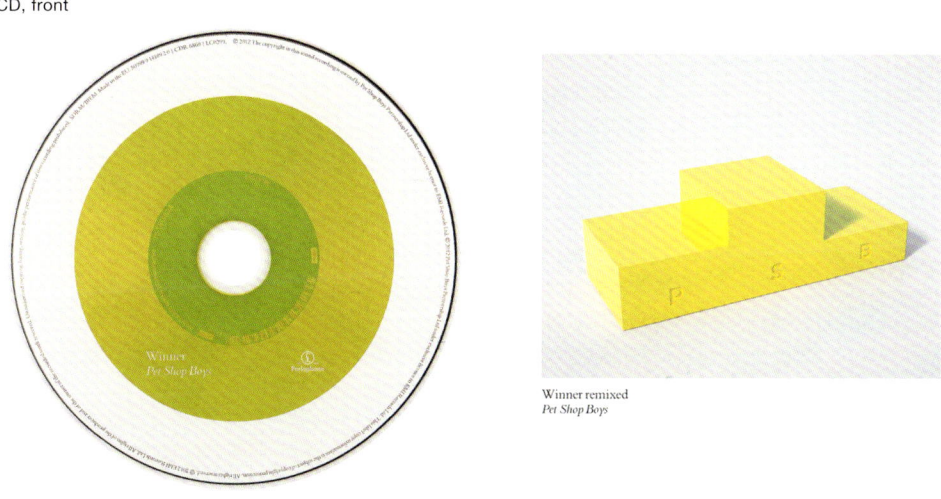

Winner remixed
Pet Shop Boys

CD, disc

Download remix

Winner 2012

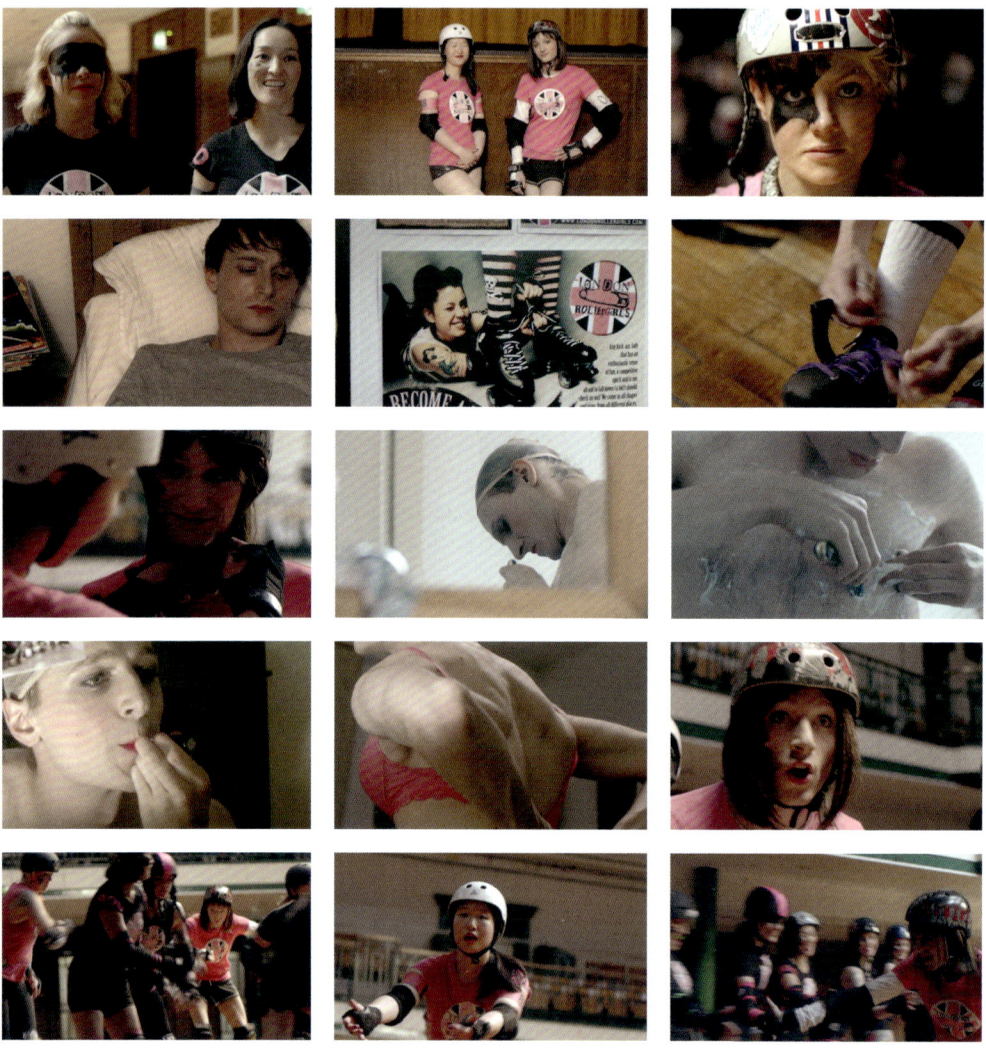

The Surrender Monkeys' video for 'Winner', selected by the Pet Shop Boys from a number of storyboard proposals solicited by Parlophone, presents the tale of a transgender boy's journey to inclusion in a roller-girl team. It focuses on the Rollergirls, an all-female, skater-owned roller derby league based in London that promotes charity, teamwork, and confidence in women by embracing everyone regardless of body shape, occupations, sexual orientation, race, or nationality. Filmed at York Hall in Bethnal Green, the video, which does not feature the Pet Shop Boys, tells the story of new team member Dirty Diana and their initiation into the group. It builds on the song's sense of winning to include not only the roller-derby team's victories, but also the personal victory of the main character's gender nonconformity and the acceptance by their teammates. Shaolynn Scarlett, Dirty Diana's rollergirl wife and mentor, says in the video: 'I want to help her grow into herself a little more while she's playing

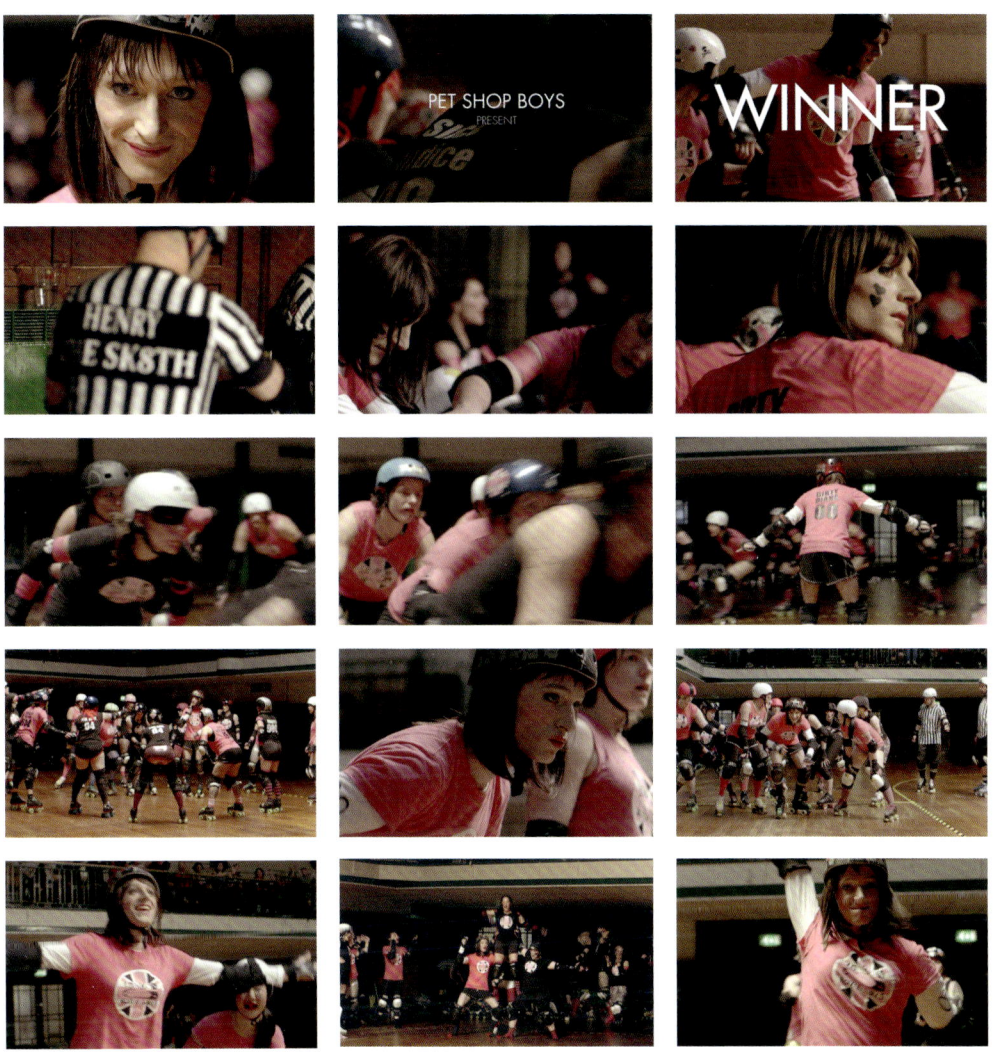

roller derby and help her to gain more confidence so she can develop into the woman she's meant to be.' 'It's got a lovely message of friendship and support', says Neil.

The Pet Shop Boys subsequently received the following unsigned email about the video: 'Thank You to the Boys for their "Winner" video, which so positively showed the transgender community who has been much maligned and battle worn for so long. Many in the trans community have been buoyed and even moved to tears by the theme of the video. The transgender community has faced great sorrow and pain in our daily lives just trying to be accepted and "fit in" because we look different. Many are forced to "go stealth" and disappear and hope no one ever finds out, because being uncovered can mean the loss of family, friends, a job, a home, and even one's life. Please pass along, if you can, this anonymous "Thank You" to all involved in the production.'

Elysium

release 5 September 2012
formats LP / double LP deluxe edition / CD / double CD deluxe edition / download
photographer Ann Summa
design and art direction Farrow / PSB

'We'd had enough of shiny pop', says Chris. 'Sick to the back teeth of it.' Trevor Horn had suggested years ago that one day the Pet Shop Boys should make 'an LA album'. 'By which', says Neil, 'he meant an album where we used excellent LA musicians to do something sort of smooth and beautiful, and in fact this idea always intrigued us.' To some degree, *Elysium* was that album. The catalyst for its title was a photo session with Ann Summa in the Los Angeles neighbourhood Elysian Park towards the end of the recording. 'And that suggested the word "Elysium". It seemed to sum up where the album was made – the sunshine – and also the dreamy quality of it.' That same day, they also posed for photos in the grounds of the rented house where they were living. In one, the gardener walked by in the background, quite by chance, and that image would appear in the album artwork. 'The gardener looks great', says Neil.

'It's fine,' says Neil, of the sleeve design, 'but it's not one of our best covers.' Proposed by Farrow, it used two different images of the natural world. 'Obviously, Elysium is the utopian place', says Gary Stillwell. 'We were trying to reflect the beauty of nature.' The standard CD used an image of dappled seawater: 'just a stock image that we found that really seemed to fit', says Stillwell. The boxed CD deluxe edition, which included an extra disc with instrumentals of the tracks, used a photograph of a sunset that Stillwell had taken on holiday in Fez, Morocco. The two vinyl versions merged both images. 'Sea and sky', summarizes Neil. 'Heaven. Paradise.' 'I remember kind of wanting to obscure the photographs with that big panel', Mark Farrow notes. 'Which is arguably too big.'

CD, inside, with booklet and disc

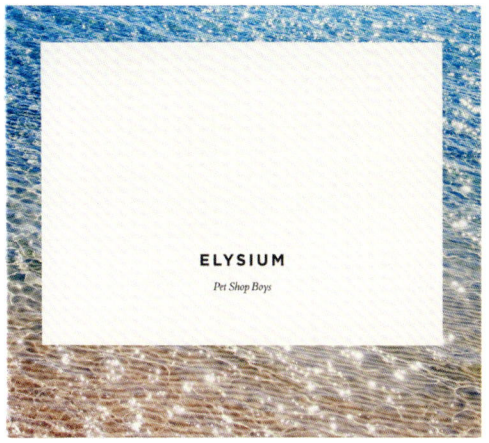
CD, front

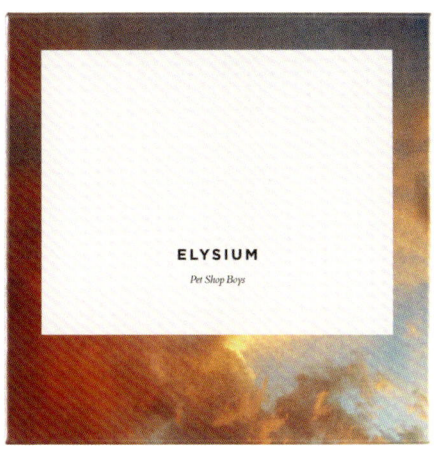
Double CD deluxe edition, front

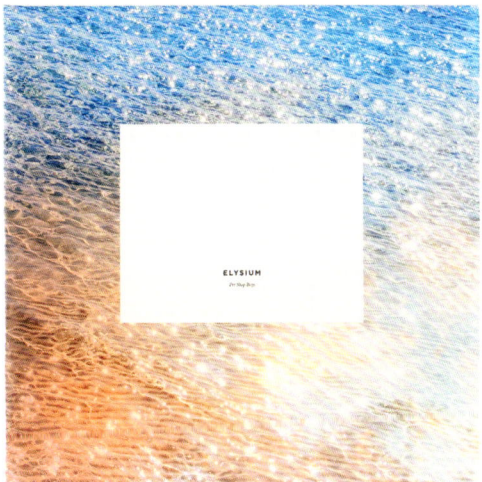
Double LP deluxe edition, outer sleeve, front

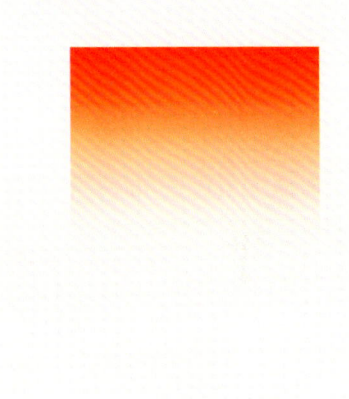
Double LP deluxe edition, inner sleeve, Record One, front

Double CD deluxe edition, booklet, front

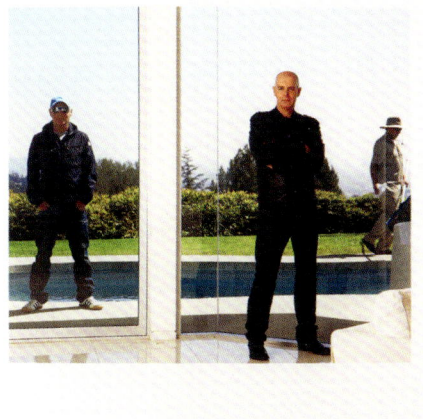
Double CD deluxe edition, booklet, inside page

Leaving

release 12 October 2012
formats 7" / 12" / CD × 2 / CD remix /
CD-R promo × 4 / download × 4
photographer Pelle Crépin
design and art direction Farrow / PSB
video David Lopez-Edwards

The artwork for 'Leaving', 'a song about death', used various black-and-white portraits from a photo session with Pelle Crépin. Chris wore a distinctive hat by J. W. Anderson, and Neil partially covered his face in deliberate imitation of an iconic movie star image. 'I'm copying Marilyn Monroe', he says. 'I know it's a ridiculous thing to say, but nonetheless. I literally thought "I'll do the Marilyn Monroe thing." Emphasize my eyes.' 'That was one of those nice ones where they just went, "There are some photographs coming over", and you're like, "Wow, these *are* great"', says Mark Farrow. They used the picture of Chris for the front sleeves of the seven-inch single and the CD, and as a picture label on the twelve inch, while the photo of Neil appeared on the front sleeves of the twelve-inch single and the remix CD, and as the picture label on the seven-inch single. The inner sleeve of the twelve-inch single featured another picture of the sky by Gary Stillwell.

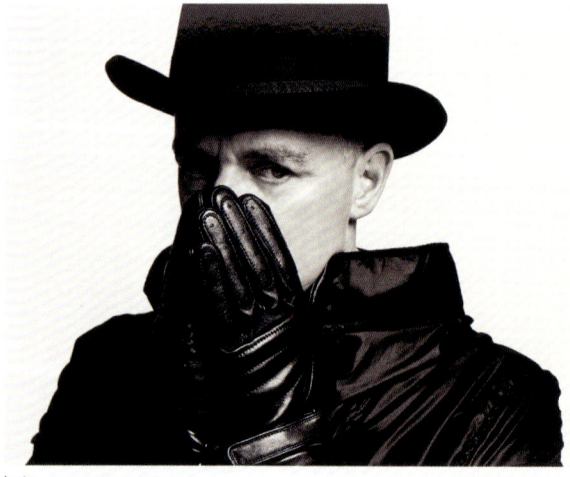 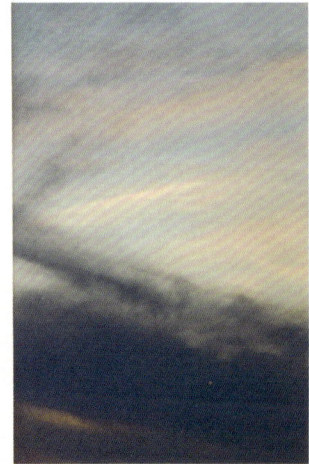

12", outer sleeve, front, and inner sleeve

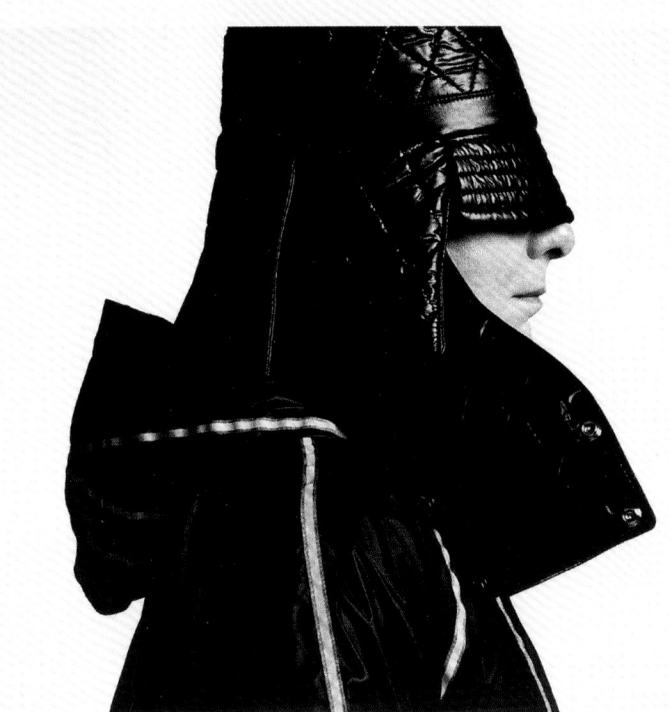

Leaving
Pet Shop Boys

7", front

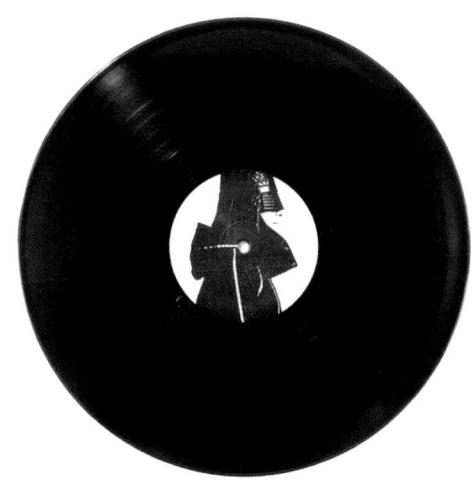

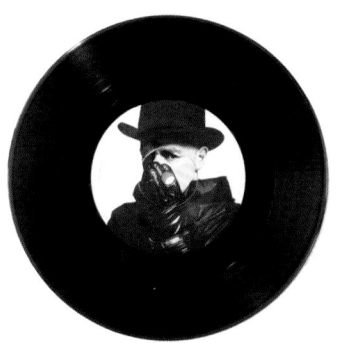

12", Side A

7", Side A

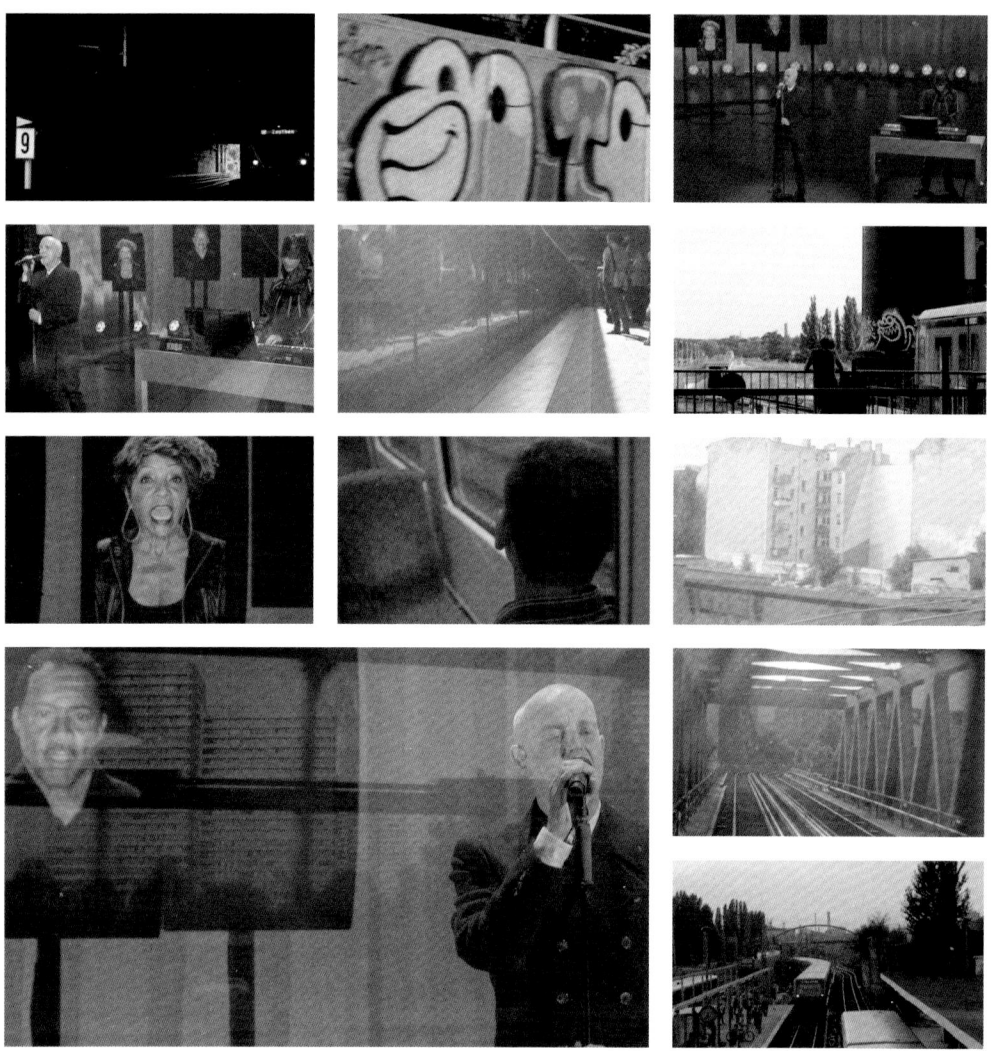

The video for 'Leaving' was inspired by the opening sequence of the 1981 German film *Christiane F*, in which a girl gets on the S-Bahn train and travels into the centre of Berlin. Shots of the S-Bahn – 'It fits with the idea of "Leaving": you're leaving on the train' – were juxtaposed with footage from the *Elysium* album launch concert at Berlin's Hau 1. 'I think it's really gorgeous this video', says Neil. 'Yes', concurs Chris.

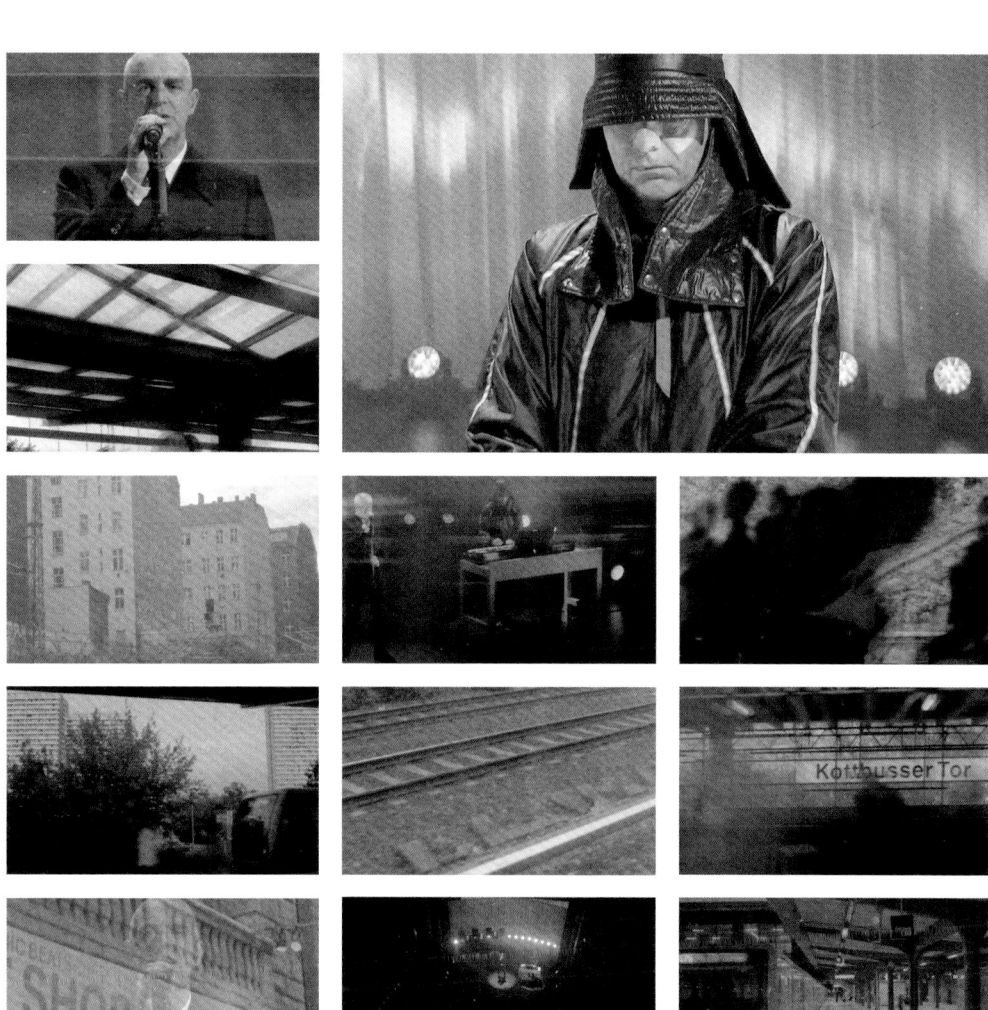

Leaving 2012

Memory of the future

release 31 December 2012
formats CD / CD remix / CD promo × 2 / CD-R promo × 2 / download × 2 / download remix
photographer Pelle Crépin
design and art direction Farrow / PSB
video David Lopez-Edwards

In this song, released as a single in Stuart Price's substantially remixed version of the *Elysium* track, 'you're remembering something that hasn't happened yet,' says Neil. 'So the idea is that future happiness seems so inevitable that you can already remember it.' A photo-session was done specifically for its sleeve. 'It is a controversial artwork in the Pet Shop Boys catalogue,' says Neil, 'because the only ones who like it are us. We had the idea. In fact, Chris had the idea.' 'Me?' Chris protests. 'No! I'm not taking the blame for this!' 'It was one of us', Neil says. 'I don't think it was me. I like it.' 'A bit weird, this one, isn't it?' says Chris. 'What's not to like?' asks Neil. The way they look in the photographs is loosely based on the 1964 movie *Children of the Damned*. 'It's a science-fiction image,' says Neil, 'so it's meant to be the future. I just quite like the fact that you can do something that changes the way you look. We had to wear blond wigs. And of course, there's a lot of retouching to make us look a lot younger. Our eyes have been changed.' Initially, the plan was to have each Pet Shop Boy's full face on their own sleeve. In the final version, their faces are bisected so that each complete face can be seen only by aligning the two CD singles next to each other. There was also an innovative promo CD, without photos, where the front of the sleeve was truncated so that the disc was visible at the top. 'It was like: We've got to do a promo – let's make it like something from the future', says Mark Farrow. 'We've always enjoyed playing with the format, and trying to push it into being something new, and this just felt like an opportunity. I was really happy with it. This was us running riot.'

CD promo, outer sleeve

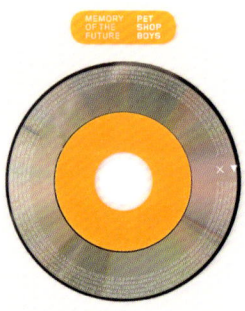

CD promo, disc

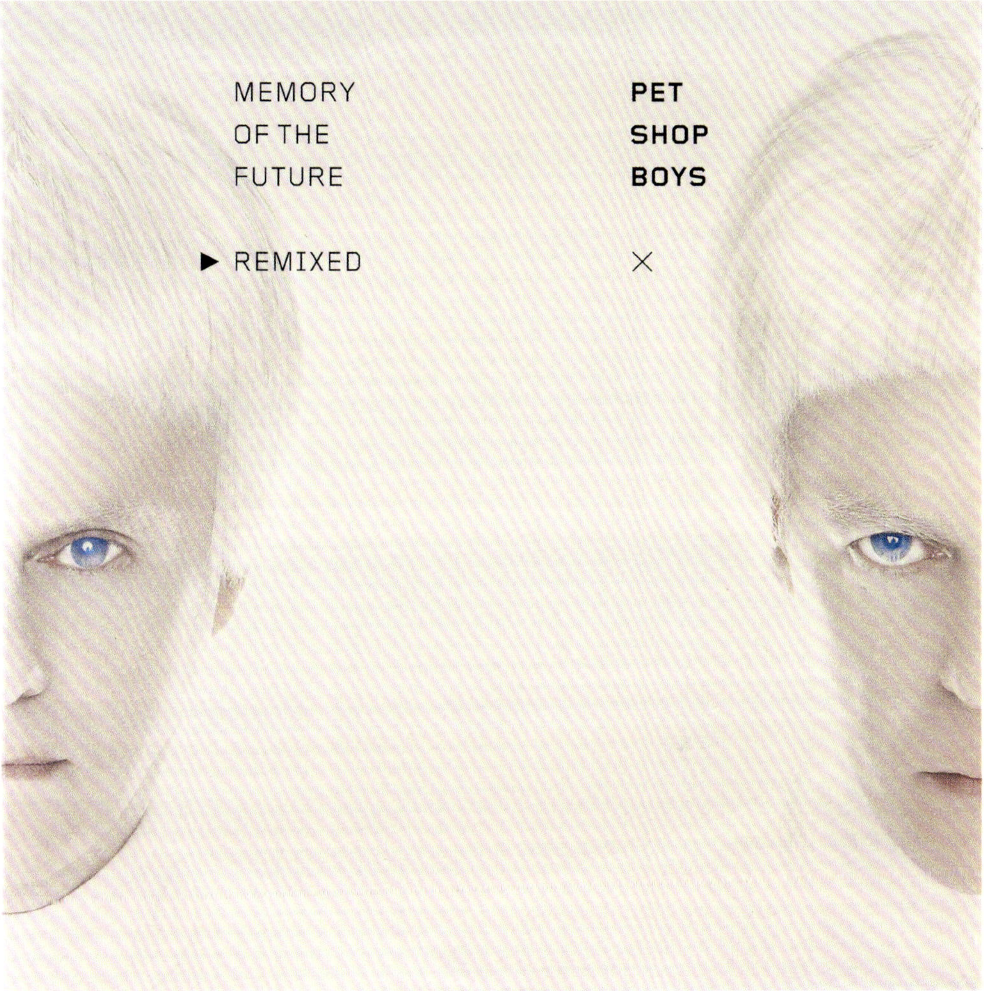

CD remix, front

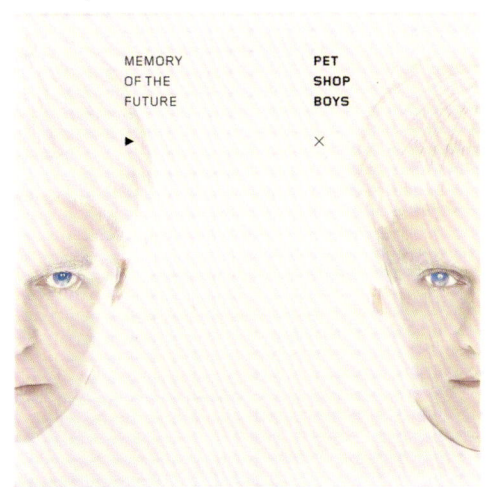

CD, front

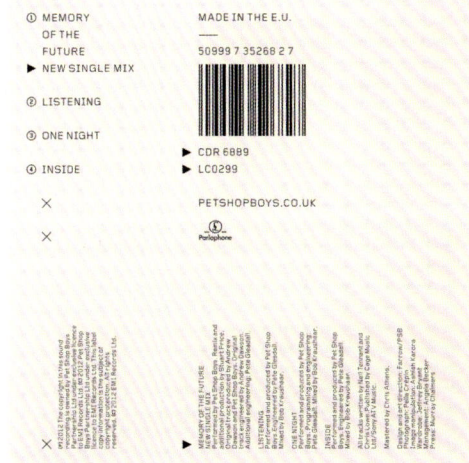

CD, back

Memory of the future 2012 399

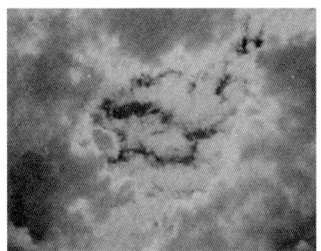
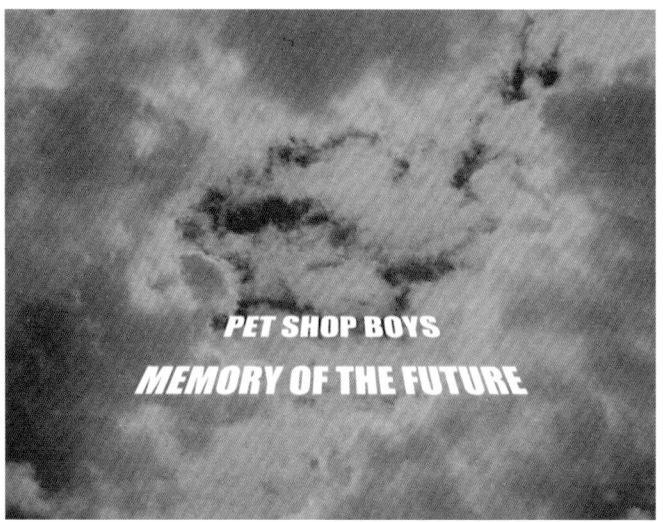
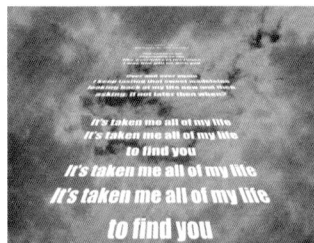
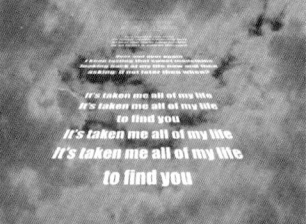
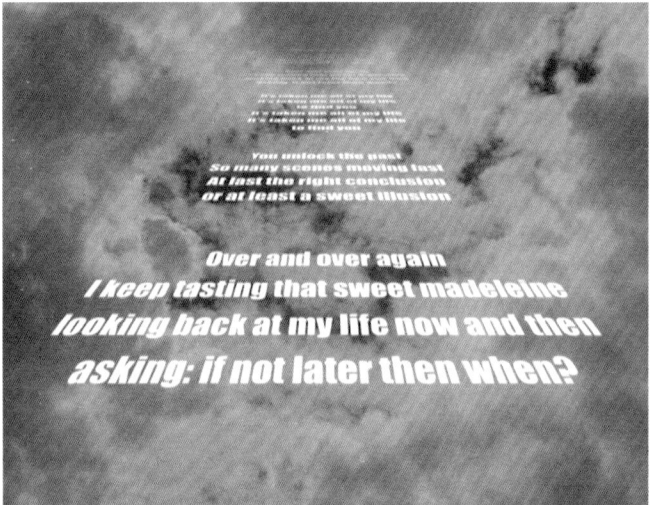
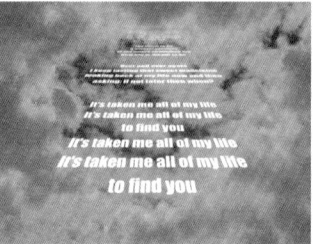

A lyric video was made for the song, which, at Chris's suggestion, uses the kind of emerging and surging type seen at the beginning of *Star Wars*. 'The fad of doing lyric videos had started', says Neil. 'The issue really is that the money isn't being generated to spend on videos, but you still want to have a video. Because social media demands that you do.'

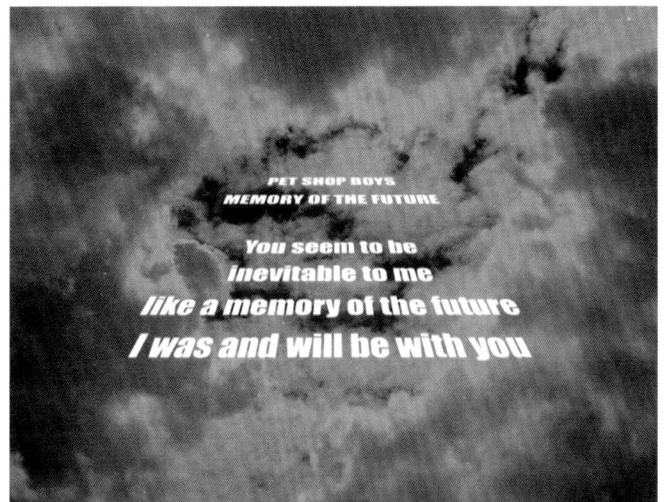
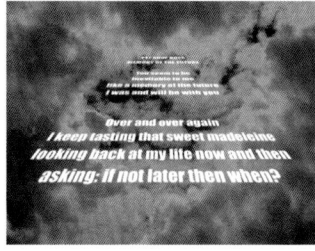
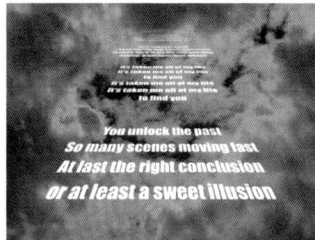
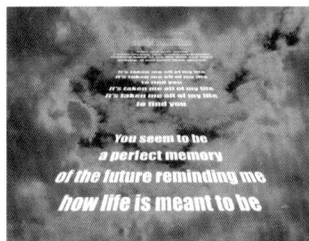
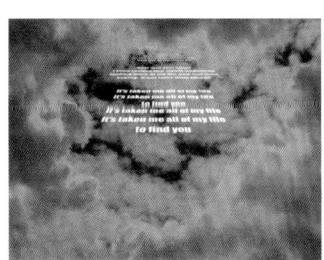
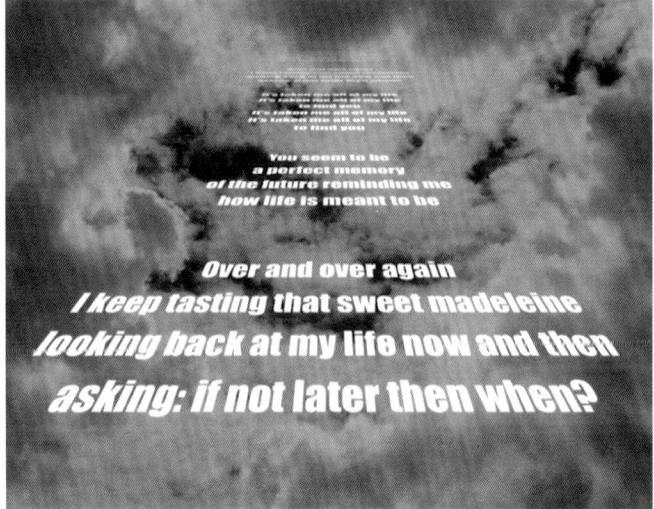

Memory of the future 2012

Electric tour

dates 22 March 2013 – 15 August 2015
set design and creative direction Es Devlin
lighting Rob Sinclair
video projections Luke Halls
choreography Lynne Page
costumes Jeffrey Bryant

The first iteration of the *Electric* tour premiered ahead of the album bearing the same name, before its full launch in St Petersburg, Russia, in June 2013. Like the album, the design of the performance leaned into a particular aspect of the Pet Shop Boys' aesthetic. One trigger for the forthcoming album had been a comment that Chris had read online when *Elysium* was out. 'They said', Neil recalls, '"Pet Shop Boys should be more banging and lasers."' The album would reflect this rubric in spirit; its accompanying tour would embody it more literally: it would be the first Pet Shop Boys tour to actually use lasers.

Once again, Es Devlin was the designer. She later wrote that Pet Shop Boys 'suggested that analogue chaos should pervade the presentation of their ecstatically electronic new album', and explained how she used the 'architecture of the printed circuit boards at the heart of the band's synthesizers', as demonstrated to her by their programmer Pete Gleadall, in both the wider visuals and the mazes etched into the Minotaur headpieces that Neil and Chris wore (pages 28 and 405), as they were flanked by dancers with more organic Minotaur heads. They appeared on stage as through from a tunnel, wearing costumes designed and hand-adorned by Jeffrey Bryant (opposite and pages 29, 410–11, and 415). 'They're both made out of 3,500 plastic straws, individually sewn on by him', says Neil. 'When you put them on the first time, it felt toxic, this plasticky smell. And it was so sharp. But of course it looked fantastic on stage so we went with it.' Later in the show, Neil wore a mirrorball hat and Chris, a full-head spherical mirrorball helmet (page 405).

Stuart Price again worked on the arrangements, and the set was informally split into four conceptual parts: 'Electric' ('because it was all super-electric music'), 'Run with the dogs tonight', 'Love etc.' ('basically love songs, ending with "Miracles"'), and finally 'Party' ('all up four-on-the floor tracks'). The tour programme included an interview with Andrew Harrison, and photography by John Ross documenting the rehearsals and production, often overlaid by Farrow's *Electric*-themed graphics (pages 404–5).

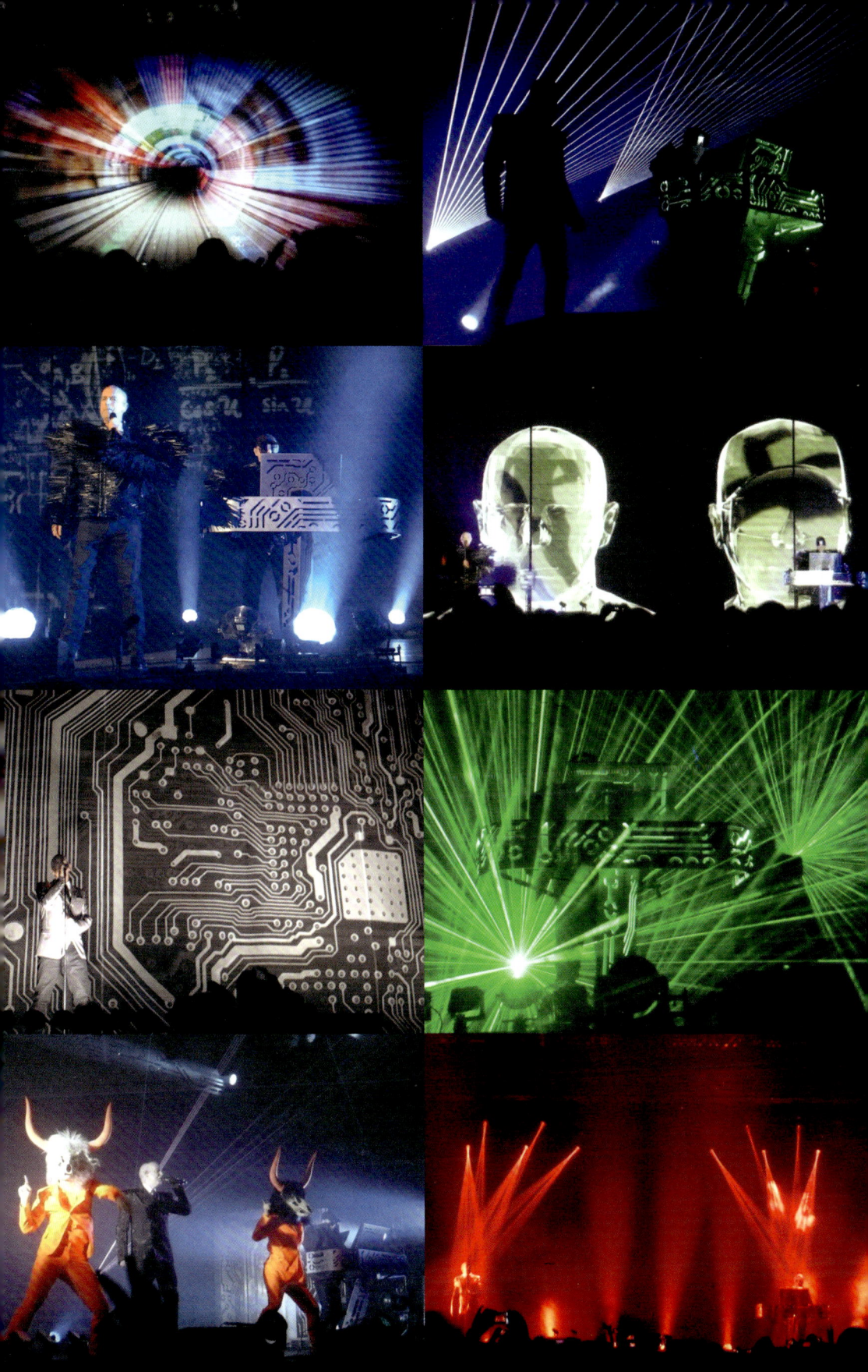

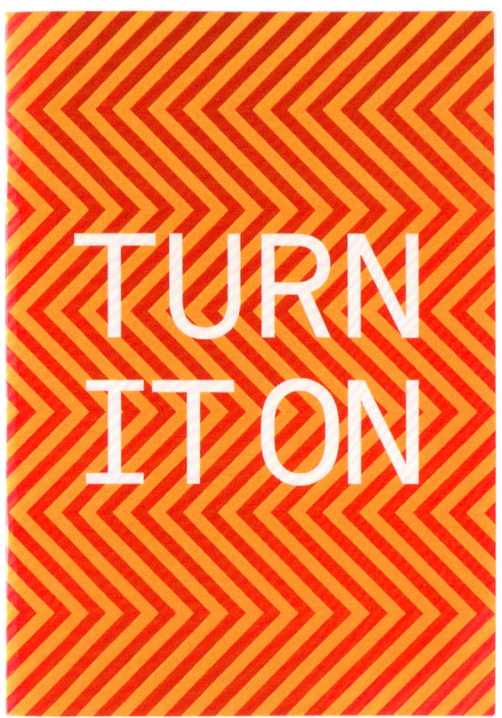

Tour programme, front

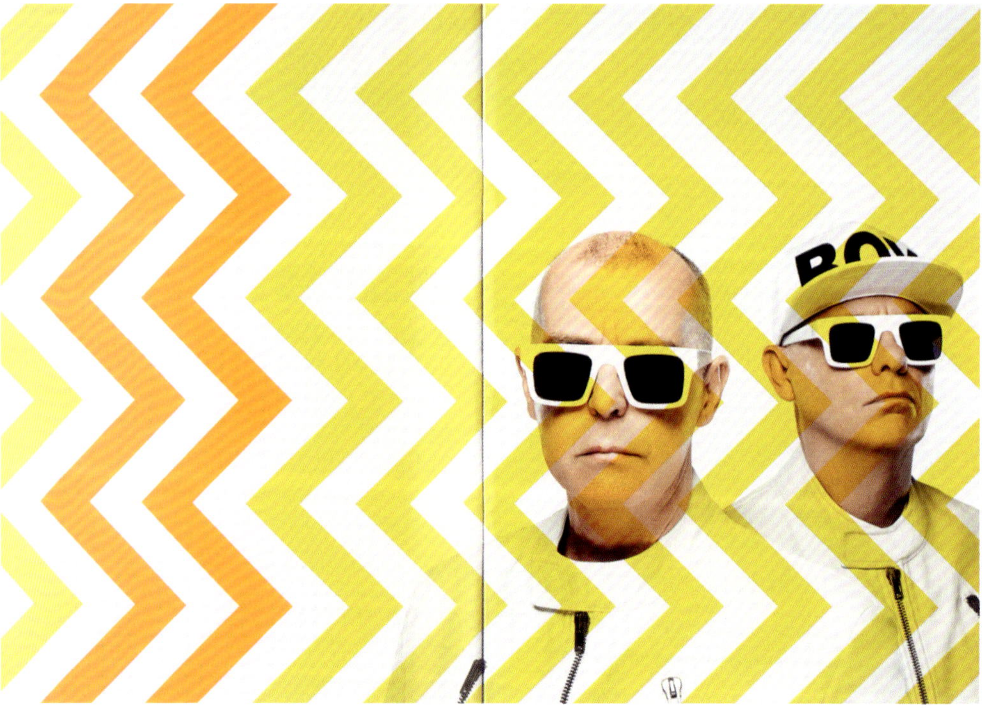

Tour programme, inside pages

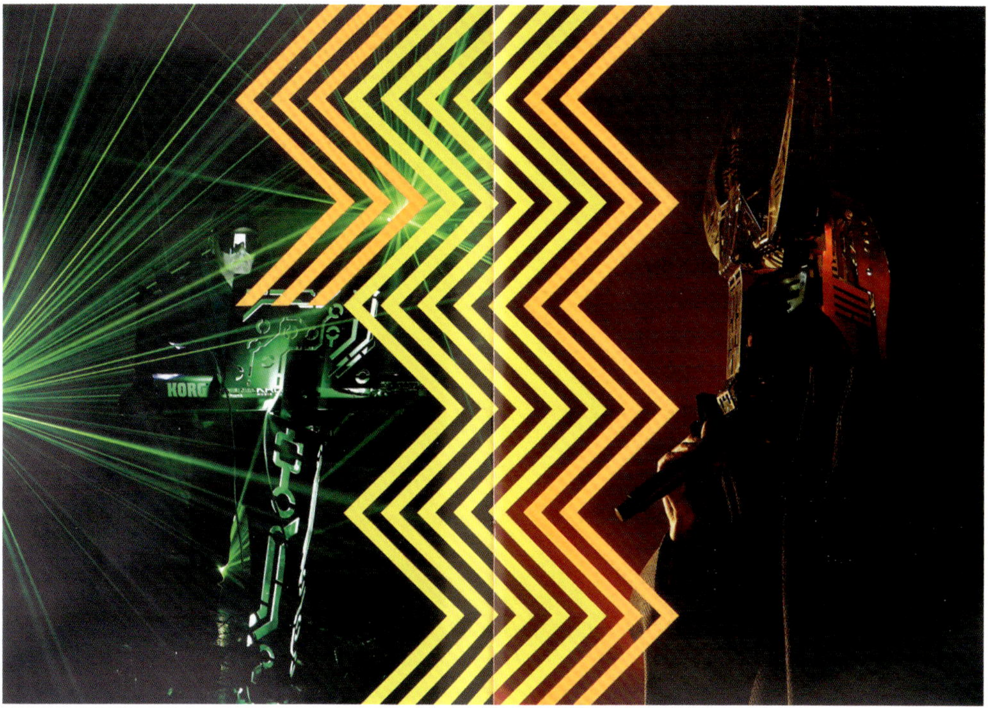

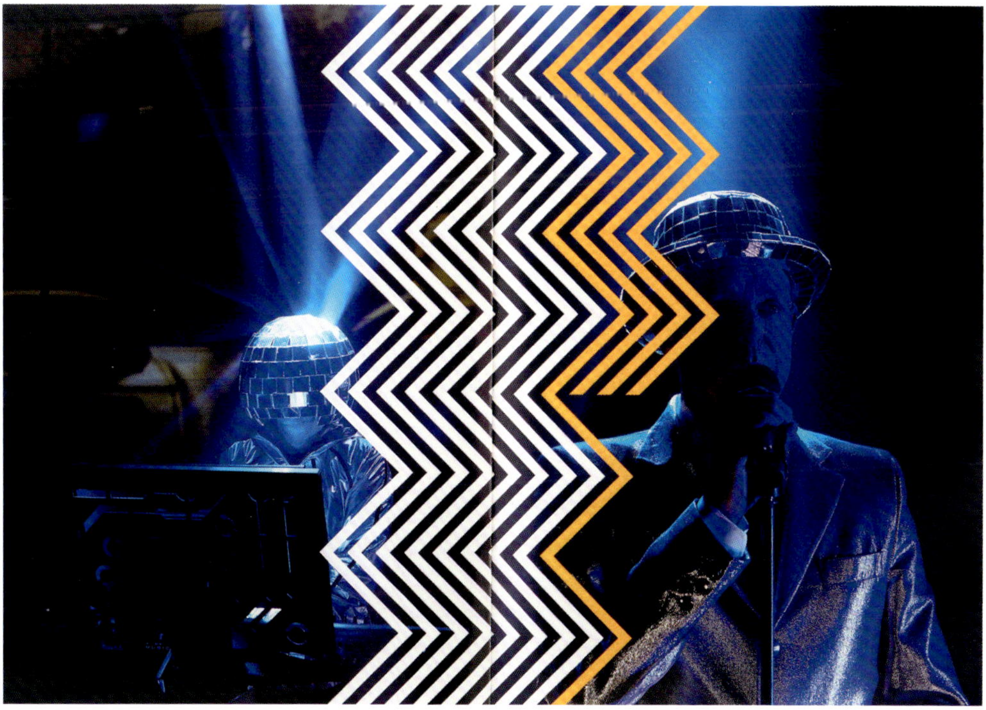

Tour programme, inside pages

Axis

release 1 May 2013
formats 12" / CD promo / download × 2 / download remix
design and art direction Farrow / PSB
video Jude Greenaway and Luke Halls

Initially released as a download-only single, 'Axis' was inspired, says Chris, by time spent at 'a really good Italo-disco night in Berlin'. 'All of the lyrics', says Neil, 'have a sort of vague double entendre.' Neil and Chris had originally suggested 'an electrical flash coming through the darkness' as the sleeve of the *Electric* album, and that concept was developed. 'The idea was that you would have this slit in the front of the sleeve – physically have a slit,' explains Mark Farrow, 'and we would have a mirrored holographic that you would see shining through.' When they moved on to a different idea for the album artwork, this idea mutated into the 'Axis' download sleeve. The specific vertical image was inspired by the beginning of Jude Greenaway and Luke Halls' video for the song (following pages), which was originally shot as the opening of the *Electric* tour (and also so used). 'So there's us bouncing off Es Devlin in this instance,' Farrow says, 'as opposed to the other way around.' The download sleeve version of the slit image was created in Photoshop. A horizontal variant was used for the remix download. 'Two axes, basically', Farrow points out. The twelve inch had a generic blue x2 sleeve – pronounced 'times two' – being the record company that Pet Shop Boys established after leaving Parlophone. 'Axis' was the first release on the new label.

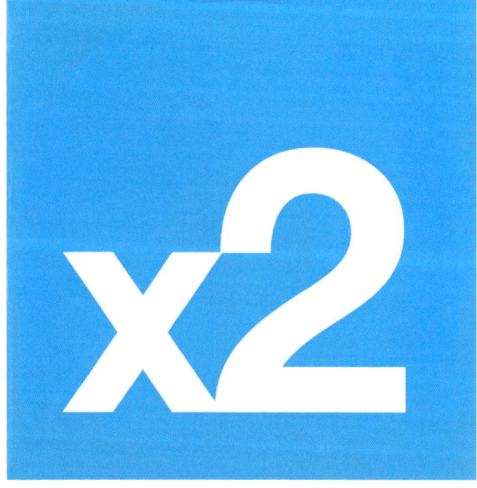

12", front

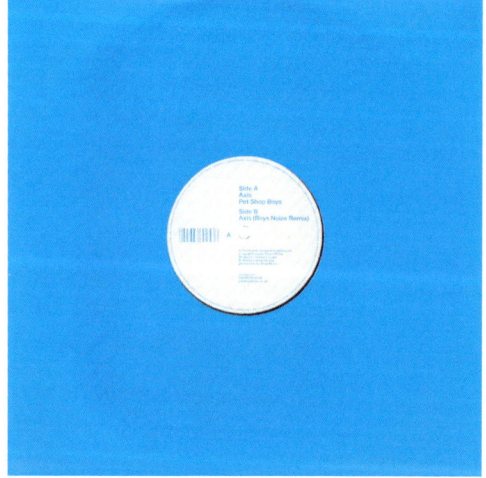

12", back

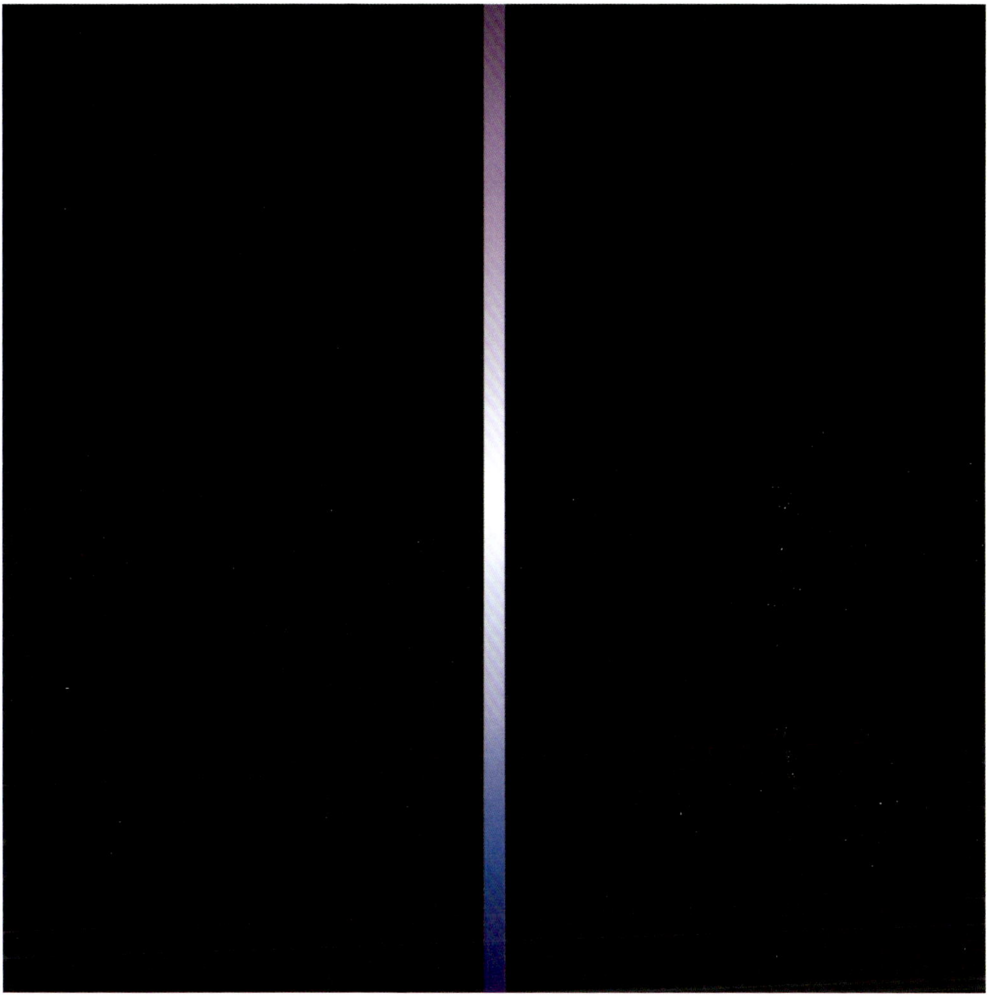

Download

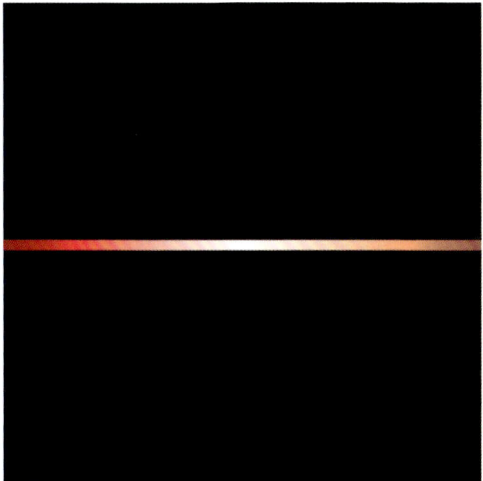

Download remix

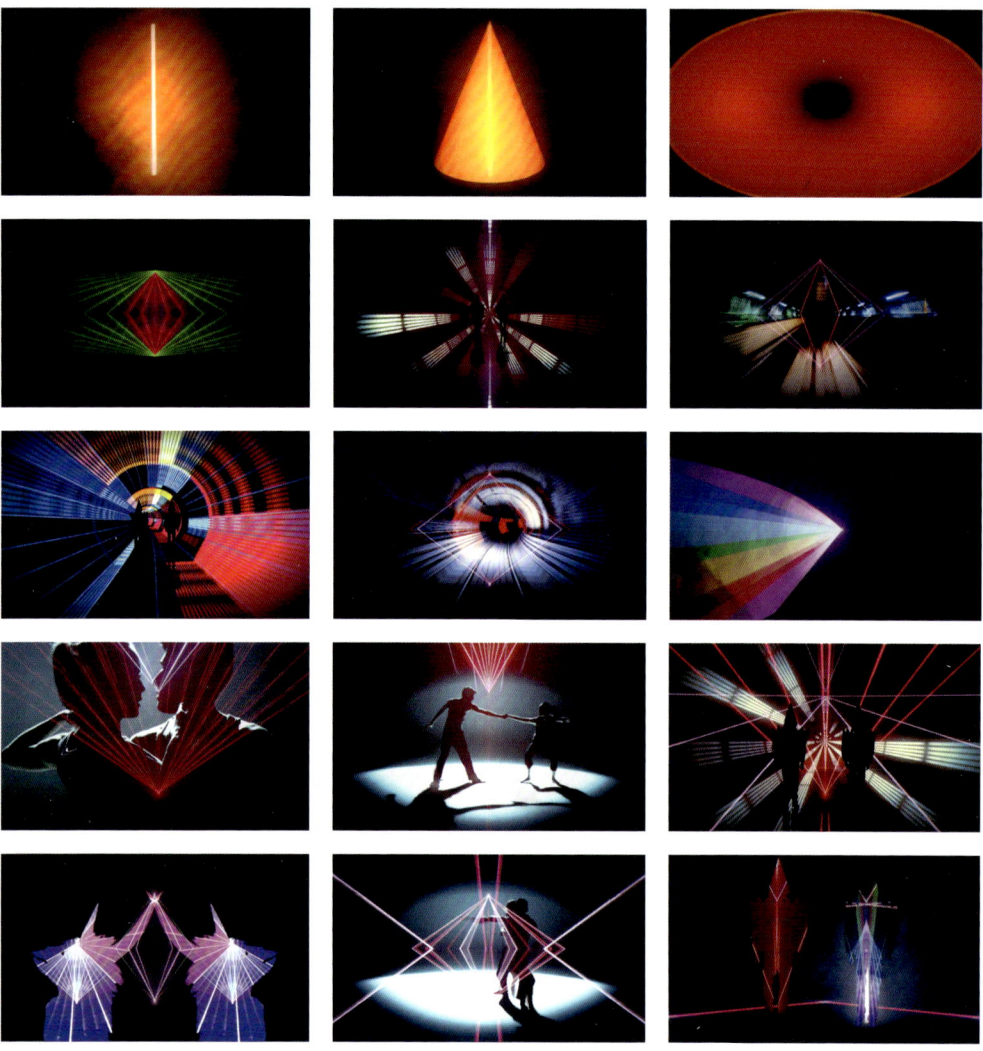

The video for 'Axis' is edited from footage shot for the projected film that opened the *Electric* tour, in which the Pet Shop Boys emerged from a pulsing, swirling, surging tunnel of light. For this, Neil and Chris had been filmed in a studio in Battersea on 10 February 2013, walking forwards, side by side, in the sculptural costumes they would wear at the start of the show. These included the black pointy hats designed by Gareth Pugh that they had first worn during their performance of 'West End girls' in the closing ceremony of the London Olympics on 12 August 2012. For the song's video, that opening footage was melded with, and augmented by, filmed elements from later in the show featuring the tour's dancers, Tom Herron and Merry Holden, sometimes human, sometimes Minotaur. 'It gave a taste of the album and, indeed, of the tour', says Neil. 'To set out the stall for the whole *Electric* project.' From now on, this kind of pragmatic cross-collateralization, where the same

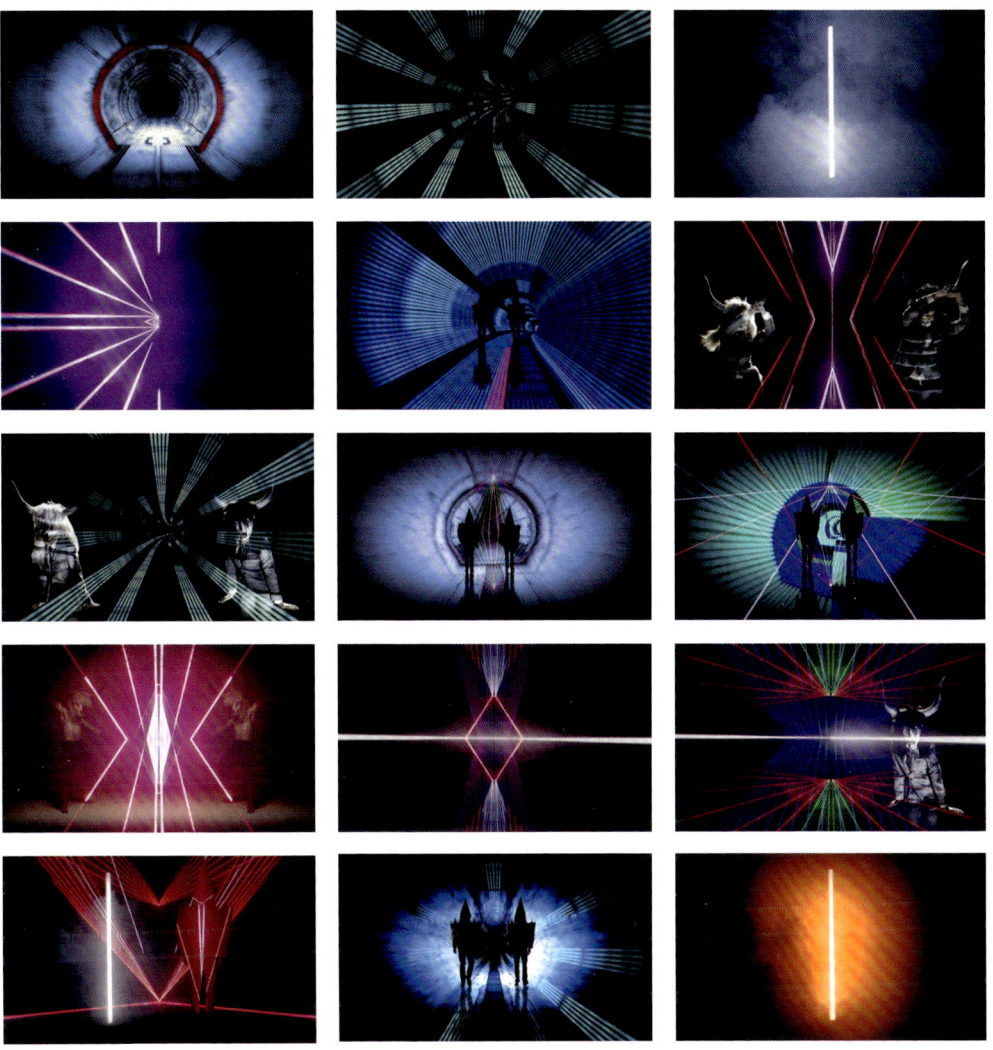

imagery might be used for both promotional videos and tour video content, would become normal. 'We made a policy decision that we would shoot videos for the shows that could also be used for promotion for songs as required', Neil adds. 'This was when we were first with Kobalt, and in a world of reduced budgets, we could split the budget between the record and the tour. I think this was the first example of that.'

Vocal

release **1 May 2013**
formats **Double 12" / CD / CD remix / CD promo / download × 3 / download remix**
photographer **John Ross**
design and art direction **Farrow / PSB**
video **Joost Vandebrug**

Released digitally ahead of *Electric*, 'Vocal' announced, says Neil, that 'this is a dance album'. A song both of and about the dancefloor, 'Vocal' had first been recorded during the sessions for *Elysium*, but had now been reimagined by Stuart Price. It was partly inspired by the recollection of nights out during the 1994 *Discovery* tour in South America 'and a lot of other memories like that, being on a dancefloor, the sense of community', says Neil. 'I like the story that emerges, too, of the singer who is lonely and strange.' Its sleeves uses photographs taken by John Ross of Neil and Chris in their Jeffrey Bryant plastic-straw costumes during rehearsals for the *Electric* tour in London. 'Farrow put them together so they're always upside down, or always the right way round, like a playing card', says Neil.

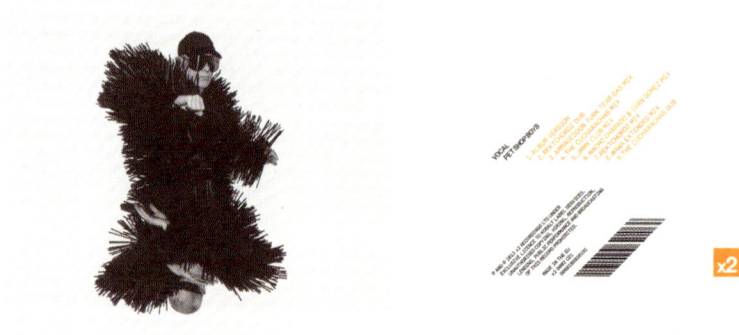

CD remix, outer sleeve, front   CD remix, outer sleeve, back

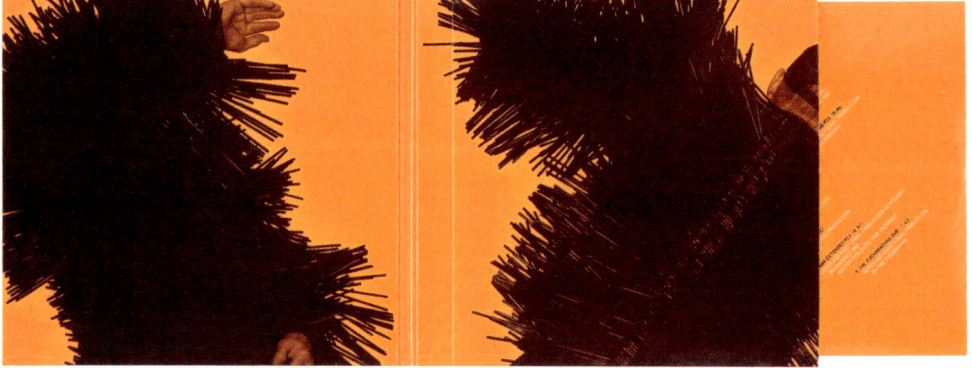

CD remix, outer sleeve, inside, and inner sleeve

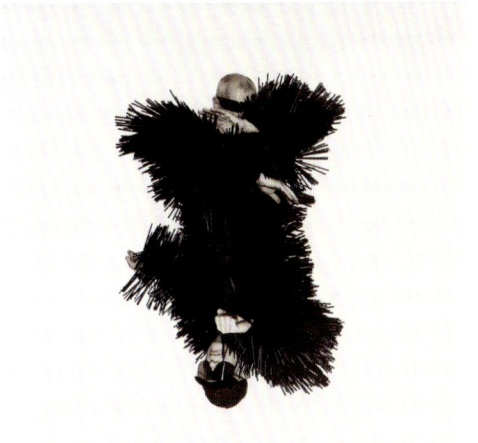

Double 12", outer sleeve, front

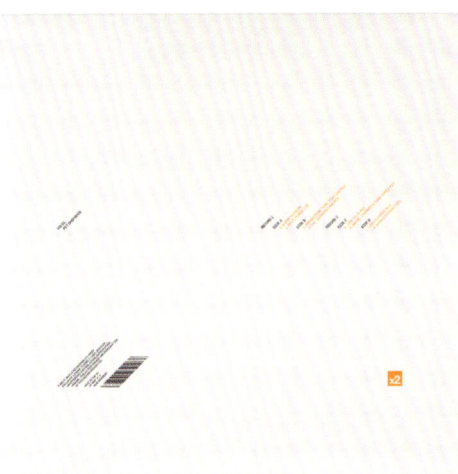

Double 12", outer sleeve, back

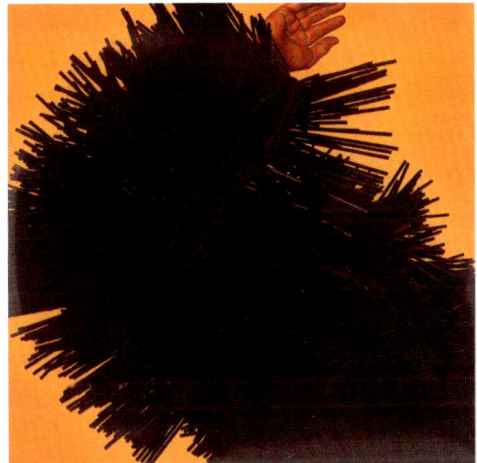

Double 12", inner sleeve, Record One, front

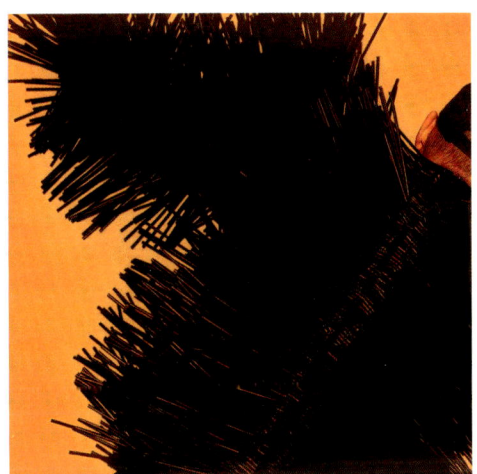

Double 12", inner sleeve, Record Two, front

Double 12", inner sleeve, Record One, back

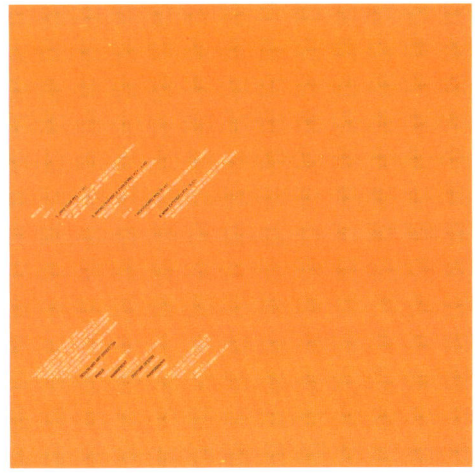

Double 12", inner sleeve, Record Two, back

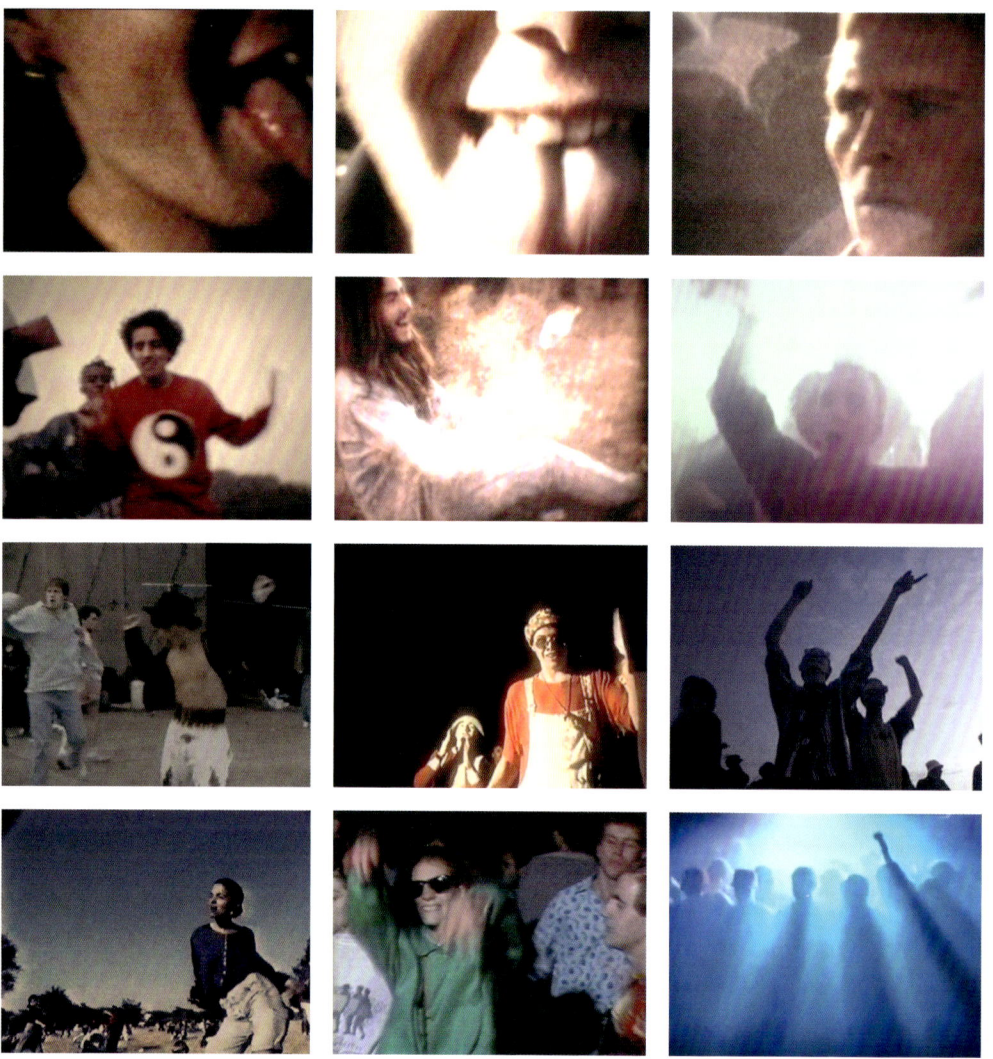

The 'Vocal' video was directed by Joost Vandebrug. He had promised the Pet Shop Boys that it would 'be a tribute to the spirit of the late Eighties raves and its awesome fashion'. He edited Super 8 footage filmed at raves and at the Hacienda in the late Eighties and the early Nineties. 'We just loved it immediately', says Neil. 'It visualizes exactly what the song's about.' 'It brought back a lot of memories', says Chris. 'The curtain haircuts! And the clothes are so different from now. It looks quite historic, doesn't it? I still think of it as being yesterday.'

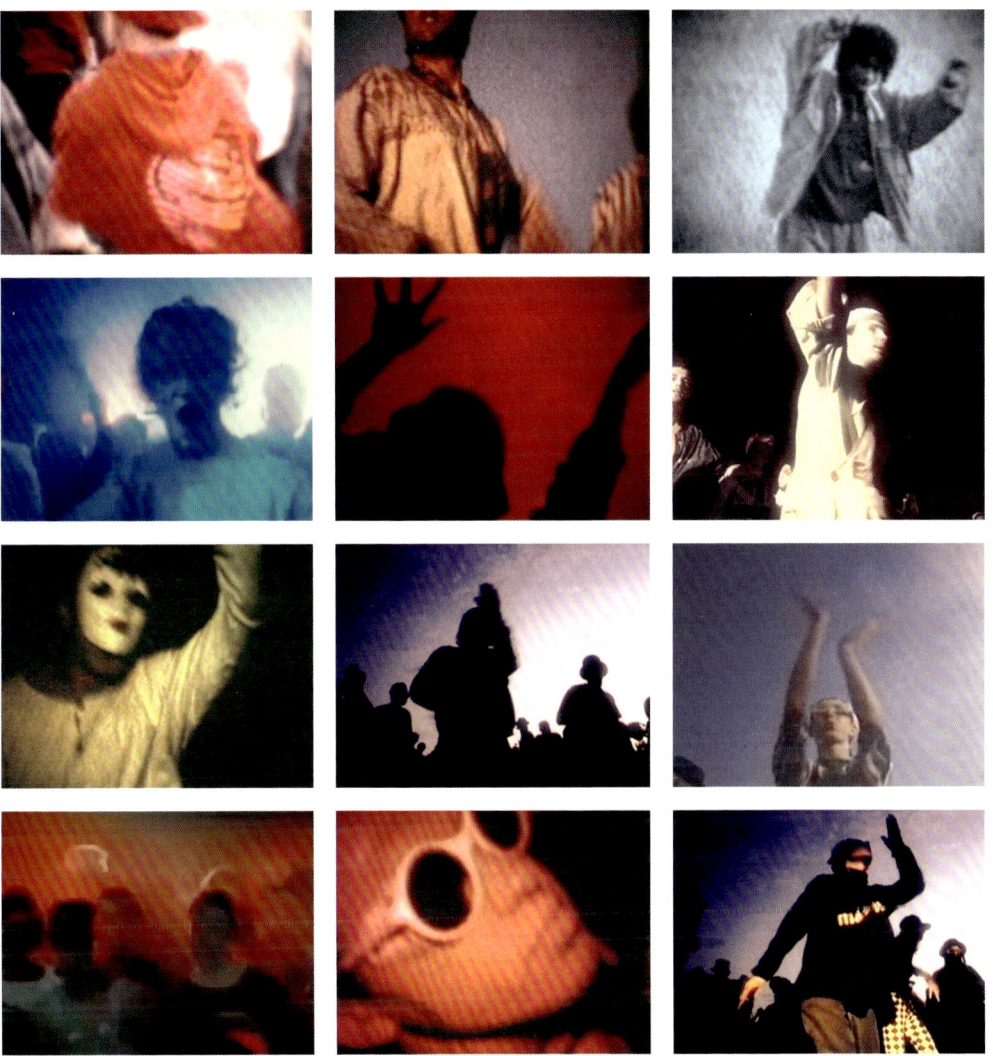

Electric

release 12 July 2013
formats Double LP / five-disc limited-edition LP /
CD / download
costumes Jeffrey Bryant
photographer John Ross
design and art direction Farrow / PSB

Asked upon its release why this new album was called *Electric*, Chris replied: 'Because it's not acoustic.' As Neil and Chris finished *Elysium*, they had talked about swiftly following up with a record that would sit in sharp contrast to it. Ten months later, the Stuart Price-produced *Electric* was the result – the moment, Neil would later reflect, where 'we turn into an electronic duo for the first time in our career, really'. As previously mentioned, one key catalyst was a fan's comment that they should be 'more banging and lasers'. 'This was a rebirthing album', says Neil. 'Chris constructed this idea of doing something called *Electric* with all the songs that we had lying around that we hadn't done, which I thought weren't necessarily that great. And yet I think the record is one of our best. It has songs that were in a way insubstantial but became really gorgeous.'

Electric's sleeve – 'the pattern is a lightning shock extended', says Chris – was devised by Farrow. 'It was only ever going to be a graphic sleeve', Mark Farrow recalls. 'We were messing about with these op-art patterns. The starting point was the electric strike, danger-of-death kind of thing. And then that developed into the zig-zag pattern, which was rather op-arty, and we quite liked that. At first, we were doing everything full bleed, with the idea that it would kind of fuck with your eyes a bit when you looked at it. But then I was walking past Fred [Ross]'s desk, and he was repositioning the electric image – it was in a fluorescent colour at that point – but he happened to put it inside the edges of the sleeve. It was one of those moments. I went, "Woah! Woah! There! That!" It was that straightforward. Done in a moment.'

'A brilliant cover', Neil says. 'I remember that we went in to see them in their office and Mark had a spiel about all that really mattered now was the little square on your phone. And he was absolutely right.' (This time around, Farrow's argument that there was no need for the artist name or title on the image was heeded.) Just one final adjustment was required. 'Neil and Chris really liked it', Farrow recalls. 'But Neil said, "It should be blue."' In explaining why, Neil quoted the lyrics of David Bowie's 'Sound and vision': 'Blue, blue, electric blue, that's the colour of my room.' Unusually for the regular album, as opposed to a remix album, for the vinyl LP, the nine tracks were presented on two records. The two inner sleeves featured enlarged and cropped versions of John Ross's photographs of Neil and Chris wearing their plastic-straw costumes designed by Jeffrey Bryant that had appeared on the sleeve of 'Vocal'.

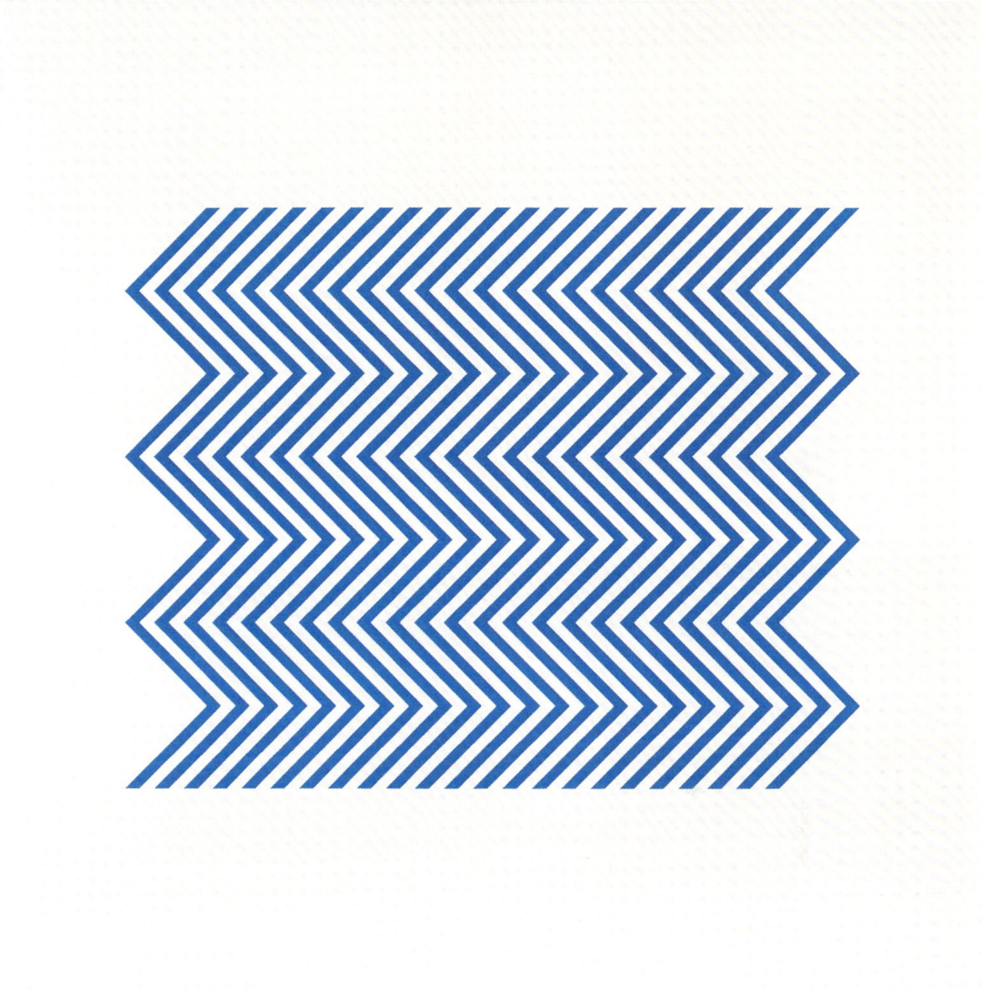

Double LP, outer sleeve, front

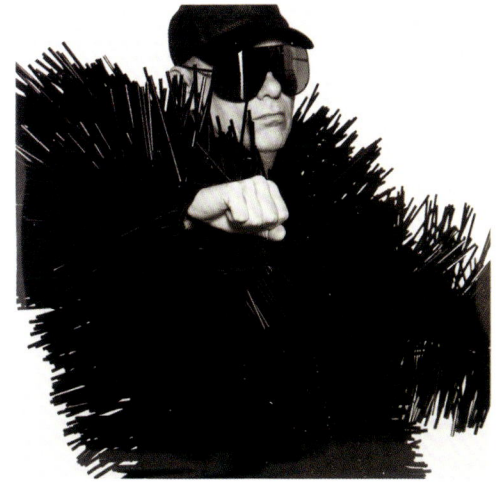

Double LP, inner sleeve, Record One, front

Double LP, outer sleeve, back

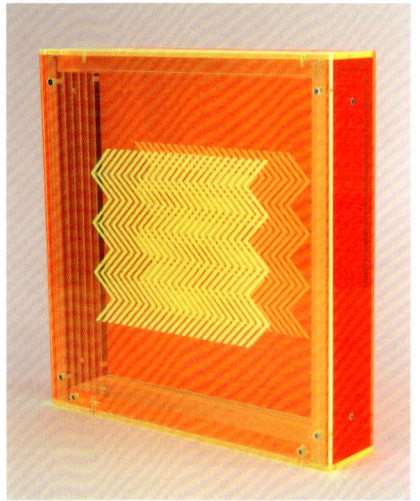
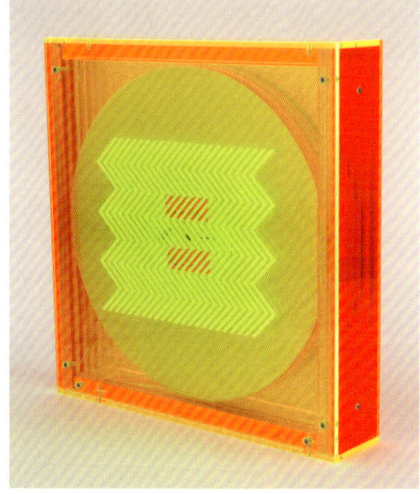

Five-disc limited-edition LP, outer box empty and with discs

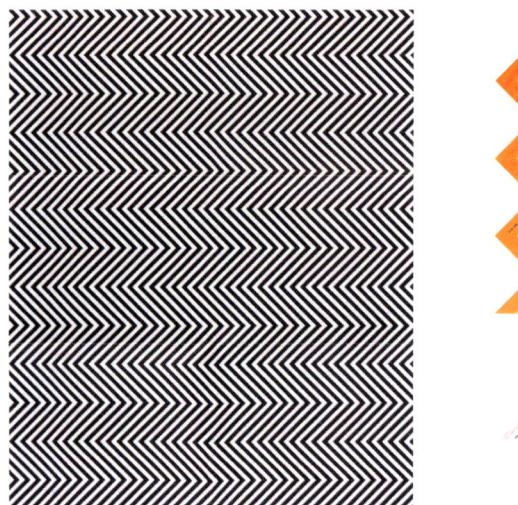
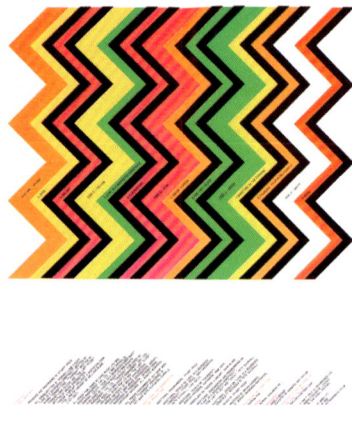

Five-disc limited-edition LP, insert with track listings and credits

The Vinyl Factory also released a limited edition of 300 signed copies: five discs inside a transparent box, complete with assembly instructions and white handling gloves. 'It looks absolutely gorgeous', says Neil. 'Each one was a different fluorescent disk', says Farrow. 'We didn't want sleeves. We wanted it to be this self-contained thing. The idea was that it would just glow. And then when you take the records out, they also glow. It had this glow-edged fluorescent plastic, so it's like a prism – it sucks in all the light, which comes out concentrated on the edges.' The five discs contain the album's nine songs, and there was debate about what should go on the reverse of the fifth disc. A remix? An etching? In the end, it was decided that all the options seemed less than leaving it be. 'The blank side's rather exciting, I think', says Neil. 'It's my favourite side', says Chris.

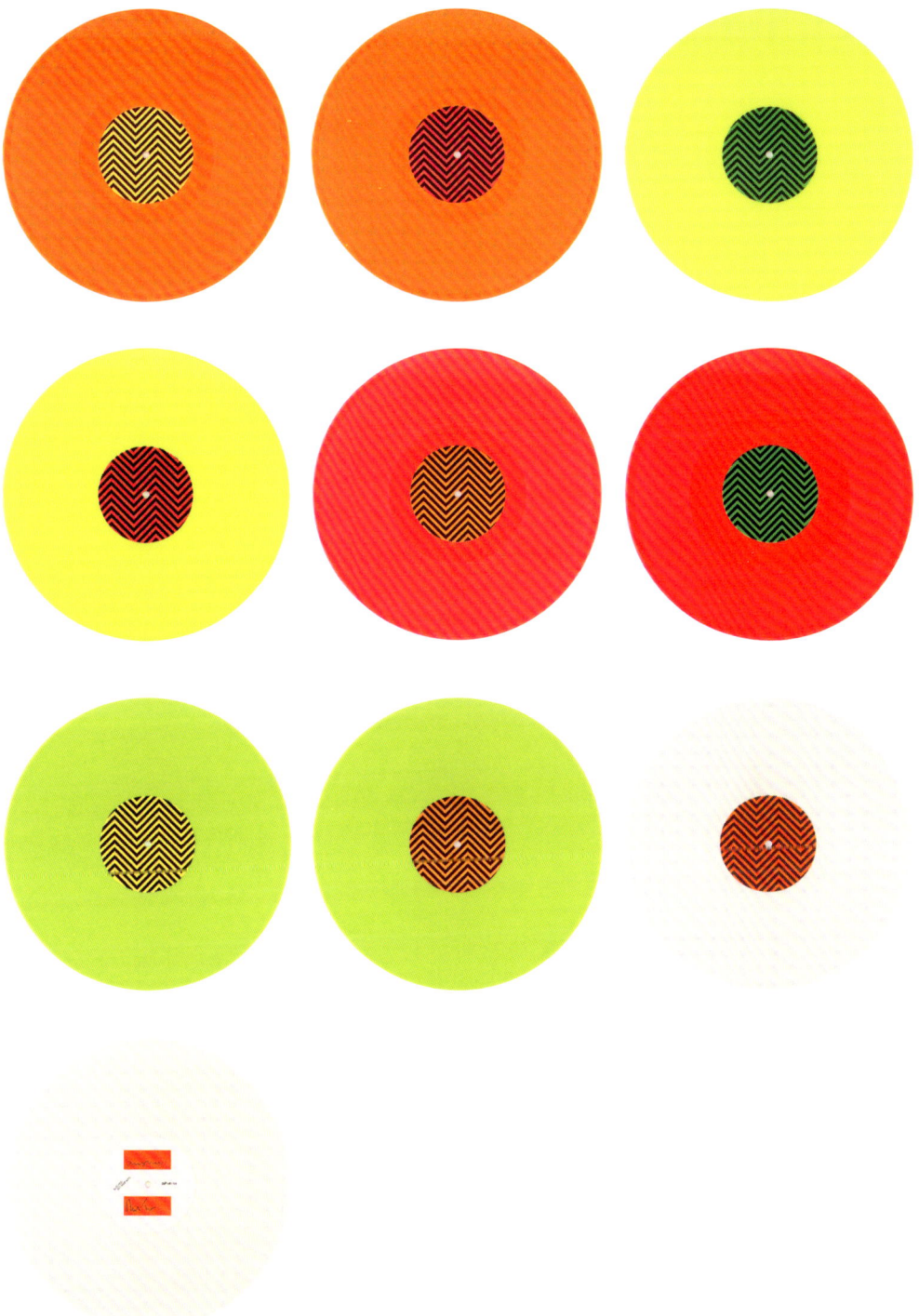

Five-disc limited-edition LP, discs:
Disc One – Orange; Disc Two – Yellow;
Disc Three – Pink; Disc Four – Green
Disc Five – White

Love is a bourgeois construct

release **1 September 2013**
formats **2 × 12" / 2 × CD / CD promo × 2 / download × 2**
design and art direction **Farrow / PSB**

This song's twin seeds were the phrase 'love is a bourgeois construct', which Neil had written in his phone after reading David Lodge's novel *Nice Work*, and Chris's suggestion that they create something based upon Michael Nyman's 'Chasing sheep is best left to shepherds'. Its sleeve, a purely graphic one, has conceptually appropriate constructivist type. 'And we don't even approve of constructivist type', Chris notes. 'We think it's been overdone in pop music', explains Neil. 'It was done in the late Seventies, by people like Kraftwerk, then more recently by Franz Ferdinand. But actually it looked really good.' They considered making a video, but they felt the song necessitated something quite extravagant. 'We got a load of treatments in', says Neil, 'and we didn't like any of them.'

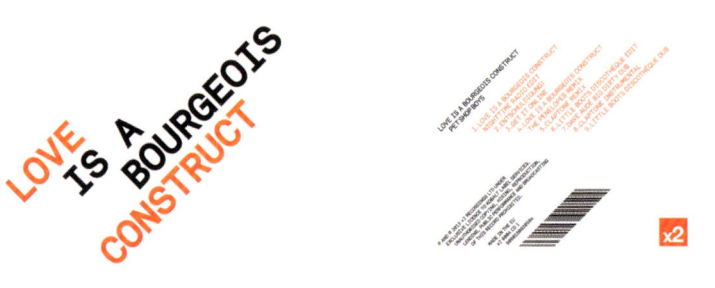

2 × CD, outer sleeve, front   2 × CD, outer sleeve, back

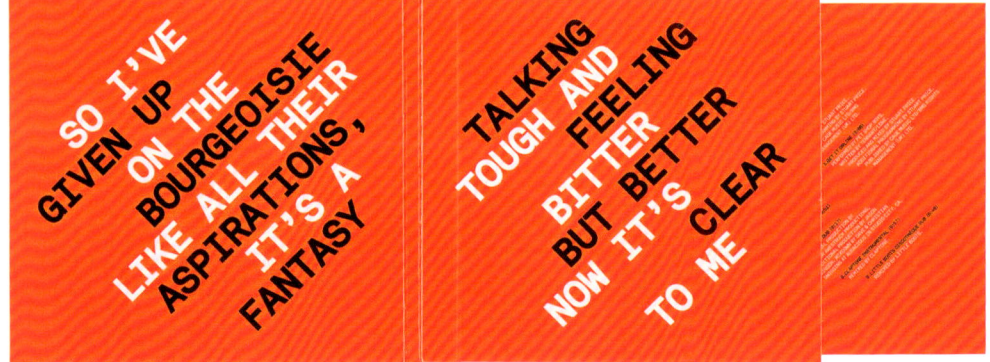

2 × CD, outer sleeve, inside, and inner sleeve

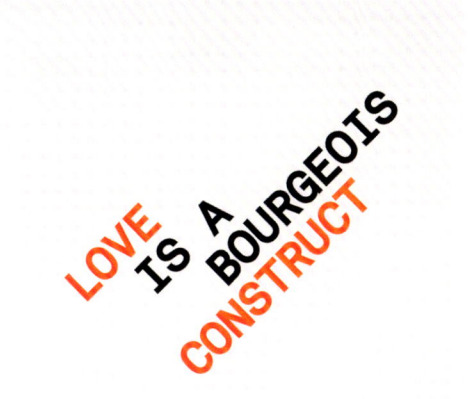

2 × 12", outer sleeve, front

2 × 12", outer sleeve, back

2 × 12", inner sleeve, Record One, front

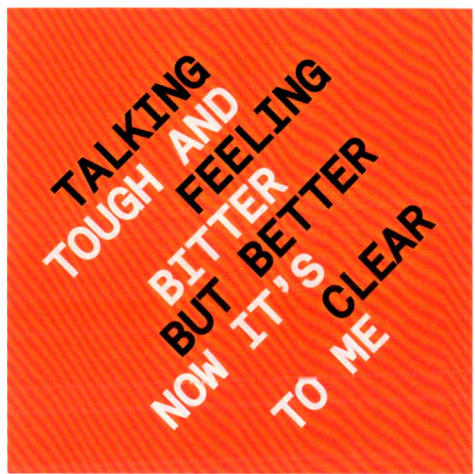

2 × 12", inner sleeve, Record Two, front

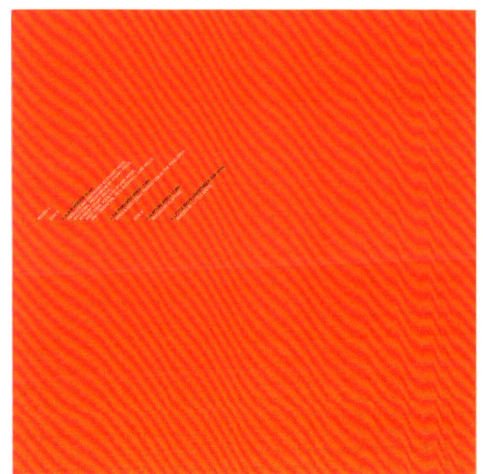

2 × 12", inner sleeve, Record One, back

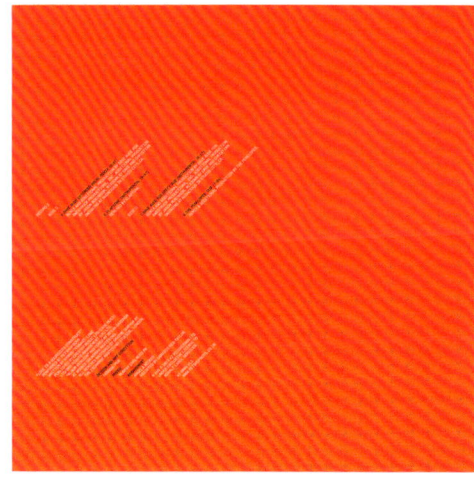

2 × 12", inner sleeve, Record Two, back

Thursday

release 4 November 2013
formats 12" / CD / CD promo / CD remix promo × 2 /
download × 2 / download remix
photographer John Ross
design and art direction Farrow / PSB
video Justyn Field

Of 'Thursday', Neil says, 'God, it's like a real pop lyric. I'm always impressed when I come up with something utterly banal because I think it's a very difficult thing to come up with.' The various sleeves all used the same image of Chris in his mirrorball helmet from the *Electric* tour, shot by John Ross for the tour programme (where it appeared, on page 5, largely covered by a red-orange-black zigzag flash), a decision they do not remember labouring. 'Farrow said, "Well, we may as well have this, don't you think?"' says Neil. 'To which we said, "Yes."' As is true throughout the *Electric* releases, all of the text was on a diagonal, mirroring the angle of the blue electric flash. 'There's nothing that's horizontal at all', says Gary Stillwell. 'That's the sort of stupid trick we'd pull', notes Mark Farrow.

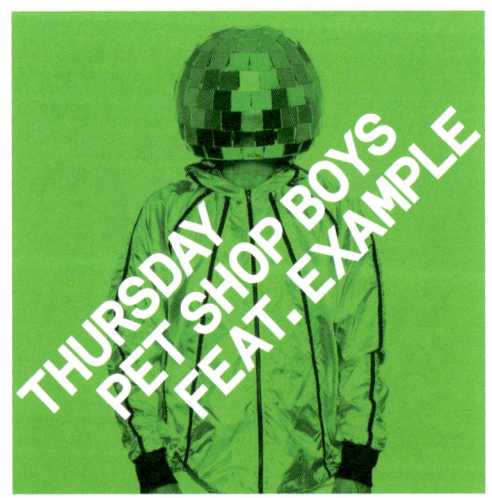

Download

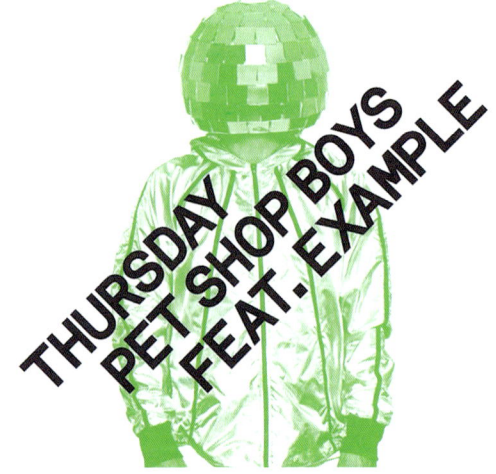

Download remix

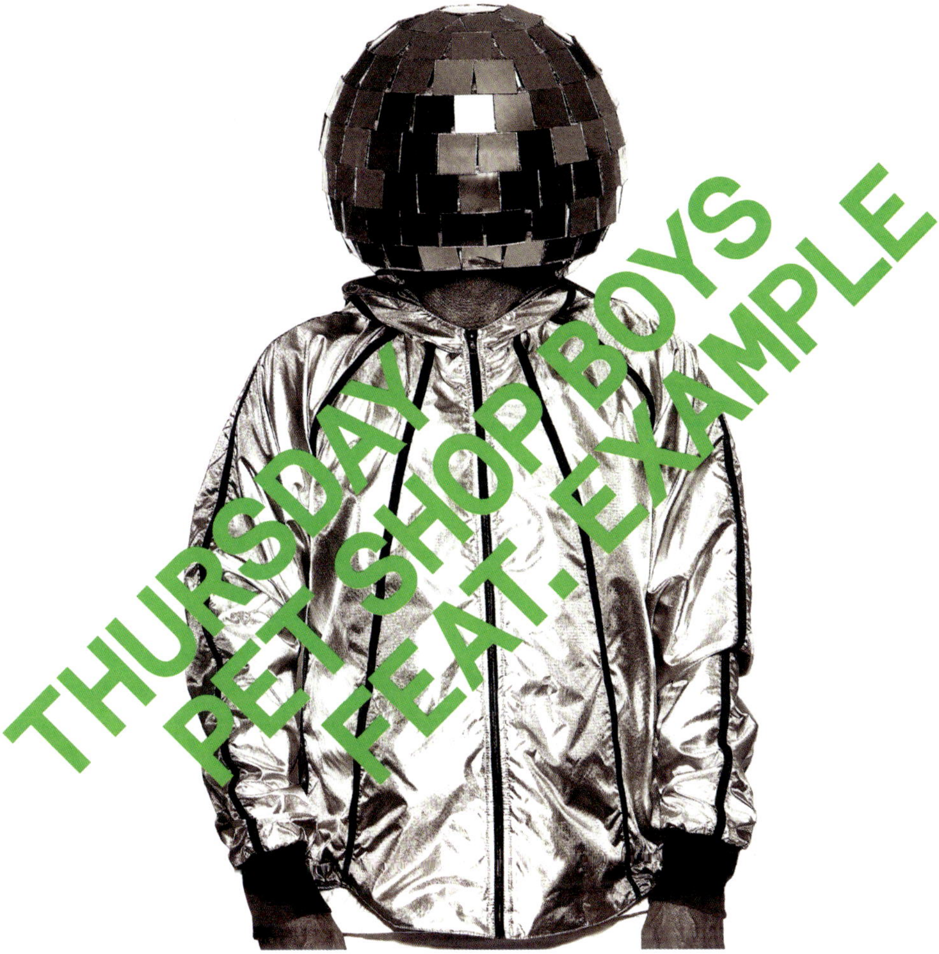

THURSDAY
PET SHOP BOYS
FEAT. EXAMPLE

12", front

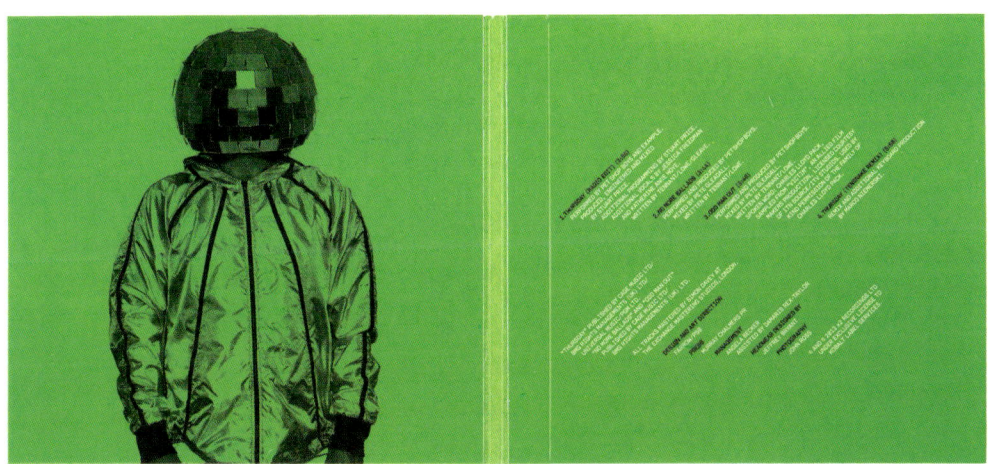

CD, inside

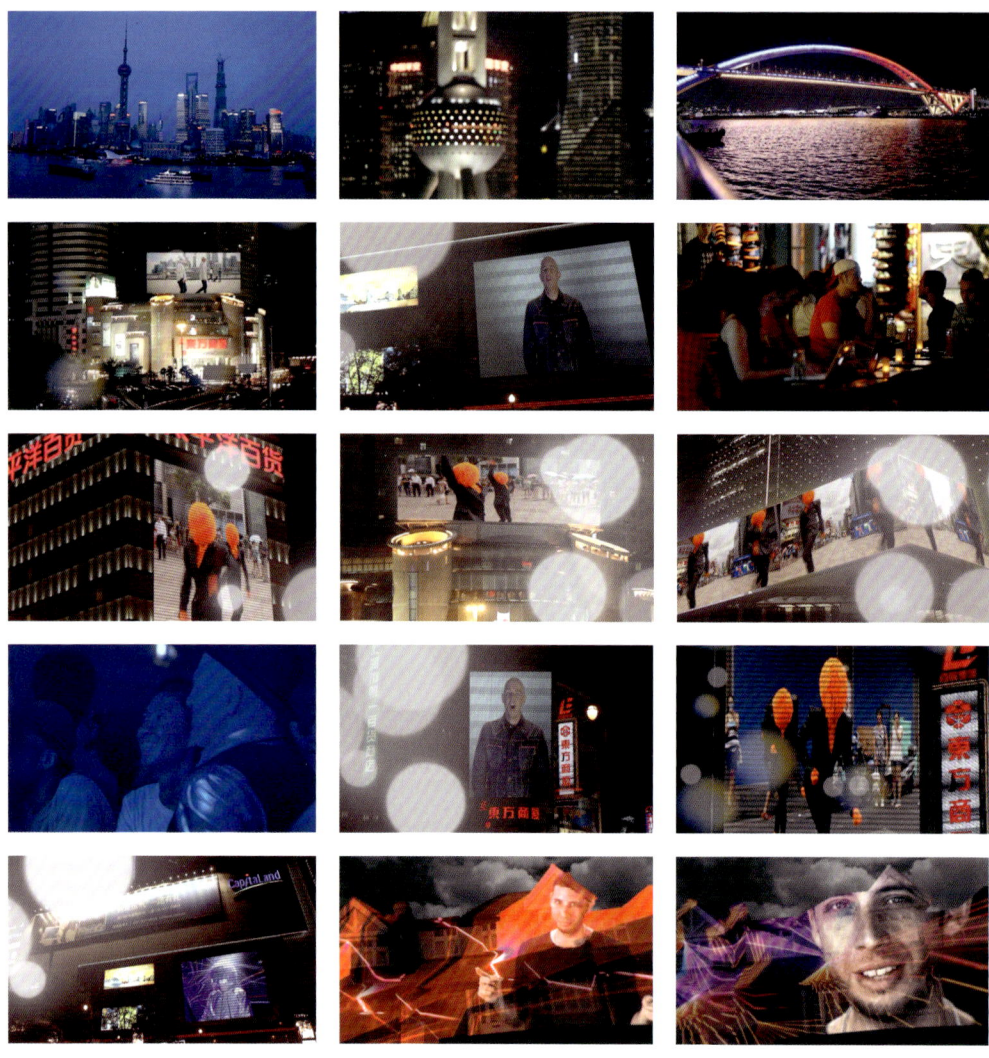

The video for 'Thursday' was filmed in Shanghai in August 2013 when Pet Shop Boys were playing two dates in China. 'Originally it was going to be a live video with audience shots,' says Neil, 'and then we decided we'd wander round Shanghai with Chris wearing the disco ball.' 'We made it all night-time', says Chris. When they saw the live footage, they decided that they didn't like that, and so would ultimately use only audience-reaction shots. 'Then,' says Neil, 'Justyn Field, the director, put Example on one of the buildings in Shanghai, and as soon as we saw that we wanted it all the way through – we wanted all of the song on the buildings outside.'

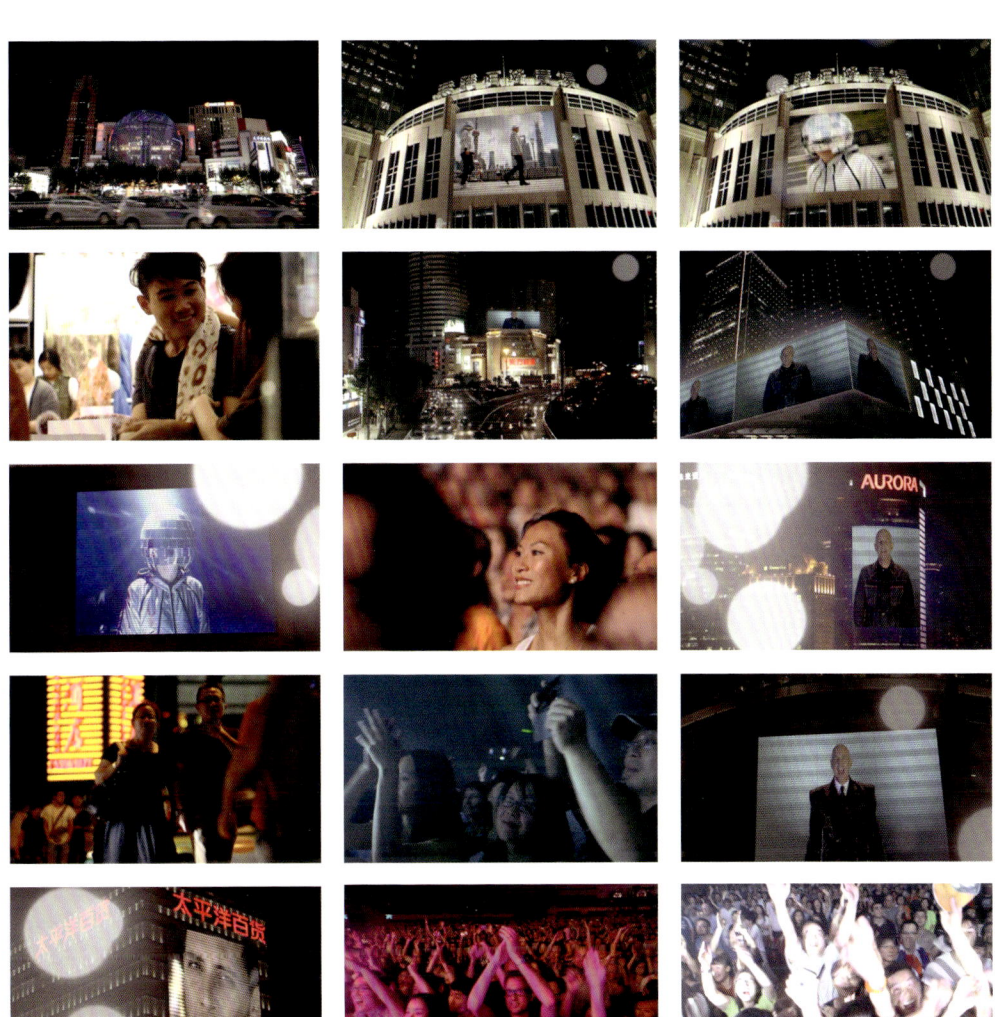

Fluorescent

release 19 April 2014
formats 12"
design Farrow / PSB

'Fluorescent' was based on a demo Chris wrote at home one evening – 'Sometimes when I'm a bit bored and there's absolutely nothing on television – and there has to be literally nothing on television, not even *Newsnight* – I might go down to the basement and knock something up if I feel like it' – around which Neil fashioned a narrative 'about a model like Kate Moss, a very glamorous person'. For Record Store Day 2014, Pet Shop Boys released a twelve-inch single of what were credited as remixes but which were effectively re-recordings done by Neil and Chris in Berlin; the mix names, 'Cali' and 'Indio' referred to the Coachella festival, at which the Pet Shop Boys were appearing for the first time that month. Its sleeve was again a generic x2 sleeve, like the 'Axis' twelve-inch single (page 406). 'One side of it was the logo, and the other side has a hole', says Mark Farrow. 'The logo is a square with "times two" in it.' 'I remember there was a little bit of a debate about the fact that the multiplication symbol is different from a letter "x"', says Gary Stillwell. Design won out over pure orthographic logic: 'It ended up being an "x" in the end.'

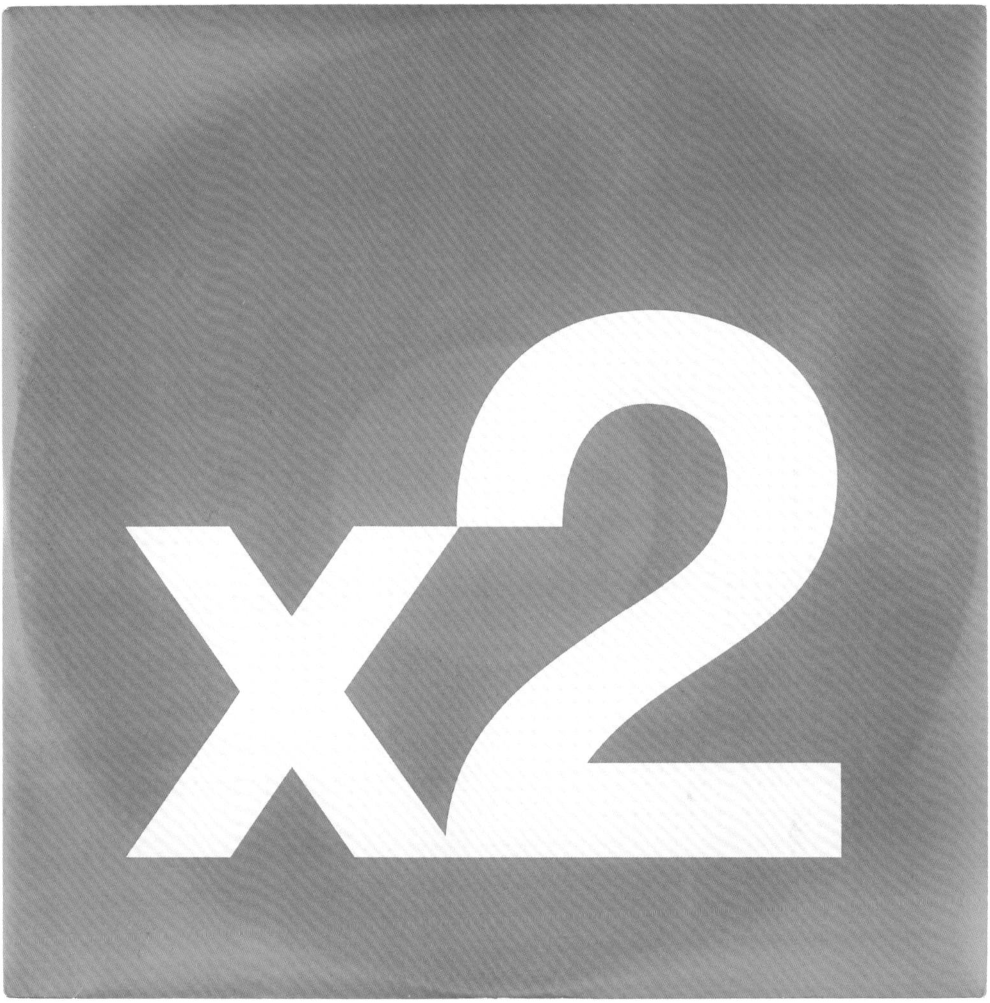

12", front

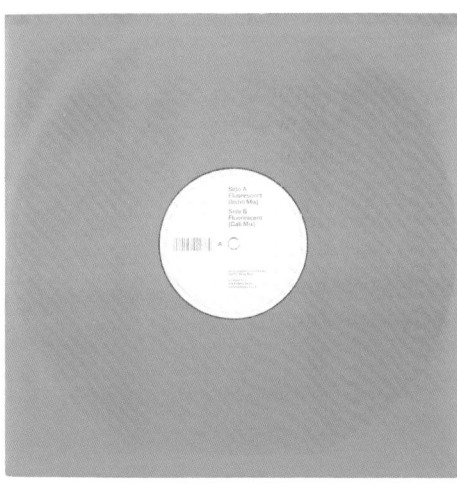

12", back

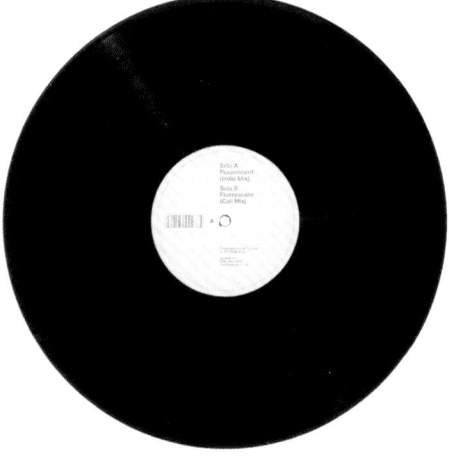

12", disc

Fluorescent 2014 425

A Man from the Future

date 23 July 2014
location Royal Albert Hall, London

In 2011, first Chris and then Neil watched a Channel 4 docudrama, *Codebreaker*, about the British scientist Alan Turing, a pioneer in computing who had been instrumental in cracking Nazi wartime codes, but who was later prosecuted for then-illegal homosexual acts, and who died at the age of forty-one by what an inquest adjudged was suicide. They both also subsequently read Andrew Hodges' 1981 biography *Alan Turing: The Enigma*. Initially, they considered Turing's story for a potential new ballet. Neil remembers that at times Hodges' book seemed bafflingly mathematical, but that nonetheless 'I went through with a biro and underlined what I thought were beautiful phrases. One of which, for example, was "He dreamed of machines": "In Grantchester that summer, lying in a meadow, Alan Turing dreamed of machines." I thought, "Oh, that's really gorgeous." Also, I couldn't believe no one had written a song called "He dreamed of machines".' Someone now would.

Neil and Chris started work on an interlinked series of songs about Turing's life and work, eventually titled *A Man from the Future*. As they did so, their goals were not purely musical. 'The point is to get him pardoned', said Chris in the autumn of 2012. A campaign to this effect was ongoing, and bills had been introduced in the British parliament, but their prospects were still unclear until, in December 2013, Queen Elizabeth II unilaterally signed a royal pardon. In the meantime, the Pet Shop Boys had begun a collaboration with Hodges, who by happenstance was a fan: in his 2008 book *One to Nine: The Inner Life of Numbers*, he had illustrated mathematical points with references to Pet Shop Boys' songs (for instance: 'As usual the Pet Shop Boys are right on target with "Two Divided by Zero': there is a problem'; or 'For an aural image of this final chapter, hear the Pet Shop Boys end their *Introspective*, suggesting how the music will go on and on and on and on.'). In July 2014, at the Royal Albert Hall, as part of the BBC Proms, and following their first live performance of 'Overture to Performance' from the 1991 *Performance* tour, and four Pet Shop Boys songs arranged by Angelo Badalamenti and sung by Chrissie Hynde, *A Man from the Future* was performed for the first time, Neil and Chris appearing with the BBC Singers and the BBC Concert Orchestra, conducted by Dominic Wheeler, with live narration from the actress Juliet Stevenson.

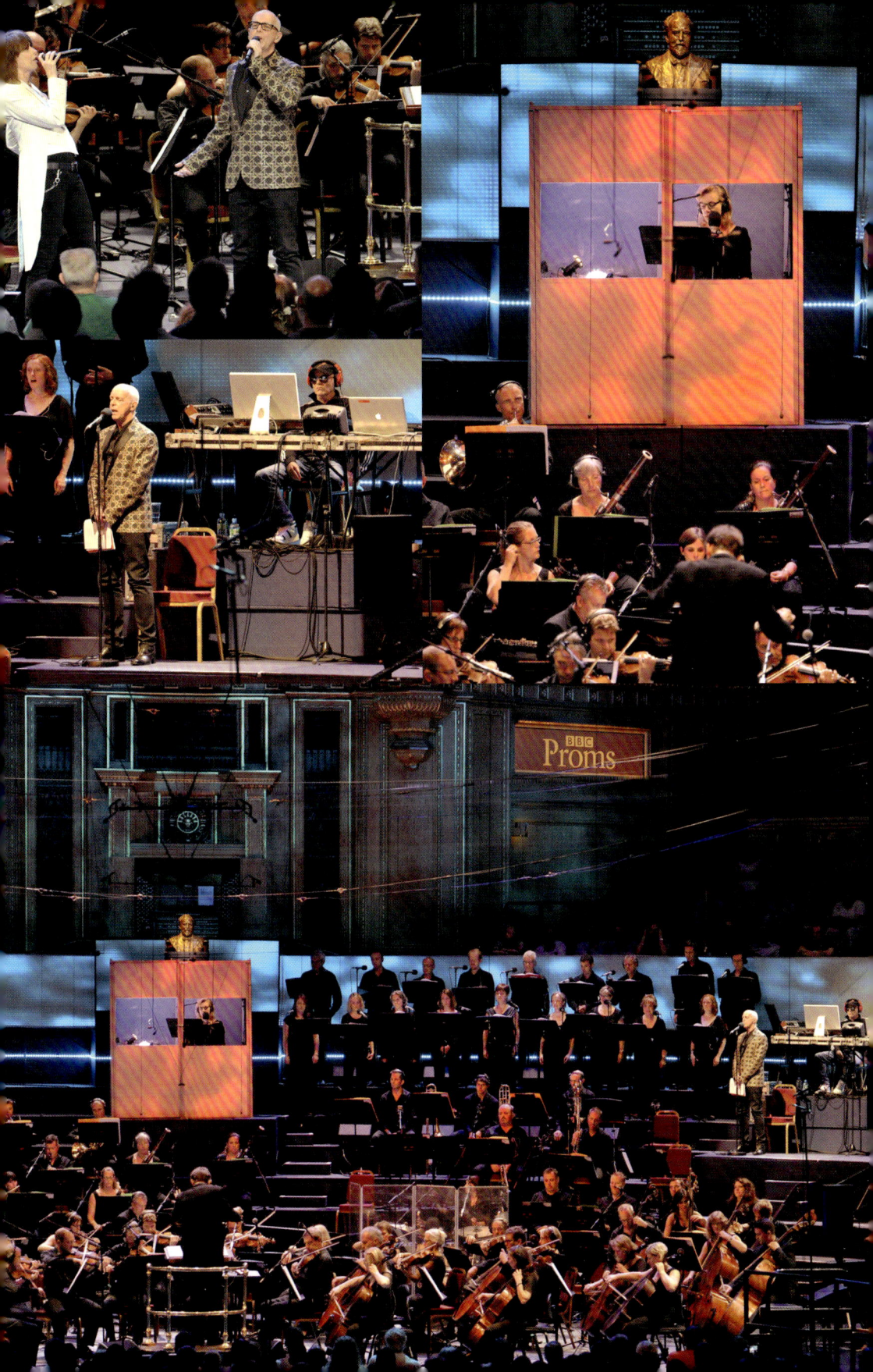

The pop kids

release 18 March 2016
formats 12" / CD / CD remix / CD promo × 3 /
download × 2 / download remix
design and art direction Farrow / PSB
live performance design Es Devlin

The first single from the forthcoming album *Super* was based on a track that Chris had written during the Take That tour in 2011. For the lyrics, says Neil, 'I had this idea based on a friend of mine who indeed went to university in London in the early '90s, and he made friends with a girl and they did what it says it in the song: they used to go out clubbing all the time, and they loved pop music and dance music, and people at university used to call them "the pop kids".' The song offers a fictional tale, but also some more abstract and eternal values: 'It's celebrating what the song "Vocal" celebrates: euphoria, and camaraderie, and friendship, and all those things you can get out of pop music. Also, it's celebrating people who take something trivial seriously. Pop music, which is ostensibly trivial, is also very important. We've always thought that. So it's celebrating the type of person who thinks that.'

    The sleeve previews the circle motif of the artwork for *Super*. The images behind the title are taken from a promotional video set to the song 'Inner sanctum'. 'We were launching the Royal Opera House shows,' says Neil, 'and we made a short film with Lynne Page choreographing dancers. It's just people jumping up and down.' 'We took stills from the video', says Gary Stillwell, 'and then we just overlaid different images – layered them all up and coloured them in.'

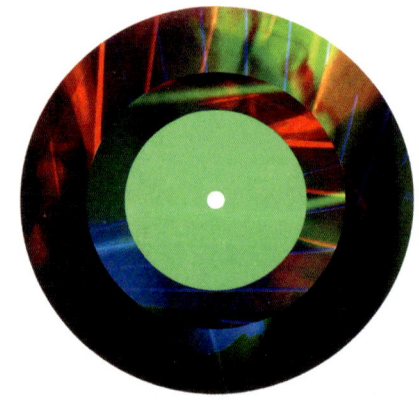

CD, inside

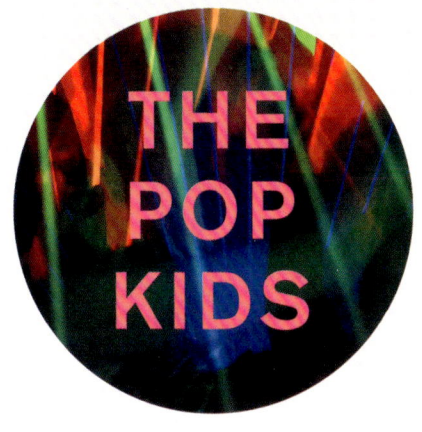

12", outer sleeve, front

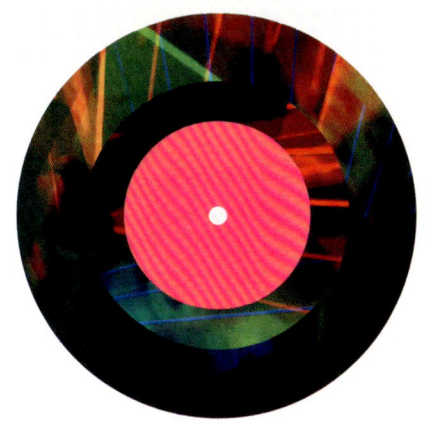

12", inner sleeve, back

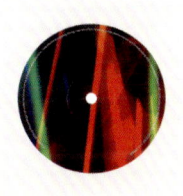

12", Side A

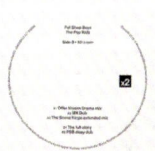

12", Side B

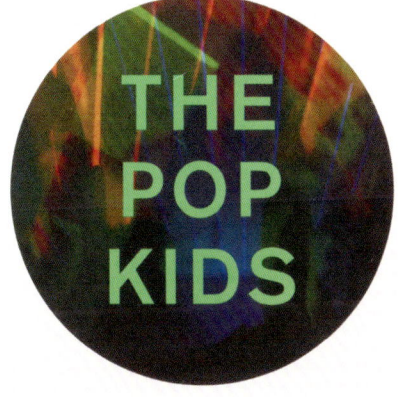

CD, front

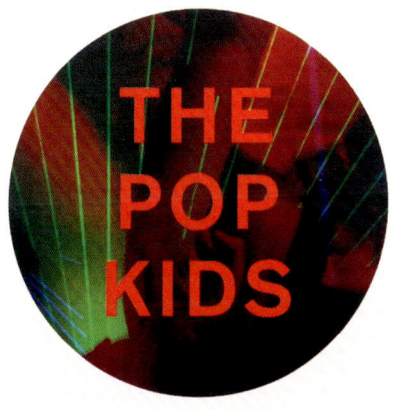

CD promo 3, front

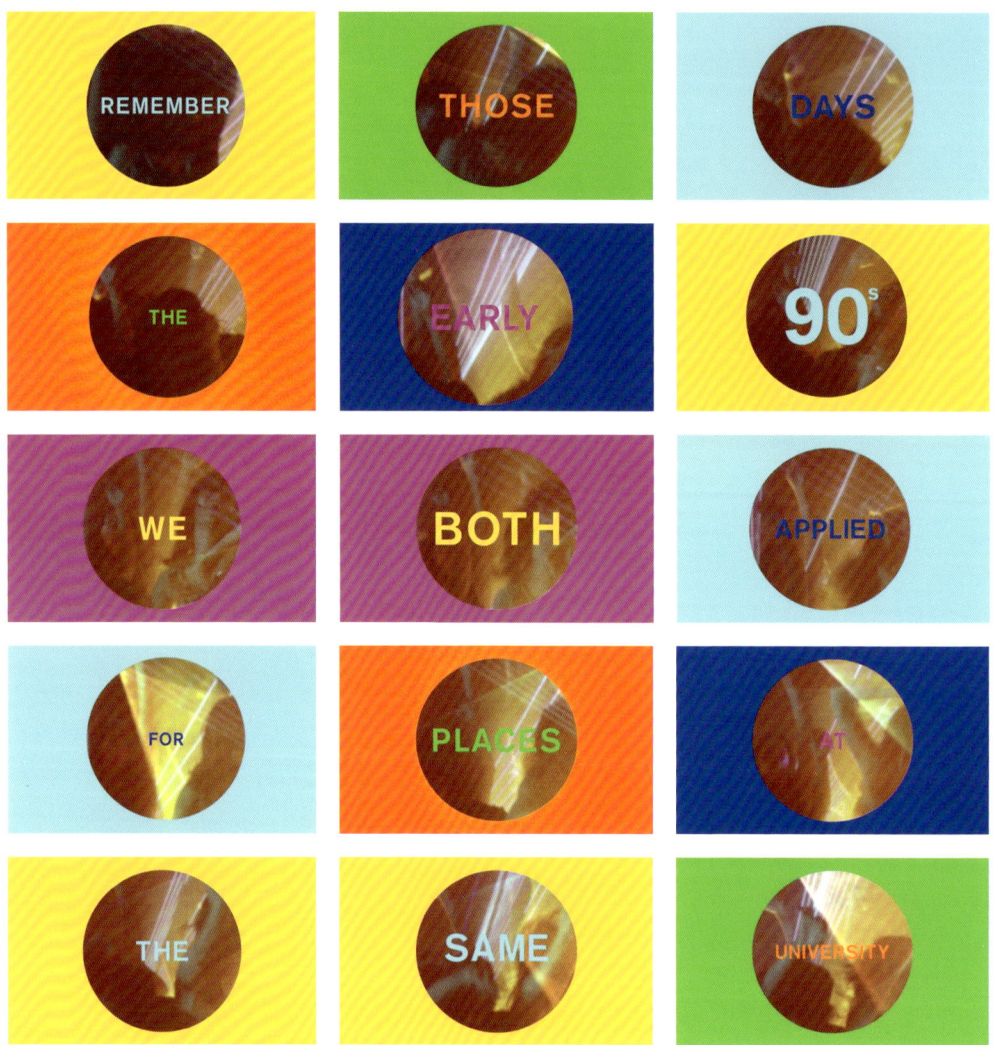

A lyric video expands on the same idea, using the same circle and typeface as the sleeve, with the Royal Opera House footage in the background. 'We didn't make a proper video', says Neil. 'I don't remember why, but a lot of the time it was budget issues. Though we did more or less get a video for "The pop kids" when we performed it on *The Graham Norton Show* on BBC1 because that was totally designed by Es Devlin – a whole setting that reflected the graphic approach of Farrow. It goes to the whole design concept. In many ways, that was the video. It was like we'd done a performance video – we just performed it live on *Graham Norton*.' 'Though the best video for it', notes Chris, 'was the unofficial one that an Israeli DJ made himself' ['The Pop Kids Offer Nissim Remix Purim Tribute']. 'It's brilliant', Neil concurs. 'I watch it all the time', says Chris.

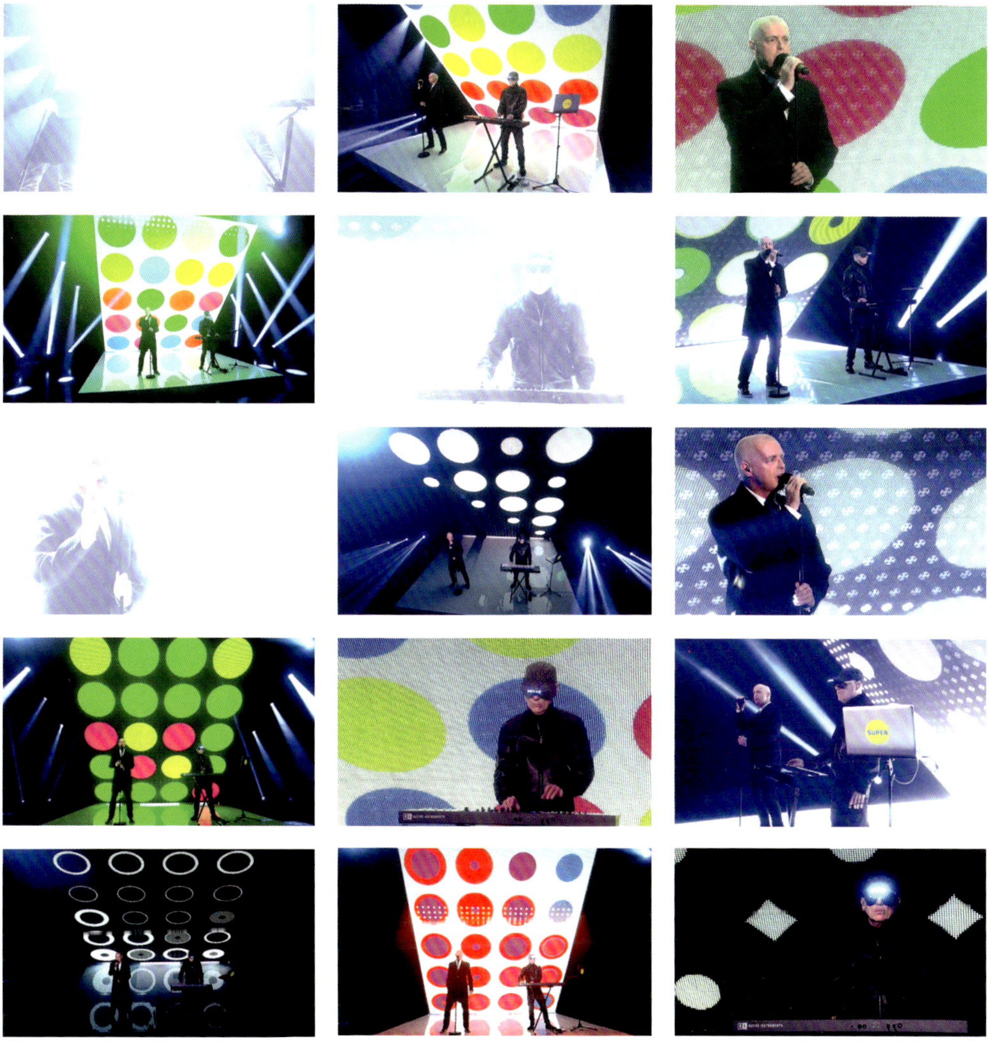

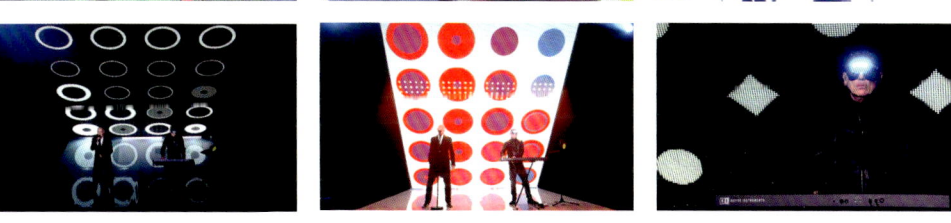

Super

release 1 April 2016
formats LP / CD / download
photographer Pelle Crépin
design and art direction Farrow / PSB

Neil and Chris considered *Super*, their second Stuart Price-produced album, an evolution from its predecessor: 'Whereas *Electric* was super-dance, this has got a lot of dancey tracks but what links it together is sort of its electronic-ness.' The title was Chris's: 'I was walking to our studio in London one day and it just came into my head. I don't know why.' 'It seemed to fit this mood of the album', says Neil. 'It's a great word. It sounds like one of our albums.'

    It was decided early on that the album would have a typographic sleeve using the album title. 'So it'd be a bit like a piece of pop art', says Chris. 'It started with Chris literally going, "I want something that's really gauche and loud and shouty"', says Mark Farrow. 'I just remember him, right from the off, going: it should just be really loud.' The path to the final design was nonetheless a meandering one. An important catalyst was a hat with a circle on it that Chris bought at a West Hollywood clothes shop, H. Lorenzo, while they were recording the album. 'That was when the SUPER in a circle idea came through', says Neil. But meanwhile Neil and Chris also did a photo session, much of it with heavy make-up. 'And when they did it, they just hated them', says Farrow. 'I was at the session, and as far as I remember, it was more or less scrapped before we'd finished taking the photographs. It just looked kind of like the Casanova period: beauty spots and the white face.' Less made-up photos from that session would appear within the album artwork (part-covered with circles of various sizes and colours). But that was not to be the front sleeve.

    For a time, says Gary Stillwell, they explored using images from the Hubble deep field telescope. 'A super expanse of space and all that sort of thing', explains Farrow. 'It was all looking very nice', says Stillwell. 'Then I think at some point, someone just said, "But is it as big and bold as we want it to be?" And I think we all decided it wasn't.' They eventually seemed to have settled on a white SUPER inside a coloured circle, but there was one more important change to be made. Chris suggested that the word SUPER, too, could be different colour. 'Which kind of just finished it all off', says Stillwell. Different combinations of colours were designed not just for each physical format, but for different streaming services: one for Apple Music / iTunes, one for Spotify, and one for miscellaneous other streamers. 'The idea was basically', says Stillwell, 'that wherever you saw the album, it would be a different colour.'

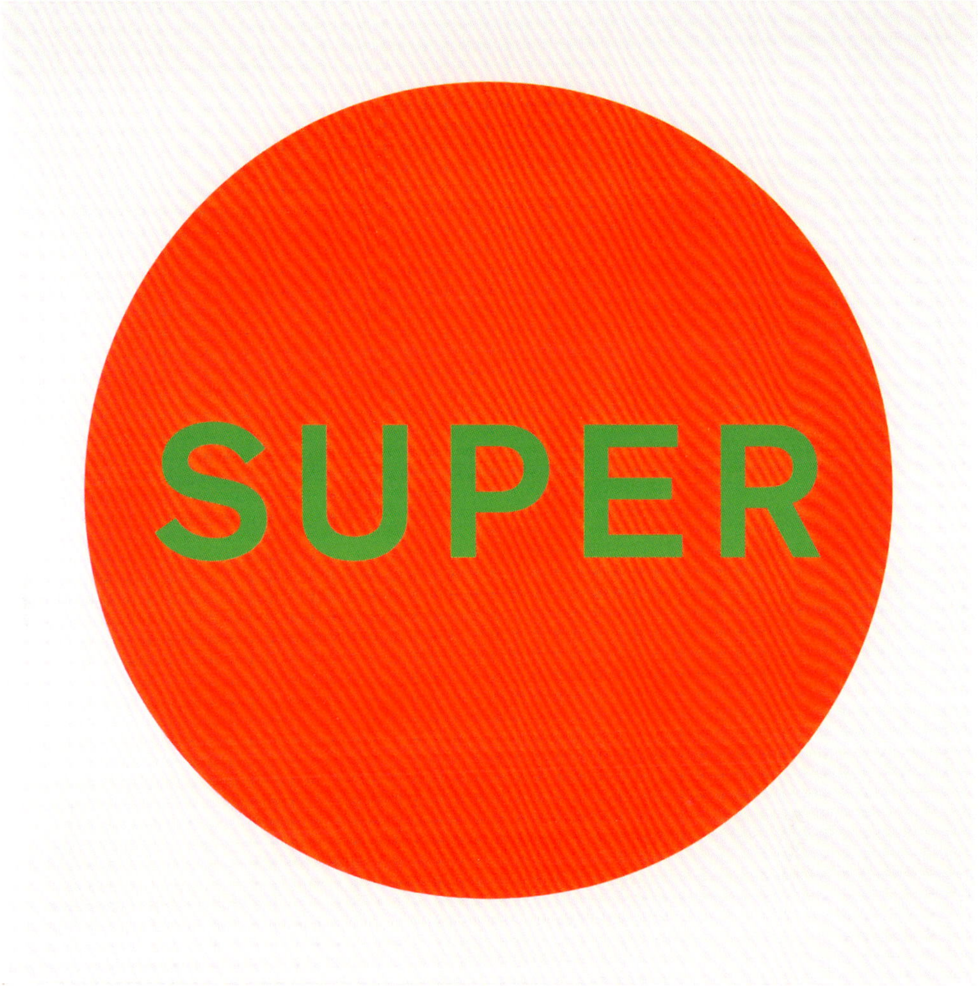

LP, outer sleeve, front

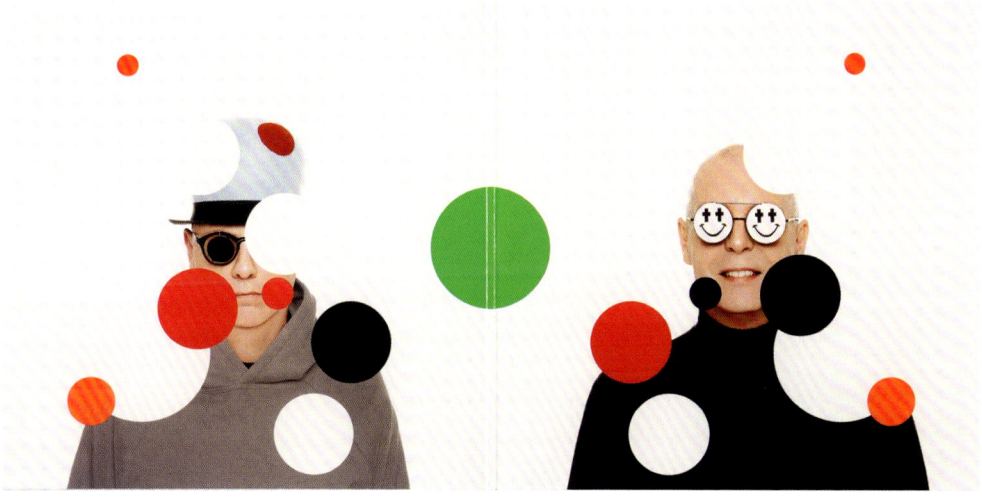

LP, inner sleeve, inside

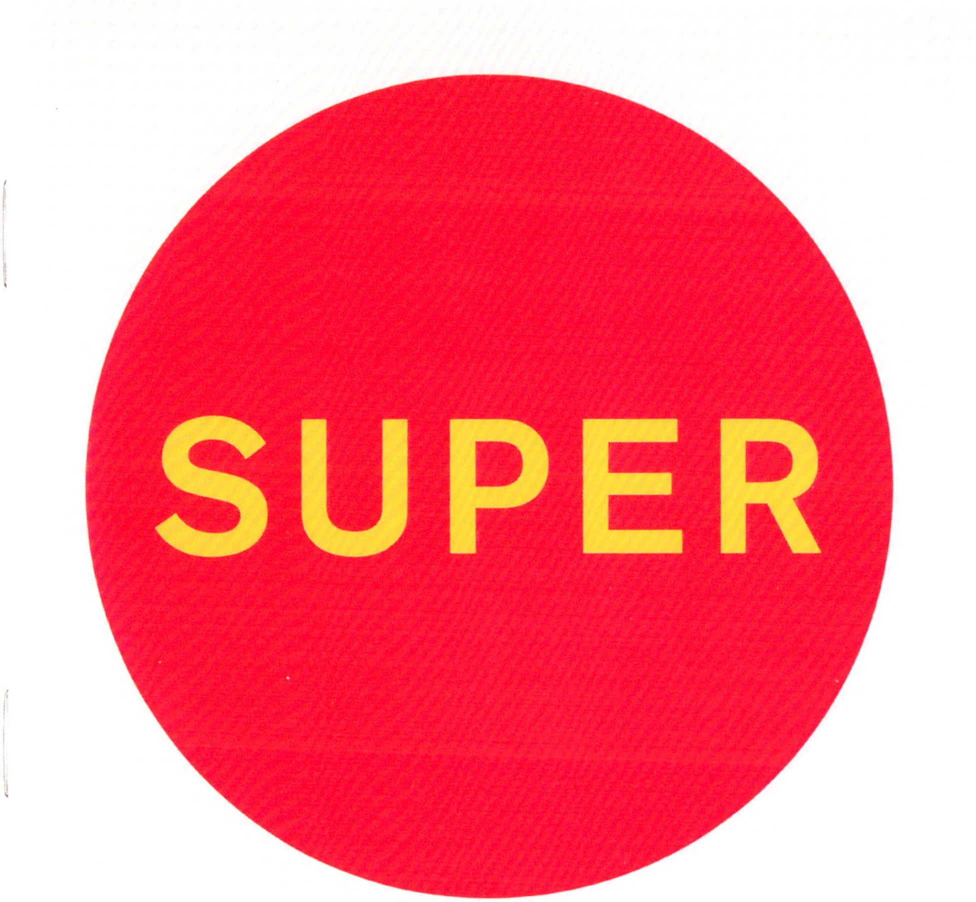

CD, booklet, front

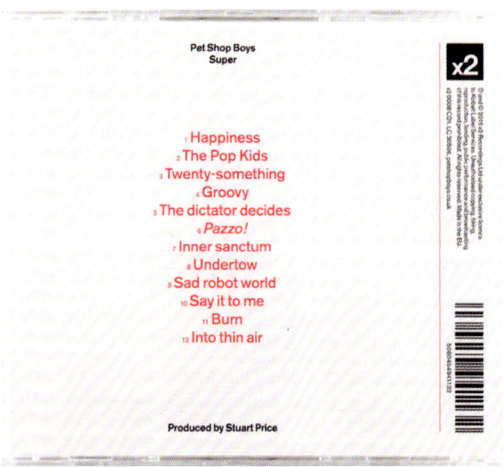

CD, back

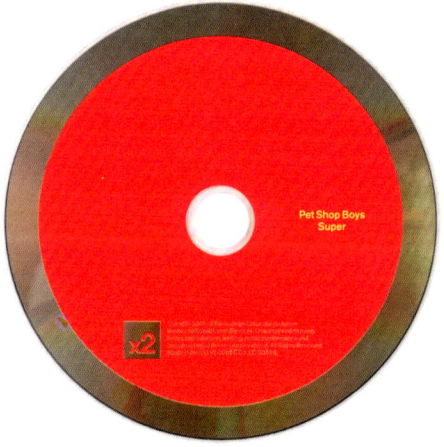

CD, disc

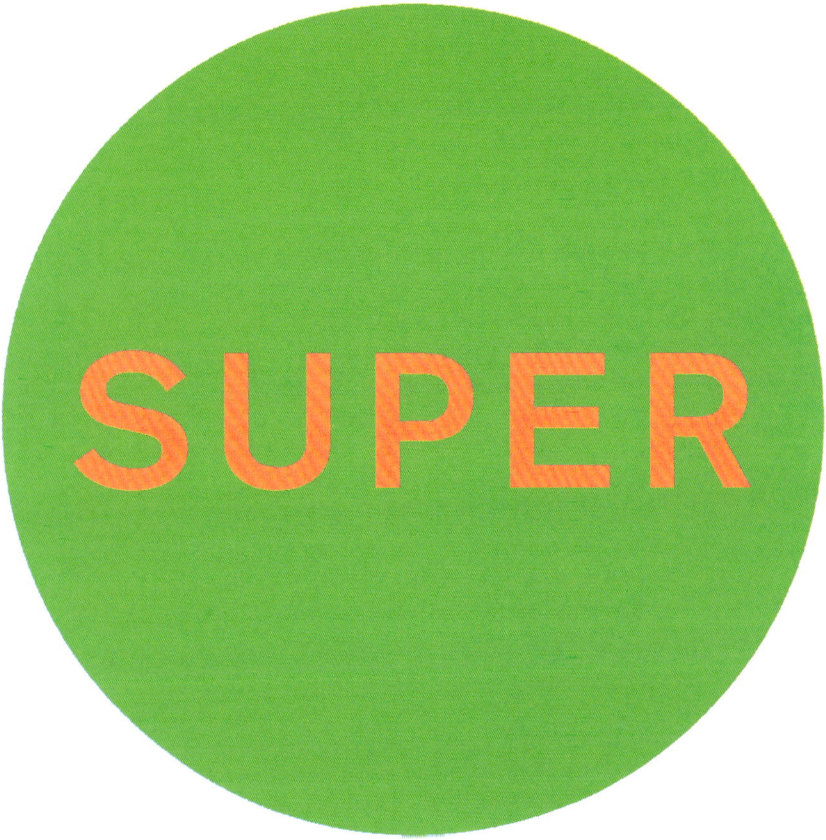

Download, Spotify

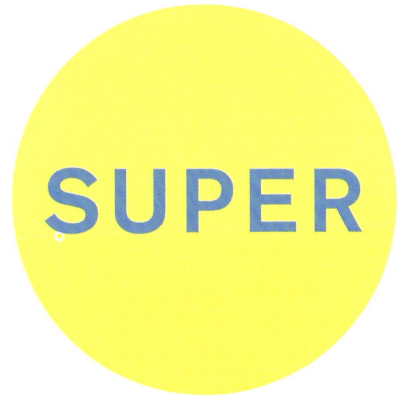

Download, Apple

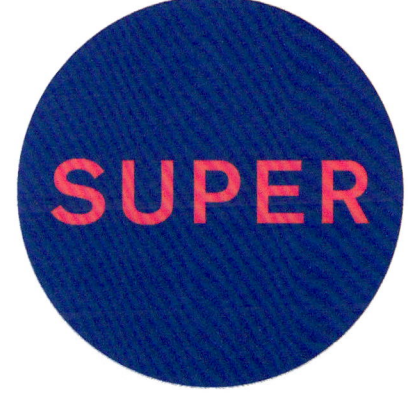

Download, other

Twenty-something

release 24 June 2016
formats CD / CD promo / download
design and art direction Farrow / PSB
video Gavin Filipiak

The music of 'Twenty-something' was inspired by a Reggaeton rhythm the Pet Shop Boys heard on the top floor of a club in Colombia in 2013, and by a Henry Purcell piece that Chris came across in the same opera from which Michael Nyman's 'Chasing sheep is best left to shepherds' was derived. For its lyrics, says Neil, 'I was thinking about what a hard life it is for people in London who are twenty-something.' 'Social commentary, everyone, to a disco beat', comments Chris. 'It's also really a song about London', says Neil. 'It's also suggesting how fleeting youth is.'

Its sleeve also uses the circle format adopted for the *Super* album, while the black-and-white images within are taken from the song's video. The director of the video was American film-maker Gavin Filipiak, of whom Neil and Chris first became aware when he made a video for a San Diego goth-rap group called Prayers, who had recorded a version of 'West End girls'.

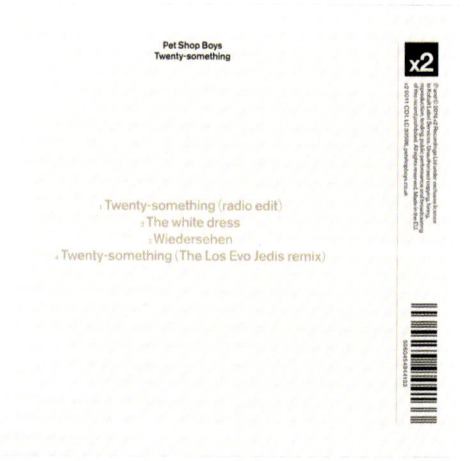

CD, back

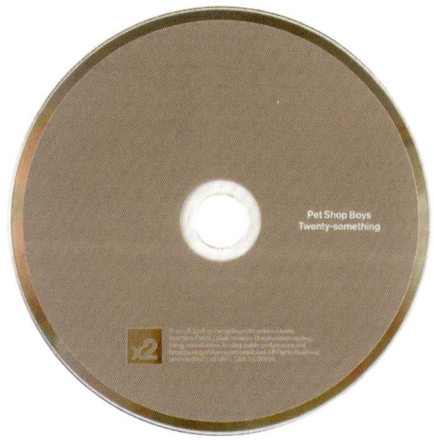

CD, disc

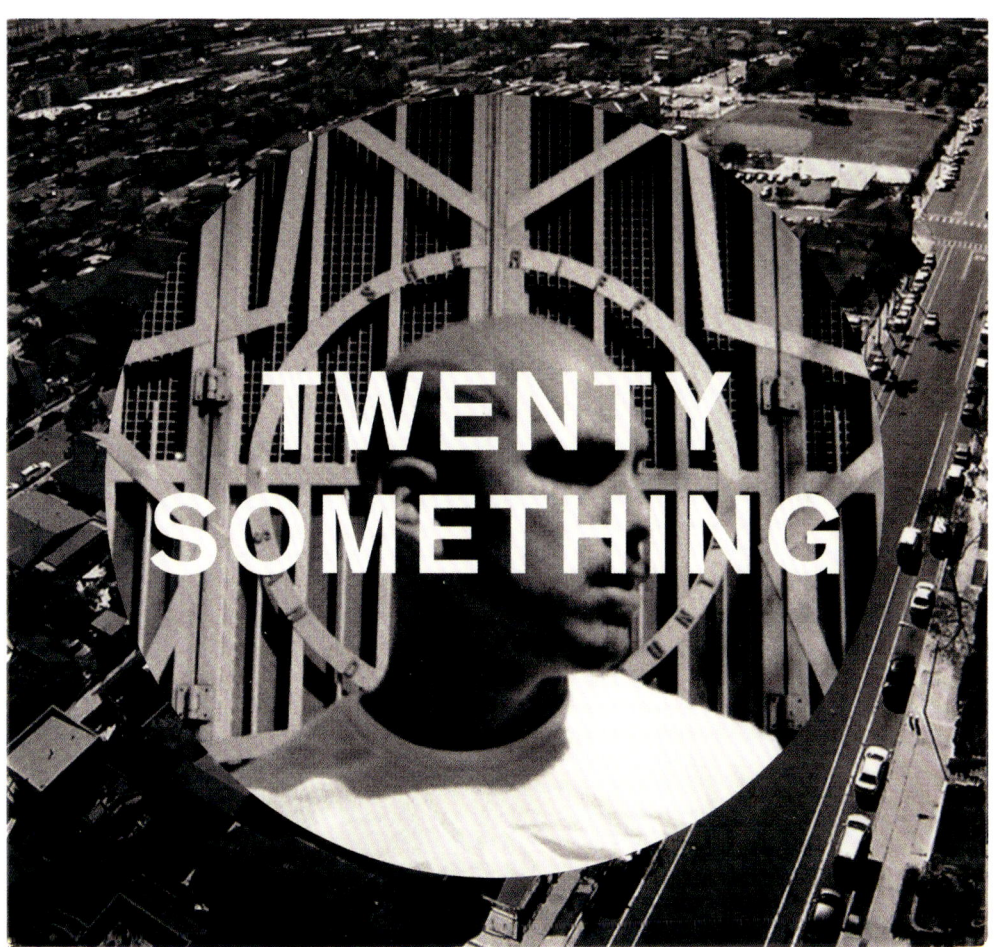

CD, front

CD, inside

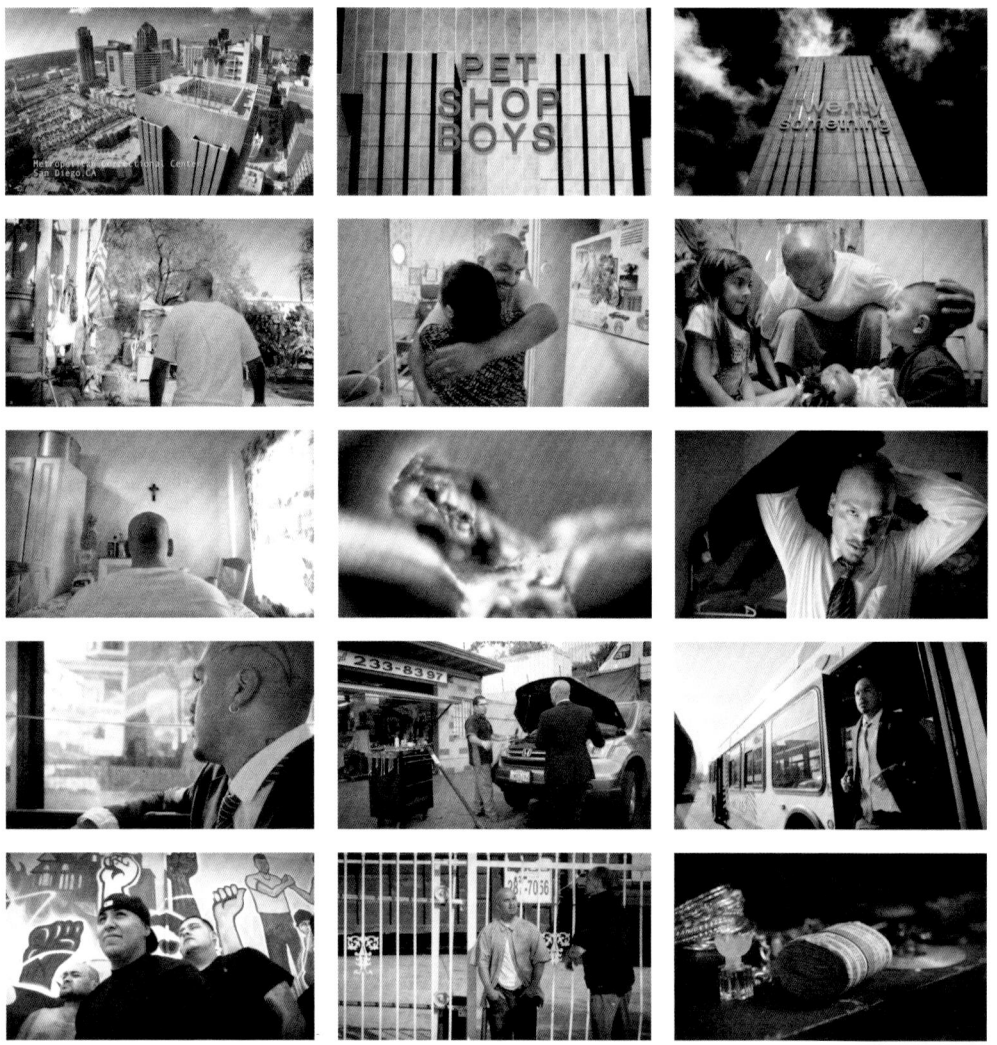

For Gavin Filipiak's video for 'Twenty-something', instead of depicting the lives of twenty-somethings in London, Neil and Chris decided that setting it amongst a Hispanic community in San Diego 'would emphasize the Hispanic or Latin rhythmic base of the Reggaeton baseline'. Chris's one stipulation, given Filipiak's evident fondness in his previous work for people blowing smoke, was that there be no smoking. 'We liked it', says Neil. 'He has a very strong visual style. And it's a bit alien – it's not what you expect from us.'

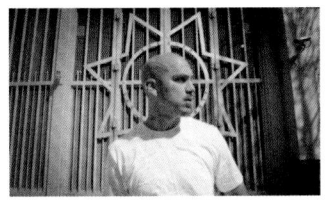 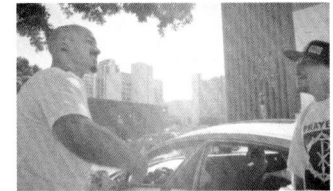 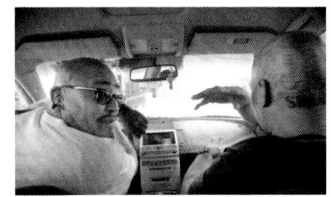
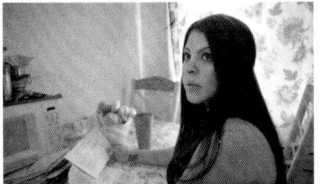 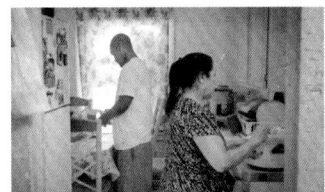 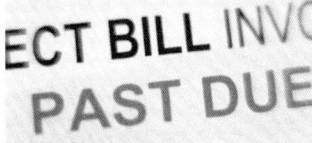
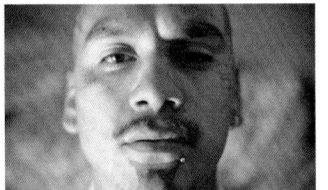 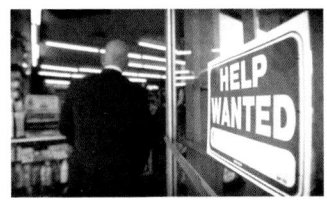 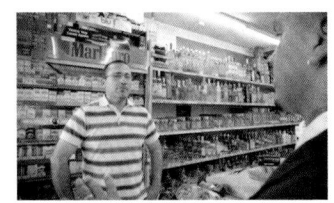
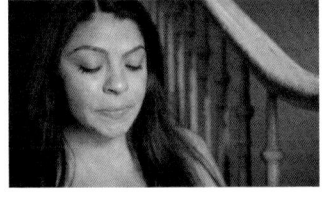 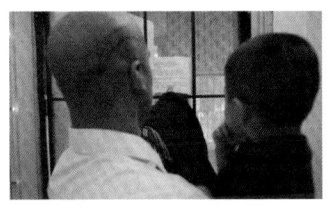 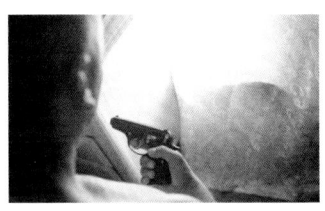
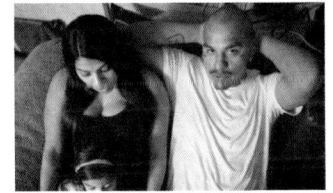 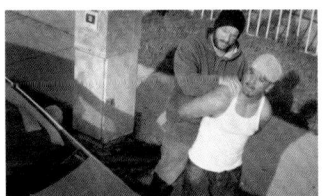 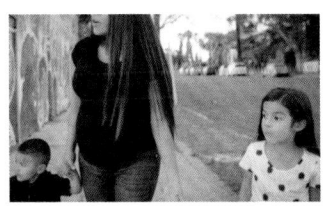

Super tour

dates 20 July 2016 – 2 April 2019
set design and creative direction Es Devlin
lighting Rob Sinclair and Ben Cash
stage direction and choreography Lynne Page
costumes Jeffrey Bryant

The first incarnation of what would become the *Super* tour was the Pet Shop Boys' *Inner Sanctum* residency at the Royal Opera House at Covent Garden, London, from 20 to 23 July 2016. 'I really liked the relationship between the lasers and the ornate Baroque interior of the opera house', notes Es Devlin. 'It provided an incredible opportunity.' The full *Super* production, which debuted on 13 October in Santiago, Chile, further pivoted in multiple ways on the album's circle motif. 'The idea behind the *Super* shows', says choreographer Lynne Page, 'was about finding surface through depth.' On this tour, the Pet Shop Boys were joined by three other musicians (Afrika Green, Christina Hizon, and Simon Tellier) and a new self-ascribed set of rules. 'The rationale for the *Super* tour – because we always have a rationale for everything – was that there were going to be no samples of acoustic instruments', says Neil. 'And that's what determined the arrangements.' Conceptually, says Neil, 'the idea of the show was that the sun fell, rose, and fell again.'

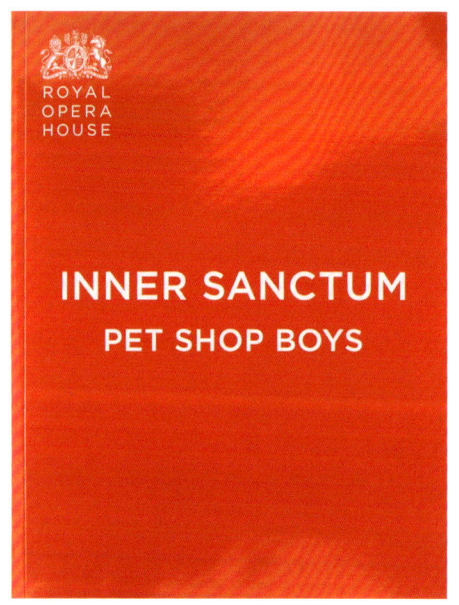

The Royal Opera House-designed programme for the *Inner Sanctum* residency, front

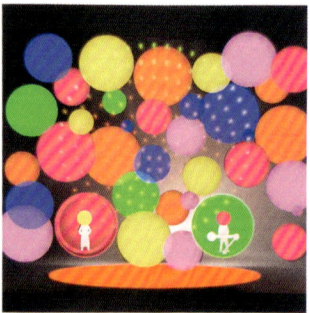

Inside page showing one of Es Devlin's initial designs for the *Super* tour

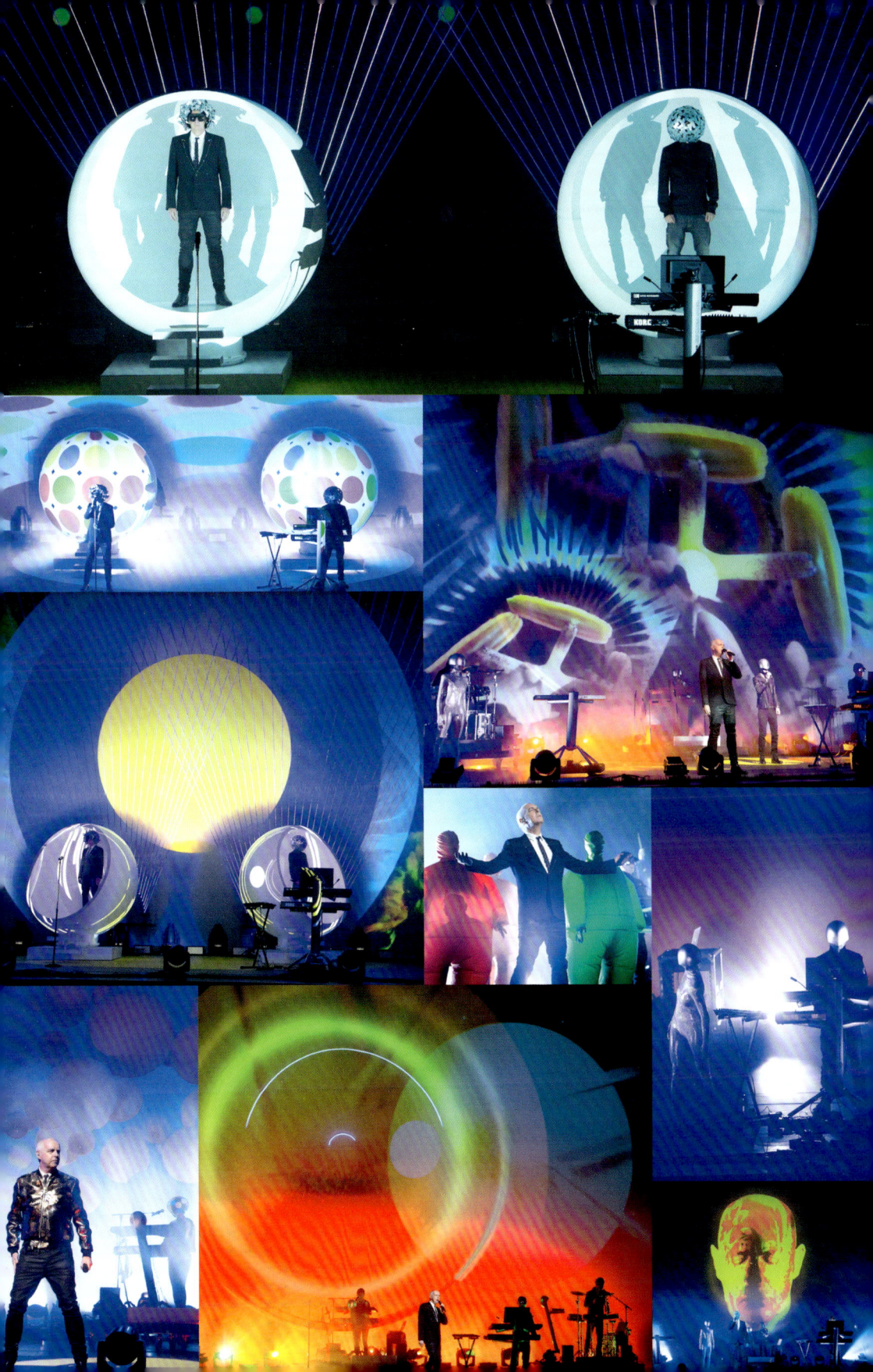

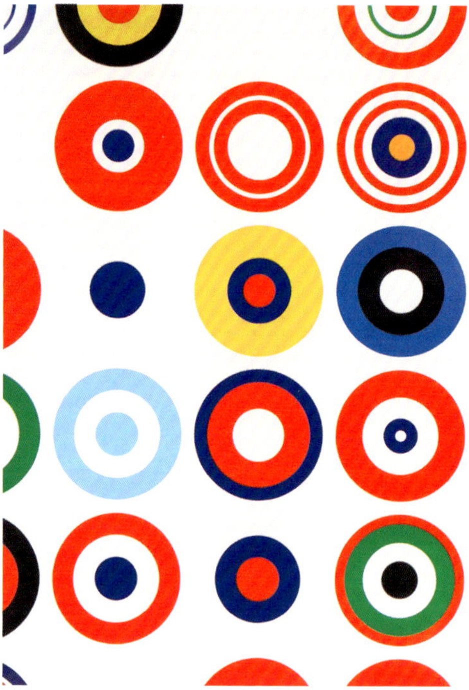

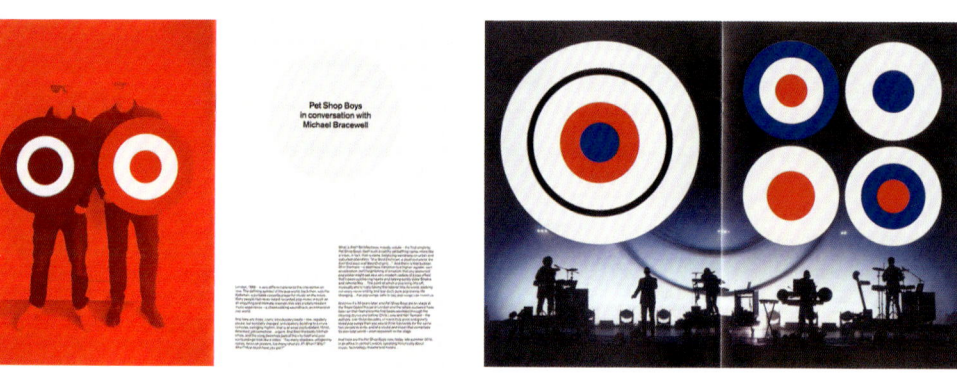

Tour programme, front cover

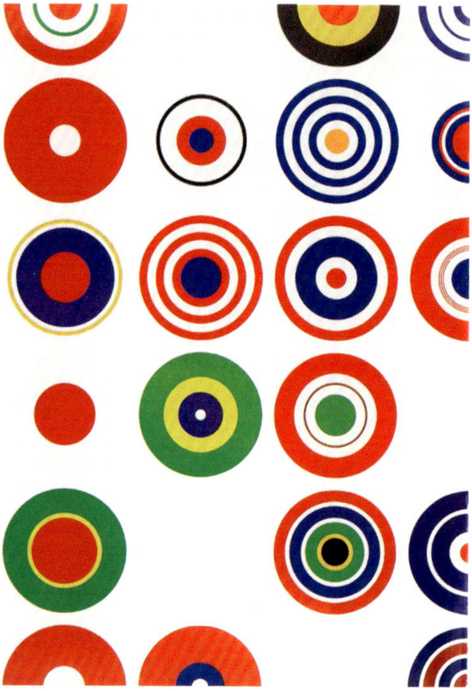

Tour programme, inside front cover

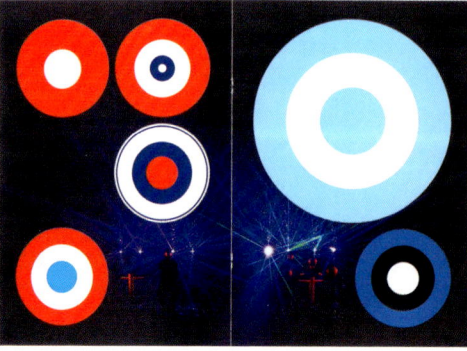
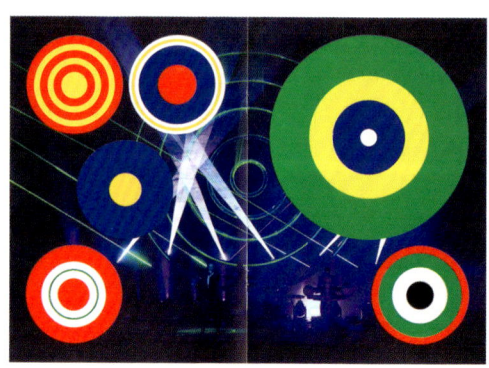

Tour programme, inside pages

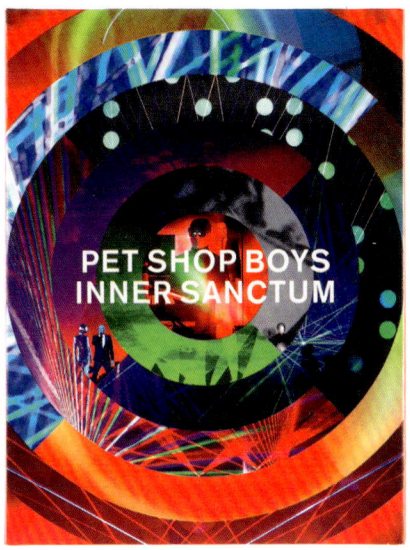

Inner Sanctum, DVD and CD set, front

The cover for the programme, which included an interview with Michael Bracewell, was a series of *Super*-style target circles in a variety of colours. These were not random. Inside, as demonstrated in detail in the illustrated listing of Pet Shop Boys' concerts between 1984 and 2017, it explains that each circle is constructed from the colours of the flag of a country where they have performed. 'Just that completeness thing', notes Mark Farrow.

The *Super* show was filmed two years later on 27 and 28 July 2018, during the Pet Shop Boys' second residency at the Royal Opera House, and released on DVD as *Inner Sanctum*, also including a film of their *Rock in Rio* performance from 17 September 2017, as well as two CDs of the music from the full Royal Opera House show.

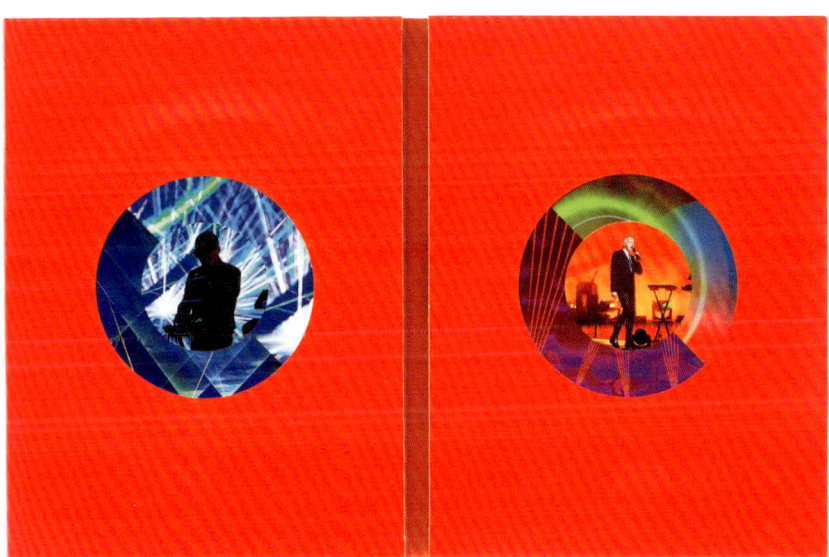

Inner Sanctum, DVD and CD set, inside gatefold (closed)

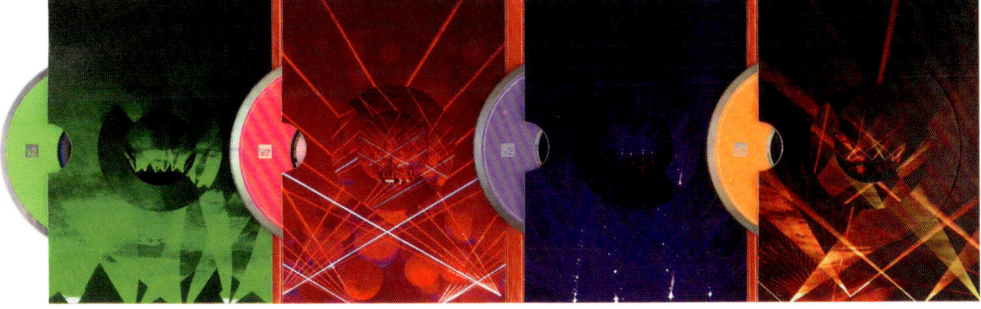

Inner Sanctum, DVD and CD set, inside gatefold (open)

Inner sanctum

release 22 July 2016
formats 12" / CD promo / download
design and art direction Farrow / PSB

The song 'Inner sanctum' was initially released as a vinyl-only four-track twelve-inch single, for exclusive sale at the Royal Opera House and through the Pet Shop Boys' website. 'Stuart Price described a lot of the songs as being vignettes', says Chris. 'This is a vignette.' 'I just thought of the inner sanctum of a club,' says Neil, 'when you're in the little bar behind the DJ booth.' The sleeve, in keeping with all *Super*-related releases, shows a circle. 'But it's a very little circle', says Neil. 'Because that is the inner sanctum on this huge white sleeve.' 'The joy is pulling the inner sleeve out', says Chris. 'The inner sleeve is sensational', Neil agrees. 'You're allowed into the inner sanctum.' 'It's everything I imagined the inner sanctum would be', says Chris.

This was one of those occasions when artist and designer found themselves at loggerheads. Farrow favoured a design that much more directly mirrored the other *Super* singles, and they were particularly against the un-centred placement of the front cover circle. 'I mean, sometimes you look back at stuff where they've gone, "What about doing this?"' considers Mark Farrow. 'And you hate the idea in the moment, but then you end up looking back on it and saying to yourself, "Well, actually, fair enough – they were probably right on that." But not always.'

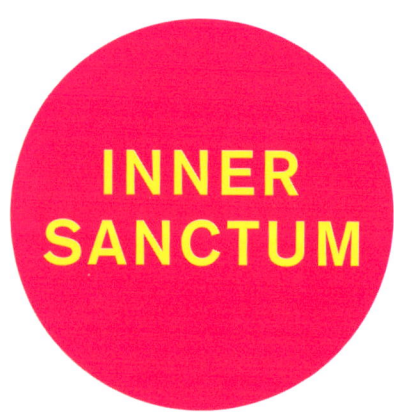

Download

12", outer sleeve, front

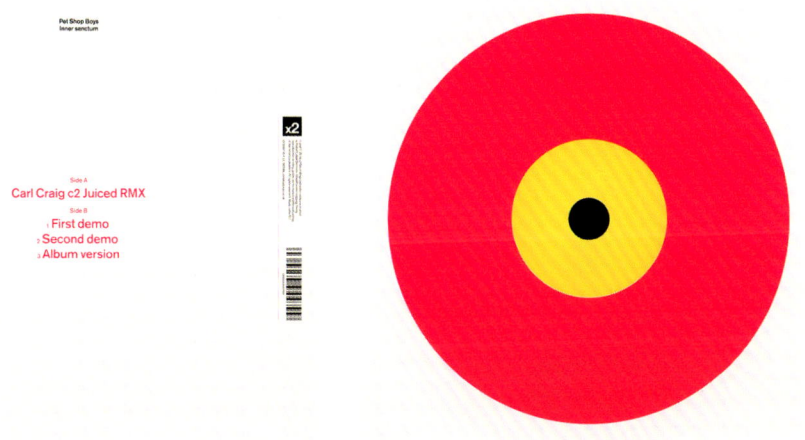

12", outer sleeve, back

12", inner sleeve, front

Say it to me

release 16 September 2016
formats 12" / CD / CD promo /
download / download remix
design and art direction Farrow / PSB

Chris had suggested that they write a song based around a single repeated phrase, like Caribou's 'Our love' or 'Can't do without you'. 'And I came up with "Say it to me"', says Neil. 'But our track is a bit moody – it doesn't really sound a bit like Caribou.' The sleeve is a further iteration of the *Super* design concept. 'That felt a good way to go', says Mark Farrow. 'Still a circle', says Chris. 'To be fair, it's clever', says Neil. 'A speech bubble.' Inside the CD single and on the inner sleeve of the twelve inch, answer-bubbles in reverse colours offer variant responses to the title's prompt, both taken from the song's lyric: 'What do you want?, What do you need?'

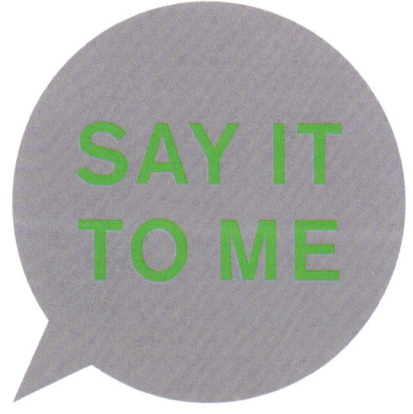

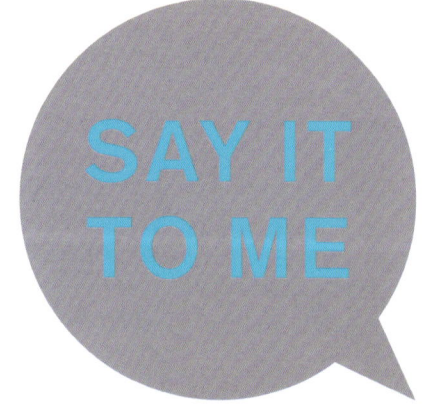

Download   Download remix

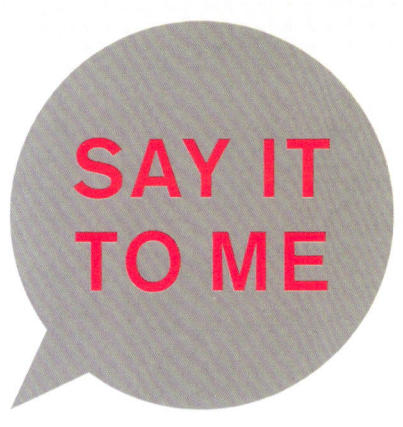

CD, front

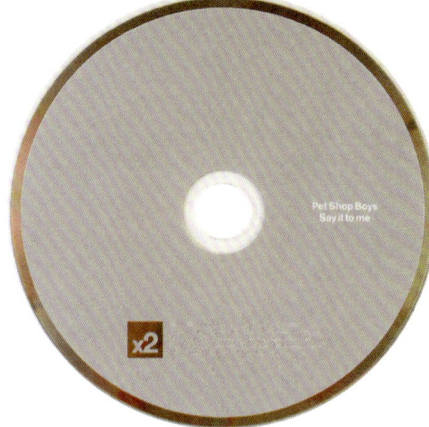

CD, disc

CD, inside

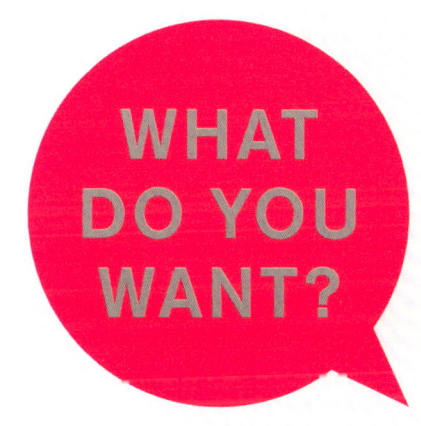

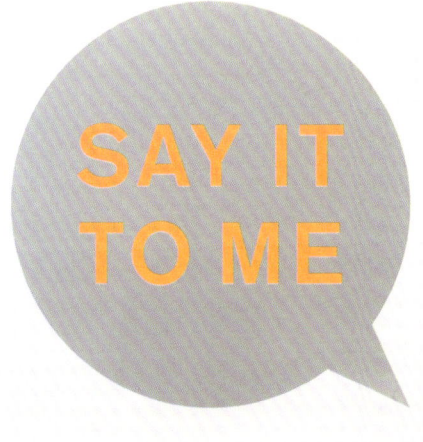

12", outer sleeve, front

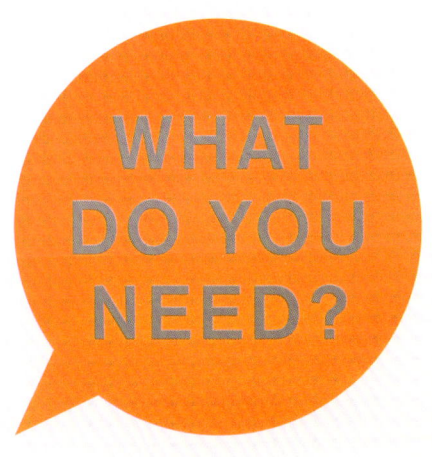

12", inner sleeve, front

Pet Shop Boys Catalogue 1999–2012

release July – October 2017
formats CD × 5
photographers Eric Watson, Dan Forbes, and John Ross
design Farrow / PSB

These remastered CD versions of five previous Pet Shop Boys albums mirrored the release of the expanded reissues of the first six studio albums in June 2001 (pages 276–7). It was determined that the words 'Pet Shop Boys' would go in front of the album title in the first three releases, and that the title would come first in the final two. Also, this time, in the case of *Nightlife*, *Release*, and *Yes*, there was so much appropriate additional material to include that two 'Further Listening' discs were required. For *Release*, the full-coloured orange poppy image, from the original LP's inner sleeve and as well as some previous international CD versions, was chosen as the new cover image, in preference to the embossed grey-tone version of the original sleeve. As before, for each album where the title was part of the original cover (in this case, all but *Release*), the title was removed from the central image. Each CD was accompanied in the slipcase by a booklet containing the lyrics of each song, a track commentary by Pet Shop Boys, and photographs of Neil and Chris from the particular period.

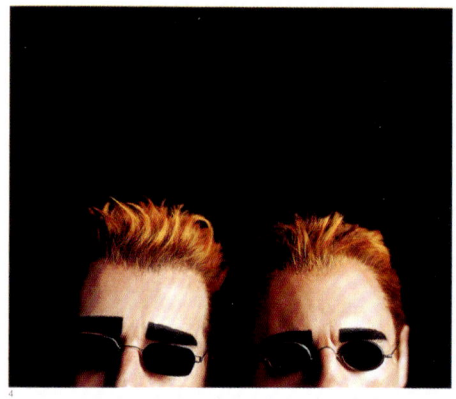

Nightlife, booklet, inside pages

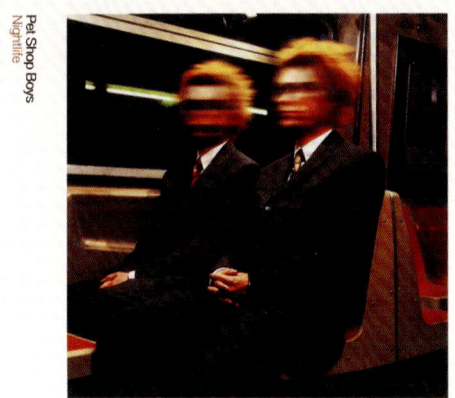

Nightlife, front

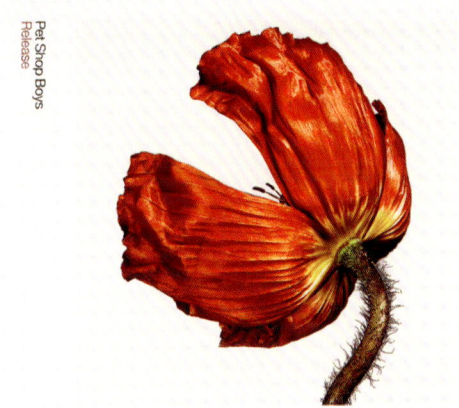

Release, front

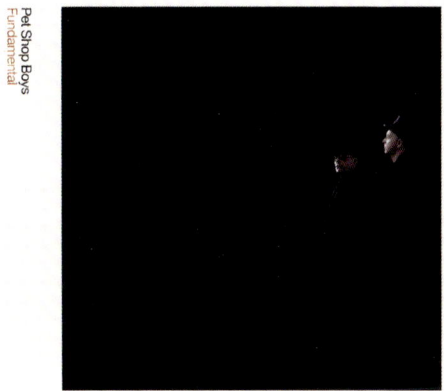

Fundamental, front

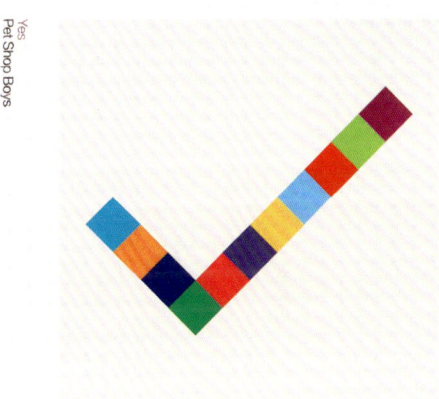

Yes, front

Elysium, front

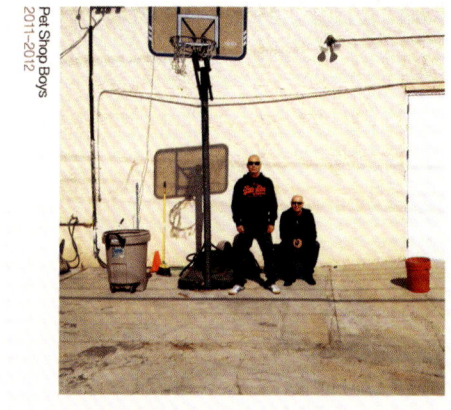

Elysium, booklet, front

Undertow

release 1 April 2017
formats 12" / CD / download
design and art direction Farrow / PSB

The final single from Super had been inspired by a stray comment one day in Berlin from Pet Shop Boys' friend Joel Gibb, the singer of the Hidden Cameras, who, in describing a recent clubbing experience, remarked 'Oh, there was an undertow.' Neil and Chris wrote this song that same week. 'It's about someone getting into a relationship they know is going to be bad for them', says Neil, 'and they just can't help it.' The illustration on the sleeve shows one final evolution of the Super design motif to fit the single's title. 'We just came up with the idea of a circular vortex', says Gary Stillwell. 'A whirlpool', says Mark Farrow. 'So it's the circle, but as this soft, blurred circle.'

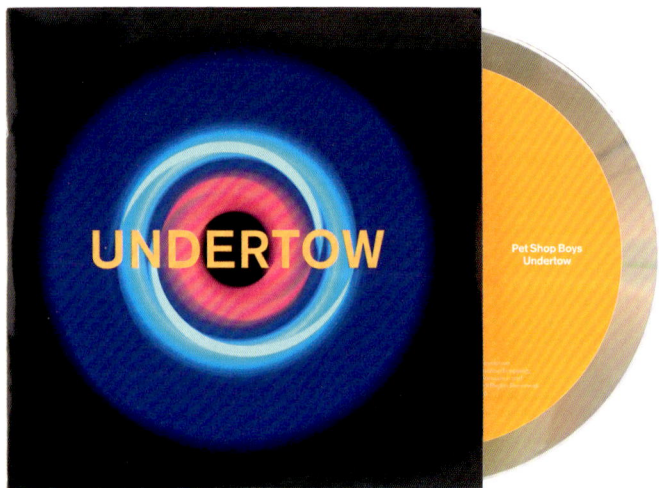

CD, front and disc

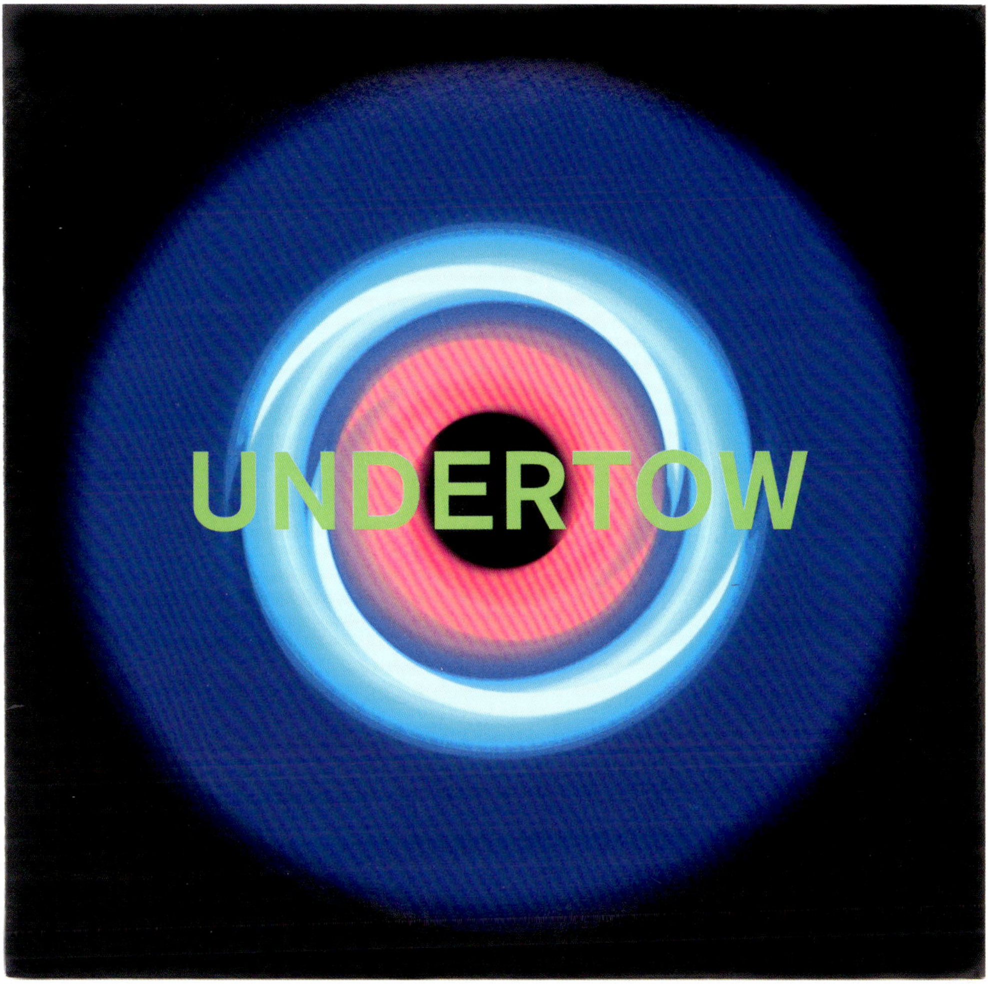

12", outer sleeve, front

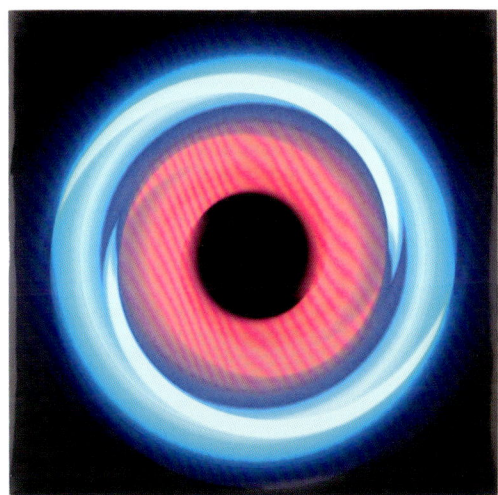

12", inner sleeve, front

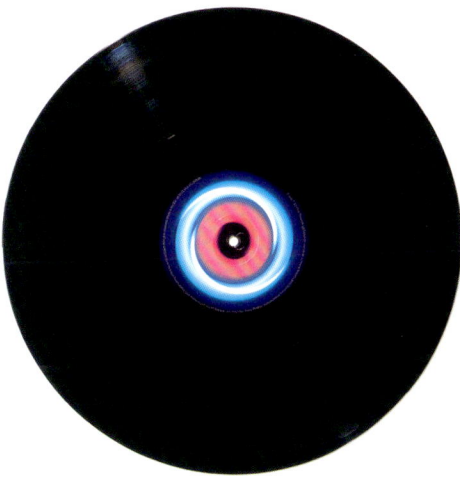

12", Side A

Agenda

release 5–8 February 2019
formats 12" / CD / download × 4
design and art direction Farrow / PSB

The four songs on the *Agenda* EP – 'Give stupidity a chance', 'On social media', 'What are we going to do about the rich?', and 'The forgotten child' – were released digitally on four consecutive days in February 2019. A twelve inch followed on 12 April, and a CD single was available exclusively as part of that year's *Annually*. These were songs that Neil and Chris realized had something in common with each other but might not fit comfortably on the next Pet Shop Boys album. 'Three satirical songs and one rather sad song', says Neil, 'but they all have, broadly speaking, political themes.' The sleeve – 'Farrow at his best', says Chris – came after they decided that 'the agitprop direction' didn't work. 'So I had the idea of going in the opposite direction – going super-gloss, glamour', says Chris. '"What are we going to do about the rich?" – that's what that photograph reference is', says Mark Farrow. 'It's just a stock image – a girl on a lavish yacht.' 'Taking a selfie', says Chris. 'So it sort of makes the point. It's satirical.' 'Just a statement on consumerism and richness and wealth', says Farrow. 'And then we deliberately went with the big, strong, powerful type over it.' Each song also had its own purely graphic digital sleeve, with the song's title in the same red type against a section of the sky taken from the yacht image.

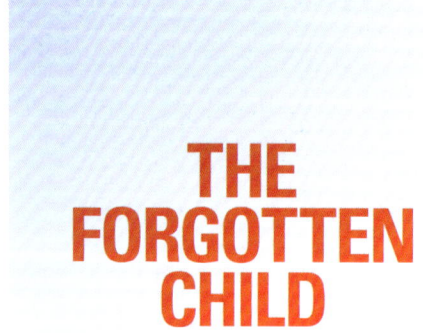

'The forgotten child', download

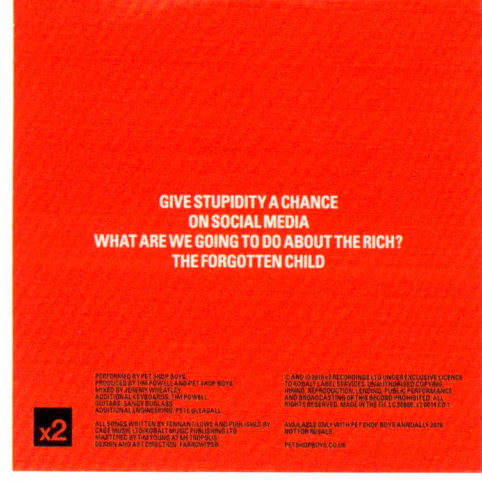

CD, back

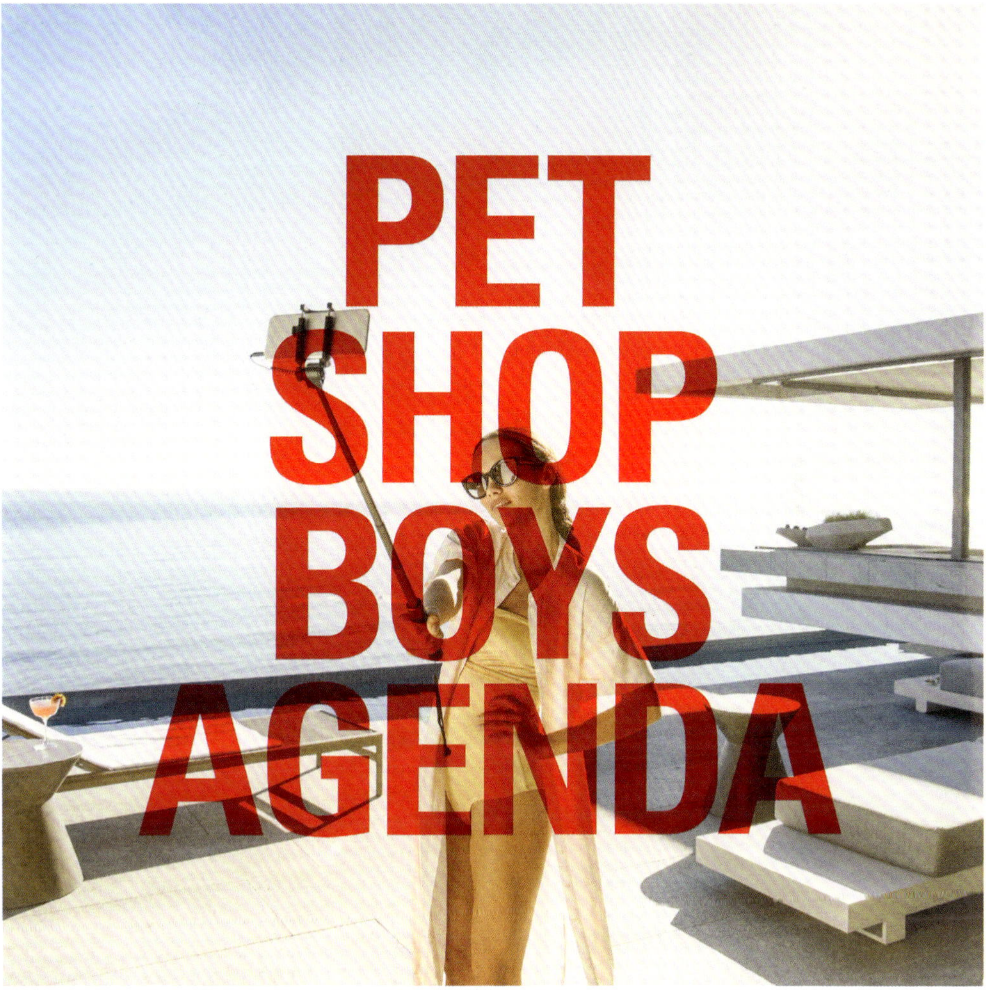

12", outer sleeve, front

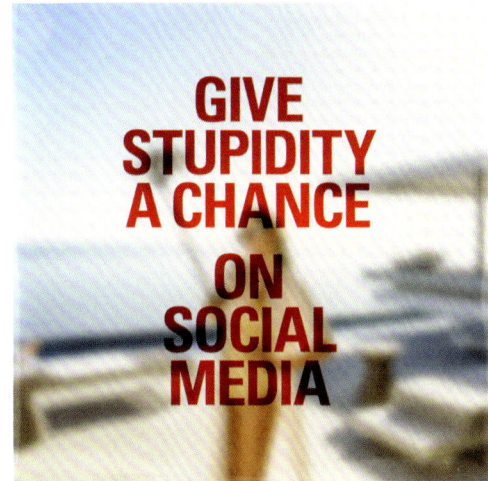

12", Record A, inner sleeve, front

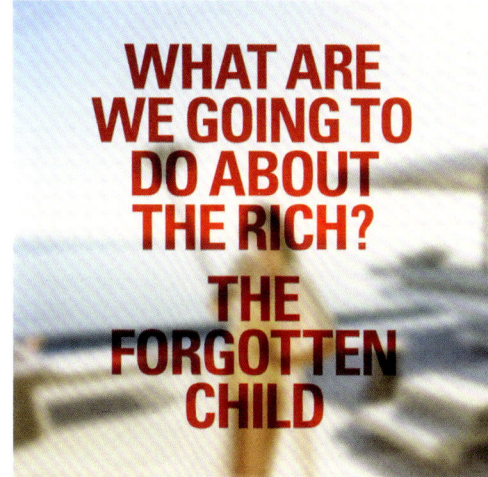

12", Record B, inner sleeve, front

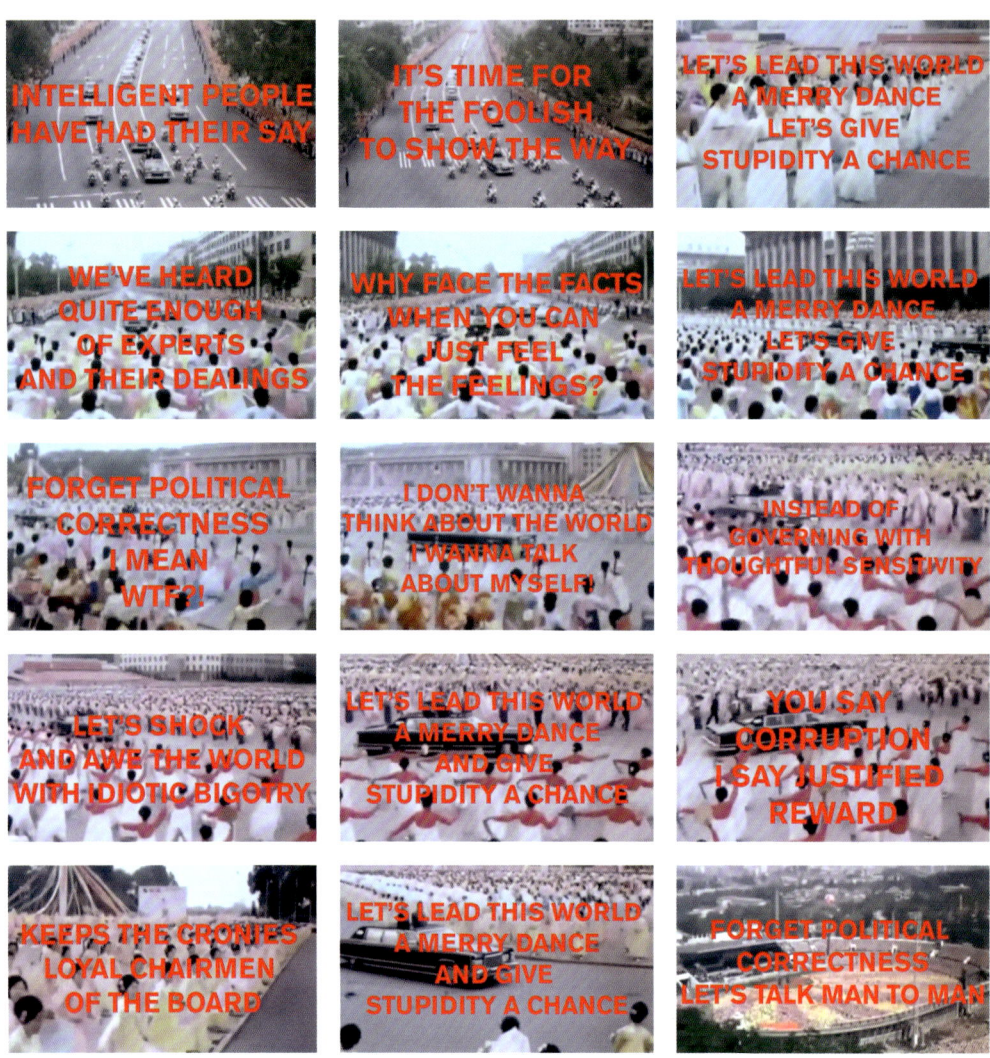

All four songs on *Agenda* had their own lyric video, three of which use the same red block capital type for the superimposed lyrics as the original sleeves. The footage in 'Give stupidity a chance' was suggested by Neil: 'It was Ceausescu, visiting Pyongyang, alongside Kim Il Sung – an event that's always fascinated me in the history of Communism, because it's when Ceausescu goes there and sees the regimentation of society, then goes back to Romania and decides he wants to make Romania like that. It had a profound effect on that country. Another thing, you've got to hand it to North Korea – they can really put on a spectacle. The traditional Korean dancing is incredible. And the costumes – for a Communist country, they're quite flamboyant. At the time, China would have just had you in Mao suits. The whole thing is so crazy. So it fits with the idea of "give stupidity a chance", even though that line was fundamentally about Nigel Farage and Trump.'

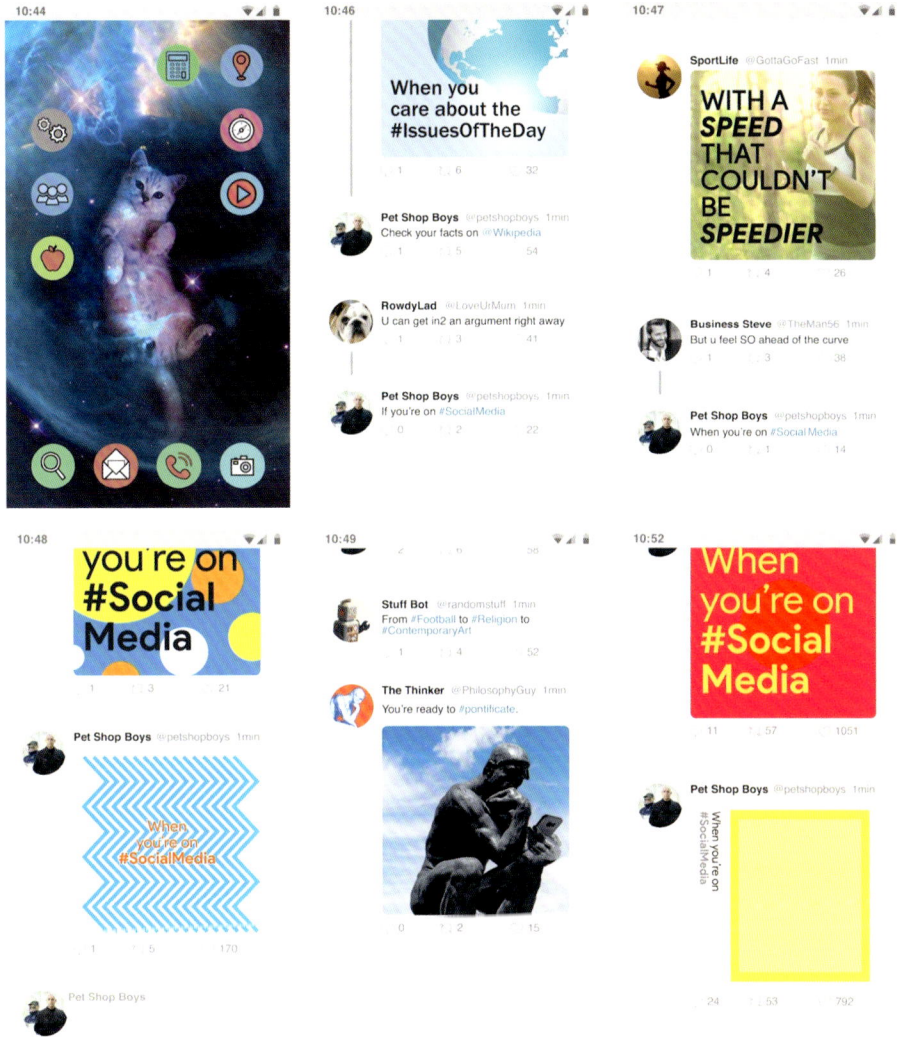

The second video – the only one not to use the red type – is for 'On social media'. 'A brilliant video', says Neil. 'It was nothing to do with us. Our product manager Nathan Liddle-Hulme at Kobalt commissioned it. It's incredibly clever – by far the best lyric video we've ever done. I also think it's one of the funniest videos ever done. I like the fact that it's in the shape of a phone screen because of the subject matter of the song, and it expresses the subject match of the song absolutely perfectly. And sarcastically. It's a brilliant piece of satire. But we can take no credit for it.'

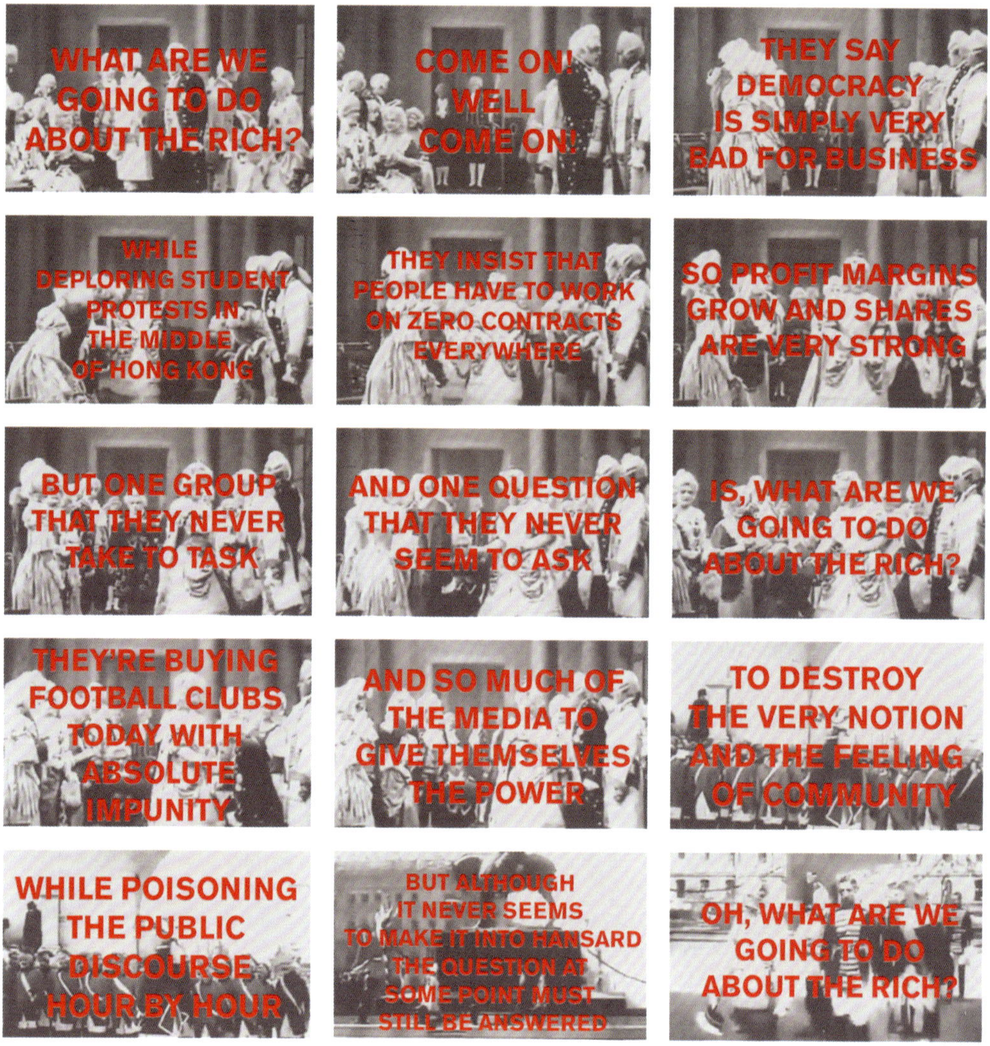

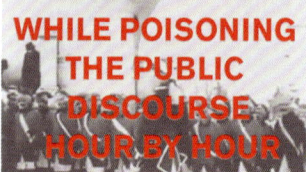 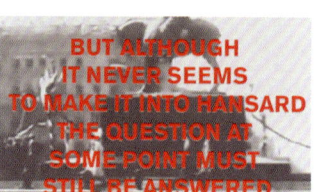 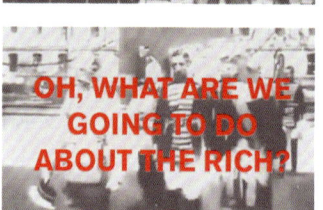

The third video from *Agenda*, 'What are we going to do about the rich?', uses, says Neil, 'an out-of-copyright silent film from the 1920s, or maybe even earlier than that. We suggested something depicting the French Revolution because in the French Revolution they worked out what to do about the rich: they guillotined them.'

The final video, for the fourth song on *Agenda*, 'The forgotten child', was partly inspired by a tragic recent incident where the body of a three-year-old Syrian migrant child had been found dead on a beach in Turkey. 'That's why the video is just the sea', says Neil.

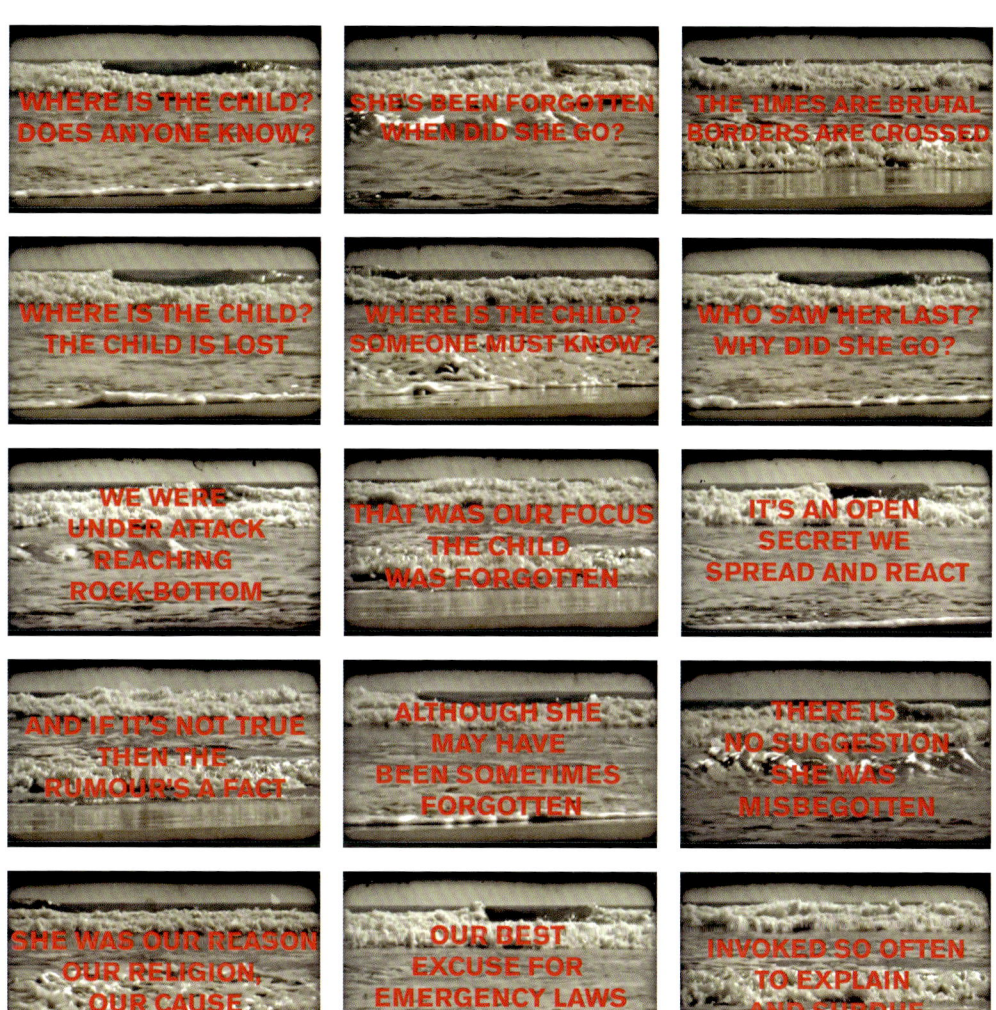

Musik

release 6 August 2019
format Download
design Farrow / PSB

Musik is a one-woman theatrical 'cabaret' in which Frances Barber reprieved the role of Billie Trix from the musical *Closer to Heaven* (pages 278–9), further detailing the often-indistinguishable triumphs and calamities of her life. 'Chris and I liked the character of Billie Trix and we thought that Jonathan Harvey wrote for her so well', says Neil. 'We'd thought for ages "Wouldn't it be good to have a show where she just talks and sings a few songs?" Frances always wanted to do it, but Jonathan didn't. Then he changed his mind.' The day after the show's premiere at the Assembly Rooms in Edinburgh on 5 August 2019, a six-song soundtrack EP was released digitally – five songs recently recorded at Pet Shop Boys' London studio (four new songs and a new recording of 'Friendly fire') alongside 'Run girl run', remixed from the 2001 seven-inch Billie Trix single sold exclusively at the theatre during *Closer to Heaven*'s first run. The EP's artwork, using an image of Billie Trix from the original poster campaign for *Closer to Heaven*, was adapted from the new show's poster.

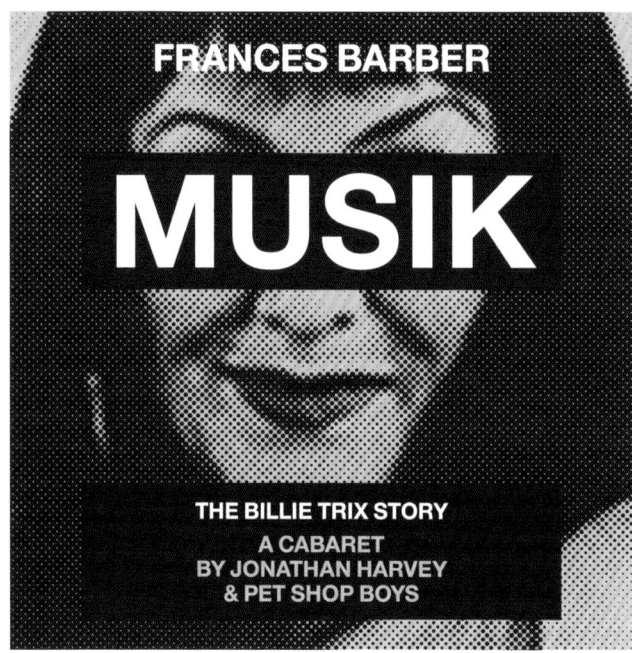

Download

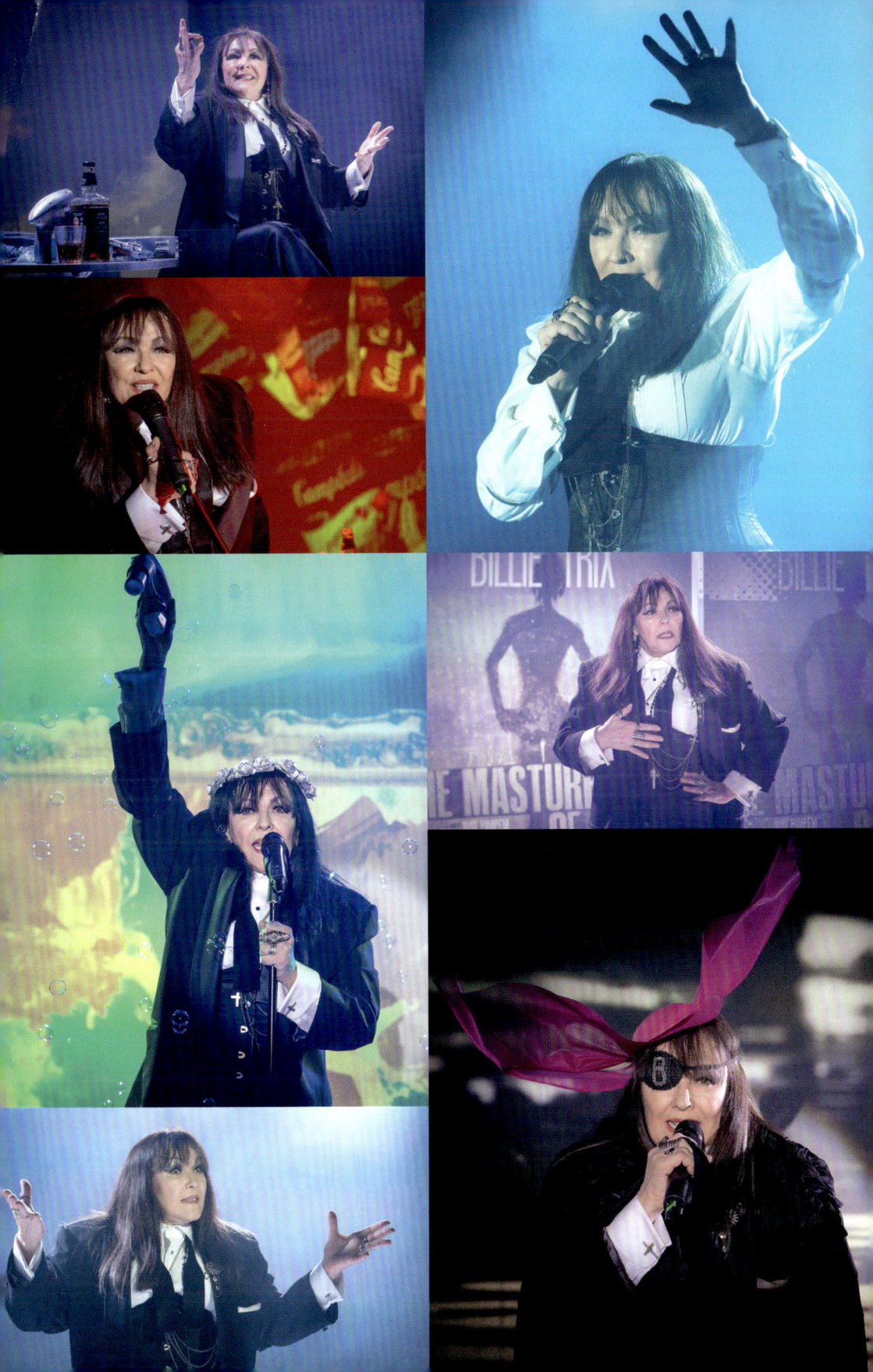

Dreamland

release 11 September 2019
formats 7" blue vinyl disc / 12" / CD / download × 2 / download remix
photographer JVP and Phil Fisk (7" blue vinyl disc)
design and art direction Farrow / PSB
video RMV Productions

Originally written with Olly Alexander for prospective use by Years & Years, 'Dreamland' became the first single from the forthcoming Pet Shop Boys album *Hotspot*. Ahead of time, Neil and Chris had advised Farrow that the album, recorded in Berlin, would have a German title. Based on this, they began working, says Mark Farrow, on 'this idea of photographing every U-Bahn station in the city, because their names are all in different typefaces, and putting each song title in a different typeface from that station.' 'Dreamland', which is based on the typeface for Alexanderplatz station – photographed by a friend of Neil and Chris's – was to have been just the first example. There was also a special collectors' seven-inch disc on blue vinyl for exclusive sale through the German magazine *Musikexpress*.

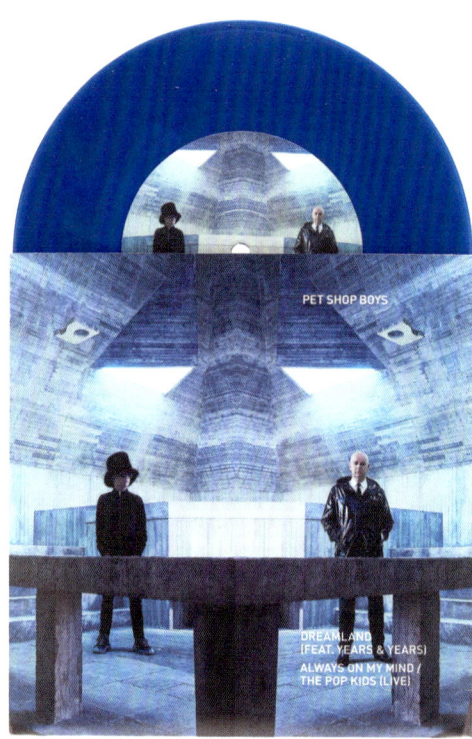

7" blue vinyl disc, front and disc

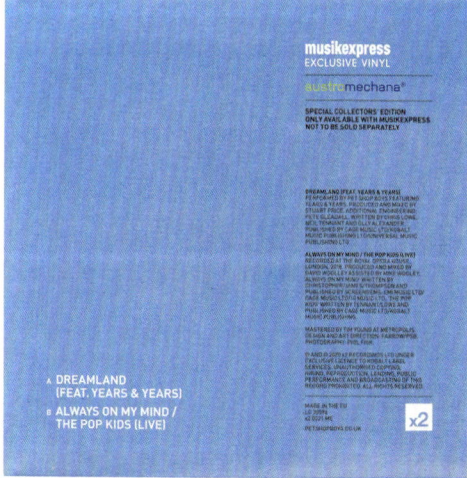

7" blue vinyl disc, back

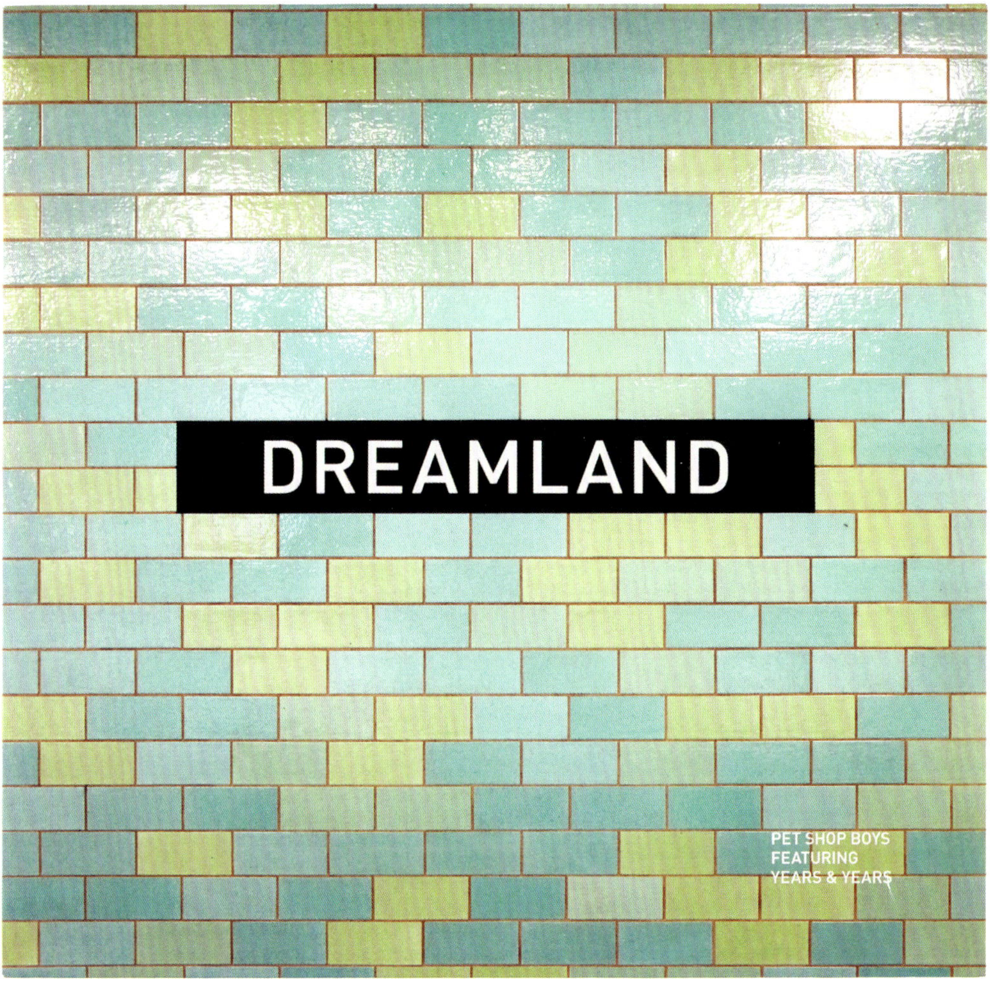

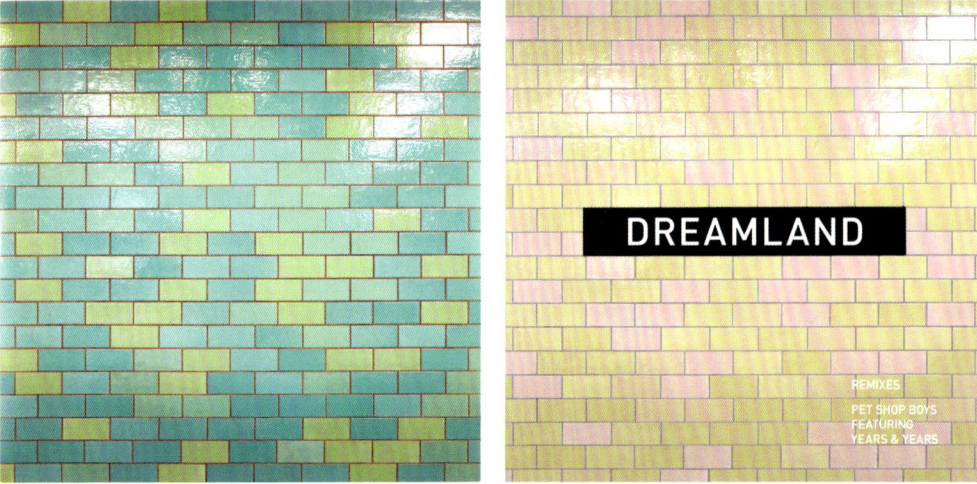

12", outer sleeve, front

12", inner sleeve, front

Download remix

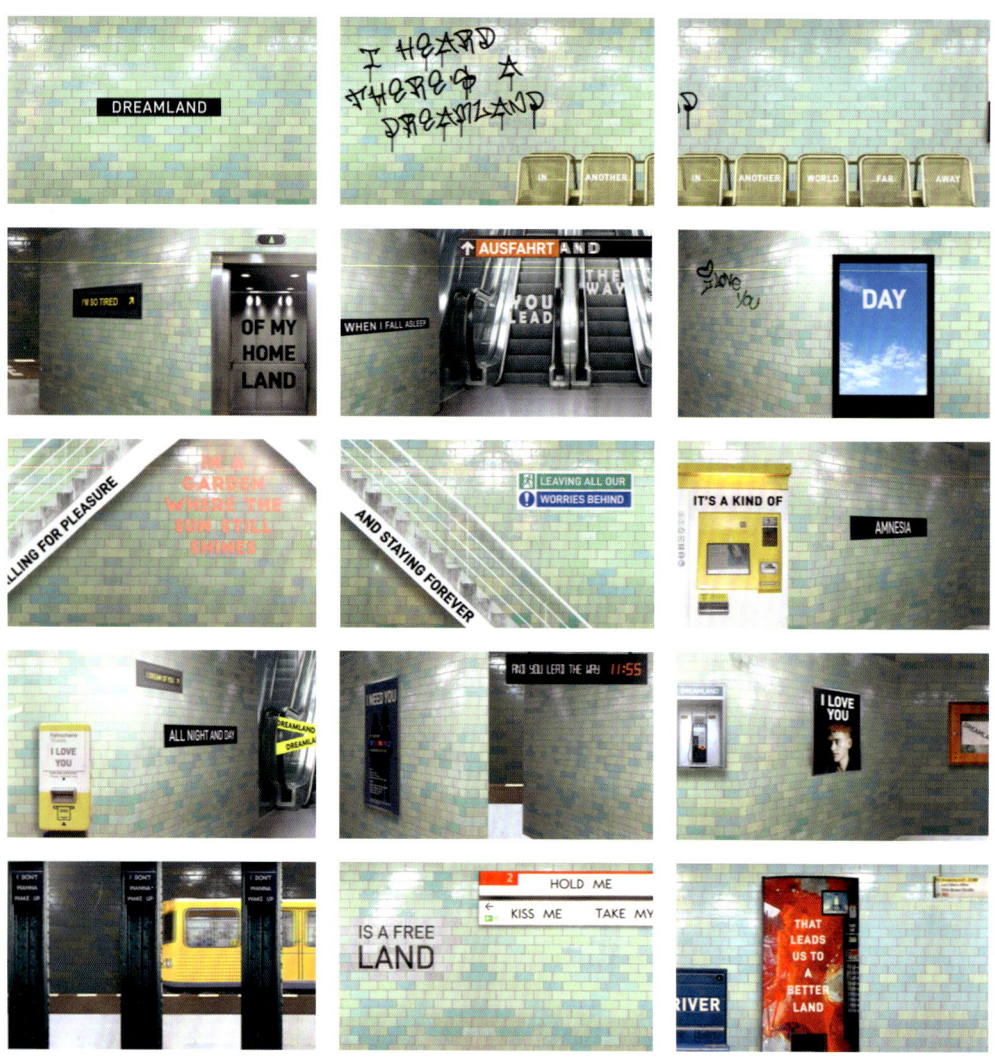

A lyric video was made for 'Dreamland'. 'For some reason, we didn't make a video with Olly', says Neil. 'I think he wasn't available.' The lyric video expands upon the idea of the sleeve, as the lyrics become apparent at the necessary moment on the walls of the Alexanderplatz station: in its sign, the advertising posters, the graffiti, the LED screens, the words on the platform edge, and the train itself, the escalator steps, the no smoking sign, the photo booth, the route map, the toilets, some safety tape, and on and on. 'Again, like with "On social media", it's brilliantly done', says Neil.

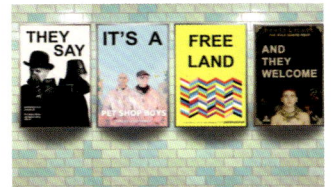 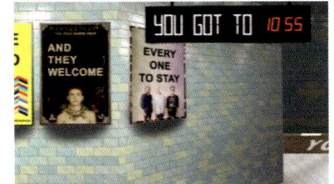 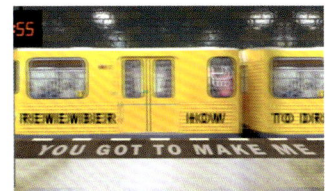
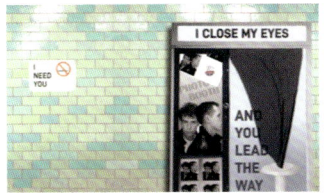 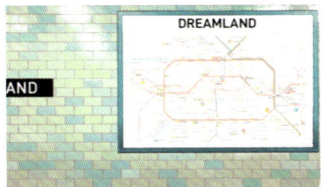 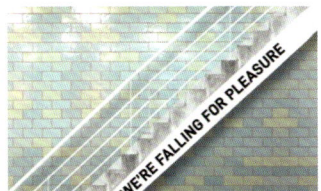
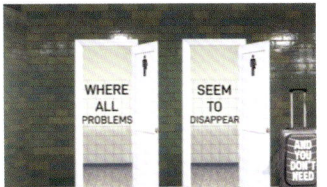 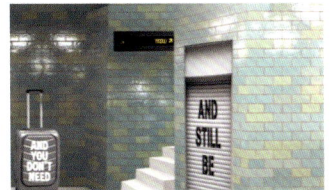 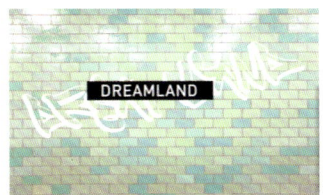
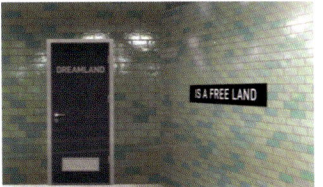 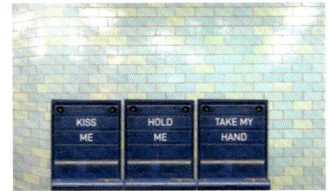 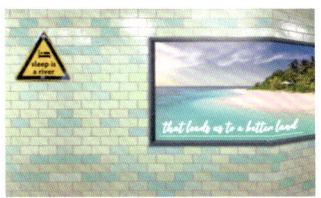
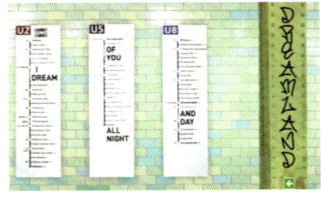 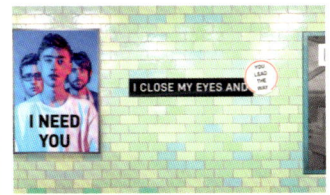 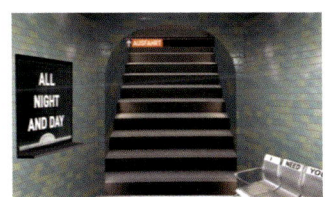

Burning the heather

release 14 November 2019
formats 7" / download × 2
photographer PSB
design and art direction Farrow / PSB
video RMV Productions

'The chorus melody, it's not like one of our tunes, really', says Neil of 'Burning the heather', *Hotspot*'s second single. 'It's almost folky. It's what we used to call at *Smash Hits* "a scarf-waver".' By now the Berlin U-Bahn station idea had been abandoned. Instead, artwork for the *Hotspot* and related releases would be based around photographs already taken by Neil and Chris. Generally, these would be photographs taken in Berlin, but 'Burning the heather' was an exception because its sleeve image depicted the very particular non-German event alluded to in the song's title. 'The idea came from when I lived in County Durham and they used to burn the heather – you do it to stimulate the growth of the heather', says Neil. 'Actually, there are two burning the heather seasons. And I've since discovered that the burning of the heather itself is controversial. But you quite often used to see it. And one day I took this photo – there was a very beautiful blue sky in autumn, so you've got this blue sky with smoke it, and of course the moors are very desolate.'

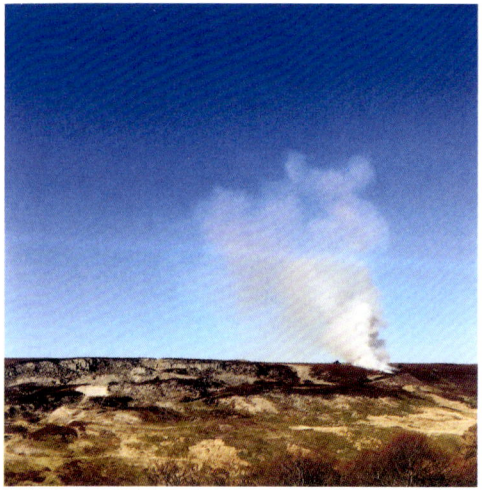

7", inner sleeve, front

7", outer sleeve, front

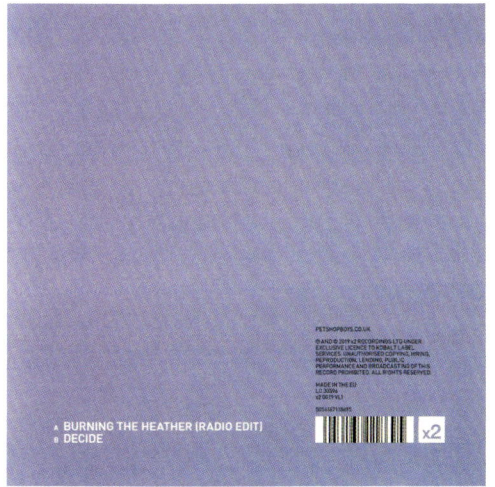

7", outer sleeve, back

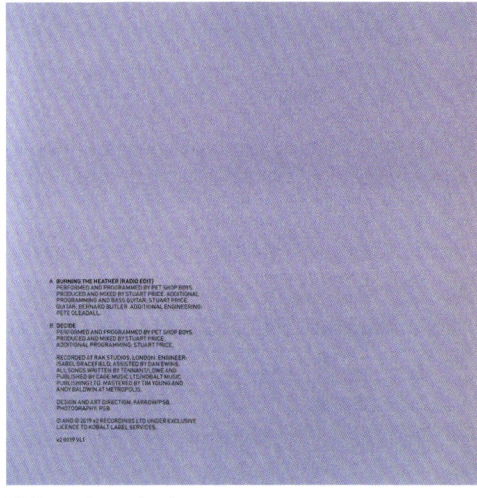

7", inner sleeve, back

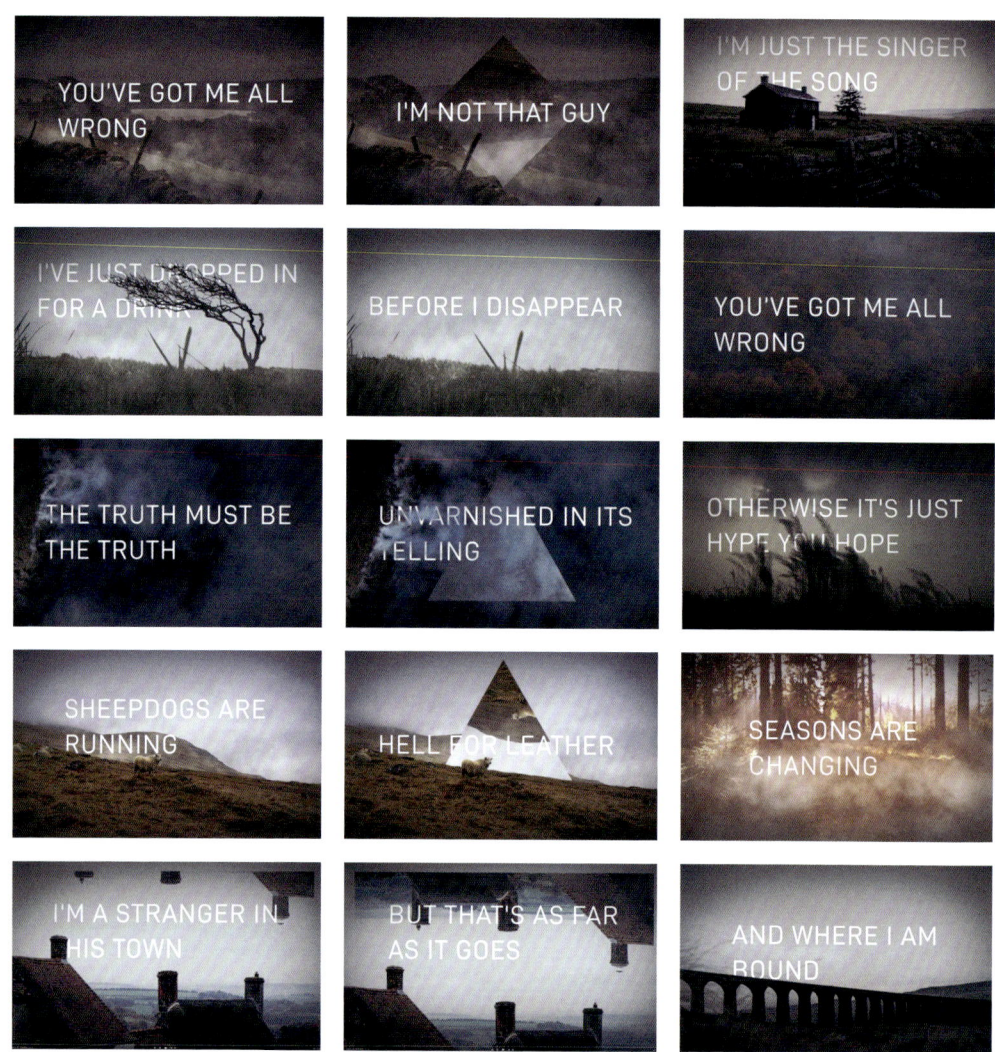

'We had nothing whatsoever to do with the lyric video', says Neil, 'and I don't remember anything about the process of it being done, but we probably said it should look like that. It's very County Durham. Just over halfway through, there's a famous railway viaduct.'

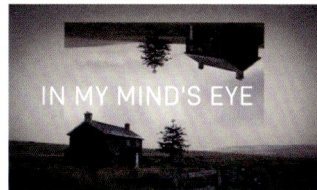
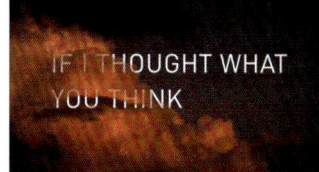
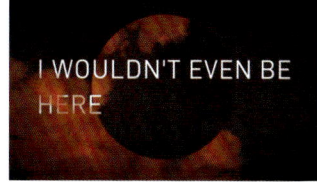
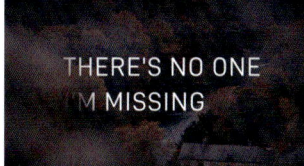
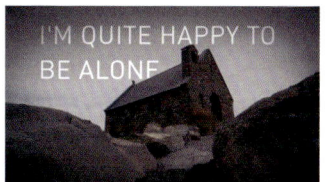
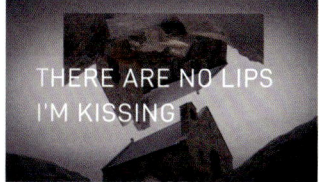
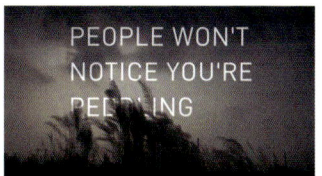
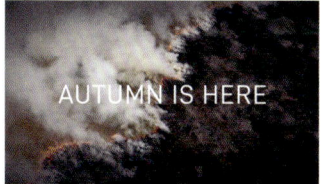
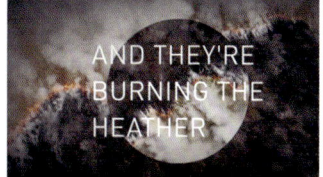
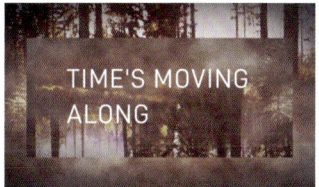
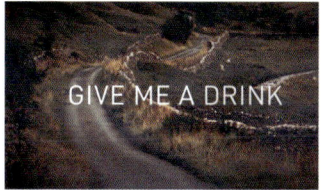
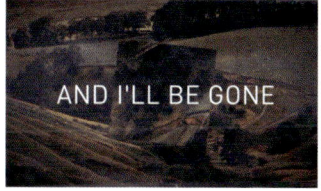
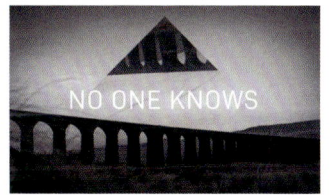
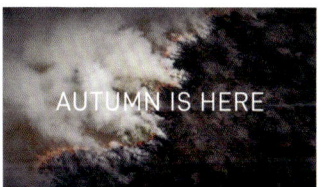
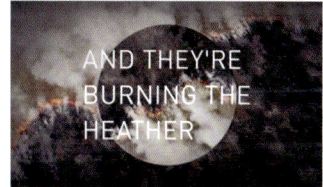

Monkey business

release 2 January 2020
formats 12" / CD / download × 2
photographer PSB
design Farrow / PSB
video Vaughan Arnell

Hotspot's third single was written in Berlin back in 2014, inspired by meeting a businessman in a Nashville backstreet who told them 'I'm looking for monkey business – just playing around.' Its sleeve photo was taken by Chris. 'I think it was in Friedrichshain in east Berlin', says Neil. 'Chris and I went on a Saturday morning to look at some art galleries for some reason. And he took that picture of me coming down the stairs.' 'The thought there was that it was Neil coming down some backstairs with his sunglasses on, I think, and it looks like he's up to monkey business', suggests Gary Stillwell. The one commonality between the design of these first three *Hotspot* singles is the position and font of the type towards the bottom-right corner. 'The type was always in the same place exactly', says Mark Farrow. 'It became the only constant because the photographs were so random.' The twelve inch was a picture disc with the same photograph of Neil as its label. The inner sleeve of the twelve inch and inside the card CD case was a second photograph taken by Neil, of the word '*Eingang!*' ('Entrance!') on a Berlin wall.

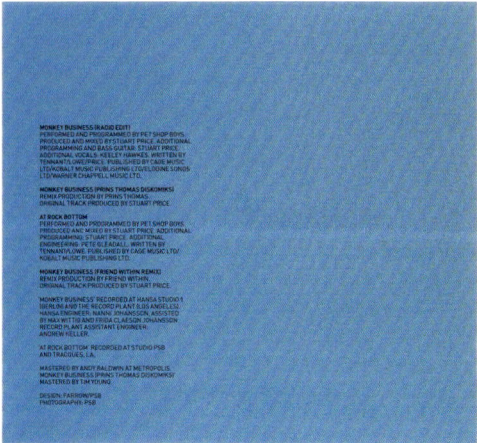 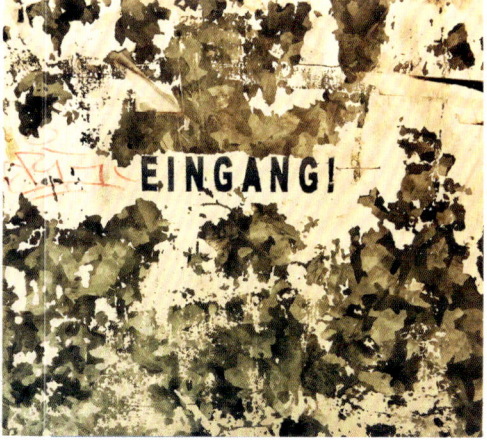

CD, inside

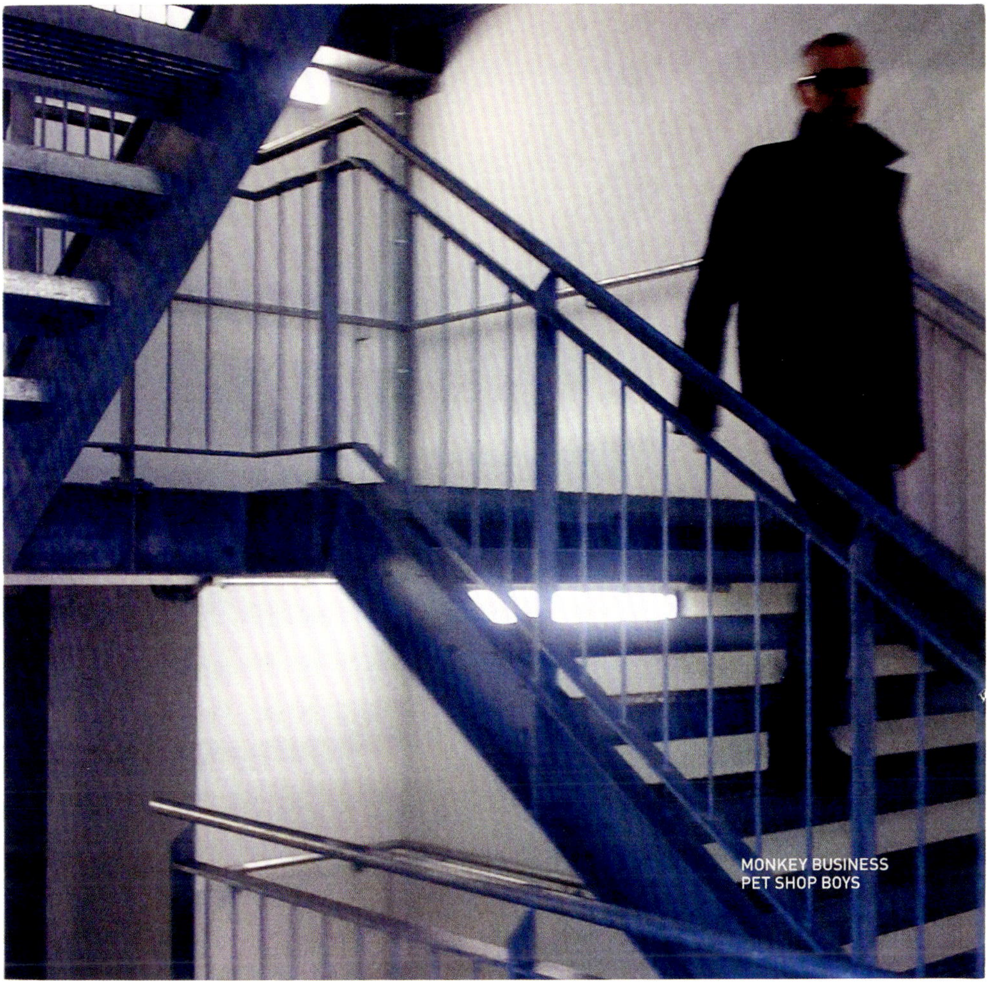

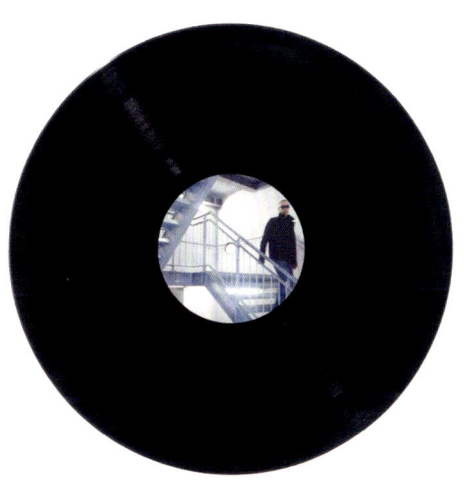

12", outer sleeve, front

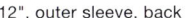

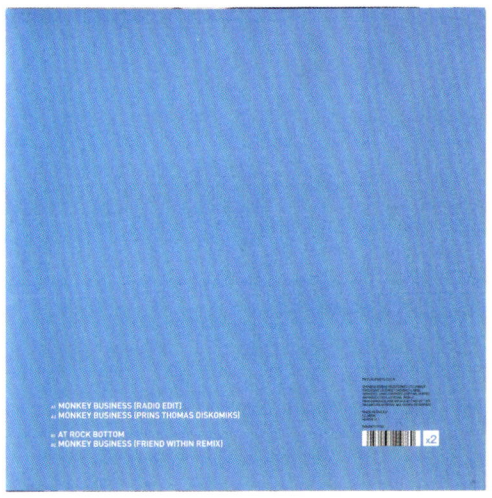

12", outer sleeve, back

12", Side A

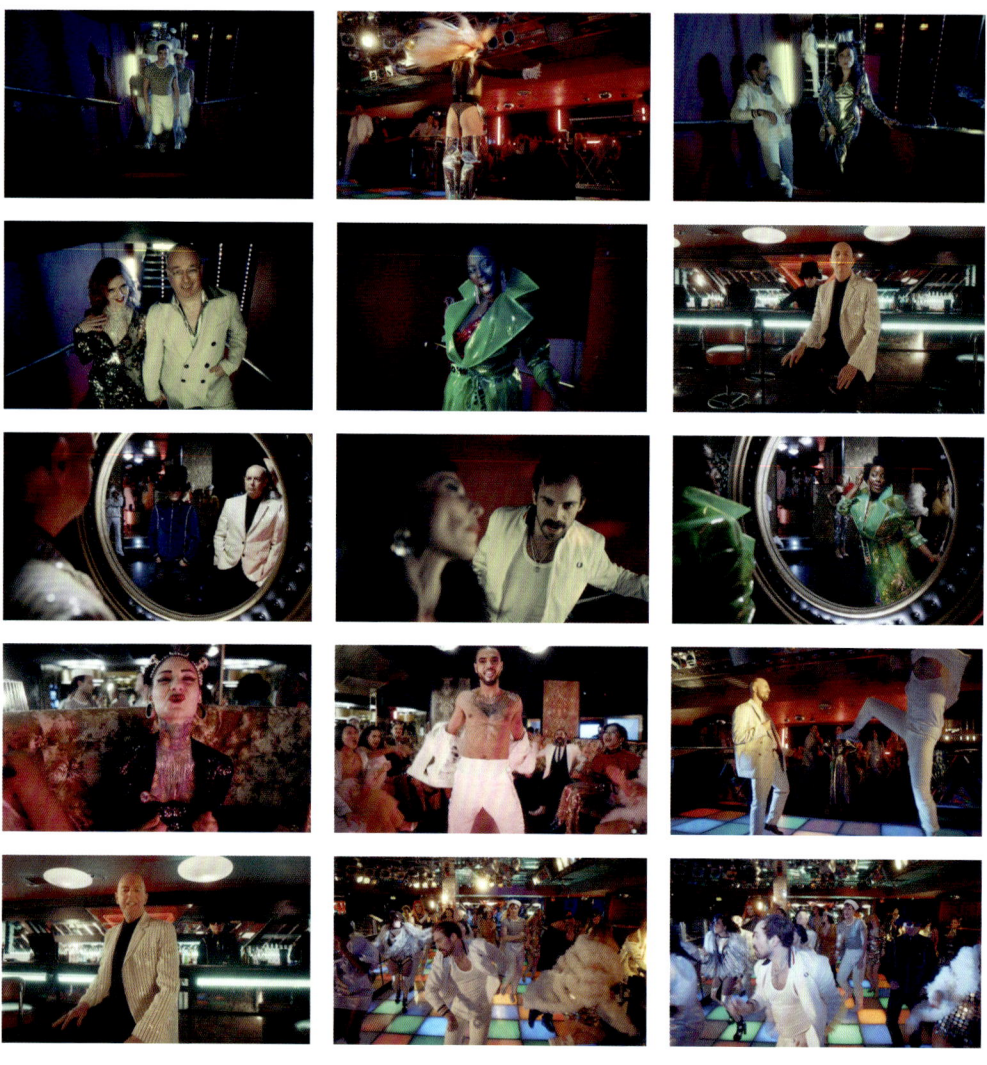

Vaughan Arnell's video for 'Monkey business', in which Neil and Chris played a central role for the first time in several years, depicted a night of 'hedonism and glamour' and was shot in Pryzm nightclub in Watford. According to the synopsis synthesized by choreographer Lynne Page from pre-production conversations: 'Neil and Chris are the curators of this evening. They know there is monkey business going on. Like the gods in Greek mythology, they are the orchestrators of everyone's fate.' Towards the end, all turns to carnage: 'Everyone's inner rebel child is out; it is unconstructed dangerous mayhem.' In the finished video, the two Pet Shop Boys, whether culpable or not of what is going on around them, remain characteristically impassive in the face of all that they may have wrought.

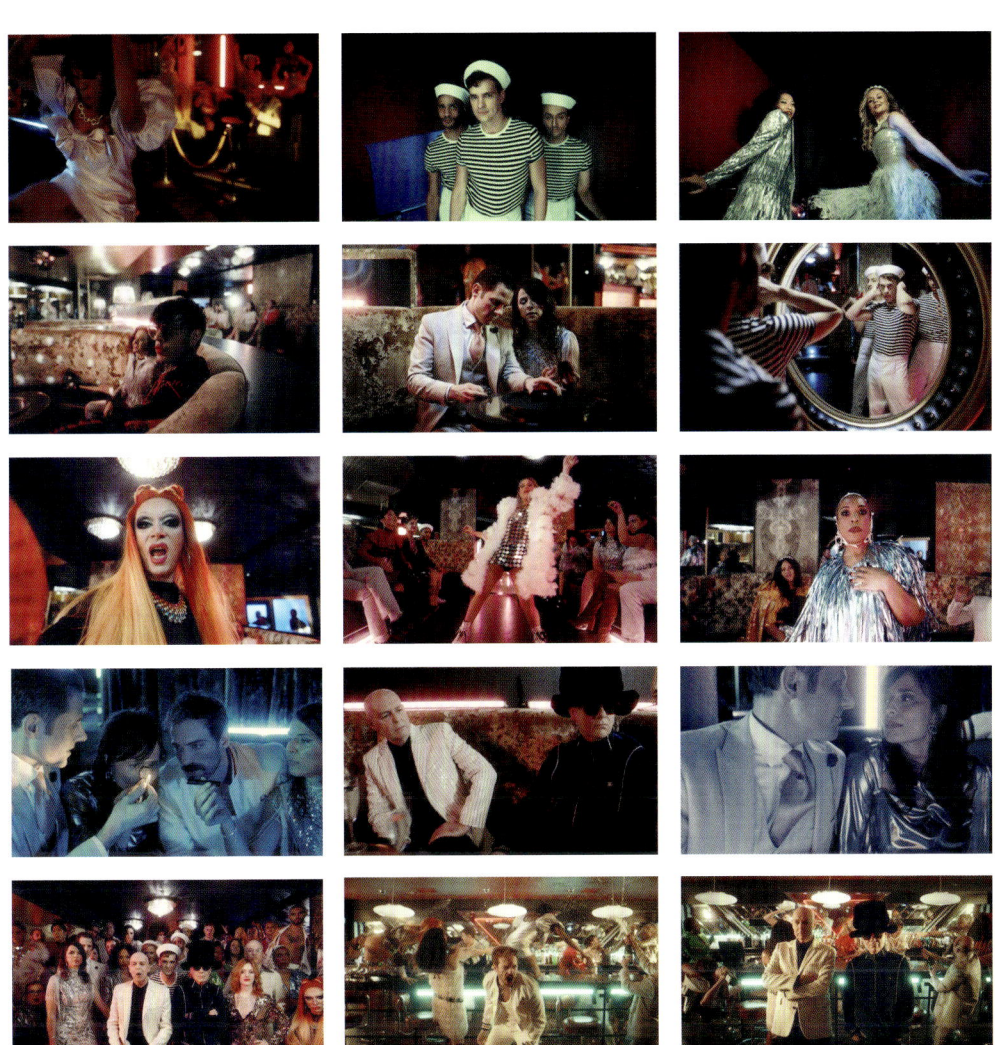

Hotspot

release 24 January 2020
formats LP / cassette / CD / 2 × CD / download
photographer Tennant / Lowe
design and art direction Farrow / PSB

Hotspot, the third in the trilogy of albums made with Stuart Price – but also, says Chris 'an album in transition' – is the first album to show Neil and Chris on its sleeve since *Fundamental*, though only obliquely. It was triggered by an image they saw when they attended the opening of the Olafur Eliasson show at Tate Modern. 'I said, "Why don't we have something like that?"' Chris relates. 'Then Neil said, "Oh, I've got something just like that in my phone"' – a photograph that he had taken of himself and Chris reflected in a mirror in a Berlin art gallery.

Initially they had planned to call the album by a different name. 'We nearly called it "Von Pet Shop Boys"', says Neil. 'The reason we didn't is because we mentioned it to two friends of ours in Germany, one of them being Wolfgang Tillmans. We thought it was hilarious. And we got complete stone faces from both of them.' 'Which in itself is funny', Chris notes. 'I still think it's a better album title than *Hotspot*', says Neil. Farrow mocked up several sleeve ideas under this earlier title. After the name changed, still pursuing the U-Bahn station sign idea, they mocked up a cover based on the Hansaplatz station sign, with HOTSPOT in its centre in the Hansaplatz font. Neil notes that throughout this process, once that they had settled on *Hotspot* as the album's title, they were hampered in one very specific way: 'It was an unfortunate thing in terms of graphics, because *Hotspot* obviously implies a circle, but we'd already done that. *Super*, it had all been circles.' Eventually they settled on the image of the reflected Pet Shop Boys. Mark Farrow has some misgivings about the final version: 'I felt that this somehow needed a nice type treatment for it to really work. That's how Neil liked it. He just thought it looked good, simple in the corner there. And I didn't agree. I was never happy with it. I thought we'd done some better versions, but that's how it ended up.' The album was released in several formats. For the first time since *Nightlife* in 1999, these included a cassette, alongside a vinyl LP, a CD, and a special edition with a second CD of instrumental versions of the *Hotspot* tracks.

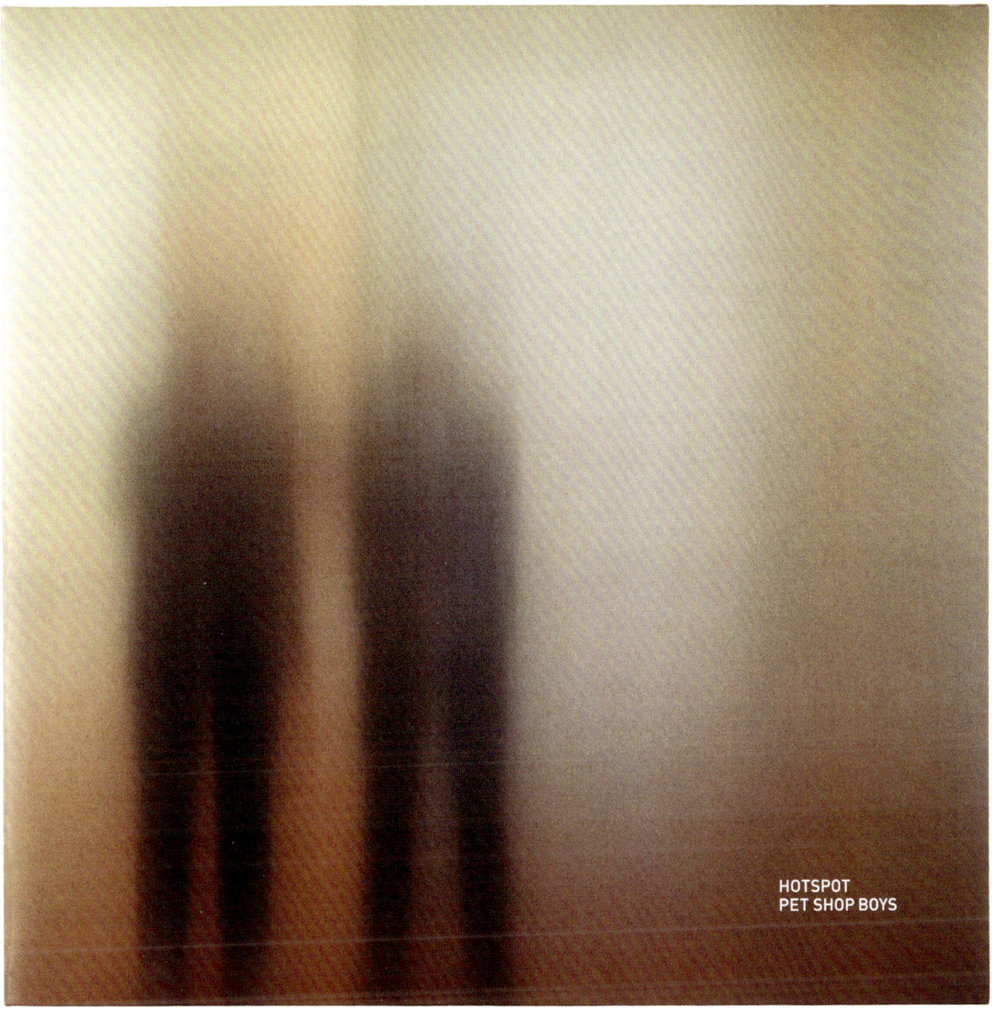

LP, outer sleeve, front

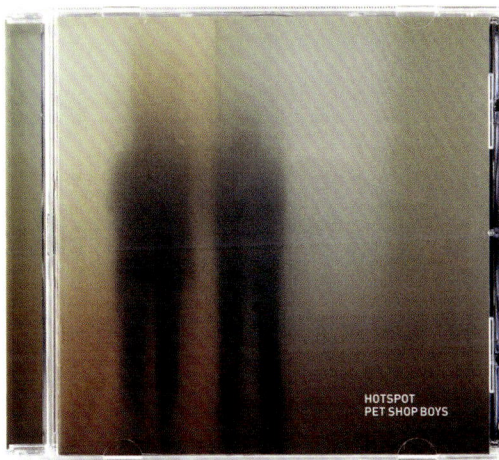

CD, front

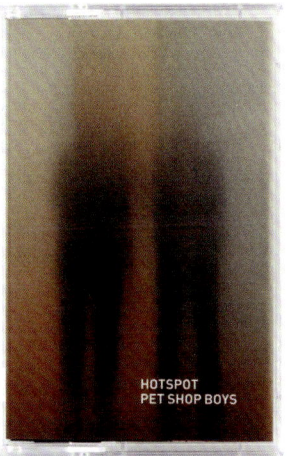

Cassette, front

Inside the various album formats were other photos taken in Berlin by Neil and Chris. These appeared in the CD booklet, on the outer and inner sleeves of the vinyl LP, and (in detail form) on the cassette sleeve. 'I think we wanted moody abstract pictures', says Neil. Here is an annotated guide: Rain/condensation on glass – 'That's taken by me. I think that's probably taken from the S-Bahn in Berlin.' (Neil). Outdoor scene – 'That's taken in woods in Berlin, in the Tiergarten. I think it's taken by me. I'm always taking pictures in the Tiergarten, actually.' (Neil). Blue – 'I don't know what it is. Very abstract, though, isn't it? Oh, do you know what, it would probably be in a club. It could be a club toilet, even.' (Chris). Cranes – 'There's a lot of building going on in Berlin. All my favourite buildings have been demolished.' (Chris). Internal view of industrial roof – 'Looks like sort of the thing I would take. I don't know where it is.' (Chris). View through glass – 'That is going to the toilet in a restaurant in West Berlin. In the corridor as you walk down to it, that glass is there and you can see the courtyard through it. Quite a common Berlin sight.' (Neil). Red – 'Well, that could be a toilet as well. I don't know what they are. They're abstract, aren't they? They're the sort of thing that Nick Rhodes would take pictures of.' (Chris).

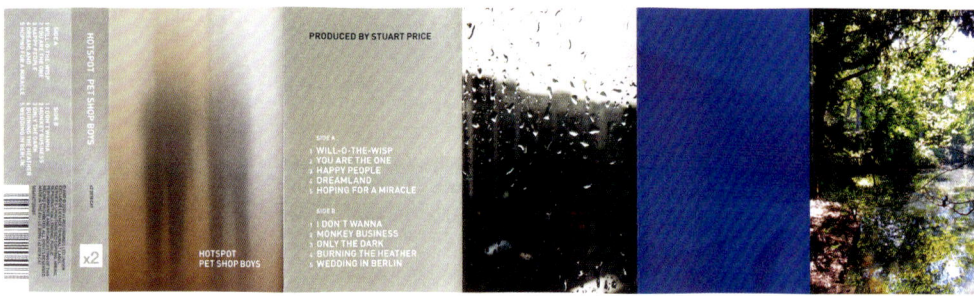

Cassette, sleeve (open), front

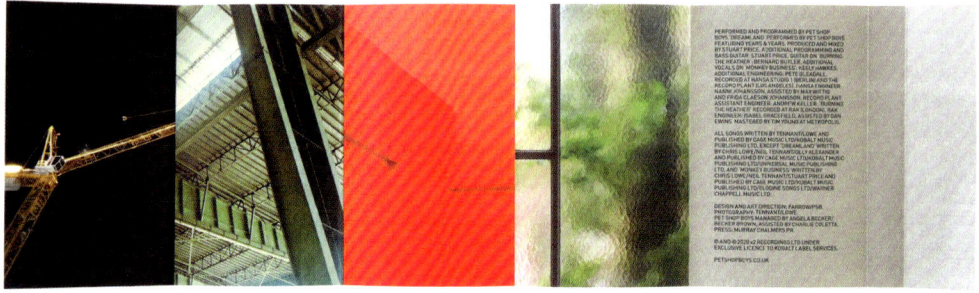

Cassette, sleeve (open), back

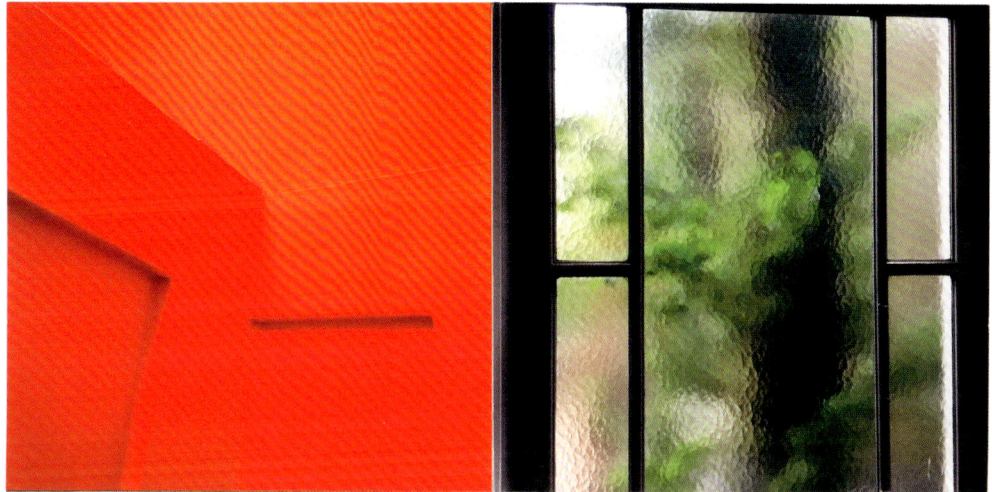

LP, outer sleeve (open), inside

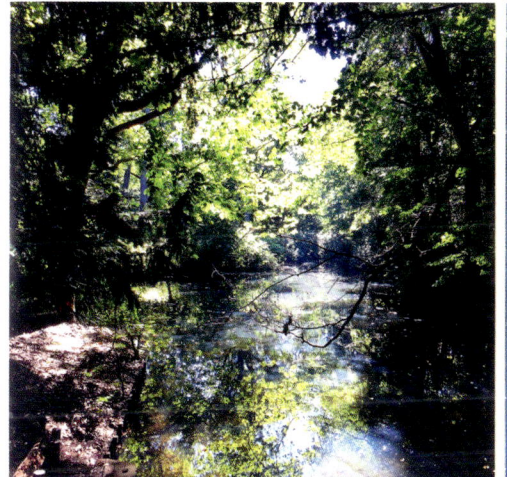

LP, inner sleeve, front

LP, inner sleeve, back

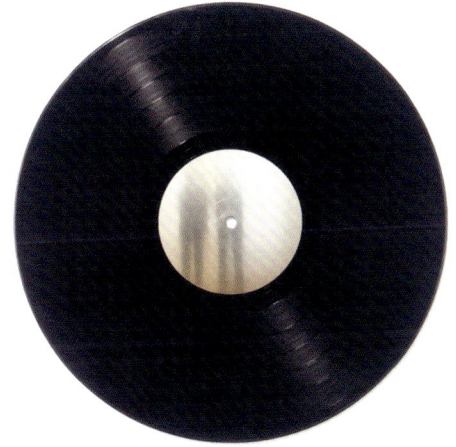

LP, Side A

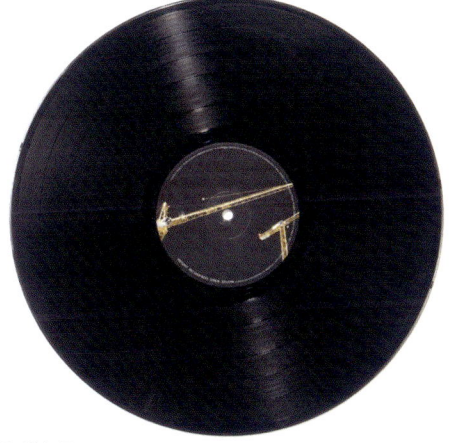

LP, Side B

Two books about Pet Shop Boys

release 19 March 2020
formats 384-page hardback and 304-page hardback book
author Chris Heath
photographers Eric Watson
design Farrow / PSB

The reissues of Chris Heath's *Pet Shop Boys, Literally* from 1990 and *Pet Shop Boys versus America* from 1993 came about, to some degree, by a quirk of circumstance. 'I was talking to Sonny Marr, Johnny Marr's daughter, who works in book publishing', says Neil. 'She was working for Heinemann, and when she said they were part of the same group as Penguin, I said, "Well, you could reissue those books."' And so it was. Neil and Chris wrote new introductions, Chris Heath wrote new afterwords, and Farrow designed new covers, using the Eric Watson photos that originally appeared on the sleeves for 'Jealousy'. 'The classic one-each idea', says Neil. 'I always loved the original *…versus America* book cover,' says Mark Farrow, 'but it felt like they should match each other. It's Pet Shop Boys, there's two of them … one should be on each. It's just very logical in that respect.' Neil chose the books' new format, with the photos printed directly onto the cover. 'I never liked the original formats of either of those books – I thought they should be more readable', he says. 'Sonny gave me a dummy of a book they had with the picture printed on the cover, and it was perfect. I quite like that format because I think it's readable.' Farrow proposed a half-width dust jacket covering part of the cover, but that was not done. They also originally mocked up covers with each full 'Jealousy' image on each cover. 'Chris had that "I don't like that photograph" thing', says Farrow. 'Which is why there's only half.' 'They look really beautiful', says Neil. 'I prefer them to the original covers.' 'It is nice to get to do a book that looks good', Farrow concurs, 'because most books don't, let's face it. It's a sea of mediocrity when you walk into a bookshop.' There was also a special edition, with both books inside a grey slipcase bearing the title *Two books about Pet Shop Boys*, with the photographs printed on the inside of the box. A subsequent 2021 Spanish paperback edition of the first book, *Pet Shop Boys, literalmente*, adapted the same design, using the photo of Neil on the front, Chris on the back.

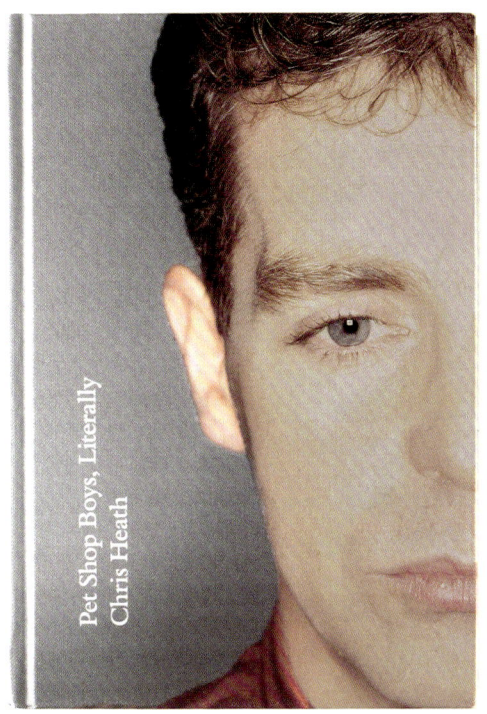

Pet Shop Boys, Literally

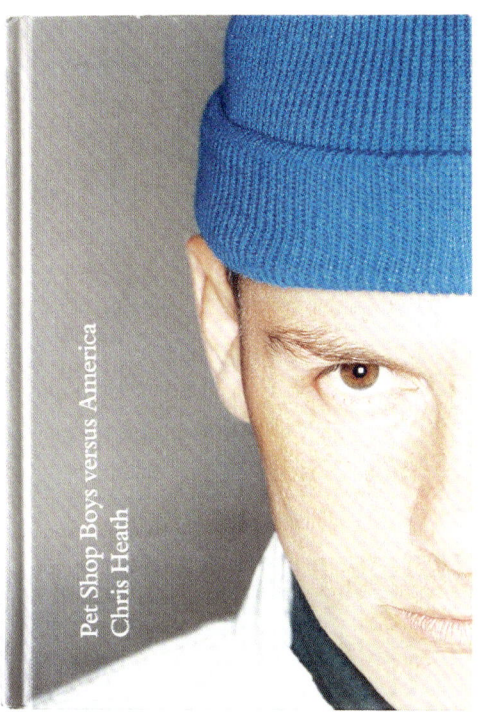

Pet Shop Boys versus America

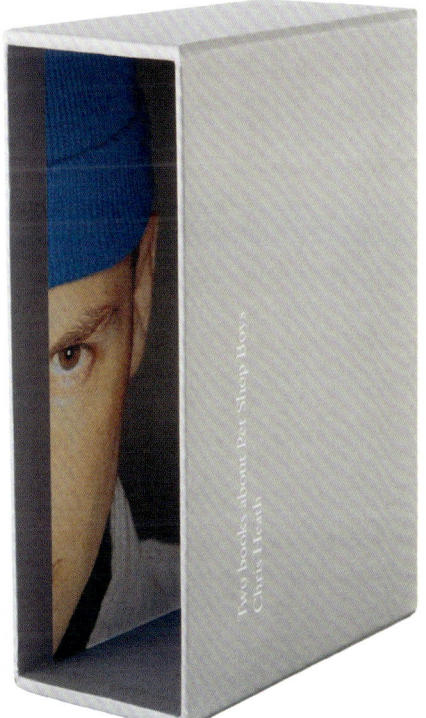

Slipcase

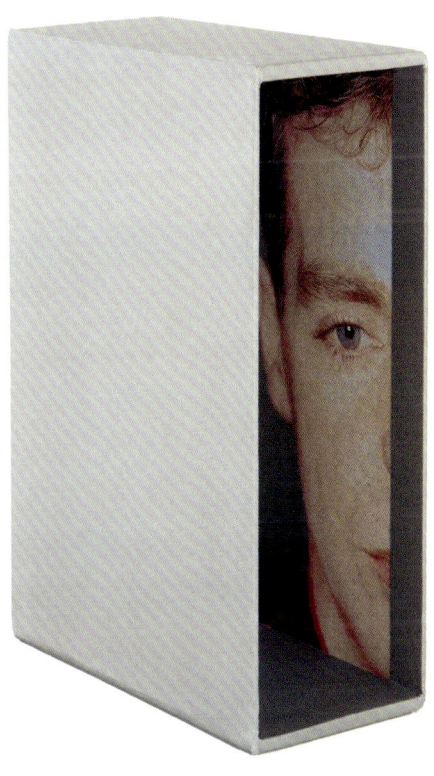

My Beautiful Laundrette

release 17 April 2020
formats CD / download
design Farrow / PSB

In early 2019, the author, film-maker, and playwright Hanif Kureishi approached Pet Shop Boys via their mutual friend Jon Savage, explaining that he and director Nikolai Foster were staging a theatrical version of his 1985 film *My Beautiful Laundrette* at the Leicester Curve theatre, requesting to use some old Pet Shop Boys songs, and also asking whether Neil and Chris would write some new instrumental music. They agreed. The eventual production, which began previews on 20 September 2019, used 'West End girls', 'I get excited (you get excited too)', 'Left to my own devices', 'Hit music', 'In the night', 'Opportunities', 'Later tonight', 'Tonight is forever', and 'Paninaro', as well as seven new pieces of music recorded by Pet Shop Boys, two with vocals by Neil. These new recordings were released on a CD available exclusively with that year's *Annually*, as well as a digital download. The CD's front cover showed two washing machines; its back showed two different baskets of miscellaneous laundry. 'That was just funny', says Mark Farrow. 'Pet Shop Boys represented by two washing machines. The eternal recurring theme of two of them.' 'With Bembo at the top', points out Gary Stillwell, referring to the typeface, 'so it's like *Actually*.' 'It's Farrow's idea', says Neil. 'It's a funny idea. Obviously, it's a piss-take of Pet Shop Boys, *Actually*.' 'I would have said we should have had a washing machine and a tumble dryer', says Chris, adding 'I would be the tumble dryer.' 'I would have said that, too', Neil agrees. 'Because I'd have been after Neil', rationalizes Chris. 'You do the washing first, so Neil's in front, followed by the tumble dryer.' 'Anyway,' says Neil, 'it's a very successful cover.' 'It's a bit "The truck-driver and his mate"', notes Chris.

Pet Shop Boys
My Beautiful Laundrette

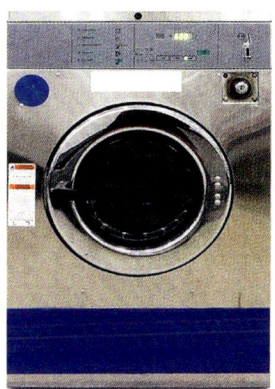
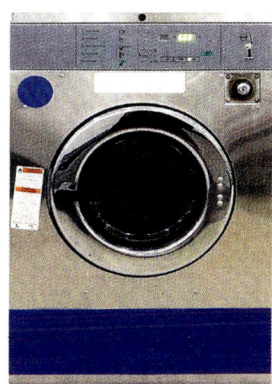

CD, front

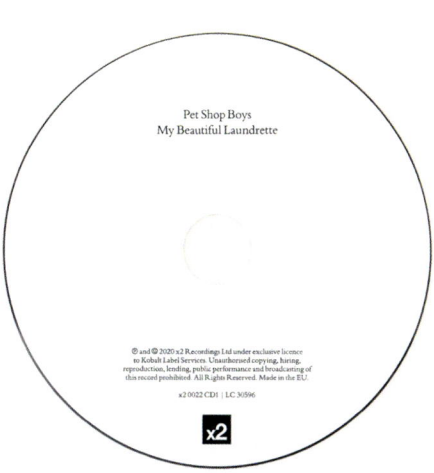

CD, back

CD, disc

I don't wanna

release 24 April 2020
formats 12" / CD / download
design Farrow / PSB
video RMV Productions

'I don't wanna' is 'a song about how listening to a pop song inspires someone', its music inspired by Tracey Thorn's 'Dancefloor' – a song which itself had been inspired by the Pet Shop Boys' 'Vocal'. 'So there you go', says Chris. 'It just goes round in circles.' 'I don't wanna' had already been scheduled as *Hotspot*'s final single before the emergent pandemic, but in this unexpected new world, the Pet Shop Boys were naturally aware of the strange concurrence between its chorus – 'I don't wanna go out' – and the circumstances in which people were now living. The idea for its sleeve – 'I think it was ours', says Neil – was that someone had texted the narrator of the song saying, 'Are you coming out tonight?' and he has now just replied, as shown, 'I don't wanna.' 'Apple iMessage', notes Mark Farrow. 'Some people get it and go, "Ah, I see what you've done there." Other people just think it's a bit of a nothing sleeve. But, I mean, it was kind of clever.' The different formats offer the alternate ways the song's chorus completes this thought: 'Go out' (the CD single) and 'Go dancing' (the twelve inch).

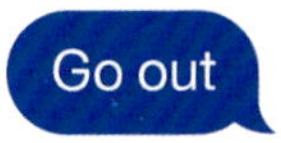

CD, inside

I don't wanna

12", outer sleeve, front

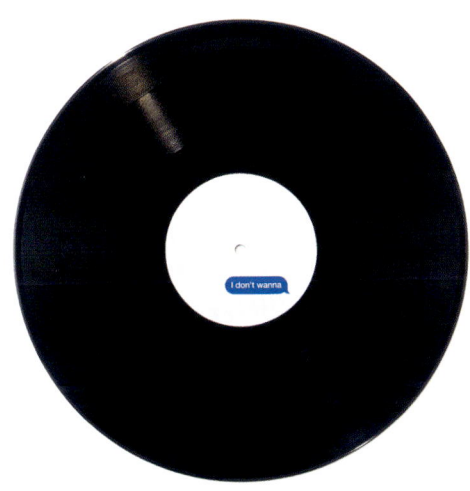

Go dancing

12", inner sleeve, front
12", Side A

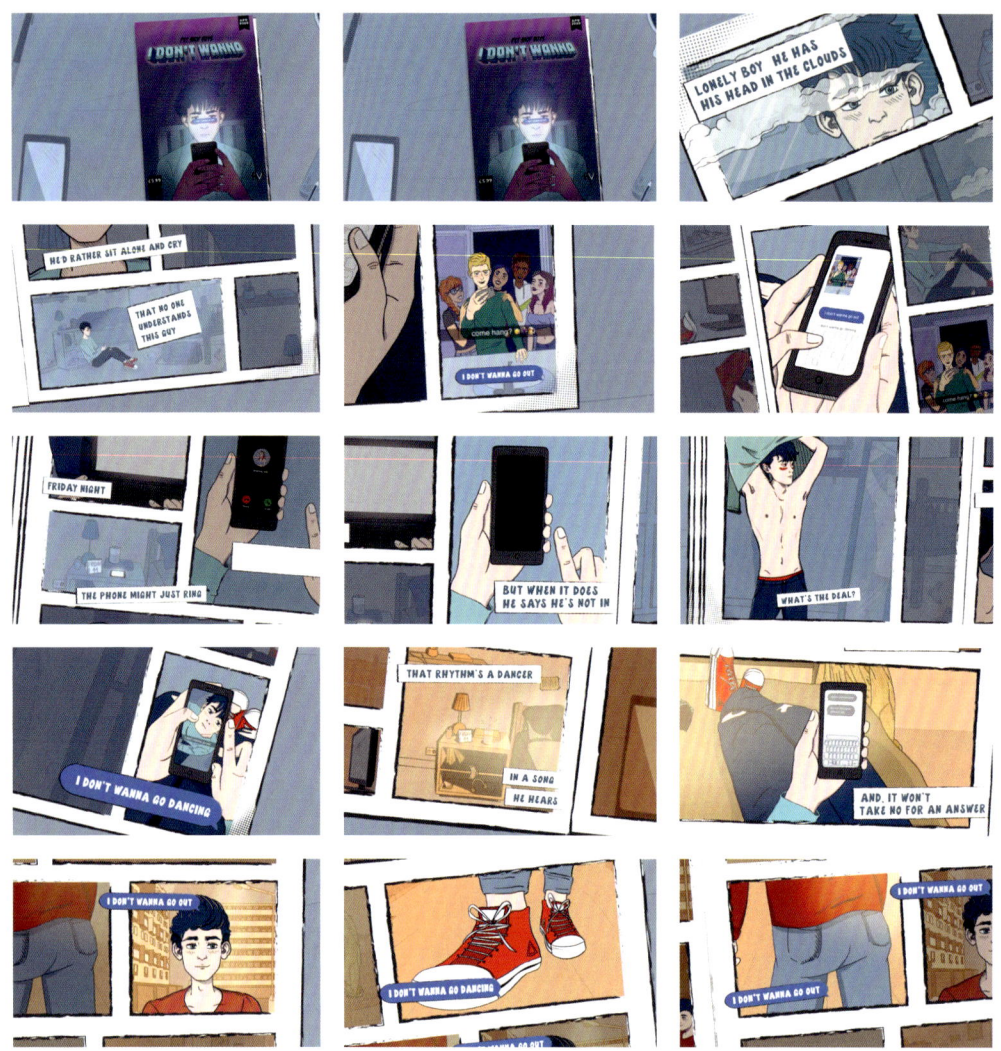

A lyric video in the style of a comic strip dramatizes, panel by panel, the song's lonely boy as he rebuffs text message exhortations until he finally, as only hinted by the song itself, transcends his fears and joins the world of people.

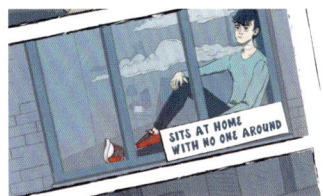
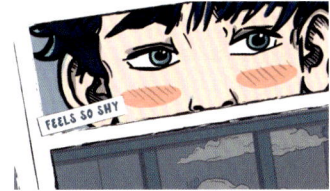
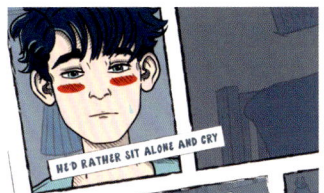
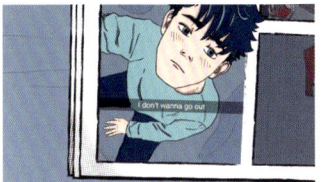
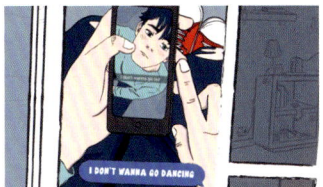
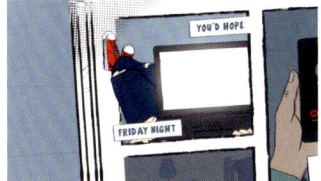
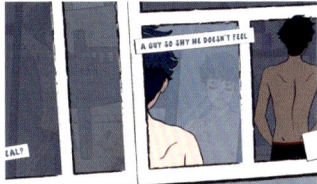
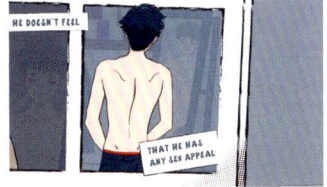
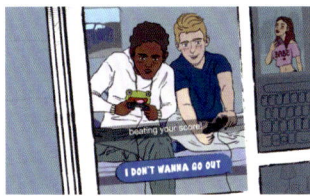
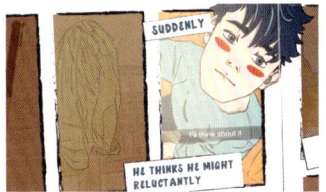
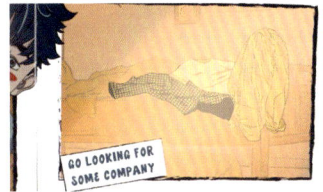
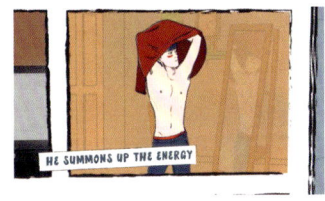
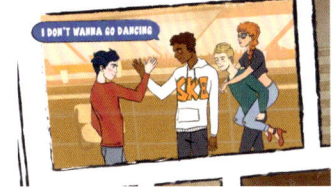
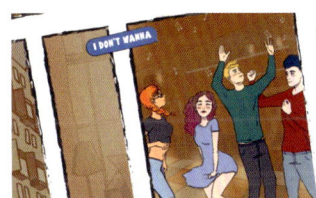
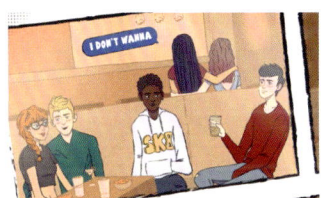

Cricket wife

release 7 May 2021
formats CD / download
design and art direction Farrow / PSB

The ten-minute 'Cricket wife', the longest Pet Shop Boys song to date, was written during the Covid-19 lockdowns. 'My mum asked me if I would write a piece of classical music for her', Chris explains. 'I thought, "Well, I've got nothing else better to do." "Classical" in inverted commas, obviously – I'm no classical composer. In the style of classical music.' After Chris sent this music to Neil, he was surprised to receive it back only two days later with an added vocal relaying an intricate lyric. The words were based on a poem Neil had written several years earlier. 'It's really about my parents', he says. 'My father played cricket for many years.' It was released physically as the first track on a two-track CD single, available only with *Annually 2021*. 'I think it was my idea to do the cricket jumper', says Mark Farrow. 'It was just a stock picture.' says Gary Stillwell. 'And Neil suggested that typeface. He sent something in with it and said "What is it?" And I found it.'

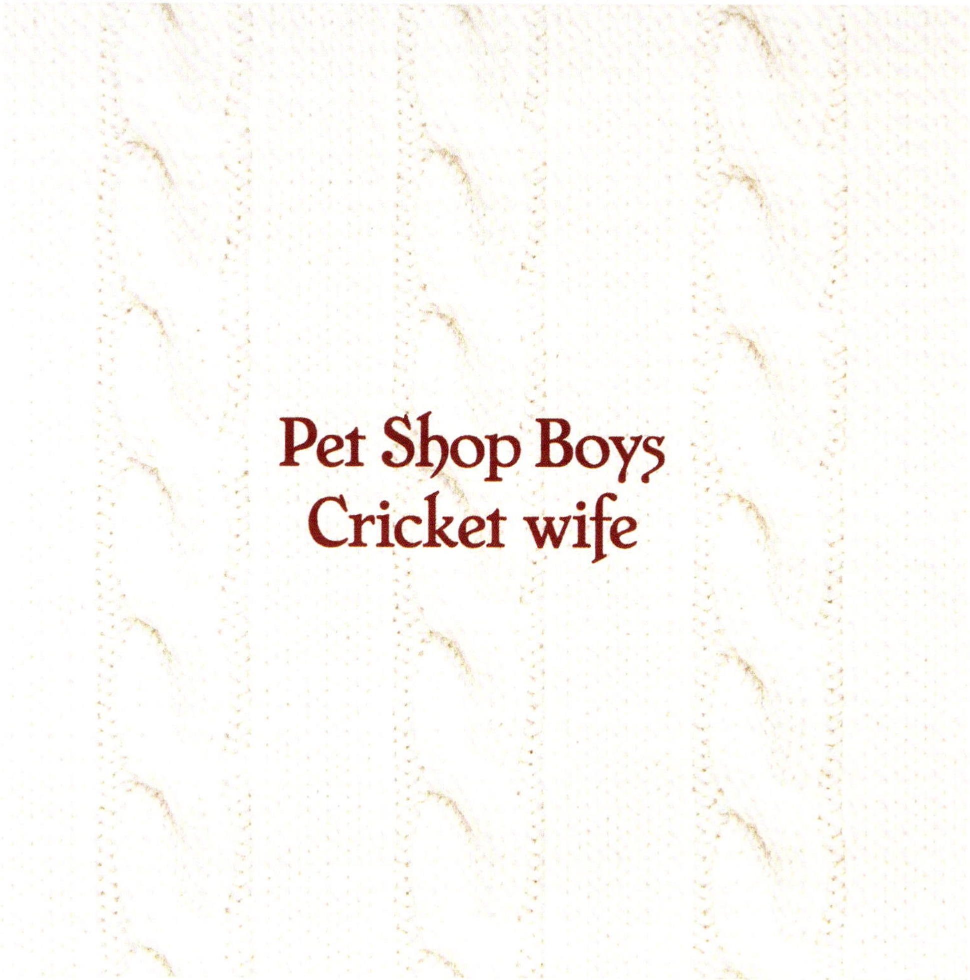

CD, front

Pet Shop Boys
Cricket wife

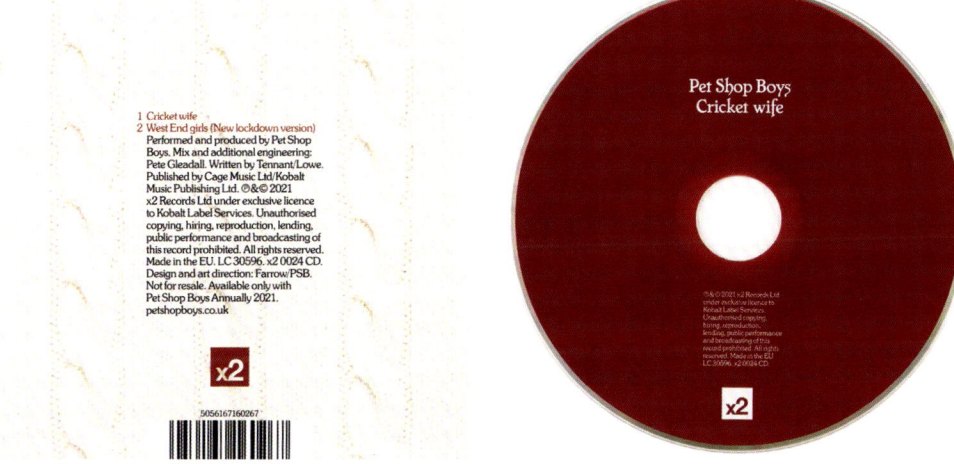

CD, back

1 Cricket wife
2 West End girls (New lockdown version)
Performed and produced by Pet Shop Boys. Mix and additional engineering: Pete Gleadall. Written by Tennant/Lowe. Published by Cage Music Ltd/Kobalt Music Publishing Ltd. ℗&© 2021 x2 Records Ltd under exclusive licence to Kobalt Label Services. Unauthorised copying, hiring, reproduction, lending, public performance and broadcasting of this record prohibited. All rights reserved. Made in the EU. LC 30596. x2 0024 CD. Design and art direction: Farrow/PSB. Not for resale. Available only with Pet Shop Boys Annually 2021.
petshopboys.co.uk

x2

5056167160267

CD, disc

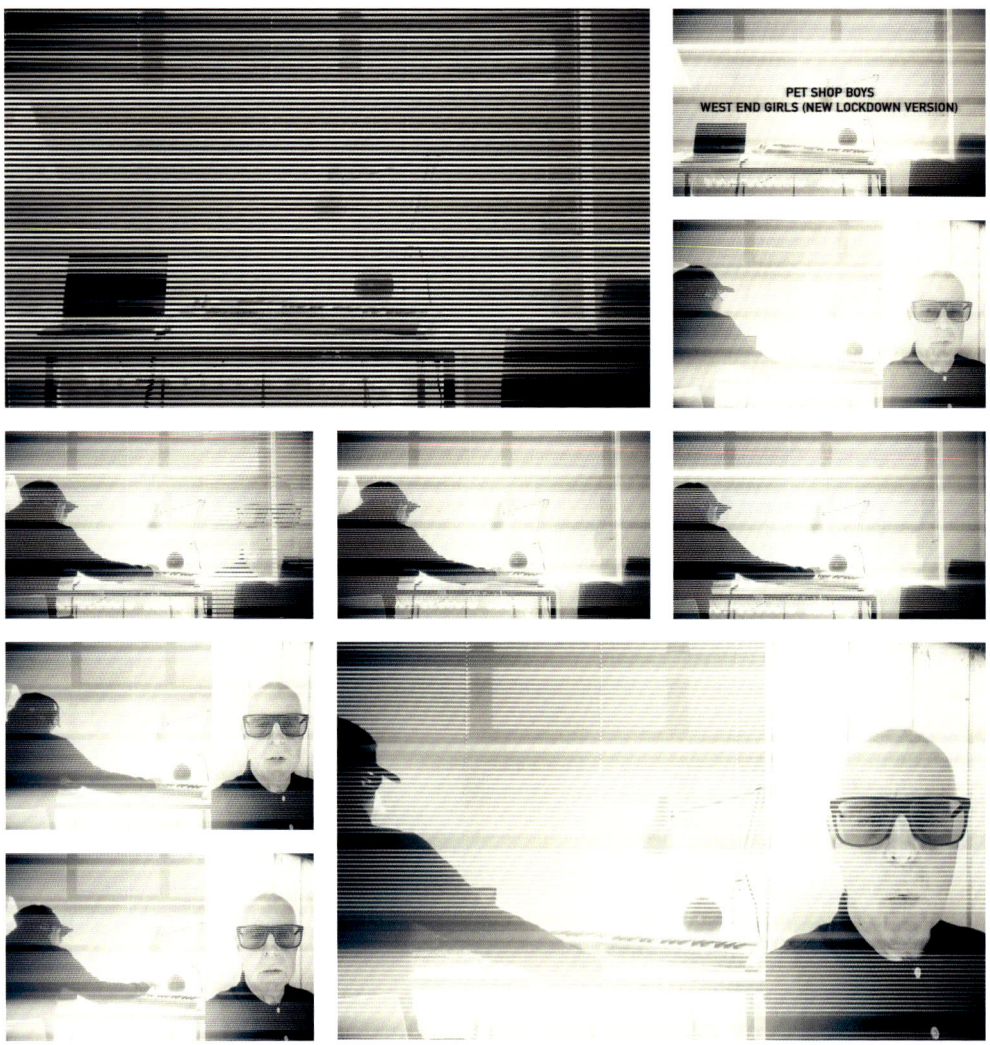

Also on the same CD was 'West End girls (New lockdown version)'. In May 2020, Pet Shop Boys were contacted by the American cultural institution the Smithsonian, which was planning an online gay pride event. It was Chris's suggestion to revisit 'West End girls'. 'My idea was to take out the chorus,' he says, 'so you don't get the bassline in the chorus. That was the big idea.' Separated under lockdown restrictions, Neil and Chris recorded their parts separately, then each filmed themselves on an iPhone for the accompanying video – Chris at home playing the keyboard, Neil outside his garage. The footage, combined by Luke Halls, served as the finale of the two-hour *Smithsonian Presents: Project Pride* on 31 May 2020.

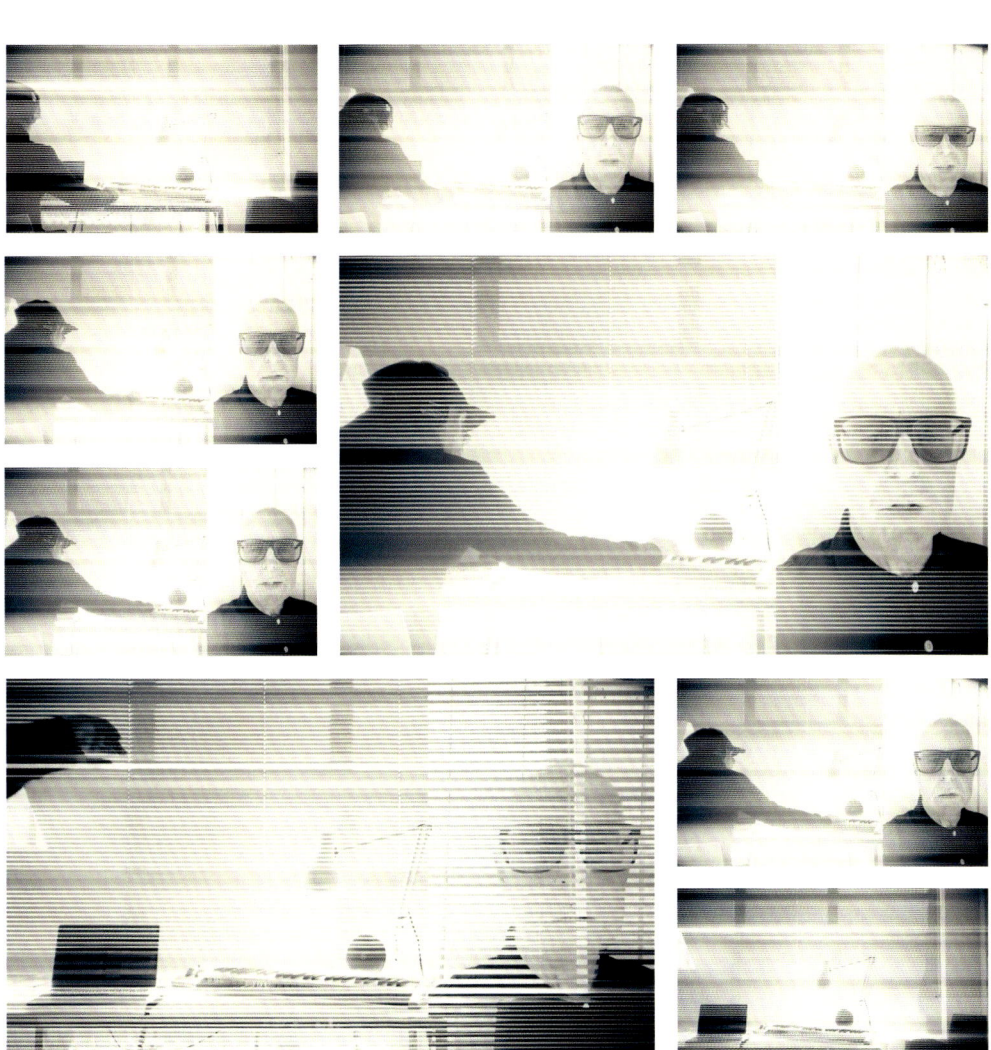

Dreamworld tour

dates 10 May 2022 – ongoing
creative direction, set, and costume design Tom Scutt
video projections Luke Halls and Jenny Rush
lighting Bruno Poet and Matthew Daw
stage direction Lynne Page

Dreamworld was conceived as the first Pet Shop Boys tour to be explicitly billed as a greatest hits show. Planning started in 2019. After Neil had been impressed by the design of the play *A Very Expensive Poison*, about the Alexander Litvinenko poisoning, at the Old Vic theatre in London, he and Chris met with the designer Tom Scutt, and subsequently asked him to design this new tour. 'We wanted to produce something that feels like a new piece of art, but also envelops their whole back catalogue and acknowledges the weight of their legacy', Scutt explains. 'Something that I do in theatre is try to reduce all the themes and ideas to a simple, visual, graphic expression, and with this tour that ended up being the shape of a line. So there's visual iconography that starts with a single line that splits into more lines, and more lines and more lines and more lines – the idea of which is that it takes you on a journey with Pet Shop Boys: from suburbia to London, then global, then to different planets, then back down to Earth.' As on recent tours, the music was produced by Stuart Price. 'The theme here', Price says, 'is a history of ideas, and assembling that into an experience that shows you the depth and the breadth of the journey Neil and Chris have been on.'

The tour was scheduled to begin on 1 May 2020 in Berlin, but as the severity of the Covid-19 pandemic became clearer, it kept being delayed. In the interim, the show evolved. After Neil and Chris guested on Olly Alexander's BBC TV New Year's Eve show in 2021, Chris realized how much he liked being positioned in the middle of the stage, further back, in what he calls the 'God is a DJ position', and so it was now arranged that he would spend much of *Dreamworld* like this. The original design also included multiple physical lamp posts, but they decided to streamline this so that there were only two. Pet Shop Boys appeared on stage wearing Scutt's 'tuning fork' masks that would become a key part of *Dreamworld*'s iconography, Neil's eyes visible (page 490), Chris's eyes covered (page 491). Between 17 September and 16 October 2022, they performed a version of this set on the *Unity* tour of North America with New Order, a concept that Chris had suggested some years earlier: 'I just thought it would be something I'd like to go and see', he says. A *Dreamworld* tour programme comprehensively documented the full Pet Shop Boys production, with photographs by Erik Weiss and interviews by Peter Robinson. A film of the show shot in Copenhagen's Royal Arena on 7 July 2023, *Dreamworld: The Greatest Hits Live*, directed by David Barnard, premiered in cinemas around the world on 31 January 2024.

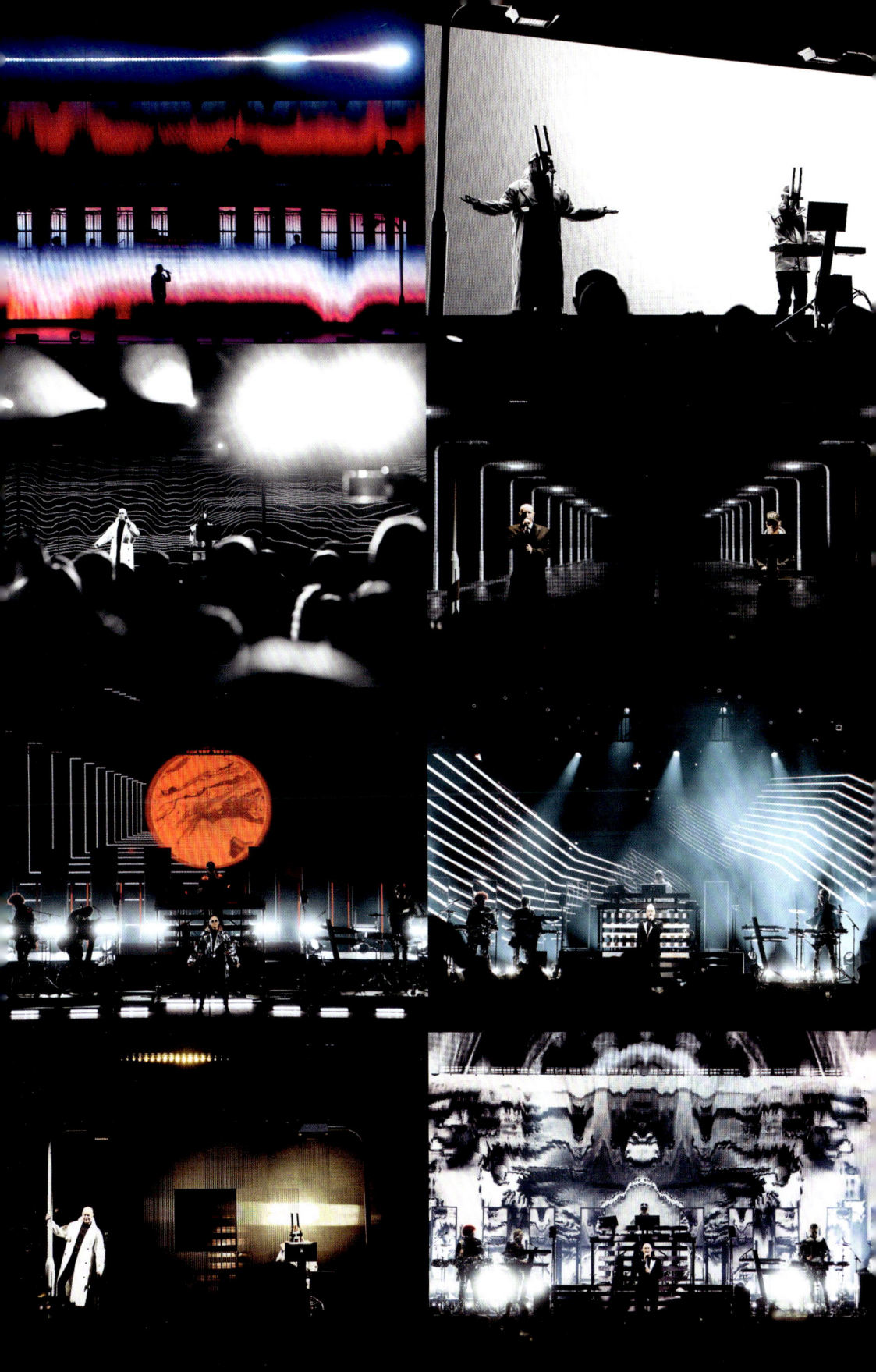

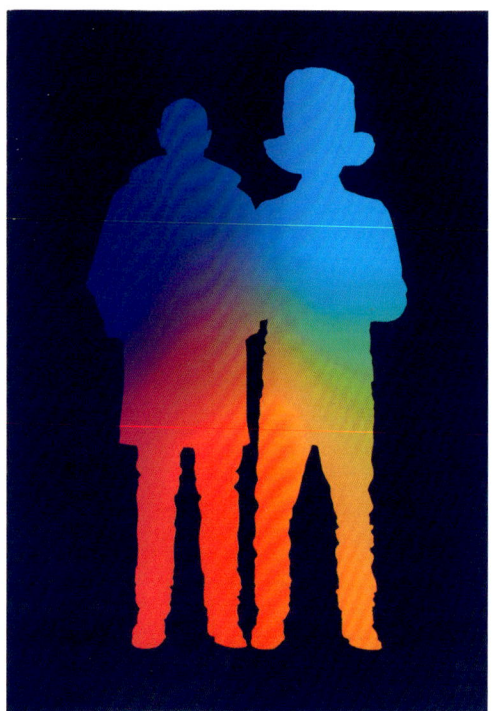

2022 tour programme, front

2022 tour programme, back

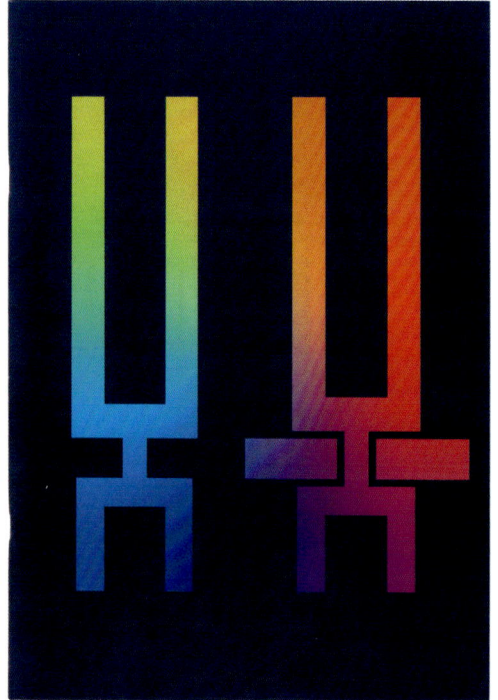

2024 tour programme, front

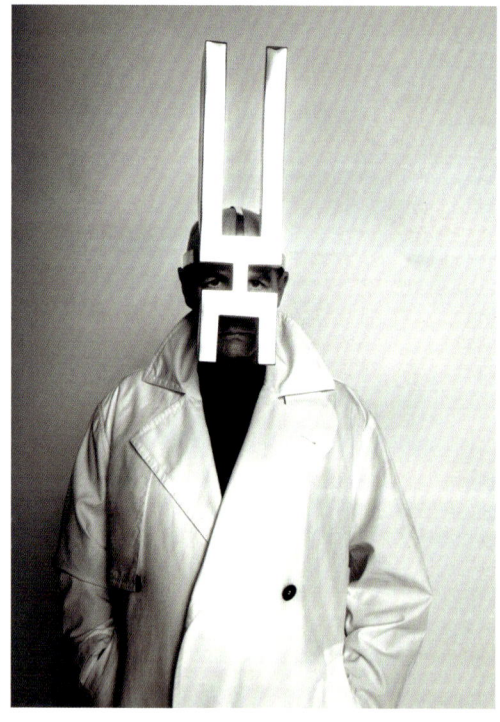

2024 tour programme, inside page

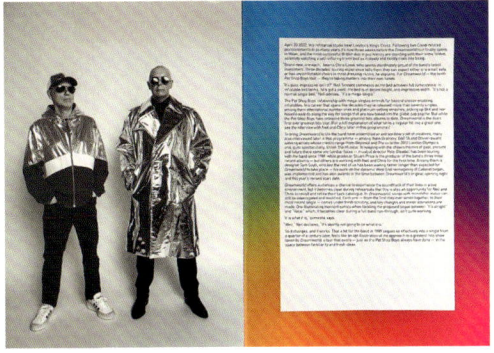
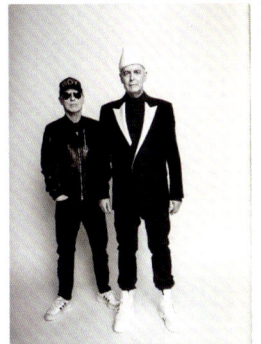
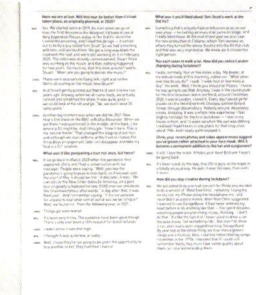

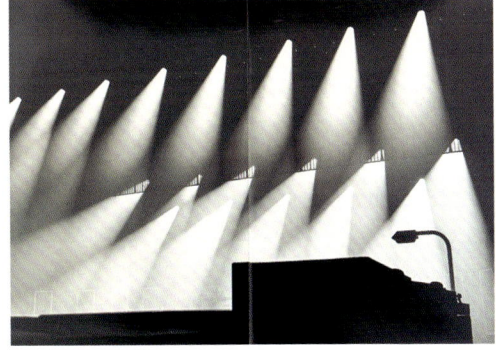
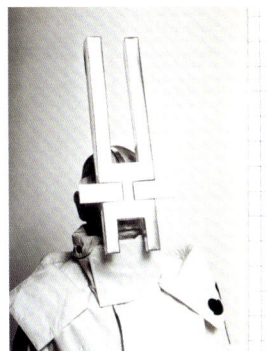
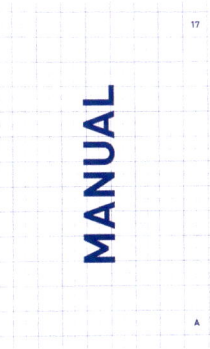

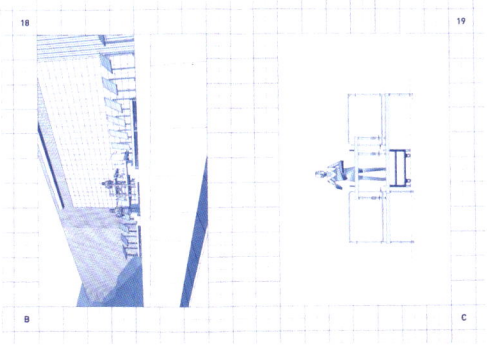
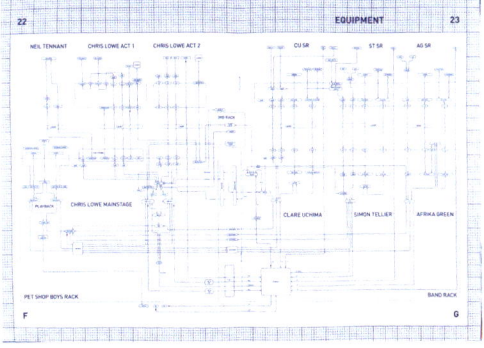

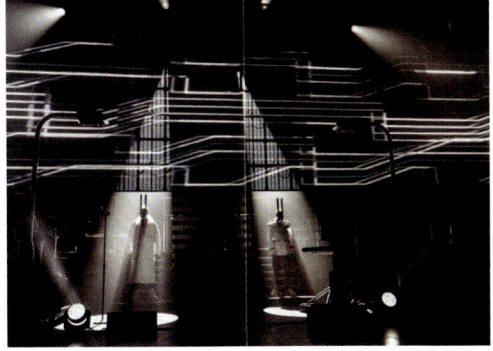
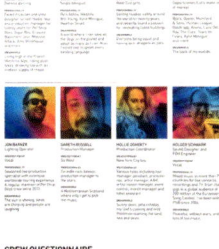
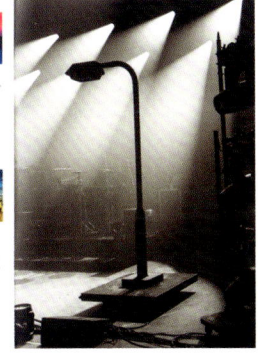

Tour programme, inside pages

Dreamworld tour   2022–ongoing

Lost

release 14 April 2023
formats CD / download
photographer Gary Stillwell
design and art direction Farrow / PSB

Lost was an EP of four songs demoed in 2015 for potential inclusion on *Super*, now belatedly released as a CD with *Annually 2023*, alongside a fifth last-minute digital-only addition. 'It wasn't that we didn't like them,' says Neil of the original four songs, 'it was just that they didn't fit into the album.' If these songs had a common theme, he says, it was that they directly or indirectly concerned 'fascism and Putinism', issues that had now been thrown into a new light by the Russian invasion of Ukraine in February 2022. The fifth song, 'Living in the past', written by Neil on his piano at home, related directly to this new history, and its raw version had been swiftly posted on social media. 'We were following the John Lennon principle', he says, 'of songs coming out, like newspapers, commenting on what was happening right at that moment.'

The EP's opening track, 'The lost room', was based on German director Volker Schlöndorff's 1966 film *Young Törless*, about cruelty and abuse at a 1900s Austrian boarding school. The sleeve of *Lost* has the look of the film, and echoes its typeface, although the actual black-and-white photograph on the front was taken in London's Victoria Park by Gary Stillwell. 'The film's opening title sequence is over kind of a field, so I wanted to try and replicate something like that', he says. 'I remember standing there and waiting for the dog walkers to walk past so I could get fields rather than people drinking espresso. I showed it to Neil and remember him saying, "Yes, that looks suitably bleak."'

Chris edited an initial video for 'The lost room' by combining some footage of *Young Törless* that he found on YouTube. Later on, Pet Shop Boys got official permission from the original producers, and Stillwell did a further edit. The video was online for only a year following the terms of the agreement with the *Young Törless* producers.

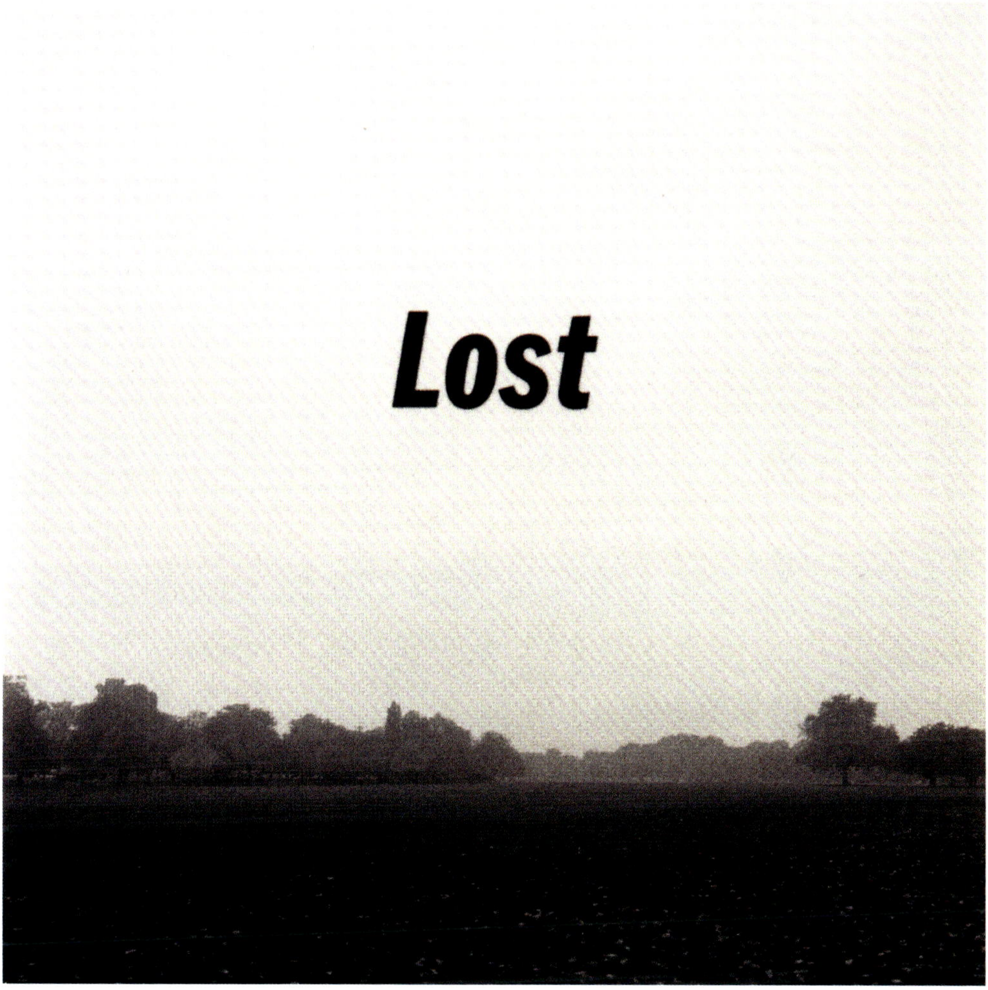

CD, front

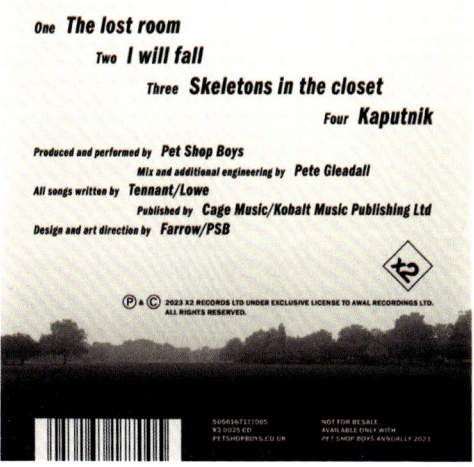

CD, back

CD, disc

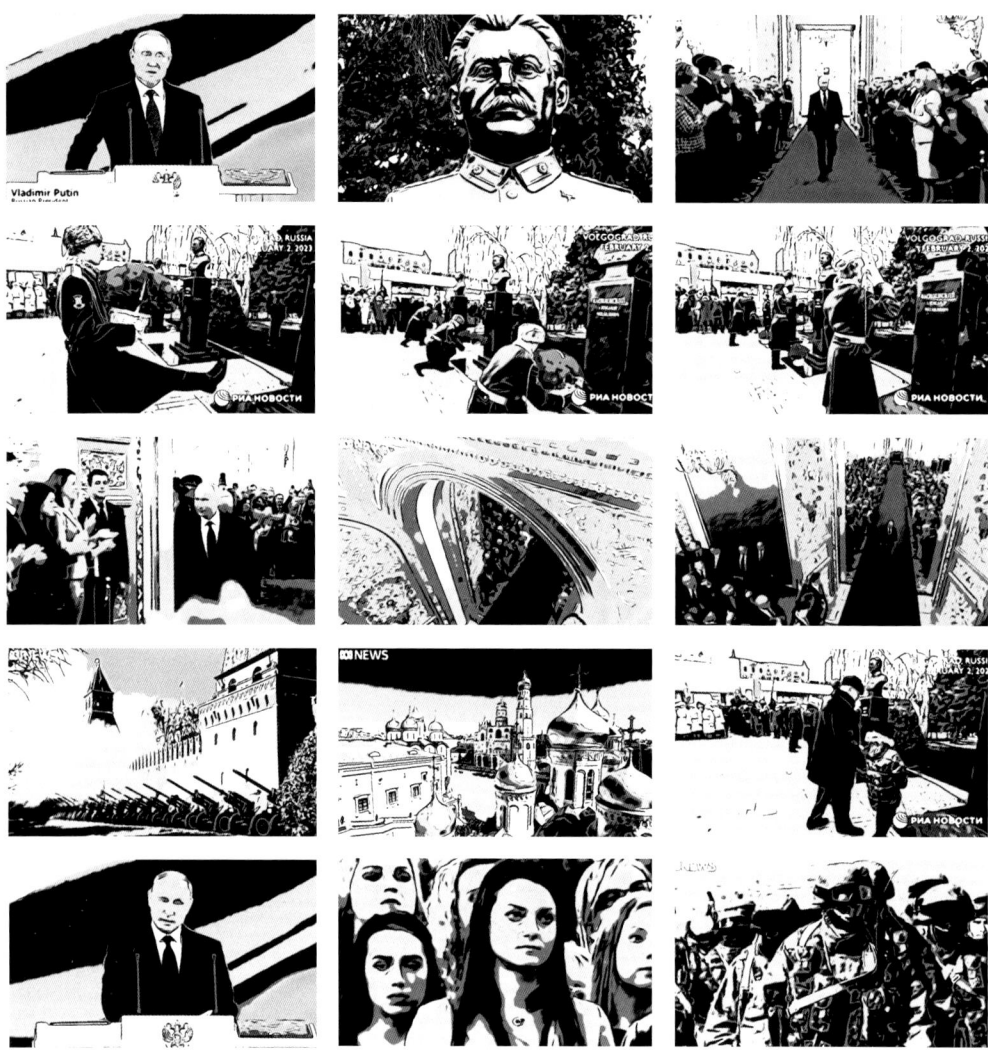

For the instant release of 'Living in the past', Chris made a video using stock footage that he edited on his phone using iMovie, in which at the end Vladimir Putin's face morphs into Joseph Stalin's.

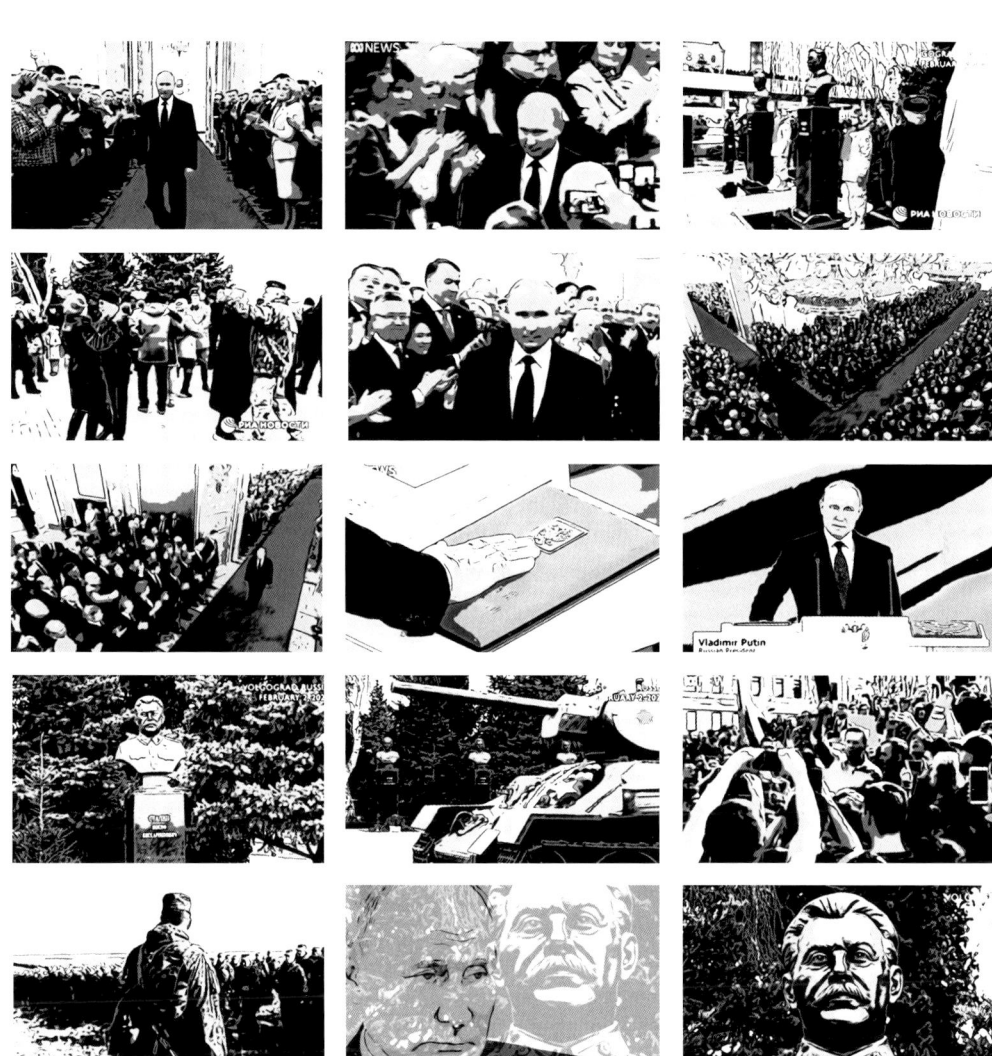

Smash

release 16 June 2023
formats Six-disc LP / limited-edition triple cassette / three-disc CD / three-disc CD + two-disc BluRay / download
design and art direction Farrow / PSB

The title of the new compilation of fifty-five Pet Shop Boys singles in chronological order was suggested by Chris: 'It seemed very Roy Lichtenstein: Pow! Wham! Smash! And there's also, "It's a smash!" – that's what people used to say about singles. And there's the connection with Neil and *Smash Hits*.' Previously, the release had been through various iterations. 'The original idea for this project came out of the notion of *Discography* being reissued,' says Neil, 'and I suggested we did *Discography* One, Two, and Three. And they mocked them up.' After a time, it was decided to release a new standalone compilation instead. For a while, this was to have been called *Hit Music*. Meanwhile, the visual treatment also took some time to coalesce. At one point, says Mark Farrow, 'There was an idea of doing a portrait of them behind fluted glass.' 'It was a bit like *Super* – we were going around in circles', says Neil. 'We actually went to Gary Stillwell's flat', Chris recalls. 'We had to have a crisis summit.' At either this meeting or a later one, says Stillwell, Neil suggested 'trying a really bold typeface.' Eventually, the designers came up with an idea – and, ironically, given how well it would conceptually fit the final title, this was when it was still to be called *Hit Music* – that they could take the original artwork of the fifty-five singles and combine them using a computer program. 'It was like: so what if we smashed all the sleeves into each other?' says Farrow. 'It was like creating art from a piece of art, from all the sleeves.' Once Chris came up with the new title *Smash* – 'It was in America, in a hotel, in somewhere like Chicago', Chris recalls – this all made even better sense. Not only does the image on the front cover really include elements from all fifty-five original singles – 'They genuinely are all in there', says Stillwell – but, characteristically, Farrow then pushed the concept even further: the six individual sleeves of the vinyl release (three black and three white records) each bore their own smashed image including only elements of the original sleeves whose songs were on that particular disc. Furthermore, they also took a series of iconic portraits of Pet Shop Boys and put these singly 'though the same filters that we used to create the smash effect', something that was strikingly effective. 'They just really invigorated these old classic images', says Farrow. I love the blurred images of the pointy hats', says Chris. A deluxe version also included BluRay discs with fifty-three videos matching the songs on the audio discs (the two exceptions are 'Love is a bourgeois construct' and 'Say it to me'), as well as thirteen further videos.

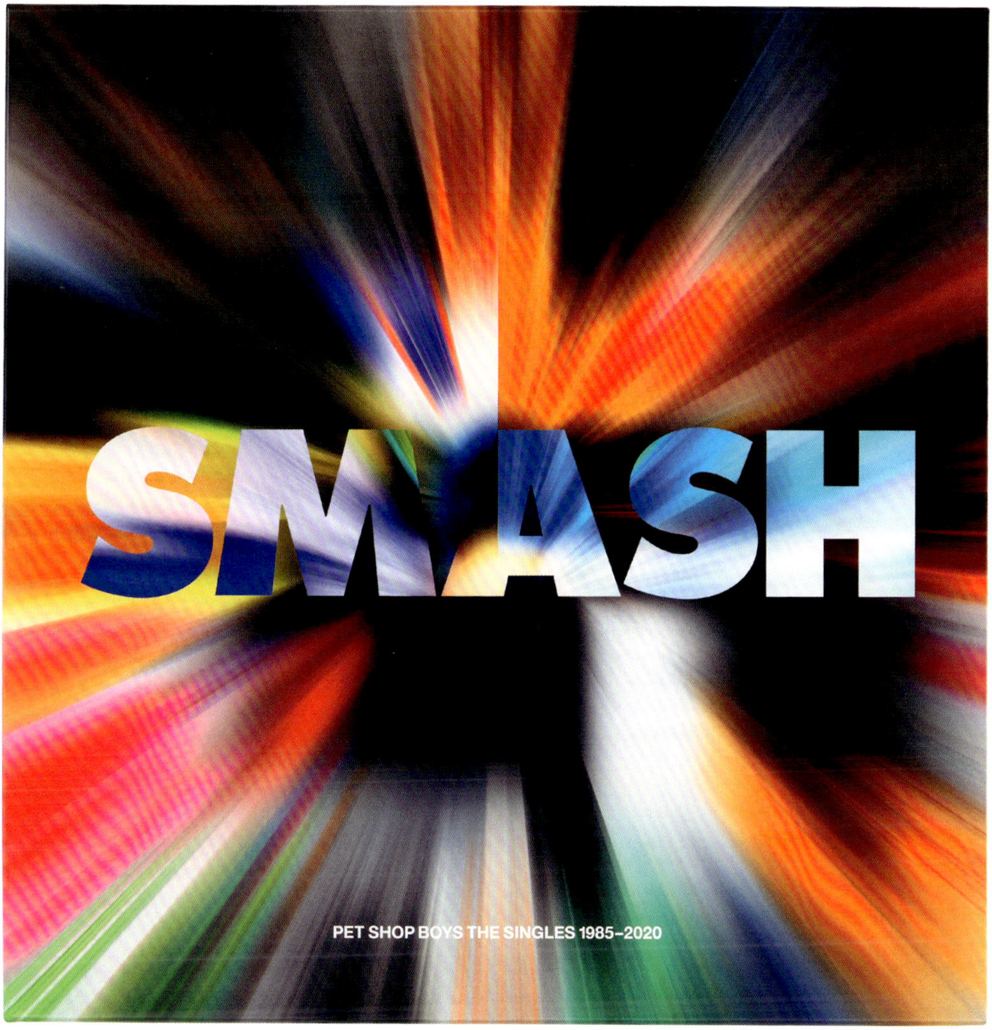

Six-disc LP, box, front

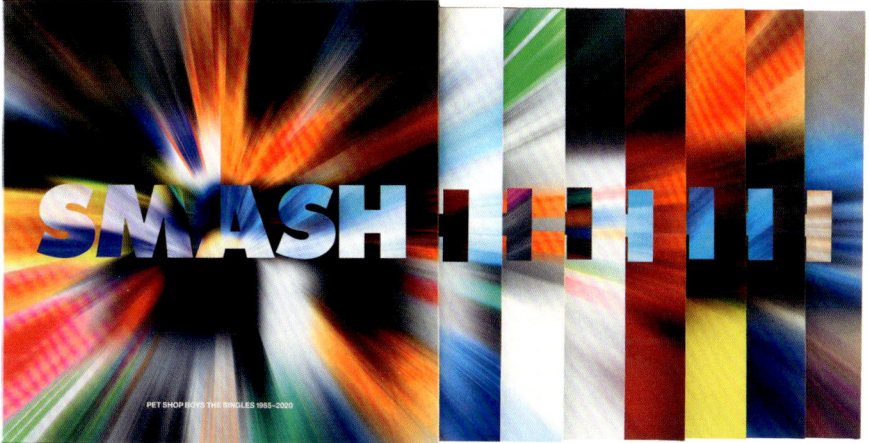

Six-disc LP, box, front, and outer sleeves and booklet

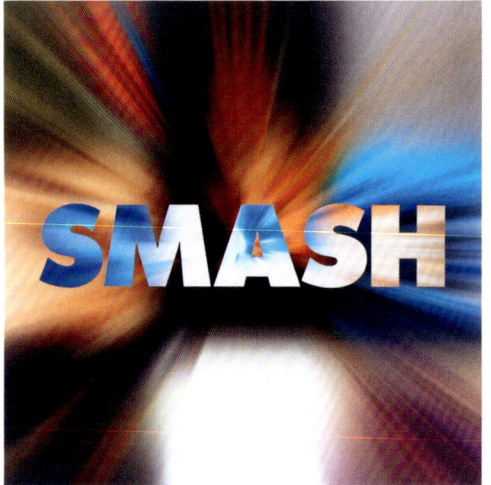
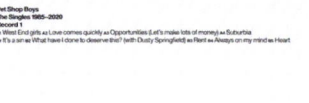
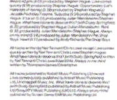

Six-disc LP, Record 1, outer sleeve, front

Six-disc LP, Record 1, outer sleeve, back

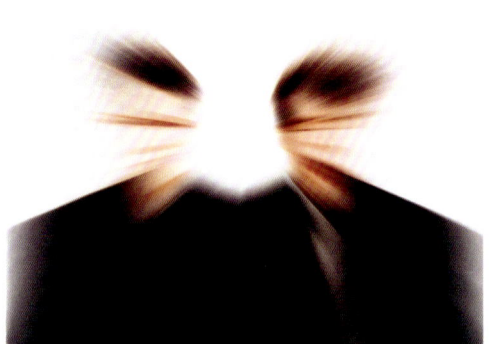
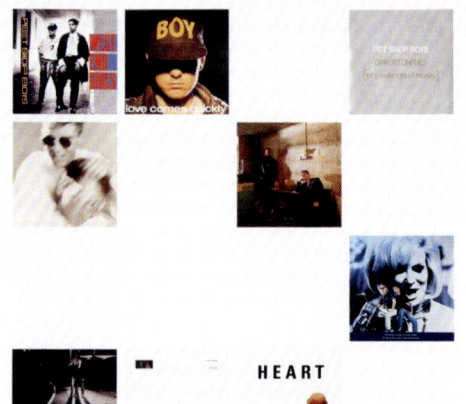

Six-disc LP, Record 1, inner sleeve, front

Six-disc LP, Record 1, inner sleeve, back

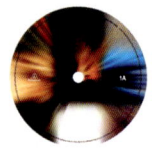
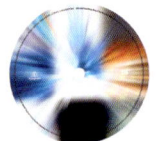

Six-disc LP, Record 1, Side A

Six-disc LP, Record 1, Side B

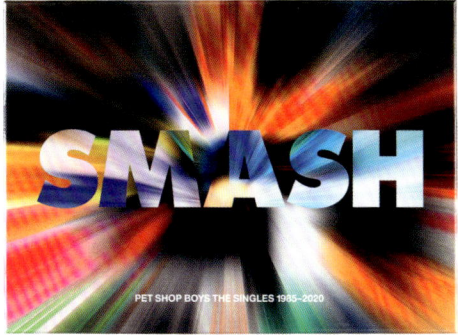

Limited-edition triple cassette, outer box, front

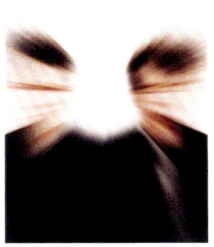

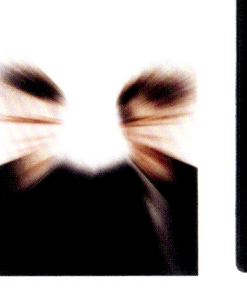

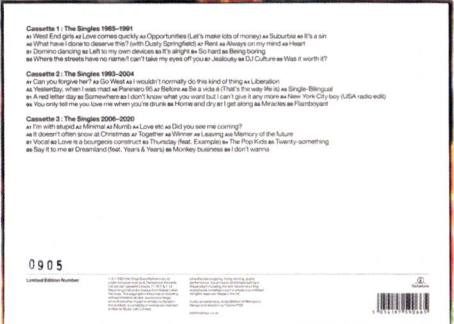

Limited-edition triple cassette, outer box, back

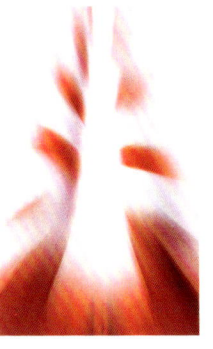

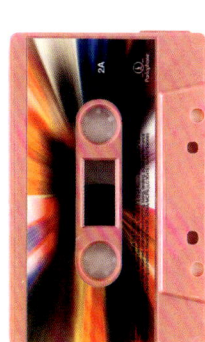

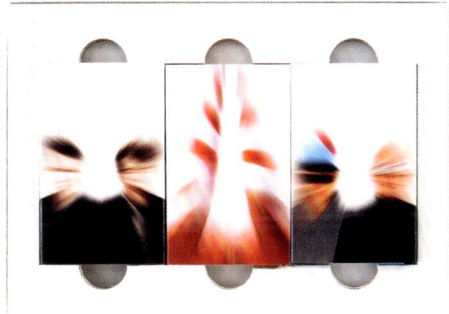

Limited-edition triple cassette, inside box

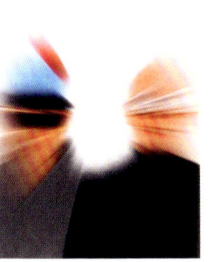

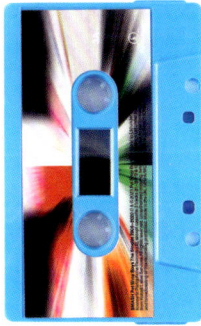

Limited-edition triple cassette, sleeves and cassettes

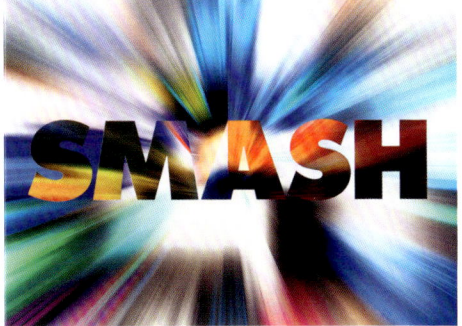

Limited-edition triple cassette, booklet, front

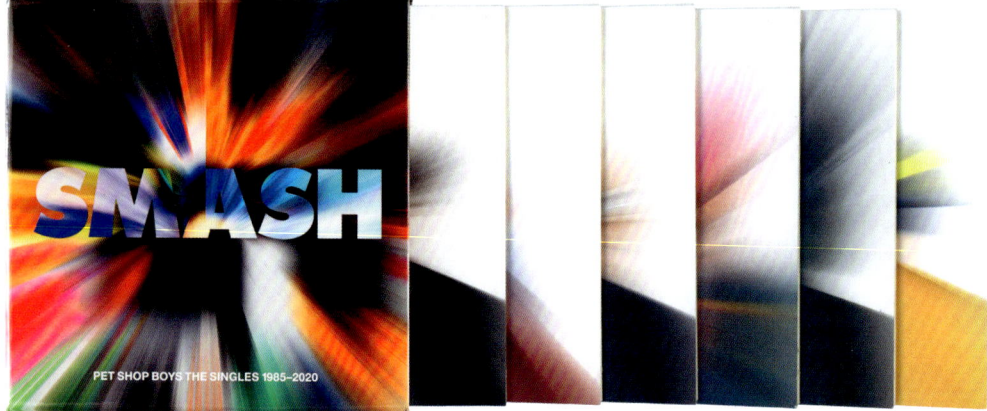

Three-disc CD + two-disc BluRay, box, front, and sleeves

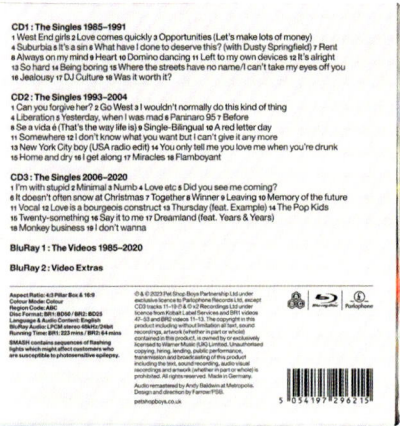

Three-disc CD + two-disc BluRay, box, back

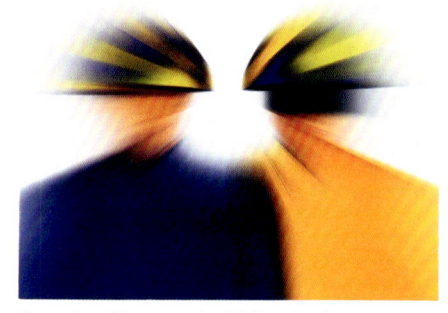

Three-disc CD + two-disc BluRay, booklet

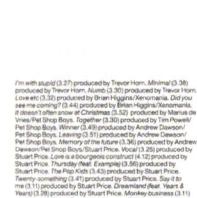

Three-disc CD + two-disc BluRay, CD3, sleeve (open)

Smash 2023

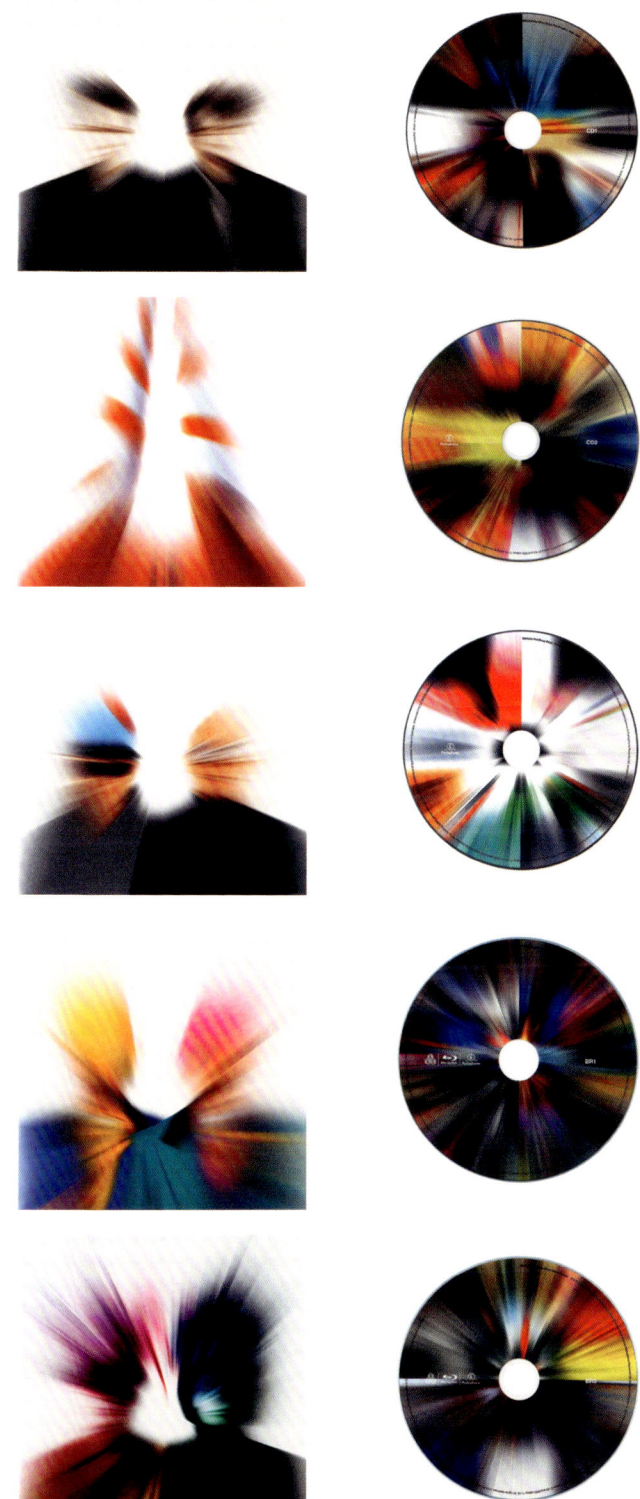

from top

Three-disc CD + two-disc BluRay
CD1, sleeve, front, and disc
CD2, sleeve, front, and disc
CD3, sleeve, front, and disc
BR1, sleeve, front, and disc
BR2, sleeve, front, and disc

Relentless

release 20 October 2023
formats LP / CD / download
design and art direction Farrow / PSB
videos Luke Halls Studios

Almost exactly thirty years after its appearance as the second half of the *Very Relentless* limited edition, *Relentless* was released as a standalone album for the first time. Its artwork adapted the original helmeted photos by Chris Nash from *Very*. 'I think Chris said "Can you make us look like an early video game?"' recalls Mark Farrow. 'Actually, he said, "Can we make it look like Eighties TV screens?"' adds Gary Stillwell. 'Kind of like CRT TV. In fact, I think he actually sent an image he'd found online.' 'A kind of teletext thing', says Farrow. 'So it's just this idea of using glitchy Eighties TV screens', explains Stillwell. 'Then Mark came back and said, "What if you did something that's a bit more like Space Invaders?" Essentially, we took the original images into Photoshop, and put a pixelated effect on it. Then we redrew each of those squares to make it a proper graphic logo.'

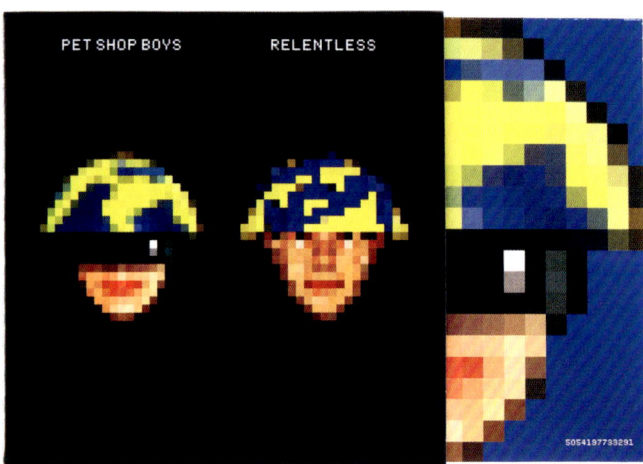

CD, front and inner sleeve

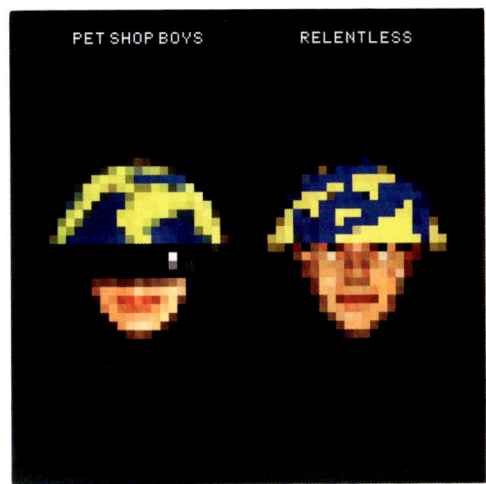

LP, outer sleeve, front

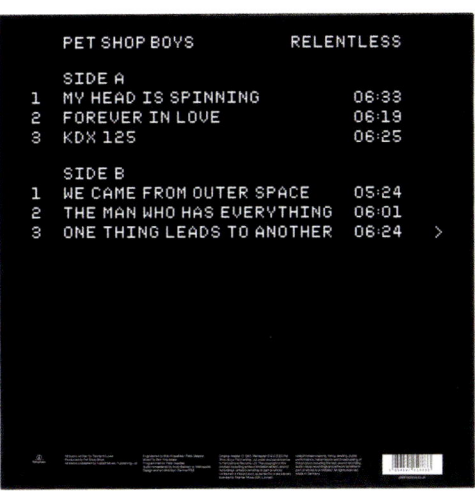

LP, outer sleeve, back

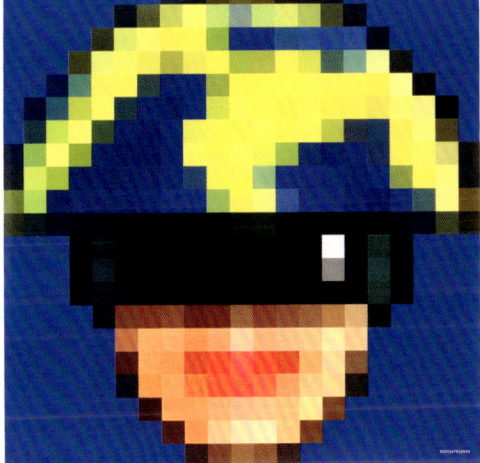

LP, inner sleeve, front

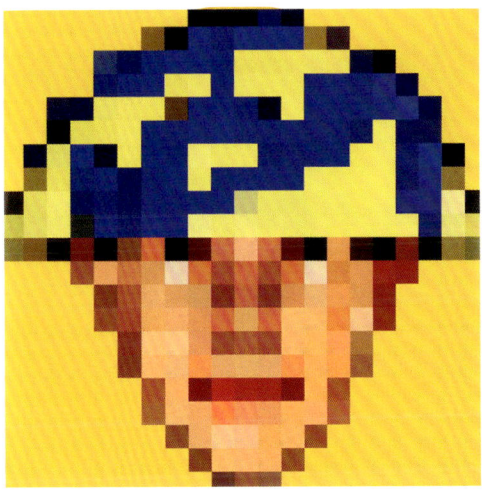

LP, inner sleeve, back

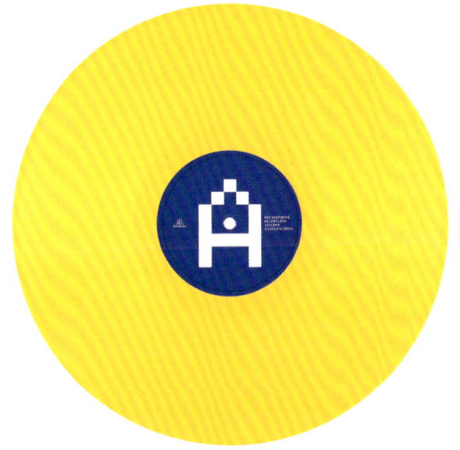

LP, Side A

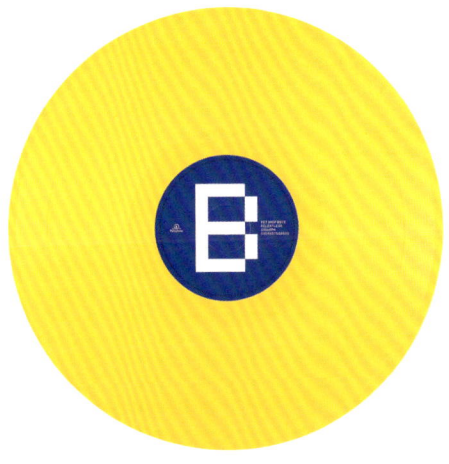

LP, Side B

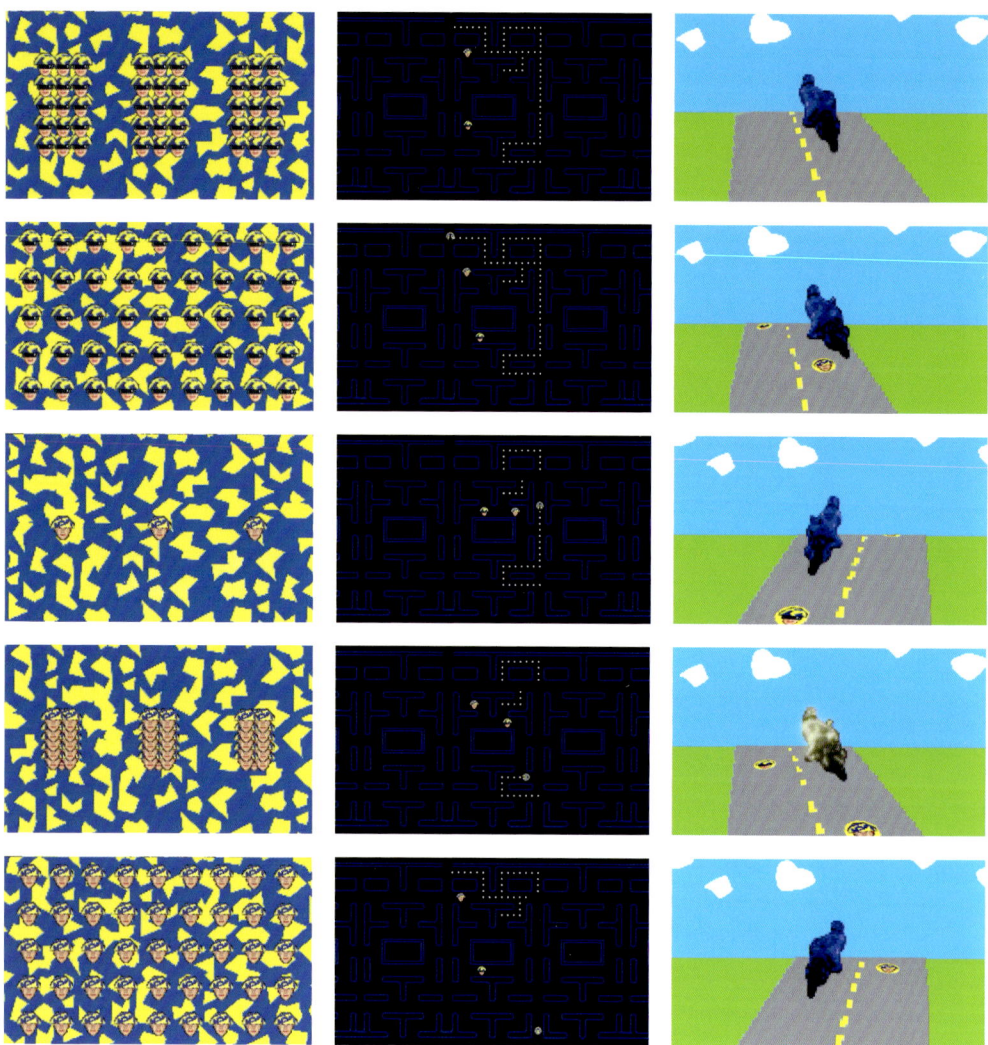

There were also newly commissioned videos for each song on *Relentless* made by Luke Halls Studios, who regularly work on projected content for the Pet Shop Boys live shows. Seen from left to right above, they are 'My head is spinning', 'Forever in love', 'KDX125', 'We came from outer space', 'The man who has everything', and 'One thing leads to another'. 'Based on old video games like Pacman', says Chris. 'They're really great', Neil agrees. 'The Space Invaders one is just brilliant', says Chris. 'That was the best thing about this whole project.'

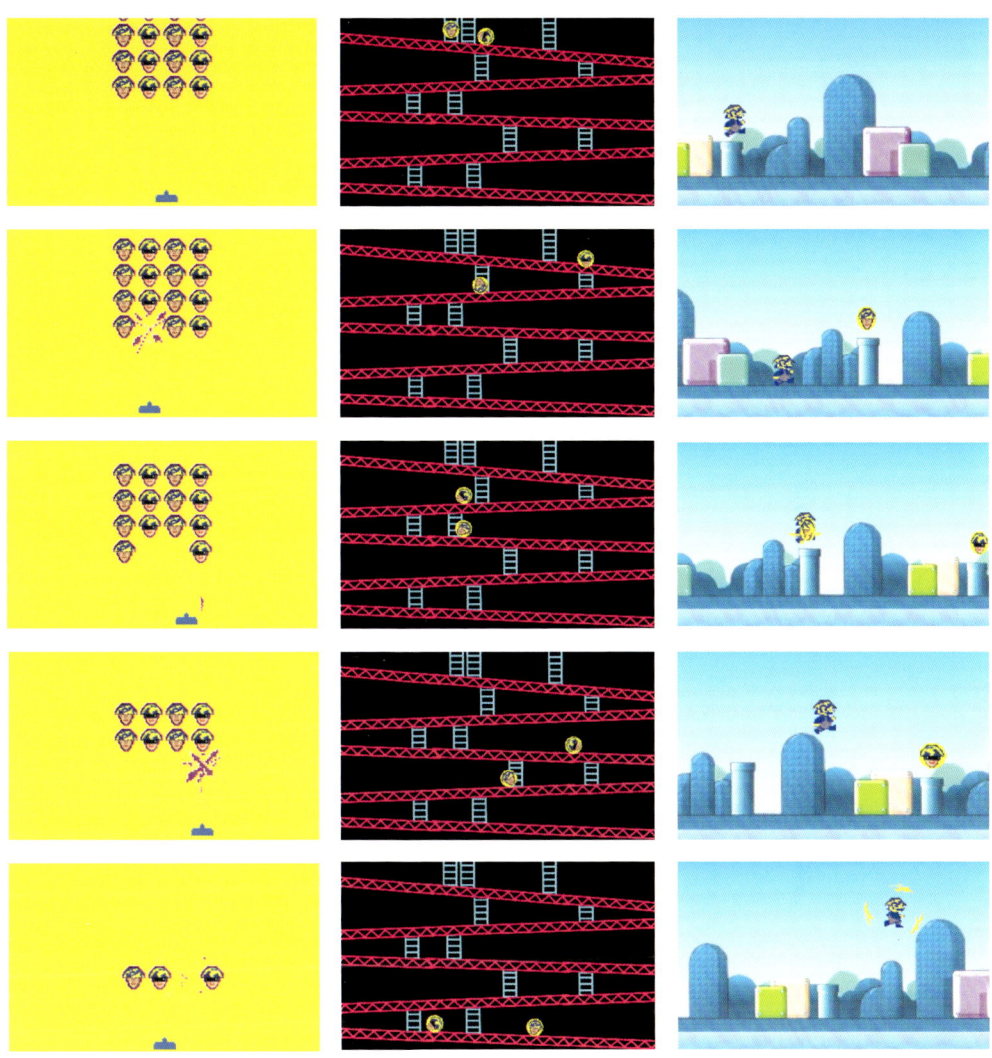

Loneliness

release 31 January 2024
formats CD / download
photographer Tim Walker
design Farrow / PSB
video Alasdair McLellan

The first single from the forthcoming *Nonetheless* album, a song that evolved out of something Chris had taken to playing during 'Love comes quickly' in the *Dreamworld* shows, was characterized by Neil as 'ultimately a cry for help'. Its sleeve image came from a photo shoot that Neil and Chris did with the photographer Tim Walker in his London studio on the final day of October 2023. Walker had originally approached them about appearing in a body of work that he was preparing for a major forthcoming exhibition. Initially, they had misgivings about that idea, but as discussions evolved, it was agreed that Walker would do a shoot that might provide the new Pet Shop Boys album cover. Ahead of time, Neil and Chris already had one concept that they liked: 'an idea of us wearing blindfolds based on a painting we had seen, like in a firing squad'. On the day of the shoot, as Neil and Chris posed blindfolded, Walker asked them to improvise with their hands. First, Neil leaned his head and framed it with his hands ('that's Judy Garland', Neil explained). Then Walker suggested that they put their hands in front of their face. 'Like what?' Chris asked. 'Like, "I don't want to be photographed by the paparazzi"', Neil suggested. 'My left or right hand?' Chris considered. 'Right hand', decided Neil. 'Because that's the hand you'd use.' At which point both of them – instinctively, although they could not see each other – assumed the same pose. That was when Walker took the photograph that would be chosen, not for the album cover, but for this introductory single.

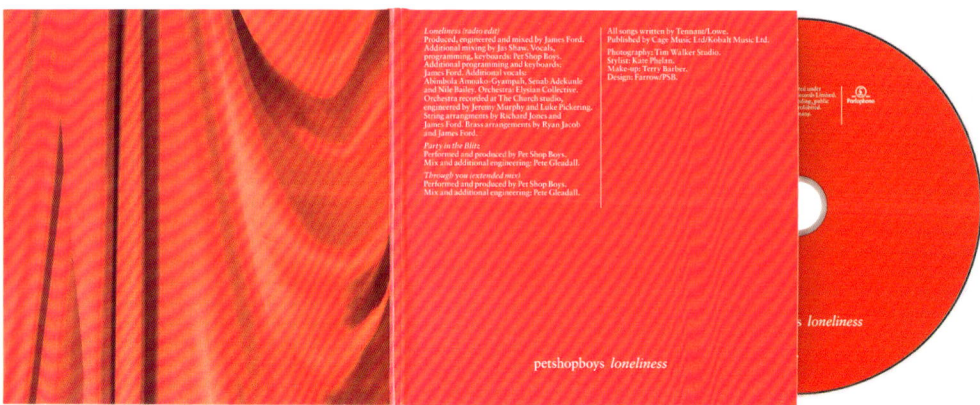

CD, front and inner sleeve

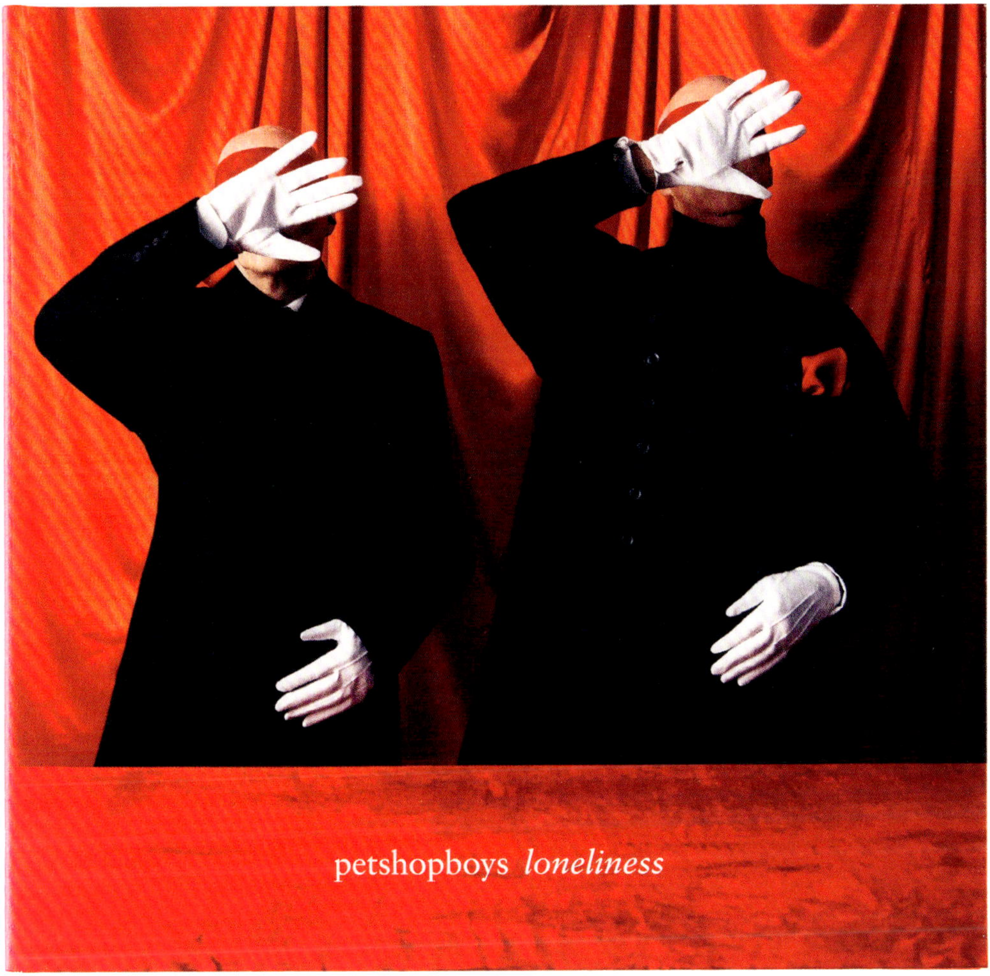

CD, front

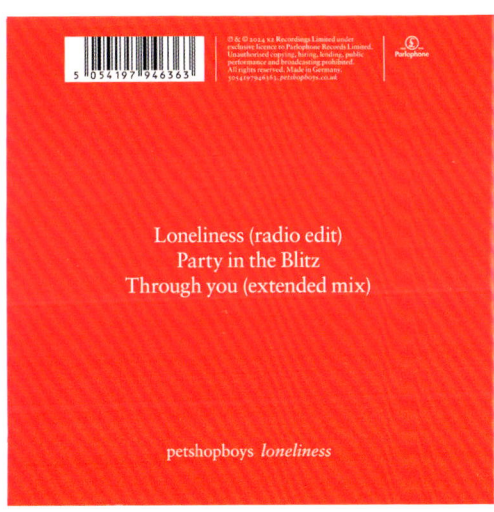

CD, back

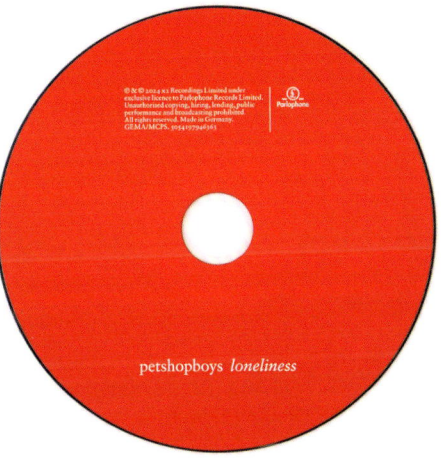

CD, disc

Loneliness 2024   507

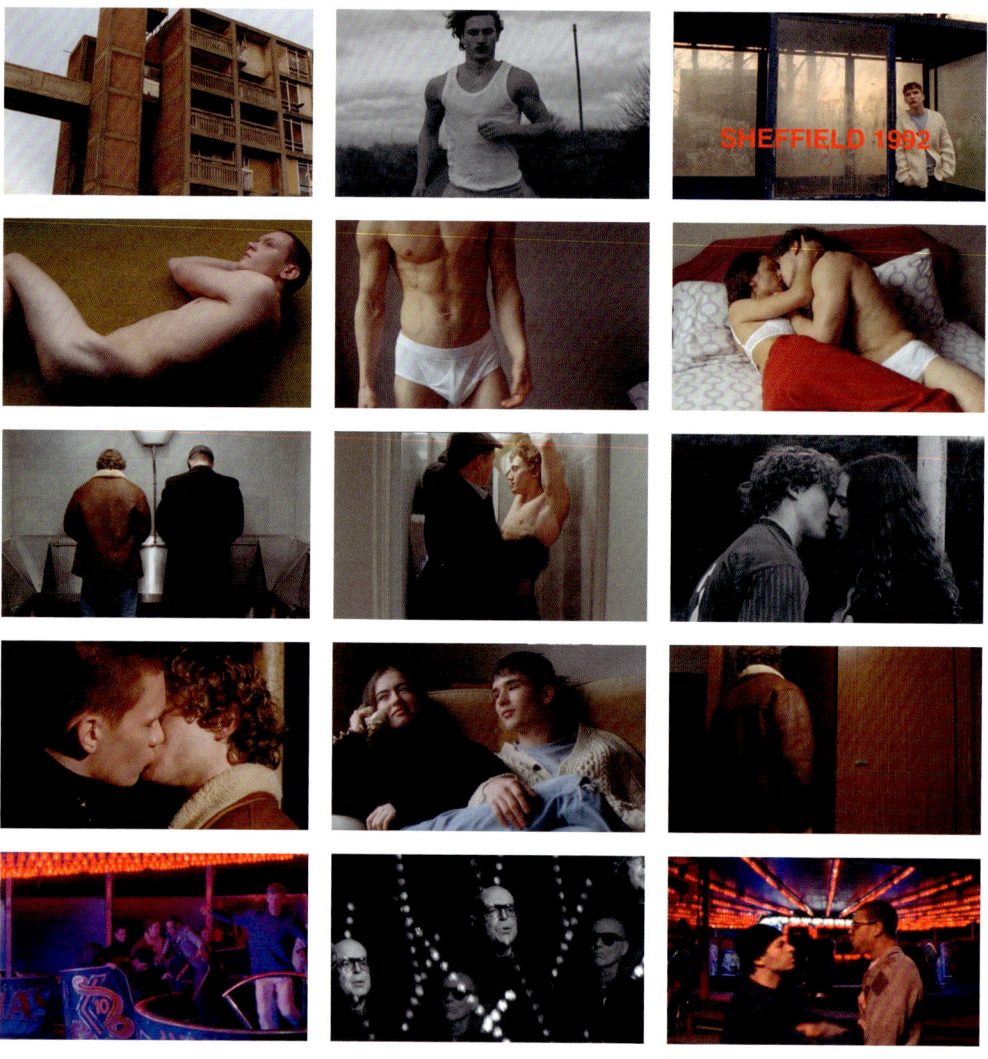

The video for 'Loneliness', directed by Alasdair McLellan, was a narrative about a young man in 1992 Sheffield struggling with his sexuality. 'He goes drinking with his mates down the pub and everything,' says Chris, 'but he has a secret double-life where he goes cruising for sex, and things like that.' In the second half of the video, set at a fairground, the Pet Shop Boys appear, as so often, intermittently within the frame but not as part of the narrative. 'Just me lip-syncing,' says Neil, 'and Chris being there.'

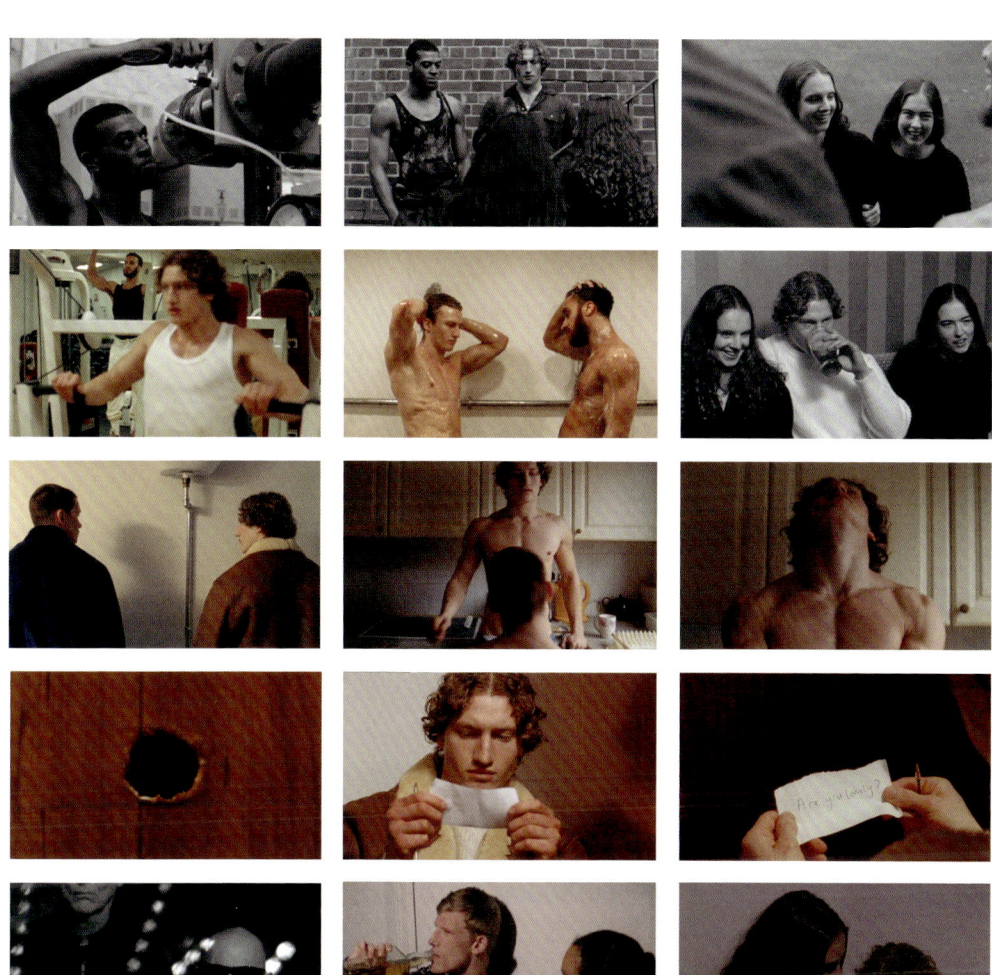

Loneliness 2024

Dancing star

release 3 April 2024
formats CD / CD promo / download
photographer Donald Southern
design Farrow / PSB
video Luke Halls Studios

The subject of 'Dancing star' is Rudolf Nureyev, the Russian ballet dancer who at the beginning of the 1960s defected into a second life and career. On the single sleeve, he is captured mid-leap by the photographer Donald Southern in 1962, the year after his defection from the Soviet Union, on stage at the London Royal Opera House – the same stage on which the Pet Shop Boys would perform for multiple nights in 2016, 2018, and 2024. 'It was very difficult to get a good picture of him dancing, actually, believe it or not', says Neil. 'We got this one from the Royal Opera House because we'd announced our dates. It was nice doing that, knowing that you were singing about him on the stage he used to dance on.' To create the sleeve image, Nureyev needed to be separated from the onstage action. 'He was quite small within the photograph, and the photograph in turn was quite small, so it wouldn't have held up', explains Mark Farrow. 'We took the background out, we isolated him and then put some colours through it', adds Gary Stillwell. 'Essentially, we just tried to make it a bit more graphic.'

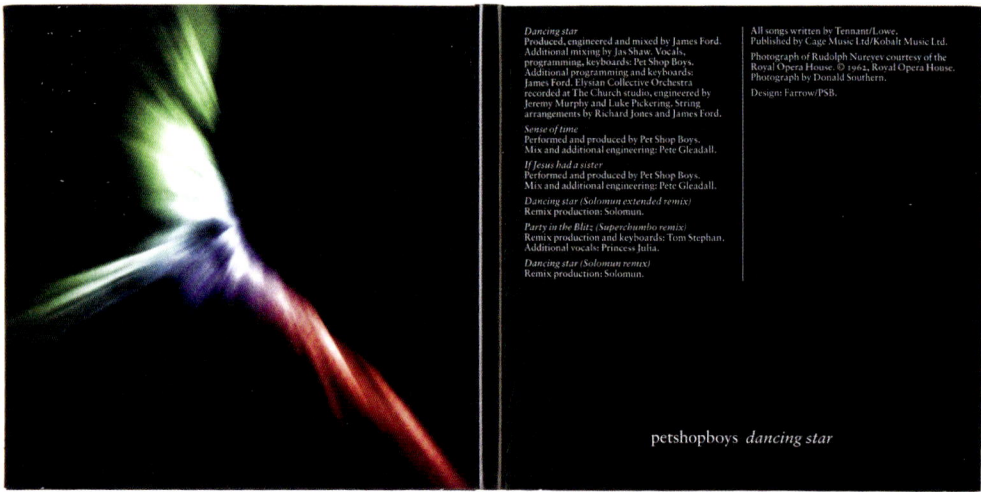

CD, inside

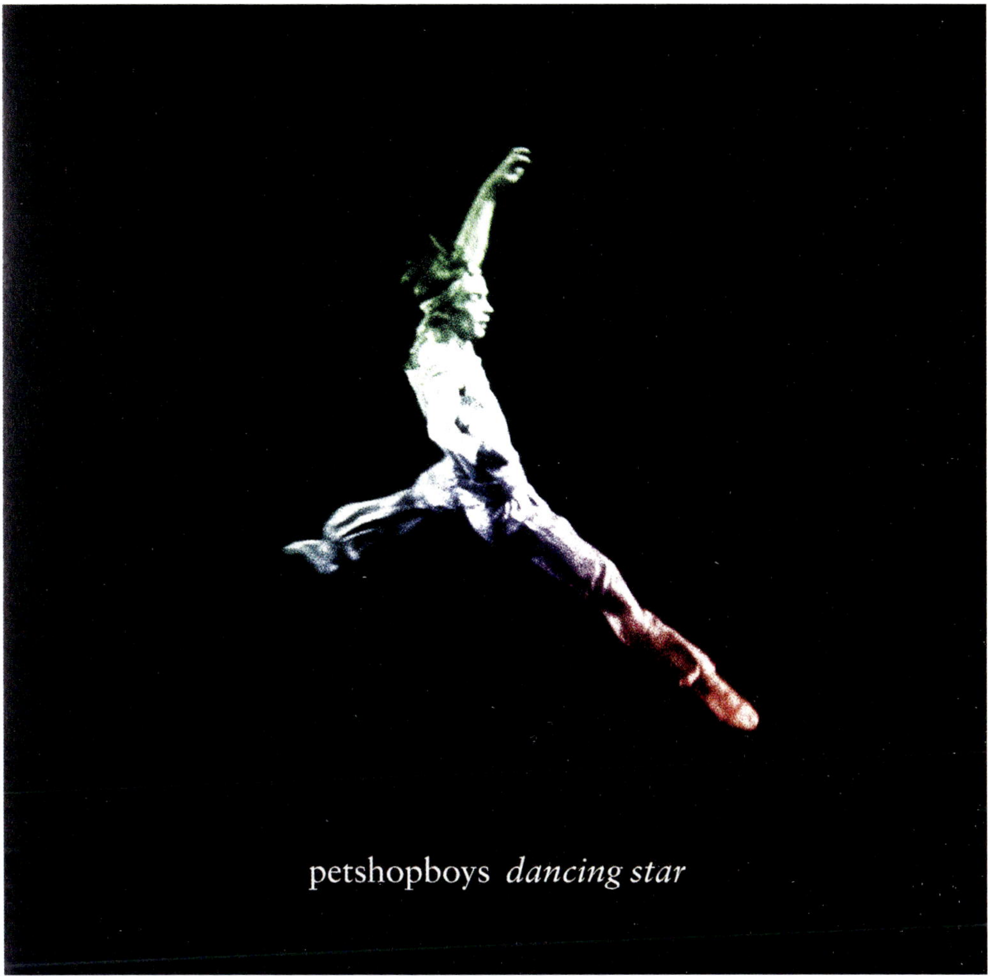

CD, front

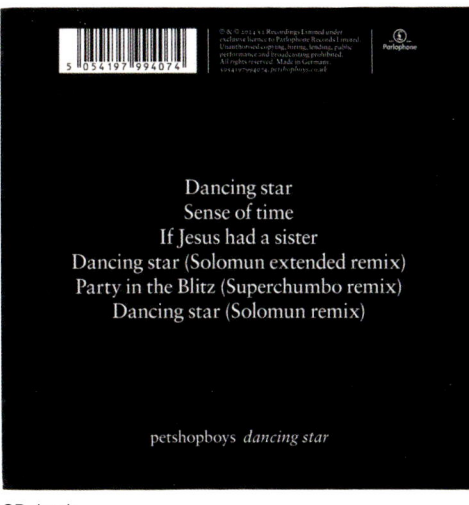

CD, back

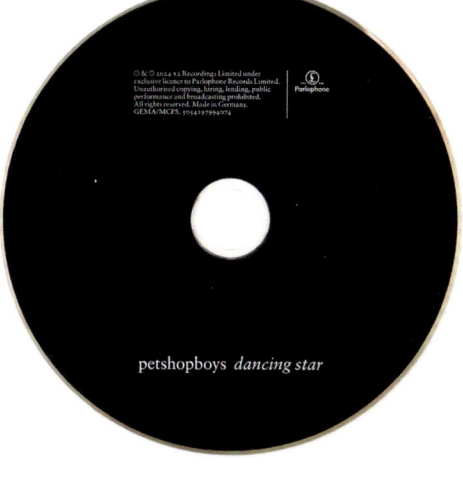

CD, disc

Dancing star 2024

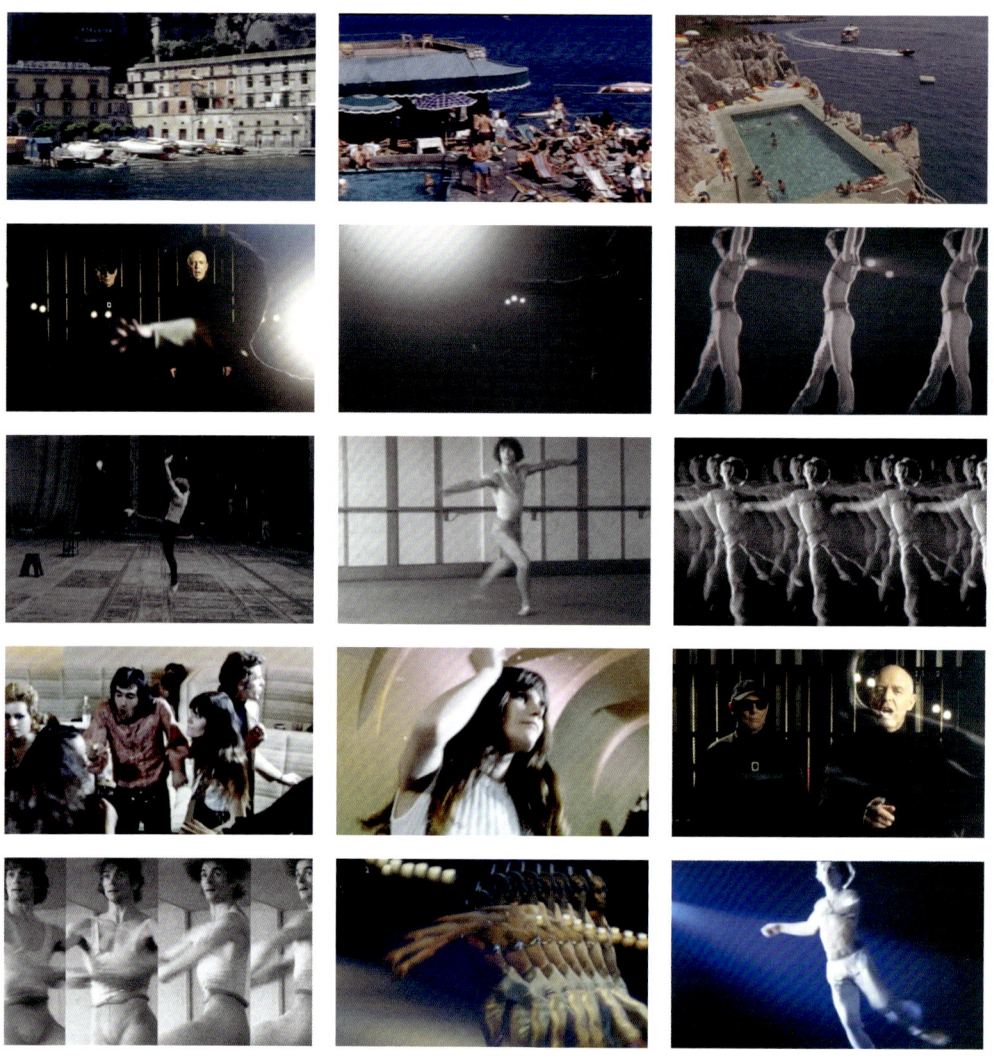

In Luke Halls' video, archive footage of Rudolf Nureyev, and of the world described in the song, is intercut with brief shots of Neil singing the song, Chris standing slightly behind him and off to one side. 'We also got the film of him dancing from the Royal Opera House', says Neil. 'It's nice having the video of him dancing on that stage', says Chris. 'Luke Halls shot us by the side of the stage as though we're looking at Nureyev', Neil explains. 'And then he got a dancer from the Royal Ballet [Stanisław Węgrzyn] to kind of play Nureyev.'

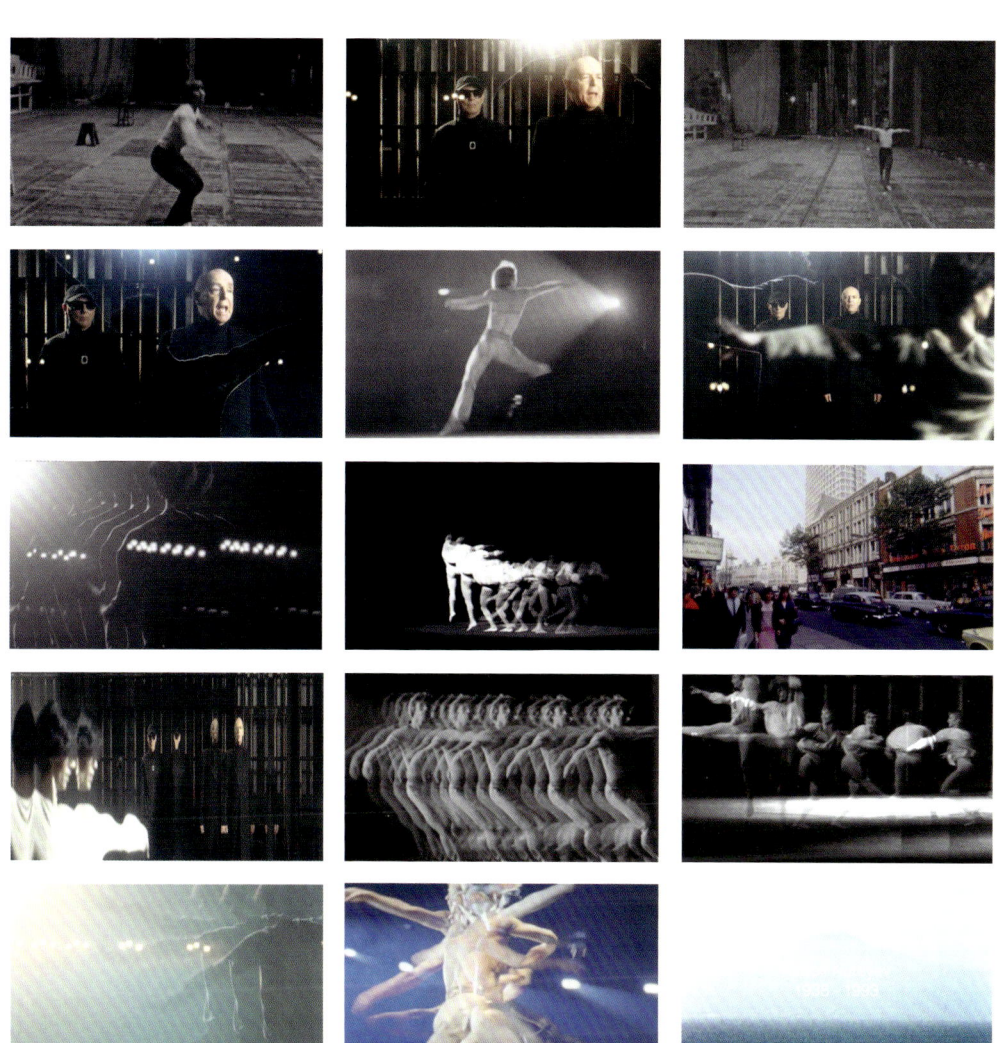

Nonetheless

release 27 April 2024
formats LP × 4 / limited-edition two-disc LP / three-disc expanded-edition LP / cassette / CD / limited-edition two-disc CD / two-disc expanded-edition CD / BluRay / download × 2
photographer Tim Walker
design Farrow / PSB

Nonetheless, produced by James Ford, was a contrast to the previous three Stuart Price albums: 'More "natural",' says Neil, 'although there are still tons of electronics in it.' Its title just seemed to fit. 'I think it's a beautiful album and it's a beautiful word', says Neil. 'The songs are beautiful and reflective, and "nonetheless" is a beautiful and reflective word.' Also, he notes, 'You could say that it's a sort of comment on carrying on regardless through the whole pandemic lockdown era.'

An idea that Pet Shop Boys had brought to their Tim Walker photo session became the 'Loneliness' sleeve (page 507); an idea of Walker's, in which they posed with torches in their mouths, became the cover of *Nonetheless*. It was a set-up that belied Walker's reputation for using elaborate scenarios and props. 'This time he decided to strip himself', says Neil. 'Just the light coming out of our mouths. It's a simple and iconic image.' That morning, as soon as Neil and Chris looked at the result, seconds after it had been shot, they immediately knew that it worked. 'You thought, "Oh well, there's the album cover done"', says Neil. 'I think Chris said "And it's not even lunchtime yet."' 'We could have gone home', Chris says. 'It sort of goes with the album – don't even know why really', says Neil, of the photo. 'You could certainly have theories about what it meant. Light in the darkness, maybe.' 'It's a bit Gilbert and George-y, but in the future and not in the past', says Chris. 'Also, we're not trying to be young.' (It would be the first time they appeared on the front of a new album – *Hotspot*'s blur aside – for nearly eighteen years.)

'It felt, as a lot of people describe it, like a classic Pet Shop Boys album cover', says Mark Farrow. 'It's very strong. That white table in front of them gives you a logical place to put the type. It was like: it's done itself, this, and we should stop fighting it, really, and just accept that it's this simple. But it did have an elegance to it. And it somehow nodded back to *Actually* in my head.' During its design, the one potential snag was with the uncomfortable unbalanced way that the words 'Pet Shop Boys' and 'nonetheless' sat together. 'The type wasn't looking that good', says Farrow. He suggested a solution: that 'petshopboys' be allowed to be printed as a single word. (Gary Stillwell further bolstered the suggestion, albeit by a kind of reverse logic, by pointing out that historically 'nonetheless' used to be written more commonly as 'none the less'). The change was made. 'That felt like a clincher to me', says Farrow, 'because even though it was very, very simple, there was that symmetry there.'

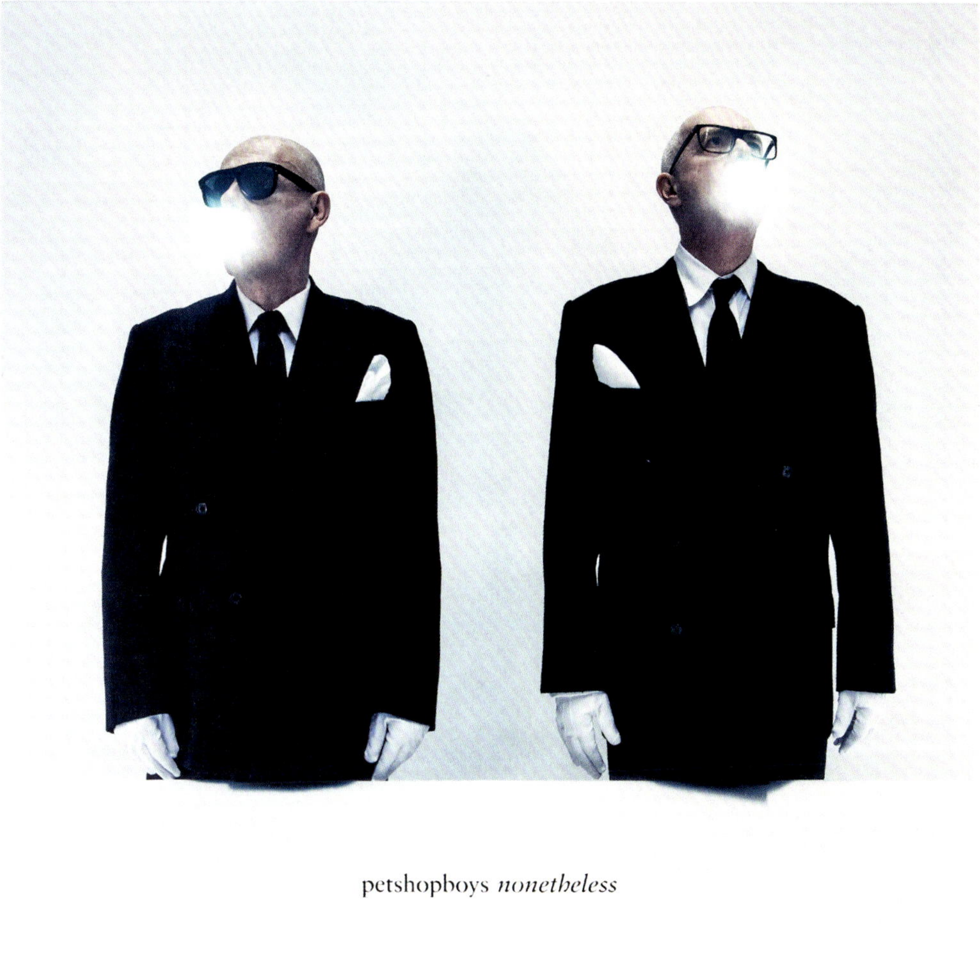

petshopboys *nonetheless*

LP, outer sleeve, front

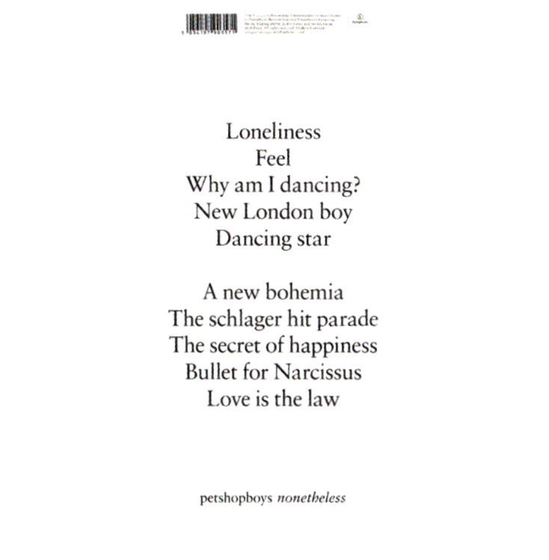

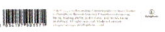

Loneliness
Feel
Why am I dancing?
New London boy
Dancing star

A new bohemia
The schlager hit parade
The secret of happiness
Bullet for Narcissus
Love is the law

petshopboys *nonetheless*

LP, outer sleeve, back

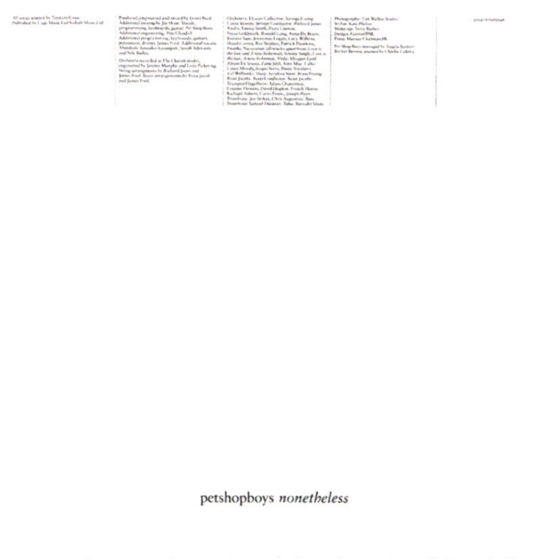

petshopboys *nonetheless*

LP, inner sleeve, back

The LP of the album was issued in four versions of vinyl: standard black, transparent, grey, and a zoetrope picture disc with the words 'Everybody needs time to think / Nobody can live without love', taken from the lyrics of 'Loneliness'. A limited-edition CD and vinyl of *Nonetheless* came with a bonus EP, entitled *Furthermore*. At first glance, its sleeve image – Chris standing, Neil seated – might appear to be a close variant of the parent album image, though in fact the photograph was taken much later on the same day (after lunch): the suits are different, as are the pocket handkerchiefs and the make-up.

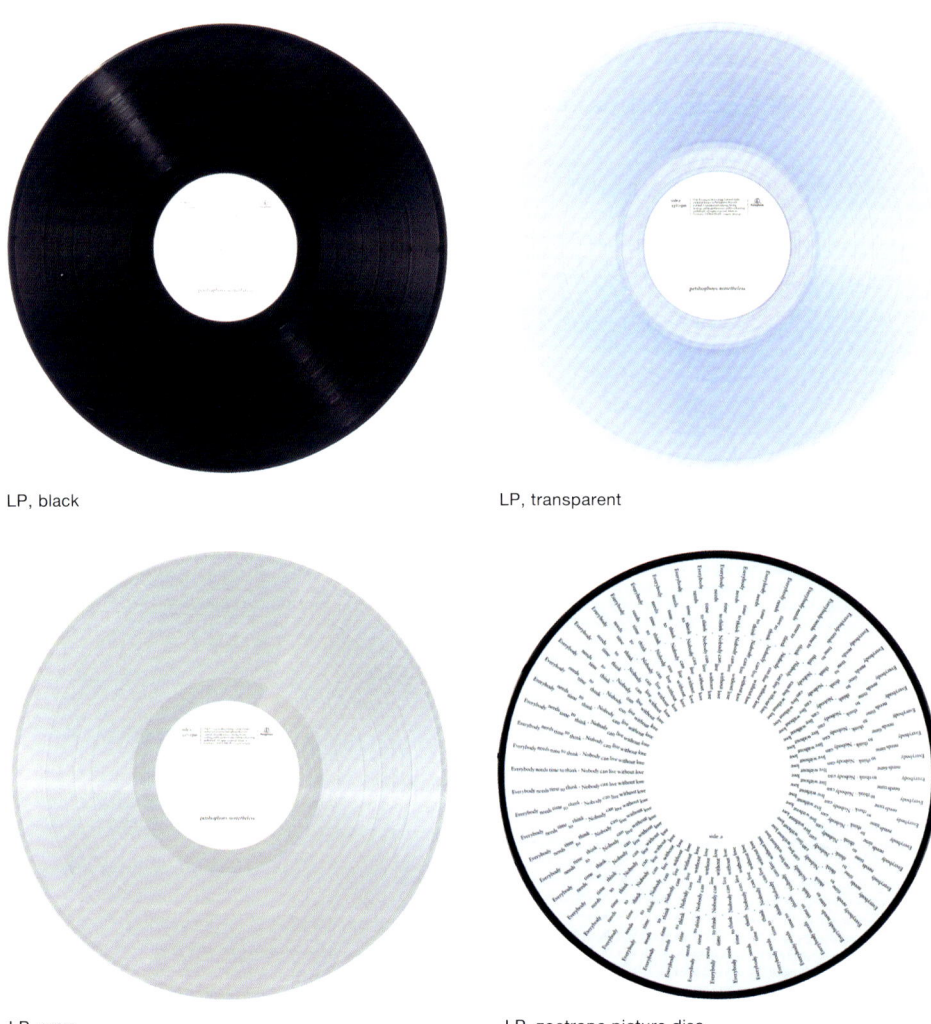

LP, black

LP, transparent

LP, grey

LP, zoetrope picture disc

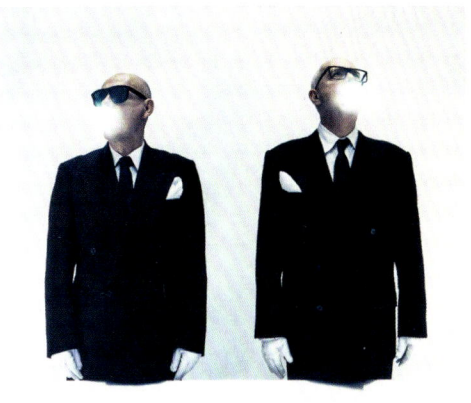

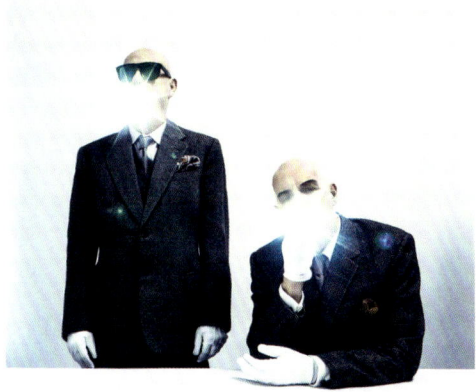

Limited-edition two-disc LP, outer sleeve, front

Furthermore EP, inner sleeve, front

Limited-edition two-disc LP, outer sleeve, gatefold (open)

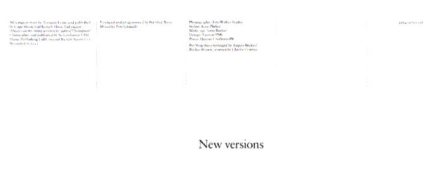

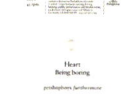

Furthermore EP, inner sleeve, back

Furthermore EP, Side A

In November 2024, *Nonetheless expanded edition* was released, including four extra songs and the demo versions of the original album tracks. The triple-vinyl outer sleeve (opposite) could be opened up and laid out, with the three inner record sleeves below it, combining to form a larger version of the album sleeve image. Similarly, but differently, the two-CD gatefold sleeve (below) could be opened – this time with Chris and Neil further apart – and the bottom half of each Pet Shop Boy's body completed by placing the two CD inner sleeves on the left and right.

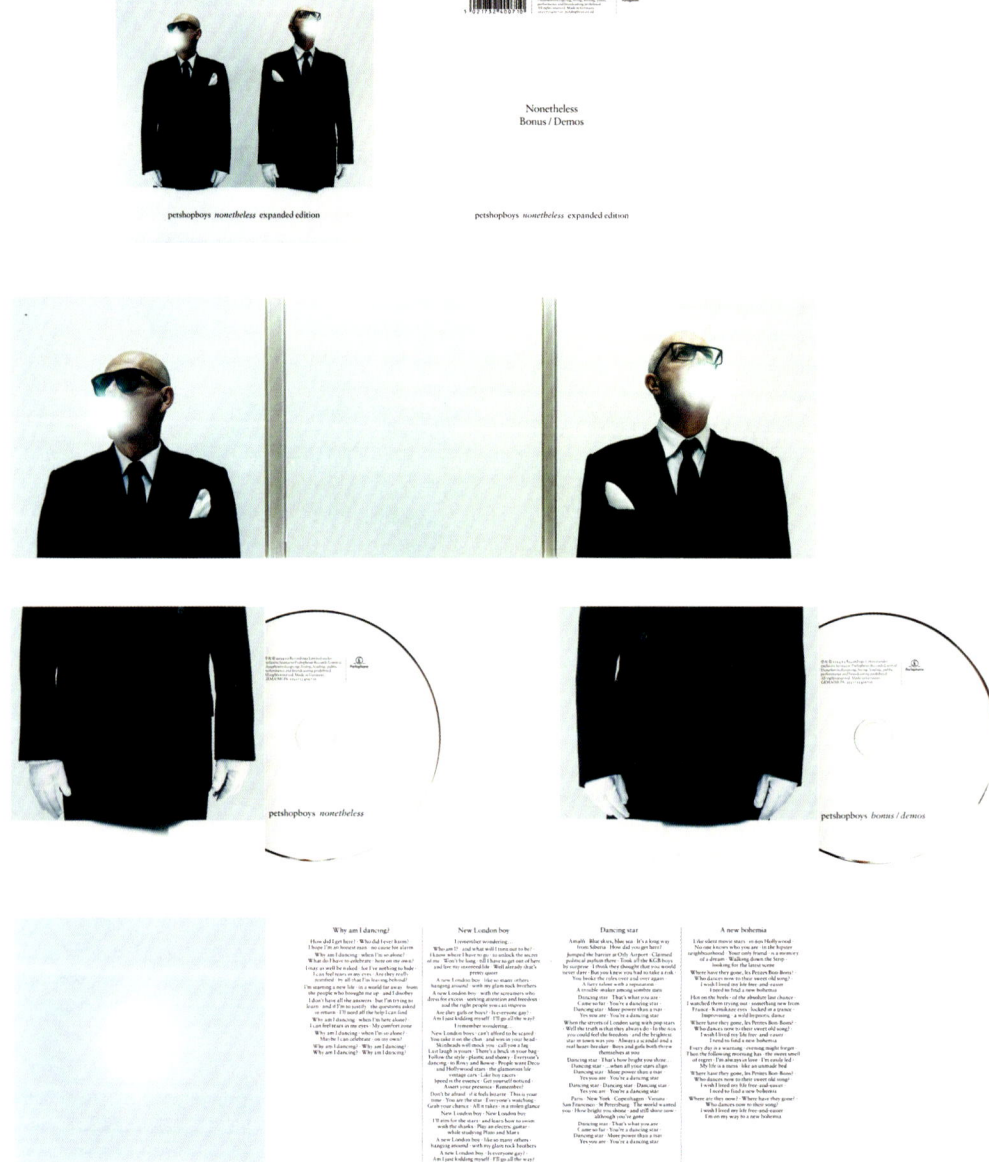

Nonetheless expanded edition two-disc CD, outer sleeve, outer sleeve inside gatefold, inner sleeves and discs, and booklet

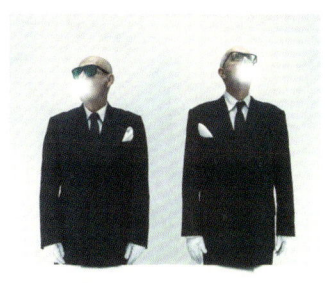
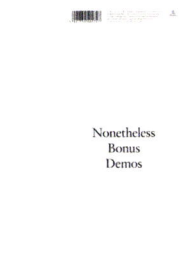

Nonetheless
Bonus
Demos

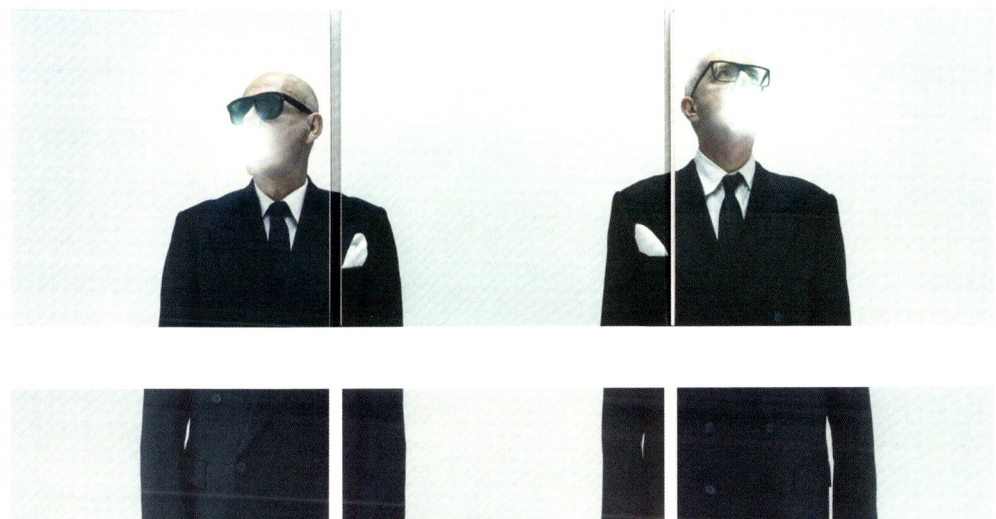

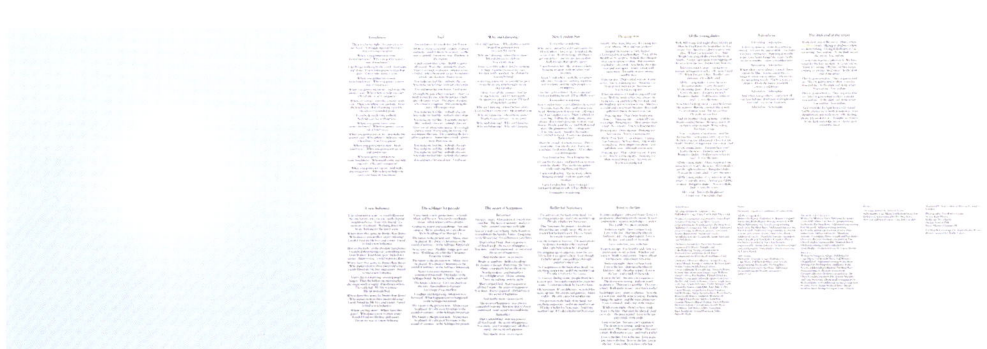

Nonetheless expanded edition three-disc LP, outer sleeve, outer sleeve inside gatefold, inner sleeves, and booklet

A new bohemia

release 4 June 2024
formats CD / download
photographer Vita Spalding
design Farrow / PSB
video Andrew Haigh

The third single from *Nonetheless* explored a particular kind of yearning. 'We were having a conversation about how we weren't really part of a scene any more', says Neil. 'We were just very lucky, really, to be in the right place for that in the Nineties', Chris concurs. 'We were regretting this fact', says Neil, 'and some of that went into the song.' For its sleeve, initially Farrow started working on some ideas based around the stickers made by the early Seventies conceptual-art collective Les Petites Bon-Bons, who are mentioned in the song's lyric. 'I don't even know if they saw that', says Gary Stillwell. 'But then, while we were looking at that, they sent over these pictures, saying "We had these done on the video shoot".' Around the same time, Farrow also realized that what they had been working on might be problematically similar to an album sleeve by French group Phoenix. Anyway, they now had a better option: the two Pet Shop Boys in front of a distressed concrete lido sign on the seafront at Margate. As Mark Farrow puts it: 'It's a bit of a classic "Domino dancing" vibe Pet Shop Boys single sleeve.'

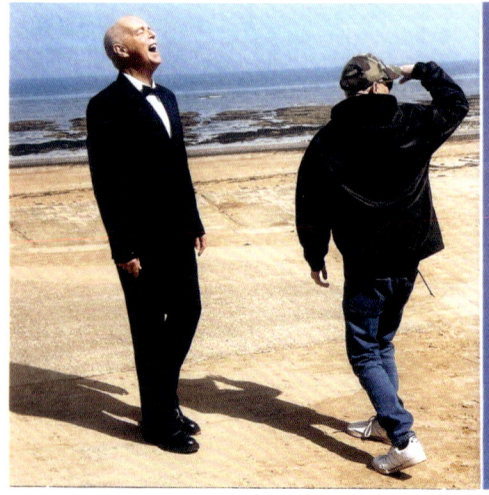 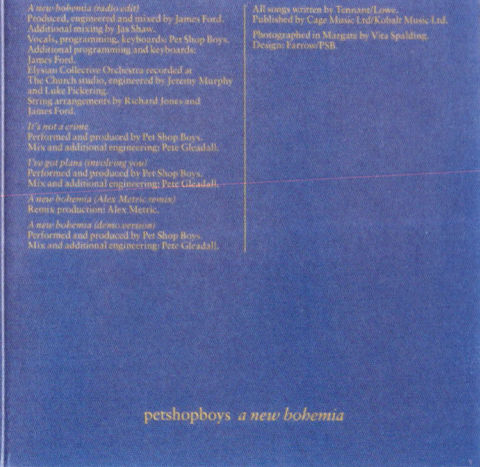

CD, front and inner sleeve

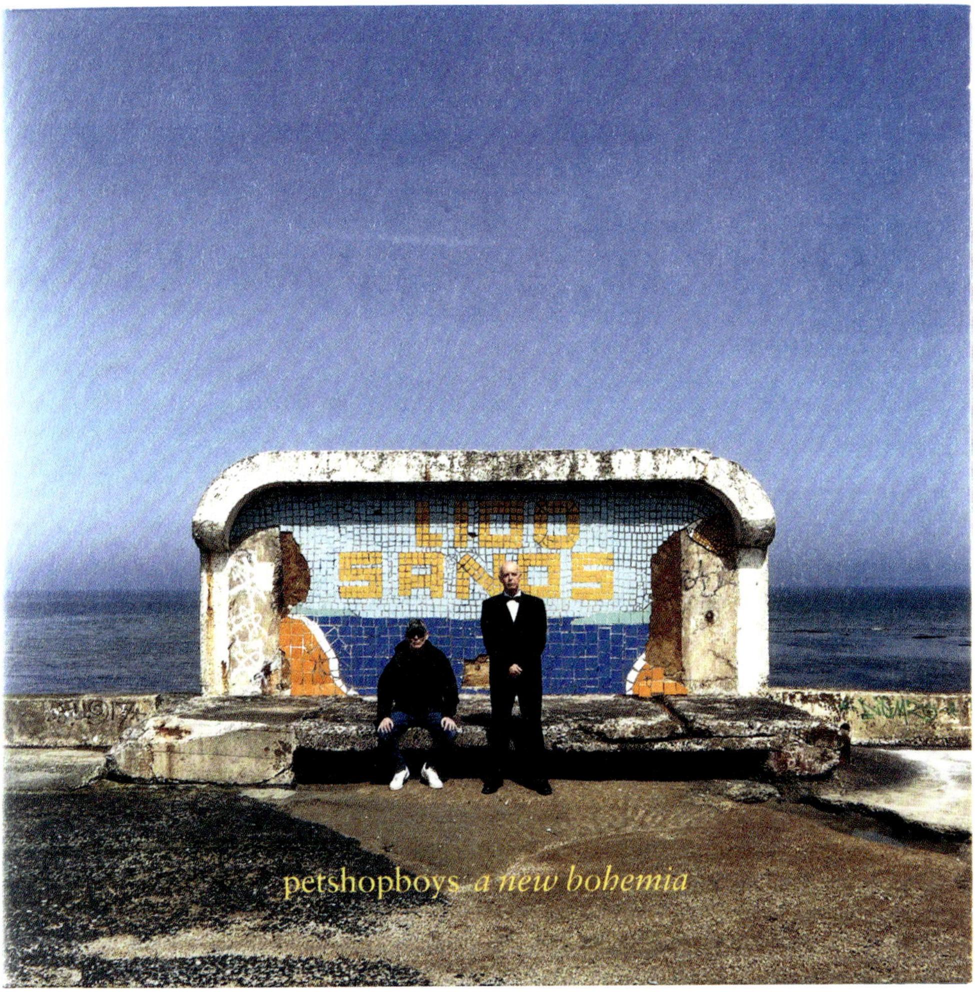

CD, front

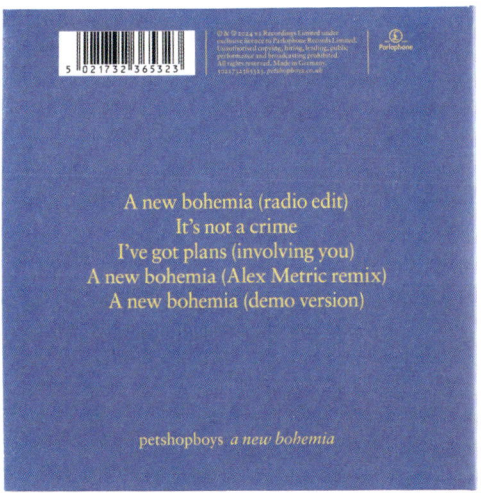

CD, back

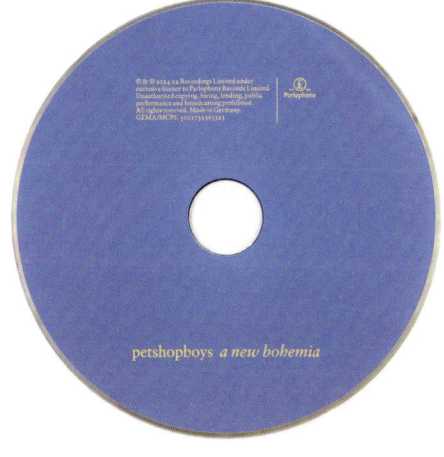

CD, disc

A new bohemia 2024

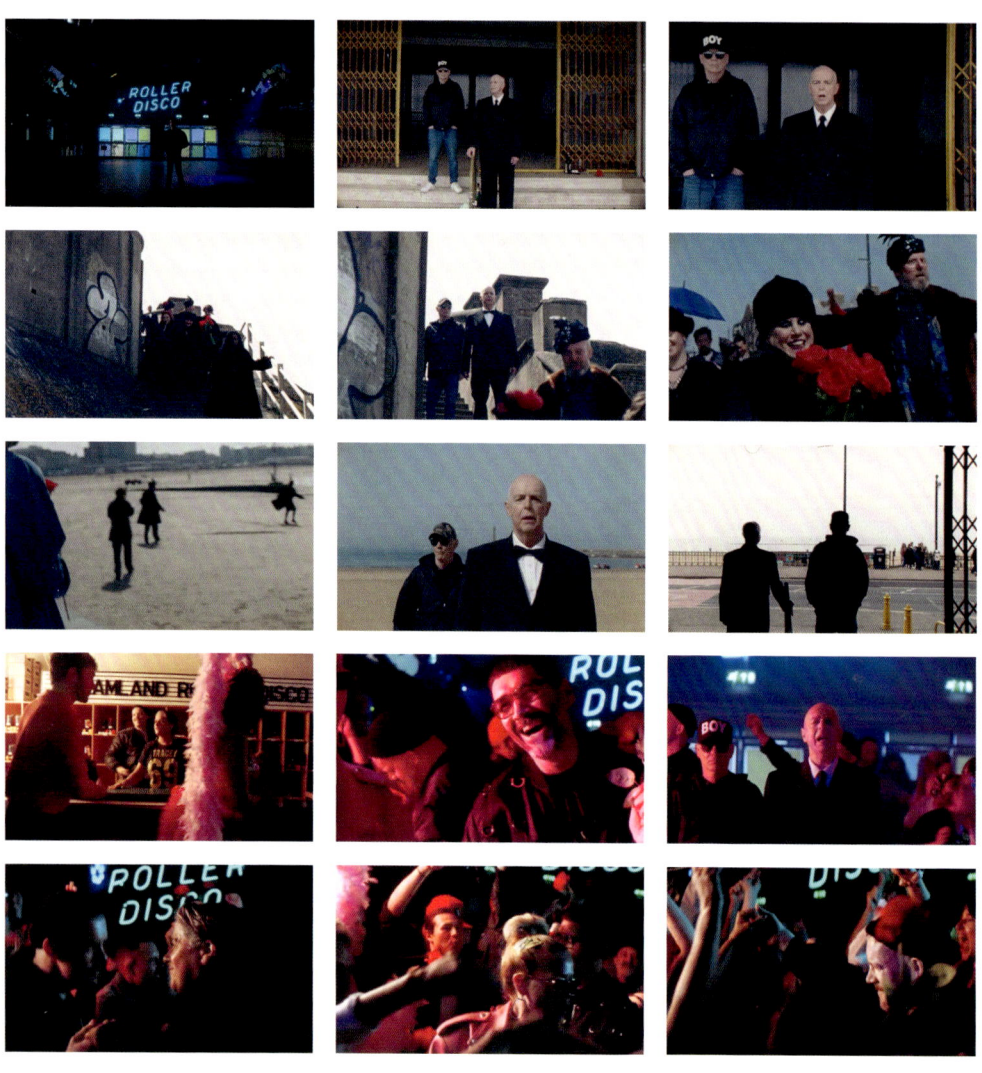

The video was made by the director Andrew Haigh, whose most recent movie, *All of Us Strangers*, had made memorable use of Pet Shop Boys' 'Always on my mind'. The idea was suggested by Parlophone. 'Actually, Andrew had phoned them up and asked if he could do a video for us', remembers Neil, who says that they had been on the verge of asking someone else. 'And we thought wow, that'd be good. It was a low budget, but he still wanted to do it. And he had the idea of doing it in Margate. It was great, actually. It was one day. Very relaxed.' 'We were very lucky with the weather', says Chris. 'It had been pouring with rain the day before, and poured the day afterwards, and then we had this gorgeous day of lovely sunshine. And we stayed at a very nice hotel. Actually it was like being on holiday.' 'We were finished by 8 o'clock', says Neil. The video idea was entirely Haigh's. 'He brought in the actor Russell Tovey, whom we know anyway', says Neil. 'And then Russell brought in Tracey Emin, who

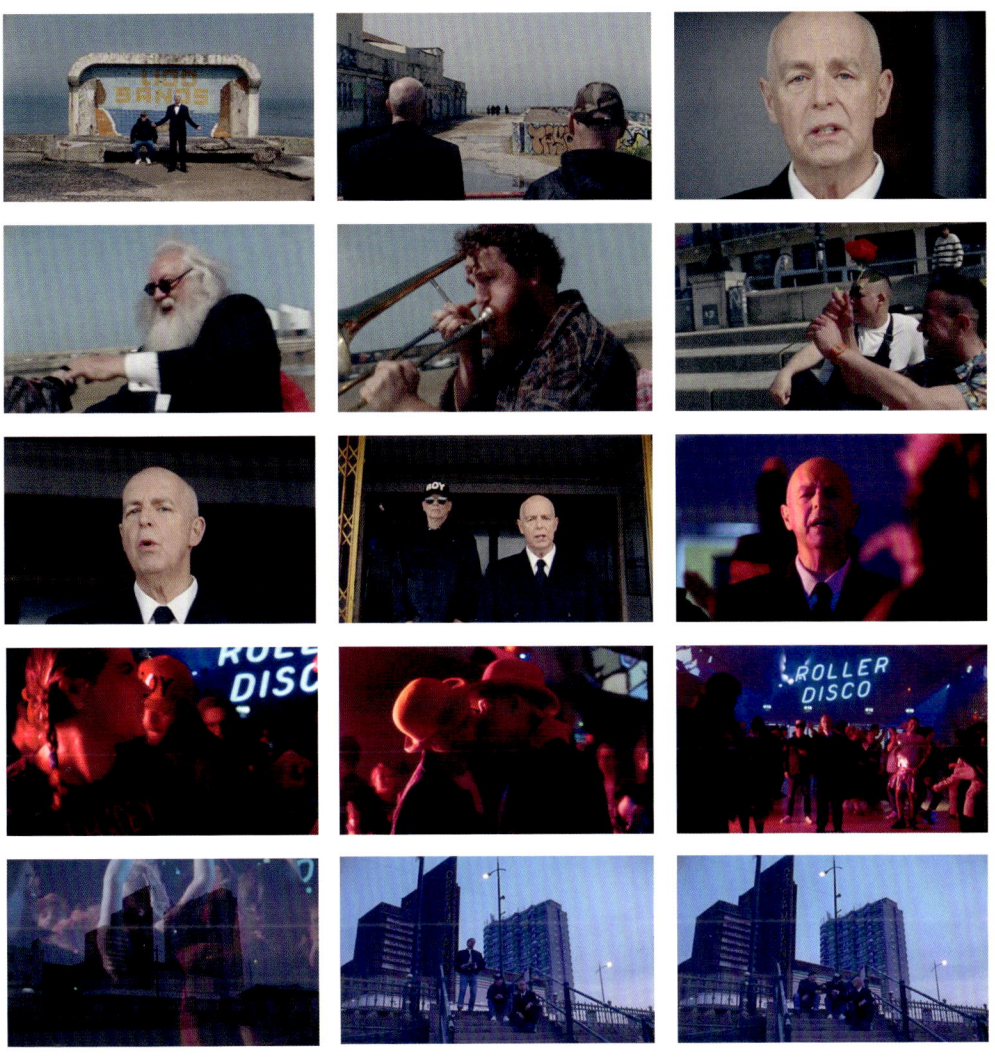

lives in Margate – that was great. And also a guy called Robert Diament, who lives and works in the art world in Margate, and he brought a lot more people in. Andrew's idea was, as a PSB fan, to have us then and us now. So that's why I'm wearing a bow tie and Chris is wearing a BOY cap. Although, in the end, I don't think we followed that idea through as strictly as he wanted. But it's sort of reasonably literal: we find a new bohemia in Margate. I love the way it starts with Russell roller skating all by himself. It carries the mood of the song really, really well. And my favourite bit is where Tracey's dancing.' 'Oh, I love Tracey in this', Chris agrees. 'And then when Russell offers us a chip at the end – I choose mine very particularly – it's actually very sweet, I think', says Neil. 'It was a proper video', Chris summarizes. 'We made a proper video with us in it.' 'We're walking, and Chris is behind me', says Neil. 'A proper Pet Shop Boys video.' 'The odd skip to try and keep up with Neil – the classic!' Chris adds.

Feel

release 20 August 2024
formats CD / download
photographer Corbin Shaw
design Farrow / PSB
video Corbin Shaw

The fourth single from *Nonetheless* was a song 'about visiting someone in prison' whose chorus had been written way back in 2003. As with 'A new bohemia', its sleeve was taken on location during the song's video shoot, though this time Neil and Chris were not present. And as with the previous single, the video photo – an old BMW with the number plate F33L, doors wide open, the sea behind it – trumped other plans for the sleeve that were in motion. 'It was going to be a couple of live pictures of them until Neil sent that photo through', says Mark Farrow. 'And then it was just "This should be the sleeve".'

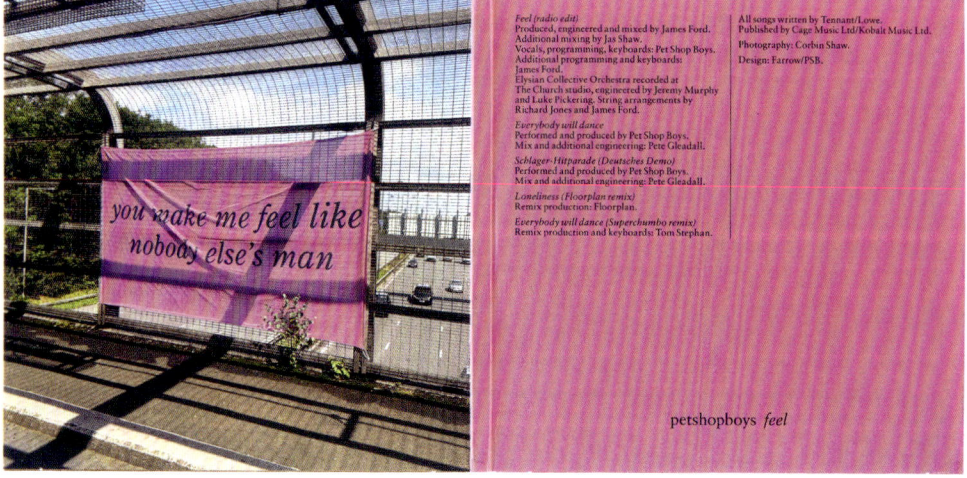

CD, front and inner sleeve

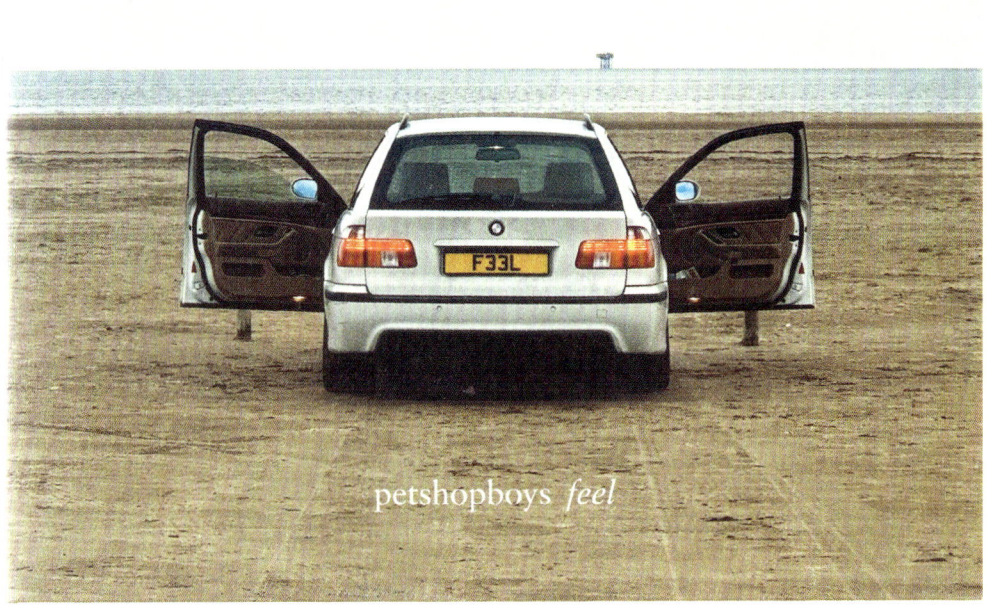

CD, front

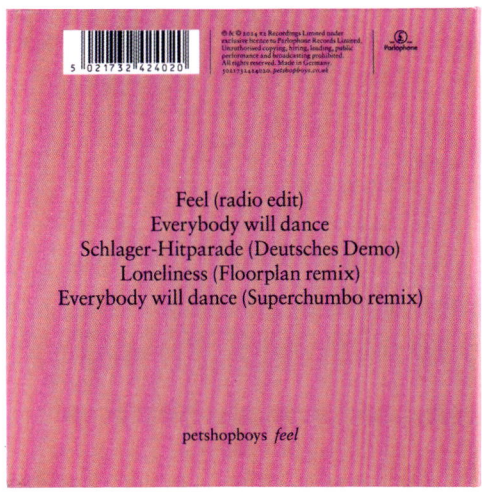

CD, back

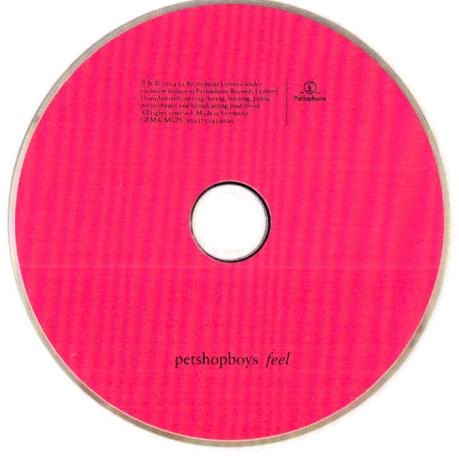

CD, disc

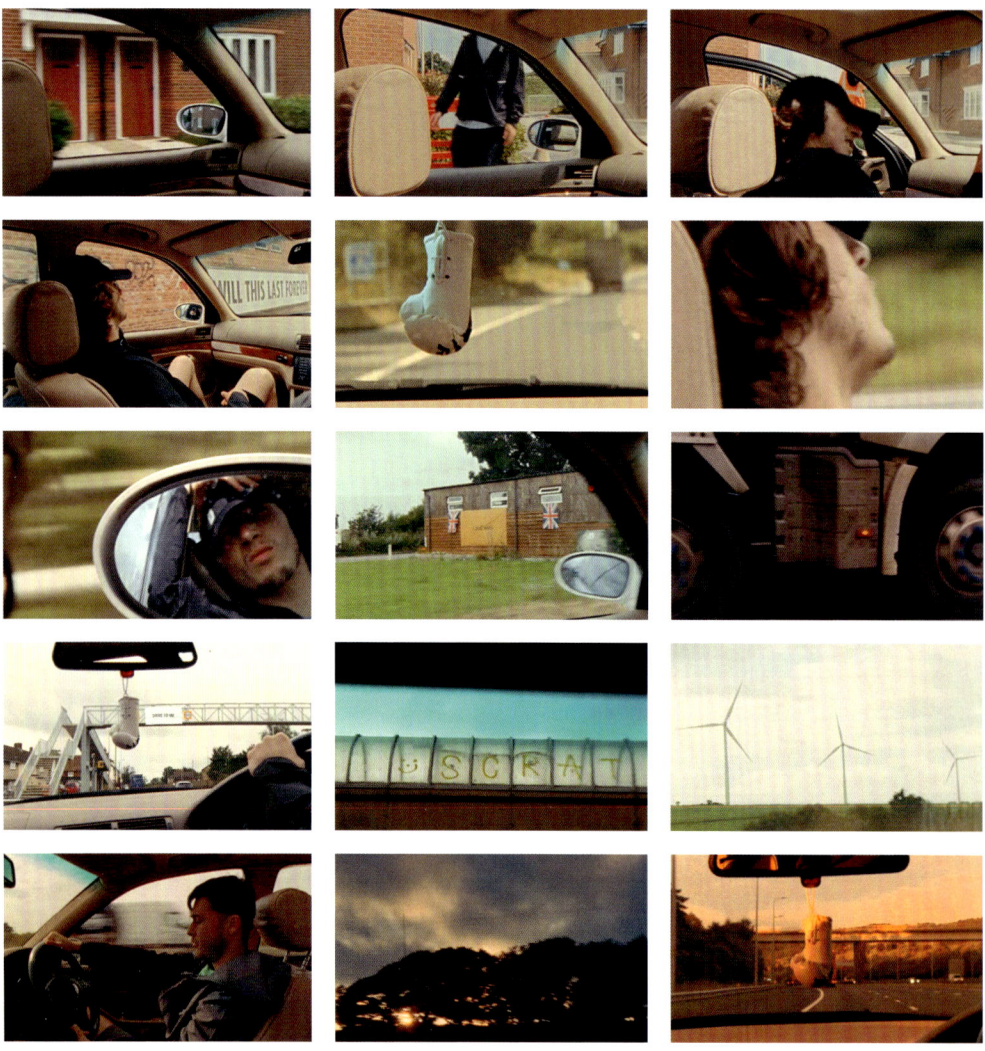

Neil met the artist Corbin Shaw at a show he had at Incubator gallery in London, where one of his films was screened. 'We thought, why don't we get him to do it?' says Neil. The video's concept was Shaw's. 'It's two guys, friends – I don't see it as being gay, by the way', says Neil. 'No, it's not at all', Chris agrees. 'It's about friendship, isn't it?' says Neil. 'About the closeness. And about being young. They drive to the beach and they run up to the sea. I like the whole feeling of it. It's got that young enthusiasm.' 'The only thing is', says Chris, 'I wish you could read the slogans better. Because that's Corbin Shaw's thing. It'd have been good if they'd zoomed in on them.' For the record, the slogans in the video included: on a brick wall billboard 'WILL THIS LAST FOREVER'; on an orange flagged pinned to a building 'I will wait'; on a tank in a field 'NOWHERE': on a poster pinned to an overpass 'DRIVE TO ME'; graffiti on an overpass 'SCRAT'; on another overpass 'ESCAPISM'; and on a billboard in a field 'ADOPTED NOSTALGIA'.

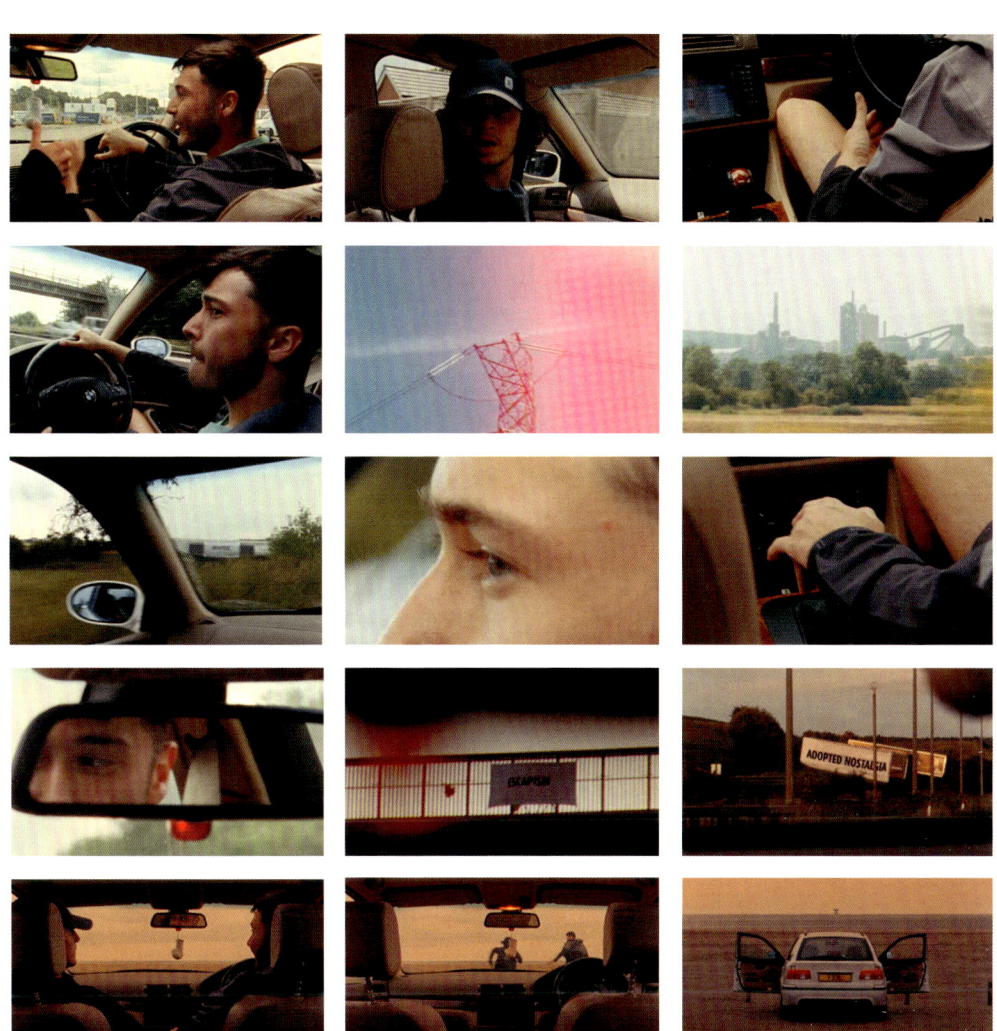

New London boy / All the young dudes

release 7 November 2024
formats CD / CD remix / download / download remix
photographer Neil Tennant and Chris Burscough
design Farrow / PSB
video Slava Mogutin

The final single from *Nonetheless*, 'New London boy', was released as a double A-side along with Pet Shop Boys' version of the 1972 song that David Bowie gave to Mott the Hoople, 'All the young dudes', which Neil and Chris first performed when they had to choose a cover version to play on the BBC's *The Piano Room* earlier in the year. It was Chris's choice. 'I've always loved it', he says. 'It just captures the spirit of youth. I don't know why it affected me – it always has done. And it makes me feel nostalgic towards Seventies Britain. Which I actually liked – I enjoyed the Seventies.' '"All the young dudes" seemed to dovetail perfectly with "New London boy",' Neil says, 'because in "New London boy", I am moving down to London with my glam rock brothers. And this is a song from the same time, 1972. So we thought it would make a good double A-side.'

    The complementary sleeves of the CD and remix CD show each Pet Shop Boy in their youth. 'This came about because we were talking on the phone about what the sleeve should be', says Neil. 'Chris had just been sent a picture of himself as a student. And we thought, "Oh!" So I went to look for an old picture of me.' Neil points out that people from their generation, from a time not just before iPhones but before digital photography of any kind, do not tend to have that many old photographs of themselves. But he went searching anyway 'in a photo album I have lurking in the basement' and found a photograph he had forgotten about: 'a picture taken in a photo booth at Leicester Forest East service station in the autumn of 1972 when I was travelling back on the bus to London from Newcastle for the weekend. I can only assume that I needed a photo for something. I'm eighteen in that picture. It's perfect because it's literally in the glam rock period. Remember, it's taken more than fifty years ago! I find it difficult to relate to that person. I'm wearing a tie because I don't want to dress like a student. That's the coat I was wearing when my friend Chris Dowell and I got thrown out of the Regent Palace Hotel because the manager thought we were rent boys. Which we were thrilled to pieces by.'

    Chris's photo had been sent to him by a friend's son, who had just come across it. He doesn't know when or where it was taken. 'It must have been around when I first came to London', he says. 'I think you're older than me than I am in mine', says Neil. 'I think you're twenty-one. Because I think when I first met you, you had the top you're wearing. But we're both northerners going to London. We're both new London boys, really.'

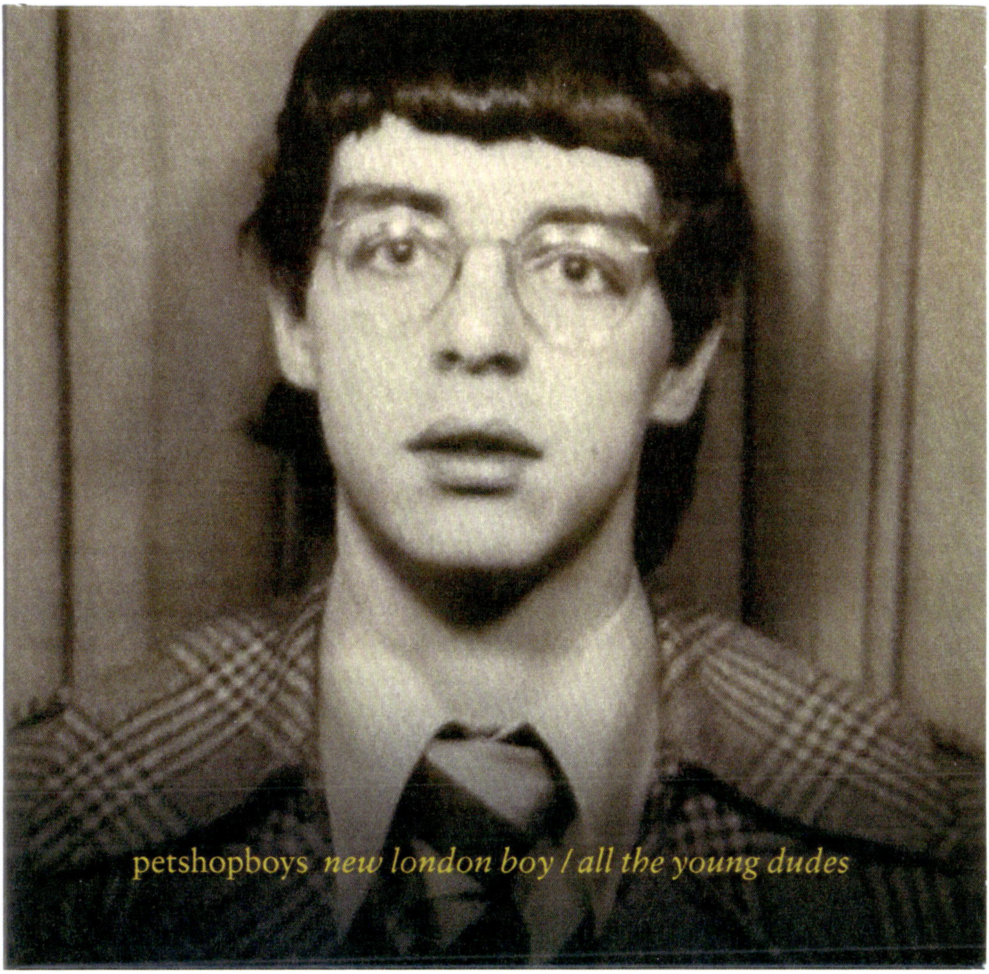

CD, front

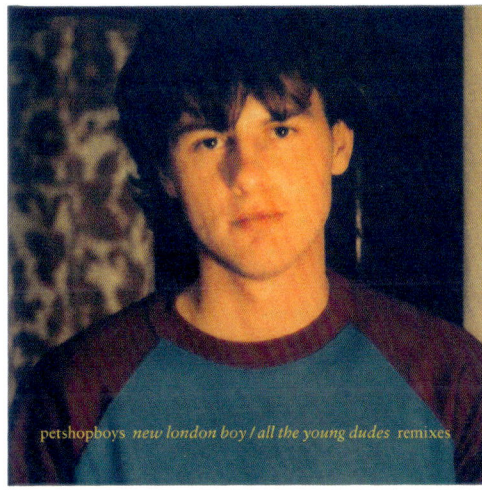
CD remix, front

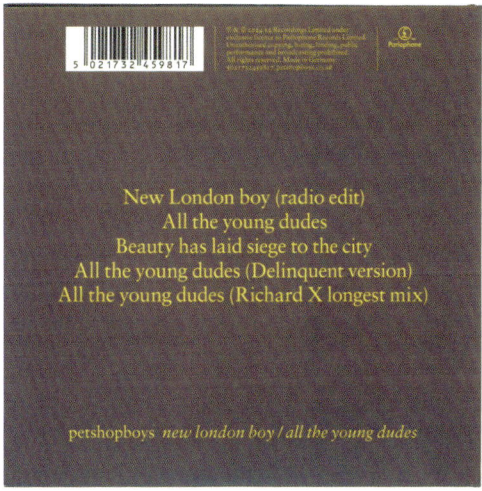
CD, back

New London boy / All the young dudes 2024

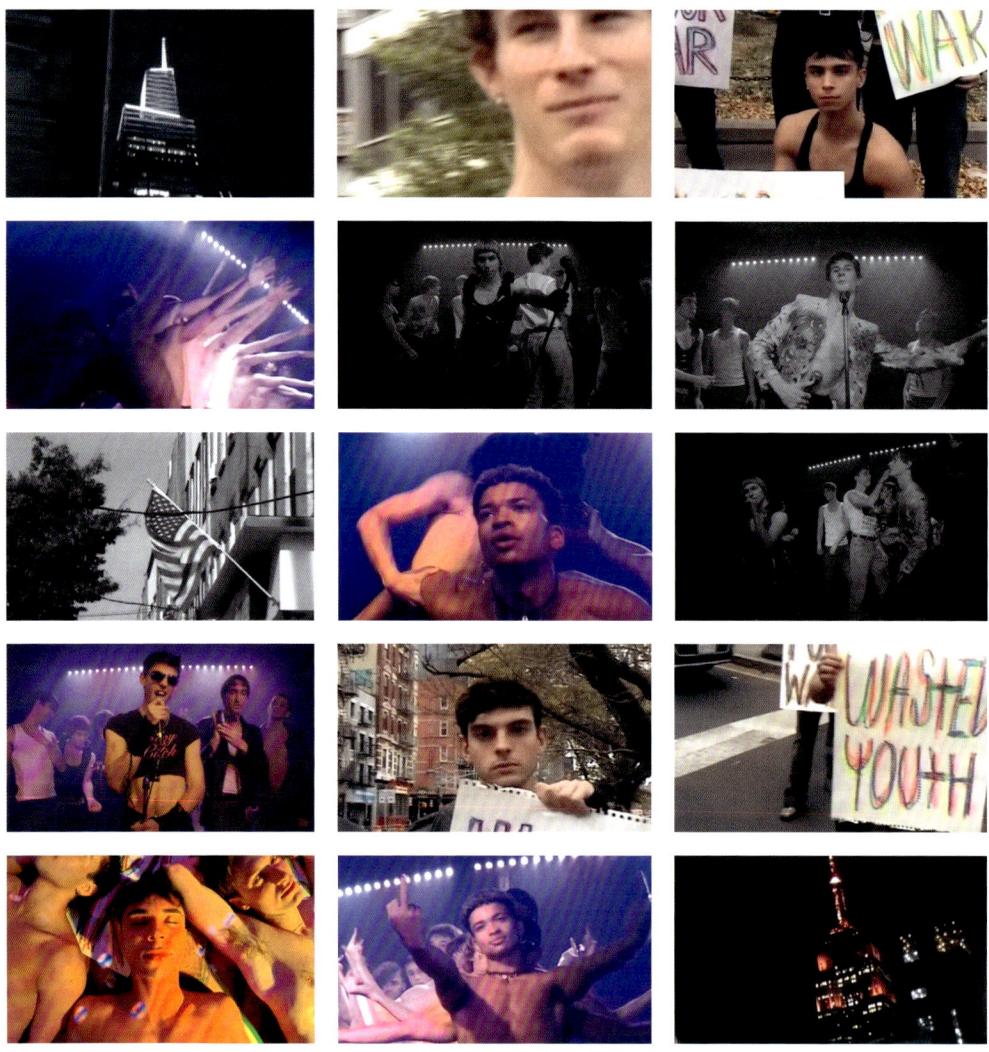

A video for 'All the young dudes' was filmed in New York by the director Slava Mogutin. 'Before we even re-signed to Parlophone,' says Neil, 'the managing director Jennifer Ivory said she thought we should make a video with Slava Mogutin. Chris and I were familiar with his work. He's a gay Russian émigré photographer artist who is based, and has been for a long time, in New York, and his work is very homoerotic. We were quite astonished that the record company head was suggesting we work with someone like him.' 'Because in the old days,' Chris points out, 'they would have been horrified! How the tables have turned in forty years of being in the record industry.' 'Slava was originally going to make the "Dancing star" video,' Neil explains, 'but when the video for "Loneliness" was so sort of homoerotic, we thought if we had that for the second one, it would be repetitious. But when we decided to do "All the young dudes" as a single, we thought it would fit his aesthetic.

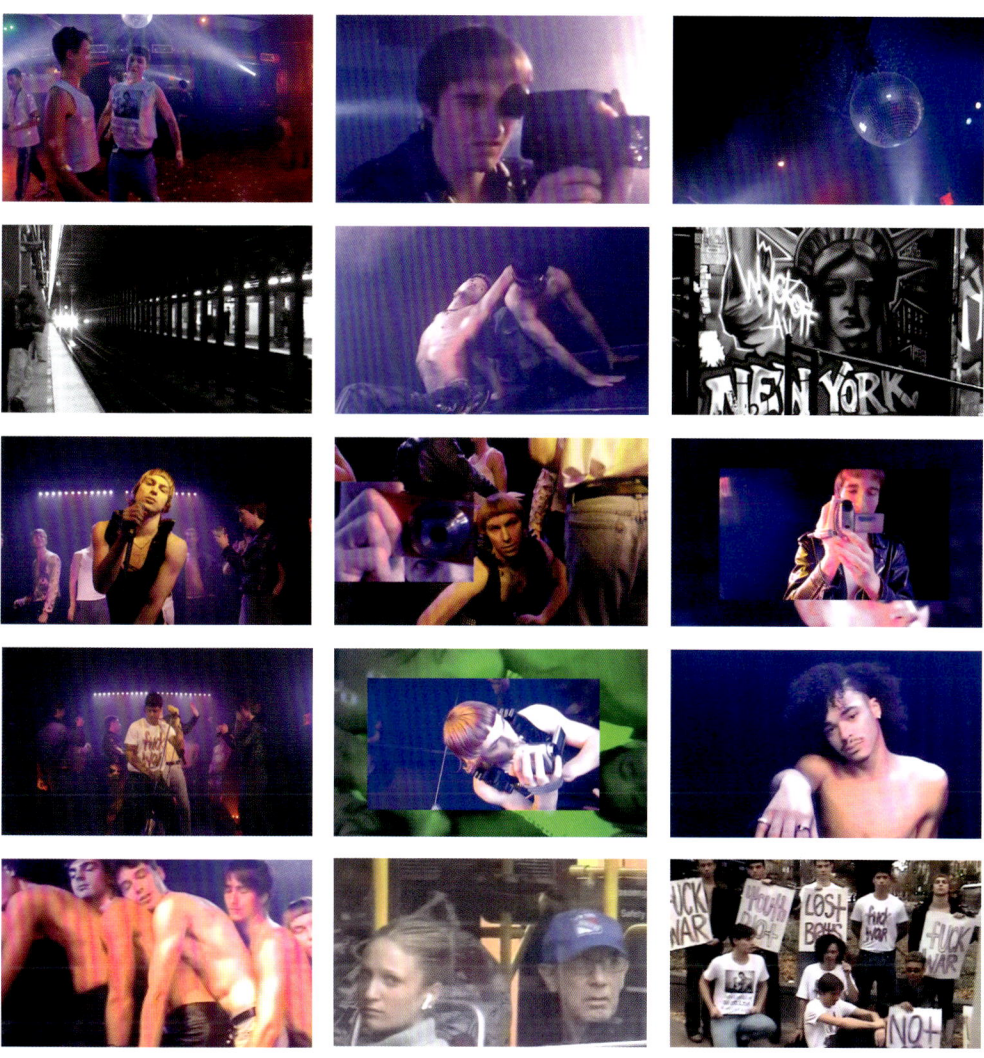

He just did it with a bunch of guys in New York.' 'I think it's a great video', says Chris. 'It looks very Slava Mogutin-y', says Neil. 'It also looks quite New York. It reminds me, actually, of the film *Velvet Goldmine*, which of course is set in the glam rock era, particularly the guy miming to the song. The idea of the song comes out in the video.' 'When you watch the video,' says Chris, 'I think you like the song more – which is really great if a video can achieve that.' 'I felt that, actually, with all of the videos for this album', says Neil. 'Also, I think we made five proper videos', says Chris, 'which is amazing.' 'And three of them we were in', Neil notes. 'As usual, in all of them observing.'

Christmas cards

Since 1986, Pet Shop Boys have sent out specially designed Christmas cards to their friends (and, since 1989, to members of their fan clubs). All but one have been designed by Mark Farrow. They imaginatively adapt key sleeve designs from the preceding year, as well as Christmas themes. In 1991, for example, the card was a pop-out mobile of the 'Was it worth it?' dolls of Neil and Chris. The pop-up 1993 card took the 'Go west' portraits of the group, turning the helmets into Christmas puddings.

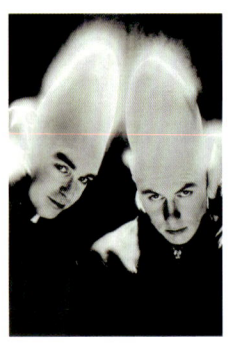

1986

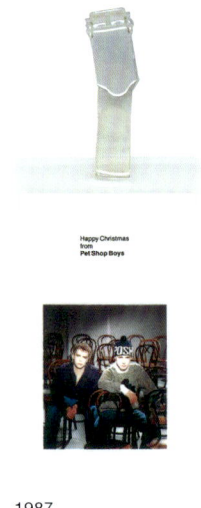

1987

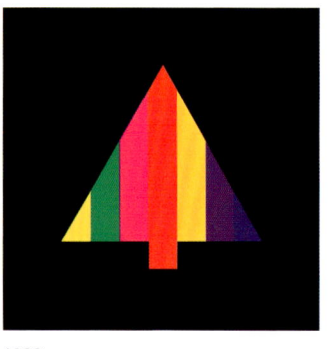

1988

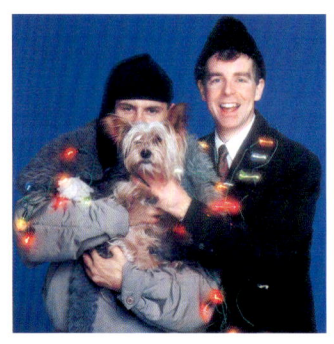

1989

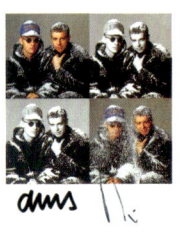

1990

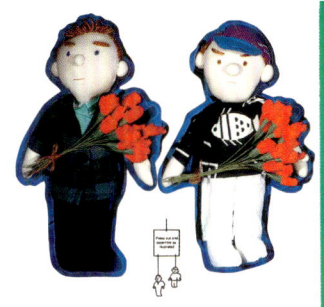 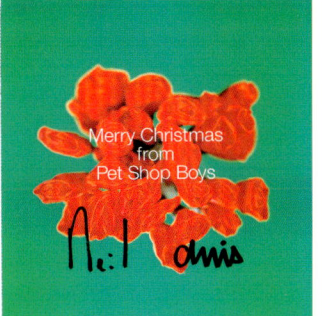 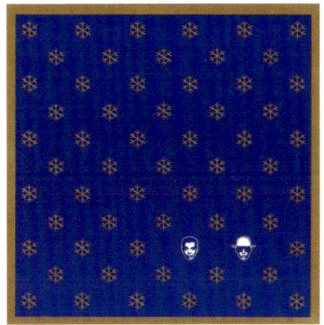

1991   1992

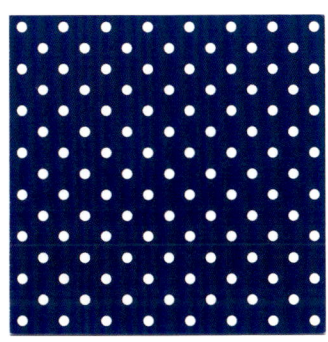 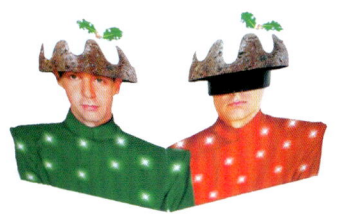

1993

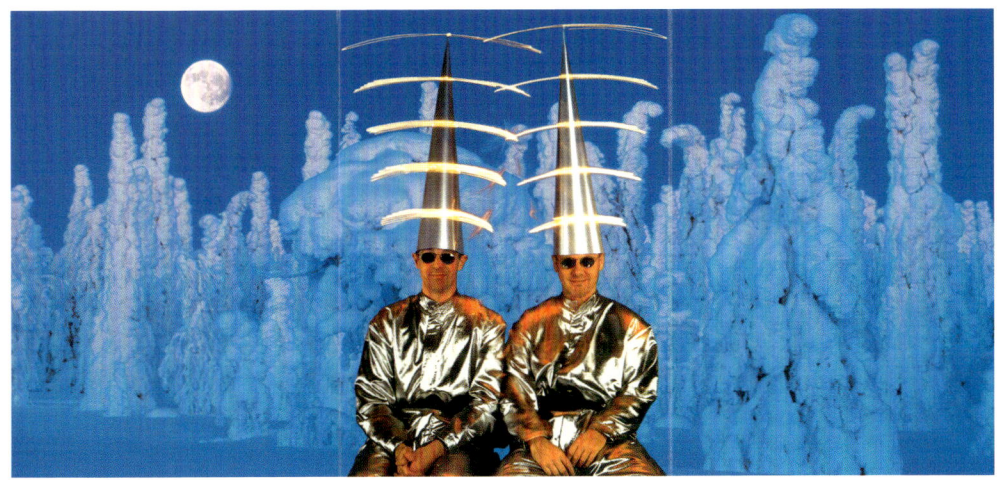

1994

Christmas cards   533

The 1995 card featured two informal photographs of Pet Shop Boys in light-hearted mood, taken by Chris Heath on the South American *Discovery* tour: Neil wears a bunch of bananas on his head, while Chris is seen in a long blond wig. The following year's card was designed as a traditional Advent calendar. Each day's window opened to reveal a recent photograph of the group, many of which had appeared on the sleeves of releases from that year's album, *Bilingual*. The 1997 'card' was in fact a clear CD of a song specially recorded for the occasion, 'It doesn't often snow at Christmas', packaged in a silver bubble-wrap sleeve. The following year, the card featured illustrations of Neil and Chris as Christmas angels, complete with haloes. The figures were designed to be punched out and to sit on the top of the recipient's Christmas tree. The 1999 card was again an object designed to be used. This time, it was a party hat in the style of the *Nightlife* orange shock wigs, to be worn when eating Christmas lunch.

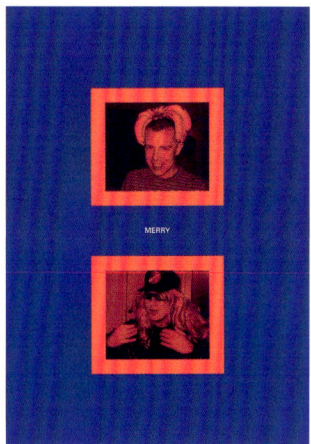

1995

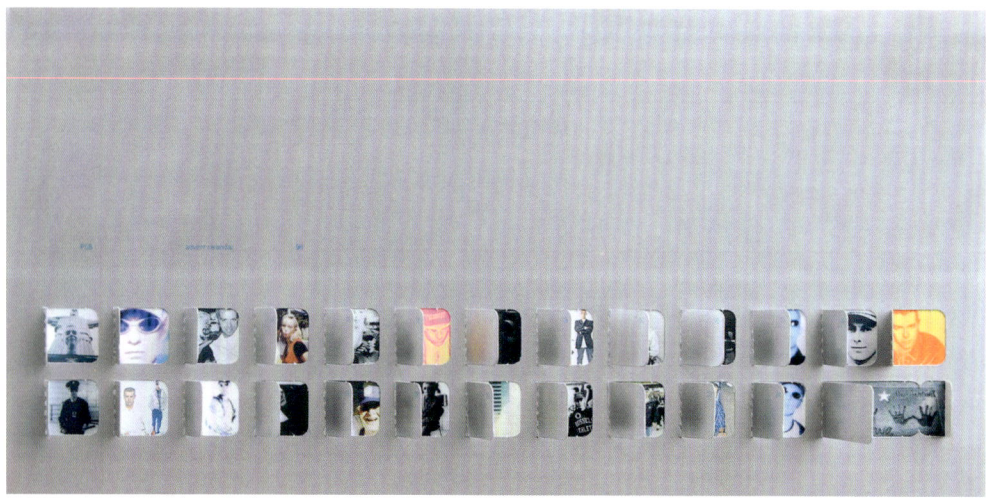

1996

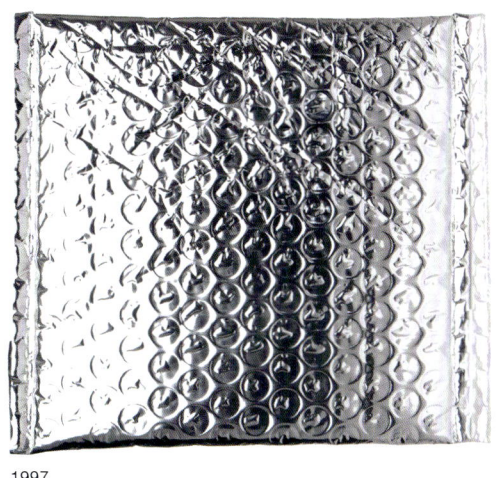
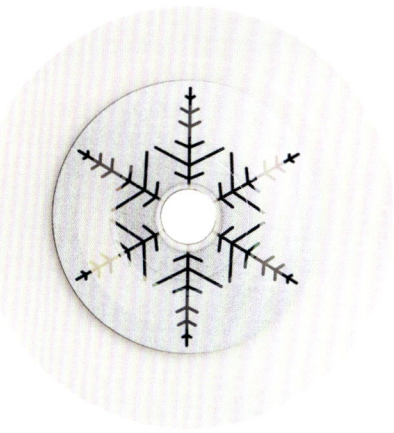

1997

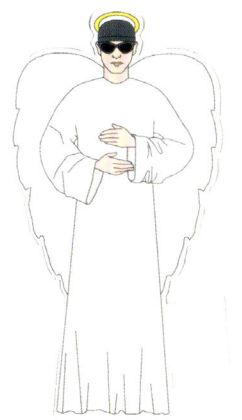
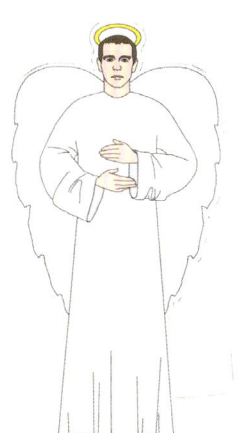

1998

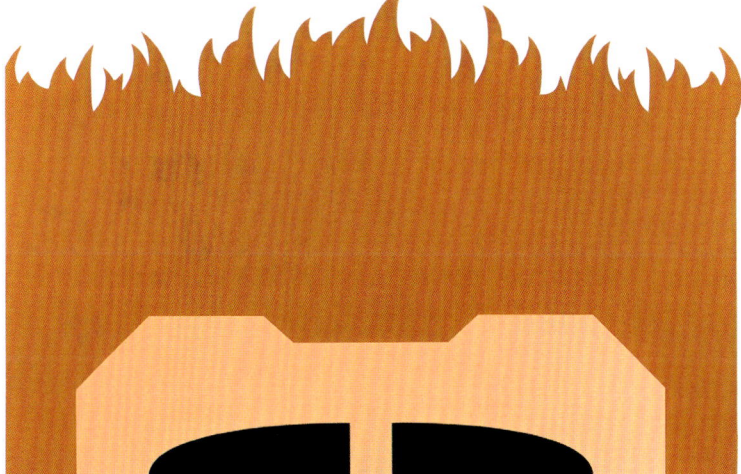

1999

Christmas cards

The following year was an all-text card showing an interview between Neil and Chris and Chris Heath, in which Pet Shop Boys talked about their Christmas memories and rituals. The 2001 card was designed in the style of the publicity for the group's *Closer to Heaven* musical of that year. That was followed in 2002 by the only card not to be designed by Mark Farrow. In the run-up to the second Gulf War, Scott King designed an anti-war card that featured portraits of Neil and Chris in rabbit heads, taken by their programmer Pete Gleadall. The 'Miracles' sleeve design was the inspiration for the 2003 card. The die-cut silhouettes of that release were repeated side by side, through which can be seen a snowy landscape that is fully revealed when the card is opened.

2000

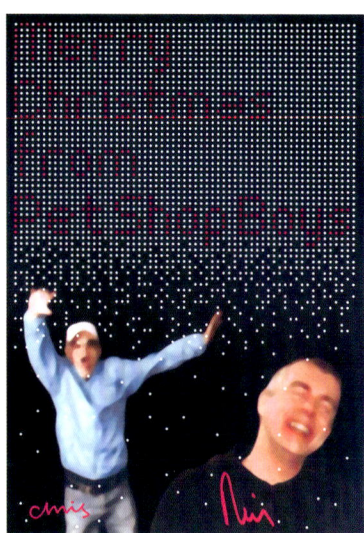

2001

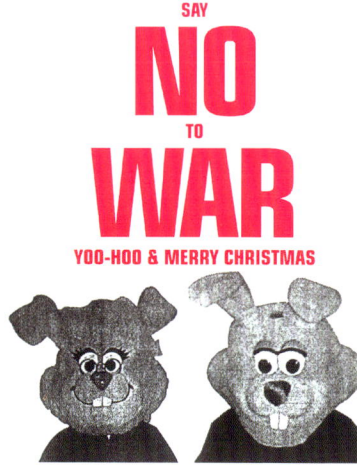

2002

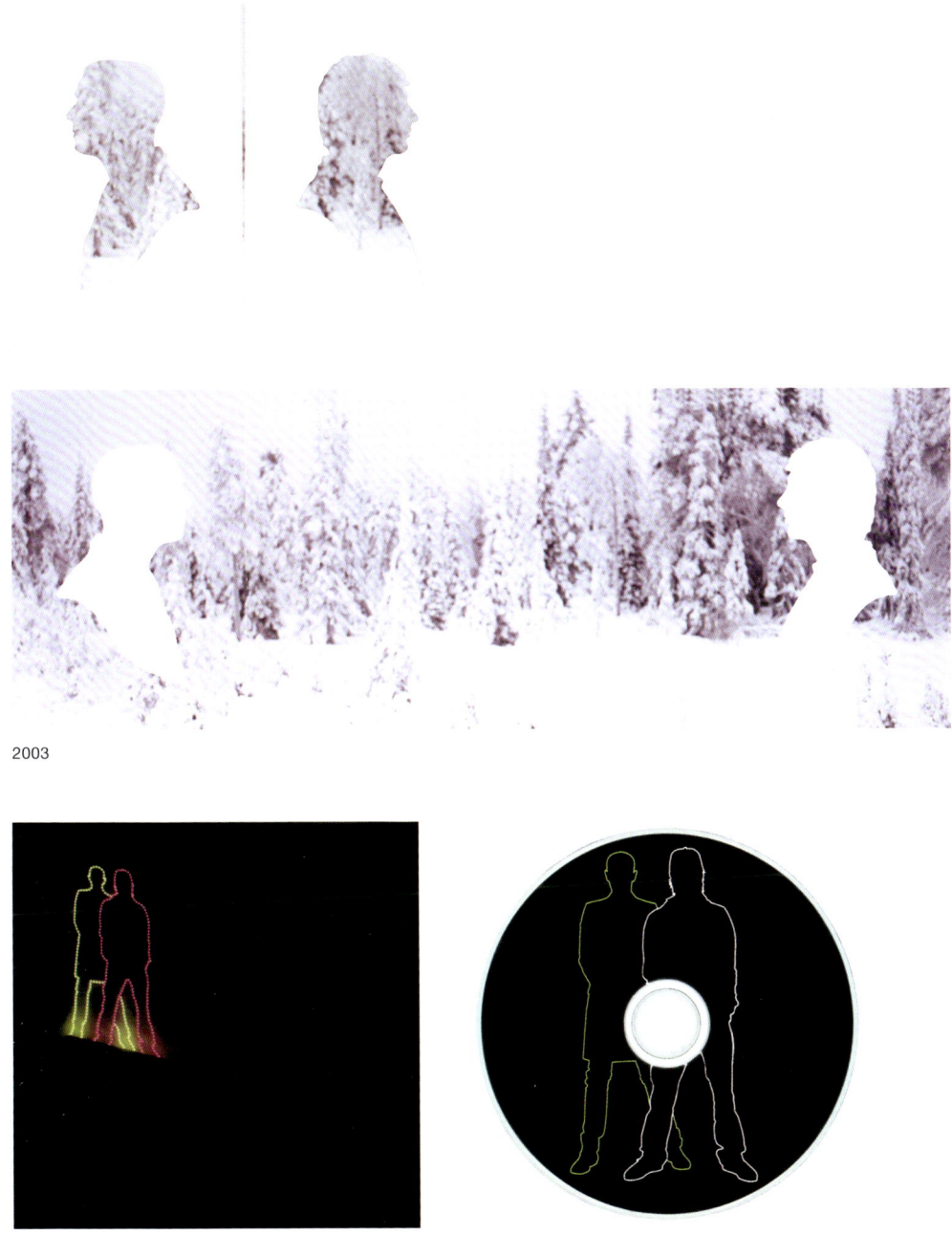

2003

2004

In 2004, the 'card' was again nothing of the sort. Instead, Pet Shop Boys sent out a DVD with highlights of their *Battleship Potemkin* performance in Trafalgar Square the previous September. The figures on the sleeve and printed on the disc were illuminated silhouettes of Neil and Chris seen standing on the square's one empty plinth, known as the 'Fourth Plinth'.

Christmas cards 537

The 2005 card adapted the portrait illustrations of the group that had appeared on their *Back To Mine* CD, which had been released earlier in the year. Here, though, they have become choir boys. Opening the card reveals an assembled host of cassocked Neils and Chrises singing 'We wish you a Merry Christmas and a Happy New Year'. The following year's offering was adapted from the cover of 'I'm with stupid', except with neon sprigs of mistletoe instead of the original red and blue arrows. In 2007, the cover of *Disco Four* provided the inspiration, its neon strip lights being replaced by a set of Christmas tree lights. The 2008 card was a simple play on words, with Neil and Chris inserting their surnames into festive greetings. And the following year's card used one of Pelle Crépin's photographs of Neil and Chris on balloons seen on the two recent releases *Pet Shop Boys Party* and *Pet Shop Boys Christmas*.

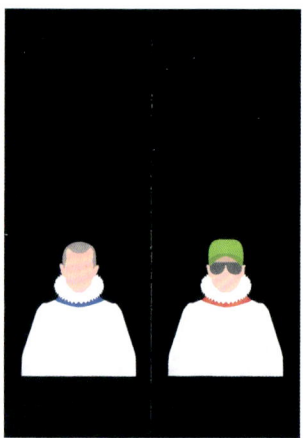 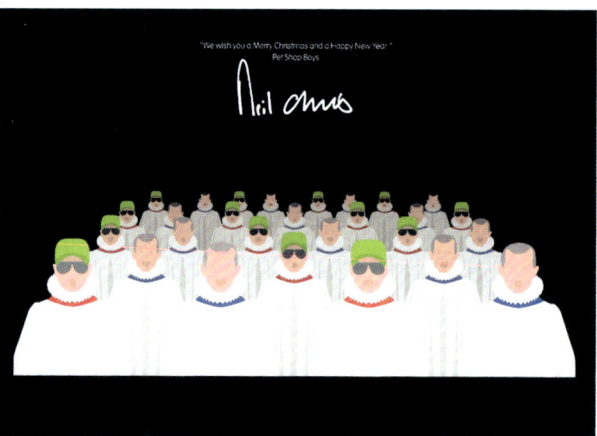

2005

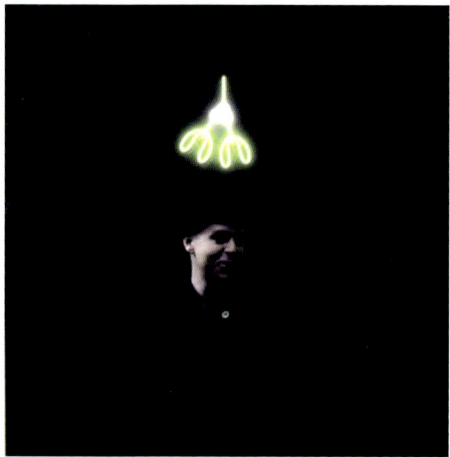 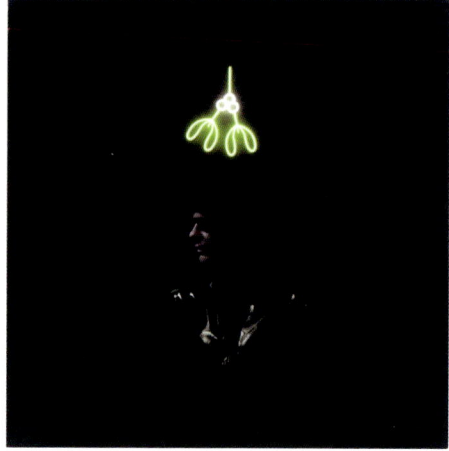

2006

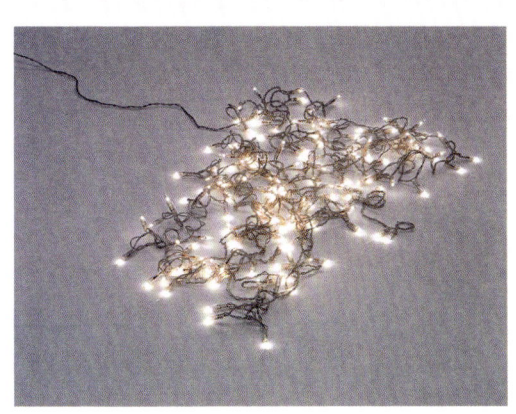

Joyeux
Noël
Tennant

Merry
Christmas
Lowe

2007   2008

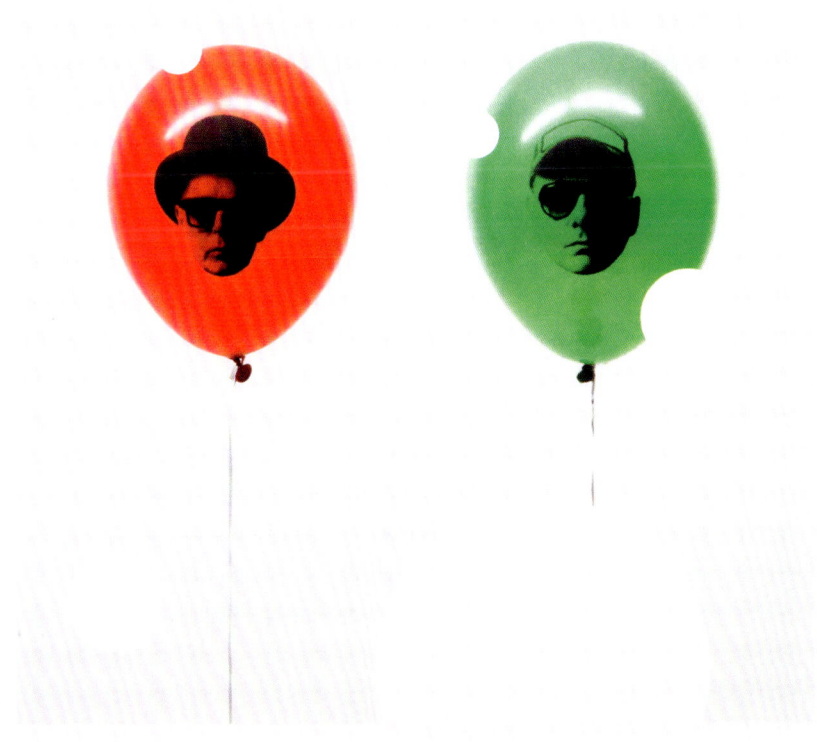

2009

Christmas cards   539

The 2010 card showed Pelle Crépin's photographs of Neil and Chris in the Michael Costiff hats that were used in the CD booklet of the greatest hits album *Ultimate* that year and worn in the *Pandemonium* tour. In 2011, they took the artwork for the album of their ballet *The Most Incredible Thing* as their inspiration, the cutout dancer appearing atop a Christmas tree. The 2012 card, on the other hand, did not refer to any recent Pet Shop Boys project but made use of a photograph taken during a session for a style magazine. The photographer's dog, Jumble, joins Neil and Chris wearing a pair of sunglasses the stylist had brought to the studio.

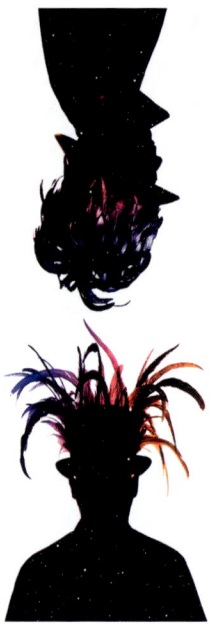
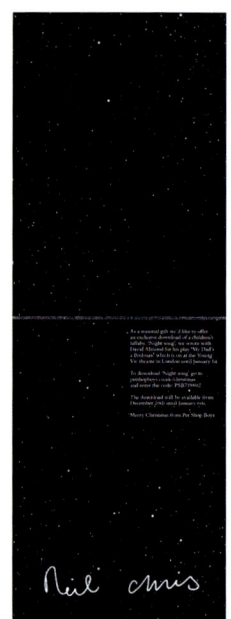

2010

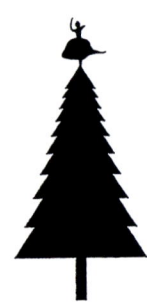
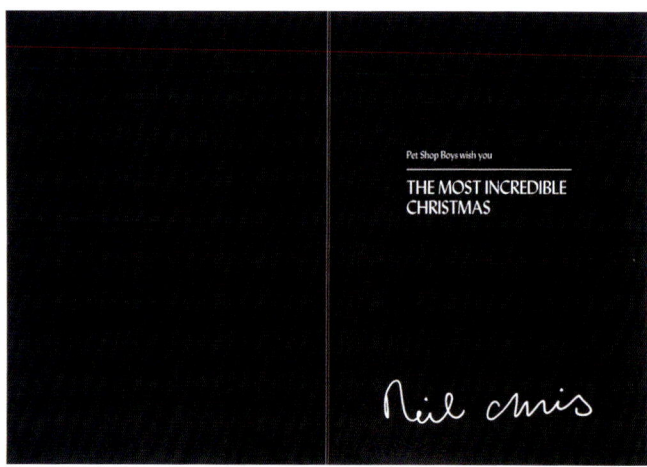

2011

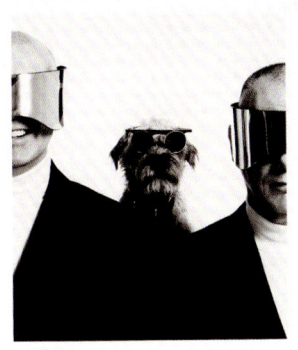

Merry Christmas
from Pet Shop Boys

2012

In 2013, the card took the wave pattern from that year's *Electric* album and converted it into a line of undecorated evergreen trees. The following year continued the green theme with a biblical Star of Bethlehem resembling a Christmas tree and evoking both the lasers of Pet Shop Boys' *Electric* tour that continued throughout 2014 and into the next year, as well as the video of 'Axis' from the associated album. In 2015, we are treated to Neil and Chris snowmen whose circular forms look forward to the artwork of the forthcoming *Super* album and the related singles.

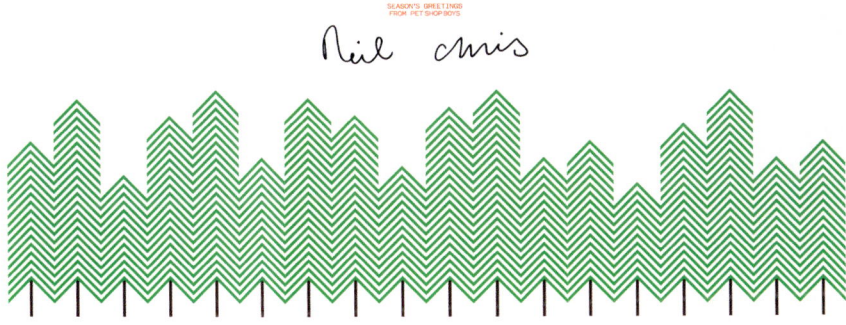

2013

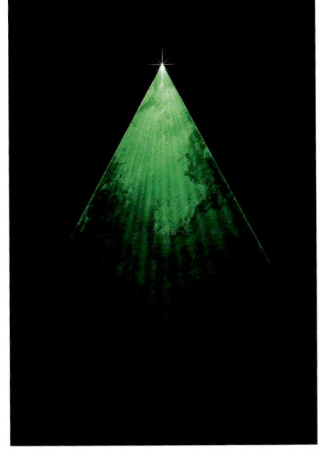

2014

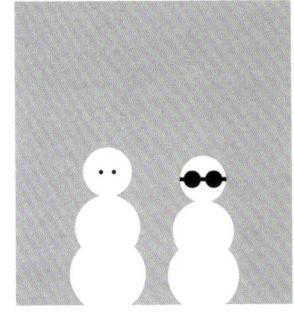

2015

Christmas cards 541

The following two years' cards developed the circular motif, this time referring explicitly to the *Super* album and the subsequent tour, respectively. The 2018 card was a festive celebration of Pet Shop Boys' history, with a pile of Christmas presents wrapped in gift paper that quotes the artwork from the past albums *Introspective*, *Very*, *Bilingual*, *PopArt*, *Yes*, and *Electric*. In 2019, a photograph of a curious-looking goose made oblique reference, through its aesthetic and the typography and positioning of the 'Happy Christmas from Pet Shop Boys' message, to the forthcoming album *Hotspot*, which would be released the following month.

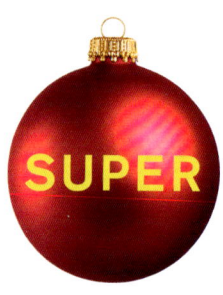

2016

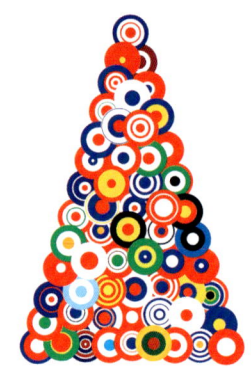

2017

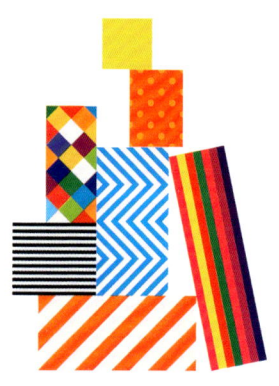

2018

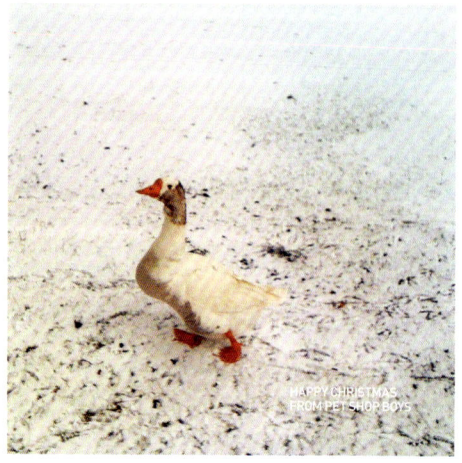

2019

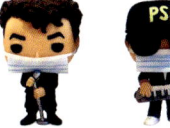

2020

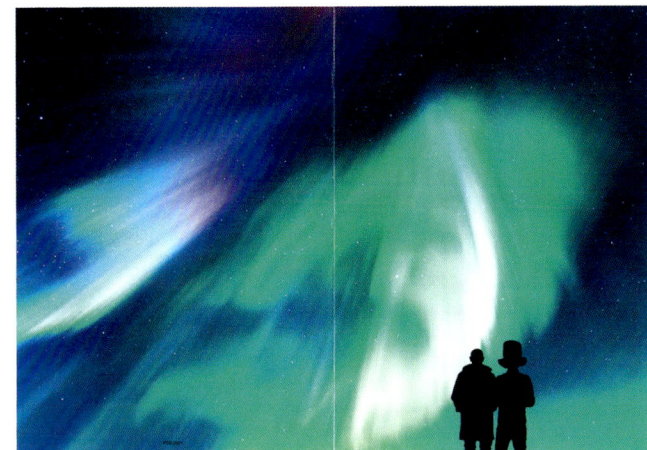

2021

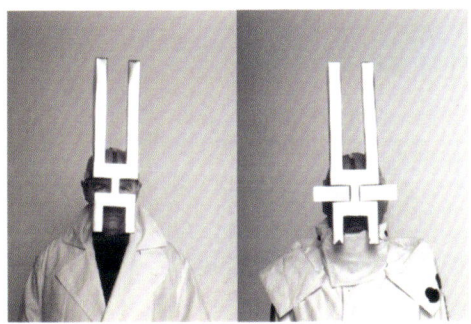

2022

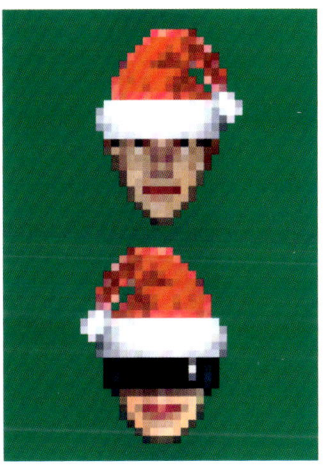

2023

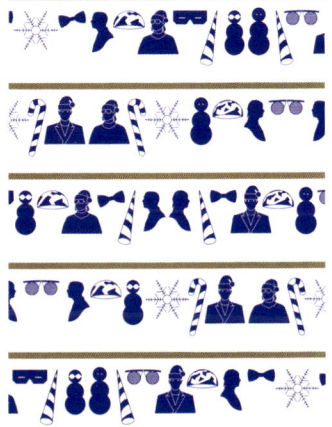

2024

Pandemic year, 2020, was commemorated with a card featuring two figurines of Neil and Chris recently released by the American company Funko, which manufactures pop-culture collectibles, only here wearing Covid-19 masks. The following year showed them in their *Dreamworld* tour silhouettes against a backdrop of the Northern Lights. In 2022, they continued the *Dreamworld* theme with Neil and Chris wearing their tuning-fork masks from the tour. The pixellated faces from the artwork of the new release of *Relentless* as a standalone album provided the inspiration in 2023, the famous 'Go west' helmets changed to Santa Claus hats, while the next year featured a festive version of the pattern of Pet Shop Boys motifs that appeared on their 'Pet Shop Boys since 1984' commemorative china tea set, released just before Christmas 2024.

Literally / Annually

Written by Chris Heath and Pet Shop Boys, and designed by Jaqui Doyle, the fan-club magazine *Literally* was published every few months, with the occasional extended gap, from July 1989 until October 2014. The covers featured recent images, many taken from record sleeves, deliberately reproduced in photocopy style. Its design and brown-paper cover were inspired by a catalogue from Cordings, a London clothing shop. In a very Pet Shop Boys way, it adopted high production values and was published with a care unprecedented for such a publication. *Literally* included in-depth reportage, exclusive photographs of Pet Shop Boys' more recent activities, and interviews with their collaborators, as well as news and Neil and Chris's answers to their fans' queries, replies that often turn into lengthy, revealing debates between the pair themselves.

In 2016, after forty-two issues, the duo decided to cease the magazine in its then format, choosing instead to publish a larger annual hardback book entitled *Annually*, the first issue of which appeared in April 2017. Since 2020, it has been designed by Valentina Verc. Just like its paperback predecessor, *Annually* features news, tour diaries, interviews, fans' letters, behind-the-scenes photographs, and archive material. Some issues are accompanied by CDs of exclusive recordings.

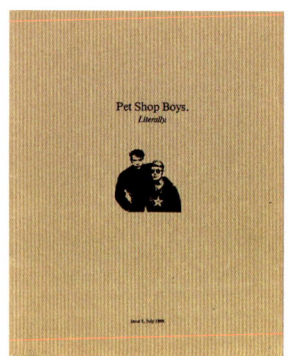
Issue 1, July 1989

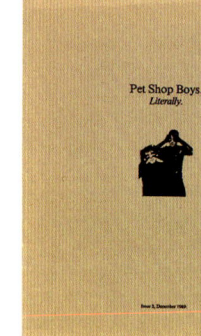
Issue 2, December 1989

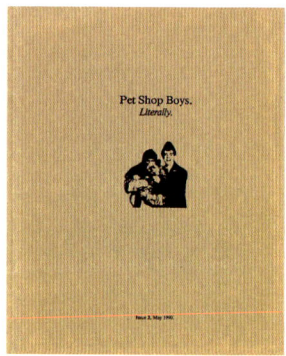
Issue 3, May 1990

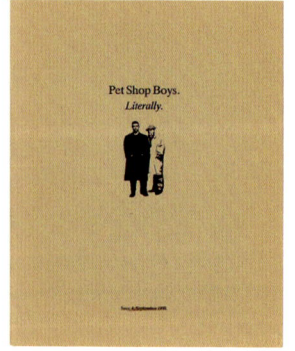
Issue 4, September 1990

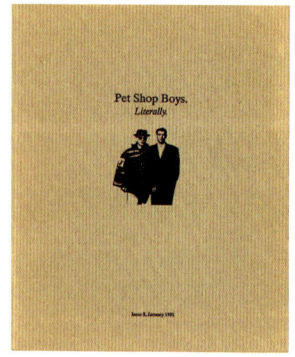
Issue 5, January 1991

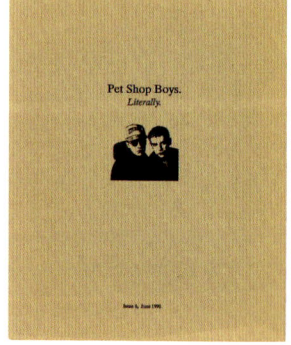
Issue 6, June 1990

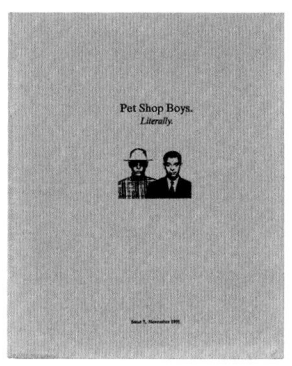
Issue 7, November 1991

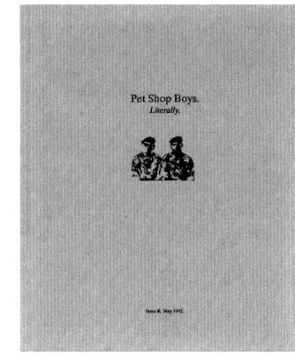
Issue 8, May 1992

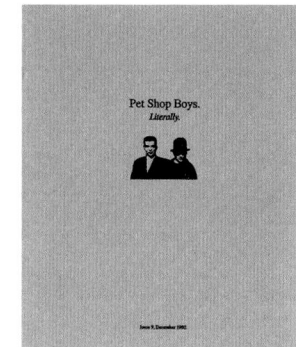
Issue 9, December 1992

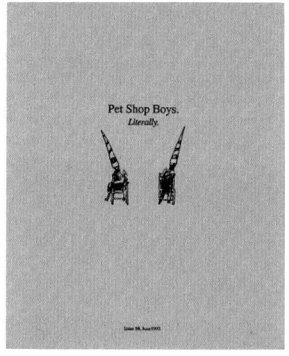
Issue 10, June 1993

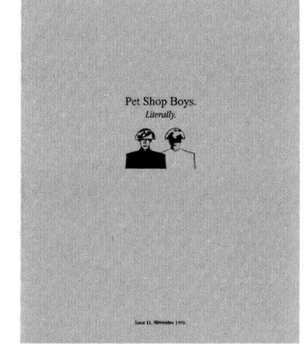
Issue 11, November 1993

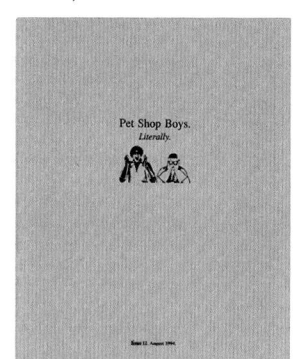
Issue 12, August 1994

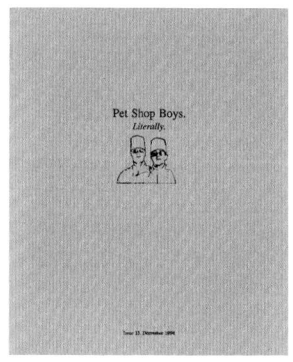
Issue 13, December 1994

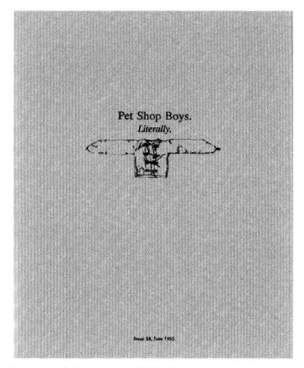
Issue 14, June 1995

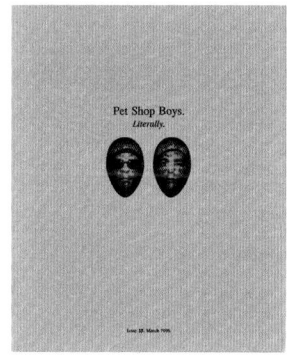
Issue 15, March 1996

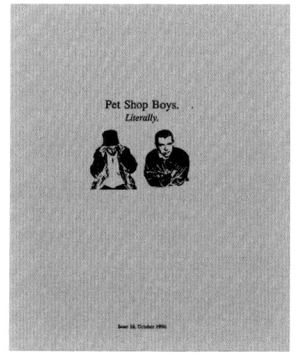
Issue 16, October 1996

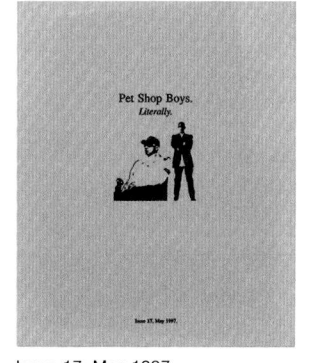
Issue 17, May 1997

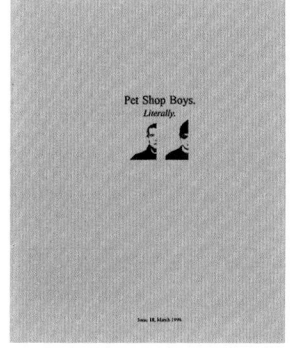
Issue 18, March 1998

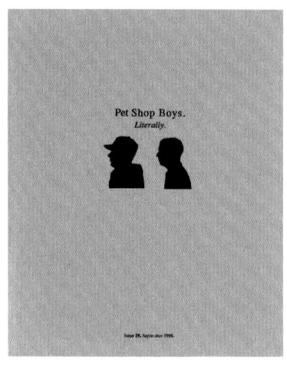
Issue 19, September 1998

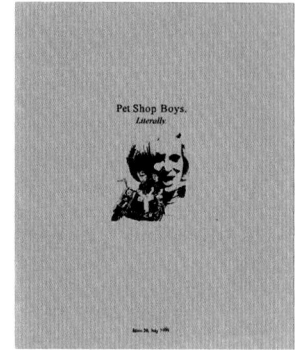
Issue 20, July 1999

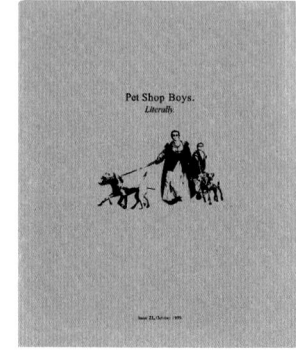
Issue 21, October 1999

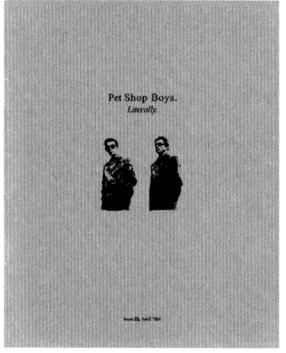
Issue 22, April 2000

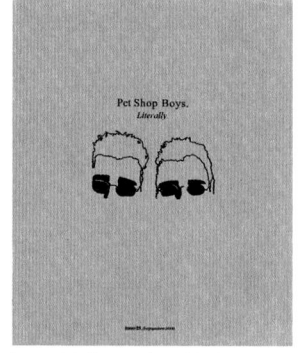
Issue 23, September 2000

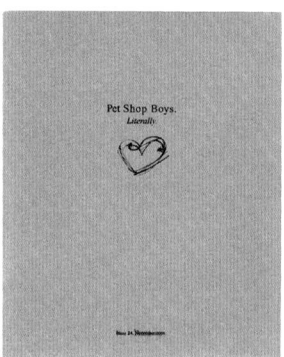
Issue 24, November 2001

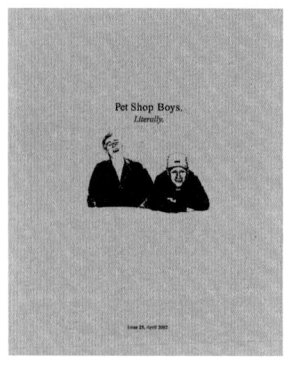
Issue 25, April 2002

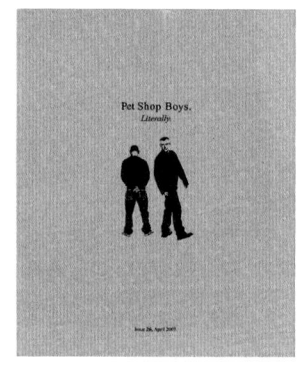
Issue 26, April 2003

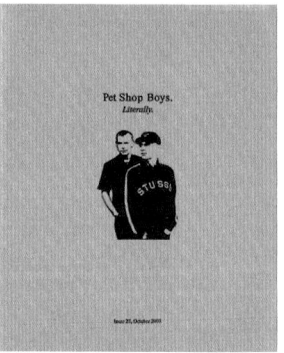
Issue 27, October 2003

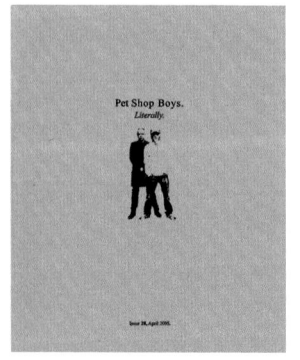
Issue 28, April 2005

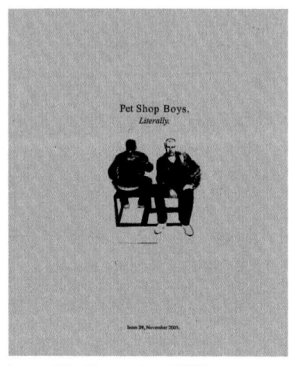
Issue 29, November 2005

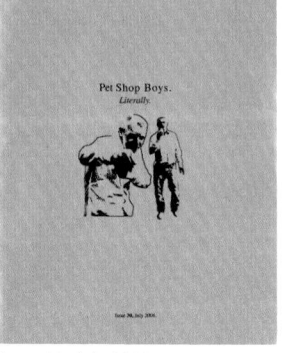
Issue 30, July 2006

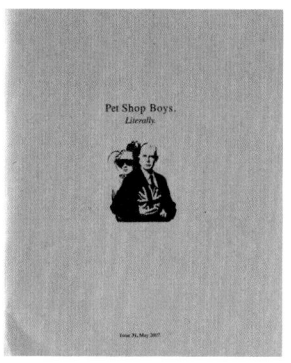
Issue 31, May 2007

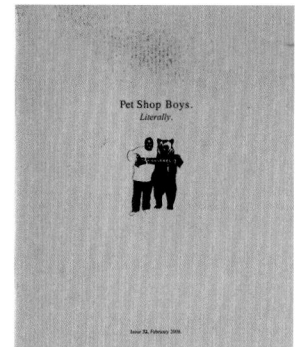
Issue 32, February 2008

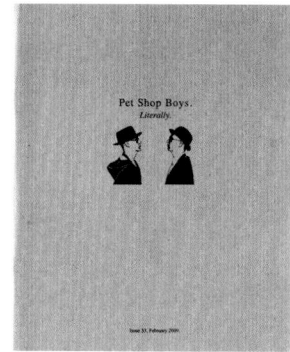
Issue 33, February 2009

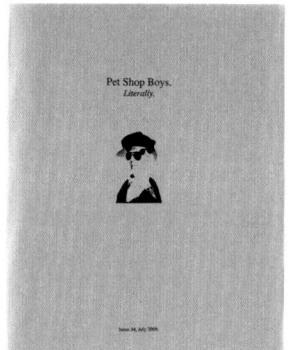
Issue 34, July 2009

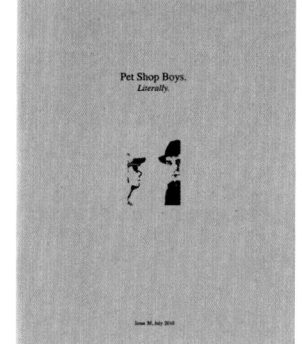
Issue 35, July 2010

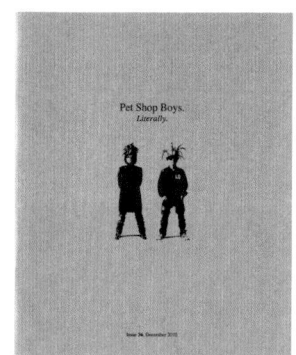
Issue 36, December 2010

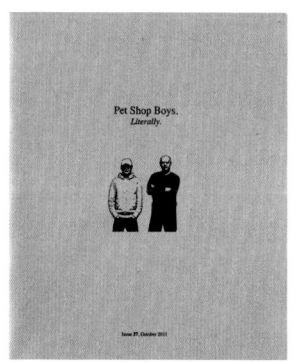
Issue 37, October 2011

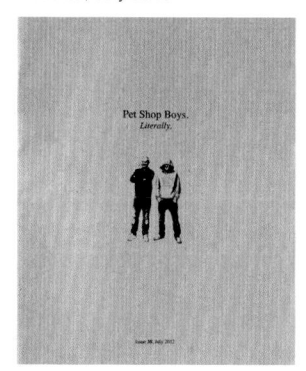
Issue 38, July 2012

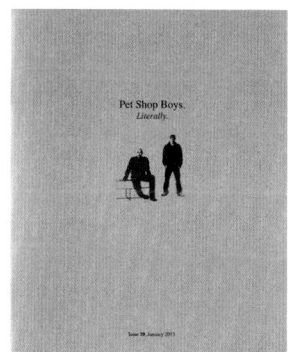
Issue 39, January 2013

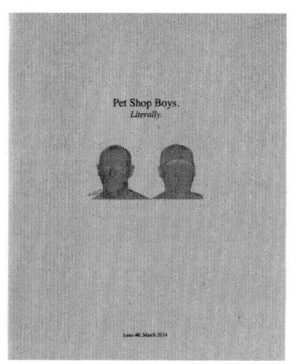
Issue 40, March 2014

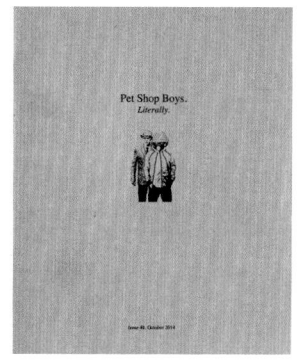
Issue 41, October 2014

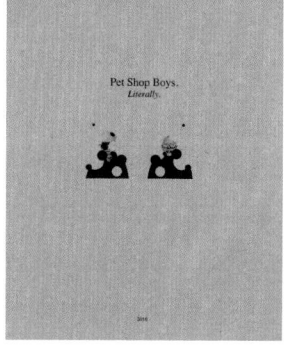
Issue 42, May 2016

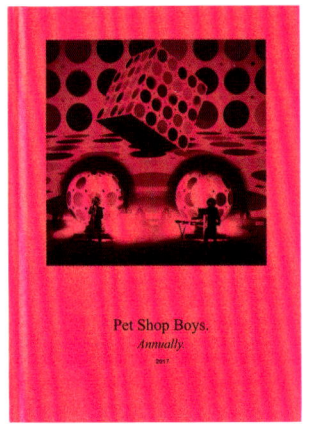
Annually 2017 (issue 43)

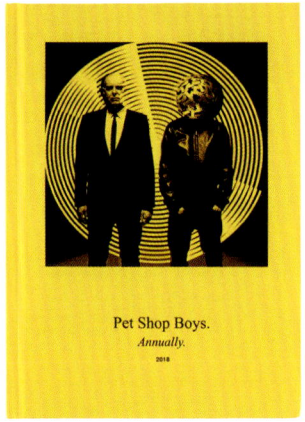
Annually 2018 (issue 44)

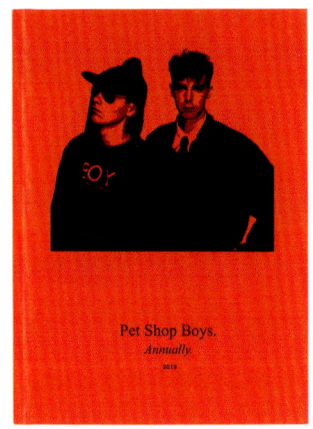
Annually 2019 (issue 45)

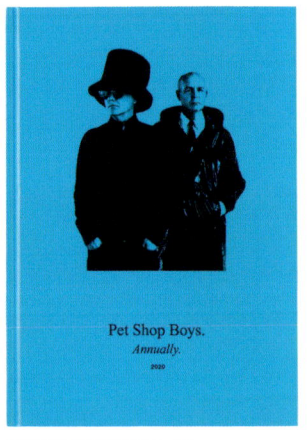
Annually 2020 (issue 46)

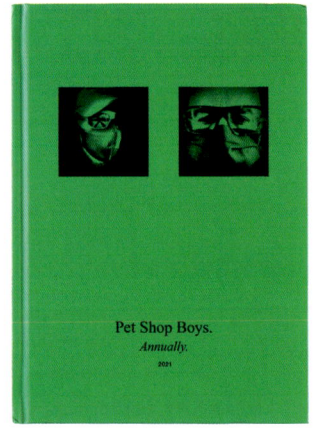
Annually 2021 (issue 47)

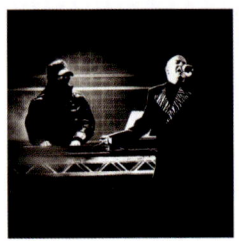
Annually 2022 (issue 48)

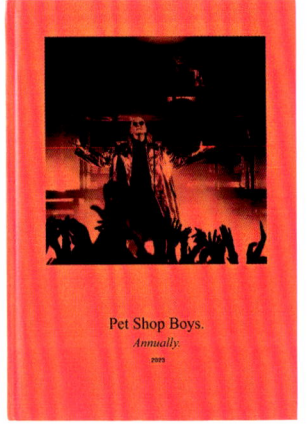
Annually 2023 (issue 49)

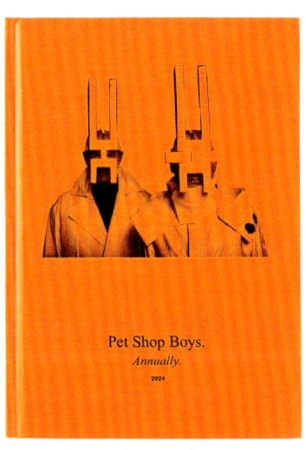
Annually 2024 (issue 50)

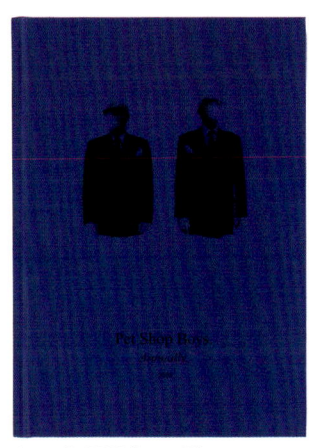
Annually 2025 (issue 51)

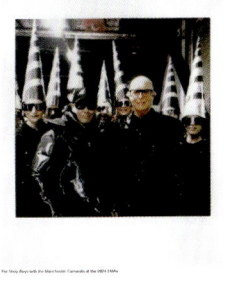
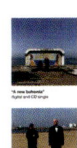
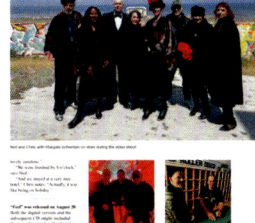
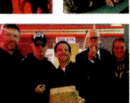
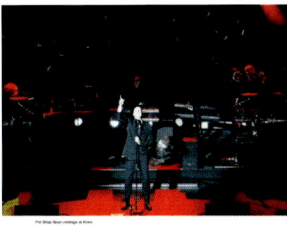
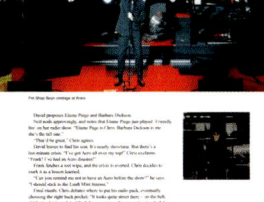
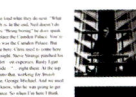

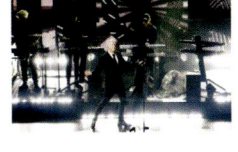

Annually 2025, inside pages

Pet Shop Boys in conversation
with Chris Heath, April 2006

When you look back over this entire visual history, what strikes you most?

Neil: How many records we've put out. Over a twenty-year period, there's always something going on. I think there are highs and lows within it, but you're very much aware that there's always a lot of effort gone into it – that it's never become routine. We've never lost our energy for working on it, for trying to change things. The visual side was always regarded by us as being of not quite but almost equal importance.

Chris: What's interesting is that we look just as young now as when we started.

Neil: I don't think that's absolutely true. But we viewed the whole project, as you would now say, as a whole. Of course, in the Eighties the visual side was very, very important anyway, and I guess that's something I had coming from *Smash Hits* as well, though I personally think we would have had it anyway. Also, I think working with Eric Watson, we shared between the three of us an idea of doing pop photographs that weren't in the style of pop photographs. Part of the inspiration of Pet Shop Boys has always been to bring things from outside pop music into pop music. Eric had a lot of photographic theories and history that he was interested in, that he wanted to bring to this, some of which we probably wouldn't even be aware of. I think you can particularly see it in those early photo sessions for 'Opportunities', where we spent two days doing photographs in the East End and in Eric's studio – we definitely wanted to do something that would make us stand apart from other pop groups at the time. When we were doing those photographs in Limehouse it was just before Live Aid, in the time of Wham! and Frankie Goes To Hollywood and Spandau Ballet and Duran Duran. Pop music seemed in a very imperial phase at this point – it had gone epic and worldwide. I think we wanted to do something that seemed to come from a completely different direction, that had a kind of quality of seriousness and a sort of dignity about it. Even a kind of puritanism about it, maybe. Those pictures of me in the Homburg hat or whatever it is, they have a sort of puritan quality and that's quite deliberate. We're partly in the East End because we'd written 'West End girls ... East End boys', but I think we're more in the East End because it expresses a disassociation from the glamour of mid-Eighties pop music.

Which was mostly happening in the West End and Notting Hill Gate.

Neil: Yes, exactly. It followed through in the music – Chris and I were fascinated by having real sounds in the music. 'West End girls' begins with someone walking down the street and then the strings come in, so it sounds to us like the start of a film. And in the imagery we wanted to look like stills from some kind of weird Italian film. There's a shop on

Brewer Street where you can buy film stills, and when I worked just round the corner at *Smash Hits*, I often used to go in and flick through the old magazines and stills.

Do you remember what you didn't want to look like?

Chris: We didn't want to look like a happy smiley pop band, pulling faces for the camera. I don't think it was in our basic nature to do that, apart from anything else.

Neil: It might have been to do with my age. When we were doing those first photographs, I was thirty. George Michael at that point was twenty-one or twenty-two. I'd met some of those groups through interviewing them and I was aware that I was older than them, and yet we were going to come along and follow them.

Chris: We thought it was very unnatural to smile and jump around in a photo session when that's not how you're feeling. We wanted the photographs to represent how we felt at the time they were taken, rather than switching on some sort of personality.

Neil: And we didn't have those performance skills. We didn't have any live performance background in music.

But although you didn't want to fake stupid pop emotion, there's nonetheless a great amount of artifice even in these early photos.

Neil: Tons of artifice. We put on clothes for the photographs, which is what we still do to this day. I was always wearing this coat by Stephen Linard. Eric bought it for himself, and he said to me, 'I think you should wear this coat.' I think he thought we looked good when we looked serious and dignified. And, actually, even morose. No one was doing moroseness. If they were morose, they didn't have pictures of themselves on the sleeves.

Chris: We were mainly driven by a desire to do things differently from anyone else.

Neil: Also, it's a self-consciousness. We always used to say – and it was true – that we didn't want to *pretend*. When we were on *Top of the Pops* or something like that, we wanted to look like ourselves. But, even so, we're not *just* like that – we laugh and joke, and the public wouldn't get to see that side, not at the beginning. In the introduction to this book, there's the quote from Noël Coward about masks – what we do is take *part* of our personality and make a mask out of it, and it masks the rest of it.

So in other words it's been the struggle to find an honest way of pretending rather than a dishonest way of pretending?

Neil: That's a good way of putting it – an honest way of pretending. And if you've got to be in public and give some kind of performance, I've always felt much more comfortable, and sort of empowered, to put on the outfit and the make-up to do that.

Chris: I go through phases. Sometimes I feel like that, and sometimes I don't at all.

Do you remember the first time you had to decide how Pet Shop Boys would represent themselves?

Chris: Wasn't it on that trip to Belgium? A radio programme was having some sort of do.

Neil: In Ostend. 'So, Neil, what do you think of our Ostend girls?' This was around the first release of 'West End girls'. We'd done one photo session by then – the eyes and the tennis racket. When Chris and I came back from New York, we'd bought a lot of Nike gear and we thought it looked terribly hip hop and were very excited about that. And there was also a vogue for wearing cycling trousers, and I used to quite like those black stretchy cycling trouser things – in

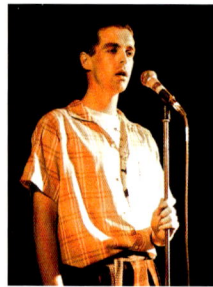
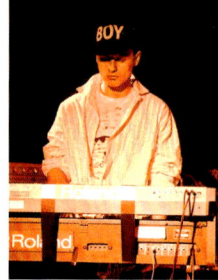
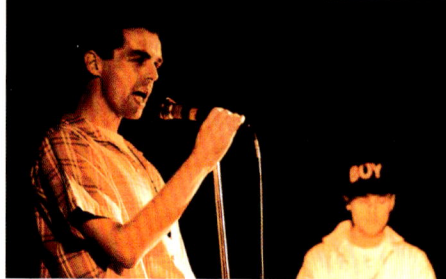

The first Pet Shop Boys gig, at the Fridge, Brixton, 24 September 1984 (photos: Chris Burscough)

fact, I wore those right into the second version of 'West End girls', under the black coat. When we went to Belgium, I was wearing a sweatshirt and those trousers, and trainers of some description, and we both wore the BOY caps. But we didn't know we were going to do a performance, and when they said that I nearly fainted.

Chris: We didn't have an act.

Neil: Anyway, it was quite interesting. Chris remarked afterwards that I moved like David Bowie.

Chris: All those hours practising in front of the mirror paid off.

Neil: So that was actually our first performance – performing in front of an audience on the radio, miming. The first TV show we did, on RTL Luxembourg, some big Saturday night show, we had Tom Watkins by then and he'd sent us out with Iain R. Webb, the stylist, so we had 'the outfit' that we wore for a while, the same outfit we wore when we performed at the Fridge in 1984, our first proper gig.

Chris: There's a fantastic picture of Neil looking like Ian Curtis.

Neil: I'm wearing tartan trousers and a checked shirt and my hair's swept back, and Chris is wearing the BOY cap and a shirt with a T-shirt under showing the BOY head. He didn't have the glasses yet.

That was really a gift, being the Pet Shop Boys, that we could have these things saying BOY. I lived over the road from the BOY shop.

Do you remember how you began to work out 'this is what we look like, this is what we do'?

Neil: Yes, but it wasn't really developed by then. The thing that made the big difference was when Chris wore the cap and the glasses, and I had the coat. The coat cost so much – it was the single most expensive garment I'd ever had in my life, £400 or something, which I suppose was borrowed from EMI – that it was going to have to earn its keep, basically. So it was worn in two videos and our first TV appearances for EMI. But when we were doing those photos with Eric, we were absolutely trying to make an image. Eric used to say, 'The important thing about a group is to make a kind of myth out of it.'

And did you go as far as knowing what kind of myth it was you were making?

Neil: No, I don't think Chris and I quite bought that. Because to us, 'myth', even at that point, meant U2 or Echo and the Bunnymen, and that's not the kind of thing we wanted to be. Nonetheless, we sort of knew what he meant – that the photographs would be kind of quasi-historical …

Chris: … enigmatic …

Neil: Precisely.

Were you comfortable having your photo taken?

Neil: It's a very odd thing, the first time you have your photograph taken. The first time I ever had my photograph taken by a professional photographer was when we did the Smash Hits Yearbook 1983 – probably the first time for Chris as well – and we modelled T-shirts. I remember standing in front of the camera and feeling incredibly self-conscious, thinking how terrifying it was.

Chris: I don't remember being terrified. I found it exciting. You've got an image of David Bailey taking photos in the Sixties, so to be the subject of it all was quite interesting.

Neil: Of course it wasn't like David Bailey because Eric's endlessly getting the light right – his big skill was that he was brilliant at the lighting. He wasn't just taking 'snappy pics', as this guy we knew from Newcastle once referred to it. 'Still taking lovely snappy pics?' I thought Eric was going to kill him. But we liked the very serious approach to the whole thing. We admire that. And we had it too.

Did you suddenly realize that you had 'an image'? Presumably you don't know for sure the particular things the public will fix on until it happens.

Neil: The thing that fixed in people's imagination was of us walking down the street in the 'West End girls' video, Chris walking behind me.

Chris: Which you can see any day of the week in London for real, if you just happen to catch us out of the car window.

Neil: Because I walk faster than Chris.

Chris: Because Neil walks faster. And I have to do a hop, skip, and a jump to catch up every now and then.

Neil: See, that's a really truthful example of us being us. Chris and I have such different bearings. Typically, I stride sternly ahead …

Chris: … chin up. And I mope with chin down.

Neil: Exactly.

That became a strong part of the way Pet Shop Boys were perceived – Chris seeming stoic and almost reluctant.

Neil: I don't know about stoic but reluctant, certainly. It was a non-participating thing.

Chris: Well, it was embarrassing making the 'West End girls' video, for instance. Walking through the streets of London with a camera crew. Particularly Waterloo Station, coming up the escalators. I didn't really want to be there. And I had a dental appointment that I had to cancel.

Neil: No, that was 'Opportunities'. You complained all day long.

Chris: I thought it was 'West End girls'. I probably moved the appointment to the day the 'West End girls' video happened to be, so I had to cancel two. That wouldn't surprise me.

The other issue for pop groups is whether they want to present themselves as sexy.

Chris: Well, that just came naturally. Didn't really have to work on that.

Neil: I don't think we thought about it. The only sexy thing we've ever done is that Chris decided that he wanted to be on the cover of My Guy, the girls' magazine. This was before we had a hit. And he was duly photographed, and looked very convincing. Then when we did have a hit, Chris was at least twice in Just 17 magazine by himself. I always felt rather proud of him, really.

Chris: Who'd have thought?

Why did you want to be on the cover of My Guy?

Chris: Because I could.

Neil: Why did you though?

Chris: I just thought it would be funny. One minute you're a student, the next minute … I'm a cover guy!

Neil: The difference is, though, in doing photographs of Pet Shop Boys, he would do the morose thing, but my recollection of the cover of *My Guy* is that he's smiling, the male model kind of thing. So in fact he had reserves of professionalism and performance that he can draw on that he had kept very quiet, but that, I have learned to realize, will just suddenly appear every now and then. Like when he suddenly announces he's going to do a dance routine in the video for 'What have I done to deserve this?' or he suddenly announces he's going to take his clothes off on the *Performance* tour.

Chris: Then it vanishes again.

Neil: Anyway, it's always an exciting moment when his performance skills arrive. Like when he played the organ at Newcastle City Hall on the *Release* tour. He has such a strong self-conscious feeling of potential shame, but sometimes that just gets pushed aside.

Chris: If something's a lot of fun, I'll do it.

That sense of shame is very important to the way Pet Shop Boys have presented themselves, isn't it?

Neil: When I first met Chris, I remember we went to the Café Picasso and I opened the door the wrong way – you had to pull and I pushed, or the other way round – and Chris then refused to go in. I was really bewildered. He goes, 'You've really shamed us.' I suppose people might have looked up and seen this ghastly social error happening and might snigger at us when we went in. I just didn't really get it, to be honest. But I learned to live with it.

Chris: This concept, this way of thinking, came from a friend from Preston. He once came down to see me in London and he got out of Euston Station but he wouldn't look at his map because he didn't want anyone to think he was a tourist, so he set off and didn't know where he was going. Also, he couldn't allow himself to do a 180-degree turn on the pavement in case anyone was watching. And so he walked miles the wrong way. A lot of it stems from him, actually, this feeling of shame.

How do you apply it being a Pet Shop Boy?

Chris: You don't want to embarrass yourself, do you?

And you found an awful lot of what most pop stars did embarrassing?

Chris: Yes. Like what people did in videos – running down corridors, looking a bit paranoid. Things like that. We have done acting since then, but in the beginning we didn't want to do acting in videos. We wanted to be more naturalistic. A lot of it was trying to avoid cliché. I think all the images of me in the book are because of me being embarrassed by me being a pop star.

Was it difficult to work out what to do in videos?

Neil: When you're in a video no one ever tells you what to do. They say, 'OK … action!' But Eric didn't want you to do anything. Eric used to like it when I looked right in the camera and raised an eyebrow.

Chris: One thing we realized was that when you don't actually move a lot, the camera comes in a lot closer on you. On television if there's a lot of movement, or a lot of dancers and musicians, you just get a wide shot and you don't get the same kind of impact. So actually it pays to do less.

Neil: I always got the impression Tom Watkins used to slightly despair.

What did he think? That you weren't really trying?

Neil: I think everyone thought that. We were introduced on *Top of the Pops* the first time by Steve Wright saying we were a very unusual duo, or a strange duo. And then the camera pans to us and you sort of think, 'Yeah, I know what he means.' I remember the first time I saw us on *Top of the Pops* – I was at EMI for some reason – I felt sort of horrified. Eric was around and seemed to make it clear he wasn't very impressed either. And even I, at that point, had the self-consciousness thing of 'Oh my God, you're on television' at a time when *Top of the Pops* was watched by a lot of people. It's vaguely alarming in a way.

Chris: It's an odd feeling, putting yourself into the public eye. You can often feel soiled. You can go to bed that evening thinking 'what have I done?'

Neil: Then, as with anyone, a cliché develops. And as Andrew Harrison pointed out in *Word* magazine, we were 'the grumpiest men in pop'. Well, we were quite happy to be that.

Chris: We still are grumpy, actually.

Neil: And as he pointed out, when I 'came out' in *Attitude* magazine, grumpy became gay. I think I preferred grumpy, really. But the gay thing is a more powerful cliché.

Over the years, where has fashion fitted into what you do visually?

Neil: Well, the Stephen Linard coat began life as fashion. But it's not really worn as fashion, it's worn as costume. There's a sort of debate in Pet Shop Boys of costume versus fashion. I probably represent costume and Chris represents fashion. But it's a good tension. It's in expressing the differences between us that we create the image of Pet Shop Boys.

Chris: Also, I think it has to do with if there's anything exciting happening in fashion. Fashion, like music, goes in waves. Sometimes fashion's great, and sometimes it's not. When it's great, it's an inspiration, it's something to get excited about. But when you don't like the fashion, then I think that's when you decide to go outside it.

How involved were you in the sleeve designs to begin with?

Neil: Tom Watkins' Massive Management was the same company as XL Design, and we used to go in there, but they had the opinion that 'We're the designers, thank you.' That writing down the side of the first 'Opportunities' sleeve, that's very XL. We've never liked meaningless design. It's like we don't like pointless symbolism in videos.

Do you remember meeting Mark Farrow?

Neil: I remember going into the office and there was a cheeky Northerner there who made sarcky comments to us, and we made sarcky comments back. When he did the 'West End girls' remix cover, we thought it was a masterpiece; as soon as that happened, we loved Mark. And when he showed us the *Please* sleeve, we thought it was brilliant.

Chris: It looked a lot different from most record sleeves at the time. I liked all the white – plenty of space to sign your autograph.

Neil: If you compared it with the other records coming out then, at the beginning of 1986, it just looked like the future to me. There was always a desire to have iconic imagery of us. For people who really didn't want to be in the public eye, we were very strangely and strongly committed to having pictures of ourselves on just about every record that we brought out. I remember with the Chris 'Love comes quickly' sleeve thinking that we'd achieved exactly what we wanted to do – to be a visual trademark without giving anything away. I thought it was absolutely perfect, and if I look at it now I still think that. And then when we did 'Suburbia', I thought it was fantastic. It's the simplicity of it, and the beauty and strength of the picture. And with *Actually*, when Mark dropped the background out and put the white in and the words 'Pet Shop Boys, actually', it immediately looked like a classic album sleeve. And then we got more confident. By the following year, Eric had met Pierre LaRoche, famously Bowie's make-up artist for *Aladdin Sane*, on an advertising job, and we were very excited about the idea of working with him. Pierre told me to undo my top two shirt buttons. Eric would never have suggested that.

I remember you were thrilled by those photos.

Neil: I still am thrilled by them. I just liked the fact that I thought we looked gorgeous in them, and that we'd worked out how to look gorgeous. I always remember Morten Harket of A-ha saying he didn't think he was attractive but that he knew how to fake it. Actually, of course, he was a handsome guy, but I thought, 'Oh yeah, I know what you mean – we've learned that.' They're very imperial, those pictures: the make-up, the depth of the colours. They were a complete and utter change of aesthetic from what we'd been doing two years earlier.

And by then you'd started making your 'costume drama' videos. Were you just fed up with being the Pet Shop Boys in videos?

Neil: I think we must have been. And I think the epic-ness of the record of 'It's a sin' suggested it. Also, I'd had the idea for ages that I should be burnt at the stake, because I'd always loved that film about Joan of Arc. Derek Jarman thought it was impractical.

Chris: That's a shame, isn't it? So close. Maybe we can get that into the next tour.

Neil: I think I've moved on.

Chris: Oh. You've let go.

Neil: It's funny, all these things that come out of your childhood subconscious. I used to joke – although it was sort of serious – that when I was a boy I wanted to be the pope. It's no accident that in the *MCMLXXXIX* tour I'm dressed as the pope, in Wembley Arena.

With those videos, did you enjoy opening the dressing-up box?

Neil: I think it was part of the 'being in disguise made you feel confident'. And we felt it was going to have an entertainment value.

Chris: Also, it was the first time we'd worked with people from the theatre and we immediately liked the way they worked, and thought, and organized, and planned, and intellectualized about everything. That's something you don't really get in the music industry in the same way – intellectual referencing …

Neil: … thinking of the meaning of the song.

Chris: And we liked all the people doing wigs, costumes, make-up, all coming together to produce something. I think we both really got off on that.

Why did it always appeal to you to bring in people from outside pop music?

Neil: It seems to renew everything, that someone comes with a completely different take on what you're doing, and does something that you don't know how to do or have never thought of. And they're normally, on a personal level, interesting to meet. You feel your horizons are expanded, and that's always been quite important to us – not to be boxed in. And we take a lot of the influences of the songs from outside music, so to bring in people from outside music seems to me to be the equivalent of that. Also, there's always a Pet Shop Boys tradition of doing things the difficult way, which continues to exhaust me but just seems to be an instinct. And sometimes, by going through a difficult process, you end up somewhere where you didn't expect to be but you're glad you're there.

Chris: With lighting, say, rock music people don't start with what effect they want the lights to have; they start with the gear and what the gear can do. It's done completely the wrong way round. People in the theatre don't think that way – they start with what it is that you want to do and then you go on to how to achieve it. I just like experiencing how artists in different fields work. It's an amazing experience to be photographed by Robert Mapplethorpe, to have gone through that process with this amazing photographer and to have been the subject of it. How he moves you slowly … well, actually, almost mesmerizes you during the taking of the photograph. It was very, very calm and relaxed and effortless but you're almost hypnotized, and I think you can see that quality in a lot of his photographs. Also, there's an excitement you get from these things. Bruce Weber agreeing to do a video for you is really exciting, apart from anything else.

Your first two tours were maybe the most extreme expression of the Pet Shop Boys aesthetic, but they were also the most real because by necessity you both had to really do it – to actually act it out on stage.

Neil: It was a big challenge. But it was a fun challenge. I think we thought, as ever, our performance skills are so limited that we've got to throw everything at this. And I think a lot of it really worked. The second tour was the kind you can only do once. I remember once asking Paul McCartney whether he thought that *Sergeant Pepper* was a cul-de-sac and that you couldn't go any further, and that's why the *White Album* was just stripped-down songs. He didn't really answer, but I always thought it was a pretty good question. You could do any number of types of the *Performance* tour, visualizing the songs with costumes and dancers, but ultimately you'd be doing the same thing with different people. So the next statement we made was the *Somewhere* show at the Savoy, designed for the particular venue and highly conceptualized. Sam Taylor-Wood came up with a strong idea that gives the whole structure to the show. It's a brilliantly simple idea. I think one is always looking for a brilliantly simple idea. And you want to feel something special is going on. That is another basic Pet Shop Boys ethos – that you're seeing something that you're only going to get from Pet Shop Boys. Whether it succeeds or not, that is definitely one of our major ideals: that you get something you only get from us. And there are, ultimately, very few performers or artists in music that you get that from.

How have you learned to best collaborate?

Chris: I think you've got to let them get on with it, really.

Neil: Trusting them. If you work with a theatre director, say, let him or her get on with what they do, because you're not a theatre director. It's good to know when to stand back. Though they'll ask you whether you have ideas, and sometimes the talented amateur, as we can be in those things, can come up with something quite good. On the *Performance* tour we forced them to have the two kid dancers, Mark and Trevor, and no one in the entire production wanted them at first – the director didn't want them, the choreographer didn't want them.

Chris: But we did.

Neil: We did, and we were right. Because they lightened the whole thing – they brought a kind of street thing into this almost high-culture show. But the only time we made a mistake in trusting people was with *Closer to Heaven*, where we thought: we don't know anything about doing a musical so we should trust the Really Useful Group. And, actually, we should have stood up for our own aesthetic. We let their aesthetic take over in some ways. Specifically the posters and the graphic design. I can never quite believe we allowed that to happen.

Chris: Amazing that we did.

Neil: It really unbelievably bugs me when I think of the poster that Mark Farrow came up with, which was perfect. They were, 'Oh, it's too gay.' Anyhow …

When during your career did the weight of what you'd done visually before begin to feel like something you also had to escape?

Neil: I think quite early on. That's probably why we worked with Derek Jarman, because we felt we had to find a new way of walking down the street, Chris walking three paces behind me.

Chris: You can only take that so far. We'd reached a cul-de-sac. It was our *Sergeant Pepper*.

Do you easily agree with each other on visual things?

Neil: In terms of design, yes.

Chris: We do.

Neil: We and Mark don't. We gang up on Mark.

Chris: But generally we and Mark do have the same aesthetic.

Neil: But we always believe that each single from an album should be redesigned not to look like part of the album project – it should look like a new exciting thing, not some secondhand derived product. It should have new B-sides and new mixes and new pictures. That's not the designer way of looking at it. And the more singles you put out the harder it gets.

Is the visual side of being a pop group an opportunity and a joy, or does it feel like a chore?

Neil: It's an opportunity and a joy.

Chris: It can be quite stressful because sometimes you don't feel that there's going to be a solution and you know you've got to get there.

Neil: The *Introspective* sleeve seemed completely like that. It went on for ages.

Chris: It feels like a miracle when something comes along.

The single biggest change of aesthetic was when you moved into the Very *era.*

Neil: I think we were thinking, coming out of *Behaviour* and the greatest hits album, that we were going to reinvent Pet Shop Boys as a radical new thing. We were reacting against the time – grunge and Nirvana, and the visual dreariness of rave music. Rave music had become rigidly visualized by 1992 in a way that hasn't changed since – it's become very conservative in the way that the hippie thing became very conservative very quickly. We'd always talked about creating our own world and we thought, let's create the world.

Chris: Computer games had become really advanced.

Neil: We were aware that technology could enable you to become like digital cartoons, and we thought that was a great idea. Probably because we were getting older.

Was there also a sense that it didn't seem enough, at that point, just to stand there and be yourselves?

Neil: Yes, definitely.

Chris: Yeah.

Neil: Because by this point we'd been going for eight years or so, and the longer you go on, the more you've got to fight. And you've got to capture people's imaginations. But it took a lot of nerve to do it.

Chris: The thing that took the most nerve was doing *Top of the Pops* in those costumes. It was fine doing it in an unreal environment, but taking it into the real world – in the *Top of the Pops* studio dancing around an egg, or walking through Red Square dressed up in a blue or yellow jumpsuit, or doing a press conference wearing pointy hats, fielding serious questions dressed ridiculously – that's when it becomes odd.

Neil: There was a sense we were drawing attention to ourselves, and we were, but it was quite a good way of drawing attention to ourselves, and we really saw it through. And also we were prepared to see the humour in it.

Then, with Bilingual, *you went straight back to reality.*

Neil: It's a *Sergeant Pepper* thing.

Chris: The Pets had hit another cul-de-sac. Where now? Back to the crossroads.

Neil: No, you've taken that thing and you've done it and you've learned from it.

Chris: I think there's a dilemma between wanting to be you and wanting to be something else, and you're constantly jumping from one to the other. I know I am. I'm always bouncing between being me and not me. And a costume is one way of not being yourself. But then you think, no, I want to raise my ugly head again. But the funny thing is, the real me is also the mask me [laughs]. I'm still searching for the real me. I think I'll find him wearing a baseball cap and sunglasses, wherever 'he' is. What's that good Bowie lyric that I've based my life on? 'Don't believe in yourself.' That really is the philosophy of my life.

For the following album, Nightlife, *you flipped back towards disguise.*

Chris: Wigs.

Neil: We were thinking of rebranding the image of Pet Shop Boys. The really important thing for us about the actual look was the eyebrows and the mouth – we were thinking that if you had these big eyebrows and the almost rectangular mouth then three lines could be a symbol of the Pet Shop Boys, and we really liked that idea. I don't think we ever got that, in fact, but I guess we were looking to find a new visual trademark.

Chris: Do you know what? You don't really go on a journey – you just keep going round a roundabout and taking different exits, don't you?

Neil: That's quite good.

Chris: It's true, when you think about it.

With Release *you stopped working with Mark Farrow. I remember you both saying at the time that you wanted to change everything.*

Neil: Yes. I would regard a lot of the *Release* things as driven by Chris – I liked it, but I think of it as very driven by him. The *University* tour was totally his idea. We wanted to do something where everything was a bit *grittier*. It was an idea of not doing glamorous pop – instead of doing artificial, making it super-real. We'd worked with Mark Farrow on every sleeve since 'Love comes quickly', and it's possible to feel over the years that people you work with have sort of got bored with you. We stopped working with Eric Watson primarily because we felt he'd lost interest in us. With Mark, we felt that we knew in advance what we'd get.

Chris: Sometimes change is good just for the sake of change, isn't it? And what came out of it is that Mark Farrow came back and did some really good work.

Neil: I think having had a break from him was a good idea, because I think he and us felt re-energized about working together, and that has carried on.

When you see all this visual material gathered together, what do you think you've achieved with it?

Neil: Often you think with pop groups that as they go on they lose interest, and I don't think you have that feeling with Pet Shop Boys.

Chris: We didn't sort of give up halfway through. It would have been easy to give up.

Neil: You can see different phases – changing, changing back, doing things in a different way – and the various graphics give you a flavour of the time and a changing iconography of us, but there's been an aesthetic as well that's always there. A slightly bleak aesthetic. There is never design for the sake it. It's never flowery. There's also a separate marketing overview – all of these things are also marketing, and normally we're challenging the record-marketing conventions at the time. But you have to take it back to the fact that it's pop music, and all the time you're trying to keep people interested. That's what you're doing, really. And keeping yourself interested. And creating something at all times that you think is beautiful in some way or another. In the beginning we made a decision – and it was in our EMI contract – that we would have control over how everything worked; that obviously the songs mattered hugely, but that the way they were presented was going to matter hugely as well; and that we were never going to give up on that.

And why does that matter?

Neil: It gives you sort of an aura – that the music itself isn't just something that's been thrown off for contractual reasons. It's all very special. That has been the point of it all, from start to finish, and that is how we judge it as well – how special it seems. That Pet Shop Boys are a unique project, a unique duo in pop music, and that everything they do is special. I think that's what we've tried to do since day one.

Chris: We've managed to do something that has our imprint on it. That's just us, unique. That says as much about us as our music does.

From the beginning, you always talked about wanting to create your own Pet Shop Boys world. What did you think that world would be like?

Neil: I thought it was going to be a world where everything was really perfect and beautiful. It was going to be a beautiful representation of why everything was wrong. It's a way of not dealing with the reality of what we're part of – a way of hermetically sealing us from becoming tragically naff, and not shaming ourselves.

And are you still trying to create a world?

Neil: Yes.

Chris: [laughs] We've had no new ideas.

Neil: Once you've embarked on that, you're obviously always going to stay with it, because it's really, really important. To stop creating the world would be to start doing something utterly ordinary. It's a life less ordinary we're trying to create. When I was a kid, I made a pact with myself that I wasn't going to have a dull suburban life. That was really, really important to me. Well, I have avoided it, thus far.

Chris: I've always wanted a dull suburban life.

Neil: I knew you were going to say that.

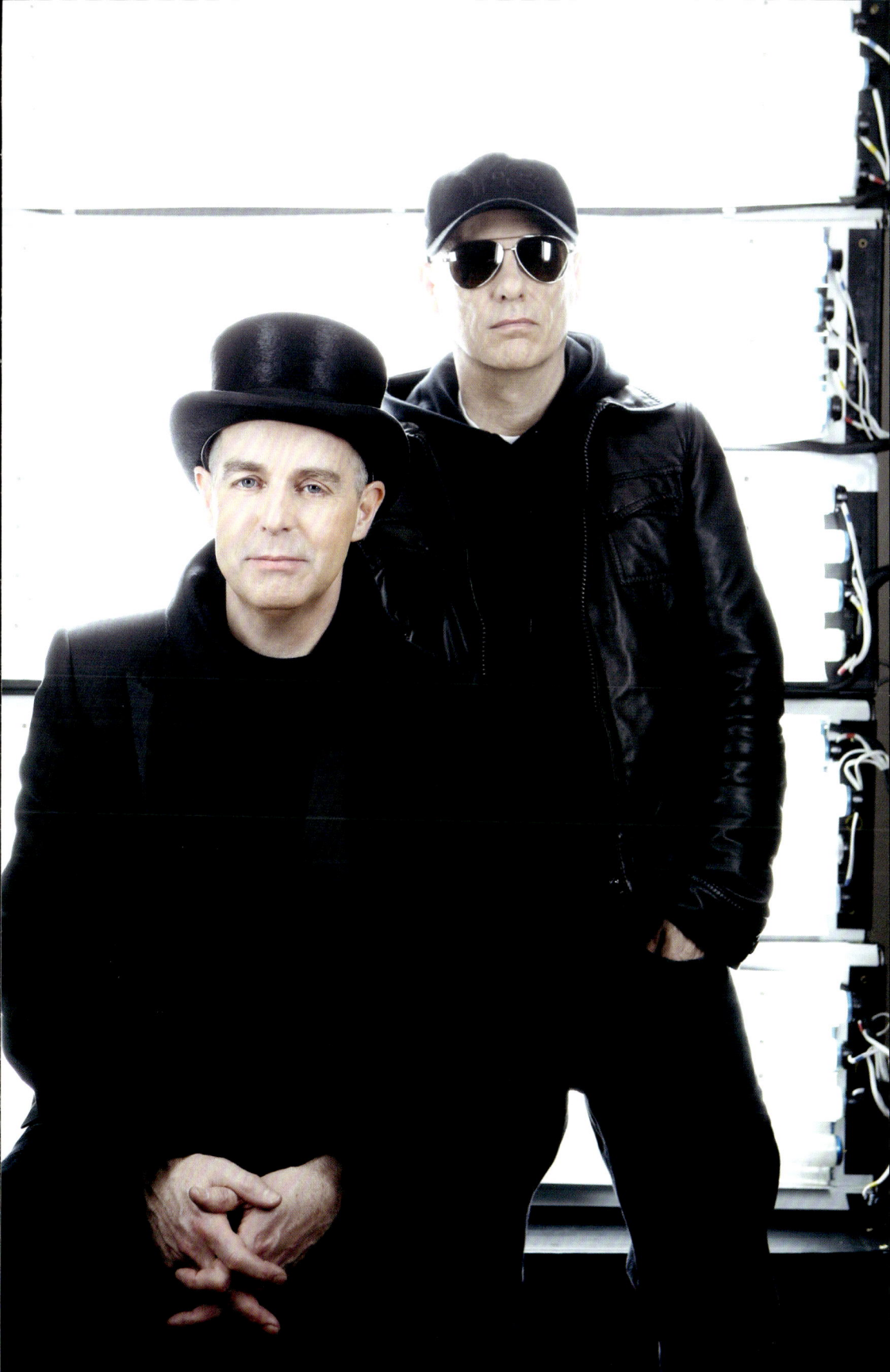

A further conversation
with Chris Heath, October 2024

So as we were saying …

Chris: Well, it's still true! I never wanted an extraordinary life.

Neil: Chris would be quite happy living with someone in suburbia.

Chris: When you said that, I just got a real pang. I'd like the suburban life. Quite a nice car. Sports car. Actually, my sister's got some friends who have got the life I want. They spend all day playing golf, going to watch Arsenal, going on holidays, tennis, socializing.

Neil: Drinking white wine.

Chris: A sip of white wine. They've a rather glamorous life. Is that too much to ask for?

Neil: [laughs] Apparently, yes.

And this has been a terrible second best that you've stumbled into?

Chris: Well, I think this has only happened because I wanted something different. Because that's what he's like, isn't he?

So, just to clarify: God punished you by giving you the Pet Shop Boys' career?

Chris: [laughs] It's been one long punishment! Why do you think I've looked so miserable the entire time? Did I show you the advert for someone to play me in a tribute band? [He finds the advert on his phone. It is for a replacement member for the band Pet Shop Boys, Actually. The advert reads 'We're on the lookout for our next Chris Lowe – could that be you?', then lists the three essential qualifications for the job: 'A love of PSB', 'Under 6ft 2in', and 'A miserable disposition'.]

Neil, would you like to offer a counterbalance?

Neil: Well, in the eighteen years since the previous conversation, I think we have carried on with expanding the world that we were talking about.

And you, unlike your partner in music, have been glad to be doing this?

Neil: Yes, absolutely. I think my partner in music has also been quite glad to, really. The problem with Chris is that he thinks he wants a normal life, but he's not a normal person.

Chris: [laughing] How dare you!

Neil: No, but that's the problem. He's actually not a normal person in any way, shape, or form. That's why the suburban life was doomed. He's a creative person who doesn't really follow a lot of the normal rules of behaviour or pursue the way of life that would have led to that. Remember, Chris left college with a lot of student debts – which were considerable; shockingly large! – and paid them off by becoming a pop star.

Chris: It's not cheap when you're doing architecture. It's not just pen and paper, like historians. We have costs.

Neil: I mean, it seemed inconceivable he would get a job as an architect, which could have led to the suburban bliss.

Chris: No, I don't think I'd have been very good at architecture.

Neil: Well, it's too much responsibility. Something you can't bear.

Chris: I know. You can't have someone like me in the office.

Neil: You can't even ask someone for a piece of bread in a restaurant!

Chris: [laughing] 'Neil, are you going to get some bread?'

Neil: I mean, that person can never be an architect.

Chris: Well, I just don't like making decisions.

Do you recognize Neil's description of you?

Chris: Yeah.

So maybe it's good this happened?

Chris: Looking back, it probably is.

Did you imagine in 2006 that we would be having this conversation again now?

Neil: If you'd suggested to me that we might be doing that, I'd have said I thought it was quite likely. I mean, let's face it, we're still alive.

Chris: Which is something. Which is a start.

I guess the broader question is: did you conceive – and I guess hope – when 'West End girls' came out, that you might be doing this, in this way, forty years later?

Neil: No. I mean, our answer to that question has always been – because people have asked that question in various ways – that we never really look ahead. We think about what we're doing at the moment, and maybe what the next thing is. And that's still completely true. We've got no ambitions for five years' time, for instance. So we just take care of the present, and maybe the next thing.

And do you reflect much on what you've achieved?

Neil: Not hugely. When it's relevant to something. When you're doing a back catalogue thing, you might look back at it. Or doing this book.

Chris: No, I'm often very aware that other people are far more familiar with what you've done than you are. I saw a Dave Hepworth clip where he had a copy of *Abbey Road* and he was with Paul McCartney. And McCartney had to look at the album to see what the track listing was. Dave Hepworth made the point that quite often the artist who's made a record isn't as familiar with, or as obsessive about, the product as the consumer is.

Neil: Because the artist moves on.

Chris: The artist moves on, but the listener probably listens to the record a lot more than the artist has done in the making of it. Anyway, I love the idea of Paul McCartney thinking 'What's on *Abbey Road* again?' That would be me.

What do you think you have achieved since Catalogue *came out?*

Neil: From 2006 to 2024 – that's like a whole other career really. Creatively, in a way, there's no change, but we've carried on expanding this world into new songs and shows. I mean, if we were being negative about our career, we probably felt, eighteen years ago, that from a commercial point of view we had been struggling a bit. In 2006, we first worked with Es Devlin on a live show – that was a turning point. In London, for instance, I think we played two nights at the Tower of London on that tour. And then not long afterwards we're starting to play arenas, and we also started headlining festivals regularly. And so we gradually developed the live shows – playing the Royal Opera House and doing these huge tours. That's probably the big change – that the business side of what we do shifted to the live thing. Also, I think over the years, the shows have improved.

Chris: And you've become a very good performer.

Neil: I've certainly been more of a performer than I was.

Chris: Yeah. I didn't see that coming!

Neil: See, I'm not even insulted by that. When I was at the youth theatre, they always used to tell you that you have to relax. We used to do relaxation exercises. Well, it took me years – decades – to relax on stage. And it's when you can relax and not feel self-conscious …

Chris: It's like when we saw Frank Sinatra performing at the Royal Albert Hall and it felt like you were in his living room.

Neil: Yes.

Chris: And actually you get to that point.

Neil: You can. In the right venue. It's by being relaxed, yeah.

How did that come?

Neil: Practice. Confidence.

Chris: A lot of therapy.

Neil: No, I've never had therapy. But you have to have a kind of mental picture of the stage with you on it – an idea of what it all looks like, and where you should be. But it's basically being relaxed.

Is there a particular moment that sticks in your mind when you realize something had changed and that you now had that?

Chris: Roskilde?

Neil: That was earlier than this, but, yes, that was a big moment. That was in 1997. We were headlining Roskilde on a Saturday night. It was an enormous audience. And there was me, Chris, Sylvia Mason-James, and Les Child dancing.

Chris: I don't remember us having much of a production, either.

Neil: We didn't. And we were in front of tens of thousands of people.

Chris: As far as the eye could see. And it was quite an empty big stage.

Neil: Yeah. And it was just you, the keyboard, and Sylvia. And Les did the occasional thing – 'zhushed' across the stage. We basically did the Savoy show with some more hits. And as we walked to the stage, Chris said, 'What are you going to do?', and I said, 'I don't know.' Then we went on stage and I ended up saying 'Roskilde!' in this sort of rock-starry voice. [They both laugh] You've just got to get on with it, really – run around the stage and deliver the songs. And it went down really well. I was quite surprised. God, talk about being thrown in the deep end.

Pop music shows have become much more elaborate, and even theatrical, over the years, haven't they?

Neil: Yes, that's something that's also developed enormously over the last eighteen years.

Is it at all a struggle to find ways of presenting yourself that still seem individual?

Neil: No. We still always work with a theatre designer. On the latest tour, it was with a new guy, Tom Scutt, because Es wasn't available. And you create memorable moments, with staging of masks and costumes. I think over time we've developed a reputation for it.

Chris: We did go against it once when we were being a rock band.

Neil: The *Release* tour.

Chris: But even then we had Ian MacNeil do it.

Neil: Yes, and it was pointed out at the time that this was as much a theatrical conceit as being theatrical, because it was as though we were playing a rock band. And it very much was like that, actually. I thought that was a very good point: that we were actually just pretending to be a rock band.

Chris: Yeah. [laughs] Has the whole thing been artifice?

Neil: The whole thing has been artifice, there's no question about that. I mean, we celebrate artifice.

Chris: We don't approve of authenticity.

Neil: We don't. Because we think it's only a style.

In our previous discussion, we talked about how you've tried to present yourselves as pretending in an honest way.

Neil: Well, that's called giving a performance.

And you're still doing that?

Neil: Yes. Chris doesn't pretend quite as much, I don't think.

Chris: Well, my role model, if I had one, has always been Nina Simone.

Can you maybe fill that out a tiny bit?

Chris: Well, as I've mentioned before now, the most memorable concert I ever went to was Nina Simone at the Barbican, where she was in a very bad mood. She wouldn't play any of her hits. Who does that remind you of? Who never wants to play any of their hits in the show? Me! She started to play 'Baltimore', slammed the piano lid down and went off stage. I don't think she came back. And the show ended with a slow handclap from the audience. What was left of the audience. Because people had been leaving during the show. And I just thought it was absolutely fantastic. I thought, 'Fair enough, she's in a bad mood. Why should she have to pretend?' That's my template.

Thank goodness you haven't acted on it too literally too often.

Neil: Well …

I said 'too often' …

Chris: No. Well, I'm obviously quite enjoying it.

You talked before about how Neil's evolved as a performer. How have you evolved?

Chris: I don't think I have. It's exactly the same. Actually, I think I might do slightly less than I did. Looking back at old *Top of the Pops* performances, I think I gave it a bit more then.

Neil: No, I think you went through a phase of giving less. Now I think you give more again. Because actually when you come on at the end of this current show and play 'West End girls', it's a pretty similar attitude to *Top of the Pops* forty years ago.

Chris: Oh, is it? Okay.

Neil: Because you kind of really bang the notes down.

Chris: Yeah.

Neil: And also it's so loud, the bass.

Chris: It is loud, isn't it? When I hit that low E, the whole place rattles. I'm always taken aback by how loud that bass is.

Neil: We've got the film of us back then behind us, and you don't look really that much different.

Chris: Well, I don't think fundamentally my performances have changed that much, really. Whereas yours are noticeably different.

Neil: Yeah, I guess some people might think it's changed too much and it's more appropriate to be self-conscious.

Chris: You're giving too much?

Neil: It's taken me decades to do this [he waves an upraised arm from side to side].

Chris: It works, though, doesn't it?

Neil: It works. Though my arm hurts.

Is it a pressure or exciting to have to keep coming up with different ways to present yourself?

Chris: Well, I always think: how many more times can we visualize 'It's a sin'?

Neil: An infinite number of times, to be honest.

Chris: Actually it's normally so far back towards the end of the show, we just rely on lights now, don't we?

Neil: We do, yeah. I don't come on dressed as the pope any more. No, it's fun putting a show together. Also, the less physical it is, the better it is, I think. I don't believe you need that many props and stuff. For this current *Dreamworld* show, the designer Tom Scutt originally had twenty-four lamp posts on the stage and we said, 'Can't you just make it look like that rather than actually have it?' And in the end we just had two, which is perfect, because the two represent us as well. But I like doing a new show. It's always a bit nerve-racking at the start, mainly because of the expense, but we have a phenomenal team of people.

Do you think the early Eighties version of you would be astonished that at the centre of what you do now is live performance?

Neil: Yes.

Chris: [nods] Mmmm.

Neil: Definitely. But the mid-Eighties person would be pleased that we actually set out to do theatre and we've achieved it. I watched some of our recent BBC Radio 2 show in Preston on the television, and even I thought, 'Wow, we've become this big thing.' All these people watching. I was sort of amazed, really, looking at it, thinking, 'Did we actually set out to do that?' I suppose we did.

More broadly, what do you think has changed in your approach over the years and what hasn't?

Neil: The basic approach has never changed. In that we want what we want, and we don't really want what anyone else wants. We still have similar taste, in design and in music. We're still seeking euphoria, but also a new way of saying things. As a lyricist, I'm still seeking to sort of develop that voice, as it were. So I guess we've developed. We've grown from the talents that we have had since the beginning. I think it's possible with music actually to get better as you get older. If you were a classical composer, people would probably assume that. In pop music, it's difficult because it's about youth or something. And also energy. Maybe you have more energy when you're younger. But I still think we've kept it sounding fresh.

Chris: I think with pop music, there's always the sound of pop at any particular moment. Whereas we are very much ourselves. So there's a conformity, in a way, to what we do, because we're not just working with a team of songwriters and producers of the moment who've got the latest sound.

Neil: Although we do use ... you know, we worked with Xenomania. With James Ford.

Chris: We do. But I think that our musical personality is so strong.

Neil: Yes, when we make a Xenomania record, Xenomania end up making a Pet Shop Boys record.

Chris: That's what I mean. Also we have a certain melodic sensibility that is constant. I think there's a constancy to our stuff.

Neil: There is, yeah.

Chris: Which, if you like it, is great.

Neil: Also, something that's happened in

the course of these eighteen years, in the latter years, is that it's possible to have lost interest in a lot of contemporary pop music. To have stopped finding the pleasure and consolation in it that one would have found even ten years ago.

Chris: I know – that's a real shame, isn't it?

Neil: It is a real shame.

Chris: I would love to love pop music at the moment. Actually, the trouble is I'm not in the car enough to listen to the radio, and I don't go out to clubs. So I have a disconnection now.

Do you think the real disconnect is in your lives, or in what pop music is like, or both?

Neil: Well, I think at the age of seventy to like the music that a fourteen-year-old likes is … I mean, I think it's possible, to be honest, but it's sort of unlikely. Because they're hearing something for the first time and you come with the weight of history behind you. And so it's difficult to come to it fresh. So you tend to look at things as a sort of – I do anyway – as a sort of phenomenon.

It seems to me that in long continuous careers, no matter what someone does creatively, there's this sort of inevitable arc, where for quite a lot of years in the middle, everything can seem uphill. And then, eventually, the gradient changes.

Neil: It does. Then everyone always liked you.

It goes from, 'Are you still doing that …?'

Chris: Or 'Why are you still doing that?' That's the main question. 'Why are you still doing that? You must have made enough money to retire now.'

Neil: That's the assumption!

Chris: That you only did it for the money.

Neil: And that's never been a primary motive. But there is a sort of a trajectory. I think two things happen. One is that you start to acquire different young generations of listener who maybe know you because of their parents or something like that. Or maybe just find out about you somehow. And then there's the strange phenomenon that ABBA is the best example of, I think, where suddenly everyone always liked you. If you went back to the late Seventies, a lot of people positively despised ABBA. I think people can now admit that we have contributed, and have made quite a lot of good records over the years. And when released from our specific time period, we can still sound fresh today. 'West End girls' is still an unusual-sounding record that people like to hear on the radio around the world.

Chris: Yeah.

Neil: And another reason to keep going is to comment on what's happening at the time, if only obliquely. There is a way of looking at the Pet Shop Boys catalogue as a social history of the times, from 1984 to now. 'The forgotten child' – and the whole *Agenda* EP actually – is a good example of that. That was partly inspired by the awful instance where that migrant child was found dead on the seashore. I don't know that anyone else is really doing that, and all the way through we've done this – this commentary on the world around us going on.

Do you feel like that gets noticed, or missed?

Neil: I think some people notice. I think it might get noticed more than it used to. I think if you were someone else, if you were a more 'important' artist, you'd never hear the end of it. But because it's us, and it's also got a sense of humour, which unnerves people a bit, it just gets slightly overlooked, I think.

Throughout this whole era, it seems like you've gone back and forth with your interest, or comfort, or whatever it is, in having your own photos on the records.

Neil: Sometimes you don't feel that you have a statement about the way you look that you want to make. And also, of course, something else we're dealing with – as you always are, I suppose – is the ageing process. So you go through a phase of not wanting to be photographed. But then I always think in life, particularly if you're a public figure of any kind, you have the various eras of what you look like and people get used to you. So they might say, 'Oh God, he's got no hair', but then they're used to it – that's the you that they're now used to. They expect you to look like that, so therefore you sort of feel more comfortable about it.

Chris: If someone said to me now 'You've got to do a photo session for a new album sleeve', my heart would sink at the very thought of it. But on the last album, Nonetheless, when we worked with Tim Walker, as soon as he took that first shot I thought it was great. It was such a strong idea. But great strong ideas like that don't always come along. It's good if you get a good image, but there's nothing worse than a not very good image of you on an album – I'd rather it was totally graphic in that case. As for the age thing, I like us to be timeless. So being presented as just two old blokes, I've never liked that. But I do think you can also look good old as well. You can look iconic. Which I think we do on the sleeve for the new album. I think that's a really good, strong old look.

Neil: It's not trying to look young.

Chris: It's not. It's embracing age in a good way. You can look old and cool.

Neil: You can, yes. You also always want a visual that's going to go with the music. I mean, Yes is one of my favourite album covers by us. We went into Farrow with a postcard from the Gerhard Richter show at the Serpentine Gallery, all these works based on squares of colour, and they had the brilliant idea of the tick.

Chris: Actually, it was a stroke of genius.

Neil: A stroke of genius. Possibly our best album cover, or certainly our best abstract one. I'd say our best album covers are Yes and Actually – Actually, you can't sort of deny that.

And why does Yes *work?*

Neil: Well, apart from the fact that it says the title graphically, and the number of squares are the number of tracks on the album, it's a pop album and the sleeve is super pop. Colours, squares – I think it's a genuine piece of pop art. It's cheerful, it's elegant, it's fun even. And it's got a classic Pet Shop Boys white background. It's actually perfect. It's a perfect album cover for us. And it's also memorable.

Chris: Yeah, I can remember that one without even having to look it up on Spotify. Which means it's worked.

In this later period, on pretty much every physical object, you've worked with Farrow throughout.

Neil: We have, yes.

How has that relationship evolved, and how does it work?

Neil: It's difficult to say that it's evolved because it's never really changed. It's the same now as it was right at the beginning. Sometimes it's more them than us. Sometimes it's more us than them. But between us, we normally manage to come up with an idea. I mean, if you look at this book, there's a lot of ideas in it. And it's good that between us, we can come up with them. Also, to have been creating a graphic identity for the same musical brand for such a long time, doing something that changes but is still recognizably them, I think part of the 'recognizably them' is actually recognizably Farrow.

Chris: Generally, we have a shared liking of minimalism. And a passion for Helvetica.

Neil: Do we? I'm always trying to get a different typeface.

It feels like you've got an interesting relationship where you've always disagreed about loads of things, but fundamentally, for the most part, completely agree on where you get to.

Neil: Well, you know when it's right. But when we don't know what we're doing, it goes on for ever and it's extremely frustrating. I remember *Super* seemed to go on for ever. To get something really extremely simple! But to get simple often is a long process. But we don't give up. And it's great when you go in and they've just got it, like *Electric*. All laid out and everything. 'Great!'

So, looking back at all that's covered in this book, in summary …

Neil: Very good fun. Mostly.

Chris: I guess it ends with the pictures of us as youngsters. It's gone full circle, hasn't it? We've ended where we began.

Neil: Yes.

Chris: We've regressed. We'll end up as babies.

Neil: That's a good idea.

Chris: Actually, it's what happens in life as well, isn't it?

Neil: Well, it's the seven ages of man. Shakespeare.

Chris: You start off helpless, dependent on other people, and ultimately, that's how you end up. I've already planned where I want to go: that care home for actors. Is it in north London somewhere? I'm hoping that, having acted in *It couldn't happen here*, I can get in there somehow.

I like the idea of being in a care home with a load of actors telling their stories of making films. Ian McKellen holding court in the lounge! I think that would be quite good fun, actually.

One of the most unusual things Pet Shop Boys have done in their career is just carry on. Are you aware of how unusual that is?

Neil: Well, we carry on because we have the energy and the will and the desire to do it.

Chris: What's the alternative? I mean, that's really the question. What's the alternative? Sitting on one's laurels?

Neil: Right at the beginning of our career, I think you always wondered how long you could do this for. Tom Watkins famously always used to say 'You're going to last three years', which actually was a fair enough point because he was sort of right about most people.

Do you remember what you thought when he said that?

Chris: I probably wouldn't have thought too much of it. I wouldn't have thought that there was an alternative path other than doing what we were doing.

Neil: I thought, 'Well, we'll see about that.'

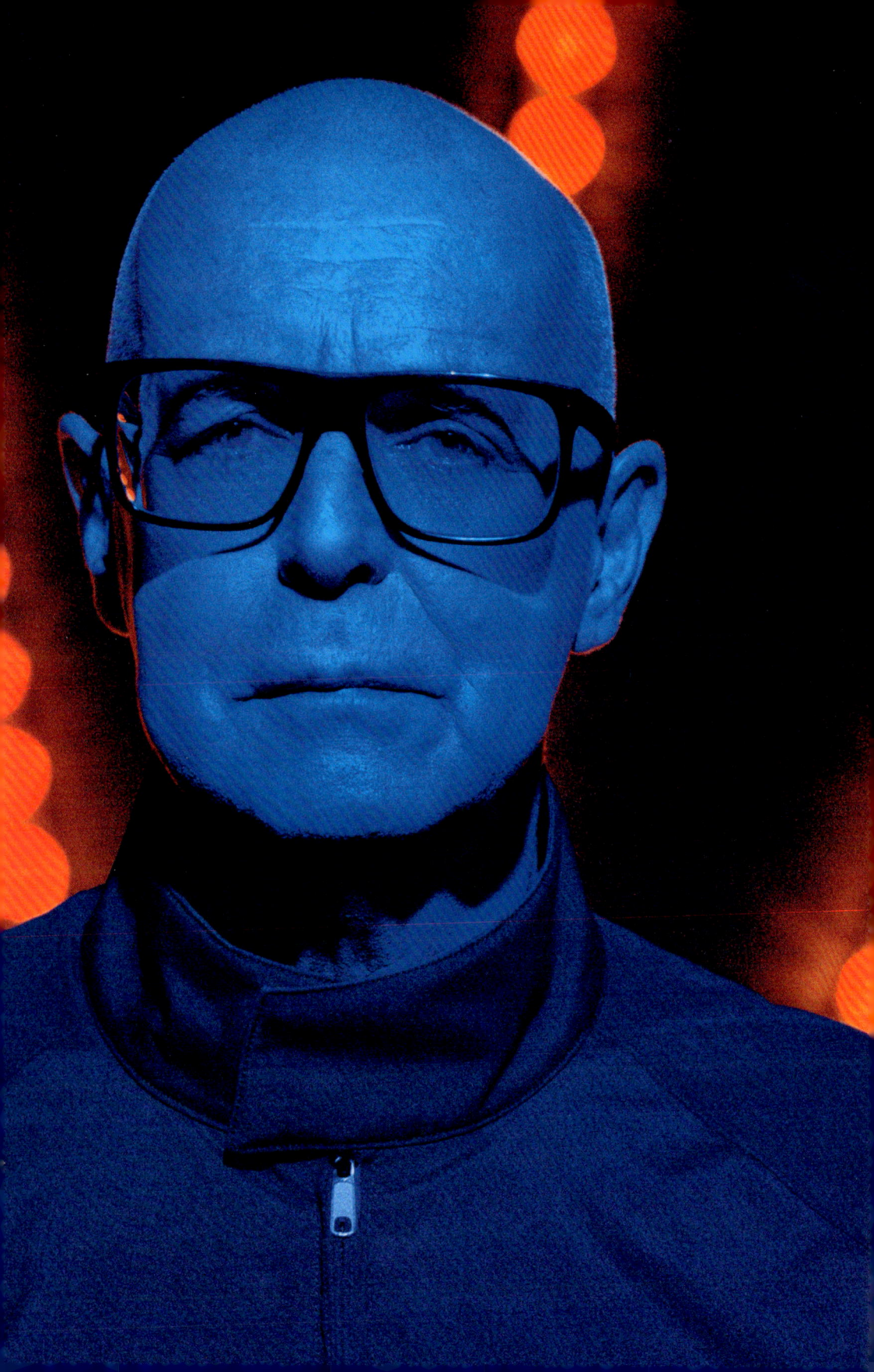

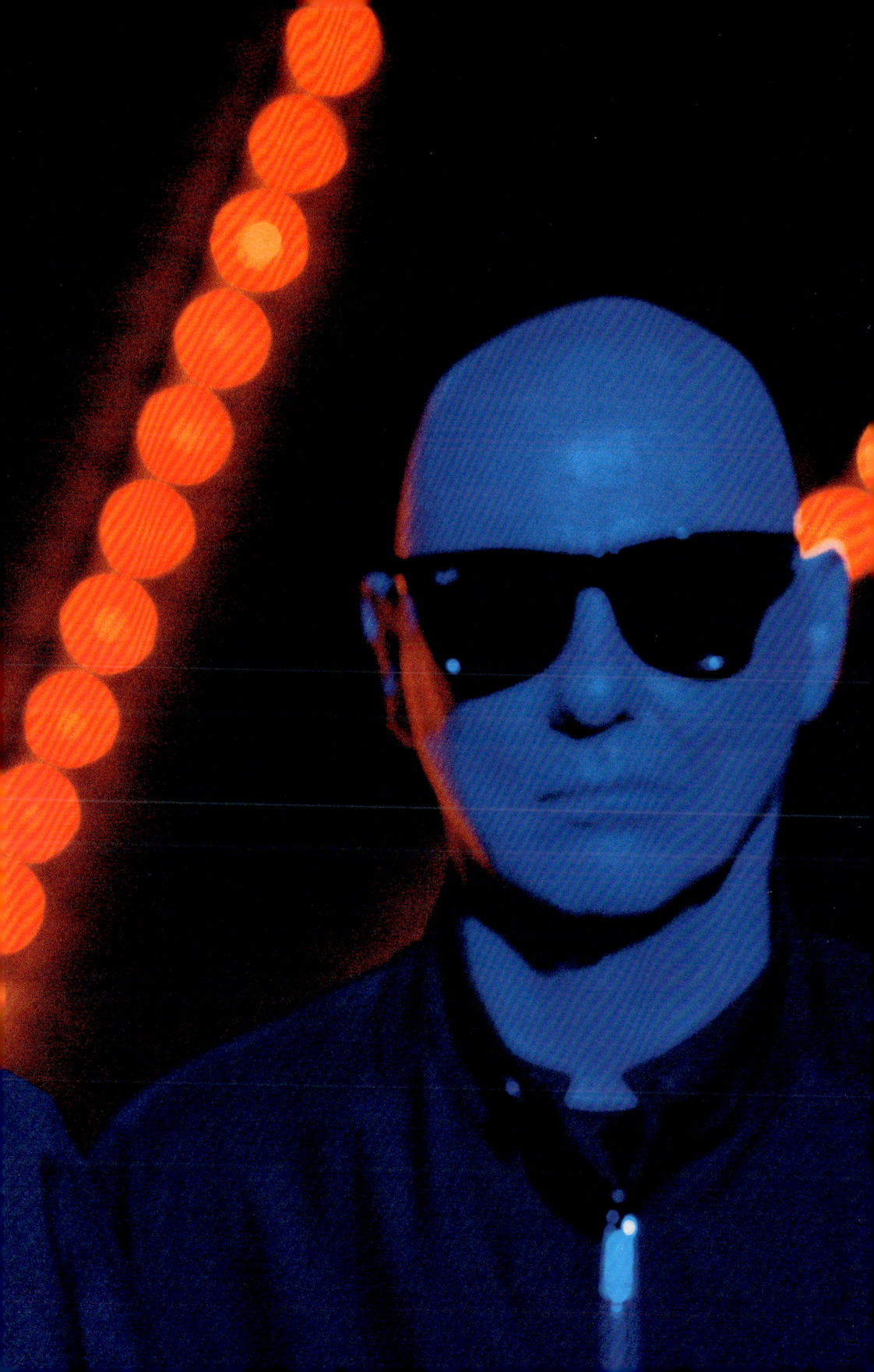

Discography

ALBUMS

Please 24/03/1986
Two divided by zero
West End girls
Opportunities (let's
 make lots of money)
Love comes quickly
Suburbia
Opportunities (Reprise)
Tonight is forever
Violence
I want a lover
Later tonight
Why don't we live together?

Disco 17/11/1986
In the night
Suburbia (the full horror)
Opportunities
Paninaro
Love comes quickly
West End girls

Actually 07/09/1987
One more chance
What have I done to
 deserve this?
Shopping
Rent
Hit music
It couldn't happen here
It's a sin
I want to wake up
Heart
King's Cross

Introspective 10/10/1988
Left to my own devices
I want a dog
Domino dancing
I'm not scared
Always on my mind /
 In my house
It's alright

In Depth (Japan) 01/06/1989
It's alright
One of the crowd
Your funny uncle
Always on my mind
Domino dancing
Left to my own devices

Behaviour 22/10/1990
Being boring
This must be the place
I waited years to leave
To face the truth
How can you expect to
 be taken seriously?
Only the wind
My October symphony
So hard
Nervously
The end of the world
Jealousy

Discography 04/11/1991
West End girls
Love comes quickly
Opportunities (let's
 make lots of money)
Suburbia
It's a sin
What have I done to
 deserve this?
Rent
Always on my mind
Heart
Domino dancing
Left to my own devices
It's alright
So hard
Being boring
Where the streets have
 no name (I can't take
 my eyes off you)
Jealousy
DJ culture
Was it worth it?

Very 27/09/1993
Can you forgive her?
I wouldn't normally do
 this kind of thing
Liberation
A different point of view
Dreaming of the queen
Yesterday, when I was
 mad
The theatre
One and one make five
To speak is a sin
Young offender
One in a million
Go west

Very Relentless
 27/09/1993

Disc 1
Can you forgive her?
I wouldn't normally do
 this kind of thing
Liberation
A different point of view
Dreaming of the queen
Yesterday, when I was
 mad
The theatre
One and one make five
To speak is a sin
Young offender
One in a million
Go west

Disc 2
My head is spinning
Forever in love
KDX 125
We came from outer space
The man who has
 everything
One thing leads to another

Disco 2 12/09/1994
Absolutely fabulous (Rollo our
 tribe tongue-in-cheek mix)
I wouldn't normally do this
 kind of thing (Beatmasters
 extended nude mix)
I wouldn't normally do this
 kind of thing (DJ Pierre
 wild pitch mix)
Go west (Farley & Heller mix)
Liberation (E Smoove 12" mix)
So hard (David Morales
 red zone mix)
Can you forgive her?
 (Rollo dub)
Yesterday, when I was mad
 (Junior Vasquez fabulous
 dub)
Absolutely fabulous (Rollo our
 tribe tongue-in-cheek mix)
Yesterday, when I was mad
 (Coconut 7" mix)
Yesterday, when I was mad
 (Jam & Spoon mix)
We all feel better in the dark
 (Brothers in Rhythm
 after hours climax mix)

Alternative 07/08/1995

Disc 1
In the night
A man could get arrested
That's my impression
Was that what it was?
Paninaro
Jack the lad
You know where you
 went wrong
A new life
I want a dog
Do I have to?
I get excited (you get
 excited too)
Don Juan
The sound of the atom
 splitting
One of the crowd
Your funny uncle

Disc 2
It must be obvious
We all feel better in the dark
Bet she's not your girlfriend
Losing my mind
Music for boys
Miserablism
Hey, headmaster
What keeps mankind alive?
Shameless
Too many people
Violence (Haçienda version)
Decadence
If love were all
Euroboy
Some speculation

Bilingual 02/09/1996
Discoteca
Single
Metamorphosis
Electricity
Se a vida é (that's the
 way life is)
It always comes as a
 surprise
A red letter day
Up against it
The survivors
Before
To step aside
Saturday night forever

Bilingual Special Edition
 07/07/1997

Disc 1
Discoteca
Single
Metamorphosis
Electricity
Se a vida é (that's the
 way life is)
It always comes as a
 surprise
A red letter day
Up against it
The survivors
Before
To step aside
Saturday night forever

Disc 2
Somewhere (extended mix)
A red letter day (Trouser
 Enthusiasts autoerotic
 decapitation mix)
To step aside (Brutal Bill mix)
Before (classic paradise mix)
The boy who couldn't
 keep his clothes on
 (international club mix)
Se a vida é (pink noise mix)
Discoteca (Trouser
 Enthusiasts adventure
 beyond the stellar
 empire mix)

Essential (US, Japan)
 31/03/1998
Domino dancing
 (alternative version)
West End girls (dance mix)
Opportunities (let's make
 lots of money) (original
 7" version)
Paninaro (7" version)
That's my impression
 (7" version)
We all feel better in the dark
 (extended mix)
It couldn't happen here
 (LP version)

It's alright (7" version)
Left to my own devices
    (7" version)
In the night (remix)
Two divided by zero
    (LP version)
Love comes quickly
    (dance mix)
Being boring (extended
    version)

Nightlife 11/10/1999
For your own good
Closer to Heaven
I don't know what you
    want but I can't give
    it any more
Happiness is an option
You only tell me you love
    me when you're drunk
Vampires
Radiophonic
The only one
Boy strange
In denial
New York City boy
Footsteps

Mini (Japan) 23/02/2000
Closer to Heaven
Screaming
Lies
Sail away
You only tell me you love me
    when you're drunk (live)
Always on my mind (live)
Being boring (live)
New York City boy (the
    Morales club mix)

Please / Further listening 1984–1986 04/06/2001

Please
Two divided by zero
West End girls
Opportunities (let's
    make lots of money)
Love comes quickly
Suburbia
Opportunities (reprise)
Tonight is forever
Violence
I want a lover
Later tonight
Why don't we live together?

Further listening 1984–1986
A man could get arrested
    (12" B-side)
Opportunities (let's
    make lots of money)
    (full length original 7")
In the night
Opportunities (let's make
    lots of money) (original
    12" mix)
Why don't we live together?
    (original New York mix)
West End girls (dance mix)
A man could get arrested
    (7" B-side)

Love comes quickly
    (dance mix)
That's my impression
    (disco mix)
Was that what it was?
Suburbia (the full horror)
Jack the lad
Paninaro (Italian mix)

Actually / Further listening 1987–1988 04/06/2001

Actually
One more chance
What have I done to
    deserve this?
Shopping
Rent
Hit music
It couldn't happen here
It's a sin
I want to wake up
Heart
King's Cross

Further listening 1987–1988
I want to wake up
    (breakdown mix)
Heart (Shep Pettibone version)
You know where you went
    wrong
One more chance (7" mix)
It's a sin (disco mix)
What have I done to deserve
    this? (extended mix)
Heart (disco mix)
A new life
Always on my mind
    (demo version)
Rent (7" mix)
I want a dog
Always on my mind
    (extended dance mix)
Do I have to?
Always on my mind (dub mix)

Introspective / Further listening 1988–1989 04/06/2001

Introspective
Left to my own devices
I want a dog
Domino dancing
I'm not scared
Always on my mind /
    In my house
It's alright

Further listening 1988–1989
I get excited (you get
    excited too)
Don Juan (demo version)
Domino dancing
    (demo version)
Domino dancing
    (alternative version)
The sound of the atom splitting
What keeps mankind alive?
Don Juan (disco mix)
Losing my mind (disco mix)
Nothing has been proved
    (demo for Dusty)

So sorry, I said
    (demo for Liza)
Left to my own devices
    (7" mix)
It's alright (10" version)
One of the crowd
It's alright (7" version)
Your funny uncle

Behaviour / Further listening 1990–1991 04/06/2001

Behaviour
Being boring
This must be the place
    I waited years to leave
To face the truth
How can you expect to be
    taken seriously?
Only the wind
My October symphony
So hard
Nervously
The end of the world
Jealousy

Further listening 1990–1991
It must be obvious
So hard (extended dance mix)
Miserablism
Being boring (extended mix)
Bet she's not your girlfriend
We all feel better in the dark
    (extended mix)
Where the streets have no
    name (I can't take my eyes
    off you) (extended mix)
Jealousy (extended mix)
Generic jingle
DJ culture (extended mix)
Was it worth it? (12" mix)
Music for boys (ambient mix)
DJ culture (7" mix)

Very / Further listening 1992–1994 04/06/2001

Very
Can you forgive her?
I wouldn't normally do this
    kind of thing
Liberation
A different point of view
Dreaming of the queen
Yesterday, when I was mad
The theatre
One and one make five
To speak is a sin
Young offender
One in a million
Go west

Further listening 1992–1994
Go west (1992 12" mix)
Forever in love
Confidential (demo for Tina)
Hey, headmaster
Shameless
Too many people
I wouldn't normally do this
    kind of thing (7" version)
Violence (Haçienda version)
Falling (demo for Kylie)
Decadence

If love were all
Absolutely fabulous
    (single version)
Euroboy
Some speculation
Yesterday, when I was mad
    (single version)
Girls and boys (live in Rio)

Bilingual / Further listening 1995–1997 4/06/2001

Bilingual
Discoteca
Single
Metamorphosis
Electricity
Se a vida é (that's the
    way life is)
It always comes as a surprise
A red letter day
Up against it
The survivors
Before
To step aside
Saturday night forever

Further listening 1995–1997
Paninaro '95
In the night (1995)
The truck-driver and his mate
Hit and miss
How I learned to hate
    rock 'n' roll
Betrayed
Delusions of grandeur
Discoteca (single version)
The calm before the storm
Discoteca (new version)
The boy who couldn't keep
    his clothes on
A red letter day (expanded
    single version)
The view from your balcony
Disco potential
Somewhere (extended mix)

Release 01/04/2002
Home and dry
I get along
Birthday boy
London
E-mail
The samurai in autumn
Love is a catastrophe
Here
The night I fell in love
You choose

Disco 3 03/02/2003
Time on my hands
Positive role model
Try it (I'm in love with
    a married man)
London (thee radikal
    blaklite edit)
Somebody else's business
Here (PSB new extended mix)
If looks could kill
Sexy northerner
    (Superchumbo mix)
Home and dry
    (Blank & Jones remix)
London (genuine piano mix)

PopArt 24/11/2003

Pop (CD 1)
Go west
Suburbia (video edit)
Se a vida é
What have I done to deserve this?
Always on my mind
I wouldn't normally do this kind of thing
Home and dry
Heart
Miracles
Love comes quickly
It's a sin
Domino dancing
Before
New York City boy (US radio edit)
It's alright
Where the streets have no name (I can't take my eyes off you)
A red letter day

Art (CD 2)
Left to my own devices
I don't know what you want but I can't give it any more
Flamboyant
Being boring
Can you forgive her?
West End girls
I get along (radio edit)
So hard
Rent
Jealousy
DJ culture
You only tell me you love me when you're drunk
Liberation
Paninaro '95
Opportunities (let's make lots of money)
Yesterday, when I was mad
Single-Bilingual
Somewhere

Mix (bonus CD with limited edition)
Can you forgive her? (Rollo mix)
So hard (David Morales red zone mix)
What have I done to deserve this? (Shep Pettibone mix)
West End girls (Sasha mix)
Miserablism (Moby electro mix)
Before (Love to infinity classic paradise mix)
I don't know what you want but I can't give it any more (Peter Rauhofer New York mix)
New York City boy (the Lange mix)
Young offender (Jam & Spoon trip-o-matic fairy tale mix)
Love comes quickly (Blank & Jones mix)

Fundamental 22/05/2006
Psychological
The Sodom and Gomorrah show
I made my excuses and left
Minimal
Numb
God willing
Luna Park
I'm with stupid
Casanova in Hell
Twentieth century
Indefinite leave to remain
Integral

Fundamentalism 22/05/2006
Fugitive (Richard X extended mix)
Sodom (Trentemøller mix)
Psychological (Alter Ego remix)
Flamboyant (Michael Mayer kompakt mix)
I'm with stupid (Melnyk heavy petting mix)
In private (Stuart Crichton club mix)
Minimal (Lobe remix)
Gomorrah (Dettinger remix)

Concrete 23/10/2006
Left to my own devices
Rent
You only tell me you love me when you're drunk
The Sodom and Gomorrah show
Casanova in Hell (sung by Rufus Wainwright)
After all
Friendly fire (sung by Frances Barber)
Integral
Numb
It's alright
Luna Park
Nothing has been proved
Jealousy (sung by Robbie Williams)
Dreaming of the queen
It's a sin
Indefinite leave to remain
West End girls

Disco Four 08/10/2007
The Killers: Read my mind (PSB stars are blazing mix)
David Bowie with Pet Shop Boys: Hallo Spaceboy (PSB extended mix)
Pet Shop Boys: Integral (PSB perfect immaculate mix)
Yoko Ono: Walking on thin ice (PSB electro mix)
Madonna: Sorry (PSB maxi-mix)
Atomizer: Hooked on radiation (PSB orange alert mix)
Rammstein: Mein teil (PSB there are no guitars on this mix)
Pet Shop Boys: I'm with stupid (PSB maxi-mix)

Pet Shop Boys Story 08/03/2009
West End girls (10" mix)
Paninaro (7" mix)
It's a sin (disco mix)
What have I done to deserve this? (7" mix)
Jealousy (7" mix)
Being boring (7" mix)
Go west (7" mix)
Before (7" mix)
Home and dry (7" mix)
Flamboyant (7" mix)
Did you see me coming?

Yes 23/03/2009
Love etc.
All over the world
Beautiful people
Did you see me coming?
Vulnerable
More than a dream
Building a wall
King of Rome
Pandemonium
The way it used to be
Legacy

Yes etc. 23/03/2009

Yes
Love etc.
All over the world
Beautiful people
Did you see me coming?
Vulnerable
More than a dream
Building a wall
King of rome
Pandemonium
The way it used to be
Legacy

Etc.
This used to be the future
More than a dream (Magical dub)
Pandemonium (The stars and the sun dub)
The way it used to be (Left at love dub)
All over the world (This is a dub)
Vulnerable (Public eye dub)
Love etc. (Beautiful dub)

Yes limited-edition LP 21/05/2009
Love etc.
Love etc. (instrumental)
All over the world
All over the world (instrumental)
Beautiful people
Beautiful people (instrumental)
Did you see me coming?
Did you see me coming? (instrumental)
Vulnerable
Vulnerable (instrumental)
More than a dream
More than a dream (instrumental)
Building a wall
Building a wall (instrumental)
King of Rome
King of Rome (instrumental)
Pandemonium
Pandemonium (instrumental)
The way it used to be
The way it used to be (instrumental)
Legacy
Legacy (instrumental)

Pet Shop Boys Party 13/11/2009
West End girls (10" mix)
Love comes quickly
Paninaro (7" mix)
It's a sin (disco mix)
What have I done to deserve this?
Always on my mind (extended dance version)
Domino dancing
It's alright (7" version)
Being boring
Go west
Before (single edit)
New York City boy (album version)
Home and dry (radio edit)
Minimal (radio edit)
Love etc.
King of Rome

Ultimate 01/11/2010
West end girls
Suburbia
It's a sin
What have I done to deserve this?
Always on my mind
Heart
Domino dancing
Left to my own devices
Being boring
Where the streets have no name (I can't take my eyes off you)
Go west
Before
Se a vida é (that's the way life is)
New York City boy
Home and dry
Miracles
I'm with stupid
Love etc.
Together (Ultimate mix)

DVD (BBC TV performances)
West End girls (Top of the Pops 15/12/85)
Love comes quickly (Top of the Pops 20/03/86)
Opportunities (let's make lots of money) (Whistle Test 29/04/86)
Suburbia (Top of the Pops 02/10/86)

It's a sin (Top of the Pops 25/06/87)
Rent (Top of the Pops 22/10/87)
Always on my mind (Top of the Pops 10/12/87)
What have I done to deserve this? (Brit Awards 08/02/88)
Heart (Wogan 30/03/88)
Domino dancing (Top of the Pops 22/09/88)
Left to my own devices (Top of the Pops 01/12/88)
So hard (Wogan 28/09/90)
Being boring (Top of the Pops 29/11/90)
Can you forgive her? (Top of the Pops 10/06/93)
Liberation (Top of the Pops 07/04/94)
Paninaro '95 (Top of the Pops 03/08/95)
Se a vida é (Top of the Pops 2 02/12/03)
A red letter day (Top of the Pops 28/03/97)
Somewhere (Top of the Pops 04/07/97)
I don't know what you want but I can't give it any more (Top of the Pops 30/07/99)
New York City boy (Top of the Pops 08/10/99)
You only tell me you love me when you're drunk (Top of the Pops 14/01/00)
Home and dry (Top of the Pops 29/03/02)
I get along (Top of the Pops 2 17/04/02)
Miracles (Top of the Pops 14/11/03)
Flamboyant (Top of the Pops 19/03/04)
I'm with stupid (Top of the Pops 23/04/06)
Live at Glastonbury 2010:
  More than a dream / Heart
  Did you see me coming?
  Love etc.
  Building a wall
  Go west
  Two divided by zero
  Why don't we live together?
  New York City boy
  Always on my mind
  Closer to Heaven / Left to my own devices
  Do I have to?
  King's Cross
  Jealousy
  Suburbia
  What have I done to deserve this?
  All over the world
  Se a vida é / Discoteca
  Domino dancing / Viva la vida
  It's a sin
  Being boring

The Most Incredible Thing 14/03/2011

Acts 1 and 2
Prologue
The grind
The challenge
Help me
Risk
Physical jerks
The competition
The meeting
The clock 1/2/3
The clock 4/5/6
The clock 7/8/9
The clock 10/11/12
The winner
Destruction

Act 3
Back to the grind
The miracle – ceremony
The miracle – revolution
The miracle – resurrection
The miracle – colour and light
The miracle – the meeting (reprise)
The wedding

Format 03/02/2012

CD 1
The truck driver and his mate
Hit and miss
In the night 1996
Betrayed
How I learned to hate rock 'n' roll
Discoteca (new version)
The calm before the storm
Confidential (demo version)
The boy who couldn't keep his clothes on (international club mix)
Delusions of grandeur
The view from the balcony
Disco potential
Silver age
Screaming
The ghost of myself
Casting a shadow
Lies
Sexy northerner

CD 2
Always
Nightlife
Searching for the face of Jesus
Between two islands
Friendly fire
We're the Pet Shop Boys (full length version)
Transparent
I didn't get where I am today
The resurrectionist
Girls don't cry
In private (Stuart Crichton 7" mix)
Blue on blue
No time for tears
Bright young things
Party song

We're all criminals now
Gin and jag
After the event
The former enfant terrible
Up and down

Elysium 05/09/2012
Leaving
Invisible
Winner
Your early stuff
A face like that
Breathing space
Ego music
Hold on
Give it a go
Memory of the future
Everything means something
Requiem in denim and leopardskin

Deluxe edition
LP / CD 1
Leaving
Invisible
Winner
Your early stuff
A face like that
Breathing space
Ego music
Hold on
Give it a go
Memory of the future
Everything means something
Requiem in denim and leopardskin

LP / CD 2
Leaving (instrumental)
Invisible (instrumental)
Winner (instrumental)
Your early stuff (instrumental)
A face like that (instrumental)
Breathing space (instrumental)
Ego music (instrumental)
Hold on (instrumental)
Give it a go (instrumental)
Memory of the future (instrumental)
Everything means something (instrumental)
Requiem in denim and leopardskin (instrumental)

Electric 12 July 2013
Axis
Bolshy
Love is a bourgeois construct
Fluorescent
Inside a dream
The last to die
Shouting in the evening
Thursday
Vocal

Super 01/04/2016
Happiness
The pop kids
Twenty-something
Groovy
The dictator decides
Pazzo!

Inner sanctum
Undertow
Sad robot world
Say it to me
Burn
Into thin air

Nightlife / Further listening 1996–2000 28/07/2017

Nightlife (CD 1)
For your own good
Closer to Heaven
I don't know what you want but I can't give it any more
Happiness is an option
You only tell me you love me when you're drunk
Vampires
Radiophonic
The only one
Boy strange
In denial
New York City boy
Footsteps

Further listening 1996–2000
CD 2
Vampires (demo)
For all of us (demo)
Call me old-fashioned (demo)
Friendly fire
Believe / Song For Guy (featuring Elton John)
Sail away
It doesn't often snow at Christmas (fan club mix)
Nightlife
Playing in the streets
Tall thin men
Radiophonic (demo)

CD3
Somebody else's business
Silver age
Screaming
For all of us
The ghost of myself
Casting a shadow
I don't know what you want but I can't give it any more (the PSB extension)
Was it worth it? (live)
Lies
Paris city boy (full French)
Positive role model
Somebody else's business (extended mix)

Release / Further listening 2001–2004 28/07/2017

Release (CD 1)
Home and dry
I get along
Birthday boy
London
E-mail
The samurai in autumn
Love is a catastrophe
Here
The night I fell in love
You choose

Further listening 2001–2004
CD 2
Between two islands
Searching for the face
 of Jesus
Time on my hands
Motoring (demo)
Love life
Transparent
Sexy Northerner
The night is a time to explore
 who you are (demo)
Closer to Heaven
 (slow version)
Run, girl, run (demo)
I didn't get where I am today
Always
Home and dry (ambient mix)
Bright young things (demo)
Kazak
A powerful friend
 (John Peel version)
If looks could kill
 (John Peel version)

CD3
Try it (I'm in love with
 a married man)
Here (PSB new extended mix)
If looks could kill
A powerful friend
Party song
No excuse (demo)
Blue on blue
Jack and Jill party (demo)
Baby (demo)
Flamboyant (original demo)
Miracles
Flamboyant (7" mix)
Numb (demo)
In private
Alone again, naturally
Reunion (electro mix)
Bright young things
We're the Pet Shop Boys

**Fundamental / Further
 listening 2005–2007
 28/07/2017**

Fundamental (CD 1)
Psychological
The Sodom and
 Gomorrah show
I made my excuses and left
Minimal
Numb
God willing
Luna Park
I'm with stupid
Casanova in Hell
Twentieth century
Indefinite leave to remain
Integral

Further listening 2005–2007
CD 2
Fugitive (Richard X
 extended mix)
Ring road (demo)
The performance of
 my life (demo)
One-way street (demo)
Girls don't cry
The resurrectionist
The Sodom and
 Gomorrah show
Dancing in the dusk (demo)
After the event
The former enfant terrible
No time for tears
 (orchestral mix)
God willing (original
 full-length mix)
I'm with stupid
 (PSB maxi-mix)
Answer the phone!
 (ringtone)
Where are you? (ringtone)
Water (ringtone)
Numb (single edit)
One night
A certain 'Je ne sais quoi'
Transfer (Visionaire mix)
Integral (PSB perfect
 immaculate 7" mix)
Integral (PSB perfect
 immaculate mix)

**Yes / Further listening
 2008–2010 20/10/2017**

Yes (CD 1)
Love etc.
All over the world
Beautiful people
Did you see me coming?
Vulnerable
More than a dream
Building a wall
King of rome
Pandemonium
The way it used to be
Legacy

Further listening 2008–2010
CD 2
Gin and Jag
This used to be the future
We're all criminals now
Gin and Jag (frisky mix)
Beautiful people (demo)
My girl
The loving kind (monitor mix)
Love etc. (PSB mix)
Did you see me coming?
 (PSB possibly more mix)
The former enfant terrible
 (PSB bring it on mix)
Up and down
Brits medley

CD3
I cried for us
It doesn't often snow at
 Christmas (new version)
All over the world
 (new version)
Viva la vida / Domino dancing
 (Christmas EP mix)
My girl (our house mix)
Leaving (demo)
Together
Glad all over
The dumpling song (demo
 from My Dad's a Birdman)
Wings and faith (demo from
 My Dad's a Birdman)
Night song

**Elysium / Further listening
 2011–2012 20/10/2017**

Elysium (CD 1)
Leaving
Invisible
Winner
Your early stuff
A face like that
Breathing space
Ego music
Hold on
Give it a go
Memory of the future
Everything means something
Requiem in denim and
 leopardskin

Further listening 2011–2012
CD 2
Vocal (demo)
She pops (demo)
Inside
In slow motion (demo)
Listening
Hell
I started a joke
In his imagination
Leaving (believe in PSB mix)
Leaving (side by side remix)
Leaving (freedom remix)
Memory of the future
 (new single mix)

Hotspot 24/01/2020
Will-o'-the-wisp
You are the one
Happy people
Dreamland
Hoping for a miracle
I don't wanna
Monkey business
Only the dark
Burning the heather
Wedding in Berlin

Special edition
CD 1
Will-o'-the-wisp
You are the one
Happy people
Dreamland
Hoping for a miracle
I don't wanna
Monkey business
Only the dark
Burning the heather
Wedding in Berlin

CD 2
Will-o'-the-wisp (instrumental)
You are the one (instrumental)
Happy people (instrumental)
Dreamland (instrumental)
Hoping for a miracle
 (instrumental)
I don't wanna (instrumental)
Monkey business
 (instrumental)
Only the dark (instrumental)
Burning the heather
 (instrumental)
Wedding in Berlin
 (instrumental)

Smash 16/06/2023
West End girls
Love comes quickly
Opportunities (let's
 make lots of money)
Suburbia
It's a sin
What have I done to
 deserve this?
Rent
Always on my mind
Heart
Domino dancing
Left to my own devices
It's alright
So hard
Being boring
Where the streets have
 no name (can't take
 my eyes off you)
Jealousy
DJ culture
Was it worth it?
Can you forgive her?
Go west
I wouldn't normally do this
 kind of thing
Liberation
Yesterday, when I was mad
Paninaro '95
Before
Se a vida é (that's the
 way life is)
Single-Bilingual
A red letter day
Somewhere
I don't know what you want
 but I can't give it any more
New York City boy
You only tell me you love me
 when you're drunk
Home and dry
I get along
Miracles
Flamboyant
I'm with stupid
Minimal
Numb
Love etc.
Did you see me coming?
It doesn't often snow at
 Christmas
Together
Winner
Leaving
Memory of the future
Vocal
Love is a bourgeois construct
Thursday
The pop kids
Twenty-something
Say it to me
Dreamland
Monkey business
I don't wanna

BluRay discs (videos)

Disc 1
West End girls
Love comes quickly
Opportunities (let's make lots of money) (second version)
Suburbia
It's a sin
What have I done to deserve this?
Rent
Always on my mind
Heart
Domino dancing
Left to my own devices
It's alright
So hard
Being boring
Where the streets have no name (can't take my eyes off you)
Jealousy
DJ culture
Was it worth it?
Can you forgive her?
Go west
I wouldn't normally do this kind of thing
Liberation
Yesterday, when I was mad
Paninaro '95
Before
Se a vida é (that's the way life is)
Single-Bilingual
A red letter day
Somewhere
I don't know what you want but I can't give it any more
New York City boy
You only tell me you love me when you're drunk
Home and dry
I get along / E-mail
Miracles
Flamboyant
I'm with stupid
Minimal
Numb
Love etc.
Did you see me coming?
It doesn't often snow at Christmas (live at the O2 Arena 2009)
Together
Winner
Leaving
Memory of the future
Vocal
Thursday
The pop kids
Twenty-something
Say it to me
Dreamland (lyric video)
Monkey business
I don't wanna

Disc 2
Opportunities (let's make lots of money) (original version)
Paninaro (1986 video)
Domino dancing (extended version)
So hard (extended version)
How can you expect to be taken seriously?
Go west (extended version)
London
Integral
All over the world (live at the O2 Arena 2009)
Invisible
Axis
On social media (lyric video)
Burning the heather (lyric video)

Relentless 20/10/2023
My head is spinning
Forever in love
KDX 125
We came from outer space
The man who has everything
One thing leads to another

Nonetheless 27/04/2024
Loneliness
Feel
Why am I dancing?
New London boy
Dancing star
A new bohemia
The schlager hit parade
The secret of happiness
Bullet for Narcissus
Love is the law

Nonetheless Furthermore 27/04/2024

LP / CD 1
Loneliness
Feel
Why am I dancing?
New London boy
Dancing star
A new bohemia
The schlager hit parade
The secret of happiness
Bullet for Narcissus
Love is the law

LP / CD 2
Heart (new version)
Being boring (new version)
Always on my mind (new version)
It's a sin (new version)

Nonetheless expanded edition 22/11/2024
Loneliness
Feel
Why am I dancing?
New London boy
Dancing star
A new bohemia
The schlager hit parade
The secret of happiness
Bullet for Narcissus
Love is the law
All the young dudes
Adrenaline
The dark end of the street
Miserere
Loneliness (demo version)
Feel (demo version)
Why am I dancing? (demo version)
New London boy (demo version)
Dancing star (demo version)
A new bohemia (demo version)
The schlager hit parade (demo version)
The secret of happiness (demo version)
Bullet for Narcissus (demo version)
Love is the law (demo version)

SINGLES AND EPs

The following list includes all official single releases, exclusive of promos. Promos are listed only where no other formats were produced.

West End girls (first release) 09/04/1984
7"
West End girls (original 7" version)
Pet Shop Boys
12"
West End girls (extended mix)
Pet Shop Boys (extended version)

One more chance Autumn 1984 (exact date unknown)
7" (Sweden)
One more chance (Kordak mix)
One more chance (Bobby 'O' remix)
12" (Belgium, Denmark)
One more chance (Kordak mix)
One more chance (Bobby 'O' remix)

Opportunities (first release) 01/07/1985
7"
Opportunities (let's make lots of money)
In the night
12" (1)
Opportunities (let's make lots of money) (dance mix)
Opportunities (dub for money)
12" (2)
Opportunities (let's make lots of money) (version latina)
Opportunities (dub for money)
In the night
12" promo
Opportunities (let's make lots of money) (dance mix)
In the night

West End girls (second release) 28/10/1985
7" and cassette
West End girls
A man could get arrested
10"
West End girls (10" mix)
A man could get arrested (alternative version)
12" (1)
West End girls (dance mix)
A man could get arrested (alternative version)
West End girls (7" mix)
12" (2)
West End girls (Shep Pettibone mastermix)
West End dub
A man could get arrested (alternative version)
12" (3)
West End girls (extended dance mix)
A man could get arrested (7" mix)
West End girls (dub version)

Love comes quickly 24/02/1986
7"
Love comes quickly
That's my impression
10"
Love comes quickly (dance mix)
That's my impression (disco mix)
12"
Love comes quickly (dance mix)
That's my impression (disco mix)

Opportunities (second release) 19/05/1986
7" and cassette
Opportunities (let's make lots of money) (edit)
Was that what it was?
12"
Opportunities (let's make lots of money) (Shep Pettibone mastermix)
Opportunities (let's make lots of money) (reprise)
Opportunities (let's make lots of money) (original dance mix)
Was that what it was?

Suburbia 22/09/1986
7" and cassette
Suburbia
Paninaro
7" gatefold
Suburbia (new version)
Paninaro
Love comes quickly (Shep Pettibone mastermix)
Jack the lad
Suburbia part two

Discography 577

12"
Suburbia (the full horror)
Paninaro
Jack the lad

Paninaro Autumn 1986 (exact date unknown)
12"
Paninaro (Pet Shop Boys mix)
Paninaro (Ian Levine mix)

It's a sin 15/06/1987
7"
It's a sin
You know where you went wrong
12" and CD
It's a sin (7" version)
You know where you went wrong
It's a sin (disco mix)
12" remix
It's a sin (remix)
You know where you went wrong (rough mix)

What have I done to deserve this? 10/08/1987
7"
What have I done to deserve this?
A new life
12" and CD
What have I done to deserve this? (extended mix)
A new life
What have I done to deserve this? (disco mix)
12" double A-side (US)
What have I done to deserve this? (Shep Pettibone remix)
What have I done to deserve this? (dub)
Rent (extended mix)
I want a dog
Cassette
What have I done to deserve this?
A new life
What have I done to deserve this? (disco mix)

Rent 12/10/1987
7" and cassette
Rent
I want a dog
12" and CD
Rent (extended mix)
Rent (dub mix)
I want a dog

Always on my mind 30/11/1987
7"
Always on my mind
Do I have to?
12", cassette, and CD
Always on my mind (extended dance version)
Do I have to?
Always on my mind (7" version)

12" remix
Always on my mind (remix)
Do I have to?
Always on my mind (dub version)

Heart 21/03/1988
7"
Heart
I get excited (you get excited too)
12", cassette, and CD
Heart (disco mix)
I get excited (you get excited too)
Heart (dance mix)
12" remix
Heart (12" remix)
Heart (dub mix)
I get excited (you get excited too)

Domino dancing 12/09/1988
7"
Domino dancing
Don Juan
12", cassette, and CD
Domino dancing (disco mix)
Don Juan (disco mix)
Domino dancing (alternative mix)
12" remix
Domino dancing (base mix)
Don Juan (demo)
Domino dancing (demo)

Left to my own devices 14/11/1988
7"
Left to my own devices
The sound of the atom splitting (extended version)
12" and CD
Left to my own devices (disco mix)
Left to my own devices
The sound of the atom splitting
Cassette
Left to my own devices
Left to my own devices (disco mix)
The sound of the atom splitting

It's alright 26/06/1989
7"
It's alright
One of the crowd
10"
It's alright (alternative mix)
It's alright (extended dance mix)
12"
It's alright (extended disco mix)
One of the crowd
Your funny uncle
12" remix
It's alright (Tyree mix)
It's alright (Sterling Void mix)
CD

It's alright (7" version)
One of the crowd
Your funny uncle
It's alright (extended disco mix)
Cassette
It's alright
One of the crowd
Your funny uncle

So hard 24/09/1990
7" and cassette
So hard
It must be obvious
12"
So hard (extended dance mix)
It must be obvious
So hard (dub mix)
12" remix
So hard (KLF vs. PSB)
It must be obvious (ufo mix)
CD
So hard
It must be obvious
So hard (extended dance mix)

Being boring 12/11/1990
7" and cassette
Being boring
We all feel better in the dark
12"
Being boring (extended mix)
We all feel better in the dark (extended mix)
12" remix
Being boring (Marshall Jefferson remix)
We all feel better in the dark (Brothers in Rhythm after hours climax mix)
We all feel better in the dark (ambient mix)
CD
Being boring
We all feel better in the dark
Being boring (extended mix)

Where the streets have no name (I can't take my eyes off you) / How can you expect to be taken seriously? 11/03/1991
7" and cassette
Where the streets have no name (I can't take my eyes off you)
How can you expect to be taken seriously? (7" mix)
12"
Where the streets have no name (I can't take my eyes off you) (extended mix)
How can you expect to be taken seriously? (extended mix)
Bet she's not your girlfriend
12" remix
Where the streets have no name (I can't take my eyes off you) (red zone mix)
How can you expect to be taken seriously? (mo mo mix)

How can you expect to be taken seriously? (ragga zone mix)
CD
Where the streets have no name (I can't take my eyes off you) (7" full length mix)
How can you expect to be taken seriously? (extended mix)
Bet she's not your girlfriend
How can you expect to be taken seriously? (classical reprise)

Jealousy 28/05/1991
7" and cassette
Jealousy
Losing my mind
12"
Jealousy (extended mix)
Losing my mind (disco mix)
CD 1
Jealousy (7" version)
Losing my mind (disco mix)
Jealousy (extended mix)
CD 2 (gatefold)
Jealousy (extended mix)
This must be the place I waited years to leave (extended mix)
So hard (eclipse mix)

DJ culture 14/10/1991
7" and cassette
DJ culture
Music for boys
CD
DJ culture
Music for boys
DJ culture (extended mix)
12"
DJ culture (extended mix)
Music for boys
Music for boys (part 2)

DJ culturemix 23/11/1991
12" remix, cassette remix, and CD remix
DJ culturemix
Music for boys (part 3)
Overture to Performance

Was it worth it? 09/12/1991
7" and cassette
Was it worth it?
Miserablism
12"
Was it worth it? (12" remix)
Was it worth it? (dub version)
Miserablism (electro mix)
CD
Was it worth it?
Miserablism
Was it worth it? (12")
Was it worth it? (dub)

Can you forgive her? 31/05/1993
7" and cassette
Can you forgive her?
Hey, headmaster

12" remix
Can you forgive her?
(Rollo remix)
Can you forgive her?
(Rollo dub)
Can you forgive her?
(MK remix)
Can you forgive her? (MK dub)
12" and cassette (US)
Can you forgive her?
(Rollo remix)
Can you forgive her?
(Rollo dub)
Can you forgive her?
Can you forgive her?
(MK remix)
Can you forgive her? (MK dub)
CD 1
Can you forgive her?
Hey, headmaster
Can you forgive her?
(Rollo remix)
Can you forgive her?
(Rollo dub)
CD 2
Can you forgive her?
(MK remix)
I want to wake up
(1993 remix)
What keeps mankind alive?
Can you forgive her? (MK dub)

Go west 06/09/1993
7" and cassette
Go west (album version)
Shameless
12"
Go west (ming's gone west
first and second movement)
Go west (Farley and Heller
disco mix)
Go west (Kevin Saunderson
tribe mix)
CD 1
Go west
Shameless
Go west (Ming's gone west
first and second movement)
CD 2
Go west
Go west (Farley and Heller
disco mix)
Go west (Kevin Saunderson
tribe mix)

I wouldn't normally do this kind of thing 15/11/1993
7" and cassette
I wouldn't normally do this kind
of thing (Beatmasters 7")
Too many people
12"
I wouldn't normally do this kind
of thing (extended nude mix)
I wouldn't normally do this kind
of thing (grandballroom mix)
West End girls (Sasha remix)
West End girls (Sasha dub)
12" remix
I wouldn't normally do this
kind of thing (wild pitch mix)
I wouldn't normally do this kind
of thing (wild tribal beats)

I wouldn't normally do this
kind of thing (club mix)
I wouldn't normally do this kind
of thing (wild pitch dub)
CD 1
I wouldn't normally do this kind
of thing (Beatmasters 7")
I wouldn't normally do this kind
of thing (extended nude mix)
I wouldn't normally do this
kind of thing (wild pitch mix)
I wouldn't normally do this kind
of thing (grandballroom mix)
I wouldn't normally do this
kind of thing (wild pitch dub)
CD 2
I wouldn't normally do this
kind of thing (album mix)
Too many people
Violence (Haçienda version)
West End girls (Sasha remix)

Liberation 04/04/1994
7" and cassette
Liberation
Decadence
12"
Liberation (E Smoove 7" edit)
Liberation (Murk
deepstrumental mix)
Liberation (Oscar G's
dopeassdub mix)
Liberation (Murk dirty club mix)
Young offender (Jam & Spoon
trip-o-matic fairy tale mix)
Young offender (remix no. 2)
CD 1
Liberation
Decadence
Liberation (E Smoove mix)
Liberation (E Smoove 7" edit)
CD 2
Liberation (Murk
deepstrumental mix)
Liberation (Oscar G'S
dopeassdub mix)
Young offender (Jam & Spoon
trip-o-matic fairy tale mix)
Decadence (unplugged mix)

Yesterday, when I was mad 29/08/199
12"
Yesterday, when I was mad
(Jam & Spoon mix)
Yesterday, when I was mad
(Junior Vasquez fabulous
dub)
Yesterday, when I was mad
(raf zone mix)
CD 1
Yesterday, when I was mad
If love were all
Can you forgive her?
(swing version)
Yesterday, when I was mad
(Jam & Spoon mix)
CD 2
Yesterday, when I was mad
(coconut 1 mix)
Some speculation
Yesterday, when I was mad
(Junior Vasquez factory dub)

Yesterday, when I was mad
(raf zone dub)
Cassette
Yesterday, when I was mad
(single mix)
Euroboy

Paninaro '95 31/07/1995
12" (part one)
Paninaro '95 (Tracy's 12" mix)
Paninaro '95 (Sharon's sexy
boyz dub)
Paninaro '95 (Tin Tin Out mix)
Paninaro '95 (Pet Shop Boys
extended remix)
12" (part two)
Paninaro '95 (Angel Moraes
deep dance mix)
Paninaro '95 (Angel Moraes
girls boys in dub)
Paninaro '95 (Angel Moraes
the hot n spycy dub)
12" remix 1
Paninaro '95 (Tracy's 12" mix)
Paninaro '95 (Sharon's sexy
boyz dub)
Paninaro '95 (Tin Tin Out mix)
Paninaro '95 (Pet Shop Boys
extended remix)
12" remix 2
Paninaro '95 (Angel Moraes
deep dance mix)
Paninaro '95 (Angel Moraes
girls boys in dub)
Paninaro '95 (Angel Moraes
the hot n spycy dub)
CD 1
Paninaro '95 (Pet Shop Boys
extended mix)
Paninaro '95 (Tin Tin Out mix)
Paninaro '95 (Tracy's 12" mix)
Paninaro '95 (Sharon's sexy
boyz dub)
Paninaro '95 (Angel Moraes
deep dance mix)
CD 2
Paninaro '95
In the night
Girls and boys (live in Rio)
CD remix
Paninaro '95
Paninaro '95 (Angel Moraes
deep dance mix)
Paninaro '95 (Angel Moraes
girls boys in dub)
Paninaro '95 (Tin Tin Out mix)
Paninaro '95 (Tracy's 12" mix)
Limited-edition cassette
Paninaro '95
In the night (Arthur Baker
remix)
Paninaro '95 (Pet Shop Boys
extended remix)

Before 22/04/1996
12"
Before (underground mix)
Before (bonus dub)
Before (underground
instrumental)
Before (bonus beats)
Before (classic paradise mix)
Before (aphrodisiac mix)

Before (hed boys mix)
Before (dub)
Before (extended mix)
CD 1
Before
The truck-driver and his mate
Hit and miss
In the night 1995
CD 2
Before (classic paradise mix)
Before (aphrodisiac mix)
Before (hed boys mix)
Before (extended mix)
Before (underground mix)
Cassette
Before
The truck-driver and his mate

Se a vida é (That's the way life is) 12/08/1996
12"
Se a vida é (that's the way
life is) (Mark Picchiotti's
deep and dark vocal)
Se a vida é (that's the way
life is) (Mark Picchiotti's
deep and dark instrumental)
Se a vida é (that's the way
life is) (Mark Picchiotti's
shelter dub)
Se a vida é (that's the way
life is) (Deep Dish liquid mix)
Se a vida é (that's the way
life is) (pink noise mix)
Se a vida é (that's the way
life is) (Deep Dish dub)
Se a vida é (that's the way
life is) (radio mix)
CD 1
Se a vida é (that's the
way life is)
Betrayed
How I learned to hate
rock 'n' roll
Se a vida é (pink noise mix)
CD 2
Se a vida é (Mark Picchiotti's
deep and dark vocal)
Se a vida é (Mark Picchiotti's
shelter dub)
Se a vida é (Deep Dish
liquid remix)
Se a vida é (Deep Dish dub)
Cassette
Se a vida é (that's the
way life is)

Single-Bilingual 11/11/1996
CD 1
Single-Bilingual (7")
Discoteca (new version)
The calm before the storm
Discoteca (Trouser Enthusiasts
adventures beyond the
stellar empire mix)
CD 2
Discoteca
(PSB extended mix)
Confidential (1992 demo
for Tina Turner)
Single-Bilingual
(Baby Doc mix)
Discoteca (Baby Doc mix)

Cassette
Single-Bilingual (7")
Discoteca (new version)

A red letter day 17/03/1997
12"
A red letter day
 (Basement Jaxx nite dub)
A red letter day (congo
 dongo dubstramental)
The boy who couldn't
 keep his clothes on
 (the far away dub)
CD 1
A red letter day
The boy who couldn't keep
 his clothes on
Delusions of grandeur
A red letter day
 (Moscow mix)
CD 2
A red letter day (Trouser
 Enthusiasts autoerotic
 decapitation mix)
A red letter day (Motiv-8
 twelve-inch master mix)
A red letter day
 (Basement Jaxx vocal mix)
A red letter day
 (PSB extended edit)
A red letter day (Trouser
 Enthusiasts congo dongo
 dubstramental)

Somewhere 23/06/1997
CD 1
Somewhere
The view from your balcony
To step aside (Ralphi's old
 school dub)
Somewhere (Forthright
 vocal mix)
CD 2
Somewhere
 (orchestral version)
Disco potential
Somewhere (Trouser
 Enthusiasts mix)
Somewhere (Forthright dub)
Cassette
Somewhere (7" version)
Somewhere
 (orchestral version)
The view from your balcony

**I don't know what you
 want but I can't give it
 any more** 19/07/1999
12"
I don't know what you want
 but I can't give it any more
 (the Morales remix)
I don't know what you want
 but I can't give it any more
 (the Morales dub mix)
I don't know what you want
 but I can't give it any more
 (the Morales radio fade)
I don't know what you want
 but I can't give it any more
 (thee maddkatt courtship
 80 witness mix)
I don't know what you want
 but I can't give it any more
 (thee drum drum mix)
I don't know what you want
 but I can't give it any more
 (thee 2 blak ninja mix)
CD 1
I don't know what you want
 but I can't give it any more
I don't know what you want
 but I can't give it any more
 (the Morales remix)
Silver age
Screaming
Multimedia: I don't know
 what you want but I can't
 give it any more (video)
CD 2
I don't know what you want
 but I can't give it any more
 (the Morales remix)
I don't know what you want
 but I can't give it any more
 (thee Maddkatt Courtship
 80 witness mix)
Je t'aime ... moi non plus
Cassette
I don't know what you want
 but I can't give it any more
 (radio edit)
Silver age
Screaming

New York City boy
27/09/1999
Limited-edition two-disc 12"
New York City boy
 (the Morales club mix)
New York City boy
 (the Almighty man on
 a mission mix)
New York City boy
 (the Lange mix)
New York City boy
 (Thunderpuss 2000
 club mix)
New York City boy
 (Superchumbo's
 downtown dub)
CD 1
New York City boy (radio edit)
The ghost of myself
New York City boy (the
 Almighty definitive mix)
Multimedia: New York City
 boy (video)
CD 2
New York City boy
 (album version)
Casting a shadow
New York City boy
 (Superchumbo's
 uptown mix)
Multimedia: Casting
 a shadow (video)
Cassette
New York City boy (radio edit)
The ghost of myself
New York City boy
 (the Almighty definitive
 mix – edit)

**You only tell me you love
 me when you're drunk**
03/01/2000
12"
You only tell me you love
 me when you're drunk
 (Brother Brown's newt mix)
You only tell me you love
 me when you're drunk
 (Attaboy still love you
 when you're sober mix)
You only tell me you love
 me when you're drunk
 (the T-total mix)
You only tell me you love
 me when you're drunk
 (Brother Brown's newt dub)
CD 1
You only tell me you love
 me when you're drunk
Lies
Sail away
Multimedia: You only tell me
 you love me when you're
 drunk (video)
CD 2
You only tell me you love
 me when you're drunk
 (the T-Total mix)
You only tell me you love
 me when you're drunk
 (Brother Brown's newt mix)
You only tell me you love
 me when you're drunk
 (Attaboy still love you
 when you're sober mix)
CD 3
You only tell me you love me
 when you're drunk (live)
Always on my mind (live)
Being boring (live)

Break 4 love 12/2001
12" promo
Break 4 love (classic club mix)
Break 4 love (Mike Monday
 kit kat dub)
Break 4 love (Friburn & Urik
 hi-pass mix)
Break 4 love (Friburn & Urik
 tribal mix)
Break 4 love (Ralphi's dub
 for love)
Home and dry
 (accapella version)

Home and dry 18/03/2002
CD 1
Home and dry (radio edit)
Sexy northerner
Always
CD 2
Home and dry (ambient mix)
Break 4 love (UK radio edit)
Break 4 love (Friburn & Urik
 Hi-Pass mix)
DVD
Home and dry (video)
Nightlife
Break 4 love (USA club mix)

I get along 15/07/2002
CD 1
I get along (radio edit)
Searching for the face
 of Jesus
Between two islands
Multimedia: I get along (video)
CD 2
I get along (live)
A red letter day (live)
Love comes quickly (live)
DVD
I get along / E-mail (video)
Friendly fire
Home and dry (Blank &
 Jones vocal)

London 14/10/2002
CD 1
London (Berlin radio mix)
Positive role model
London (geniune piano mix)
CD 2
London (Westbam in Berlin
 remix)
London (thee radical
 blacklite remix)
London (thee radical dub)

Miracles 17/11/2003
12"
Miracles (extended mix)
Miracles (Lemon Jelly remix)
Miracles (Eric Prydz remix)
CD 1
Miracles
We're the Pet Shop Boys
CD 2
Miracles (extended mix)
Miracles (Lemon Jelly remix)
Transparent

Flamboyant 29/03/2004
12"
Flamboyant (DJ Hell mix)
Flamboyant (Scissor Sisters
 Silhouettes and Shadows
 mix)
West End girls (DJ Hell remix)
CD 1
Flamboyant (new single mix)
I didn't get where I am today
CD 2
Flamboyant (Tomcraft
 extended mix)
Flamboyant (Scissor Sisters
 silhouettes and shadows
 mix)
Flamboyant (DJ Hell remix)
Flamboyant (original demo)
Multimedia: Flamboyant
 (video)

I'm with stupid 08/05/2006
7"
I'm with stupid
Girls don't cry
12" (US)
I'm with stupid
 (Melnyk heavy petting mix)
I'm with stupid
 (Max Tundra mix)

I'm with stupid (album edit)
I'm with stupid
   (PSB maxi-mix)
I'm with stupid
   (Abe Duque mix)
CD 1
I'm with stupid
The resurrectionist
CD 2
I'm with stupid
The resurrectionist
   (Goetz B. extended mix)
Girls don't cry
DVD
I'm with stupid
The resurrectionist
   (Goetz B. extended mix)
Girls don't cry
I'm with stupid (video)
Download 1
I'm with stupid
   (Max Tundra mix)
I'm with stupid
   (Abe Duque mix)
I'm with stupid
   (Melnyk heavy petting mix)
The resurrectionist
   (Goetz B. extended mix)
Download 2
I'm with stupid
   (PSB maxi-mix)
Girls don't cry
I'm with stupid (instrumental)
The resurrectionist

Minimal 24/07/2006
7" and CD 1
Minimal (radio edit)
In private (Stuart Crichton
   7" mix)
12"
Minimal (Tocadisco's Sunday
   at space remix)
Minimal (M Factor mix)
CD 2
Minimal (radio edit)
Minimal (Tocadisco's Sunday
   at space remix)
Minimal (M Factor mix)
Enhanced CD
Minimal (radio edit)
Minimal (Tocadisco's Sunday
   at space remix)
Minimal (M Factor mix)
CD-ROM content:
   Minimal (U-myx format)
DVD
Minimal (Telex hell remix)
Blue on blue
No time for tears (7" mix)
Minimal (video)
Download 1
Minimal (radio edit)
Blue on blue
Minimal (M Factor dub)
Minimal (Superchumbo's light
   and shade dub)
Minimal (Tiga m-i-n-i-m-a-l
   dub)
No time for tears (7" mix)
Download 2
Minimal (Telex heaven remix)

Minimal (Tiga m-i-n-i-m-a-l
   remix)
In private (Stuart Crichton
   7" mix)
Minimal (M Factor mix)
Minimal (Tocadisco's Sunday
   at space remix)
Minimal (Telex hell remix)

Numb 16/10/2006
7"
Numb (new radio version)
Party song
12"
Numb (album version)
Numb (accapella)
Psychological (Ewan Pearson
   vocal remix)
CD
Numb (new radio version)
West End girls (live at the
   Mermaid Theatre)
Enhanced CD
Numb (original demo)
Party song
Bright young things
Multimedia: Numb (video)
Download
Numb (new radio version)
Bright young things
Numb (original demo)
Party song
Numb (accapella)
Psychological (Ewan Pearson
   vocal remix)

Integral 04/10/2007
CD
Integral (PSB perfect
   immaculate mix)
Integral (PSB perfect
   immaculate 7")
Download
Integral (PSB perfect
   immaculate mix)
Integral (Dave Spoon mix)

Love etc. 17/03/2009
CD
Love etc.
Gin and jag
CD remix
Love etc.
Love etc. (Pet Shop Boys mix)
Love etc. (Gui Boratto remix)
Love etc. (Kurd Maverick
   remix)
Love etc. (Frankmusik star
   and garter dub)
Love etc. (Kurd Maverick dub)
Download 1
Love etc.
We're all criminals now
Download 2
Love etc. (Pet Shop Boys mix)
Love etc. (Gui Boratto remix)
Love etc. (Kurd Maverick
   remix)
Love etc. (Frankmusik star
   and garter dub)

Did you see me coming?
   01/06/2009
12" remix
Did you see me coming?
   (PSB possibly more mix)
Did you see me coming?
   (Unicorn Kid mix)
The way it used to be
   (Richard X mix)
CD 1
Did you see me coming?
   (album version)
After the event
CD 2
Did you see me coming?
   (PSB possibly more mix)
The former enfant terrible
Up and down
CD 3
Did you see me coming?
   (album version)
After the event
The former enfant terrible
Up and down
Download
Did you see me coming?
   (album version)
Brit Award 2009 medley
   (studio version)
Did you see me coming?
   (Unicorn Kid mix)
The way it used to be
   (Richard X mix)
Did you see me coming?
   (PSB possibly more mix)
The former enfant terrible
   (bring it on mix)

Beautiful people
   02/10/2009
CD
Beautiful people
Beautiful people (demo)
Fugitive (Richard X 7" mix)
Up and down (Tom Stephan
   vocal remix)

Pet Shop Boys Christmas
   14/12/2009
CD
It doesn't often snow at
   Christmas (new version)
My girl (studio version)
All over the world
   (new version)
Viva la vida / Domino dancing
   (studio version)
My girl (our house mix)

Love life 17/04/2010
7"
Love life
A powerful friend

Together 24/10/2010
CD 1 and Download 2
Together (ultimate mix)
Glad all over
I cried for us
Together (extended mix)
CD 2 and Download 3
Together (radio mix)
West End girls (Grum remix)

Download 1
Together (ultimate mix)
Download 4
Together (Pepptalk mix)
Together (Ultrabeat remix)
West End girls
   (Grum dub mix)
Download 5
Together (video)

Winner 06/08/2012
CD 1 and Download 2
Winner (album version)
A certain 'Je ne sais quoi'
Way through the woods
   (long version)
I started a joke
Download 1
Winner
Download 3
Winner (Andrew Dawson
   happy hour remix)
Winner (John Dahlback remix)
Winner (Niki and the Dove
   remix)
Winner (Andrew Dawson
   extended happy sad remix)
Download 4
Winner (Wideboys remix)
Winner (Wideboys dub)
Winner (Wideboys radio edit)

Leaving 12/10/2012
7"
Leaving
Leaving (demo)
12"
Leaving (lost her love remix)
Leaving (happysad remix)
Leaving (happyhour remix)
CD 1
Leaving
Leaving (instrumental)
CD 2 and Download 2
Leaving
Hell
In his imagination
Baby (2003 demo)
CD remix
Leaving (lost her love remix)
Leaving (happysad remix)
Leaving (demo)
Download 1
Leaving
Download 3
Leaving (lost her love remix)
Leaving (believe in
   PSB remix)
Leaving (demo)
Download 4
Leaving (PSB side-by-side
   remix)
Leaving (happysad remix)
Leaving (PSB freedom remix)

Memory of the future
   31/12/2012
CD and Download 2
Memory of the future
   (new single mix)
Listening (demo)
One night
Inside

Discography   581

CD remix and
  Download remix
Memory of the future
  (Stuart Price extended
  mix)
Memory of the future
  (Ulrich Schnauss remix)
Memory of the future
  (DJ Waldo squash remix)
Memory of the future
  (Digital Dog club remix)
Memory of the future
  (Digital Dog dub)
Download 1
Memory of the future
  (new single mix)

Axis 01/05/2013
12"
Axis
Axis (Boys Noize remix)
Download 1
Axis (album version)
Download 2
Axis (video)
Download remix
Axis (Boys Noize remix)

Vocal 01/05/2013
12"
Vocal (album version)
Vocal (Rektchordz dub)
Vocal (Armageddon Turk
  tear gas extended remix)
Vocal (The Cucharachas mix)
Vocal (JRMX club remix)
Vocal (Nacho Chapado &
  Ivan Gomez mix)
Vocal (Rektchordz mix)
Vocal (WAWA extended mix)
CD and Download 2
Vocal (radio edit)
Vocal (album version)
Vocal (instrumental)
CD remix and
  Download remix
Vocal (album version)
Vocal (Rektchordz dub)
Vocal (Armageddon Turk
  tear gas extended remix)
Vocal (The Cucharachas mix)
Vocal (JRMX club remix)
Vocal (Nacho Chapado &
  Ivan Gomez mix)
Vocal (Rektchordz mix)
Vocal (WAWA extended mix)
Vocal (The Cucarachas dub)
Download 1
Vocal (album version)
Download 3
Vocal (Flashmob remix)
Vocal (Flashmob instrumental)

**Love is a bourgeois
  construct** 01/09/2013
12"
Love is a bourgeois construct
  (album version)
Love is a bourgeois construct
  (The Penelopes remix)
Love is a bourgeois construct
  (Claptone remix)

Love is a bourgeois construct
  (Little Boots discothèque
  dub)
Love is a bourgeois construct
  (Dave Audé extended vocal)
Love is a bourgeois construct
  (Claptone instrumental)
Love is a bourgeois construct
  (Dave Audé big dirty
  dub mix)
Love is a bourgeois construct
  (The Penelopes dub)
CD
Love is a bourgeois construct
  (nighttime radio edit))
Entschuldigung!
Get it online
Love is a bourgeois construct
  (The Penelopes remix)
Love is a bourgeois construct
  (Claptone remix)
Love is a bourgeois construct
  (Little Boots discothèque
  edit)
Love is a bourgeois construct
  (Dave Audé big dirty
  dub mix)
Love is a bourgeois construct
  (Claptone instrumental)
Love is a bourgeois construct
  (Little Boots discothèque
  dub)
Download 1
Love is a bourgeois construct
  (nighttime radio edit))
Entschuldigung!
Get it online
Love is a bourgeois construct
  (The Penelopes remix
  – radio edit)
Download 2
Love is a bourgeois construct
  (The Penelopes remix)
Love is a bourgeois construct
  (Claptone remix)
Love is a bourgeois construct
  (Little Boots discothèque
  edit)
Love is a bourgeois construct
  (Dave Audé big dirty
  dub mix)
Love is a bourgeois construct
  (Claptone instrumental)

Thursday 01/09/2013
12"
Thursday (album mix)
Thursday (Eddie Amador
  main remix)
Thursday (Tensnake remix)
CD and Download 2
Thursday (radio edit)
No more ballads
Odd man out
Thursday (Tensnake remix)
Download 1
Thursday
Download remix
Thursday (no rap radio edit)
Thursday (Eddie Amador
  main remix)
Thursday (Mindskap mix)

Fluorescent 19/04/2014
12"
Fluorescent (Indio mix)
Fluorescent (Cali mix)

The pop kids 18/03/2016
12"
The pop kids (Offer Nissim
  drama remix)
The pop kids (MK dub)
The pop kids (Scene Kings
  extended)
The pop kids (the full story)
The pop kids (PSB deep dub)
Download 1
The pop kids (radio edit)
CD and Download 2
The pop kids (radio edit)
In bits
One-hit wonder
The pop kids (PSB deep dub)
The pop kids (the full story)
Download remix
The pop kids (Offer Nissim
  drama remix)
The pop kids (MK dub
  radio edit)
The pop kids (PSB deep dub
  radio edit)
The pop kids (MK dub)

Twenty-something
  24/06/2016
CD
Twenty-something (radio edit)
The white dress
Wiedersehen
Twenty-something
  (the Los Evo Jedis remix)
Download
Twenty-something (radio edit)
The white dress
Wiedersehen
Twenty-something
  (the Los Evo Jedis remix)
Twenty-something
  (Kornél Kovács remix)

Inner sanctum 22/07/2016
12"
Inner sanctum (Carl Craig
  c2 juiced RMX)
Inner sanctum (first demo)
Inner sanctum (second demo)
Inner sanctum (album version)
Download
Inner sanctum (Carl Craig
  c2 juiced RMX)

Say it to me 16/09/2016
12"
Say it to me (Real Lies remix)
Say it to me (Tom Demac
  remix)
Say it to me (Offer Nissim
  remix)
Say it to me (Stuart Price
  alternative mix)
CD
Say it to me (new radio edit)
A cloud in a box
The dead can dance

Say it to me (Stuart Price
  alternative mix)
Inner sanctum (Carl Craig
  c2 juiced RMX)
Download
Say it to me (new radio edit)
A cloud in a box
The dead can dance
Say it to me (Stuart Price
  alternative mix)
Download remix
Say it to me (Tom Demac
  remix)
Say it to me (Real Lies remix)
Say it to me (Offer Nissim
  remix)

Undertow 01/04/2017
12"
Undertow (Tuff City
  Kids remix)
Left to my own devices
  (Super tour version)
Burn (Baba Stiltz remix)
Undertow (Tuff City Kids dub)
CD and Download
Undertow (Tuff City
  Kids remix)
Left to my own devices
  (Super tour version)
Burn (Baba Stiltz remix)

Agenda 05–08/02/2019
12", and CD
Give stupidity a chance
On social media
What are we going to
  do about the rich
The forgotten child
Download 1
Give stupidity a chance
Download 2
On social media
Download 3
What are we going to
  do about the rich
Download 4
The forgotten child

Dreamland 11/09/2019
7"
Dreamland
Always on my mind /
  The pop kids (live)
12" and Download remix
Dreamland (PSB remix)
Dreamland (TWD vocal remix)
Dreamland (TWD dub)
Dreamland (Jacques Renault
  remix)
CD
Dreamland
An open mind
No boundaries
Dreamland (PSB remix)
Dreamland (TWD vocal remix)
Download 1
Dreamland
Download 2
Dreamland
An open mind
No boundaries

Burning the heather 14/11/2019
7"
Burning the heather
 (radio edit)
Decide
Download 1
Burning the heather
 (radio edit)
Download 2
Burning the heather
 (radio edit)
Decide
Decide (CYA remix)

Monkey business
 02/01/2020
12", CD, and Download 2
Monkey business (radio edit)
Monkey business
 (Prins Thomas diskomiks)
At rock bottom
Monkey business
 (Friend Within remix)
Download 1
Monkey business (radio edit)

My Beautiful Laundrette
 17/04/2020
CD and Download
Omar's theme
Angelic thug
Johnny's dark side
Night sings (Popa's theme)
Johnny's theme
Beautiful laundrette
No boundaries

I don't wanna 24/04/2020
12", CD, and Download
I don't wanna (radio edit)
New boy
I don't wanna
 (Mano Le Tough remix)
I don't wanna
 (David Jackson remix one)
I don't wanna
 (David Jackson remix two)

Cricket wife 07/05/2021
CD and Download
Cricket wife
West End girls (new
 lockdown version)

Lost 14/04/2023
CD
The lost room
I will fall
Skeletons in the closet
Kaputnik
Download
The lost room
I will fall
Skeletons in the closet
Kaputnik
Living in the past

Loneliness 31/01/2024
CD
Loneliness (radio edit)
Party in the Blitz
Through you (extended mix)

Download
Loneliness (radio edit)
Loneliness (album version)
Party in the Blitz
Through you (extended mix)

Dancing star 03/04/2024
CD and Download
Dancing star
Sense of time
If Jesus had a sister
Dancing star (Solomun
 extended remix)
Party in the Blitz
 (Superchumbo remix)
Dancing star
 (Solomun remix)

A new bohemia 04/06/2024
CD and Download
A new bohemia (radio edit)
It's not a crime
I've got plans (involving you)
A new bohemia
 (Alex Metric remix)
A new bohemia
 (demo version)

Feel 20/08/2024
CD and Download
Feel (radio edit)
Everybody will dance
The schlager hit parade
 (Deutsche demo)
Loneliness (Floorplan remix)
Everybody will dance
 (Superchumbo remix)

New London boy /
 All the young dudes
 07/11/2024
CD and Download
New London boy (radio edit)
All the young dudes
Beauty has laid siege to
 the city
All the young dudes
 (Delinquent version)
All the young dudes
 (Richard X longest mix)
CD remix and
 Download remix
All the young dudes
 (Richard X edit)
New London boy
 (Boy Harsher remix)
Clean air hybrid electric bus
All the young dudes
 (I. Jordan remix)

VIDEOS

Television 01/12/1986
Opportunities (let's make lots
 of money) (first version)
West End girls
Love comes quickly
Opportunities (let's make lots
 of money) (second version)
Suburbia
Paninaro

Showbusiness 01/12/1988
It's a sin
What have I done to
 deserve this?
Rent
Always on my mind
Heart
Domino dancing
 (disco version)

I like it here, wherever it is
 01/12/1988
Actually TV commercial
It's a sin
What have I done to
 deserve this?
Rent
Always on my mind

It couldn't happen here
 01/12/1989
It couldn't happen here
Suburbia (video mix)
It's a sin (disco mix)
West End girls
Always on my mind
Rent
Two divided by zero
What have I done to deserve
 this? (extended version)
King's Cross
One more chance
I want to wake up

Highlights 03/12/1990
The sound of the atom
 splitting
It's a sin
Shopping
Love comes quickly
Domino dancing
Rent
King's Cross
It's alright

Promotion 03/06/1991
Left to my own devices
It's alright
So hard
Being boring
How can you expect to
 be taken seriously?
Where the streets have
 no name
Jealousy

Videography 04/11/1991
West End girls
Love comes quickly
Opportunities (let's
 make lots of money)
Suburbia
It's a sin
What have I done to
 deserve this?
Rent
Always on my mind
Heart
Domino dancing
Left to my own devices
It's alright
So hard
Being boring

How can you expect to
 be taken seriously?
Where the streets have
 no name (I can't take
 my eyes off you)
Jealousy
DJ culture

Performance 28/09/1992
This must be the place
 I waited years to leave
It's a sin
Losing my mind
What have I done to
 deserve this?
My October symphony
I'm not scared
We all feel better in the dark
So sorry, I said
Suburbia
So hard
Opportunities (let's
 make lots of money)
How can you expect to
 be taken seriously?
Rent
Where the streets have
 no name
West End girls
Jealousy
Always on my mind
Your funny uncle
DVD released 27/09/2005

Projections 01/12/1993
Opportunities (tour film)
Heart (tour film)
Paninaro (tour film)
It's a sin (tour film)
Domino dancing
 (alternative mix) (tour film)
King's Cross (tour film)
Always on my mind (tour film)
Violence (Haçienda version)
 (film 'A Garden in Luxor')
Being boring
 (film 'Studio Bankside')

Various 06/03/1995
Can you forgive her?
Go west
I wouldn't normally do this
 kind of thing
Liberation
Yesterday, when I was mad
Absolutely fabulous
Go west (part 2)

Discovery 07/08/1995
Tonight is forever
I wouldn't normally do this
 kind of thing
Always on my mind
Domino dancing
To speak is a sin
One in a million / Mr Vain
Paninaro
Rent
Suburbia
King's Cross
So hard
Left to my own devices /
 Rhythm of the night

Discography   583

Absolutely fabulous
Liberation
West End girls
Can you forgive her?
Girls and boys
It's a sin / I will survive
Go west / Go west (reprise)
Being boring

Somewhere – Live at the Savoy 24/11/1997
Yesterday, when I was mad
The truck-driver and his mate
Se a vida é (that's the way life is)
Hallo spaceboy
To step aside
Go west
The theatre
It's a sin / I will survive
Discoteca
Can you forgive her?
Somewhere
Rent
Being boring
Left to my own devices

Montage 12/11/2001
West End girls
Discoteca
Being boring
Closer to Heaven
Can you forgive her?
Only the wind
What have I done to deserve this?
New York City boy
Left to my own devices
Young offender
Vampires
You only tell me you love me when you're drunk
Was it worth it?
Se a vida é (that's the way life is)
I don't know what you want but I can't give it any more
Always on my mind
Shameless
Opportunities (let's make lots of money)
It's a sin
It's alright
Footsteps
Go west

PopArt 24/11/2003
Opportunities (let's make lots of money) (first release)
West End girls
Love comes quickly
Opportunities (let's make lots of money) (second release)
Suburbia
Paninaro
It's a sin
What have I done to deserve this?
Rent
Always on my mind
Heart

Domino dancing
Left to my own devices
It's alright
So hard
Being boring
How can you expect to be taken seriously?
Where the streets have no name
Jealousy
DJ culture
Was it worth it?
Can you forgive her?
Go west
I wouldn't normally do this kind of thing
Liberation
Yesterday, when I was mad
Paninaro '95
Before
Se a vida é (that's the way life is)
Single-Bilingual
A red letter day
Somewhere
I don't know what you want but I can't give it any more
New York City boy
You only tell me you love me when you're drunk
Home and dry
I get along / E-mail
London
Domino dancing (extended version)
So hard (extended version)
Go west (extended version)

A Life in Pop 23/10/2006
The beginning
Two divided by zero
London
The first meeting
West End girls
Image
The best was yet to come
Serious songwriting
Live at last
Behaviour
Pop or rock
Going west
Latin influence
Closer to Heaven
Release and Potemkin
Depth through surface
Videos:
Miracles
Flamboyant
I'm with stupid
Minimal
Numb
West End girls (live on *Hit des Clubs*)
What have I done to deserve this (live 1998 Brit Awards)
Go west (live 1994 Brit Awards)

Cubism 21/05/2007
Psycho intro
God willing
Psychological

Left to my own devices
I'm with stupid
Suburbia
Can you forgive her?
Minimal
Shopping
Rent
Dreaming of the queen
Heart
Opportunities
Integral
Numb
Se a vida é
Domino dancing
Flamboyant
Home and dry
Always on my mind
Where the streets have no name
West End girls
The Sodom and Gomorrah show
So hard
It's a sin
Go west
Extras

Pandemonium 15/02/2010
CD
More than a dream (dub) / Heart
Did you see me coming?
Pandemonium / Can you forgive her?
Love etc.
Go west / Paninaro
Two divided by zero
Why don't we live together?
New YorkCity boy
Always on my mind
Closer to Heaven / Left to my own devices
Do I have to?
King's Cross
Suburbia
Se a vida é / Discoteca / Domino dancing / Viva la vida
It's a sin
Being boring
West end girls
DVD
More than a dream / Heart
Did you see me coming?
Pandemonium / Can you forgive her?
Love etc.
Building a wall
Go west
Two divided by zero
Why don't we live together?
New York City boy
Always on my mind
Closer to Heaven / Left to my own devices
Do I have to?
King's Cross
The way it used to be
Jealousy
Suburbia
What have I done to deserve this?
All over the world

Se a vida é / Discoteca / Domino dancing / Viva la vida
It's a sin
Being boring
West End girls
DVD extras
My girl (live at The O2)
It doesn't often snow at Christmas (live at The O2)
Love etc. (video)
Did you see me coming? (video)
All over the world (video)
2009 Brit Awards performance (with Lady Gaga and Brandon Flowers)
(Audio commentary by Pet Shop Boys and Es Devlin)

Inner Sanctum 12/04/2019
Inner sanctum
Opportunities (let's make lots of money)
The pop kids / In the night / Burn
Love is a bourgeois construct
New York City boy
Se a vida é (that's the way life is)
Love comes quickly
Love etc.
The dictator decides / Inside a dream
West End girls
Home and dry / The Enigma
Vocal / The Sodom and Gomorrah show
It's a sin
Left to my own devices
Heart / Go west
Domino dancing
Always on my mind
The pop kids (reprise)
Bonus video
Pet Shop Boys live at Rock in Rio, 17 September 2017

BOOKS

Pet Shop Boys, annually 08/1988 (exact date unknown)
ISBN 0-7235-6842-1

Pet Shop Boys, Literally 12/11/1990
ISBN 0-306-80494-8

Pet Shop Boys versus America 04/11/1993
ISBN 1-886894-31-0

Catalogue 16/10/2006
ISBN 0-500-51307-4

Two books about Pet Shop Boys 19/03/2020
Pet Shop Boys, Literally
ISBN 1-785-15236-X
Pet Shop Boys versus America
ISBN 1-785-15235-1

Biographies

David Alden
Born in New York, Alden decided at sixteen that he wanted to direct opera and has done so to widespread acclaim since the late 1970s, creating productions for companies such as New York's Metropolitan Opera, the English National Opera, Netherlands Opera, and the New Israel Opera, many in association with designer David Fielding.

Arma Andon
Pet Shop Boys' manager in the United States between 1990 and 1998. He spent six decades in the music business. After working as an assistant to The Beatles, he moved to Columbia Records, where he became vice-president of marketing. As well as Pet Shop Boys, he managed acts such as Cathy Dennis, Wilson Phillips, Extreme, and Donna Lewis.

Vaughan Arnell
Arnell is a British music video and television commercial director. He has directed numerous music videos, including Dead or Alive's 'You spin me round (like a record)', George Michael's 'Fastlove', Terence Trent D'Arby's 'Sign your name', All Saints' 'Pure shores', Spice Girls' 'Say you'll be there', and One Direction's 'Kiss you'. He often collaborates with Robbie Williams.

David Barnard
Barnard is an award-winning independent film-maker best known for music films and live multi-camera broadcasting. He has made films for Gorillaz, Nick Cave and the Bad Seeds, and Radiohead, among many other musical acts.

Angela Becker
Pet Shop Boys' longest-serving manager, California-born Becker has held that role since 2008. She started her career in the film division at United Talent Agency. In 2004, she became Madonna's manager, working with her for the next four years. In 2024, Becker and Pet Shop Boys were honoured at the Artist & Manager Awards for their shared pioneering impact on music and culture.

Nico Beyer
German video and commercials director Beyer has shot award-winning work for Audi, BMW, Canon, Coca-Cola, Ford, Nike, Siemens, Suzuki, and many other brands. He has also produced videos for acts such as Swing Out Sister, Suzanne Vega, The Verve, Erasure, and Dee-lite.

Jack Bond
Bond was a British film and television writer, director, and producer. His many credits included *Separation* (1967), *The Other Side of the Underneath* (1972), *Anti-Clock* (1980), *The Wickedest Man in the World* (2002) – a documentary about infamous devil-worshipper Aleister Crowley – and *Broken Morning* (2003), a docu-drama about French writer Albert Camus.

Jeffrey Bryant
Bryant is a Welsh costume designer who has worked with musical acts including Duran Duran, Tina Turner, George Michael, Mick Jagger, and Westlife. After moving to London at the height of the Blitz scene in the early 1980s, he started making outré clothes for the nightclub elite of drag queens and club promoters.

Don Cameron
Cameron is an Australian director, designer, photographer, and visual artist. He has created iconic videos for artists including Garbage, Blur, and Pet Shop Boys. As a photographer, he works primarily in architectural photography, his images acting as a starting point for creating furniture.

Jill Carrington
Carrington's first job was in a pet shop, but at nineteen she became a temp receptionist at K-Tel Records. Within ten years she was marketing manager of EMI Records, and was soon asked to run Parlophone. She was then appointed marketing director of Polydor Records, working with Van Morrison and Paul Weller, before becoming Pet Shop Boys' second manager from 1989 to 1998.

Ben Cash
Cash is director of Flare Lighting, a lighting and show design company specializing in illuminating live concerts, tours, and corporate entertainment. As well as Pet Shop Boys' *Inner Sanctum*, he has worked on live shows by Sam Smith, Sleaford Mods, Fatboy Slim, and Mark Ronson.

Les Child
Child has been a ground-breaking choreographer and dancer since the 1980s. He has worked with dancers and acts such as Michael Clark, Leigh Bowery, Erasure, Sinead O'Connor, Robbie Williams, U2, Scissor Sisters, Dizzee Rascal, and REM. He was mother of the legendary House of Child, the original London voguing house, and choreographer on the hit musical *Taboo*, about the life of Bowery and starring Boy George, and on the drag-queen comedy *Kinky Boots* (2005).

Mitch Clark
Clark first met Neil Tennant and Chris Lowe in the early 1990s in her job as promotions manager at EMI International, where she rose to vice-president. Pet Shop Boys asked her to become their manager in 1998, and she continued in that role until 2003.

Pelle Crépin
Crépin is a London-based Swedish fashion photographer, known for his elegant and refined aesthetic and meticulous attention to detail.

Matthew Daw
Daw is a London-based lighting designer working internationally in theatre, art, live music, film, and events. Recent work includes lighting for productions by the Royal Shakespeare Company and the National Theatre, as well as live performances by Alicia Keys, Lorde, Arcade Fire, and Sigur Rós.

Jeremy Deller
Deller is an artist based in London, known for his collaborative work that often has a political aspect. He won the Turner Prize in 2004 and represented Britain at the 55th Venice Biennale in 2013. He is the author of *Art is Magic*.

Es Devlin
Devlin trained in music and fine art before studying stage design. Her work for the RSC, National Theatre, Royal Court, Broadway, and other theatre and opera companies has won several prestigious awards. As well as designing tours for Pet Shop Boys, she has produced stage designs for Beyoncé, Kanye West, Adele, U2, The Weeknd, and Lorde. In 2022, she was appointed a CBE by HM Queen Elizabeth II for services to design.

David Dorrell
Pet Shop Boys' manager between 2003 and 2008 (and manager of Bush, UNKLE, Dirty Vegas, and Sasha, among others), Dorrell is a former journalist on the *NME*. A successful DJ and producer, he had a number one in 1987 with 'Pump up the volume' and has remixed and produced for U2, De La Soul, and Tina Turner.

The Douglas Brothers
British brothers Andrew and Stuart Douglas work at the threshold of art and commercial photography. Their distinctive, natural style has gained them critical acclaim and numerous awards,

and they have shot for the magazine, music, and advertising industries on both sides of the Atlantic. In 1991, they began to direct music videos and commercials. In 2004, Andrew Douglas was nominated as best commercial director by the Directors Guild of America. He directed an award-winning documentary and the 2005 remake of *The Amityville Horror*. Stuart has directed award-winning commercials for numerous clients.

Jaqui Doyle
Doyle is a creative director and graphic designer based in London. She has helped launch and visually brand music television shows and has produced factual entertainment programmes. She designed the Pet Shop Boys fanzine *Literally* and its successor publication, *Annually*, from 1989 until 2019.

Andy Earl
Photographer and film-maker Earl attended Worthing College of Art and Trent Polytechnic in the 1970s. In 1978, he had a one-person show at the Photographers' Gallery in London, which resulted in Malcolm McClaren's commission to shoot a controversial nude image for a Bow Wow Wow sleeve. A year later, he represented Britain at the Venice Biennale. A successful career in international music business followed, and Earl has shot for dozens of sleeves and directed many videos for artists such as the Rolling Stones.

Mark Farrow
Born in Manchester, Farrow began designing sleeves for Factory Records in the early 1980s, where he worked with Peter Saville, before moving to London to join XL Design. He designed his first Pet Shop Boys sleeve in 1985, and has been the group's principal designer ever since. Voted 'the most important graphic designer working today' in design magazine *Creative Review*'s peer poll in 2004, he has won numerous D&AD design awards, and received Grammy Award nominations in 1993 and 1995 for his sleeve designs. He has also produced high-profile restaurant, bar, nightclub, and gallery design, and his work has been exhibited in the Design Museum and the Victoria & Albert Museum, both in London. In 2009 he was named a Royal Designer for Industry (RDI) by the Royal Society of Arts.

Chiara Ferrari
Ferrari is an Italian product, interiors, and exhibition designer based in Mallorca.

Justyn Field
Field is an Australian executive producer and director of photography for film, event, and multimedia campaigns. He was cinematographer on David Lynch's 2010 short *Lady Blue Shanghai Poem: 'It Holds the Love'*.

David Fielding
Fielding is an award-winning international director and stage and costume designer. He studied at the Central School of Art and Design in London under acclaimed theatre designer Ralph Koltai. He has worked in opera, ballet, and theatre over three decades for companies in Britain, Europe, and the United States, designing both sets and costumes, often in collaboration with David Alden. He has also directed a number of theatre and opera productions.

Gavin Filipiak
Filipiak is a film director and editor in San Diego. He has directed several music videos in the past decade, including a cover of 'West End girls' by Mexican-American cholo goth duo Prayers.

Phil Fisk
Over the last twenty years, award-winning London-based portrait photographer and film-maker Fisk has photographed dozens of figures from the worlds of stage and screen, music, and art for magazines, newspapers, and cultural and corporate clients across the world. His portrait of Paul Weller was featured in *Portrait of Britain 2021*.

Dan Forbes
Forbes is an award-winning still-life photographer based in New York.

Elliott Franks
Franks is a press photographer in the UK covering news, politics, and the arts.

Julian Gibbs
Gibbs is a British director of film, music videos, and commercials. He works with creative director Julian House at creative agency Intro, and with motion designer Chris Sayer.

Carisa Glucksman
Glucksman is an American actress and costume designer.

Jude Greenaway
Greenaway is an artist, musician, and animator, working in motion graphics, film direction, sound design, and live audio performance.

Howard Greenhalgh
Yorkshire-born Greenhalgh studied at the Royal College of Art in London in the 1980s before becoming a video and commercials director. His many commercial credits include Bacardi, Vauxhall, Adidas, BBC, Stella Artois, Citroën, Ford, Renault, Rimmel, Reebok, AT&T, Lexus, and Smirnoff. He has produced dozens of music videos for acts such as A-ha, Culture Club, Steps, Faithless, S Club 7, Melanie C, Keane, Placebo, Underworld, Muse, Morcheeba, George Michael, Puff Daddy, Sting, Elton John, Meat Loaf, Soundgarden, and Suede. He has won numerous awards, including an MTV Video Award and a Cannes Gold Lion. He was nominated for a D&AD award and a Grammy for the 'Go west' video.

Annie Griffin
Griffin is an American writer and director. Originally from Buffalo, New York, Griffin came to Britain in 1981 to pursue her ambitions as an experimental actor. In the early 1990s, she was invited to direct animated inserts for MTV Europe before going on to produce short films and television documentaries, and creating the acclaimed Channel 4 drama series *The Book Group* and the movie *Festival*.

Tim Gutt
Gutt is a London-based fashion photographer known for his surreal, conceptual imagery. He has worked with publications such as *Vogue*, *Elle*, and *Harper's Bazaar*.

Zaha Hadid
Hadid was an award-winning Iraqi-born British architect and designer. Born in Baghdad, she studied mathematics in Beirut and then architecture at the Architectural Association, London. She worked with her former teacher Rem Koolhas before establishing her own practice in 1979. Her realized buildings include the London Aquatics Centre, Queen Elizabeth Olympic Park, London; Zaragoza Bridge Pavilion, Zaragoza; National Museum of Arts of the 21st Century (MAXXI), Rome; Vitra Fire Station, Weil an Rhein; Rosental Center for Contemporary Art, Cincinnati; and the BMW Centre, Leipzig. In 2004, she became the first woman to win the prestigious Pritzker Architecture Prize, and was appointed a CBE in the same year.

Andrew Haigh
Haigh is an award-winning English film-maker. He wrote and directed the films *Weekend* (2011), *45 Years* (2015), *Lean on Pete* (2017), and *All of Us Strangers* (2023). He has also worked in television, serving as an executive producer and lead writer-director on HBO's *Looking*.

Luke Halls
Halls has been producing video design and animation for more than a decade, specializing in opera, theatre, art, dance, and live performance. He has worked for many artists, creating video designs and animations for tours by Adele, Beyoncé, U2, and Rihanna, among others.

Douglas Hart
Hart is a Scottish musician and music video and commercials director, and founding member of The Jesus and Mary Chain. As well as Pet Shop Boys, he has directed videos for The Stone Roses, Babyshambles, Paul Weller, and Primal Scream, among others.

Alexei Hay
Based in New York, Hay is a fashion and art photographer and jewelry designer. Known for his innovative, expressionistic visuals and acidic realism, he has shot campaigns for Gucci, Baby Phat, and Armani Exchange, among others. His photographs have appeared in publications such as *i-D*, *Dazed & Confused*, *Another Magazine*, *The Face*, *Purple Sex*, *New York Times Magazine*, *Spin*, *Dutch*, and the *Independent*. His work also appeared in the 2004 Whitney Biennial Exhibition in New York.

Chris Heath
Chris Heath is an acclaimed writer and journalist. His first job was at *Smash Hits* magazine and he has collaborated with Pet Shop Boys since the 1980s. He is the author of *Pet Shop Boys, Literally* and *Pet Shop Boys versus America*, two best-selling biographies of Robbie Williams, and the 2024 book *No Road Leading Back: An Improbable Escape from the Nazis and the Tangled Way We Tell the Story of the Holocaust*. He currently writes for *The Atlantic*, *GQ*, *Esquire*, *Vanity Fair*, *New York*, *Telegraph Magazine*, *Fantastic Man*, *The Gentlewoman*, and the *Smithsonian* magazine.

Philip Hoare
Philip Hoare is a writer and curator. He is the author of ten acclaimed books, including biographies of Stephen Tennant and Noël Coward, and *Leviathan or, The Whale*, which won the BBC Samuel Johnson Prize. His most recent books include *Albert and the Whale*, on the German artist Albrecht Dürer, and *William Blake and the Sea Monsters of Love* (2025).

Han Hoogerbrugge
Hoogerbrugge is a Dutch digital artist and one of the pioneers of internet animation. He is known for producing films, drawings, and prints in a dry, surrealistic comic style.

Julian House
House is a creative director and partner at creative agency Intro along with Julian Gibbs. He works across all media, from print to film to sound design, in music, publishing, arts, and advertising projects.

Derek Jarman
A celebrated British painter, theatre designer, and film-maker, Jarman designed sets and costumes for the theatre in the 1960s, including *Jazz Calendar* with Frederick Ashton and *The Rake's Progress* with Ken Russell. His films spanned the 1970s to the 1990s, and included *Sebastiane* (1976), *Jubilee* (1977), *Caravaggio* (1986), *The Garden* (1990), and *Blue* (1993). His published works include *Dancing Ledge* (1984), *The Last of England* (1987), *Modern Nature* (1991), and, posthumously, *Derek Jarman's Garden* (1995).

Liam Kan
Now part of directing duo Who? (with Grant Hodgson), Kan began as a film editor and then director of music videos for the likes of The Beautiful South, Take That, Wet Wet Wet, and Alison Moyet. With Hodgson, he has shot award-winning commercials for Peugeot, Ripolin, Rover, Opel, Schweppes, Kellogg's, Bacardi, Camel, Virgin, and Volkswagen. In March 2005, they completed their first documentary, *The Steve Plan*, about Steven Lesser, the head of the emergency unit at Charity Hospital, New Orleans, and his struggle to realize the artist within.

Scott King
King trained as a graphic designer and worked as art director of *i-D* before going on to become creative director of *Sleazenation*, for which he was awarded 'Best Cover' and 'Best Designed Feature of the Year' prizes. His graphic design clients have included Morrissey, Malcolm McLaren, Michael Clark Dance Company, Sony Music, Diesel, Selfridges, and Benetton. He now works primarily as an artist and has exhibited in many international galleries, including the Institute of Contemporary Arts and Cubitt in London; Kunst-Werke in Berlin; Portikus in Frankfurt; and White Columns and the Museum of Modern Art in New York.

Pierre LaRoche
LaRoche, from the House of Arden, was David Bowie's personal make-up artist in the early 1970s. It was he who applied the famous lightning-bolt motif to Bowie's face for the *Aladdin Sane* album cover photo in 1973 and the astral sphere on Bowie's forehead, and who created the make-up for the Ziggy Stardust persona. He also created the cover girl make-up on Roxy Music's *Stranded* album and designed the make-up for *The Rocky Horror Picture Show*. He was make-up artist to both Mick and Bianca Jagger and to Freddie Mercury, among others.

Rob Leggatt
Leggatt is a British screenwriter and film-maker. With partner Leigh Marling, working together as Blue Source, he has produced and directed several commercials for brands including Lynx, Pizza Hut, and Travelocity, and music videos for acts such as Fatboy Slim, New Order, and Dirty Vegas.

David Lopez-Edwards
Lopez-Edwards is a London-based director and videographer with twenty-five years' experience in the music industry. After a decade at EMI Music, he founded Dynamic Cut Films Ltd, a boutique video production outfit in east London.

Alasdair McLellan
McLellan is a British photographer and film-maker renowned for his sensitive approach to photography in all of its forms. Whether fashion, portraiture, landscape, or documentary, his work displays a range of emotions and often reflects issues around gender, sexuality, and identity. He has had several solo exhibitions, including at the Institute of Contemporary Arts in London. He has produced music videos for The xx and Saint Etienne, as well as Pet Shop Boys.

Ian MacNeil
MacNeil has worked extensively in theatre, notably as costume designer for Stephen Daldry's production of *An Inspector Calls* in London and New York. He first collaborated with Pet Shop Boys on concepts and costumes for the *Nightlife* album and tour. He has since worked extensively in theatre and opera design, including Daldry's production of *Billy Elliot*. He won a Tony Award for 'Best Scenic Design of a Musical' for *Billy Elliot the Musical*.

Merck Mercuriadis
Mercuriadis was Pet Shop Boys' manager in the United States between 1998 and 2003, which he describes as a 'fabulous time'. He worked for more than twenty years at artist management company Sanctuary Group, eventually becoming chief executive officer. In that time, he managed multiple acts, including Elton John, Morrissey, Guns 'n' Roses, Destiny's Child, Beyoncé, Lou Reed, and Joss Stone. He then became, with Nile Rodgers, a founder of Hipgnosis Songs Fund Limited, a music IP investment company.

Slava Mogutin
Born in Siberia, Mogutin is a New York-based Russian artist and author who works across photography, video, text, installation, sculpture, and painting. He is exiled from Russia for his outspoken writing and activism. Since 1999, his photography has been exhibited internationally and featured in a wide range of publications. He is the author of several critically acclaimed monographs of photography, *Lost Boys*, *NYC Go-Go*, and *Bros & Brosephines*, and seven books of writings in Russian. His poetry, fiction, essays, and interviews have appeared in numerous publications and anthologies, and he won the 2000 Andrei Belyi Prize for Literature.

Andy Morahan
London-born Morahan studied graphic design and film at St Martin's School of Art, and has directed more than two hundred music videos. MTV has twice named him 'Best Director'. He has also directed commercials for brands such as Carling, Bacardi, Lynx, BT, Pepsi, Kelloggs, Nescafé, Rimmel, Mitsubishi,

and Fanta. In 1996, he gained worldwide acclaim with his Guess? Jeans 'Cheat' campaign featuring Juliette Lewis and Harry Dean Stanton, which won more than sixty awards.

Chris Nash

Award-winning dance photographer Nash took his first dance photograph in 1977 and is now recognized as one of the most creative photographers of his generation. He has worked with a number of world-renowned companies and choreographers, including the Rambert Dance Company, and has held more than forty exhibitions of his work in sixteen countries and published several volumes of photographs. He was appointed an MBE in the 2022 New Year's Honours List for services to dance and photography.

Hakeem Onibudo

Onibudo is an award-winning choreographer, performer, and CEO of Impact Dance, a hip-hop theatre company in London that he established in 1995.

Lynne Page

British choreographer Page works internationally in film and television, opera, theatre, musicals, commercials, and music. Her theatre work includes *The Cherry Orchard* and *The Merchant of Venice* at the National Theatre in London, while her extensive opera credits include productions at the Royal Opera House, Metropolitan Opera, New York, and La Scala in Milan. In 2020, Page choreographed *Lyssa*, her first work for the Royal Ballet. As well as Pet Shop Boys, she has worked with Stormzy and Jess Glynne at the BRIT Awards, and with Kanye West, Ellie Goulding, Imogen Heap, and Duffy.

Cindy Palmano

London-based fashion photographer and art director Palmano has photographed and made videos for a number of music acts, notably Tori Amos, with whom she has collaborated many times. Her work has featured in several publications such as *i-D*, and appears in the National Portrait Gallery, London.

Martin Parr

Arguably the most influential figure in British social documentary photography, Parr's work takes a critical look at modern society, specifically consumerism, foreign travel and tourism, motoring, the family and relationships, and food. He is known for his lurid, and sometimes shocking, use of colour, and for the humorous and incisive nature of his vision. His work has been widely exhibited in Europe and the United States and acquired by a large number of major public and private collections. He has shot several films and has made a television documentary, *Think of England*. In 2014, Parr was elected president of Magnum Photos International, a post he held until 2017. He has been awarded numerous lifetime achievement honours and was appointed a CBE for services to photography in the 2021 Queen's Birthday Honours.

Valerie Phillips

New York-born fashion and fine-art photographer Phillips is based in London. Her commercial clients include Nike, Doc Martens, Puma, Reebok, Paul Smith, Virgin Atlantic, Sony PlayStation, and Selfridges. Her work has appeared in *W*, *Big*, *Details*, *Nylon*, *Dazed & Confused*, and *Vogue*. She produced an acclaimed and controversial two-year faux documentary campaign for the Liverpool club Cream, and works regularly with P. J. Harvey. Her books include *Amber is for Caution*, *Another Girl Another Planet*, *Look at Me, I'm Lacy*, *One More Minute for Courtney, Please*, and *Monika Monster, Future First Woman on Mars*.

Bruno Poet

Poet is a London-based award-winning lighting designer working internationally in music, theatre, opera, festivals, and events. Recent work includes *Don Giovanni* at Houston Grand Opera (designed by Es Devlin), Andrew Lloyd Webber's *Bad Cinderella*, *Tina: The Tina Turner Musical*, and Björk's *Cornucopia*.

Peeter Rebane

Rebane is an Estonian film director and producer. He has directed the feature films *Firebird* (2021) and *Robbie Williams: Fans Journey to Tallinn* (2014), as well as numerous music videos. He has produced hundreds of shows in the Baltic region for artists including Elton John, Bob Dylan, Madonna, Sting, Lady Gaga, Metallica, and Queen.

Paul Rider

London-based portrait photographer Rider began his career in the British music press. At *Smash Hits*, he met and worked with Neil Tennant. He went on to photograph Pet Shop Boys as well as many other bands and musicians. He currently works in advertising, publishing, theatre, and editorial.

RMV Productions

RMV Productions was a British company established by video and animation producer Pete Reeve, specializing in video production and animation for music videos, television, and live events.

Michael Roberts

Born in Britain of a British father and St Lucian mother, Roberts attended art school in High Wycombe and emerged into swinging London in 1968. He was fashion editor at the *Sunday Times* in the late 1970s before assuming the same post at *Tatler* in the 1980s. He then became style editor at the *New Yorker*. He was also the fashion and style director of *Vanity Fair* magazine and the design director of British *Vogue*. He produced four books of his illustrations. In 2005, he published *The Snippy World of New Yorker Fashion Artist Michael Roberts*. He was appointed a CBE by HM Queen Elizabeth II in the 2022 New Year's Honours for services to fashion.

Pedro Romhanyi

British video and commercials director Romhanyi worked as a video commissioner at London Records before going on to direct videos for such artists as Blur, Pulp, Travis, Suede, The Propellerheads, Paul McCartney, Robbie Williams, Kylie Minogue, Manic Street Preachers, Paul Weller, The Beautiful South, OMD, Bryan Ferry, and The Sugarcubes.

John Ross

Ross is an award-winning, London-based photographer. His commercial work includes projects for Nokia, Nike, Honda, V&A, Bollinger, and Ferrari. As well as photographing for Pet Shop Boys on numerous occasions, he has photographed music acts such as Stormzy, Spiritualized, Kylie Minogue, and Manic Street Preachers.

Jenny Rush

Rush is Head of Production at Luke Halls Studio. Her credits include projects for Dua Lipa, Take That, Louis Vuitton, and the V&A.

Zbigniew Rybczynski

Born in Poland, Rybczynski has worked as a film director and teacher in Europe and the United States since the early 1970s. He has created music videos for artists such as The Art of Noise, Mick Jagger, Simple Minds, Yoko Ono, Lou Reed, Supertramp, Rush, Propaganda, and John Lennon. Having won an Oscar for 'Best Animated Short' in 1983 for his film *Tango*, he has gone on to receive dozens of prestigious industry awards. He has also won an Emmy, the Prix Italia, three MTV awards (together with the MTV 'Video Vanguard Award' for his role as a 'visionary in the field of music video'), and numerous awards at international film festivals.

Chris Sayer

Sayer is an award-winning British freelance motion designer. He frequently works with Julian Gibbs and Julian House to create music videos and commercials.

Tom Scutt

Scutt is a multiple award-winning British director, scenic, and costume designer, working across theatre, opera, dance, exhibition, and live music. He regularly works in London's major theatres and on Broadway, and has created shows and events for Christine and the Queens, Sam Smith, Apple Music, and MTV.

Libby Sellers
Sellers is a design historian, curator, and writer. Formerly a curator at the Design Museum in London, she ran her eponymous design gallery for a decade. She is the author of *Women Design: Pioneers from the Twentieth Century to Today*. In 2014, she was awarded Woman of Achievement in the Arts by the Women of the Year awards.

Corbin Shaw
Shaw is a British artist originally from Sheffield in South Yorkshire but now based in east London. His work, which is often tinged with humour or heart-breaking pathos, focuses on definitions of class, masculinity, and geographical divides, and the complex, shifting nature of identity and its relationship to place and community.

Rob Sinclair
Sinclair is a multiple award-winning lighting and production designer based in California. His many music concert credits include shows for Madonna, Human League, Shania Twain, Kylie Minogue, and Pulp.

Pennie Smith
Born in London, Smith studied graphics and fine art at Twickenham Art School in the late 1960s. She worked on *Friendz* magazine with Barney Bubbles and Nick Kent, and her first major commission was to cover Led Zeppelin's tours of the early 1970s. She was staff photographer for *NME* until the 1980s, producing many iconic cover images, particularly of The Clash. Her 1980 book *The Clash, Before and After* was a bestseller. She still lives and works in the railway station she bought and converted as a student. She was appointed an MBE in the 2024 King's Birthday Honours for services to photography.

Vita Spalding
Spalding is a British photographer based in London.

Gary Stillwell
Stillwell is an award-winning designer, photographer, and partner at Farrow, where he has worked for more than twenty years.

Ann Summa
Based in Los Angeles and Mexico, Summa is an award-winning American photographer who specializes in documentary, travel, and environmental portraiture.

Surrender Monkeys
Surrender Monkeys is a London-based group of directors, creatives, and designers. They have directed videos for The Kooks, Duke Dumont, and Pet Shop Boys.

Sam Taylor-Johnson (née Taylor-Wood)
One of the most successful of the young British artists generation, Taylor-Johnson worked at the Royal Opera House and Camden Palace after university. Her solo exhibitions include *Killing Time* (1994), *Travesty of a Mockery* (1995), *Pent-Up* (1996), *Five Revolutionary Seconds* (1997), *Mute* (2001), a major show at the Hayward Gallery in 2002, and a retrospective survey at the Baltic Centre for Contemporary Art in Gateshead in 2006. In 2008, she directed *Nowhere Boy*, a biopic about the childhood of John Lennon. She also directed the 2015 adaptation of E. L. James's novel *Fifty Shades of Grey* and the 2024 *Back to Black*, a biopic based on the life of British singer Amy Winehouse. She has made celebrated film and video work with Elton John, David Beckham, and Robert Downey Jr., as well as recording vocals (as Kiki Kokova) for the Pet Shop Boys-produced songs 'Je t'aime ... moi non plus', 'Love to love you, baby', and 'I'm in love with a German film star'. She was appointed OBE in the 2011 Queen's Birthday Honours for services to the arts.

Wolfgang Tillmans
German-born Tillmans's street-fashion photographs were first published in *i-D* and other magazines in the late 1980s. From 1990 to 1992, he studied at Bournemouth and Poole College before moving to London and then New York, photographing musicians, artists, and film directors such as Moby, Damon Albarn, and John Waters. He has had major solo shows in Zurich, Wolfsburg, Madrid, Cologne, Tokyo, Paris, London, and New York. He has been the subject of large-scale retrospectives at the Museum of Modern Art, Tate, Moderna Museet, and Centre Pompidou and dozens of monographs of his work have been published. He has received numerous awards and honours, including, in 2000, the Turner Prize and, in 2018, the Order of Merit of the Federal Republic of Germany. In 2023, he was named one of the most influential people in the world by *Time*.

Joost Vandebrug
Vandebrug is a Dutch artist working with photography and film. His acclaimed 2018 documentary film, *Bruce Lee and the Outlaw*, in which he follows a group of adolescents for six years as they inhabit abandoned tunnels in Bucharest, was screened in more than fifty film festivals around the world.

Valentina Verc
Verc is a Slovenian graphic designer, art director, and illustrator based in London.

Tim Walker
Walker is an internationally celebrated British fashion and portrait photographer and film-maker based in London. He rose to prominence in the mid-1990s with his highly imaginative and fantastical photographs inspired by fairy tales. He is acclaimed around the world for his lavish tableaux and narrative-driven images. He shot his first fashion story for *Vogue* at the age of twenty-five, and has photographed regularly for the British, Italian, and American editions. He has also shot notable covers for multiple international magazines. There have been several important exhibitions and books of his work, including three published by Thames & Hudson. His first film, the 2010 short *The Lost Explorer* won Best Short Film at the Chicago United Film Festival. His music work includes a video for Björk and shooting the album art for Kate Bush's *Director's Cut* and Harry Styles' *Fine Line*.

Tom Watkins
Pet Shop Boys' first manager, from 1984 to 1989, Watkins' Massive Management managed several pop acts, including Bros and East 17.

Eric Watson
Newcastle-born Watson attended Hornsey School of Art from 1977 to 1980, gaining a degree in fine art and art history. After college, he assisted the Rembrandt Brothers (Gered Mankowitz and Red Saunders) before working for Stiff Records, where he created cover images for Madness. From 1981 to 1987, he photographed for *Smash Hits*. He subsequently directed many videos for Rod Stewart, Chris Rea, Holly Johnson, and Dusty Springfield, among others.

Bruce Weber
American photographer and film-maker Weber came to public recognition in the early 1980s with his iconoclastic fashion spreads, and, in 1983, his black-and-white portraits of 250 Olympic hopefuls. A frequent contributor to Andy Warhol's *Interview* magazine, he later became famous for his campaigns for Calvin Klein, Abercrombie & Fitch, and Ralph Lauren. His editorial work has appeared in *Vogue*, *GQ*, *Vanity Fair*, *Elle*, *Life*, and *Rolling Stones* magazines. He has made five feature-length films to date, the most recent of which, the 2022 *The Treasure of His Youth*, focuses on the prominent Italian photojournalist Paolo Di Paolo.

Erik Weiss
Weiss is a German music and portrait photographer based in Berlin.

Index

Figures in **bold** refer to a main entry;
figures in *italics* refer to illustrations.

A Life in Pop **342–3**, 584
A Man from the Future **426–7**
'A new bohemia' **520–3**
'A powerful friend' 376
'A red letter day' **240–3**
About Pet Shop Boys 244, *247*
'Absolutely fabulous' 211, 212
Ackland, Joss *102–3*, 104, *105*, 116
Actually 20, 80, **90–3**, 104, 110, 142, 158, 168, 276, *277*, 478, 514, 556, 568
Agenda **452–7**, 567
Alden, David 16, 154, *155*, 157
Alexander, Olly 460, 462, 488
'All the young dudes' **528–31**
Allsopp, Robert 28
Alternative 214, **220–1**, 386
'Always on my mind' **98–103**, 106, 120, *121*, *135*, 522
Andon, Arma 166, 174
Andreas, Peter 94, *112–13*, 118, *120*, 160
Annually 452, 478, 484, 492, 544, **548–9**
A1 Designs 324
Aris, Brian *60–1*
Arnell, Vaughan 468, *470–1*
'Axis' **406–9**, 424, 541

Back To Mine: Pet Shop Boys **318–19**, 538
Badalamenti, Angelo 426
Barber, Frances 278, 344, 458, *459*
Barnard, David 328, 368, 488
Battleship Potemkin **314–17**, 384, 537
BBC Concert Orchestra 314, 344, 426
BBC Singers 426
Beatles, The 19, 136, 194, 294, 557
'Beautiful people' **372–3**
Beckett, Paul 286
'Before' **222–5**, 226
Behaviour **142–3**, 144, 148, 158, 170, 276, *277*, 558
'Being boring' **144–7**, 151
Beyer, Nico 310, *312–13*
Bilingual 16, 222, **234–5**, 240, 244, 276, *277*, 534, 542, 559
Blitz club / Blitz Kids 29, 48, 172
Blitz magazine 11, 38, 44
Bond, Jack 98, *102–3*, 104, 106, *108–9*, 244
Borden, Harry *272–3*
Bowie, David 12, 98, 130, 284, 350, 414, 528, 552, 556, 559
Bracewell, Michael 11, 15, 52, 154, 252, *254–5*, 268, 288, 443
Branson, Brad *222–3*
'Break 4 love' 280, *281*, 296
Bryant, Jeffrey 24, 29, 368, *369*, 402, *403*, 410, *411*, 414, *415*, 440, *441*
Burbridge, Richard *202–3*, *220–1*
Burnett, Carl 284, *285*, 288, *289*
'Burning the heather' **464–7**
Burscough, Chris *60–1*, *528*, *529*, 552

Cameron, Don 332, *334–5*
'Can you forgive her?' 22, 23, 154, **174–9**, 200, 212, 268, 306
Cash, Ben 440, *441*
Catlin, Andrew 91
Cea, José 234, *235*
Cecchetto, Flavio 240, *241*

Child, Les 208, 244, 264, *265*, 564
Churilla, Lynda 226, *227–31*
Clarke, Margi *96–7*
Closer to Heaven **278–9**, 328, 458, 536, 558
Cohen, Lester 269, *271*, *272*, *273*
Concrete **344–5**
Connell, Dainton *140–1*, *160–1*, *173*, 243, *250–1*
Costiff, Gerlinda 172
Costiff, Michael 172, *382–3*, 540
Coward, Noël 11, 17, 551
Creamfields **264–5**
Crépin, Pelle *8*, 368, *371*, 374, *375*, *382–3*, *394–5*, 398, *399*, 432, *433*, 538, *539*, 540
'Cricket wife' **484–5**
Cubism 328, *331*

'Dancing star' **510–13**
Daw, Matthew 488, *489*
Devlin, Es 24, *27–8*, 278, 328, *329*, 368, *369*, 402, *403*, 406, 428, 430, *431*, 440, *441*, 563
Dickson, Neil *102*, 104, *105*
'Did you see me coming?' **364–7**
Disco **78–9**, 80, 206, 276
Disco 2 **206–7**, 211, 276
Disco 3 **300–1**
Disco Four 346, **350–1**, 538
Discography **168–9**, 174, 382, 496
'Discoteca' **236–9**
Discovery tour 28, **208–11**, 212, 214, 234, 410, 534
'DJ culture' **164–7**
'Domino dancing' **112–15**, 116, *120*, *135*, 141, 520
Domeisen, Oliver 268, *269*
Dorrell, David 346
Douglas Brothers, The *136*, 144, *145*, 151
Doyle, Jaqui 110, *111*, *544–8*
'Dreamland' **460–3**
Dreamworld tour 27, 28, 29, *30–1*, **488–91**, 506, 543, 556
Dresdner Sinfoniker 314, *315*, *316*
Duffy, Patrick *280–1*
Duran Duran 12, 74, 550

Earl, Andy *194–5*, *210–1*, *212–13*, *234*, *235*, 244, *246*, *249*, 533
Eastman, Claire 208, *209*, 244, *245*
Eisenstein, Sergei 314, *315*, *316*
Electric 20, 402, 406, 408, 410, **414–17**, 420, 432, 541, 542, 569
Electric tour *27–8*, *28*, *29*, **402–5**, 406, *4908–9*, 410, 420, 541
Elysium 388, **392–3**, 396, 398, 402, 410, 414, *449*
'E-mail' *294–5*
EMI Records 47, 382, 552, 555, 560; *see also* Parlophone Records
Emin, Tracey *522–3*
Epic Records 34, 38, 48
Example **422–3**

Face, The 14, 15, 19, 44, 66, 133, *179*, 180
Factory Records 14, 47, 58, 62, 112, 142
'Feel' **524–7**
Ferrari, Chiara 388, *389*
Field, Justyn 420, *422–3*
Fielding, David 16, 154, *155*, 157, *174–9*, *184–91*, *198–9*
Fields, Duggie 84, 85
Filipiak, Gavin 436, *438–9*
Fisk, Phil 460

Fitzgerald, Zelda 147
'Flamboyant' **310–13**
Flavin, Dan 324, 350
'Fluorescent' **424–5**
Foley, Greg *286–7*, *449*
Forbes, Dan *286–7*, 448, *449*
Ford, James 514, 566
'Forever in love' 504
Format **386–7**
Foster, Nikolai 478
Frankie Goes To Hollywood 14, 15, 550
Franks, Elliott *344–5*
Fundamental 20, 320, **324–7**, 332, 338, 342, 350, 358, *449*, 472
Fundamental tour 27, **328–31**, 368
Fundamentalism 324, *326–7*
Furthermore 516, *517*

Gascoigne, Anna Marie *140–1*
Gaz, Tatiana *286–7*, *449*
Gibb, Joel 450
Gibbs, Julian 338, *340–1*, 346, *348–9*
Gilbert and George 15, 82, 154, 196, 514
Gilbert Scott, Sir George 254, 256
'Give stupidity a chance' **452–4**
Gleadall, Pete 402, *536*
Glucksman, Carisa 368, *369*
Gowabs, Christophe 118
Graham Norton Show, The 430, *431*
Greenaway, Jude 406, *408–9*
Greenhalgh, Howard 23, 174, *178–9*, 180, *182–3*, 194, *196–7*, 198, *200–1*, 202, *204–5*, 214, *218–19*, 222, *224–5*, 236, *238–9*, 240, *242–3*, 258, *262–3*, 302, *304–5*
Griffin, Annie 244, *247*, 248, *250–1*
Griggs, Paul Wesley 278
Groupe **278–9**
Gutt, Tim 328, *330*

Hadid, Zaha 16, 268, *269*
Haigh, Andrew 520, *522–3*
Halls, Luke 25, 26, 28, 402, *403*, 406, *408–9*, *486–7*, 488, *489*, 502, *504–5*, 510, *512–13*
Harrison, Andrew 402, 555
Hart, Douglas 364, *366–7*
Harvey, Jonathan 278, 372, 458
Hay, Alexei *266–7*, *270*
'Heart' **106–9**, 110, 134, *135*
Heath, Chris 23, *110–11*, 132, 133, *136–7*, *156*, 157, *192–3*, 234, *235*, 328, *336–7*, *476–7*, 534, *535*, *544–9*, 550–69
Helbig, Sven *316*
Henry, Trevor *150–3*, 557
Hepworth, Dave 563
Herron, Tom *408–9*
Highlights 133
'Hit music' 478
Hoare, Philip 10–17, 20, 26, 288, 336
Hochhaussinfonie 316
Hodges, Andrew 426
Holden, Merry *408–9*
Holmes, Abigail Rosen 208, *209*, 244, *245*
'Home and dry' *280–3*, 296
Hoogerbrugge, Han 354, *356–7*
Hooton, Ian *60–1*
Horn, Trevor 14, 15, 320, 332, 344, 392
Hotspot 460, 464, 468, **472–5**, 480, 514, 542
House, Julian 338, *340–1*, 346, *348–9*

'How can you expect to be taken seriously?' 148, *149*, *150–1*, 152
Hunt, Gareth *102–3*, 104, *105*
Hynde, Chrissie 426, *427*

i-D 12, 44, 74
'I don't know what you want but I can't give it any more' **252–7**, 258, 271, 336
'I don't wanna' **480–3**
'I get along' **292–5**
'I get excited (you get excited too)' 478
I like it here, wherever it is **116–17**
'I want a dog' 120
'I wouldn't normally do this kind of thing' 23, **194–7**
'I'm not scared' *120*, 121
'I'm with stupid' **320–3**, 538
In Depth 133
'In the night' 478
'Inner sanctum' 428, **444–5**
Inner Sanctum (Royal Opera House residency) 440, *443*
Institute of Contemporary Arts, London (ICA) 17, 89, 314
Integral **346–9**
Interview 266
Introspective **118–21**, 133, *276–7*, 269, 358, 426, 542, 558
It couldn't happen here 98, *99*, *102–3*, **104–5**, 116, 569
'It's alright' *121*, **126–9**, 133, *136*, 164
'It's a sin' 15, **82–5**, 106, 109, 116, 130, *135*, 256, 566

Jarman, Derek 15, 26, 27, 82, *84–5*, 94, *96–7*, 130, *131*, 133, 134, *135*, 208, 224, 556, 558
'Jealousy' **158–61**, 162, 476
Joy Division 20; *see also* New Order

Kan, Liam 148, *150–3*
'KDX125' 504
Key, Trevor 184, *185*, *210*, *212–13*
King, Scott *280–1*, 288, *290–1*, *292–3*, *296–7*, *300–1*, *536*
'King's Cross' *135*
Kinky Gerlinky 29, *172–3*, 382
Kraftwerk 9, 11, 201, 418
Kubrick, Stanley 85, 256, 264
Kureishi, Hanif 478

LaRoche, Pierre 98, *100–1*, *120–1*, 126, *127*, 556
'Later tonight' 478
'Leaving' **394–7**
Lebec, Pascal 140
'Left to my own devices' 14, 25, *120*, 121, **122–5**, 162, 478
Leggatt, Rob 320, *322–3*
Les Petites Bon-Bons 520
Leston, Kimberley 14–15
'Liberation' **198–201**, 206, 211, 322
Life magazine 192
Linard, Stephen 28, *85*, 551, 555
Lipson, Steve 344
Literally 82, 110, 136, 234, **544–9**
'Living in the past (home demo)' 25, 492, *494–5*
'London' **296–9**
'Loneliness' **506–9**, 514, 516, 530
Lopez-Edwards, David 394, *396–7*, 398, *400–1*
Lost **492–5**
'Love comes quickly' **52–7**, 506, 555–6, 559
'Love etc.' **354–7**

590

'Love is a bourgeois construct' **418–19**, 496
'Love life' **376–7**
Lucas, Matt *322–3*
Lynch, David 42, 170, 264

McBurney, Simon 314
McCabe, Jake *286–7*
McCartney, Paul 557, 563
McKellen, Ian *108–9*, 569
McLellan, Alasdair 358, *359–62*, *364–5*, 506, *508–9*, *570–1*
MacNeil, Ian 16, 252, *253–7*, *259*, *262–3*, *265*, 268, 269, 328, 564
Madonna 34, 74, 106, 140, 350
Mapplethorpe, Robert 52, *54–5*, 128, 557
Marley, Jacob *166–7*
Marr, Johnny 244, 476
Marr, Sonny 476
Martin, Mark *150–3*, 557
Mason-James, Sylvia *250–1*, 264, *265*, 564
Mauder, Pete *220–1*
MCMLXXXIX tour 26, 126, **130–3**, *134*, *135*, 136, 148, 556
'Memory of the future' **398–401**
Meneely, Warren 271
Mini 271
'Minimal' **332–5**
'Miracles' 20, **302–5**, 310, 536
Miyake, Issey 66, 76, 256
Mogutin, Slava 528, *530–1*
'Monkey business' **468–71**
Montage 271
Moody, Ron 85
Morahan, Andy 38, *42–3*, 44, *50–1*, *52*, *56–7*
Mott, George 148, 154, *155*, *158*
MTV 147, 182, 283
Muir, Alastair 278, *279*
Musik **458–9**
Musikexpress 460
My Beautiful Laundrette **478–9**
'My head is spinning' *504*
Myers, Terry 336

Nash, Chris 22, 23, *174–7*, *180–1*, *184–7*, *188–91*, *210*, *212–13*, *502–3*
Nauman, Bruce 268, 324
'New London boy' **528–31**
New Order 20, 44, 488
'New York City boy' **258–63**, *264*, *266*, 271, 272
Nightlife 16, 252, **266–7**, 271, 448, *449*, 472, 534, 559
Nightlife tour 16, **268–71**, 272, 274
Nirvana 16, 174, 158
Nonetheless 20, 506, **514–19**, 520, *524*, 528, 552, 568
Nonetheless expanded edition *518–19*
'Numb' 310, **338–41**
Nureyev, Rudolf *510–11*

'On social media' *452–3*, *455*, 462
'One more chance' 15, **36–7**
'One thing leads to another' 504, *505*
Onibudo, Hakeem 328
'Opportunities' (let's make lots of money) (first release) 15, **38–43**, 120, 550, 553, 555
'Opportunities' (let's make lots of money) (second release) **62–5**, *72*, *135*, 151, 170, 236, 478
Orlando, Bobby (Bobby 'O') 12, 34, 44, 244, 342

Page, Lynne 368, *369*, 402, *403*, 428, 440, *441*, *470–1*, 488, *489*
Palmano, Cindy 90, *91–3*, 116, *117*, *121*, 126, *133*, 276, *277*
Palmer, Tony 121
Pandemonium tour 24, **368–71**, 382, 540

'Paninaro' **74–7**, 78, 80, 130, 133, *135*
'Paninaro '95' **214–9**
Parlophone Records 38, 376, 390, 406, 522, 530; *see also* EMI Records
Parr, Martin 296, *298–9*
Pentagram *184–5*, *188–9*
Performance tour 15–16, *18*, 19, 73, 106, 150, **154–7**, 158, 166, 174, 176, 192, 278, 426, 554, 557
Petrie, Rob *168–9*, *210–11*, *220–1*
Pet Shop Boys, annually **110–11**
Pet Shop Boys Catalogue 20, 23, **336–7**
'Pet Shop Boys Catalogue 1986–1996' **276–7**, 448
'Pet Shop Boys Catalogue 1999–2012' **448–9**
Pet Shop Boys, Literally **136–7**, *476*, *477*
Pet Shop Boys Party/Pet Shop Boys Christmas **374–5**, 538
Pet Shop Boys Story **352–3**
'Pet Shop Boys: Then and Now' (BBC *Imagine*) 27
Pet Shop Boys versus America **192–3**, *476*, *477*
Phillips, Valerie 288, *290–1*
Please **58–61**, 80, 90, 98, 142, 276, *277*, 555
PopArt **306–9**, 310, 338, 382, 542
Poet, Bruno 488, *489*
Presley, Elvis 98, 104, 151, 243
Price, Stuart 368, 398, 402, 410, 414, 432, 444, 472, 488, 514
Projections 130, **134–5**, 208
Promotion **162–3**
Pugh, Gareth 364, 408
Putin, Vladimir 25, *494–5*
Putrov, Ivan 384

Rammstein 314
Rasch, Torsten 314
Rauhofer, Peter 280
Rebane, Peeter 378, *380–1*
Release 280, **286–7**, 288, 292, 300, 306, 448, *449*, 559
Release tour 17, **288–91**, 376, 554, 556
Relentless 25, 188, **502–5**, 543
Renner, Bettina 316
'Rent' 87, 90, **94–7**, 256
Richter, Gerhard 23, 24, 354, 358, *364*, 568
Rider, Paul 40, *60–1*, *148*
Ridgers, Derek *18*, *19*, *157*
Rimmer, Dave 15, 180
Rindt, Markus 316
Ripley & Ripley (Rip) 318, *561*
RMV Productions 460, *462–3*, 464, *465–6*, 480, *482–3*
Roberts, Michael 118, *120*, 121, 122, *123*
Robinson, Peter 488
Robotnik, Alexander 120
Rollergirls *390–1*
Romhanyi, Pedro 252, *254–5*, 272, *274–5*
Ross, Fred 414
Ross, John 320, *321*, 324, *325–7*, *332–3*, *344–5*, *350–1*, *374–5*, *378–9*, 402, *405*, *410–11*, 414, *415*, *420–1*, 448, *449*
Royal Opera House 9, 428, 430, *440*, *443*, 444, 510, 512, 563
Rush, Jenny 488, *489*
Rybczynski, Zbigniew 62, *64–5*

Sadler's Wells 384
Savage, Jon 220, 386, 478
Saville, Peter 14, 20, 44
'Say it to me' **446–7**, 496
Sayer, Chris 338, *340–1*, 346, *348–9*

Schlöndorff, Volker 492
Scott, George *342–3*
Scutt, Tom 27, 28, 29, *30–1*, 488, *489–91*, 564, 566
'Se a vida é (That's the way life is)' **226–33**
Shackleton, Robert *170–1*, *533*
Shaw, Corbin 524, *526–7*
SheBoom *238–9*
Showbusiness **116–17**
Shutter, Joe *60–1*
Sims, Phil *210*, *220–1*
Sinclair, Rob 368, *369*, 402, *403*, *440*, *441*
'Single-Bilingual' **236–9**
Smash **496–501**
Smash Hits 12, 34, 44, 90, 91, 464, 496, 550, 551, 553
Smith, Maggi *336–7*
Smith, Pennie *10–17*, *155*, *192–3*, *240–1*, 286
'So hard' **138–41**, 144
'Somewhere' **248–51**
Somewhere – in concert at the Savoy Theatre 16, **244–7**, 248, *250–1*, 264, 557
Sondheim, Stephen 248
Sottsass, Ettore 47
Southern, Donald *510–11*
Spalding, Vita *520–1*
Spandau Ballet 12, 74, 550
Spheeris, Penelope 66, 72
Springfield, Dusty 86, *87–9*, 244, 342
Stevenson, Juliet 426, *427*
Stillwell, Gary 306, 310, *311*, 318, *319*, 324, *325–7*, 332, 338, 350, 352, *353*, 358, 368, 382, 384, 386, 388, 392, *393*, *394*, 420, 424, 428, 432, 440, 468, 478, 484, 492, *493*, 496, 502, 510, 514, 520
Stockhammer, Jonathan 316
Stoddard, John *60–1*
Street-Porter, Janet 268
'Suburbia' 15, **66–73**, 74, 76, 78, 112, 298, 306, 336, 556
Summa, Ann 392, *393*, *449*
Sumner, Bernard 244
Super **432–5**, 436, 440, 443, 444, 446, 450, 472, 492, 496, 541, 542, 569
Super tour 29, **440–3**
Surrender Monkeys 388, *390–1*

Taboo 29, 172
Tada, Toshima *170–1*
Take That 368, 428
Talk 244
Taylor-Johnson (née Taylor-Wood), Sam 16, *244–5*, *338–9*, 557
Television **80–1**, 116
The Most Incredible Thing **384–5**
'The pop kids' **428–31**
'The forgotten child' 452, *453*, 456, *457*, 567
'The lost room' 492, *493*
'The man who has everything' 504, *505*
The Most Incredible Thing **384–5**, 540
'The truck-driver and his mate' 222, *223*, 478
'Thursday' **420–3**
Tillmans, Wolfgang 280, *282–3*, 286, 300, *301*, 472
'Together' **378–81**
'Tonight is forever' 478
Top of the Pops 20, 26, 94, 176, 179, 180, 322, 551, 555, 559, 565
Tovey, Russell *522–3*
Turing, Alan 426
'Twenty-something' **436–9**
Two books about Pet Shop Boys **476–7**

Ultimate 378, **382–3**, 540
'Undertow' **450–1**
Unity tour 488
University tour 17, **284–5**, 288, 559

Vale, Michael 244, *245*
Vandebrug, Joost 410, *412–13*
Various **212–13**
Verc, Valentina 544, *548–9*
Very 20, 23, 25, 170, 174, **184–7**, 188, 194, 196, 198, 211, 212, 276, *277*, 306, 502, 542, 558
Very Relentless **188–91**, 194, 502
Videography 168, *169*
Village People 16, 180
Villiers, Jonathan de *296–7*
Vinyl Factory, The *25*, 360, *361*, *384*, *385*, *416–17*
Visionaire *286–7*
'Vocal' **410–13**, 414, 480
Vodianova, Natalia *294–5*

Walker, Tim 20, *506–7*, 514, *515*, *517–19*, 568
Walliams, David *322–3*
Warhol, Andy 12, 70, 128, 172, 222, 244, 262, 336
Warren, Diane 338
'Was it worth it?' *170–3*, 532
Watkins, Tom 15, 47, 48, 50, 118, 552, 554, 555, 569
Watson, Eric *6–7*, 15, 20, 21, *34–5*, *36–7*, *38–43*, *44–51*, *52–3*, *56–7*, *58–61*, *66–73*, *82–3*, *86–9*, *91*, *92*, *94–5*, *98–101*, *106–7*, *110*, *114–15*, *118*, *120–1*, *124–5*, *127–9*, *137*, *139–41*, *142–3*, *157*, *159–61*, *165–7*, *168–9*, *172–3*, *214–15*, 220, *253*, *256–7*, *259*, *270*, *336*, *337*, *532*, 550, 551, 552, 553, 554, 555, 556, 559
Watson, Lawrence 130, *131*, *136*, 148, *149*
Watt, Alison 90, *92*
Webb, Iain R. 48, 552
Weber, Bruce 16, 26, 122, 144, *146–7*, 226, *232–3*, 292, *294–5*, 557
'We came from outer space' 504, *505*
Węgrzyn, Stanisław *512–13*
Weil, Daniel *184–5*, *188–9*
Weiss, Erik 488, *490–1*
'West End girls' (first release) **34–5**, 36, 551
'West End girls' (second release) 38, **44–51**, 52, 62, 106, 278, 342, 388, 408, 436, 478, 550, 551, 552, 553, 555, 563, 565, 567
'West End girls' (New lockdown version) *486–7*
Wham! 15, 36, 50, 496, 550
'What are we going to do about the rich?' *452–3*, *456*
'What have I done to deserve this?' *86–9*, 90, *92–3*, 94, 102, 116, 342, 554
Wheeler, Dominic 426
'Where the streets have no name (I can't take my eyes off you)' **148–53**, 162
Wilmer, Val 86, *87*
Windsor, Barbara *103*, 104, *105*
'Winner' **388–91**

x2 *406*, 424, *425*
Xenomania 354, 566
XL Design 14, *34–5*, *38–9*, *44–7*, 555

Yes 23, *24–5*, 352, 354, **358–63**, 368, 372, 448, *449*, 542, 568
'Yesterday, when I was mad' **202–5**, 211, 212
'You only tell me you love me when you're drunk' 271, **272–5**

Index 591

Photographers' credits

p. 2: Eva Pentel
pp. 6–7: Eric Watson
p. 8: Pelle Crépin
p. 27: Es Devlin
p. 28: Katja Ogrin/Alamy Stock Photo
p. 29: AP Photo/MTI, Tibor Illyes/Alamy Stock Photo
pp. 30–1: Martin Thomas Photography
p. 131: Lawrence Watson
p. 155: Pennie Smith
p. 269: Oliver Domeisen and Lester Cohen
p. 289: Steve Jennings, unless otherwise stated below
p. 289 top row, left: James Nielsen/Houston Chronicle via Getty Images
p. 289 second row, second right: Rob Verhorst/Redferns/Getty Images
p. 289 third row, left: Carlos Alvarez/Getty Images
p. 289 bottom row, right: Getty Images
p. 315: Hayley Madden
p. 316: Dresdner Sinfoniker
p. 329: Es Devlin Studio and Mark Snyder (Remark)
p. 369: Larissa Szymanek
p. 403: Larissa Szymanek and Mark Snyder (Remark)
p. 427: Chris Christodoulou
p. 441: Ken McKay
p. 489: Steve Kyle
p. 561: Rip
pp. 570–1: Alasdair McLellan

Product photography on pp. 34–319, 520–38, 544–6 by Andrew Brown

Product photography on pp. 24–5, 320–519, 539–43, 547–8 by Simon Pask

Video stills by Andrew Brown

The publishers and Pet Shop Boys would like to thank Robin Dashwood for kindly allowing us to photograph his copy of the limited edition of *Yes*.

Our thanks go to Sonny Marr for allowing us to photograph her copy of the slipcase edition of *Two books about Pet Shop Boys*.

Finally, we thank Mark Snyder (Remark) for generously providing his photographs of the *Fundamental* and *Electric* tours.

First published in the United Kingdom in 2006 under the title *Pet Shop Boys Catalogue* by Thames & Hudson Ltd, 6–24 Britannia Street, London WC1X 9JD

First published in the United States of America in 2006 under the title *Pet Shop Boys Catalogue* by Thames & Hudson Inc., 500 Fifth Avenue, New York, New York 10110

This revised and expanded edition published in 2026 under the title *Pet Shop Boys Volume*

Pet Shop Boys Catalogue © 2006 Thames & Hudson Ltd, London

Pet Shop Boys Volume © 2026 Thames & Hudson Ltd, London

Original text © 2006 Chris Heath and Philip Hoare
Updated text © 2026 Chris Heath
Foreword for this revised and expanded edition by Jeremy Deller
Introduction for this revised and expanded edition by Libby Sellers

Photographs and artwork © 2006 and 2026 Pet Shop Boys, unless otherwise stated

Jacket and cover designed by Farrow

Edited and designed by Andrew Brown

All Rights Reserved. No part of this publication may be reproduced or transmitted in any form or by any means, electronic or mechanical, including photocopy, recording or any other information storage and retrieval system, without prior permission in writing from the publisher.

EU Authorized Representative: Interart S.A.R.L.
19 rue Charles Auray, 93500 Pantin, Paris, France
productsafety@thamesandhudson.co.uk
interart.fr

A CIP catalogue record for this book is available from the British Library

Library of Congress Control Number 2025947630

ISBN 978-0-500-02747-9
01

Printed and bound in China by C & C Offset Printing Co. Ltd

Be the first to know about our new releases, exclusive content and author events by visiting
thamesandhudson.com
thamesandhudsonusa.com
thamesandhudson.com.au

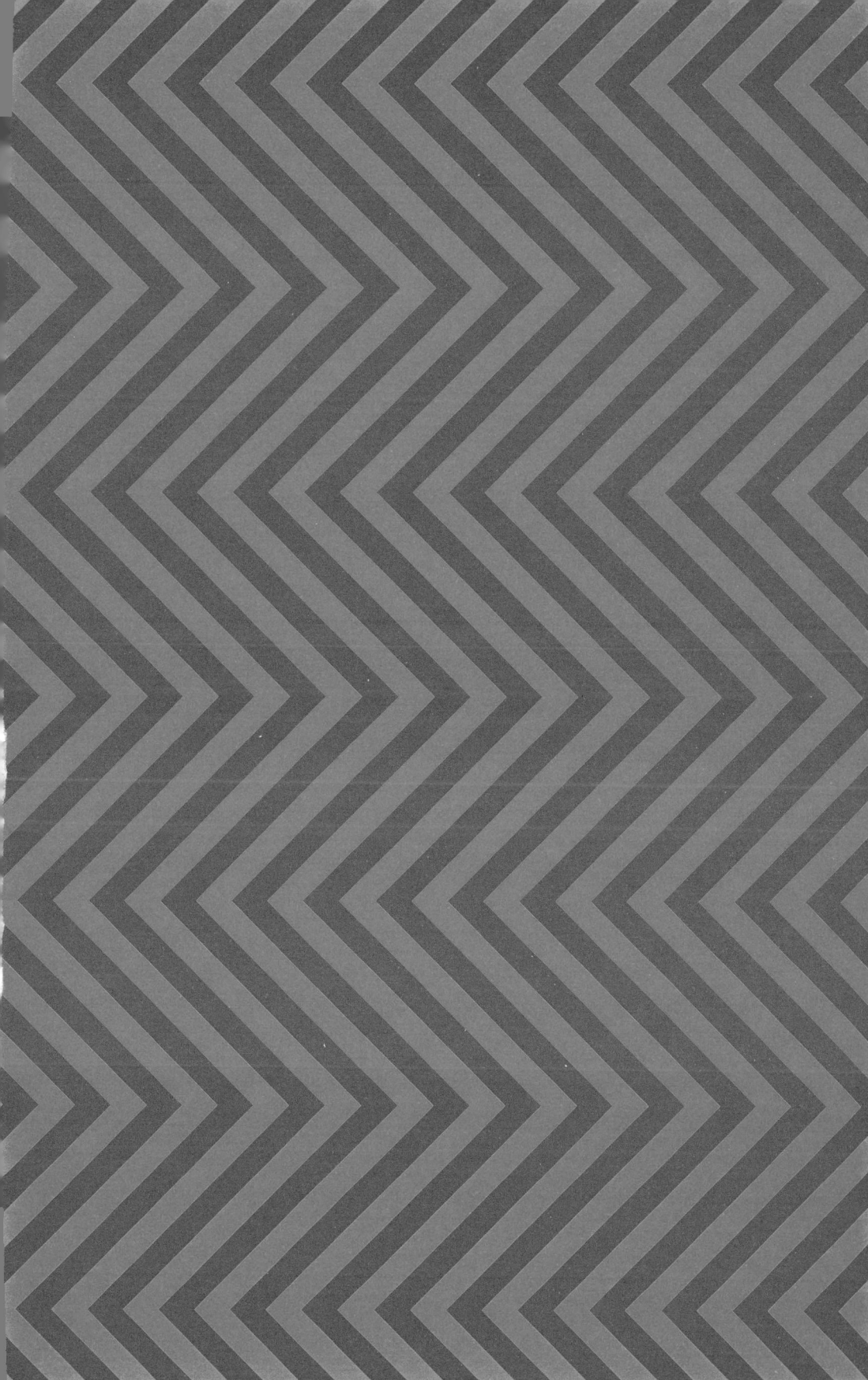

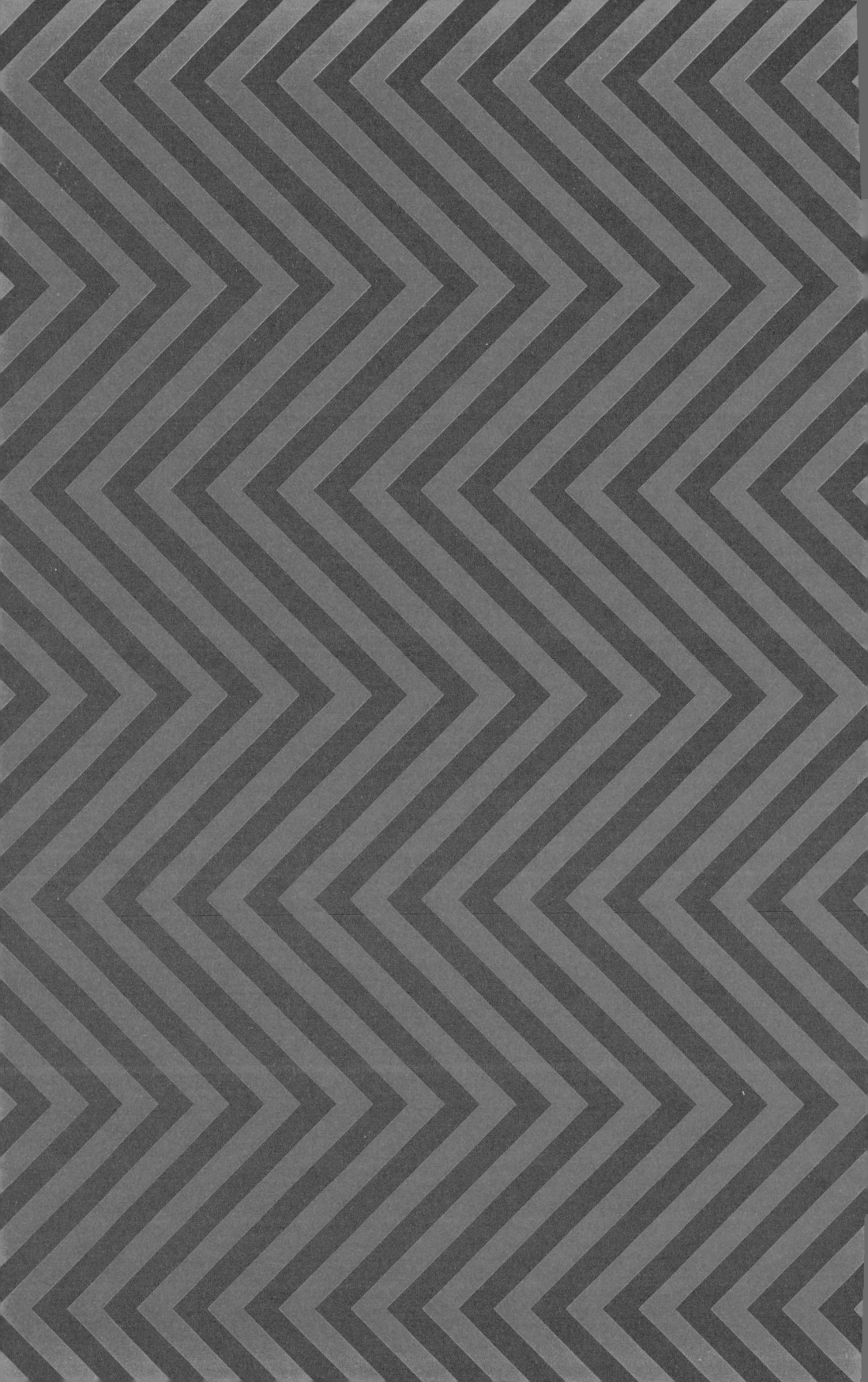